# MODERN BIOLOGY®

**John H. Postlethwait**
**Janet L. Hopson**

**HOLT, RINEHART AND WINSTON**

A Harcourt Education Company

Orlando • **Austin** • New York • San Diego • Toronto • London

# ABOUT THE AUTHORS

The legacy of *Modern Biology* extends from 1921, when the first edition was published under the title *Biology for Beginners*. The original author was Truman Moon, a high school teacher in Middletown, New York. Moon believed that a strong grounding in the basic concepts and vocabulary of biology was the best way to prepare students for college biology. Paul Mann, a science teacher in New York City, shared Moon's passion for teaching biology and later became a coauthor.

In the mid-1940s, James Otto, a biology teacher from George Washington High School in Indianapolis, took over authorship of the book, which by then was titled *Modern Biology*. Otto added another hallmark to the program—an emphasis on the latest developments in biology at a level appropriate for young learners. In 1958, Dr. Albert Towle, a professor of biology at San Francisco State University, was added to the program as a coauthor. After the death of Otto in 1972, Towle remained the primary author until he completed the 2002 edition after which he passed away.

Now, to continue the legacy of more than eight decades of exceptional authorship, *Modern Biology* adds two more distinguished authors: John Postlethwait and Janet Hopson.

### John H. Postlethwait

John Postlethwait received his Ph.D. in developmental genetics from Case Western Reserve University and completed his postdoctoral fellowship in genetics at Harvard University. During a teaching career that has spanned more than 30 years, he has received several research awards and the Ersted Distinguished Teaching Award. Dr. Postlethwait now teaches general biology, embryology, and genetics at the University of Oregon and, is the coauthor of several college-level textbooks.

### Janet L. Hopson

Jan Hopson received her B.A. in biology from Southern Illinois University and her M.A. in science writing from the University of Missouri. Ms. Hopson has taught science writing at two campuses of the University of California and has authored and coauthored several college-level biology textbooks and popular science books. She won the Russell L. Cecil Award for magazine writing. Ms. Hopson's news and feature articles have appeared in publications such as *Science News*, *Smithsonian*, *Newsweek*, *Psychology Today*, and *Science Digest*.

**On the cover:** The white-faced owl is found in most regions of Africa south of the Sahara. Recent DNA research suggests that the owl differs significantly from members of the genus *Otus*, to which it was once assigned. As a result, taxonomists have reclassified this owl into two species: the Southern white-faced owl—*Ptilopsis granti* and the Northern white-faced owl—*Ptilopsis leucotis*.

Printed in the United States of America

ISBN 0-03-065178-6     4 5 6 7 8 9  048  09 08 07 06

# ACKNOWLEDGMENTS

## Contributing Writers

**Barbara Christopher**
*Science Writer*
Austin, Texas

**Christena M. Cox, Ph.D.**
*Freelance Science Editor and Writer*
Columbus, Ohio

**Linda K. Gaul, Ph.D., MPH**
*Epidemiologist*
Department of State Health
  Services
Austin, Texas

**Charlotte W. Luongo, MSc**
*Science Writer*
Austin, Texas

**Annette Ratliff**
*Science Writer and Assessment
  Specialist*
Austin, Texas

**Linda B. Thornhill, M.S.**
*Science Writer*
Columbus, Ohio

## Inclusion Specialist

**Joan Altobelli**
*Special Education Director*
Austin Independent School District
Austin, Texas

## Teacher Edition Development

**Christena M. Cox, Ph.D.**
*Freelance Science Editor and Writer*
Columbus, Ohio

**Alan Eagy**
*Biology Teacher*
Columbia Gorge High School
The Dalles, Oregon

**Charlotte W. Luongo, MSc**
*Science Writer*
Austin, Texas

**Annette Ratliff**
*Science Writer and Assessment
  Specialist*
Austin, Texas

**Linda B. Thornhill, M.S.**
*Science Writer*
Columbus, Ohio

## Biology Field Testers

**Adam Ashby**
*Biology Teacher*
Cactus High School
Glendale, Arizona

**Collette E. Baughman**
*Teacher*
Wichita Heights High School
Wichita, Kansas

**Jessica Bolson**
Washington Irving High School
Brooklyn, New York

**Aruna Chopra**
*Biology Teacher*
Benjamin Franklin High School
Philadelphia, Pennsylvania

**Dora Coleman**
*Department Chair*
G. W. Carver High School
Memphis, Tennessee

**Christy C. Collins**
*Science Department Chair*
Charles B. Aycock High School
Pikeville, North Carolina

**Beau Gee**
*Biology Teacher*
Waccamaw High School
Pawleys Island, South Carolina

**Bissoon Jarawar**
*Teacher*
William H. Taft High School
Bronx, New York

**Mary E. Kelley**
*Teacher*
Bethel High School
Hampton, Virginia

**Chris Mante**
*Teacher*
Science Department
Parma Senior High School
Parma Ohio

**Diane McKinney**
*Biology Teacher*
Cloudland High School
Roan Mountain, Tennessee

**Dr. L. Eugene Morton**
*Teacher*
South Stanly High School
Norwood, North Carolina

**Babtunde Oronti**
*Teacher*
Olney High School
Philadelphia, Pennsylvania

**Gail Porter**
*Teacher*
Chipley High School
Chipley, Florida

**Terry Smith**
*Teacher*
Bradford County High School
Starke, Florida

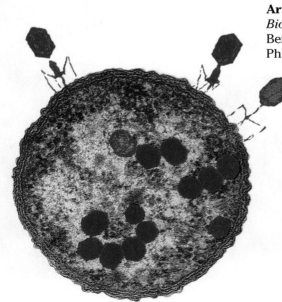

## Biology Field Testers
*(continued)*

**Mike Trimble**
*Teacher*
Corona Del Sol High School
Tempe, Arizona

**Barry Tucker**
*Teacher*
Colerain High School
Cincinnati, Ohio

**Lois G. Walsh**
*Teacher*
A.D. Harris High School
Panama City, Florida

**Janet F. Washington**
*Teacher*
Hunters Lane High School
Nashville, Tennessee

**Jacqueline M. Wilson**
*Teacher*
Sidney Lanier High School
Montgomery, Alabama

**Patricia E. Wrocklage**
*Teacher*
Hayden High School
Topeka, Kansas

## Academic Reviewers

**Renato J. Aguilera, Ph.D.**
*Professor and Director of the
  Graduate Program in Biology*
University of Texas at El Paso
El Paso, Texas

**David M. Armstrong**
*Professor*
Ecology and Evolutionary Biology
University of Colorado
Boulder, Colorado

**Nigel Atkinson, Ph.D.**
*Associate Professor of Neurobiology*
Section of Neurobiology
University of Texas at Austin
Austin, Texas

**Jerry Baskin**
*Professor of Biology*
Biology Department
University of Kentucky
Lexington, Kentucky

**Sonal S. D. Blumenthal, Ph.D.**
*Life Science Consultant*
Austin, Texas

**Joe W. Crim, Ph.D.**
*Professor of Cellular Biology*
Cellular Biology Department
University of Georgia
Athens, Georgia

**James F. Curran, Ph.D.**
*Professor*
Biology Department
Wake Forest University
Winston-Salem, North Carolina

**James Denbow, Ph.D.**
*Associate Professor*
Department of Anthropology
University of Texas at Austin
Austin, Texas

**Linda K. Gaul, Ph.D., MPH**
*Epidemiologist*
Department of State Health
  Services
Austin, Texas

**Herbert Grossman, Ph.D.**
*Associate Professor of Botany and
  Biology* (retired)
Biology
Pennsylvania State University
University Park, Pennsylvania

**William B. Guggino, Ph.D.**
*Professor of Physiology and
  Pediatrics*
Physiology Department
Johns Hopkins University School
  of Medicine
Baltimore, Maryland

**David Haig**
*Professor of Biology*
Organismic and Evolutionary
  Biology
Harvard University
Cambridge, Massachusetts

**John E. Hoover, Ph.D.**
*Professor of Biology*
Department of Biology
Millersville University
Millersville, Pennsylvania

**Joan E. N. Hudson, Ph.D.**
*Associate Professor of Biology*
Biological Sciences
Sam Houston State University
Huntsville, Texas

*(continued on p. 1127)*

# CONTENTS IN BRIEF

# CONTENTS

## UNIT 5   Ecology     356

## UNIT 6 Microbes, Protists, and Fungi 458

## UNIT 7  Plants                                                542

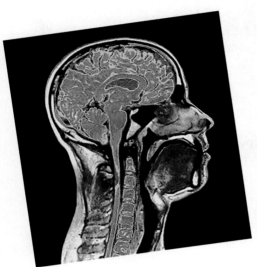

# LABS & ACTIVITIES

## Quick Labs

**Quick Labs provide hands-on experience, require few materials, and reinforce key concepts.**

## SCIENTIFIC AMERICAN PROJECT IDEAS

**Advanced project ideas from *Scientific American's* "Amateur Scientist" allow you to explore more on your own.**

# CHAPTER LABS

*Inquiry Labs* allow you to form hypotheses and draw conclusions based on your work.

*Exploration Labs* allow you to model a phenomenon.

*Skills Practice Labs* teach you lab skills used by biologists.

# FEATURE ARTICLES

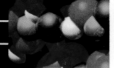

# internet connect

**Maintained by the National Science Teachers Association**

**The *SciLinks* topics below take you to more resources on the topic.**
**Go to *www.scilinks.org* and type in the keyword found on the pages indicated below.**

# HOW TO USE YOUR TEXTBOOK

## Your Roadmap for Success with *Modern Biology*

## Read for Meaning

Read the **Objectives** at the beginning of each section because they will tell you what you'll need to learn. **Vocabulary** terms are also listed for each section. Each Vocabulary term is highlighted in the text and defined in text and in the **Glossary** in the **Appendix.**

After reading each chapter, turn to the **Chapter Highlights** page and review the **key concepts,** which are brief summaries of the chapter's main ideas. You may want to do this even before you read the chapter.

**STUDY TIP** If you don't understand a definition, reread the page on which the term was introduced. The surrounding text should help make the definition easier to understand.

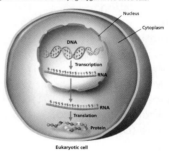

### SECTION 4

#### OBJECTIVES

- **Outline** the flow of genetic information in cells from DNA to protein.
- **Compare** the structure of RNA with that of DNA.
- **Summarize** the process of transcription.
- **Describe** the importance of the genetic code.
- **Compare** the role of mRNA, rRNA, and tRNA in translation.
- **Identify** the importance of learning about the human genome.

#### VOCABULARY

ribonucleic acid (RNA)
transcription
translation
protein synthesis
ribose
messenger RNA (mRNA)
ribosomal RNA (rRNA)
transfer RNA (tRNA)
RNA polymerase
promoter
termination signal
genetic code
codon
anticodon
genome

## PROTEIN SYNTHESIS

*Characteristics such as hair color are largely determined by genetic factors. But how does inheriting a particular form of a gene result in the appearance of a specific hair color? The structure of DNA helps explain how genes function in making proteins that determine traits in organisms.*

### FLOW OF GENETIC INFORMATION

A gene is a segment of DNA that is located on a chromosome and that codes for a hereditary character. For example, a gene in hair follicle cells determines a person's hair color. The gene directs the making of the protein called *melanin* (a pigment) through an intermediate—the nucleic acid called **ribonucleic acid,** or **RNA.**

Figure 10-12 summarizes the flow of genetic information in a eukaryotic cell. During **transcription,** DNA acts as a template for the synthesis of RNA. In **translation,** RNA directs the assembly of proteins. Forming proteins based on information in DNA and carried out by RNA is called **protein synthesis,** or gene expression. This central concept can be symbolized as *DNA* ➞ *RNA* ➞ *protein.* Proteins do important work in cells, such as protecting the body against infections and carrying oxygen in red blood cells.

**FIGURE 10-12**
DNA contains the instructions for building a protein. DNA transfers the instructions to an RNA molecule in a process called transcription. The RNA moves out into the cytoplasm, where its instructions are read and the protein is assembled in a process called *translation.*

Nucleus
Cytoplasm
DNA
Transcription
RNA
RNA
Translation
Protein
Eukaryotic cell

**204** CHAPTER 10

---

## Be Resourceful—Use the Web

**SciLinks** boxes in your textbook take you to resources that you can use for science projects, reports, and research papers. Go to **scilinks.org,** and type in the **SciLinks code** to get information on a topic.

**Visit go.hrw.com**
Find resources and reference materials that go with your textbook at **go.hrw.com.** Enter the keyword **HM6 Home** to access the home page for your textbook.

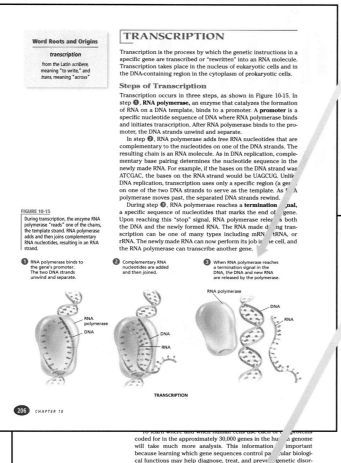

**Word Roots and Origins**

*transcription*

from the Latin *scribere*, meaning "to write," and *trans*, meaning "across"

# TRANSCRIPTION

Transcription is the process by which the genetic instructions in a specific gene are transcribed or "rewritten" into an RNA molecule. Transcription takes place in the nucleus of eukaryotic cells and in the DNA-containing region in the cytoplasm of prokaryotic cells.

## Steps of Transcription

Transcription occurs in three steps, as shown in Figure 10-15. In step ❶, **RNA polymerase**, an enzyme that catalyzes the formation of RNA on a DNA template, binds to a promoter. A **promoter** is a specific nucleotide sequence of DNA where RNA polymerase binds and initiates transcription. After RNA polymerase binds to the promoter, the DNA strands unwind and separate.

In step ❷, RNA polymerase adds free RNA nucleotides that are complementary to the nucleotides on one of the DNA strands. The resulting chain is an RNA molecule. As in DNA replication, complementary base pairing determines the nucleotide sequence in the newly made RNA. For example, if the bases on the DNA strand was ATCGAC, the bases on the RNA strand would be UAGCUG. Unlike DNA replication, transcription uses only a specific region (a gene) on one of the two DNA strands to serve as the template. As RNA polymerase moves past, the separated DNA strands rewind.

During step ❸, RNA polymerase reaches a **termination signal,** a specific sequence of nucleotides that marks the end of a gene. Upon reaching this "stop" signal, RNA polymerase releases both the DNA and the newly formed RNA. The RNA made during transcription can be one of many types including mRNA, tRNA, or rRNA. The newly made RNA can now perform its job in the cell, and the RNA polymerase can transcribe another gene.

**FIGURE 10-15**
During transcription, the enzyme RNA polymerase "reads" one of the chains, the template strand. RNA polymerase adds and then joins complementary RNA nucleotides, resulting in an RNA strand.

❶ RNA polymerase binds to the gene's promoter. The two DNA strands unwind and separate.

❷ Complementary RNA nucleotides are added and then joined.

❸ When RNA polymerase reaches a termination signal in the DNA, the DNA and new RNA are released by the polymerase.

RNA polymerase

DNA

RNA

RNA polymerase

DNA

DNA

RNA

**TRANSCRIPTION**

206 CHAPTER 10

To learn where and when human cells use each of the proteins coded for in the approximately 30,000 genes in the human genome will take much more analysis. This information is important because learning which gene sequences control particular biological functions may help diagnose, treat, and prevent genetic disorders, cancer, and infectious diseases in the future.

### SECTION 4 REVIEW

1. Summarize the flow of genetic information.

2. List the four ways in which the structure of RNA differs from that of DNA.

3. Describe the structure and function of each of the three types of RNA.

4. Sequence the main steps of transcription.

5. What is the genetic code?

6. Compare the roles of the three different types of RNA during translation.

7. Describe the significance of identifying the entire sequence of the human genome.

**CRITICAL THINKING**

8. **Making Comparisons** How does the role of RNA polymerase in transcription differ from that of DNA polymerase in DNA replication?

9. **Applying Information** What amino acids would translation of the mRNA with the sequence UAACAAGGAGCAUCC produce?

10. **Analyzing Processes** Discuss why it is important which of the two DNA strands serves as a template during transcription.

11. **Drawing Conclusions** How does the structure of tRNA relate to its function in translation?

210 CHAPTER 10

# Use the Illustrations and Photos

Art shows complex ideas and processes. Learn to analyze the art so that you better understand the material in the text.

Tables and graphs display important information in an organized way to help you see relationships.

A picture is worth a thousand words. Look at the photographs to see relevant examples of science concepts that you are reading about.

# Prepare for Tests

**Section Reviews** and **Chapter Reviews** test your knowledge of the main points of the chapter. **Critical Thinking** items challenge you to think about the material in different ways and in greater depth. The **Standardized Test Preparation** that is located after each Chapter Review helps you sharpen your test-taking abilities.

**STUDY TIP** Reread the Objectives and Chapter Highlights when studying for a test to be sure you know the material.

# Use the Appendix

The **Appendix** contains a variety of resources designed to enhance your learning experience. These resources include **Using a Compound Light Microscope, Using SI Units for Measurement,** and **Analyzing Word Parts.** The Appendix also contains reference materials that will be useful in your exploration of biology, such as **Biologist's Guide to the Periodic Table, Classification,** and **Geologic Time Scale.**

**Visit Holt Online Learning**
If your teacher gives you a special password to log onto the **Holt Online Learning** site, you'll find your complete textbook on the Web. In addition, you'll find some great learning tools and practice quizzes. You'll be able to see how well you know the material from your textbook.

For advanced-level project ideas from *Scientific American,* visit **go.hrw.com** and type in the keyword **HM6SAX.**

# FOUNDATIONS OF BIOLOGY

66 *Our ideas are only instruments which we use to break into phenomena; we must change them when they have served their purpose, as we change a blunt lancet that we have used long enough.* 99

Claude Bernard

*Organisms living in this taiga ecosystem are adapted to dry, cold weather and to reduced availability of food in winter.*

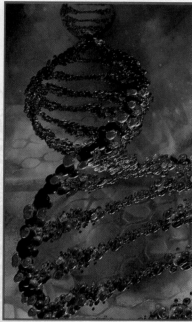

DNA is responsible for transmitting genetic information to offspring.

This giant panda gets its energy by eating bamboo leaves. The Amazon water lily, above left, lives in shallow eutrophic ponds.

Red-eyed tree frog

# THE SCIENCE OF LIFE

Snowy owls are keen hunters that live in Arctic forests and on open tundra. These juveniles of the species *Nyctea scandiaca* hatched on a flower-filled alpine meadow.

# THE WORLD OF BIOLOGY

*O*wls, such as the young snowy owls on the previous page, have for centuries been symbols of both wisdom and mystery. To many cultures their piercing eyes have conveyed a look of intelligence. Their silent flight through darkened landscapes in search of prey has projected an air of power or wonder. For this chapter and this book, owls are an engaging example of a living organism from the world of biology—the study of life.

## BIOLOGY AND YOU

Living in a small town, in the country, or at the edge of the suburbs, one may be lucky enough to hear an owl's hooting. This experience can lead to questions about where the bird lives, what it hunts, and how it finds its prey on dark, moonless nights. **Biology,** or the study of life, offers an organized and scientific framework for posing and answering such questions about the natural world. Biologists study questions about how living things work, how they interact with the environment, and how they change over time. Biologists study many different kinds of living things ranging from tiny organisms, such as bacteria, to very large organisms, such as elephants.

Each day, biologists investigate subjects that affect you and the way you live. For example, biologists determine which foods are healthy. As shown in Figure 1-1, everyone is affected by this important topic. Biologists also study how much a person should exercise and how one can avoid getting sick. Biologists also study what your air, land, and food supply will be like in the near future.

### OBJECTIVES

- **Relate** the relevance of biology to a person's daily life.
- **Describe** the importance of biology in human society.
- **List** the characteristics of living things.
- **Summarize** the hierarchy of organization within complex multicellular organisms.
- **Distinguish** between homeostasis and metabolism and between growth, development, and reproduction.

### VOCABULARY

**biology**
**organization**
**cell**
**unicellular**
**multicellular**
**organ**
**tissue**
**organelle**
**biological molecule**
**homeostasis**
**metabolism**
**cell division**
**development**
**reproduction**
**gene**

**FIGURE 1-1**

Biology, the study of life, directly applies to your health, life, and future in ways as simple as daily food choices.

## Biology and Society

By studying biology you can make informed decisions on issues that impact you and our society. Every day newspapers, television, and the Internet contain issues that relate to biology. For example, you may read that your local water or air supply is polluted. How will that pollution affect your health and the health of other living things? You may hear about new technologies or tools that biologists have invented. How will we control how those technologies and tools are used? Biologists actively work to solve these and other real-world issues and problems, including improving our food supply, curing diseases and preserving our environment.

# CHARACTERISTICS OF LIFE

The world is filled with familiar objects, such as tables, rocks, plants, pets, and automobiles. Which of these objects are living or were once living? What are the criteria for assigning something to the living world or the nonliving world? Biologists have established that living things share seven characteristics of life. These characteristics are organization and the presence of one or more cells, response to a stimulus (plural, *stimuli*), homeostasis, metabolism, growth and development, reproduction, and change through time.

## Organization and Cells

**Organization** is the high degree of order within an organism's internal and external parts and in its interactions with the living world. For example, compare an owl to a rock. The rock has a specific shape, but that shape is usually irregular. Furthermore, different rocks, even rocks of the same type, are likely to have different shapes and sizes. In contrast, the owl is an amazingly organized individual, as shown in Figure 1-2. Owls of the same species have the same body parts arranged in nearly the same way and interact with the environment in the same way.

**FIGURE 1-2**

Every living organism has a level of organization. The different levels of organization for a complex multicellular organism, such as an owl, are shown in the figure below.

**ORGANISM**
(Barn Owl)

**ORGAN**
(Owl's Ear)

**TISSUE**
(Nervous Tissue Within the Ear)

**CELL**
(Nerve Cell)

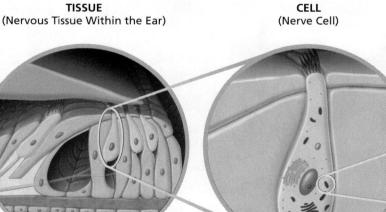

All living organisms, whether made up of one cell or many cells, have some degree of organization. A **cell** is the smallest unit that can perform all life's processes. Some organisms, such as bacteria, are made up of one cell and are called **unicellular** (YOON-uh-SEL-yoo-luhr) organisms. Other organisms, such as humans or trees, are made up of multiple cells and are called **multicellular** (MUHL-ti-SEL-yoo-luhr) organisms. Complex multicellular organisms have the level of organization shown in Figure 1-2. In the highest level, the organism is made up of *organ systems,* or groups of specialized parts that carry out a certain function in the organism. For example, an owl's nervous system is made up of a brain, sense organs, nerve cells, and other parts that sense and respond to the owl's surroundings.

Organ systems are made up of organs. **Organs** are structures that carry out specialized jobs within an organ system. An owl's ear is an organ that allows the owl to hear. All organs are made up of tissues. **Tissues** are groups of cells that have similar abilities and that allow the organ to function. For example, nervous tissue in the ear allows the ear to detect sound. Tissues are made up of cells. A cell must be covered by a membrane, contain all genetic information necessary for replication, and be able to carry out all cell functions.

Within each cell are organelles. **Organelles** are tiny structures that carry out functions necessary for the cell to stay alive. Organelles contain **biological molecules,** the chemical compounds that provide physical structure and that bring about movement, energy use, and other cellular functions. All biological molecules are made up of *atoms.* Atoms are the simplest particle of an element that retains all the properties of a certain element.

## Response to Stimuli

Another characteristic of life is that an organism can respond to a *stimulus*—a physical or chemical change in the internal or external environment. For example, an owl dilates its pupils to keep the level of light entering the eye constant. Organisms must be able to respond and react to changes in their environment to stay alive.

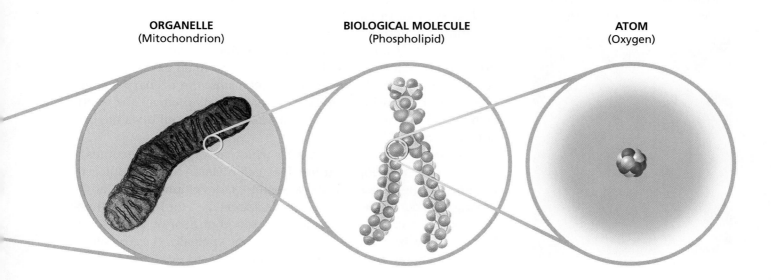

**ORGANELLE**
(Mitochondrion)

**BIOLOGICAL MOLECULE**
(Phospholipid)

**ATOM**
(Oxygen)

## Quick Lab

### Observing Homeostasis

**Materials** 500 mL beakers (3), wax pen, tap water, thermometer, ice, hot water, goldfish, small dip net, watch or clock with a second hand

**Procedure**

1. Use a wax pen to label three 500 mL beakers as follows: 27°C (80°F), 20°C (68°F), 10°C (50°F). Put 250 mL of tap water in each beaker. Use hot water or ice to adjust the temperature of the water in each beaker to match the temperature on the label.

2. Put the goldfish in the beaker of 27°C water. Record the number of times the gills move in 1 minute.

3. Move the goldfish to the beaker of 20°C water. Repeat observations. Move the goldfish to the beaker of 10°C. Repeat observations.

**Analysis** What happens to the rate at which gills move when the temperature changes? Why? How do gills help fish maintain homeostasis?

**FIGURE 1-3**

This unicellular organism, *Escherichia coli,* inhabits the human intestines. *E. coli* reproduces by means of cell division, during which the original cell splits into two identical offspring cells.

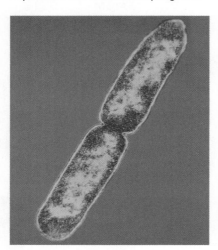

## Homeostasis

All living things, from single cells to entire organisms, have mechanisms that allow them to maintain stable internal conditions. Without these mechanisms, organisms can die. For example, a cell's water content is closely controlled by the taking in or releasing of water. A cell that takes in too much water will rupture and die. A cell that doesn't get enough water will also shrivel and die.

**Homeostasis** (HOH-mee-OH-STAY-sis) is the maintenance of a stable level of internal conditions even though environmental conditions are constantly changing. Organisms have regulatory systems that maintain internal conditions, such as temperature, water content, and uptake of nutrients by the cell. In fact, multicellular organisms usually have more than one way of maintaining important aspects of their internal environment. For example, an owl's temperature is maintained at about 40°C (104°F). To keep a constant temperature, an owl's cells burn fuel to produce body heat. In addition, an owl's feathers can fluff up in cold weather. In this way, they trap an insulating layer of air next to the bird's body to maintain its body temperature.

## Metabolism

Living organisms use energy to power all the life processes, such as repair, movement, and growth. This energy use depends on metabolism (muh-TAB-uh-LIZ-uhm). **Metabolism** is the sum of all the chemical reactions that take in and transform energy and materials from the environment. For example, plants, algae, and some bacteria use the sun's energy to generate sugar molecules during a process called *photosynthesis*. Some organisms depend on obtaining food energy from other organisms. For instance, an owl's metabolism allows the owl to extract and modify the chemicals trapped in its nightly prey and use them as energy to fuel activities and growth.

## Growth and Development

All living things grow and increase in size. Some nonliving things, such as crystals or icicles, grow by accumulating more of the same material of which they are made. In contrast, the growth of living things results from the division and enlargement of cells. **Cell division** is the formation of two new cells from an existing cell, as shown in Figure 1-3. In unicellular organisms, the primary change that occurs following cell division is cell enlargement. In multicellular life, however, organisms mature through cell division, cell enlargement, and development.

**Development** is the process by which an organism becomes a mature adult. Development involves cell division and cell differentiation, or specialization. As a result of development, an adult organism is composed of many cells specialized for different functions, such as carrying oxygen in the blood or hearing. In fact, the human body is composed of trillions of specialized cells, all of which originated from a single cell, the fertilized egg.

## Reproduction

All organisms produce new organisms like themselves in a process called **reproduction.** Reproduction, unlike other characteristics, is not essential to the survival of an individual organism. However, because no organism lives forever, reproduction is essential for the continuation of a species. Glass frogs, as shown in Figure 1-4, lay many eggs in their lifetime. However, only a few of the frogs' off-spring reach adulthood and successfully reproduce.

During reproduction, organisms transmit hereditary information to their offspring. Hereditary information is encoded in a large molecule called *deoxyribonucleic acid,* or *DNA*. A short segment of DNA that contains the instructions for a single trait of an organism is called a **gene.** DNA is like a large library. It contains all the books—genes—that the cell will ever need for making all the structures and chemicals necessary for life.

Hereditary information is transferred to offspring during two kinds of reproduction. In *sexual reproduction,* hereditary information recombines from two organisms of the same species. The resulting offspring are similar but not identical to their parents. For example, a male frog's sperm can fertilize a female's egg and form a single fertilized egg cell. The fertilized egg then develops into a new frog.

In *asexual reproduction,* hereditary information from different organisms is not combined; thus the original organism and the new organism are genetically the same. A bacterium, for example, reproduces asexually when it splits into two identical cells.

**FIGURE 1-4**

Like many animal species, this glass frog, *Centrolenella* sp., produces and lays a large number of eggs. However, a high percentage of these eggs die. In contrast, the offspring of animals that give birth to just a few live offspring typically have a high rate of survival.

## Change Through Time

Although individual organisms experience many changes during their lifetime, their basic genetic characteristics do not change. However, populations of living organisms *evolve* or change through time. The ability of populations of organisms to change over time is important for survival in a changing world. This factor is also important in explaining the diversity of life-forms we see on Earth today.

---

## SECTION 1 REVIEW

1. How does biology affect a person's daily life?

2. How does biology affect society?

3. Name the characteristics shared by living things.

4. Summarize the hierarchy of organization found in complex multicellular organisms.

5. What are the different functions of homeostasis and metabolism in living organisms?

6. How does the growth among living and nonliving things differ?

7. Why is reproduction an important characteristic of life?

**CRITICAL THINKING**

8. **Applying Information** Crystals of salt grow and are highly organized. Why don't biologists consider them to be alive?

9. **Analyzing Models** When a scientist designs a space probe to detect life on a distant planet, what kinds of things should it measure?

10. **Making Comparisons** Both cells and organisms share the characteristics of life. How are cells and organisms different?

- **Identify** three important themes that help explain the living world.
- **Explain** how life can be diverse, yet unified.
- **Describe** how living organisms are interdependent.
- **Summarize** why evolution is an important theme in biology.

## VOCABULARY

domain
kingdom
ecology
ecosystem
evolution
natural selection
adaptation

# THEMES IN BIOLOGY

*A* snowy owl, with all its beauty and complexity, is just one species among the millions of species on Earth. How can one understand so many different living organisms? Important unifying themes help explain the living world and are part of biology. These themes are found within this book and include the diversity and unity of life, the interdependence of living organisms, and the evolution of life.

## DIVERSITY AND UNITY OF LIFE

The *diversity,* or variety, of life, is amazing. For example, there are single-celled organisms that thrive inside thick Antarctic ice that never thaws. There are whales that contain about 1,000 trillion cells that can easily cruise the Pacific and migrate each year from Alaska to Mexico. There are even plants that can capture and eat insects. Biologists have identified more than 1.5 million species on Earth. And there may be many more species that remain to be identified.

### Unity in the Diversity of Life

Life is so diverse, yet life is also characterized by *unity,* or features that all living things have in common. One feature is the *genetic code,* the rules that govern how cells use the hereditary information in DNA. Another unifying feature is the presence of organelles that carry out all cellular activities.

The "tree of life" shown in Figure 1-5 is a model of the relationships by ancestry among organisms. All living things share certain genes, yet no two types of organisms have the same full sets of genes. One way biologists build a "tree of life" is to place organisms that have more similar sets of genes on closer branches, or *lineages,* of the "tree." They place the more distantly related organisms on more distant branches. The placement of all kinds of organisms produces a "tree" that relates and unites life's diversity.

**FIGURE 1-5**

This "tree of life," is a model of the relationships by ancestry among all major groups of organisms. The model is based on comparisons of organisms' characteristics, including body structures and genetic information. For updates on such "trees," visit **go.hrw.com** and enter the keyword **HM6 Phylo.**

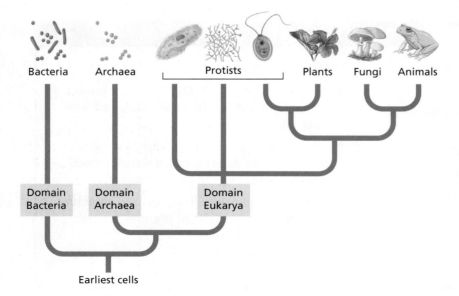

Bacteria    Archaea    Protists    Plants    Fungi    Animals

Domain Bacteria    Domain Archaea    Domain Eukarya

Earliest cells

So, how does the "tree of life" represent the unity in the diversity of life? Scientists think that all living things have descended with modification from a single common ancestor. Thus, all of life is connected. Yet, there are many different lineages representing different species. This diversity stems from the fact that genetic changes accumulate over the years. Also, organisms change as they become suited to their own special environments.

## Three Domains of Life

Notice in Figure 1-5 that the "tree" has three main branches. Biologists call these major subdivisions of all organisms **domains.** The three domains are Bacteria, Archaea, and Eukarya. Bacteria and Archaea have less complex cells than those of Eukarya. Later chapters describe these domains in more detail. Notice that the largest and most familiar organisms, the animals, plants, and fungi, occupy parts of the Eukarya branch of the "tree."

Another system of grouping organisms divides all life into six major categories called **kingdoms.** The six kingdoms consist of four kingdoms within the domain Eukarya (the Kingdoms Animalia, Plantae, Fungi, and Protista), one kingdom in the domain Archaea (Kingdom Archaea) and one kingdom in the domain Bacteria (Kingdom Bacteria). Many biologists recognize these six kingdoms and three domains, but some biologists use other systems of grouping.

**Word Roots and Origins**

*ecosystem*

from the Greek word, *eco,* meaning "house," and *system,* meaning "ordered parts in a whole"

# INTERDEPENDENCE OF ORGANISMS

Organisms interact with each other throughout the living world. **Ecology** is the branch of biology that studies organisms interacting with each other and with the environment. Ecologists study single species as well as ecosystems (EK-oh-SIS-tuhmz). **Ecosystems** are communities of living species and their physical environments. Such studies reveal that organisms depend on each other as well as on minerals, nutrients, water, gases, heat, and other elements of their physical surroundings. For example, a panther eats a bird, which eats nuts from trees. The tree needs carbon dioxide and water. Carbon dioxide is a main byproduct of all animals.

Scientists now recognize the huge effect that humans have had on the world's environment. For millions of years, tropical rain forests, as shown in Figure 1-6, have existed as stable—but fragile—environments. These forests play a vital role in the global environment. Humans have cleared vast areas of these forests in recent years. The destruction of these forests, in addition to other ecological changes in other regions, could impact all life on Earth.

**FIGURE 1-6**

Tropical rain forests, such as this one in the Amazon River basin in Ecuador, support an extraordinary variety and number of plants and animals, which are all on top of a very thin layer of fertile topsoil.

# EVOLUTION OF LIFE

Individual organisms change during their lifetime, but their basic genetic characteristics do not change. However, populations of living organisms do change through time, or evolve. **Evolution,** or descent with modification, is the process in which the inherited characteristics within populations change over generations, such that genetically distinct populations and new species can develop.

Evolution as a theme in biology helps us understand how the various branches of the "tree of life" came into existence and have changed over time. It also explains how organisms alive today are related to those that lived in the past. Finally, it helps us understand the mechanisms that underlie the way organisms look and behave.

## Natural Selection

The ability of populations of organisms to change over time is important for survival in a changing world. According to the theory of evolution by **natural selection,** organisms that have certain favorable traits are better able to survive and reproduce successfully than organisms that lack these traits.

One product of natural selection is the adaptation of organisms to their environment. **Adaptations** are traits that improve an individual's ability to survive and reproduce. For example, rabbits with white fur and short ears in a snowy place, such as the one in Figure 1-7a, may avoid predators and frostbitten ears more often than those with dark fur and long ears. Thus, the next generation of rabbits will have a greater percentage of animals carrying the genes for white fur and short ears. In contrast, the brown, long-eared rabbit, as shown in Figure 1-7b, would survive and reproduce more successfully in a hot desert environment.

The survival and reproductive success of organisms with favorable traits cause a change in populations of organisms over generations. This descent with modification is an important factor in explaining the diversity of organisms we see on Earth today.

(a)

(b)

**FIGURE 1-7**

(a) This short-eared arctic hare, *Lepus arcticus,* is hidden from predators and protected from frostbite in a snowy environment. (b) The mottled brown coats of desert rabbits blend in with the dirt and dry grasses, and their long ears help them radiate excess heat and thus avoid overheating.

## SECTION 2 REVIEW

1. Name three unifying themes found in biology.

2. How is the unity and diversity in the living world represented?

3. Identify the three domains and the kingdoms found in each domain.

4. How are organisms interdependent?

5. Describe why evolution is important in explaining the diversity of life.

6. Distinguish between evolution and natural selection.

**CRITICAL THINKING**

7. **Applying Information** Assign the various toppings you put on pizza to the appropriate domains and kingdoms of life.

8. **Analyzing Graphics** According to the "tree" in Figure 1-5, which of these pairs are more closely related: Archaea:Bacteria or Archaea:Eukarya?

9. **Making Hypotheses** Fossil evidence shows that bats descended from shrewlike organisms that could not fly. Write a hypothesis for how natural selection might have led to flying bats.

# THE STUDY OF BIOLOGY

*Curiosity leads us to ask questions about life. Science provides a way of answering such questions about the natural world. Science is a systematic method that involves forming and testing hypotheses. More importantly, science relies on evidence, not beliefs, for drawing conclusions.*

## SECTION 3

### OBJECTIVES

- **Outline** the main steps in the scientific method.
- **Summarize** how observations are used to form hypotheses.
- **List** the elements of a controlled experiment.
- **Describe** how scientists use data to draw conclusions.
- **Compare** a scientific hypothesis and a scientific theory.
- **State** how communication in science helps prevent dishonesty and bias.

### VOCABULARY

**scientific method**
**observation**
**hypothesis**
**prediction**
**experiment**
**control group**
**experimental group**
**independent variable**
**dependent variable**
**theory**
**peer review**

## SCIENCE AS A PROCESS

Science is characterized by an organized approach, called the **scientific method,** to learn how the natural world works. The methods of science are based on two important principles. The first principle is that events in the natural world have natural causes. For example, the ancient Greeks believed that lightning and thunder occurred because a supernatural god Zeus hurled thunderbolts from the heavens. By contrast, a scientist considers lightning and thunder to result from electric charges in the atmosphere. When trying to solve a puzzle from nature, all scientists, such as the one in Figure 1-8, accept that there is a natural cause to solve that puzzle.

A second principle of science is uniformity. *Uniformity* is the idea that the fundamental laws of nature operate the same way at all places and at all times. For example, scientists assume that the law of gravity works the same way on Mars as it does on Earth.

### Steps of the Scientific Method

Although there is no single method for doing science, scientific studies involve a series of common steps.

1. The process of science begins with an observation. An **observation** is the act of perceiving a natural occurrence that causes someone to pose a question.
2. One tries to answer the question by forming hypotheses (singular, *hypothesis*). A **hypothesis** is a proposed explanation for the way a particular aspect of the natural world functions.
3. A **prediction** is a statement that forecasts what would happen in a test situation if the hypothesis were true. A prediction is recorded for each hypothesis.
4. An **experiment** is used to test a hypothesis and its predictions.
5. Once the experiment has been concluded, the data are analyzed and used to draw conclusions.
6. After the data have been analyzed, the data and conclusions are communicated to scientific peers and to the public. This way others can verify, reject, or modify the researcher's conclusions.

**FIGURE 1-8**

All researchers, such as the one releasing an owl above, use the scientific method to answer the questions they have about nature.

# OBSERVING AND ASKING QUESTIONS

The scientific method generally begins with an unexplained observation about nature. For example, people have noticed for thousands of years that owls can catch prey in near total darkness. As shown in steps ❶ and ❷ of Figure 1-9, an observation may then raise questions. The owl observation raises the question: How does an owl detect prey in the dark?

# FORMING A HYPOTHESIS

After stating a question, a biologist lists possible answers to a scientific question—hypotheses. Good hypotheses answer a question and are testable in the natural world. For example, as shown in step ❸ Figure 1-9, there are several possible hypotheses for the question of how owls hunt at night: (a) owls hunt by keen vision in the dark; (b) owls hunt by superb hearing; or (c) owls hunt by detecting the prey's body heat.

## Predicting

To test a hypothesis, scientists make a prediction that logically follows from the hypothesis. A prediction is what is expected to happen if each hypothesis were true. For example, if hypothesis (a) is true, (owls hunt by keen night vision) then one can predict that the owl will pounce only on the mouse in either a light or a dark room. If hypothesis (b) is true (owls hunt by hearing), then one can predict that in a lighted room, the owl will pounce closer to the mouse's head. But, in a dark room, the owl should pounce closer to a rustling leaf attached to the mouse. Finally, if hypothesis (c) is true (owls hunt by sensing body heat), then an owl would strike only the prey no matter the room conditions, because owls hunt by detecting the prey's body heat.

**FIGURE 1-9**

A scientific study includes observations, questions, hypotheses, predictions, experiments, data analysis, and conclusions. A biologist can use the scientific method to set up an experiment to learn how an owl captures prey at night.

❶ **OBSERVATION**
Owls capture prey on dark nights.

❷ **QUESTION**
How do owls detect prey on dark nights?

❸ **HYPOTHESES**

a) Owls hunt in the dark by vision.

b) Owls hunt in the dark by hearing.

c) Owls hunt in the dark by sensing body heat.

Notice that these predictions make it difficult to distinguish between the vision and body heat hypotheses. The reason is that both hypotheses predict that the owl could grab the mouse in a dark room. Also, these three hypotheses do not eliminate all other factors that could influence how the owl finds its prey. However, testing predictions can allow one to begin rejecting hypotheses and thus to get closer to determining the answer(s) to a question.

# DESIGNING AN EXPERIMENT

Biologists often test hypotheses by setting up an experiment. Step ❹ in Figure 1-9 outlines an experiment to test the hypotheses about how an owl hunts at night. First, experimenters set up a room with an owl perch high on one side and a small trap door on the other side for releasing mice. Then, they tied a leaf to each mouse's tail with a string and released each mouse into the room. Next, each mouse ran silently across the room, but the leaf trailed behind, making a rustling noise. During half of the trials, the lights were on. During the other half, the room was dark. Technicians videotaped all the action in the chamber with an infrared light, which owls cannot see. The researchers then viewed the videos and measured the position of the owl's strike relative to each mouse's head.

## Performing the Experiment

Many scientists use a controlled experiment to test their hypotheses. A *controlled experiment* compares an experimental group and a control group and only has one variable. The **control group** provides a normal standard against which the biologist can compare results of the experimental group. The **experimental group** is identical to the control group except for one factor, the **independent variable.** The experimenter manipulates the independent variable, sometimes called the *manipulated variable.*

❹ **EXPERIMENT**

Test predictions of the three hypotheses.

**Control:** In the light    **Experimental:** In the dark

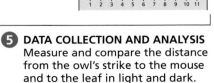

❺ **DATA COLLECTION AND ANALYSIS**
Measure and compare the distance from the owl's strike to the mouse and to the leaf in light and dark.

❻ **CONCLUSION**
Data supported the hearing hypothesis: Owls hunt in the dark by hearing.

The independent variable in the owl experiment is the presence or absence of light. In the owl experiment, the control group hunts in the light, and the experimental group hunts in the dark. In addition to varying the independent variable, a scientist observes or measures another factor called the **dependent variable,** or *responding variable,* because it is affected by the independent variable. In the owl experiment, the dependent variable is distance from the owl's strike to the mouse's head.

### Testing the Experiment

Some controlled experiments are conducted "blind." In other words, the biologist who scores the results is unaware of whether a given subject is part of the experimental or control group. This factor helps eliminate experimenter bias. Experiments should also be repeated, because living systems are variable. Moreover, scientists must collect enough data to find meaningful results.

# COLLECTING AND ANALYZING DATA

Most experiments measure a variable—the dependent variable. This measurement provides *quantitative data,* data measured in numbers. For example, in the experiment above, scientists measured the distance of an owl's strike from the prey's head in centimeters, as shown in step **5** of Figure 1-9. An event's duration in milliseconds is also an example of quantitative data.

Biologists usually score the results of an experiment by using one of their senses. They might see or hear the results of an experiment. Scientists also extend their senses with a microscope for tiny objects or a microphone for soft sounds. In the owl experiment, biologists extended their vision with infrared cameras.

### Analyzing and Comparing Data

After collecting data from a field study or an experiment and then organizing it, biologists then analyze the data. In analyzing data, the goal is to determine whether the data are reliable, and whether they support or fail to support the predictions of the hypothesis. To do so, scientists may use statistics to help determine relationships between the variables involved.

They can then compare their data with other data that were obtained in other similar studies. It is also important at this time to determine possible sources of error in the experiment just performed. Scientists usually display their data in tables or graphs when analyzing it. For the owl study, biologists could have made a bar graph such as the one in Figure 1-10, which shows the average distance from the owl's strike relative to the mouse's head or the leaf in the light and in the dark.

**FIGURE 1-10**

The data below are hypothetical results that might occur from the described owl experiment. The independent variable is the darkness of the room, and the dependent variable is how far the owl struck from the mouse's head. The data show that the owl strikes more accurately at the mouse in the light but strikes more accurately at the leaf in the dark.

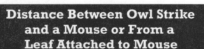

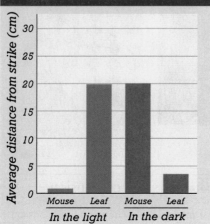

# DRAWING CONCLUSIONS

Biologists analyze their tables, graphs, and charts to draw conclusions about whether or not a hypothesis is supported, as shown in step ❻ of Figure 1-9. The hypothetical owl data show that in the light, owls struck with greater accuracy at the mouse than at the leaf, but in the dark, owls struck with greater accuracy at the leaf than the mouse. Thus, the findings support the hearing hypothesis, but not the vision hypothesis.

An experiment can only disprove, not prove, a hypothesis. For example, one cannot conclude from the results that the hearing hypothesis is *proven* to be true. Perhaps the owl uses an unknown smell to strike at the mouse. One can only reject the vision hypothesis because it did not predict the results of the experiment correctly.

Acceptance of a hypothesis is always tentative in science. The scientific community revises its understanding of phenomena, based on new data. Having ruled out one hypothesis, a biologist will devise more tests to try to rule out any remaining hypotheses.

## Making Inferences

Scientists often draw inferences from data gathered during a field study or experiment. An *inference* (IN-fuhr-uhns) is a conclusion made on the basis of facts and previous knowledge rather than on direct observations. Unlike a hypothesis, an inference is not directly testable. In the owl study, it is inferred that the owl detects prey from a distance rather than by direct touch.

## Applying Results and Building Models

As shown in Figure 1-11, scientists often apply their findings to solve practical problems. They also build models to represent or describe things. For example in 1953, James Watson and Francis Crick used cardboard balls and wire bars to build physical models of atoms in an attempt to understand the structure of DNA. Mathematical models are sets of equations that describe how different measurable items interact in a system. The experimenter can adjust variables to better model the real-world data.

**FIGURE 1-11**

Biologists often apply their knowledge of the natural world to practical problems. Studies on the owl's keen ability to locate sounds in space despite background noise are helping biotechnologists and bioengineers develop better solutions for people with impaired hearing, such as the people shown in this picture.

# CONSTRUCTING A THEORY

When a set of related hypotheses is confirmed to be true many times, and it can explain a great amount of data, scientists often reclassify it as a **theory.** Some examples include the quantum theory, the cell theory, or the theory of evolution. People commonly use the word "theory" in a different way than scientists use the word. People may say "It's just a theory" suggesting that an idea is untested, but scientists view a theory as a highly tested, generally accepted principle that explains a vast number of observations and experimental data.

# COMMUNICATING IDEAS

An essential aspect of scientific research is scientists working together. Scientists often work together in research teams or simply share research results with other scientists. This is done by publishing findings in scientific journals or presenting them at scientific meetings, as shown in Figure 1-12. Sharing information allows others working independently to verify findings or to continue work on established results. For example, Roger Payne published the results of his owl experiments in a journal in 1971. Then, other biologists could repeat it for verification or use it to study the mechanisms introduced by the paper. With the growing importance of science in solving societal issues, it is becoming increasingly vital for scientists to be able to communicate with the public at large.

## Publishing a Paper

Scientists submit research papers to scientific journals for publication. A typical research paper has four sections. First, the *Introduction* poses the problem and hypotheses to be investigated. Next, the *Materials and Methods* describe how researchers proceeded with the experiment. Third, the *Results* state the findings the experiment presented, and finally, the *Discussion* gives the significance of the experiment and future directions the scientists will take.

## Careers in BIOLOGY

# Forensic Biologist

**Job Description** Forensic biologists are scientists who study biological materials to investigate potential crimes and other legal issues against humans and animals. Forensic scientists have knowledge in areas of biology, such as DNA and blood pattern analysis, and work in private sector and public laboratories.

**Focus On a Forensic Biologist**
As a law enforcement forensic specialist for the Texas Parks and Wildlife Department, Beverly Villarreal assists the game warden in investigations of fish and wildlife violations, such as illegal hunting and fishing. Villarreal analyzes blood and tissue samples to identify species of animals such as fish, birds, and reptiles. Her work helps game wardens as they enforce state laws regarding hunting and fishing. Most people think of forensic scientists as the glamorous crime investigators on TV, but according to Villarreal real forensic scientists "spend a great deal of time at a lab bench running analysis after analysis." Many of the methods used in animal forensics, such as DNA sequencing, are also used in human forensics.

**Education and Skills**
- **High school**—three years of science courses and four years of math courses.

- **College**—bachelor of science in biology, including course work in zoology and genetics, plus experience in performing DNA analyses.
- **Skills**—patience, attention to detail, and ability to use fine tools.

For more about careers, visit **go.hrw.com** and type in the keyword **HM6 Careers.**

After scientists submit their papers to a scientific journal, the editors of that journal will send the paper out for peer review. In a **peer review,** scientists who are experts in the field anonymously read and critique that research paper. They determine if a paper provides enough information so that the experiment can be duplicated and if the author used good experimental controls and reached an accurate conclusion. They also check if the paper is written clearly enough for broad understanding. Careful analysis of each other's research by fellow scientists is essential to making scientific progress and preventing scientific dishonesty.

**FIGURE 1-12**

Scientists present their experiments in various forms. The scientists above are presenting their work in the form of a poster at a scientific meeting.

# HONESTY AND BIAS

The scientific community depends on both honesty and good science. While designing new studies, experimenters must be very careful to prevent previous ideas and biases from tainting both the experimental process and the conclusions. Scientists have to keep in mind that they are always trying to disprove their favorite ideas. Scientists repeat experiments to verify previous findings. This allows for science to have a method for self-correction and it also keeps researchers honest and credible to their peers in the field.

## Conflict of Interest

For most scientists, maintaining a good reputation for collecting and presenting valid data is more important than temporary prestige or income. So, scientists try to avoid any potential conflicts of interest. For example, a scientist who owns a biotechnology company and manufactures a drug would not be the best researcher to critically test that drug's safety and effectiveness. To avoid this potential conflict of interest, the scientist allows an unaffected party, such as a research group, to test the drug's effectiveness. The threat of a potential scandal based on misleading data or conclusions is a powerful force in science that helps keep scientists honest and fair.

## SECTION 3 REVIEW

1. What two principles make the scientific method a unique process?

2. Define the roles of observations and hypotheses in science.

3. Summarize the parts of a controlled experiment.

4. Summarize how we make conclusions about the results of an experiment.

5. Why is the phrase, "it's just a theory" misleading?

6. Give another example of a conflict of interest.

**CRITICAL THINKING**

7. **Making Hypotheses** On a nocturnal owl's skull, one ear points up, and the other ear points down. Suggest a hypothesis for this observation.

8. **Designing Experiments** Design an experiment to establish if owls hunt by keen sight or hunt by heat seeking.

9. **Calculating Information** What was the average distance between the owl's strike and the mouse if the recorded differences in this experiment were 25, 22, 19, 19, and 15?

# SCIENCE ON THE INTERNET: A New Information Age

In the past, students researching a science topic would typically begin their research by visiting a library to use printed reference materials, such as encyclopedias. Today, most students research topics by using a computer and searching for information on the Internet.

The Internet can provide students with a wealth of information. But which Web sites have accurate information, and which Web sites do not?

### Checking Web Addresses

Students should use the Web address, or *URL,* to establish the Web site's credibility. Usually, the domain name can suggest who has published the Web site. Web sites can be published by governmental agencies (ends in "dot gov" or .gov), by educational institutions (ends in "dot edu" or .edu), by organizations (ends in "dot org" or .org), or by commercial businesses (ends in "dot com" or .com).

Government Web sites are usually reliable. Examples of credible governmental Web sites are the National Institutes of Health (NIH) and the Food and Drug Administration (FDA). University and medical school sites are also reliable sources of information. Many organizations that research and teach the public about specific diseases and conditions can also provide reliable information. Examples of such organizations are the American Cancer Society and the American Heart Association.

### Evaluating Web Sites

The credibility of the author of the Web site should also be checked. Make sure the author is not trying to sell anything and is established in his or her field. For example, a health Web site's author should be a medical professional.

It is also important to check the date that the information was posted on the Web to ensure that the information is current. Also, the Web site should provide references from valid sources, such as scientific journals or government publications.

Finally, the student should always double-check information between several reliable Web sites. If two or three reliable sites provide the same information, the student can feel confident in using that information.

### Web Sites for Students

The Internet Connect boxes in this textbook have all been reviewed by professionals at the National Science Teachers Association (NSTA). Students can trust that these sites are reliable sources for science- or health-related topics.

*The Internet can provide a wealth of scientific information for a report, but the information may not always be credible or accurate. You can use the methods above to check the accuracy and credibility of your sources.*

## REVIEW

1. Which types of Web addresses are the most reliable?
2. List four important features to evaluate when using a Web site for research.
3. **Supporting Reasoned Opinions** Why do you think a Web site that is advertising a product may not offer accurate information?

internet connect

www.scilinks.org
**Topic: Using the Internet**
**Keyword: HM61589**

SC*i*LINKS. Maintained by the National Science Teachers Association

# TOOLS AND TECHNIQUES

*With proper equipment and good methods, biologists can see, manipulate, and understand the natural world in new ways. Microscopes are one of many useful tools used to unlock nature's biological secrets.*

## MICROSCOPES AS TOOLS

*Tools* are objects used to improve the performance of a task. *Microscopes* are tools that extend human vision by making enlarged images of objects. Biologists use microscopes to study organisms, cells, cell parts, and molecules. Microscopes reveal details that otherwise might be difficult or impossible to see.

### Light Microscopes

To see small organisms and cells, biologists typically use a light microscope, such as the one shown in Figure 1-13. A **compound light microscope** is a microscope that shines light through a specimen and has two lenses to magnify an image. To use this microscope, one first mounts the specimen to be viewed on a glass slide. The specimen must be thin enough for light to pass through it. For tiny pond organisms, such as the single-celled paramecium, light passing through the organism is not a problem. For thick objects, such as plant stems, biologists must cut thin slices for viewing. There are four major parts of a compound light microscope. For further description of the parts of a microscope, see the Appendix.

1. **Eyepiece** The **eyepiece (ocular** (AHK-yoo-luhr) **lens)** magnifies the image, usually 10 times.
2. **Objective Lens** Light passes through the specimen and then through the objective lens, which is located directly above the specimen. The **objective lens** enlarges the image of the specimen. Scientists sometimes use stains to make the image easier to see.
3. **Stage** The **stage** is a platform that supports a slide holding the specimen. The slide is placed over the opening in the stage of the microscope.
4. **Light Source** The **light source** is a light bulb that provides light for viewing the image. It can be either light reflected with a mirror or an incandescent light from a small lamp.

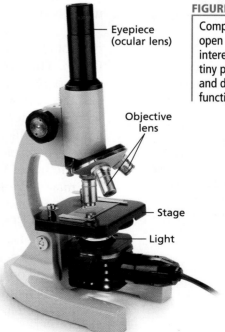

Eyepiece
(ocular lens)

Objective
lens

Stage

Light

**FIGURE 1-13**

Compound light microscopes open the human eye to an interesting world including tiny pond organisms, healthy and diseased cells, and the functioning of cell parts.

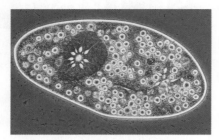

**(a)** *Paramecium* (light microscope)

**(b)** *Paramecium* (scanning electron microscope)

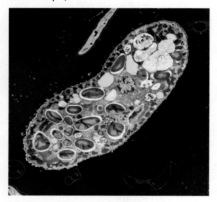

**(c)** *Paramecium* (transmission electron microscope)

**FIGURE 1-14**

The images above show a *Paramecium* as viewed under three different types of microscopes. (a) Light microscopes can produce an image that is up to 1,000 times larger than the actual specimen. (b) Scanning electron microscopes produce images up to 100,000 times larger than the specimen. SEMs provide a view of surface features. (c) Transmission electron microscopes produce images up to 200,000 times larger than the actual specimen.

## Magnification and Resolution

Microscopes vary in powers of magnification and resolution. **Magnification** is the increase of an object's apparent size. Revolving the **nosepiece,** the structure that holds the set of objective lens, rotates these lenses into place above the specimen. In a typical compound light microscope, the most powerful objective lens produces an image up to 100 times (100×) the specimen's actual size. The degree of enlargement is called the *power of magnification* of the lens. The standard ocular lens magnifies a specimen 10 times (10×). To compute the power of magnification of a microscope, the power of magnification of the strongest objective lens (in this case, 100×) is multiplied by the power of magnification of the ocular lens (10×). The result is a total power of magnification of 1000×.

**Resolution** (REZ-uh-LOO-shuhn) is the power to show details clearly in an image. The physical properties of light limit the ability of light microscopes to resolve images, as shown in Figure 1-14a. At powers of magnification beyond about 2,000×, the image of the specimen becomes fuzzy. For this reason, scientists use other microscopes to view very small cells and cell parts.

## Electron Microscopes

To examine cells in more detail or to view cell parts or viruses, scientists can use other microscopes, such as an electron microscope. In an *electron microscope,* a beam of electrons produces an enlarged image of the specimen. Electron microscopes are more powerful in magnification and resolution than light microscopes. Some electron microscopes can even show the contours of individual atoms in a specimen. Electron microscope images are always in black and white. However, scientists can use computers to add artificial colors to help identify structures in the image. Also, the specimen must be placed in a vacuum chamber. Because cells cannot survive in a vacuum, electron microscopes cannot be used to view living specimens.

There are two main types of electron microscopes. The first type of electron microscope is the **scanning electron microscope (SEM).** The SEM passes a beam of electrons over the specimen's surface. SEMs provide three-dimensional images of the specimen's surface, as shown in Figure 1-14b. First, the specimen is sprayed with a fine metal coating. Then, a beam of electrons is aimed at the specimen, which causes the metal coating to emit a shower of electrons. These electrons project onto a fluorescent screen or photographic plate. The result is an image of the object's surface. SEMs can magnify objects up to 100,000 times.

The second type is the **transmission electron microscope (TEM).** The TEM transmits a beam of electrons through a very thinly sliced specimen. Magnetic lenses enlarge the image and focus it on a screen or photographic plate. The result is an image such as the one shown in Figure 1-14c. Note the great resolution of the paramecium's internal structure. Transmission electron microscopes can magnify objects up to 200,000 times.

## TABLE 1-1 *SI Base Units*

| Base quantity | Name | Abbreviation |
|---|---|---|
| Length | meter | m |
| Mass | kilogram | kg |
| Time | second | s |
| Electric current | ampere | A |
| Thermodynamic temperature | kelvin | K |
| Amount of substance | mole | mol |
| Luminous (light) intensity | candela | cd |

## TABLE 1-2 *Some SI prefixes*

| Prefix | Abbreviation | Factor of base unit |
|---|---|---|
| giga | G | 1,000,000,000 ($10^9$) |
| mega | M | 1,000,000 ($10^6$) |
| kilo | k | 1,000 ($10^3$) |
| hecto | h | 100 ($10^2$) |
| deka | da | 10 ($10^1$) |
| base unit | | 1 |
| deci | d | 0.1 ($10^{-1}$) |
| centi | c | 0.01 ($10^{-2}$) |
| milli | m | 0.001 ($10^{-3}$) |
| micro | μ | 0.000001 ($10^{-6}$) |
| nano | n | 0.000000001 ($10^{-9}$) |
| pico | p | 0.000000000001 ($10^{-12}$) |

# UNITS OF MEASUREMENT

Scientists use a common measurement system so that they can compare their results. Scientists use a single, standard system of measurement, called the **metric system.** The metric system is a decimal system and thus is based on powers of 10. The official name of this measurement system is *Système International d'Unités*. The English translation of this French title is the International System of Units, or simply SI. Biology students use SI while making measurements in the laboratory.

## Base and Other Units

The SI has seven fundamental **base units** that describe length, mass, time, and other quantities, as shown in Table 1-1. Multiples of a base unit (in powers of 10) are designated by prefixes, as shown in Table 1-2. For example, the base unit for length is the meter. One kilometer (km) is equal in length to 1,000 meters (m).

Although the base units in Table 1-1 are extremely useful, they can't be applied to certain measurements, such as surface area or velocity. Scientists use other important units called derived units for these types of quantities. *Derived units* are produced by the mathematical relationship between two base units or between two derived units. Table 1-3 shows some common derived units. There are some additional units of measurement that are not part of the SI but that can be used with SI units such as units of time, volume, and mass, as shown in Table 1-3.

## TABLE 1-3 *Some Derived and Other Units*

| Quantity | Name | Abbreviation |
|---|---|---|
| Area | square meter | $m^2$ |
| Volume | cubic meter | $m^3$ |
| Density | kilogram per cubic meter | $kg/m^3$ |
| Specific volume | cubic meter per kilogram | $m^3/kg$ |
| Celsius temperature | degree Celsius | °C |
| Time | minute | 1 min = 60 s |
| Time | hour | 1 h = 60 min |
| Time | day | 1 d = 24 h |
| Volume | liter | 1 L = 1,000 $cm^3$ |
| Mass | kilogram metric ton | 1,000 g = 1 kg 1 t = 1,000 kg |

# SAFETY

**FIGURE 1-15**

Good laboratory practice involves protecting yourself and others by being safe.

Studying living things is interesting, fun, and rewarding, but it can be hazardous. The hazards can be chemical, physical, radiological, or biological and can vary between the the lab and the field. For example, getting splashed in the eye with a blinding chemical is more likely to occur in the laboratory, but falling down a cliff or getting bitten by a poisonous spider is more likely to occur in the field.

## Good Laboratory Practice

Lab safety involves good laboratory practice, which means establishing safe, common-sense habits, as shown in Figure 1-15. Never work alone in the lab or without proper supervision by the teacher, and always ask your teacher before using any equipment. The diagram below shows the safety symbols used in this book. More information on lab safety and the safety symbols can be found in the Appendix.

 Eye Safety

 Hand Safety

 Safety with Gases

 Sharp-Object Safety

 Clothing Protection

 Animal Care and Safety

 Heating Safety

 Hygienic Care

 Glassware Safety

 Proper Waste Disposal

 Electrical Safety

 Plant Safety

 Chemical Safety

## SECTION 4 REVIEW

1. List the four major parts of a compound light microscope.

2. What is the difference between the magnification and resolution of an image under a microscope?

3. Compare the function of a transmission electron microscope with that of a scanning electron microscope.

4. What is the importance of scientists using a common SI system of measurement?

5. How would you convert kilometers to millimeters?

6. Name the safety symbols used in this textbook.

**CRITICAL THINKING**

7. **Applying Information** A biologist thinks a virus, which is much smaller than a cell, is likely to cause a disease. Which type of microscope is most likely to be used to view the internal structure of a virus?

8. **Calculating Information** How would you convert cubic meters to cubic centimeters?

9. **Calculating Information** On a light microscope, an objective lens magnifies the view of some pond water 25 times, and the ocular lens magnifies it 10 times further. What is the final magnification of the image?

## SECTION 1 — The World of Biology

- Biology is the study of life and can be used to both solve societal problems and explain aspects of our daily lives.
- Living things share the same 7 characteristics: organization and cells, response to stimuli, homeostasis, metabolism, growth and development, reproduction, and evolution.
- Multicellular organisms show a hierarchy of organization going from the organism to the atom.
- To stay alive, living things must maintain homeostasis, obtain and use energy, and pass on hereditary information from parents to offspring, also called reproduction.

**Vocabulary**

| | | | |
|---|---|---|---|
| biology (p. 5) | multicellular (p. 7) | biological molecule (p. 7) | development (p. 8) |
| organization (p. 6) | organ (p. 7) | homeostasis (p. 8) | reproduction (p. 9) |
| cell (p. 7) | tissue (p. 7) | metabolism (p. 8) | gene (p. 9) |
| unicellular (p. 7) | organelle (p. 7) | cell division (p. 8) | |

## SECTION 2 — Themes in Biology

- Three themes in biology are the unity of life's diversity, the interdependence of organisms, and evolution of life.
- Living organisms show diversity and can be classified into domains and kingdoms.
- Organisms live in interdependent communities and interact with both organisms and the environment.
- Evolution helps to explain how species came to exist, have changed over time, and adapt to their environment.

**Vocabulary**

| | | | |
|---|---|---|---|
| domain (p. 11) | ecology (p. 11) | evolution (p. 12) | adaptation (p. 12) |
| kingdom (p. 11) | ecosystem (p. 11) | natural selection (p. 12) | |

## SECTION 3 — The Study of Biology

- The scientific method involves making observations, asking questions, forming hypotheses, designing experiments, analyzing data, and drawing conclusions.
- Trying to answer questions about observations helps scientists form hypotheses.
- A controlled experiment has a control and experimental group, and tests independent and dependent variables.
- Scientists analyze data to draw conclusions about the experiment performed.
- A theory is a set of related hypotheses confirmed to be true many times.
- Communication between scientists about their methods and results helps prevent dishonesty and bias in science.

**Vocabulary**

| | | | |
|---|---|---|---|
| scientific method (p. 13) | prediction (p. 13) | experimental group (p. 15) | dependent variable (p. 16) |
| observation (p. 13) | experiment (p. 13) | independent | theory (p. 17) |
| hypothesis (p. 13) | control group (p. 15) | variable (p. 15) | peer review (p. 19) |

## SECTION 4 — Tools and Techniques

- Four major parts of a compound light microscope are the ocular lens, objective lens, stage, and light source.
- Transmission and scanning electron microscopes provide greater magnification than light microscopes.
- Scientists use the metric system to take scientific measurements.
- Lab safety is a good laboratory practice.

**Vocabulary**

| | | | |
|---|---|---|---|
| compound light microscope (p. 21) | objective lens (p. 21) | nosepiece (p. 22) | transmission electron microscope (TEM) (p. 22) |
| eyepiece (ocular lens) (p. 21) | stage (p. 21) | resolution (p. 22) | metric system (p. 23) |
| | light source (p. 21) | scanning electron microscope (SEM) (p. 22) | base unit (p .23) |
| | magnification (p. 22) | | |

## USING VOCABULARY

1. For each pair of terms, explain how the meanings of the terms differ.
   a. *unicellular* and *multicellular*
   b. *homeostasis* and *metabolism*
   c. *natural selection* and *adaptation*
   d. *hypothesis* and *theory*
   e. *magnification* and *resolution*

2. Explain the relationship between an independent variable and a dependent variable.

3. Use the following terms in the same sentence: *observation, hypothesis, prediction,* and *experiment.*

4. **Word Roots and Origins** The word *magnification* is derived from the Latin *magnificus* or *magnus,* which means "large" or "great." Using this information, explain why the term *magnification* is a good name for the function it describes.

## UNDERSTANDING KEY CONCEPTS

5. **Describe** why learning about biology is relevant to a person's life.

6. **Describe** one way in which biology affects our society.

7. **Summarize** the characteristics of living things.

8. **List** the hierarchy of organization in a snowy owl.

9. **Explain** how homeostasis and metabolism are interrelated.

10. **Compare** the processes of growth, development, and reproduction.

11. **State** three major themes found in biology.

12. **Identify** how the "tree of life" can help explain both the unity and diversity of life.

13. **Describe** the interdependence of living organisms.

14. **Summarize** how evolution helps explain the diversity of life.

15. **Sequence** the main steps of the scientific method.

16. **Explain** how observations are used to form hypotheses.

17. **Summarize** how biologists set up controlled experiments.

18. **State** the purpose of analyzing data that are collected during an experiment.

19. **Summarize** how a hypothesis becomes a theory.

20. **Describe** two types of scientific models.

21. **Identify** how a peer review keeps scientists honest.

22. **Name** the part of the compound light microscope denoted by each letter in the figure below.

23. **Differentiate** between the scanning electron microscope and the transmission electron microscope.

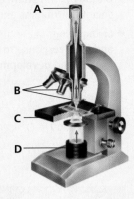

24. **Describe** the relationship between a kilometer, meter, and micrometer.

25. **Explain** why scientists throughout the world use the SI system.

26. **List** three safety symbols used in this textbook.

27. 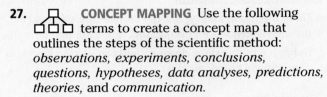 **CONCEPT MAPPING** Use the following terms to create a concept map that outlines the steps of the scientific method: *observations, experiments, conclusions, questions, hypotheses, data analyses, predictions, theories,* and *communication.*

## CRITICAL THINKING

28. **Forming Hypotheses** Go to a window or outside, and observe a bird's behavior for a few minutes. Record your observations, and write down one question about bird behavior and one hypothesis that answers the question.

29. **Analyzing Concepts** One of the most important parts of any scientific publication is the part called Methods and Materials, in which the scientist describes the procedure used in the experiment. Why do you think such details are so important?

30. **Making Calculations** Determine the number of liters that are in 150 kiloliters.

31. **Making Comparisons** Look at the photographs below. The TEM (left) is a photo of a paramecium. The SEM (right) is also a photo of a paramecium. Compare and contrast what each electron micrograph reveals to you about this organism.

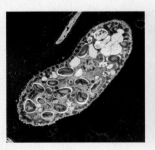 

# Standardized Test Preparation

**DIRECTIONS:** Choose the letter of the answer choice that best answers the question.

1. Which of the following does evolution help explain?
   A. how organisms reproduce
   B. how organisms grow and develop
   C. how organisms are related to each other
   D. how organisms obtain and metabolize energy

2. Which of the following is the hereditary material in most living things?
   F. DNA
   G. lipids
   H. oxygen
   J. carbon dioxide

3. Which of the following does the hierarchy of organization within an organism describe?
   A. metabolism
   B. homeostasis
   C. internal structures
   D. relationship to the physical environment

4. To which of the following does the resolution of a microscope refer?
   F. its ability to show detail clearly
   G. its power to scan the surface of an object
   H. its series of interchangeable objective lenses
   J. its power to increase an object's apparent size

**INTERPRETING GRAPHICS:** The graph below shows the distance it takes an owl to strike a mouse under different conditions. Use the graph to answer the question that follows.

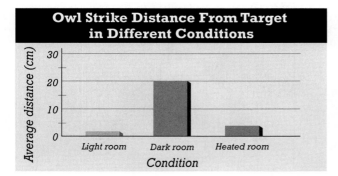

Owl Strike Distance From Target in Different Conditions

5. An owl strikes a mouse more closely and on target in which of the following rooms?
   A. dark room
   B. light room
   C. heated room
   D. dark and lighted rooms

**DIRECTIONS:** Complete the following analogy.

6. compound light microscope : light :: TEM:
   F. tissues
   G. electrons
   H. organelles
   J. organ systems

**INTERPRETING GRAPHICS:** The figure below shows a newspaper clipping. Use the figure to answer the question that follows.

7. Which of the following terms most accurately reflects the use of the term theory in the newspaper headline above?
   A. law
   B. fact
   C. hypothesis
   D. experiment

## SHORT RESPONSE

Dolly was cloned from mammary cells from an adult female sheep. She was an exact genetic copy of her mother.

Explain whether Dolly represents a product of sexual reproduction or asexual reproduction.

## EXTENDED RESPONSE

Life is so diverse, yet it is characterized by a unity. The tree of life can relate life's unity and diversity.

*Part A* Describe the relationship between animals, plants, fungi, protists, bacteria, and archaea in the "tree of life."

*Part B* Explain how the "tree of life" represents and relates both the unity and diversity of life.

**Test TIP** When faced with similar answers, define the answer choices and then use that definition to narrow down the choices on a multiple-choice question.

# Using SI Units

## OBJECTIVES

- Express measurements in SI units.
- Read a thermometer.
- Measure liquid volume using a graduated cylinder.
- Measure mass using a balance.
- Determine the density (mass-to-volume ratio) of two different liquids.

## PROCESS SKILLS

- measuring
- calculating

## MATERIALS

- 75 mL light-colored sand
- 75 mL dark-colored sand
- 1 100 mL graduated cylinder
- Celsius thermometers, alcohol filled (2)
- 5 oz plastic cups (4)
- graph paper
- heat-protective gloves
- light source
- stopwatch or clock
- ring stand or lamp support
- 25 mL corn oil
- 25 mL water
- clear-plastic cup
- balance

### Background

1. What does the abbreviation *SI* stand for?
2. List the seven SI base units.

### PART A  Measuring Temperature

1. In your lab report, prepare a data table similar to Table A, above right.
2. Using a graduated cylinder, measure 75 mL of light-colored sand and pour it into one of the small plastic cups. Repeat this procedure with the dark-colored sand and another plastic cup.
3. Level the sand by placing the cup on your desk and sliding the cup back and forth.

### TABLE A  *SAND TEMPERATURE*

| Time (min) | Temperature (°C) | |
| --- | --- | --- |
| | Dark-colored sand | Light-colored sand |
| Start | | |
| 1 | | |
| 2 | | |
| 3 | | |
| 4 | | |
| 5 | | |
| 6 | | |
| 7 | | |
| 8 | | |
| 9 | | |
| 10 | | |

4. Insert one thermometer into each cup. The zero line on the thermometer should be level with the sand, as shown in the figure below. Re-level the sand if necessary.

**5.** ⚠ **CAUTION Wear heat-protective gloves when handling the lamp. The lamp will become very hot and may burn you.** Using a ring stand or lamp support, position the lamp approximately 9 cm from the top of the sand, as shown in the figure on p. 28. Make sure the lamp is evenly positioned between the two cups.

**6.** Before turning on the lamp, record the initial temperature of each cup of sand in your data table.

**7.** Note the time or start the stopwatch when you turn on the lamp. The lamp will become hot and warm the sand. Check the temperature of the sand in each container at one-minute intervals for 10 minutes. Record the temperature of the sand after each minute in your data table.

**PART B** **Comparing the Density of Oil and Water**

**8.** In your lab report, prepare a data table similar to Table B below.

### TABLE B  *DENSITY OF TWO LIQUIDS*

| | | |
|---|---|---|
| **a. Mass of empty oil cup** | _____ | **g** |
| **b. Mass of empty water cup** | _____ | **g** |
| **c. Mass of cup and oil** | _____ | **g** |
| **d. Mass of cup and water** | _____ | **g** |
| **e. Volume of oil** | **25 mL** | |
| **f. Volume of water** | **25 mL** | |
| **Calculating Actual Mass** | | |
| **Oil** Item c − Item a = | _____ | **g** |
| **Water** Item d − Item b = | _____ | **g** |
| **g. Density of oil** | _____ | **g/ml** |
| **h. Density of water** | _____ | **g/ml** |

**9.** Label one clean plastic cup "oil," and label another "water." Using a balance, measure the mass of each plastic cup, and record the value in your data table.

**10.** Using a clean graduated cylinder, measure 25 mL of corn oil and pour it into the plastic cup labeled "oil." Using a balance, measure the mass of the plastic cup containing the corn oil, and record the mass in your data table.

**11.** Using a clean graduated cylinder, measure 25 mL of water and pour it into the plastic cup labeled "water." Using a balance, measure the mass of the plastic cup containing the water, and record the mass in your data table.

**12.** To find the mass of the oil, subtract the mass of the empty cup from the mass of the cup and the oil together.

**13.** To find the density of the oil, divide the mass of the oil by the volume of the oil, as shown in the equation below:

$$\text{Density of oil} = \frac{\text{mass of oil}}{\text{volume of oil}} = \underline{\hspace{2cm}} \text{ g/mL}$$

**14.** To find the mass of water, subtract the mass of the empty cup from the mass of the cup and the water together.

**15.** To find the density of the water, divide the mass of the water by the volume of the water, as shown in the equation below:

$$\text{Density of water} = \frac{\text{mass of water}}{\text{volume of water}} = \underline{\hspace{2cm}} \text{ g/mL}$$

**16.** Combine the oil and water in the clear cup, and record your observations in your lab report.

**17.** ⚠ ⚠ Clean up your materials, and wash your hands before leaving the lab.

### Analysis and Conclusions

**1.** Graph the data you collected in Part A. Plot time on the *x*-axis and temperature on the *y*-axis.

**2.** Based on your data from Part A, what is the relationship between color and heat absorption?

**3.** How might the color of the clothes you wear affect how warm you are on a sunny 90° day?

**4.** In Part B, what did you observe when you combined the oil and water in the clear cup? Relate your observation to the densities that you calculated.

**5.** What could you infer about the value for the density of ice if you observe it to float in water?

**6.** How would your calculated values for density be affected if you misread the volume measurement on the graduated cylinder?

### Further Inquiry

Pumice is a volcanic rock that has a density less than 1.00 g/cm³. How would you prove this if you did not have a balance to weigh the pumice? (Hint: The density of water is 1.00 g/cm³.)

# CHEMISTRY OF LIFE

All living things are made of the same basic materials: carbon, hydrogen, oxygen, and nitrogen. Living things, such as this jellyfish, *Pseudorhiza haeckeli,* are made of cells that are composed primarily of water. The chemical reactions of life occur in the aqueous environment of the cell.

**SECTION 1** *Composition of Matter*

**SECTION 2** *Energy*

**SECTION 3** *Water and Solutions*

# COMPOSITION OF MATTER

*E*arth supports an enormous variety of organisms. The structure and function of all living things are governed by the laws of chemistry. An understanding of the basic principles of chemistry will give you a better understanding of living things and how they function.

## SECTION 1

### OBJECTIVES

- **Define** the term *matter.*
- **Explain** the relationship between elements and atoms.
- **Draw** and label a model of the structure of an atom.
- **Explain** how compounds affect an atom's stability.
- **Contrast** covalent and ionic bonds.

### VOCABULARY

matter
mass
element
atom
nucleus
proton
neutron
atomic number
mass number
electron
orbital
isotope
compound
chemical bond
covalent bond
molecule
ion
ionic bond

## MATTER

Everything in the universe is made of matter. **Matter** is anything that occupies space and has mass. **Mass** is the quantity of matter an object has. Mass and weight are not the same; *weight* is defined as the force produced by gravity acting on mass. The same mass would have less weight on the moon than it would on Earth because the moon exerts less force on the object than the Earth does.

Chemical changes in matter are essential to all life processes. Biologists study chemistry because all living things are made of the same kinds of matter that make up nonliving things. By learning how changes in matter occur, you will gain an understanding of the life processes of the organisms you will study.

## ELEMENTS AND ATOMS

**Elements** are substances that cannot be broken down chemically into simpler kinds of matter. More than 100 elements have been identified, though fewer than 30 are important to living things. In fact, more than 90 percent of the mass of all kinds of living things is composed of combinations of just four elements: oxygen, carbon, hydrogen, and nitrogen.

Information about the elements is summarized on a chart known as the *periodic table,* which appears in the Appendix. Each element has a different chemical symbol. A chemical symbol consists of one, two, or three letters, as shown in Figure 2-1. In most cases, the symbol derives from the first letter or other letters in the name of the element, such as Cl for chlorine. Most of the other symbols are derived from the Latin names of elements. One example is sodium's symbol, Na, from the Latin word *natrium.*

**FIGURE 2-1**

The periodic table lists information about the elements, including the atomic number, the chemical symbol, and the atomic mass for each element. A complete periodic table can be found in the Appendix.

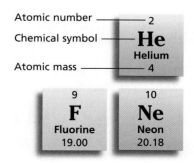

Atomic number ———— 2
Chemical symbol ———— **He**
Helium
Atomic mass ———— 4

| 9 | 10 |
| **F** | **Ne** |
| Fluorine | Neon |
| 19.00 | 20.18 |

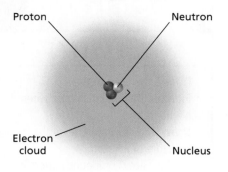

**Helium-3**

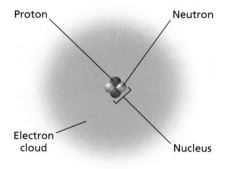

**Helium-4**

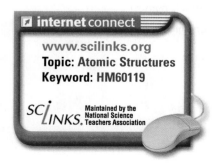

The simplest particle of an element that retains all of the properties of that element is an **atom.** The properties of different kinds of atoms determine the structure and properties of the matter they compose. Atoms are so small that their structure cannot be directly observed. However, scientists have developed models that describe the structure of the atom. One model is shown in Figure 2-2.

## The Nucleus

The central region, or **nucleus,** makes up the bulk of the mass of the atom and consists of two kinds of subatomic particles, a **proton** and a neutron. The proton is positively charged and the neutron has no charge. The number of protons in an atom is called the **atomic number** of the element. In the periodic table of elements, the atomic number generally appears directly above the chemical symbol, as shown in Figure 2-1. The atomic number of fluorine is 9, which indicates that each atom of the element fluorine has nine protons. The **mass number** of an atom is equal to the total number of protons and neutrons of the atom. The mass number of fluorine is 19, which indicates that each atom of fluorine has 10 neutrons.

## Electrons

In an atom, the number of positively charged protons is balanced by an equal number of small, negatively charged particles called **electrons.** The net electrical charge of an atom is zero. Electrons are high-energy particles that have very little mass. They move about the nucleus at very high speeds and are located in orbitals. An **orbital** is a three-dimensional region around a nucleus that indicates the probable location of an electron. Electrons in orbitals that are farther away from the nucleus have greater energy than electrons that are in orbitals closer to the nucleus. When all orbitals are combined, there is a cloud of electrons surrounding the nucleus, as shown in Figure 2-2.

Orbitals correspond to specific energy levels. Each energy level corresponds to a group of orbitals that can hold only a certain, total number of electrons. For example, the orbital that corresponds to the first energy level can hold only two electrons. The first energy level is the highest energy level for the elements hydrogen and helium. There are four orbitals in the second energy level, and that energy level can hold up to eight total electrons, with a maximum of two electrons in each orbital.

## Isotopes

All atoms of an element have the same number of protons. However, all atoms of an element do not necessarily have the same number of neutrons. Atoms of the same element that have a different number of neutrons are called **isotopes.** Additional neutrons change the mass of the element. Most elements are made up of a mixture of isotopes, as shown in Figure 2-2. The *average atomic mass* of an element takes into account the relative amounts of each isotope in the element, and this average is the mass found in the periodic table.

# COMPOUNDS

Under natural conditions, most elements do not exist alone; atoms of most elements can readily combine with the same or different atoms or elements to make compounds. **Compounds** are made up of atoms of two or more elements in fixed proportions. A chemical formula shows the kinds and proportions of atoms of each element that forms a particular compound. For example, water's chemical formula, $H_2O$, shows that the atoms always combine in a proportion of two hydrogen (H) atoms to one oxygen (O) atom.

The physical and chemical properties differ between the compounds and elements that compose them. In nature, the elements oxygen and hydrogen are usually found as gases with the formulas $O_2$ and $H_2$. However, when oxygen gas and hydrogen gas combine at room temperature, they form liquid $H_2O$. How elements combine and form compounds depends on the number and arrangement of electrons in their orbitals. An atom is chemically stable when the orbitals that correspond to its highest energy level are filled with the maximum number of electrons. Some elements, such as helium and neon, consist of atoms that have the maximum number of electrons in the orbitals of their highest energy levels. These elements, also called *noble* or *inert elements,* do not react with other elements under normal conditions.

Most atoms are not stable in their natural state, so they tend to react with other atoms in different ways to become more stable. Carbon, nitrogen, and oxygen atoms have unfilled orbitals that correspond to their highest energy levels. Similar to these elements, most elements tend to interact with other atoms to form chemical bonds. **Chemical bonds** are the attractive forces that hold atoms together.

## Covalent Bonds

A **covalent bond** forms when two atoms share one or more pairs of electrons. For example, water is made up of one oxygen atom and two hydrogen atoms held together by covalent bonds. In Figure 2-3, step ❶, an atom of hydrogen needs a second electron to achieve stability. Having two electrons in the orbital that corresponds to hydrogen's highest energy level allows the atom to be more stable. The oxygen atom needs two more electrons to give it a stable arrangement of eight electrons, which fill oxygen's orbitals to its highest energy level. Thus, hydrogen atoms and oxygen atoms share pairs of electrons in a ratio of two atoms of hydrogen to one atom of oxygen. The resulting stable compound, $H_2O$ (water), is shown in step ❷.

A **molecule** is the simplest part of a substance that retains all of the properties of that substance and can exist in a free state. For example, one molecule of the compound water is $H_2O$, and one molecule of oxygen gas is $O_2$. Some molecules that biologists study are large and complex.

**Word Roots and Origins**

*compound*

from the Latin *componere,* meaning "to put together"

**FIGURE 2-3**

Two atoms of hydrogen and one atom of oxygen share electrons in covalent bonds and thus become stable. Covalent bonding results in the formation of molecules.

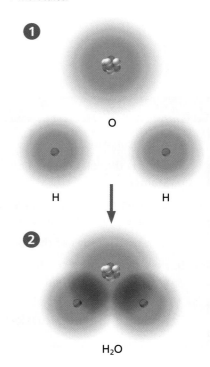

FIGURE 2-4

By losing its outermost electron (e⁻), a sodium atom becomes a Na⁺ ion. By gaining one electron, a chlorine atom becomes a Cl⁻ ion. Because of their opposite charges, the Na⁺ and Cl⁻ ions are attracted to each other and form an ionic bond.

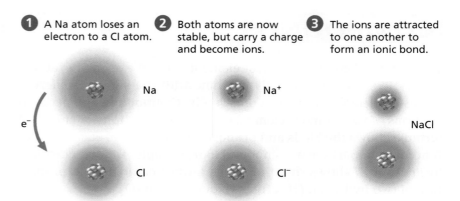

**1** A Na atom loses an electron to a Cl atom.

**2** Both atoms are now stable, but carry a charge and become ions.

**3** The ions are attracted to one another to form an ionic bond.

Na

Na⁺

e⁻

Cl

Cl⁻

NaCl

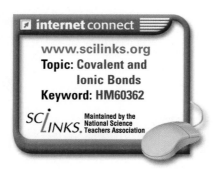

**internet** connect

**www.scilinks.org**
**Topic: Covalent and Ionic Bonds**
**Keyword: HM60362**

SCI*LINKS*. Maintained by the National Science Teachers Association

## Ionic Bonds

In Figure 2-4, step **1**, both sodium and chlorine atoms have unfilled outermost energy levels and are therefore reactive. Both atoms achieve stability in the presence of one another. The one outer electron (e⁻) of a sodium atom is transferred to a chlorine atom. This transfer makes both atoms more stable than they were before. The orbitals that correspond to the sodium atom's new outermost energy level are filled with eight electrons. But it also results in a sodium atom with a net positive electrical charge. The sodium atom has 11 protons (11 positive charges) balanced by only 10 electrons (10 negative charges). An atom or molecule with an electrical charge is called an **ion.** The sodium ion is written as Na⁺.

Chlorine, in step **2**, gained an electron from a sodium atom. The chlorine atom now has eight electrons in its orbitals that correspond to its outermost energy level. This makes the chlorine atom more stable. With this additional electron, chlorine becomes a negatively charged ion which is abbreviated as Cl⁻.

Because positive and negative electrical charges attract each other, the sodium ion and the chloride ion attract each other. This attraction is called an **ionic bond.** The resulting compound, sodium chloride, NaCl, shown in step **3**, is an ionic compound and is familiar to you as common table salt.

## SECTION 1 REVIEW

1. What is matter?

2. What is the relationship between elements and atoms?

3. Describe the arrangement within energy levels of the six electrons of an atom of carbon.

4. How are isotopes of the same element alike?

5. How can we predict which elements are reactive under normal conditions and which are unreactive?

6. Distinguish between covalent and ionic bonds.

**CRITICAL THINKING**

7. **Distinguishing Differences** Explain why the terms *mass* and *weight* should not be used interchangeably.

8. **Applying Information** Classify each of the following as an element or a compound: HCl, $CO_2$, Cl, Li, and $H_2O$.

9. **Applying Information** Given that elements are pure substances, how many types of atoms make up the structure of a single element? Explain your answer.

# ENERGY

*All living things use energy. The amount of energy in the universe remains the same over time, but energy can change from one form to another. It is the transfer of energy—from the sun to and through almost every organism on Earth—that biologists seek to understand when they study the chemistry of living things.*

## ENERGY AND MATTER

Scientists define **energy** as the ability to do work. Energy can occur in various forms, and one form of energy can be converted to another form. In a light bulb's filament, electrical energy is converted to radiant energy (light) and thermal energy (heat). Some forms of energy important to biological systems include chemical energy, thermal energy, electrical energy, and mechanical energy. Inside any single organism, energy may be converted from one form to another. For example, after you eat a meal, your body changes the chemical energy found in food into thermal and mechanical energy, among other things.

### States of Matter

Although it is not apparent when we observe matter, all the atoms and molecules in any substance are in constant motion. The motion of and spacing between atoms or molecules of a substance determine the substance's state: solid, liquid, or gas, as shown in Figure 2-5. In general, the atoms or molecules of a solid are more closely linked together than in a liquid or gas. Water is an exception to this, as will be described later. Solids move less rapidly than the particles that make up a liquid or a gas. A solid maintains a fixed volume and shape. A liquid maintains a fixed volume, but its particles move more freely than those of a solid, which gives a liquid its ability to flow and to conform to the shape of any container. Particles of a gas move the most rapidly. Gas particles have little or no attraction to each other, and they fill the volume of the container they occupy. Thermal energy must be added to the substance to cause a substance to change states.

**FIGURE 2-5**

Matter exists as solids, liquids, and gases as shown below with water.

Gas

Solid

Liquid

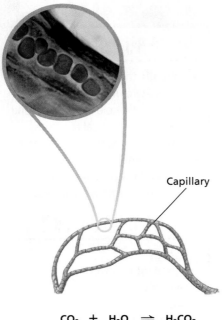

Capillary

$$CO_2 \;+\; H_2O \;\rightleftharpoons\; H_2CO_3$$
Carbon    Water    Carbonic
dioxide                acid

**FIGURE 2-6**

Chemical reactions occur in the human body. The chemical reaction shown above takes place in capillaries. Because the products of the reaction remain in the blood, the reaction is reversible and is written as: $CO_2 + H_2O \rightleftharpoons H_2CO_3$.

# ENERGY AND CHEMICAL REACTIONS

In a **chemical reaction,** one or more substances change to produce one or more different substances. Energy is absorbed or released when chemical bonds are broken and new ones are formed. Living things undergo many thousands of chemical reactions every day. Reactions can vary from highly complex to very simple. The chemical reaction in Figure 2-6 takes place in your blood. Carbon dioxide is taken up from body cells and into the blood when it crosses the thin capillary walls. The carbon dioxide reacts with water in the blood to form carbonic acid. Carbon dioxide is then released into the lung's alveoli and exhaled when the carbonic acid breaks down to carbon dioxide and water.

If the reaction proceeds in only one direction, the **reactants** are shown on the left side of the equation. In the reaction in Figure 2-6, the reactants are carbon dioxide ($CO_2$) and water ($H_2O$). In a chemical reaction, bonds present in the reactants are broken, the elements are rearranged, and new compounds are formed as the products. The **products** of this reaction are shown on the right side. In this reaction, the product is carbonic acid ($H_2CO_3$). Notice that the number of each kind of atom must be the same on either side of the arrow. Some chemical reactions can proceed in either direction and a two-direction arrow ($\rightleftharpoons$) is used. For example, the equation in Figure 2-6 is reversible and can be written as $CO_2 + H_2O \rightleftharpoons H_2CO_3$.

The energy your body needs is provided by the sugars, proteins, and fats found in foods. Your body continuously undergoes a series of chemical reactions in which these energy-supplying substances are broken down into carbon dioxide, water, and other products. In this process, energy is released for use by your body to build and maintain body cells, tissues, and organs. **Metabolism** (MUH-TAB-uh-LIZ-uhm) is the term used to describe all of the chemical reactions that occur in an organism.

## Activation Energy

For most chemical reactions to begin, energy must be added to the reactants. In many chemical reactions, the amount of energy needed to start the reaction, called **activation energy,** is large. Figure 2-7 shows the activation energy for a hypothetical chemical reaction.

Certain chemical substances, known as **catalysts** (KAT-uh-LISTS), reduce the amount of activation energy that is needed for a reaction to take place, as shown in Figure 2-7. A reaction in the presence of the correct catalyst will proceed spontaneously or with the addition of a small amount of energy. In living things enzymes act as catalysts. An **enzyme** is a protein or RNA molecule that speeds up metabolic reactions without being permanently changed or destroyed.

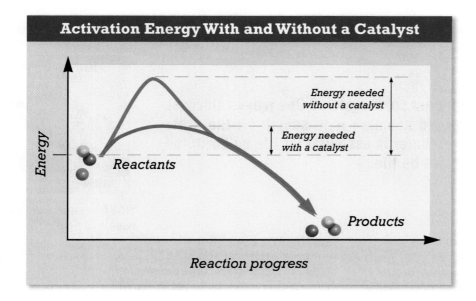

## Activation Energy With and Without a Catalyst

*Energy needed without a catalyst*

*Energy needed with a catalyst*

*Reactants*

*Products*

*Reaction progress*

Energy

**FIGURE 2-7**

The blue curve shows the activation energy that must be supplied before this reaction can begin. The activation energy can be reduced, as shown by the red curve, by adding a catalyst.

## Oxidation Reduction Reactions

You know that there is a constant transfer of energy into and throughout living things. Many of the chemical reactions that help transfer energy in living things involve the transfer of electrons. These reactions in which electrons are transferred between atoms are known as oxidation reduction reactions, or **redox reactions.** In an **oxidation** (AHKS-i-DAY-shuhn) **reaction,** a reactant loses one or more electrons, thus becoming more positive in charge. For example, remember that a sodium atom loses an electron to achieve stability when it forms an ionic bond, as shown in Figure 2-4. Thus, the sodium atom undergoes oxidation to form a $Na^+$ ion. In a **reduction reaction,** a reactant gains one or more electrons, thus becoming more negative in charge. When a chlorine atom gains an electron to form a $Cl^-$ ion, the atom undergoes reduction. Redox reactions always occur together. An oxidation reaction occurs, and the electron given up by one substance is then accepted by another substance in a reduction reaction.

 **Quick Lab**

### Modeling Ionic Bonds

**Materials** toothpicks, small and large marshmallows, and raisins

**Procedure**
Use large marshmallows to represent chlorine, small marshmallows to represent sodium, raisins to represent electrons, and toothpicks to represent bonds or orbital place holders. Make models of Na, Cl, $Na^+$, $Cl^-$, and NaCl (sodium chloride).

**Analysis** Use your models to identify each of the following: a sodium atom, a sodium ion, a chlorine atom, a chloride ion, an ionic bond, and a particle of sodium chloride.

## SECTION 2 REVIEW

1. Name and describe the physical properties of the three states of matter.

2. Explain the roles of reactants and products in a chemical reaction.

3. Describe the effect of an enzyme on the activation energy in a chemical reaction.

4. Enzymes are biological catalysts. Explain what they do in living systems.

5. Why does a reduction reaction always accompany an oxidation reaction?

**CRITICAL THINKING**

6. **Analyzing Concepts** Living things need a constant supply of energy. Explain why.

7. **Analyzing Graphics** Carbonic anhydrase is the enzyme that catalyzes the chemical reaction illustrated in Figure 2-6. What effect might a molecule that interferes with the action of carbonic anhydrase have on your body?

8. **Analyzing Information** In a reduction reaction, the reduced atom gains one or more electrons. Why is this reaction called a reduction?

# Science in Action

## Is There Water on Mars?

Do other living organisms share our solar system? One way to discover a possible answer to this age-old question is to search for the presence of water on other planets. Water is essential for life on Earth, so where there is water, there might be life.

**NASA's exploration rover *Opportunity***

**HYPOTHESIS: Water Exists on Mars**

Scientists at the National Aeronautics and Space Administration (NASA) have sent orbiters, (reusable spacecraft designed to transport people and cargo) between Earth and Mars. Recent orbiters to be sent to Mars include NASA's *Mars Global Surveyor (MGS)* and *Mars Odyssey*. These missions revealed boulders, dust, canyons, and tall volcanic peaks. Some of the most exciting images revealed gullies carved into the Martian landscape. The appearance of these gullies led geologists to hypothesize that the gullies had been carved by running water within the past few million years.

Why is the presence of water on Mars so intriguing? On our planet, where there is water, there is life. For now, scientists are assuming that life-forms on Mars would have the same dependence on water.

**METHODS: Image and Analyze Martian Rock Samples**

In the summer of 2003, NASA scientists launched *Spirit* and *Opportunity*, two Mars exploration rovers. The job of these two rovers was to take small-scale geologic surveys of surrounding rocks and soil and to search for ancient traces of water. These rovers landed in regions near the Martian equator that may have held water at one time.

**RESULTS: Water and Minerals That Can Form in Water Are Present on Mars**

The images sent back by the *Odyssey* and *MGS* orbiters reveal that water covers large areas of Mars' polar regions as well as some large areas at its equator. The water is almost certainly frozen in the form of dusty snowpacks, which may occur largely as an icy soil layer. These icepacks may resemble the permafrost of Earth's polar regions.

In addition, *Opportunity* detected the presence of hematite at its landing site, the Meridiani Planum, an area on Mars that was thought to have been a shallow lake at one time. Hematite is a mineral that often forms in pools of standing water on Earth but can also form as a result of volcanic activity.

*Opportunity* also found strong evidence that the rocks at Meridiani Planum were once sediments that were laid down by liquid water. This discovery also gives greater weight to the hypothesis that Mars was once a habitat for microbial life.

**CONCLUSION: Mars Once Had Water**

Chances are that the current mission to Mars will not determine whether life ever started on the planet, but scientists are hopeful that they will have an answer someday. Human exploration of Mars is already being planned. Astronauts would be able to carry out many experiments that robots cannot do.

*This picture was taken by one of the rovers that explored Mars.*

### REVIEW

1. Why did geologists initially hypothesize that there might have been water on Mars?

2. What did the images sent back by the NASA orbiters and the exploration rovers in 2003 reveal?

3. **Critical Thinking** Explain why the existence of hematite may not be the best indicator of water on Mars.

internet connect

www.scilinks.org
**Topic:** Mars
**Keyword:** HM60913

SCLINKS Maintained by the National Science Teachers Association

# WATER AND SOLUTIONS

*Compare the body of a jellyfish with your own body. A jellyfish would die if it was removed from its watery environment. Yet you can live on the driest parts of Earth. Jellyfish and humans seem unlike each other, yet the bodies of both are made of cells that consist mostly of water. The chemical reactions of all living things take place in the aqueous environment of the cell. Water has several unique properties that make it one of the most important compounds found in living things.*

## SECTION 3

### OBJECTIVES

- **Describe** the structure of a water molecule.
- **Explain** how water's polar nature affects its ability to dissolve substances.
- **Outline** the relationship between hydrogen bonding and the different properties of water.
- **Identify** the roles of solutes and solvents in solutions.
- **Differentiate** between acids and bases.

### VOCABULARY

polar
hydrogen bond
cohesion
adhesion
capillarity
solution
solute
solvent
concentration
saturated solution
aqueous solution
hydroxide ion
hydronium ion
acid
base
pH scale
buffer

## POLARITY

Many of water's biological functions stem from its chemical structure. Recall that in the water molecule, $H_2O$, the hydrogen and oxygen atoms share electrons to form covalent bonds. However, these atoms do not share the electrons equally. The oxygen atom has a greater ability to attract electrons to it because it pulls hydrogen's electrons towards its nucleus. As a result, as shown in Figure 2-8, the region of the molecule where the oxygen atom is located has a partial negative charge, denoted with a $\delta^-$, while the regions of the molecule where each of the two hydrogen atoms are located have partial positive charges, each of which are denoted with a $\delta^+$. Thus, even though the total charge on a water molecule is neutral, the charge is unevenly distributed across the water molecule. Because of this uneven distribution of charge, water is called a **polar** compound.

Notice also in Figure 2-8 that the three atoms in a water molecule are not arranged in a straight line as you might expect. Rather, the two hydrogen atoms bond with the single oxygen atom at an angle.

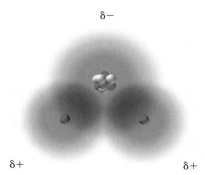

**(a)** Electron cloud model

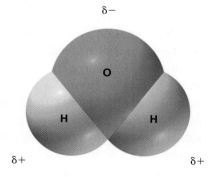

**(b)** Space-filling model

**FIGURE 2-8**

The oxygen region of the water molecule is weakly negative, and the hydrogen regions are weakly positive. Notice the different ways to represent water, $H_2O$. You are familiar with the electron cloud model (a). The space-filling model (b) shows the three-dimensional structure of a molecule.

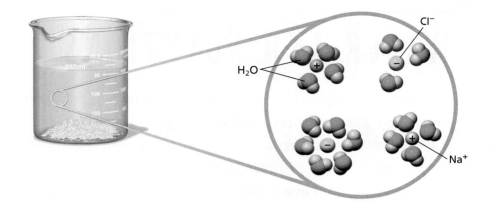

**FIGURE 2-9**

The positive region of a water molecule attracts the negative region of an ionic compound, such as the $Cl^-$ portion of NaCl. Similarly, the negative region of the water molecule attracts the positive region of the compound—the $Na^+$ portion of NaCl. As a result, NaCl breaks apart, or dissolves, in water.

## Solubility of Water

The polar nature of water allows it to dissolve polar substances, such as sugars, ionic compounds, and some proteins. Water does not dissolve nonpolar substances, such as oil because a weaker attraction exists between polar and nonpolar molecules than between two polar molecules. Figure 2-9 shows how water dissolves the ionic compound sodium chloride, NaCl. In your body, ions, such as sodium and chloride, are essential to bodily functions, such as muscle contraction and transmission of impulses in the nervous system. In fact, dissolved, or dissociated ions, are present in all of the aqueous solutions found in living things and are important in maintaining normal body functions.

# HYDROGEN BONDING

**FIGURE 2-10**

The dotted lines in this figure represent hydrogen bonds. A hydrogen bond is a force of attraction between a hydrogen atom in one molecule and a negatively charged region or atom in a second molecule.

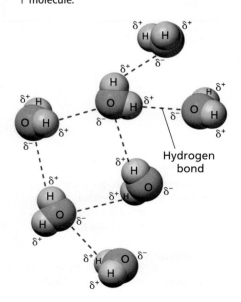

The polar nature of water also causes water molecules to be attracted to one another. As is shown in Figure 2-10, the positively charged region of one water molecule is attracted to the negatively charged region of another water molecule. This attraction is called a hydrogen bond. A **hydrogen bond** is the force of attraction between a hydrogen molecule with a partial positive charge and another atom or molecule with a partial or full negative charge. Hydrogen bonds in water exert an attractive force strong enough so that water "clings" to itself and some other substances.

Hydrogen bonds form, break, and reform with great frequency. However, at any one time, a great number of water molecules are bonded together. The number of hydrogen bonds that exist depends on the state that water is in. If water is in its solid state all its water molecules are hydrogen bonded and do not break. As water liquifies, more hydrogen bonds are broken than are formed, until an equal number of bonds are formed and broken. Hydrogen bonding accounts for the unique properties of water, some of which we will examine further. These properties include cohesion and adhesion, the ability of water to absorb a relatively large amount of energy as heat, the ability of water to cool surfaces through evaporation, the density of ice, and the ability of water to dissolve many substances.

## Cohesion and Adhesion

Water molecules stick to each other as a result of hydrogen bonding. An attractive force that holds molecules of a single substance together is known as **cohesion.** Cohesion due to hydrogen bonding between water molecules contributes to the upward movement of water from plant roots to their leaves.

Related to cohesion is the *surface tension* of water. The cohesive forces in water resulting from hydrogen bonds cause the molecules at the surface of water to be pulled downward into the liquid. As a result, water acts as if it has a thin "skin" on its surface. You can observe water's surface tension by slightly overfilling a drinking glass with water. The water will appear to bulge above the rim of the glass. Surface tension also enables small creatures such as spiders and water-striders to run on water without breaking the surface.

**Adhesion** is the attractive force between two particles of different substances, such as water molecules and glass molecules. A related property is **capillarity** (KAP-uh-LER-i-tee), which is the attraction between molecules that results in the rise of the surface of a liquid when in contact with a solid. Together, the forces of adhesion, cohesion, and capillarity help water rise through narrow tubes against the force of gravity. Figure 2-11 shows cohesion and adhesion in the water-conducting tubes in the stem of a flower.

## Temperature Moderation

Water has a high heat capacity, which means that water can absorb or release relatively large amounts of energy in the form of heat with only a slight change in temperature. This property of water is related to hydrogen bonding. Energy must be absorbed to break hydrogen bonds, and energy is released as heat when hydrogen bonds form. The energy that water initially absorbs breaks hydrogen bonds between molecules. Only after these hydrogen bonds are broken does the energy begin to increase the motion of the water molecules, which raises the temperature of the water. When the temperature of water drops, hydrogen bonds reform, which releases a large amount of energy in the form of heat.

Therefore, during a hot summer day, water can absorb a large quantity of energy from the sun and can cool the air without a large increase in the water's temperature. At night, the gradually cooling water warms the air. In this way, the Earth's oceans stabilize global temperatures enough to allow life to exist. Water's high heat capacity also allows organisms to keep cells at an even temperature despite temperature changes in the environment.

As a liquid evaporates, the surface of the liquid that remains behind cools down. A relatively large amount of energy is absorbed by water during evaporation, which significantly cools the surface of the remaining liquid. Evaporative cooling prevents organisms that live on land from overheating. For example, the evaporation of sweat from a person's skin releases body heat and prevents overheating on a hot day or during strenuous activity.

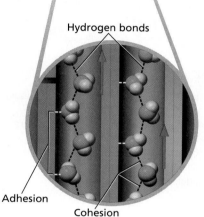

Hydrogen bonds

Adhesion

Cohesion

**FIGURE 2–11**

Cohesion, adhesion, and capillarity contribute to the upward movement of water from the roots of plants.

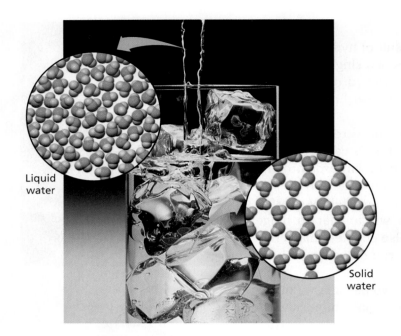

Liquid water

Solid water

### Density of Ice

Unlike most solids, which are denser than their liquids, solid water is less dense than liquid water. This property is due to the shape of the water molecule and hydrogen bonding. The angle between the hydrogen atoms is quite wide. So, when water forms solid ice, the angles in the molecules cause ice crystals to have large amounts of open space, as shown in Figure 2-12. This open space lattice structure causes ice to have a low density.

Because ice floats on water, bodies of water such as ponds and lakes freeze from the top down and not the bottom up. Ice insulates the water below from the cold air, which allows fish and other aquatic creatures to survive under the icy surface.

**FIGURE 2-12**

Ice (solid water) is less dense than liquid water because of the structure of ice crystals. The water molecules in ice are bonded to each other in a way that creates large amounts of open space between the molecules, relative to liquid water.

### Word Roots and Origins

*solvent*

from the Latin *solvere*, meaning "to loosen"

# SOLUTIONS

A **solution** is a mixture in which one or more substances are uniformly distributed in another substance. Solutions can be mixtures of liquids, solids, or gases. For example, plasma, the liquid part of blood, is a very complex solution. It is composed of many types of ions and large molecules, as well as gases, that are dissolved in water. A **solute** (SAHL-YOOT) is a substance dissolved in the solvent. The particles that compose a solute may be ions, atoms, or molecules. The **solvent** is the substance in which the solute is dissolved. For example, when sugar, a solute, and water, a solvent, are mixed, a solution of sugar water results. Though the sugar dissolves in the water, neither the sugar molecules nor the water molecules are altered chemically. If the water is boiled away, the sugar molecules remain and are unchanged.

Solutions can be composed of various proportions of a given solute in a given solvent. Thus, solutions can vary in concentration. The **concentration** of a solution is the amount of solute dissolved in a fixed amount of the solution. For example, a 2 percent saltwater solution contains 2 g of salt dissolved in enough water to make 100 mL of solution. The more solute dissolved, the greater is the concentration of the solution. A **saturated solution** is one in which no more solute can dissolve.

**Aqueous** (AY-kwee-uhs) **solutions**—solutions in which water is the solvent—are universally important to living things. Marine microorganisms spend their lives immersed in the sea, an aqueous solution. Most nutrients that plants need are in aqueous solutions in moist soil. Body cells exist in an aqueous solution of intercellular fluid and are themselves filled with fluid; in fact, most chemical reactions that occur in the body occur in aqueous solutions.

# ACIDS AND BASES

One of the most important aspects of a living system is the degree of its acidity or alkalinity. What do we mean when we use the terms *acid* and *base*?

## Ionization of Water

As water molecules move about, they bump into one another. Some of these collisions are strong enough to result in a chemical change: one water molecule loses a proton (a hydrogen nucleus), and the other gains this proton. This reaction really occurs in two steps. First, one molecule of water pulls apart another water molecule, or dissociates, into two ions of opposite charge:

$$H_2O \rightleftharpoons H^+ + OH^-$$

The $OH^-$ ion is known as the **hydroxide ion.** The free $H^+$ ion can react with another water molecule, as shown in the equation below.

$$H^+ + H_2O \rightleftharpoons H_3O^+$$

The $H_3O^+$ ion is known as the **hydronium ion.** Acidity or alkalinity is a measure of the relative amounts of hydronium ions and hydroxide ions dissolved in a solution. If the number of hydronium ions in a solution equals the number of hydroxide ions, the solution is said to be neutral. Pure water contains equal numbers of hydronium ions and hydroxide ions and is therefore a neutral solution.

## Acids

If the number of hydronium ions in a solution is greater than the number of hydroxide ions, the solution is an **acid.** For example, when hydrogen chloride gas, HCl, is dissolved in water, its molecules dissociate to form hydrogen ions, $H^+$, and chloride ions, $Cl^-$, as is shown in the equation below.

$$HCl \rightleftharpoons H^+ + Cl^-$$

These free hydrogen ions combine with water molecules to form hydronium ions, $H_3O^+$. This aqueous solution contains many more hydronium ions than it does hydroxide ions, making it an acidic solution. Acids tend to have a sour taste; however, never taste a substance to test it for acidity. In concentrated forms, they are highly corrosive to some materials, as you can see in Figure 2-13.

## Bases

If sodium hydroxide, NaOH, a solid, is dissolved in water, it dissociates to form sodium ions, $Na^+$, and hydroxide ions, $OH^-$, as shown in the equation below.

$$NaOH \rightleftharpoons Na^+ + OH^-$$

**FIGURE 2-13**

Sulfur dioxide, $SO_2$, which is produced when fossil fuels are burned, reacts with water in the atmosphere to produce acid precipitation. Acid precipitation, or acid rain, can make lakes and rivers too acidic to support life and can even corrode stone, such as the face of this statue.

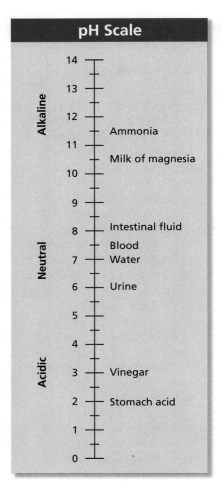

## pH Scale

14 —
13 —
12 —
11 — Ammonia
10 — Milk of magnesia
9 —
8 — Intestinal fluid
7 — Blood
   — Water
6 — Urine
5 —
4 —
3 — Vinegar
2 — Stomach acid
1 —
0 —

Alkaline / Neutral / Acidic

**FIGURE 2-14**

Some of your body fluids are acidic, and others are alkaline. A solution with a pH above 7 is alkaline, and a solution with a pH below 7 is acidic. Each unit on the pH scale reflects a 10-fold change in acidity or alkalinity.

This solution then contains more hydroxide ions than hydronium ions and is therefore defined as a **base.** The adjective *alkaline* refers to bases. Bases have a bitter taste; however, never taste a substance to test for alkalinity. They tend to feel slippery because the OH⁻ ions react with the oil on our skin to form a soap. In fact, commercial soap is the product of a reaction between a base and a fat.

## pH

Scientists have developed a scale for comparing the relative concentrations of hydronium ions and hydroxide ions in a solution. This scale is called the **pH scale,** and it ranges from 0 to 14, as shown in Figure 2-14. A solution with a pH of 0 is very acidic, a solution with a pH of 7 is neutral, and a solution with a pH of 14 is very basic. A solution's pH is measured on a logarithmic scale. That is, the change of one pH unit reflects a 10-fold change in the acidity or alkalinity. For example, urine has 10 times the $H_3O^+$ ions at a pH of 6 than water does at a pH of 7. Vinegar, has 1,000 times more $H_3O^+$ ions at a pH of 3 than urine at a pH of 6, and 10,000 times more $H_3O^+$ ions than water at a pH of 7. The pH of a solution can be measured with litmus paper or with some other chemical indicator that changes color at various pH levels.

## Buffers

The control of pH is important for living systems. Enzymes can function only within a very narrow pH range. The control of pH in organisms is often accomplished with buffers. **Buffers** are chemical substances that neutralize small amounts of either an acid or a base added to a solution. As Figure 2-14 shows, the composition of your internal environment—in terms of acidity and alkalinity—varies greatly. Some of your body fluids, such as stomach acid and urine, are acidic. Others, such as intestinal fluid and blood, are basic or alkaline. Complex buffering systems maintain the pH values in a normal healthy body.

## SECTION 3 REVIEW

1. Illustrate the structure of a water molecule by drawing a space-filling model.

2. Why is water called a polar molecule?

3. Identify the properties of water that are important for life to be able to exist.

4. Identify the solute and solvent in a hot chocolate solution that is made of chocolate syrup and warm milk.

5. Why does pure water have a neutral pH?

6. Outline a reason why the control of pH is important in living systems.

**CRITICAL THINKING**

7. **Recognizing Relationships** What is the relationship among hydrogen bonds and the forces of cohesion, adhesion, and capillarity?

8. **Applying Information** The active ingredient in aspirin is acetylsalicylic acid. Why would doctors recommend buffered aspirin, especially for those with a "sensitive" stomach?

9. **Analyzing Graphics** All units on the pH scale in Figure 2-14 look equivalent, but they are not. Why is the scale drawn as though they are?

## SECTION 1 — Composition of Matter

- Matter is anything that occupies space and has mass.

- Elements are made of a single kind of atom and cannot be broken down by chemical means into simpler substances.

- Atoms are composed of protons, neutrons, and electrons. Protons and neutrons make up the nucleus of the atom. Electrons move about the nucleus in orbitals.

- Compounds consist of atoms of two or more elements that are joined by chemical bonds in a fixed proportion.

- Most elements react to form chemical bonds so that their atoms become stable. An atom achieves stability when the orbitals that correspond to its highest energy level are filled with the maximum number of electrons.

- A covalent bond is formed when two atoms share electrons.

- An ionic bond is formed when one atom gives up an electron to another. The positive ion is then attracted to a negative ion to form the ionic bond.

### Vocabulary

| | | | |
|---|---|---|---|
| matter (p. 31) | proton (p. 32) | orbital (p. 32) | molecule (p. 33) |
| mass (p. 31) | neutron (p. 32) | isotope (p. 32) | ion (p. 34) |
| element (p. 31) | atomic number (p. 32) | compound (p. 33) | ionic bond (p. 34) |
| atom (p. 32) | mass number (p. 32) | chemical bond (p. 33) | |
| nucleus (p. 32) | electron (p. 32) | covalent bond (p. 33) | |

## SECTION 2 — Energy

- Addition of energy to a substance can cause its state to change from a solid to a liquid and from a liquid to a gas.

- Reactants are substances that enter chemical reactions. Products are substances produced by chemical reactions.

- Enzymes lower the amount of activation energy necessary for a reaction to begin in living systems.

- A chemical reaction in which electrons are exchanged between atoms is called an oxidation-reduction reaction.

### Vocabulary

| | | | |
|---|---|---|---|
| energy (p. 35) | product (p. 36) | catalyst (p. 36) | oxidation reaction (p. 37) |
| chemical reaction (p. 36) | metabolism (p. 36) | enzyme (p. 36) | reduction reaction (p. 37) |
| reactant (p. 36) | activation energy (p. 36) | redox reaction (p. 37) | |

## SECTION 3 — Water and Solutions

- The two hydrogen atoms and one oxygen atom that make up a water molecule are arranged at an angle to one another.

- Water is a polar molecule. The electrons in the molecule are shared unevenly between hydrogen and oxygen. This polarity makes water effective at dissolving other polar substances.

- Hydrogen bonding accounts for most of the unique properties of water.

- The unique properties of water include the ability to dissolve many substances, cohesion and adhesion, the ability to absorb a relatively large amount of energy as heat, the ability to cool surfaces through evaporation, and the low density of ice.

- A solution consists of a solute dissolved in a solvent.

- Water ionizes into hydronium ions and hydroxide ions.

- Acidic solutions contain more hydronium ions than hydroxide ions. Basic solutions contain more hydroxide ions than hydronium ions.

- Buffers are chemicals that neutralize the effects of adding small amounts of either an acid or a base to a solution.

### Vocabulary

| | | | |
|---|---|---|---|
| polar (p. 39) | solution (p. 42) | aqueous solution (p. 42) | pH scale (p. 44) |
| hydrogen bond (p. 40) | solute (p. 42) | hydroxide ion (p. 43) | buffer (p. 44) |
| cohesion (p. 41) | solvent (p. 42) | hydronium ion (p. 43) | |
| adhesion (p. 41) | concentration (p. 42) | acid (p. 43) | |
| capillarity (p. 41) | saturated solution (p. 42) | base (p. 44) | |

## USING VOCABULARY

1. For each pair of terms, explain how the meanings of the terms differ.
   a. *oxidation* and *reduction*
   b. *reactants* and *products*
   c. *acid* and *base*

2. Explain the relationship between electrons, neutrons, and protons.

3. Choose the term that does not belong in the following group, and explain why it does not belong: *element, compound, chemical bonds,* and *adhesion*.

4. **Word Roots and Origins** The term *catalyst* comes from the Greek *katalysis,* meaning "dissolution." Give reasons that this term is appropriate in describing the function of enzymes.

## UNDERSTANDING KEY CONCEPTS

5. **Differentiate** between the mass and the weight of an object.

6. **Name** the subatomic particles that are found in the nucleus of an atom.

7. **Describe** the arrangement within energy levels of the seven electrons of an atom of nitrogen.

8. **Describe** how compounds affect an atom's stability.

9. **Differentiate** between covalent and ionic bonds.

10. **Compare** the motion and spacing of the molecules in a solid to the motion and spacing of the molecules in a gas.

11. **Identify** the reactants and the products in the following chemical reaction.

$$A + B \longrightarrow C + D$$

12. **Explain** the relationship between enzymes and activation energy.

13. **Explain** oxidation and reduction in terms of electron transfer and charge.

14. **Describe** the structure of a water molecule.

15. **Outline** what happens when water ionizes.

16. **Describe** how water behaves at its surface and the role hydrogen bonding plays in this behavior.

17. **Identify** the solute(s) and solvent(s) in a cup of instant coffee with sugar.

18. **Name** two ions that are the products of the dissociation of water.

19. **Compare** an acid to a base in terms of the hydroxide ion concentration.

20. **CONCEPT MAPPING** Use the following terms to create a concept map that shows how the properties of water help it rise in plants: *water, hydrogen bonds, cohesion, adhesion, capillarity,* and *plants*.

## CRITICAL THINKING

21. **Analyzing Concepts** In nature, the elements oxygen and hydrogen are usually found as gases with the formulas $O_2$ and $H_2$. Why? Are they compounds? Are they molecules?

22. **Analyzing Data** The table below shows melting and boiling points at normal pressure for five different elements or compounds. Above the boiling point, a compound or element exists as a gas. Between the melting point and the boiling point, a compound or element exists as a liquid. Below the melting point, a compound or element exists as a solid. Use the table to answer the following questions:
   a. At 20°C and under normal pressure conditions, which substances exist as solids? as liquids? as gases?
   b. Which substance exists as a liquid over the broadest range of temperature?
   c. Which substance exists as a liquid over the narrowest range of temperature?
   d. Which one of the substances are you least likely to encounter as a gas?

### Melting and Boiling Points at Normal Pressure

| Substance | Melting point (°C) | Boiling point (°C) |
|-----------|--------------------|--------------------|
| Aluminum  | 658                | 2,330              |
| Argon     | −190               | −186               |
| Chlorine  | −104               | −34                |
| Mercury   | −39                | 357                |
| Water     | 0                  | 100                |

23. **Recognizing Relationships** Cells contain mostly water. What would happen to the stability of an organism's internal temperature with respect to environmental temperature changes if cells contained mostly oil, which does not have extensive hydrogen bonding?

# Standardized Test Preparation

**DIRECTIONS:** Choose the letter of the answer choice that best answers the question.

1. The way in which elements bond to form compounds depends on which of the following?
   **A.** the model of the atom
   **B.** the structural formula of the compound
   **C.** the dissociation of the ions in the compound
   **D.** the number and arrangement of electrons in the atoms of the elements

2. If an atom is made up of 6 protons, 7 neutrons, and 6 electrons, what is its atomic number?
   **F.** 6
   **G.** 7
   **H.** 13
   **J.** 19

**INTERPRETING GRAPHICS:** The graph below shows the energy in a chemical reaction as the reaction progresses. Use the graph to answer the questions that follow.

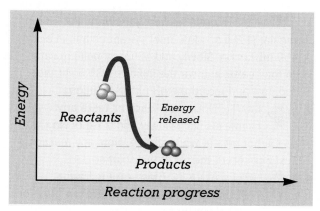

3. The amount of energy needed for this chemical reaction to begin is shown by the line rising from the reactants. What is this energy called?
   **A.** chemical energy
   **B.** electrical energy
   **C.** activation energy
   **D.** mechanical energy

4. Suppose that this reaction needs a catalyst to proceed. In the absence of a catalyst, the activation energy would be which of the following?
   **F.** larger than what is shown
   **G.** the same as what is shown
   **H.** smaller than what is shown
   **J.** not much different from what is shown

5. What is an aqueous solution that contains more hydroxide ions than hydronium ions called?
   **A.** a gas
   **B.** a base
   **C.** a solid
   **D.** an acid

**DIRECTIONS:** Complete the following analogy.

6. Oxidation : loss :: reduction :
   **F.** win
   **G.** gain
   **H.** take
   **J.** forfeit

**INTERPRETING GRAPHICS:** The illustration below is a space-filling model of water. Use the model to answer the following question.

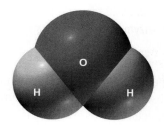

7. The water molecule above has partial positive charges on the hydrogen atoms and a partial negative charge on the oxygen atom. What can you conclude from this information and the diagram of the water molecule?
   **A.** Water is an ion.
   **B.** Water is a polar molecule.
   **C.** Water needs a proton and two electrons to be stable.
   **D.** Oxygen atoms and hydrogen atoms have opposite charges.

## SHORT RESPONSE

Covalent bonding is a sharing of electrons between atoms. Why do some atoms share electrons?

## EXTENDED RESPONSE

Pure water contains equal numbers of hydronium ions and hydroxide ions and is therefore a neutral solution.

*Part A* What is the initial cause of the dissociation of water molecules into hydrogen and hydroxide ions? Explain the process.

*Part B* After water dissociates, hydronium ions are formed. Explain this process.

# Measuring the Activity of Enzymes in Detergents

## OBJECTIVES

■ Recognize the function of enzymes in laundry detergents.

■ Relate the factors of temperature and pH to the activity of enzymes.

## PROCESS SKILLS

■ designing an experiment
■ making observations
■ measuring volume, mass, and pH

■ graphing
■ analyzing data
■ making conclusions

## MATERIALS

■ safety goggles
■ lab apron
■ balance
■ graduated cylinder
■ glass stirring rod
■ 150 mL beaker
■ 18 g regular instant gelatin or 1.8 g sugar-free instant gelatin
■ 0.7 g Na$_2$CO$_3$, sodium carbonate
■ tongs or a hot mitt
■ 50 mL boiling water

■ thermometer
■ pH paper
■ 6 test tubes
■ test-tube rack
■ pipet with bulb
■ plastic wrap
■ tape
■ 50 mL beakers (6)
■ 50 mL distilled water
■ 1 g each of 5 brands of laundry detergent
■ wax pencil
■ metric ruler

## Background

1. Write a definition for the term *enzyme.*
2. From what you know about enzymes, why might enzymes be added to detergents?

## Procedure

**PART A  Making a Protein Substrate**

1. CAUTION  **Always wear safety goggles and a lab apron to protect your eyes and clothing.** Put on safety goggles and a lab apron.

2. CAUTION  **Use tongs or a hot mitt to handle heated glassware.** Put 18 g of regular (1.8 g of sugar-free) instant gelatin in a 150 mL beaker. Slowly add 50 mL of boiling water to the beaker, and stir the mixture with a stirring rod. Test and record the pH of this solution.

3. CAUTION  **Do not touch or taste any chemicals.** Very slowly add 0.7 g of Na$_2$CO$_3$ to the hot gelatin while stirring. Note any reaction. Test and record the pH of this solution.

4. CAUTION  **Glassware is fragile. Notify the teacher of broken glass or cuts. Do not clean up broken glass or spills with broken glass unless the teacher tells you to do so. Remember to use tongs or a hot mitt to handle heated glassware.** Place 6 test tubes in a test-tube rack. Pour 5 mL of the gelatin-Na$_2$CO$_3$ mixture into each tube. Use a pipet to remove any bubbles from the surface of the mixture in each tube. Cover the tubes tightly with plastic wrap and tape. Cool the tubes, and store them at room temperature until you begin Part C. Complete step 11 in Part C.

## PART B  Designing Your Experiment

5. Based on the objectives for this lab, write a question you would like to explore about enzymes in detergents. To explore the question, design an experiment that uses the materials listed for this lab.

6. Write a procedure for your experiment. Make a list of all the safety precautions you will take. Have your teacher approve your procedure and safety precautions before you begin the experiment.

## PART C  Conducting Your Experiment

7.  **CAUTION Always wear safety goggles and a lab apron to protect your eyes and clothing.** Put on safety goggles and a lab apron.

8. Make a 10 percent solution of each laundry detergent by dissolving 1 g of detergent in 9 mL of distilled water.

9. Set up your experiment. Repeat step 11.

10. Record your data after 24 hours in a data table similar to the one below.

 **CAUTION Know the location of the emergency shower and eyewash station and how to use them. If you get a chemical on your skin or clothing, wash it off at the sink while calling to the teacher. Notify the teacher**

of a spill. Spills should be cleaned up promptly, according to your teacher's directions. Dispose of solutions, broken glass, and gelatin in the designated waste containers. Do not pour chemicals down the drain or put lab materials in the trash unless your teacher tells you to do so.

11. Clean up your work area and all lab equipment. Return lab equipment to its proper place. Wash your hands thoroughly before leaving the lab and after finishing all work.

## Analysis and Conclusions

1. Suggest a reason for adding $Na_2CO_3$ to the gelatin solution.

2. Make a bar graph of your data. Plot the amount of gelatin broken down (change in the depth of the gelatin) on the $y$-axis and the type of detergent on the $x$-axis. Use a separate sheet of graph paper.

3. What conclusions did your group infer from the results? Explain.

## Further Inquiry

Research other household products that contain enzymes, and find out their role in each of the products.

| DATA TABLE | | |
|---|---|---|
| Solution | Date | Observations |
|  |  |  |
|  |  |  |
|  |  |  |
|  |  |  |
|  |  |  |
|  |  |  |
|  |  |  |
|  |  |  |

# CHAPTER 3 BIOCHEMISTRY

All living organisms, such as those seen in this photo, are made up of molecules that contain primarily carbon atoms.

**SECTION 1** *Carbon Compounds*

**SECTION 2** *Molecules of Life*

# CARBON COMPOUNDS

*Although water is the primary medium for life on Earth, most of the molecules from which living organisms are made are based on the element carbon. Carbon's ability to form large and complex molecules has contributed to the great diversity of life.*

## CARBON BONDING

All compounds can be classified in two broad categories: organic compounds and inorganic compounds. **Organic compounds** are made primarily of carbon atoms. Most matter in living organisms that is not water is made of organic compounds. *Inorganic compounds,* with a few exceptions, do not contain carbon atoms.

A carbon atom has four electrons in its outermost energy level. Most atoms become stable when their outermost energy level contains eight electrons. A carbon atom therefore readily forms four covalent bonds with the atoms of other elements. Unlike other elements, however, carbon also readily bonds with other carbon atoms, forming straight chains, branched chains, or rings, as shown in Figure 3-1. This tendency of carbon to bond with itself results in an enormous variety of organic compounds.

In the symbolic shorthand of chemistry, each line shown in Figure 3-1 represents a covalent bond formed when two atoms share a pair of electrons. A bond formed when two atoms share one pair of electrons is called a *single bond.*

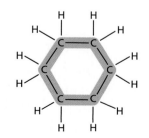

**(a)** Straight carbon chain

**(c)** Carbon ring

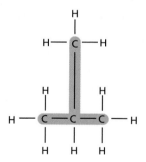

**(b)** Branched carbon chain

**(d)** Simplified view of a carbon ring

**FIGURE 3-1**

Carbon can bond in a number of ways to produce molecules of very different shapes, including straight chains (a), branched chains (b), and rings (c) and (d). These structures form the backbone of many different kinds of organic molecules. The carbon ring is shown with all of its atoms (c), and in a simplified version (d) commonly used in this textbook and elsewhere.

FIGURE 3-2

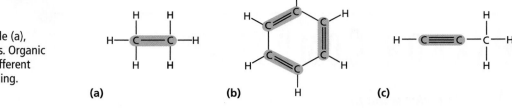

**FIGURE 3-2**

Carbon atoms can form single (a), double (b), or triple (c) bonds. Organic molecules can have many different shapes and patterns of bonding.

(a)       (b)       (c)

A carbon atom can also share two or even three pairs of electrons with another atom. Figure 3-2b shows a model for an organic compound in which six carbon atoms have formed a ring. Notice that each carbon atom forms four covalent bonds: a single bond with another carbon atom, a single bond with a hydrogen atom, and a double bond with a second carbon atom. In a *double bond*—represented by two parallel lines—atoms share two pairs of electrons. A *triple bond*, the sharing of three pairs of electrons, is represented by three parallel lines in Figure 3-2c.

# FUNCTIONAL GROUPS

In most organic compounds, clusters of atoms, called **functional groups,** influence the characteristics of the molecules they compose and the chemical reactions the molecules undergo. For example, one functional group important to living things, the hydroxyl group, —OH, can make the molecule it is attached to polar. Polar molecules are *hydrophilic* (HIE-droh-FIL-ik), or soluble in water. An *alcohol* is an organic compound with a hydroxyl group attached to one of its carbon atoms. The hydroxyl group makes an alcohol a polar molecule. The alcohol illustrated in the first row in Table 3-1 is ethanol. Other functional groups important to living things are shown in Table 3-1. These functional groups include a carboxyl group, an amino group, and a phosphate group.

**Quick Lab**

**Demonstrating Polarity**

**Materials** disposable gloves; lab apron; safety goggles; 3 test tubes; test-tube rack; 6 mL each of cooking oil, ethanol, and water

**Procedure**
1. Put on disposable gloves, a lab apron, and safety goggles, and then label the test tubes "A," "B," and "C."
2. In test tube A, put 3 mL of water and 3 mL of oil.
3. In test tube B, put 3 mL of ethanol and 3 mL of oil.
4. In test tube C, put 3 mL of water and 3 mL of ethanol.
5. With your middle finger, flick each test tube to mix the contents, and allow each to sit for 10–15 minutes. Record your observations.

**Analysis** Polar molecules are soluble in water. How does this activity demonstrate polarity of molecules that contain the —OH group?

**TABLE 3-1** *Common Functional Groups*

| Functional group | Structural formula | Example |
|---|---|---|
| Hydroxyl | —OH | ethanol structure ending in OH |
| Carboxyl | O‖—C—OH | amino-substituted carboxylic acid structure |
| Amino | H\|—N—H | amino acid structure |
| Phosphate | O‖—O—P—OH\|OH | phosphate-substituted structure |

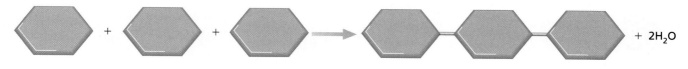

Monomers                                         Polymer + 2H₂O

# LARGE CARBON MOLECULES

Many carbon compounds are built up from smaller, simpler molecules known as **monomers** (MAH-ne-mers), such as the ones shown in Figure 3-3. As you can also see in Figure 3-3, monomers can bond to one another to form polymers (PAWL-eh-mer). A **polymer** is a molecule that consists of repeated, linked units. The units may be identical or structurally related to each other. Large polymers are called **macromolecules.** There are many types of macromolecules, such as carbohydrates, lipids, proteins and nucleic acids.

Monomers link to form polymers through a chemical reaction called a **condensation reaction.** Each time a monomer is added to a polymer, a water molecule is released. In the condensation reaction shown in Figure 3-4, two sugar molecules, glucose and fructose, combine to form the sugar sucrose, which is common table sugar. The two sugar monomers become linked by a C—O—C bridge. In the formation of that bridge, the glucose molecule releases a hydrogen ion, $H^+$, and the fructose molecule releases a hydroxide ion, $OH^-$. The $OH^-$ and $H^+$ ions that are released then combine to produce a water molecule, $H_2O$.

In addition to building polymers through condensation reactions, living organisms also have to break them down. The breakdown of some complex molecules, such as polymers, occurs through a process known as hydrolysis (hie-DRAHL-i-sis). In a **hydrolysis** reaction, water is used to break down a polymer. The water molecule breaks the bond linking each monomer. Hydrolysis is the reverse of a condensation reaction. The addition of water to some complex molecules, including polymers, under certain conditions can break the bonds that hold them together. For example, in Figure 3-4 reversing the reaction will result in sucrose breaking down into fructose and glucose.

**FIGURE 3-3**

A polymer is the result of bonding between monomers. In this example, each monomer is a six-sided carbon ring. The starch in potatoes is an example of a molecule that is a polymer.

**FIGURE 3-4**

The condensation reaction below shows how glucose links with fructose to form sucrose. One water molecule is produced each time two monomers form a covalent bond.

Glucose        Fructose                              Sucrose        + H₂O

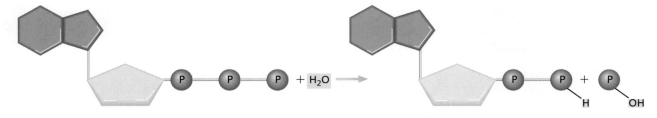

Adenosine triphosphate (ATP)

Adenosine diphosphate (ADP) and
inorganic phosphate

**FIGURE 3-5**

The hydrolysis of ATP yields adenosine diphosphate (ADP) and inorganic phosphate. In hydrolysis, a hydrogen ion from a water molecule bonds to one of the new molecules, and a hydroxide ion bonds to the other new molecule. Most hydrolysis reactions release energy.

**Word Roots and Origins**

*phosphate*

from the Latin *phosphor,* meaning "morning star," (morning stars are very bright, similar to phosphorus when it burns) and *ate,* meaning "salt"

# ENERGY CURRENCY

Life processes require a constant supply of energy. This energy is available to cells in the form of certain compounds that store a large amount of energy in their overall structure. One of these compounds is **adenosine** (uh-DEN-uh-SEEN) **triphosphate,** more commonly referred to by its abbreviation, **ATP.**

The left side of Figure 3-5 shows a simplified ATP molecule structure. The 5-carbon sugar, ribose, is represented by the blue carbon ring. The nitrogen-containing compound, adenine, is represented by the 2 orange rings. The three linked phosphate groups, $-PO_4^-$, are represented by the blue circles with a "P." The phospate groups are attached to each other by covalent bonds.

The covalent bonds between the phosphate groups are more unstable than the other bonds in the ATP molecule because the phosphate groups are close together and have negative charges. Thus, the negative charges make the bonds easier to break. When a bond between the phosphate groups is broken, energy is released. This hydrolysis of ATP is used by the cell to provide the energy needed to drive the chemical reactions that enable an organism to function.

## SECTION 1 REVIEW

1. How do inorganic and organic compounds differ?

2. How do carbon's bonding properties contribute to the existence of a wide variety of biological molecules?

3. Name four types of functional groups.

4. What role do functional groups play in the molecules in which they are found?

5. How are monomers, polymers, and macromolecules related to each other?

6. How is a polymer broken down?

7. Why is ATP referred to as the "energy currency" in living things?

**CRITICAL THINKING**

8. **Analyzing Concepts** Humans are about 65 percent water, and tomatoes are about 90 percent water. Yet, water is not a major building block of life. Explain.

9. **Analyzing Concepts** Carbon dioxide, $CO_2$, contains carbon, yet it is considered to be inorganic. Explain.

10. **Relating Information** Condensation reactions are also referred to as dehydration synthesis. Explain how the name *dehydration synthesis* is descriptive of the process.

# MOLECULES OF LIFE

*Four main classes of organic compounds are essential to the life processes of all living things: carbohydrates, lipids, proteins, and nucleic acids. You will see that although these compounds are built primarily from carbon, hydrogen, and oxygen, these atoms occur in different ratios in each class of compound. Each class of compounds has different properties.*

## SECTION 2

### OBJECTIVES

- **Distinguish** between monosaccharides, disaccharides, and polysaccharides.
- **Explain** the relationship between amino acids and protein structure.
- **Describe** the induced fit model of enzyme action.
- **Compare** the structure and function of each of the different types of lipids.
- **Compare** the nucleic acids DNA and RNA.

### VOCABULARY

carbohydrate
monosaccharide
disaccharide
polysaccharide
protein
amino acid
peptide bond
polypeptide
enzyme
substrate
active site
lipid
fatty acid
phospholipid
wax
steroid
nucleic acid
deoxyribonucleic acid (DNA)
ribonucleic acid (RNA)
nucleotide

## CARBOHYDRATES

**Carbohydrates** are organic compounds composed of carbon, hydrogen, and oxygen in a ratio of about one carbon atom to two hydrogen atoms to one oxygen atom. The number of carbon atoms in a carbohydrate varies. Some carbohydrates serve as a source of energy. Other carbohydrates are used as structural materials. Carbohydrates can exist as monosaccharides, disaccharides, or polysaccharides.

### Monosaccharides

A monomer of a carbohydrate is called a **monosaccharide** (MAHN-oh-SAK-uh-RIED). A monosaccharide—or simple sugar—contains carbon, hydrogen, and oxygen in a ratio of 1:2:1. The general formula for a monosaccharide is written as $(CH_2O)_n$, where $n$ is any whole number from 3 to 8. For example, a six-carbon monosaccharide, $(CH_2O)_6$, would have the formula $C_6H_{12}O_6$.

The most common monosaccharides are glucose, fructose, and galactose, as shown in Figure 3-6. Glucose is a main source of energy for cells. Fructose is found in fruits and is the sweetest of the monosaccharides. Galactose is found in milk.

Notice in Figure 3-6 that glucose, fructose, and galactose have the same molecular formula, $C_6H_{12}O_6$, but differing structures. The different structures determine the slightly different properties of the three compounds. Compounds like these sugars, with a single chemical formula but different structural forms, are called *isomers* (IE-soh-muhrz).

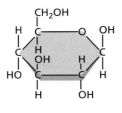

Glucose

Fructose

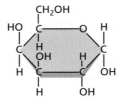

Galactose

**FIGURE 3-6**

Glucose, fructose, and galactose have the same chemical formula, but their structural differences result in different properties among the three compounds.

## Disaccharides and Polysaccharides

In living things, two monosaccharides can combine in a condensation reaction to form a double sugar, or **disaccharide** (die-SAK-e-RIED). For example in Figure 3-4, the monosaccharides fructose and glucose can combine to form the disaccharide sucrose.

A **polysaccharide** is a complex molecule composed of three or more monosaccharides. Animals store glucose in the form of the polysaccharide *glycogen.* Glycogen consists of hundreds of glucose molecules strung together in a highly branched chain. Much of the glucose that comes from food is ultimately stored in your liver and muscles as glycogen and is ready to be used for quick energy.

Plants store glucose molecules in the form of the polysaccharide *starch.* Starch molecules have two basic forms—highly branched chains that are similar to glycogen and long, coiled, unbranched chains. Plants also make a large polysaccharide called *cellulose.* Cellulose, which gives strength and rigidity to plant cells, makes up about 50 percent of wood. In a single cellulose molecule, thousands of glucose monomers are linked in long, straight chains. These chains tend to form hydrogen bonds with each other. The resulting structure is strong and can be broken down by hydrolysis only under certain conditions.

# PROTEINS

**Proteins** are organic compounds composed mainly of carbon, hydrogen, oxygen, and nitrogen. Like most of the other biological macromolecules, proteins are formed from the linkage of monomers called **amino acids.** Hair and horns, as shown in Figure 3-7a, are made mostly of proteins, as are skin, muscles and many biological catalysts (enzymes).

## Amino Acids

There are 20 different amino acids, and all share a basic structure. As Figure 3-7b shows, each amino acid contains a central carbon atom covalently bonded to four other atoms or functional groups. A single hydrogen atom, highlighted in blue in the illustration, bonds at one site. A carboxyl group, —COOH, highlighted in green, bonds at a second site. An amino group, —$NH_2$, highlighted in yellow, bonds at a third site. A side chain called the *R group,* highlighted in red, bonds at the fourth site.

The main difference among the different amino acids is in their R groups. The R group can be complex or it can be simple, such as the $CH_3$ group shown in the amino acid alanine in Figure 3-7b. The differences among the amino acid R groups gives different proteins very different shapes. The different shapes allow proteins to carry out many different activities in living things. Amino acids are commonly shown in a simplified way such as balls, as shown in Figure 3-7c.

**FIGURE 3-7**

(a) Many structures, such as hair and horns are made of proteins. (b) Proteins are made up of amino acids. Amino acids differ only in the type of R group (shown in red) they carry. Polar R groups can dissolve in water, but nonpolar R groups cannot. (c) Amino acids have complex structures, so, in this and other textbooks, they are often simplified into balls.

**(a)**

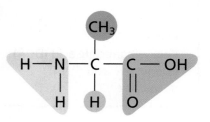

**(b)** Alanine (an amino acid)

**(c)** Simplified version of amino acid

## Dipeptides and Polypeptides

Figure 3-8a shows how two amino acids bond to form a *dipeptide* (die-PEP-TIED). In this condensation reaction, the two amino acids form a covalent bond, called a **peptide bond** (shaded in blue in Figure 3-8a) and release a water molecule.

Amino acids often form very long chains called **polypeptides** (PAHL-i-PEP-TIEDZ). Proteins are composed of one or more polypeptides. Some proteins are very large molecules, containing hundreds of amino acids. Often, these long proteins are bent and folded upon themselves as a result of interactions—such as hydrogen bonding—between individual amino acids. Protein shape can also be influenced by conditions such as temperature and the type of solvent in which a protein is dissolved. For example, cooking an egg changes the shape of proteins in the egg white. The firm, opaque result is very different from the initial clear, runny material.

## Enzymes

**Enzymes**—RNA or protein molecules that act as biological catalysts—are essential for the functioning of any cell. Many enzymes are proteins. Figure 3-9 shows an induced fit model of enzyme action.

Enzyme reactions depend on a physical fit between the enzyme molecule and its specific **substrate,** the reactant being catalyzed. Notice that the enzyme has folds, or an **active site,** with a shape that allows the substrate to fit into the active site. An enzyme acts only on a specific substrate because only that substrate fits into its active site. The linkage of the enzyme and substrate causes a slight change in the enzyme's shape. The change in the enzyme's shape weakens some chemical bonds in the substrate, which is one way that enzymes reduce activation energy, the energy needed to start the reaction. After the reaction, the enzyme releases the products. Like any catalyst, the enzyme itself is unchanged, so it can be used many times.

An enzyme may not work if its environment is changed. For example, change in temperature or pH can cause a change in the shape of the enzyme or the substrate. If such a change happens, the reaction that the enzyme would have catalyzed cannot occur.

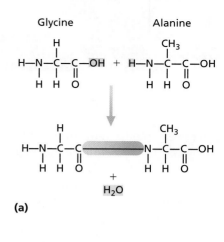

**(a)**

**(b)**

**FIGURE 3-8**

(a) The peptide bond (shaded blue) that binds amino acids together to form a polypeptide results from a condensation reaction that produces water. (b) Polypeptides are commonly shown as a string of balls in this textbook and elsewhere. Each ball represents an amino acid.

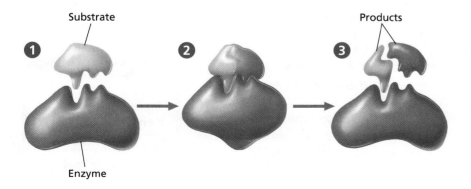

**FIGURE 3-9**

❶ In the induced fit model of enzyme action, the enzyme can attach only to a substrate (reactant) with a specific shape. ❷ The enzyme then changes and reduces the activation energy of the reaction so reactants can become products. ❸ The enzyme is unchanged and is available to be used again.

# TREATING AND PREVENTING DIABETES

**P**roteins play many important roles in living organisms. The hormone *insulin* is a protein that stimulates cells to take up glucose. More than 18 million Americans have *diabetes,* an inability of the body to make or respond to insulin.

When the body cannot make or respond to insulin, the body's cells must switch to burning mainly fat as their fuel. The resulting high levels of fat in the blood can cause cardiovascular disease. In addition, the glucose that accumulates in the blood causes other problems. For example, diabetes can have serious complications, including kidney disease, heart failure, blindness, and amputation of the lower limbs. Some symptoms of diabetes include increased thirst, frequent urination, fatigue, and weight loss.

*Regular physical activity can help reduce the risk of developing type 2 diabetes.*

### Type 1 Diabetes

Between 5 and 10 percent of people who suffer from diabetes have type 1 diabetes, which usually starts in childhood. The body's immune system mistakenly attacks cells in the pancreas that make insulin. If untreated, type 1 diabetes is usually fatal.

### Treating Type 1 Diabetes

People with type 1 diabetes require a carefully monitored diet, physical activity, home blood glucose testing several times a day, and multiple daily insulin injections. In the past, insulin was delivered by shots. Now, there are pumps that regularly deliver small amounts of insulin. The pumps can be implanted surgically and refilled periodically by injection.

### Type 2 Diabetes

The majority of people who suffer from diabetes have type 2 diabetes, which can begin at any age. A diet high in sugars and fats, a sedentary lifestyle, and being overweight can each increase the chances of developing this type of diabetes. Type 2 diabetes occurs when the pancreas cannot keep up with the demand for insulin or the cells become resistant to insulin's effects.

### Treating Type 2 Diabetes

For type 2 diabetes, treatment typically includes a healthy diet, regular exercise, and home blood glucose testing. Some people must also take oral medication and/or insulin.

About 40 percent of people with type 2 diabetes require insulin injections.

### Preventing Diabetes

There is currently not a way to prevent type 1 diabetes. But exercise, a healthy diet, and insulin injections can allow a person to lead a normal life. Ways to prevent type 2 diabetes include exercising regularly and eating a healthy diet.

### Future Treatments for Diabetes

Medical researchers are working on devices that can monitor blood sugar better. Other researchers are trying to improve the delivery of insulin by using timed-release drugs or by developing smaller implants. Some researchers are working on improving organ transplant surgery and finding genes linked to diabetes.

### REVIEW

1. Distinguish between type 1 and type 2 diabetes.
2. Why is insulin important?
3. **Critical Thinking** A friend asks, "Why should I worry? By the time I'm old, they'll have diabetes cured anyway." What is your opinion? Defend your answer.

internet connect

www.scilinks.org
**Topic: Diabetes**
**Keyword: HM60400**

SCiLINKS. Maintained by the National Science Teachers Association

# LIPIDS

**Lipids** are large, nonpolar organic molecules. They do not dissolve in water. Lipids include triglycerides (trie-GLIS-uhr-IEDZ), phospholipids, steroids, waxes, and pigments. Lipid molecules have a higher ratio of carbon and hydrogen atoms to oxygen atoms than carbohydrates have. Because lipid molecules have larger numbers of carbon-hydrogen bonds per gram than other organic compounds do, they store more energy per gram.

## Fatty Acids

**Fatty acids** are unbranched carbon chains that make up most lipids. Figure 3-10 shows that a fatty acid contains a long carbon chain (from 12 to 28 carbons) with a carboxyl group, —COOH, attached at one end. The two ends of the fatty-acid molecule have different properties. The carboxyl end is polar and is thus *hydrophilic* or attracted to water molecules. In contrast, the hydrocarbon end of the fatty-acid molecule is nonpolar. This end tends not to interact with water molecules and is said to be *hydrophobic* (HIE-droh-FOH-bik), or "water fearing."

In saturated fatty acids, such as palmitic acid, which is shown in Figure 3-10, each carbon atom is covalently bonded to four atoms. The carbon atoms are in effect full, or *saturated*. In contrast, linoleic acid, also shown in Figure 3-10, has carbon atoms that are not bonded to the maximum number of atoms to which they can bond. Instead, they have formed double bonds within the carbon chain. This type of fatty acid is said to be *unsaturated*.

## Triglycerides

Three classes of lipids important to living things contain fatty acids: triglycerides (fats), phospholipids, and waxes. A *triglyceride* is composed of three molecules of fatty acid joined to one molecule of the alcohol glycerol. Saturated triglycerides are composed of saturated fatty acids. They typically have high melting points and tend to be hard at room temperature. Common dietary saturated triglycerides include butter and fats in red meat. In contrast, unsaturated triglycerides are composed of unsaturated fatty acids and are usually soft or liquid at room temperature. Unsaturated triglycerides are found primarily in plant seeds where they serve as an energy and carbon source for germinating plants.

## Phospholipids

**Phospholipids** have two, rather than three, fatty acids attached to a molecule of glycerol. They have a phosphate group attached to the third carbon of the glycerol. As shown in Figure 3-11, the cell membrane is made of two layers of phospholipids, called the *lipid bilayer*. The inability of lipids to dissolve in water allows the membrane to form a barrier between the inside and outside of the cell.

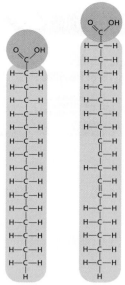

Palmitic acid   Linoleic acid

**FIGURE 3-10**

Fatty acids have a polar carboxyl head, highlighted in purple, and a nonpolar hydrocarbon tail, highlighted in green.

**FIGURE 3-11**

The lipid bilayer of a cell membrane is a double row of phospholipids. The "tails" face each other. The "head" of a phospholipid, which contains a phosphate group, is polar and hydrophilic. The two tails are two fatty acids and are nonpolar and hydrophobic.

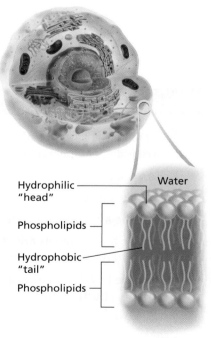

Hydrophilic "head"

Water

Phospholipids

Hydrophobic "tail"

Phospholipids

Water

## Waxes

A **wax** is a type of structural lipid consisting of a long fatty-acid chain joined to a long alcohol chain. Waxes are waterproof, and in plants, form a protective coating on the outer surfaces. Waxes also form protective layers in animals. For example, earwax helps prevent microorganisms from entering the ear canal.

## Steroids

Unlike most other lipids, which are composed of fatty acids, **steroid** molecules are composed of four fused carbon rings with various functional groups attached to them. Many animal hormones, such as the male hormone testosterone, are steroid compounds. One of the most familiar steroids in humans is cholesterol. Cholesterol is needed by the body for nerve and other cells to function normally. It is also a component of the cell membrane.

**FIGURE 3-12**

DNA as shown below, and RNA, are very large molecules formed from nucleotides linked together in a chain. A nucleotide consists of a phosphate group, a five-carbon sugar, and a ring-shaped nitrogenous base.

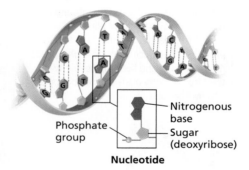

Phosphate group

Nitrogenous base

Sugar (deoxyribose)

**Nucleotide**

# NUCLEIC ACIDS

**Nucleic acids** are very large and complex organic molecules that store and transfer important information in the cell. There are two major types of nucleic acids: deoxyribonucleic acid and ribonucleic acid.

   **Deoxyribonucleic acid,** or **DNA,** contains information that determines the characteristics of an organism and directs its cell activities. **Ribonucleic** (RIE-boh-noo-KLEE-ik) **acid,** or **RNA,** stores and transfers information from DNA that is essential for the manufacturing of proteins. RNA molecules can also act as enzymes. Both DNA and RNA are polymers, composed of thousands of linked monomers called *nucleotides* (NOO-klee-uh-TIEDS). As shown in Figure 3-12, each **nucleotide** is made of three main components: a phosphate group, a five-carbon sugar, and a ring-shaped nitrogenous base.

## SECTION 2 REVIEW

1. Compare the structure of monosaccharides, disaccharides, and polysaccharides.

2. How are proteins constructed from amino acids?

3. How do amino acids differ from one another?

4. Describe a model of enzyme action.

5. Why do phospholipids orient in a bilayer when in a watery environment, such as a cell?

6. Describe how the three major types of lipids differ in structure from one another.

7. What are the functions of the two types of nucleic acids?

### CRITICAL THINKING

8. **Applying Information** Before a long race, runners often "carbo load." This means that they eat substantial quantities of carbohydrates. How might this help their performance?

9. **Recognizing Relationships** High temperatures can weaken bonds within a protein molecule. How might this explain the effects of using a hot curling iron or rollers in one's hair?

10. **Applying Information** You want to eat more unsaturated than saturated fats. Name examples of foods you would eat more of and less of.

# CHAPTER HIGHLIGHTS

## SECTION 1    Carbon Compounds

- Organic compounds contain carbon atoms and are found in living things. Most inorganic compounds do not contain carbon atoms.

- Carbon atoms can readily form four covalent bonds with other atoms including other carbon atoms. The carbon bonds allow the carbon atoms to form a wide variety of simple and complex organic compounds.

- Functional groups are groups of atoms that influence the properties of molecules and the chemical reactions in which the molecules participate.

- Condensation reactions join monomers (small simple molecules) to form polymers. A condensation reaction releases water as a by-product. In a hydrolysis reaction, water is used to split polymers into monomers.

- Adenosine triphosphate (ATP) stores and releases energy during cell processes enabling organisms to function.

### Vocabulary

| | | | |
|---|---|---|---|
| organic compound (p. 51) | polymer (p. 53) | condensation reaction (p. 53) | adenosine triphosphate |
| functional group (p. 52) | macromolecule (p. 53) | hydrolysis (p. 53) | (ATP) (p. 54) |
| monomer (p. 53) | | | |

## SECTION 2    Molecules of Life

- There are four main classes of organic compounds: carbohydrates, proteins, lipids, and nucleic acids.

- Carbohydrates are made up of monomers called monosaccharides. Two monosaccharides join to form a double sugar called a disaccharide. A complex sugar, or polysaccharide, is made of three or more monosaccharides.

- Carbohydrates such as glucose, are a source of energy and are used as structural materials in organisms.

- Proteins have many functions including structural, defensive, and catalytic. Proteins are made up of monomers called amino acids. The sequence of amino acids determines a protein's shape and function. A long chain of amino acids is called a polypeptide, which is made up of amino acids joined by peptide bonds.

- Enzymes speed up chemical reactions and bind to specific substrates. The binding of a substrate with an enzyme causes a change in the enzyme's shape and reduces the activation energy of the reaction.

- Lipids are nonpolar molecules that store energy and are an important part of cell membranes. Most lipids contain fatty acids, molecules that have a hydrophilic end and a hydrophobic end.

- There are three kinds of lipids: Triglycerides consist of three fatty acids and one molecule of glycerol. Phospholipids, which make up cell membranes, consist of two fatty acids and one glycerol molecule. A wax is made of one long fatty acid chain joined to one long alcohol.

- The nucleic acid, deoxyribonucleic acid (DNA), contains all the genetic information for cell activities. Ribonucleic acid (RNA) molecules play many key roles in building of proteins and can act as enzymes.

### Vocabulary

| | | | |
|---|---|---|---|
| carbohydrate (p. 55) | peptide bond (p. 57) | fatty acid (p. 59) | deoxyribonucleic acid (DNA) |
| monosaccharide (p. 55) | polypeptide (p. 57) | triglyceride (p. 59) | (p. 60) |
| disaccharide (p. 56) | enzyme (p. 57) | phospholipid (p. 59) | ribonucleic acid |
| polysaccharide (p. 56) | substrate (p. 57) | wax (p. 60) | (RNA) (p. 60) |
| protein (p. 56) | active site (p. 57) | steroid (p. 60) | nucleotide (p. 60) |
| amino acid (p. 56) | lipid (p. 59) | nucleic acid (p. 60) | |

# CHAPTER REVIEW

## USING VOCABULARY

1. For each pair of terms, explain how the meanings of the terms differ.
   a. *monomer* and *polymer*
   b. *functional group* and *macromolecule*
   c. *monosaccharide* and *disaccharide*
   d. *polypeptide* and *protein*
   e. *nucleic acid* and *nucleotide*

2. For each pair of terms, explain the relationship between the terms.
   a. *fatty acid* and *triglyceride*
   b. *substrate* and *enzyme*

3. Use the following terms in the same sentence: *monomer, polymer, condensation reaction,* and *hydrolysis.*

4. **Word Roots and Origins** The word *organic* is derived from the Greek *organikos,* which means "organ." Explain how the word *organic* is descriptive of most carbon compounds.

## UNDERSTANDING KEY CONCEPTS

5. **Differentiate** between organic and inorganic compounds.

6. **Relate** the properties of carbon to the formation of organic compounds.

7. **Summarize** how functional groups help determine the properties of organic compounds.

8. **Compare** how organic compounds are built to how they are broken down.

9. **Explain** the role of ATP in cellular activities.

10. **List** the four major classes of organic compounds.

11. **Describe** the general structure of carbohydrates.

12. **Define** the term *isomer.*

13. **Summarize** the differences between simple sugars, double sugars, and complex sugars.

14. **Describe** how a protein's structure is determined by the arrangement of amino acids.

15. **State** the basic structure of an amino acid.

16. **Compare** the processes used in the formation of a dipeptide and a disaccharide.

17. **Summarize** the induced fit model of enzyme activity.

18. **Differentiate** between saturated and unsaturated triglycerides.

19. **Compare** the structures of triglycerides, phospholipids, and steroids.

20. **State** how steroids differ from other lipids.

21. **Identify** an important characteristic of waxes in living organisms.

22. **Compare** two kinds of nucleic acids.

23. **Name** the three parts of a nucleotide.

24. **CONCEPT MAPPING** Use the following terms to create a concept map that describes the different types of organic compounds: *dipeptide, triglycerides, RNA, phospholipids, carbohydrates, monosaccharide, amino acid, disaccharide, polypeptide, polysaccharide, proteins, DNA, lipids, nucleic acids, steroids,* and *waxes.*

## CRITICAL THINKING

25. **Applying Information** What is the chemical formula for a monosaccharide that has three carbons?

26. **Analyzing Concepts** Starch easily dissolves in water. Cellulose does not. Both substances, however, consist of chains of glucose molecules. What structural difference between starch and cellulose might account for their different behavior in water?

27. **Interpreting Graphics** Identify the type of organic molecule shown below. Identify each of the functional groups shaded in yellow, red, and green.

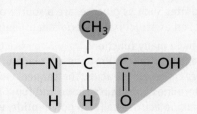

28. **Making Inferences** Analysis of an unknown substance showed that it has the following characteristics: It contains carbon, hydrogen, and oxygen and it is soluble in oil but not water. Predict what kind of substance it might be. Explain your answer.

29. **Applying Information** Many birds store significant amounts of energy to power flight during winter migration. What type of organic molecule might be best suited for energy storage? Explain.

# Standardized Test Preparation

**DIRECTIONS:** Choose the letter of the answer choice that best answers the question.

1. Which of the following is not a function of polysaccharides?
   A. energy source
   B. energy storage
   C. structural support
   D. storage of genetic information

2. Which of the following statements is false?
   F. A wax is a lipid.
   G. Starch is a lipid.
   H. Saturated fats are solid at room temperature.
   J. Unsaturated fats are liquid at room temperature.

3. Which of the following molecules stores hereditary information?
   A. ATP
   B. DNA
   C. protein
   D. carbohydrates

4. What is the name of the molecule in plants that stores sugars?
   F. starch
   G. protein
   H. cellulose
   J. glycogen

**INTERPRETING GRAPHICS:** The figure below illustrates the basic structure of a cell membrane. Use the figure to answer the questions that follow.

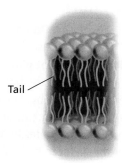

Tail

5. Which of the following molecules make up the basic structure of a cell membrane?
   A. waxes
   B. steroids
   C. fatty acids
   D. phospholipids

6. The "tails" of the molecules in the figure orient away from water. Which of the following describes the tail's movement away from water?
   F. polar
   G. adhesive
   H. hydrophilic
   J. hydrophobic

**DIRECTIONS:** Complete the following analogy.

7. simple sugars : carbohydrates :: amino acids :
   A. lipids
   B. proteins
   C. nucleic acids
   D. amino groups

**INTERPRETING GRAPHICS:** The figure below represents the structural formula of a molecule. Use the figure to answer the question that follows.

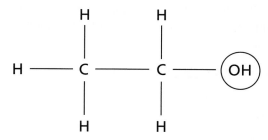

8. What is the name of the functional group circled in the structural formula above?
   F. amino
   G. hydroxyl
   H. phosphate
   J. carboxyl

## SHORT RESPONSE

Proteins are affected by environmental conditions such as heat and pH.

Explain why the process of cooking an egg cannot be reversed.

## EXTENDED RESPONSE

Enzymes are essential for the functioning of all cells.

*Part A* Explain what enzymes do that is essential for cell function.

*Part B* Explain the induced fit model of enzyme action.

**Test TIP** When writing an answer to an extended response question, make an outline of what you plan to write before writing your answer. Although it may take a little more time, the answer will be easier to write.

# Identifying Organic Compounds in Foods

## OBJECTIVES

- Determine whether specific nutrients are present in a solution of unknown composition.
- Perform chemical tests using substances called *indicators.*

## PROCESS SKILLS

- experimenting
- observing
- identifying
- measuring

## MATERIALS

- lab apron
- safety goggles
- disposable gloves
- 500 mL beaker
- hot plate
- 9 test tubes
- labeling tape
- marker
- 10 mL graduated cylinder
- Benedict's solution
- 9 dropping pipets
- glucose solution
- unknown solution
- distilled water
- 9 glass stirring rods
- tongs or test-tube holder
- test-tube rack
- albumin solution
- sodium hydroxide solution
- copper sulfate solution
- vegetable oil
- Sudan III solution

## Background

1. Carbohydrates, proteins, and lipids are nutrients that make up all living things. Some foods, such as table sugar, contain only one of these nutrients. Most foods, however, contain mixtures of proteins, carbohydrates, and lipids. You can confirm this fact by reading the information in the Nutrition Facts box found on any food label.

2. In this investigation, you will use chemical substances, called *indicators,* to identify the presence of specific nutrients in an unknown solution. By comparing the color change an indicator produces in the unknown food sample with the change it produces in a sample of known composition, you can determine whether specific organic compounds are present in the unknown sample.

3. Benedict's solution is used to determine the presence of monosaccharides, such as glucose. A mixture of sodium hydroxide and copper sulfate determines the presence of some proteins. This procedure is called the biuret test. Sudan III is used to determine the presence of lipids.

## Procedure

   **CAUTION Put on a lab apron, safety goggles, and gloves. In this lab, you will be working with chemicals that can harm your skin and eyes or stain your skin and clothing. If you get a chemical on your skin or clothing, wash it off at the sink while calling to your teacher. If you get a chemical in your eyes, immediately flush it out at the eyewash station while calling to your teacher.** As you perform each test, record your data in your lab report, organized in a table such as the one on the next page.

## Test 1: Monosaccharides

1. **CAUTION Do not touch the hot plate. Use tongs to move heated objects. Turn off the hot plate when not in use. Do not plug in or unplug the hot plate with wet hands.** Make a water bath by filling a 500 mL beaker half full with water. Then, put the beaker on a hot plate, and bring the water to a boil.

2. While you wait for the water to boil, label one test tube "1-glucose," label the second test tube "1-unknown," and label the third test tube "1-water." Using the graduated cylinder, measure 5 mL of Benedict's solution, and add it to the "1-glucose" test tube. Repeat the procedure, adding 5 mL of Benedict's solution each to the "1-unknown" test tube and "1-water" test tube.

3. Using a dropping pipet or eyedropper, add 10 drops of glucose solution to the "1-glucose" test tube. Using a second dropping pipet, add 10 drops of the unknown solution to the "1-unknown" test tube.

## IDENTIFICATION OF SPECIFIC NUTRIENTS BY CHEMICAL INDICATORS

| Test | Nutrient in test solution | Nutrient category (protein, lipid, etc.) | Result for known sample | Result for unknown sample | Result for distilled water |
|------|---------------------------|------------------------------------------|-------------------------|----------------------------|----------------------------|
| 1 | | | | | |
| 2 | | | | | |
| 3 | | | | | |

Using a third dropping pipet, add 10 drops of distilled water to the "1-water" test tube. Mix the contents of each test tube with a clean stirring rod. (**It is important not to contaminate test solutions by using the same dropping pipet or stirring rod in more than one solution. Use a different dropping pipet and stirring rod for each of the test solutions.**)

4. When the water boils, use tongs to place the test tubes in the water bath. Boil the test tubes for 1 to 2 minutes.

5. **CAUTION** Do not touch the test tubes with your hands. They will be very hot. Use tongs to remove the test tubes from the water bath and place them in the test-tube rack. As the test tubes cool, an orange or red precipitate will form if large amounts of glucose are present. If small amounts of glucose are present, a yellow or green precipitate will form. Record your results in your data table.

### Test 2: Proteins

6. Label one clean test tube "2-albumin," label a second test tube "2-unknown," and label a third test tube "2-water." Using a dropping pipet, add 40 drops of albumin solution to the "2-albumin" test tube. Using a second dropping pipet, add 40 drops of unknown solution to the "2-unknown" test tube. Using a third dropping pipet, add 40 drops of water to the "2-water" test tube.

7. Add 40 drops of sodium hydroxide solution to each of the three test tubes. Mix the contents of each test tube with a clean stirring rod.

8. Add a few drops of copper sulfate solution, one drop at a time, to the "2-albumin" test tube. Stir the solution with a clean stirring rod after each drop. Note the number of drops required to cause the color of the solution in the test tube to change. Then, add the same number of drops of copper sulfate solution to the "2-unknown" and "2-water" test tubes.

9. Record your results in your data table.

### Test 3: Lipids

10. Label one clean test tube "3-vegetable oil," label a second test tube "3-unknown," and label a third test tube "3-water." Using a dropping pipet, add 5 drops of vegetable oil to the "3-vegetable oil" test tube. Using a second dropping pipet, add 5 drops of the unknown solution to the "3-unknown" test tube. Using a third dropping pipet, add 5 drops of water to the "3-water" test tube.

11. **CAUTION** Sudan III solution will stain your skin and clothing. Promptly wash off spills to minimize staining. Do not use Sudan III solution in the same room with an open flame. Using a clean dropping pipet, add 3 drops of Sudan III solution to each test tube. Mix the contents of each test tube with a clean stirring rod.

12. Record you results in your data table.

13. Clean up your materials, and wash your hands before leaving the lab.

### Analysis and Conclusions

1. Based on the results you recorded in your data table, identify the nutrient or nutrients in the unknown solution.

2. What are the experimental controls in this investigation?

3. Explain how you were able to use the color changes of different indicators to determine the presence of specific nutrients in the unknown substance.

4. List four potential sources of error in this investigation.

### Further Inquiry

Is there a kind of macromolecule that the tests in this lab did not test for? If so, list the kinds of macromolecules not tested for, and give one reason why they were not tested for.

# CELL BIOLOGY

❝ *The cell is the natural granule of life in the same way as the atom is the natural granule of simple, elemental matter. If we are to take the measure of the transit to life and determine its precise nature, we must try to understand the cell.* ❞

From "The Advent of Life," from *The Phenomenon of Man*, by Pierre Teilhard de Chardin. Copyright © 1955 by Editions du Seuil. English translation copyright © 1959 by William Collins Sons & Co. Ltd., London and Harper & Row Publishers, Inc., New York. Reproduced by permission of **HarperCollins Publishers, Inc.** and electronic format by permission of **Georges Borchardt, Inc.**

References to *Scientific American* project ideas are located throughout this unit.

**internet** connect

National Science Teachers Association *sci* LINKS Internet resources are located throughout this unit.

*sci* LINKS. Maintained by the National Science Teachers Association

*Eukaryotic cells contain a number of complex internal structures.*

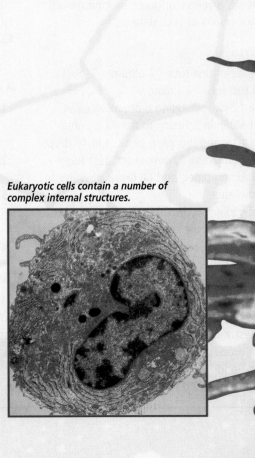

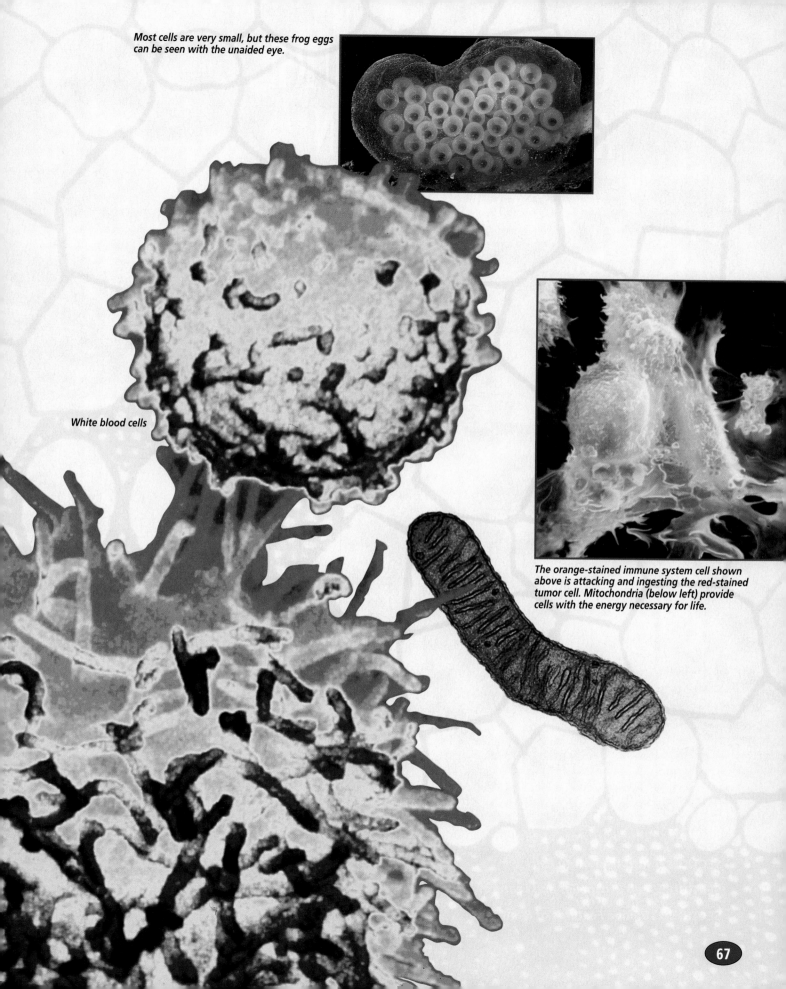

Most cells are very small, but these frog eggs can be seen with the unaided eye.

White blood cells

The orange-stained immune system cell shown above is attacking and ingesting the red-stained tumor cell. Mitochondria (below left) provide cells with the energy necessary for life.

# CELL STRUCTURE AND FUNCTION

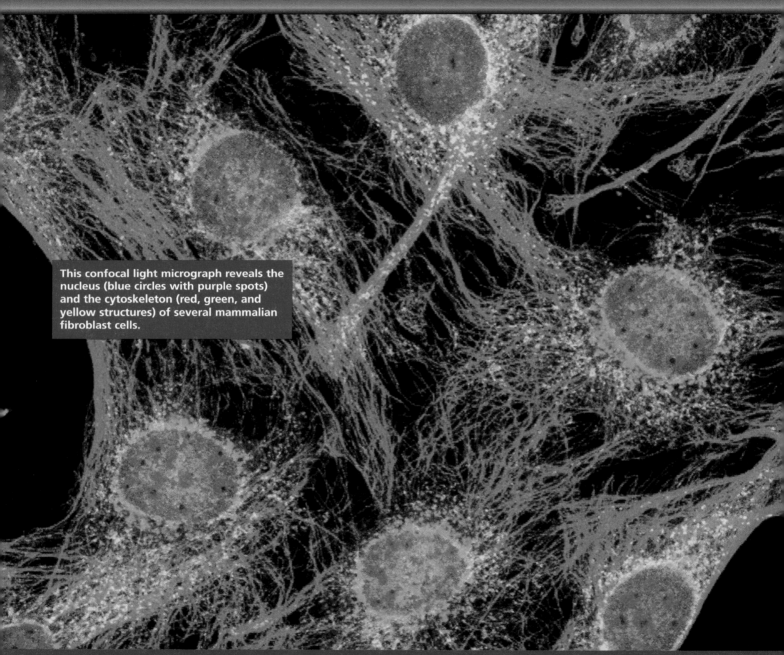

This confocal light micrograph reveals the nucleus (blue circles with purple spots) and the cytoskeleton (red, green, and yellow structures) of several mammalian fibroblast cells.

Unit 1—Cell Transport and Homeostasis
Topics 1–2

# THE HISTORY OF CELL BIOLOGY

*Both living and nonliving things are made of atoms, molecules, and compounds. How are living and nonliving things different? The discovery of the cell was an important step toward answering this question.*

## THE DISCOVERY OF CELLS

All living things are made up of one or more cells. A **cell** is the smallest unit that can carry on all of the processes of life. Beginning in the 17th century, curious naturalists were able to use microscopes to study objects too small to be seen with the unaided eye. Their studies led them to propose the cellular basis of life.

### Hooke

In 1665, English scientist Robert Hooke studied nature by using an early *light microscope,* such as the one in Figure 4-1a. A light microscope is an instrument that uses optical lenses to magnify objects by bending light rays. Hooke looked at a thin slice of cork from the bark of a cork oak tree. "I could exceedingly plainly perceive it to be all perforated and porous," Hooke wrote. He described "a great many little boxes" that reminded him of the cubicles or "cells" where monks live. When Hooke focused his microscope on the cells of tree stems, roots, and ferns, he found that each had similar little boxes. The drawings that Hooke made of the cells he saw are shown in Figure 4-1b. The "little boxes" that Hooke observed were the remains of dead plant cells, such as the cork cells shown in Figure 4-1c.

**FIGURE 4-1**

Robert Hooke used an early microscope (a) to see cells in thin slices of cork. His drawings of what he saw (b) indicate that he had clearly observed the remains of cork cells (300×) (c).

(a)

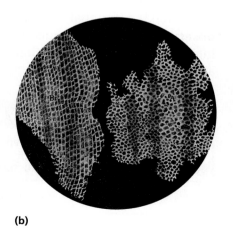

(b)

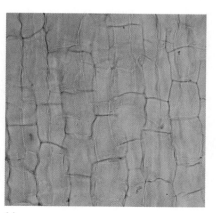

(c)

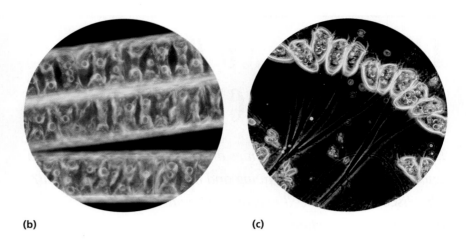

(b)　　　　　　　　　　　　　　　　　　　(c)

## Leeuwenhoek

The first person to observe living cells was a Dutch trader named Anton van Leeuwenhoek. Leeuwenhoek made microscopes that were simple and tiny, but he ground lenses so precisely that the magnification was 10 times that of Hooke's instruments. In 1673, Leeuwenhoek, shown in Figure 4-2a, was able to observe a previously unseen world of microorganisms. He observed cells with green stripes from an alga of the genus *Spirogyra*, as shown in Figure 4-2b, and bell-shaped cells on stalks of a protist of the genus *Vorticella*, as shown in Figure 4-2c. Leeuwenhoek called these organisms *animalcules.* We now call them *protists.*

**FIGURE 4-2**

Anton van Leeuwenhoek (1632–1723) is shown here with one of his hand-held lenses (a). Leeuwenhoek observed an alga of the genus *Spirogyra* (b) and a protist of the genus *Vorticella* (c).

(a)

# THE CELL THEORY

Although Hooke and Leeuwenhoek were the first to report observing cells, the importance of this observation was not realized until about 150 years later. At this time, biologists began to organize information about cells into a unified understanding. In 1838, the German botanist Matthias Schleiden concluded that all plants were composed of cells. The next year, the German zoologist Theodor Schwann concluded the same thing for animals. And finally, in his study of human diseases, the German physician Rudolf Virchow (1821–1902) noted that all cells come from other cells. These three observations were combined to form a basic theory about the cellular nature of life. The **cell theory** has three essential parts, which are summarized in Table 4-1.

internet connect

www.scilinks.org
**Topic:** Cell Theory
**Keyword:** HM60241

SCLINKS Maintained by the National Science Teachers Association

| TABLE 4-1 *The Cell Theory* |
|---|
| All living organisms are composed of one or more cells. |
| Cells are the basic units of structure and function in an organism. |
| Cells come only from the reproduction of existing cells. |

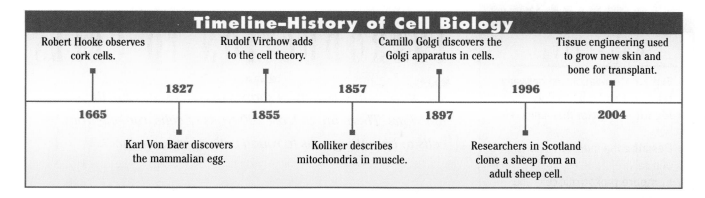

## Timeline–History of Cell Biology

Robert Hooke observes cork cells.

Rudolf Virchow adds to the cell theory.

Camillo Golgi discovers the Golgi apparatus in cells.

Tissue engineering used to grow new skin and bone for transplant.

**1827**  **1857**  **1996**

**1665**  **1855**  **1897**  **2004**

Karl Von Baer discovers the mammalian egg.

Kolliker describes mitochondria in muscle.

Researchers in Scotland clone a sheep from an adult sheep cell.

## Developments in Cell Biology

The discovery of cells and the development of the cell theory happened at the beginning of a revolutionary time in the history of science. Before the invention of the microscope, many questions about what makes up living and nonliving things could not be answered. Once cells could be observed, these questions could be explored. Scientists could then turn their attention to finding out how cells function. Figure 4-3 lists some of the major events in the history of cell biology.

## The Cellular Basis of Life

Microscopes helped biologists clarify our definition of life. All living things share several basic characteristics. All living things consist of organized parts, obtain energy from their surroundings, perform chemical reactions, change with time, respond to their environments, and reproduce.

In addition, living things must be able to separate their relatively constant internal environment from the ever-changing external environment. The ability to maintain a constant internal environment, called *homeostasis,* will be discussed later. Finally, all living things share a common history. All cells share characteristics that indicate that cells are related to other living things.

**FIGURE 4-3**

The study of cell biology began with the discovery of the cell by Robert Hooke in 1665. Since then, constantly improving technology has allowed scientists to unlock the secrets of the cell.

## SECTION 1 REVIEW

1. Describe the major contributions of Hooke and Leeuwenhoek to cell biology.

2. Identify the advance that enabled Leeuwenhoek to view the first living cells.

3. Describe the research that led to the development of the cell theory.

4. State the three fundamental parts of the cell theory.

5. List three major events in the history of cell biology.

6. Name eight characteristics that all living things share.

**CRITICAL THINKING**

7. **Applying Concepts** If you could go back in time, how would you explain the cell theory to someone who had never heard of cells?

8. **Making Calculations** A biologist photographs a cell in a microscope magnified at 40 times. The cell in the photo is 2 mm in diameter. What is the true diameter of the cell in micrometers (μm)?

9. **Justifying Conclusions** If organisms exist on other planets, would they consist of cells? Defend your answer.

## OBJECTIVES

- **Explain** the relationship between cell shape and cell function.
- **Identify** the factor that limits cell size.
- **Describe** the three basic parts of a cell.
- **Compare** prokaryotic cells and eukaryotic cells.
- **Analyze** the relationship among cells, tissues, organs, organ systems, and organisms.

## VOCABULARY

plasma membrane
cytoplasm
cytosol
nucleus
prokaryote
eukaryote
organelle
tissue
organ
organ system

# INTRODUCTION TO CELLS

*Cells come in a variety of shapes and sizes that suit their diverse functions. There are at least 200 types of cells, ranging from flat cells to branching cells to round cells to rectangular cells.*

## CELL DIVERSITY

Cells of different organisms and even cells within the same organism are very diverse in terms of shape, size, and internal organization. One theme that occurs again and again throughout biology is that form follows function. In other words, a cell's function influences its physical features.

### Cell Shape

The diversity in cell shapes reflects the different functions of cells. Compare the cell shapes shown in Figure 4-4. The long extensions that reach out in various directions from the nerve cell shown in Figure 4-4a allow the cell to send and receive nerve impulses. The flat, platelike shape of skin cells in Figure 4-4b suits their function of covering and protecting the surface of the body. As shown below, a cell's shape can be simple or complex depending on the function of the cell. Each cell has a shape that has evolved to allow the cell to perform its function effectively.

**FIGURE 4-4**

Cells have various shapes. (a) Nerve cells have long extensions. (b) Skin cells are flat and platelike. (c) Egg cells are spherical. (d) Some bacteria are rod shaped. (e) Some plant cells are rectangular.

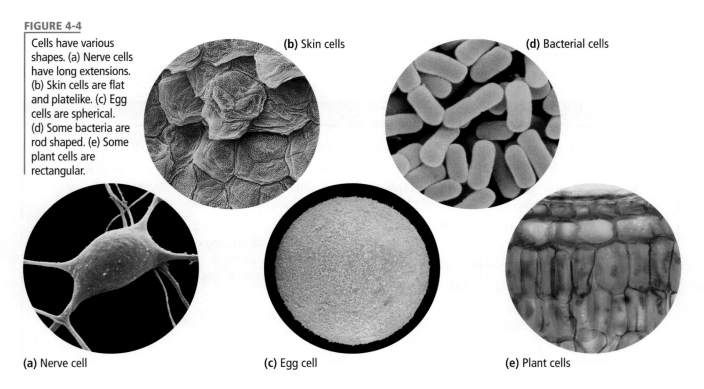

**(b)** Skin cells

**(d)** Bacterial cells

**(a)** Nerve cell

**(c)** Egg cell

**(e)** Plant cells

## Cell Size

Cells differ not only in their shape but also in their size. A few types of cells are large enough to be seen by the unaided human eye. For example, the nerve cells that extend from a giraffe's spinal cord to its foot can be 2 m (about 6 1/2 ft) long. A human egg cell is about the size of the period at the end of this sentence. Most cells, however, are only 10 to 50 μm in diameter, or about 1/500 the size of the period at the end of this sentence.

The size of a cell is limited by the relationship of the cell's outer surface area to its volume, or its *surface area–to-volume ratio*. As a cell grows, its volume increases much faster than its surface area does, as shown in Figure 4-5. This trend is important because the materials needed by a cell (such as nutrients and oxygen) and the wastes produced by a cell (such as carbon dioxide) must pass into and out of the cell through its surface. If a cell were to become very large, the volume would increase much more than the surface area. Therefore, the surface area would not allow materials to enter or leave the cell quickly enough to meet the cell's needs. As a result, most cells are microscopic in size.

### Quick Lab

#### Comparing Surface Cells

**Materials** microscope, prepared slides of plant (dicot) stem and animal (human) skin, pencil, paper

**Procedure** Examine slides by using medium magnification (100×). Observe and draw the surface cells of the plant stem and the animal skin.

**Analysis** How do the surface cells of each organism differ from the cells beneath the surface cells? What is the function of the surface cells? Explain how surface cells are suited to their function based on their shape.

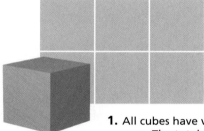

**1.** All cubes have volume and surface area. The total surface area is equal to the sum of the areas of each of the six sides (area = length X width).

**FIGURE 4-5**

Small cells can exchange substances more readily than large cells because small objects have a higher surface area–to-volume ratio.

**2.** If you split the first cube into eight smaller cubes, you get 48 sides. The volume remains constant, but the total surface area doubles.

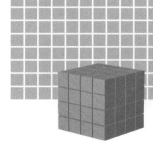

**3.** If you split each of the eight cubes into eight smaller cubes, you have 64 cubes that together contain the same volume as the first cube. The total surface area, however, has doubled again.

# BASIC PARTS OF A CELL

Despite the diversity among cells, three basic features are common to all cell types. All cells have an outer boundary, an interior substance, and a control region.

## Plasma Membrane

The cell's outer boundary, called the **plasma membrane** (or the *cell membrane*), covers a cell's surface and acts as a barrier between the inside and the outside of a cell. All materials enter or exit through the plasma membrane. The surface of a plasma membrane is shown in Figure 4-6a.

## Cytoplasm

The region of the cell that is within the plasma membrane and that includes the fluid, the cytoskeleton, and all of the organelles except the nucleus is called the **cytoplasm.** The part of the cytoplasm that includes molecules and small particles, such as ribosomes, but not membrane-bound organelles is the **cytosol.** About 20 percent of the cytosol is made up of protein.

## Control Center

Cells carry coded information in the form of DNA for regulating their functions and reproducing themselves. The DNA in some types of cells floats freely inside the cell. Other cells have a membrane-bound organelle that contains a cell's DNA. This membrane-bound structure is called the **nucleus.** Most of the functions of a eukaryotic cell are controlled by the cell's nucleus. The nucleus is often the most prominent structure within a eukaryotic cell. It maintains its shape with the help of a protein skeleton called the *nuclear matrix.* The nucleus of a typical animal cell is shown in Figure 4-6b.

**FIGURE 4-6**

Most animal cells have a cell membrane, a nucleus, and a variety of other organelles embedded in a watery substance. The surface of the cell membrane can be seen in (a). The organelles inside the cell are labeled in the diagram (b).

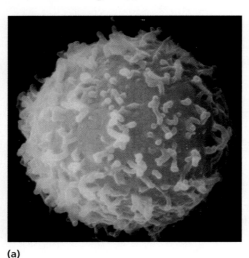

(a)

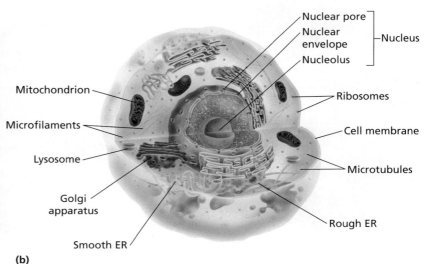

(b)

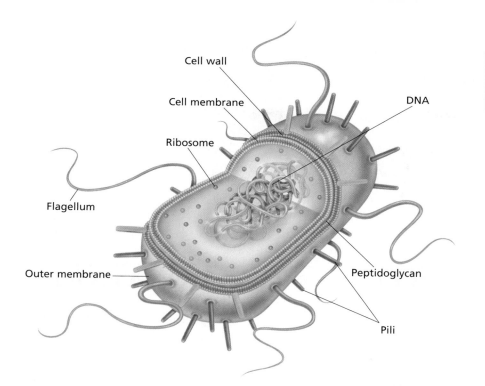

Cell wall

Cell membrane

Ribosome

Flagellum

DNA

Outer membrane

Peptidoglycan

Pili

**FIGURE 4-7**

A prokaryotic cell lacks a membrane-bound nucleus and membrane-bound organelles. Most prokaryotic cells are much smaller than eukaryotic cells are.

# TWO BASIC TYPES OF CELLS

Fossil evidence suggests that the earliest cells on Earth were simple cells similar to some present-day bacteria. As cells evolved, they differentiated into two major types: prokaryotes and eukaryotes.

## Prokaryotes

**Prokaryotes** (proh-KAR-ee-OHTS) are organisms that lack a membrane-bound nucleus and membrane-bound organelles. Although prokaryotic cells lack a nucleus, their genetic information—in the form of DNA—is often concentrated in a part of the cell called the *nucleoid*. Figure 4-7 shows a typical prokaryotic cell. Prokaryotes are divided into two domains: Bacteria and Archaea (ahr-KEE-uh). The domain Bacteria includes organisms that are similar to the first cellular life-forms. The domain Archaea includes organisms that are thought to be more closely related to eukaryotic cells found in all other kingdoms of life.

## Eukaryotes

Organisms made up of one or more cells that have a nucleus and membrane-bound organelles are called **eukaryotes** (yoo-KAR-ee-OHTS). Eukaryotic cells also have a variety of subcellular structures called **organelles,** well-defined, intracellular bodies that perform specific functions for the cell. Many organelles are surrounded by a membrane. The organelles carry out cellular processes just as a person's pancreas, heart, and other organs carry out a person's life processes. Eukaryotic cells are generally much larger than prokaryotic cells, as seen in Figure 4-8, which shows a white blood cell (eukaryote) destroying tiny bacterial cells (prokaryotes).

**FIGURE 4-8**

A white blood cell (eukaryotic) changes shape as it attacks purple-stained bacterial cells that are much smaller (prokaryotic).

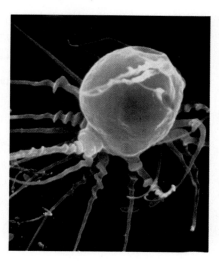

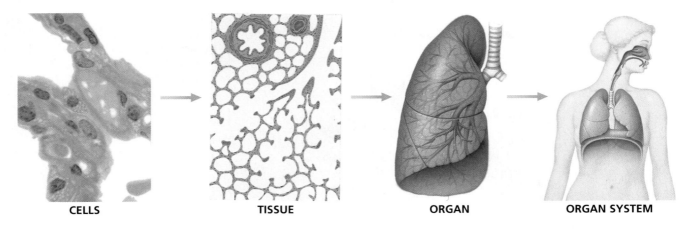

| CELLS | TISSUE | ORGAN | ORGAN SYSTEM |

**FIGURE 4-9**

In a multicellular eukaryotic organisms, cells organize into tissues. Tissues organize into organs. Organs are part of organ systems, in which organs work together to perform body functions.

# CELLULAR ORGANIZATION

Over time, cells began to form groups that functioned together. Some cells retained the ability to live outside a group. Others became dependent on each other for survival.

## Colonies

A *colonial organism* is a collection of genetically identical cells that live together in a connected group. Colonial organisms are not truly multicellular because few cell activities are coordinated.

## True Multicellularity

As organisms evolved, their cells became more specialized and eventually were unable to survive independently. Groups of cells took on specific roles within the organism. A group of similar cells and their products that carry out a specific function is called a **tissue.** Groups of tissues that perform a particular job in an organism are called **organs.** An **organ system** is a group of organs that accomplish related tasks. The stomach and liver are organs that are part of the digestive system. Finally, several organ systems combine to make up an organism. This hierarchical organization found in multicellular organisms is shown in Figure 4-9.

## SECTION 2 REVIEW

1. Describe the relationship between a cell's shape and its function.

2. Explain the factor that limits cell size.

3. Identify and describe three basic parts of a cell.

4. Summarize the differences between prokaryotic cells and eukaryotic cells.

5. List four levels of organization that combine to form an organism.

**CRITICAL THINKING**

6. **Making Calculations** If a cube-shaped cell grew from 1 cm per side to 3 cm per side, how much would its volume change?

7. **Forming Reasoned Opinions** Why do you think there are three basic structures common to all cell types? Support your answer.

8. **Analyzing Processes** How are the functions of prokaryotic cells controlled without a nucleus?

# CELL ORGANELLES AND FEATURES

*Eukaryotic cells have many membrane systems. These membranes divide cells into compartments that function together to keep a cell alive.*

### OBJECTIVES

- **Describe** the structure and function of a cell's plasma membrane.
- **Summarize** the role of the nucleus.
- **List** the major organelles found in the cytosol, and describe their roles.
- **Identify** the characteristics of mitochondria.
- **Describe** the structure and function of the cytoskeleton.

### VOCABULARY

phospholipid bilayer
chromosome
nuclear envelope
nucleolus
ribosome
mitochondrion
endoplasmic reticulum
Golgi apparatus
lysosome
cytoskeleton
microtubule
microfilament
cilium
flagellum
centriole

## PLASMA MEMBRANE

The plasma membrane (also called the *cell membrane*) has several functions. For example, it allows only certain molecules to enter or leave the cell. It separates internal metabolic reactions from the external environment. In addition, the plasma membrane allows the cell to excrete wastes and to interact with its environment.

### Membrane Lipids

The plasma membrane, as well as the membranes of cell organelles, is made primarily of phospholipids. Phospholipids have a polar, hydrophilic ("water-loving") phosphate head and two nonpolar, hydrophobic ("water-fearing") fatty acid tails. Water molecules surround the plasma membrane. The phospholipids line up so that their heads point outward toward the water and their tails point inward, away from water. The result is a double layer called a **phospholipid bilayer,** as shown in Figure 4-10. The cell membranes of eukaryotes also contain lipids, called *sterols,* between the tails of the phospholipids. The major membrane sterol in animal cells is cholesterol. Sterols in the plasma membrane make the membrane more firm and prevent the membrane from freezing at low temperatures.

**FIGURE 4-10**

Cell membranes are made of a phospholipid bilayer. Each phospholipid molecule has a polar "head" and a two-part nonpolar "tail."

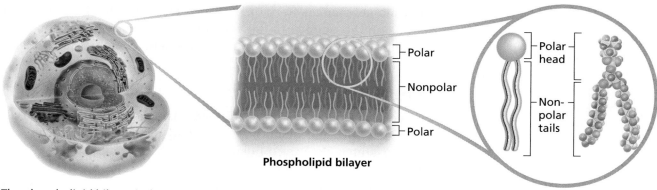

**Phospholipid bilayer**

The phospholipid bilayer is the foundation of the cell membrane.

The arrangement of phospholipids in the bilayer makes the cell membrane selectively permeable.

A phospholipid's "head" is polar, and its two fatty acid "tails" are nonpolar.

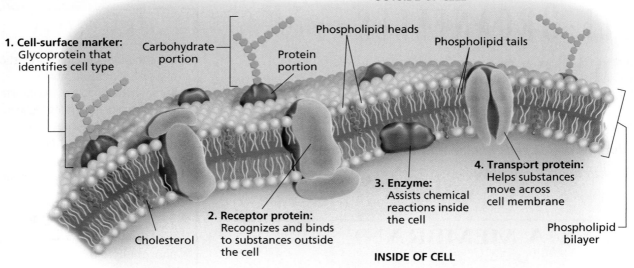

**OUTSIDE OF CELL**

**1. Cell-surface marker:** Glycoprotein that identifies cell type

Carbohydrate portion

Phospholipid heads

Protein portion

Phospholipid tails

**4. Transport protein:** Helps substances move across cell membrane

**3. Enzyme:** Assists chemical reactions inside the cell

**2. Receptor protein:** Recognizes and binds to substances outside the cell

Cholesterol

Phospholipid bilayer

**INSIDE OF CELL**

**FIGURE 4-11**

Cell membranes often contain proteins. Integral proteins include cell-surface markers, receptor proteins, and transport proteins. Enzymes are examples of peripheral proteins.

## Membrane Proteins

Plasma membranes often contain specific proteins embedded within the lipid bilayer. These proteins are called *integral proteins*. Figure 4-11 shows that some integral proteins, such as cell surface markers, emerge from only one side of the membrane. Others, such as receptor proteins and transport proteins, extend across the plasma membrane and are exposed to both the cell's interior and exterior environments. Proteins that extend across the plasma membrane are able to detect environmental signals and transmit them to the inside of the cell. *Peripheral proteins,* such as the enzyme shown in Figure 4-11, lie on only one side of the membrane and are not embedded in it.

As Figure 4-11 shows, integral proteins exposed to the cell's external environment often have carbohydrates attached. These carbohydrates can act as labels on cell surfaces. Some labels help cells recognize each other and stick together. Viruses can use these labels as docks for entering and infecting cells.

Integral proteins play important roles in actively transporting molecules into the cell. Some act as channels or pores that allow certain substances to pass. Other integral proteins bind to a molecule on the outside of the cell and then transport it through the membrane. Still others act as sites where chemical messengers such as hormones can attach.

## Fluid Mosaic Model

A cell's plasma membrane is surprisingly dynamic. Scientists describe the cell membrane as a fluid mosaic. The *fluid mosaic model* states that the phospholipid bilayer behaves like a fluid more than it behaves like a solid. The membrane's lipids and proteins can move laterally within the bilayer, like a boat on the ocean. As a result of such lateral movement, the pattern, or "mosaic," of lipids and proteins in the cell membrane constantly changes.

# NUCLEUS

Most of the functions of a eukaryotic cell are controlled by the nucleus, shown in Figure 4-12. The nucleus is filled with a jellylike liquid called the *nucleoplasm,* which holds the contents of the nucleus and is similar in function to a cell's cytoplasm.

The nucleus houses and protects the cell's genetic information. The hereditary information that contains the instructions for the structure and function of the organism is coded in the organism's DNA, which is contained in the nucleus. When a cell is not dividing, the DNA is in the form of a threadlike material called *chromatin.* When a cell is about to divide, the chromatin condenses to form **chromosomes.** Chromosomes are structures in the nucleus made of DNA and protein.

The nucleus is the site where DNA is transcribed into ribonucleic acid (RNA). RNA moves through nuclear pores to the cytoplasm, where, depending on the type of RNA, it carries out its function.

## Nuclear Envelope

The nucleus is surrounded by a double membrane called the **nuclear envelope.** The nuclear envelope is made up of two phospholipid bilayers. Covering the surface of the nuclear envelope are tiny, protein-lined holes, which are called *nuclear pores.* The nuclear pores provide passageways for RNA and other materials to enter and leave the nucleus.

## Nucleolus

Most nuclei contain at least one denser area, called the **nucleolus** (noo-KLEE-uh-luhs). The nucleolus (plural, *nucleoli*) is the site where DNA is concentrated when it is in the process of making ribosomal RNA. **Ribosomes** (RIE-buh-SOHMZ) are organelles made of protein and RNA that direct protein synthesis in the cytoplasm.

**FIGURE 4-12**

The nucleus of a cell is surrounded by a double membrane called the nuclear envelope. The nucleus stores the cell's DNA.

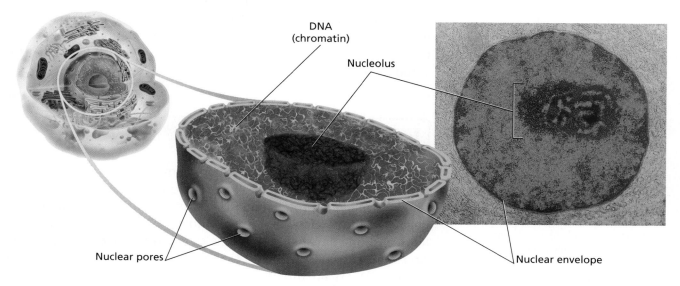

DNA (chromatin)

Nucleolus

Nuclear pores

Nuclear envelope

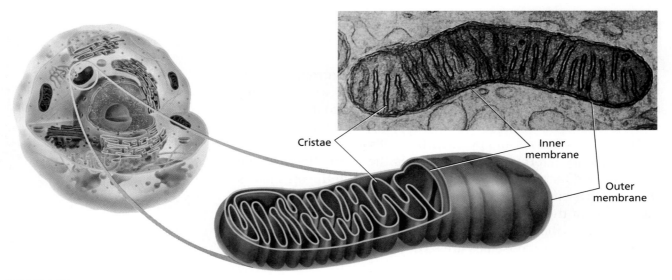

Cristae

Inner membrane

Outer membrane

**FIGURE 4-13**

Mitochondria convert organic molecules into energy for the cell. Mitochondria have an inner membrane and an outer membrane. The folds of the inner membrane, called *cristae*, are the site of energy conversion.

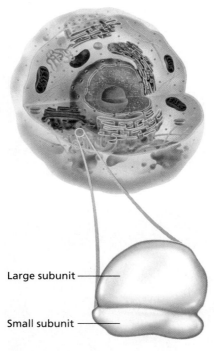

Large subunit

Small subunit

**FIGURE 4-14**

Ribosomes are the organelles responsible for building protein. Ribosomes have a large and small subunit, each made of protein and ribosomal RNA. Some ribosomes are free in the cell. Others are attached to the rough endoplasmic reticulum.

# MITOCHONDRIA

**Mitochondria** (MIET-oh-KAHN-dree-uh) (singular, *mitochondrion*) are tiny organelles that transfer energy from organic molecules to adenosine triphosphate (ATP). ATP ultimately powers most of the cell's chemical reactions. Highly active cells, such as muscle cells, can have hundreds of mitochondria. Cells that are not very active, such as fat-storage cells, have few mitochondria.

Like a nucleus, a mitochondrion has an inner and an outer phospholipid membrane, as shown in Figure 4-13. The outer membrane separates the mitochondrion from the cytosol. The inner membrane has many folds, called *cristae* (KRIS-tee). Cristae contain proteins that carry out energy-harvesting chemical reactions.

## Mitochondrial DNA

Mitochondria have their own DNA and can reproduce only by the division of preexisting mitochondria. Scientists think that mitochondria originated from prokaryotic cells that were incorporated into ancient eukaryotic cells. This symbiotic relationship provided the prokaryotic invaders with a protected place to live and provided the eukaryotic cell with an increased supply of ATP.

# RIBOSOMES

Ribosomes are small, roughly spherical organelles that are responsible for building protein. Ribosomes do not have a membrane. They are made of protein and RNA molecules. Ribosome assembly begins in the nucleolus and is completed in the cytoplasm. One large and one small subunit come together to make a functioning ribosome, shown in Figure 4-14. Some ribosomes are free within the cytosol. Others are attached to the rough endoplasmic reticulum.

# ENDOPLASMIC RETICULUM

The **endoplasmic reticulum** (EN-doh-PLAZ-mik ri-TIK-yuh-luhm), abbreviated ER, is a system of membranous tubes and sacs, called *cisternae* (sis-TUHR-nee). The ER functions primarily as an intracellular highway, a path along which molecules move from one part of the cell to another. The amount of ER inside a cell fluctuates, depending on the cell's activity. There are two types of ER: rough and smooth. The two types of ER are thought to be continuous.

## Rough Endoplasmic Reticulum

The rough endoplasmic reticulum is a system of interconnected, flattened sacs covered with ribosomes, as shown in Figure 4-15. The rough ER produces phospholipids and proteins. Certain types of proteins are made on the rough ER's ribosomes. These proteins are later exported from the cell or inserted into one of the cell's own membranes. For example, ribosomes on the rough ER make digestive enzymes, which accumulate inside the endoplasmic reticulum. Little sacs or vesicles then pinch off from the ends of the rough ER and store the digestive enzymes until they are released from the cell. Rough ER is most abundant in cells that produce large amounts of protein for export, such as cells in digestive glands and antibody-producing cells.

## Smooth Endoplasmic Reticulum

The smooth ER lacks ribosomes and thus has a smooth appearance. Most cells contain very little smooth ER. Smooth ER builds lipids such as cholesterol. In the ovaries and testes, smooth ER produces the steroid hormones estrogen and testosterone. In skeletal and heart muscle cells, smooth ER releases calcium, which stimulates contraction. Smooth ER is also abundant in liver and kidney cells, where it helps detoxify drugs and poisons. Long-term abuse of alcohol and other drugs causes these cells to produce more smooth ER. Increased amounts of smooth ER in liver cells is one of the factors that can lead to drug tolerance. As Figure 4-15 shows, rough ER and smooth ER form an interconnected network.

**Word Roots and Origins**

*reticulum*

from the Latin *rete,* meaning "net"; *reticulum* means "little net"

**FIGURE 4-15**

The endoplasmic reticulum (ER) serves as a site of synthesis for proteins, lipids, and other materials. The dark lines in the photo represent the membranes of the ER, and the narrow lighter areas between the dark lines show the channels and spaces (cisternae) inside the ER.

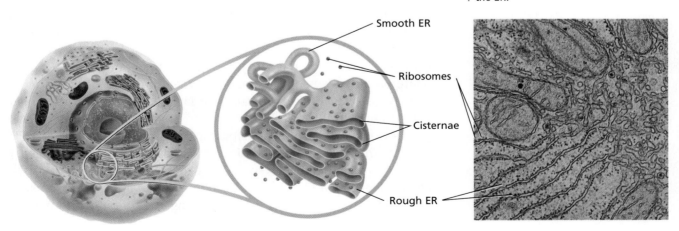

Smooth ER

Ribosomes

Cisternae

Rough ER

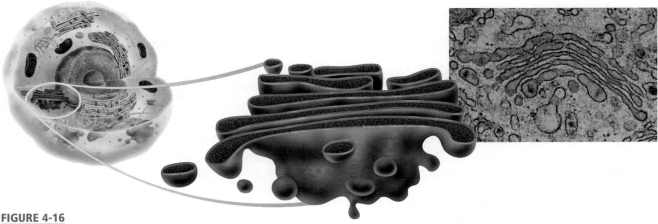

**FIGURE 4-16**

The Golgi apparatus modifies many cellular products and prepares them for export.

# GOLGI APPARATUS

The **Golgi apparatus,** shown in Figure 4-16, is another system of flattened, membranous sacs. The sacs nearest the nucleus receive vesicles from the ER containing newly made proteins or lipids. Vesicles travel from one part of the Golgi apparatus to the next and transport substances as they go. The stacked membranes modify the vesicle contents as they move along. The proteins get "address labels" that direct them to various other parts of the cell. During this modification, the Golgi apparatus can add carbohydrate labels to proteins or alter new lipids in various ways.

# VESICLES

Cells contain several types of vesicles, which perform various roles. Vesicles are small, spherically shaped sacs that are surrounded by a single membrane and that are classified by their contents. Vesicles often migrate to and merge with the plasma membrane. As they do, they release their contents to the outside of the cell.

## Lysosomes

**Lysosomes** (LIE-suh-SOHMZ) are vesicles that bud from the Golgi apparatus and that contain digestive enzymes. These enzymes can break down large molecules, such as proteins, nucleic acids, carbohydrates, and phospholipids. In the liver, lysosomes break down glycogen in order to release glucose into the bloodstream. Certain white blood cells use lysosomes to break down bacteria. Within a cell, lysosomes digest worn-out organelles in a process called *autophagy* (aw-TAHF-uh-jee).

Lysosomes are also responsible for breaking down cells when it is time for the cells to die. The digestion of damaged or extra cells by the enzymes of their own lysosomes is called *autolysis* (aw-TAHL-uh-sis). Lysosomes play a very important role in maintaining an organism's health by destroying cells that are no longer functioning properly.

## Peroxisomes

Peroxisomes are similar to lysosomes but contain different enzymes and are not produced by the Golgi apparatus. Peroxisomes are abundant in liver and kidney cells, where they neutralize free radicals (oxygen ions that can damage cells) and detoxify alcohol and other drugs. Peroxisomes are named for the hydrogen peroxide, $H_2O_2$, they produce when breaking down alcohol and killing bacteria. Peroxisomes also break down fatty acids, which the mitochondria can then use as an energy source.

## Other Vesicles

Specialized peroxisomes, called *glyoxysomes,* can be found in the seeds of some plants. They break down stored fats to provide energy for the developing plant embryo. Some cells engulf material by surrounding it with plasma membrane. The resulting pocket buds off to become a vesicle inside the cell. This vesicle is called an *endosome.* Lysosomes fuse with endosomes and digest the engulfed material. Food vacuoles are vesicles that store nutrients for a cell. Contractile vacuoles are vesicles that can contract and dispose of excess water inside a cell.

## Protein Synthesis

One of the major functions of a cell is the production of protein. The path some proteins take from synthesis to export can be seen in Figure 4-17. In step **1**, proteins are assembled by ribosomes on the rough ER. Then, in step **2**, vesicles transport proteins to the Golgi apparatus. In step **3**, the Golgi modifies proteins and packages them in new vesicles. In step **4**, vesicles release proteins that have destinations outside the cell. In step **5**, vesicles containing enzymes remain inside the cell as lysosomes, peroxisomes, endosomes, or other types of vesicles.

**FIGURE 4-17**

The rough ER, Golgi apparatus, and vesicles work together to transport proteins to their destinations inside and outside the cell.

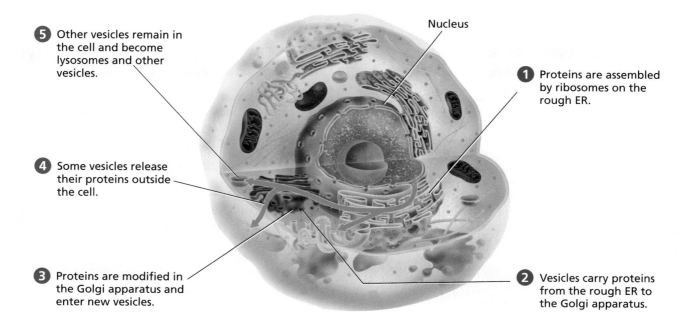

**5** Other vesicles remain in the cell and become lysosomes and other vesicles.

Nucleus

**1** Proteins are assembled by ribosomes on the rough ER.

**4** Some vesicles release their proteins outside the cell.

**3** Proteins are modified in the Golgi apparatus and enter new vesicles.

**2** Vesicles carry proteins from the rough ER to the Golgi apparatus.

# CYTOSKELETON

The **cytoskeleton** is a network of thin tubes and filaments that crisscrosses the cytosol. The tubes and filaments give shape to the cell from the inside in the same way that tent poles support the shape of a tent. The cytoskeleton also acts as a system of internal tracks, shown in Figure 4-18, on which items move around inside the cell. The cytoskeleton's functions are based on several structural elements. Three of these are microtubules, microfilaments, and intermediate filaments, shown and described in Table 4-2.

## Microtubules

**Microtubules** are hollow tubes made of a protein called *tubulin*. Each tubulin molecule consists of two slightly different subunits. Microtubules radiate outward from a central point called the *centrosome* near the nucleus. Microtubules hold organelles in place, maintain a cell's shape, and act as tracks that guide organelles and molecules as they move within the cell.

## Microfilaments

Finer than microtubules, **microfilaments** are long threads of the beadlike protein actin and are linked end to end and wrapped around each other like two strands of a rope. Microfilaments contribute to cell movement, including the crawling of white blood cells and the contraction of muscle cells.

## Intermediate Filaments

*Intermediate filaments* are rods that anchor the nucleus and some other organelles to their places in the cell. They maintain the internal shape of the nucleus. Hair-follicle cells produce large quantities of intermediate filament proteins. These proteins make up most of the hair shaft.

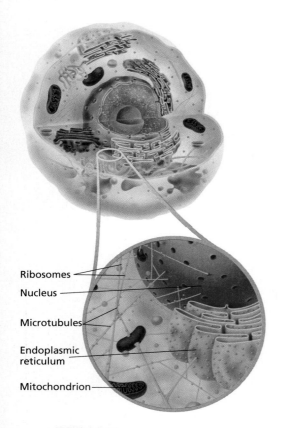

Ribosomes
Nucleus
Microtubules
Endoplasmic reticulum
Mitochondrion

**FIGURE 4-18**

Microtubules provide a path for organelles and molecules as they move throughout the cell.

| Property | Microtubules | Microfilaments | Intermediate filaments |
|---|---|---|---|
| **TABLE 4-2** *The Structure of the Cytoskeleton* | | | |
| Structure | hollow tubes made of coiled protein | two strands of intertwined protein | protein fibers coiled into cables |
| Protein subunits | tubulin, with two subunits: α and β tubulin | actin | one of several types of fibrous proteins |
| Main function | maintenance of cell shape; cell motility (in cilia and flagella); chromosome movement; organelle movement | maintenance and changing of cell shape; muscle contraction; movement of cytoplasm; cell motility; cell division | maintenance of cell shape; anchor nucleus and other organelles; maintenance of shape of nucleus |
| Shape | | | |

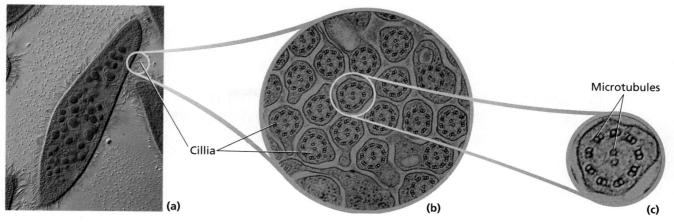

(a)                                                                    (b)                                                    (c)

## Cilia and Flagella

**Cilia** (SIL-ee-uh) and **flagella** (fluh-JEL-uh) are hairlike structures that extend from the surface of the cell, where they assist in movement. Cilia are short and are present in large numbers on certain cells, whereas flagella are longer and are far less numerous on the cells where they occur. Cilia and flagella have a membrane on their outer surface and an internal structure of nine pairs of microtubules around two central tubules, as Figure 4-19 shows.

Cilia on cells in the inner ear vibrate and help detect sound. Cilia cover the surfaces of many protists and "row" the protists through water like thousands of oars. On other protists, cilia sweep water and food particles into a mouthlike opening. Many kinds of protists use flagella to propel themselves, as do human sperm cells.

## Centrioles

**Centrioles** consist of two short cylinders of microtubules at right angles to each other and are situated in the cytoplasm near the nuclear envelope. Centrioles occur in animal cells, where they organize the microtubules of the cytoskeleton during cell division, as shown in Figure 4-20. Plant cells lack centrioles. Basal bodies have the same structure that centrioles do. Basal bodies are found at the base of cilia and flagella and appear to organize the development of cilia and flagella.

**FIGURE 4-19**

A SEM of a paramecium shows cilia on the surface of the cell (a). A TEM of a cross section of those cilia (b) reveals the internal structure of the cilia. The characteristic 9+2 configuration of microtubules can be clearly seen (c).

**FIGURE 4-20**

During cell division, centrioles organize microtubules that pull the chromosomes (orange) apart. The centrioles are at the center of rays of microtubules, which have been stained green with a fluorescent dye.

## SECTION 3 REVIEW

1. Explain how the fluid mosaic model describes the plasma membrane.

2. List three cellular functions that occur in the nucleus.

3. Describe the organelles that are found in a eukaryotic cell.

4. Identify two characteristics that make mitochondria different from other organelles.

5. Contrast three types of cytoskeletal fibers.

**CRITICAL THINKING**

6. **Relating Concepts** If a cell has a high energy requirement, would you expect the cell to have many mitochondria or few mitochondria? Why?

7. **Analyzing Information** How do scientists think that mitochondria originated? Why?

8. **Analyzing Statements** It is not completely accurate to say that organelles are floating freely in the cytosol. Why not?

# Science in Action

## How Do Cells Secrete Proteins?

The invention of electron microscopes allowed biologists to see the detail of the tiny structures inside cells. But it was clever experimentation by George Palade that revealed how those tiny structures help a cell survive.

George Palade

### HYPOTHESIS: Membranous Organelles Secrete Proteins

Six years after he graduated from medical school in Romania, George Palade began conducting research at the Rockefeller Institute for Medical Research in New York City. He studied the network of membranous organelles in cells of the guinea pig pancreas. This network included the rough endoplasmic reticulum (ER), the smooth ER, the Golgi apparatus, lysosomes, and secretory granules.

Palade knew about the structure of these organelles. He also knew that ribosomes on the rough ER were associated with making proteins. But what Palade and other scientists did not know was how the proteins were secreted from cells once they were made on the ribosomes. Palade suspected that the membranous organelles played a role.

### METHODS: Track Proteins

Part of Palade's genius was inventing a way to make thin slices of tissue from a guinea pig's pancreas and keep the cells of the tissue alive. He also developed a way to track newly made proteins, a method called the *pulse-chase technique*. With this technique, Palade added "labeled" amino acids (made with radioactive atoms) to the pancreas cells for a fixed amount of time. This was the "pulse." The cells used the labeled amino acids and their own "unlabeled" amino acids (without radioactive atoms) to make proteins. Palade would then "chase" out any labeled amino acid that the cells had not used to build proteins by adding an excess of unlabeled amino acid.

### RESULTS: Black Dots Move as Time Passes

At first, the black dots that represented labeled amino acids were found in the rough ER. Photos taken at later time periods showed the black dots in vesicles close to smooth ER, then in smooth ER, then in the Golgi apparatus, and finally in vesicles close to the edge of the cell.

### CONCLUSION: Secreted Proteins Follow a Specific Path

Palade concluded that secreted proteins move from the rough ER to the smooth ER in vesicles that are pinched off from the rough ER membrane. The proteins then move from the smooth ER to the Golgi apparatus (again, in vesicles). From the Golgi apparatus, the proteins move in vesicles to the edge of the cell. Finally, the vesicles fuse with the plasma membrane.

### Further Experiments and a Nobel Prize

Palade published the work in 1964. In 1974, George Palade and two other researchers, Albert Claude and Christian De Duve, were awarded the Nobel Prize in medicine for their discoveries about the organization of the cell.

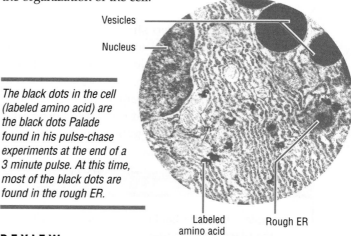

Vesicles

Nucleus

Labeled amino acid

Rough ER

*The black dots in the cell (labeled amino acid) are the black dots Palade found in his pulse-chase experiments at the end of a 3 minute pulse. At this time, most of the black dots are found in the rough ER.*

### REVIEW

1. What did the pulse-chase experiments allow Palade to observe?

2. Summarize the results of Palade's pulse-chase experiments.

3. **Critical Thinking** Was it important to use living tissue for the experiments?

**internet** connect

**www.scilinks.org**
**Topic:** Exocytosis and Endocytosis
**Keyword:** HM60554

SCLINKS. Maintained by the National Science Teachers Association

# UNIQUE FEATURES OF PLANT CELLS

*Plant cells have three kinds of structures that are not found in animal cells and that are extremely important to plant survival: plastids, central vacuoles, and cell walls.*

## PLANT CELLS

Most of the organelles and other parts of the cell just described are common to all eukaryotic cells. However, plant cells have three additional kinds of structures that are extremely important to plant function: cell walls, large central vacuoles, and plastids.

To understand why plant cells have structures not found in animal cells, consider how a plant's lifestyle differs from an animal's. Plants make their own carbon-containing molecules directly from carbon taken in from the environment. Plant cells take carbon dioxide gas from the air, and in a process called *photosynthesis,* they convert carbon dioxide and water into sugars. The organelles and structures in plant cells are shown in Figure 4-21.

### OBJECTIVES

- **List** three structures that are present in plant cells but not in animal cells.
- **Compare** the plasma membrane, the primary cell wall, and the secondary cell wall.
- **Explain** the role of the central vacuole.
- **Describe** the roles of plastids in the life of a plant.
- **Identify** features that distinguish prokaryotes, eukaryotes, plant cells, and animal cells.

### VOCABULARY

cell wall
central vacuole
plastid
chloroplast
thylakoid
chlorophyll

**FIGURE 4-21**

In addition to containing almost all of the types of organelles that animal cells contain, plant cells contain three unique features. Those features are the cell wall, the central vacuole, and plastids, such as chloroplasts.

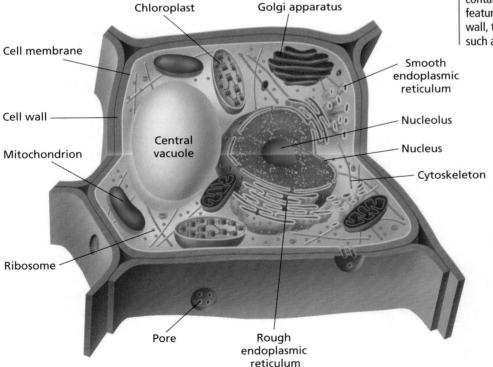

# CELL WALL

The **cell wall** is a rigid layer that lies outside the cell's plasma membrane. Plant cell walls contain a carbohydrate called *cellulose*. Cellulose is embedded in a matrix of proteins and other carbohydrates that form a stiff box around each cell. Pores in the cell wall allow water, ions, and some molecules to enter and exit the cell.

## Primary and Secondary Cell Walls

The main component of the cell wall, cellulose, is made directly on the surface of the plasma membrane by enzymes that travel along the membrane. These enzymes are guided by microtubules inside the plasma membrane. Growth of the primary cell wall occurs in one direction, based on the orientation of the microtubules. Other components of the cell wall are made in the ER. These materials move in vesicles to the Golgi and then to the cell surface.

Some plants also produce a secondary cell wall. When the cell stops growing, it secretes the secondary cell wall between the plasma membrane and the primary cell wall. The secondary cell wall is very strong but can no longer expand. The wood in desks and tabletops is made of billions of secondary cell walls. The cells inside the walls have died and disintegrated.

# CENTRAL VACUOLE

Plant cells may contain a reservoir that stores large amounts of water. The **central vacuole** is a large, fluid-filled organelle that stores not only water but also enzymes, metabolic wastes, and other materials. The central vacuole, shown in Figure 4-22, forms as other smaller vacuoles fuse together. Central vacuoles can make up 90 percent of the plant cell's volume and can push all of the other organelles into a thin layer against the plasma membrane. When water is plentiful, it fills a plant's vacuoles. The cells expand and the plant stands upright. In a dry period, the vacuoles lose water, the cells shrink, and the plant wilts.

## Other Vacuoles

Some vacuoles store toxic materials. The vacuoles of acacia trees, for example, store poisons that provide a defense against plant-eating animals. Tobacco plant cells store the toxin nicotine in a storage vacuole. Other vacuoles store plant pigments, such as the colorful pigments found in rose petals.

**FIGURE 4-22**

The central vacuole occupies up to 90 percent of the volume of some plant cells. The central vacuole stores water and helps keep plant tissue firm.

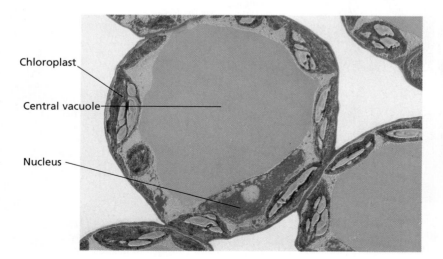

Chloroplast

Central vacuole

Nucleus

# PLASTIDS

Plastids are another unique feature of plant cells. **Plastids** are organelles that, like mitochondria, are surrounded by a double membrane and contain their own DNA. There are several types of plastids, including chloroplasts, chromoplasts, and leucoplasts.

## Chloroplasts

**Chloroplasts** use light energy to make carbohydrates from carbon dioxide and water. As Figure 4-23 shows, each chloroplast contains a system of flattened, membranous sacs called **thylakoids.** Thylakoids contain the green pigment **chlorophyll,** the main molecule that absorbs light and captures light energy for the cell. Chloroplasts can be found not only in plant cells but also in a wide variety of eukaryotic algae, such as seaweed.

Chloroplast DNA is very similar to the DNA of certain photosynthetic bacteria. Plant cell chloroplasts can arise only by the division of preexisting chloroplasts. These facts may suggest that chloroplasts are descendants of ancient prokaryotic cells. Like mitochondria, chloroplasts are also thought to be the descendants of ancient prokaryotic cells that were incorporated into plant cells through a process called *endosymbiosis*.

## Chromoplasts

*Chromoplasts* are plastids that contain colorful pigments and that may or may not take part in photosynthesis. Carrot root cells, for example, contain chromoplasts filled with the orange pigment carotene. Chromoplasts in flower petal cells contain red, purple, yellow, or white pigments.

## Other Plastids

Several other types of plastids share the general features of chloroplasts but differ in content. For example, amyloplasts store starch. Chloroplasts, chromoplasts, and amyloplasts arise from a common precursor, called a *proplastid*.

**Word Roots and Origins**

*chloroplast*

from the Greek *chloros*, meaning "pale green," and *plastos*, meaning "formed"

**FIGURE 4-23**

A chloroplast captures energy from sunlight and uses that energy to convert carbon dioxide and water into sugar and other carbohydrates.

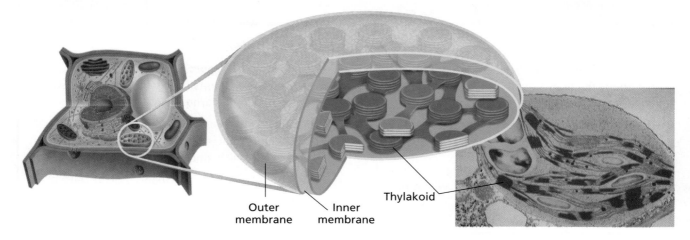

Outer membrane    Inner membrane    Thylakoid

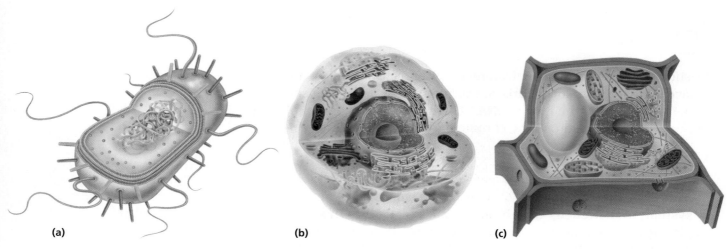

(a)　　　　　　　　　　　　　(b)　　　　　　　　　　　　　(c)

**FIGURE 4-24**

Prokaryotes (a) can be distinguished from eukaryotes (b and c) in that prokaryotes lack a nucleus and membrane-bound organelles. Plant cells (c) have the same organelles that animal cells do and have a cell wall, a central vacuole, and plastids.

# COMPARING CELLS

All cells share common features, such as a cell membrane, cytoplasm, ribosomes, and genetic material. But there is a high level of diversity among cells, as shown in Figure 4-24. There are significant differences between prokaryotes and eukaryotes. In addition, plant cells have features that are not found in animal cells.

## Prokaryotes Versus Eukaryotes

Prokaryotes differ from eukaryotes in that prokaryotes lack a nucleus and membrane-bound organelles. Prokaryotes have a region, called a *nucleoid,* in which their genetic material is concentrated. However, prokaryotes lack an internal membrane system.

## Plant Cells Versus Animal Cells

Three unique features distinguish plant cells from animal cells. One is the production of a cell wall by plant cells. Plant cells contain a large central vacuole. Third, plant cells contain a variety of plastids, which are not found in animal cells. Cell walls, central vacuoles, and plastids are unique features that are important to plant function.

**internet** connect

**www.scilinks.org**
**Topic: Plant Cells**
**Keyword: HM61157**

*SCI*
*LINKS*® Maintained by the
National Science
Teachers Association

---

## SECTION 4 REVIEW

1. Identify three unique features of plant cells.

2. List the differences between the plasma membrane, the primary cell wall, and the secondary cell wall.

3. Identify three functions of plastids.

4. Name three things that may be stored in vacuoles.

5. Describe the features that distinguish prokaryotes from eukaryotes and plant cells from animal cells.

**CRITICAL THINKING**

6. **Evaluating Viewpoints** One student says vacuoles keep plants from wilting. Another says cell walls do this. Who is right? Explain.

7. **Making Comparisons** If you discovered a new cell, what characteristics would you use to determine which kind of cell it is? Explain.

8. **Analyzing Information** Tobacco plant cells contain a toxic chemical. Why don't tobacco plant cells poison themselves? Explain.

# CHAPTER HIGHLIGHTS

SECTION 1
## SECTION 1  The History of Cell Biology

- All living things are made up of one or more cells. Robert Hooke discovered cells. Anton van Leeuwenhoek was the first to observe living cells.
- The cell theory states all living organisms are made of one or more cells, cells are the basic units of structure and function, and cells come only from pre-existing cells.

- All living things are made of organized parts, obtain energy from their surroundings, perform chemical reactions, change with time, respond to their environment, and reproduce.

### Vocabulary
cell (p. 69)    cell theory (p. 70)

## SECTION 2  Introduction to Cells

- A cell's shape reflects its function.
- Cell size is limited by a cell's surface area–to-volume ratio.
- The three basic parts of a cell are the plasma membrane, the cytoplasm, and the nucleus.

- Prokaryotes are organisms that lack a nucleus or membrane-bound organelles.
- In multicellular eukaryotes, cells organize into tissues, organs, organ systems, and finally organisms.

### Vocabulary
plasma membrane (p. 74)    nucleus (p. 74)    organelle (p. 75)    organ system (p. 76)
cytoplasm (p. 74)    prokaryote (p. 75)    tissue (p. 76)
cytosol (p. 74)    eukaryote (p. 75)    organ (p. 76)

## SECTION 3  Cell Organelles and Features

- Cell membranes are made of two phospholipid layers and proteins.
- The nucleus directs the cell's activities and stores DNA.
- Mitochondria harvest energy from organic compounds and transfer it to ATP.
- Ribosomes are either free or attached to the rough ER and play a role in protein synthesis.

- The rough ER prepares proteins for export or insertion into the cell membrane. The smooth ER builds lipids and participates in detoxification of toxins.
- The Golgi processes and packages proteins.
- Vesicles are classified by their contents.
- The cytoskeleton is made of protein fibers that help cells move and maintain their shape.

### Vocabulary
phospholipid bilayer (p. 77)    ribosome (p. 79)    lysosome (p. 82)    cilium (p. 85)
chromosome (p. 79)    mitochondrion (p. 80)    cytoskeleton (p. 84)    flagellum (p.85)
nuclear envelope (p. 79)    endoplasmic reticulum (p. 81)    microtubule (p. 84)    centriole (p. 85)
nucleolus (p. 79)    Golgi apparatus (p. 82)    microfilament (p. 84)

## SECTION 4  Unique Features of Plant Cells

- Plant cells have cell walls, central vacuoles, and plastids.
- In plant cells, a rigid cell wall covers the cell membrane and provides support and protection.
- Large central vacuoles store water, enzymes, and waste products and provide support for plant tissue.

- Plastids store starch and pigments. The chloroplast converts light energy into chemical energy by photosynthesis.
- Prokaryotes, animal cells, and plant cells can be distinguished from each other by their unique features.

### Vocabulary
cell wall (p. 88)    plastid (p. 89)    thylakoid (p. 89)
central vacuole (p. 88)    chloroplast (p. 89)    chlorophyll (p. 89)

# CHAPTER REVIEW

## USING VOCABULARY

1. For each pair of terms, explain how the meanings of the terms differ.
   a. *nucleolus* and *nucleus*
   b. *cell wall* and *cell membrane*
   c. *ribosomes* and *endoplasmic reticulum*
   d. *chromatin* and *chromosomes*
   e. *mitochondria* and *chloroplast*

2. Explain the relationship between cilia and flagella.

3. Use the following terms in the same sentence: *rough ER, smooth ER, Golgi apparatus, vesicle,* and *ribosome.*

4. **Word Roots and Origins** The word root *eu* means "true," *pro* means "before," and *kary* means "nucleus." Using this information, explain what the terms *eukaryote* and *prokaryote* suggest about their evolution.

## UNDERSTANDING KEY CONCEPTS

5. **Name** the scientist that first observed nonliving cells.

6. **Discuss** the roles of Schleiden, Schwann, and Virchow in the development of the cell theory.

7. **Analyze** the three parts of the cell theory.

8. **Identify** the characteristics shared by all living organisms.

9. **State** the relationship between cell shape and cell function.

10. **Identify** the factors that limit the growth of cells.

11. **Draw** the three major parts of a eukaryotic cell.

12. **Compare** the structure of a prokaryotic cell with that of a eukaryotic cell.

13. **Sequence** the relationship between organs, cells, organ systems, and tissues.

14. **Explain** why a cell membrane is called a *fluid mosaic.*

15. **Describe** the parts of a nucleus.

16. **Propose** why muscle cells have more mitochondria than other kinds of eukaryotic cells have.

17. **Describe** the role of ribosomes in cells.

18. **Compare** the functions of the Golgi apparatus with those of the ER.

19. **Discuss** the structure and function of vesicles.

20. **Describe** the structures that make up the cytoskeleton.

21. **Summarize** the differences between plant cells and animal cells.

22. **Propose** how the cell wall helps give support to a plant cell.

23. **Compare** primary and secondary cell walls.

24. **Predict** what would happen to a plant with a genetic defect that produced no central vacuole.

25. **Compare** mitochondria and chloroplasts.

26. **CONCEPT MAPPING** Use the following terms to create a concept map that compares animal cells with plant cells: *cell membrane, cell wall, central vacuole, chloroplasts,* and *mitochondria.*

## CRITICAL THINKING

27. **Interpreting Graphics** Answer the following questions based on the figure below.
    a. Identify the structures labeled A in the micrograph.
    b. Explain the significance of the shape of these structures.

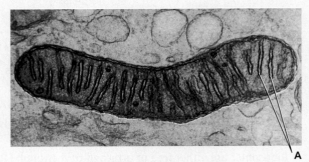

A

28. **Applying Concepts** Using your knowledge of the relationship between surface area and volume, explain why small pieces of a food cook faster than larger pieces of the same food.

29. **Making Comparisons** The coils of a radiator provide a large surface area from which heat is radiated into a room. Which cell organelles have a structure similar to that of a radiator? How is their structure related to their function?

30. **Evaluating Differences** Explain why colonial organisms are not considered multicellular. What features make colonial organisms different from multicellular organisms?

31. **Applying Information** Write a report summarizing the roles of different types of cell-membrane proteins in the preservation of body organs donated for transplant.

# Standardized Test Preparation

**DIRECTIONS:** Choose the letter of the answer choice that best answers the question.

1. The eukaryotic nucleus houses all of the following except the
   A. RNA
   B. DNA
   C. nucleolus
   D. endoplasmic reticulum

2. Which structure contributes to support and movement within a cell?
   F. crista
   G. cell wall
   H. ribosome
   J. microfilament

3. Which of the following statements about RNA is true?
   A. RNA is found only in proteins.
   B. RNA is found only in the nucleus.
   C. RNA is found only in the cytoplasm.
   D. RNA is found in the nucleus and cytoplasm.

**INTERPRETING GRAPHICS:** The graph below shows the relationship between cell size and surface area–to–volume ratio. Use the graph below to answer the questions that follow.

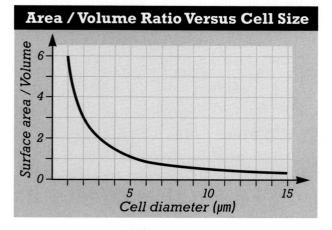

**Area / Volume Ratio Versus Cell Size**

4. By what percentage does the surface area–to–volume ratio change when a cell grows from 1 μm to 2 μm in diameter?
   F. 10 percent
   G. 20 percent
   H. 50 percent
   J. 90 percent

5. What is the maximum diameter that this cell could attain before the surface area–to–volume ratio would fall below 1?
   A. 2 μm
   B. 5 μm
   C. 10 μm
   D. 15 μm

**DIRECTIONS:** Complete the following analogy.

6. Mitochondria : energy release :: ribosome :
   F. cell support
   G. protein synthesis
   H. cellular digestion
   J. cellular transport

**INTERPRETING GRAPHICS:** The figure below shows a diagram of a cell. Use the figure to answer the question that follows.

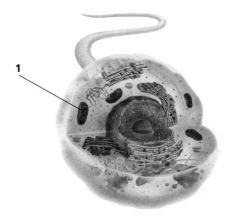

7. What is the function of the structure labeled 1?
   A. to make ATP
   B. to make proteins
   C. to make carbohydrates
   D. to move proteins through the cell

**SHORT RESPONSE**

A cell's shape is generally related to its function.

Skin cells are flat and platelike. Nerve cells have long extensions. Explain the relationship between the shape of skin and nerve cells and their function in the body.

**EXTENDED RESPONSE**

Despite the diversity among cells, eukaryotic cells share many common features.

*Part A*   Describe the structure and function of the organelles found in an animal cell.

*Part B*   Summarize the differences that distinguish animal cells from bacteria and plant cells.

**Test TIP** For short-response and essay questions that ask you to compare and contrast, be sure to include both the shared characteristics (compare) and unique characteristics (contrast) for each item.

# Comparing Animal and Plant Cells

## OBJECTIVES

■ Examine the similarities and differences between the structure of cells in animals and the structure of cells in plants.

## PROCESS SKILLS

■ hypothesizing
■ classifying
■ observing

## MATERIALS

■ lab apron
■ safety goggles
■ compound light microscope
■ forceps
■ microscope slides and coverslips
■ dropper bottle of Lugol's iodine solution
■ prepared slides of human epithelial cells
■ sprigs of *Elodea*
■ prepared slides of three unknowns

## Background

**1.** In this investigation, you will use a compound light microscope to observe cells from animals and plants. First, you will view a prepared slide of human epithelial cells taken from the skin lining the mouth. Then, you will make your own slide of a leaf from *Elodea,* a pond weed shown in the photograph on the next page.

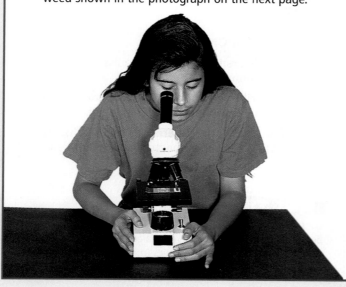

**2.** Based on your observations of human epithelial cells and *Elodea* leaf cells, you will be asked to classify three slides of unknown cells as either animal or plant cells.

**3.** Before you examine any cells, list the structural characteristics that distinguish animal cells from plant cells.

## PART A  Animal Cells

**1.** ⚠ CAUTION  **Handle glass microscope slides carefully. Dispose of broken glass separately in a container designated by your teacher.**

**2.** ⚠ CAUTION  **Do not use electrical equipment with wet hands or near water.**

**3.** Examine a prepared slide of epithelial cells under low, power. Locate cells that are separate from each other, and place them in the center of the field of view. Examine the cells under high power. Adjust the diaphragm to reduce the light intensity and achieve greater clarity.

**4.** In your lab report, make a drawing of two or three cells as they appear under high power. Identify and label the cell membrane, the cytoplasm, the nuclear envelope, and the nucleus of one of the cells in your drawing.

## PART B  Plant Cells

**5.** Carefully tear off a small leaf near the top of an *Elodea* sprig. Using forceps, place the whole leaf in a drop of water on a slide. Place a coverslip on top of the leaf.

**6.** Observe the leaf under low power. The outermost part of the cell is the cell wall. The many small, green organelles in the cells are chloroplasts.

**7.** Locate a cell that you can see clearly, and move the slide so that the cell is in the center of the field of view. Examine this cell under high power, and use the fine adjustment to bring the cell into focus.

**8.** Find an *Elodea* cell that is large enough to allow you to see the cell wall and the chloroplasts clearly. In your lab report, make a drawing of this cell. Label the cell wall and at least one chloroplast in your drawing.

**12.** Observe the stained cells under low and high power. Make a drawing of a stained *Elodea* cell in your lab report. Label the central vacuole, nucleus, nucleolus, chloroplasts, cell wall, and cell membrane if they are visible.

**PART C** Identifying Unknown Cells

**13.** Make a data table like the one below to record your observations of the unknown specimens.

**14.** Obtain prepared slides of three unknown specimens from your teacher.

**15.** Observe each specimen under low and high power. In your data table, record the code number assigned to each unknown, each specimen's classification as plant or animal, and your reasons for classifying each specimen.

**16.**  Clean up your materials, and wash your hands before leaving the lab.

## Analysis and Conclusions

**1.** According to your observations in this investigation, list several ways that plant and animal cells are structurally similar and several ways that they are different.

**2.** What do you think might be the function of cytoplasmic streaming in a plant cell? Lugol's iodine solution causes cytoplasmic streaming to stop. Why do you think this happens?

**3.** Which organelles that you read about in this chapter did you not see in this investigation? Why do you think you were unable to see these organelles in your slides?

## Further Inquiry

Use library resources to locate electron micrographs of cell structures that you were unable to see with the compound light microscope.

**9.** The chloroplasts may be moving in some of the cells. If you observe no movement, warm the slide in your hand or shine a bright lamp on it for a minute or two. Then, reexamine the slide under high power, and look for the movement of the cell's contents. This movement is called *cytoplasmic streaming.*

**10.** Because the cell membrane is pressed against the cell wall, you may not see it. Also, the abundance of chloroplasts may hide other organelles in the cells. You can make the cell membrane, vacuole, nucleus, and nucleolus more visible by making a stained wet-mount slide of *Elodea.*

**11.**  Put on a lab apron and safety goggles. Prepare a wet-mount slide of *Elodea* as you did in step 4, but substitute Lugol's iodine solution for the water. Allow the iodine solution to diffuse throughout the leaf.

| CLASSIFICATION OF UNKNOWN SPECIMENS | | |
|---|---|---|
| **Unknown (code number)** | **Classification (plant or animal)** | **Reasons for classification** |
| | | |
| | | |

# CHAPTER 5

# HOMEOSTASIS AND CELL TRANSPORT

The process of phagocytosis is just one of the many ways cells transport materials in and out of the cell. An example of phagocytosis is shown here as a macrophage engulfs a human tumor cell. (SEM 3,520×)

SECTION 1 *Passive Transport*

SECTION 2 *Active Transport*

BIOLOGY INTERACTIVE TUTOR

Unit 1—Cell Transport and Homeostasis
Topics 3–6

# PASSIVE TRANSPORT

*Cell membranes help organisms maintain homeostasis by controlling what substances may enter or leave cells. Some substances can cross the cell membrane without any input of energy by the cell in a process known as **passive transport**.*

## DIFFUSION

The simplest type of passive transport is diffusion. **Diffusion** is the movement of molecules from an area of higher concentration to an area of lower concentration. This difference in the concentration of molecules across a distance is called a **concentration gradient.** Consider what happens when you add a sugar cube to a beaker of water. As shown in Figure 5-1, the sugar cube sinks to the bottom of the beaker. This sinking makes the concentration of sugar molecules greater at the bottom of the beaker than at the top. As the cube dissolves, the sugar molecules begin to diffuse slowly through the water, moving towards the lower concentration at the top.

Diffusion is driven entirely by the molecules' kinetic energy. Molecules are in constant motion because they have kinetic energy. Molecules move randomly, traveling in a straight line until they hit an object, such as another molecule. When they hit something, they bounce off and move in a new direction, traveling in another straight line. If no object blocks their movement, they continue on their path. Thus, molecules tend to move from areas where they are more concentrated to areas where they are less concentrated, or "down" their concentration gradient.

In the absence of other influences, diffusion will eventually cause the molecules to be in **equilibrium**—the concentration of molecules will be the same throughout the space the molecules occupy. Returning to the example in Figure 5-1, if the beaker of water is left undisturbed, at some point the concentration of sugar molecules will be the same throughout the beaker. The sugar concentration will then be at equilibrium.

### OBJECTIVES

- **Explain** how an equilibrium is established as a result of diffusion.
- **Distinguish** between diffusion and osmosis.
- **Explain** how substances cross the cell membrane through facilitated diffusion.
- **Explain** how ion channels assist the diffusion of ions across the cell membrane.

### VOCABULARY

passive transport
diffusion
concentration gradient
equilibrium
osmosis
hypotonic
hypertonic
isotonic
contractile vacuole
turgor pressure
plasmolysis
cytolysis
facilitated diffusion
carrier protein
ion channel

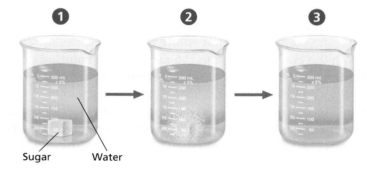

Sugar    Water

**FIGURE 5-1**

Sugar molecules, initially in a high concentration at the bottom of a beaker, ❶, will move about randomly through diffusion, ❷, and eventually reach equilibrium, ❸. At equilibrium the sugar concentration will be the same throughout the beaker. Diffusion occurs naturally because of the kinetic energy the molecules possess.

It is important to understand that even at equilibrium the random movement of molecules continues. But because there is an equal concentration of molecules everywhere, molecules are just as likely to move in one direction as in any other. The random movements of many molecules in many directions balance one another, and equilibrium is maintained.

## Diffusion Across Membranes

Cell membranes allow some molecules to pass through, but not others. If a molecule can pass through a cell membrane, it will diffuse from an area of higher concentration on one side of the membrane to an area of lower concentration on the other side. Diffusion across a membrane is also called *simple diffusion,* and only allows certain molecules to pass through the membrane.

The simple diffusion of a molecule across a cell membrane depends on the size and type of molecule and on the chemical nature of the membrane. A membrane can be made, in part, of a phospholipid bilayer, and certain proteins can form pores in the membrane. Molecules that can dissolve in lipids may pass directly through the membrane by diffusion. For example, because of their nonpolar nature, both carbon dioxide and oxygen dissolve in lipids. Molecules that are very small but not soluble in lipids may diffuse across the membrane by moving through the pores in the membrane.

## OSMOSIS

A solution is composed of a solute dissolved in a solvent. In the sugar water described in Figure 5-1, the solute was sugar and the solvent was water, and the solute molecules diffused through the solvent. It is also possible for solvent molecules to diffuse. In the case of cells, the solutes are organic and inorganic compounds, and the solvent is water. The process by which water molecules diffuse across a cell membrane from an area of higher concentration to an area of lower concentration is called **osmosis** (ahs-MOH-sis). Because water is moving from a higher to lower concentration, osmosis does not require cells to expend energy. Therefore, osmosis is the passive transport of water.

### Direction of Osmosis

The net direction of osmosis depends on the relative concentration of solutes on the two sides of the membrane. Examine Table 5-1. When the concentration of solute molecules outside the cell is *lower* than the concentration in the cytosol, the solution outside is **hypotonic** to the cytosol. In this situation, water diffuses *into* the cell until equilibrium is established. When the concentration of solute molecules outside the cell is *higher* than the concentration in the cytosol, the solution outside is **hypertonic** to the cytosol. In this situation, water diffuses *out of* the cell until equilibrium is established.

## TABLE 5-1 Direction of Osmosis

| Condition | Net movement of water | |
|---|---|---|
| External solution is hypotonic to cytosol | into the cell | $H_2O \rightarrow \quad \leftarrow H_2O$ |
| External solution is hypertonic to cytosol | out of the cell | $H_2O \leftarrow \quad \rightarrow H_2O$ |
| External solution is isotonic to cytosol | none | $H_2O \leftrightarrows \quad \leftrightarrows H_2O$ |

When the concentrations of solutes outside and inside the cell are equal, the outside solution is said to be **isotonic** to the cytosol. Under these conditions, water diffuses into and out of the cell at equal rates, so there is no net movement of water.

Notice that the prefixes *hypo-, hyper-,* and *iso-* refer to the relative solute concentrations of two solutions. Thus, if the solution outside the cell is *hypo*tonic to the cytosol, then the cytosol must be *hyper*tonic to that solution. Conversely, if the solution outside is *hyper*tonic to the cytosol, then the cytosol must be *hypo*tonic to the solution. Water tends to diffuse from hypotonic solutions to hypertonic solutions.

## How Cells Deal with Osmosis

Cells that are exposed to an isotonic external environment usually have no difficulty keeping the movement of water across the cell membrane in balance. This is the case with the cells of vertebrate animals on land and of most other organisms living in the sea. In contrast, many cells function in a hypotonic environment. Such is the case for unicellular freshwater organisms. Water constantly diffuses into these organisms. Because they require a relatively lower concentration of water in the cytosol to function normally, unicellular organisms must rid themselves of the excess water that enters by osmosis.

Some of them, such as the paramecia shown in Figure 5-2, do this with **contractile vacuoles** (kon-TRAK-til VAK-yoo-OL), which are organelles that remove water. Contractile vacuoles collect the excess water and then contract, pumping the water out of the cell. Unlike diffusion and osmosis, this pumping action is not a form of passive transport because it requires the cell to expend energy.

**FIGURE 5-2**

The paramecia shown below live in fresh water, which is hypotonic to their cytosol. (a) Contractile vacuoles collect excess water that moves by osmosis into the cytosol. (b) The vacuoles then contract, returning the water to the outside of the cell. (LM 315×)

**(a)**

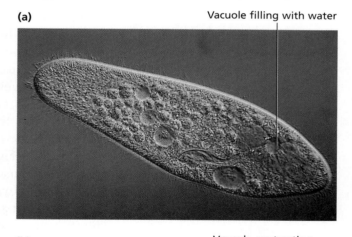

Vacuole filling with water

**(b)**

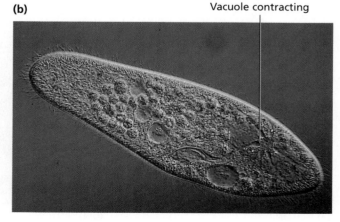

Vacuole contracting

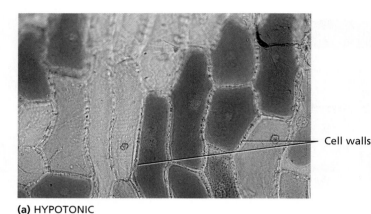

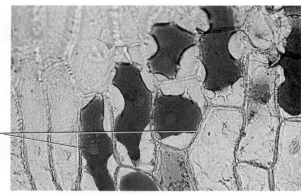

Cell walls

**(a)** HYPOTONIC

**(b)** HYPERTONIC

**FIGURE 5-3**

These two photographs show cells in the skin of a red onion. (a) In a hypotonic environment, the cells are pressed against the cell walls. (b) In a hypertonic environment, the cells contract and pull away from the cell walls.

**Word Roots and Origins**

*cytolysis*

from the Greek *kytos,* meaning "hollow vessel," and *lysis,* meaning "loosening"

**FIGURE 5-4**

(a) In an environment that is isotonic to the cytosol, a human red blood cell keeps its normal shape—round and dimpled. (b) In a hypotonic environment, the cell gains water and swells. (c) In a hypertonic environment, the cell loses water and becomes shriveled.

Other cells, including many of those in multicellular organisms, respond to hypotonic environments by pumping solutes out of the cytosol. This lowers the solute concentration in the cytosol, bringing it closer to the solute concentration in the environment. As a result, water molecules are less likely to diffuse into the cell.

Most plant cells, like animal cells, live in a hypotonic environment. In fact, the cells that make up plant roots may be surrounded by water. This water moves into plant cells by osmosis. These cells swell as they fill with water until the cell membrane is pressed against the inside of the cell wall, as Figure 5-3a shows. The cell wall is strong enough to resist the pressure exerted by the water inside the expanding cell. The pressure that water molecules exert against the cell wall is called **turgor pressure** (TER-GOR PRESH-er).

In a hypertonic environment, water leaves the cells through osmosis. As shown in Figure 5-3b, the cells shrink away from the cell walls, and turgor pressure is lost. This condition is called **plasmolysis** (plaz-MAHL-uh-sis), and is the reason that plants wilt if they don't receive enough water.

Some cells cannot compensate for changes in the solute concentration of their environment. Red blood cells in humans, for instance, lack contractile vacuoles, solute pumps, and cell walls. As shown in Figure 5-4, these cells lose their normal shape when they are exposed to an environment that is not isotonic to their cytosol. In a hypertonic environment, water leaves the cells, making them shrink and shrivel. In a hypotonic environment, water diffuses into the cells, causing them to swell and eventually burst. The bursting of cells is called **cytolysis** (sie-TAHL-uh-sis).

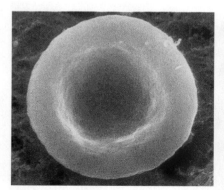

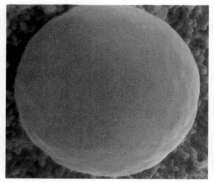

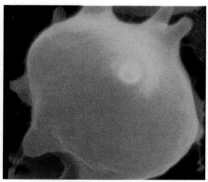

**(a)** ISOTONIC

**(b)** HYPOTONIC

**(c)** HYPERTONIC

# FACILITATED DIFFUSION

Another type of passive transport is called **facilitated diffusion.** This process is used for molecules that cannot readily diffuse through cell membranes, even when there is a concentration gradient across the membrane. Such molecules may not be soluble in lipids, or they may be too large to pass through the pores in the membrane. In facilitated diffusion, the movement of these kinds of molecules across the cell membrane is assisted by specific proteins in the membrane. These proteins are known as **carrier proteins.**

The carrier proteins that serve in facilitated diffusion transport molecules from an area of higher concentration on one side of the membrane to an area of lower concentration on the other side. Because the molecules are moving from a higher to lower concentration, which does not require any additional energy, facilitated diffusion is passive transport.

Figure 5-5 shows a model of how facilitated diffusion is thought to work. According to the model, a molecule binds to a specific carrier protein that transports it. As soon as the molecule binds to the carrier protein, the carrier protein then changes shape. This altered shape may shield the molecule from the hydrophobic interior of the lipid bilayer. Once shielded, the molecule can be transported through the cell membrane. On the other side of the membrane, the molecule is released from the carrier protein, and the protein returns to its original shape. The carrier protein is now free to bind to another molecule.

A good example of facilitated diffusion is the transport of glucose. Many cells depend on glucose for much of their energy needs. But glucose molecules are too large to diffuse easily across cell membranes. When the level of glucose within a cell is lower than the level of glucose outside the cell, carrier proteins transport glucose into the cell.

**FIGURE 5-5**

Facilitated diffusion occurs in four steps. ❶ A molecule, such as glucose, binds to a carrier protein on one side of the cell membrane. ❷ The carrier protein changes shape, shielding the molecule from the interior of the membrane. ❸ The molecule is released on the other side of the membrane. ❹ The carrier protein then returns to its original shape.

**FACILITATED DIFFUSION**

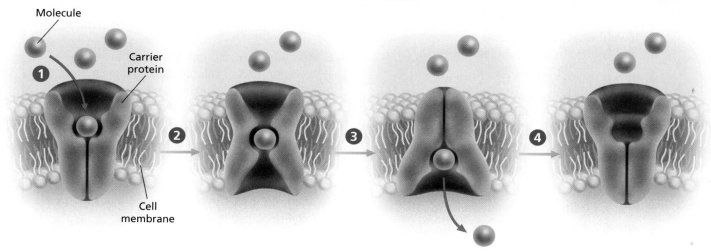

The tendency for water molecules to diffuse across membranes can be used to extract pure water from a mixture of water and solutes. If a dilute solution is separated from a more concentrated solution by a selectively permeable membrane, osmosis will occur, as water molecules diffuse from the dilute solution to the concentrated solution. However, if enough external pressure is applied to the concentrated solution, the opposite will happen: water molecules will diffuse from the concentrated solution to the dilute solution. This process, called *reverse osmosis,* effectively moves most of the water to one side of the membrane and leaves most of the solutes on the other side.

Reverse osmosis was initially developed for desalination plants, which produce fresh water from sea water. It is now also used to purify polluted water from a variety of sources, including manufacturing facilities and sanitary landfills. After the polluted water from these sources is purified through reverse osmosis, it is clean enough to be returned safely to the environment.

The transport of glucose illustrates two important properties of facilitated diffusion. First, facilitated diffusion can help substances move either into or out of a cell, depending on the concentration gradient. Thus, when the level of glucose is higher inside a cell than it is outside the cell, facilitated diffusion speeds the diffusion of glucose out of the cell. Second, the carrier proteins involved in facilitated diffusion are each specific for one type of molecule. For example, the carrier protein that helps with the diffusion of glucose and other simple sugars does not assist with the diffusion of amino acids.

# DIFFUSION THROUGH ION CHANNELS

Another type of transport involves membrane proteins known as **ion channels.** When ion channels transport ions from higher to lower concentrations they are a form of passive transport. Ion channels transport ions such as sodium ($Na^+$), potassium ($K^+$), calcium ($Ca^{2+}$), and chloride ($Cl^-$). These ions are important for a variety of cell functions. Because they are not soluble in lipids, however, ions cannot diffuse across the phospholipid bilayer without assistance. Ion channels provide small passageways across the cell membrane through which ions can diffuse. Each type of ion channel is usually specific for one type of ion. For example, sodium channels will allow $Na^+$ ions to go through, but will not allow $Ca^{2+}$ ions or $Cl^-$ to enter the cell.

Some ion channels are always open. Others have "gates" that open to allow ions to pass or close to stop their passage. The gates may open or close in response to three kinds of stimuli: stretching of the cell membrane, electrical signals, or chemicals in the cytosol or external environment. These stimuli therefore control the ability of specific ions to cross the cell membrane.

## SECTION 1 REVIEW

1. Toward what condition does diffusion eventually lead, in the absence of other influences?

2. How is osmosis related to diffusion?

3. If the concentration of solute molecules outside a cell is lower than the concentration in the cytosol, is the external solution hypotonic, hypertonic, or isotonic to the cytosol?

4. What role do carrier proteins play in facilitated diffusion?

5. How is facilitated diffusion similar to diffusion through ion channels?

**CRITICAL THINKING**

6. **Applying Information** Sea water has a higher concentration of solutes than do human body cells. Why might drinking large amounts of sea water be dangerous for humans?

7. **Relating Concepts** What would happen to a grape placed in a bowl with highly concentrated sugar water?

8. **Applying Information** Using what you know about osmosis, explain what would happen to a jellyfish placed in a freshwater lake.

# ACTIVE TRANSPORT

*In many cases, cells must move materials from an area of lower concentration to an area of higher concentration, or "up" their concentration gradient. Such movement of materials is known as **active transport**. Unlike passive transport, active transport requires a cell to expend energy.*

## SECTION 2

### OBJECTIVES

- **Distinguish** between passive transport and active transport.
- **Explain** how the sodium-potassium pump operates.
- **Compare** endocytosis and exocytosis.

### VOCABULARY

active transport
sodium-potassium pump
endocytosis
vesicle
pinocytosis
phagocytosis
phagocyte
exocytosis

## CELL MEMBRANE PUMPS

Ion channels and carrier proteins not only assist in passive transport but also help with some types of active transport. The carrier proteins that serve in active transport are often called *cell membrane "pumps"* because they move substances from lower to higher concentrations.

Carrier proteins involved in facilitated diffusion and those involved in active transport are very similar. In both, the molecule first binds to a specific kind of carrier protein on one side of the cell membrane. Once it is bound to the molecule, the protein changes shape, shielding the molecule from the hydrophobic interior of the phospholipid bilayer. The protein then transports the molecule through the membrane and releases it on the other side. However, cell membrane pumps require energy. Most often the energy needed for active transport is supplied directly or indirectly by ATP.

### Sodium-Potassium Pump

One example of active transport in animal cells involves a carrier protein known as the **sodium-potassium pump.** As its name suggests, this protein transports $Na^+$ ions and $K^+$ ions up their concentration gradients. To function normally, some animal cells must have a higher concentration of $Na^+$ ions outside the cell and a higher concentration of $K^+$ ions inside the cell. The sodium-potassium pump maintains these concentration differences.

Follow the steps in Figure 5-6 to see how the sodium-potassium pump operates. First, three $Na^+$ ions bind to the carrier protein on the cytosol side of the membrane, as shown in step **❶**. At the same time, the carrier protein removes a phosphate group from a molecule of ATP. As you can see in step **❷**, the phosphate group from the ATP molecule binds to the carrier protein. Step **❸** shows how the removal of the phosphate group from ATP supplies the energy needed to change the shape of the carrier protein. With its new shape, the protein carries the three $Na^+$ ions through the membrane and then forces the $Na^+$ ions outside the cell where the $Na^+$ concentration must remain high.

🖪 internet connect

www.scilinks.org
**Topic:** Active Transport
**Keyword:** HM60018

SCI LINKS. Maintained by the National Science Teachers Association

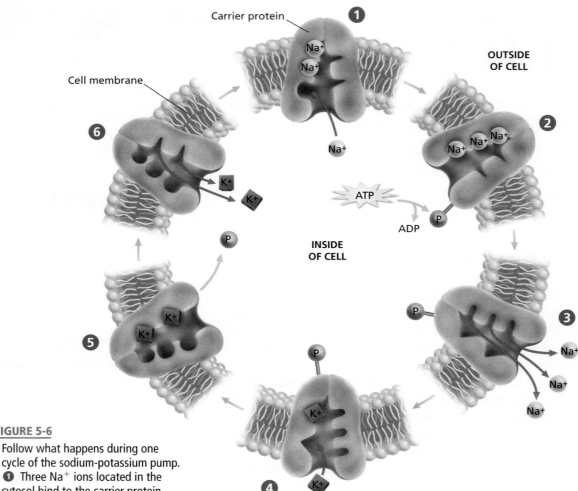

Carrier protein

Cell membrane

**OUTSIDE OF CELL**

**INSIDE OF CELL**

ATP

ADP

Na+

K+

P

**FIGURE 5-6**

Follow what happens during one cycle of the sodium-potassium pump.
❶ Three Na+ ions located in the cytosol bind to the carrier protein.
❷ A phosphate group, represented by the letter P in the diagram, is removed from ATP and bound to the carrier protein. ❸ The binding of the phosphate group changes the shape of the carrier protein, allowing the three Na+ ions to be released into the cell's environment. ❹ Two K+ ions located outside the cell bind to the carrier protein. ❺ The phosphate group is released, restoring the original shape of the carrier protein. ❻ The two K+ ions are released into the cytosol, and the cycle is ready to repeat.

At this point, the carrier protein has the shape it needs to bind two K+ ions outside the cell, as step ❹ shows. When the K+ ions bind, the phosphate group is released, as indicated in step ❺, and the carrier protein restores its original shape. As shown in step ❻ this time, the change in shape causes the carrier protein to release the two K+ ions inside the cell. At this point the carrier protein is ready to begin the process again. Thus, a complete cycle of the sodium-potassium pump transports three Na+ ions out of the cell and two K+ ions into the cell. At top speed, the sodium-potassium pump can transport about 450 Na+ ions and 300 K+ ions per second.

The exchange of three Na+ ions for two K+ ions creates an electrical gradient across the cell membrane. That is, the outside of the membrane becomes positively charged relative to the inside of the membrane, which becomes relatively negative. In this way, the two sides of the cell membrane are like the positive and negative terminals of a battery. This difference in charge is important for the conduction of electrical impulses along nerve cells. The sodium-potassium pump is only one example of a cell membrane pump. Other pumps work in similar ways to transport important metabolic materials across cell membranes.

# MOVEMENT IN VESICLES

Some substances, such as macromolecules and nutrients, are too large to pass through the cell membrane by the transport processes you have studied so far. Cells employ two other transport mechanisms—endocytosis and exocytosis—to move such substances into or out of cells. Endocytosis and exocytosis are also used to transport large quantities of small molecules into or out of cells at a single time. Both endocytosis and exocytosis require cells to expend energy. Therefore, they are types of active transport.

## Endocytosis

**Endocytosis** (EN-doh-sie-TOH-sis) is the process by which cells ingest external fluid, macromolecules, and large particles, including other cells. As you can see in Figure 5-7, these external materials are enclosed by a portion of the cell's membrane, which folds into itself and forms a pouch. The pouch then pinches off from the cell membrane and becomes a membrane-bound organelle called a **vesicle.** Some of the vesicles fuse with lysosomes, and their contents are digested by lysosomal enzymes. Other vesicles that form during endocytosis fuse with other membrane-bound organelles.

Two main types of endocytosis are based on the kind of material that is taken into the cell: **pinocytosis** (PIEN-oh-sie-TOH-sis) involves the transport of solutes or fluids, and **phagocytosis** (FAG-oh-sie-TOH-sis) is the movement of large particles or whole cells. Many unicellular organisms feed by phagocytosis. In addition, certain cells in animals use phagocytosis to ingest bacteria and viruses that invade the body. These cells, known as **phagocytes,** allow lysosomes to fuse with the vesicles that contain the ingested bacteria and viruses. Lysosomal enzymes then destroy the bacteria and viruses before they can harm the animal.

internet connect

www.scilinks.org
**Topic:** Endocytosis
**Keyword:** HM60505

SC*LINKS.* Maintained by the National Science Teachers Association

**Word Roots and Origins**

*vesicle*

from the Latin *vesicula,* meaning "bladder" or "sac"

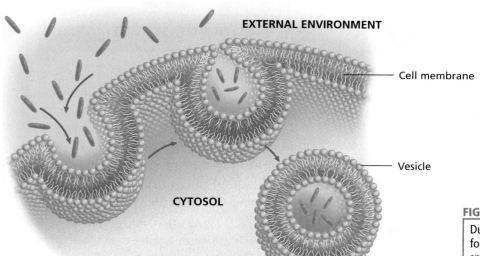

EXTERNAL ENVIRONMENT

—— Cell membrane

—— Vesicle

CYTOSOL

**FIGURE 5-7**

During endocytosis, the cell membrane folds around food or liquid and forms a small pouch. The pouch then pinches off from the cell membrane to become a vesicle.

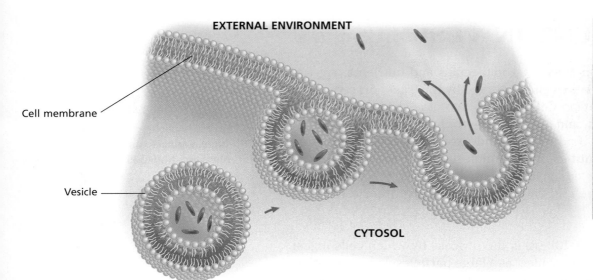

EXTERNAL ENVIRONMENT

Cell membrane

Vesicle

CYTOSOL

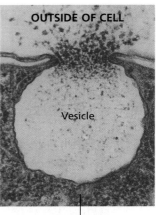

OUTSIDE OF CELL

Vesicle

INSIDE OF CELL

**FIGURE 5-8**

During exocytosis, a vesicle moves to the cell membrane, fuses with it, and then releases its contents to the outside of the cell.

## Exocytosis

**Exocytosis** (EK-soh-sie-TOH-sis) is the process by which a substance is released from the cell through a vesicle that transports the substance to the cell surface and then fuses with the membrane to let the substance out of the cell. This process, illustrated in Figure 5-8, is basically the reverse of endocytosis. During exocytosis, vesicles release their contents into the cell's external environment. Figure 5-8 also shows a photo of a vesicle during exocytosis.

Cells may use exocytosis to release large molecules such as proteins, waste products, or toxins that would damage the cell if they were released within the cytosol. Recall that proteins are made on ribosomes and packaged into vesicles by the Golgi apparatus. The vesicles then move to the cell membrane and fuse with it, delivering the proteins outside the cell. Cells in the nervous and endocrine systems also use exocytosis to release small molecules that control the activities of other cells.

## SECTION 2 REVIEW

1. Explain the difference between passive transport and active transport.

2. What functions do carrier proteins perform in active transport?

3. What provides the energy that drives the sodium-potassium pump?

4. Explain the difference between pinocytosis and phagocytosis.

5. Describe the steps involved in exocytosis.

6. How do endocytosis and exocytosis differ? How can that difference be seen?

**CRITICAL THINKING**

7. **Analyzing Information** During intense exercise, potassium tends to accumulate in the fluid surrounding muscle cells. What membrane protein helps muscle cells counteract this tendency? Explain your answer.

8. **Evaluating Differences** How does the sodium-potassium pump differ from facilitated diffusion?

9. **Relating Concepts** The vesicles formed during pinocytosis are much smaller than those formed during phagocytosis. Explain.

## SECTION 1    Passive Transport

- Passive transport involves the movement of molecules across the cell membrane without an input of energy by the cell.

- Diffusion is the movement of molecules from an area of higher concentration to an area of lower concentration, driven by the molecules' kinetic energy until equilibrium is reached.

- Molecules can diffuse across a cell membrane by dissolving in the phospholipid bilayer or by passing through pores in the membrane.

- Osmosis is the diffusion of water across a membrane. The net direction of osmosis is determined by the relative solute concentrations on the two sides of the membrane.

- When the solute concentration outside the cell is lower than that in the cytosol, the solution outside is hypotonic to the cytosol, and water will diffuse into the cell.

- When the solute concentration outside the cell is higher than that in the cytosol, the solution outside is hypertonic to the cytosol, and water will diffuse out of the cell.

- When the solute concentrations outside and inside the cell are equal, the solution outside is isotonic, and there will be no net movement of water.

- To remain alive, cells must compensate for the water that enters the cell in hypotonic environments and leaves the cell in hypertonic environments.

- In facilitated diffusion, a molecule binds to a carrier protein on one side of the cell membrane. The carrier protein then changes its shape and transports the molecule down its concentration gradient to the other side of the membrane.

- Ion channels are proteins, or groups of proteins, that provide small passageways across the cell membrane through which specific ions can diffuse.

### Vocabulary

passive transport (p. 97)    osmosis (p. 98)    contractile vacuole (p. 99)    facilitated diffusion (p. 101)
diffusion (p. 97)    hypotonic (p. 98)    turgor pressure (p. 100)    carrier protein (p. 101)
concentration gradient (p. 97)    hypertonic (p. 98)    plasmolysis (p. 100)    ion channel (p. 102)
equilibrium (p. 97)    isotonic (p. 99)    cytolysis (p. 100)

## SECTION 2    Active Transport

- Active transport moves molecules across the cell membrane from an area of lower concentration to an area of higher concentration. Unlike passive transport, active transport requires cells to expend energy.

- Some types of active transport are performed by carrier proteins called cell membrane pumps.

- One example of a cell membrane pump is the sodium-potassium pump. It moves three $Na^+$ ions into the cell's external environment for every two $K^+$ ions it moves into the cytosol. ATP supplies the energy that drives the pump.

- Endocytosis and exocytosis are active transport mechanisms in which large substances enter or leave cells inside vesicles.

- In endocytosis, the cell membrane folds around something in the external environment and forms a pouch. The pouch then pinches off and becomes a vesicle in the cytoplasm.

- Endocytosis includes pinocytosis, in which the vesicle contains solutes or fluids, and phagocytosis, in which the vesicle contains large particles or cells.

- In exocytosis, vesicles made by the cell fuse with the cell membrane, releasing their contents into the external environment.

### Vocabulary

active transport (p. 103)    endocytosis (p. 105)    pinocytosis (p. 105)    phagocyte (p. 105)
sodium-potassium pump (p. 103)    vesicle (p. 105)    phagocytosis (p. 105)    exocytosis (p. 106)

## USING VOCABULARY

1. For each pair of terms, explain how the meanings of the terms differ.
   a. *diffusion* and *facilitated diffusion*
   b. *hypotonic* and *hypertonic*
   c. *plasmolysis* and *cytolysis*
   d. *pinocytosis* and *phagocytosis*

2. Explain the relationship between plasmolysis and turgor pressure in plant cells.

3. Use the following terms in the same sentence: *carrier protein, concentration gradient, facilitated diffusion,* and *passive transport.*

4. **Word Roots and Origins** The prefix *pino-* means "to drink," *phago-* means "to eat," and *cyto-* means "cell." Using this information, explain why the words *pinocytosis* and *phagocytosis* are good names for the processes they describe.

## UNDERSTANDING KEY CONCEPTS

5. **Explain** why diffusion eventually results in equilibrium.

6. **Identify** whether all molecules diffuse through all cell membranes. Explain your answer.

7. **Distinguish** between diffusion and osmosis.

8. **Describe** what it means to say that two solutions are isotonic.

9. **Define** the term *contractile vacuole.* What is a contractile vacuole's function?

10. **Determine** how hypotonic, hypertonic and turgor pressure are interrelated.

11. **Summarize** the factors that determine the direction of net movement of water across a cell membrane.

12. **Determine** how the phospholipid bilayer of a membrane forms a barrier to molecules.

13. **Explain** how substances cross a cell membrane through facilitated diffusion.

14. **Describe** how ion channels assist in the diffusion of ions through a cell membrane.

15. **Distinguish** between passive transport and active transport.

16. **Explain** how a cell that consumes glucose can speed up its intake of glucose from the environment.

17. **Identify** how ATP is involved in maintaining the sodium and potassium gradients across a cell membrane.

18. **Distinguish** between the processes of endocytosis and exocytosis.

19. **CONCEPT MAPPING** Use the following terms to create a concept map that shows how cells maintain homeostasis: *active transport, carrier protein, cell transport, concentration gradient, diffusion, endocytosis, exocytosis, facilitated diffusion, homeostasis, osmosis, passive transport,* and *sodium-potassium pump.*

## CRITICAL THINKING

20. **Making Comparisons** There is a higher concentration of air molecules inside an inflated balloon than there is outside the balloon. Because of their constant random motion, the molecules inside press against the balloon and keep it taut. How is the pressure exerted by these air molecules similar to turgor pressure? How is it different?

21. **Comparing Concepts** Sometimes, water seeps through the concrete wall of a basement after a heavy rain, and the homeowner must remove the water with a sump pump. How can this situation be compared to the action of a unicellular non-photosynthetic organism that lives in a pond?

22. **Predicting Results** If a cell were exposed to a poison that blocked the cell's ability to manufacture ATP, what effect would that have on the cell membrane's transport processes?

23. **Interpreting Graphics** The drawing below shows a plant cell after the solute concentration of its environment has been changed. How would you describe the new external environment?

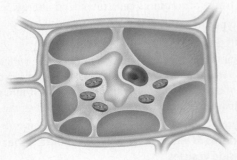

24. **Analyzing Information** Write a report summarizing the roles of osmosis and diffusion in the preservation of body organs donated for transplants. Why must organs be preserved in special solutions prior to a transplant? Find out what kinds of substances these solutions contain.

# Standardized Test Preparation

**DIRECTIONS:** Choose the letter of the answer choice that best answers the question.

1. During diffusion, molecules tend to move in what direction?
   - **A.** the molecules involved in diffusion never move
   - **B.** in a direction that doesn't depend on the concentration gradient
   - **C.** from an area of lower concentration to an area of higher concentration
   - **D.** from an area of higher concentration to an area of lower concentration

2. Ion channels aid the movement of which substances?
   - **F.** ions across a cell membrane
   - **G.** water across a cell membrane
   - **H.** molecules up a concentration gradient
   - **J.** carrier proteins within the lipid bilayer

3. The sodium-potassium pump transports which of the following?
   - **A.** both $Na^+$ and $K^+$ into the cell
   - **B.** both $Na^+$ and $K^+$ out of the cell
   - **C.** $Na^+$ into the cell and $K^+$ out of the cell
   - **D.** $Na^+$ out of the cell and $K^+$ into the cell

4. Which process do some animal cells use to engulf, digest, and destroy invading bacteria?
   - **F.** exocytosis
   - **G.** pinocytosis
   - **H.** phagocytosis
   - **J.** All of the above

**INTERPRETING GRAPHICS:** The graph below shows the rate of glucose transport across a cell membrane versus the concentration gradient. Use the graph that follows to answer the question.

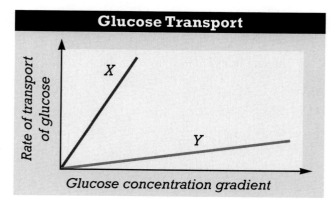

**Glucose Transport**

Rate of transport of glucose (vertical axis)

*X*

*Y*

*Glucose concentration gradient* (horizontal axis)

5. Which line represents the diffusion of glucose through the lipid bilayer?
   - **A.** line *X*
   - **B.** line *Y*
   - **C.** both lines *X* and *Y*
   - **D.** neither line *X* nor *Y*

**DIRECTIONS:** Complete the following analogy.

6. passive transport : osmosis :: active transport :
   - **F.** cytolysis
   - **G.** diffusion
   - **H.** ion channel
   - **J.** endocytosis

**INTERPRETING GRAPHICS:** The diagram below shows one form of cellular transport. Use the diagram to answer the question that follows.

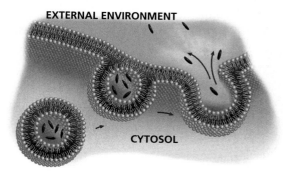

**EXTERNAL ENVIRONMENT**

**CYTOSOL**

7. What form of cellular transport is being illustrated in the above diagram?
   - **A.** osmosis
   - **B.** exocytosis
   - **C.** facilitated diffusion
   - **D.** a cell membrane pump

**SHORT RESPONSE**

When a cell takes in substances through endocytosis, the outside of the cell membrane becomes the inside of the vesicle.

What might this suggest about the structure of the cell membrane?

**EXTENDED RESPONSE**

Some cells have carrier proteins that transport sugar molecules and hydrogen ions into the cytosol at the same time. These proteins move sugar up their gradient as hydrogen ions move down their gradient.

*Part A* How would the transport of sugar into these cells affect the pH of the cells' external environment?

*Part B* What would happen to the transport of sugar if hydrogen ions were removed from the external environment?

**Test TIP** Pay close attention to questions that contain words such as *not, only, rather,* and *some,* because these words can often help you eliminate answer choices.

# Analyzing the Effect of Cell Size on Diffusion

## OBJECTIVES

- **Relate** a cell's size to its surface area-to-volume ratio.
- **Predict** how the surface area-to-volume ratio of a cell will affect the diffusion of substances into the cell.

## PROCESS SKILLS

- making observations
- using scientific methods
- designing an experiment
- collecting data
- organizing data
- graphing
- analyzing data

## MATERIALS

- safety goggles
- lab apron
- disposable gloves
- block of phenolphthalein agar (3 × 6 cm)
- plastic knife
- metric ruler
- 250 mL beaker
- 150 mL vinegar
- plastic spoon
- paper towel

## Background

1. Substances enter and leave a cell in several ways including by diffusion.
2. Describe the process of diffusion.
3. Define the terms *surface area* and *volume.*
4. How efficiently a cell can exchange substances depends on the surface area-to-volume ratio. Surface area-to-volume ratio can be calculated by dividing surface area by volume of the cell (surface area ÷ volume of cell).

## PART A  Designing an Experiment

1. Using the materials listed for this lab, design an experiment to test how the surface area-to-volume ratio affects the diffusion of a substance into a cell.

### You Choose

As you design your experiment, decide the following:
   a. what question you will explore
   b. what hypothesis you will test
   c. how many "cells" (agar cubes) you will have and what sizes they will be
   d. how long to leave the "cells" in the vinegar
   e. how to determine how far the vinegar diffused into a "cell"
   f. how to prevent contamination of agar cubes as you handle them
   g. what data to record in your data table

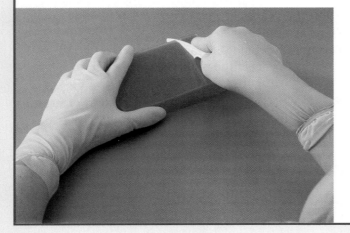

2. Write a procedure for your experiment. Make a list of all the safety precautions you will take. Have your teacher approve your procedure and safety precautions before you begin the experiment.

**PART B** Conducting Your Experiment

3. **CAUTION Always wear safety goggles and a lab apron to protect your eyes and clothing. Put on safety goggles, a lab apron, and disposable gloves. Do not touch or taste any chemicals.** Carry out the experiment you designed. Record your observations in your data table.

4. **CAUTION Know the location of the emergency shower and eyewash station and how to use them.** If you get a chemical on your skin or clothing, wash it off at the sink while calling to the teacher. Notify the teacher of a spill. Spills should be cleaned up promptly, according to your teacher's directions.

5. **CAUTION Glassware is fragile.** Notify the teacher of broken glass or cuts. Do not clean up broken glass or spills with broken glass unless the teacher tells you to do so.

6. Clean up your work area and all lab equipment. Return lab equipment to its proper place. Dispose of solutions, broken glass, and agar in the designated waste containers. Do not pour chemicals down the drain or put lab materials in the trash unless your teacher tells you to do so. Wash your hands thoroughly before you leave the lab and after you finish all work.

**Analysis and Conclusions**

1. Describe any changes in the appearance of the cubes.
2. Make a graph using your group's data. Plot "Diffusion distance (mm)" on the vertical axis. Use graph paper to plot "Surface area-to-volume ratio" on the horizontal axis.
3. Using the graph you made in item 2, make a statement about the relationship between the surface area-to-volume ratio and the distance a substance diffuses.
4. Make a graph using your group's data. Use graph paper to plot "Rate of diffusion (mm/min)" (distance vinegar moved time) on the vertical axis. Plot "Surface area-to-volume ratio" on the horizontal axis.
5. Using the graph you made in item 4, make a statement about the relationship between the surface area-to-volume ratio and the rate of diffusion of a substance.
6. In what ways do your agar models simplify or fail to simulate the features of real cells?
7. Calculate the surface area and volume of a cube with a side length of 5 cm. Calculate the surface area and volume of a cube with a side length of 10 cm. Determine the surface area-to-volume ratio of each of these cubes. Which cube has the greater surface area-to-volume ratio?
8. How does the size of a cell affect the diffusion of substances into the cell?

**Further Inquiry**

Write a new question about cell size and diffusion that also explores hypotonic and hypertonic solutions that could be explored with another investigation.

# PHOTOSYNTHESIS

Alfalfa, corn, and soybeans are growing on this farmland in Pennsylvania. Through photosynthesis, these plants obtain energy from the sun and store it in organic compounds. Humans and other living organisms depend on organic compounds—and therefore on photosynthesis—to obtain the energy necessary for living.

**SECTION 1** *The Light Reactions*

**SECTION 2** *The Calvin Cycle*

**BIOLOGY** Unit 2—Photosynthesis
INTERACTIVE TUTOR Topics 1–6

# THE LIGHT REACTIONS

*All organisms use energy to carry out the functions of life. Where does this energy come from? Directly or indirectly, almost all of the energy in living systems comes from the sun. Energy from the sun enters living systems when plants, algae, some unicellular protists, and some prokaryotes absorb sunlight and use it to make organic compounds.*

### OBJECTIVES

- **Explain** why almost all organisms depend on photosynthesis.
- **Describe** the role of chlorophylls and other pigments in photosynthesis.
- **Summarize** the main events of the light reactions.
- **Explain** how ATP is made during the light reactions.

### VOCABULARY

autotroph
photosynthesis
heterotroph
light reactions
chloroplast
thylakoid
granum
stroma
pigment
chlorophyll
carotenoid
photosystem
primary electron acceptor
electron transport chain
chemiosmosis

## OBTAINING ENERGY

Organisms can be classified according to how they get energy. Organisms that use energy from sunlight or from chemical bonds in inorganic substances to make organic compounds are called **autotrophs** (AWT-oh-TROHFS). Most autotrophs use the process of **photosynthesis** to convert light energy from the sun into chemical energy in the form of organic compounds, primarily carbohydrates.

The tree in Figure 6-1 is an autotroph because it converts light energy from the sun into organic compounds. The tree uses these compounds for energy. The caterpillar also depends on the tree for energy, as it cannot manufacture organic compounds itself. Animals and other organisms that must get energy from food instead of directly from sunlight or inorganic substances are called **heterotrophs** (HEHT-uhr-oh-TROHFS). The bird is also a heterotroph. The food that fuels the bird originates with an autotroph (the tree), but it passes indirectly to the bird through the caterpillar. In similar ways, almost all organisms ultimately depend on autotrophs to obtain the energy necessary to carry out the processes of life.

Photosynthesis involves a complex series of chemical reactions in which the product of one reaction is consumed in the next reaction. A series of chemical reactions linked in this way is referred to as a *biochemical pathway*.

**FIGURE 6-1**

The tree depends on the sun for energy. Like all heterotrophs, the caterpillar and bird depend on an autotroph (the tree and its leaves) for energy.

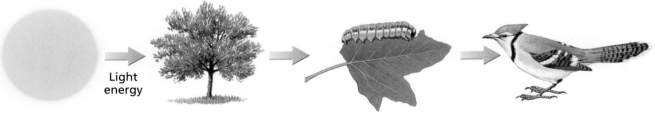

Light energy

Plants convert light energy to chemical energy.

Caterpillars get energy by eating plants.

Birds get energy by eating caterpillars.

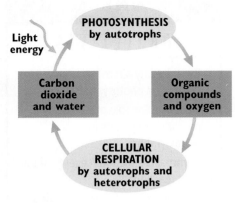

FIGURE 6-2

Many autotrophs produce organic compounds and oxygen through photosynthesis. Both autotrophs and heterotrophs produce carbon dioxide through cellular respiration.

# OVERVIEW OF PHOTOSYNTHESIS

Figure 6-2 shows how autotrophs use photosynthesis to produce organic compounds from carbon dioxide ($CO_2$) and water. The oxygen ($O_2$) and some of the organic compounds produced are then used by cells in a process called *cellular respiration*. During cellular respiration, $CO_2$ and water are produced. Thus, the products of photosynthesis are reactants in cellular respiration. Conversely, the products of cellular respiration are reactants in photosynthesis.

Photosynthesis can be divided into two stages:

1. **Light Reactions** Light energy (absorbed from the sun) is converted to chemical energy, which is temporarily stored in ATP and the energy carrier molecule *NADPH*.
2. **Calvin Cycle** Organic compounds are formed using $CO_2$ and the chemical energy stored in ATP and NADPH.

Photosynthesis can be summarized by the following equation:

$$6CO_2 + 6H_2O \xrightarrow{\text{light energy}} C_6H_{12}O_6 + 6O_2$$

This equation, however, does not explain how photosynthesis occurs. It is helpful to examine the two stages separately in order to better understand the overall process of photosynthesis.

# CAPTURING LIGHT ENERGY

The first stage of photosynthesis includes the **light reactions,** so named because they require light to happen. The light reactions begin with the absorption of light in **chloroplasts,** organelles found in the cells of plants and algae. Most chloroplasts are similar in structure. As shown in Figure 6-3, each chloroplast is surrounded by a pair of membranes. Inside the inner membrane is another system of membranes called **thylakoids** (THIE-luh-koydz) that are arranged as flattened sacs. The thylakoids are connected and layered to form stacks called **grana** (GRAY-nuh) (singular, **granum**). Surrounding the grana is a solution called the **stroma** (STROH-muh).

FIGURE 6-3

Photosynthesis in eukaryotes occurs inside the chloroplast. The light reactions of photosynthesis take place in the thylakoids, which are stacked to form grana.

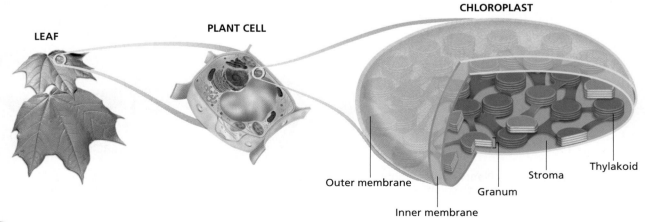

LEAF

PLANT CELL

CHLOROPLAST

Outer membrane

Inner membrane

Granum

Stroma

Thylakoid

## Light and Pigments

To understand how chloroplasts absorb light in photosynthesis, it is important to understand some of the properties of light. Light from the sun appears white, but it is actually made of a variety of colors. As shown in Figure 6-4, white light can be separated into its component colors by passing the light through a prism. The resulting array of colors, ranging from red at one end to violet at the other, is called the *visible spectrum.*

When white light strikes an object, its component colors can be reflected, transmitted, or absorbed by the object. Many objects contain **pigments,** compounds that absorb light. Most pigments absorb certain colors more strongly than others. By absorbing certain colors, a pigment subtracts those colors from the visible spectrum. Therefore, the light that is reflected or transmitted by the pigment no longer appears white. For example, the lenses in green-tinted sunglasses contain a pigment that reflects and transmits green light and absorbs the other colors. As a result, the lenses look green.

## Chloroplast Pigments

Located in the membrane of the thylakoids are several pigments, the most important of which are called **chlorophylls** (KLAWR-uh-FILZ). There are several different types of chlorophylls. The two most common types are known as chlorophyll *a* and chlorophyll *b*. As Figure 6-5 shows, chlorophyll *a* absorbs less blue light but more red light than chlorophyll *b* absorbs. Neither chlorophyll *a* nor chlorophyll *b* absorbs much green light. Instead, they allow green light to be reflected or transmitted. For this reason, leaves and other plant structures that contain large amounts of chlorophyll look green.

Only chlorophyll *a* is directly involved in the light reactions of photosynthesis. Chlorophyll *b* assists chlorophyll *a* in capturing light energy, and therefore chlorophyll *b* is called an accessory pigment. Other compounds found in the thylakoid membrane, including the yellow, orange, and brown **carotenoids** (kuh-RAHT'n-OYDZ), also function as accessory pigments. Looking again at Figure 6-5, notice that the pattern of light absorption of one of the carotenoids differs from the pattern of either type of chlorophyll. By absorbing colors that chlorophyll *a* cannot absorb, the accessory pigments enable plants to capture more of the energy in light.

In the leaves of a plant, the chlorophylls are generally much more abundant and therefore mask the colors of the other pigments. But in the nonphotosynthetic parts of a plant, such as fruits and flowers, the colors of the other pigments may be quite visible. During the fall, many plants lose their chlorophylls, and their leaves take on the rich hues of the carotenoids.

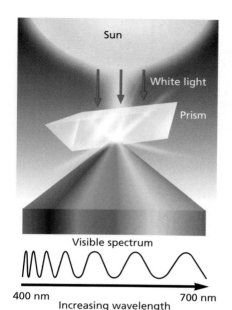

**FIGURE 6-4**

White light contains a variety of colors called the *visible spectrum.* Each color has a different wavelength, measured in nanometers.

**FIGURE 6-5**

The three curves on this graph show how three pigments involved in photosynthesis differ in the colors of light they absorb. Where a curve has a peak, much of the light at that wavelength is absorbed. Where a curve has a trough, much of the light at that wavelength is reflected or transmitted.

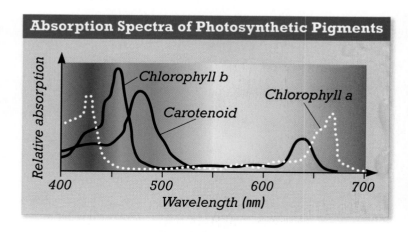

# CONVERTING LIGHT ENERGY TO CHEMICAL ENERGY

Once the pigments in the chloroplast have captured light energy, the light energy must then be converted to chemical energy. The chemical energy is temporarily stored in ATP and NADPH. During these reactions, $O_2$ is given off. The chlorophylls and carotenoids are grouped in clusters of a few hundred pigment molecules in the thylakoid membrane. Each cluster of pigment molecules and the proteins that the pigment molecules are embedded in are referred to collectively as a **photosystem.** Two types of photosystems are known: *photosystem I* and *photosystem II.* They contain similar kinds of pigments, but they have different roles in the light reactions.

The light reactions begin when accessory pigment molecules in both photosystems absorb light. By absorbing light, those molecules acquire some of the energy carried by the light. In each photosystem, the acquired energy is passed quickly to the other pigment molecules until it reaches a specific pair of chlorophyll *a* molecules. Chlorophyll *a* can also absorb light. The events that occur next can be divided into five steps, as shown in Figure 6-6.

In step ❶, light energy forces electrons to enter a higher energy level in the two chlorophyll *a* molecules of photosystem II. These energized electrons are said to be "excited."

**FIGURE 6-6**

The light reactions, which take place in the thylakoid membrane, use energy from sunlight to produce ATP, NADPH, and oxygen.

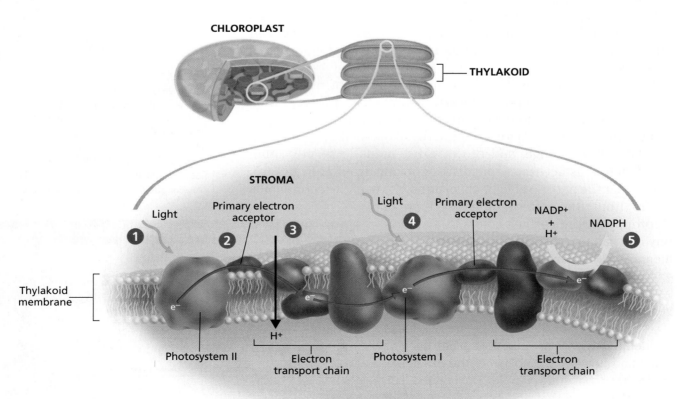

The excited electrons have enough energy to leave the chlorophyll *a* molecules. Because they have lost electrons, the chlorophyll *a* molecules have undergone an oxidation reaction. Remember that each oxidation reaction must be accompanied by a reduction reaction. So, some substance must accept the electrons that the chlorophyll *a* molecules have lost, as shown in step ❷. The acceptor of the electrons lost from chlorophyll *a* is a molecule in the thylakoid membrane called the **primary electron acceptor.**

In step ❸, the primary electron acceptor donates the electrons to the first of a series of molecules located in the thylakoid membrane. These molecules are called an **electron transport chain** because they transfer electrons from one molecule to the next. As the electrons pass from molecule to molecule in the chain, they lose most of the energy that they acquired when they were excited. The energy they lose is used to move protons ($H^+$) into the thylakoid.

In step ❹, light is absorbed by photosystem I. This happens at the same time that light is absorbed by photosystem II. Electrons move from a pair of chlorophyll *a* molecules in photosystem I to another primary electron acceptor. The electrons lost by these chlorophyll *a* molecules are replaced by the electrons that have passed through the electron transport chain from photosystem II.

The primary electron acceptor of photosystem I donates electrons to a different electron transport chain. This chain brings the electrons to the side of the thylakoid membrane that faces the stroma. There the electrons combine with a proton and $NADP^+$, an organic molecule that accepts electrons during oxidation/reduction reactions. As you can see in step ❺, this reaction causes $NADP^+$ to be reduced to NADPH.

## Replacing Electrons in Light Reactions

In step ❹, electrons from chlorophyll molecules in photosystem II replace electrons that leave chlorophyll molecules in photosystem I. If this replacement did not occur, both electron transport chains would stop, and photosynthesis would not happen. The replacement electrons for photosystem II are provided by water molecules. As Figure 6-7 shows, an enzyme inside the thylakoid splits water molecules into protons, electrons, and oxygen. The following equation summarizes the reaction:

$$2H_2O \longrightarrow 4H^+ + 4e^- + O_2$$

For every two molecules of water that are split, four electrons become available to replace those lost by the chlorophyll molecules in photosystem II. The protons that are produced are left inside the thylakoid, and the oxygen diffuses out of the chloroplast and can then leave the plant. Thus, oxygen is not needed for photosynthesis to occur but is essential for cellular respiration in most organisms, including plants themselves.

**FIGURE 6-7**

The splitting of water inside the thylakoid releases electrons, which replace the electrons that leave photosystem II.

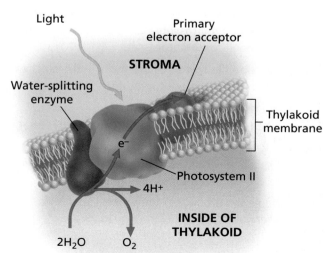

Light

Primary electron acceptor

STROMA

Water-splitting enzyme

Thylakoid membrane

$e^-$

Photosystem II

$4H^+$

INSIDE OF THYLAKOID

$2H_2O$     $O_2$

FIGURE 6-8

During chemiosmosis, the movement of protons into the stroma of the chloroplast releases energy, which is used to produce ATP.

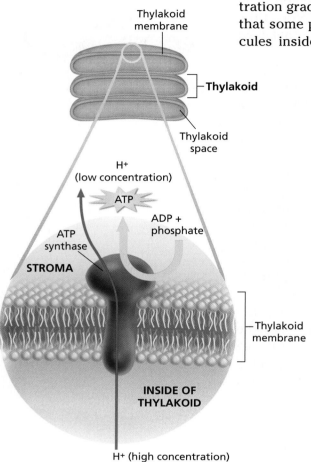

Thylakoid membrane

Thylakoid

Thylakoid space

H+ (low concentration)

ATP

ADP + phosphate

ATP synthase

STROMA

Thylakoid membrane

INSIDE OF THYLAKOID

H+ (high concentration)

# Making ATP in Light Reactions

ATP is the main energy currency of cells. An important part of the light reactions is the synthesis of ATP through a process called **chemiosmosis** (KEM-i-ahs-MOH-sis). Chemiosmosis relies on a concentration gradient of protons across the thylakoid membrane. Recall that some protons are produced from the splitting of water molecules inside the thylakoid. Other protons are pumped from the stroma to the interior of the thylakoid. The energy required to pump these protons is supplied by the excited electrons as they pass along the electron transport chain of photosystem II. Both of these mechanisms act to build up a concentration gradient of protons. That is, the concentration of protons is higher inside the thylakoid than in the stroma.

The concentration gradient of protons represents potential energy. That energy is harnessed by an enzyme called *ATP synthase,* which is located in the thylakoid membrane, as Figure 6-8 shows. ATP synthase makes ATP by adding a phosphate group to adenosine diphosphate, or ADP. The energy driving this reaction is provided by the movement of protons from inside the thylakoid to the stroma through the ATP synthase complex. Thus, ATP synthase converts the potential energy of the proton concentration gradient into chemical energy stored in ATP. As you learned earlier, some of the protons in the stroma are used to make NADPH from NADP$^+$ at the end of the electron transport chain of photosystem I. Together, NADPH and ATP provide energy for the second set of reactions in photosynthesis, which are described in the next section.

## SECTION 1 REVIEW

1. Explain why both autotrophs and heterotrophs depend on photosynthesis to obtain the energy they need for life processes.

2. Describe the role of chlorophylls in the biochemical pathways of photosynthesis.

3. List the three substances that are produced when water molecules are broken down during the light reactions.

4. Explain why the splitting of water is important to the continuation of the light reactions.

5. Name the product of the process known as *chemiosmosis.*

**CRITICAL THINKING**

6. **Making Comparisons** Thinking about the main role of pigments in photosynthesis, explain how the pigments in colored objects such as clothes differ from plant pigments.

7. **Analyzing Information** The molecule that precedes the electron transport chains of both photosystem I and photosystem II is an electron acceptor. What is the original molecule that is the electron donor for both of these systems?

8. **Predicting Results** Explain how the light reactions would be affected if there were no concentration gradient of protons across the thylakoid membrane.

# Science in Action

## How Can Scientists Replicate Photosynthesis in the Lab?

**Life on Earth is powered by the sun's energy. The chloroplasts found in plants and some other organisms can efficiently capture and convert solar energy to sugars through a process known as *photosynthesis*. Now, scientists have developed an artificial photosystem that may one day allow for solar-powered food or fuel production in the lab.**

Dr. Darius Kuciauskas

### HYPOTHESIS: Synthetic Compounds Can Imitate a Photosynthetic System

In nature, a photosystem contains pigments and proteins embedded in a linear sequence in the membrane of a chloroplast. This arrangment allows for effective capture and orderly transfer of electrons from one photosystem to another and eventually to a final electron acceptor for powering synthesis of sugar.

Dr. Darius Kuciauskas (koo-si-AHS-kuhs) of Virginia Commonwealth University and his colleagues thought they could produce an artificial photosystem that carried out the initial steps of photosynthesis. Kuciauskas and his team predicted that when they shined light on four pigment molecules with energy-conducting chemical bonds, the pigment molecules would capture and channel light energy through the "wirelike" bonds. The electrons traveling through the bonds would then pass to, and electrically charge, an acceptor molecule that was placed at the center of the pigment complex.

*Kuciauskas and his colleagues use laser systems such as this one to study light absorption in molecules that might one day be used in an artificial photosystem.*

### METHODS: Design and Build a Pigment-Protein Light-Harvesting Complex

Kuciauskas and his team set out to create the photosystem. The team started with purple pigment molecules called *porphyrins*. These molecules absorb light energy and are related to naturally occurring chlorophyll. The scientists joined four of the porphyrins to each other. To the center-most porphyrin, they attached a ball-shaped cluster of 60 carbon atoms called $C_{60}$, or *fullerene*.

### RESULTS: The Artificial Photosystem Captured and Transferred Electrons

The four porphyrin pigments captured light energy, and the bonds passed electrons to the $C_{60}$ acceptor molecule. The acceptor held the charge for only one microsecond—about one millionth of a second.

### CONCLUSION: Artificial Photosystems Are Possible

The Kuciauskas team concluded that their complex does act as an artificial photosystem, at least for a fleeting instant. Kuciauskas and his colleagues have continued their work, aiming to modify the complex further so it can hold its energy longer. Ultimately, they hope their photosystem can power chemical reactions for making important organic molecules that serve as food or fuel.

### REVIEW

1. What are the essential parts of a photosystem?
2. Describe the method by which the Kuciauskas team built an artificial photosystem.
3. **Critical Thinking** Review the methods that Kuciauskas and his team used to test their hypothesis. Determine one variable the scientists might change to modify their results.

**internet** connect

**www.scilinks.org**
Topic: Plant Photosynthetic Pigments
Keyword: HM61164

SCILINKS. Maintained by the National Science Teachers Association

OBJECTIVES

- **Summarize** the main events of the Calvin cycle.
- **Describe** what happens to the compounds that are made in the Calvin cycle.
- **Distinguish** between $C_3$, $C_4$, and CAM plants.
- **Summarize** how the light reactions and the Calvin cycle work together to create the continuous cycle of photosynthesis.
- **Explain** how environmental factors influence photosynthesis.

VOCABULARY

Calvin cycle
carbon fixation
stomata
$C_4$ pathway
CAM pathway

# THE CALVIN CYCLE

*In the second set of reactions in photosynthesis, plants use the energy that was stored in ATP and NADPH during the light reactions to produce organic compounds in the form of sugars. These organic compounds are then consumed by autotrophs and heterotrophs alike for energy. The most common way that plants produce organic compounds is called the Calvin cycle.*

## CARBON FIXATION

The **Calvin cycle** is a series of enzyme-assisted chemical reactions that produces a three-carbon sugar. In the Calvin cycle, carbon atoms from $CO_2$ in the atmosphere are bonded, or "fixed," into organic compounds. This incorporation of $CO_2$ into organic compounds is called **carbon fixation.** A total of three $CO_2$ molecules must enter the Calvin cycle to produce each three-carbon sugar that will be used to make the organic compounds. The Calvin cycle occurs within the stroma of the chloroplast. Figure 6-9 shows the events that occur when three $CO_2$ molecules enter the Calvin cycle.

In step **1**, $CO_2$ diffuses into the stroma from the surrounding cytosol. An enzyme combines each $CO_2$ molecule with a five-carbon molecule called *ribulose bisphosphate* (RuBP). The six-carbon molecules that result are very unstable, and they each immediately split into two three-carbon molecules. These three-carbon molecules are called *3-phosphoglycerate* (3-PGA).

**FIGURE 6-9**

The Calvin cycle, in which carbon is fixed into organic compounds, takes place in the stroma of the chloroplast.

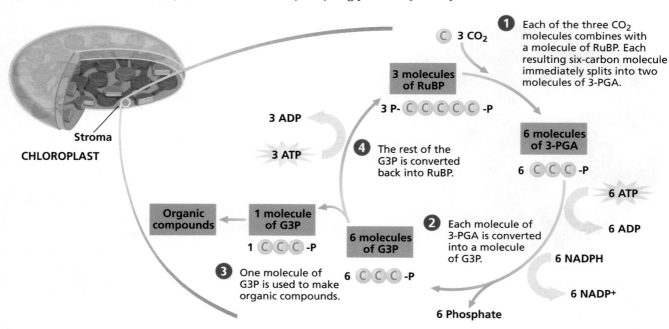

**Stroma**

**CHLOROPLAST**

**1** Each of the three $CO_2$ molecules combines with a molecule of RuBP. Each resulting six-carbon molecule immediately splits into two molecules of 3-PGA.

3 molecules of RuBP

3 P- C C C C C -P

3 CO₂  C  3 CO₂

**4** The rest of the G3P is converted back into RuBP.

3 ADP

3 ATP

6 molecules of 3-PGA

6 C C C -P

6 ATP

6 ADP

6 NADPH

6 NADP+

**2** Each molecule of 3-PGA is converted into a molecule of G3P.

6 molecules of G3P

6 C C C -P

6 Phosphate

Organic compounds

1 molecule of G3P

1 C C C -P

**3** One molecule of G3P is used to make organic compounds.

In step ❷, each molecule of 3-PGA is converted into another three-carbon molecule, glyceraldehyde 3-phosphate (G3P), in a two-part process. First, each 3-PGA molecule receives a phosphate group from a molecule of ATP. The resulting compound then receives a proton ($H^+$) from NADPH and releases a phosphate group, producing G3P. The ADP, $NADP^+$, and phosphate that are also produced can be used again in the light reactions to make more ATP and NADPH.

In step ❸, one of the G3P molecules leaves the Calvin cycle and is used to make organic compounds (carbohydrates) in which energy is stored for later use.

In step ❹, the remaining G3P molecules are converted back into RuBP through the addition of phosphate groups from ATP molecules. The resulting RuBP molecules then enter the Calvin cycle again.

The Calvin cycle (named for Melvin Calvin, the American biochemist who worked out the chemical reactions in the cycle) is the most common pathway for carbon fixation. Plant species that fix carbon exclusively through the Calvin cycle are known as $C_3$ plants because of the three-carbon compound that is initially formed in this process.

# ALTERNATIVE PATHWAYS

Many plant species that evolved in hot, dry climates fix carbon through alternative pathways. Under hot and dry conditions, plants can rapidly lose water to the air through small pores called **stomata** (STOH-muh-tuh). Stomata (singular, *stoma*), shown in Figure 6-10, are usually located on the undersurface of the leaves. Plants can reduce water loss by partially closing their stomata when the air is hot and dry.

Stomata are the major passageways through which $CO_2$ enters and $O_2$ leaves a plant. When a plant's stomata are partly closed, the level of $CO_2$ in the plant falls as $CO_2$ is consumed in the Calvin cycle. At the same time, the level of $O_2$ in the plant rises as the light reactions generate $O_2$. Both a low $CO_2$ level and a high $O_2$ level inhibit carbon fixation by the Calvin cycle. Alternative pathways for carbon fixation help plants deal with this problem.

**Word Roots and Origins**

*stomata*

from the Greek *stoma*, meaning "mouth"

**(a) OPEN STOMA**

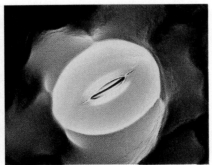

**(b) CLOSED STOMA**

**FIGURE 6-10**

These photos show stomata in the leaf of a tobacco plant, *Nicotiana tabacum.* (a) When a stoma is open, water, carbon dioxide, and other gases can pass through it to enter or leave a plant (814×). (b) When a stoma is closed, passage through it is greatly restricted (878×).

## The C₄ Pathway

One alternative pathway enables certain plants to fix $CO_2$ into four-carbon compounds. This pathway is thus called the **C₄ pathway,** and plants that use it are known as *C₄ plants.* During the hottest part of the day, C₄ plants have their stomata partially closed. However, certain cells in C₄ plants have an enzyme that can fix $CO_2$ into four-carbon compounds even when the $CO_2$ level is low and the $O_2$ level is high. These compounds are then transported to other cells, where $CO_2$ is released and enters the Calvin cycle. C₄ plants include corn, sugar cane, and crab grass. Such plants lose only about half as much water as C₃ plants when producing the same amount of carbohydrates. Many plants that use the C₄ pathway evolved in tropical climates.

## The CAM Pathway

Cactuses, pineapples, and certain other plants have a different adaptation to hot, dry climates. Such plants fix carbon through a pathway called the **CAM pathway.** CAM is an abbreviation for *crassulacean acid metabolism,* because this water-conserving pathway was first discovered in plants of the family Crassulaceae, such as the jade plant. Plants that use the CAM pathway open their stomata at night and close them during the day—just the opposite of what other plants do. At night, CAM plants take in $CO_2$ and fix it into a variety of organic compounds. During the day, $CO_2$ is released from these compounds and enters the Calvin cycle. Because CAM plants have their stomata open at night, when the temperature is lower, they grow fairly slowly. However, they lose less water than either C₃ or C₄ plants.

## Eco Connection

**Photosynthesis and the Global Greenhouse**

With the beginning of the Industrial Revolution around 1850, the atmospheric concentration of $CO_2$ started to increase. This increase has resulted largely from the burning of fossil fuels, which releases $CO_2$ as a byproduct. You might expect plants to benefit from the buildup of $CO_2$ in the atmosphere. In fact, the rise in $CO_2$ levels may harm photosynthetic organisms more than it helps them. $CO_2$ and other gases in the atmosphere retain some of the Earth's heat, causing the Earth to become warmer. This warming could reduce the amount of worldwide precipitation, creating deserts that would be inhospitable to most plants.

# A SUMMARY OF PHOTOSYNTHESIS

Photosynthesis happens in two stages, both of which occur inside the chloroplasts of plant cells and algae.

1. The light reactions—Energy is absorbed from sunlight and converted into chemical energy, which is temporarily stored in ATP and NADPH.
2. The Calvin cycle—Carbon dioxide and the chemical energy stored in ATP and NADPH are used to form organic compounds.

Photosynthesis itself is an ongoing cycle: the products of the light reactions are used in the Calvin cycle, and some of the products of the Calvin cycle are used in the light reactions. The other products of the Calvin cycle are used to produce a variety of organic compounds, such as amino acids, lipids, and carbohydrates. Many plants produce more carbohydrates than they need. These extra carbohydrates can be stored as starch in the chloroplasts and in structures such as roots and fruits. These stored carbohydrates provide the chemical energy that both autotrophs and heterotrophs depend on.

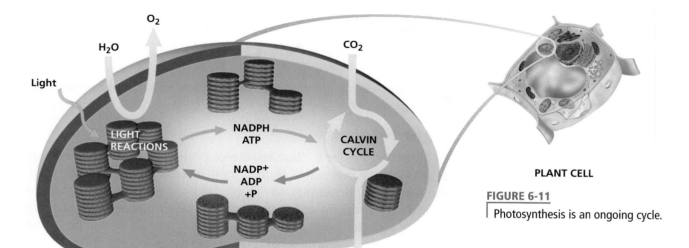

**O₂**

**H₂O**

**Light**

**LIGHT REACTIONS**

**NADPH ATP**

**NADP+ ADP +P**

**CALVIN CYCLE**

**CO₂**

**CHLOROPLAST**

**Organic compounds**

**PLANT CELL**

**FIGURE 6-11**

Photosynthesis is an ongoing cycle.

Figure 6-11 above illustrates how the light reactions in the thylakoid and the Calvin cycle in the stroma actually work together as one continuous cycle—photosynthesis. Amazingly, this complicated process can occur in every one of the thousands of chloroplasts present in a plant if the conditions are right.

Recall that water is split during the light reactions, yielding electrons, protons, and oxygen as a byproduct. Thus, the simplest overall equation for photosynthesis, including both the light reactions and the Calvin cycle, can be written as follows:

$$CO_2 + H_2O \xrightarrow{\text{light energy}} (CH_2O) + O_2$$

In the equation above, $(CH_2O)$ represents the general formula for a carbohydrate. It is often replaced in this equation by the carbohydrate glucose, $C_6H_{12}O_6$, giving the following equation:

$$6CO_2 + 6H_2O \xrightarrow{\text{light energy}} C_6H_{12}O_6 + 6O_2$$

However, glucose is not actually a direct product of photosynthesis. Glucose is often included in the equation mainly to emphasize the relationship between photosynthesis and cellular respiration, in which glucose plays a key role. Just as the light reactions and the Calvin cycle together create an ongoing cycle, photosynthesis and cellular respiration together also create an ongoing cycle.

The light reactions are sometimes referred to as *light-dependent reactions,* because the energy from light is required for the reactions to occur. The Calvin cycle is sometimes referred to as the *light-independent reactions* or the *dark reactions,* because the Calvin cycle does not require light directly. But the Calvin cycle usually proceeds during daytime, when the light reactions are producing the materials that the Calvin cycle uses to fix carbon into organic compounds.

## Quick Lab

### Analyzing Photosynthesis

**Materials** disposable gloves, lab apron, safety goggles, 250 mL Erlenmeyer flasks (3), bromothymol blue, 5 cm sprigs of elodea (2), water, drinking straw, plastic wrap, 100 mL graduated cylinder

**Procedure**

1. Put on your disposable gloves, lab apron, and safety goggles.
2. Label the flasks "1," "2," and "3." Add 200 mL of water and 20 drops of bromothymol blue to each flask.
3. Put the drinking straw in flask 1, and blow into the blue solution until the solution turns yellow. Repeat this step with flask 2.
4. Put one elodea sprig in flask 1. Do nothing to flask 2. Put the other elodea sprig in flask 3.
5. Cover all flasks with plastic wrap. Place the flasks in a well-lighted location, and leave them overnight. Record your observations.

**Analysis** Describe your results. Explain what caused one of the solutions to change color. Why did the other solutions not change color? Which flask is the control in this experiment?

# FACTORS THAT AFFECT PHOTOSYNTHESIS

Photosynthesis is affected by the environment. Three factors with the most influence are light intensity, $CO_2$ level, and temperature.

## Light Intensity

As shown in Figure 6-12a, the rate of photosynthesis increases as light intensity increases. Higher light intensity excites more electrons in both photosystems. Thus, the light reactions occur more rapidly. However, at some point all of the available electrons are excited, and the maximum rate of photosynthesis is reached. The rate stays level regardless of further increases in light intensity.

## Carbon Dioxide Levels

Increasing levels of $CO_2$ also stimulate photosynthesis until the rate of photosynthesis levels off. Thus, a graph of the rate of photosynthesis versus $CO_2$ concentration would resemble Figure 6-12a.

## Temperature

Increasing temperature accelerates the chemical reactions involved in photosynthesis. As a result, the rate of photosynthesis increases as temperature increases, over a certain range. This effect is illustrated by the left half of the curve in Figure 6-12b. The rate peaks at a certain temperature, at which many of the enzymes that catalyze the reactions become ineffective. Also, the stomata begin to close, limiting water loss and $CO_2$ entry into the leaves. These conditions cause the rate of photosynthesis to decrease when the temperature is further increased, as shown by the right half of the curve in Figure 6-12b.

**FIGURE 6-12**

Environmental factors affect the rate of photosynthesis in plants. (a) As light intensity increases, the rate of photosynthesis increases and then levels off at a maximum. (b) As temperature increases, the rate of photosynthesis increases to a maximum and then decreases with further rises in temperature.

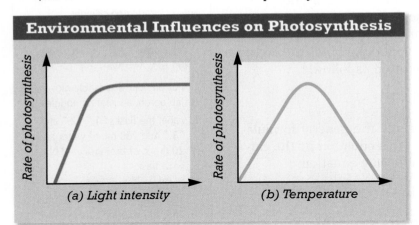

**Environmental Influences on Photosynthesis**

(a) Light intensity

(b) Temperature

---

## SECTION 2 REVIEW

1. Name the part of the chloroplast where the Calvin cycle takes place.

2. Describe what can happen to the three-carbon molecules made in the Calvin cycle.

3. Distinguish between $C_3$, $C_4$, and CAM plants.

4. Explain why the light reactions and the Calvin cycle are dependent on each other.

5. Explain why increased light intensity might not result in an increased rate of photosynthesis.

**CRITICAL THINKING**

6. **Predicting Results** What would happen to photosynthesis if all of the three-carbon sugars produced in the Calvin cycle were used to make organic compounds?

7. **Inferring Relationships** Explain how a global temperature increase could affect plants.

8. **Evaluating Differences** Explain how the world would be different if $C_4$ plants and CAM plants had not evolved.

## SECTION 1    The Light Reactions

- Photosynthesis converts light energy into chemical energy through series of reactions known as biochemical pathways. Almost all life depends on photosynthesis.

- Autotrophs use photosynthesis to make organic compounds from carbon dioxide and water. Heterotrophs cannot make their own organic compounds from inorganic compounds and therefore depend on autotrophs.

- White light from the sun is composed of an array of colors called the visible spectrum. Pigments absorb certain colors of light and reflect or transmit the other colors.

- The light reactions of photosynthesis begin with the absorption of light by chlorophyll *a* and accessory pigments in the thylakoids.

- Excited electrons that leave chlorophyll *a* travel along two electron transport chains, resulting in the production of NADPH. The electrons are replaced when water is split into electrons, protons, and oxygen in the thylakoid. Oxygen is released as a byproduct of photosynthesis.

- As electrons travel along the electron transport chains, protons move into the thylakoid and build up a concentration gradient. The movement of protons down this gradient of protons and through ATP synthase results in the synthesis of ATP through chemiosmosis.

### Vocabulary

| | | | |
|---|---|---|---|
| autotroph (p. 113) | thylakoid (p. 114) | carotenoid (p. 115) | electron transport |
| photosynthesis (p. 113) | granum (p. 114) | photosystem (p. 116) | chain (p. 117) |
| heterotroph (p. 113) | stroma (p. 114) | primary electron | chemiosmosis (p. 118) |
| light reactions (p. 114) | pigment (p. 115) | acceptor (p. 117) | |
| chloroplast (p. 114) | chlorophyll (p. 115) | | |

## SECTION 2    The Calvin Cycle

- The ATP and NADPH produced in the light reactions drive the second stage of photosynthesis, the Calvin cycle. In the Calvin cycle, $CO_2$ is incorporated into organic compounds, a process called carbon fixation.

- The Calvin cycle produces a compound called G3P. Most G3P molecules are converted into RuBP to keep the Calvin cycle operating. However, some G3P molecules are used to make other organic compounds, including amino acids, lipids, and carbohydrates.

- Plants that fix carbon using only the Calvin cycle are known as $C_3$ plants. Some plants that evolved in hot, dry climates fix carbon through alternative pathways—the $C_4$ and CAM pathways. These plants carry out carbon fixation and the Calvin cycle either in different cells or at different times.

- Photosynthesis occurs in two stages. In the light reactions, energy is absorbed from sunlight and converted into chemical energy; in the Calvin cycle, carbon dioxide and chemical energy are used to form organic compounds.

- The rate of photosynthesis increases and then reaches a plateau as light intensity or $CO_2$ concentration increases. Below a certain temperature, the rate of photosynthesis increases as temperature increases. Above that temperature, the rate of photosynthesis decreases as temperature increases.

### Vocabulary

| | | |
|---|---|---|
| Calvin cycle (p. 120) | stomata (p. 121) | CAM pathway (p. 122) |
| carbon fixation (p. 120) | $C_4$ pathway (p. 122) | |

## USING VOCABULARY

1. For each pair of terms, explain the relationship between the terms.
   a. *electron transport chain* and *primary electron acceptor*
   b. *photosystem* and *pigment*
   c. *thylakoid* and *stroma*
   d. *carbon fixation* and $C_4$ *pathway*

2. Use the following terms in the same sentence: *photosynthesis, light reactions, pigment,* and *photosystem.*

3. Choose the term that does not belong in the following group, and explain why it does not belong: *electron transport chain, chemiosmosis, Calvin cycle,* and *photosystem II.*

4. **Word Roots and Origins** The prefix *chloro-* is derived from the Greek word that means "green." Using this information, explain why the chlorophylls are well named.

## UNDERSTANDING KEY CONCEPTS

5. **Distinguish** between autotrophs and heterotrophs.

6. **Identify** the primary source of energy for humans.

7. **Relate** the types of pigments involved in photosynthesis and their roles.

8. **Compare** the different roles of photosystem I and photosystem II in photosynthesis.

9. **Describe** what happens to the extra energy in excited electrons as they pass along an electron transport chain in a chloroplast.

10. **Explain** how oxygen is generated in photosynthesis.

11. **Summarize** the events of chemiosmosis.

12. **State** the three major steps of the Calvin cycle.

13. **Explain** what happens to the 3-carbon compounds that do not leave the Calvin cycle to be made into organic compounds.

14. **Propose** what might happen to photosynthesis if ATP were not produced in the light reactions.

15. **Relate** the rate of photosynthesis to carbon dioxide levels.

16. **Unit 2–Photosynthesis**

    BIOLOGY Many plants have stomata that take in $CO_2$ at night and release it during the day. Write a report about these types of plants, and summarize why this adaptation is an advantage for plants living in a hot, dry climate.

17. **CONCEPT MAPPING** Create a concept map that shows the steps of photosynthesis. Include the following terms in your concept map: *light reactions, Calvin cycle, photosystem I, photosystem II, carbon fixation, accessory pigment, chlorophyll, electron transport chain, ATP synthase, chemiosmosis,* and *photosynthesis.*

## CRITICAL THINKING

18. **Predicting Results** When the $CO_2$ concentration in the cells of a $C_3$ plant is low compared with the $O_2$ concentration, an enzyme combines RuBP with $O_2$ rather than with $CO_2$. What effect would this enzymatic change have on photosynthesis? Under what environmental conditions would it be most likely to occur?

19. **Evaluating Information** All of the major components of the light reactions, including the pigment molecules clustered in photosystems I and II, are located in the thylakoid membrane. What is the advantage of having these components confined to the same membrane rather than dissolved in the stroma or the cytosol?

20. **Inferring Relationships** When the sun's rays are blocked by a thick forest, clouds, or smoke from a large fire, what effect do you think there will be on photosynthesis? How might it affect the levels of atmospheric carbon dioxide and oxygen? What experiments could scientists conduct in the laboratory to test your predictions?

21. **Interpreting Graphics** The graph below shows how the percentage of stomata that are open varies over time for two different plants. One curve represents the stomata of a geranium, and the other curve represents the stomata of a pineapple. Which curve corresponds to the pineapple stomata? Explain your reasoning.

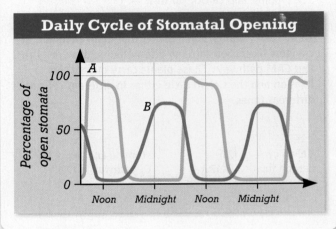

**Daily Cycle of Stomatal Opening**

# Standardized Test Preparation

**DIRECTIONS:** Choose the letter of the answer choice that best answers the question.

1. Which of the following is a reactant in the Calvin cycle?
   - **A.** $O_2$
   - **B.** $CO_2$
   - **C.** $H_2O$
   - **D.** $C_6H_{12}O_6$

2. Which of the following statements is correct?
   - **F.** Accessory pigments are not involved in photosynthesis.
   - **G.** Accessory pigments add color to plants but do not absorb light energy.
   - **H.** Accessory pigments absorb colors of light that chlorophyll *a* cannot absorb.
   - **J.** Accessory pigments receive electrons from the electron transport chain of photosystem I.

3. Oxygen is produced at what point during photosynthesis?
   - **A.** when $CO_2$ is fixed
   - **B.** when water is split
   - **C.** when ATP is converted into ADP
   - **D.** when 3-PGA is converted into G3P

**INTERPRETING GRAPHICS:** The diagram below shows a portion of a chloroplast. Use the diagram to answer the question that follows.

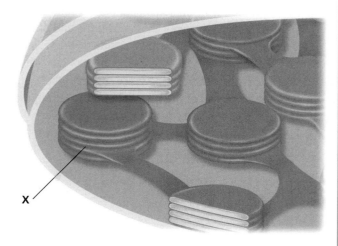

4. Which of the following correctly identifies the structure marked *X* and the activities that take place there?
   - **F.** stroma—Calvin cycle
   - **G.** stroma—light reactions
   - **H.** thylakoid—Calvin cycle
   - **J.** thylakoid—light reactions

**DIRECTIONS:** Complete the following analogy.

5. light reactions : ATP :: Calvin cycle :
   - **A.** $H^+$
   - **B.** $O_2$
   - **C.** G3P
   - **D.** $H_2O$

**INTERPRETING GRAPHICS:** The diagram below shows a step in the process of chemiosmosis. Use the diagram to answer the question that follows.

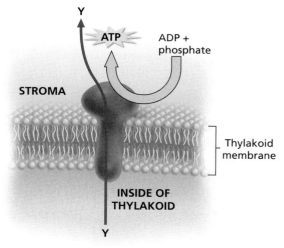

6. What is the substance identified as *Y* in the image?
   - **F.** $H^+$
   - **G.** $NAD^+$
   - **H.** NADPH
   - **J.** ADP synthase

## SHORT RESPONSE

Chloroplasts are organelles with areas that conduct different specialized activities.

Where in the chloroplast do the light reactions and the Calvin cycle occur?

## EXTENDED RESPONSE

The reactions of photosynthesis make up a biochemical pathway.

*Part A* What are the reactants and products for both the light reactions and the Calvin cycle?

*Part B* Explain how the biochemical pathway of photosynthesis recycles many of its own reactants, and identify the recycled reactants.

**Test TIP** For a question involving a biochemical pathway, write out all of the reactants and products of each step *before* answering the question.

# Measuring the Rate of Photosynthesis

## OBJECTIVES

- Measure the amount of oxygen produced by an elodea sprig.
- Determine the rate of photosynthesis for elodea.

## PROCESS SKILLS

- making observations
- measuring
- collecting data
- graphing

## MATERIALS

- 500 mL of 5% baking-soda-and-water solution
- 600 mL beaker
- 20 cm long elodea sprigs (2–3)
- glass funnel
- test tube
- metric ruler

## Background

1. Summarize the main steps of photosynthesis.
2. State the source of the oxygen produced during photosynthesis.
3. Identify factors that can affect the rate of photosynthesis.

## Procedure

 **PART A** **Setting Up the Experiment**

**CAUTION** Always wear safety goggles and a lab apron to protect your eyes and clothing. Glassware is fragile. Notify the teacher of broken glass or cuts. Do not clean up broken glass or spills with broken glass unless the teacher tells you to do so. Wear disposable polyethylene gloves when handling any plant. Do not eat any part of a plant or plant seed used in the lab. Wash hands thoroughly after handling any part of a plant.

1. Add 450 mL of baking-soda-and-water solution to a beaker.
2. Put two or three sprigs of elodea in the beaker. The baking soda will provide the elodea with the carbon dioxide it needs for photosynthesis.
3. Place the wide end of the funnel over the elodea. The end of the funnel with the small opening should be pointing up. The elodea and the funnel should be completely under the solution.
4. Fill a test tube with the remaining baking-soda-and-water solution. Place your thumb over the end of the test tube. Turn the test tube upside down, taking care that no air enters. Hold the opening of the test tube under the solution, and place the test tube over the small end of the funnel. Try not to let any solution leak out of the test tube as you do this.
5. Place the beaker setup in a well-lighted area near a lamp or in direct sunlight.

## PART B Collecting Data

6. Create a data table like the one below.
7. Record that there was 0 mm gas in the test tube on day 0. (If you were unable to place the test tube without getting air in the tube, measure the height of the column of air in the test tube in millimeters. Record this value for day 0.) In this lab, change in gas volume is indicated by a linear measurement expressed in millimeters.
8. For days 1 through 5, measure the amount of gas in the test tube. Record the measurements in your data table under the heading "Total amount of gas present (mm)."
9. Calculate the amount of gas produced each day by subtracting the amount of gas present on the previous day from the amount of gas present today. Record these amounts under the heading "Amount of gas produced per day (mm)."

### Analysis and Conclusions

1. Using the data from your table, prepare a graph.
2. Using information from your graph, describe what happened to the amount of gas in the test tube.
3. How much gas was produced in the test tube after day 5?
4. Write the equation for photosynthesis. Explain each part of the equation. For example, which ingredients are necessary for photosynthesis to take place? Which substances are produced by photosynthesis? Which gas is produced that we need in order to live?

5. What may happen to the oxygen level if an animal, such as a snail, were put in the beaker with the elodea sprig while the elodea sprig was making oxygen?

### Further Inquiry

Design an experiment for predicting the effects of temperature on the amount of oxygen produced or rate of photosynthesis by elodea.

## AMOUNT OF GAS PRESENT IN THE TEST TUBE

| Days of exposure to light | Total amount of gas present (mm) | Amount of gas produced per day (mm) |
|---|---|---|
| 0 | | |
| 1 | | |
| 2 | | |
| 3 | | |
| 4 | | |
| 5 | | |

# CELLULAR RESPIRATION

Like other heterotrophs, the giant panda, *Ailuropoda melanoleuca,* obtains organic compounds by consuming other organisms. Biochemical pathways within the panda's cells transfer energy from those compounds to ATP.

**SECTION 1** *Glycolysis and Fermentation*

**SECTION 2** *Aerobic Respiration*

**Unit 3—Cellular Respiration**
Topics 1–6

For project ideas from *Scientific American,* visit go.hrw.com and type in the keyword **HM6SAA.**

# GLYCOLYSIS AND FERMENTATION

*Most foods contain usable energy, stored in complex organic compounds such as proteins, carbohydrates, and fats. All cells break down organic compounds into simpler molecules, a process that releases energy to power cellular activities.*

## HARVESTING CHEMICAL ENERGY

**Cellular respiration** is the complex process in which cells make adenosine triphosphate (ATP) by breaking down organic compounds. Recall that autotrophs, such as plants, use photosynthesis to convert light energy from the sun into chemical energy, which is stored in organic compounds. Both autotrophs and heterotrophs undergo cellular respiration to break these organic compounds into simpler molecules and thus release energy. Some of the energy is used to make ATP. The energy in ATP is then used by cells to do work.

### Overview of Cellular Respiration

Figure 7-1 shows that autotrophs and heterotrophs use cellular respiration to make carbon dioxide ($CO_2$) and water from organic compounds and oxygen ($O_2$). ATP is also produced during cellular respiration. Autotrophs then use the $CO_2$ and water to produce $O_2$ and organic compounds. Thus, the products of cellular respiration are reactants in photosynthesis. Conversely, the products of photosynthesis are reactants in cellular respiration. Cellular respiration can be divided into two stages:

1. **Glycolysis** Organic compounds are converted into three-carbon molecules of **pyruvic** (pie-ROO-vik) **acid,** producing a small amount of ATP and **NADH** (an electron carrier molecule). Glycolysis is an **anaerobic** (AN-uhr-oh-bik) process because it does not require the presence of oxygen.
2. **Aerobic Respiration** If oxygen is present in the cell's environment, pyruvic acid is broken down and NADH is used to make a large amount of ATP through the process known as **aerobic** (uhr-OH-bik) **respiration** (covered later).

Pyruvic acid can enter other pathways if there is no oxygen present in the cell's environment. The combination of glycolysis and these anaerobic pathways is called *fermentation*.

## OBJECTIVES

- **Identify** the two major steps of cellular respiration.
- **Describe** the major events in glycolysis.
- **Compare** lactic acid fermentation with alcoholic fermentation.
- **Calculate** the efficiency of glycolysis.

## VOCABULARY

cellular respiration
pyruvic acid
NADH
anaerobic
aerobic respiration
glycolysis
$NAD^+$
fermentation
lactic acid fermentation
alcoholic fermentation
kilocalorie

**FIGURE 7-1**

Both autotrophs and heterotrophs produce carbon dioxide and water through cellular respiration. Many autotrophs produce organic compounds and oxygen through photosynthesis.

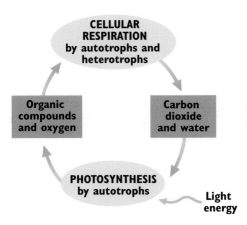

CELLULAR RESPIRATION by autotrophs and heterotrophs

Organic compounds and oxygen

Carbon dioxide and water

PHOTOSYNTHESIS by autotrophs

Light energy

**FIGURE 7-2**

Organisms use cellular respiration to harness energy from organic compounds in food. (a) Glycolysis, the first stage of cellular respiration, produces a small amount of ATP. Most of the ATP produced in cellular respiration results from aerobic respiration, which is the second stage of cellular respiration. (b) In some cells, glycolysis may result in fermentation if oxygen is not present.

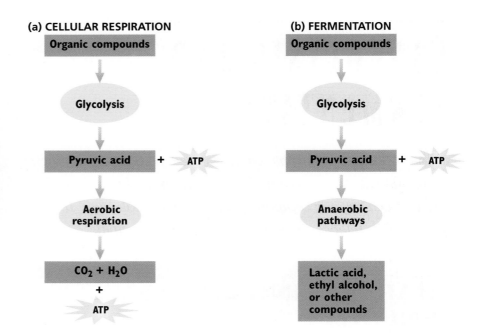

Many of the reactions in cellular respiration are redox reactions. Recall that in a *redox reaction,* one reactant is oxidized (loses electrons) while another is reduced (gains electrons). Although many kinds of organic compounds can be oxidized in cellular respiration, it is customary to focus on the simple sugar called *glucose* ($C_6H_{12}O_6$). The following equation summarizes cellular respiration:

$$C_6H_{12}O_6 + 6O_2 \xrightarrow{\text{enzymes}} 6CO_2 + 6H_2O + \text{energy (ATP)}$$

This equation, however, does not explain how cellular respiration occurs. It is useful to examine each of the two stages, summarized in Figure 7-2a. (Figure 7-2b illustrates the differences between cellular respiration and fermentation.) The first stage of cellular respiration is glycolysis.

# GLYCOLYSIS

**Glycolysis** is a biochemical pathway in which one six-carbon molecule of glucose is oxidized to produce two three-carbon molecules of pyruvic acid. Like other biochemical pathways, glycolysis is a series of chemical reactions catalyzed by specific enzymes. All of the reactions of glycolysis take place in the cytosol and occur in four main steps, as illustrated in Figure 7-3 on the next page.

In step ❶, two phosphate groups are attached to one molecule of glucose, forming a new six-carbon compound that has two phosphate groups. The phosphate groups are supplied by two molecules of ATP, which are converted into two molecules of ADP in the process.

In step ❷, the six-carbon compound formed in step ❶ is split into two three-carbon molecules of glyceraldehyde 3-phosphate (G3P). Recall that G3P is also produced by the Calvin cycle in photosynthesis.

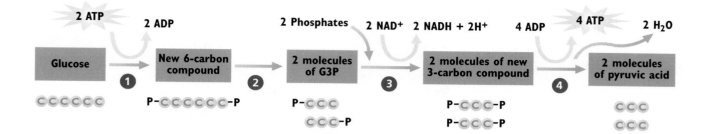

In step ❸, the two G3P molecules are oxidized, and each receives a phosphate group. The product of this step is two molecules of a new three-carbon compound. As shown in Figure 7-3, the oxidation of G3P is accompanied by the reduction of two molecules of nicotinamide adenine dinucleotide ($NAD^+$) to NADH. $NAD^+$ is similar to $NADP^+$, a compound involved in the light reactions of photosynthesis. Like $NADP^+$, $NAD^+$ is an organic molecule that accepts electrons during redox reactions.

In step ❹, the phosphate groups added in step ❶ and step ❸ are removed from the three-carbon compounds formed in step ❸. This reaction produces two molecules of pyruvic acid. Each phosphate group is combined with a molecule of ADP to make a molecule of ATP. Because a total of four phosphate groups were added in step ❶ and step ❸, four molecules of ATP are produced.

Notice that two ATP molecules were used in step ❶, but four were produced in step ❹. Therefore, glycolysis has a net yield of two ATP molecules for every molecule of glucose that is converted into pyruvic acid. What happens to the pyruvic acid depends on the type of cell and on whether oxygen is present.

**FIGURE 7-3**

Glycolysis takes place in the cytosol of cells and involves four main steps. A net yield of two ATP molecules is produced for every molecule of glucose that undergoes glycolysis.

# FERMENTATION

When oxygen is present, cellular respiration continues as pyruvic acid enters the pathways of aerobic respiration. (Aerobic respiration is covered in detail in the next section.) In anaerobic conditions (when oxygen is absent), however, some cells can convert pyruvic acid into other compounds through additional biochemical pathways that occur in the cytosol. The combination of glycolysis and these additional pathways, which regenerate $NAD^+$, is known as **fermentation.** The additional fermentation pathways do not produce ATP. However, if there were not a cellular process that recycled $NAD^+$ from NADH, glycolysis would quickly use up all the $NAD^+$ in the cell. Glycolysis would then stop. ATP production through glycolysis would therefore also stop. The fermentation pathways thus allow for the continued production of ATP.

There are many fermentation pathways, and they differ in terms of the enzymes that are used and the compounds that are made from pyruvic acid. Two common fermentation pathways result in the production of lactic acid and ethyl alcohol.

**Word Roots and Origins**

*fermentation*

from the Latin *fermentum*, meaning "leaven" or anything that causes baked goods to rise, such as yeast

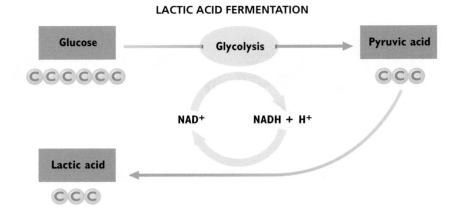

**FIGURE 7-4**

Some cells engage in lactic acid fermentation when oxygen is absent. In this process, pyruvic acid is reduced to lactic acid and NADH is oxidized to NAD$^+$.

**LACTIC ACID FERMENTATION**

## Lactic Acid Fermentation

In **lactic acid fermentation,** an enzyme converts pyruvic acid made during glycolysis into another three-carbon compound, called lactic acid. As Figure 7-4 shows, lactic acid fermentation involves the transfer of one hydrogen atom from NADH and the addition of one free proton (H$^+$) to pyruvic acid. In the process, NADH is oxidized to form NAD$^+$. The resulting NAD$^+$ is used in glycolysis, where it is again reduced to NADH. Thus, the regeneration of NAD$^+$ in lactic acid fermentation helps to keep glycolysis operating.

Lactic acid fermentation by microorganisms plays an essential role in the manufacture of many dairy products, as illustrated in Figure 7-5. Milk will ferment naturally if not refrigerated properly or consumed in a timely manner. Such fermentation of milk is considered "spoiling." But ever since scientists discovered the microorganisms that cause this process, fermentation has been used in a controlled manner to produce cheese, buttermilk, yogurt, sour cream, and other cultured dairy products. Only harmless, active microorganisms are used in the fermentation of dairy products.

Lactic acid fermentation also occurs in your muscle cells during very strenuous exercise, such as sprinting. During this kind of exercise, muscle cells use up oxygen more rapidly than it can be delivered to them. As oxygen becomes depleted, the muscle cells begin to switch from cellular respiration to lactic acid fermentation. Lactic acid accumulates in the muscle cells, making the cells' cytosol more acidic. The increased acidity may reduce the capacity of the cells to contract, resulting in muscle fatigue, pain, and even cramps. Eventually, the lactic acid diffuses into the blood and is transported to the liver, where it can be converted back into pyruvic acid.

**FIGURE 7-5**

In cheese making, fungi or bacteria are added to large vats of milk. The microorganisms carry out lactic acid fermentation, converting some of the sugar in the milk to lactic acid.

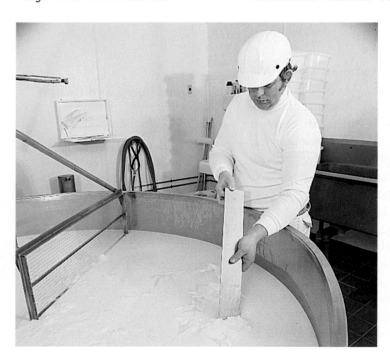

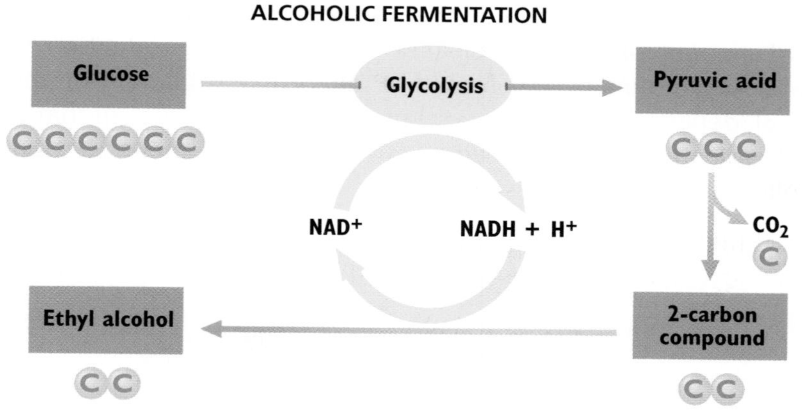

ALCOHOLIC FERMENTATION

FIGURE 7-6

Some cells engage in alcoholic fermentation, converting pyruvic acid into ethyl alcohol. Again, NADH is oxidized to $NAD^+$.

## Alcoholic Fermentation

Some plant cells and unicellular organisms, such as yeast, use a process called **alcoholic fermentation** to convert pyruvic acid into ethyl alcohol. After glycolysis, this pathway requires two steps, which are shown in Figure 7-6. In the first step, a $CO_2$ molecule is removed from pyruvic acid, leaving a two-carbon compound. In the second step, two hydrogen atoms are added to the two-carbon compound to form ethyl alcohol. As in lactic acid fermentation, these hydrogen atoms come from NADH and $H^+$, regenerating $NAD^+$ for use in glycolysis.

Alcoholic fermentation by yeast cells such as those in Figure 7-7 is the basis of the wine and beer industry. Yeasts are a type of fungi. These microorganisms cannot produce their own food. But supplied with food sources that contain sugar (such as fruits and grains), yeast cells will perform the reactions of fermentation, releasing ethyl alcohol and carbon dioxide in the process. The ethyl alcohol is the 'alcohol' in alcoholic beverages. To make table wines, the $CO_2$ that is generated in the first step of fermentation is allowed to escape. To make sparkling wines, such as champagne, $CO_2$ is retained within the mixture, "carbonating" the beverage.

Bread making also depends on alcoholic fermentation performed by yeast cells. In this case, the $CO_2$ that is produced by fermentation makes the bread rise by forming bubbles inside the dough, and the ethyl alcohol evaporates during baking.

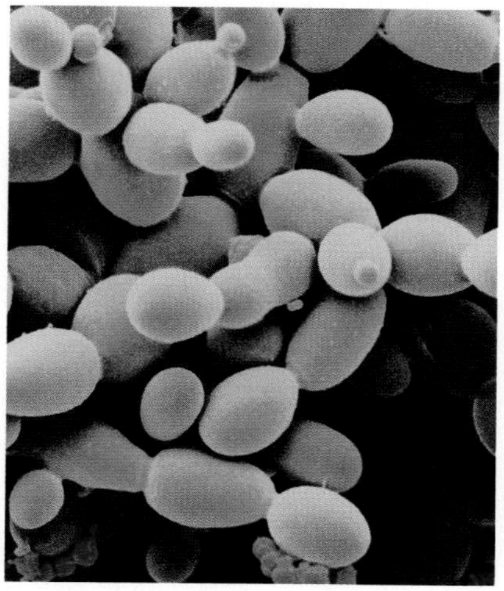

FIGURE 7-7

The yeast *Saccharomyces cerevisiae* is used in alcohol production and bread making.

# EFFICIENCY OF GLYCOLYSIS

How efficient is glycolysis in obtaining energy from glucose and using it to make ATP from ADP? To answer this question, one must compare the amount of energy available in glucose with the amount of energy contained in the ATP that is produced by glycolysis. In such comparisons, energy is often measured in units of **kilocalories** (kcal). One kilocalorie equals 1,000 calories (cal).

**Word Roots and Origins**

*kilocalorie*

from the Greek *chilioi,* meaning "thousand," and the Latin *calor,* meaning "heat"

Scientists have calculated that the complete oxidation of a standard amount of glucose releases 686 kcal. The production of a standard amount of ATP from ADP absorbs a minimum of about 7 kcal, depending on the conditions inside the cell. Recall that two ATP molecules are produced from every glucose molecule that is broken down by glycolysis.

$$\text{Efficiency of glycolysis} = \frac{\text{Energy required to make ATP}}{\text{Energy released by oxidation of glucose}}$$

$$= \frac{2 \times 7 \text{ kcal}}{686 \text{ kcal}} \times 100\% = 2\%$$

You can see that the two ATP molecules produced during glycolysis receive only a small percentage of the energy that could be released by the complete oxidation of each molecule of glucose. Much of the energy originally contained in glucose is still held in pyruvic acid. Even if pyruvic acid is converted into lactic acid or ethyl alcohol, no additional ATP is synthesized. It's clear that glycolysis alone or as part of fermentation is not very efficient in transferring energy from glucose to ATP.

Organisms probably evolved to use glycolysis very early in the history of life on Earth. The first organisms were bacteria, and they produced all of their ATP through glycolysis. It took more than a billion years for the first photosynthetic organisms to appear. The oxygen they released as a byproduct of photosynthesis may have stimulated the evolution of organisms that make most of their ATP through aerobic respiration.

By themselves, the anaerobic pathways provide enough energy for many present-day organisms. However, most of these organisms are unicellular, and those that are multicellular are very small. All of them have limited energy requirements. Larger organisms have much greater energy requirements that cannot be satisfied by glycolysis alone. These larger organisms meet their energy requirements with the more efficient pathways of aerobic respiration.

## SECTION 1 REVIEW

1. Explain the role of organic compounds in cellular respiration.

2. For each six-carbon molecule that begins glycolysis, identify how many molecules of ATP are used and how many molecules of ATP are produced.

3. Distinguish between the products of the two types of fermentation discussed in this section.

4. Calculate the efficiency of glycolysis if 12 kcal of energy are required to transfer energy from glucose to ATP.

**CRITICAL THINKNG**

5. **Applying Information** A large amount of ATP in a cell inhibits the enzymes that drive the first steps of glycolysis. How will this inhibition of enzymes eventually affect the amount of ATP in the cell?

6. **Predicting Results** How might the efficiency of glycolysis change if this process occurred in only one step? Explain your answer.

7. **Relating Concepts** In what kind of environment would you expect to find organisms that carry out fermentation?

# AEROBIC RESPIRATION

*In most cells, glycolysis does not result in fermentation. Instead, when oxygen is available, pyruvic acid undergoes aerobic respiration, the pathway of cellular respiration that requires oxygen. Aerobic respiration produces nearly 20 times as much ATP as is produced by glycolysis alone.*

### OBJECTIVES

- **Relate** aerobic respiration to the structure of a mitochondrion.
- **Summarize** the events of the Krebs cycle.
- **Summarize** the events of the electron transport chain and chemiosmosis.
- **Calculate** the efficiency of aerobic respiration.
- **Contrast** the roles of glycolysis and aerobic respiration in cellular respiration.

### VOCABULARY

mitochondrial matrix
acetyl CoA
Krebs cycle
oxaloacetic acid
citric acid
FAD

## OVERVIEW OF AEROBIC RESPIRATION

Aerobic respiration has two major stages: the Krebs cycle and the electron transport chain, which is associated with chemiosmosis (using the energy released as protons move across a membrane to make ATP). In the Krebs cycle, the oxidation of glucose that began with glycolysis is completed. As glucose is oxidized, $NAD^+$ is reduced to NADH. In the electron transport chain, NADH is used to make ATP. Although the Krebs cycle also produces a small amount of ATP, most of the ATP produced during aerobic respiration is made through the activities of the electron transport chain and chemiosmosis. The reactions of the Krebs cycle, the electron transport chain, and chemiosmosis occur only if oxygen is present in the cell.

In prokaryotes, the reactions of the Krebs cycle and the electron transport chain take place in the cytosol of the cell. In eukaryotic cells, however, these reactions take place inside mitochondria rather than in the cytosol. The pyruvic acid that is produced in glycolysis diffuses across the double membrane of a mitochondrion and enters the mitochondrial matrix. The **mitochondrial matrix** is the space inside the inner membrane of a mitochondrion. Figure 7-8 illustrates the relationships between these mitochondrial parts. The mitochondrial matrix contains the enzymes needed to catalyze the reactions of the Krebs cycle.

**FIGURE 7-8**

In eukaryotic cells, the reactions of aerobic respiration occur inside mitochondria. The Krebs cycle takes place in the mitochondrial matrix, and the electron transport chain is located in the inner membrane.

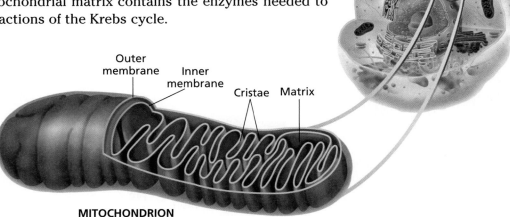

Outer membrane  Inner membrane  Cristae  Matrix

**MITOCHONDRION**

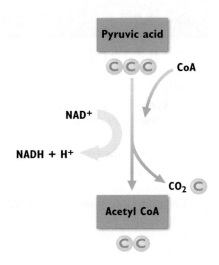

**FIGURE 7-9**

Glycolysis yields two molecules of pyruvic acid. In aerobic respiration, each molecule of pyruvic acid reacts with coenzyme A (CoA) to form a molecule of acetyl CoA. Notice that $CO_2$, NADH, and $H^+$ are also produced in this reaction.

When pyruvic acid enters the mitochondrial matrix, it reacts with a molecule called coenzyme A to form acetyl (uh-SEET-uhl) coenzyme A, abbreviated **acetyl CoA** (uh-SEET-uhl KOH-AY). This reaction is illustrated in Figure 7-9. The acetyl part of acetyl CoA contains two carbon atoms, but as you learned earlier, pyruvic acid is a three-carbon compound. The carbon atom that is lost in the conversion of pyruvic acid to acetyl CoA is released in a molecule of $CO_2$. This reaction reduces a molecule of $NAD^+$ to NADH.

# THE KREBS CYCLE

The **Krebs cycle** is a biochemical pathway that breaks down acetyl CoA, producing $CO_2$, hydrogen atoms, and ATP. The reactions that make up the cycle were identified by Hans Krebs (1900–1981), a German biochemist. The Krebs cycle has five main steps. In eukaryotic cells, all five steps occur in the mitochondrial matrix. Examine Figure 7-10 as you read about the steps in the Krebs cycle.

In step ❶, a two-carbon molecule of acetyl CoA combines with a four-carbon compound, **oxaloacetic** (AHKS-uh-loh-uh-SEET-ik) **acid,** to produce a six-carbon compound, **citric** (SI-trik) **acid.** Notice that this reaction regenerates coenzyme A.

In step ❷, citric acid releases a $CO_2$ molecule and a hydrogen atom to form a five-carbon compound. By losing a hydrogen atom with its electron, citric acid is oxidized. The electron in the hydrogen atom is transferred to $NAD^+$, reducing it to NADH.

**FIGURE 7-10**

The Krebs cycle takes place in the mitochondrial matrix and involves five main steps.

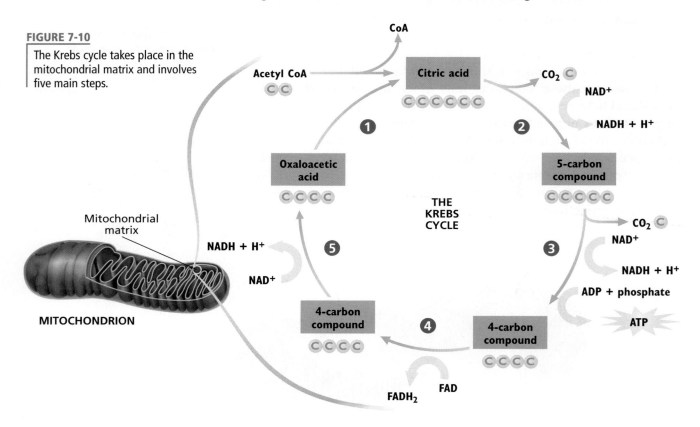

In step ❸, the five-carbon compound formed in step ❷ also releases a $CO_2$ molecule and a hydrogen atom, forming a four-carbon compound. Again, $NAD^+$ is reduced to NADH. Notice that in this step a molecule of ATP is also synthesized from ADP.

In step ❹, the four-carbon compound formed in step ❸ releases a hydrogen atom to form another four-carbon compound. This time, the hydrogen atom is used to reduce FAD to $FADH_2$. **FAD,** or flavin adenine dinucleotide, is a molecule very similar to $NAD^+$. Like $NAD^+$, FAD accepts electrons during redox reactions.

In step ❺, the four-carbon compound formed in step ❹ releases a hydrogen atom to regenerate oxaloacetic acid, which keeps the Krebs cycle operating. The electron in the hydrogen atom reduces $NAD^+$ to NADH.

Recall that in glycolysis one glucose molecule produces two pyruvic acid molecules, which can then form two molecules of acetyl CoA. Thus, one glucose molecule is completely broken down in two turns of the Krebs cycle. These two turns produce four $CO_2$ molecules, two ATP molecules, and hydrogen atoms that are used to make six NADH and two $FADH_2$ molecules. The $CO_2$ diffuses out of the cells and is given off as waste. The ATP can be used for energy. But note that each glucose molecule yields only two molecules of ATP through the Krebs cycle—the same number as in glycolysis.

The bulk of the energy released by the oxidation of glucose still has not been transferred to ATP. Glycolysis of one glucose molecule produces two NADH molecules, and the conversion of the two resulting molecules of pyruvic acid to acetyl CoA produces two more. Adding the six NADH molecules from the Krebs cycle gives a total of 10 NADH molecules for every glucose molecule that is oxidized. These 10 NADH molecules and the two $FADH_2$ molecules from the Krebs cycle drive the next stage of aerobic respiration. That is where most of the energy transfer from glucose to ATP actually occurs.

 **Quick Lab**

## Comparing $CO_2$ Production

**Materials** disposable gloves, lab apron, safety goggles, 250 mL flask, 100 mL graduated cylinder, phenolphthalein solution, pipet, drinking straw, water, clock, sodium hydroxide solution

**Procedure**

1. Put on your disposable gloves, lab apron, and safety goggles.
2. Add 50 mL of water and four drops of phenolphthalein to the flask.
3. Use the straw to gently blow into the solution for 1 minute. Add the sodium hydroxide one drop at a time, and gently swirl the flask. Record the number of drops you use.
4. When the liquid turns pink, stop adding drops.
5. Empty and rinse your flask as your teacher directs, and repeat step 2. Walk vigorously for 2 minutes, and repeat steps 3 and 4.

**Analysis** Which trial produced the most carbon dioxide? Which trial used the most energy?

# ELECTRON TRANSPORT CHAIN AND CHEMIOSMOSIS

The electron transport chain, linked with chemiosmosis, constitutes the second stage of aerobic respiration. Recall that the *electron transport chain* is a series of molecules in a membrane that transfer electrons from one molecule to another. In eukaryotic cells, the electron transport chain and the enzyme ATP synthase are embedded in the inner membrane of the mitochondrion in folds called *cristae*. In prokaryotes, the electron transport chain is in the cell membrane. ATP is produced by the electron transport chain when NADH and $FADH_2$ release hydrogen atoms, regenerating $NAD^+$ and FAD. To understand how ATP is produced, you must follow what happens to the electrons and protons that make up these hydrogen atoms.

internet connect

**www.scilinks.org**
**Topic: Krebs Cycle**
**Keyword: HM60842**

SCLINKS. Maintained by the National Science Teachers Association

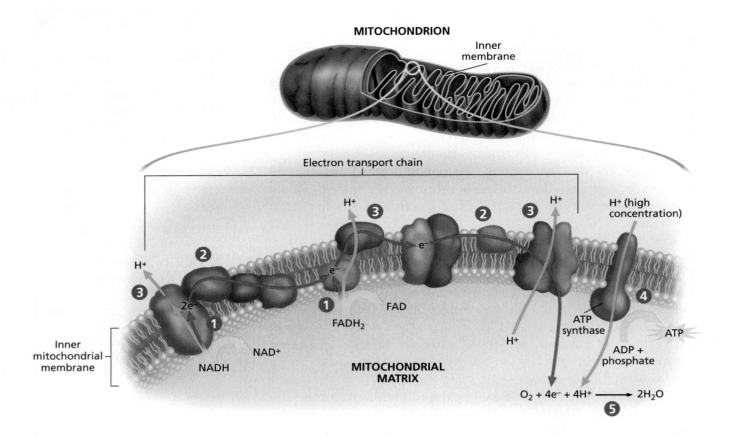

MITOCHONDRION

Inner membrane

Electron transport chain

H⁺

H⁺ (high concentration)

Inner mitochondrial membrane

NADH

NAD⁺

FADH₂

FAD

MITOCHONDRIAL MATRIX

ATP synthase

ADP + phosphate

ATP

$O_2 + 4e^- + 4H^+ \longrightarrow 2H_2O$

**FIGURE 7-11**

Electron transport and chemiosmosis take place along the inner mitochondrial membrane and involve five steps.

The electrons in the hydrogen atoms from NADH and FADH₂ are at a high energy level. In the electron transport chain, these electrons are passed along a series of molecules embedded in the inner mitochondrial membrane, as shown in Figure 7-11. In step ❶, NADH and FADH₂ give up electrons to the electron transport chain. NADH donates electrons at the beginning, and FADH₂ donates them farther down the chain. These molecules also give up protons (hydrogen ions, H⁺). In step ❷, the electrons are passed down the chain. As they move from molecule to molecule, they lose energy. In step ❸, the energy lost from the electrons is used to pump protons from the matrix, building a high concentration of protons between the inner and outer membranes. Thus, a concentration gradient of protons is created across the inner membrane. An electrical gradient is also created, as the protons carry a positive charge.

In step ❹, the concentration and electrical gradients of protons drive the synthesis of ATP by chemiosmosis, the same process that generates ATP in photosynthesis. ATP synthase molecules are embedded in the inner membrane, near the electron transport chain molecules. As protons move through ATP synthase and down their concentration and electrical gradients, ATP is made from ADP and phosphate. In step ❺, oxygen is the final acceptor of electrons that have passed down the chain. Oxygen also accepts protons that were part of the hydrogen atoms supplied by NADH and FADH₂. The protons, electrons, and oxygen all combine to form water, as shown by the equation in step ❺.

# MITOCHONDRIA: Many Roles in Disease

Every cell contains very small organelles that are known as *mitochondria*. Mitochondria generate almost all of the ATP that fuels the activity in living organisms. Scientists have known for years that certain diseases are directly caused by mitochondrial dysfunction. However, new research shows that mitochondria may play roles in the symptoms of aging and may contribute to the development of Alzheimer's disease and cancer.

## Mitochondrial Diseases

Mitochondria are very unusual organelles, because they have their own DNA. Mutations in mitochondrial DNA are responsible for several rare but serious disorders. Examples include *Leigh's syndrome,* a potentially deadly childhood disease that causes loss of motor and verbal skills, and *Pearson's syndrome,* which causes childhood bone marrow dysfunction and pancreatic failure.

## Mitochondria in Aging

Mitochondria may play a role in causing some problems associated with aging. Chemical reactions of the Krebs cycle and electron transport chain sometimes release stray electrons that "leak out" of mitochondria into the cell. These electrons can combine with oxygen to form free radicals. Free radicals are especially reactive atoms or groups of atoms with one or more unpaired electrons. Free radicals quickly react with other molecules, such as DNA and protein; these reactions may disrupt cell activity. Biologists think that many characteristics of human aging, from wrinkles to mental decline, may be brought on partly by the damage caused by free radicals.

## Mitochondria in Other Diseases

Recent research also shows that mitochondria may be important in diseases related to *apoptosis,* or programmed cell death. Scientists have shown that signals from the mitochondria are instrumental in starting and/or continuing the apoptosis process. Yet sometimes, mitochondria mistakenly push or fail to push the "self-destruct button" in cells. In cases of stroke and Alzheimer's disease, for example, mitochondria may cause too many cells to die, which may lead to mental lapses and other symptoms. In the case of cancer, mitochondria may fail to initiate apoptosis. This failure could allow tumor cells to grow and invade healthy tissues.

## Promise of New Treatments

Researchers are now investigating mitochondria as targets for drug treatments to prevent or treat a variety of conditions. Conversely, researchers are also studying how certain conditions impair mitochondrial function. One day, scientists may use knowledge about mitochondria to help ease the symptoms of aging and to cure or prevent many diseases.

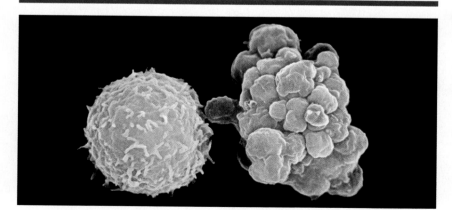

*Mitochondria may play a role in programmed cell death, or apoptosis. A white blood cell undergoing apoptosis (right) looks very different from a normal white blood cell (left). (SEM 2,600×)*

## REVIEW

1. How do mitochondria contribute to free radical formation?
2. How could research on mitochondria be helpful to society?
3. **Critical Thinking** Evaluate the following statement: Mitochondria—we can't live with them; we can't live without them.

**internet** connect

www.scilinks.org
**Topic: Cancer Cells**
**Keyword: HM60209**

SCILINKS. Maintained by the National Science Teachers Association

## The Importance of Oxygen

ATP can be synthesized by chemiosmosis only if electrons continue to move from molecule to molecule in the electron transport chain. The last molecule in the electron transport chain must pass electrons on to a final electron acceptor. Otherwise, the electron transport chain would come to a halt. Consider what would happen if cars kept entering a dead-end, one-way street. At some point, no more cars could enter the street. Similarly, if the last molecule could not "unload" the electrons it accepts, then no more electrons could enter the electron transport chain and ATP synthesis would stop. By accepting electrons from the last molecule in the electron transport chain, oxygen allows additional electrons to pass along the chain. As a result, ATP can continue to be made through chemiosmosis.

# EFFICIENCY OF CELLULAR RESPIRATION

How many ATP molecules are made in cellular respiration? Refer to Figure 7-12 as you calculate the total. Recall that glycolysis and the Krebs cycle each produce two ATP molecules directly for every glucose molecule that is oxidized. Furthermore, each NADH molecule that supplies the electron transport chain can generate three ATP molecules, and each $FADH_2$ molecule can generate two ATP molecules. Thus, the 10 NADH and two $FADH_2$ molecules made through glycolysis, conversion of pyruvic acid to acetyl CoA, and the Krebs cycle can produce up to 34 ATP molecules by the electron transport chain and chemiosmosis. Adding the four ATP molecules from glycolysis and the Krebs cycle gives a maximum yield of 38 ATP molecules per molecule of glucose.

**FIGURE 7-12**

Follow each pathway to see how one glucose molecule can generate up to 38 ATP molecules in cellular respiration when oxygen is present.

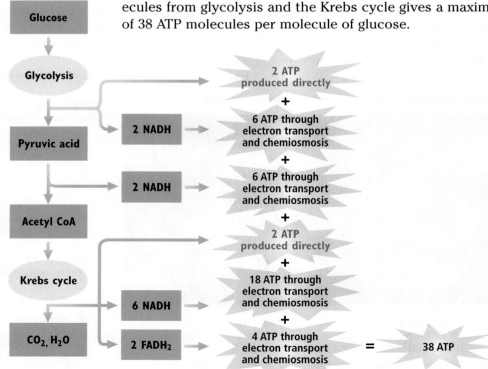

The actual number of ATP molecules generated through cellular respiration varies from cell to cell. In most eukaryotic cells, the NADH that is made in the cytosol during glycolysis cannot diffuse through the inner membrane of the mitochondrion. Instead, it must be actively transported into the mitochondrial matrix. The active transport of NADH consumes ATP. As a result, most eukaryotic cells produce only about 36 ATP molecules per glucose molecule.

The efficiency of cellular respiration can vary depending on conditions in the cell. In general, the efficiency when 38 ATP molecules are generated can be estimated as shown below:

$$\frac{\text{Efficiency of}}{\text{cellular respiration}} = \frac{\text{Energy required to make ATP}}{\text{Energy released by oxidation of glucose}}$$

$$= \frac{38 \times 7 \text{ kcal}}{686 \text{ kcal}} \times 100\% = 39\%$$

Thus, cellular respiration is nearly 20 times more efficient than glycolysis alone. In fact, the efficiency of cellular respiration is quite impressive compared with the efficiency of machines that humans have designed, such as the car shown in Figure 7-13. An automobile engine, for example, is only about 25 percent efficient in extracting energy from gasoline to move a car. Most of the remaining energy released from gasoline is lost as heat.

**FIGURE 7-13**

Through cellular respiration, cells are more efficient at generating energy than many machines—including cars.

# A SUMMARY OF CELLULAR RESPIRATION

Cellular respiration occurs in two stages, as listed below and shown in Figure 7-14:
1. Glycolysis—Glucose is converted into pyruvic acid, producing a small amount of ATP and NADH.
2. Aerobic respiration—Pyruvic acid is converted into $CO_2$ and water in the presence of oxygen, producing a large amount of ATP.

**FIGURE 7-14**

Cellular respiration occurs in two stages: glycolysis and aerobic respiration (which includes the conversion of pyruvic acid to acetyl CoA, the Krebs cycle, the electron transport chain, and chemiosmosis).

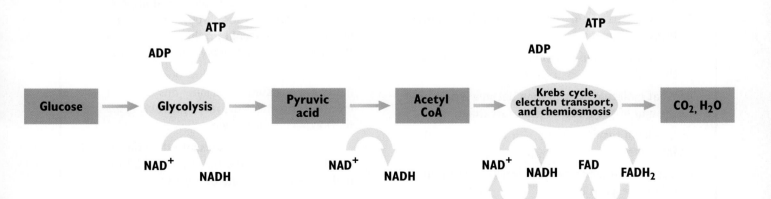

The following equation summarizes the complete oxidation of glucose in cellular respiration:

$$C_6H_{12}O_6 + 6O_2 \longrightarrow 6CO_2 + 6H_2O + energy\ (ATP)$$

In addition to glucose, many other compounds can be used as fuel in cellular respiration. Molecules derived from the breakdown of fats, proteins, and carbohydrates can enter glycolysis or the Krebs cycle at various points in order to yield more energy to an organism.

The equation above can be considered the opposite of the overall equation for photosynthesis, if glucose is considered to be a product of photosynthesis:

$$6CO_2 + 6H_2O \xrightarrow{\text{light energy}} C_6H_{12}O_6 + 6O_2$$

That is, the products of photosynthesis are reactants in celluar respiration, and the products of cellular respiration are reactants in photosynthesis. However, cellular respiration is not the reverse of photosynthesis. These two processes involve different biochemical pathways and occur at different sites inside cells.

## Another Role of Cellular Respiration

Cellular respiration provides the ATP that all cells need to support the activities of life. But providing cells with ATP is not the only important function of cellular respiration. Cells also need specific organic compounds from which to build the macromolecules that compose their own structures. Some of these specific compounds may not be contained in the food that a heterotroph consumes.

The molecules formed at different steps in glycolysis and the Krebs cycle are often used by cells to make the compounds that are missing in food. Compounds formed during glycolysis and the Krebs cycle can be diverted into other biochemical pathways in which the cell makes the molecules it requires. For example, approximately 10 of the amino acids needed by the human body can be made with compounds diverted from the Krebs cycle.

■ internet connect ═══

www.scilinks.org
Topic: Cellular Respiration
Keyword: HM60244

SC/LINKS. Maintained by the National Science Teachers Association

## SECTION 2 REVIEW

1. In what part of a mitochondrion does the Krebs cycle occur?

2. In what part of a mitochondrion is the electron transport chain located?

3. What four-carbon compound is regenerated at the end of the Krebs cycle?

4. What molecule does oxygen become a part of at the end of the electron transport chain?

5. Is cellular respiration more or less efficient than fermentation?

6. List the two processes that together result in cellular respiration.

**CRITICAL THINKING**

7. **Predicting Results** Sometimes protons leak out of a cell or are used for purposes other than ATP production. How would this loss of protons affect the production of ATP in aerobic respiration?

8. **Inferring Relationships** How does the arrangement of the cristae in the inner membrane of mitochondria affect the rate of aerobic respiration? Explain your answer.

9. **Making Calculations** Calculate the efficiency of cellular respiration if a cell generates 32 ATP molecules per molecule of glucose.

# CHAPTER HIGHLIGHTS

SECTION 1 Glycolysis and Fermentation

- Cellular respiration is the process by which cells break down organic compounds to produce ATP.

- Cellular respiration begins with glycolysis, which takes place in the cytosol of cells. During glycolysis, one glucose molecule is oxidized to form two pyruvic acid molecules. Glycolysis results in a net production of two ATP molecules and two NADH molecules.

- If oxygen is not present, glycolysis may lead to anaerobic pathways in which pyruvic acid is converted into other organic molecules in the cytosol. Glycolysis combined with these anaerobic pathways is called *fermentation*. Fermentation does not produce ATP, but it does regenerate $NAD^+$, which helps keep glycolysis operating.

- In lactic acid fermentation, an enzyme converts pyruvic acid into lactic acid.

- In alcoholic fermentation, other enzymes convert pyruvic acid into ethyl alcohol and $CO_2$.

- Through glycolysis, only about 2 percent of the energy available from the oxidation of glucose is captured as ATP.

### Vocabulary
cellular respiration (p.131)
pyruvic acid (p. 131)
NADH (p. 131)
anaerobic (p. 131)
aerobic respiration (p. 131)
glycolysis (p.132)
$NAD^+$ (p. 133)
fermentation (p. 133)
lactic acid fermentation (p. 134)
alcoholic fermentation (p. 135)
kilocalorie (p. 135)

SECTION 2 Aerobic Respiration

- In eukaryotic cells, the processes of aerobic respiration occur inside the mitochondria. The Krebs cycle occurs in the mitochondrial matrix. The electron transport chain is embedded in the inner mitochondrial membrane.

- In the mitochondrial matrix, pyruvic acid produced in glycolysis is converted into acetyl CoA. Then, acetyl CoA enters the Krebs cycle. Each turn of the Krebs cycle generates three NADH, one $FADH_2$, one ATP, and two $CO_2$ molecules.

- NADH and $FADH_2$ donate electrons to the electron transport chain in the inner mitochondrial membrane. These electrons are passed from molecule to molecule in the transport chain.

- As electrons pass along the electron transport chain, protons donated by NADH and $FADH_2$ are pumped into the space between the inner and outer mitochondrial membranes. This pumping creates a concentration gradient of protons and a charge gradient across the inner mitochondrial membrane. As protons move through ATP synthase, down their concentration and charge gradients, and back into the mitochondrial matrix, ATP is produced.

- During aerobic respiration, oxygen accepts both protons and electrons from the electron transport chain. As a result, oxygen is converted to water.

- Cellular respiration can produce up to 38 ATP molecules from the oxidation of a single molecule of glucose. Thus, up to 39 percent of the energy released by the oxidation of glucose can be transferred to ATP. However, most eukaryotic cells produce only about 36 ATP molecules per molecule of glucose.

- Cellular respiration uses the processes of glycolysis and aerobic respiration to obtain energy from organic compounds.

### Vocabulary
mitochondrial matrix (p. 137)
acetyl CoA (p. 138)
Krebs cycle (p. 138)
oxaloacetic acid (p. 138)
citric acid (p. 138)
FAD (p. 139)

## USING VOCABULARY

1. For each pair of terms, explain the relationship between the terms.
   a. *alcoholic fermentation* and *lactic acid fermentation*
   b. *glycolysis* and *pyruvic acid*
   c. *mitochondrial matrix* and *Krebs cycle*

2. Use the following terms in the same sentence: *acetyl CoA*, *citric acid*, and *oxaloacetic acid*.

3. Explain the difference between the terms *fermentation* and *cellular respiration*.

4. **Word Roots and Origins** The word *glycolysis* is derived from the Greek words *glykys*, which means "sweet," and *lysis*, which means "loosening." Using this information, explain why the term *glycolysis* is a good name for the biological process it describes.

## UNDERSTANDING KEY CONCEPTS

5. **Compare** the two stages of cellular respiration.

6. **Explain** why the net yield of ATP molecules in glycolysis is two, even though four ATP molecules are produced.

7. **Describe** what causes your muscles to become fatigued and sometimes develop cramps when you exercise too strenuously.

8. **Calculate** the efficiency of glycolysis if the number of ATP molecules produced during glycolysis were 5 times greater.

9. **Name** the two areas of the mitochondrion where the major stages of aerobic respiration occur.

10. **Explain** the importance of the cyclical nature of the Krebs cycle.

11. **Define** the specific role that oxygen plays in the electron transport chain.

12. **Summarize** the process of electron transport and chemiosmosis, including where the electron transport chain is located, what structures make up the electron transport chain, where the electrons come from and their characteristics, what happens to them as they move along the electron transport chain and as they reach the end of the chain, and what is accomplished by this process.

13. **Explain** why most eukaryotic cells produce fewer than 38—the maximum number possible—ATP molecules for every glucose molecule that is oxidized by cellular respiration.

14. **Compare** the efficiency of glycolysis alone with the efficiency of cellular respiration.

15. **Unit 3—Cellular Respiration**
    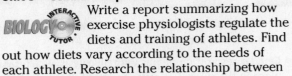
    Write a report summarizing how exercise physiologists regulate the diets and training of athletes. Find out how diets vary according to the needs of each athlete. Research the relationship between exercise and metabolism.

16. **CONCEPT MAPPING** Use the following terms to create a concept map that shows the activities of fermentation: *alcoholic fermentation, anaerobic pathway, fermentation, glycolysis, lactic acid fermentation,* and *pyruvic acid.*

## CRITICAL THINKING

17. **Evaluating Results** Some yeast can use fermentation or cellular respiration. If oxygen is present, these yeast cells consume glucose much more slowly than if oxygen is absent. Explain this observation.

18. **Inferring Relationships** How does cellular respiration ultimately depend on photosynthesis?

19. **Predicting Results** Some eukaryotic cells must use ATP to move NADH into the mitochondrial matrix. Would you expect cellular respiration to be more or less efficient in prokaryotic cells than in eukaryotic cells? Explain your answer.

20. **Interpreting Graphics** The graph below shows the rate of ATP production by a culture of yeast cells over time. At the time indicated by the dashed line, cyanide was added to the culture. Cyanide blocks the flow of electrons to $O_2$ from the electron transport chain in mitochondria. Explain why adding cyanide affects ATP production in the way indicated by the graph.

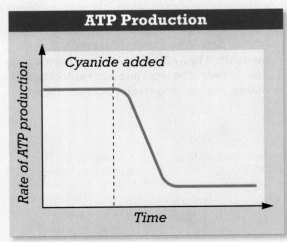

ATP Production

# Standardized Test Preparation

**DIRECTIONS:** Choose the letter of the answer choice that best answers the question.

1. Which of the following must pyruvic acid be converted into before the Krebs cycle can proceed?
   A. NADH
   B. glucose
   C. citric acid
   D. acetyl CoA

2. Which of the following occurs in lactic acid fermentation?
   F. Oxygen is consumed.
   G. Lactic acid is converted into pyruvic acid.
   H. $NAD^+$ is regenerated for use in glycolysis.
   J. Electrons pass through the electron transport chain.

3. Which of the following is not a product of the Krebs cycle?
   A. $CO_2$
   B. ATP
   C. $FADH_2$
   D. ethyl alcohol

4. In which way is cellular respiration similar to photosynthesis?
   F. They both make G3P.
   G. They both involve ATP.
   H. They both involve chemiosmosis.
   J. all of the above

5. ATP is synthesized in chemiosmosis when which of the following moves across the inner mitochondrial membrane?
   A. NADH
   B. oxygen
   C. protons
   D. citric acid

**INTERPRETING GRAPHICS:** The illustration shows part of a biochemical pathway. Use the illustration to answer the question that follows.

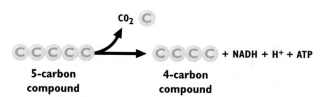

6. This reaction occurs during which of the following processes?
   F. Krebs cycle
   G. acetyl CoA formation
   H. alcoholic fermentation
   J. lactic acid fermentation

**DIRECTIONS:** Complete the following analogy.

7. glycolysis : pyruvic acid :: Krebs cycle :
   A. $O_2$
   B. ATP
   C. lactic acid
   D. acetyl CoA

**INTERPRETING GRAPHICS:** The illustration below shows some stages and reactants of cellular respiration. Use the illustration to answer the question that follows.

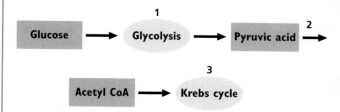

8. At which of the points is ATP, the main energy currency of the cell, produced?
   F. 1 only
   G. 2 only
   H. 1 and 3
   J. 1, 2, and 3

## SHORT RESPONSE

The inner membrane of a mitochondrion is folded; these folds are called *cristae*.

How might cellular respiration be different if the inner mitochondrial membrane were not folded?

## EXTENDED RESPONSE

Oxygen is produced during the reactions of photosynthesis, and it is used in the reactions of cellular respiration.

*Part A* How does oxygen get into or out of chloroplasts and mitochondria?

*Part B* What are the roles of oxygen in the processes of photosynthesis and cellular respiration, and how are the roles similar?

**Test TIP** Make sure you get plenty of rest the night before the test. Eat a healthy breakfast the day of the test and wear comfortable clothing.

# Observing Cellular Respiration

## OBJECTIVES

■ Measure the rate of cellular respiration in germinating seeds.
■ Compare cellular respiration rates in germinating and nongerminating seeds.

## PROCESS SKILLS

■ experimenting
■ collecting data
■ analyzing data

## MATERIALS

■ volumeter jar and screw-on lid
■ tap water at room temperature
■ ring stand with support ring
■ 8.5 in. × 11 in. piece of cardboard
■ 8.5 in. × 11 in. sheet of white paper
■ cellophane tape
■ 40 germinating corn or pea seeds
■ 40 nongerminating corn or pea seeds
■ 100 mL graduated cylinder
■ glass or plastic beads
■ 3 plastic or paper cups
■ 3 volumeters
■ cotton
■ 3 soda-lime packets
■ forceps
■ Pasteur pipet
■ colored water
■ ruler with millimeter markings

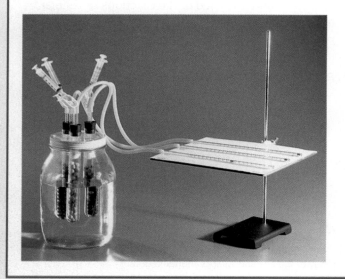

## Background

1. When glucose is oxidized in cellular respiration, what other substance is consumed and what substances are produced?
2. Write the balanced equation for the complete oxidation of glucose in cellular respiration.

### PART A Setting Up the Apparatus

1. Pour water into the volumeter jar until the jar is about two-thirds full. Screw on the lid.
2. Place the cardboard on top of the ring stand support ring, and tape a sheet of white paper to the cardboard. Adjust the support ring so that the cardboard is level, as shown in the illustration below.
3. **CAUTION** **Put on a lab apron, safety goggles, and protective gloves. Keep the seeds, which may have been treated with a fungicide, away from your skin.** Place 40 germinating seeds in a graduated cylinder and measure their volume. Do the same for the 40 nongerminating seeds.
4. Add beads to the seeds that have the smaller volume until the combined volume is the same as the volume of the other group of seeds. Then transfer both groups to separate cups. To a third cup, add a volume of beads equal to the volume of each of the other two cups.
5. Remove the stopper assemblies from three volumeter tubes and transfer the contents of the three cups to separate tubes. Place a 2 cm plug of dry cotton into each tube, leaving a gap of about 1 cm between the cotton and the seeds or beads.
6. **CAUTION** **Soda lime is corrosive. Do not touch it. If it gets on your skin or clothing, wash it off at the sink. If it gets in your eyes, immediately flush it out at the eyewash station while calling to your teacher.** Using forceps, place a packet of soda lime wrapped in gauze on top of the cotton plug in each tube. Soda lime absorbs the $CO_2$ that is produced as a result of respiration.
7. Gently but firmly press the stopper assembly into each volumeter tube. Insert the tubes into the volumeter jar through the large holes in the lid.

**8.** Use a Pasteur pipet to place a small drop of colored water into the three capillary tubes. Tilt two of the tubes slightly until the drops are lined up with the outermost calibration mark. Carefully attach these tubes to the latex tubing on the two volumeter tubes containing seeds. Position the drop in the third capillary tube near the middle of the tube. Attach this tube to the volumeter tube that contains only beads. This volumeter is the control volumeter. Tape all three capillary tubes to the paper on the ring stand.

**9.** Wait 5 min for the temperature to become uniform throughout the volumeter jar. While you wait, make a data table like the one shown below. Then return the drops in the capillary tubes to their original positions by using the syringes to inject air into or withdraw air from the volumeter tubes, if necessary.

**PART B** **Measuring Respiration Rates**

**10.** On the paper beneath the capillary tubes, mark the position of one end of each drop of colored water. Note the time. Repeat this procedure every 5 min for 20 min. If respiration is rapid, you may have to reposition the drops as you did in Step 9. In which direction would you expect a drop to move if respiration in the volumeter tube were causing it to move?

**11.** Remove the paper from the ring stand and use a ruler to measure the distance moved by the drops during each time interval. If you repositioned any drops in Step 10, be sure to add this adjustment when you measure the distances. Enter the measurements in the "Uncorrected" columns in your data table.

**12.** Clean up your materials and wash your hands before leaving the lab.

## Analysis and Conclusions

**1.** No respiration should have occurred in the control volumeter, which contained only beads. Therefore, any movement of the drop in the control volumeter must have been caused by changes in the temperature of the volumeter jar or the air pressure in the classroom. Since these changes would have affected all three volumeters to the same extent, you must subtract the distance you measured for the control volumeter from the distances you measured for the other two volumeters. Do this calculation for each time interval, and enter the results in the "Corrected" columns in your data table.

**2.** Each capillary tube has a capacity of 0.063 mL between each 1 cm mark on the tube. Use this information to calculate the volume of $O_2$ consumed by the germinating and nongerminating seeds during each time interval. Enter these results in your data table.

**3.** Prepare a graph to show the volume of $O_2$ consumed versus time; use different symbols or colors to distinguish the points for the germinating seeds from those for the nongerminating seeds. Make sure each point represents the cumulative volume of $O_2$ consumed. For example, the point plotted for the 15–20 min interval should represent the volume consumed during that interval plus the volume consumed during all of the preceding intervals. Draw the best-fit line through the points for each group of seeds. From the slope of this line, calculate the average rate of respiration in milliliters of $O_2$ per minute for both groups of seeds.

**4.** Which group of seeds had the higher average rate of respiration? What is the significance of this difference in terms of a seed's ability to survive for long periods?

### MEASUREMENTS OF CELLULAR RESPIRATION

| Time interval (min) | Distance moved by drops in volumeters (mm) | | | | | Volume of $O_2$ consumed (mL) | |
| --- | --- | --- | --- | --- | --- | --- | --- |
| | Control | Germinating seeds | | Nongerminating seeds | | Germinating | Nongerminating |
| | | Uncorrected | Corrected | Uncorrected | Corrected | | |
| 0–5 | | | | | | | |
| 5–10 | | | | | | | |
| 10–15 | | | | | | | |
| 15–20 | | | | | | | |

# CHAPTER
# 8
# CELL REPRODUCTION

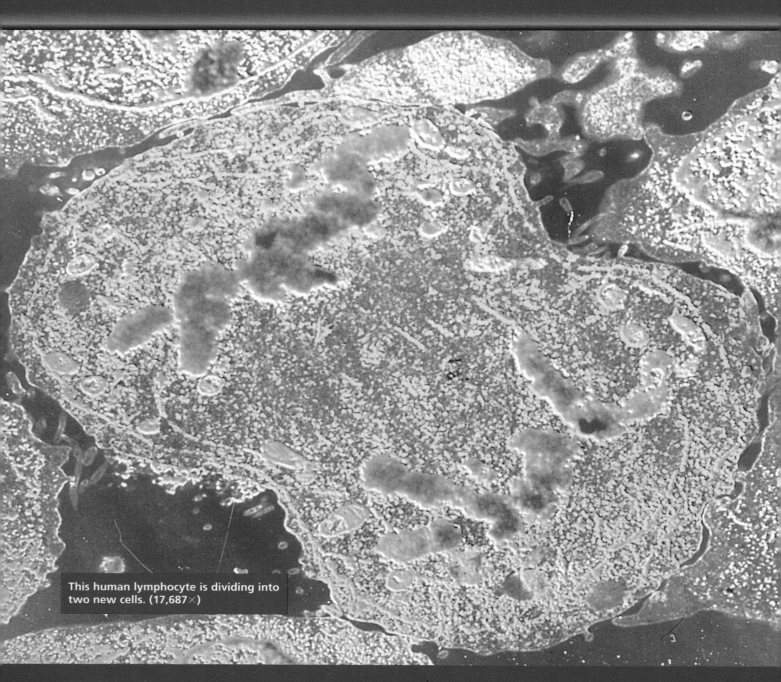

This human lymphocyte is dividing into two new cells. (17,687×)

**SECTION 1** *Chromosomes*

**SECTION 2** *Cell Division*

**SECTION 3** *Meiosis*

**Unit 4—Cell Reproduction**
Topics 1–6

# CHROMOSOMES

*Recall that DNA is a long, thin molecule that stores genetic information. The DNA in a human cell is estimated to consist of three billion nucleotides. To visualize the enormity of three billion nucleotides, imagine increasing a cell nucleus to the size of a basketball. Then, imagine taking the DNA out of the basketball-sized nucleus and stretching it into a straight line. That line of DNA would stretch for more than 20 miles. How can a nucleus hold so much DNA? Inside the nucleus, the DNA is coiled and packed in a complicated yet organized manner. As a cell prepares to divide, the DNA coils even further into tightly compacted structures.*

## OBJECTIVES

- **Describe** the structure of a chromosome.
- **Identify** the differences in structure between prokaryotic chromosomes and eukaryotic chromosomes.
- **Compare** the numbers of chromosomes in different species.
- **Explain** the differences between sex chromosomes and autosomes.
- **Distinguish** between diploid and haploid cells.

## VOCABULARY

chromosome
histone
chromatid
centromere
chromatin
sex chromosome
autosome
homologous chromosome
karyotype
diploid
haploid

## CHROMOSOME STRUCTURE

During cell division, the DNA in a eukaryotic cell's nucleus is coiled into very compact structures called chromosomes. **Chromosomes** are rod-shaped structures made of DNA and proteins. In Figure 8-1, you can see the many levels of DNA coiling required to form a chromosome.

The chromosomes of stained eukaryotic cells undergoing cell division are visible as darkened structures inside the nuclear membrane. Each chromosome is a single DNA molecule associated with proteins. The DNA in eukaryotic cells wraps tightly around proteins called **histones.** Histones help maintain the shape of the chromosome and aid in the tight packing of DNA. Nonhistone proteins are generally involved in controlling the activity of specific regions of the DNA.

**FIGURE 8-1**

As a cell prepares to divide, its DNA coils around histones and twists into rod-shaped chromosomes.

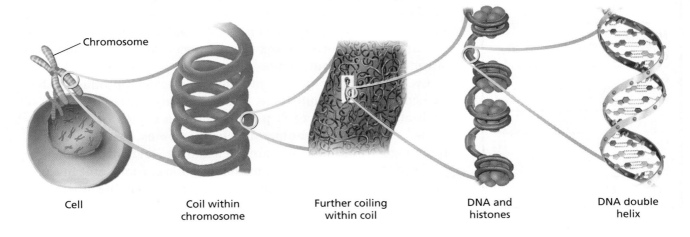

| Cell | Coil within chromosome | Further coiling within coil | DNA and histones | DNA double helix |

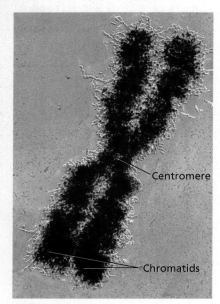

Centromere

Chromatids

**FIGURE 8-2**

Chromosomes, such as this one isolated from a dividing human cell, consist of two identical chromatids. (TEM 12,542×)

Figure 8-2 shows a chromosome that was isolated from a dividing cell. Notice that the chromosome consists of two identical halves. Each half of the chromosome is called a **chromatid.** Chromatids form as the DNA makes a copy of itself before cell division. When the cell divides, each of the two new cells will receive one chromatid from each chromosome. The two chromatids of a chromosome are attached at a point called a **centromere.** The centromere holds the two chromatids together until they separate during cell division. As you will learn in the next section, centromeres are especially important for the movement of chromosomes during cell division.

Between cell divisions, DNA is not so tightly coiled into chromosomes. Regions of DNA uncoil in between cell divisions so they can be read and so the information can be used to direct the activities of the cell. The less tightly coiled DNA-protein complex is called **chromatin.**

As you might expect, chromosomes are simpler in prokaryotes than in eukaryotes. The DNA of most prokaryotes consists of only one chromosome, which is attached to the inside of the cell membrane. Prokaryotic chromosomes consist of a circular DNA molecule. As with eukaryotic chromosomes, prokaryotic chromosomes must be very compact to fit into the cell.

# CHROMOSOME NUMBERS

Each species has a characteristic number of chromosomes in each cell. Table 8-1 lists the number of chromosomes found in some organisms. Some species of organisms have the same number of chromosomes. For example, potatoes, plums, and chimpanzees all have 48 chromosomes in each cell.

## Sex Chromosomes and Autosomes

Human and animal chromosomes are categorized as either sex chromosomes or autosomes. **Sex chromosomes** are chromosomes that determine the sex of an organism, and they may also carry genes for other characteristics. In humans, sex chromosomes are either X or Y. Females normally have two X chromosomes, and males normally have an X and a Y chromosome. All of the other chromosomes in an organism are called **autosomes.** Two of the 46 human chromosomes are sex chromosomes, and the remaining 44 chromosomes are autosomes.

Every cell of an organism produced by sexual reproduction has two copies of each autosome. The organism receives one copy of each autosome from each parent. The two copies of each autosome are called **homologous chromosomes,** or *homologues.* Homologous chromosomes are the same size and shape and carry genes for the same traits. For example, if one chromosome in a pair of homologues contains a gene for eye color, so will the other chromosome in the homologous pair.

| TABLE 8-1 Chromosome Numbers of Various Species | |
| --- | --- |
| **Organism** | **Number of chromosomes** |
| Adder's tongue fern | 1,262 |
| Carrot | 18 |
| Cat | 32 |
| Chimpanzee | 48 |
| Dog | 78 |
| Earthworm | 36 |
| Fruit fly | 8 |
| Garden pea | 20 |
| Gorilla | 48 |
| Horse | 64 |
| Human | 46 |
| Lettuce | 18 |
| Orangutan | 48 |
| Sand dollar | 52 |

Figure 8-3 shows a **karyotype,** which is a photomicrograph of the chromosomes in a normal dividing cell found in a human. Notice that the 46 human chromosomes exist as 22 homologous pairs of autosomes and 2 sex chromosomes (XY in males and XX in females).

## Diploid and Haploid Cells

Cells having two sets of chromosomes are **diploid.** Diploid cells have two autosomes for each homologous pair. Diploid cells also have two sex chromosomes in animals, including humans, and in many other organisms that have sex chromosomes. All human cells, except reproductive cells (sperm cells and egg cells), are normally diploid cells. Diploid is commonly abbreviated as $2n$. In humans, the diploid, or $2n$, number of chromosomes is 46—22 pairs of homologous autosomes and 2 sex chromosomes.

Sperm cells and egg cells are **haploid** cells, which contain only one set of chromosomes. Haploid cells have half the number of chromosomes that are present in diploid cells. Thus, haploid cells have only one autosome of each homologous pair and only one sex chromosome (23 total). Haploid is abbreviated as $1n$. When a sperm cell ($1n$) and an egg cell ($1n$) combine to create the first cell of a new organism, the new cell will be diploid ($2n$). If the reproductive cells were diploid, the new cell would have too many chromosomes and would not be functional.

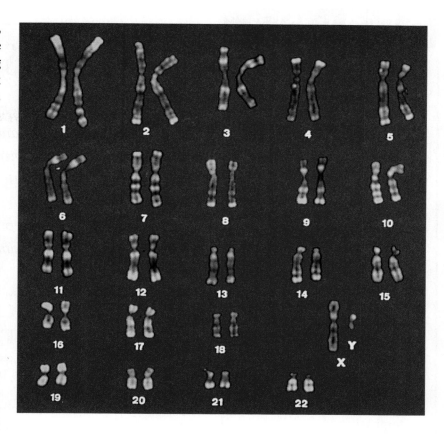

**FIGURE 8-3**

Karyotypes, such as this one, are used to examine an individual's chromosomes. Karyotypes are made from a sample of a person's blood. White blood cells from the sample are treated chemically to stimulate mitosis and to arrest mitosis in metaphase. The chromosomes are then photographed, cut out, and arranged by size and shape into pairs.

## SECTION 1 REVIEW

1. Name the proteins that DNA wraps around to form a chromosome in eukaryotic cells.

2. How do the structure and location of a prokaryotic chromosome differ from that of a eukaryotic chromosome?

3. Does chromosome number indicate whether an organism is a plant or an animal? Explain.

4. Contrast sex chromosomes with autosomes.

5. Using Table 8-1, list the haploid and diploid number of chromosomes for each organism.

**CRITICAL THINKING**

6. **Forming Reasoned Opinions** Is there a correlation between the number of chromosomes and the complexity of an organism? Give support for your answer.

7. **Predicting Results** What would be the consequence for future generations of cells if sperm and egg cells were normally diploid?

8. **Interpreting Graphics** What is the sex of the person whose chromosomes are shown in Figure 8-3 above? Explain your answer.

## OBJECTIVES

- **Describe** the events of cell division in prokaryotes.
- **Name** the two parts of the cell that are equally divided during cell division in eukaryotes.
- **Summarize** the events of interphase.
- **Describe** the stages of mitosis.
- **Compare** cytokinesis in animal cells with cytokinesis in plant cells.
- **Explain** how cell division is controlled.

## VOCABULARY

binary fission
mitosis
asexual reproduction
meiosis
gamete
interphase
cytokinesis
prophase
spindle fiber
metaphase
anaphase
telophase
cell plate

# CELL DIVISION

*Approximately 2 trillion cells—about 25 million cells per second—are produced by an adult human body every day. All cells come from the division of preexisting cells. Cell division (also called cell reproduction) is the process by which cells produce offspring cells. Cell division differs in prokaryotes and eukaryotes. But cell reproduction in both prokaryotes and eukaryotes produces the same result—two cells from one.*

## CELL DIVISION IN PROKARYOTES

Prokaryotes have cell walls but lack nuclei and membrane-bound organelles. A prokaryote's single DNA molecule is not coiled around proteins to form chromosomes. Instead, a prokaryote's DNA is a circular chromosome attached to the inner surface of the plasma membrane like a rope attached to the inner wall of a tent. For most prokaryotes, cell division takes place through a process called binary fission.

**Binary fission** is the division of a prokaryotic cell into two off-spring cells, as shown in Figure 8-4. The DNA is copied, resulting in two identical chromosomes attached to the inside of the prokaryote's inner cell membrane. A new cell membrane then begins to develop between the two DNA copies. The cell grows until it reaches approximately twice the cell's original size. As new material is added, the growing cell membrane pushes inward and the cell is constricted in the center, like a balloon being squeezed in the middle. A new cell wall forms around the new membrane. Eventually, the dividing prokaryote is split into two independent cells. Each cell contains one of the identical chromosomes that resulted from the copying of the original cell's chromosome.

**FIGURE 8-4**

Most prokaryotes reproduce by binary fission, in which two identical cells are produced from one cell.

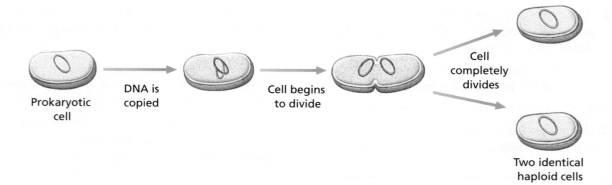

Prokaryotic cell → DNA is copied → Cell begins to divide → Cell completely divides → Two identical haploid cells

# CELL DIVISION IN EUKARYOTES

In eukaryotic cell division, both the cytoplasm and the nucleus divide. There are two kinds of cell division in eukaryotes. The first type of cell division that you will learn about is called mitosis. **Mitosis** results in new cells with genetic material that is identical to the genetic material of the original cell. Mitosis occurs in organisms undergoing growth, development, repair, or asexual reproduction. **Asexual reproduction** is the production of offspring from one parent.

The second type of cell division that you will learn about (in the next section) is called meiosis. **Meiosis** occurs during the formation of **gametes,** which are haploid reproductive cells. Meiosis reduces the chromosome number by half in new cells. Each new cell has the potential to join with another haploid cell to produce a diploid cell with a complete set of chromosomes.

## The Cell Cycle

The *cell cycle* is the repeating set of events in the life of a cell. Cell division is one phase of the cycle. The time between cell divisions is called **interphase.** Interphase is divided into three phases, and cell division is divided into two phases, as shown in Figure 8-5.

During cell division, the chromosomes and cytoplasm are equally divided between two offspring cells. Cell division consists of mitosis and cytokinesis. During mitosis, the nucleus of a cell divides. **Cytokinesis** is the division of the cell's cytoplasm.

## Interphase

Notice in Figure 8-5 that cells spend most of the cell cycle in interphase. Following cell division, offspring cells are approximately half the size of the original cell. During the first stage of interphase—called the $G_1$ *phase*—offspring cells grow to mature size. $G_1$ stands for the time gap following cell division and preceding DNA replication. After cells have reached a mature size, many proceed into the next phase of interphase, called the *S phase.* During the S phase, the cell's DNA is copied (synthesized). The $G_2$ *phase* represents the time gap following DNA synthesis (S phase) and preceding cell division. The $G_2$ phase is a time during which the cell prepares for cell division.

Cells can also exit the cell cycle (usually from the $G_1$ phase) and enter into a state called the $G_0$ *phase*. During the $G_0$ phase, cells do not copy their DNA and do not prepare for cell division. Many cells in the human body are in the $G_0$ phase. For example, fully developed cells in the central nervous system stop dividing at maturity and normally never divide again.

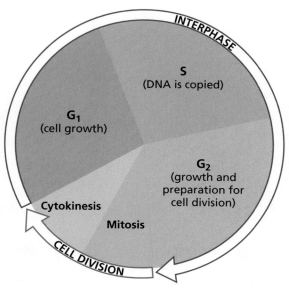

**FIGURE 8-5**

The cell cycle consists of interphase and cell division. Phases of growth, DNA synthesis, and preparation for cell division make up interphase. Cell division is divided into mitosis (division of the nucleus) and cytokinesis (division of the cytoplasm).

**internet** connect

www.scilinks.org
Topic: Cell Cycle
Keyword: HM60235

*SCI*LINKS. Maintained by the National Science Teachers Association

*CELL REPRODUCTION* **155**

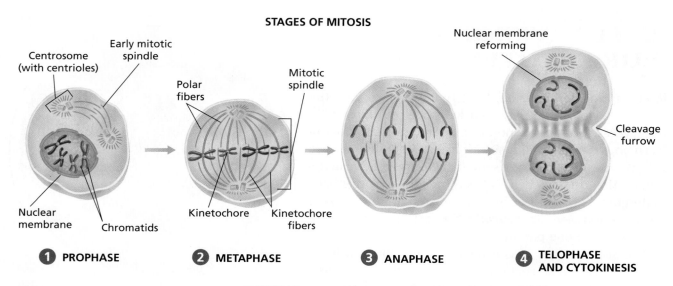

**Centrosome (with centrioles)**
**Early mitotic spindle**
**Polar fibers**
**Mitotic spindle**
**Nuclear membrane reforming**
**Nuclear membrane**
**Chromatids**
**Kinetochore**
**Kinetochore fibers**
**Cleavage furrow**

**1 PROPHASE**    **2 METAPHASE**    **3 ANAPHASE**    **4 TELOPHASE AND CYTOKINESIS**

**FIGURE 8-6**

❶ During prophase, the copied DNA coils into chromosomes. ❷ During metaphase, the chromosomes line up along the midline of the dividing cell. ❸ During anaphase, the chromatids of each chromosome begin moving toward opposite poles of the cell. ❹ During telophase, the chromosomes reach opposite poles of the cell, and a cleavage furrow is formed. Cytokinesis follows.

# STAGES OF MITOSIS

Mitosis is the division of the nucleus, which occurs during cell division. Mitosis is a continuous process that allows for the organized distribution of a cell's copied DNA to offspring cells. The process of mitosis is usually divided into four phases for ease of understanding: prophase, metaphase, anaphase, and telophase.

## Prophase

**Prophase** is the first phase of mitosis. Prophase, shown in step ❶ of Figure 8-6, begins with the shortening and tight coiling of DNA into rod-shaped chromosomes that can be seen with a light microscope. Recall that during the S phase, each chromosome is copied. The two copies of each chromosome—the chromatids—stay connected to one another by the centromere. At this time, the nucleolus and the nuclear membrane break down and disappear.

Two pairs of dark spots called *centrosomes* appear next to the disappearing nucleus. In animal cells, each centrosome contains a pair of small, cylindrical bodies called *centrioles*. The centrosomes of plant cells lack centrioles. In both animal and plant cells, the centrosomes move toward opposite poles of the cell during prophase.

As the centrosomes separate, **spindle fibers** made of microtubules radiate from the centrosomes in preparation for metaphase. This array of spindle fibers is called the *mitotic spindle*, which serves to equally divide the chromatids between the two offspring cells during cell division. Two types of spindle fibers make up the mitotic spindle: kinetochore fibers and polar fibers. *Kinetochore fibers* attach to a disk-shaped protein—called a *kinetochore*—that is found in the centromere region of each chromosome. Kinetochore fibers extend from the kinetochore of each chromatid to one of the centrosomes. *Polar fibers* extend across the dividing cell from centrosome to centrosome but do not attach to the chromosomes.

## Word Roots and Origins

### kinetochore

from the Greek *kinetos,* meaning "moving," and *choros,* meaning "place"

Spindle microtubules

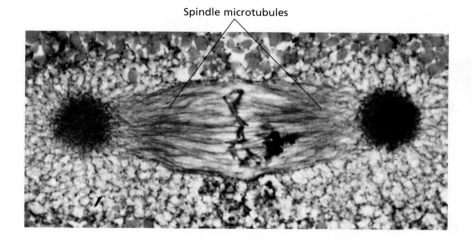

**FIGURE 8-7**

This micrograph of the spindle apparatus during metaphase shows the kinetochore fibers moving the chromosomes to the center of the dividing cell. The wormlike structures in the center are the chromosomes. (LM 1,080×)

## Metaphase

**Metaphase,** as shown in step ❷ of Figure 8-6, is the second phase of mitosis. During metaphase, chromosomes are easier to identify by using a microscope than during other phases; thus, karyotypes are typically made from photomicrographs of chromosomes in metaphase. As shown in Figure 8-7 above, the kinetochore fibers move the chromosomes to the center of the dividing cell during metaphase. Once in the center of the cell, each chromosome is held in place by the kinetochore fibers.

## Anaphase

During **anaphase,** shown in step ❸ of Figure 8-6 on the previous page, the chromatids of each chromosome separate at the centromere and slowly move, centromere first, toward opposite poles of the dividing cell. After the chromatids separate, they are considered to be individual chromosomes.

## Telophase

**Telophase** is shown in step ❹ in Figure 8-6 on the previous page. After the chromosomes reach opposite ends of the cell, the spindle fibers disassemble, and the chromosomes return to a less tightly coiled chromatin state. A nuclear envelope forms around each set of chromosomes, and a nucleolus forms in each of the newly forming cells.

Cleavage furrow

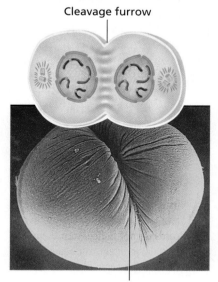

Cleavage furrow

**FIGURE 8-8**

In animal cells, such as this frog cell, the cell membrane pinches in at the center of the dividing cell, eventually dividing the cell into two offspring cells. (SEM 78×)

# CYTOKINESIS

During telophase, the cytoplasm begins dividing by the process of cytokinesis. In animal cells, cytokinesis begins with a pinching inward of the cell membrane midway between the dividing cell's two poles, as shown in Figure 8-8. The area of the cell membrane that pinches in and eventually separates the dividing cell into two cells is called the *cleavage furrow.* The cleavage furrow pinches the cell into two cells through the action of microfilaments.

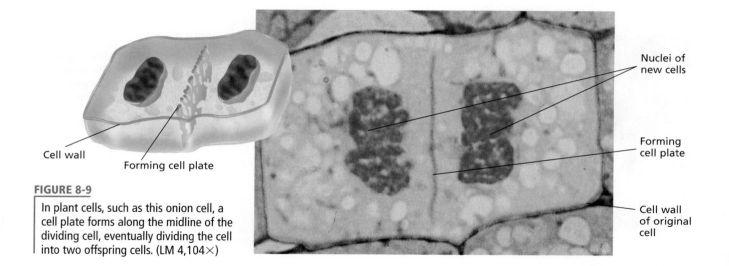

Cell wall

Forming cell plate

Nuclei of new cells

Forming cell plate

Cell wall of original cell

**FIGURE 8-9**

In plant cells, such as this onion cell, a cell plate forms along the midline of the dividing cell, eventually dividing the cell into two offspring cells. (LM 4,104×)

## Quick Lab

### Identifying Prefixes and Suffixes

**Materials** dictionary, 3 × 5 in. index cards (18), pencil

**Procedure**
1. Write each of the following prefixes and suffixes on separate cards: *pro-, meta-, ana-, telo-, cyto-, oo-, inter-, -kinesis,* and *-genesis.*

2. Use a dictionary to find the definition of each prefix and suffix. Write the definitions on cards.

3. Play "Memory" with a partner. Mix the cards, and place each one face down on the table. Turn over two cards. If the two cards consist of a prefix or suffix and its definition, pick up the cards, and take another turn. If the two cards do not match, turn them face down again, and leave them in the same place.

4. Repeat step 3 until no cards remain on the table. The player with the most pairs wins.

**Analysis** How does knowing the meaning of a prefix or suffix help you understand a word's meaning?

Figure 8-9 shows cytokinesis in plant cells. In plant cells, vesicles from the Golgi apparatus join together at the midline of the dividing cell to form a **cell plate.** A cell wall eventually forms from the cell plate at the midline, dividing the cell into two cells.

In both animal cells and plant cells, offspring cells are approximately equal in size. Each offspring cell receives an identical copy of the original cell's chromosomes and approximately one-half of the original cell's cytoplasm and organelles.

# CONTROL OF CELL DIVISION

Recall that a cell spends most of its time in interphase, the time between cell divisions. What triggers a cell to leave interphase and begin dividing? In eukaryotes, proteins regulate the progress of cell division at certain checkpoints. This system of checkpoints can be thought of as a kind of "traffic signal" for the cell. Certain feedback signals from the cell can trigger the proteins to initiate the next phase of the cell cycle, much as a green light signals traffic to move forward. Other feedback signals from the cell can trigger the proteins to halt the cycle, just as a red light signals traffic to stop.

Control occurs at three main checkpoints. These checkpoints are illustrated in Figure 8-10 on the next page.
1. **Cell growth ($G_1$) checkpoint.** Proteins at this checkpoint control whether the cell will divide. If the cell is healthy and has grown to a suitable size during the $G_1$ phase, proteins will initiate DNA synthesis (the S phase). The cell copies its DNA during this phase. If conditions are not favorable for DNA synthesis, the cell cycle will stop at this point. The cell cycle may also stop at this checkpoint if the cell needs a rest period. Certain cells pass into the $G_0$ phase at this checkpoint. Many cells that have passed into the $G_0$ phase will never divide again.

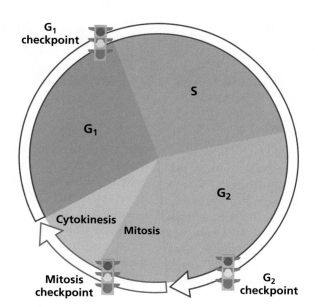

G₁ checkpoint

S

G₁

G₂

Cytokinesis

Mitosis

Mitosis checkpoint

G₂ checkpoint

FIGURE 8-10

The cell cycle in eukaryotes is controlled at three inspection points, or checkpoints. Many proteins are involved in the control of the cell cycle.

2. **DNA synthesis (G₂) checkpoint.** At this point in the $G_2$ phase, DNA repair enzymes check the results of DNA replication. If this checkpoint is passed, proteins will signal the cell to begin the molecular processes that will allow the cell to divide mitotically.

3. **Mitosis checkpoint.** If a cell passes this checkpoint, proteins signal the cell to exit mitosis. The cell then enters into the $G_1$ phase, the major growth phase of the cell cycle, once again.

## When Control Is Lost: Cancer

The proteins that regulate cell growth and division are coded for by genes. If a mutation occurs in one of these genes, the proteins may not function properly. Cell growth and division may be disrupted as a result. Such a disruption could lead to *cancer*, the uncontrolled growth of cells. Cancer cells do not respond normally to the body's control mechanisms. Some mutations cause cancer by overproducing growth-promoting molecules, which can lead to increased cell division. Other mutations may interfere with the ability of control proteins to slow or stop the cell cycle.

---

## SECTION 2 REVIEW

1. Name the process by which prokaryotic cells divide.

2. What is the name of the process by which the cell's cytoplasm divides?

3. During which of the phases of interphase does an offspring cell grow to mature size?

4. During which phase of mitosis do chromatids separate to become chromosomes?

5. Explain the main difference between cytokinesis in animal cells and cytokinesis in plant cells.

6. Which type of molecule controls the cell cycle?

**CRITICAL THINKING**

7. **Predicting Results** What would happen if cytokinesis took place before mitosis?

8. **Applying Information** What would result if chromosomes did not replicate during interphase?

9. **Evaluating Information** Why are individual chromosomes more difficult to see during interphase than during mitosis?

# STEM CELLS: Promise and Difficulty

**S**tem cells are unspecialized cells that give rise to the different types of cells that make up the human body. Scientists researching stem cells hope someday to be able to use them to replace damaged or diseased cells in the body. There are two general types of stem cells: embryonic stem cells and adult stem cells.

### Embryonic Stem Cells

Embryonic stem cells seem to show more promise in medical treatment than do adult stem cells. Embryonic stem cells are easier to find than are adult stem cells. Embryonic stem cells can reproduce indefinitely in culture and have the potential to grow into any cell type. However, embryonic stem cells would be genetically different from the cells of a transplant recipient. The recipient's immune system could reject the cells, causing transplant failure.

### Adult Stem Cells

Some stem cells remain in the body into adulthood. These adult stem cells naturally produce just one or a few types of cells. For example, bone marrow stem cells give rise only to new blood cells. Studies have shown some success in coaxing adult stem cells into becoming other cell types. Using a person's own stem cells for cell transplant would avoid a possible immune response. However, because there are so few adult stem cells, they can be difficult to find. Adult stem cells also have a limited life span in the lab, which gives rise to questions about the life span of any transplant done with adult stem cells.

### Stem Cell Controversy

Despite the possibilities of stem cell use, research on them has been controversial. Embryonic stem cells are harvested from human embryos that are unused for fertility treatment. When embryonic stem cells are harvested, the embryo is destroyed. Many people believe it is unethical to destroy embryos that have the potential to develop into babies. The harvesting of adult stem cells causes no lasting harm to the donor, but the potential for the cells may be limited.

Stem cell transplants might one day be used routinely to treat diseases and disorders such as Alzheimer's disease, diabetes, cancer, and spinal cord injuries. We may even be able to grow complete new organs from stem cells. Funding will be one factor that affects the direction of research. Federal, state, and private funding set the landscape for the future of stem cell research. While the promise of stem cells seems unlimited, major advances will only be achieved through years of intensive research.

*In 2004, New York Mets coach Don Baylor (center) enjoyed his first day back with the team after receiving stem cell replacement therapy for cancer.*

## REVIEW

1. How do adult stem cells differ from embryonic stem cells?
2. Why is stem cell research controversial?
3. **Critical Thinking** What do you think are the strongest reasons for and against further research? Based on these two points, would you propose stem cell research be regulated? If so, how?

**internet** connect

**www.scilinks.org**
**Topic: Differentiation of Cells**
**Keyword: HM60404**

SC*LINKS* Maintained by the National Science Teachers Association

# MEIOSIS

*M*eiosis is a process of nuclear division that reduces the number of chromosomes in new cells to half the number in the original cell. The halving of the chromosome number counteracts a joining of cells later in the life cycle of the organism.

### OBJECTIVES

- **Compare** the end products of meiosis with those of mitosis.
- **Summarize** the events of meiosis I.
- **Explain** crossing-over and how it contributes to the production of unique individuals.
- **Summarize** the events of meiosis II.
- **Compare** spermatogenesis and oogenesis.
- **Define** *sexual reproduction.*

### VOCABULARY

synapsis
tetrad
crossing-over
genetic recombination
independent assortment
spermatogenesis
oogenesis
polar body
sexual reproduction

## FORMATION OF HAPLOID CELLS

In animals, meiosis produces gametes, which are haploid reproductive cells. Human gametes are sperm cells and egg cells. Sperm and egg cells each contain 23 ($1n$) chromosomes. The fusion of a sperm and an egg results in a zygote that contains 46 ($2n$) chromosomes.

Cells preparing to divide by meiosis undergo the $G_1$, S, and $G_2$ phases of interphase. During interphase, the cell grows to a mature size and copies its DNA. Thus, cells begin meiosis with a duplicate set of chromosomes, just as cells beginning mitosis do. Because cells undergoing meiosis divide twice, diploid ($2n$) cells that divide meiotically result in four haploid ($1n$) cells rather than two diploid ($2n$) cells. The stages of the first cell division are called *meiosis I,* and the stages of the second cell division are called *meiosis II.*

## MEIOSIS I

While reading about each phase of meiosis I, shown in Figure 8-11 on the next page, notice how these phases compare with the corresponding phases that occur in mitosis.

### Prophase I

In prophase I (step ❶), DNA coils tightly into chromosomes. As in the prophase of mitosis, spindle fibers appear. Then, the nucleolus and nuclear membrane disassemble. Notice that every chromosome lines up next to its homologue. The pairing of homologous chromosomes, which does not occur in mitosis, is called **synapsis.** Each pair of homologous chromosomes is called a **tetrad.** In each tetrad, chromatids of the homologous chromosomes are aligned lengthwise so that the genes on one chromosome are adjacent to the corresponding genes on the other chromosome.

### Word Roots and Origins

**tetrad**

from the Greek *tetras,* meaning "four"

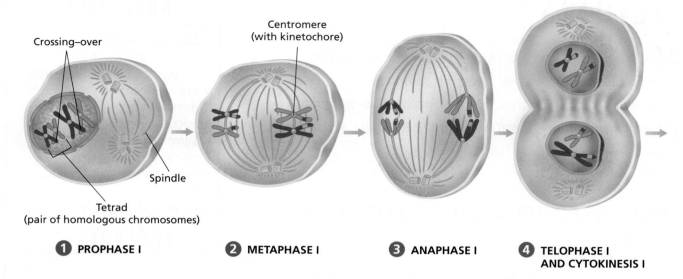

Centromere (with kinetochore)

Crossing–over

Spindle

Tetrad
(pair of homologous chromosomes)

**1** PROPHASE I    **2** METAPHASE I    **3** ANAPHASE I    **4** TELOPHASE I
AND CYTOKINESIS I

**FIGURE 8-11**

Meiosis occurs in diploid reproductive cells. Before meiosis begins, the DNA of the diploid reproductive cells is copied. Meiosis I results in two haploid cells. Meiosis II results in four haploid offspring cells.

During synapsis, the chromatids within a homologous pair twist around one another, as shown in Figure 8-12. Portions of chromatids may break off and attach to adjacent chromatids on the homologous chromosome—a process called **crossing-over.** This process permits the exchange of genetic material between maternal and paternal chromosomes. Thus, **genetic recombination** results, because a new mixture of genetic material is created.

## Metaphase I

During metaphase I (step **2**), the tetrads line up randomly along the midline of the dividing cell, as shown in Figure 8-11. The orientation of the pair of chromosomes is random with respect to the poles of the cell. Spindle fibers from one pole attach to the centromere of one homologous chromosome. Spindle fibers from the opposite pole attach to the other homologous chromosome of the pair.

## Anaphase I

During anaphase I (step **3**), each homologous chromosome (consisting of two chromatids attached by a centromere) moves to an opposite pole of the dividing cell. The random separation of the homologous chromosomes is called **independent assortment.** Independent assortment results in genetic variation.

## Telophase I and Cytokinesis I

During telophase I (step **4**), the chromosomes reach the opposite ends of the cell, and cytokinesis begins. Notice that the new cells contain a haploid number of chromosomes.

During meiosis I, the original cell produces two new cells, each containing one chromosome from each homologous pair. The new cells contain half the number of chromosomes of the original cell. However, each new cell contains two copies (as chromatids), because the original cell copied its DNA before meiosis I.

**FIGURE 8-12**

Crossing-over occurs when chromosomes that make up a tetrad exchange portions of their chromatids during synapsis. Crossing-over results in an exchange of genes and in new combinations of genes.

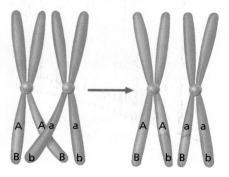

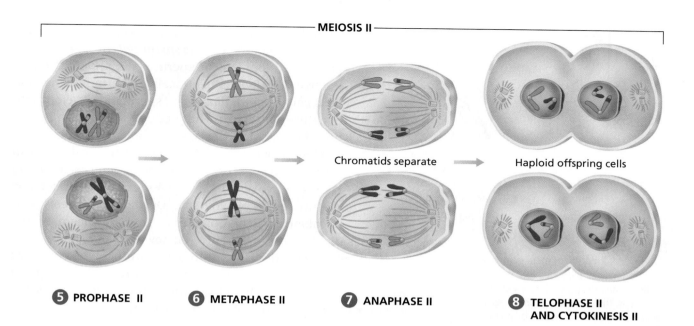

Chromatids separate

Haploid offspring cells

**5** PROPHASE II

**6** METAPHASE II

**7** ANAPHASE II

**8** TELOPHASE II AND CYTOKINESIS II

# MEIOSIS II

Meiosis II occurs in each cell formed during meiosis I and is not preceded by the copying of DNA. The events of meiosis II are shown above. In some species, meiosis II begins after the nuclear membrane re-forms in the new cells. In other species, meiosis II begins immediately following meiosis I.

## Prophase II, Metaphase II, and Anaphase II

During prophase II (step **5**), spindle fibers form and begin to move the chromosomes toward the midline of the dividing cell. In metaphase II (step **6**), the chromosomes move to the midline of the dividing cell, with each chromatid facing opposite poles of the dividing cell. In anaphase II (step **7**), the chromatids separate and move toward opposite poles of the cell.

## Telophase II and Cytokinesis II

In telophase II (step **8**), a nuclear membrane forms around the chromosomes in each of the four new cells. Cytokinesis II then occurs, resulting in four new cells, each of which contains half of the original cell's number of chromosomes.

# DEVELOPMENT OF GAMETES

In animals, the only cells that divide by meiosis are those that produce gametes within the reproductive organs. However, organisms vary in timing and structures associated with gamete formation. In humans, meiosis occurs in the testes (males) and the ovaries (females). Figure 8-13 shows a male human gamete joining with a female human gamete.

**FIGURE 8-13**

When the female gamete (the egg) joins with a male gamete (sperm), the genetic instructions from the male and female are combined, and a new individiual is formed. (SEM 1,225×)

Egg

Sperm

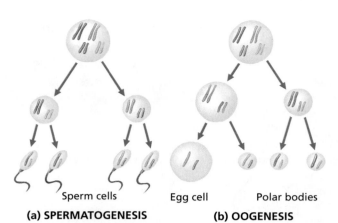

Sperm cells          Egg cell          Polar bodies

**(a) SPERMATOGENESIS**          **(b) OOGENESIS**

**FIGURE 8-14**

(a) In the formation of male gametes, the original cell produces four sperm cells by meiosis. (b) In the formation of egg cells, the original cell produces one egg and three polar bodies by meiosis. The egg cell receives most of the original cell's cytoplasm.

In the testes, meiosis is involved in the production of male gametes known as *sperm cells* or *spermatozoa.* In the development of sperm cells, a diploid reproductive cell divides meiotically to form four haploid cells called *spermatids.* Each spermatid develops into a mature sperm cell. The production of sperm cells is called **spermatogenesis,** shown in Figure 8-14a.

**Oogenesis** (OH-oh-JEN-uh-sis) is the production of mature egg cells, or ova. During oogenesis, a diploid reproductive cell divides meiotically to produce one mature egg cell (ovum). During cytokinesis and cytokinesis II of oogenesis, the cytoplasm of the original cell is divided unequally between new cells. As Figure 8-14b shows, one cell, which develops into a mature egg cell, receives most of the cytoplasm of the original cell. As a result, one egg cell is produced by meiosis. The other three products of meiosis, called **polar bodies,** eventually will degenerate.

# SEXUAL REPRODUCTION

**Sexual reproduction** is the production of offspring through meiosis and the union of a sperm and an egg. Offspring produced by sexual reproduction are genetically different from the parents because genes are combined in new ways in meiosis. In fact, except in the case of identical twins, sexually produced offspring contain unique combinations of their parents' genes. The evolutionary advantage of sexual reproduction is that it enables species to adapt rapidly to new conditions. For example, if disease strikes a crop of grain, a few plants may have genetic variations that make them resistant to the disease. Although many individuals may die, these few resistant plants survive and reproduce.

## SECTION 3 REVIEW

1. How do the end products of meiosis differ from the end products of mitosis?

2. How does anaphase I in meiosis differ from anaphase in mitosis?

3. Explain the role of crossing-over in ensuring genetic variation.

4. During which stage of meiosis is the diploid number of chromosomes reduced to the haploid number of chromosomes?

5. Describe the differences between spermatogenesis and oogenesis.

6. Why is meiosis essential to sexual reproduction?

**CRITICAL THINKING**

7. **Applying Information** Explain why the chromosomes in the haploid cells that are produced by meiosis I look different from those produced by meiosis II.

8. **Relating Concepts** Explain how it might happen that a human offspring with 47 chromosomes could be produced.

9. **Distinguishing Relevant Information** In humans, the egg is larger than the sperm. Explain how it is possible that a child inherits equally from its mother and father.

# CHAPTER HIGHLIGHTS

Chromosomes

- Chromosomes are tightly coiled DNA molecules. In eukaryotes, proteins called *histones* help maintain the compact structure of chromosomes.

- Chromosomes in prokaryotes are simpler than chromosomes in eukaryotes.

- Each species has a characteristic number of chromosomes in each cell.

- Sex chromosomes are chromosomes that determine the sex of an organism. All of the other chromosomes in an organism are autosomes.

- Cells having two sets of chromosomes are diploid ($2n$). Haploid cells ($1n$) have half the number of chromosomes that are present in diploid cells.

### Vocabulary

| | | | |
|---|---|---|---|
| chromosome (p. 151) | centromere (p. 152) | autosome (p. 152) | karyotype (p. 153) |
| histone (p. 151) | chromatin (p. 152) | homologous | diploid (p. 153) |
| chromatid (p. 152) | sex chromosome (p. 152) | chromosome (p. 152) | haploid (p. 153) |

---

**SECTION 2** Cell Division

- Cell division is the process by which cells reproduce themselves. Binary fission is the process of cell division in prokaryotes.

- The cell cycle is the repeating set of events in the life of a cell. The cell cycle consists of cell division and interphase.

- Cell division in eukaryotes includes nuclear division (mitosis) and the division of cytoplasm (cytokinesis).

- Interphase consists of growth ($G_1$), DNA replication (S), and preparation for cell division ($G_2$).

- Mitosis is divided into prophase, metaphase, anaphase, and telophase. Mitosis results in two offspring cells that are genetically identical to the original cell.

- During cytokinesis in animal cells, a cleavage furrow pinches in and eventually separates the dividing cell into two cells. In plant cells, a cell plate separates the dividing cell into two cells.

- Cell division in eukaryotes is controlled by many proteins. Control occurs at three main checkpoints. Cancer may result if cells do not respond to control mechanisms.

### Vocabulary

| | | | |
|---|---|---|---|
| binary fission (p. 154) | gamete (p. 155) | prophase (p. 156) | anaphase (p. 157) |
| mitosis (p. 155) | interphase (p. 155) | spindle fiber (p. 156) | telophase (p. 157) |
| asexual reproduction (p. 155) | cytokinesis (p. 155) | metaphase (p. 157) | cell plate (p. 158) |
| meiosis (p. 155) | | | |

---

**SECTION 3** Meiosis

- Meiosis is a process of nuclear division that reduces the number of chromosomes in new cells to half the number in the original cell. Meiosis produces gametes.

- Cells undergoing meiosis divide twice. Diploid cells that divide meiotically result in four haploid cells rather than two diploid cells as in mitosis.

- Meiosis I includes prophase I, metaphase I, anaphase I, and telophase I. Crossing-over during prophase I results in genetic recombination.

- Meiosis II includes prophase II, metaphase II, anaphase II, and telophase II. Four new haploid cells result.

- Spermatogenesis is the process by which sperm cells are produced. Oogenesis is the process that produces egg cells.

- Sexual reproduction is the formation of offspring through the union of a sperm and an egg. Offspring produced by sexual reproduction are genetically different from the parents.

### Vocabulary

| | | | |
|---|---|---|---|
| synapsis (p. 161) | genetic recombination (p. 162) | spermatogenesis (p. 164) | polar body (p. 164) |
| tetrad (p. 161) | independent assortment (p. 162) | oogenesis (p. 164) | sexual reproduction (p. 164) |
| crossing-over (p. 162) | | | |

## USING VOCABULARY

1. For each pair of terms, explain how the meanings of the terms differ.
   a. *autosome* and *sex chromosome*
   b. *synapsis* and *crossing-over*
   c. *haploid* and *diploid*

2. Explain the relationship between the terms *chromosome* and *homologous chromosomes*.

3. Use the following terms in the same sentence: *mitosis*, *meiosis*, and *cytokinesis*.

4. **Word Roots and Origins** The word *oogenesis* is derived from the Greek *oion*, which means "egg," and *geneia*, which means "birth." Using this information, explain why the term *oogenesis* is a good name for the biological process it describes.

## UNDERSTANDING KEY CONCEPTS

5. **Describe** the structure of a chromosome.

6. **Compare** prokaryotic chromosomes with eukaryotic chromosomes.

7. **State** the number of chromosomes in normal human cells.

8. **Identify** the type of chromosome that determines the sex of an organism.

9. **Distinguish** between haploid cells and diploid cells.

10. **Define** the term *binary fission*. In what type of organism does this type of cell division occur?

11. **Differentiate** mitosis from cytokinesis.

12. **Describe** the events that occur in the $G_0$, $G_1$, and $G_2$ phases.

13. **Summarize** the phases of mitosis.

14. **Describe** the process of cytokinesis in plant cells.

15. **List** the three main checkpoints at which the cell cycle is controlled.

16. **Identify** the type of nuclear division that results in haploid cells.

17. **Compare** the phases of meiosis I with those of meiosis II.

18. **Name** the meiotic process that results in genetic recombination.

19. **Summarize** the major characteristics of spermatogenesis and oogenesis.

20. **Identify** the relationship between sexual reproduction and genetic variation.

21. **Unit 4—Cell Reproduction**
    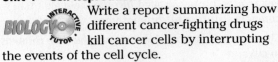
    Write a report summarizing how different cancer-fighting drugs kill cancer cells by interrupting the events of the cell cycle.

22. **CONCEPT MAPPING** Use the following terms to create a concept map that shows the connection between cellular division in prokaryotes and eukaryotes: *binary fission, cell cycle, cytokinesis, eukaryote, mitosis,* and *prokaryote.*

## CRITICAL THINKING

23. **Predicting Results** Can mitosis occur in the absence of cytokinesis? Support your answer. If your answer is yes, describe how the new cell would appear in the $G_1$ phase.

24. **Making Calculations** If you consider the mass of DNA in a sperm (a haploid cell) to be 1, what would the relative value be for the DNA mass of a cell in the $G_2$ phase of the cell cycle?

25. **Applying Information** Does a cell in metaphase II have the same mass of DNA as a diploid cell in the $G_1$ phase? Assume that both cells are from the same animal. Explain your answer.

26. **Analyzing Information** The events of mitosis in plants and animals are very similar, with the exception of the absence of centrioles in plants. How has the absence of centrioles in plant cells influenced scientists' thinking about the function of centrioles in mitosis?

27. **Interpreting Graphics** The photograph below shows cell division in a grasshopper testis. The offspring cells are gametes. Do you think the photograph shows mitosis or meiosis? Explain your answer.

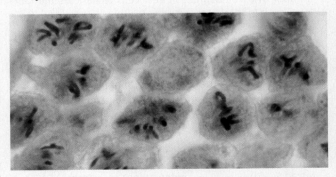

# Standardized Test Preparation

**DIRECTIONS:** Choose the letter of the answer choice that best answers the question.

1. Which of the following statements about prokaryotic chromosomes is true?
   - **A.** Prokaryotes have at least two chromosomes.
   - **B.** Prokaryotic chromosomes consist of a circular DNA molecule.
   - **C.** Prokaryotic chromosomes include histone and nonhistone proteins.
   - **D.** Prokaryotic chromosomes are made of DNA wrapped tightly around histone proteins.

2. Crossing-over occurs during which process?
   - **F.** mitosis
   - **G.** meiosis I
   - **H.** meiosis II
   - **J.** interphase

**INTERPRETING GRAPHICS:** The graph below shows the relative mass of DNA and chromosome number for a cell undergoing mitosis. Use the graph to answer the questions that follow.

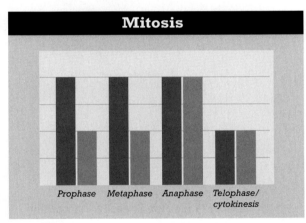

**Mitosis**

- ■ DNA mass
- ■ Chromosome number

Prophase   Metaphase   Anaphase   Telophase/cytokinesis

3. In which phase of mitosis do chromatids separate and become individual chromosomes?
   - **A.** prophase
   - **B.** metaphase
   - **C.** anaphase
   - **D.** telophase/cytokinesis

4. What process occurs that leads to the decrease in the cell's DNA mass?
   - **F.** prophase
   - **G.** metaphase
   - **H.** anaphase
   - **J.** telophase/cytokinesis

**DIRECTIONS:** Complete the following analogy.

5. prokaryote : binary fission :: eukaryote :
   - **A.** mitosis
   - **B.** cytokinesis
   - **C.** crossing-over
   - **D.** genetic recombination

**INTERPRETING GRAPHICS:** The diagram below shows a model of cell division. Use the diagram to answer the question that follows.

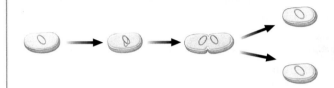

6. Which type of cell division is shown in the diagram?
   - **F.** mitosis
   - **G.** meiosis
   - **H.** binary fission
   - **J.** sexual reproduction

## SHORT RESPONSE

Human cells are either diploid or haploid. All human cells with 46 chromosomes are diploid.

Would a human cell with *any* 23 chromosomes be haploid? Explain your answer.

## EXTENDED RESPONSE

For a cell to function efficiently, its surface area must exceed that of its volume.

*Part A* Explain how cell division maintains the relationship between surface area and volume.

*Part B* How does a stable ratio between surface area and volume help maintain proper cell functioning?

**Test TIP** To help you learn the stages of mitosis and meiosis, make a note card describing each stage, mix the cards up, and practice reordering the stages.

# Observing Mitosis in Plant Cells

## OBJECTIVES

- Examine the dividing root-tip cells of an onion.
- Identify the phase of mitosis that different cells in an onion root tip are undergoing.
- Determine the relative length of time each phase of mitosis takes in onion root-tip cells.

## PROCESS SKILLS

- observing
- classifying
- collecting
- organizing
- analyzing data
- calculating

## MATERIALS

- compound light microscope
- prepared microscope slide of a longitudinal section of *Allium* (onion) root tip

## Background

1. Mitosis is divided into four phases: prophase, metaphase, anaphase, and telophase.
2. Interphase is not considered a part of mitosis.
3. List the visible characteristics of each phase of mitosis.
4. In many plants, there are growth regions called *meristems* where mitosis is ongoing. Meristems are found in the tips of plant roots and shoots.

## PART A  Identifying the Phases of Mitosis

1. Look at the photograph below of a longitudinal section of an onion root tip. Find the meristem on the photograph. As you can see, the meristem is located just behind the root cap.

**ONION ROOT TIP**

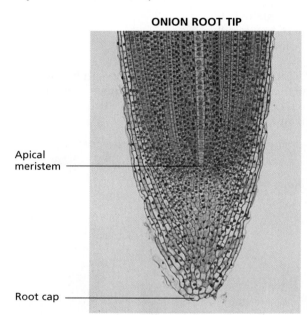

Apical meristem

Root cap

2. **CAUTION  Slides break easily. Use caution when handling them.** Using low power on your microscope, bring the meristem region on your slide into focus.

### TABLE A  *RELATIVE DURATION OF EACH PHASE OF MITOSIS*

| Phase of mitosis | Tally marks | Count | Percentage | Time (in minutes) |
|------------------|-------------|-------|------------|-------------------|
| Prophase | | | | |
| Metaphase | | | | |
| Anaphase | | | | |
| Telophase | | | | |

## TABLE B  DATA COLLECTED BY THE ENTIRE CLASS

| Phase of mitosis | Count | Percentage | Time (in minutes) |
|---|---|---|---|
| Prophase | | | |
| Metaphase | | | |
| Anaphase | | | |
| Telophase | | | |

3. In your lab report, prepare a data table like Table A.

4. Examine the meristem carefully. Choose a sample of about 50 cells. Look for a group of cells that appear to have been actively dividing at the time that the slide was made. The cells will appear in rows, so it should be easy to keep track of them. The dark-staining bodies are the chromosomes.

5. For each of the cells in your sample, identify the stage of mitosis and place a mark in the "Tally marks" column beside the appropriate phase.

### PART B  Calculating the Relative Length of Each Phase

6. When you have classified each cell in your sample, count the tally marks for each phase and fill in the "Count" column. In which phase of mitosis were the greatest number of cells? In which phase were the fewest number of cells?

7. Calculate the percentage of cells found in each phase. Divide the number of cells in a phase by the total number of cells in your sample, and multiply by 100 percent. Enter the figures under "Percentage."

8. The percentage of cells found in each phase can be used as a measure of how long each phase lasts. For example, if 25 percent of the cells are in prophase, then prophase takes 25 percent of the total time it takes for a cell to undergo mitosis. Mitosis in onion cells takes about 80 minutes. Calculate the actual time for each phase using this information and the percentage you have just determined.

Duration of phase (in minutes) =

$$\frac{\text{percentage}}{100} \times 80 \text{ minutes}$$

9. Record the actual time for each phase in your data table.

10. Make another data table, similar to Table B, shown above. Collect and record the count for each phase of mitosis for the entire class. Fill in the percentage and time information using the data collected by the entire class.

11. Clean up your materials before leaving the lab.

### Analysis and Conclusions

1. What color are the chromosomes stained?

2. How can you distinguish between early and late anaphase?

3. According to your data table, which phase of mitosis lasts the longest? Why might this phase require more time than other phases of mitosis?

4. According to your data table, which phase takes the least amount of time?

5. How do your results compare with those of the entire class?

6. In this investigation, you assumed that the percentage of the total time that any given phase takes is equal to the percentage of cells in that phase at any moment. Why might this not be true for very small samples of cells?

### Further Inquiry

1. Given the rate of mitosis in a type of animal cells, how could you determine how long each phase of mitosis takes in those cells?

2. Cancerous tissue is composed of cells undergoing uncontrolled, rapid cell division. How could you develop a procedure to identify cancerous tissue by counting the number of cells undergoing mitosis?

# GENETICS AND BIOTECHNOLOGY

> ❝ . . . [G]enetics has come to occupy an important position at the center of the sciences of life . . . genetics became allied with biochemistry; it revolutionized bacteriology, played a major role in the emergence of the molecular biology of the fifties, resisted the challenge of ecology, took hold of cancer research and is even now reaching out to revolutionize taxonomy and its old rival embryology. ❞

From "Mendel, Mendelism and Genetics," by Robert C. Olby from *The NetSpace Foundation, Inc.* web site, accessed July 2, 1997 at http://www.netspace.org/MendelWeb/MWolby.html. Copyright © 1997 by **Robert C. Olby**. Reproduced by permission of the author.

References to *Scientific American* project ideas are located throughout this unit.

**internet** connect

National Science Teachers Association *sci* LINKS Internet resources are located throughout this unit.

SCI LINKS. Maintained by the National Science Teachers Association

These tiger cub siblings look very similar to one another because they have inherited characteristics from their parents.

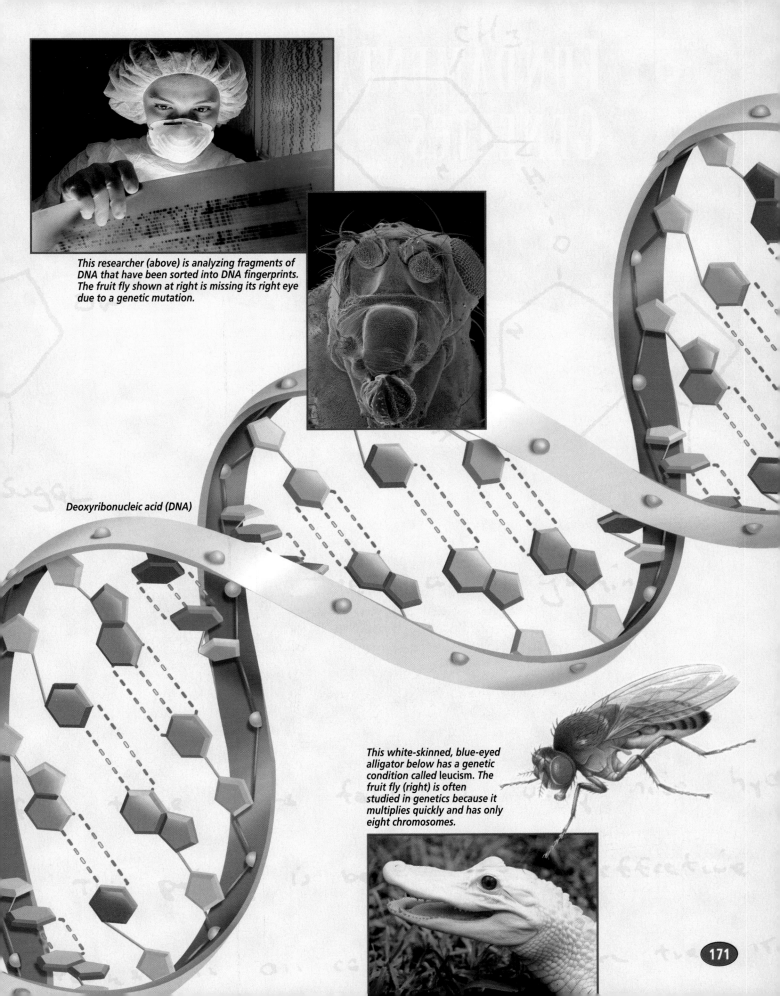

This researcher (above) is analyzing fragments of DNA that have been sorted into DNA fingerprints. The fruit fly shown at right is missing its right eye due to a genetic mutation.

Deoxyribonucleic acid (DNA)

This white-skinned, blue-eyed alligator below has a genetic condition called leucism. The fruit fly (right) is often studied in genetics because it multiplies quickly and has only eight chromosomes.

# FUNDAMENTALS OF GENETICS

The unique appearance of this white-skinned, blue-eyed alligator is the result of a genetic condition.

**SECTION 1**  *Mendel's Legacy*

**SECTION 2**  *Genetic Crosses*

**BIOLOGY** INTERACTIVE TUTOR

Unit 5—Heredity
Topics 1–6

# MENDEL'S LEGACY

*Genetics* is the field of biology devoted to understanding how characteristics are transmitted from parents to offspring. Genetics was founded with the work of Gregor Johann Mendel. This section describes Mendel's experiments and the principles of genetics that resulted from them.

## GREGOR MENDEL

In 1843, at the age of 21, Gregor Mendel, shown in Figure 9-1, entered a monastery in Brunn, Austria. His task of tending the garden gave him time to think and to observe the growth of many plants. In 1851, he entered the University of Vienna to study science and mathematics. His mathematics courses included training in the then-new field of statistics. Mendel's knowledge of statistics later proved valuable in his research on **heredity**—the transmission of characteristics from parents to offspring. When Mendel returned to the monastery, he taught in a high school and also kept a garden plot. Although he studied many plants, he is remembered most for his experiments with *Pisum sativum,* a species of garden peas.

### Mendel's Garden Peas

Mendel observed seven characteristics of pea plants. A characteristic is a heritable feature, such as flower color. Each characteristic occurred in two contrasting traits. A **trait** is a genetically determined variant of a characteristic, such as yellow flower color. The pea characteristics that Mendel observed were *plant height* (traits: long and short), *flower position along stem* (traits: axial and terminal), *pod color* (traits: green and yellow), *pod appearance* (traits: inflated and constricted), *seed texture* (traits: round and wrinkled), *seed color* (traits: yellow and green), and *flower color* (traits: purple and white). Mendel used his knowledge of statistics to analyze his observations of these seven characteristics.

## SECTION 1

### OBJECTIVES

- **Describe** how Mendel was able to control how his pea plants were pollinated.
- **Describe** the steps in Mendel's experiments on true-breeding garden peas.
- **Distinguish** between dominant and recessive traits.
- **State** two laws of heredity that were developed from Mendel's work.
- **Describe** how Mendel's results can be explained by scientific knowledge of genes and chromosomes.

### VOCABULARY

genetics
heredity
trait
pollination
self-pollination
cross-pollination
true-breeding
P generation
$F_1$ generation
$F_2$ generation
dominant
recessive
law of segregation
law of independent assortment
molecular genetics
allele

**FIGURE 9-1**

Gregor Johann Mendel lived from 1822 to 1884. Mendel's experiments with garden peas led to his discovery of the basic principles of genetics.

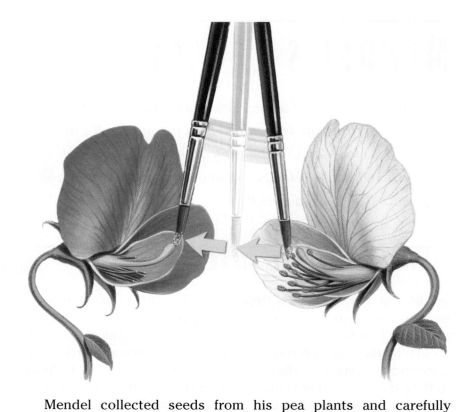

**FIGURE 9-2**

Mendel controlled the breeding of his pea plants and tracked the inheritance of traits by transferring pollen from the anthers of one plant to the stigma of another plant.

Mendel collected seeds from his pea plants and carefully recorded each plant's traits and seeds. The next year, he planted the seeds. He observed that purple-flowering plants grew from most of the seeds obtained from purple-flowering plants but that white-flowering plants grew from some of the seeds of purple-flowering plants. And when experimenting with the characteristic of plant height, he observed that while tall plants grew from most of the seeds obtained from tall plants, short plants grew from some of the seeds obtained from tall plants. Mendel wanted to find an explanation for such variations.

## Mendel's Methods

Mendel was able to observe how traits were passed from one generation to the next by carefully controlling how pea plants were pollinated. **Pollination** occurs when pollen grains produced in the male reproductive parts of a flower, called the *anthers*, are transferred to the female reproductive part of a flower, called the *stigma*.

**Self-pollination** occurs when pollen is transferred from the anthers of a flower to the stigma of either that flower or another flower on the same plant. **Cross-pollination** occurs between flowers of two plants. Pea plants normally reproduce through self-pollination.

Self-pollination can be prevented by removing all of the anthers from the flowers of a plant. Then, cross pollination can be performed by manually transferring pollen from the flower of a second plant to the stigma of the antherless plant, as Figure 9-2 shows. By preventing self pollination and manually cross-pollinating pea plants, Mendel selected parent plants that had specific traits and observed the traits that appeared in the offspring.

■ **internet** connect

**www.scilinks.org**
**Topic:** Gregor Mendel
**Keyword:** HM60698

*SCi*LINKS. Maintained by the National Science Teachers Association

# MENDEL'S EXPERIMENTS

Mendel initially studied each characteristic and its contrasting traits individually. He began by growing plants that were true-breeding for each trait. Plants that are **true-breeding,** or pure, for a trait always produce offspring with that trait when they self-pollinate. For example, pea plants that are true-breeding for the trait of yellow pods self-pollinate to produce offspring that have yellow pods. Mendel produced true-breeding plants by self-pollinating the pea plants for several generations, as Figure 9-3 shows. He eventually obtained 14 true-breeding plant types, one for each of the 14 traits observed.

Mendel cross-pollinated pairs of plants that were true-breeding for contrasting traits of a single characteristic. He called the true-breeding parents the **P generation.** He cross-pollinated by transferring pollen from the anthers of one plant to the stigma of another plant. For example, if he wanted to cross a plant that was true-breeding for the trait of yellow pods with one that was true-breeding for the trait of green pods, he first removed the anthers from the plant that produced green pods. Then, he dusted the pollen from a yellow-podded plant onto the stigma of a green-podded plant and allowed the seeds to develop.

When the plants matured, Mendel recorded the number of each type of offspring produced by each cross. He called the offspring of the P generation the first filial generation, or **F₁ generation.** He then allowed the flowers from the $F_1$ generation to self-pollinate and collected the seeds. Mendel called the plants in this generation the second filial generation, or **F₂ generation.** Following this process, Mendel performed hundreds of crosses and documented the results of each by counting and recording the observed traits of every cross. Table 9-1 summarizes the results of many of Mendel's crosses.

**FIGURE 9-3**

Mendel bred plants for several generations that were true breeding for specific traits. These plants he called the P generation. He then observed the passage of these specific traits through successive generations.

**THREE STEPS OF MENDEL'S EXPERIMENTS**

① **Producing a true-breeding P generation**

② **Producing an F₁ generation**

③ **Producing an F₂ generation**

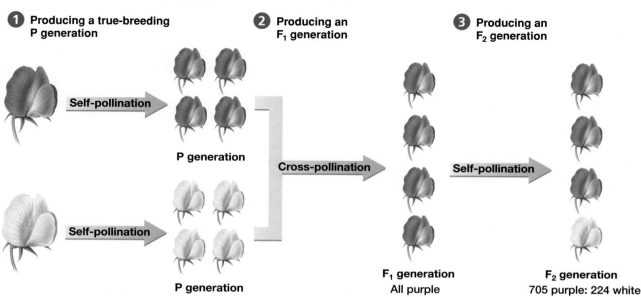

Self-pollination

P generation

Self-pollination

P generation

Cross-pollination

Self-pollination

F₁ generation
All purple

F₂ generation
705 purple: 224 white

TABLE 9-1 *Mendel's Crosses and Results*

| Characteristic | P generation | F₁ generation | F₂ generation | Observed ratio | Predicted ratio |
|---|---|---|---|---|---|
| Position of flowers along stem | axial × terminal | all axial | 651 axial 207 terminal | 3.14:1 | 3:1 |
| Height of plant | tall × short | all tall | 787 tall 277 short | 2.84:1 | 3:1 |
| Pod appearance | inflated × constricted | all inflated | 882 inflated 299 constricted | 2.95:1 | 3:1 |
| Pod color | green × yellow | all green | 428 green 152 yellow | 2.82:1 | 3:1 |
| Seed texture | round × wrinkled | all round | 5,474 round 1,850 wrinkled | 2.96:1 | 3:1 |
| Seed color | yellow × green | all yellow | 6,022 yellow 2,001 green | 3.01:1 | 3:1 |
| Flower color | purple × white | all purple | 705 purple 224 white | 3.15:1 | 3:1 |

# MENDEL'S RESULTS AND CONCLUSIONS

In one of his experiments, Mendel crossed a plant true-breeding for green pods with one true-breeding for yellow pods, as shown in Figure 9-4. The resulting seeds produced an $F_1$ generation that had only green-podded plants. No yellow pods developed even though one parent had been true-breeding for yellow pods. Only one of the two traits found in the P generation appeared in the $F_1$ generation.

Next, Mendel allowed the $F_1$ plants to self-pollinate and planted the resulting seeds. When the $F_2$ generation plants grew, he observed that about three-fourths of the $F_2$ plants had green pods and about one-fourth had yellow pods.

His observations and careful records led Mendel to hypothesize that something within the pea plants controlled the characteristics observed. He called these controls *factors*. Mendel hypothesized that each trait was inherited by means of a separate factor. Because the characteristics studied had two alternative forms, he reasoned that a *pair* of factors must control each trait.

## Recessive and Dominant Traits

Whenever Mendel crossed strains, one of the P traits failed to appear in the $F_1$ plants. In every case, that trait reappeared in a ratio of about 3:1 in the $F_2$ generation. This pattern emerged in thousands of crosses and led Mendel to conclude that one factor in a pair may prevent the other from having an effect. Mendel hypothesized that the trait appearing in the $F_1$ generation was controlled by a **dominant** factor because it masked, or dominated, the factor for the other trait in the pair. He thought that the trait that did not appear in the $F_1$ generation but reappeared in the $F_2$ generation was controlled by a **recessive** factor.

Thus, a trait controlled by a recessive factor had no observable effect on an organism's appearance when that trait was paired with a trait controlled by a dominant factor.

## The Law of Segregation

Mendel concluded that the paired factors separate during the formation of reproductive cells. That is, each reproductive cell, or gamete, receives one factor of each pair. When two gametes combine during fertilization, the offspring have two factors for each characteristic. The **law of segregation** states that a pair of factors is segregated, or separated, during the formation of gametes.

## The Law of Independent Assortment

Mendel also crossed plants that differed in two characteristics, such as flower color and seed color. The data from these more-complex crosses showed that traits produced by dominant factors do not necessarily appear together. A green seed pod produced by a dominant factor could appear in a white-flowering pea plant.

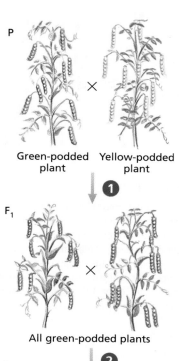

P

Green-podded plant    Yellow-podded plant

❶

$F_1$

All green-podded plants

❷

$F_2$

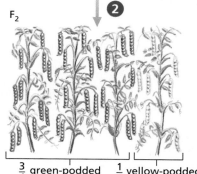

$\frac{3}{4}$ green-podded plants    $\frac{1}{4}$ yellow-podded plants

**FIGURE 9-4**

❶ True-breeding green-podded pea plants crossed with true-breeding yellow-podded pea plants produce only green-podded plants. ❷ Yet when the $F_1$ generation is permitted to self-pollinate, about one-fourth of the plants of the $F_2$ generation are yellow-podded plants.

## Word Roots and Origins

**recessive**

from the Latin *recessus*, meaning "to recede"

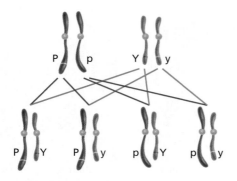

**FIGURE 9-5**

Independent assortment of these two pairs of homologous chromosomes (Pp and Yy) would result in gametes that contain the allele combinations shown above. *P* denotes the dominant purple flower color, and *p* denotes the recessive white flower color. *Y* denotes yellow seed color, and *y* denotes green seed color.

Mendel concluded that the factors for individual characteristics are not connected. Recall that the random separation of homologous chromosomes is called *independent assortment.* The **law of independent assortment** states that factors separate independently of one another during the formation of gametes.

# SUPPORT FOR MENDEL'S CONCLUSIONS

Most of Mendel's findings agree with what biologists now know about molecular genetics. **Molecular genetics** is the study of the structure and function of chromosomes and genes. A chromosome is a threadlike structure made up of DNA. A gene is the segment of DNA on a chromosome that controls a particular hereditary trait. Because chromosomes occur in pairs, genes also occur in pairs. Each of two or more alternative forms of a gene is called an **allele.** Mendel's *factors* are now called *alleles.*

Letters are used to represent alleles. Capital letters refer to dominant alleles, and lowercase letters refer to recessive alleles. For example, the dominant allele for the trait of purple flower color may be represented by *P,* and the recessive allele for the trait of white flower color may be represented by *p,* as is shown in Figure 9-5. Whether a letter is capitalized or lowercased is important. The actual letter selected to represent an allele is typically the first letter of the dominant trait. During meiosis, gametes receive one chromosome from each homologous pair of chromosomes. Thus, when the gametes combine in fertilization, the offspring receives from each parent one allele for a given trait.

Mendel's law of independent assortment is supported by the independent segregation of chromosomes to gametes during meiosis. Therefore, the law of independent assortment is observed only for genes located on separate chromosomes or located far apart on the same chromosome.

---

## SECTION 1 REVIEW

1. Describe what a *true-breeding* plant is.

2. Outline how Mendel produced plants that had genes for both contrasting traits of a characteristic.

3. Define the terms *dominant* and *recessive*.

4. State in modern terminology the two laws of heredity that resulted from Mendel's work.

5. Differentiate genes from alleles.

**CRITICAL THINKING**

6. **Evaluating Results** How did Mendel's F₁ generation plants differ from his F₂ generation plants?

7. **Recognizing Relationships** Many inherited disorders of humans appear in children of parents who do not have the disorder. How can you explain this?

8. **Applying Information** During meiosis, what allows genes located on the same chromosome to separate independently of one another?

# Science in Action

## Do Genes Jump?

The rediscovery of Mendel's work in 1900 is said to mark the birth of the science of genetics. Barbara McClintock, born in 1902, devoted her life to this new science. Ironically, certain assumptions about genetics—which were strongly believed but wrong—prevented early acceptance of McClintock's exciting conclusions.

**Barbara McClintock**

### HYPOTHESIS: Genes Can Move

The prevailing opinion among most geneticists in Barbara McClintock's time was that genes were lined up on chromosomes in an unchanging way, much like beads on a string. However, observations from her experiments with maize (*Zea mays*) told McClintock otherwise.

As a graduate student at Cornell, McClintock developed new staining techniques and discovered that each of the 10 maize chromosomes could be distinguished under the microscope. She noted that some changes in the appearance of the corn kernels and plants were coupled with changes in the shape of one or more of the maize chromosomes. She also noted that kernels that had been exposed to X rays germinated and grew into seemingly normal plants but that the shapes of some of their chromosomes had changed. She proposed that the maize genome had a dynamic chromosome repair system that allowed for growth even after major chromosome damage that X rays had caused. Geneticists at the time assumed that a mutated gene was dead and could not be reactivated. McClintock's findings, however, challenged this belief.

### METHODS: Analyze Maize Chromosomes

McClintock wanted to examine more closely the results of growing maize that contained broken chromosomes. So during the winter of 1944–1945, she planted self-pollinated kernels that were the product of many generations of inbreeding and self-fertilization. She hoped to track chromosome repairs by observing changes in chromosome shapes.

### RESULTS: Unexpected Changes

When the plants germinated, McClintock was astounded at the results. The leaves had odd patches that lacked the normal green coloration. These patches occurred regularly along the leaf blades. She compared chromosomes of these plants with those of the parent plants under the microscope and concluded that parts of the offspring plants' chromosomes had changed position.

### CONCLUSION: Genes Have the Ability to "Jump"

The changes that McClintock saw in these plants and their chromosomes led her to conclude that genes are not stable within the chromosome but can move to a new place on a chromosome or to a new chromosome entirely. McClintock called these movable genes *controlling elements*. They were later called *transposons*.

McClintock observed two kinds of transposons: dissociators and activators. Dissociators could jump to a new chromosomal location when signaled by activators. The dissociators would then cause changes in nearby genes on the chromosome and in the color of the kernels and leaves in the maize. McClintock verified her conclusions through repeated experiments.

McClintock summarized her findings in 1951 at a Cold Spring Harbor symposium, but her work was not well received. After many years, recognition of the value of her work grew and she was awarded the Nobel Prize in medicine or physiology in 1983.

*The colorful maize plant* Zea mays *was harvested at Cornell University during the late 1920s and early 1930s to study its genetics. The varied colors of its kernels worked as a multicolored spreadsheet of genetic data.*

### REVIEW

1. What was the purpose of exposing the maize kernels to X rays?

2. What is a transposon?

3. **Critical Thinking** Why was it important that McClintock used self-fertilized kernels in her experiments?

- **Differentiate** between the genotype and the phenotype of an organism.
- **Explain** how probability is used to predict the results of genetic crosses.
- **Use** a Punnett square to predict the results of monohybrid and dihybrid genetic crosses.
- **Explain** how a testcross is used to show the genotype of an individual whose phenotype expresses the dominant trait.
- **Differentiate** a monohybrid cross from a dihybrid cross.

### VOCABULARY

genotype
phenotype
homozygous
heterozygous
probability
monohybrid cross
Punnett square
genotypic ratio
phenotypic ratio
testcross
complete dominance
incomplete dominance
codominance
dihybrid cross

# GENETIC CROSSES

*T*oday, geneticists rely on Mendel's work to predict the likely outcome of genetic crosses. In this section, you will learn how to predict the probable genetic makeup and appearance of offspring resulting from specified crosses.

## GENOTYPE AND PHENOTYPE

An organism's genetic makeup is its **genotype** (JEEN-uh-TIEP). The genotype consists of the alleles that the organism inherits from its parents. For example, the genotype of the white-flowering pea plant in Figure 9-6 consists of two recessive alleles for white flower color, represented as *pp*. The genotype of a purple-flowering pea plant may be either *PP* or *Pp*. Either of these two genotypes would result in a pea plant that has purple flowers because the P allele is dominant.

An organism's appearance is its **phenotype** (FEE-noh-TIEP). The phenotype of a *PP* or a *Pp* pea plant is purple flowers, whereas the phenotype of a *pp* pea plant is white flowers. As this example shows, a phenotype does not always indicate genotype. In addition to recessive alleles, certain environmental factors can affect phenotype. For example, lack of proper nutrition can cause a genetically tall plant to remain short.

**FIGURE 9-6**

The flower color genotype of the pea plant on the left is *pp*. The plant's phenotype is white flowers. The flower color phenotype of the pea plant on the right is purple flowers. The plant's genotype is either *Pp* or *PP*.

When both alleles of a pair are alike, the organism is said to be **homozygous** (HOH-moh-ZIE-guhs) for that characteristic. An organism may be homozygous dominant or homozygous recessive. For example, a pea plant that is homozygous dominant for flower color has the genotype *PP*. A pea plant that is homozygous recessive for flower color has the genotype *pp*. When the two alleles in the pair are different, the organism is **heterozygous** (HET-uhr-OH-ZIE-guhs) for that characteristic. A pea plant that is heterozygous for flower color has the genotype *Pp*.

# PROBABILITY

**Probability** is the likelihood that a specific event will occur. A probability may be expressed as a decimal, a percentage, or a fraction. Probability is determined by the following equation:

$$\text{Probability} = \frac{\text{number of times an event is expected to happen}}{\text{number of times an event could happen}}$$

For example, in Mendel's experiments, the dominant trait of yellow seed color appeared in the $F_2$ generation 6,022 times. The recessive trait of green seed color appeared 2,001 times. The total number of individuals was 8,023 (6,022 + 2,001). Using the probability equation above we can determine that the probability that the dominant trait will appear in a similar cross is

$$\frac{6,022}{8,023} = 0.75$$

Expressed as a percentage, the probability is 75 percent. Expressed as a fraction, the probability is 3/4.

The probability that the recessive trait will appear in an $F_2$ generation is

$$\frac{2,001}{8,023} = 0.25$$

Expressed as a percentage, the probability is 25 percent. Expressed as a fraction, the probability is 1/4. Fractions can also be expressed as ratios. For example, the ratio 1:3 represents the same probability that 1/4 does. Probability tells us that there are three chances in four that an offspring of two heterozygous individuals will have the dominant trait and one chance in four that the offspring will have only the recessive trait.

The results predicted by probability are more likely to occur when there are many trials. For example, many coin tosses should yield a result of heads 50 percent of the time and tails 50 percent of the time. However, if you toss a coin only a few times, you might not get this result. But *each* time a coin is tossed, the probability of landing tails is 50 percent. Only after many, many tries would you be *likely* to get the percentage of heads predicted on the basis of probability, that is, 50 percent heads and 50 percent tails.

## Quick Lab

### Calculating Probability

**Materials** paper sack containing 20 jelly beans of three different colors (with an unknown number of each color)

**Procedure**

1. Obtain a sack of 20 jelly beans from your teacher. Do not look into the sack. Do not eat the jelly beans. There are three possible colors of jelly beans that can be pulled from the sack. Pull one jelly bean out, and record the color. Return the jelly bean to the sack, and shake the bag to mix the jelly beans.

2. Repeat step 1 until you have examined 20 jelly beans.

3. Determine the probability of getting a jelly bean of a specific color with a single draw. Do this for each of the three colors of jelly beans. Compare your results with those of the rest of the class.

**Analysis** Does anyone have the same probabilities that you do? Are any probabilities very close to yours? Are any probabilities very different from yours? From these observations, determine how many jelly beans of each color are in your sack.

**(pp)**

**(PP)**

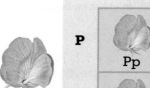

**FIGURE 9-7**

A pea plant homozygous for purple flowers that is crossed with a pea plant homozygous for white flowers will produce only purple-flowering offspring. Note that all of the offspring, called *monohybrids,* are heterozygous for flower color.

**FIGURE 9-8**

Crossing a guinea pig homozygous for black coat color with one heterozygous for black coat color produces all black-coated monohybrid offspring. Note that half of the monohybrid offspring are predicted to be homozygous for coat color.

**(Bb)**

**(BB)**

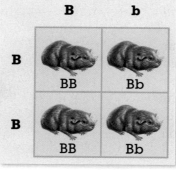

# PREDICTING RESULTS OF MONOHYBRID CROSSES

A cross in which only one characteristic is tracked is a **monohybrid** (MAHN-oh-HIE-brid) **cross.** The offspring of a monohybrid cross are called *monohybrids*. A cross between a pea plant that is true-breeding for producing purple flowers and one that is true-breeding for producing white flowers is an example of a monohybrid cross. Biologists use a diagram called a **Punnett** (PUHN-uht) **square,** such as the one shown in Figure 9-7, to aid them in predicting the probable distribution of inherited traits in the offspring. The following examples show how a Punnett square can be used to predict the outcome of different types of crosses.

## Example 1: Homozygous × Homozygous

Figure 9-7 shows a cross between a pea plant homozygous for purple flower color (*PP*) and a pea plant homozygous for white flower color (*pp*). The alleles carried in gametes of the homozygous dominant parent are represented by *P*'s on the left side of the Punnett square. The alleles carried in gametes of the homozygous recessive parent are represented by *p*'s across the top of the Punnett square. Each box within the Punnett square is filled in with the letters, or alleles, that are above it and at left of it outside the square. The combinations of alleles in the four boxes indicate the possible genotypes that can result from the cross. The predicted genotype is *Pp* in every case. Thus, there is a 100 percent probability that the offspring will have the genotype *Pp* and thus the phenotype purple flower color.

## Example 2: Homozygous × Heterozygous

Figure 9-8 shows a cross between a guinea pig that is homozygous dominant for the trait of black coat color (*BB*) and a guinea pig that is heterozygous for this trait (*Bb*). The letter *b* stands for the recessive allele. Genotype *bb* results in a brown coat. Notice that two possible genotypes can result from this cross: *BB* or *Bb*. The probability of an offspring having the genotype *BB* is 2/4, or 50 percent. The probability of an offspring having the genotype *Bb* is also 2/4, or 50 percent. You could expect about 50 percent of the offspring resulting from this cross to be homozygous dominant for the black coat and about 50 percent to be heterozygous dominant for a black coat. The probable phenotype is black coat color in every case; thus, 4/4, or 100 percent, of the offspring are expected to have a black coat. What would happen if the homozygous guinea pig were homozygous recessive for coat color? The homozygote would have the genotype *bb*. Crossing a *bb* guinea pig with a *Bb* guinea pig is likely to produce about 50 percent *Bb* offspring and about 50 percent *bb* offspring.

**(Bb)**

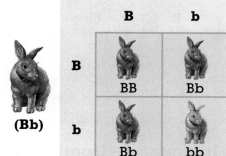

**(Bb)**

|   | **B** | **b** |
|---|-------|-------|
| **B** | BB | Bb |
| **b** | Bb | bb |

**FIGURE 9-9**

The probable results of crossing two rabbits that are heterozygous for black coat color are 50 percent heterozygous black individuals, 25 percent homozygous black individuals, and 25 percent homozygous brown individuals.

## Example 3: Heterozygous × Heterozygous

In rabbits, the allele for black coat color (*B*) is dominant over the allele for brown coat color (*b*). The Punnett square in Figure 9-9 shows the predicted results of crossing two rabbits that are heterozygous (*Bb*) for coat color. As you can see, 1/4 (25 percent) of the offspring are predicted to have the genotype *BB*, 1/2 (50 percent) are predicted to have the genotype *Bb*, and 1/4 (25 percent) are predicted to have the genotype *bb*. Thus, 3/4 (75 percent) of the offspring resulting from this cross are predicted to have a black coat. One-fourth (25 percent) of the offspring are predicted to have a brown coat.

The ratio of the genotypes that appear in offspring is called the **genotypic ratio.** The probable genotypic ratio of the monohybrid cross represented in Figure 9-9 is 1 *BB* : 2 *Bb* : 1 *bb*. The ratio of the offspring's phenotypes is called the **phenotypic ratio.** The probable phenotypic ratio of the cross represented in Figure 9-9 is 3 black : 1 brown.

## Example 4: Testcross

Recall that in guinea pigs, both *BB* and *Bb* result in a black coat. How might you determine whether a black guinea pig is homozygous (*BB*) or heterozygous (*Bb*)? You could perform a **testcross,** in which an individual of unknown genotype is crossed with a homozygous recessive individual. A testcross can determine the genotype of any individual whose phenotype expresses the dominant trait. You can see from Figure 9-10 that if the black guinea pig of unknown genotype is homozygous black, all offspring will be black. If the individual with the unknown genotype is heterozygous black, about half of the offspring will be black. In reality, if the cross produced any brown offspring, the genotype of the black-coated parent is likely to be heterozygous.

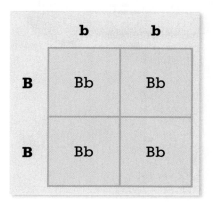

|   | **b** | **b** |
|---|-------|-------|
| **B** | Bb | Bb |
| **B** | Bb | Bb |

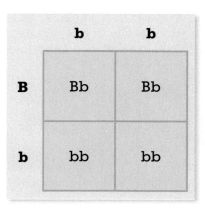

|   | **b** | **b** |
|---|-------|-------|
| **B** | Bb | Bb |
| **b** | bb | bb |

**FIGURE 9-10**

If a black guinea pig is crossed with a brown guinea pig and even one of the offspring is brown, the black guinea pig is heterozygous for coat color.

**FIGURE 9-11**

When red-flowering four o'clocks are crossed with white-flowering four o'clocks, all of the $F_1$ offspring produce pink flowers, an intermediate between the two parental phenotypes. When the $F_1$ generation is interbred, red-flowering, pink-flowering, and white-flowering plants are produced because the trait for red flower color has incomplete dominance over the trait for white flower color.

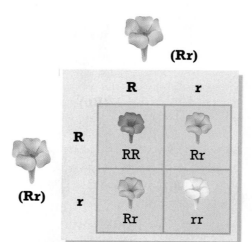

internet connect

www.scilinks.org
Topic: Dominance
Keyword: HM60422

SCiLINKS. Maintained by the National Science Teachers Association

## Example 5: Incomplete Dominance

Recall that in Mendel's pea-plant crosses, one allele was completely dominant over another, a relationship called **complete dominance.** In complete dominance, heterozygous plants and homozygous dominant plants are indistinguishable in phenotype. For example, both pea plants *PP* and *Pp* for flower color have purple flowers.

Sometimes, however, the $F_1$ offspring will have a phenotype in between that of the parents, a relationship called **incomplete dominance.** Incomplete dominance occurs when the phenotype of a heterozygote is intermediate between the phenotypes determined by the dominant and recessive traits. In four o'clocks, for example, both the allele for red flowers (*R*) and the allele for white flowers (*r*) influence the phenotype. Neither allele is completely dominant over the other allele. When four o'clocks self-pollinate, red-flowering plants produce only red-flowering offspring and white-flowering plants produce only white-flowering offspring. However, when red four o'clocks are crossed with white four o'clocks, all of the $F_1$ offspring have *pink* flowers. One hundred percent of the offspring of this cross have the *Rr* genotype, which results in a pink phenotype.

What would be the result of crossing two pink-flowering (*Rr*) four o'clocks? As the Punnett square in Figure 9-11 shows, the probable genotypic ratio is 1 *RR* : 2 *Rr* : 1 *rr*. Given that neither the allele for red flowers (*R*) nor the allele for white flowers (*r*) is completely dominant, the probable phenotypic ratio is 1 red : 2 pink : 1 white.

## Example 6: Codominance

**Codominance** occurs when both alleles for a gene are expressed in a heterozygous offspring. In codominance, neither allele is dominant or recessive, nor do the alleles blend in the phenotype.

For example, the three human MN blood types, M, N, and MN, are determned by two alleles, $L^M$, and $L^N$. The letters M and N refer to two molecules on the surface of the red blood cell. The genotype of a person with blood type MN is $L^M L^N$, and neither allele is dominant over the other. Type MN blood cells cary both M- and N-types of molecules on their surface.

# PREDICTING RESULTS OF DIHYBRID CROSSES

A **dihybrid** (die-HIE-brid) **cross** is a cross in which two characteristics are tracked. The offspring of a dihybrid cross are called *dihybrids.* Predicting the results of a dihybrid cross is more complicated than predicting the results of a monohybrid cross because more combinations of alleles are possible. For example, to predict the results of a cross in which both seed texture and seed color are tracked, you have to consider how four alleles from each parent can combine.

## Homozygous × Homozygous

Suppose that you want to predict the results of a cross between a pea plant that is homozygous for round, yellow seeds and one that is homozygous for wrinkled, green seeds. In pea plants, the allele for round seeds (*R*) is dominant over the allele for wrinkled seeds (*r*), and the allele for yellow seeds (*Y*) is dominant over the allele for green seeds (*y*).

As Figure 9-12 shows, the Punnett square used to predict the results of a cross between a parent of the genotype *RRYY* and a parent of the genotype *rryy* will contain 16 boxes. Alleles are carried by the male and female gametes (pollen and ovule). The independently sorted alleles from one parent—*RY, RY, RY,* and *RY*—are listed along the left side of the Punnett square. The independently sorted alleles from the other parent—*ry, ry, ry,* and *ry*—are listed along the top of the Punnett square. Each box is filled with the letters that are above it and to the left of it outside the square. Notice that the genotype of all of the offspring of this cross will be heterozygous for both traits (*RrYy*); therefore, all of the offspring will have round, yellow seed phenotypes.

### Quick Lab

**Determining Genotypes**

**Materials** pencil and paper

**Procedure** The ability to roll the tongue upward from the sides is a dominant, inherited trait. In one family, both parents and three children are tongue rollers, while one child is not. Determine the genotype and phenotype of each parent.

**Analysis** Are the parents homozygous or heterozygous? Are the children homozygous or heterozygous?

rryy

RRYY

| | ry | ry | ry | ry |
|---|---|---|---|---|
| RY | RrYy | RrYy | RrYy | RrYy |
| RY | RrYy | RrYy | RrYy | RrYy |
| RY | RrYy | RrYy | RrYy | RrYy |
| RY | RrYy | RrYy | RrYy | RrYy |

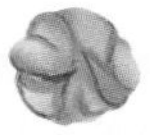

**FIGURE 9-12**

This Punnett square shows a dihybrid cross between a pea plant that is homozygous recessive for wrinkled, green seeds (*rryy*) and a pea plant that is homozygous dominant for round, yellow seeds (*RRYY*).

## Heterozygous × Heterozygous

The same procedure is used to determine the results of crossing two pea plants heterozygous for round, yellow seeds. As Figure 9-13 shows, the offspring of this dihybrid cross are likely to have nine different genotypes. These nine genotypes will result in pea plants that have the following four phenotypes:

- 9/16 that have round, yellow seeds (genotypes *RRYY, RRYy, RrYY,* and *RrYy*)
- 3/16 that have round, green seeds (genotypes *RRyy* and *Rryy*)
- 3/16 that have wrinkled, yellow seeds (genotypes *rrYY* and *rrYy*)
- 1/16 that have wrinkled, green seeds (genotype *rryy*)

**FIGURE 9-13**

A dihybrid cross of two individuals heterozygous for both traits of interest is likely to result in nine different genotypes and four different phenotypes.

**RrYy**

**RrYy**

|  | **RY** | **Ry** | **rY** | **ry** |
|---|---|---|---|---|
| **RY** | RRYY | RRYy | RrYY | RrYy |
| **Ry** | RRYy | RRyy | RrYy | Rryy |
| **rY** | RrYY | RrYy | rrYY | rrYy |
| **ry** | RrYy | Rryy | rrYy | rryy |

## SECTION 2 REVIEW

1. Explain why a phenotype might not always indicate genotype.

2. Identify the equation used to determine probability.

3. Explain how you might go about determining the genotype of a purple-flowering plant.

4. Illustrate in the form of a Punnett square the results of crossing a pink-flowering four o'clock with a white-flowering four o'clock.

5. Explain the difference between a monohybrid cross and a dihybrid cross and give an example of each.

**CRITICAL THINKING**

6. **Analyzing Concepts** The offspring of two short-tailed cats have a 25 percent chance of having no tail, a 25 percent chance of having a long tail, and a 50 percent chance of having a short tail. Using this information, what can you hypothesize about the genotypes of the parents and the way in which tail length is inherited?

7. **Inferring Relationships** If you crossed two purple-flowering pea plants and all of the F₁ offspring were purple-flowering, what could you say about the genotypes of the parents? If some of the F₁ offspring were white-flowering, what could you say about the genotypes of the parents?

# CHAPTER HIGHLIGHTS

## SECTION 1 — Mendel's Legacy

- The study of how characteristics are transmitted from parents to offspring is called *genetics*.

- Mendel observed seven characteristics of pea plants. Each characteristic occurred in two contrasting traits.

- Self-pollination, in which pollen is transferred from the anthers of a flower to either the stigma of the same flower or the stigma of another flower on the same plant, normally occurs in pea plants. Cross-pollination occurs when pollen is transferred between flowers of two different plants.

- Mendel concluded that inherited characteristics are controlled by factors that occur in pairs. In his experiments on pea plants, one factor in a pair masked the other. The trait that masked the other was called the *dominant trait*. The trait that was masked was called the *recessive trait*.

- The law of segregation states that a pair of factors is segregated, or separated, during the formation of gametes. Two factors for a characteristic are then combined when fertilization occurs and a new offspring is produced.

- The law of independent assortment states that factors for individual characteristics are distributed to gametes independently. The law of independent assortment is observed only for genes that are located on separate chromosomes or are far apart on the same chromosome.

- We now know that the factors that Mendel studied are alleles, or alternative forms of a gene. Each of two or more alternative forms of a gene is called an *allele.* One allele for each trait is passed from each parent to the offspring.

### Vocabulary

genetics (p. 173)
heredity (p. 173)
trait (p. 173)
pollination (p. 174)
self-pollination (p. 174)

cross-pollination (p. 174)
true-breeding (p. 175)
P generation (p. 175)
$F_1$ generation (p. 175)
$F_2$ generation (p. 175)

dominant (p. 177)
recessive (p. 177)
law of segregation (p. 177)
law of independent
  assortment (p. 178)

molecular genetics (p. 178)
allele (p. 178)

## SECTION 2 — Genetic Crosses

- The genotype is the genetic makeup of an organism. The phenotype is the appearance of an organism.

- Probability is the likelihood that a specific event will occur. A probability may be expressed as a decimal, a percentage, or a fraction.

- A Punnett square can be used to predict the outcome of genetic crosses.

- A cross in which one characteristic is tracked is a monohybrid cross. The offspring of a monohybrid cross are called *monohybrids.*

- A testcross, in which an individual of unknown genotype is crossed with a homozygous recessive individual, can be used to determine the genotype of an individual whose phenotype expresses the dominant trait.

- Complete dominance occurs when heterozygous individuals and dominant homozygous individuals are indistinguishable in phenotype.

- Incomplete dominance occurs when two or more alleles influence the phenotype and results in a phenotype intermediate between the dominant trait and the recessive trait.

- Codominance occurs when both alleles for a gene are expressed in a heterozygous offspring. Neither allele is dominant or recessive, nor do the alleles blend in the phenotype as they do in incomplete dominance.

- A cross in which two characteristics are tracked is a dihybrid cross. The offspring of a dihybrid cross are called *dihybrids.*

### Vocabulary

genotype (p. 180)
phenotype (p. 180)
homozygous (p. 181)
heterozygous (p.181)

probability (p. 181)
monohybrid cross (p. 182)
Punnett square (p. 182)
genotypic ratio (p. 183)

phenotypic ratio (p. 183)
testcross (p. 183)
complete dominance
  (p. 184)

incomplete dominance
  (p. 184)
codominance (p. 184)
dihybrid cross (p. 185)

# CHAPTER REVIEW

## USING VOCABULARY

1. For each pair of terms, explain how the meanings of the terms differ.
   a. *homozygous* and *heterozygous*
   b. *law of segregation* and *law of independent assortment*
   c. *genetics* and *heredity*

2. Use the following terms in the same sentence: *pollination, self-pollination,* and *cross-pollination.*

3. For each pair of terms, explain the relationship between the terms.
   a. *genotype* and *phenotype*
   b. *monohybrid cross* and *dihybrid cross*
   c. *allele* and *trait*

4. **Word Roots and Origins** The word *dominant* comes from the Latin *dominari,* which means "to rule." Using this information, explain why the term *dominant* is a good name for the genetic phenomenon that the term describes.

## UNDERSTANDING KEY CONCEPTS

5. **Relate** why Mendel began his experiments by allowing pea plants to self-pollinate for several generations.

6. **Explain** the difference between dominant and recessive traits.

7. **Describe** the differences between the P generation, the $F_1$ generation, and the $F_2$ generation.

8. **Relate** why it is not necessary, when the dominant and recessive traits are known, to use the term *homozygous* when referring to the genotype of an individual that has a recessive phenotype.

9. **State** the difference between a monohybrid cross and a dihybrid cross.

10. **Propose** how crossing-over during meiosis might affect the segregation of genes that are on the same chromosome.

11. **Relate** the events of meiosis to the law of segregation.

12. **Summarize** how a gardener who has a pea plant that produces round seeds can determine whether the plant is homozygous or heterozygous for the allele that determines seed texture. (In pea plants, round seed texture is dominant over wrinkled seed texture.)

13. **Relate** probability to the study of genetics.

14. **Predict** the results of a cross between a rabbit homozygous dominant for black coat color (*BB*) and a rabbit homozygous recessive for brown coat color (*bb*).

15. **CONCEPT MAPPING** Use the following terms to create a concept map that illustrates information related to Mendel's experiments: *pea plants, heredity, self-pollination, cross-pollination, $F_1$ generation, $F_2$ generation, trait,* and *true-breeding.*

## CRITICAL THINKING

16. **Interpreting Graphics** Use the Punnett square below to answer the questions that follow.
    a. Does the Punnett square demonstrate a monohybrid cross or a dihybrid cross?
    b. List the genotypes of the parents.
    c. Give the genotypic ratio predicted by the Punnett square for the cross.

|      | QT   | Qt   | qT   | qt   |
|------|------|------|------|------|
| **QT** | QQTT | QQTt | QqTT | QqTt |
| **Qt** | QQTt | QQtt | QqTt | Qqtt |
| **qT** | QqTT | QqTt | qqTT | qqTt |
| **qt** | QqTt | Qqtt | qqTt | qqtt |

17. **Predicting Results** In rabbits, the allele for black coat color (*B*) is dominant over the allele for brown coat color (*b*). Predict the results of a cross between a rabbit homozygous for black coat color (*BB*) and a rabbit homozygous for brown coat color (*bb*).

18. **Applying Information** Write a report summarizing how an understanding of heredity allows animal breeders to develop animals that have desirable traits. Find out what kinds of animals are bred for special purposes.

# Standardized Test Preparation

**DIRECTIONS:** Choose the letter of the answer choice that best answers the question.

1. What is a procedure in which an individual of unknown genotype is crossed with a homozygous recessive individual to determine the genotype of the unknown individual called?
   A. a monohybrid cross
   B. a dihybrid cross
   C. a hybrid cross
   D. a testcross

2. In a monohybrid cross of two heterozygous parents (*Pp*), what would the expected genotypes of the offspring be?
   F. 1 *PP* : 2 *Pp* : 1 *pp*
   G. 1 *pp* : 3 *PP*
   H. 3 *Pp* : 1 *pp*
   J. all *Pp*

3. Which of the following is an example of a genotype of a heterozygous individual?
   A. *p*
   B. *YY*
   C. *Zz*
   D. *rr*

**INTERPRETING GRAPHICS:** Use the diagrams of chromosomes below to answer the question that follows. The single chromosome below has two genes, both of which carry a dominant allele *Q* and *R*.

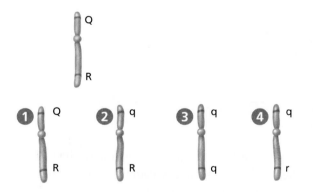

4. Homologous chromosomes are chromosomes that carry genes for the same characteristics, such as eye color or hair color. Which of the chromosomes in the bottom row could not be the homologous chromosome for the single chromosome in the top row?
   F. 1
   G. 2
   H. 3
   J. 4

**DIRECTIONS:** Complete the analogy below:

5. *Rr* : genotype :: red :
   A. F$_1$ generation
   B. heterozygote
   C. phenotype
   D. dominant

**INTERPRETING GRAPHICS:** Use the diagram of a Punnett square below to answer the question that follows.

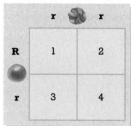

The Punnett square above shows the expected results of a cross between two pea plants. *R* and *r* represent the alleles for round seed and wrinkled seed traits, respectively.

6. What would the seed texture phenotype of the plant in box 4 be?
   F. round
   G. *Rr*
   H. wrinkled
   J. *rr*

## SHORT RESPONSE

Mendel was able to observe certain traits as they were passed on by carefully controlling how the pea plants were pollinated. Explain why Mendel began his experiments by allowing pea plants to self-pollinate for several generations.

## EXTENDED RESPONSE

A cross between two pea plants that have axial flowers and inflated pods gives the following offspring: 20 that have axial flowers and inflated pods, 7 with axial flowers and constricted pods, and 5 that have terminal flowers and inflated pods.

*Part A* Identify the most probable genotype of the two parents.

*Part B* Use a Punnett square to explain the results.

**Test TIP** Before answering word problems that are genetics questions, write the problem down by using letters to symbolize genotypes.

# Modeling Monohybrid Crosses

## OBJECTIVES

- Predict the genotypic and phenotypic ratios of offspring resulting from the random pairing of gametes.
- Calculate the genotypic ratio and phenotypic ratio among the offspring of a monohybrid cross.

## PROCESS SKILLS

- predicting
- organizing
- analyzing data
- calculating

## MATERIALS

- lentils
- green peas
- 2 Petri dishes

## Background

1. How many traits are involved in a monohybrid cross? How many alleles are involved?
2. What prevents the expression of a recessive allele?
3. When gametes form, what happens to the alleles for each trait?

## PART A Simulating a Monohybrid Cross

1. You will model the random pairing of alleles by choosing lentils and peas from Petri dishes. These dried seeds will represent the alleles for seed color. A green pea will represent *G*, the dominant allele for green seeds, and a lentil will represent *g*, the recessive allele for yellow seeds.
2. The seeds in each Petri dish will represent the alleles from a single parent. Label one Petri dish "female gametes" and the other Petri dish "male gametes." Place one green pea and one lentil in the Petri dish labeled "female gametes," and place one green pea and one lentil in the Petri dish labeled "male gametes."

3. Each parent contributes one allele to each offspring. Model a cross between these two parents by choosing a random pairing of the dried seeds from the two containers. Do so by simultaneously picking one seed from each container *without looking*. Place the pair of seeds together on the lab table. The pair of seeds represents the genotype of one offspring.
4. Record the genotype of the first offspring in your lab report in a table like Table A, shown below.

### TABLE A *GAMETE PAIRINGS*

| Trial | Offspring genotype | Offspring phenotype |
|-------|--------------------|--------------------|
| 1 | | |
| 2 | | |
| 3 | | |
| 4 | | |
| 5 | | |
| 6 | | |
| 7 | | |
| 8 | | |
| 9 | | |
| 10 | | |

5. Return the seeds to their original dishes, and repeat step 3 nine more times. Record the genotype of each offspring in your data table.
6. Based on each offspring's genotype, determine and record each offspring's phenotype. Assume that the allele for green seeds, *G*, is completely dominant over the allele for yellow seeds, *g*.

## PART B  Calculating Genotypic and Phenotypic Ratios

7. In your lab report, prepare a data table similar to Table B, shown below.

8. Determine the genotypic and phenotypic ratios among the offspring. First, count and record the number of homozygous dominant, heterozygous, and homozygous recessive individuals recorded in Table A. Then, record the number of offspring that produce green seeds and the number that produce yellow seeds under "Phenotypes" in your data table.

9. Calculate the genotypic ratio for each genotype by using the following equation:

$$\text{Genotypic ratio} = \frac{\text{number of offspring with a given genotype}}{\text{total number of offspring}}$$

10. Calculate the phenotypic ratio for each phenotype by using the following equation:

$$\text{Phenotypic ratio} = \frac{\text{number of offspring with a given phenotype}}{\text{total number of offspring}}$$

11. Now, pool the data for the whole class, and record the data in your lab report in a table like Table C.

12. Compare your class's sample with your small sample of 10. Calculate and record in your data table the genotypic and phenotypic ratios for the class data.

13. Construct a Punnett square showing the parents and their offspring in your lab report.

14. Clean up your materials before leaving the lab.

## Analysis and Conclusions

1. What characteristic is being studied in this investigation?

2. What are the genotypes of the parents? Describe the genotypes of both parents by using the terms *homozygous*, *heterozygous*, or both.

3. What does each seed in the Petri dish represent?

4. When the seeds were selected and paired, what did the pairs represent?

5. Did Tables B and C reflect a classic monohybrid-cross phenotypic ratio of 3:1?

6. When the class data were tabulated, did a classic monohybrid-cross phenotypic ratio of 3:1 result?

7. If a genotypic ratio of 1:2:1 is observed, what must the genotypes of both parents be?

8. Show what the genotypes of the parents would be if 50 percent of the offspring were green and 50 percent of the offspring were yellow.

9. Construct a Punnett square for the cross of a heterozygous black guinea pig and an unknown guinea pig whose offspring include a recessive white-furred individual. What are the possible genotypes of the unknown parent?

## Further Inquiry

Design a model to demonstrate a dihybrid cross of two parents that are heterozygous for two characteristics. Construct and complete a Punnett square for this cross.

### TABLE B  OFFSPRING RATIOS

| Genotypes | Total | Genotypic ratio |
|---|---|---|
| Homozygous dominant (*GG*) | | |
| Heterozygous (*Gg*) | | |
| Homozygous recessive (*gg*) | | ____ : ____ : ____ |
| **Phenotypes** | | **Phenotypic ratio** |
| Green seeds | | |
| Yellow seeds | | ____ : ____ |

### TABLE C  OFFSPRING RATIOS (Entire Class)

| Genotypes | Total | Genotypic ratio |
|---|---|---|
| Homozygous dominant (*GG*) | | |
| Heterozygous (*Gg*) | | |
| Homozygous recessive (*gg*) | | ____ : ____ : ____ |
| **Phenotypes** | | **Phenotypic ratio** |
| Green seeds | | |
| Yellow seeds | | ____ : ____ |

# DNA, RNA, AND PROTEIN SYNTHESIS

DNA has a spiral staircase shape, as shown in this model. DNA contains the instructions for making the proteins necessary for life.

**SECTION 1** *Discovery of DNA*

**SECTION 2** *DNA Structure*

**SECTION 3** *DNA Replication*

**SECTION 4** *Protein Synthesis*

*BIOLOGY*

**Unit 6—Gene Expression**
Topics 1–6

For project ideas from *Scientific American*, visit go.hrw.com and type in the keyword **HM6SAB**.

# DISCOVERY OF DNA

*From his studies with pea plants, Mendel concluded that hereditary factors determine many of an organism's traits. But what were these hereditary factors? How did these molecules store hereditary information? Scientists believed that if they could answer these questions, they could understand how cells pass on characteristics to their descendants. The answers to these questions began to emerge during an epidemic of pneumonia in London in the 1920s.*

### OBJECTIVES

- **Relate** how Griffith's bacterial experiments showed that a hereditary factor was involved in transformation.
- **Summarize** how Avery's experiments led his group to conclude that DNA is responsible for transformation in bacteria.
- **Describe** how Hershey and Chase's experiment led to the conclusion that DNA, not protein, is the hereditary molecule in viruses.

### VOCABULARY

virulent
transformation
bacteriophage

## GRIFFITH'S EXPERIMENTS

In 1928, British medical officer Frederick Griffith was studying a bacterium called *Streptococcus pneumoniae* (abbreviated *S. pneumoniae*). Some types, or strains, of this bacterium can cause the lung disease pneumonia in mammals. Griffith was trying to develop a vaccine against a disease-causing, or **virulent** (VIR-yoo-luhnt) strain of the bacterium.

As shown in Figure 10-1, each virulent bacterium is surrounded by a capsule made of polysaccharides that protects it from a body's defense systems. The bacteria in a virulent strain grow as **s**mooth-edged colonies when grown in a Petri dish and are called the *S* strain. In contrast, a second strain of *S. pneumoniae* does not cause pneumonia and lacks a capsule. The second strain is called the *R* strain because it grows into **r**ough colonies. The *R* strain is also shown in Figure 10-1.

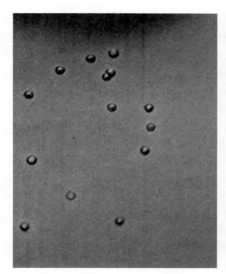

Colonies of the harmful (*S*) strain

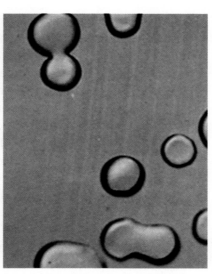

Colonies of the harmless (*R*) strain

**FIGURE 10-1**

Griffith studied *S. pneumoniae* bacteria. The *S* strain can cause pneumonia. The *R* strain does not cause pneumonia.

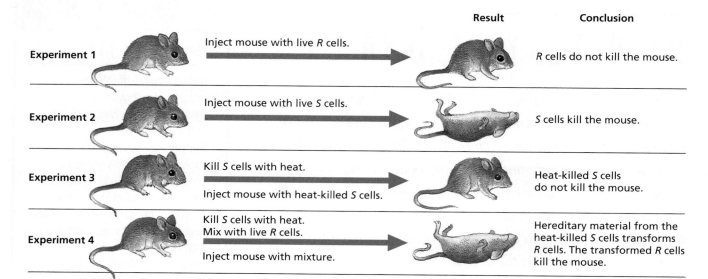

|  |  | Result | Conclusion |
|---|---|---|---|
| **Experiment 1** | Inject mouse with live *R* cells. | | *R* cells do not kill the mouse. |
| **Experiment 2** | Inject mouse with live *S* cells. | | *S* cells kill the mouse. |
| **Experiment 3** | Kill *S* cells with heat. Inject mouse with heat-killed *S* cells. | | Heat-killed *S* cells do not kill the mouse. |
| **Experiment 4** | Kill *S* cells with heat. Mix with live *R* cells. Inject mouse with mixture. | | Hereditary material from the heat-killed *S* cells transforms *R* cells. The transformed *R* cells kill the mouse. |

**FIGURE 10-2**

Frederick Griffith used virulent (*S*) and nonvirulent (*R*) bacterial cells to show that the hereditary material can pass from cell to cell.

**Word Roots and Origins**

*transformation*

from the Latin *trans,* meaning "across," and *forma,* meaning "a form": to change the condition, character, or function of something

Griffith used the two strains of *S. pneumoniae* bacteria in a series of four experiments, shown in Figure 10-2. These experiments provide insight about the nature of the hereditary material. In Experiments 1 and 2, Griffith injected either live *R* or live *S* cells into mice. He found that only *S* cells killed the mice. In Experiment 3, he injected heat-killed *S* bacteria into mice and found that the mice survived. In his fourth experiment, he injected mice with both heat-killed *S* cells and live *R* cells. He found that the mice died.

Griffith concluded from his four experiments that heat-killed virulent bacterial cells release a hereditary factor that transfers the disease-causing ability to the live harmless cells. This type of transfer of genetic material from one cell to another cell or from one organism to another organism is called **transformation.**

# AVERY'S EXPERIMENTS

In the early 1940s, American researcher Oswald Avery and his colleagues set out to test whether the transforming agent in Griffith's experiment was protein, RNA, or DNA. The scientists used enzymes to separately destroy each of the three molecules in heat-killed *S* cells. They used a protease enzyme to destroy protein in heat-killed cells in the first experiment, an enzyme called RNase to destroy RNA in the second experiment, and an enzyme called DNase to destroy DNA in the third experiment. Then, they separately mixed the three experimental batches of heat-killed *S* cells with live *R* cells and injected mice with the mixtures.

Avery and his group found that the cells missing protein and RNA were able to transform *R* cells into *S* cells and kill the mice. However, cells missing DNA did not transform *R* cells into *S* cells, and therefore the mice survived. They concluded that DNA is responsible for transformation in bacteria.

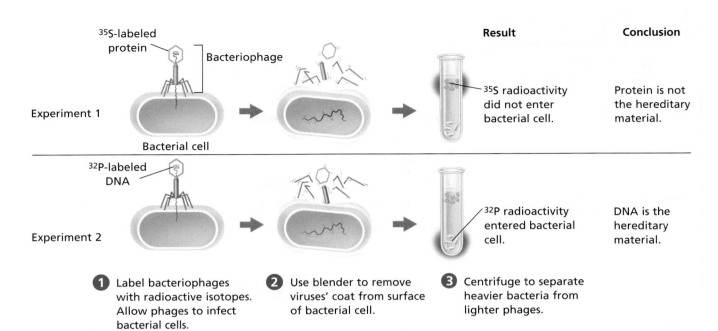

| | | Result | Conclusion |
|---|---|---|---|
| Experiment 1 | ³⁵S-labeled protein / Bacteriophage / Bacterial cell | ³⁵S radioactivity did not enter bacterial cell. | Protein is not the hereditary material. |
| Experiment 2 | ³²P-labeled DNA | ³²P radioactivity entered bacterial cell. | DNA is the hereditary material. |

**1** Label bacteriophages with radioactive isotopes. Allow phages to infect bacterial cells.

**2** Use blender to remove viruses' coat from surface of bacterial cell.

**3** Centrifuge to separate heavier bacteria from lighter phages.

# HERSHEY-CHASE EXPERIMENT

**FIGURE 10-3**

The experiment of Hershey and Chase showed that DNA carries hereditary information from bacteriophages into the bacteria they infect.

In 1952, two American researchers, Martha Chase and Alfred Hershey, set out to test whether DNA or protein was the hereditary material viruses transfer when viruses enter a bacterium. Viruses that infect bacteria are called **bacteriophages,** or just *phages.* As shown in Figure 10-3 in step **1**, Hershey and Chase used radioactive isotopes to label the protein and DNA in the phage. They used radioactive sulfur ($^{35}$S) to label protein and radioactive phosphorus ($^{32}$P) to label DNA. Then, they allowed protein-labeled and DNA-labeled phage to separately infect *Escherischia coli* (abbreviated *E. coli*) bacteria. In step **2**, they removed the phage coats from the cells in a blender. They then used a centrifuge in step **3** to separate the phage from the *E. coli.* They found that all of the viral DNA and little of the protein had entered *E. coli* cells. They concluded that DNA is the hereditary molecule in viruses.

## SECTION 1 REVIEW

1. How did Griffith's experiments show that a hereditary factor was involved in bacterial transformation?

2. Describe how the contributions of Avery and his colleagues revealed that DNA is responsible for transformation in bacteria.

3. How did the Hershey and Chase experiment produce evidence that DNA, and not protein, is the hereditary material in viruses?

**CRITICAL THINKING**

4. **Analyzing Methods** Why did heat kill Griffith's *S* bacteria?

5. **Analyzing Results** What were the essential differences between the methods and results of Griffith and Avery's experiments?

6. **Applying Information** What might Hershey and Chase have concluded if they had found both $^{32}$P and $^{35}$S in the bacterial cells?

## OBJECTIVES

- **Evaluate** the contributions of Franklin and Wilkins in helping Watson and Crick discover DNA's double helix structure.
- **Describe** the three parts of a nucleotide.
- **Summarize** the role of covalent and hydrogen bonds in the structure of DNA.
- **Relate** the role of the base-pairing rules to the structure of DNA.

## VOCABULARY

nucleotide
deoxyribose
nitrogenous base
purine
pyrimidine
base-pairing rules
complementary base pair
base sequence

# DNA STRUCTURE

*By the early 1950s, most biologists accepted DNA as the hereditary material. However, they still lacked an understanding of DNA's structure or how this molecule could replicate, store, and transmit hereditary information and direct cell function. These mysteries would soon begin to unravel at Cambridge University in England.*

## DNA DOUBLE HELIX

In the 1950s, a young American biologist, James Watson, teamed up with British graduate student Francis Crick at Cambridge University in England to try to determine the structure of DNA. By 1953, they had put together a model for the structure of DNA as shown in Figure 10-4. They proposed that DNA is made of two chains that wrap around each other in the shape of a double helix, a shape similar to a winding spiral staircase. Their final model was correct and was remarkable because it explained how DNA could replicate.

Watson and Crick relied on other scientists' work to develop their DNA model. Part of that work was X-ray diffraction photographs of DNA crystals, such as the one shown in Figure 10-5. The photographs and crystals were produced by researchers Rosalind Franklin, shown in Figure 10-5, and Maurice Wilkins, at King's College in London.

In 1962, Watson, Crick, and Wilkins received the Nobel Prize in Medicine for their work on DNA. Rosalind Franklin died in 1958 and so could not be named in the award. However, an important genetics institute in Cambridge now bears her name, and her contribution is recognized around the world.

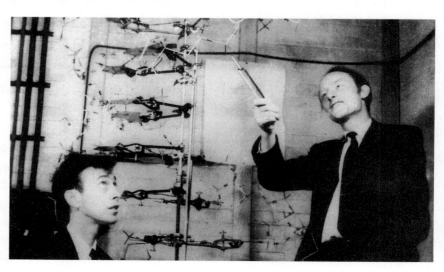

**FIGURE 10-4**

James Watson (left) and Francis Crick stand beside their tin-and-wire model of DNA.

# DNA NUCLEOTIDES

DNA is a nucleic acid made of two long chains (also called strands) of repeating subunits called nucleotides (NOO-klee-oh-TIEDZ). Each **nucleotide** consists of three parts: a five-carbon sugar, a phosphate group, and a nitrogenous base. The three parts of a DNA nucleotide are illustrated in Figure 10-6. The five-carbon sugar in a DNA nucleotide is called **deoxyribose** (dee-AHKS-ee-RIE-bohs). The phosphate group consists of a phosphorus (P) atom bonded to four oxygen (O) atoms. The **nitrogenous** (nie-TRAHJ-uh-nuhs) **base** contains nitrogen (N) atoms and carbon (C) atoms and is a base (accepts hydrogen ions).

## Bonds Hold DNA Together

The DNA double helix is similar to a spiral staircase, as Figure 10-6 shows. The alternating sugar and phosphate molecules form the side "handrails" of the staircase. Nucleotides along each strand are connected by covalent bonds between the sugar of one nucleotide and the phosphate group of the next nucleotide. Each full turn of the DNA helix has 10 nucleotide pairs.

The nitrogenous bases (called "bases" for short) face toward the center of the DNA molecule. The bases on one strand of DNA face—and form bonds called *hydrogen bonds* with—the bases on the other strand. Nitrogenous bases are bonded in pairs between the two strands by two or three hydrogen bonds. The base pairs form the "steps" of the staircase. The base pairs are of uniform width because, in each pair one base has a two-ring structure and the other base has a single-ring structure.

In Figure 10-6, dashed lines indicate the locations of the hydrogen bonds. Hydrogen bonds between the bases help hold the two chains of the DNA double helix together.

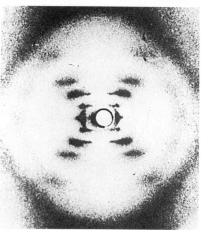

**FIGURE 10-5**

Rosalind Franklin and her X-ray diffraction photo of DNA helped reveal the characteristic shape of a double helix.

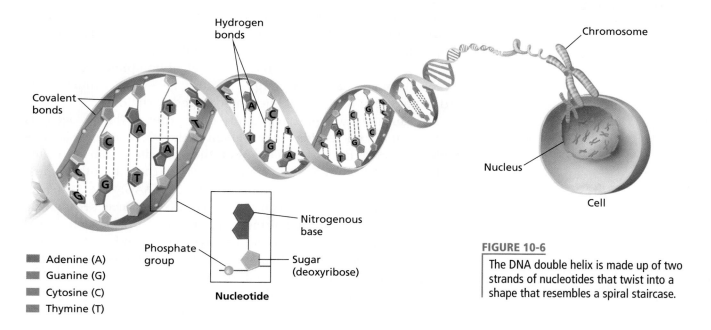

Adenine (A)
Guanine (G)
Cytosine (C)
Thymine (T)

Hydrogen bonds

Covalent bonds

Nitrogenous base

Phosphate group

Sugar (deoxyribose)

**Nucleotide**

Chromosome

Nucleus

Cell

**FIGURE 10-6**

The DNA double helix is made up of two strands of nucleotides that twist into a shape that resembles a spiral staircase.

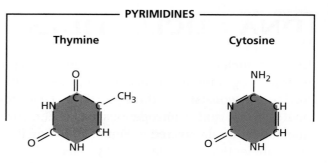

PURINES — PYRIMIDINES

Adenine    Guanine    Thymine    Cytosine

**FIGURE 10-7**

Each nucleotide in a DNA molecule is made of a deoxyribose sugar, a phosphate group, and one of the four nitrogenous bases shown above: thymine, cytosine, adenine, or guanine.

## Nitrogenous Bases

The sugar and phosphate group are identical in all DNA nucleotides. However, the nitrogenous base may be any one of four different kinds—thymine (THIE-MEEN), cytosine (SIET-oh-SEEN), adenine (AD-uh-NEEN), or guanine (GWAH-NEEN). The nitrogenous bases and their chemical structures, called *rings,* are shown above in Figure 10-7. The nitrogenous bases are often represented by the first letter of their name—T (thymine), C (cytosine), A (adenine), and G (guanine).

Nitrogenous bases that have a double ring of carbon and nitrogen atoms, such as adenine and guanine, are called **purines** (PYUR-EENZ). Nitrogenous bases that have a single ring of carbon and nitrogen atoms, such as cytosine and thymine, are called **pyrimidines** (pi-RIM-uh-DEENZ).

### Word Roots and Origins

*deoxyribose*

from the Latin *de,* meaning "away from," the Greek *oxys,* meaning "sharp, or acid" (as in oxygen), and *ribose,* a type of sugar

# COMPLEMENTARY BASES

In 1949, American biochemist Erwin Chargaff observed that the percentage of adenine equals the percentage of thymine, and the percentage of cytosine equals that of guanine in the DNA of a variety of organisms. This observation was key to understanding the structure of DNA because it meant bases pair by **base-pairing rules**—in DNA, cytosine on one strand pairs with guanine on the opposite strand, and adenine pairs with thymine, as shown in Figure 10-8. These pairs of bases are called **complementary base pairs.** Notice that each complementary base pair contains one double-ringed purine and one single-ringed pyrimidine.

Because of the base-pairing rules, the order of the nitrogenous bases on the nucleotides in one chain of the DNA molecule is complementary to the order of bases on the opposite chain. For example, if a DNA chain has the sequence ATTC, then the other chain must have the complementary sequence TAAG. The order of nitrogenous bases on a chain of DNA is called its **base sequence.**

Complementary base pairing is important in DNA structure and function for two reasons. First, the hydrogen bonds between the base pairs help hold the two strands of a DNA molecule together. Second, the complementary nature of DNA helps explain how DNA replicates before a cell divides. One strand of a DNA molecule can serve as a template for making a new complementary strand.

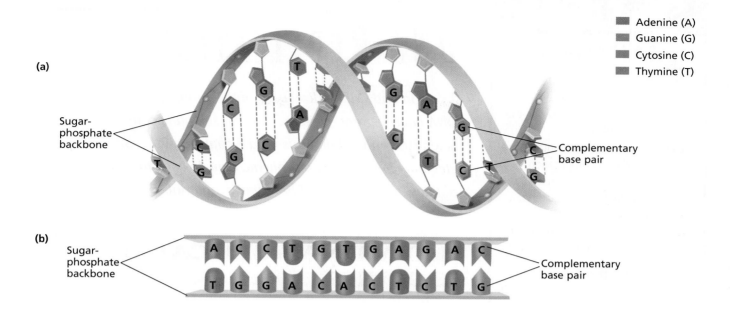

(a)

Sugar-phosphate backbone

Complementary base pair

(b)

Sugar-phosphate backbone

| A | C | C | T | G | T | G | A | G | A | C |

| T | G | G | A | C | A | C | T | C | T | G |

Complementary base pair

## DNA Models

The structure of DNA is often simplified when it is drawn or modeled. For example, the DNA double helix is often illustrated as a straight ladder, as shown at the bottom of Figure 10-8. The sugar-phosphate "handrails" are drawn as a straight line so that the base-pair "steps" between the DNA strands are easier to see. Notice that simplifying the DNA structure highlights the complementary base pairs in each of the DNA nucleotides. In some cases the structure of DNA is simplified even more by just writing the first letter of each of the nitrogenous bases in the DNA nucleotides. For example, the DNA in Figure 10-8b would be represented by

A C C T G T G A G A C
T G G A C A C T C T G

**FIGURE 10-8**

The DNA double helix resembles a spiral staircase (a), but it is often shown as a straight ladder (b) to more easily show the base pairs.

---

## SECTION 2 REVIEW

1. What piece of information did Franklin and Wilkins have that helped Watson and Crick determine the double helix structure of DNA?

2. Name the three parts of a nucleotide.

3. Summarize the locations of covalent bonds and hydrogen bonds in a DNA molecule.

4. Describe why the two strands of the double helix are considered to be complementary.

5. State the base-pairing rules in DNA.

6. How do the base-pairing rules relate to the structure of DNA?

**CRITICAL THINKING**

7. **Making Predictions** If 2.2 picograms of DNA could be extracted from a certain number of human muscle cells, about how many picograms of DNA could be extracted from the same number of human gamete cells?

8. **Applying Information** Use the base-pairing rules to determine the base sequence that is complementary to the sequence C-G-A-T-T-G.

9. **Making Calculations** A plant's DNA has nucleotides that are 20 percent thymine. What percentage of guanine would be present?

- **Summarize** the process of DNA replication.
- **Identify** the role of enzymes in the replication of DNA.
- **Describe** how complementary base pairing guides DNA replication.
- **Compare** the number of replication forks in prokaryotic and eukaryotic cells during DNA replication.
- **Describe** how errors are corrected during DNA replication.

## VOCABULARY

DNA replication
helicase
replication fork
DNA polymerase
semi-conservative replication
mutation

# DNA REPLICATION

*Watson and Crick's discovery of the double helix structure of DNA caused great excitement in the scientific community. Scientists realized that this model could explain simply and elegantly how DNA can replicate exactly each time a cell divides, a key feature of hereditary material.*

## HOW DNA REPLICATION OCCURS

**DNA replication** is the process by which DNA is copied in a cell before a cell divides by mitosis, meiosis, or binary fission. During DNA replication, the two nucleotide strands of the original double helix separate along the strands. Because the two strands are complementary, each strand serves as a template to make a new complementary strand. After replication, the two identical double-stranded DNA molecules separate and move to the new cells formed during cell division, as shown in Figure 10-9.

### Steps of DNA Replication

The process of DNA replication is shown in Figure 10-10. In step **❶**, enzymes called **helicases** separate the DNA strands. Helicases move along the DNA molecule, breaking the hydrogen bonds between the complementary nitrogenous bases. This action allows the two DNA strands of the double helix to separate from each other. The Y-shaped region that results when the two strands separate is called a **replication fork.**

During step **❷**, enzymes called **DNA polymerases** add complementary nucleotides, found floating freely inside the nucleus, to each of the original strands. As the nucleotides on the newly forming strand are added, covalent bonds form between the adjacent nucleotides. Covalent bonds form between the deoxyribose sugar of one nucleotide and the phosphate group of the next nucleotide on the growing strand. Hydrogen bonds form between the complementary nitrogenous bases on the original and new strands.

By step **❸**, DNA polymerases finish replicating the DNA and fall off. The result is two separate and identical DNA molecules that are ready to move to new cells in cell division.

In each new DNA double helix, one strand is from the original molecule, and one strand is new. This type of replication is called **semi-conservative replication** because each of the new DNA molecules has kept (or conserved) one of the two (or semi) original DNA strands.

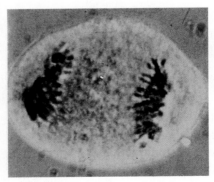

**FIGURE 10-9**

Before a cell divides, its DNA is copied in a process called *DNA replication.* One copy of each chromosome moves to each new cell. In the photo above, the chromosomes (seen as the blue rods on each side of the cell) were in the process of moving during cell division.

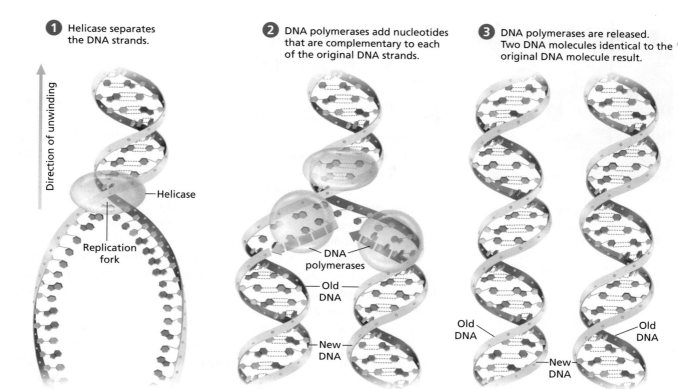

**①** Helicase separates the DNA strands.

**②** DNA polymerases add nucleotides that are complementary to each of the original DNA strands.

**③** DNA polymerases are released. Two DNA molecules identical to the original DNA molecule result.

Direction of unwinding

Helicase

Replication fork

DNA polymerases

Old DNA

New DNA

**ORIGINAL DNA MOLECULE**

Old DNA

Old DNA

New DNA

**TWO IDENTICAL DNA MOLECULES**

## Action at the Replication Fork

DNA synthesis occurs in different directions on each strand, as shown by the arrows near the replication fork in step **②** of Figure 10-10. As the replication fork moves along the original DNA, synthesis of one strand follows the movement of the replication fork. Synthesis on the other strand, however, moves in the opposite direction, away from the replication fork, which leaves gaps in the newly synthesized strand. The gaps are later joined together by an enzyme called DNA *ligase*.

## Prokaryotic and Eukaryotic Replication

In prokaryotic cells, which have one circular chromosome, replication begins at one place along the chromosome. Two replication forks are formed and proceed in opposite directions, like two zippers opening in opposing directions. Replication continues along each fork until they meet and the entire molecule is copied.

In eukaryotic cells, each chromosome is long, but not circular. At the rate that DNA polymerase adds nucleotides (about 50 nucleotides per second in eukaryotic cells), it would take 53 days to replicate the largest human chromosome. Instead, replication begins at many points or *origins* along the DNA. As with prokaryotes, at each origin, two replication forks move in opposite directions. For example, in a fruit fly chromosome, replication begins simultaneously at about 3,500 sites in a DNA molecule. Only simultaneous replication along chromosomes could allow rapid enough copying of the organism's entire DNA.

**FIGURE 10-10**

During DNA replication, the two strands separate, and each strand serves as a template. DNA polymerases add complementary nucleotides. At the end of replication, there are two identical copies of the original DNA molecule.

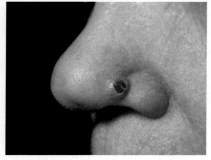

**FIGURE 10-11**

Skin cancer can be the result of a DNA mutation in a skin cell that received too much ultraviolet radiation from sunlight. Exposure to harmful radiation from the Sun can be reduced by using sunscreen lotion.

# DNA ERRORS IN REPLICATION

DNA replication usually occurs with great accuracy. Only about one error occurs for every billion paired nucleotides added. That's the equivalent of typing this book 1,000 times and making only one typing error. What accounts for this accuracy? DNA polymerases have repair functions that "proofread" DNA in the same way a friend might check a term paper for spelling errors. For example, if an adenine pairs with a cytosine instead of a thymine, DNA polymerase can repair the error by removing the mispaired cytosine and replacing it with a thymine.

When mistakes in DNA replication do occur, the base sequence of the newly formed DNA differs from the base sequence of the original DNA. A change in the nucleotide sequence of a DNA molecule is called a **mutation.** Mutations can have serious effects on the function of an important gene and disrupt an important cell function.

Some errors escape repair. In addition, chemicals and ultraviolet radiation from the sun can damage DNA. Some mutations can lead to cancer, such as the one shown in Figure 10-11. Thus, an effective mechanism for the repair of damaged DNA is very important to the survival of an organism.

## DNA Replication and Cancer

DNA replication is an elegant process in which genetic information is passed from cell to cell for thousands of generations. It also explains how mutations can arise and lead to altered cells and organisms. Sometimes, the changes allow individuals to survive and reproduce better, so these variations increase in the population over many generations. Sometimes, mutations that are not repaired can cause diseases such as cancer. For example, mutations that affect genes that control how a cell divides can lead to an abnormal mass of cells called a *tumor.* Studying DNA replication is one promising avenue to understanding and treating various types of human cancers.

## SECTION 3 REVIEW

1. Describe what happens at a DNA replication fork during replication.

2. Describe the role of helicases and DNA polymerases during DNA replication.

3. State why DNA replication is a semi-conservative process.

4. Compare the number of replication forks in prokaryotic and eukaryotic DNA during replication.

5. How are replication errors corrected?

**CRITICAL THINKING**

6. **Analyzing Concepts** Why are there two DNA polymerases at one replication fork?

7. **Drawing Conclusions** Why are DNA repair enzymes important to an organism's survival?

8. **Evaluating Information** Is a mutation that occurs during the formation of an egg cell or sperm cell more significant than a mutation that occurs in a body cell? Explain.

# DNA REPAIR AND SKIN CANCER

Sometimes, the errors that occur during DNA replication are not fixed by DNA repair enzymes. These unrepaired errors can lead to mutations. Cancer can occur if the mutations happen within genes that control cell growth and cell division. Scientists hope that by studying DNA replication and DNA repair, they can develop treatments or even cure various types of cancers.

## Ultraviolet Light and Skin Cancer

Ultraviolet light, the most energetic part of sunlight, is the main cause of mutations that trigger skin cancer. Skin cancer is the most common type of cancer in the United States. Each year, about 1 million Americans get skin cancer.

When UV light reaches the DNA inside a skin cell, thymine bases that are next to each other on the same strand of DNA can become linked by a covalent bond, as shown in the figure below. Linked thymine pairs are called *thymine dimers*. Thymine dimers are usually detected by enzymes moving along the DNA strand because the dimers cause a kink in the DNA, as shown in the figure below. Dimers that are not repaired during DNA replication can cause mutations in genes that control cell division. The mutation can trigger a skin cell to become cancerous.

## DNA Repair Enzymes and Skin Cancer Treatments

Some organisms do not get skin cancer. One reason is that these organisms have a DNA repair enzyme called *photolyase* (FOH-toh-LIE-AYS). Photolyase is activated by light and can repair thymine dimers caused by UV radiation. Human skin cells can correct UV-induced dimers by a complex process known as *excision repair* that involves other enzymes. But photolyase uses a more direct and effective mechanism for DNA repair than excision repair. Scientists have already developed a sunscreen containing photolyase to repair the UV-induced DNA damage that occurs when a person is sunburned.

Some researchers want to try to use gene therapy to insert the gene for photolyase in people that are at high risk for skin cancer. Gene therapy is a technique in which a defective gene is replaced with a normal version of the gene. Ongoing studies of DNA repair enzymes may help develop gene therapy and other types of cancer treatments in humans.

*It is important to guard against skin cancer. For example, apply sunscreen before prolonged exposure to sunlight.*

## REVIEW

1. How can errors during DNA replication lead to cancer?
2. How does the DNA repair enzyme photolyase prevent skin cancer?
3. **Supporting Reasoned Opinions** Would you buy a sunscreen that contains photolyase? Why or why not?

**internet** connect

**www.scilinks.org**
**Topic: Cancer Gene**
**(Oncogenes)**
**Keyword: HM60210**

SCiLINKS. Maintained by the National Science Teachers Association

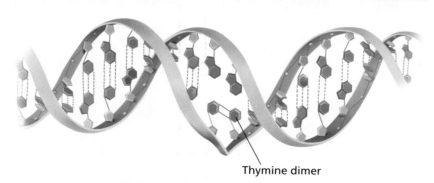

Thymine dimer

*Unrepaired DNA damage can prevent accurate copying of the DNA and can lead to mutations. One example of DNA damage is covalent cross-linking between two thymine bases, which is called a thymine dimer.*

# PROTEIN SYNTHESIS

*Characteristics such as hair color are largely determined by genetic factors. But how does inheriting a particular form of a gene result in the appearance of a specific hair color? The structure of DNA helps explain how genes function in making proteins that determine traits in organisms.*

## FLOW OF GENETIC INFORMATION

A gene is a segment of DNA that is located on a chromosome and that codes for a hereditary character. For example, a gene determines a person's hair color. The gene directs the making of the protein called *melanin* (a pigment) in hair follicle cells through an intermediate—the nucleic acid called **ribonucleic acid,** or **RNA.**

Figure 10-12 summarizes the flow of genetic information in a eukaryotic cell. During **transcription,** DNA acts as a template for the synthesis of RNA. In **translation,** RNA directs the assembly of proteins. Forming proteins based on information in DNA and carried out by RNA is called **protein synthesis,** or gene expression. This central concept can be symbolized as *DNA* ⟶ *RNA* ⟶ *protein.* Proteins do important work in cells, such as protecting the body against infections and carrying oxygen in red blood cells.

**FIGURE 10-12**

DNA contains the instructions for building a protein. DNA transfers the instructions to an RNA molecule in a process called transcription. The RNA moves out into the cytoplasm, where its instructions are read and the protein is assembled in a process called *translation.*

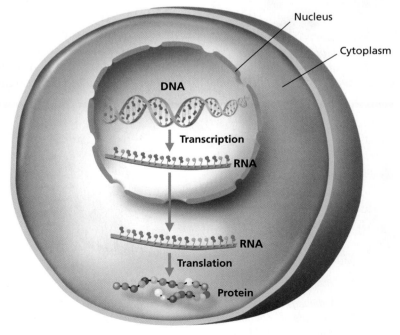

**Eukaryotic cell**

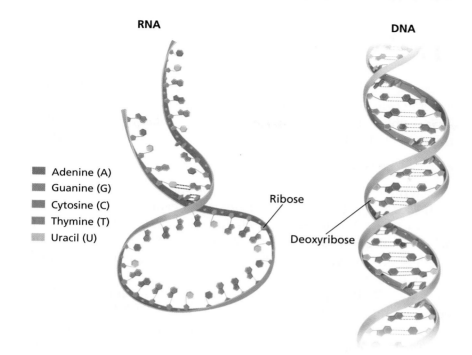

**RNA**  **DNA**

■ Adenine (A)
■ Guanine (G)
■ Cytosine (C)
■ Thymine (T)
■ Uracil (U)

Ribose

Deoxyribose

**FIGURE 10-13**

The structure of RNA is different from the structure of DNA. Each of the three major types of RNA—mRNA, tRNA, and rRNA—play a different role during protein synthesis.

# RNA STRUCTURE AND FUNCTION

Like DNA, RNA is a nucleic acid made up of nucleotides. However, as shown in Figure 10-13, the structure of RNA differs from that of DNA in four basic ways. First, RNA contains the sugar **ribose,** not the sugar deoxyribose found in DNA. Second, RNA contains the nitrogenous base *uracil* instead of the nitrogenous base thymine found in DNA. Third, RNA is usually single stranded rather than double stranded like DNA. However, within a single-stranded RNA molecule, some regions fold to form short double-stranded sections. In the double-stranded regions, guanine forms base pairs with cytosine, and uracil forms base pairs with adenine. Fourth, RNA is usually much shorter in length than DNA (about the length of one gene). On the other hand, DNA is usually long, containing hundreds or thousands of genes.

## Types of RNA

Cells have three major types of RNA, as shown in Figure 10-14. Each type of RNA plays a different role in protein synthesis. The first type of RNA is **messenger RNA (mRNA),** a single-stranded RNA molecule that carries the instructions from a gene to make a protein. In eukaryotic cells, mRNA carries the genetic "message" from DNA in the nucleus to the ribosomes in the cytosol. The second type of RNA is **ribosomal RNA (rRNA),** which is part of the structure of ribosomes. Ribosomes are organelles in the cell where protein synthesis occurs. Ribosomes are made of rRNAs and many proteins. Figure 10-14 shows a model of a ribosome. The third type of RNA is **transfer RNA (tRNA),** which transfers amino acids to the ribosome to make a protein. Although the entire tRNA is made of nucleotides linked together, only three are emphasized in Figure 10-14.

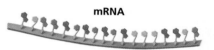

mRNA

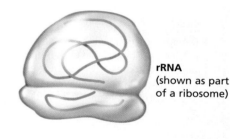

rRNA
(shown as part of a ribosome)

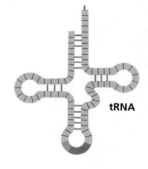

tRNA

**FIGURE 10-14**

Each of the three major types of RNA differs in its structure. Messenger RNA (mRNA) is typically drawn as a relatively straight chain. Ribosomal RNA (rRNA) is shown as part of the structure of a ribosome. Transfer RNA's (tRNA) two-dimensional structure is typically shown with only three of its many nucleotides emphasized.

# TRANSCRIPTION

Transcription is the process by which the genetic instructions in a specific gene are transcribed or "rewritten" into an RNA molecule. Transcription takes place in the nucleus of eukaryotic cells and in the DNA-containing region in the cytoplasm of prokaryotic cells.

## Steps of Transcription

Transcription occurs in three steps, as shown in Figure 10-15. In step ❶, **RNA polymerase,** an enzyme that catalyzes the formation of RNA on a DNA template, binds to a promoter. A **promoter** is a specific nucleotide sequence of DNA where RNA polymerase binds and initiates transcription. After RNA polymerase binds to the promoter, the DNA strands unwind and separate.

In step ❷, RNA polymerase adds free RNA nucleotides that are complementary to the nucleotides on one of the DNA strands. The resulting chain is an RNA molecule. As in DNA replication, complementary base pairing determines the nucleotide sequence in the newly made RNA. For example, if the bases on the DNA strand was ATCGAC, the bases on the RNA strand would be UAGCUG. Unlike DNA replication, transcription uses only a specific region (a gene) on one of the two DNA strands to serve as the template. As RNA polymerase moves past, the separated DNA strands rewind.

During step ❸, RNA polymerase reaches a **termination signal,** a specific sequence of nucleotides that marks the end of a gene. Upon reaching this "stop" signal, RNA polymerase releases both the DNA and the newly formed RNA. The RNA made during transcription can be one of many types including mRNA, tRNA, or rRNA. The newly made RNA can now perform its job in the cell, and the RNA polymerase can transcribe another gene.

**FIGURE 10-15**

During transcription, the enzyme RNA polymerase "reads" one of the chains, the template strand. RNA polymerase adds and then joins complementary RNA nucleotides, resulting in an RNA strand.

❶ RNA polymerase binds to the gene's promoter. The two DNA strands unwind and separate.

❷ Complementary RNA nucleotides are added and then joined.

❸ When RNA polymerase reaches a termination signal in the DNA, the DNA and new RNA are released by the polymerase.

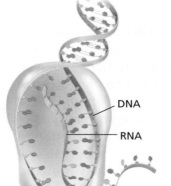

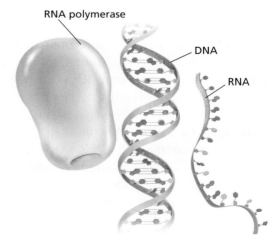

**TRANSCRIPTION**

# THE GENETIC CODE

During the next process of gene expression, amino acids are assembled based on instructions encoded in the sequence of nucleotides in the mRNA. The **genetic code** is the term for the rules that relate how a sequence of nitrogenous bases in nucleotides corresponds to a particular amino acid. In the genetic code, three adjacent nucleotides ("letters") in mRNA specify an amino acid ("word") in a polypeptide. Each three-nucleotide sequence in mRNA that encodes an amino acid or signifies a start or stop signal is called a **codon.**

Table 10-1 lists the 64 mRNA codons and the amino acids they encode in most organisms. For example, the codon *GCU* specifies the amino acid *alanine* in the genetic code. The genetic code is nearly universal to all life on Earth and supports the idea that all organisms share an ancient common ancestor.

Some amino acids are encoded by two, three, or more different codons, as shown in Table 10-1. These codons often differ from one another by only one nucleotide. No codon encodes more than one amino acid. One special codon, AUG, acts as a start codon. A *start codon* is a specific sequence of nucleotides in mRNA that indicates where translation should begin. The start codon encodes the amino acid methionine. Certain sequences of nucleotides in mRNA (UAA, UAG, or UGA), called *stop codons,* do not code for amino acids, but instead signal for translation to end.

internet connect

www.scilinks.org
Topic: Genetic Code
Keyword: HM60648

SC*LINKS.* Maintained by the National Science Teachers Association

## TABLE 10-1  *Codons in mRNA*

| First base | Second base | | | | Third base |
|---|---|---|---|---|---|
| | **U** | **C** | **A** | **G** | |
| **U** | UUU UUC } Phenylalanine<br>UUA UUG } Leucine | UCU UCC UCA UCG } Serine | UAU UAC } Tyrosine<br>UAA UAG } Stop | UGU UGC } Cysteine<br>UGA } Stop<br>UGG } Tryptophan | U<br>C<br>A<br>G |
| **C** | CUU CUC CUA CUG } Leucine | CCU CCC CCA CCG } Proline | CAU CAC } Histidine<br>CAA CAG } Glutamine | CGU CGC CGA CGG } Arginine | U<br>C<br>A<br>G |
| **A** | AUU AUC AUA } Isolecine<br>AUG } Methionine (Start) | ACU ACC ACA ACG } Threonine | AAU AAC } Asparagine<br>AAA AAG } Lysine | AGU AGC } Serine<br>AGA AGG } Arginine | U<br>C<br>A<br>G |
| **G** | GUU GUC GUA GUG } Valine | GCU GCC GCA GCG } Alanine | GAU GAC } Aspartic acid<br>GAA GAG } Glutamic acid | GGU GGC GGA GGG } Glycine | U<br>C<br>A<br>G |

# TRANSLATION

Although the instructions for making a protein are copied from DNA to mRNA, all three major types of RNA are involved in translation—the making of a protein.

## Protein Structure

Every protein is made of one or more polypeptides. Polypeptides are chains of amino acids linked by peptide bonds. There are 20 different amino acids found in the proteins of living things. Each polypeptide chain may consist of hundreds or thousands of the 20 different amino acids, arranged in a sequence specific to each protein. The amino acid sequence determines how the polypeptides will twist and fold into the three-dimensional structure of the protein. The shape of the protein is critical to its function.

## Steps of Translation

The translation or decoding of the genetic instructions to form a polypeptide involves five main steps, as shown in Figure 10-16. In step **❶**, two ribosomal subunits, tRNA, and an mRNA join together. Enzymes first attach a specific amino acid to one end of each tRNA according to the genetic code. The other end of each tRNA contains the **anticodon,** three nucleotides on the RNA that are complementary to the sequence of a codon in mRNA.

**FIGURE 10-16**

During translation, amino acids are assembled from information encoded in mRNA. As the mRNA codons move through the ribosome, tRNAs add specific amino acids to the growing polypeptide chain. The process continues until a stop codon is reached and the newly made protein is released.

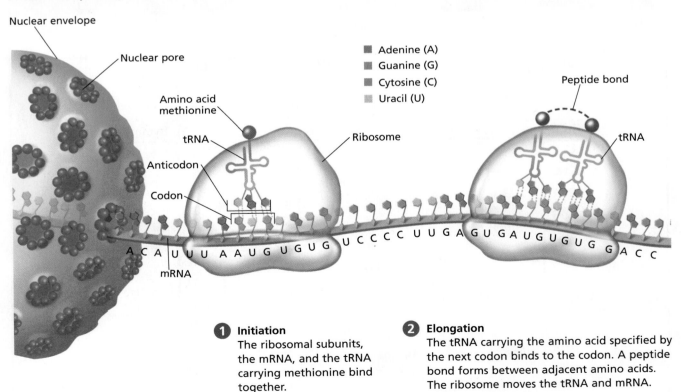

❶ **Initiation**
The ribosomal subunits, the mRNA, and the tRNA carrying methionine bind together.

❷ **Elongation**
The tRNA carrying the amino acid specified by the next codon binds to the codon. A peptide bond forms between adjacent amino acids. The ribosome moves the tRNA and mRNA.

A tRNA carrying the amino acid methionine at one end and the anticodon UAC at the other end pairs with the start codon AUG on the mRNA. The first amino acid in nearly all polypeptides is methionine, but this amino acid may be removed later.

In step ❷, the polypeptide chain is put together. A tRNA carrying the appropriate amino acid pairs its anticodon with the second codon in the mRNA. The ribosome then detaches methionine from the first tRNA, and a peptide bond forms between methionine and the second amino acid. The first tRNA then exits the ribosome. The ribosome then moves a distance of one codon along the mRNA.

During step ❸, the polypeptide chain continues to grow as the mRNA moves along the ribosome. A new tRNA moves in, carrying an amino acid for the next mRNA codon. The growing polypeptide chain moves from one tRNA to the amino acid attached to the next tRNA.

The polypeptide grows one amino acid at a time until step ❹. At this step, the ribosome reaches the stop codon. The newly made polypeptide falls off.

During step ❺, the components of translation come apart. The last tRNA leaves the ribosome, and the ribosome moves away from the mRNA. The translation machinery is now free to translate the same or another mRNA.

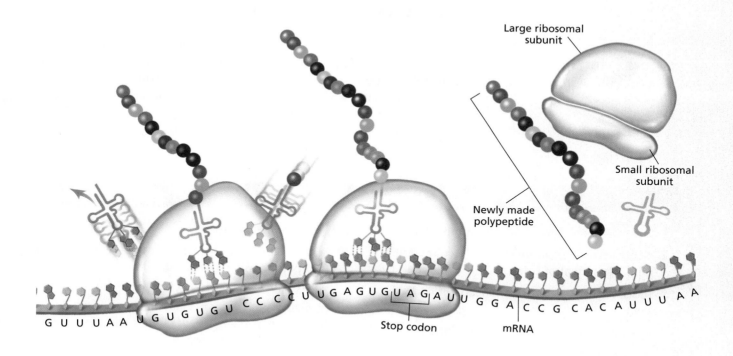

❸ **Elongation (continued)**
The first tRNA detaches and leaves its amino acid behind. Elongation continues. The polypeptide chain continues to grow.

❹ **Termination**
The process ends when a stop codon is reached. A stop codon is one for which there is no tRNA that has a complementary anticodon.

❺ **Disassembly**
The ribosome complex falls apart. The newly made polypeptide is released.

## Translating Many Ribosomes at Once

Because a new ribosome begins translating mRNA almost as soon as the preceding ribosome has moved aside, several ribosomes may translate the same mRNA transcript at the same time. In fact, prokaryotes lack a nuclear envelope separating their DNA from ribosomes in the cytosol, thus translation can begin on an mRNA even before transcription of the mRNA has finished. In eukaryotes, translation of an mRNA occurs only after transcription is finished.

# THE HUMAN GENOME

In the years since Watson and Crick discovered the structure of DNA, biologists have achieved a milestone in applying this knowledge to human biology. The entire gene sequence of the human **genome,** the complete genetic content, is now known. Biologists have deciphered the order of the 3.2 billion base pairs in the 23 human chromosomes. The human genome is so large that it would take a person almost 10 years to read the total sequence aloud.

The challenge now is to learn what information the DNA sequences actually encode. An important new field called *bioinformatics* uses computers to compare different DNA sequences. Scientists can program computers to help interpret most DNA sequences and predict where genes lie along the DNA.

To learn where and when human cells use each of the proteins coded for in the approximately 30,000 genes in the human genome will take much more analysis. This information is important because learning which gene sequences control particular biological functions may help diagnose, treat, and prevent genetic disorders, cancer, and infectious diseases in the future.

## SECTION 4 REVIEW

1. Summarize the flow of genetic information.

2. List the four ways in which the structure of RNA differs from that of DNA.

3. Describe the structure and function of each of the three types of RNA.

4. Sequence the main steps of transcription.

5. What is the genetic code?

6. Compare the roles of the three different types of RNA during translation.

7. Describe the significance of identifying the entire sequence of the human genome.

**CRITICAL THINKING**

8. **Making Comparisons** How does the role of RNA polymerase in transcription differ from that of DNA polymerase in DNA replication?

9. **Applying Information** What amino acids would translation of the mRNA with the sequence UAACAAGGAGCAUCC produce?

10. **Analyzing Processes** Discuss why it is important which of the two DNA strands serves as a template during transcription.

11. **Drawing Conclusions** How does the structure of tRNA relate to its function in translation?

# CHAPTER HIGHLIGHTS

**Discovery of DNA**

- Griffith's experiments showed that hereditary material can pass from one bacterial cell to another. This is called transformation.

- Avery's work showed that DNA is the hereditary material that transfers information between bacterial cells.

- Hershey and Chase confirmed that DNA, and not protein, is the hereditary material.

**Vocabulary**

virulent (p. 193)  transformation (p. 194)  bacteriophage (p. 195)

---

**SECTION 2** **DNA Structure**

- Watson and Crick created a model of DNA by using Franklin's and Wilkins's DNA diffraction X-rays.

- DNA is made of two nucleotide strands that wrap around each other in the shape of a double helix.

- A DNA nucleotide is made of a deoxyribose sugar, a phosphate group, and one of four nitrogenous bases: adenine (A), guanine (G), cytosine (C), or thymine (T).

- Nucleotides along each DNA strand are linked by covalent bonds. Complementary nitrogenous bases are bonded by hydrogen bonds.

- Hydrogen bonding between the complementary base pairs, G-C and A-T, holds the two strands of a DNA molecule together.

**Vocabulary**

nucleotide (p. 197)  nitrogenous base (p. 197)  pyrimidine (p. 198)  complementary base pair (p. 198)
deoxyribose (p. 197)  purine (p. 198)  base-pairing rules (p. 198)  base sequence (p. 198)

---

**SECTION 3** **DNA Replication**

- DNA replication is the process by which DNA is copied in a cell before a cell divides.

- Replication begins with the separation of the DNA strands by helicases. Then, DNA polymerases form new strands by adding complementary nucleotides to each of the original strands.

- Each new DNA molecule is made of one strand of nucleotides from the original DNA molecule and one new strand.

- Changes in DNA are called mutations. Proofreading and repair prevent many replication errors.

**Vocabulary**

DNA replication (p. 200)  replication fork (p. 200)  semi-conservative  mutation (p. 202)
helicase (p. 200)  DNA polymerase (p. 200)  replication (p. 200)

---

**SECTION 4** **Protein Synthesis**

- The flow of genetic information can be symbolized as DNA → RNA → protein.

- RNA has the sugar ribose instead of deoxyribose and uracil in place of thymine. RNA is single stranded and is shorter than DNA.

- During transcription, DNA acts as a template for directing the synthesis of RNA.

- The genetic code identifies the specific amino acids coded for by each mRNA codon.

- The RNA called mRNA carries the genetic "message" from the nucleus to the cytosol; rRNA is the major component of ribosomes; tRNA carries specific amino acids, helping to form polypeptides.

**Vocabulary**

ribonucleic acid (RNA) (p. 204)  ribose (p. 205)  transfer RNA (tRNA) (p. 205)  genetic code (p. 207)
transcription (p. 204)  messenger RNA  RNA polymerase (p. 206)  codon (p. 207)
translation (p. 204)  (mRNA) (p. 205)  promoter (p. 206)  anticodon (p. 208)
protein synthesis (p. 204)  ribosomal RNA (rRNA) (p. 205)  termination signal (p. 206)  genome (p. 210)

## USING VOCABULARY

1. For each pair of terms, explain how the meanings of the terms differ.
   a. *purine* and *pyrimidine*
   b. *ribosome* and *ribosomal RNA*
   c. *messenger RNA* and *transfer RNA*
   d. *termination signal* and *stop codon*
   e. *transcription* and *translation*

2. Explain the relationship between *codon* and *gene*.

3. Use the following terms in the same sentence: *DNA replication, replication fork, helicase,* and *DNA polymerase.*

4. **Word Roots and Origins** The word *transcription* is derived from the Latin *scribere,* which means "to write." The prefix *trans* means "across." Using this information, explain why the term transcription is a good name for the biological process it describes.

## UNDERSTANDING KEY CONCEPTS

5. **Summarize** Griffith's transformation experiments.

6. **Describe** how Avery's experiments led to the understanding of DNA as the molecule of heredity in bacteria.

7. **Describe** the contributions of Hershey and Chase to the understanding that DNA is the hereditary molecule in viruses.

8. **State** how Watson and Crick were able to build a structural model of DNA.

9. **Identify** the components of a nucleotide.

10. **Name** the bonds that link the nucleotides along a DNA strand.

11. **List** the rules of complementary base pairing.

12. **Summarize** the major steps that occur during DNA replication.

13. **Name** the function of DNA polymerase during DNA replication.

14. **State** how complementary base pairing is important in the replication of DNA.

15. **Differentiate** the number of replication forks in prokaryotic and eukaryotic DNA.

16. **Describe** the importance of repair enzymes for the identification of errors during DNA replication.

17. **Outline** the flow of genetic information in cells.

18. **Compare** the structure of RNA to that of DNA.

19. **Summarize** how RNA is formed from a gene during the process of transcription.

20. **Identify** the function of the genetic code.

21. **Differentiate** the functions of the three types of RNA involved in protein synthesis.

22. **Sequence** the major steps of translation.

23. **Discuss** the importance of learning about the human genome.

24. **Unit 6—Gene Expression**

     Write a report summarizing how antibiotics inhibit protein synthesis in bacteria. How do some antibiotics interfere with translation?

25. **CONCEPT MAPPING** Use the following terms to create a concept map that describes the structure of DNA and how it is copied: *nucleotides, phosphate group, deoxyribose, nitrogenous base, double helix, replication, purine, pyrimidine, DNA polymerases,* and *genes.*

## CRITICAL THINKING

26. **Analyzing Information** Why is it unlikely that any particular mutation would have any noticeable effect in a population?

27. **Interpreting Graphics** A segment of DNA has the following sequence:

    | T | A | C | G | G | T | C | T | C | A | G | C |

    Write the mRNA transcript from this sequence of DNA. Next, write the tRNA anticodons that would pair with the mRNA transcript. Use Table 10-1 to write the names of the amino acids coded for by the mRNA transcript.

28. **Analyzing Concepts** A DNA molecule replicates to produce two new DNA molecules. Both of the two new DNA molecules then replicate to form four more new DNA molecules. Are any nucleotide chains from the original DNA present in the last four new DNA molecules? If so, how many?

29. **Analyzing Current Research** Scientists have determined essentially all of the 3 billion or so nucleotides that spell out the human genome. This genetic information will revolutionize the diagnosis, prevention, and treatment of many human diseases. Propose why this information is important for research on human disease.

30. **Applying Information** List all codons in the genetic code that could be changed into a stop codon by a single nucleotide mutation.

# Standardized Test Preparation

**DIRECTIONS:** Choose the letter of the answer choice that best answers the question.

1. For which of the following is DNA responsible?
   A. directing RNA to make lipids
   B. directing RNA to produce glucose
   C. encoding information for making proteins
   D. encoding information for changing the genetic code

2. Where is RNA found?
   F. only in proteins
   G. only in the nucleus
   H. only in the cytoplasm
   J. in the nucleus and cytoplasm

3. What is the basic unit of DNA called?
   A. sugar
   B. nucleotide
   C. phosphate
   D. nucleic acid

4. Which of the following nucleic acids is involved in translation?
   F. DNA only
   G. mRNA only
   H. DNA and mRNA
   J. mRNA and tRNA

**INTERPRETING GRAPHICS:** The table below shows the percentage of bases in some organisms. Use the table to answer the questions that follow.

| Percentage of Each Nitrogenous Base in Different Organisms | | | | |
|---|---|---|---|---|
| | A | T | G | C |
| E. coli | 24.7 | 23.6 | 26.0 | 25.7 |
| Human | 30.4 | 30.1 | 19.6 | 19.9 |
| Wheat | 27.3 | 27.1 | 22.7 | 22.8 |

5. What is the ratio of purines to pyrimidines for these organisms?
   A. about 1:1
   B. about 1:2
   C. about 1:3
   D. about 1:4

6. Within each organism, which nucleotides are found in similar percentages?
   F. A and T, G and C
   G. A and C, G and T
   H. A and C, G and U
   J. A and G, T and U

**DIRECTIONS:** Complete the following analogy.

7. mRNA : uracil :: DNA :
   A. guanine
   B. thymine
   C. adenine
   D. cytosine

**DIRECTIONS:** The model below represents a DNA molecule undergoing DNA replication. Use the model to answer the question that follows.

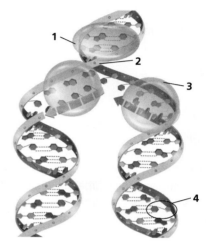

8. Which part of the model represents DNA helicase?
   F. 1
   G. 2
   H. 3
   J. 4

## SHORT RESPONSE

DNA is made up of two strands of subunits called nucleotides. The two strands are twisted around each other in a double helix shape.

Explain why the structure of a DNA molecule is sometimes described as a zipper.

## EXTENDED RESPONSE

DNA can be damaged by mistakes made during its replication. The mistakes are called mutations.

*Part A* Explain eukaryotic DNA replication.

*Part B* Explain how a mutation during replication can affect a protein that is synthesized.

> **Test TIP** Test questions may not be arranged in order of increasing difficulty. If you are unable to answer a question, mark it and move on to other questions.

# Modeling DNA Replication and Protein Synthesis

## OBJECTIVES

- Construct and analyze a model of DNA.
- Use a model to simulate the process of replication.
- Use a model to simulate the process of protein synthesis.

## PROCESS SKILLS

- demonstrating
- identifying
- manipulating a model

## MATERIALS

- plastic soda straws of two different colors, cut into 3 cm sections (54)
- metric ruler
- scissors
- permanent marker
- 54 pushpins (12 red, 12 blue, 12 yellow, 12 green, and 6 white)
- 54 paper clips
- 3 in. × 5 in. note cards
- oval-shaped card

## Background

1. Describe the structure of DNA.
2. State the base-pairing rules.
3. List the steps involved in the copying of DNA before cell division.

4. What are the roles of mRNA, rRNA and tRNA in protein synthesis?
5. Describe the process of transcription and the process of translation.

## PART A  Making a Model of DNA

1. **CAUTION  Sharp or pointed objects may cause injury. Handle pushpins carefully.** Insert a pushpin midway along the length of each straw segment of one color, as shown in the figure below. Push a paper clip into one end of each straw segment until the clip touches the pin.

2. Keeping the pins in a straight line, insert the paper clip from a blue-pushpin segment into the open end of a red-pushpin segment. Add additional straw segments to the red-segment end in the following order: green, yellow, blue, yellow, blue, yellow, green, red, red, and green. Use the permanent marker to label the blue-segment end "top." This chain of segments is one-half of your first model.
3. Assign nucleotides to the corresponding pushpin colors as follows: red = adenine, blue = guanine, yellow = cytosine, and green = thymine.
4. Construct the other half of your first model. Begin with a yellow segment across from the blue pushpin at the top of your first model. Keep the pins in a straight line. Link segments together in this second strand of DNA according to the base-pairing rules.
5. When you have completed your model of one DNA segment, make a sketch of the model in your lab report. Use colored pencils or pens to designate the pushpin colors. Include a key that indicates which nucleotide each color represents in your sketch.

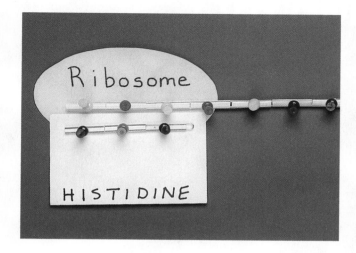

**PART B** Modeling DNA Replication

6. Place the chains parallel to each other on the table. The "top" blue pin of the first chain should face the "top" yellow pin of the second chain.

7. Demonstrate replication by simulating a replication fork at the top pair of pins. Add the remaining straw segments to complete a new DNA model. Be sure to follow the base-pairing rules.

8. Sketch the process of DNA replication in your lab report. Label the replication fork, the segments of original DNA, and the segments of new DNA in your sketch.

**PART C** Modeling Protein Synthesis

9. Place the chains of one of the DNA models parallel to each other on the table.

10. Repeat step 1, but use the straw segments of the second color.

11. Assign the uracil nucleotide to the white pushpins. Using the available pushpins and the second set of straw segments, construct a model of an mRNA transcript of the DNA segment. Begin by separating the two chains of DNA and pairing the mRNA nucleotides with the left strand of DNA as you transcribe from the top of the segment to the bottom of the segment.

12. In your lab report, sketch the mRNA model that you transcribed from the DNA segment.

13. Refer to Table 10-1 on page 207 and the photo at the left. Label the note cards with amino acids that you will need to translate your mRNA model. Use the "ribosome" oval cards to model translation.

14. In your lab report, write the sequence of amino acids that resulted from the translation.

15. Clean up your materials before leaving the lab.

### Analysis and Conclusions

1. Write the base-pair order for the DNA molecule you created by using the following code: red = adenine, blue = guanine, yellow = cytosine, and green = thymine.

2. How does the replicated model of DNA compare with the original model of DNA?

3. Predict what would happen if the nucleotide pairs in the replicated model were not in the same sequence as the pairs in the original model.

4. What is the relationship between the anticodon of a tRNA and the amino acid the tRNA carries?

5. Write the mRNA transcript of the DNA sequence presented below.

CTG TTC ATA ATT

Next, write the tRNA anticodons that would pair with the mRNA transcript. Use Table 10-1 to write the amino acids coded for by the mRNA transcript.

6. If you transcribed the "wrong" side of the DNA molecule, what would the result be? How might the proteins that the organism produced be affected?

7. What are the advantages of having DNA remain in the nucleus of eukaryotic cells?

### Further Inquiry

Design models to represent a eukaryotic and a prokaryotic cell. Use these models along with the models you constructed in this investigation to demonstrate where replication, transcription, and the steps of protein synthesis occur.

# GENE EXPRESSION

This fruit fly has only one eye as the result of a mutation in a gene that regulates development.

**SECTION 1** *Control of Gene Expression*

**SECTION 2** *Gene Expression in Development and Cell Division*

Unit 6—Gene Expression
Topics 1–6

# CONTROL OF GENE EXPRESSION

*Cells use information in genes to build several thousands of different proteins, each with a unique function. But not all proteins are required by the cell at any one time. By regulating gene expression, cells are able to control when each protein is made.*

## ROLE OF GENE EXPRESSION

**Gene expression** is the activation or "turning on" of a gene that results in transcription and the production of mRNA. Most of the mRNA produced in cells is translated into proteins. But cells do not always need to produce all of the proteins for which their genes contain instructions. Recall that proteins have many different functions. Some proteins play a structural role. Others are enzymes that act as catalysts in chemical reactions. Mechanisms to control gene expression have evolved so that each protein is produced only when it is needed.

The complete genetic material contained in an individual is called the **genome** (JEE-NOHM). By regulating gene expression, cells are able to control which portion of the genome will be expressed and when. Most gene expression occurs at two steps, transcription and translation. Gene expression begins when the enzyme RNA polymerase transcribes the DNA nucleotide sequence of a gene into a specific mRNA. During translation, this mRNA then migrates to a ribosome, where it is translated into a specific protein.

## GENE EXPRESSION IN PROKARYOTES

Scientists first studied gene expression in prokaryotes. Much of our initial knowledge of gene expression came from the work of French scientists François Jacob (1920–) and Jacques Monod (1910–1976) at the Pasteur Institute in Paris. In the early 1960s, Jacob and Monod discovered how genes control the metabolism of the sugar lactose in *Escherichia coli,* a bacterium that lives in the intestines of mammals. Jacob and Monod won the Nobel Prize in 1965 for their discoveries.

### OBJECTIVES

- **Explain** why cells regulate gene expression.
- **Discuss** the role of operons in prokaryotic gene expression.
- **Determine** how repressor proteins and inducers affect transcription in prokaryotes.
- **Describe** the structure of a eukaryotic gene.
- **Compare** the two ways gene expression is controlled in eukaryotes.

### VOCABULARY

gene expression
genome
structural gene
operator
operon
*lac* operon
repressor protein
regulator gene
inducer
euchromatin
intron
exon
pre-mRNA
transcription factor
enhancer

**Word Roots and Origins**

*genome*

from the words *gene* and *chromosome*

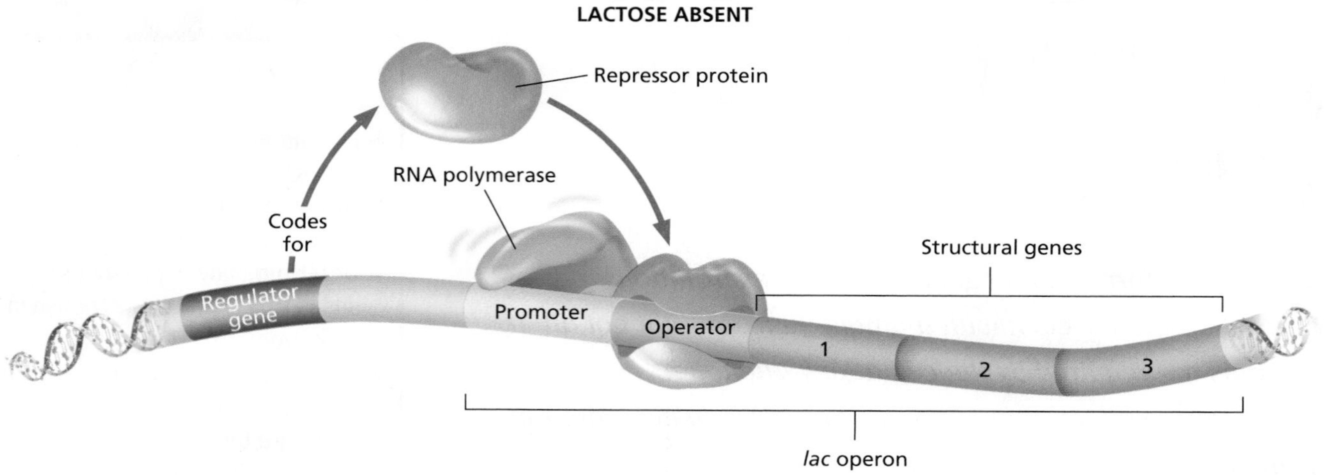

**LACTOSE ABSENT**

*lac* operon

## FIGURE 11-1

In the *lac* operon of *E. coli,* three structural genes code for the enzymes needed to utilize lactose. When lactose is absent, a repressor protein attaches to the operator. The presence of the repressor protein on the operator blocks the advancement of RNA polymerase.

Lactose is a disaccharide that is composed of the two monosaccharides glucose and galactose. When *E. coli* bacteria are in the presence of lactose, the lactose induces *E. coli* to produce three enzymes. These three enzymes control metabolism of lactose. The production of these enzymes is regulated by three elements found within the DNA of *E. coli:*

- **Structural Genes** Genes that code for polypeptides are called **structural genes.** The structural genes studied by Jacob and Monod code for enzymes that allow *E. coli* to metabolize lactose. The three structural genes that code for these three enzymes are located next to each other on the chromosome.

- **Promoter** Recall that a promoter is a DNA segment that is recognized by the enzyme RNA polymerase. This enzyme then initiates transcription.

- **Operator** An **operator** is a DNA segment that serves as a kind of "switch" by controlling the access of RNA polymerase to the promoter. Thus, the operator controls the ability of RNA polymerase to move along the structural genes.

The structural genes, the promoter, and the operator collectively form an operon. An **operon** (AHP-uhr-AHN) is a series of genes that code for specific products and the regulatory elements that control these genes. Researchers have found that the clustered arrangement of genes that form an operon is a pattern that occurs commonly among bacteria. Jacob and Monod named the operon that they studied the ***lac* operon** because its structural genes coded for the enzymes that regulate lactose metabolism. The *lac* operon, shown in Figure 11-1 above, includes the entire segment of DNA required to produce the enzymes involved in lactose metabolism.

Jacob and Monod found that the genes for the enzymes for lactose utilization were expressed only when lactose was present. How were the bacteria able to shut off these genes when lactose was absent? Their research showed that gene activation in the *lac* operon depends on whether the operon is "turned off" or "turned on."

## Operon "Turned Off"

In the absence of lactose, a protein called a *repressor* attaches to the operator. A **repressor protein** is a protein that inhibits genes from being expressed. Repressor proteins are coded for by **regulator genes,** which are located some distance from the operators they affect. The attachment of the repressor protein to the operator physically blocks the advancement of RNA polymerase toward the structural genes and thus inhibits transcription. Figure 11-1 shows how the attachment of the repressor protein to the operator (the "switch") causes the *lac* operon to "turn off."

## Operon "Turned On"

When lactose is present in the *E. coli* cell, lactose binds to the repressor protein. This binding changes the shape of the repressor protein. The change in shape causes the repressor protein to detach from the operator ("the switch"), as shown in Figure 11-2 below. RNA polymerase is no longer blocked from transcribing the structural genes of the *lac* operon. The operon—including the three structural genes—is now "turned on," so all three enzymes required for lactose metabolism are produced. Because it activates, or induces, transcription, lactose acts as an inducer. An **inducer** is a molecule that initiates gene expression.

The *lac* operon illustrates in simple terms the great advantage of regulating gene expression. Cells of *E. coli* are able to "turn off" or "turn on" lactose metabolism depending on whether lactose is present. Because lactose acts as an inducer, the *lac* operon is "turned on" only in the presence of lactose. As a result, lactose induces its own metabolism. When the level of lactose drops, the repressor protein again attaches to the operator, which "turns off" the *lac* operon. Therefore, the three enzymes used in lactose metabolism are not produced when lactose is not present. By controlling gene expression, *E. coli* bacteria conserve resources and produce only those proteins that are needed.

**FIGURE 11-2**

When lactose is present in an *E. coli* cell, lactose acts as an inducer by binding to the repressor protein. The repressor protein then changes shape and detaches. The detachment of the repressor protein allows the transcription of the three structural genes to proceed, and mRNA is produced.

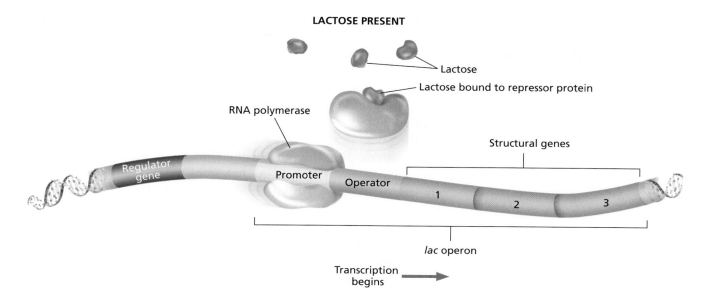

**LACTOSE PRESENT**

Lactose

Lactose bound to repressor protein

RNA polymerase

Structural genes

Regulator gene

Promoter

Operator

1  2  3

*lac* operon

Transcription begins

# GENE EXPRESSION IN EUKARYOTES

Eukaryotes are vastly different from prokaryotes. Their genomes are much larger than those of prokaryotes. In addition, the DNA of eukaryotic cells is located in several individual chromosomes instead of in the single circular chromosome that occurs in prokaryotes. Finally, most eukaryotes are multicellular organisms made of specialized cells. Although each cell type contains a complete set of the organism's genes, only some of these genes are expressed at a given time. Different cell types produce different proteins. Not surprisingly, the control of gene expression in eukaryotes is far more complex than it is in prokaryotes. Although operons are common in prokaryotes, they have not been found often in eukaryotes.

## Structure of a Eukaryotic Gene

Much of the control of gene expression in eukaryotes occurs at the level of the individual chromosome. In eukaryotes, gene expression is partly related to the coiling and uncoiling of DNA within each chromosome. Recall that eukaryotic DNA is organized as fibers of chromatin wrapped around small specialized proteins called *histones*. Prior to mitosis or meiosis, the DNA and histones coil tightly, forming the structures we recognize as chromosomes. After mitosis or meiosis, certain regions of the DNA coils relax, thus making transcription possible. This uncoiled form, known as **euchromatin** (yoo-KROH-muh-tin), is the site of active transcription of DNA into RNA. However, some portions of the chromatin in specific cells remain permanently coiled, so their genes can never be transcribed. Thus, the degree to which DNA is uncoiled indicates the degree of gene expression.

As in prokaryotes, the promoter is the binding site of RNA polymerase in eukaryotes. In the eukaryotic gene, there are two kinds of segments beyond the promoter: introns and exons. **Introns** (IN-trahnz) are sections of a structural gene that are transcribed but are not translated. **Exons** (EK-sahnz) are the sections of a structural gene that, when expressed, are transcribed and translated.

The benefits of the intron-exon pattern of gene organization are not yet fully understood. For many years, scientists were uncertain of the role of introns in the cell. However, recent research suggests that the noncoding RNA transcribed from introns performs important functions even though it is not translated. Some of these functions include regulating RNA that *is* translated, interacting with this coding RNA to influence gene expression, and acting as "switches" that allow protein production only when "turned on" by the presence of certain chemical targets. Scientists continue to explore the role of introns and noncoding RNA. For example, some researchers are investigating medicines that work by affecting the actions of introns and noncoding RNA.

### Word Roots and Origins

*intron* and *exon*

The "int" in the word *intron* comes from the "int" in the word *intervening*. The "ex" in the word *exon* comes from the "ex" in the word *expressed*.

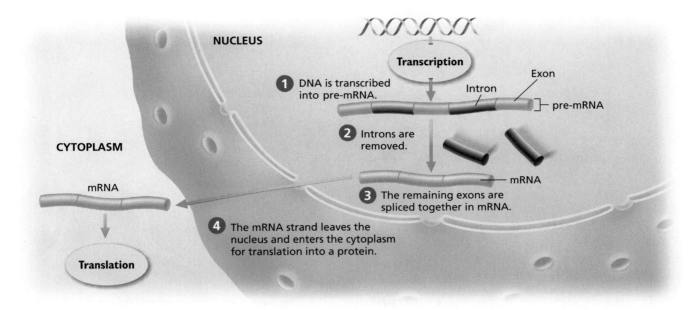

NUCLEUS

Transcription

1 DNA is transcribed into pre-mRNA.

Intron

Exon

pre-mRNA

2 Introns are removed.

CYTOPLASM

mRNA

mRNA

3 The remaining exons are spliced together in mRNA.

4 The mRNA strand leaves the nucleus and enters the cytoplasm for translation into a protein.

Translation

## Control After Transcription

In prokaryotes, transcription and translation occur within the cytoplasm. In eukaryotes, however, transcription occurs in the nucleus, and then mRNA passes through the nuclear envelope and into the cytoplasm, where translation occurs. The physical separation of transcription and translation by the nuclear envelope gives eukaryotes more opportunities to regulate gene expression.

Unlike prokaryotes, eukaryotes can control gene expression by modifying RNA after transcription. When transcription occurs, both introns and exons are transcribed, as shown in step ❶ of Figure 11-3. The result is a large molecule known as pre-mRNA. **Pre-mRNA** is a form of messenger RNA (mRNA) that contains both introns and exons. (Note that the terms *intron* and *exon* can be used to describe both DNA segments and the RNA segments that are transcribed.) A molecule of mRNA is formed when introns are removed (step ❷) from pre-mRNA and the remaining exons are spliced (joined) to one another (step ❸). Complex assemblies of RNA and protein called *spliceosomes* split the pre-mRNA at each end of an intron and join the exons. The end result is an mRNA molecule containing only the exons. The mRNA strand leaves the nucleus and enters the cytoplasm to begin the manufacture of a protein on the ribosomes (step ❹). The nucleotides in the removed introns can be used again during the transcription of additional pre-mRNA. Similar RNA splicing occurs following the transcription of transfer RNA and ribosomal RNA.

The removal of introns and splicing of an mRNA molecule have also been found to occur in another way. Scientists have discovered that RNA molecules can act as biological catalysts. RNA itself can act as a catalyst to remove introns from mRNA molecules as they form in the nucleus. Until this discovery, it was thought that all enzymes were proteins. RNA molecules that act as enzymes are called *ribozymes*.

**FIGURE 11-3**

Both introns and exons are transcribed to form pre-mRNA. Spliceosomes cut out the introns and join the remaining exons together, forming mRNA.

## Quick Lab

### Modeling Post-Transcription Control

**Materials** felt-tip markers, paper, scissors, tape

**Procedure**

1. Write a sentence that contains only three-letter words and makes sense.

2. Hide the words in random places in a long sequence of letters. This sequence should contain random letters and other three-letter words that make no sense in the sentence you are hiding. Print the sequence of letters all the same size, equally spaced, and with no breaks between them.

3. Trade papers with another team. Use scissors to cut out the "introns." Find the message, and reassemble it with tape.

**Analysis** What represents pre-mRNA in this activity? What represents mRNA?

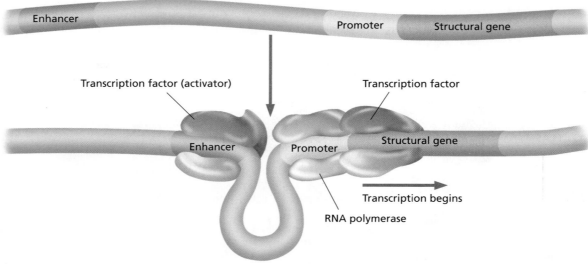

**FIGURE 11-4**

Many enhancers are located far (thousands of nucleotide bases) away from the genes they activate. Transcription factors facilitate transcription by binding to the enhancer and to the promoter.

## Control at the Onset of Transcription

Most gene regulation in eukaryotes occurs when RNA polymerase binds to a gene—the onset of transcription. Eukaryotic cells, like prokaryotic cells, have regulatory genes. But eukaryotic gene regulation involves more proteins, and the interactions are more complicated. Regulatory proteins in eukaryotes are known as **transcription factors.**

Transcription factors help in the placement of RNA polymerase at the correct area on the promoter, as shown in Figure 11-4. Many different transcription factors may influence one gene.

Transcription factors may also bind sequences of DNA called **enhancers.** In general, enhancers are located at a position far—thousands of nucleotide bases away—from the promoter. A loop in the DNA may bring the enhancer and its *activator* (the attached transcription factor) into contact with the RNA polymerase and transcription factors at the promoter. Transcription factors bound to enhancers can activate transcription factors bound to promoters, as shown in Figure 11-4.

---

## SECTION 1 REVIEW

1. Why is it beneficial for organisms to control gene expression?

2. Describe the role of operons in prokaryotic organisms.

3. How does lactose affect the functioning of the *lac* operon?

4. Name the sections of eukaryotic genes that are transcribed and translated.

5. Distinguish between pre-mRNA and mRNA.

**CRITICAL THINKING**

6. **Making Comparisons** What region of a prokaryotic gene is analogous to the enhancer region of a eukaryotic gene?

7. **Predicting Results** How would RNA polymerase be affected if the repressor protein were not bound to the proper site on a gene?

8. **Relating Concepts** How might the absence of a nuclear envelope in prokaryotes prevent prokaryotes from controlling gene expression by modifying RNA after transcription?

# GENE EXPRESSION IN DEVELOPMENT AND CELL DIVISION

*The control of gene expression plays an important role in the growth of eukaryotes as different cells become specialized to perform different tasks. When the expression of genes is altered—by mutations, for example—abnormalities and even cancer can result.*

### OBJECTIVES

- **Summarize** the role of gene expression in an organism's development.
- **Describe** the influence of homeotic genes in eukaryotic development.
- **State** the role of the homeobox in eukaryotic development.
- **Summarize** the effects of mutations in causing cancer.
- **Compare** the characteristics of cancer cells with those of normal cells.

### VOCABULARY

cell differentiation
homeotic gene
homeobox
proto-oncogene
oncogene
tumor
cancer
tumor-suppressor gene
metastasis
carcinogen
carcinoma
sarcoma
lymphoma
leukemia

## GENE EXPRESSION IN DEVELOPMENT

All multicellular, sexually reproducing organisms begin life as a fertilized egg, or zygote. Although every cell in the developing zygote contains all of the organism's genes, only a small number of the genes are expressed. Certain genes are turned on and off as various proteins are needed at different times during the organism's life. For example, as eukaryotes grow, cells become specialized to perform different tasks. Muscle cells specialize in movement, and liver cells specialize in making enzymes that break down fat. The development of cells that have specialized functions is known as **cell differentiation** (DIF-uhr-EN-shee-AY-shuhn). As organisms grow and develop, organs and tissues develop to produce a characteristic form. This development of form in an organism is called *morphogenesis* (MOR-foh-JEN-uh-sis).

### Homeotic Genes

**Homeotic** (HOH-mee-AH-tik) **genes** are regulatory genes that determine where certain anatomical structures, such as appendages, will develop in an organism during morphogenesis. Homeotic genes seem to be master genes of development that determine the overall body organization of multicellular organisms.

When a homeotic gene is transcribed and translated, regulatory proteins are formed. It is thought that these proteins regulate development by switching groups of developmental genes on or off. Such control of gene expression increases or decreases the rates of cell division in various areas of the developing organism. The resultant variation in growth rates in specific areas of the organism produces specific patterns of structural development.

---

**Word Roots and Origins**

*homeotic*

from the Greek *homoioun,* meaning "to make like"

---

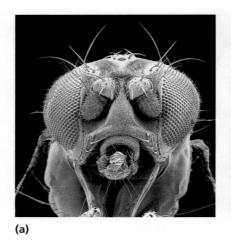

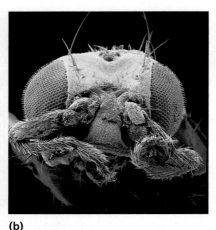

**(a)**                    **(b)**

**FIGURE 11-5**

(a) Homeotic genes are expressed normally in this fruit fly. (b) This fruit fly has legs growing out of its head. This abnormality is caused by a homeotic mutation.

## Homeobox Sequences

One of the best-known examples of homeotic genes is found in fruit flies of the genus *Drosophila*, shown in Figure 11-5a. Each homeotic gene of this fruit fly shares a common DNA sequence of 180 nucleotide pairs. This specific DNA sequence within a homeotic gene is called a **homeobox,** and the homeobox codes for proteins that regulate patterns of development. As the fruit fly embryo becomes an elongated larva, specific homeoboxes control the morphogenesis of specific regions in the larva. Each of these homeoboxes will also control a specific part of the adult fruit fly. As Figure 11-5b shows, a mutation in a homeotic gene can lead to abnormalities. The same or very similar homeobox sequences have been found in homeotic genes of many eukaryotic organisms. It is thought that all organisms may have similar homeoboxes that code for their anatomy.

## Tracking Changes in Gene Expression

The control of gene expression is important not only in the development of an organism but throughout the organism's life. Only a fraction of an organism's genes are expressed in any one cell. And cells constantly switch genes on and off. In the 1990s, researchers developed a tool for tracking gene expression called a *DNA chip.*

DNA chips contain a microscopic grid with thousands of known DNA fragments that are "tagged" with a fluorescent compound. A sample of mRNA from the organism being studied is spread over the grid. When spots on the grid light up, as shown in Figure 11-6, mRNA segments from the sample have linked with complementary sequences of DNA on the chip. Scientists can use this information to determine at once which genes are being expressed.

DNA chips have many practical applications but will likely have a significant impact in medicine. In fact, the technology is already being used to better understand gene expression in cancer.

**FIGURE 11-6**

The lighted spots on this grid of a DNA chip indicate to scientists which genes are being expressed in the cells being studied.

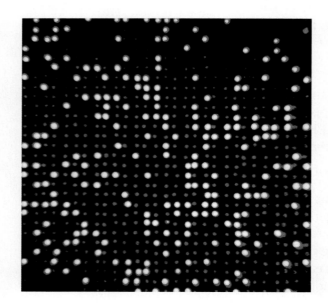

# GENE EXPRESSION, CELL DIVISION, AND CANCER

**internet** connect

www.scilinks.org
**Topic: Cancer Gene (Oncogenes)**
**Keyword: HM60210**

SCI LINKS. Maintained by the National Science Teachers Association

The division of cells is regulated by many genes, including genes called **proto-oncogenes** (PROHT-oh-AHNG-kuh-JEENZ), which regulate cell growth, cell division, and the ability of cells to adhere to one another. These genes code for regulatory proteins that ensure that the events of cell division occur in the proper sequence and at the correct rate.

A mutation in a proto-oncogene can change the gene into an **oncogene,** a gene that can cause uncontrolled cell proliferation. The mutation may lead to the overexpression of proteins that initiate cell division or to the expression of such proteins at inappropriate times during the cell cycle. These conditions can lead to uncontrolled cell division.

## Tumor Development

A **tumor** is an abnormal proliferation of cells that results from uncontrolled, abnormal cell division. The cells that make up a *benign* (bi-NIEN) *tumor* remain within a mass. Benign tumors generally pose no threat to life unless they are allowed to grow until they compress vital organs. Examples of benign tumors are the fibroid cysts that can occur in a woman's breasts or uterus. Most benign tumors can be removed by surgery if necessary.

In a *malignant* (muh-LIG-nuhnt) *tumor,* the uncontrolled dividing cells may invade and destroy healthy tissues elsewhere in the body. This uncontrolled growth of cells that can invade other parts of the body is called **cancer.**

Some genes act as "brakes" to suppress tumor formation. **Tumor-suppressor genes** code for proteins that prevent cell division from occurring too often. In cancer, these tumor-suppressor genes are damaged, and a decrease in the activity of tumor-suppressing proteins can increase the rate of cell division. Cells have three types of tumor-suppressing genes, all of which must be damaged before cancer can occur. Figure 11-7 illustrates how mutations in proto-oncogenes and tumor-suppressor genes may lead to cancer.

**FIGURE 11-7**

Mutations in proto-oncogenes or tumor-suppressor genes can destroy normal gene functioning, possibly resulting in cancer. A mutation in a proto-oncogene may cause the gene to become an oncogene, a gene that can trigger cancer.

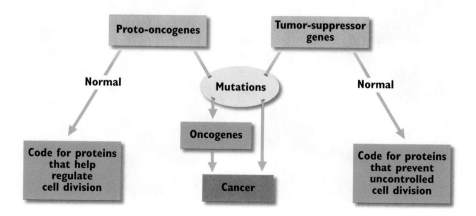

## Gene Expression in Cancer

The expression of oncogenes and mutated tumor-suppressor genes causes cancer cells to behave differently than normal cells. A normal cell must be attached to other cells, to a membrane, or to fibers between cells in order to divide. Also, normal mammalian cells will stop dividing after about 40 cell divisions—or sooner if they become too crowded. Cancer cells, however, continue to divide indefinitely, even when they are very densely packed, seemingly ignoring the normal cellular message to stop dividing. They also continue dividing even after they are no longer attached to other cells, a trait that facilitates the spread of cancer cells throughout the body. The spread of cancer cells beyond their original site is called **metastasis** (muh-TAS-tuh-sis). When metastasis occurs, cancer cells can invade healthy tissues and begin forming new tumors.

## Causes of Cancer

The mutations that alter the expression of genes coding for cell-regulating proteins can occur spontaneously but are more likely to occur as a result of the organism's exposure to a carcinogen (kahr-SIN-uh-juhn). A **carcinogen** is any substance that can induce or promote cancer. Most carcinogens are *mutagens* (MYOOT-uh-JUHNZ), agents that cause mutations to occur within a cell.

Well-known carcinogens include the chemicals in tobacco smoke, asbestos, and ionizing radiation, such as X rays or ultraviolet light from the sun. For example, tobacco smoke, shown in Figure 11-8, has been found to be the cause of more than 85 percent of all lung cancers. Certain viruses can cause cancer. Many viral genes are actually oncogenes. Viruses can also stimulate uncontrolled growth in host cells by causing mutations in proto-oncogenes or tumor-suppressor genes, thus accelerating the rate of cell division in the host cell. Or they may activate the cell's own oncogenes. Viruses have been found to cause some cancers in blood-forming tissues, and the human papilloma virus has been shown to cause cervical cancer.

**FIGURE 11-8**

Tobacco smoke contains more than 60 known carcinogens, including cyanide, formaldehyde, and lead.

# MILESTONES
## IN Recent DNA Research

*Watson and Crick's model of the DNA double helix, established in 1953, has served as a foundation for the ever-growing body of DNA research. In the relatively brief time since the structure of DNA was first determined, several groundbreaking discoveries—many of them very recent—have expanded greatly our knowledge of DNA.*

### Timeline

**1983** The polymerase chain reaction is invented.

**1990** The Human Genome Project is launched.

**1992** The first DNA chip patent is issued.

**1997** Dolly, a successful clone of an adult sheep, is born.

**1998** The first genome sequence of a multicellular organism, the roundworm, is completed.

**2002** Mouse genome sequencing is completed, one year ahead of schedule.

**2003** Sequencing of the human genome is completed.

**2003** Gene linked to heart attacks is discovered.

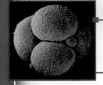

**2004** Korean scientists report the cloning of human embryos.

One area in which many developments have been made in recent years is genetic technology. One of the most important of these was the development of the polymerase chain reaction (PCR) in 1983. PCR allows researchers to quickly make billions of copies of a specific segment of DNA. The ability to copy DNA in mass quantities has made the study of DNA much easier. Another important technological development is the DNA chip, patented in 1992. The DNA chip can be used to track gene expression in organisms. Other recent technological developments include fluorescence in-situ hybridization (FISH), a method used to identify specific parts of a chromosome, and spectral karyotyping (SKY), a form of FISH used to study complex changes in genetic material.

An enormous amount of research has been done in recent years to map the genomes of various organisms, including humans. The Human Genome Project was a cooperative, 13-year effort to map the human genome. The Human Genome Project was funded by the United States Government, contributions from several other countries, and private corporations. By the completion of sequencing in 2003, the U.S. government had spent over 437 million dollars. The project determined the sequence of the 3 billion base pairs that make up human DNA. Remarkably, all goals of the project were completed on time, and at a significantly lower cost than projected. As a result of the Human Genome Project, more than 1,400 genes related to disease have been identified.

Since 1995, scientists have sequenced the genomes of more than 150 organisms. In 1998, the first full sequencing of a genome in a multicellular organism—the roundworm—was completed. In 2002, sequencing of the mouse genome was completed. The mouse genome has its own version of nearly every human gene.

Along with all this recent DNA research come many difficult ethical questions. In 1997, the first successful cloning of an organism from differentiated cells resulted in the birth of Dolly the sheep. Since then many animals have been cloned. But Dolly began to suffer early from conditions normally found only in older sheep, raising questions about possible problems of premature aging in clones. Dolly was euthanized in 2003.

### Review

1. Name a practical application of the Human Genome Project.
2. **Critical Thinking** Why might it be useful to study the genomes of other organisms besides humans?
3. **Critical Thinking** Why might clones such as Dolly the sheep suffer from premature aging?

**internet** connect

**www.scilinks.org**
**Topic: Genetic Tools**
**Keyword: HM60657**

SCILINKS. Maintained by the National Science Teachers Association

227

FIGURE 11-9

The top photo shows a healthy lung. The bottom photo shows carcinomas in a diseased lung. Lung cancer is one of the deadliest forms of cancer; 87 percent of lung cancer patients die within five years of diagnosis.

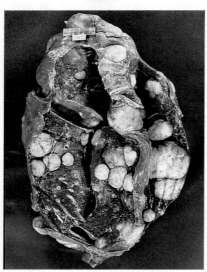

## Risks of Developing Cancer

Whether a person actually develops cancer seems to depend on many factors. Some families exhibit higher-than-average rates of certain cancers, leading researchers to determine that some people have a genetic predisposition to these types of cancer. With regard to cancers caused by mutagens, the number of exposures to the carcinogen and the amount of carcinogen in each exposure are significant factors. Mutations in gametes (egg or sperm cells) are especially important because these mutations are passed along to offspring.

Usually, more than one mutation is needed to produce a cancer cell. Perhaps this helps to explain why the cancer risk increases with the number of exposures to carcinogens and with the age of the individual. The longer an individual lives, the more mutations he or she will accumulate. But according to the National Cancer Institute in 2003, heightened awareness of the causes of cancer, combined with improved detection and treatment of the disease, has resulted in a decline in the number of deaths in the United States caused by the four most common cancers. The death rate for all cancers combined has also stabilized.

## Kinds of Cancer

Malignant tumors can be categorized according to the types of tissues affected. **Carcinomas** (KAHR-suh-NOH-muhz) grow in the skin and the tissues that line the organs of the body. Lung cancer, shown in Figure 11-9, and breast cancer are examples of carcinomas. **Sarcomas** (sahr-KOH-muhz) grow in bone and muscle tissue. **Lymphomas** (lim-FOH-muhz) are solid tumors that grow in the tissues of the lymphatic system. Tumors in blood-forming tissues may cause **leukemia** (loo-KEE-mee-uh), the uncontrolled production of white blood cells. Usually, it takes several years for cancer to develop. However, when a vital organ, such as the liver or pancreas, is involved, the symptoms caused by organ dysfunction due to cancer may develop more rapidly.

## SECTION 2 REVIEW

1. How can morphogenesis be affected by the control of gene expression?

2. What is the role of homeotic genes in fruit flies of the genus *Drosophila?*

3. Explain the relationship between a homeobox and a homeotic gene.

4. Describe how mutations in proto-oncogenes or tumor-suppressor genes can lead to cancer.

5. List three ways in which cancer cells differ from normal cells.

**CRITICAL THINKING**

6. **Relating Concepts** Why might X rays be more dangerous to an ovary than to muscle tissue?

7. **Predicting Patterns** Tobacco products were first introduced in Europe in the late 1500s. Draw a graph showing a possible pattern of lung cancer rates in Europe over the past 1000 years.

8. **Inferring Relationships** What does the presence of similar homeobox sequences among many eukaryotic organisms suggest about the possible evolutionary relationships between these organisms?

# CHAPTER HIGHLIGHTS

**Control of Gene Expression**

- Gene expression is the activation of a gene that results in transcription and the production of mRNA. Only a fraction of any cell's genes are expressed at any one time.

- A promoter and an operator regulate the transcription of structural genes. In prokaryotes, the structural genes, the promoter, and the operator collectively form an operon.

- A promoter is the segment of DNA that is recognized by the enzyme RNA polymerase, which then initiates transcription. An operator is the segment of DNA that acts as a "switch" by controlling the access of RNA polymerase to the promoter.

- A repressor protein can inhibit genes from being expressed. Repressor proteins are coded for by regulator genes. A repressor protein attaches to the operator, physically blocking the advancement of RNA polymerase.

- An inducer is a molecule that initiates gene expression. In *E. coli*, lactose serves as an inducer. An inducer binds to the repressor protein. As a result, the shape of the repressor protein changes, and the repressor protein detaches from the operator. RNA polymerase can then advance to the structural genes.

- Eukaryotes do not have operons. The genomes of eukaryotes are larger and more complex than those of prokaryotes.

- Eukaryotic genes are organized into noncoding sections, called *introns,* and coding sections, called *exons.*

- In eukaryotes, gene expression can be controlled after transcription—through the removal of introns from pre-mRNA—or at the onset of transcription—through the action of transcription factors.

**Vocabulary**

| | | | |
|---|---|---|---|
| gene expression (p. 217) | operon (p. 218) | inducer (p. 219) | pre-mRNA (p. 221) |
| genome (p. 217) | *lac* operon (p. 218) | euchromatin (p. 220) | transcription factor (p. 222) |
| structural gene (p. 218) | repressor protein (p. 219) | intron (p. 220) | enhancer (p. 222) |
| operator (p. 218) | regulator gene (p. 219) | exon (p. 220) | |

**Gene Expression in Development and Cell Division**

- The development of specialized cells is called *cell differentiation.* The development of form in an organism is called *morphogenesis.* Both cell differentiation and morphogenesis are governed by gene expression.

- Homeotic genes are regulatory genes that determine where anatomical structures will be placed during development.

- Within each homeotic gene, a specific DNA sequence known as the *homeobox* regulates patterns of development. The homeoboxes of many eukaryotic organisms appear to be very similar.

- Mutations of proto-oncogenes or tumor-suppressor genes may lead to cancer. Cancer is the uncontrolled growth of abnormal cells.

- A carcinogen is any substance that can induce or promote cancer. Most carcinogens are mutagens, substances that cause mutations.

- Unlike normal cells, cancer cells continue to divide indefinitely, even if they become densely packed. Cancer cells will also continue dividing even if they are no longer attached to other cells.

**Vocabulary**

| | | | |
|---|---|---|---|
| cell differentiation (p. 223) | oncogene (p. 225) | tumor-suppressor gene (p. 225) | carcinoma (p. 228) |
| homeotic gene (p. 223) | tumor (p. 225) | metastasis (p. 226) | sarcoma (p. 228) |
| homeobox (p. 224) | cancer (p. 225) | carcinogen (p. 226) | lymphoma (p. 228) |
| proto-oncogene (p. 225) | | | leukemia (p. 228) |

## USING VOCABULARY

1. For each pair of terms, explain how the meanings of the terms differ.
   a. *operator* and *operon*
   b. *proto-oncogene* and *oncogene*
   c. *intron* and *exon*
   d. *homeotic gene* and *homeobox*

2. Explain the relationships between carcinogen and mutagen.

3. Use the following terms in the same sentence: *gene, gene expression, regulator gene,* and *repressor protein.*

4. **Word Roots and Origins** The word *morphogenesis* is derived from the Greek *morphe,* which means "shape," and the Latin *genus,* which means "birth." Using this information, explain why the term *morphogenesis* is a good name for the biological process that the term describes.

## UNDERSTANDING KEY CONCEPTS

5. **Identify** the term that describes the activation of a gene that results in transcription and the production of mRNA.

6. **Name** the kind of organism in which gene expression was first observed.

7. **Describe** how *E. coli* benefit by making enzymes to utilize lactose only when lactose is in the cellular environment.

8. **Explain** what causes the *lac* operon to "turn off" and "turn on."

9. **Compare** pre-mRNA with mRNA.

10. **Describe** the role of enhancers in the control of gene expression.

11. **Evaluate** the relationship between gene expression and morphogenesis.

12. **Identify** the role of homeoboxes in morphogenesis.

13. **Compare** the roles of proto-oncogenes and tumor-suppression genes.

14. **State** the unusual characteristic of cancer cells that can lead to metastasis.

15. **Define** *carcinogen.*

16. **Unit 6—Gene Expression**

    Write a report describing the influence of homeotic genes on an organism's development.

17. **CONCEPT MAPPING** Use the following terms to create a concept map that shows how a mutated gene can lead to cancer: *exon, gene expression, intron, mutagen, oncogene, proto-oncogene, tumor-suppressor gene,* and *tumor.*

## CRITICAL THINKING

18. **Analyzing Information** Kwashiorkor is a disease in children caused by a diet high in carbohydrates but lacking in complete protein. When children with kwashiorkor are put on a diet rich in protein, they may become very ill with ammonia poisoning, and some even die. The high level of ammonia in their blood is due to the inadequate metabolism of protein. What does this tell you about the enzymes that metabolize protein?

19. **Relating Concepts** Fruit flies of the genus *Drosophila* feed on fermenting fruit, which often contains a large amount of alcohol. If these fruit flies are fed a diet that has a high alcohol content, the amount of the enzyme that metabolizes alcohol in the digestive tract increases. What does this increase tell you about the enzyme?

20. **Interpreting Graphics** Study the diagram of the *lac* operon shown below.
    a. Describe the role of the following elements shown in the diagram: promoter, operator, and structural genes.
    b. What does it mean to say that an operon is "turned on"?
    c. Is the operon "turned on" in the diagram shown below?

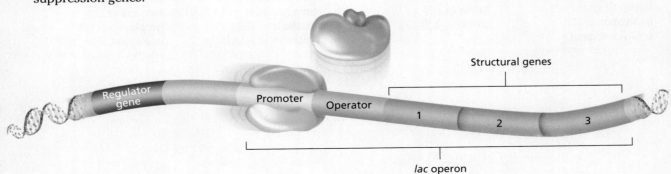

Regulator gene

Promoter

Operator

Structural genes

1    2    3

*lac* operon

# Standardized Test Preparation

**DIRECTIONS:** Choose the letter of the answer choice that best answers the question.

1. Which of the following codes for a repressor protein?
   A. enhancer
   B. promoter
   C. regulator gene
   D. structural gene

2. Which component of an operon controls the advancement of RNA polymerase?
   F. exon
   G. operator
   H. promoter
   J. structural gene

3. Pre-mRNA contains which of the following?
   A. exons only
   B. introns only
   C. both introns and exons
   D. neither introns nor exons

**INTERPRETING GRAPHICS:** The graph below shows the number of cigarettes smoked per capita per year between 1920 and 2000 and the annual incidence of lung cancer among women. Use the graph to answer the question that follows.

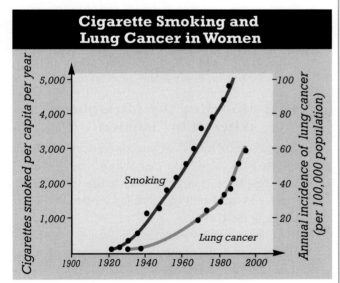

4. What was the relationship between number of cigarettes smoked and incidence of lung cancer?
   F. There was no relationship between cigarette smoking and lung cancer.
   G. As the number of cigarettes smoked decreased, the incidence of lung cancer increased.
   H. As the number of cigarettes smoked increased, the incidence of lung cancer increased.
   J. As the number of cigarettes smoked increased, the incidence of lung cancer decreased.

**DIRECTIONS:** Complete the following analogy.

5. skin : carcinoma :: blood-forming tissue :
   A. sarcoma
   B. leukemia
   C. lymphoma
   D. carcinogen

**INTERPRETING GRAPHICS:** The diagram below shows how mutations in certain genes can lead to cancer. Use the diagram to answer the questions that follow.

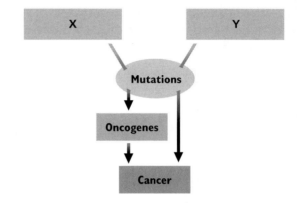

6. What does *X* represent?
   F. mutagens
   G. carcinogens
   H. proto-oncogenes
   J. tumor-suppressor genes

7. What does *Y* represent?
   A. mutagens
   B. carcinogens
   C. proto-oncogenes
   D. tumor-suppressor genes

## SHORT RESPONSE

A biologist isolates mRNA from a mouse brain and liver and finds that the two types of mRNA differ.

Can these results be correct, or has the biologist made an error? Explain your answer.

## EXTENDED RESPONSE

Mutations may occur in gametes or in body cells.

*Part A* In which cell type could a mutation cause genetic variation in a population?

*Part B* Explain how genetic variation could result from a mutation in this cell type.

**Test TIP** When using a graph to answer a question, make sure you know what variables are represented on the *x*- and *y*-axes before answering.

# Modeling Gene Expression in the *lac* Operon

## OBJECTIVES

- Make a model of the *lac* operon.
- Demonstrate the mechanisms that regulate gene expression in the *lac* operon of *Escherichia coli*.
- Simulate the transcription of the structural genes in the *lac* operon.

## PROCESS SKILLS

- comparing and contrasting
- identifying
- demonstrating
- manipulating a model

## MATERIALS

- pipe cleaner
- large colored beads, 6
- colored modeling clay in three colors
- labeling tape
- marking pen
- pencil
- paper

## Background

1. Define *gene*.
2. What is the role of RNA polymerase in protein synthesis?
3. Where does protein synthesis occur? What is the function of mRNA in protein synthesis?
4. What is the role of ribosomes during protein synthesis?
5. What are the roles of the operator, promoter, and structural genes within the *lac* operon?
6. How does the presence or absence of lactose affect the *lac* operon?
7. What is a regulator gene?

### PART A  Making a Model of the *lac* Operon

1. In this investigation, you will use the materials provided to make a model of a *lac* operon. Allow the pipe cleaner to represent the portion of DNA that constitutes the *lac* operon.
2. Thread the pipe cleaner through three beads of similar size, shape, and color. These three beads represent the structural genes of the *lac* operon.
3. Add one bead to represent the operator portion of the *lac* operon. Also, add beads to represent the promoter and the regulator gene, respectively.
4. Using labeling tape and a marking pen, label each of the beads you have placed on the pipe cleaner. This represents a model of the *lac* operon.
5. Compare the sequence of the labeled beads on the pipe cleaner with the sequence of segments in the diagram of the *lac* operon in the chapter. When your model of the *lac* operon correctly reflects the parts of the *lac* operon in the figure, proceed to Part B.

### PART B  Modeling the *lac* Operon When It Is "Turned Off"

6. Choose one color of modeling clay to represent the enzyme RNA polymerase, and choose another color to represent the repressor molecule. Use the modeling clay to mold an RNA polymerase molecule and a repressor molecule.
7. Using the molecules you made out of clay in step 6, modify your model of the *lac* operon so that it shows the *lac* operon when it is "turned off."
8. In your lab report, draw your model of the *lac* operon when it is "turned off." Label all parts of your drawing. How does the presence of the repressor molecule prevent transcription of the structural genes?

## PART C Modeling the *lac* Operon When It Is "Turned On"

9. Choose a third color of modeling clay to represent the inducer molecule. Use the modeling clay to form an inducer molecule.

10. Using the inducer molecule you made out of clay, modify your model of the *lac* operon so that it shows the *lac* operon when it is "turned on."

11. Simulate the activation of the *lac* operon and the transcription of the structural genes.

12. In your lab report, prepare a diagram of your model that shows the expression of the structural genes in the *lac* operon. Include ribosomes and mRNA in your diagram. Label all parts of your diagram.

13. The graphic organizer below shows the sequence of steps that occurs after lactose enters *E. coli* cells. Copy this graphic organizer in your lab report. Complete the graphic organizer by describing what takes place during step 2 and step 3. Explain how the end product affects the events shown in the graphic organizer.

14. Clean up your materials before leaving the lab.

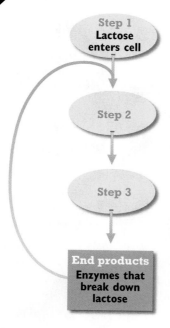

Step 1
Lactose enters cell

Step 2

Step 3

End products
Enzymes that break down lactose

## Analysis and Conclusions

1. What substance serves as an inducer in the *lac* operon?
2. How might a mutation in the regulator gene affect the *lac* operon?
3. Look at the diagram you made in step 12. Refer to your diagram, and predict what will happen when the inducer is no longer present.
4. How would the loss of the promoter site from the operon affect the production of the enzymes needed to utilize lactose?
5. In homes and apartments, a consistent temperature is maintained by means of a thermostat, which regulates when heating (or air conditioning) is turned on or off. In what way does the *lac* operon function like a thermostat?
6. Biological processes often take place in a series of sequential steps called a *biochemical pathway*. Many biochemical pathways are controlled by feedback inhibition. In feedback inhibition, a pathway's end product affects an earlier step in the pathway and causes the pathway to stop. Explain how the function of the *lac* operon is similar to the process of feedback inhibition.

## Further Inquiry

1. Use classroom or library references to find examples of feedback inhibition in biology. Describe why models of feedback inhibition are sometimes called *feedback loops*.
2. The products of the *lac* operon are produced when lactose is present. In this way, the presence of a specific molecule stimulates transcription of the structural genes. In contrast, some operons are repressed when a specific molecule is present. Use classroom or library references to find out how the *trp* operon functions in *E. coli*. Then, compare the function of the *trp* operon with the function of the *lac* operon.

# INHERITANCE PATTERNS AND HUMAN GENETICS

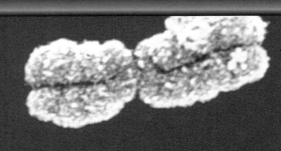
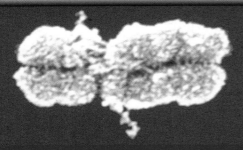
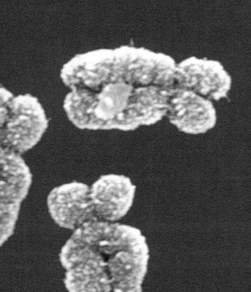

Almost every human body cell except a sperm or an egg has 23 pairs of chromosomes. Each chromosome contains thousands of genes that play an important role in how a person develops, functions, and grows.

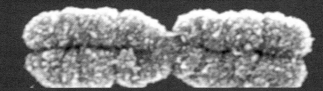

**SECTION 1** *Chromosomes and Inheritance*

**SECTION 2** *Human Genetics*

BIOLOGY INTERACTIVE TUTOR

**Unit 5—Heredity**
Topics 1–6

# CHROMOSOMES AND INHERITANCE

*Francis Collins and his lab group discovered the gene responsible for cystic fibrosis (CF). Cystic fibrosis often is a fatal genetic disorder. Thick, sticky mucus builds up and blocks ducts in the pancreas and intestines and causes difficulty in breathing. In this chapter, you will learn how diseases, such as CF, and characteristics, such as eye color, are inherited and expressed.*

## CHROMOSOMES

Jeff Pinard, a student in Collins's lab, studied more about how CF is inherited. Pinard, shown in Figure 12-1, has CF. Pinard and the rest of Collins's group were able to study the CF gene in part because of work carried out by geneticists in the early 1900s.

### Early Work

In the early 1900s, researcher Thomas Hunt Morgan began experimenting with the small fruit fly *Drosophila melanogaster*. Morgan observed that the flies have four pairs of chromosomes. He also observed that three of the pairs were identical in both females and males, but one pair differed in size and shape. In females, the fourth pair had two identical chromosomes, now called *X chromosomes*. In males, the fourth pair had one X chromosome, but also a shorter chromosome, now called a *Y chromosome*. Today, geneticists call the X and Y chromosomes *sex chromosomes*.

### OBJECTIVES

- **Distinguish** between sex chromosomes and autosomes.
- **Explain** the role of sex chromosomes in sex determination.
- **Describe** how an X- or Y-linked gene affects the inheritance of traits.
- **Explain** the effect of crossing-over on the inheritance of genes in linkage groups.
- **Distinguish** between chromosome mutations and gene mutations.

### VOCABULARY

sex chromosome
autosome
sex-linked trait
linked gene
chromosome map
map unit
germ-cell mutation
somatic-cell mutation
lethal mutation
deletion
inversion
translocation
nondisjunction
point mutation
substitution
frameshift mutation
insertion mutation

**FIGURE 12-1**

Student Jeff Pinard uses molecular techniques to learn about the genetic variation that causes his symptoms of cystic fibrosis (CF).

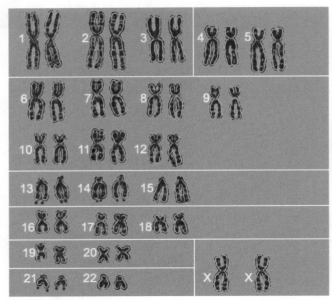

**(a)** Female karyotype

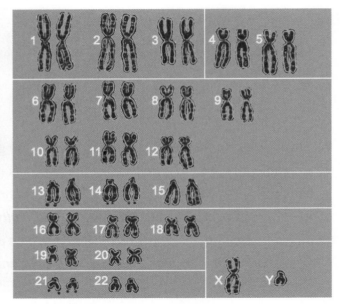

**(b)** Male karyotype

**FIGURE 12-2**

Human female and male karyotypes have in common 22 chromosome pairs, called *autosomes.* The karyotype of females (a) differs from that of males (b) in only the 23rd pair, which consists of the sex chromosomes. The 23rd chromosome pair has two X chromosomes in females and one X chromosome and one Y chromosome in males.

---

**Word Roots and Origins**

*autosome*

from the Greek *autos,* meaning "self," and *soma,* meaning "a body"

---

## Sex Chromosomes and Autosomes

The **sex chromosomes** contain genes that determine the sex (gender) of an individual. The remaining chromosomes that are not directly involved in determining the sex of an individual are called **autosomes.** As in fruit flies, human males have an X and a Y chromosome, and human females have two X chromosomes. Figure 12-2a shows an example of the 23 pairs of human chromosomes from a female; Figure 12-2b shows an example of chromosomes from a male. In certain organisms, such as chickens and moths, males have two identical sex chromosomes, and females have two different sex chromosomes. Most plants and some fish lack sex chromosomes entirely.

## Sex Determination

Like other homologous chromosomes, sex chromosomes pair during meiosis I. As meiosis proceeds, the paired chromosomes separate and move to different cells. As a result, a sperm cell has an equal chance of receiving an X chromosome or a Y chromosome. Each egg, however, receives only an X chromosome. This system of sex determination results in a one-to-one ratio of males to females. Each egg and sperm cell also receives a single copy of each autosome.

In mammals, when an egg that carries an X chromosome is fertilized by a sperm carrying a Y chromosome, the offspring has an XY pair and is male. Likewise, when an egg is fertilized by a sperm cell carrying an X chromosome, the offspring has an XX pair and is female. In a male mammal, the Y chromosome contains a gene called *SRY* for **S**ex-determining **R**egion **Y.** This gene codes for a protein that causes the gonads of an embryo to develop as testes. Because female embryos do not have the *SRY* gene, the gonads develop as ovaries.

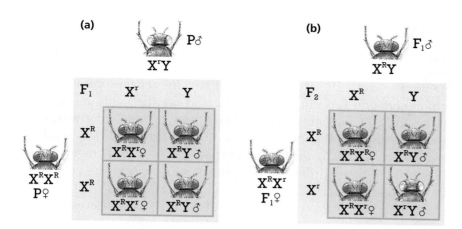

**FIGURE 12-3**

Eye color is a sex-linked trait in fruit flies, as these two Punnett squares show. (a) A male (♂) with white eyes mated to a female (♀) with red eyes yields all red-eyed $F_1$ offspring. (b) An $F_1$ cross results in an $F_2$ generation in which all females are red-eyed, half of the males are red-eyed, and half of the males are white-eyed.

# EFFECTS OF GENE LOCATION

When Morgan was doing his research with fruit flies, one of the lab members noticed that a single male fruit fly had white eyes instead of the red eyes that are normally found in the flies. Morgan crossed this white-eyed male with a normal red-eyed female, and found that all the $F_1$ offspring had red eyes, as shown in Figure 12-3a. This demonstrated that the red-eye trait is dominant to the white-eye trait. Morgan next crossed $F_1$ males with $F_1$ females, as shown in Figure 12-3b. The resulting $F_2$ generation showed the expected ratio of three red-eyed flies to one white-eyed fly. Unexpectedly, however, all of the white-eyed flies were male.

## Sex-Linked Genes and Traits

Based on this surprising observation, Morgan hypothesized that the gene for eye color is carried on the X chromosome and that the Y chromosome lacks an allele for the eye-color gene. An X chromosome carries a gene for eye color, either $X^R$ (red-eye allele) or $X^r$ (white-eye allele). In a cross of an $X^RX^R$ female (red-eyed) with an $X^rY$ male (white-eyed), all of the $F_1$ females will be $X^RX^r$ (red-eyed), and all of the $F_1$ males will be $X^RY$ (red-eyed).

In the $F_2$ generation, half of the females will be $X^RX^R$, and the other half will be $X^RX^r$. Because all have the dominant allele *R*, all will be red-eyed. In the $F_2$ males, however, half will be $X^RY$ (red-eyed), but the other half will be $X^rY$ (white-eyed).

The results of these experiments showed Morgan not only that genes reside on chromosomes but also that the red eye-color gene resides on the X chromosome. Morgan called genes located on the X chromosome *X-linked genes*. He called genes on the Y chromosome, such as *SRY* in humans, *Y-linked genes*. The term **sex-linked trait** refers to a trait that is coded for by an allele on a sex chromosome. The X chromosome is much larger than the Y chromosome, so there are more X-linked than Y-linked traits. Most X-linked alleles have no homologous counterpart on the Y chromosome. Because males have only one X chromosome, a male who carries a recessive allele on the X chromosome will exhibit the sex-linked trait.

### Quick Lab

#### Modeling Linkage

**Materials** Two kinds of candy, toothpicks, pencil, paper

**Procedure** Use two kinds of candy, each kind of which has two colors, to represent genes for two traits. Long noses are dominant over short noses. Large ears are dominant over small ears. One color of candy will represent the dominant allele, and a different color candy will represent the recessive allele. Use these materials to determine the outcome of a cross between two individuals, each heterozygous for both traits. Your teacher will tell you if the genes are linked or not.

1. Draw a Punnett square. Use the appropriate alleles to make gametes for each individual. Then place the allele combinations in each square representing the possible zygotes from that cross.

2. If your genes are linked, you must use toothpicks to link the genes together before you arrange gametes on your Punnett square.

**Analysis** What is the phenotypic ratio in the offspring when the genes are not linked? What is the phenotypic ratio when the genes are linked? Explain the difference.

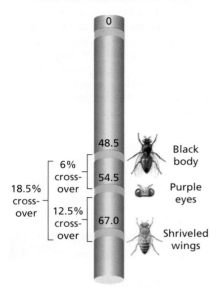

**FIGURE 12-4**

The cross-over frequency between the gene for black body and the gene for purple eyes is 6 percent, so these two genes are 6 map units apart. The cross-over frequency between the purple-eye gene and the shriveled-wing gene is 12.5 percent, which is equivalent to 12.5 map units. The black-body gene and the shriveled-wing gene are 18.5 map units apart.

**HUMAN X CHROMOSOME**

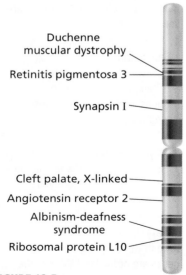

**FIGURE 12-5**

The locations of a few genes on the X chromosome are shown here.

# Linked Genes

Morgan and other geneticists hypothesized that if genes are inherited together, the reason is that they occur on the same chromosome. For example, Morgan studied two fly genes—one for body color and one for wing length—located on the same autosome. Gray body, *G,* was dominant to black body, *g,* and long wings, *L,* were dominant to short wings, *l.* Morgan crossed gray-bodied, long-winged (*GGLL*) flies with black-bodied, short-winged (*ggll*) flies. All the $F_1$ offspring had the genotype *GgLl* and were gray with long wings.

Morgan then crossed members of the $F_1$ generation with one another (*GgLl* × *GgLl*) to produce an $F_2$ generation. The flies in the $F_2$ generation occurred in a phenotypic ratio of three gray, long-winged flies to one black, short-winged fly. If the alleles of the two genes had been located on different chromosomes, they would have assorted independently and produced an $F_2$ generation with a phenotypic ratio of 9:3:3:1 as in Mendel's peas. Morgan called pairs of genes that tend to be inherited together **linked genes,** and he called a set of linked genes a *linkage group*.

Morgan hypothesized that genes are linked because they are found on the same chromosome. An unexpected observation helped confirm this hypothesis. His $F_2$ crosses produced a few offspring unlike either parent, with gray bodies and short wings (*Ggll*) or black bodies and long wings (*ggLl*). Morgan realized mutations are too rare to explain all the exceptions he saw. Morgan thus inferred that the natural rearrangement process during crossing-over must be responsible. Recall that *crossing-over* is the exchange of pieces of DNA between homologous chromosomes. Crossing-over during the first division of meiosis does not create new genes or delete old ones. Instead, it rearranges allele combinations.

# Chromosome Mapping

The farther apart two genes are located on a chromosome, the more likely a cross-over will occur. The greater the percentage of $F_2$ offspring showing recombinant traits, the farther apart the genes for those traits must lie on a chromosome.

Researchers conduct breeding experiments and use the resulting data to prepare a chromosome map. A **chromosome map** is a diagram that shows the linear order of genes on a chromosome. Alfred H. Sturtevant, one of Morgan's students, made the first chromosome map for flies, as shown in Figure 12-4. To prepare his map, Sturtevant compared the frequency of crossing-over for several genes. The percentage of crossing-over for two traits is proportional to the distance between them on a chromosome. Sturtevant defined one **map unit** as a frequency of crossing-over of 1 percent.

Today, researchers have new techniques to map genes. A simplified map of the human X chromosome, made by using these new techniques, is shown in Figure 12-5.

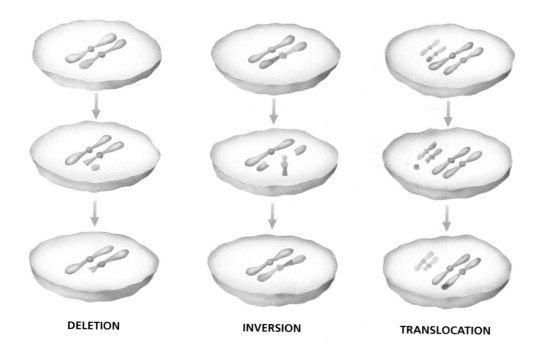

DELETION          INVERSION          TRANSLOCATION

# MUTATIONS

Cystic fibrosis results from a mutation. A *mutation* is a change in the nucleotide-base sequence of a gene or DNA molecule. **Germ-cell mutations** occur in an organism's gametes. Germ-cell mutations do not affect the organism itself, but they can be passed on to offspring. **Somatic-cell** (soh-MAT-ik SEL) **mutations** take place in an organism's body cells and can therefore affect the organism. For example, certain types of human skin cancer and leukemia result from somatic-cell mutations. Somatic-cell mutations cannot be inherited.

**Lethal mutations** cause death, often before birth. Some mutations, however, result in phenotypes that are beneficial to the individual. Organisms with beneficial mutations have a better chance of surviving and reproducing, and therefore have an evolutionary advantage. Mutations provide the variation upon which natural selection acts. Mutations can involve an entire chromosome or a single DNA nucleotide.

## Chromosome Mutations

Chromosome mutations involve changes in the structure of a chromosome or the loss or gain of a chromosome. Three types of chromosome mutations are shown in Figure 12-6. A **deletion** is the loss of a piece of a chromosome due to breakage. In an **inversion,** a chromosomal segment breaks off, flips around backward, and reattaches. In a **translocation,** a piece of one chromosome breaks off and reattaches to a nonhomologous chromosome. In **nondisjunction** (NAHN-dis-JUNGK-shuhn), a chromosome fails to separate from its homologue during meiosis. One gamete receives an extra copy of a chromosome, and another gamete receives no copies. An example of nondisjunction that results in Down syndrome is shown in Figure 12-7.

**FIGURE 12-6**

In some types of mutations, chromosomes break. In a deletion, a piece of a chromosome is lost. In an inversion, a piece flips and reattaches. In a translocation, a broken piece attaches to a nonhomologous chromosome.

**FIGURE 12-7**

Some chromosome mutations are the loss or gain of entire chromosomes. The mutation that gives a person three copies of chromosome 21 results in Down Syndrome.

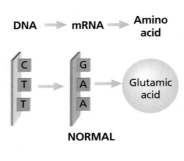

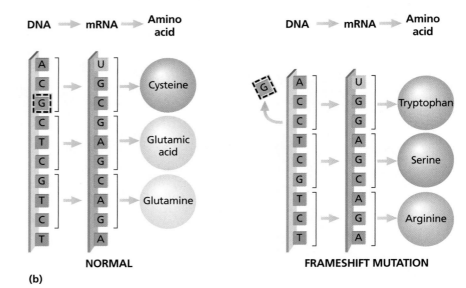

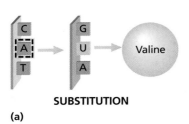

NORMAL

SUBSTITUTION

(a)

NORMAL

FRAMESHIFT MUTATION

(b)

**FIGURE 12-8**

(a) In a substitution mutation, one nucleotide replaces another, forming a new codon that may signal the insertion of the wrong amino acid.
(b) Deleting a nucleotide causes all subsequent codons to be incorrectly read, resulting in a frameshift mutation. Adding a nucleotide shifts the codon grouping too, and causes misreading.

## Gene Mutations

The substitution, addition, or removal of a single nucleotide is a **point mutation,** which is a change that occurs within a single gene or other segment of DNA on a chromosome. In a **substitution,** one nucleotide replaces another, as shown in Figure 12-8a. If this substitution occurs in a codon, the amino acid can be changed. In a deletion mutation, one or more nucleotides in a gene are lost. This loss can cause incorrect grouping of the remaining codons, called a **frameshift mutation,** making all amino acids downstream change. A frameshift mutation is shown in Figure 12-8b. This mutation, in turn, can have a disastrous effect on the protein's function. In **insertion mutations,** one or more nucleotides are added to a gene, which can also result in a frameshift mutation.

## SECTION 1 REVIEW

1. Compare sex chromosomes with autosomes.

2. How does the inheritance of sex chromosomes result in approximately equal numbers of males and females among the offspring of fruit flies?

3. Explain why Morgan did not find white-eyed female *D. melanogaster* in the F₂ generation when he crossed white-eyed males with red-eyed females.

4. How do sex linkage and crossing-over show that genes are found on chromosomes?

5. How can crossing-over between two alleles be used to map their locations on chromosomes?

6. Describe how nondisjunction can change chromosome number.

**CRITICAL THINKING**

7. **Predicting Results** What cross could Morgan have performed to make the first white-eyed female fruit fly?

8. **Analyzing Concepts** Three genes (A, B, and C) are on the same chromosome. However, only C and A are usually expressed together in the same phenotype. Explain this result and describe the relative positions of A, B, and C on the chromosome.

9. **Relating Concepts** Chromosome mutations most often occur during nuclear division. Explain why this is a true statement.

# HUMAN GENETICS

*This section investigates how geneticists analyze genetic data from families to track the inheritance of human genes. It also explores the genetic and environmental factors that influence human genetic traits and disorders, and discusses how geneticists detect and treat human genetic disorders.*

## INHERITANCE OF TRAITS

Geneticists can study human genetic traits and trace genetic diseases from one generation to the next by studying the phenotypes of family members in a pedigree.

### Pedigrees

A **pedigree** is a diagram that shows how a trait is inherited over several generations. Figure 12-9 is a pedigree of a family that has several cases of cystic fibrosis. In a pedigree, squares stand for males and circles stand for females. A filled symbol means that the person has the trait or condition. An empty symbol means that the person does not have the trait or condition. A horizontal line joining a male and female indicates a mating. A vertical line indicates offspring arranged from left to right in order of their birth. Roman numerals label different generations.

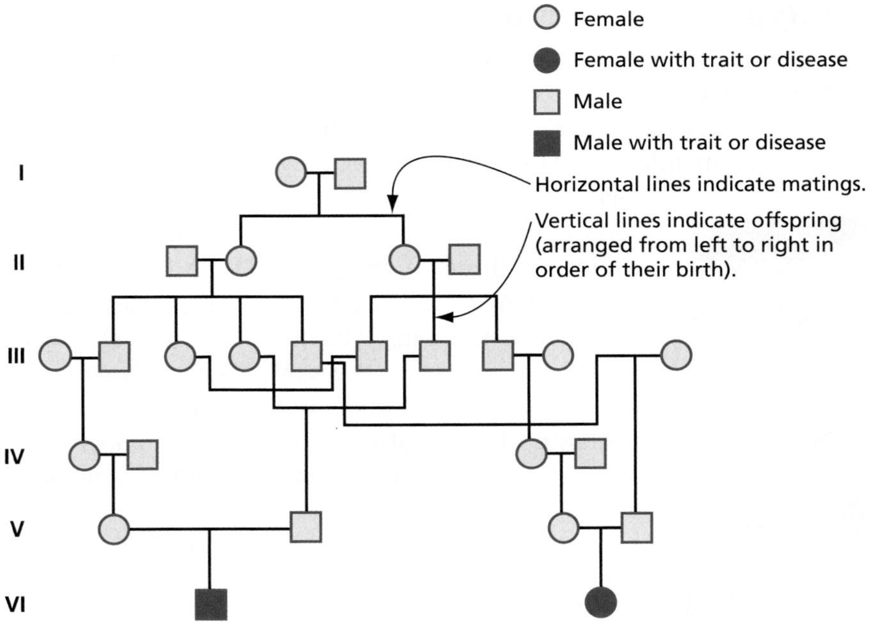

### OBJECTIVES

- **Analyze** pedigrees to determine how genetic traits and genetic disorders are inherited.
- **Summarize** the different patterns of inheritance seen in genetic traits and genetic disorders.
- **Explain** the inheritance of ABO blood groups.
- **Compare** sex-linked traits with sex-influenced traits.
- **Explain** how geneticists can detect and treat genetic disorders.

### VOCABULARY

pedigree
carrier
genetic disorder
polygenic
complex character
multiple allele
codominance
incomplete dominance
sex-influenced trait
Huntington's disease
amniocentesis
chorionic villi sampling
genetic counseling
gene therapy

- ◯ Female
- ● Female with trait or disease
- ☐ Male
- ■ Male with trait or disease

Horizontal lines indicate matings.

Vertical lines indicate offspring (arranged from left to right in order of their birth).

**FIGURE 12-9**

This pedigree for cystic fibrosis (CF) shows that each of the two affected individuals in the sixth generation has unaffected parents. Note that a cystic fibrosis allele from the first generation passed unexpressed through the next four generations. Marriages within the family during those four generations resulted in affected individuals who had two copies of the recessive disease allele for the CF gene.

## Patterns of Inheritance

Biologists learn about genetic diseases by analyzing *patterns of inheritance,* the expression of genes over generations. Pedigrees help to interpret patterns of inheritance. For example, if a trait is autosomal, it will appear in both sexes equally. If a trait is sex-linked, it is usually seen only in males. Most sex-linked traits are recessive.

If a trait is autosomal dominant, every individual with the trait will have a parent with the trait. If the trait is recessive, an individual with the trait can have one, two, or neither parent exhibit the trait.

If individuals with autosomal traits are homozygous dominant or heterozygous, their phenotype will show the dominant characteristic. If individuals are homozygous recessive, their phenotype will show the recessive characteristic. Two people who are heterozygous carriers of a recessive mutation will not show the mutation, but they can produce children who are homozygous for the recessive allele.

The pedigree in Figure 12-9 shows that the condition of cystic fibrosis is inherited as an autosomal recessive. Individuals such as the four people in the fifth generation in the pedigree are called **carriers** because they have one copy of the recessive allele but do not have the disease. Although carriers do not express the recessive allele, they can pass it to their offspring.

**FIGURE 12-10**

Many characters, such as height, weight, hair color, and skin color, are polygenic. Often, the environment strongly influences polygenic characters.

# GENETIC TRAITS AND DISORDERS

Genes controlling human traits show many patterns of inheritance. Some of these genes cause genetic disorders. **Genetic disorders** are diseases or disabling conditions that have a genetic basis.

## Polygenic Inheritance

Single genes having two or more alleles can determine traits, such as blood type or cystic fibrosis. Geneticists have learned, however, that most human characteristics are **polygenic** (PAHL-ee-JEHN-ik) characters: they are influenced by several genes. Polygenic characters show many degrees of variation, as seen in Figure 12-10. Skin color, for example, results from the additive effects of three to six genes. These genes control the amount of the brownish-black pigment called *melanin* in the skin. The more melanin skin cells produce, the darker the skin. Each of three to six genes has an allele that produces low amounts of melanin and another allele that makes high amounts of melanin. The final amount of melanin in a person's skin that is not exposed to sunlight comes from the number of high-melanin alleles among these few skin-color genes. Eye color, height, and hair color are also polygenic characters.

## Complex Characters

Many human conditions are **complex characters**—characters that are influenced strongly both by the environment and by genes. Skin color is both polygenic and complex. Exposure to sunlight generally causes the skin to become darker, no matter what the skin-color genotype is. Human height is another polygenic character that is controlled by an unknown number of genes that influence the growth of the skeleton. Height, however, is also influenced by environmental factors, such as nutrition and disease.

Other complex characters play a role in diseases or conditions such as breast cancer, diabetes, heart disease, stroke, and schizophrenia. Most breast cancer, for example, occurs in people with no familial history of the disease. But breast cancer also runs in some families.

Geneticist Marie-Claire King studied the genetics of breast cancer in families in which several individuals had the disease at younger ages than the average breast cancer patient does. Figure 12-11 shows the pedigrees of two of the families she studied. In Family A, each affected person has an affected parent, which is the inheritance pattern of a dominant trait. Family B demonstrates that additional genetic and environmental factors can influence whether or not a person expresses a trait. In Family B, a female, individual III-A, does not develop breast cancer herself but has a child who goes on to develop breast cancer. Notice also, individual III-B in Family B is a male who has breast cancer. This again shows that many factors in addition to the central gene influence the onset of a genetic disease.

Biologists hope that by identifying the environmental components that contribute to a disease, they can educate people in ways that minimize their risk of developing the disease. For breast cancer, for example, non-genetic risk factors include a diet high in saturated fat.

**FIGURE 12-11**

These diagrams show the pedigrees of families in which there is hereditary breast cancer.

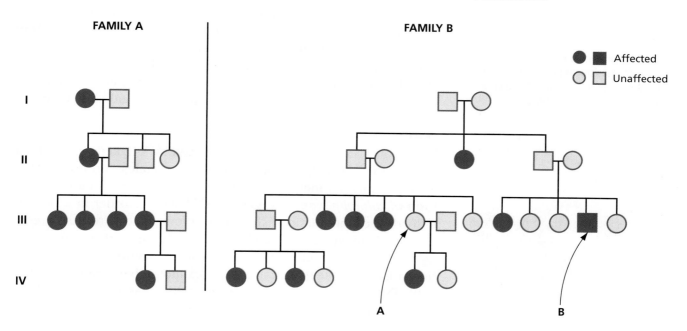

| Phenotype | | |
|---|---|---|
| Blood type | Molecule on red blood cell surface | Genotype |
| A | | $I^A I^A$ or $I^A i$ |
| B | | $I^B I^B$ or $I^B i$ |
| AB | | $I^A I^B$ |
| O | Neither A nor B | $ii$ |

**(a) Blood Types**

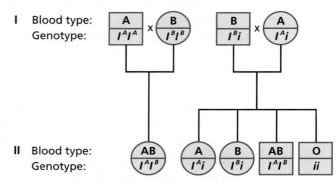

I Blood type:
Genotype:

II Blood type:
Genotype:

**(b) Inheritance of Blood Type Alleles**

FIGURE 12-12

The ABO gene has three alleles (a). Allele $I^A$ causes a type A sugar to appear on the surface of red blood cells. Allele $I^B$, causes red blood cells to display a type B sugar. The third allele, *i*, does not cause the display of any sugars. In (b), a pedigree shows two examples of how blood type can be inherited.

FIGURE 12-13

A person who has a red-green colorblindness might not be able to see the number 5 in the center of the circle in this color-vision test chart.

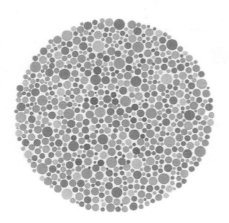

## Multiple Alleles

Many genes have more than three alleles. Genes with three or more alleles are said to have **multiple alleles.** For example, in humans, the ABO blood groups (blood types) are controlled by the three alleles $I^A$, $I^B$, and *i*. The alleles $I^A$ and $I^B$ are codominant. In **codominance,** both alleles are expressed in the phenotype of a heterozygote. Both $I^A$ and $I^B$ are dominant to the recessive *i* allele. The $I^A$ and $I^B$ alleles encode variants of an enzyme that cause two different sugar molecules to appear on the surface of red blood cells. The *i* allele lacks the activity of the enzyme entirely, so neither of the sugars appear on the red blood cell surface. Figure 12-12a shows how combinations of the three different alleles can produce four different blood types—A, B, AB, and O. Notice that a person who inherits two *i* alleles has type O blood. Figure 12-12b shows how blood type can be inherited.

## Incomplete Dominance

Sometimes, an individual displays a trait that is intermediate between the two parents, a condition known as **incomplete dominance.** For example, in Caucasians, the child of a straight-haired parent and a curly-haired parent would have wavy hair. Straight hair and curly hair are homozygous traits. Wavy hair is heterozygous and is intermediate between straight and curly hair.

## X-Linked Traits

Some complex characters are determined by X-linked genes, and a pedigree will usually reveal many affected males and no affected females. A male inherits his X chromosome from his mother. One form of *colorblindness* is a recessive X-linked disorder in which an individual cannot distinguish certain colors, such as red and green. Several X-linked genes encode proteins that absorb red or green light in the eye. Red-green colorblindness occurs because mutations disrupt these genes, so the eye cannot absorb some colors of light. Eye doctors often test for colorblindness by using a chart similar to the one in Figure 12-13.

## Sex-Influenced Traits

**Sex-influenced traits** are involved in other complex characters. Males and females can show different phenotypes even when they share the same genotype. Sex-influenced traits are usually autosomal. For example, an allele that is dominant in males but recessive in females controls pattern baldness, the type of baldness usually found in men. The difference is due to higher levels of the hormone testosterone in men, which interacts with the genotype to produce pattern baldness.

## Single-Allele Traits

A single allele of a gene controls single-allele traits. Geneticists have discovered that more than 200 human traits are governed by single dominant alleles. **Huntington's disease** (HD) is an autosomal dominant condition characterized by forgetfulness and irritability. It develops as an affected person reaches 30 or 40 years of age and progresses to muscle spasms, severe mental illness, and, finally, death. Because a dominant gene exists in every HD heterozygote, each affected person has at least one affected parent. Unfortunately, many HD patients have already had children by the time their symptoms appear. Direct DNA testing is beginning to allow for earlier diagnosis of the HD allele.

**FIGURE 12-14**

Geneticists can use fetal cells obtained by amniocentesis or by chorionic villi sampling to prepare fetal karyotypes that might display chromosome mutations. This allows physicians to diagnose chromosomal abnormalities before a child's birth.

# DETECTING GENETIC DISEASE

Many people with a family history of genetic disease seek genetic screening before having children. *Genetic screening* is an examination of a person's genetic makeup. It may involve karyotypes, blood tests for certain proteins, or direct tests of DNA. Physicians can now also detect more than 200 genetic disorders in the fetus. The technique called **amniocentesis** (AM-nee-oh-sen-TEE-sis), shown in Figure 12-14, allows a physician to remove some amniotic fluid from the amnion, the sac that surrounds the fetus, between the 14th and 16th week of pregnancy. Geneticists can analyze fetal cells for genetic disease by examining chromosomes and proteins in the fluid.

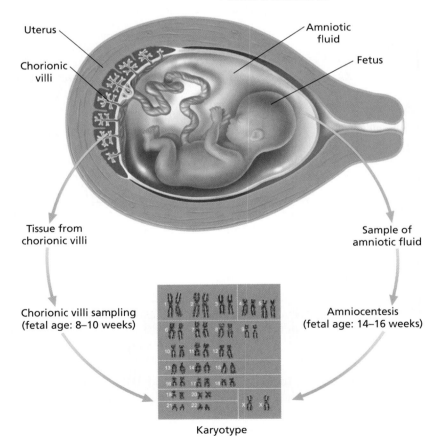

Uterus

Chorionic villi

Amniotic fluid

Fetus

Tissue from chorionic villi

Chorionic villi sampling (fetal age: 8–10 weeks)

Sample of amniotic fluid

Amniocentesis (fetal age: 14–16 weeks)

Karyotype

In **chorionic villi** (KAWR-ee-AHN-ik VIL-ie) **sampling,** also shown in Figure 12-14, the physician takes a sample of the chorionic villi—cells derived from the zygote that grow between the mother's uterus and the placenta—between the 8th and 10th week. Both procedures allow technicians to analyze fetal cells, chromosomes, proteins and detect genetic disease.

Table 12-1 lists some important genetic disorders, symptoms, and their patterns of inheritance.

## TABLE 12-1  *Some Important Genetic Disorders*

| Disorder (Gene) | Symptom | Normal protein; function; effect | Pattern of inheritance and chromosome location | Frequency among human births |
|---|---|---|---|---|
| Huntington's disease (gene HD) | gradual deterioration of brain tissue in middle age; shortened life expectancy | huntingtin protein; involved in movement of vesicles in nerve cells; mutation causes extra copies of the codon CAG in the gene | autosomal dominant on chromosome 4 | 1 in 10,000 |
| Cystic fibrosis (gene CFTR) | mucus clogs lungs and pancreas; victims today live to early adulthood or longer | cystic fibrosis transmembrane conductance regulator; regulates the transport of chloride ions in epithelial cells | autosomal recessive on chromosome 7 | Up to 1 in 900 French Canadians; 1 in 2000 Europeans |
| Sickle cell anemia (gene HBB) | organ damage due to impaired blood flow | beta globin; carries oxygen in blood; mutation causes red blood cells to change shape and clog capillaries | autosomal recessive on chromosome 11 | 1 in 500 African Americans |
| Tay-Sachs disease (gene HEXA) | deterioration of central nervous system in infancy; death in early childhood | hexosaminidase A; breaks down cellular wastes in lysosome; mutation allows waste buildup, causing nerve-cell death | autosomal recessive on chromosome 15 | 1 in 600 Jews of European descent |
| Phenylketonuria (gene PAH) | infant brain fails to develop normally; death in childhood | phenylalanine hydroxylase; catalyzes change of the amino acid phenylalanine to tyrosine; without the enzyme, a toxic substance accumulates | autosomal recessive on chromosome 12 | 1 in 18,000 Americans |
| Marfan syndrome (gene FBN1) | long limbs, loose joints, deformed vertebral column, crowded teeth, rupture of large arteries | fibrillin-1; a major component of connective tissue; lack of this protein causes weakness of ligaments and blood-vessel sheaths | autosomal dominant on chromosome 15 | 1 in 20,000 Americans |
| Breast cancer (gene BRCA1) | malignant tumors in breast tissue | breast cancer-1; inhibits growth of breast and ovarian tumors, probably by encouraging repair of DNA damage | autosomal dominant on chromosome 17 | About 8 percent of breast cancer patients |
| Hemophilia (gene F8) | prolonged bleeding due to ineffective blood clotting | coagulation factor 8; helps cause blood to clot; the mutant protein does not function in clotting | X-linked recessive on chromosome X | 1 in 7,000 |

# Genetic Counselor

### Job Description

A genetic counselor is a health professional who has a specialized graduate degree and experience in the areas of medical genetics and counseling.

### Focus On a Genetic Counselor

Robin Bennett is a senior genetic counselor and clinic manager at the Medical Genetics Clinic of the University of Washington. Individuals and couples who seek genetic counseling include people whose family members have birth defects or genetic disorders and people who may be at risk for an inherited condition. Clients may be expecting a child or considering parenthood, or they may

have been recently diagnosed with a disease. "The whole family becomes your patient," says Bennett. At the first meeting with a client, Bennett usually draws up a pedigree, obtains medical records of affected relatives, and, in some cases, orders blood tests. "After the appointment, I send the client a written report, which helps patients and their families and healthcare providers to understand the information."

### Education and Skills

- **High school**—a focus on science and math courses
- **College**—bachelor's degree, including course work in genetics, chemistry, statistics, psychology, and developmental biology; M.S. degree in genetic counseling; national certification is available
- **Skills**—strong verbal skills, emotional stability, and strong writing skills

For more about careers, visit **go.hrw.com** and type in the keyword **HM6 Careers.**

## Genetic Counseling

Many people with a family history of a genetic disease also undergo **genetic counseling,** the process of informing a person or couple about their genetic makeup. Genetic counseling is a form of medical guidance that informs individuals about problems that might affect their offspring. By studying the data from genetic screening tests and the family's pedigree, a genetic counselor can predict the likelihood that a couple will produce an affected child. For diseases that have both genetic and environmental influences, such as diabetes, physicians and counselors can advise families on how to lower risk factors.

## TREATING GENETIC DISEASE

Physicians can treat genetic diseases in several ways. For many diseases they can treat just the symptoms. For example, an individual with the genetic disease phenylketonuria (PKU) lacks an enzyme that converts the amino acid phenylalanine into the amino acid tyrosine. Phenylalanine builds up in the body and causes severe mental retardation. Physicians prescribe strict food regimens for phenylketonuria (PKU) patients to eliminate the amino acid phenylalanine from their diets. PKU can be detected by means of a blood test administered to infants during the first few days of life.

**FIGURE 12-15**

Jeff Pinard discusses with a colleague the results of his DNA analyses of cystic fibrosis.

For cystic fibrosis patients, physicians prescribe 45-minute-long sessions of pounding on the back and chest to dislodge sticky mucus.

For some diseases, physicians can implement symptom-prevention measures. For example, a physician might prescribe insulin injections to patients with diabetes. For patients with hemophilia, a doctor might prescribe injections of a missing blood-clotting protein. Physicians can even do some types of surgery to correct genetic defects in a fetus before birth.

## Gene Therapy

Another level of treatment currently in development involves replacing the defective gene. This type of therapy, called **gene therapy,** is a technique that places a healthy copy of a gene into the cells of a person whose copy of the gene is defective. Gene therapy relies on knowing gene sequences like the one Pinard is viewing in Figure 12-15. Medical researchers place a functional allele of the gene, such as the *CFTR* gene, into the DNA of a virus. They then introduce the modified virus into a patient's lungs where the virus infects the cells and brings along the functional gene. This improves the patient's symptoms, but only until the infected cells slough off. Then the patient must undergo the procedure again. Researchers are working to increase the effectiveness of gene therapy.

Gene therapy, in which only body cells are altered, is called *somatic cell gene therapy*. This contrasts with *germ cell gene therapy,* the attempt to alter eggs or sperm. Bioethicists, who study ethical issues in biological research, generally view somatic cell gene therapy as an extension of normal medicine to improve patients' health. Germ cell gene therapy, however, poses more risks and ethical issues because future generations could be affected in unpredictable ways.

## SECTION 2 REVIEW

1. A husband and wife have a son with cystic fibrosis. Their second child, a daughter, does not. Prepare a pedigree for this family.

2. Explain the difference between a polygenic character and a complex character.

3. A husband and wife have the ABO blood group genotypes $I^A I^B$ and *ii*. What ABO blood types can their children have?

4. Use Table 12-1 to compare Huntington's disease with sickle cell anemia.

5. Describe the methods physicians can use to detect genetic diseases in an unborn fetus.

**CRITICAL THINKING**

6. **Predicting Patterns** A woman with cystic fibrosis marries a man who is heterozygous for cystic fibrosis. What is the likelihood that their children will have cystic fibrosis?

7. **Applying Information** Why is colorblindness less common among females?

8. **Analyzing Patterns** A man with blood type B marries a woman with blood type A. Their first child is blood type O. What is the probability their next child will be blood type AB? blood type B?

# CHAPTER HIGHLIGHTS

Chromosomes and Inheritance

- Genes reside on chromosomes. Sex chromosomes contain genes that determine an organism's sex. The remaining chromosomes that are not directly involved in determining the sex of an individual are called autosomes.

- In mammals, an individual carrying two X chromosomes is female. An individual carrying an X and a Y chromosome is male.

- Genes found on the X chromosome are X-linked genes. A sex-linked trait is a trait whose allele is located on a sex chromosome. Because males have only one X chromosome, a male who carries a recessive allele on the X or Y chromosome will exhibit the sex-linked condition.

- Pairs of genes that tend to be inherited together are called linked genes. They occur close to each other on the same chromosome. The farther apart two genes are located on a chromosome, the more likely a cross-over will occur. Researchers use recombinant percentages to construct chromosome maps showing relative gene positions.

- Germ-cell mutations occur in gametes and can be passed on to offspring. Somatic-cell mutations occur in body cells and affect only the individual organism.

- Chromosome mutations are changes in the structure of a chromosome or the loss or gain of an entire chromosome. Gene mutations are changes in one or more of the nucleotides in a gene.

### Vocabulary

sex chromosome (p. 236)
autosome (p. 236)
sex-linked trait (p. 237)
linked gene (p. 238)
chromosome map (p. 238)

map unit (p. 238)
germ-cell mutation (p. 239)
somatic-cell
  mutation (p. 239)
lethal mutation (p. 239)

deletion (p. 239)
inversion (p. 239)
translocation (p. 239)
nondisjunction (p. 239)
point mutation (p. 240)

substitution (p. 240)
frameshift mutation (p. 240)
insertion mutation (p. 240)

Human Genetics

- Geneticists use pedigrees to trace diseases or traits through families. Pedigrees reveal inheritance patterns of genes.

- A carrier has one copy of a recessive allele but does not express the trait.

- Polygenic characters, such as skin color, are controlled by two or more genes.

- Complex characters, such as height, are influenced by both genes and environment.

- Multiple-allele characters, such as ABO blood groups, are controlled by three or more alleles of a gene.

- The gene for colorblindness, an X-linked recessive, is found on the X chromosome.

- A sex-influenced trait, such as pattern baldness, is expressed differently in men than in women even if it is on an autosome and both sexes have the same genotype.

- Genetic screening examines a person's genetic makeup and potential risks of passing disorders to offspring. Amniocentesis and chorionic villi sampling help physicians test a fetus for the presence of genetic disorders.

- Genetic counseling informs screened individuals about problems that might affect their offspring.

- Genetic disorders are treated in various ways. Among the treatments are symptom-relieving treatments and symptom-prevention measures, such as insulin injections for diabetes.

- Gene therapy is a type of treatment under development. In gene therapy, a defective gene is replaced with a copy of a healthy gene.

- Somatic cell gene therapy alters only body cells. Germ cell gene therapy attempts to alter eggs or sperm.

### Vocabulary

pedigree (p. 241)
carrier (p. 242)
genetic disorder (p. 242)
polygenic (p. 242)

complex character (p. 243)
multiple allele (p. 244)
codominance (p. 244)

incomplete
  dominance (p. 244)
sex-influenced trait (p. 245)
Huntington's disease (p. 245)

amniocentesis (p. 245)
chorionic villi sampling (p. 246)
genetic counseling (p. 247)
gene therapy (p. 248)

## USING VOCABULARY

1. For each pair of terms, explain how the meanings of the terms differ.
   a. *germ-cell mutation* and *somatic-cell mutation*
   b. *multiple-allele* and *polygenic*
   c. *sex-linked trait* and *sex-influenced trait*
   d. *amniocentesis* and *chorionic villi sampling*

2. Explain the relationship between a *chromosome map* and a *map unit*.

3. Use the following terms in the same sentence: *point mutation, substitution,* and *frameshift mutation.*

4. **Word Roots and Origins** The word *somatic* is derived from the Greek *somatikos,* which means "body." Using this information, explain why the term *somatic-cell mutation* is a good name for what the term describes.

## UNDERSTANDING KEY CONCEPTS

5. **Compare** sex chromosomes and autosomes.

6. **Identify** the evidence that led Morgan to hypothesize that the gene for eye color in *Drosophila melanogaster* is carried on the X chromosome.

7. **Describe** where the human *SRY* gene resides and its significance.

8. **Relate** how X-linked genes affect the inheritance of sex-linked traits.

9. **Evaluate** the relationship between crossing over, recombinant types, and chromosome mapping.

10. **Differentiate** between a chromosome mutation and a point mutation.

11. **Differentiate** between nondisjunction and translocation mutations.

12. **State** the type of information that is obtained by analyzing a pedigree.

13. **Describe** the pattern of inheritance in Huntington's disease.

14. **Predict** the possible genotypes for a person whose ABO blood group is type A.

15. **Summarize** two ways in which geneticists can detect genetic disorders.

16. **Describe** how gene therapy is used to treat genetic disorders.

17. **Unit 5—Heredity**

    BIOLOGY·INTERACTIVE·TUTOR Write a report summarizing the latest findings on treating a genetic disorder with gene therapy. What obstacles still need to be overcome?

18. **CONCEPT MAPPING** Use the following terms to create a concept map that describes the ways that changes in DNA occur: *mutation, chromosome mutation, substitution, deletion, point mutation, death, inversion, translocation, nondisjunction, germ-cell mutation, lethal mutation,* and *gametes.*

## CRITICAL THINKING

19. **Analyzing Data** In *Drosophila* the genes for body color and wing length are on the same chromosome. Gray body (*G*) is dominant to black body (*g*), and long wings (*L*) are dominant to short wings (*l*). Assume that both dominant alleles are on the same chromosome. Draw a Punnett square representing the cross *GgLl* × *GgLl*. Write the phenotypic and genotypic ratios that would be expected among the offspring, assuming that crossing-over does not occur.

20. **Relating Concepts** Individuals who are heterozygous for sickle cell anemia should avoid extreme conditions that severely reduce the amount of oxygen available to the body, such as playing vigorous sports at high elevations. Explain why this would be advisable.

21. **Inferring Relationships** A 20-year-old man with cystic fibrosis has a sister who is soon to be married. If you were the man, how would you explain your sister's likelihood of having children with cystic fibrosis?

22. **Interpreting Graphics** The individual shown in blue (third from the left, bottom row) in the pedigree below is affected by a genetic disorder. State the pattern of inheritance for the disorder and whether the disorder is autosomal or sex-linked. Explain your answer.

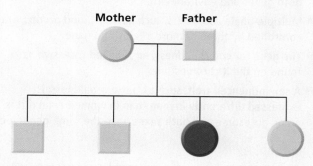

23. What advice might a genetic counselor give to the unaffected brothers and sister shown in the pedigree in question 22?

# Standardized Test Preparation

**DIRECTIONS:** Choose the letter of the answer choice that best answers the question.

1. Which can a chromosomal map show?
   **A.** the sex of the individual
   **B.** the presence of mutant alleles
   **C.** the positions of genes on a chromosome
   **D.** whether a gene is autosomal or recessive

2. Which can result from the deletion of a single nucleotide?
   **F.** trisomy
   **G.** a translocation
   **H.** nondisjunction
   **J.** a frameshift mutation

3. At the present time amniocentesis cannot reveal which of the following?
   **A.** eye color
   **B.** genetic disease
   **C.** sex of the fetus
   **D.** chromosomal abnormalities

4. A geneticist working with the fruit fly *Drosophila melanogaster* discovers a mutant phenotype that appears only in males who are offspring of males of the same phenotype. What does this information suggest about the mutant phenotype?
   **F.** The trait is X-linked.
   **G.** The trait is Y-linked.
   **H.** The trait is autosomal dominant.
   **J.** The trait is autosomal recessive.

**INTERPRETING GRAPHICS:** The table below shows the genotypes and phenotypes of pattern baldness. Use the table to answer the question that follows.

| Genotypes and Phenotypes of Pattern Baldness | | |
|---|---|---|
| | **Phenotype** | |
| **Genotype** | **Female** | **Male** |
| BB | Bald | Bald |
| Bb | Not bald | Bald |
| bb | Not bald | Not bald |

5. Which statement best explains why men and women express the *Bb* genotype differently?
   **A.** The trait is polygenic.
   **B.** The trait has multiple alleles.
   **C.** Pattern baldness is a sex-linked trait.
   **D.** Pattern baldness is a sex-influenced trait.

**DIRECTIONS:** Complete the following analogy.

6. translocation : chromosome mutation :: substitution :
   **F.** gene mutation
   **G.** point mutation
   **H.** germ-cell mutation
   **J.** somatic-cell mutation

**INTERPRETING GRAPHICS:** The image below is a pedigree showing the inheritance of hemophilia in a family. Use the pedigree to answer the question that follows.

**A Pedigree of Hemophilia**

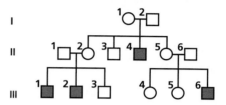

7. Which type of inheritance pattern is associated with hemophilia?
   **A.** autosomal recessive
   **B.** sex-linked dominant
   **C.** sex-linked recessive
   **D.** autosomal dominant

## SHORT RESPONSE

Consider a couple about to get married. The woman has cystic fibrosis, but the man does not.

What benefit would they gain by seeing a genetic counselor?

## EXTENDED RESPONSE

Colorblindness is a recessive, sex-linked trait. A woman and a man, both with normal vision, have three daughters with normal vision. One of the daughters marries a man with normal vision, and they have a son who is colorblind.

*Part A* Which parent of the son is the carrier of the trait? Explain your answer.

*Part B* What is the likelihood that the children of a woman heterozygous for colorblindness and a colorblind man will express the trait? Explain your answer.

> **Test TIP** Test questions are not necessarily arranged in order of increasing difficulty. If you are unable to answer a question, mark it and move on to another question.

# Analyzing Karyotypes

## OBJECTIVES

- **Make** a human karyotype by arranging chromosomes in order by length, centromere position, and banding pattern.
- **Identify** a karyotype as normal or abnormal.
- **Identify** any genetic disorder that is present and describe the effect of the genetic disorder on the individual.

## PROCESS SKILLS

- Identifying
- Describing
- Analyzing
- Modeling

## MATERIALS

- chromosome spread
- human karyotyping form
- metric ruler
- photomicrograph of chromosomes
- scissors
- transparent tape

## Background

1. Define and describe a human karyotype.
2. Compare the two procedures used to obtain the cells needed for preparing a fetal karyotype.
3. List four types of chromosomal mutations that can be identified by preparing a fetal karyotype.
4. Name the disorder that occurs in people who have an extra copy of chromosome 21.

## Procedure

1. Obtain a photomicrograph and note the letter identifying which person the cells were taken from.
2. ◆ CAUTION **Always cut in a direction away from your face and body.** Carefully cut apart the chromosomes on each photomicrograph. Be sure to leave a slight margin around each chromosome.

3. Arrange the chromosomes in homologous pairs. The members of each pair will be the same length and will have their centromeres located in the same area. Use the ruler to measure the length of the chromosome and the position of the centromere. The banding patterns of homologous chromosomes will be similar and may also help you pair the chromosomes.

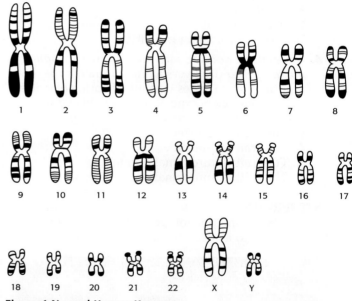

**Figure 1 Normal Human Karyotype**

4. Arrange the pairs according to their length. Begin with the largest chromosomes and move to the smallest.
5. Tape each pair of homologous chromosomes to a human karyotyping form. Place the centromeres on the lines provided. Place the longest chromosome at position 1, and the shortest at position 22. Place the two sex chromosomes at position 23.
6. The diagram you have made is a karyotype, as in Figure 1. Analyze your karyotype to determine the sex of the individual. Use the information in Table 1 to guide your analysis.

## TABLE 1 GENETIC DISORDERS CAUSED BY AN ABNORMAL CHROMOSOME NUMBER

| Name of abnormality | Chromosome affected | Description of abnormality |
|---|---|---|
| Down syndrome, or Trisomy 21 | #21 | 47 chromosomes; mental retardation with specific characteristic features; may have heart defects and respiratory problems |
| Edwards' syndrome, or Trisomy 18 | #18 | 47 chromosomes; severe mental retardation; very characteristic malformations of the skull, pelvis, and feet, among others; die in early infancy |
| Patau syndrome, or Trisomy 13 | #13 | 47 chromosomes; abnormal brain function that is very severe; many facial malformations; usually die in early infancy |
| Turner's syndrome | Single X in female (XO) | 45 chromosomes; in females only; missing an X chromosome; do not develop secondary sex characteristics; are infertile |
| Klinefelter's syndrome | Extra X in male (XXY) | 47 chromosomes; in males only; sterile, small testicles; otherwise normal appearance |
| XYY syndrome | Extra Y in male (XYY) | 47 chromosomes; in males only; low mental ability; otherwise normal appearance |
| Triple X syndrome | Extra X in female (XXX) | 47 chromosomes; sterility sometimes occurs; normal mental ability |

7. Create a data table like the example below, and record your results. Pool your data with that from the rest of the class.

### TABLE 2 POOLED CLASS DATA

| Letter identifier | Sex | Condition | Chromosome abnormality |
|---|---|---|---|
| A | | | |
| B | | | |
| C | | | |
| D | | | |
| E | | | |
| F | | | |
| G | | | |
| H | | | |
| I | | | |

8. Clean up your materials and wash your hands before leaving the lab.

## Analysis and Conclusions

1. Is the fetus represented by your karyotype male or female? How do you know?
2. Does the fetus have a genetic disorder? Explain.

3. Assume that two students started with the same photomicrograph. One student concluded that the individual had Down syndrome. The other student concluded that the individual had Edwards' syndrome. Explain how this could happen.
4. How is sex determined in a person who has more than two sex chromosomes? Explain your answer.
5. In this lab, you examined karyotypes for the presence of abnormal chromosome numbers in both autosomes and sex chromosomes. Which condition seems to have a greater influence on a person's health—trisomy of an autosome or trisomy of a sex chromosome?
6. Assume that an individual has a deletion mutation in one of their chromosomes. What would the karyotype look like in this situation?
7. How might banding patterns be important to detecting an inversion mutation?
8. Some medical labs make karyotypes from several of an individual's cells before drawing conclusions about the individual's health. Do you think this is necessary? Why or why not?

## Further Inquiry

Trisomy occurs when an individual has three copies of the same chromosome. Monosomy occurs when an individual has only one copy of a chromosome. In this lab, you examined a fetal karyotype for the presence of three different trisomies. Find out why monosomies are rarely detected.

# GENE TECHNOLOGY

Using DNA technology called a *microarray,* researchers are able to see which genes are being actively transcribed in a cell. In the microarray seen on the computer screen, each spot corresponds to a different gene within the cell being studied.

**SECTION 1** *DNA Technology*

**SECTION 2** *The Human Genome Project*

**SECTION 3** *Genetic Engineering*

**Unit 6—Gene Expression**
Topics 1–6

For project ideas from *Scientific American,* visit go.hrw.com and type in the keyword **HM6SAC**.

# DNA TECHNOLOGY

*Today, scientists manipulate DNA for many practical purposes by using techniques collectively called DNA technology. For example, DNA technology can be used as evidence in a criminal case by providing positive identification of DNA left at the scene of a crime. Scientists also use DNA technology to improve food crops, to determine if a person has the genetic information for certain diseases before symptoms appear, and to do research on treatments and cures for genetic diseases. This chapter discusses the tools of DNA technology, how scientists apply these tools to study entire genomes, and how they use them to improve human lives.*

## DNA IDENTIFICATION

Except for identical twins, no two people in the world are genetically alike. A majority of DNA is actually the same in all humans, but about 0.10 percent of the human genome (the complete genetic material in an individual) varies from person to person. Because of the 0.10 percent variation, scientists are able to identify people based on their DNA. DNA identification compares DNA samples in regions of a chromosome that differ. DNA identification is useful for many purposes, including determining a person's paternity, identifying human remains, tracing human origins, and providing evidence in criminal cases.

### Noncoding DNA

Amazingly, about 98 percent of our genetic makeup does not code for any protein. The regions of DNA that do not code for proteins are called *noncoding DNA.* Noncoding DNA contains many **length polymorphisms,** or variations in the length of the DNA molecule between known genes. Some length polymorphisms in noncoding regions come from short, repeating sequences of DNA. For example, a repeating nucleotide sequence might be CACACA, and so on. These sequences can repeat a few or many times in tandem (one "behind" another) and so are called **variable number tandem repeats (VNTR).** The number of tandem repeats at specific places (loci) in DNA varies among individuals. For each of the many VNTR loci in a person's DNA, he or she will have a certain number of repeats. Geneticists have calculated how frequently VNTR used in DNA identification occur in the general population. With these numbers, they can determine how rare a particular DNA profile is.

### OBJECTIVES

- **Explain** the significance of non-coding DNA to DNA identification.
- **Describe** four major steps commonly used in DNA identification.
- **Explain** the use of restriction enzymes, cloning vectors, and probes in making recombinant DNA.
- **Summarize** several applications of DNA identification.

### VOCABULARY

length polymorphism
variable number tandem repeats (VNTR)
polymerase chain reaction (PCR)
primer
restriction enzyme
gel electrophoresis
DNA fingerprint
genetic engineering
recombinant DNA
clone
vector
plasmid
probe

**internet** connect

www.scilinks.org
**Topic:** Genetic Engineering/ Recombinant DNA
**Keyword:** HM60655

SC*LINKS.* Maintained by the National Science Teachers Association

# STEPS IN DNA IDENTIFICATION

The main steps involved in DNA identification are (1) isolate the DNA in a sample and, if needed, make copies, (2) cut the DNA into shorter fragments that contain known VNTR areas, (3) sort the DNA by size, and (4) compare the size fragments in the unknown sample of DNA to those of known samples of DNA. If a match occurs between the unknown sample and a known sample, then a person's identity can be confirmed.

## Copying DNA: Polymerase Chain Reaction

Often, DNA that is recovered from a crime scene or from human tissues is present in very small amounts. In these cases, scientists need to make copies in order to have enough DNA to use for DNA identification. The **polymerase chain reaction (PCR)** is a technique that quickly produces many copies of a DNA fragment.

As shown in step ❶ of Figure 13-1, PCR requires a *template,* a DNA fragment containing the sequence the scientist wants to copy. PCR also requires a supply of the four DNA nucleotides, heat-tolerant DNA polymerase, and primers. **Primers** are artificially made pieces of single-stranded DNA that are 20 to 30 nucleotides long that must be present for DNA polymerase to initiate replication. Primers are complementary to the ends of the DNA fragment that is to be copied.

When all the ingredients are combined, copying can begin. Primers bind to DNA, and DNA polymerase makes a copy of both DNA strands. Heating breaks the bonds holding the template DNA to the newly made strands. After cooling, as shown in step ❷, primers can once more bind to the DNA. Then, in step ❸, DNA polymerase can copy again. In step ❹, the cycle is repeated. With each new cycle, the DNA between the two primers doubles.

**FIGURE 13-1**

In the polymerase chain reaction (PCR), a scientist chooses a DNA fragment to copy and designs primers that will bind to both ends of the fragment. DNA polymerase copies the segment between the two primers. Repeating the procedure through about 30 cycles generates millions of copies of a single piece of DNA fragment.

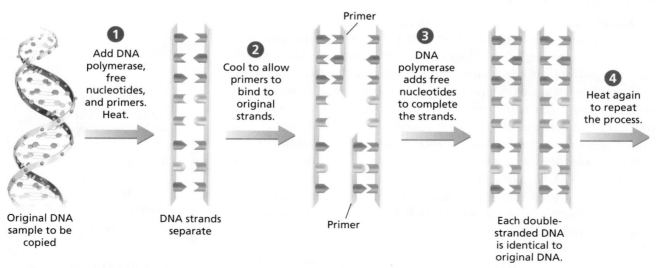

❶ Add DNA polymerase, free nucleotides, and primers. Heat.

Original DNA sample to be copied

DNA strands separate

Primer

❷ Cool to allow primers to bind to original strands.

Primer

❸ DNA polymerase adds free nucleotides to complete the strands.

Each double-stranded DNA is identical to original DNA.

❹ Heat again to repeat the process.

## Cutting DNA: Restriction Enzymes

To cut long DNA molecules into shorter pieces, biologists use bacterial proteins called **restriction enzymes.** Restriction enzymes recognize specific short DNA sequences, and cut the DNA in or near the sequence, as Figure 13-2 shows. Some restriction enzymes leave DNA overhangs that function like "sticky ends" so that other pieces of DNA with complementary sequences can bind to them.

## Sorting DNA by Size: Gel Electrophoresis

DNA fragments can be studied using a technique called **gel electrophoresis.** Gel electrophoresis separates nucleic acids or proteins according to their size and charge. As shown in step ❶ of Figure 13-3, the DNA samples are cut with a restriction enzyme. The DNA is then placed in wells made on a thick gel, as shown in step ❷. An electric current runs through the gel for a given period of time. Negatively charged DNA fragments migrate toward the positively charged end of the gel. Smaller DNA fragments migrate faster and farther than longer fragments, and this separates the fragments by size. In step ❸, the DNA is transferred to a nylon membrane and radioactive probes are added. The probes bind to complementary DNA. In step ❹, an X-ray film is exposed to the radiolabeled membrane. The resulting pattern of bands is called a **DNA fingerprint.**

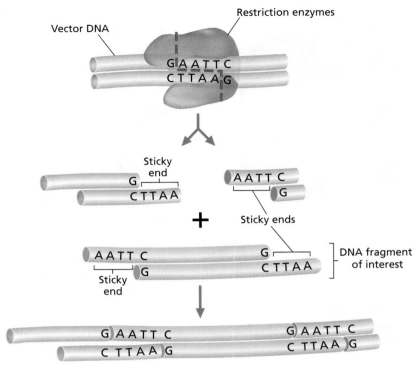

**FIGURE 13-2**

The restriction enzyme in this figure recognizes the sequence GAATTC on each DNA and cuts each chain between the G and A nucleotides. DNA fragments with sticky ends result.

**FIGURE 13-3**

In a DNA fingerprint, DNA samples are cut, transferred to a nylon membrane, and exposed to radioactive probes. Explosing X-ray film to the membrane makes the fingerprint visible.

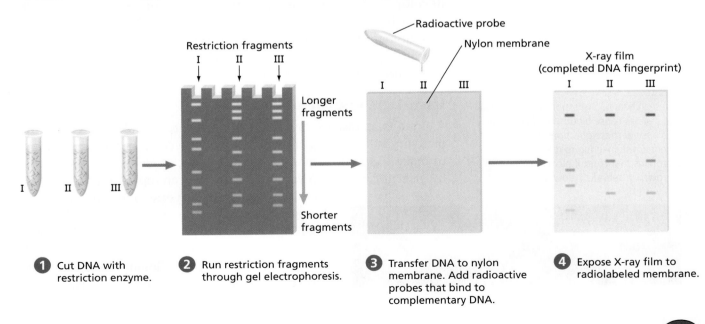

❶ Cut DNA with restriction enzyme.

❷ Run restriction fragments through gel electrophoresis.

❸ Transfer DNA to nylon membrane. Add radioactive probes that bind to complementary DNA.

❹ Expose X-ray film to radiolabeled membrane.

FIGURE 13-4

**FIGURE 13-4**

A DNA fingerprint can pinpoint subtle genetic differences that identify each individual uniquely. Identical twins share the same DNA fingerprint.

## Comparing DNA: DNA Fingerprints

To permanently preserve the DNA fingerprint, a technician can place a positively charged nylon membrane over the gel and transfer the negatively charged DNA to the membrane. To visualize specific DNA pieces, biologists can prepare a nucleic acid complementary to the DNA of interest and label it radioactively. A sheet of X-ray film placed over the gel will be exposed only where the desired DNA is on the gel, providing a DNA fingerprint. An example of a DNA fingerprint is shown in Figure 13-4.

## Accuracy of DNA Fingerprints

What makes a DNA fingerprint so powerful as an identification tool is the combined analysis of many VNTR loci. Analyzing only one VNTR locus is like having only one digit in a person's telephone number. DNA fingerprinting typically compares from five to thirteen VNTR loci. Thirteen loci, as often used by some crime labs in their criminal profiles, produce the odds that two people will share a DNA profile at about one in 100 billion. There are about 6.5 billion people on Earth, so this should be enough to remove any doubt.

# RECOMBINANT DNA

The techniques of DNA technology are sometimes used to modify the genome of a living cell or organism. The process of altering the genetic material of cells or organisms to allow them to make new substances is called **genetic engineering. Recombinant DNA** results when DNA from two different organisms is joined.

An organism with recombinant DNA is shown in Figure 13-5. To study blood vessel growth, researchers combined a jellyfish gene encoding green fluorescent protein (GFP) that glows under ultraviolet light with a zebrafish gene that is involved in blood-vessel development. They inserted the GFP/blood-vessel gene into zebrafish embryos. The fish's blood-vessel cells transcribed the recombinant DNA and made the green fluorescent proteins. As the zebrafish grew, their blood vessels glowed green, and researchers could more easily study their growth.

## Cloning Vectors

A **clone** is an exact copy of a DNA segment, a whole cell, or a complete organism. Biologists also use the term *clone* as a verb, meaning to make a genetic duplicate. Researchers can clone DNA fragments by inserting them into **vectors,** DNAs that can replicate within a cell, usually a bacterium or yeast, and that can carry foreign DNA. When the vector carrying the foreign DNA enters bacteria and the bacteria reproduce, they grow a colony of cloned cells that includes the foreign DNA. Cloning vectors include viruses that infect bacteria and plasmids.

**FIGURE 13-5**

Researchers had questions about which molecules cause blood vessels to grow. To answer these questions, they used genetic engineering to make the proteins that control blood-vessel growth in zebrafish glow green.

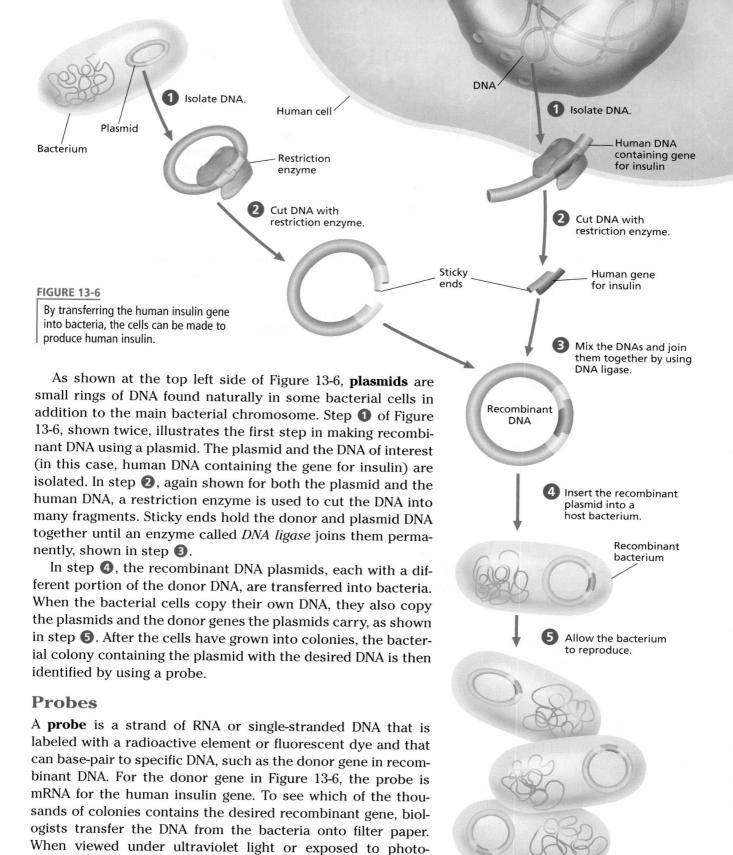

Bacterium

Plasmid

**1** Isolate DNA.

Human cell

Restriction enzyme

**2** Cut DNA with restriction enzyme.

DNA

**1** Isolate DNA.

Human DNA containing gene for insulin

**2** Cut DNA with restriction enzyme.

Sticky ends

Human gene for insulin

**3** Mix the DNAs and join them together by using DNA ligase.

Recombinant DNA

**4** Insert the recombinant plasmid into a host bacterium.

Recombinant bacterium

**5** Allow the bacterium to reproduce.

Bacteria are able to produce human insulin.

**FIGURE 13-6**

By transferring the human insulin gene into bacteria, the cells can be made to produce human insulin.

As shown at the top left side of Figure 13-6, **plasmids** are small rings of DNA found naturally in some bacterial cells in addition to the main bacterial chromosome. Step **1** of Figure 13-6, shown twice, illustrates the first step in making recombinant DNA using a plasmid. The plasmid and the DNA of interest (in this case, human DNA containing the gene for insulin) are isolated. In step **2**, again shown for both the plasmid and the human DNA, a restriction enzyme is used to cut the DNA into many fragments. Sticky ends hold the donor and plasmid DNA together until an enzyme called *DNA ligase* joins them permanently, shown in step **3**.

In step **4**, the recombinant DNA plasmids, each with a different portion of the donor DNA, are transferred into bacteria. When the bacterial cells copy their own DNA, they also copy the plasmids and the donor genes the plasmids carry, as shown in step **5**. After the cells have grown into colonies, the bacterial colony containing the plasmid with the desired DNA is then identified by using a probe.

## Probes

A **probe** is a strand of RNA or single-stranded DNA that is labeled with a radioactive element or fluorescent dye and that can base-pair to specific DNA, such as the donor gene in recombinant DNA. For the donor gene in Figure 13-6, the probe is mRNA for the human insulin gene. To see which of the thousands of colonies contains the desired recombinant gene, biologists transfer the DNA from the bacteria onto filter paper. When viewed under ultraviolet light or exposed to photographic film, the clone of cells bearing the donor DNA and its attached probe glows and reveals its location. Biologists can now grow more of the specific recombinant bacterial clone.

**Materials** ink pad, paper, pencil, scissors

**Procedure**

1. Cut four 3-in. squares of plain paper.

2. Draw lines on a full-sized sheet of paper to divide it into four equal squares.

3. Each team member will press a right thumb on the ink pad and then will quickly press the inked thumb in a square on the large sheet of paper and again on one of the small squares of paper.

4. Examine each of the thumbprints, and list the differences and similarities of the prints. Describe how each thumbprint is unique. Then, shuffle the four thumbprints on the small squares, and try to match each with its duplicate on the large sheet of paper.

**Analysis** What characteristics are common to all thumbprints? What characteristics made each thumbprint unique? How do a person's fingerprints relate to his or her DNA fingerprints?

# APPLICATIONS FOR DNA TECHNOLOGY

DNA technology has been used for many purposes. For example, DNA identification has been used in forensics to identify criminals and to free the wrongly convicted. DNA has also been used to identify human remains. For example, DNA identification techniques were used to identify Czar Nicholas II of Russia and his family, who were executed by the Bolsheviks in 1918.

In addition to forensic applications, DNA technology is of great importance in other scientific efforts. Anthropologists use DNA identification techniques to trace human origins and migrations. Environmental conservationists use the same techniques to trace migrations and movements of threatened or endangered organisms in the effort to preserve their species.

Recombinant DNA techniques give microorganisms new capabilities that have useful applications. The first recombinant DNA product to be used commercially was human insulin (for the treatment of diabetes) in 1982. A recombinant DNA molecule was made by inserting a human gene for insulin into a bacterial plasmid. These bacteria are now grown in vats, from which large amounts of human insulin are extracted and used to treat diabetes.

Since 1982, more than 30 products made using DNA technology have been approved and are being used around the world. These proteins are preferred to conventional drugs because they are highly specific and have fewer side effects. Medically important proteins include factors to treat immune-system deficiencies and anemia. Clotting factors for people with hemophilia, human growth hormone for people with growth defects, interferons for viral infections and cancer, and proteins, such as growth factors to treat burns and ulcers, are just a few other genetically engineered medicines in use today.

## SECTION 1 REVIEW

1. Summarize the significance of noncoding DNA to DNA identification.

2. Describe the steps in a polymerase chain reaction.

3. What role do restriction enzymes play in DNA technology?

4. What are "sticky ends," and in what way do they function in making recombinant DNA?

5. Explain the role cloning vectors play in making recombinant DNA.

6. List three ways that DNA technology could be used to improve the lives of humans.

**CRITICAL THINKING**

7. **Relating Concepts** Explain why the process of genetic fingerprinting uses only specific, short segments of DNA rather than the entire genome.

8. **Evaluating Conclusions** A student performing electrophoresis on a DNA sample believes that her smallest DNA fragment is the band nearest the negative pole of the gel. Do you agree with her conclusion? Explain your answer.

9. **Applying Information** Explain the statement that the genetic code is universal.

# THE HUMAN GENOME PROJECT

*One exciting application of DNA technology has been the sequencing of the entire human genome. This section discusses how researchers used modern genetic tools to sequence the human genome and what their findings mean for 21st century biology and society.*

## SECTION 2

### OBJECTIVES

- **Discuss** two major goals of the Human Genome Project.
- **Summarize** important insights gained from the Human Genome Project.
- **Explain** why animal model species are useful to study genes.
- **State** how information from the Human Genome Project will be applied to future projects.
- **Relate** bioinformatics, proteomics, and microarrays to the Human Genome Project.

### VOCABULARY

Human Genome Project
proteome
single nucleotide
    polymorphism (SNP)
bioinformatics
proteomics
two-dimensional gel
    electrophoresis

## MAPPING THE HUMAN GENOME

In 1990, geneticists around the world tackled one of the most ambitious projects in scientific history—the Human Genome Project. The **Human Genome Project** is a research effort undertaken to sequence all of our DNA and locate within it all of the functionally important sequences, such as genes. That is, the project seeks to determine the sequence of all 3.3 billion nucleotides of the human genome and to map the location of every gene on each chromosome. Information from the project will provide insight into our evolutionary past, genome organization, gene expression, and cell growth.

The Human Genome Project linked more than 20 scientific laboratories in six countries. By 2001, the draft sequence of the human genome appeared in two landmark papers in the science journals *Science* and *Nature*. The high-quality sequence was completed in 2003—two years ahead of schedule. Figure 13-7 shows an example of how the sequence of nucleotides in a piece of DNA is displayed on a computer screen.

### Important Insights

Scientists with the Human Genome Project were surprised by some of the discoveries they made, including the following:

1. Only about 2 percent of the human genome codes for proteins.
2. Chromosomes have unequal distribution of exons—sequences of nucleotides that are transcribed and translated.
3. The human genome is smaller than previously estimated. The human genome has only about 20,000 to 25,000 protein-coding genes—far fewer than the 100,000 originally estimated. Scientists now know that RNAs are not used only for translating DNA into proteins. Many RNAs are involved in regulating gene expression.

**FIGURE 13-7**

Researchers with the Human Genome Project developed automated DNA sequencing machines that could determine the order of millions of base pairs per day. The four bases are represented by different colors.

### Word Roots and Origins

*proteome*

a new, combined word from *prote* in the word *protein* and *ome* in the word *genome*

**4.** The exons of human genes are spliced in many ways, allowing the same gene to encode different versions of a protein. An organism's complete set of proteins is called its **proteome.** The human proteome is quite complex.

**5.** About half of the human genome arises from the shuffling of transposons, pieces of DNA that move from one chromosome location to another. Transposons appear to have no specific role in development or physiology.

**6.** There are about 8 million **single nucleotide polymorphisms (SNP),** unique spots where individuals differ by a single nucleotide. SNPs are important for mapping the genome in more detail, and in the identification of human disease genes.

## Model Species

In order to better understand how human genes control development and health and to explain how genes affect behaviors, biologists want to map similar genes in *model species.* Since the Human Genome Project, many other genome sequence projects have been completed, and more are underway. Some of the model species for genome sequencing, as seen in Table 13-1, include a bacterium, a roundworm, a fruit fly, a zebrafish, and a mouse. Researchers can induce mutations in each of these species to look for gene actions. Because they represent such a broad phylogenetic base, it is possible to make valid generalizations that relate to larger groups.

### TABLE 13-1  *Genome Sizes of Some Species*

| Domain/Kingdom | Organism | Common name | Genome size (million bases) | Number of genes |
|---|---|---|---|---|
| Archaea | | | | |
| Archaebacteria | *Pyrococcus furiosus* | Pyrococcus | 1.9 | 2,065 |
| Bacteria | | | | |
| Eubacteria | *Chlamydia trachomatis* | Chlamydia | 1.0 | 894 |
| | *Escherichia coli* | E. coli | 4.6 | 4,289 |
| Eukarya | | | | |
| Protista | *Dictyostelium discoideum* | Amoeba | 34 | ~9,000 |
| Fungi | *Saccharomyces cerevisiae* | Yeast | 12 | 6,000 |
| Plantae | *Arabidopsis thaliana* | Mustard | 125 | 23,174 |
| | *Lilium longiflorum* | Easter lily | 100,000 | ~25,000 |
| Animalia | *Drosophila melanogaster* | Fruit fly | 120 | 13,600 |
| | *Caenorhabditis elegans* | Roundworm | 97 | 19,049 |
| | *Xenopus tropicalis* | Frog | 1,700 | ~30,000 |
| | *Homo sapiens* | Human | 3,300 | ~20,000 |
| | *Mus musculus* | Mouse | 3,630 | ~30,000 |
| | *Danio rerio* | Zebrafish | 1,700 | ~3,000 |

*E. coli*

*D. discoideum*

*L. longiflorum*

*S. cerevisiae*

*M. musculus*

## Applications

Information from the Human Genome Project has been and will continue to be applied to different medical, industrial, commercial, and scientific purposes. For example, scientists have already discovered specific genes responsible for several genetic disorders, including cystic fibrosis, Duchenne muscular dystrophy, and colon cancer. Researchers may improve diagnoses, treatments, and therapies for the more than 4,000 human genetic disorders.

John Carpten of the National Institutes of Health, pictured in Figure 13-8, is a researcher taking such an approach to prostate cancer. Carpten knew that prostate cancer rates in men are second only to skin cancer rates and that some forms of the disease run in families. By studying male relatives with and without prostate cancer, he and his team were able to map a gene for susceptibility to prostate cancer. The gene, called *RNASEL*, occurs near a gene sequenced during the Human Genome Project. *RNASEL* encodes an RNA-digesting enzyme. Carpten isolated the *RNASEL* gene from patients, and found mutations. His discoveries may one day lead to new prostate cancer treatments.

**FIGURE 13-8**

Dr. John Carpten is a researcher at the National Human Genome Research Institute. He uses the results of the Human Genome Project to study prostate cancer.

# THE FUTURE OF GENOMICS

It is clear that although the more than 3 billion letters of the human genetic code have been sequenced, this is only the beginning of the quest to understand the human genome. New tools and fields of scientific research have arisen that enable the acquisition, analysis, storage, modeling, and distribution of the information contained within DNA and protein sequence data. Geneticists will now be able to apply their new tools to benefit human health.

## Bioinformatics

Keeping track of the billions of nucleotide base pairs in a complex genome requires substantial computer power. Much of the progress in studying genomes comes from advances in the new scientific field of bioinformatics. **Bioinformatics** combines biological science, computer science, and information technology to enable the discovery of new biological insights and unifying principles. Bioinformatics utilizes databases to store and integrate the data coming out of genomic research. One such database called the BLAST search allows rapid comparisons between a gene or protein sequence from one organism and similar sequences from all other organisms in a database at the National Center for Biotechnology Information. The BLAST tool allows a worker to find corresponding genes in different organisms. By knowing the function of a gene from a related model species such as a mouse, the researcher can then infer the function of a previously unstudied human gene.

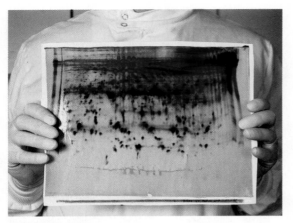

**FIGURE 13-9**

Two-dimensional gel electrophoresis separates proteins in two steps. The first dimension separates proteins according to their isoelectric points. The second dimension separates proteins according to their molecular weights.

## Proteomics

As important as genomes are, it is the proteins they encode that actually carry out the work of cells. To understand how genes work, biologists must understand proteins. **Proteomics** is the study of all of an organism's proteins, including their identities, structures, interactions, and abundances. A key tool in proteomics is **two-dimensional gel electrophoresis,** a method that separates the proteins in a sample into individual spots, as shown in Figure 13-9. A researcher can cut out a protein spot from the gel, then use special methods to determine the amino acid sequence in part of the protein. Using bioinformatics, he or she can then search the DNA of a sequenced genome and match an individual gene to that unique protein. Proteomics and bioinformatics will allow medical researchers to identify new targets for therapeutic drugs and develop new markers for diagnosing disease.

## Microarrays

An important tool of the genomic revolution is a technique called *DNA microarray,* a two-dimensional arrangement of DNA molecules representing thousands of cloned genes. A DNA microarray can show which genes are active in a cell. To prepare the DNA microarray, robotic machines arrange tiny amounts of sequences from thousands of genes on a single microscope slide. To investigate, for example, how tumor cells differ from normal cells, mRNA from the tumor is labeled with fluorescent dyes and poured onto the microarray slides. The more mRNA that binds to its complement at a particular spot on the slide, the brighter the color, indicating that this specific gene is highly active. Physicians use DNA microarray analysis to classify patients' cancers. Such classification can lead to better-informed decisions about which type of treatment is best. A DNA microarray is shown on the first page of this chapter.

## SECTION 2 REVIEW

1. Describe two major goals of the Human Genome Project.

2. Summarize four insights from the initial analysis of the complete sequence of the human genome.

3. Why are model species useful to study genes?

4. List and describe two genetic disorders that might be treated using DNA technology information gained in the Human Genome Project.

5. Distinguish between proteomics and bioinformatics.

**CRITICAL THINKING**

6. **Relating Concepts** Describe how the rapid growth of the computer technology industry in the 1990s relates to the Human Genome Project.

7. **Analyzing Models** Some people might assume that the more nucleotides in a genome, the more genes it contains. Make a graph of the data in Table 13-1. Explain why you agree or disagree.

8. **Evaluating Choices** If you were the scientist who developed the model organism list, which organisms would you include? Justify your choices.

# WHO OWNS GENES?

The very large U.S. government investment in the Human Genome Project has spurred research in genetics. Within months of the genetic map's release, researchers around the country applied for patents on thousands of different genes and parts of genes. By the end of 2004, more than three million gene-related patent applications had been filed. Most gene-related patents have been issued to the government, the University of California, and three top biotechnology companies. Some observers criticize the idea of patenting human genes. Others support it.

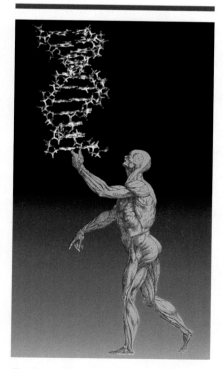

Today the public is debating whether or not patents should be awarded for human genes.

## The Patent Process

The United States Commerce Department issues patents on inventions. By proving that he or she is the first to invent something, an inventor can get exclusive rights to develop and sell products based on the invention for 20 years.

The patent office must determine that an invention is practically useful, new, clever, and creative in design, and useful to a skilled technician for the practical purpose intended.

## Gene Patents

The patent office has ruled that whole genes as they occur in nature on chromosomes are not patentable. If a person isolates a gene, however, or modifies the gene, it becomes a candidate for a patent. Most patent applications are for gene fragments that contain one or more changed base pairs and may represent gene sequences that lead to disease or new drugs.

## Arguments Against Gene Patents

One critic of human gene patents, Dr. Jonathan King, points out that the human genome mapping project came from 50 years of public investment and therefore shouldn't be patentable by private companies. Others object to patenting any part of nature. Still others argue that patenting gene fragment base-pair sequences rewards the easy part. The cost of identifying a gene is only a small fraction of the total cost of developing useful applications from genetic information. It is argued that gene patents penalize anyone (such as pharmaceutical companies) who would invest in the research for drugs or therapies derived from the gene sequence. Most critics agree that gene patenting could slow the study of the human genome.

## Arguments in Favor of Gene Patents

Some companies say patents are necessary because of high research and development costs. Companies fear they will waste millions of dollars on duplicated efforts because only patented information is made public. Unpatented information is kept secret. They point out that owning a patent draws investors, which helps fund research. The public nature of a patent reduces secrecy and allows researchers to share techniques.

## REVIEW

1. What characteristics of an invention must be present for a gene to be patented?
2. What are the arguments for and against gene patents?
3. **Critical Thinking** Are you in favor of gene patenting? Why or why not?

internet connect

www.scilinks.org
**Topic:** Genome Research
**Keyword:** HM60661

SCILINKS. Maintained by the National Science Teachers Association

### OBJECTIVES

- **Discuss** the uses of genetic engineering in medicine.
- **Summarize** how gene therapy is being used to try to cure genetic disorders.
- **Discuss** cloning and its technology.
- **Describe** two ways genetic engineering has been used to improve crop plants.
- **Discuss** environmental and ethical issues associated with genetic engineering.

### VOCABULARY

gene therapy
cloning by nuclear transfer
telomere
DNA vaccine
bioethics

# GENETIC ENGINEERING

*In addition to DNA fingerprints and genomics, genetic engineering techniques are being used in medical, industrial, commercial, and agriculture settings. This section discusses some of these applications and the ethical issues the techniques raise.*

## MEDICAL APPLICATIONS

Genetic engineering has allowed biologists to study how genes function. For example, researchers in Montreal used genetic engineering to study brain development in mice. They wanted to determine what activates the gene *Hoxd4* as the hindbrain develops in an embryo. This is important because abnormal hindbrain development may contribute to autism, a disorder that disrupts a child's ability to socialize and communicate.

The researchers combined the *Hoxd4* gene and a region adjacent to the gene with a "reporter gene." The reporter gene encodes an enzyme that can make a blue-colored product. They inserted the recombinant DNA into mouse cells, grew embryos, and found that the region adjacent to the *Hoxd4* gene could turn on the reporter gene and its blue product, as shown in Figure 13-10a. When they mutated the adjacent region, they discovered (by the lack of blue color) that it was expressed in the spinal cord, but not in the embryo's hindbrain, as shown in Figure 13-10b. They concluded that the DNA sequence adjacent to *Hoxd4* helps control hindbrain development. Experiments such as these are unraveling the mysteries of gene function during development and may eventually provide therapies for disease.

**FIGURE 13-10**

(a) DNA adjacent to the mouse *Hoxd4* gene participates in normal hindbrain development. (b) After a researcher deliberately mutates the flanking DNA, he or she can see that the *Hoxd4* gene is expressed in the spinal cord but not in the hindbrain.

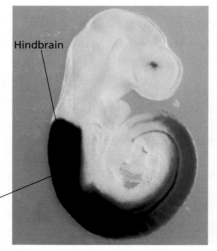

Hindbrain

Spinal cord

(a)

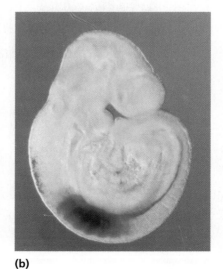

(b)

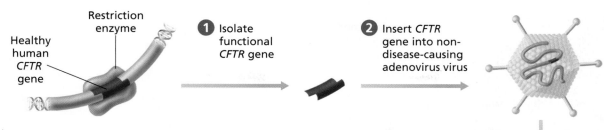

**Healthy human *CFTR* gene** **Restriction enzyme**

**1** Isolate functional *CFTR* gene

**2** Insert *CFTR* gene into non-disease-causing adenovirus virus

**3** Infect patient's airway cells with virus carrying the healthy *CFTR* gene

## Gene Therapy

Genetic engineering has also allowed biologists to try to treat genetic disorders in different ways. One method is a technique called gene therapy. In **gene therapy** a genetic disorder is treated by introducing a gene into a patient's cells. Gene therapy works best for disorders that result from the loss of a single protein. For example, the lung disease *cystic fibrosis* results from the lack of a functional gene called the *CFTR* gene. When functional, the gene encodes a protein that helps transport ions into and out of cells in the breathing passages. Without that gene, poor ion exchange causes the symptoms of cystic fibrosis, including the buildup of sticky mucus that blocks the airways.

Figure 13-11 summarizes the steps involved in gene therapy. In step **1**, researchers isolate the functional gene (such as the *CFTR* gene). In step **2**, they insert the healthy gene into a viral vector. In step **3**, they introduce the recombinant virus to the patient by infecting the patient's airway by means of a nasal spray. The healthy copy of the *CFTR* gene temporarily produces the missing protein and improves ion exchange. The traditional treatment for cystic fibrosis involves thumping sessions—clapping on the back and chest for half-hour periods several times a day to dislodge mucus.

Cystic fibrosis research has accelerated since the discovery of the *CFTR* gene in 1989. In the laboratory, researchers were able to add a healthy copy of *CFTR* into the DNA of cystic fibrosis cells. The result was an immediate return to a normal ion transport mechanism. However, trials in the laboratory are different from trials on living humans. Apparently, the cells that express the highest levels of *CFTR* are deeper in the lungs than the surface cells that current forms of gene therapy can reach. Because the cells that line the airway slough off periodically, the treatment must be repeated. In addition, patients may suffer immune reactions to the treatment. Researchers hope to overcome these obstacles and to one day provide a permanent cure.

People with certain kinds of hemophilia, acquired immunodeficiency syndrome (AIDS), or some cancers are future candidates for gene therapy. Until recombinant DNAs can be inserted into the correct cells, however, and immune reactions can be prevented, gene therapy may continue to be a short-term solution.

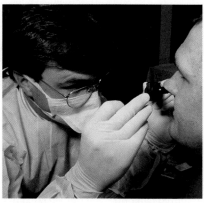

**FIGURE 13-11**

The steps in gene therapy for cystic fibrosis are summarized. The patient in the photo is receiving gene therapy for cystic fibrosis. A healthy copy of the gene responsible for cystic fibrosis is being administered through a nasal spray.

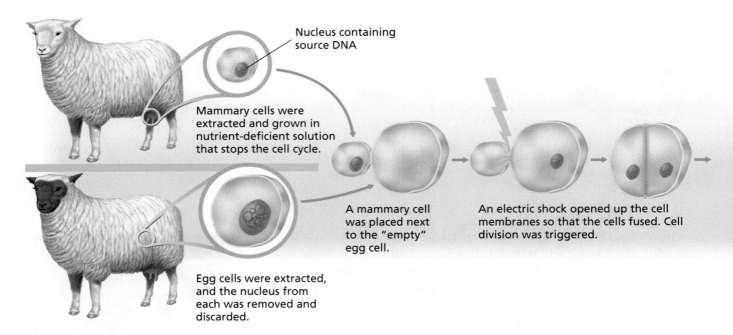

Nucleus containing source DNA

Mammary cells were extracted and grown in nutrient-deficient solution that stops the cell cycle.

Egg cells were extracted, and the nucleus from each was removed and discarded.

A mammary cell was placed next to the "empty" egg cell.

An electric shock opened up the cell membranes so that the cells fused. Cell division was triggered.

**FIGURE 13-12**

Biologists cloned a sheep by transferring a somatic cell nucleus from one animal into the egg cell of another. They implanted the resulting embryo into a surrogate mother, and the offspring that developed was a clone of the original nucleus donor.

## Cloning

In the 1990s, biologists began cloning whole organisms, such as sheep and mice. The name for this procedure is **cloning by nuclear transfer,** the introduction of a nucleus from a body cell into an egg cell to generate an organism identical to the nucleus donor. The first animal successfully cloned from an adult tissue was a sheep named Dolly in 1996.

As shown in Figure 13-12, scientists in Scotland isolated a mature, functioning mammary cell nucleus from an adult sheep. They also isolated an egg cell from a second sheep and removed the nucleus. They then fused the mammary cell with the "empty" egg cell. The egg was stimulated to divide and grew into an embryo. The researchers implanted this embryo into the uterus of a surrogate mother who gave birth to a lamb, which they called Dolly. Dolly's nuclear DNA was identical to the original donor of the mammary gland cell.

Despite the successful cloning, Dolly suffered premature aging and disease and died at age 6, only half of a normal sheep's lifespan. Researchers found that Dolly had short **telomeres,** or repeated DNA sequences at the ends of chromosomes that shorten with each round of cell division. Short telomeres may be associated with premature aging. Other cloned species, however, have not experienced similar telomere shortening.

The goal of most animal cloning is to alter the genome in some useful way. For example, researchers have altered and cloned goats so that they secrete human blood clotting factors into their milk. Cloned pigs have been altered in the hope that pig livers, hearts, and other organs might not trigger organ rejection if transplanted into human recipients. Some researchers are cloning animals as models for the study of human disease, such as cystic fibrosis.

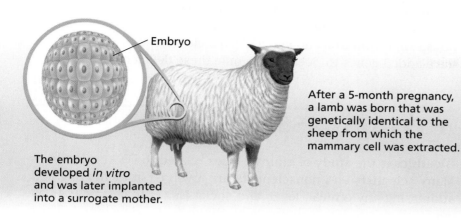

Embryo

The embryo developed *in vitro* and was later implanted into a surrogate mother.

After a 5-month pregnancy, a lamb was born that was genetically identical to the sheep from which the mammary cell was extracted.

## Vaccines

A vaccine is a substance containing all or part of a harmless version of a pathogen that physicians introduce into the body to produce immunity to disease. The immune system recognizes the pathogen's surface proteins and responds by making defensive proteins called *antibodies*. A **DNA vaccine** is a vaccine made from the DNA of a pathogen but does not have disease-causing capability. The DNA vaccine is injected into a patient where it directs the synthesis of a protein. The immune system mounts a defense against the protein. If the vaccinated person contacts the disease agent in the future, his or her new immunity should provide protection. Researchers are currently working on developing DNA vaccines to prevent AIDS, malaria, and certain cancers.

☑ internet connect

www.scilinks.org
**Topic:** Herbicides
**Keyword:** HM60737

SCI*LINKS.* Maintained by the National Science Teachers Association

# AGRICULTURAL APPLICATIONS

Plant researchers are using genetic engineering to develop new strains of plants called *genetically modified (GM) crops.* In a world of exponentially increasing human population, the need for more food with better nutritional value presents a challenge to plant biologists.

## Increasing Yields and Improving Nutrition

To feed the planet's hungry population, biologists have made crop plants that are more tolerant to environmental conditions. They have also added genes to strains of wheat, cotton, and soybeans that make the plants resistant to weed-controlling chemicals called *herbicides.* To increase the amount of food a crop will yield, researchers have transferred genes for proteins that are harmful to insects and other pests into crop plants. The plants are protected from serious damage and yield more food. Similar techniques have been used to make plants resistant to certain diseases.

### Word Roots and Origins

*herbicide*

from the Latin *herba,* meaning "plant," and *cida,* meaning "to kill"

Genetic engineers have also been able to improve the nutritional value of many crop plants. For example, in Asia many people use rice as a major food source, yet rice has low levels of iron and beta carotene, which the body uses to make vitamin A. As a result, millions suffer from iron and vitamin A deficiencies. Genetic engineers have added genes to rice to overcome these deficiencies.

# ETHICAL ISSUES

**Bioethics** is the study of ethical issues related to DNA technology. Many scientists and nonscientists are involved in identifying and addressing any ethical, legal, and social issues that may arise as genetic engineering techniques continue to be developed. They want to make sure that none of the tools turn out to be dangerous or have unwanted results and that any technology and data that arise are carefully used. Almost all scientists agree that continued restraint and oversight are needed.

For example, some people are concerned that GM food crops might harm the environment in unusual ways. What would happen if introduced genes for herbicide resistance jumped to the wild, weedy relative of a GM crop? To this end, in the mid-1970s, government agencies set standards for safety procedures and required permits and labels for certain GM products. Most biologists agree that rigorous testing should be conducted and safeguards required before farmers release GM organisms into the environment.

Most scientists currently consider gene therapy to be unethical if it involves reproductive cells that would affect future generations. Most people consider cloning of human embryos for reproduction unethical.

The welfare of each patient is most important. Confidentiality of each individual's genetic make up is vital to prohibit discrimination in the workplace. Decisions about ethical issues must be made not just by scientists but by the involvement of an informed public.

## SECTION 3 REVIEW

1. List two types of medical products that can be produced using DNA technology.

2. How have medical researchers used gene therapy to help people with cystic fibrosis?

3. What are the main steps in cloning a sheep?

4. Describe a potential safety and environmental concern with regard to genetically modified (GM) crops.

5. Relate bioethics to the continued development of genetic engineering techniques.

**CRITICAL THINKING**

6. **Forming Reasoned Opinions** Should genetically engineered food products require special labels? Why or why not?

7. **Applying Information** If you were to genetically engineer a crop, what would it be, and how would you improve it?

8. **Evaluating Information** In what way might employers discriminate against a person if his or her genome were known to them?

# CHAPTER HIGHLIGHTS

SECTION 1 DNA Technology

- DNA technology provides the tools to manipulate DNA molecules for practical purposes.

- The repeating sequences in noncoding DNA vary between individuals and thus can be used to identify an individual.

- To identify a DNA sample, scientists isolate the DNA and copy it using the polymerase chain reaction (PCR). The DNA is then cut into fragments using restriction enzymes. The fragments are separated by size using gel electrophoresis.

- The resulting pattern is compared to the pattern from a known sample of DNA treated in the same way.

- Restriction enzymes recognize and cut specific nucleotide sequences. This process creates single chains called sticky ends on the ends of each piece of DNA. The enzyme DNA ligase can rejoin sticky ends and connect DNA fragments.

- Researchers use restriction enzymes to insert DNA fragments into vectors. The resulting DNA from two different organisms is called recombinant DNA.

### Vocabulary

length polymorphism (p. 255)
variable number tandem repeats (VNTR) (p. 255)

polymerase chain reaction (PCR) (p. 256)
primer (p. 256)
restriction enzyme (p. 257)

gel electrophoresis (p. 257)
DNA fingerprint (p. 257)
genetic engineering (p. 258)
recombinant DNA (p. 258)

clone (p. 258)
vector (p. 258)
plasmid (p. 259)
probe (p. 259)

SECTION 2 The Human Genome Project

- The goals of the Human Genome Project were to determine the nucleotide sequence of the entire human genome and map the location of every gene on each chromosome. This information will advance the diagnosis, treatment, and prevention of human genetic disorders.

- The Human Genome Project yielded important information about human genes and proteins. For example, there are far fewer protein-encoding human genes than once believed but far more proteins because of the complex way they are encoded.

- The Human Genome Project included sequencing the genes of many model species to provide insights into gene function.

- Information from the Human Genome Project has been applied to medical, commercial, and scientific purposes.

- Bioinformatics uses computers to catalog and analyze genomes. Microarrays, two-dimensional arrangements of cloned genes, allow researchers to compare specific genes such as those that cause cancer. Proteomics studies the identities, structures, interactions, and abundances of an organism's proteins.

### Vocabulary

Human Genome Project (p. 261)
proteome (p. 262)

single nucleotide polymorphism (SNP) (p. 262)

bioinformatics (p. 263)
proteomics (p. 264)

two-dimensional gel electrophoresis (p. 264)

SECTION 3 Genetic Engineering

- Genetic engineering is being used to provide therapies for certain genetic diseases.

- Gene therapy refers to treating genetic disorders by correcting a defect in a gene or by providing a normal form of a gene. Researchers hope that gene therapy can be used to cure genetic disorders in the future.

- In cloning by nuclear transfer, a nucleus from a body cell of one individual is introduced into an egg cell (without

its nucleus) from another individual. An organism identical to the nucleus donor results.

- Genetic engineering is used to produce disease-resistant, pest-resistant, and herbicide-resistant crops in an effort to improve the yields and nutrition of the human food supply.

- Some people fear that the release of genetically modified organisms would pose a separate environmental risk. Many safety, environmental, and ethical issues involved in genetic engineering have not been resolved.

### Vocabulary

gene therapy (p. 267)

cloning by nuclear transfer (p. 268)

telomere (p. 268)
DNA vaccine (p. 269)

bioethics (p. 270)

## USING VOCABULARY

1. Explain the relationship between *length polymorphisms* and *variable number tandem repeats (VNTR)*.

2. For each pair of terms, explain how the meanings of the terms differ.
   a. *gel electrophoresis* and *DNA fingerprint*
   b. *restriction enzyme* and *recombinant DNA*
   c. *vector* and *plasmid*

3. Use the following terms in the same sentence: *cloning by nuclear transfer* and *telomeres*.

4. **Word Roots and Origins** The word *herbicide* derives from the Latin *herba,* meaning "plant" and *cida,* meaning "to kill." Using this information, explain how the term *herbicide* relates to an increase in food crop yields.

## UNDERSTANDING KEY CONCEPTS

5. **Describe** how variable number tandem repeats (VNTR) are used to identify DNA.

6. **Name** the four major steps used in DNA identification.

7. **Identify** the purpose for using the polymerase chain reaction (PCR).

8. **Explain** how restriction enzymes are used.

9. **Describe** how a DNA fingerprint is prepared.

10. **Relate** cloning vectors to recombinant DNA.

11. **Name** two applications of DNA identification.

12. **State** the two major goals of the Human Genome Project.

13. **Discuss** three insights gained from the Human Genome Project.

14. **Describe** the importance of sequencing the genomes of model species.

15. **State** how information from the Human Genome Project will be applied to future projects.

16. **Discuss** the role of bioinformatics in the Human Genome Project.

17. **Explain** how gene therapy has been used to treat cystic fibrosis.

18. **Describe** how biologists used cloning by nuclear transfer to clone animals.

19. **List** two ways that genetic engineering may increase crop yields.

20. **Describe** the steps scientists are taking to ensure that genetic engineering techniques are carefully used in society.

21. **CONCEPT MAPPING** Use the following terms to create a concept map about genetic engineering: *DNA of interest, vectors, recombinant DNA, plasmids, restriction enzymes,* and *sticky ends.*

## CRITICAL THINKING

22. **Applying Information** In the past, breeders developed new plant and animal varieties by selecting organisms with desirable traits and breeding them. Name an advantage and a disadvantage of genetic engineering techniques over this method.

23. **Unit 6—Gene Expression**

    The United States has regulations regarding the release of genetically engineered organisms into the environment. Write a report about reasons why people have concerns regarding the release of such organisms.

24. **Interpreting Graphics** The photograph below shows eight lanes (columns) in a gel. Several of these lanes contain DNA fingerprints of samples taken from a crime scene, a victim, and four suspects. State which suspect's DNA fingerprint matches the blood found at the crime scene. Is it likely that the blood found at the crime scene belongs to the suspect? Explain.

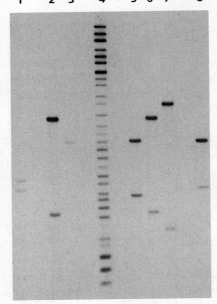

**KEY**

| | |
|---|---|
| 1 Control | 5 Suspect 1 |
| 2 Blood | 6 Suspect 2 |
| 3 Victim | 7 Suspect 3 |
| 4 Standard | 8 Suspect 4 |

# Standardized Test Preparation

**DIRECTIONS:** Choose the letter of the answer choice that best answers the question.

1. Which is a molecule containing DNA from two different organisms?
   A. vector DNA
   B. a DNA clone
   C. plasmid DNA
   D. recombinant DNA

2. Which of the following is used to cut DNA molecules in specific locations?
   F. cloning vectors
   G. cloning enzymes
   H. restriction enzymes
   J. polymerase chain reaction

3. What is the term used for inserting a healthy copy of a gene into a person who has a defective gene?
   A. cloning vector
   B. gene therapy
   C. recombinant DNA
   D. polymerase chain reaction (PCR)

4. Which is the process used in animal cloning?
   F. DNA cloning
   G. recombinant DNA
   H. polymerase chain reaction
   J. cloning by nuclear transfer

**INTERPRETING GRAPHICS:** The graphic below shows a bacterial cell. Use the graphic to answer the questions that follow.

5. Which best describes molecule A?
   A. It is an insulin gene.
   B. It is recombinant DNA.
   C. It is a bacterial plasmid.
   D. It is a disease-causing virus.

6. How is a bacterial plasmid described after donor DNA is inserted into the bacterium's DNA?
   F. vector DNA
   G. cloned DNA
   H. plasmid DNA
   J. recombinant DNA

**DIRECTIONS:** Complete the following analogy.

7. Proteomics : proteins :: genomics :
   A. lipids
   B. genes
   C. proteins
   D. carbohydrates

**INTERPRETING GRAPHICS:** The diagram below is of two pieces of DNA that were cut with the same restriction enzyme. Use the diagram to answer the question that follows.

8. Which nucleotide sequence must the sticky end labeled 2 have if it is to bond with the sticky end labeled 1?
   F. UGGCCU
   G. TCCGGA
   H. ACCGGT
   J. CTTAAG

## SHORT RESPONSE

A probe is a strand of RNA or single-stranded DNA that is labeled with a radioactive element or fluorescent dye.

How do biologists use a probe to find cloned DNA?

## EXTENDED RESPONSE

One concern about genetic engineering involves confidentiality and insurance.

*Part A*  How could the human genome be misused, relative to confidentiality issues?

*Part B*  What might people's concern be about health insurance, and why?

> **Test TIP**  Check for careless mistakes such as marking two answers for a single question.

# Analyzing DNA Using Gel Electrophoresis

### OBJECTIVES

- Use restriction enzymes to cut DNA.
- Separate DNA fragments of different sizes.

### PROCESS SKILLS

- experimenting
- analyzing
- calculating

### MATERIALS

- protective clothing
- ice, crushed
- ice bucket
- microtube rack
- microtube A—Uncut DNA
- microtube B—*Hind*III
- microtube C—*Bam*HI
- microtube D—*Eco*RI
- microtube E—Unknown
- permanent marker
- micropipetter (0.5–10 μL)
- micropipetter tips
- 10× restriction buffer for each restriction enzyme
- Lambda virus DNA (34 μL)
- water bath (37°C)
- gel-casting tray
- gel comb, 6-well
- hot-water bath (65°C)
- agarose (0.8%)
- hot mitt
- zipper-lock plastic bag
- graduated cylinder (10 mL)
- 1× TBE buffer
- freezer
- loading dye (5 μL)
- gel chamber and power supply
- WARD'S DNA stain
- staining trays
- water, distilled
- ruler, metric

### Background

1. DNA has a negative charge and flows toward the positive end of a gel during electrophoresis. Small DNA fragments move faster than larger fragments.
2. The distance that each DNA fragment moves is used to calculate the $R_f$, or relative mobility, of a fragment. The $R_f$ is used to calculate the number of base pairs in the fragment.

### PART A  Cutting DNA

1.    Wear safety goggles, gloves, and a lab apron at all times.

2. Fill an ice bucket with ice. Obtain one each of the following microtubes: A—Uncut DNA, B—*Hind*III, C—*Bam*HI, D—*Eco*RI, and E—Unknown. Microtubes B–D contain 1 μL of the indicated restriction enzyme. Place all microtubes in the ice. *Restriction enzymes MUST be kept on ice until step 6.*

3. With a permanent marker, write the initials for everyone in your group *on the top* of microtubes A–E.

4. ☠ CAUTION  **If you get a chemical on your skin or clothing, wash it off at the sink while calling to your teacher.** Set a micropipetter to 1 μL, and put a tip on the end of the micropipetter, as shown in (a) below. Using a new tip for each microtube, add 1 μL of the corresponding 10× restriction buffer to each of microtubes B–D. Place the buffer on the side of the tube. *Do not touch the micropipetter tips to the solutions in the microtubes.*

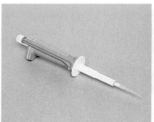 

(a) MICROPIPETTER       (b) CASTING TRAY

5. Reset the micropipetter to 8 μL. Using the micropipetter and a new tip for each microtube, add 8 μL of the Lambda virus DNA to the side of each of microtubes B–D. Gently flick the bottom of each microtube with your finger to mix the solutions. *Do not shake the microtubes!* Reset the micropipetter to 10 μL, and add 10 μL of Lambda DNA to microtube A.

6. Place all of the microtubes into a 37°C water bath. After 50–60 minutes, remove the microtubes from the water bath, and immediately put them into a freezer. If the class period ends before 50 minutes have passed, your teacher will give you further directions. While the restriction enzymes are working, go to Part B.

## PART B  Preparing an Agarose Gel

7. Set up a gel-casting tray, as shown in (b). Place a gel comb in the grooves of the gel-casting tray. Make sure that the comb does not touch the bottom of the tray. If it does, get another comb from your teacher.

8. Write the names of the members of your group on a paper towel. Carry your tray to the table with the melted agarose, and place your tray on the paper towel.

9. ⚠ Using a hot mitt, pour melted 0.8% agarose into your gel-casting tray until the agarose reaches a depth of 3 mm. Make sure that the agarose spreads evenly throughout the tray. *Do not move your gel tray before the agarose solidifies.*

10. Let the gel cool (about 20–30 minutes) until the agarose solidifies.

11. While the gel is cooling, write your name, the date, and your class period on a zipper-lock plastic bag. Pour 5 mL of $1\times$ TBE buffer into the bag.

12. When the gel has solidified, carefully remove the gel comb by pulling it straight up. If the comb does not come up easily, pour a little $1\times$ TBE buffer on the comb area. After removing the gel comb, open the plastic bag and carefully slide the gel tray into the bag. *Do not remove the gel from the gel-casting tray.* Store the gel according to your teacher's instructions.

## PART C  Running a Gel

13. Retrieve your microtubes (A–E) and your gel. If the materials in the microtubes are frozen, hold each tube in your hand until the solutions thaw.

14. Set a micropipetter to 1 µL, and place a tip on the end. Add 1µL of loading dye to each microtube. *Use a new tip for each microtube.* Gently tap each microtube on your lab table to thoroughly mix the solutions. *Do not shake the microtubes.*

15. Remove your gel (still in the gel-casting tray) from the plastic bag, and place it in a gel chamber. Orient the gel so that the wells are closest to the black wire, or anode.

16. Set a micropipetter to 10 µL, and place a new tip on the end. Open microtube A, and remove 10 µL of solution. Carefully place the solution into the well in lane 1, the left-most lane. To do this, place both elbows on the lab table, lean over the gel, and slowly lower the micropipetter tip into the opening of the well before depressing the plunger. *Do not jab the micropipetter tip through the bottom of the well.*

17. *Using a new micropipetter tip for each tube,* repeat step 16 for each of the remaining microtubes. Use lane 2 for microtube B, lane 3 for microtube C, lane 4 for microtube D, and lane 5 for microtube E.

18. Very slowly fill the gel chamber with $1\times$ TBE buffer until the level of the buffer is approximately 1–2 mm above the surface of the gel.

19. ⚠ **CAUTION Follow all of the manufacturer's precautions regarding the use of this equipment.** Close the gel chamber, and connect it to a power supply according to your teacher's instructions.

20. Allow an electric current to flow through the gel. You will see a blue line moving away from the wells. When the blue line is approximately 5 mm from the end of the gel, disconnect the power supply and remove the gel. Store the gel overnight in the plastic bag.

## PART D  Analyzing a Gel

21. To stain a gel, carefully place the gel (wells up) into a staining tray. Pour WARD'S DNA stain into the staining tray until the gel is completely covered. Cover the staining tray, and label it with your initials. Allow the stain to sit for at least 2 hours. Next, carefully pour the stain into the sink drain, and flush it down the drain with water. *Do not let the stained gel slip out of the staining tray.*

22. To destain a gel, cover the gel with distilled water by pouring water to one side of the gel. Let the gel sit overnight (or at least 8–12 hours). The bands of DNA will appear as purple lines against a light background.

23. Calculate the $R_f$ for each fragment using the following equation:
$$R_f = \frac{\text{distance in mm that DNA fragment migrated}}{\text{distance in mm from well to the dye}}$$

24. ⚠ ⚠ Dispose of your materials according to your teacher's directions, and wash your hands before leaving the lab.

## Analysis and Conclusions

1. Which two samples appear to have the same pattern of DNA bands?

2. Which restriction enzyme cut the DNA in the unknown sample? Justify your answer.

3. What are some measures that you took to prevent contamination of your DNA samples during this lab?

# EVOLUTION

" *The past, the finite greatness of the past! For what is the present, after all, but a growth out of the past.* "

Walt Whitman

Charles Darwin studied the giant tortoises (above) on the Galápagos Islands. Observations that Darwin made during his voyage on the HMS Beagle (right) led him to look for a mechanism by which evolution occurs.

internet connect

National Science Teachers Association *sci* LINKS Internet resources are located throughout this unit.

SCI LINKS. Maintained by the National Science Teachers Association

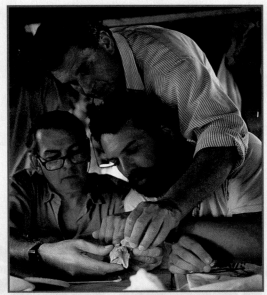

Archeologists (above) scrutinize fossilized remains of human ancestors for clues to human evolution. Darwin observed a number of finches (right) on the Galápagos Islands and found that each species was adapted to a different food source.

Australopithecus robustus

# HISTORY OF LIFE

Molten rock breaks through Earth's crust in the form of a volcano. Conditions in a volcano are similar to those thought to have been present on early Earth.

# BIOGENESIS

*T*he principle of **biogenesis** *(BIE-oh-JEN-uh-sis), which states that all living things come from other living things, seems very reasonable to us today. Before the seventeenth century, however, it was widely thought that living things could also arise from nonliving things in a process called* **spontaneous generation**. *This seemed to explain why maggots appeared on rotting meat and why fish appeared in ponds that had been dry the previous season—people thought mud might have given rise to the fish. In attempting to learn more about the process of spontaneous generation, scientists performed controlled experiments. As you read about these experiments, refer to the figures that show the experimental design.*

## SECTION 1

### OBJECTIVES

- **Compare** the principle of biogenesis with the idea of spontaneous generation.
- **Summarize** the results of experiments by Redi and by Spallanzani that tested the hypothesis of spontaneous generation.
- **Describe** how Pasteur's experiment disproved the hypothesis of spontaneous generation.

### VOCABULARY

biogenesis
spontaneous generation

## REDI'S EXPERIMENT

Flies have often been viewed as pesky creatures. Most people are too busy trying to get rid of flies to even think about studying them. In the middle of the 17th century, however, the Italian scientist Francesco Redi (1626–1697) noticed and described the different developmental forms of flies. Redi observed that tiny wormlike maggots turned into sturdy oval cases, from which flies eventually emerge. He also observed that maggots seemed to appear where adult flies had previously landed.

These observations led Redi to question the commonly held belief that flies were generated spontaneously from rotting meat. Figure 14-1 shows an experiment that Redi conducted in 1668 to test his hypothesis that meat kept away from adult flies would remain free of maggots.

**FIGURE 14-1**

In Redi's experiment, maggots were found only in the control jars because that was the only place where adult flies could reach the meat to lay eggs.

**CONTROL GROUP**     **EXPERIMENTAL GROUP**

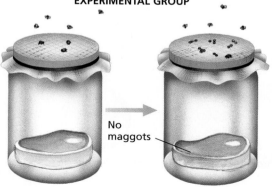

Maggots

No maggots

Redi's experimental group consisted of netting-covered jars that contained meat. The control group consisted of uncovered jars that also contained meat. The netting allowed air to enter and prevented flies from landing on the meat. After a few days, maggots were living in the meat in the open jars, but the net-covered jars remained free of maggots. Redi's experiment showed convincingly that flies come only from eggs laid by other flies. Redi's hypothesis was confirmed, and a major blow was struck against the hypothesis of spontaneous generation.

# SPALLANZANI'S EXPERIMENT

**FIGURE 14-2**

In Spallanzani's experiment, he boiled meat broth in open flasks. Then, he sealed the flasks of the experimental group by melting the glass necks of the flasks closed. The broth inside remained uncontaminated by microorganisms.

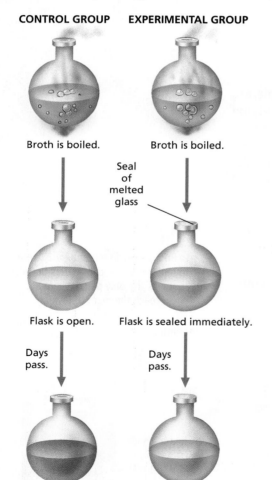

CONTROL GROUP    EXPERIMENTAL GROUP

Broth is boiled.     Broth is boiled.

Seal of melted glass

Flask is open.    Flask is sealed immediately.

Days pass.      Days pass.

Broth becomes cloudy.    Broth remains clear.

At about the same time that Redi carried out his experiment, other scientists began using a new tool—the microscope. Their observations with the microscope revealed that the world is teeming with tiny creatures. They discovered that microorganisms are simple in structure and amazingly numerous and widespread. Many investigators at the time thus concluded that microorganisms arise spontaneously from a "vital force" in the air.

In the 1700s, another Italian scientist, Lazzaro Spallanzani (1729–1799), designed an experiment to test the hypothesis of spontaneous generation of microorganisms, as shown in Figure 14-2. Spallanzani hypothesized that microorganisms formed not from air but from other microorganisms. He knew that microorganisms grew easily in food, such as broth made from boiled meat. Spallanzani reasoned that boiling broth in a flask would kill all the microorganisms in the broth, on the inside of the glass, and in the air in the flask. For his experimental group, Spallanzani boiled clear, fresh broth until the flasks filled with steam. While the broth was hot, he sealed the flasks by melting their glass necks. The control-group flasks of broth were left open. The broth in the sealed flasks remained clear and free of microorganisms, while the broth in the open flasks became cloudy because it was contaminated with microorganisms.

Spallanzani concluded that the boiled broth became contaminated only when microorganisms from the air entered the flask. Spallanzani's opponents, however, objected to his method and disagreed with his conclusions. They claimed that Spallanzani had heated the experimental flasks too long, destroying the "vital force" in the air inside them. Air lacking this "vital force," they claimed, could not generate life. Thus, those who believed in spontaneous generation of microorganisms kept the idea alive for another century.

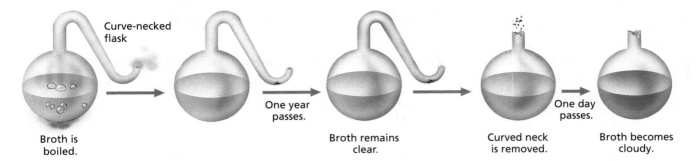

Curve-necked flask

Broth is boiled.

One year passes.

Broth remains clear.

Curved neck is removed.

One day passes.

Broth becomes cloudy.

# PASTEUR'S EXPERIMENT

By the mid-1800s, the controversy over spontaneous generation had grown fierce. The Paris Academy of Science offered a prize to anyone who could clear up the issue once and for all. The winner of the prize was the French scientist Louis Pasteur (1822–1895).

Figure 14-3 shows how Pasteur set up his prize-winning experiment. To answer objections to Spallanzani's experiment, Pasteur made a curve-necked flask that allowed the air inside the flask to mix with air outside the flask. The curve in the neck of the flask prevented solid particles, such as microorganisms, from entering the body of the flask. Broth boiled inside the experimental curve-necked flasks remained clear for up to a year. But when Pasteur broke off the curved necks, the broth became cloudy and contaminated with microorganisms within a day. Pasteur reasoned that the contamination was due to microorganisms in the air.

Those who had believed in the spontaneous generation of microorganisms gave up their fight. With Pasteur's experiment, the principle of biogenesis became a cornerstone of biology.

**FIGURE 14-3**

In Pasteur's experiment, a flask with a curved but open neck prevented microorganisms from entering. Broth boiled in the flasks became contaminated by microorganisms only when the curved necks were removed from the flasks.

## Word Roots and Origins

### biogenesis

from the Greek *bioun*, meaning "to live," and *gignesthai*, meaning "to be born"

## SECTION 1 REVIEW

1. What does the term *spontaneous generation* mean?

2. Explain how Redi's experiment disproved the hypothesis that flies formed in food by spontaneous generation.

3. What caused people to think the air contained a "vital force" that produced living organisms?

4. Describe the argument that Spallanzani's experiment failed to disprove the occurrence of spontaneous generation. Explain how Pasteur's experiment addressed these criticisms.

**CRITICAL THINKING**

5. **Making Comparisons** Spallanzani and Pasteur both used a technique that is now widely used to preserve food. What was this technique?

6. **Analyzing Methods** What would have happened if Pasteur had tipped one of his flasks so that the broth in the flask had come into contact with the curve of the neck?

7. **Analyzing Ideas** If spontaneous generation does not occur and the principle of biogenesis is true, what scientific question remains?

- **Outline** the modern scientific understanding of the formation of Earth.
- **Summarize** the concept of half-life.
- **Describe** the production of organic compounds in the Miller-Urey apparatus.
- **Summarize** the possible importance of cell-like structures produced in the laboratory.

### VOCABULARY

radiometric dating
isotope
mass number
radioactive decay
radioactive isotope
half-life
microsphere
coacervate

# EARTH'S HISTORY

*I*f spontaneous generation does not happen on Earth today, then the question remains: How did cell-based life arise in the first place? The key to answering this question lies in scientific hypotheses that conditions on early Earth were very different from present conditions. Scientists continue to form and test these hypotheses by modeling conditions and processes that could have given rise to the first cellular life on Earth.

## THE FORMATION OF EARTH

Evidence from computer models of the sun suggests that about 5 billion years ago, our solar system was a swirling mass of gas and dust, as shown in Figure 14-4. Over time, most of this material was pulled together by gravity and formed the sun. The remaining gas, dust, and debris circled the young sun. Scientists think that the planets formed through repeated collisions of this space debris. During a 400 million–year period, Earth grew larger as gravity pulled in more debris. The collisions between Earth and space debris also released a great deal of thermal energy. Some collisions would have released enough energy to melt large portions of Earth's surface.

### Earth's Age

The estimated age of Earth, more than 4 billion years, is about 700,000 times as long as the period of recorded history. It is about 50 million times as long as an average human life span. How can we determine what happened so long ago? Scientists have explored Earth's surface and examined its many layers to establish a fairly complete picture of its geologic history. Early estimates of Earth's age were made from studying layers of sedimentary rock in Earth's crust. The age of Earth could not be estimated accurately, however, until the middle of the twentieth century, when modern methods of establishing the age of materials were developed.

### Radiometric Dating

Methods of establishing the age of materials include the techniques known as **radiometric dating.** Recall that the atomic number of an element is the number of protons in the nucleus. All atoms of an element have the same atomic number, but their number of neutrons can vary. Atoms of the same element that differ in the number of neutrons they contain are called **isotopes** (IE-suh-TOHPS). Most elements have several isotopes.

The solar system began to form about 5 billion years ago.

The sun began to form a few million years later.

Earth began to form about 4.6 billion years ago and grew by colliding with space debris.

Volcanoes emitted gas, forming an atmosphere.

By 2.2 billion years ago, Earth probably appeared much as it does today.

The **mass number** of an isotope is the total number of protons and neutrons in the nucleus. The mass number of the most common carbon isotope is 12. If you recall that the atomic number of carbon is 6, you can calculate that this carbon isotope has six protons and six neutrons. Isotopes are designated by their chemical name followed by their mass number; for example, carbon exists as both *carbon-12* and *carbon-14*.

Some isotopes have unstable nuclei, which undergo **radioactive decay;** that is, their nuclei release particles or radiant energy, or both, until the nuclei become stable. Such isotopes are called **radioactive isotopes.** Rates of decay of radioactive isotopes have been determined for many isotopes. The length of time it takes for one-half of any size sample of an isotope to decay to a stable form is called the **half-life** of the isotope. Depending on the isotope, half-lives vary from a fraction of a second to billions of years.

The quantity of a particular radioactive isotope in a material can be measured to determine the material's age. This amount is compared with that of some other substance whose quantity in the material remains constant over time. For example, organic materials can be dated by comparing the amount of carbon-14, a radioactive isotope, with the amount of carbon-12, a stable isotope. Living things take carbon into their bodies constantly. Most of the carbon is in the form of carbon-12. A very small proportion of it, however, is in the form of carbon-14, which undergoes decay. This ratio of carbon-14 to carbon-12 is a known quantity for living organisms.

**FIGURE 14-4**

It took about one-half billion years for Earth to form from a swirling mass of gases. Sometime after Earth formed, living organisms began to affect the atmosphere.

## Quick Lab

### Modeling Radioactive Decay

**Materials** shoebox, 50 pennies, 50 paper clips

**Procedure** Place the pennies in the shoebox. Close the lid, shake the box, and then set the box down. Replace each face-up penny with a paper clip. Record the number of pennies and paper clips in the box. Repeat this process five times.

**Analysis** If the pennies in the box represent an unstable isotope, such as carbon-14, what do the paper clips represent? What does each shake of the box represent?

**FIGURE 14-5**

This deerskin quiver, with a wooden bow and arrows, is about 3,000 years old. Carbon-14 dating methods can be used for organic materials less than 60,000 years old.

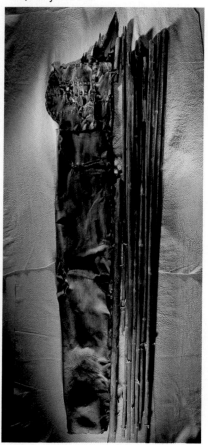

| TABLE 14-1 *Some Isotopes Used in Radiometric Dating* | |
|---|---|
| **Isotope** | **Half-life (years)** |
| Carbon-14 | 5,730 |
| Uranium-235 | 704,000,000 |
| Potassium-40 | 1,250,000,000 |
| Uranium-238 | 4,500,000,000 |

When an organism dies, its uptake of carbon stops, and decay of the existing carbon-14 continues. Thus, over time, the amount of carbon-14 declines with respect to the original amount of the stable carbon-12. After 5,730 years, half of the carbon-14 in a sample will have decayed. After another 5,730 years, half of the remaining carbon-14 in the sample likewise will have decayed. Use of carbon-14 dating is limited to organic remains less than about 60,000 years old, such as the leather quiver and wooden bow and arrows shown in Figure 14-5. Isotopes with longer half-lives are used to date older rocks.

Radioactive isotopes occur naturally in all matter. Some of the isotopes commonly used in radiometric dating procedures appear in Table 14-1. Radiometric dating is accurate within certain limits. The techniques depend on making careful measurements and obtaining samples that are uncontaminated with more recent material. Scientists compare several types of independent measurements to determine a range of plausible dates.

Scientists have estimated Earth's age by using a dating method that is based on the decay of uranium and thorium isotopes in rock crystals. Collisions between Earth and large pieces of space debris probably caused the surface of Earth to melt many times as the planet was formed. Therefore, the age of the oldest unmelted surface rock should tell us when these collisions stopped and the cooling of Earth's surface began. The oldest known rocks and crystals are about 4 billion years old. So, scientists infer that organic molecules began to accumulate about 4 billion years ago.

# FIRST ORGANIC COMPOUNDS

All of the elements found in organic compounds are thought to have existed on Earth and in the rest of the solar system when the Earth formed. But how and where were these elements assembled into organic compounds? An important hypothesis to solve this puzzle was proposed in the 1920s by two scientists: Soviet Alexander I. Oparin (1894–1980) and American John B. S. Haldane (1892–1964). They thought that the early atmosphere contained ammonia, $NH_3$; hydrogen gas, $H_2$; water vapor, $H_2O$; and compounds made of hydrogen and carbon, such as methane, $CH_4$.

According to Oparin, at high temperatures, these gases might have formed simple organic compounds, such as amino acids. When Earth cooled and water vapor condensed to form lakes and seas, these simple organic compounds would have collected in the water. Over time, these compounds could have entered complex chemical reactions, fueled by energy from lightning and ultraviolet radiation. These reactions, Oparin reasoned, ultimately would have resulted in the macromolecules essential to life, such as proteins.

## Synthesis of Organic Compounds

Oparin carefully developed his hypotheses, but he did not perform experiments to test them. So, in 1953, an American graduate student, Stanley L. Miller (1930–), and his professor, Harold C. Urey (1893–1981), set up an experiment using Oparin's hypotheses as a starting point. Their apparatus, illustrated in Figure 14-6, included a chamber containing the gases Oparin assumed were present in the young Earth's atmosphere. As the gases circulated in the chamber, electric sparks, substituting for lightning, supplied energy to drive chemical reactions. The Miller-Urey experiment, and other variations that have followed, produced a variety of organic compounds, including amino acids.

Since the 1950s, scientists have used similar experiments to test and revise hypotheses about the origin of simple organic compounds. In such experiments, scientists have combined a variety of chemicals and energy sources to produce an assortment of organic compounds, including amino acids, ATP, and nucleotides. Scientists are convinced that basic organic compounds could have formed on early Earth in many ways.

Furthermore, scientists who study planet formation have proposed new hypotheses about early Earth's atmosphere. For example, one hypothesis holds that the atmosphere of early Earth was composed largely of carbon dioxide, $CO_2$; nitrogen, $N_2$; and water vapor, $H_2O$. Laboratory simulations of these atmospheric conditions have shown that both carbon dioxide and oxygen gas interfere with the production of organic compounds. Therefore, the production of organic compounds might only have been possible in areas protected from the atmosphere, such as those that exist in undersea hot springs.

## Organic Compounds from Beyond Earth

Some scientists hypothesize that organic compounds could have been carried to Earth by debris from space. In 1970, a broad mixture of organic compounds was found in a newly fallen meteorite. Because the meteorite was recovered before it was contaminated with organic compounds from Earth, these compounds must have formed in space. So, organic compounds from space could have accumulated on the surface of early Earth.

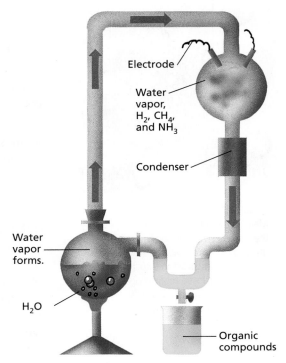

Electrode

Water vapor, $H_2$, $CH_4$, and $NH_3$

Condenser

Water vapor forms.

$H_2O$

Organic compounds

**FIGURE 14-6**

The apparatus of the Miller-Urey experiment was intended to test Oparin's hypothesis about the conditions for formation of organic molecules on early Earth. Although similar experiments and hypotheses continue to be revised and tested, the experiment was an important milestone in this area of scientific investigation.

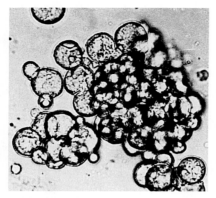

Membrane-bound structures, such as these, have been formed in the laboratory under conditions that may have existed on early Earth. Structures such as these may have enclosed replicating molecules of RNA and may have been the forerunners of the first cells.

# FROM MOLECULES TO CELL-LIKE STRUCTURES

Sidney Fox (1912–1998) and others have done extensive research on the physical structures that may have given rise to the first cells. These cell-like structures, such as the ones shown in Figure 14-7, form spontaneously in the laboratory from solutions of simple organic chemicals. The structures include **microspheres,** which are spherical in shape and are composed of many protein molecules that are organized as a membrane, and **coacervates** (coh-AS-uhr-VAYTS), which are collections of droplets that are composed of molecules of different types, including lipids, amino acids and sugars.

For many years, it had been assumed that all cell structures and the chemical reactions of life required enzymes that were specified by the genetic information of the cell. Both coacervates and microspheres, however, can form spontaneously under certain conditions. For example, the polymers that form microspheres can arise when solutions of simple organic chemicals are dripped onto the surface of hot clay. The heat vaporizes the water, encouraging polymerization. Coacervates and microspheres have a number of cell-like properties, including the ability to take up certain substances from their surroundings. Coacervates can grow, and microspheres can bud to form smaller microspheres. These properties of coacervates and microspheres show that some important aspects of cellular life can arise without direction from genes. Thus, these studies suggest that the gap between the nonliving chemical compounds and cellular life may not be quite as wide as previously thought.

However, microspheres and coacervates do not have all of the properties of life. These cell-like structures do not have hereditary characteristics. Thus, these structures cannot respond to natural selection. Scientists are still investigating hypotheses about how living cells may have formed from simpler ingredients.

## SECTION 2 REVIEW

1. Outline the major steps in the formation of Earth, as reconstructed by modern scientists.

2. If 1.0 g of a radioactive isotope had a half-life of 1 billion years, how much of it would be left after each of the following intervals of time: 1 billion years, 2 billion years, 3 billion years, and 4 billion years?

3. What are two possible sources of simple organic compounds on early Earth?

4. What properties do microspheres and coacervates share with cells?

**CRITICAL THINKING**

5. **Evaluating Conclusions** Which parts of Oparin's hypothesis were tested by the Miller-Urey experiment? Which parts were not tested?

6. **Making Inferences** Some radioactive isotopes that are used in medicine have half-lives of a few years. Would these isotopes also be useful in dating rocks? Why or why not?

7. **Designing an Experiment** Form your own hypothesis about a stage in the formation or development of early life on Earth. Describe how scientists might test this hypothesis.

# THE FIRST LIFE-FORMS

*Scientists continue to investigate many competing hypotheses about possible transitions from simple organic molecules to cellular life. A critical part of each such hypothesis is to explain how molecules could be organized into self-replicating systems, in other words, to explain the origin of heredity.*

## THE ORIGIN OF HEREDITY

Chapter 10 provides a detailed explanation of how hereditary information affects the phenotype of cells. Recall that the hereditary information contained in a DNA molecule is first transcribed into an RNA message, and then the RNA message is translated into a protein, as shown in Figure 14-8. Thus, DNA serves as the template for RNA, which in turn serves as the template for specific proteins.

In recent years, scientists have taken a closer look at the DNA-RNA-protein sequence. Why is RNA necessary for this process? Why doesn't DNA, which is a template itself, carry out protein synthesis directly? The clues to a more complete understanding of RNA function may be found in its structure. RNA molecules take on a greater variety of shapes than DNA molecules do. An example is the unique shape of transfer RNA, shown in Figure 14-8. These shapes are dictated by hydrogen bonds between particular nucleotides in an RNA molecule, much as the shapes of proteins depend on hydrogen bonds between particular amino acids. These questions and observations led to the speculation that some RNA molecules might actually behave like proteins and catalyze chemical reactions.

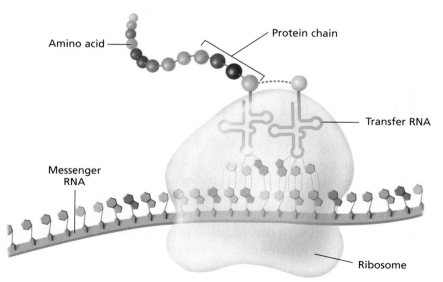

Amino acid

Protein chain

Transfer RNA

Messenger RNA

Ribosome

**FIGURE 14-8**

Messenger RNA is transcribed from a DNA template. Transfer RNA translates the three-base codons in the mRNA, assembling a protein from the specified amino acids.

Some species of archaea, such as *Methanosarcina barkeri* pictured in Figure 14-9, are referred to as methanogens. Within these curious prokaryotic cells, hydrogen gas reacts with carbon dioxide to produce methane, $CH_4$, a simple carbon compound. Methanogens are poisoned by oxygen, but they can live in watery environments where other organisms have consumed all free oxygen, such as in swamps and even the intestines of animals.

Methanogens may prove useful to humans in two significant ways: they are currently used in the cleanup of organic waste, such as sewage, and they may eventually be harnessed for large-scale production of methane for use as a fuel source.

Other species of archaea are being used in the cleanup of petroleum spills into soil, such as occur when underground gasoline tanks develop leaks. This technique, called *bioremediation,* often relies on archaeal species that are already present in the soil. These cells are stimulated by application of nutrient-rich solutions formulated to their taste. As the cells multiply, they metabolize petroleum, releasing harmless byproducts.

## Word Roots and Origins

*archaea*

from the Greek *archein,* meaning "to begin"

# THE ROLES OF RNA

In the early 1980s, researcher Thomas Cech (1947–) found that a type of RNA found in some unicellular eukaryotes is able to act as a chemical catalyst, similar to the way an enzyme acts. Cech used the term **ribozyme** (RIE-buh-ZIEM) for an RNA molecule that can act as a catalyst and promote a specific chemical reaction.

Later studies based on Cech's discovery indicated that ribozymes could act as catalysts for their own replication. In fact, self-replicating systems of RNA molecules have been created in the laboratory. These findings support the hypothesis that life could have started with self-replicating molecules of RNA.

Furthermore, other roles for RNA have been discovered. RNA plays a vital role in DNA replication, protein synthesis, and other basic biochemistry. Perhaps most or all of the chemistry and genetics of early cells were based on RNA. This model of the beginnings of life on Earth is sometimes called *the RNA world.*

Self-replicating RNA molecules might have been not only the first case of heredity but also the first case of competition. For an RNA molecule, self-replication might involve competing with other RNA molecules for a limited number of available nucleotides. A particular RNA molecule with a slightly different structure than other RNA molecules might be more successful in getting nucleotides from its environment and thus more likely to be replicated. Thus, over time, the more-efficient RNA molecules would "survive," and the "world" of RNA would slowly change.

There are several competing hypotheses about how RNA or other simple replicating systems could have evolved into modern cellular life. Some hypotheses propose that certain kinds of minerals formed a template on which organic molecules could line up and form polymers. Another hypothesis is that self-replicating RNA started to evolve inside cell-like structures such as microspheres or coacervates. The self-replicating RNA could have provided the hereditary information that the cell-like structures lack. If the RNA molecules were able to direct the assembly of the structures that carried them, a cell-like system would be formed.

# THE FIRST CELLS

Although lacking direct evidence of the first cells, scientists can make some inferences. First, many scientists think that little or no oxygen gas existed on early Earth. Second, the oldest fossils that are thought to be cells are the size and shape of some living prokaryotes. Finally, the first cells might have developed in an environment filled with organic molecules for food. Thus, the first cells were probably anaerobic, heterotrophic prokaryotes.

We can reason that a growing population of heterotrophs that depended on spontaneously formed organic molecules for food eventually would have removed most of these molecules from the environment. At this point, autotrophs would have begun to have an advantage. The first autotrophs, however, probably did not depend on photosynthesis the way that most autotrophs do today.

## Chemosynthesis

If we look for living organisms that may be similar to these early organisms, we find the archaea (ahr-KEE-uh). The **archaea** are a related group of unicellular organisms, many of which thrive under extremely harsh environmental conditions. *Methanosarcina barkeri*, the archaeon shown in Figure 14-9, lives in anaerobic environments. Many species of archaea are autotrophs that obtain energy by chemosynthesis (KEE-moh-SIN-thuh-sis) instead of photosynthesis. In the process of **chemosynthesis**, $CO_2$ serves as a carbon source for the assembly of organic molecules. Energy is obtained from the oxidation of various inorganic substances, such as sulfur.

## Photosynthesis and Aerobic Respiration

Some forms of life had become photosynthetic by 3 billion years ago. Scientists infer this from a variety of geologic evidence, such as the chemical traces of photosynthetic activity. Also, most of the oldest known fossils of cells are similar to modern **cyanobacteria** (SIE-uh-no-bak-TIR-ee-uh)—a group of photosynthetic, unicellular prokaryotes. *Lynbgya,* a genus of modern cyanobacteria, is shown in Figure 14-10a. *Lynbgya* cells often grow in colonies and form layered structures called *stromatolites,* shown in Figure 14-10b. Fossils of stromatolites as old as 3.5 billion years are known.

Oxygen, a byproduct of photosynthesis, was damaging to many early unicellular organisms. Oxygen could destroy some coenzymes essential to cell function. Within some organisms, however, oxygen bonded to other compounds, thereby preventing the oxygen from doing damage. This bonding was one of the first steps in aerobic respiration. Thus, an early function of aerobic respiration may have been to prevent the destruction of essential organic compounds by oxygen.

Many scientists think that it took a billion years or more for oxygen gas levels to reach today's levels. The oxygen gas, $O_2$, eventually reached the upper part of the atmosphere, where it was bombarded with sunlight. Some wavelengths of sunlight can split $O_2$ to form highly reactive single oxygen atoms, O. These O atoms react with $O_2$ and form **ozone,** $O_3$. Ozone is poisonous to both plant and animal life, but in the upper atmosphere, a layer of ozone absorbs much of the ultraviolet radiation from the sun. Ultraviolet radiation damages DNA, and without the protection of the ozone layer, life could not have come to exist on land.

**FIGURE 14-9**

This archaeal species, *Methanosarcina barkeri*, produces methane during metabolism. Archaea are thought to be similar to the types of cellular life that first populated Earth about 4 billion years ago.

**FIGURE 14-10**

Most of the oldest known fossils of cells are similar to modern cyanobacteria, such as members of the genus *Lygnbya* (a). Cyanobacteria such as these sometimes form large colonies that grow in layers and form stromatolites (b).

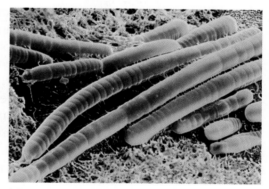

**(a)**

**(b)**

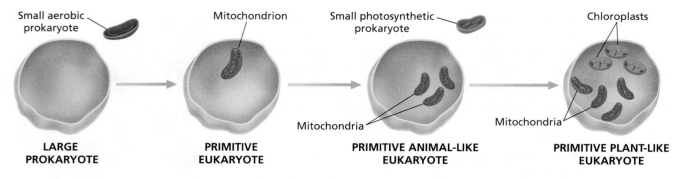

Small aerobic prokaryote

Mitochondrion

Small photosynthetic prokaryote

Chloroplasts

Mitochondria

Mitochondria

**LARGE PROKARYOTE**

**PRIMITIVE EUKARYOTE**

**PRIMITIVE ANIMAL-LIKE EUKARYOTE**

**PRIMITIVE PLANT-LIKE EUKARYOTE**

**FIGURE 14-11**

According to the theory of endosymbiosis, large prokaryotic, unicellular organisms engulfed smaller prokaryotic, unicellular organisms. Engulfed prokaryotes eventually gave rise to modern mitochondria and chloroplasts, which carry their own DNA and replicate independently from the rest of the cell that contains them.

**Word Roots and Origins**

*endosymbiosis*

from the Greek *endon,* meaning "within," *syn* meaning "together," and *biosis,* meaning "way of life"

# THE FIRST EUKARYOTES

Recall that eukaryotic cells differ from prokaryotic cells in several ways. Eukaryotic cells are larger, their DNA is organized into chromosomes in a cell nucleus, and they contain membrane-bound organelles. How did eukaryotic cells evolve? Researcher Lynn Margulis (1938–) proposed that early prokaryotic cells may have developed a mutually beneficial relationship. A large body of evidence suggests that between about 2.0 billion and 1.5 billion years ago, a type of small aerobic prokaryote was engulfed by and began to live and reproduce *inside* of a larger, anaerobic prokaryote. This theory is called **endosymbiosis** (EN-doh-SIM-bie-OH-sis) and is modeled in Figure 14-11. The eukaryotes provided a beneficial environment, and the prokaryotes provided a method of energy synthesis.

Scientists infer that endosymbiotic aerobic prokaryotes evolved into modern mitochondria, which perform aerobic respiration in eukaryotic cells. In a later case of endosymbiosis, photosynthetic cyanobacteria may have evolved into chloroplasts, which perform photosynthesis in modern eukaryotic plant and algae cells. There is compelling evidence to support these hypotheses for the origin of these organelles. Both chloroplasts and mitochondria replicate independently from the replication cycle of the cell that contains them. Moreover, chloroplasts and mitochondria contain some of their own genetic material, which differs from that of the rest of the cell. Finally, the DNA of these organelles is found in a circular arrangement that is characteristic of prokaryotic cells.

## SECTION 3 REVIEW

1. How does RNA differ from DNA?

2. Describe three major scientific inferences about the first living cells on Earth.

3. What traits make archaebacteria likely relatives of Earth's earliest organisms?

4. Explain the difference between chemosynthesis and photosynthesis.

5. Explain the theory of endosymbiosis.

**CRITICAL THINKING**

6. **Evaluating Conclusions** What evidence supports the hypothesis that mitochondria were once free-living prokaryotic cells?

7. **Identifying Relationships** How did anaerobic cells influence the development of aerobic cells?

8. **Predicting Consequences** Some forms of air pollution reduce the thickness of Earth's ozone layer. How might this change affect modern life?

# CHAPTER HIGHLIGHTS

Biogenesis

- Before the 1600s, it was generally thought that organisms could arise from nonliving material by spontaneous generation.

- Redi showed in 1668 that rotting meat kept away from flies would not produce new flies. Maggots appeared only on meat that had been exposed to flies.

- Spallanzani showed in the 1700s that microorganisms would not grow in broth when its container was heated and then sealed. He inferred that microorganisms do not arise spontaneously but, rather, are carried in the air.

- Pasteur in the 1800s used a variation of Spallanzani's design to prove that microorganisms are carried in the air and do not arise by spontaneous generation.

### Vocabulary
biogenesis (p. 279)  spontaneous generation (p. 279)

---

**SECTION 2** Earth's History

- Scientists think that Earth formed by the gravitational accumulation of dust and debris moving through space.

- Isotopes are atoms with varying numbers of neutrons. The ages of rocks and other materials can be determined by measuring the amount of radioactive decay that has occurred in radioactive isotopes found in samples of those materials. An isotope's half-life is the time that one-half of a sample of the isotope takes to decay.

- The first simple organic compounds on early Earth may have formed under conditions of high energy and in an atmosphere very different from that of today's Earth.

- Meteorites may have brought organic compounds to Earth.

- Further chemical reactions may have converted simple organic compounds into the macromolecules important to life. Lightning, ultraviolet radiation, or heat from within the Earth could have provided the energy for these reactions. These conditions have been experimentally modeled.

- Cell-like structures, including microspheres and coacervates, form spontaneously in certain kinds of solutions. These structures could have been a step in the formation of modern cells but lack hereditary material.

- Scientists continue to investigate many hypotheses about the origins of organic molecules and cells in Earth's history.

### Vocabulary
radiometric dating (p. 282)  mass number (p. 283)  radioactive isotope (p. 283)  microsphere (p. 286)
isotope (p. 282)  radioactive decay (p. 283)  half-life (p. 283)  coacervate (p. 286)

---

**SECTION 3** The First Life-Forms

- In addition to serving as a template for protein assembly, some RNA molecules can act as enzymes. Like proteins, RNA molecules can assume different shapes. These shapes depend on areas of attraction between the RNA nucleotides. For these reasons, the first molecule that held hereditary information may have been RNA rather than DNA.

- The first cells that formed on Earth were probably heterotrophic prokaryotes.

- The first autotrophic cells probably used chemosynthesis to make food. Chemosynthesis produces energy through the oxidation of inorganic substances.

- Most modern autotrophic cells use photosynthesis to make food. An important byproduct of photosynthesis is oxygen.

- Once oxygen began to accumulate on Earth, cells would need to bind oxygen to other compounds in order to prevent damage to cell enzymes. This binding function may have been a first step toward aerobic respiration in cells.

- Eukaryotic cells may have evolved from large prokaryotic cells that engulfed smaller prokaryotic cells. The engulfed prokaryotic cells may have become the ancestors of organelles such as mitochondria and chloroplasts.

### Vocabulary
ribozyme (p. 288)  chemosynthesis (p. 289)  ozone (p. 289)
archaea (p. 289)  cyanobacteria (p. 289)  endosymbiosis (p. 290)

## USING VOCABULARY

1. For each of the following pairs of terms, explain how the meanings of the terms differ.
   a. *biogenesis* and *spontaneous generation*
   b. *ribozyme* and *enzyme*
   c. *photosynthesis* and *chemosynthesis*
   d. *archaebacteria* and *cyanobacteria*

2. Explain the relationships between radioactive decay, isotopes, and half-life.

3. ____ and ____ are examples of nonliving, cell-like structures that can form in certain solutions.

4. **Word Roots and Origins** The word *biogenesis* is derived from the Greek word *gignesthai,* which means "origin." The prefix *bio* means "to be born." Using this information, explain how the meaning of *biogenesis* relates to this chapter.

## UNDERSTANDING KEY CONCEPTS

5. **Predict** what would have happened if Redi had used jars covered with netting that had very large openings in his experiment.

6. **Evaluate** Spallanzani's experiment, and explain why his results did not conclusively disprove the theory of spontaneous generation.

7. **Describe** Pasteur's experiment, and explain how it disproved spontaneous generation.

8. **Relate** the role of gravity to the early formation of Earth.

9. **Calculate** the age of a sample containing thorium-230 (whose half-life is 75,000 years) after three-fourths of the sample has decayed.

10. **Identify** the natural phenomenon that the electric spark in the Miller-Urey experiment was intended to model.

11. **Compare** the hypothesis tested in the Miller-Urey experiment with subsequent hypotheses about the conditions under which life may have first formed on Earth.

12. **Compare** microspheres and coacervates with modern, living cells.

13. **Explain** why many scientists who investigate the origin of life have focused on RNA chemistry.

14. **Describe** a hypothesis about the role of RNA in the original development of cells on early Earth.

15. **Identify** which modern organisms are thought to be most like the first forms of life on Earth.

16. **Infer** which environmental factors would probably favor the evolution of autotrophs.

17. **List** and describe two types of autotrophs. State how each makes its own food.

18. **Describe** the conditions under which the ability to bind oxygen gas is an advantage to a cell.

19. **Explain** how the formation of the ozone layer permitted organisms to colonize land.

20. **Explain** the theory of endosymbiosis.

21. **CONCEPT MAPPING** Use the following terms to create a concept map illustrating the theory of endosymbiosis: *anaerobic prokaryotes, eukaryotes, cyanobacteria, aerobic prokaryotes, endosymbiosis, mitochondria,* and *chloroplasts.*

## CRITICAL THINKING

22. **Comparing Concepts** How does the principle of biogenesis pose a scientific question regarding the origin of life on Earth?

23. **Evaluating Conclusions** People once believed fish could form from the mud in a pond that sometimes dried up. How could you demonstrate that this conclusion is false?

24. **Evaluating Methods** Why did the Miller-Urey experiment not include oxygen gas, $O_2$, in the mixture of gases simulating Earth's first atmosphere?

25. **Interpreting Graphics** The apparatus shown below is an example of the Miller-Urey experiment modeling conditions on early Earth. Explain the function of each part of the apparatus.

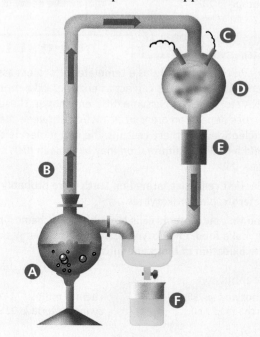

# Standardized Test Preparation

**DIRECTIONS:** Choose the letter that best answers the question.

1. In the 17th and 18th centuries, which of the following was the hypothesis of spontaneous generation used to explain?
   A. how new life started
   B. how eukaryotes evolved
   C. how simple organic compounds formed
   D. how coacervates and microspheres formed

2. Coacervates are similar to cells but lack which of the following?
   F. genetic information
   G. interior fluid
   H. complex organic molecules
   J. the chemical properties of cells

3. The planets of our solar system gained mass for a half-billion years after their formation as a result of which of the following?
   A. flames from the sun
   B. collisions with space debris
   C. tidal forces generated by moons
   D. the synthesis of organic molecules

**INTERPRETING GRAPHICS:** The graph below shows the decay of a radioactive isotope over time. Use the graph to answer the question that follows.

### Amount Remaining of Radioactive Sample

*Graph shows a decay curve starting at "All", passing through $\frac{1}{2}$, $\frac{1}{4}$, $\frac{1}{8}$, $\frac{1}{16}$ at successive half-lives. The x-axis is labeled "Half-lives" from 0 to 7.*

4. If the half-life of carbon-14 is 5,730 years, how many years would it take for $\frac{7}{8}$ of the original amount of carbon-14 in a sample to decay?
   F. 5,014 years
   G. 11,460 years
   H. 17,190 years
   J. 22,920 years

**DIRECTIONS:** Complete the following analogy.

5. chloroplasts : cyanobacteria :: mitochondria :
   A. archaea
   B. aerobic prokaryotes
   C. anaerobic eukaryotes
   D. chemosynthetic bacteria

**INTERPRETING GRAPHICS:** Use the table below to answer the questions that follow.

### Estimated Abundance of Some Elements on Earth and in Meteorites

| Element | Earth (% of total mass) | Meteorites (% of total mass) |
|---|---|---|
| Iron | 36.0 | 27.2 |
| Oxygen | 28.7 | 33.2 |
| Magnesium | 13.6 | 17.1 |
| Silicon | 14.8 | 14.3 |
| Sulfur | 1.7 | 1.9 |

6. According to the table, which element is found on Earth in a greater abundance than the element's abundance in meteorites?
   F. iron
   G. sulphur
   H. oxygen
   J. magnesium

7. If this table is typical of the relative abundance of all elements on Earth, in meteorites, and on other planets, which of the following statements would be supported?
   A. Earth and meteorites have similar origins.
   B. Earth and meteorites have different origins.
   C. All meteorites formed from parts of Earth.
   D. All elements on Earth come from meteorites.

## SHORT RESPONSE

Describe the prevailing scientific model of the original formation of Earth.

## EXTENDED RESPONSE

Little direct evidence has been found of any life that existed in the first few billion years of Earth's history.

*Part A* Describe the major steps that may have led to the development of eukaryotic organisms.

*Part B* Describe evidence that supports hypotheses about some of these steps.

> **Test TIP** For short-response and essay questions, be sure to answer the prompt as fully as possible. Include major steps, important facts, descriptive examples, and supporting details in your response.

# Making Microspheres

## OBJECTIVES

- Make microspheres from amino acids by simulating the conditions found on early Earth.
- Compare the structure of microspheres with the structure of living cells.

## PROCESS SKILLS

- observing
- comparing and contrasting
- modeling
- relating

## MATERIALS

- safety goggles
- lab apron
- heat-protective gloves
- 500 mL beaker
- hot plate
- 125 mL Erlenmeyer flasks, 2
- ring stand with clamp
- balance
- amino acid mixture (supplied by your teacher)
- glass stirring rod
- tongs
- clock or timer
- 1% sodium chloride (NaCl) solution
- 50 mL graduated cylinder
- dropper
- microscope slide
- coverslip
- compound light microscope
- 1% sodium hydroxide (NaOH) solution

## Background

1. Microspheres are very small, spherical vessels that are bounded by a membranelike layer of amino acids. Microspheres can be created in the laboratory under controlled conditions.
2. How do microspheres differ from living cells?
3. How do microspheres resemble living cells?

4. What role might have been played by microspheres or similar structures before life began on Earth?

## Procedure

1. Put on safety goggles, a lab apron, and heat-protective gloves before beginning this investigation.

2. CAUTION Do not plug in or unplug the hot plate with wet hands. Use care to avoid burns when working with the hot plate. Do not touch the hot plate. Use tongs to move heated objects. Turn off the hot plate when not in use. Fill a 500 mL beaker half full with water, and heat it on a hot plate. You will use the beaker as a hot-water bath. Leave space on the hot plate for a 125 mL Erlenmeyer flask, to be added later.

3. While waiting for the water to boil, clamp a 125 mL Erlenmeyer flask to a ring stand. Add 6 g of the amino acid mixture to the flask.

4. When the water in the beaker begins to boil, move the ring stand carefully so that the flask of amino acids sits in the hot-water bath.

5. When the amino acids have heated for 20 minutes, measure 10 mL of NaCl solution in a graduated cylinder, and pour the solution into a second Erlenmeyer flask. Place the second flask on the hot plate beside the hot-water bath.

6. When the NaCl solution begins to boil, use tongs to remove the flask containing the NaCl solution from the hot plate. Then, while holding the flask with tongs, slowly add the NaCl solution to the hot amino acids while stirring.

7. Let this NaCl–amino acid solution boil for 30 seconds.

8. Remove the solution from the water bath, and allow it to cool for 10 minutes.

9. ⚠ CAUTION **Slides break easily. Use caution when handling them.** Use a dropper to place a drop of the solution on a microscope slide, and cover the drop with a coverslip.

10. Place the slide on the microscope stage. Examine the slide under low power for tiny spherical structures. Then, examine the structures under high power. These tiny sphere-shaped objects are microspheres.

11. ☠ CAUTION **If you get the sodium hydroxide (NaOH) solution on your skin or clothing, wash it off at the sink while calling to your teacher. If you get the sodium hydroxide solution in your eyes, immediately flush your eyes at the eyewash station while calling to your teacher.** Place a drop of 1% NaOH solution at the edge of the coverslip to raise the pH as you observe the microspheres. What happens?

12. In your lab report, make a table similar to the one shown below. Based on your observations of microspheres and cells, complete your table. Consider the appearance of microspheres and cells, their method of reproduction, their interaction with their environment, and any other characteristics that you observe.

13. ⚠ ⚠ Clean up your lab materials, and wash your hands before leaving the lab.

## Analysis and Conclusions

1. Suggest how the microspheres in step 10 were formed.

2. What did you observe when the pH was raised in step 11?

3. What does this suggest about the relationship of pH to microsphere formation?

4. Compare and contrast microspheres with living cells.

5. What characteristics would microspheres have to exhibit in order to be considered living?

6. How might the conditions you created in the lab be similar to those that are thought to have existed when life first evolved on Earth?

7. Predict what would happen to microspheres if they were placed in hypotonic and hypertonic solutions.

## Further Inquiry

1. What do you think would happen if you added too much or too little heat? What happens to proteins at high temperatures? How can you test for the right amount of heat to use?

2. Do you think your microsphere experiment would have worked if you had substituted other amino acids? How can you test your hypothesis?

| COMPARING MICROSPHERES WITH CELLS | |
|---|---|
| **Cell-like characteristics** | **Characteristics that are not cell-like** |
| | |
| | |
| | |
| | |

# THEORY OF EVOLUTION

When the famous scientist Charles Darwin visited the Galápagos Islands in the early 1800s, he was intrigued by unique organisms such as these giant tortoises, *Geochelone elephantosus*. Darwin formed an important theory to explain how Earth's many unique organisms could have evolved.

# HISTORY OF EVOLUTIONARY THOUGHT

*In the 1830s, the young English naturalist Charles Darwin took a trip around the world on a ship called HMS* Beagle. *He was fascinated by diverse and unique organisms, such as the giant tortoises of the Galápagos Islands. Darwin went on to form one of the most important theories in biology.*

## THE IDEA OF EVOLUTION

After visiting the Galápagos Islands, Charles Darwin (1809–1882), shown in Figure 15-1, noted that groups of animals varied from island to island. For example, the tortoises on the same island resembled each other closely, but those from neighboring islands were different. Darwin noticed similarities and differences among many organisms as he traveled around the world. He became convinced that organisms had changed over time, and he wanted to understand why.

The development of new types of organisms from preexisting types of organisms over time is called **evolution.** Modern scientists also define evolution as a heritable change in the characteristics within a population from one generation to the next. Darwin sought to present the evidence that the evolution of new organisms occurs. Furthermore, he formed a theory to explain how evolution could occur. Others had tried to form such theories earlier, but Darwin's theory became the basis for modern explanations of evolution. Remember that in science, a *theory* is a well-supported explanation for some aspect of the natural world that incorporates many observations, inferences, and tested hypotheses. In forming his theory, Darwin took years to put together data from many sources and to take account of the ideas of other scientists of his time.

### Ideas Of Darwin's Time

In Europe in the 18th century, most scientists thought that all species were permanent and unchanging. Furthermore, they thought that the Earth was only thousands—and not billions—of years old. However, scientists began to present evidence that the species on Earth have changed over time, and that the Earth is much older than anyone had thought.

**FIGURE 15-1**

Charles Darwin first studied to be a doctor and then a minister, but was also interested in nature. At the age of 22, he set off on a five-year voyage that became an important part of the history of science.

**FIGURE 15-2**

The strata of the Grand Canyon contain evidence of the history of the area over millions of years of geologic time.

## Ideas About Geology

By the 1800s, scientists in Europe had begun to study rock layers—called **strata**—such as those shown in Figure 15-2. They found that strata are formed as new layers of rock are deposited over time. They inferred that, in general, lower strata were formed first and are thus the oldest. The scientists also found that different rock strata hold fossils of different kinds of organisms.

French anatomist Georges Cuvier (coo-VYAY) (1769–1832) spent years reconstructing the appearance of unique organisms from fossil bones. Cuvier gave convincing evidence that some organisms in the past differed greatly from any living species and that some organisms had become *extinct*, meaning the species had ceased to live after a point in time. Cuvier also found that deeper and older strata hold fossils that are increasingly different from living species. Finally, Cuvier found many "sudden" changes in the kinds of organisms found in one rock stratum compared to the next.

To explain these observations, Cuvier promoted the idea of *catastrophism* (kuh-TAS-truh-FIZ-uhm)—the idea that sudden geologic catastrophes caused the extinction of large groups of organisms at certain points in the past. Even though scientists no longer accept all of his explanations, Cuvier contributed to scientific acceptance that geologic change and extinction had occurred.

The English geologist Charles Lyell (1797–1875) shared some of Cuvier's ideas but thought that the geologic processes that have changed the shape of Earth's surface in the past continue to work in the same ways. Lyell's idea is called *uniformitarianism* (YOON-uh-FAWRM-uh-TER-ee-uhn-IZ-um). Charles Darwin read Lyell's writings while on his trip around the world. He was excited to find how well Lyell's ideas fit with his own observations and ideas. Lyell had shown evidence from geology that fit with Darwin's evidence from biology. Darwin referred to Lyell's work in many of his writings.

## Lamarck's Ideas on Evolution

The French biologist Jean Baptiste Lamarck (1744–1829) also supported the idea that populations of organisms change over time. Lamarck put forward a new idea to explain how evolution could happen, though this idea is no longer accepted among scientists. Lamarck thought that simple organisms could arise from nonliving matter. He also thought that simple forms of life inevitably develop into more complex forms. He proposed that individuals could acquire traits during their lifetimes as a result of experience or behavior, then could pass on those traits to offspring. Lamarck's idea is called the *inheritance of acquired characteristics*. Even though Darwin himself once accepted Lamarck's idea, it was rejected by many scientists of their time and has not been supported by modern scientific study of the mechanisms of inheritance.

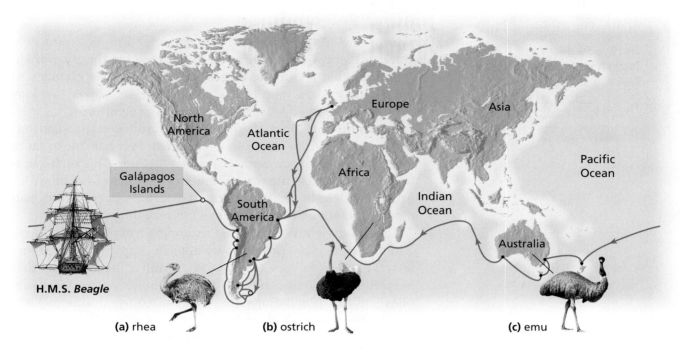

**(a)** rhea      **(b)** ostrich      **(c)** emu

# DARWIN'S IDEAS

At about the same time in the mid-1800s, both Charles Darwin and the English naturalist Alfred Russel Wallace (1823–1913) formed a new theory to explain how evolution may take place. Both Darwin and Wallace had been on sea voyages around the world; Darwin's voyage is shown in Figure 15-3. In 1858, the ideas of Darwin and Wallace were presented to a prestigious group of scientists in London. The following year, Darwin published a book entitled *On the Origin of Species by Means of Natural Selection.*

Darwin had two goals in his book: first, he wanted to present the large amount of evidence that evolution occurs; and second, he wanted to explain the variety and distribution of organisms on Earth in terms of natural processes that are observable every day.

## Descent with Modification

Darwin used the phrase *descent with modification* to describe the process of evolution. He carefully reviewed the evidence that every species—living or extinct—must have descended by reproduction from preexisting species and that species must be able to change over time. Darwin was not the first person to put forward the idea of descent with modification, but he was the first to argue that *all* species had descended from only one or a few original kinds of life.

Darwin saw the animals of the Galápagos Islands as evidence of descent with modification. For example, the islands are home to 13 similar species of finches. Each of these bird species has a beak that is best adapted for a certain kind of food. But Darwin suspected that all 13 species descended from and diverged from just a few ancestral finches. These ancestors could have flown to the Galápagos Islands from elsewhere sometime after the islands were formed.

**FIGURE 15-3**

On his voyage, Darwin noticed the locations of similar organisms around the world. The rhea (a), ostrich (b), and emu (c), for example, are clearly related species that have similar body forms and occupy similar habitats. They occur on different continents, however. Darwin wondered what causes such distributions in nature.

## Natural Selection

Darwin proposed the theory of **natural selection** as the mechanism for descent with modification. In forming his theory, Darwin thought carefully about the forces that could cause changes in organisms over time. The following summary explains the four main parts of Darwin's reasoning, as shown in Figure 15-4:

❶ **Overproduction** More offspring can be produced than can survive to maturity. For example, each female deer has one or more offspring per year for many years in a lifetime. This multiplication could increase the total number of deer in a short time. But each new deer needs food and is vulnerable to predators and disease, so not all of the deer live for very long.

Darwin drew this part of his reasoning from a popular book about human social problems by English clergyman and economist Thomas Malthus (1766–1834). Malthus pointed out that human populations can increase more quickly than food supplies and that populations are often limited by conditions such as war, disease, or lack of food. Darwin realized that the environment limits the populations of *all* organisms by causing deaths or by limiting births.

❷ **Genetic Variation** Within a population, individuals have different traits. For example, some deer may have thicker fur or longer legs than others. Also, some of this variation can be inherited. For example, deer that have thick fur tend to have offspring with thick fur. Occasionally, new traits may appear in a population.

❸ **Struggle to Survive** Individuals must compete with each other in what Darwin called a "struggle for existence." Some variations improve an individual's chance to survive and reproduce, but some variations reduce this chance. For example, deer that have thick fur may survive in the cold better than deer that have thin fur. A trait that makes an individual successful in its environment, such as thick fur in cold climates, is called an **adaptation.**

**FIGURE 15-4**

This diagram represents the process of natural selection explained by Charles Darwin as the mechanism for evolution.

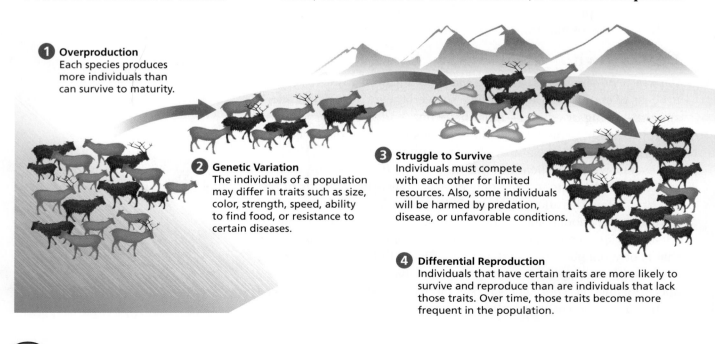

❶ **Overproduction**
Each species produces more individuals than can survive to maturity.

❷ **Genetic Variation**
The individuals of a population may differ in traits such as size, color, strength, speed, ability to find food, or resistance to certain diseases.

❸ **Struggle to Survive**
Individuals must compete with each other for limited resources. Also, some individuals will be harmed by predation, disease, or unfavorable conditions.

❹ **Differential Reproduction**
Individuals that have certain traits are more likely to survive and reproduce than are individuals that lack those traits. Over time, those traits become more frequent in the population.

**4 Differential Reproduction** Darwin concluded that organisms with the best adaptations are most likely to survive and reproduce. And through inheritance, the adaptations will become more frequent in the population. So, populations may begin to differ as they become adapted to different environments, even if they descended from the same ancestors. This conclusion is the core idea of Darwin's theory.

Darwin explained that natural selection could account for descent with modification as species become better adapted to different environments. That is, the theory of natural selection proposes that nature changes species by selecting traits. The environment "selects" the traits that may increase in a population by selecting the parents for each new generation.

Darwin sometimes used the phrase "survival of the fittest" to describe natural selection. In evolutionary terms, **fitness** is a measure of an individual's hereditary contribution to the next generation. This kind of fitness is more than simply living a long time. A fit individual is one that has offspring that also live long enough to reproduce in a given environment. For example, if thick fur is an advantage for a deer living in the mountains, then deer that have thick fur are more likely to live long enough to reproduce and pass on the genes for thick fur. If a certain trait increases an individual's fitness, the proportion of individuals with that trait is likely to increase over time. So, adaptations are those traits that increase the fitness of individuals, and populations tend to be well adapted to survive the conditions in which they live.

In evolutionary theory, the term *adaptation* is also used to describe changes in traits in populations over time. This meaning is different from that of short-term adaptation by an individual to a temporary condition. Also, long-term adaptation in populations is not the same as acclimatization in individuals. *Acclimatization* is a short-term process in which physiological changes take place in a single being in its own lifetime. An example of acclimatization is an animal adjusting to a new climate by growing thicker fur.

## Eco Connection

### Galápagos Islands

The unique ecosystems of the Galápagos Islands have been in danger since the discovery of the islands by Europeans in 1535. For 400 years, the islands were a favorite stopping place for pirates and whalers. Sailors valued the large native tortoises as a meat source because the tortoises could live for long periods aboard a ship with little or no food or water. Over the years, the number of native tortoises was severely reduced. Three of the 14 original subspecies of tortoises are now extinct. However, since 1936, the government of Ecuador and scientists from many countries have taken steps to preserve and restore the islands' native species and habitats. In 1965, the Charles Darwin Research Station began to breed and reintroduce the tortoises and other species.

## SECTION 1 REVIEW

1. Explain Darwin's use of the phrase *descent with modification* to describe the process of evolution.

2. Describe two scientists' ideas about geology that influenced ideas about evolution in the 1800s.

3. Explain the difference between an acquired characteristic and an inherited characteristic.

4. In what ways was Darwin an important scientist?

5. Describe the four parts of reasoning in Darwin's theory of evolution by natural selection. Use examples in your answer.

**CRITICAL THINKING**

6. **Inferring Meaning** Explain why some biologists say that "fitness is measured in grandchildren."

7. **Analyzing Processes** Suppose that an individual has a new trait that makes it live longer than others in its population. Does this individual have greater fitness? Explain your answer.

8. **Applying Information** What have you learned about heredity and genetics that could support Darwin's theory of natural selection?

# EVIDENCE OF EVOLUTION

*Many kinds of evidence give insight into the history of life on Earth and the patterns of change among organisms. Fossils that are different from organisms living today are strong evidence that organisms on Earth can change over time. But evidence of evolution is also found inside living organisms.*

## THE FOSSIL RECORD

A **fossil** is the remains or traces of an organism that died long ago. Fossils of many kinds of organisms can be formed under a number of different conditions, as shown in Figure 15-5. Fossils show that different types of organisms appeared at different times and places on Earth. Some fossils are of organisms that have become *extinct*, meaning the species is no longer alive. Fossils are among the most powerful evidence of evolution.

### The Age of Fossils

In 1669, Danish scientist Nicolaus Steno (1638–1686) proposed the principle of **superposition.** This principle states that if the rock strata at a location have not been disturbed, the lowest stratum was formed before the strata above it. Successive strata are newer, and the most recent stratum is on the top. Geologists in the 1700s and 1800s built on Steno's ideas by comparing strata in different places and by comparing the fossils found in different strata. The geologists began to put together a timeline for the order in which different groups of rocks and fossils were formed. This timeline is commonly known as the *geologic time scale* (a simple version of this table appears in the Appendix). Today, geologists often can tell a fossil's **relative age**—its age compared to that of other fossils—by referring to the geologic time scale and to records of known fossils.

**FIGURE 15-5**

These fossils of pterosaur bones (a), fern leaves (b), and trilobite exoskeletons (c) were buried in ancient sediment. The insect (d) was trapped in ancient tree sap. In each case, the surrounding material later became rock.

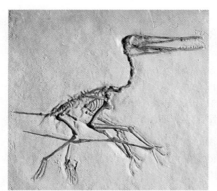
(a)

(b)

(c)

(d)

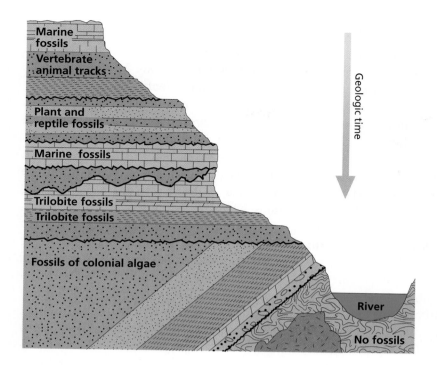

Marine fossils

Vertebrate animal tracks

Plant and reptile fossils

Marine fossils

Trilobite fossils

Trilobite fossils

Fossils of colonial algae

Geologic time

River

No fossils

For certain rocks, scientists can estimate the time since formation, or the **absolute age** of the rock, by techniques such as *radiometric dating*. Scientists use both relative and absolute dating as they compare fossils around the world. In this way, scientists try to make their history of life on Earth as precise as possible. However, the fossil record is an incomplete history of life because not all organisms have left fossil evidence. Most fossils are formed only by rare events. For example, a fossil could form if an organism died in a place where it did not fully decay and where rock later formed over the remains. Then, if the fossil escapes destruction over time, humans will discover it only by chance. Nevertheless, Earth is rich with fossil evidence of organisms that lived in the past.

## The Distribution of Fossils

A number of additional inferences can be made from the fossil record. First, we can infer that different organisms lived at different times. For example, the rock strata shown in Figure 15-6 hold different kinds of fossils in successive layers. Second, we can infer that today's organisms are different from those of the past. Trilobites, for example, were unlike any organism alive today. Third, we can infer that fossils found in adjacent layers are more like each other than to fossils found in deeper or higher layers. In other words, organisms that lived during closer time periods are more alike than organisms that lived in widely separated time periods. Different species of trilobites appear in nearby strata, whereas deeper and older strata do not hold trilobites but hold other kinds of organisms. Fourth, by comparing fossils and rocks from around the planet, we can infer when and where different organisms existed. Each fossil provides evidence about the environment in which the organism existed and for which the organism had become adapted.

internet connect

www.scilinks.org
Topic: Extinction
Keyword: HM60558

SCLINKS. Maintained by the National Science Teachers Association

## Transitional Species

Finally, we can infer from the fossil record that species have differed in a gradual sequence of forms over time. This inference is based on *transitional species,* which have features that are intermediate between those of hypothesized ancestors and later descendant species. For example, evolutionary scientists have hypothesized that modern marine mammals, such as whales, evolved from early mammals in the fossil record that walked with four legs on land. This hypothesis predicts that there should be fossils that share characteristics of both ancient land-dwelling mammals and modern whales.

Indeed, scientists have found several fossils, such as those in Figure 15-7, that form a sequence of transitional forms. Comparing these fossils with each other and with modern whales reveals a sequence of differences in the structure of the hind limbs, forelimbs, vertebrae, and skull of each species. Scientists explain these differences as increasing adaptations for life in water. For example, hind limbs were smaller in later species and are absent in modern whales except for tiny pelvic bones. The hypothesis of whale evolution from land mammals is strongly supported by these fossil finds. However, there are other groups of organisms for which fossils of hypothesized transitional species have not been found.

**FIGURE 15-7**

The fossil skeletons below form a sequence of transitional forms that support the hypothesis that whales evolved from four-legged, land-dwelling mammals.

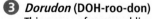
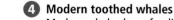

**❶** *Pakicetus* **(pak-uh-SEE-tuhs)**
Scientists think that whales evolved from land-dwelling mammals. One of these ancestors may have belonged to the genus *Pakicetus,* which lived about 50 million years ago. The fossil skeleton of a pakicetid is shown here.

**❷** *Ambulocetus* **(am-byoo-loh-SEE-tuhs)**
This genus of mammal lived in coastal waters about 49 million years ago. It could swim by kicking its legs and using its tail for balance. It could also waddle on land with its short legs.

**❸** *Dorudon* **(DOH-roo-don)**
This genus of mammal lived in the oceans about 40 million years ago. It resembled a giant dolphin and propelled itself with a massive tail. It had forelimbs that were flippers and tiny hind limbs that could not have been used for walking or swimming.

**❹** **Modern toothed whales**
Modern whales have forelimbs that are flippers. They also have tiny, nonfunctioning hip bones at the rear of their bodies.

# BIOGEOGRAPHY

**Biogeography** is the study of the locations of organisms around the world. When traveling, Charles Darwin and Alfred Russel Wallace saw evidence of evolution in the distribution of organisms. Both Darwin and Wallace observed animals that seemed closely related yet were adapted to different environments in nearby regions. However, they also observed animals that seemed unrelated but that had similar adaptations to similar environments in regions that were far apart. Again, the model of descent with modification provides an explanation for these patterns of distribution.

The mammals of the continent of Australia provide a striking example of biogeographic evidence of evolution. There are native Australian animals that resemble wolves, cats, mice, moles, or anteaters. However, most Australian mammals are marsupials, mammals that have pouches in their bodies for carrying their young. A possible explanation for this pattern is that these animals evolved in isolation on the Australian continent.

# ANATOMY AND EMBRYOLOGY

Descent with modification also predicts the findings of *anatomy*—the study of the body structure of organisms— and *embryology*—the study of how organisms develop. Look at the bones in the forelimbs of humans, penguins, alligators, and bats shown in Figure 15-8. These forelimbs are used in different ways in each animal, yet each limb has a similar bone structure. One explanation for the commonalities among the forelimb bones of the four animals is that an early ancestor shared by all these vertebrates had a forelimb with a similar bone structure. As generations passed, different populations of descendants adapted to different environments. Bones inherited from ancestors may have become modified for different tasks.

Biologists define **homologous structures** as anatomical structures that occur in different species and that originated by heredity from a structure in the most recent common ancestor of the species. Homologous organs often have a related structure even if their functions differ between species. On the other hand, **analogous structures** have closely related functions but do not derive from the same ancestral structure. For example, even though birds, bats, and moths have wings, their wings have very different underlying structures. Scientists think that wings evolved independently in each of these groups of animals.

## Word Roots and Origins

**homologous**

from the Greek *homo,* meaning "equivalent to" and *logos,* meaning "relation" or "reason"

**FIGURE 15-8**

Humans, penguins, alligators, and bats each have forelimbs with homologous parts.

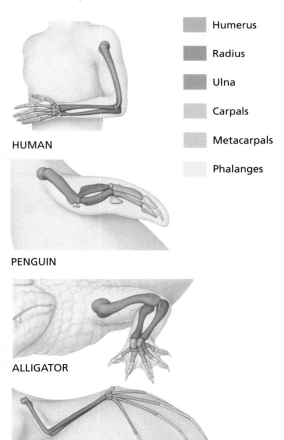

Humerus

Radius

Ulna

Carpals

Metacarpals

Phalanges

HUMAN

PENGUIN

ALLIGATOR

BAT

**(a)** dogfish, *Squalus acanthias*

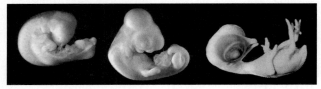

**(b)** chicken, *Gallus gallus*

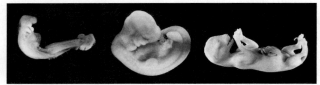

**(c)** cat, *Felis catus*

**FIGURE 15-9**

Modern analysis of vertebrate embryos shows that fish, chick, and cat embryos are remarkably similar at certain stages. This pattern would be expected if all were descended from a common ancestor. Processes occurring later in development then modify the ancestral body structures.

Further evidence of evolution is found in structures called **vestigial structures** that seem to serve no function but that resemble structures with functional roles in related organisms. For example, the human tailbone, or coccyx, is made up of four fused vertebrae that resemble the bones in an animal's tail. Other examples of vestigial structures are the pelvic bones of modern whales and the human appendix.

The development of animal embryos is also evidence of descent with modification. As shown in Figure 15-9, some stages of vertebrate embryo development are very alike, although the similarities fade as development proceeds. One possible explanation for these similarities is that vertebrates share a common ancestor and have inherited similar stages of development.

# BIOLOGICAL MOLECULES

Organisms that share many traits should have a more recent common ancestor than organisms that share fewer traits. Darwin made this prediction by studying anatomy, but modern studies of biological molecules also support this prediction. In all species, DNA and RNA are the molecular basis for inheritance of traits. Furthermore, DNA affects traits encoding the amino acid sequences that form proteins. Biologists can compare the DNA, RNA, proteins, and other biological molecules from many different organisms. Then, they can look for similarities and differences among the data for each species. The greater the number of similarities between any given species, the more closely the species are related through a common ancestor. However, because the study of biological molecules is still relatively new, scientists continue to debate how to interpret this kind of evidence.

# DEVELOPING THEORY

Not until the mid-1900s did scientists begin to integrate the theory of natural selection with new understandings of genetics. This blending has been called the *modern synthesis* of evolutionary theory. As in all areas of science, hypotheses and theories about evolution continue to be formed, challenged, and revised. Many aspects of evolution remain poorly understood, and some observations remain unexplained. Although modern evolutionary theory, like all theories in science, can never be "proven," it is widely accepted and applied by scientists because it explains the broadest range of observations and makes useful predictions.

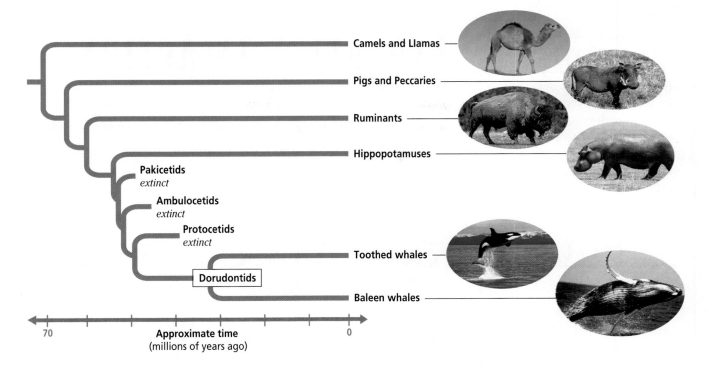

Camels and Llamas

Pigs and Peccaries

Ruminants

Hippopotamuses

**Pakicetids**
*extinct*

**Ambulocetids**
*extinct*

**Protocetids**
*extinct*

Dorudontids

Toothed whales

Baleen whales

70      **Approximate time**      0
(millions of years ago)

For example, scientists try to model **phylogeny,** the relationships by ancestry among groups of organisms. To do so, they must analyze many kinds of evidence. Sometimes, different evidence supports different models. Figure 15-10 shows a phylogenetic diagram, or "tree," which models a hypothesized phylogeny. This particular phylogeny was based on an analysis of biological molecules in animals that seem closely related to whales. The "trunk" represents a past species that could have been the ancestor of all these animals. Each "branch" over time represents a separate population or lineage. More closely related groups appear closer to each other on a branch. For example, whales are more closely related to hippopotamuses than to camels. Hypotheses such as these are supported when independent anatomical and biochemical data match the same model.

**FIGURE 15-10**

This phylogenetic diagram, or "tree," shows one hypothesis of the ancestral relationships among whales and the group of hoofed mammals known as *artiodactyls.* Scientists construct models such as these by comparing the anatomical or biochemical traits of many organisms. For updates on phylogenetic information, visit **go.hrw.com** and enter the keyword **HM6 Phylo.**

## SECTION 2 REVIEW

1. Relate several inferences about the history of life that are supported by geologic evidence.

2. What evidence supports the hypothesis that whales evolved from land-dwelling mammals?

3. Compare the concepts of homologous structures, analogous structures, and vestigial structures.

4. Explain the evidence of evolution presented by the mammals of Australia.

5. Compare the use of biological molecules to other types of analysis of phylogeny.

**CRITICAL THINKING**

6. **Analyzing Theories** Does natural selection act on vestigial structures? Support your answer.

7. **Analyzing Models** If the DNA of a whale, a hippopotamus, and a camel were compared, what finding would support the model in Figure 15-10 above?

8. **Inferring Relationships** Fly embryos and frog embryos differ from each other more than frog embryos and ape embryos do. What does this imply about how these groups may be related?

## OBJECTIVES

- **Describe** how convergent evolution can result among different species.
- **Explain** how divergent evolution can lead to species diversity.
- **Compare** artificial selection and natural selection.
- **Explain** how organisms can undergo coevolution.

## VOCABULARY

convergent evolution
divergent evolution
adaptive radiation
artificial selection
coevolution

# EVOLUTION IN ACTION

*Evolution is a continuous process. Evolution is going on today in populations of living species and can be observed, recorded, and tested. Patterns of evolution repeat in different times and places. Interactions between species, including humans, affect their ongoing evolution.*

## CASE STUDY: CARIBBEAN ANOLE LIZARDS

Often, when scientists compare groups of species, the scientists find patterns that are best explained as evolution in progress. An example is the comparison of anole lizard species (genus *Anolis*) on the Caribbean islands of Cuba, Hispaniola, Jamaica, and Puerto Rico. Among these lizards, each species' body type correlates with the habitat in which the species lives, as shown in Figure 15-11. For example, anole species that live mainly on tree trunks have stocky bodies and long legs. In contrast, those that reside on slender twigs have thin bodies, short legs and tails, and large toe pads. Grass-dwelling anoles tend to be slender and have very long tails. In all, there are at least six anole body types that are each adapted to their environment in a unique way. Also, distinct species of anoles with the same body types occur on different islands. For example, a distinct species of twig-dwelling anole is found on each island.

Many different hypotheses could explain these observations. Two possibilities are that (1) an ancestral anole species specialized for living on twigs originally lived on one island and later migrated to other islands or that (2) each twig-dwelling species evolved independently on each island from distinct ancestor anole species.

**FIGURE 15-11**

Each of these lizards is a member of the genus *Anolis* and lives on the island of Hispaniola in the Caribbean. One species (a) dwells mainly on tree trunks and on the ground and has much longer legs than a species (b) that mostly inhabits tree branches. Another species (c) stays mainly in the grass and has a long tail.

**(a)** *Anolis cybotes*

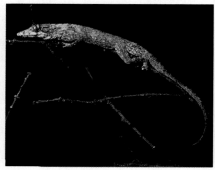

**(b)** *Anolis insolitus*

**(c)** *Anolis pulchellus*

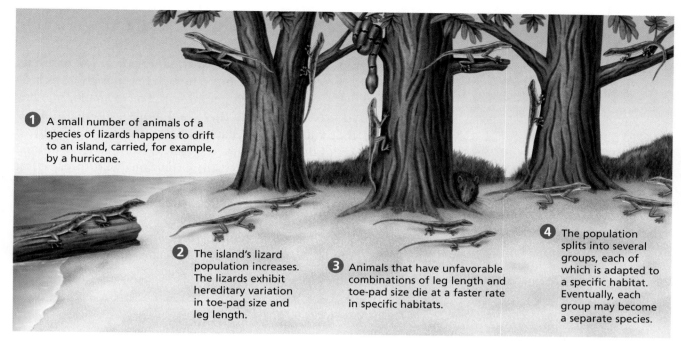

1 A small number of animals of a species of lizards happens to drift to an island, carried, for example, by a hurricane.

2 The island's lizard population increases. The lizards exhibit hereditary variation in toe-pad size and leg length.

3 Animals that have unfavorable combinations of leg length and toe-pad size die at a faster rate in specific habitats.

4 The population splits into several groups, each of which is adapted to a specific habitat. Eventually, each group may become a separate species.

Biologists tested these hypotheses by comparing DNA from various species to look for closely related species. The DNA evidence supported hypothesis 2—twig-dwelling species evolved independently on each island. In other words, each twig-dwelling species came from different ancestors but evolved similar adaptations to similar habitats. The process by which different species evolve similar traits is called **convergent evolution.** Many other examples of convergent evolution can be found in nature.

## Divergence and Radiation

A model of Caribbean anole evolution must also explain how the lizards became adapted to their particular habitats. Studies showed that long-legged trunk-dwelling species could run faster on flat surfaces than short-legged twig-dwelling species, but the twig-dwelling species could cling to twigs better and did not fall as often. However, both kinds of lizards on each island were closely related.

The best explanation for this pattern of phylogeny is that divergent evolution occurred on each island. **Divergent evolution** is a process in which the descendants of a single ancestor diversify into species that each fit different parts of the environment. Lizards with genes for large toe pads and short legs ran so slowly on the trunk and ground that predators often caught them, and lizards with long legs and small toe pads often slipped if they climbed thin branches.

Sometimes, a new population in a new environment, such as an island, will undergo divergent evolution until the population fills many parts of the environment. This pattern of divergence is called **adaptive radiation.** Figure 15-12 illustrates a possible scenario for the evolution of Caribbean anole lizards. Fossil evidence suggests many cases of adaptive radiation on the geologic time scale.

**FIGURE 15-12**

This diagram shows a possible scenario to explain, through natural selection, the evolution of a variety of anole lizard species in the Caribbean islands by descent from common ancestors.

## Quick Lab

### Observing Adaptations Around You

**Materials** paper and pencil

**Procedure** Observe organisms around your school grounds or around your home. Describe any traits that seem to be adaptations to a particular environment or way of life. Also, look for and describe variations within groups of organisms that you see. Explain your reasoning for each inference you make about adaptations.

**Analysis** Which variations in the traits that you observed might increase or decrease the fitness of the organisms? Explain your reasoning.

# ARTIFICIAL SELECTION

**FIGURE 15-13**

Recent DNA evidence shows that despite the enormous variation among domestic dogs, all varieties descended from Asian wolves. By artificially selecting the dogs that will be the parents of the next generation, people have increased the rate of divergent evolution among domestic dogs.

Darwin started his famous book with a chapter on **artificial selection.** This process occurs when a human breeder chooses individuals that will parent the next generation. For example, humans may choose to breed oat plants that yield more grain per stalk or greyhounds that run faster. Because of the immense differences among varieties of dogs, as shown in Figure 15-13, Darwin doubted that all domestic dog breeds arose from the same wild species. But in the 2000s, geneticists analyzed DNA from 654 dog breeds, including ancient dog remains. Their findings indicated that all breeds of dogs share DNA similarities with wolves in East Asia. These findings support the hypothesis that humans first selected domestic dogs from a wolf population about 15,000 years ago.

# COEVOLUTION

It is important to keep in mind that evolution is ongoing and that in a given environment, many species may be evolving at once. Each species is part of the forces of natural selection that act upon the other species. When two or more species have evolved adaptations to each other's influence, the situation is called **coevolution.**

Through coevolution, some species have evolved strategies to avoid being eaten, while the animals that eat them have evolved strategies to keep eating them. Many flowering plants have evolved such that specific insects carry pollen to other plants. Some microbes have evolved to live within certain animals, while these animals have adapted to either benefit from or avoid the microbes.

Humans are also involved in many cases of coevolution. For example, humans have developed and used antibiotics, such as penicillin, to kill disease-causing bacteria. But as antibiotic use has increased, many populations of bacteria have evolved adaptations to resist the effects of some antibiotics. This kind of adaptation is called *resistance.* Similarly, the evolution of resistance to pesticides is observed among populations of insects in agricultural settings.

## SECTION 3 REVIEW

1. Explain how the anole lizard species on Caribbean islands demonstrate both convergent and divergent evolution.

2. What are the key differences and similarities between natural selection and artificial selection?

3. Give examples of species that are likely to be coevolving. Describe how each species influences the evolution of the other species.

**CRITICAL THINKING**

4. **Inferring Meaning** What is the meaning of *radiation* as used in the term *adaptive radiation*?

5. **Constructing Models** Draw a phylogenetic tree to match each of the two proposed hypotheses for the evolution of the anole lizards.

6. **Analyzing Patterns** Propose a reason why some Caribbean islands lack lizard species.

# CHAPTER HIGHLIGHTS

History of Evolutionary Thought

- Evolution is the process of change in the inherited characteristics within populations over generations such that new types of organisms develop from preexisting types.

- Scientific understanding of evolution began to develop in the 17th and 18th centuries as geologists and naturalists compared geologic processes and living and fossil organisms around the world.

- Among geologists, Cuvier promoted the idea of catastrophism, and Lyell promoted uniformitarianism. Among naturalists, Lamarck proposed the inheritance of acquired characteristics as a mechanism for evolution.

- After making many observations and considering ideas of other scientists, both Darwin and Wallace proposed the theory of natural selection to explain evolution.

- Darwin wrote *On the Origin of Species,* in which he argued that descent with modification occurs, that all species descended from common ancestors, and that natural selection is the mechanism for evolution.

- Organisms in a population adapt to their environment as the proportion of individuals with genes for favorable traits increases. Those individuals that pass on more genes are considered to have greater fitness.

**Vocabulary**

evolution (p. 297)  natural selection (p. 300)  adaptation (p. 300)  fitness (p. 301)
strata (p. 298)

SECTION 2  Evidence of Evolution

- Evidence of evolution can be found by comparing several kinds of data, including the fossil record, biogeography, anatomy and development, and biological molecules. Evolutionary theories are supported when several kinds of evidence support similar conclusions.

- Geologic evidence supports theories about the age and development of Earth. The fossil record shows that the types and distribution of organisms on Earth have changed over time. Fossils of transitional species show evidence of descent with modification.

- Biogeography, the distribution of organisms, shows evidence of descent with modification.

- In organisms, analogous structures are similar in function but have different evolutionary origins. Homologous structures have a common evolutionary origin. A species with a vestigial structure probably shares ancestry with a species that has a functional form of the structure. Related species show similarities in embryological development.

- Similarity in the subunit sequences of biological molecules such as RNA, DNA, and proteins indicates a common evolutionary history.

- Modern scientists integrate Darwin's theory with other advances in biological knowledge. Theories and hypotheses about evolution continue to be proposed and investigated.

**Vocabulary**

fossil (p. 302)  absolute age (p. 303)  homologous structure (p. 305)  vestigial structure (p. 306)
superposition (p. 302)  biogeography (p. 305)  analogous structure (p. 305)  phylogeny (p. 307)
relative age (p. 302)

SECTION 3  Evolution in Action

- Ongoing examples of evolution among living organisms can be observed, recorded, and tested.

- In divergent evolution, related populations become less similar as they respond to different environments. Adaptive radiation is the divergent evolution of a single group of organisms in a new environment.

- In convergent evolution, organisms that are not closely related resemble each other because they have responded to similar environments.

- The great variety of dog breeds is an example of artificial selection.

- The increasing occurrence of antibiotic resistance among bacteria is an example of coevolution in progress.

**Vocabulary**

convergent evolution (p. 309)  adaptive radiation (p. 309)  artificial selection (p. 310)  coevolution (p. 310)
divergent evolution (p. 309)

## USING VOCABULARY

1. Use the following terms in the same sentence: *evolution, natural selection, adaptation,* and *fitness.*

2. For each pair of terms, explain how the meanings of the terms differ.
   a. *acquired trait* and *inherited trait*
   b. *homologous structure* and *analogous structure*
   c. *relative age* and *absolute age*
   d. *divergent evolution* and *convergent evolution*
   e. *artificial selection* and *natural selection*

3. **Word Roots and Origins** The word *radiation* is derived from the Latin *radius,* which means "rod" or "ray." Using this information, explain the meaning of *adaptive radiation.*

## UNDERSTANDING KEY CONCEPTS

4. **Define** the biological process of evolution.

5. **Contrast** Cuvier's catastrophism with Lyell's uniformitarianism.

6. **Describe** how the finch species of the Galápagos Islands illustrate descent with modification.

7. **List** the steps of reasoning that Darwin gave to explain the process of natural selection.

8. **Identify** several factors that could limit the growth of populations.

9. **Relate** the roles of adaptation and fitness in the theory of natural selection.

10. **State** several inferences about evolution that are supported by fossil evidence.

11. **Describe** evidence from biogeography that species evolve adaptations to their environments.

12. **Identify** an example of a vestigial structure.

13. **Explain** how biological molecules indicate relatedness between species.

14. **Summarize** the examples of convergent and divergent evolution seen in Caribbean lizards.

15. **Describe** an example of coevolution.

16. **Explain** why antibiotics are not consistently effective against infections of bacteria.

17. **CONCEPT MAPPING** Use the following terms to create a concept map: *struggle to survive, theory, inheritable variation, Darwin, overpopulation, natural selection,* and *successful reproduction.*

## CRITICAL THINKING

18. **Analyzing Concepts** Could a characteristic that is not controlled by heredity be subject to natural selection? Explain your answer.

19. **Making Predictions** Suppose that an island in the Pacific Ocean was just formed by a volcano. Describe a possible scenario for the kinds of species that could be found on this island over the next million years.

20. **Interpreting Graphics** The graph below shows the diversity among different groups of animals over time. Of the four eras listed, the Cenozoic era is the most recent. The changing width of the bar for each group reflects the changing number of known subgroups over geologic time. Use the graph to answer the following questions:
    a. Which group most recently evolved?
    b. Which group is or was the most diverse? the least diverse?
    c. Which group diversified rapidly soon after it first appeared?
    d. Which group(s) became extinct?

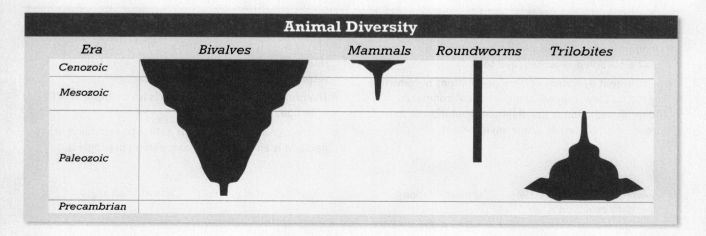

**Animal Diversity**

| Era | Bivalves | Mammals | Roundworms | Trilobites |
|-----|----------|---------|------------|------------|
| Cenozoic | | | | |
| Mesozoic | | | | |
| Paleozoic | | | | |
| Precambrian | | | | |

# Standardized Test Preparation

**DIRECTIONS:** Choose the letter of the answer choice that best answers the question.

1. What is the term for the idea that geologic processes occurring now on Earth are much the same as those that occurred long ago?
   A. catastrophism
   B. uniformitarianism
   C. adaptive radiation
   D. convergent evolution

2. What is the term for the biological process by which the kinds of organisms on Earth change over time?
   F. evolution
   G. superposition
   H. biogeography
   J. uniformitarianism

3. When the internal structures of two species are very similar, what can be inferred about both species?
   A. They share similar environments.
   B. They evolved in similar environments.
   C. They have similar external structures.
   D. They evolved from a common ancestor.

**INTERPRETING GRAPHICS:** The graph below shows the variation in average beak size in a group of finches in the Galápagos Islands over time. These finches eat mostly seeds. Use the graph to answer the question that follows.

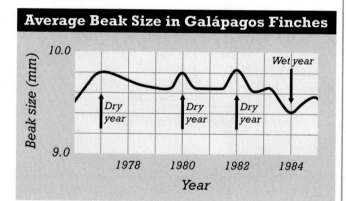

4. Beak size in these finches is correlated to the size of seeds they can eat. What can be inferred from the graph?
   F. In wet years, the finches that survive are mostly those that can eat larger seeds.
   G. In dry years, the finches that survive are mostly those that can eat larger seeds.
   H. In all years, the finches that survive are mostly those that can eat larger seeds.
   J. In all years, the finches that survive are mostly those that can eat smaller seeds.

**DIRECTIONS:** Complete the following analogy.

5. vestigial : functional :: vacated :
   A. used
   B. visceral
   C. broken
   D. occupied

**INTERPRETING GRAPHICS:** The diagram below shows possible evolutionary relationships between some organisms. Use the diagram to answer the question that follows.

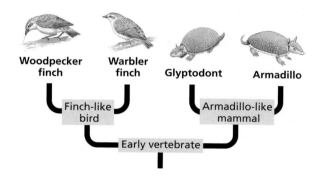

6. What does the diagram imply about warbler finches and armadillos?
   F. They are unrelated.
   G. They are equally related to glyptodonts.
   H. They share a common ancestor.
   J. They did not evolve from older forms of life.

## SHORT RESPONSE

The human body has a tailbone but no tail. It also has an organ called the appendix, which is attached to the intestines but does not serve a function in digestion.

How would an evolutionary biologist explain the presence of these structures in the human body?

## EXTENDED RESPONSE

An example of an acquired characteristic is large leg muscles built up in an individual by frequent running. An example of an inherited characteristic is the maximum height to which an individual can grow.

*Part A* Explain the difference between inherited and acquired characteristics.

*Part B* Contrast two historical theories that explained evolution, based on either acquired characteristics or inherited characteristics.

**Test TIP** When answering questions based on graphs, look for answers that are supported by evidence from the graphs.

# Modeling Selection

## OBJECTIVES

- Simulate the generation of variation.
- Model the selection of favorable traits in new generations.

## PROCESS SKILLS

- observing
- testing
- measuring

## MATERIALS

- construction paper
- cellophane tape
- soda straws
- penny, or other coin
- six-sided die
- scissors
- meterstick or tape measure
- metric ruler

## Background

1. The fictitious Egyptian origami bird (*Avis papyrus*) lives in arid regions of North Africa. Only the birds that can fly the long distances between oases live long enough to breed successfully.
2. Successful evolution requires the generation of inheritable variations by mutation and then selection by the environment of the most-fit individuals.

### PART A  Parent Generation

1. Make a "parent bird." First, cut two strips of paper, 2 cm × 20 cm each. Make a loop with one strip of paper, letting the paper overlap by 1 cm, and tape the loop closed. Repeat for the other strip. Tape one loop 3 cm from each end of the straw, as shown in the figure. Mark the front end of the bird with a felt-tip marker. This "bird" will represent the parent generation.
2. In your lab report, prepare a data table like the one shown below.

| | Coin flip (H or T) | Die throw (1–6) | Anterior wing (cm) | | | Posterior wing (cm) | | | Average distance flown (m) |
|---|---|---|---|---|---|---|---|---|---|
| **Bird** | | | **Width** | **Circum.** | **Distance from front** | **Width** | **Circum.** | **Distance from back** | |
| **Parent** | NA | NA | 2 | 19 | 3 | 2 | 19 | 3 | |
| **Generation 1** | | | | | | | | | |
| Chick 1 | | | | | | | | | |
| Chick 2 | | | | | | | | | |
| Chick 3 | | | | | | | | | |
| **Generation 2** | | | | | | | | | |
| Chick 1 | | | | | | | | | |
| Chick 2 | | | | | | | | | |
| Chick 3 | | | | | | | | | |

**DATA TABLE**

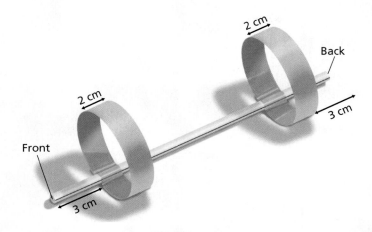

2 cm

2 cm

Back

3 cm

Front

3 cm

3. Test how far your parent bird can fly by releasing it with a gentle overhand pitch. Test the bird twice. Record the bird's average flight distance in your data table.

**PART B  First (F₁) Generation**

4. Model the breeding of offspring. Each origami bird lays a clutch of three eggs. Assume that the first chick is a clone of the parent. Fill in the table with data for this chick.

5. Assume that the next two chicks have mutations. Follow steps A–C below to determine the effects of each mutation.

    **Step A**  Flip a coin to determine which part of the bird is affected by the mutation.
    Heads = anterior (front)
    Tails = posterior (back)

    **Step B**  Throw a die to determine how the mutation affects the wing.

    (1) = The wing position moves 1 cm toward the end of the straw.

    (2) = The wing position moves 1 cm toward the middle of the straw.

    (3) = The circumference of the wing increases 2 cm.

    (4) = The circumference of the wing decreases by 2 cm.

    (5) = The width of the wing increases by 1 cm.

    (6) = The width of the wing decreases by 1 cm.

**Step C**  A mutation is lethal if it results in a wing falling off or a wing with a circumference smaller than that of the straw. If you get a lethal mutation, disregard it, and breed another chick. Record the mutations and the dimensions of each offspring in your data table. The circumference of the wings can be calculated by measuring the length of the strips of paper used to form the wings and subtracting 1 cm for the overlap.

6. Test the birds. Release each bird with a gentle overhand pitch. It is important to release the birds as uniformly as possible. Test each bird at least twice.

7. The most successful bird is the one that flies the farthest. Record the flight distance of each offspring bird in your data table.

**PART C  Subsequent Generations**

8. Assume that the most successful bird in the F₁ generation is the sole parent of the next (F₂) generation. Continue to breed, test, and record data for 8 more generations.

9. Clean up your materials before leaving the lab.

**Analysis and Conclusions**

1. Did your selection process result in birds that fly better?
2. Describe two aspects of this investigation that model evolution of biological organisms.
3. Your most successful bird may have a different lineage from the most successful bird of your neighboring groups. Compare your winning bird with those of your neighbors. How does it differ?
4. What might happen to your last bird if the environmental conditions change?
5. How might this lab help explain the observations Darwin made about finches on the Galápagos Islands?

**Further Inquiry**

A flock of origami birds is blown off the mainland and onto a very small island. These birds face little danger on the ground, but they experience significant risk when flying because they can be blown off the island. Birds that cannot fly at all are most likely to survive and reproduce. Continue the experiment for several generations, selecting birds that can't fly.

# POPULATION GENETICS AND SPECIATION

Sexual selection, which is one variation of natural selection, influences the development of extreme phenotypic traits in some species. The vibrant red stripe on the blue muzzle of this male mandrill baboon, *Mandrillus sphinx,* does not appear in females.

# GENETIC EQUILIBRIUM

*By the time of Darwin's death, in 1882, the idea of evolution by natural selection had gained wide acceptance among scientists. Within the next century, an increasing scientific understanding of genetics became strongly linked with theories of evolution and natural selection.*

### OBJECTIVES

- **Identify** traits that vary in populations and that may be studied.
- **Explain** the importance of the bell curve to population genetics.
- **Compare** three causes of genetic variation in a population.
- **Calculate** allele frequency and phenotype frequency.
- **Explain** Hardy-Weinberg genetic equilibrium.

### VOCABULARY

population genetics
microevolution
bell curve
gene pool
allele frequency
phenotype frequency
Hardy-Weinberg genetic
  equilibrium

## VARIATION OF TRAITS WITHIN A POPULATION

**Population genetics** is the study of evolution from a genetic point of view. Evolution at the genetic level is sometimes called **microevolution,** defined as a change in the collective genetic material of a population. Recall that the genetic material of organisms consists of many alleles—or variations—of many genes that code for various traits. Recall that a population consists of a group of individuals of the same species that routinely interbreed. Populations are important to the study of evolution because a population is the smallest unit in which evolution occurs.

Within a population, individuals may vary in observable traits. For example, fish of a single species in a pond may vary in size. Biologists often study variation in a trait by measuring that trait in a large sample. Figure 16-1 shows a graph of the frequency of lengths in a population of mature fish. Because the shape of the curve looks like a bell, it is called a **bell curve.** The bell curve shows that whereas a few fish in this population are very short and a few are very long, most are of average length. In nature, many quantitative traits in a population—such as height and weight—tend to show variation that follows a bell curve pattern.

**internet** connect

www.scilinks.org
**Topic:** Population
  Genetics
**Keyword:** HM61185

SC*LINKS.* Maintained by the
National Science
Teachers Association

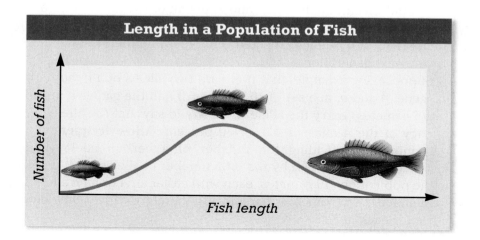

**Length in a Population of Fish**

*Number of fish*

*Fish length*

**FIGURE 16-1**

A bell curve illustrates that most members of a population have similar values for a given, measurable trait. Only a few individuals display extreme variations of the trait.

**FIGURE 16-2**

Many varied but similar phenotypes occur within families because members of a family share some alleles but not others.

## Causes of Variation

What causes variation in traits? Some variations are influenced by environmental factors, such as the amount or quality of food available to an organism. Variation is also influenced by heredity. Some variations occur as a range of phenotypic possibilities (such as a range of body sizes), whereas others occur as a set of specific phenotypes (such as two possible flower colors).

To consider variability, think about phenotypes within a single human family. Two parents, each with a distinct genotype, may produce several children. In the picture of the family in Figure 16-2, the two young-adult brothers are not identical to each other, even though their genotypes are combinations of the genotypes of the same two parents. Both young men resemble their father, though in different traits. The baby resembles his young father, his grandfather, and his uncle. Thus, these males representing three generations look similar but not identical.

What causes genes to vary? Variations in genotype arise in three main ways. (1) *Mutation* is a random change in a gene that is passed on to offspring. (2) *Recombination* is the reshuffling of genes in a diploid individual. Recall that recombination occurs during meiosis by independent assortment and crossing-over of genes on chromosomes. (3) The *random pairing of gametes* occurs because each organism produces large numbers of gametes. So, the union of a particular pair of gametes is partly a matter of chance.

Scientists are still exploring other causes of variation in traits. For example, the expression of some genes depends upon the presence or absence of other genes or factors in the environment. The net result of having many alleles of many genes is the variety of unique genotypes and phenotypes that we see in populations.

## THE GENE POOL

Population geneticists use the term **gene pool** to describe the total genetic information available in a population. It is easy to imagine genes for the next generation as existing in an imaginary pool. If you could inventory this pool and know all of the alleles that are present, then you could apply a simple set of rules based on probability theory to predict expected genotypes and their frequencies for the next generation.

Suppose, for example, that there are two alleles of a hypothetical gene, *A* and *a*, in a set of 10 gametes. If half the gametes in the set (5 gametes) carry the allele A, we would say that the allele frequency of the *A* allele is 0.5, or 50 percent. **Allele frequency** is determined by dividing the number of a certain allele (five instances of the *A* allele) by the total number of alleles of all types in the population (10 gametes, each with either an *A* or an *a* allele). Remember that a gamete is haploid and therefore carries only one allele for each gene.

# Predicting Phenotype

The population of four o'clock flowers, shown in Figure 16-3, illustrates how phenotype can change from generation to generation. Homozygous *RR* flowers are red. Homozygous *rr* flowers are white. Heterozygous *Rr* flowers are pink rather than red, as you might expect. These flowers show incomplete dominance for color, meaning heterozygotes show a trait that falls between the dominant trait and the recessive trait. Thus, homozygotes and heterozygotes can be easily identified by observing the phenotype.

Compare the parent generation with the offspring generation of the four o'clock flowers shown in Figure 16-3. There are equal numbers of plants with the *RR* genotype and the *Rr* genotype in the first generation. You can compute the phenotype frequencies from the figure. A **phenotype frequency** is equal to the number of individuals with a particular phenotype divided by the total number of individuals in the population. Phenotype frequencies in the first generation are 0.5 pink (4 pink plants out of a total of 8 plants), 0.5 red (4 red plants out of a total of 8 plants), and 0.0 white. Recall that allele frequencies are computed using the same principle: the allele frequencies in the first-generation plants are 0.75 *R* (12 *R* alleles out of a total of 16 alleles) and 0.25 *r* (4 *r* alleles out of a total of 16 alleles).

We now can predict the genotypes and phenotypes of the second generation. If a male gamete encounters a female gamete, they will produce a new four o'clock plant whose genotype is the combination of both parental gametes. Thus, an *R* male gamete combined with an *R* female gamete will produce a plant with the *RR* genotype, which has red flowers. According to the laws of probability, the chance of an *R* gamete (a single allele) meeting with another *R* gamete is the arithmetic product of their allele frequencies in the gene pool:

$$\text{frequency of } R \times \text{frequency of } R = \text{frequency of } RR \text{ pair}$$
$$0.75 \times 0.75 = 0.5625$$

The expected frequency of the *rr* genotype is then

$$\text{frequency of } r \times \text{frequency of } r = \text{frequency of } rr \text{ pair}$$
$$0.25 \times 0.25 = 0.0625$$

**FIGURE 16-3**

Although the four o'clock flowers differ phenotypically from generation to generation, the allele frequencies tend to remain the same.

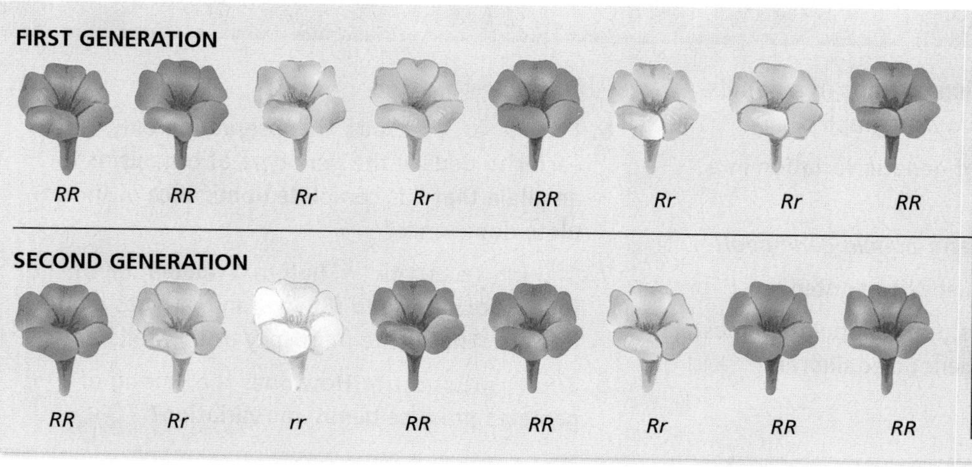

| FIRST GENERATION | | | | | | | | PHENOTYPE FREQUENCY | | ALLELE FREQUENCY |
|---|---|---|---|---|---|---|---|---|---|---|
| *RR* | *RR* | *Rr* | *Rr* | *RR* | *Rr* | *Rr* | *RR* | White 0<br>Pink 0.5<br>Red 0.5 | | *R* = 0.75<br>*r* = 0.25 |
| **SECOND GENERATION** | | | | | | | | | | |
| *RR* | *Rr* | *rr* | *RR* | *RR* | *Rr* | *RR* | *RR* | White 0.125<br>Pink 0.25<br>Red 0.625 | | *R* = 0.75<br>*r* = 0.25 |

The frequencies of all genotypes expected in the second generation must add up to 1.0, just as fractions of a whole must add up to 1. Having established the probabilities of getting an *RR* and an *rr* plant, we can compute the expected frequency of the *Rr* plants. All those plants that are neither *RR* nor *rr* will be *Rr*, so

$$1.0 - \text{frequency of } RR - \text{frequency of } rr = \text{frequency of } Rr$$
$$1.0 - 0.5625 - 0.0625 = 0.375$$

**FIGURE 16-4**

This flock of mallards, *Anas platyrhynchos*, likely violates some or all of the conditions necessary for Hardy-Weinberg genetic equilibrium.

# HARDY-WEINBERG GENETIC EQUILIBRIUM

It is clear from the example of the four o'clock flowers that phenotype frequencies can change dramatically from generation to generation. But what happens to allele frequencies over generations? A German physician, Wilhelm Weinberg (1862–1937), and a British mathematician, Godfrey Hardy (1877–1947), independently showed that genotype frequencies in a population tend to remain the same from generation to generation unless acted on by outside influences. This principle is referred to as **Hardy-Weinberg genetic equilibrium,** and it is based on a set of assumptions about an ideal hypothetical population that is not evolving:

1. No net mutations occur; that is, the alleles remain the same.
2. Individuals neither enter nor leave the population.
3. The population is large (ideally, infinitely large).
4. Individuals mate randomly.
5. Selection does not occur.

Bear in mind that true genetic equilibrium is a theoretical state. Real populations, such as the flock of mallards in Figure 16-4, may not meet all of the conditions necessary for genetic equilibrium. By providing a model of how genetic equilibrium is maintained, the Hardy-Weinberg principle allows us to consider what forces disrupt genetic equilibrium.

**Word Roots and Origins**

*equilibrium*

from the Latin *aequilibris*, meaning "equal balance"

## SECTION 1 REVIEW

1. How does the distribution of traits in a population look when displayed as a graph?

2. Describe three causes of genetic variation in a population.

3. What is meant by the term *human gene pool*?

4. How is phenotype frequency computed?

5. What are the conditions that a population must meet in order to have genetic equilibrium?

**CRITICAL THINKING**

6. **Evaluating Methods** By observation only, is it easier to deduce the genotype of organisms for an allele that has complete dominance or incomplete dominance?

7. **Making Calculations** Half of a population of four o'clocks has red flowers, and half has white flowers. What is the frequency of the *r* allele?

8. **Relating Concepts** How does the pairing of gametes produce genotypic variation?

# DISRUPTION OF GENETIC EQUILIBRIUM

*Evolution is the change in a population's genetic material over generations, that is, a change of the population's allele frequencies or genotype frequencies. Any exception to the five conditions necessary for Hardy-Weinberg equilibrium can result in evolution.*

## MUTATION

The first requirement for genetic equilibrium is that allele frequencies not change overall because of mutations. Spontaneous mutations occur constantly, at very low rates under normal conditions. But if an organism is exposed to mutagens—mutation-causing agents such as radiation and certain chemicals—mutation rates can increase significantly. Mutations can affect genetic equilibrium by producing totally new alleles for a trait. Many mutations are harmful, although some have no effect. Because natural selection operates only on genes that are expressed, it is very slow to eliminate harmful recessive mutations. In the long run, however, beneficial mutations are a vital part of evolution.

## GENE FLOW

The second requirement for genetic equilibrium is that the size of the population remains constant. If individuals move, genes move with them. **Immigration** is the movement of individuals into a population, and **emigration** is the movement of individuals out of a population.

The behavioral ecology of some animal species encourages immigration and emigration. Common baboons live on the savannas of eastern Africa in social and breeding groups called *troops*. A troop is dominated by a few adult males, and it may have from 10 to 200 members. Females tend to remain with the troop they are born into; however, younger or less dominant males leave their birth troop, eventually joining another troop. This constant movement of male animals ensures gene flow. **Gene flow** is the process of genes moving from one population to another. Gene flow can occur through various mechanisms, such as the migration of individuals or the dispersal of seeds or spores.

### Word Roots and Origins

***immigration***

from the Latin *immigrare*, meaning "to go into"

FIGURE 16-5

Genetic drift is significant only in small and medium-sized populations. In a small population, a particular allele may disappear completely over a few generations. In a larger population, a particular allele may vary widely in frequency due to chance but still be present in enough individuals to be maintained in the population. In a much larger population, the frequency of a particular allele may vary slightly by chance but remain relatively stable over generations.

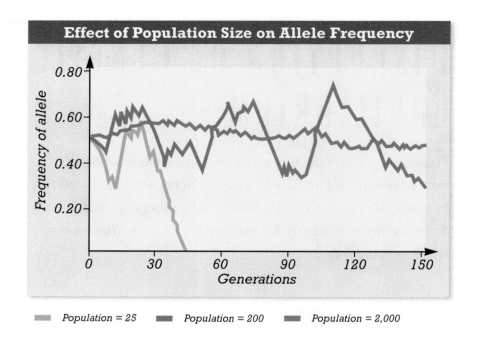

**Effect of Population Size on Allele Frequency**

Population = 25    Population = 200    Population = 2,000

FIGURE 16-6

Populations of the once nearly extinct northern elephant seal, *Mirounga angustirostris*, have lost genetic variability—individuals are homozygous for all of their genes that have been tested. This result of genetic drift could make the species vulnerable to extinction.

# GENETIC DRIFT

The third requirement of genetic equilibrium is the presence of a large population. The Hardy-Weinberg principle is based on the laws of probability, which are less applicable to smaller populations. **Genetic drift** is the phenomenon by which allele frequencies in a population change as a result of random events, or chance. In small populations, the failure of even a single organism to reproduce can significantly disrupt the allele frequency of the population, as can greater-than-normal reproduction by an individual, resulting in genetic drift. Because it can result in significant changes within a population, genetic drift is thought to be another possible mechanism for the evolution of new species.

Figure 16-5 shows a graph of genetic drift in populations of three differing sizes. Small populations can undergo abrupt changes in allele frequencies, exhibiting a large degree of genetic drift, whereas large populations retain fairly stable allele frequencies, maintaining a small degree of genetic drift. In the smallest population shown in the graph, the frequency of the example allele reaches zero at about the 45th generation. If we assume that the population started with two alleles for a trait, then only one allele is left, and every individual is homozygous for that trait. Once this change happens, the population is in danger of becoming extinct because there is no variation for natural selection to act on. For example, a natural disaster or a new disease could wipe out the entire population. For this reason, endangered species, such as the northern elephant seal, as shown in Figure 16-6, remain in peril of extinction even as their numbers increase.

# NONRANDOM MATING

The fourth requirement of genetic equilibrium is random matings, without regard to genetic makeup. However, many species do not mate randomly. Mate selection is often influenced by geographic proximity, which can result in mates with some degree of kinship. Matings of related individuals can amplify certain traits and can result in offspring with disorders caused by recessive genes, which, although rare, may be present in the genomes of related individuals.

In another example of nonrandom mating, individuals may select a mate that has traits similar to their own traits. This mate would probably have some similar genes. The selection of a mate based on similarity of traits is called *assortative mating.* Nonrandom mating affects which alleles will be combined within individuals, but it does not affect overall allele frequencies within a population.

## Sexual Selection

In many species of birds, the males are brightly colored and often heavily plumed, such as the peacock shown in Figure 16-7. These elaborately decorated males are easy for predators to see. Why would natural selection work in favor of an organism being conspicuous to a predator? Females tend to choose the males they mate with based on certain traits. This tendency is referred to as **sexual selection.** In order to leave offspring, a male must be selected by the female. The peacock's gaudy plumage increases his chances of being selected. Extreme traits, such as heavy, brightly colored plumage, may give the female an indication of the quality of the male's genes or his fitness in his environment. Remember that natural selection acts upon differences in survival *and* reproduction. Natural selection favors an increase in the genes of successful *reproducers,* rather than merely those of successful *survivors.*

**FIGURE 16-7**

Males sometimes display extreme traits, such as the large tail of this peacock, *Pavo cristatus.* This trait is favorable if it attracts females and increases the reproductive fitness of the male.

# NATURAL SELECTION

The fifth requirement of genetic equilibrium is the absence of natural selection. Natural selection is an ongoing process in nature, so it often disrupts genetic equilibrium. As you have learned, natural selection means that some members of a population are more likely than other members to survive and reproduce and thus contribute their genes to the next generation.

Recall that natural selection operates on variations of traits within a population, such as body size or color. When natural selection is at work over time, the distribution of traits in a population may change. In a graph, this kind of change would appear as a shift away from the normal bell curve. Scientists observe three general patterns of natural selection: stabilizing selection, disruptive selection, and directional selection.

## Stabilizing Selection

In **stabilizing selection,** individuals with the average form of a trait have the highest fitness. The average represents the optimum for most traits; extreme forms of most traits confer lower fitness on the individuals that have them. Consider a hypothetical species of lizard in which larger-than-average individuals might be more easily spotted, captured, and eaten by predators. On the other hand, lizards that are smaller than average might not be able to run fast enough to escape.

Figure 16-8a shows the effect of stabilizing selection on body size in these lizards. The red curve shows the initial variation in lizard size as a standard bell curve. The blue curve represents the variation in body size several generations after a new predator was introduced. This predator easily captured the large, visible lizards and the small, slower lizards. Thus, selection against these extreme body types reduced the size range of the lizards. Stabilizing selection is the most common kind of selection. It operates on most traits and results in very similar morphology between most members of a species.

## Disruptive Selection

In **disruptive selection,** individuals with either extreme variation of a trait have greater fitness than individuals with the average form of the trait. Figure 16-8b shows the effect of disruptive selection on shell color in limpets, which are marine animals. The shell color of limpets varies from pure white to dark tan. White-shelled limpets that are on rocks covered with goose barnacles, which are also white, are at an advantage. Birds that prey on limpets have a hard time distinguishing the white-shelled limpets from the goose barnacles. On bare, dark-colored rocks, dark-shelled limpets are at an advantage. Again, the limpet-eating birds have a hard time locating the dark shells against the dark background. However, the birds easily spot limpets with shells of intermediate color, which are visible against both the white and dark backgrounds.

**(a)**

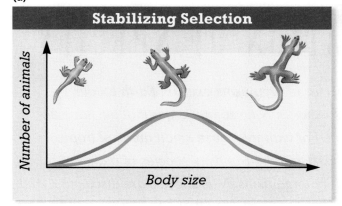

**Stabilizing Selection**

*Number of animals* (y-axis)

*Body size* (x-axis)

**(b)**

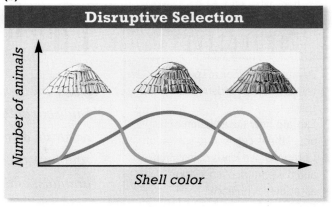

**Disruptive Selection**

*Number of animals* (y-axis)

*Shell color* (x-axis)

**(c)**

**Directional Selection**

*Number of animals* (y-axis)

*Tongue length* (x-axis)

**FIGURE 16-8**

Natural selection is evident when the distribution of traits in a population changes over time, shifting from the original bell curve (indicated in red) toward another pattern (shown in blue). Stabilizing selection (a) is a shift toward the center of the original bell curve. Disruptive selection (b) is a shift in both directions away from the center. Directional selection (c) is a shift in one direction only.

## Directional Selection

In **directional selection,** individuals that display a more extreme form of a trait have greater fitness than individuals with an average form of the trait. Figure 16-8c shows the effects of directional selection on tongue length in anteaters. Anteaters feed by breaking open termite nests, pushing their sticky tongue into the nest, and lapping up termites. Suppose that the termites in an area began to build deeper nests. Anteaters with long tongues could more effectively prey on these termites than could anteaters with short or average tongues. Thus, directional selection would act to direct the trait of tongue length away from the average and toward one extreme.

---

## SECTION 2 REVIEW

1. List five conditions that can disrupt genetic equilibrium and cause evolution to occur.

2. Explain the role of mutations in evolution.

3. Contrast gene flow with genetic drift.

4. Explain why genetic drift is more significant in smaller populations.

5. Contrast stabilizing selection, disruptive selection, and directional selection.

**CRITICAL THINKING**

6. **Making Inferences** Why might a harmful allele persist in a population for many generations?

7. **Relating Concepts** Give an example of a species that exhibits the effects of sexual selection.

8. **Applying Concepts** For each of the three patterns of natural selection, give an example of a species that exhibits the effects of that selection.

## OBJECTIVES

- **Relate** the biological species concept to the modern definition of species.
- **Explain** how the isolation of populations can lead to speciation.
- **Compare** two kinds of isolation and the pattern of speciation associated with each.
- **Contrast** the model of punctuated equilibrium with the model of gradual change.

## VOCABULARY

speciation
morphology
biological species concept
geographic isolation
allopatric speciation
reproductive isolation
prezygotic isolation
postzygotic isolation
sympatric speciation
gradualism
punctuated equilibrium

# FORMATION OF SPECIES

*How many species of organisms exist on Earth today? Undiscovered species may be so numerous that we have no accurate answer. For example, even small areas of tropical rain forests can contain thousands of species of plants, animals, and microorganisms. New species are discovered and others become extinct at an increasing rate. In this section, you will learn how one species can become two through a process called speciation.*

## THE CONCEPT OF SPECIES

You have learned that existing species are essentially changed versions of older species. The process of species formation, **speciation** (SPEE-shee-AY-shun), results in closely related species. Some are very similar to their shared ancestral species, whereas other descendant species become quite different over time.

### Morphological Concept of Species

For many years, scientists used the internal and external structure and appearance of an organism—its **morphology** (mawr-FAHL-uh-jee)—as the chief criterion for classifying it as a species. Using the morphological concept of species, scientists defined species primarily according to structure and appearance. Because morphological characteristics are easy to observe, making species designations based on morphology proved convenient.

The morphological concept of species has limitations, however. There can be phenotypic differences among individuals in a single population. Notice, for example, the variation between the two red-tailed monkeys shown in Figure 16-9. To further complicate the matter, some organisms that appear different enough to belong to different species interbreed in the wild and produce fertile offspring. In response to the capacity of dissimilar organisms to reproduce, the biological species concept arose.

**FIGURE 16-9**

The facial features of red-tailed monkeys, *Cercopithecus ascianus,* can differ from individual to individual.

## The Biological Species Concept

According to the **biological species concept,** as proposed by German-born, American biologist Ernst Mayr (1904–2005), a species is a population of organisms that can successfully interbreed but cannot breed with other groups. Although this definition is useful for living animals, the biological species concept does not provide a satisfactory definition for species of extinct organisms, whose reproductive compatibility cannot be tested. Nor is it useful for organisms that do not reproduce sexually. Thus, our modern definition of species includes components of both the morphological and biological species concepts. A species is a single kind of organism. Members of a species are morphologically similar and can interbreed to produce fully fertile offspring. The many species alive today diverged from a smaller number of earlier species.

# ISOLATION AND SPECIATION

How do species give rise to other, different species? Speciation begins with isolation. In isolation, two parts of a formerly interbreeding population stop interbreeding. Two important types of isolation frequently drive speciation.

## Geographic Isolation

**Geographic isolation** is the physical separation of members of a population. Populations may be physically separated when their original habitat becomes divided. A deep canyon could develop, a river could change course, or a drying climate in a valley could force surviving fragments of an original population into separate mountain ranges. Once the subpopulations become isolated, gene flow between them stops. Natural selection and genetic drift cause the two subpopulations to diverge, eventually making them incompatible for mating.

In pupfish, small freshwater fish shown in Figure 16-10, speciation following geographic isolation apparently took place in parts of the western United States, including the desert of Death Valley. Death Valley has a number of isolated ponds formed by springs. Each pond contains a species of fish that lives only in that one pond, but the fish species of various ponds in the area are quite similar.

How did these different populations of fish become isolated in Death Valley? Geologic evidence indicates that most of Death Valley was covered by a lake during the last ice age. When the ice age ended, the region became dry, and only small, spring-fed ponds remained. Members of a fish species that previously formed a single population in the lake may have become isolated in different ponds. The environments of the isolated ponds differ enough that the separate populations of fish diverged. Eventually, the fishes in the different ponds diverged enough to be considered separate species.

These two types of pupfish live in isolated water sources in the western United States. Both types appear to have evolved from a common ancestor after undergoing geographic isolation.

**(a)** desert pupfish, *Cyprinodon macularius*

**(b)** Amargosa pupfish, *Cyprinodon nevadensis*

**(a)** white-tailed antelope squirrel, *Ammospermophilis leucurus*

**(b)** Harris's antelope squirrel, *Ammospermophilis harrisi*

**FIGURE 16-11**

These two closely related squirrels are probably the result of allopatric speciation. The white-tailed antelope squirrel (a) is found on the north rim of the Grand Canyon, and Harris's antelope squirrel (b) is found on the south rim.

Geographic barriers can be formed by canyons, mountain ranges, bodies of water, deserts, or other geographic features that organisms cannot cross. In addition, parts of a population may be accidentally transported to new islands or slowly drift apart on separate continents. On the geologic time scale, the processes of geology frequently rearrange populations.

Whether or not a geographic barrier will isolate a particular group of organisms depends on the organisms' ability to move around. Birds, for example, can easily fly back and forth across a deep canyon. However, a canyon might be a major barrier to a small, crawling mammal. An example of such a barrier is the Grand Canyon in Arizona. The ever-deepening canyon separates the habitats of two closely related populations of squirrels, shown in Figure 16-11. These two populations are different enough to be considered separate species, but similar enough that scientists debate whether they might simply be subspecies. Because their ranges do not overlap, the two populations do not interbreed.

## Allopatric Speciation

**Allopatric speciation** happens when species arise as a result of geographic isolation. *Allopatric* means "different homelands." Populations separated by a geographic barrier no longer experience gene flow between them. So, the gene pools of each separate population may begin to differ due to genetic drift, mutations, and natural selection.

Allopatric speciation is more likely to occur in small populations because a smaller gene pool will be changed more significantly by genetic drift and natural selection. The key question in this type of speciation is whether or not the separated populations become different enough to be reproductively isolated from one another. In other words, if the geographic barrier is removed, could the two groups interbreed and produce fertile offspring?

## Reproductive Isolation

Sometimes, groups of organisms within a population become genetically isolated without being geographically isolated. **Reproductive isolation** results from barriers to successful breeding between population groups in the same area. Reproductive isolation and the species formation that follows it may sometimes arise through disruptive selection. Remember that in disruptive selection, the two extremes of a trait in a given population are selected for and the organisms begin to diverge. Once successful mating is prevented between members of the two subpopulations, the effect is the same as what would have occurred if the two subpopulations had been geographically isolated. There are two general types of reproductive isolation: prezygotic (pree-zie-GAHT-ik) isolation and postzygotic isolation. **Prezygotic isolation,** or *premating isolation,* occurs before fertilization, and **postzygotic isolation,** or *postmating isolation,* occurs after fertilization.

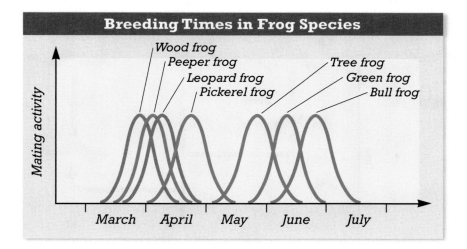

**Breeding Times in Frog Species**

*Mating activity* (y-axis)

Wood frog
Peeper frog
Leopard frog
Pickerel frog
Tree frog
Green frog
Bull frog

March  April  May  June  July

**FIGURE 16-12**

As the graph shows, frogs that share habitats may be reproductively isolated by differences in timing of mating activity.

If two potentially interbreeding species mate and fertilization occurs, success is measured by the production of healthy, fully fertile offspring. But this may be prevented by one of several types of postzygotic isolation. The offspring of interbreeding species may not develop completely and may die early, or, if healthy, they may not be fertile. From an evolutionary standpoint, if death or sterility of offspring occurs, the parent organisms have wasted their gametes producing offspring that cannot, in turn, reproduce.

In contrast, prezygotic isolating mechanisms can reduce the chance of hybrid formation. For example, a mating call that is not recognized as such by a potential mate can contribute to isolation. Differences in mating times are another type of prezygotic isolation. Both mechanisms are in effect for the frogs shown in Figure 16-12. The time of peak mating activity differs for each frog, reducing the chance of interbreeding. As a result, the wood frog and the leopard frog, shown in Figure 16-13, are reproductively isolated. Though these two frogs interbreed in captivity, they do not interbreed where their ranges overlap in the wild. The wood frog usually breeds in late March, and the leopard frog usually breeds in mid-April.

## Sympatric Speciation

**Sympatric speciation** occurs when two subpopulations become reproductively isolated within the same geographic area. Charles Darwin proposed this model of speciation in the 1850s. He hypothesized that competing individuals within a population could gain an adaptive advantage by using slightly different niches. This specialization could lead each group to become reproductively isolated from the other.

For example, a population of insects might live on a single type of plant. If some of the individuals from this population began to live on another type of plant, they might no longer interbreed with the original population. The two groups of insects would then be able to evolve independently and could eventually become two different species.

**FIGURE 16-13**

Differences in peak mating times and in mating calls appear to have led to reproductive isolation of the wood frog (a) from its close relative, the leopard frog (b).

**(a)** wood frog, *Rana sylvatica*

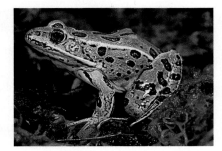

**(b)** leopard frog, *Rana pipiens*

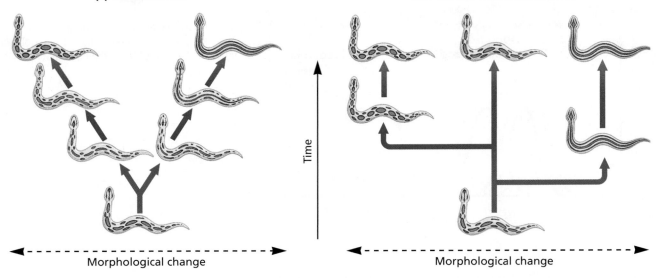

Time

Morphological change

Morphological change

**FIGURE 16-14**

In the model of speciation shown on the left, species evolve gradually, at a stable rate. In the model of speciation shown on the right, species arise abruptly and differ noticeably from the root species. These species then change little over time.

**internet** connect

**www.scilinks.org**
**Topic:** Species Formation
**Keyword:** HM61434

*SCI*LINKS. Maintained by the National Science Teachers Association

# RATES OF SPECIATION

Speciation sometimes requires millions of years. But apparently some species can form more rapidly. For example, Polynesians introduced banana trees to the Hawaiian Islands about a thousand years ago. Today, there are several species of moths that are unique to the Hawaiian Islands and that feed only on bananas. These species likely descended from ancestral moths during the past thousand years, since bananas were introduced to Hawaii.

The idea that speciation occurs at a regular, gradual rate is called **gradualism.** However, some scientists think that speciation happens in "bursts" relative to the geologic time scale. The fossil record holds evidence that many species existed without change for long periods of time, whereas in some cases a great diversity of new forms seems to have evolved rapidly. That is, change occurred in a few thousand, rather than a few million, years. Scientists call this pattern of species formation **punctuated equilibrium.** The term *punctuated* refers to sudden, rapid change, and *equilibrium* refers to periods of little change. Figure 16-14 illustrates these two contrasting models as they might apply to the evolution of snakes.

## SECTION 3 REVIEW

1. What role did Ernst Mayr play in the development of the modern biological species concept?

2. Explain how geographic isolation can lead to allopatric speciation.

3. Explain how reproductive isolation can lead to sympatric speciation.

4. Contrast the model of punctuated equilibrium with the model of gradualism.

**CRITICAL THINKING**

5. **Critiquing Explanations** What are two shortcomings of the biological species concept?

6. **Analyzing Concepts** Describe one possible scenario of postzygotic reproductive isolation in an animal species.

7. **Drawing Conclusions** How might the generation time of a population affect future speciation?

# CHAPTER HIGHLIGHTS

**Genetic Equilibrium**

- Population biologists study many different traits in populations, such as size and color.

- Traits vary and can be mapped along a bell curve, which shows that most individuals have average traits, whereas a few individuals have extreme traits.

- Variations in genotype arise by mutation, recombination, and the random fusion of gametes.

- The total genetic information available in a population is called the gene pool.

- Allele frequencies in the gene pool do not change unless acted upon by certain forces.

- The principle of Hardy-Weinberg genetic equilibrium is a theoretical model of a population in which no evolution occurs and the gene pool of the population is stable.

### Vocabulary
microevolution (p. 317)
population genetics (p. 317)
bell curve (p. 317)
gene pool (p. 318)
allele frequency (p. 318)
phenotype frequency (p. 319)
Hardy-Weinberg genetic equilibrium (p. 320)

---

**SECTION 2** **Disruption of Genetic Equilibrium**

- Evolution can take place when a population is not in a state of genetic equilibrium. Thus, evolution may take place when populations are subject to genetic mutations, gene flow, genetic drift, nonrandom mating, or natural selection.

- Emigration and immigration cause gene flow between populations and can thus affect gene frequencies.

- Genetic drift is a change in allele frequencies due to random events. Genetic drift operates most strongly in small populations.

- Mating is nonrandom whenever individuals may choose partners. Sexual selection occurs when certain traits increase an individual's success at mating. Sexual selection explains the development of traits that improve reproductive success but that may harm the individual.

- Natural selection can influence evolution in one of three general patterns. Stabilizing selection favors the formation of average traits. Disruptive selection favors extreme traits rather than average traits. Directional selection favors the formation of more-extreme traits.

### Vocabulary
immigration (p. 321)
emigration (p. 321)
gene flow (p. 321)
genetic drift (p. 322)
sexual selection (p. 323)
stabilizing selection (p. 324)
disruptive selection (p. 324)
directional selection (p. 325)

---

**SECTION 3** **Formation of Species**

- According to the biological species concept, a species is a population of organisms that can successfully interbreed but cannot breed with other groups.

- Geographic isolation results from the separation of population subgroups by geographic barriers. Geographic isolation may lead to allopatric speciation.

- Reproductive isolation results from the separation of population subgroups by barriers to successful breeding. Reproductive isolation may lead to sympatric speciation.

- In the gradual model of speciation, species undergo small changes at a constant rate. In the punctuated equilibrium model, new species arise abruptly, differ greatly from their ancestors, and then change little over long periods.

### Vocabulary
speciation (p. 326)
morphology (p. 326)
biological species concept (p. 327)
geographic isolation (p. 327)
allopatric speciation (p. 328)
reproductive isolation (p. 328)
prezygotic isolation (p. 328)
postzygotic isolation (p. 328)
sympatric speciation (p. 329)
gradualism (p. 330)
punctuated equilibrium (p. 330)

## USING VOCABULARY

1. Use each of the following terms in a separate sentence: *bell curve* and *gene flow*.

2. For each pair of terms, explain how the meanings of the terms differ.
   a. *allele frequency* and *phenotype frequency*
   b. *stabilizing selection* and *disruptive selection*
   c. *immigration* and *emigration*
   d. *geographic isolation* and *reproductive isolation*
   e. *allopatric speciation* and *sympatric speciation*
   f. *punctuated equilibrium* and *gradualism*

3. Use the following terms in the same sentence: *nonrandom mating, assortative mating,* and *sexual selection*.

4. Use the following terms in the same sentence: *genetic equilibrium, gene pool,* and *speciation*.

5. **Word Roots and Origins** The word *disrupt* is derived from the Latin *disruptus,* which means "to break apart." Using this information, explain the term *disruptive selection*.

## UNDERSTANDING KEY CONCEPTS

6. **Compare** the three main causes of variation in the genotypes of organisms.

7. **Identify** the five conditions that are necessary for Hardy-Weinberg genetic equilibrium.

8. **Identify** the five conditions that may cause evolution to occur in a population.

9. **Describe** how immigration and emigration can alter allele frequencies in a population.

10. **List** examples of how mating could be nonrandom in a population.

11. **Contrast** natural selection with sexual selection.

12. **Identify** which type of selection is happening when a population's bell curve narrows over time.

13. **Explain** why prezygotic isolating mechanisms have an advantage over postzygotic isolating mechanisms.

14. **Relate** the size of a population to the influence of genetic drift on the population's gene pool.

15. **Compare** the effects of stabilizing selection, disruptive selection, and directional selection.

16. **Model** a situation that might cause the geographic isolation of a subgroup of a population of fish living in a large river.

17. **Explain** why the biological species concept cannot be used to identify fossil organisms.

18. **Identify** the type of isolating mechanism in the following scenario: Where populations of two related species of frogs overlap geographically, their mating calls differ more than they do where the species don't overlap.

19. **Summarize** the hypothesis of punctuated equilibrium as it relates to the rate of speciation.

20. **CONCEPT MAPPING** Use the following terms to create a concept map of how new species can form: *natural selection, allele frequency, geographic isolation, reproductive isolation,* and *speciation*.

## CRITICAL THINKING

21. **Relating Concepts** Explain the relationship between evolution and natural selection.

22. **Forming Hypotheses** Propose a hypothesis about how pollutants in the environment could influence the evolution of its inhabitants.

23. **Drawing Conclusions** Freeways may provide an effective geographic isolating mechanism for some slow-moving animals. Are such artificial barriers likely to result in complete speciation?

24. **Applying Information** The common biological definition of *species* states that a species is a group of organisms that can interbreed and produce fertile offspring in nature. A mule is the offspring of a horse and a donkey. Mules are always sterile. By the definition above, do a horse and a donkey belong to the same species? Explain your answer.

25. **Interpreting Graphics** From the illustration of four o'clock flowers shown below, calculate the frequency of the *R* and *r* alleles, and state the phenotype frequency.

# Standardized Test Preparation

**DIRECTIONS:** Choose the letter of the answer choice that best answers the question.

1. What is the term for the total genetic information in a population?
   A. gene pool
   B. allele frequency
   C. distribution of traits
   D. phenotype frequency

2. Saint Bernards and Chihuahuas (two breeds of domestic dogs) cannot normally mate because they differ so much in size. Thus, they are reproductively isolated to some extent. What type of isolating mechanism is operating in this case?
   F. artificial
   G. prezygotic
   H. postzygotic
   J. geographic

3. How do mutations affect genetic equilibrium?
   A. Mutations cause emigration.
   B. Mutations cause immigration.
   C. Mutations introduce new alleles.
   D. Mutations maintain genotype frequency.

**INTERPRETING GRAPHICS:** The illustration below shows two contrasting models for rates of speciation. Use the illustration to answer the questions that follow.

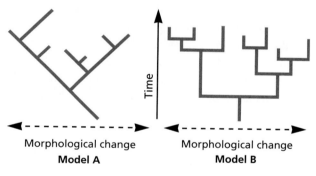

4. Which model of speciation rates is illustrated by model A in the graph?
   F. gradualism
   G. sexual selection
   H. disruptive selection
   J. punctuated equilibrium

5. Which model of speciation rates is illustrated by model B in the graph?
   A. gradualism
   B. sexual selection
   C. disruptive selection
   D. punctuated equilibrium

**DIRECTIONS:** Complete the following analogy:

6. genotype : allele :: phenotype :
   F. trait
   G. mutation
   H. gene pool
   J. population

**INTERPRETING GRAPHICS:** The illustration below shows the occurrence of variations in a particular characteristic within a population. The dark line represents an earlier point in time than the dashed line. Use the illustration to answer the question that follows.

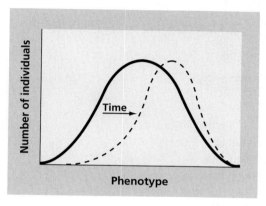

7. Which type of selection is modeled in the illustration above?
   A. sexual selection
   B. disruptive selection
   C. stabilizing selection
   D. directional selection

## SHORT RESPONSE

Explain the difference between reproductive isolation and geographic isolation.

## EXTENDED RESPONSE

The phrase *Hardy-Weinberg genetic equilibrium* refers to the frequency of genotypes in populations from generation to generation.

*Part A*  Briefly describe what this model predicts about genotype frequencies.

*Part B*  What are the set of assumptions that must be met for the Hardy-Weinberg genetic equilibrium to be valid?

**Test TIP** For multiple-choice questions, try to eliminate any answer choices that are obviously incorrect, and then consider the remaining answer choices.

# Predicting Allele Frequency

## OBJECTIVES

- Demonstrate the effect of natural selection on genotype frequencies.

## PROCESS SKILLS

- modeling
- predicting
- calculating
- analyzing

## MATERIALS

- 300 black beads
- 300 white beads
- 3 containers
- labeling tape
- marking pen

## Background

1. What is natural selection?
2. What is the result of natural selection?

## PART A  Random Mating

1. Obtain three containers, and label them "Parental," "Offspring," and "Dead."
2. Place 200 black beads and 200 white beads in the "Parental" container. Assume that each black bead represents a dominant allele for black coat *(B)* and that each white bead represents a recessive allele for white coat *(b)* in a hypothetical animal. Assume that the container holds gametes from a population of 200 of these hypothetical animals: 50 *BB*, 100 *Bb*, and 50 *bb*.
3. In your lab report, make a data table like Table A.
4. Without looking, remove two beads from the "Parental" container. What does this simulate?
5. Record the genotype and phenotype of the resulting offspring in your data table. Then, put the alleles into the "Offspring" container. Replace the beads that you removed from the "Parental" container with new beads of the same color.
6. Repeat steps 4 and 5 forty-nine times. Record the genotype and phenotype of each offspring in your data table.
7. Calculate the frequencies of alleles in the offspring. First, make a table in your lab report like Table B. Then, count and record the number of black beads in the "Offspring" container. This number divided by the total number of beads (100) and multiplied by 100% is the frequency of *B* alleles. Then, count and record the number of white beads in the "Offspring" container. Determine the frequency of *b* alleles as you did with the *B* alleles.

## TABLE A  *MATING*

| Trial | Random mating | | Nonrandom mating | |
| --- | --- | --- | --- | --- |
| | Offspring genotype | Offspring phenotype | Offspring genotype | Offspring phenotype |
| 1 | | | | |
| 2 | | | | |
| 3 | | | | |
| 4 | | | | |
| 5 | | | | |

## TABLE B  *ALLELE FREQUENCIES*

| Generation | Number of B alleles | B alleles/ total alleles | B allele frequency | Number of b alleles | b alleles/ total alleles | b allele frequency |
|---|---|---|---|---|---|---|
| Parental | 200 | 200/400 | 50% | 200 | 200/400 | 50% |
| Offspring | | | | | | |

## TABLE C  *PHENOTYPE FREQUENCIES*

| Generation | Number of black animals | Black animals/ total animals | Frequency of black animals | Number of white animals | White animals/ total animals | Frequency of white animals |
|---|---|---|---|---|---|---|
| Parental | 100 | 150/200 | 75% | 50 | 50/200 | 25% |
| Offspring | | | | | | |

**8.** Calculate the frequencies of phenotypes in the offspring. First, make a table in your lab report like Table C. Then, count and record the number of offspring with black coat color. Divide this number by the total number of offspring (50), and multiply by 100% to determine the frequency of black phenotype. Repeat this calculation to determine the frequency of white coat color among the offspring.

## PART B  Nonrandom Mating

**9.** Return the beads in the "Offspring" container to the container labeled "Parental."

**10.** Assume that animals with white-coat phenotype are incapable of reproducing. What is the genotype of animals with a white coat? To simulate this situation, remove 100 white beads from the container labeled "Parental," and set them aside.

**11.** Start by removing two beads from the container labeled "Parental," and record the results in your Table A. If the offspring has a white-coat phenotype, put its alleles in the container labeled "Dead." If the offspring has a black-coat phenotype, put its alleles in the container labeled "Offspring."

**12.** If animals with a white-coat phenotype cannot reproduce, predict what would happen to allele frequency if step 11 were repeated until the parental gene pool was empty. Write your prediction in your lab report.

**13.** Repeat step 11 until the parental gene pool is empty. Record the results of each pairing in your lab report in Table A. Compare your results with your prediction.

**14.** Transfer the beads from the "Offspring" container to the "Parental" container. Leave the beads that you have placed in the "Dead" container in that container. Do not return those beads to the parental container.

**15.** Repeat step 11 again until the parental pool is empty. Record your results in your data table.

**16.** Repeat steps 14 and 15 two more times.

**17.** Calculate the frequencies of the final genotypes produced, as you did in Part A. Compare the results with your prediction from step 12.

**18.** Clean up your materials before leaving the lab.

## Analysis and Conclusions

**1.** Compare the frequency of recessive alleles produced in Part A with that produced in Part B. Did you correctly predict the frequencies?

**2.** Did the frequency of the *b* allele change uniformly through all generations? If not, what happened?

**3.** Why did you remove 100 white beads from the "Parental" container in step 10?

**4.** How did this change the phenotype frequency of white animals in the parental generation from the original ratio of 50/200?

## Further Inquiry

If you continued Part B, would you eventually eliminate the *b* allele? Form a hypothesis and test it.

# CLASSIFICATION OF ORGANISMS

The ground pangolin, *Manis temminckii*, inhabits the forests, grasslands, and savannas of Africa. When threatened, it rolls into a tight ball, which exposes its razor-sharp scales. Its common name is *scaly anteater* because of its feeding habits, but it is not classified with other kinds of anteaters.

**SECTION 1** *Biodiversity*

**SECTION 2** *Systematics*

**SECTION 3** *Modern Classification*

# BIODIVERSITY

*Biologists have named and classified almost 2 million species. However, they estimate that the total number of species on Earth is much greater. Over time, scientists have created various systems of classification to organize their knowledge of the tremendous number of species. Each system places species into categories based on particular characteristics.*

## SECTION 1

### OBJECTIVES

- **Relate** biodiversity to biological classification.
- **Explain** why naturalists replaced Aristotle's classification system.
- **Identify** the main criterion that Linnaeus used to classify organisms.
- **List** the common levels of modern classification from general to specific.

### VOCABULARY

biodiversity
taxonomy
taxon
kingdom
domain
phylum
division
class
order
family
genus
species
binomial nomenclature
subspecies

## CLASSIFYING ORGANISMS

One important branch of biology investigates **biodiversity,** the variety of organisms considered at all levels from populations to ecosystems. In general, the scientific catalogue of all biodiversity on Earth has increased over time. The number of identified species has grown from hundreds to millions. And scientists are certain that many more remain unidentified.

Since the 1980s, ecologist Terry Erwin and others have been working to catalog insect species in plots of tropical rain forest. To do this, researchers may fog the treetops with insecticide and then catch the falling insects in a net, as shown in Figure 17-1. Then, the scientists will count and classify the insects. Using such methods, Erwin collected over 1,000 species of beetles from just 19 trees of the same species in a limited area of rain forest. Furthermore, Erwin used his data to estimate the total possible number of insect species worldwide. He proposed that there could be more than 30 million species of insects on Earth!

Every year, biologists discover thousands of new species and seek to classify them in a meaningful way. Over the centuries, classification systems for organisms have been proposed and modified to include an increasing understanding of how organisms are structured and how they evolved. Biologists are challenged to organize their knowledge of such diversity in a way that makes sense.

For example, consider the pangolin, a species that is covered with scales and catches ants on its sticky tongue. Should pangolins be grouped in a category with other scaly animals, such as lizards and crocodiles? Biologists have decided against such a classification, because pangolins share many more similarities with mammals such as dogs and cats than with lizards or crocodiles. Should pangolins be grouped in a category with other mammals that use sticky tongues to eat ants? Again, biologists have decided against this grouping, because pangolins share more similarities with dogs and cats than with the other ant-eating mammal species.

**FIGURE 17-1**

These researchers are fogging a tree with insecticide to collect the insects that live on its leaves and branches.

## Word Roots and Origins

**taxonomy**

from the Greek words *taxis,* meaning "to put in order," and *nomia,* meaning "law"

# TAXONOMY

The science of describing, naming, and classifying organisms is called **taxonomy** (taks-AHN-uh-mee). Any particular group within a taxonomic system is called a **taxon** (plural, *taxa*). Over time, scientists have created taxonomic systems that have different numbers and levels of taxa as well as different names for each taxon.

About 2,400 years ago, the Greek philosopher Aristotle classified organisms into only two taxa—either plants or animals. He grouped animals according to whether they lived on land, in water, or in air and grouped plants based on differences in their stems. As naturalists described more organisms, they realized that Aristotle's classification system was inadequate.

Early naturalists also found that common names, such as *robin* or *fir tree,* were not useful to identify organisms because common names vary from place to place and many don't accurately define a species. For example, the common name *jellyfish* is misleading. Although it has a jellylike body, a jellyfish is not a fish. Some naturalists named species by using long descriptions in Latin, but these names were difficult to remember and did not describe relationships among organisms.

## The Linnaean System

Swedish naturalist Carolus Linnaeus (1707–1778) devised a system of grouping organisms into hierarchical categories according to their form and structure. Each category represents a level of grouping from larger, more general categories to smaller, more specific categories. Linnaeus's original system had seven levels. Figure 17-2 and Table 17-1 show a modern classification of different organisms in a hierarchical system similar to that used by Linnaeus.

**FIGURE 17-2**

Under the modern Linnaean system, the classification of an organism places the organism within a nested hierarchy of taxa. The hierarchy ranges from the most general category (domain) to the most specific (species).

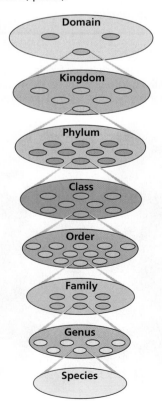

### TABLE 17-1 *Classification Hierarchy of Organisms*

|  | Pangolin | Dandelion |
|---|---|---|
| **Domain** | Eukarya | Eukarya |
| **Kingdom** | Animalia | Plantae |
| **Phylum/division** | Chordata | Magnoliophyta |
| **Class** | Mammalia | Magnoliopsida |
| **Order** | Pholidota | Asterales |
| **Family** | Manidae | Asteraceae |
| **Genus** | Manis | Taraxacum |
| **Species** | *Manis temminckii* | *Taraxacum officinale* |

# LEVELS OF CLASSIFICATION

The modern version of Linnaeus's nested hierarchy of organization is shown in Figure 17-2. His largest category was the **kingdom,** which was made up of only two kingdoms—animals and plants. Modern biologists adopted this system but added several other kingdoms as well as **domains,** which are categories above the kingdom level. Subsets below the kingdom level are called **phyla** (FIE-luh) (singular, *phylum*). Each phylum consists of **classes,** and each class contains **orders.** Still smaller groupings are the **family** and the **genus** (JEE-nuhs). The smallest grouping, which contains only a single kind of organism, is the **species** (SPEE-sheez).

## Binomial Nomenclature

Linnaeus gave an organism a species name, or scientific name, with two parts: the genus name followed by the *species identifier.* This system of two-part names is known as **binomial nomenclature** (bie-NOH-mee-uhl NOH-muhn-KLAY-chuhr). The species name for humans is *Homo sapiens.* The species name is written in italics with the genus name capitalized. Species names generally come from Latin roots and are intended to be the same for all countries and in every language.

The name of a species is often quite descriptive. One kind of amoeba, which changes its shape seemingly randomly as it crawls in a pond, is *Chaos chaos.* The ground pangolin's species identifier is *temminckii,* which commemorates C. J. Temminck, a 19th-century Dutch naturalist who first collected a specimen of this species.

Biologists refer to variations of a species that live in different geographic areas as **subspecies.** A subspecies name follows the species identifier. For example, *Terrapene carolina triunui* is a subspecies of the common eastern box turtle, *Terrapene carolina.*

## Quick Lab

### Practicing Classification

**Materials** paper, pencil

**Procedure** Using Table 17-1 as a model, classify a fruit or vegetable that you would find in a grocery store. Use all eight levels of classification.

**Analysis** At which level did you assign the least specific name? At which level did you assign the most specific name? Would Aristotle have classified your item differently? Explain your answer.

---

## SECTION 1 REVIEW

1. Explain how Earth's biodiversity relates to classification.

2. In what ways was Aristotle's classification system inadequate?

3. What criteria did Linnaeus use to classify organisms?

4. What are the eight levels of the modern classification system?

5. What are two reasons that species names are more precise than common names?

6. How is a subspecies given a scientific name?

**CRITICAL THINKING**

7. **Analyzing Models** Explain why many of Linnaeus's categories are still used.

8. **Calculating Information** Suppose that there are 67 butterfly species for every 22,000 insect species and there are 15,000 to 22,000 species of butterflies worldwide. How many insect species are there?

9. **Applying Information** Organize ten produce items from the grocery store into a hierarchy, and make up a species name for each one based on Linnaean principles.

# MILESTONES

## IN Classification of Organisms

### Timeline

**Prehistory**
Humans identify plants and animals.

**300 B.C.**
Theophrastus classifies 500 plants.

**1555** Gessner publishes *Historia Animalium.*

**1650** Ray publishes *Historia Plantarum.*

**1735** Linnaeus proposes taxonomic system.

**1866** Haeckel draws a "Tree of Life."

**1959–1969**
Whittaker proposes four-kingdom and then five-kingdom system.

**1966** Hennig proposes cladistics.

**1977–1990**
Woese names sixth kingdom and three domains.

*For uncounted millennia, humans have been observing Earth's organisms and trying to make sense of their diversity. Over time, a naming system that lumped all life-forms into "plants" or "animals" gave way to more sophisticated and accurate approaches to classification based on shared traits and ancestry. The modern approach can logically organize millions of species, including those yet to be discovered.*

Prehistoric humans survived by hunting animals and gathering plants. Their lives depended on recognizing the edible and the harmful. Indeed, native cultures have passed along a deep store of knowledge about thousands of plant and animal species organized by utility, such as edibility, toxicity, and medicinal value.

The Greek philosopher Aristotle observed and recorded nature in a scholarly way. His student Theophrastus, who lived from 370 BCE to 285 BCE, recorded 500 plant types, classified into herbs, shrubs, "pre-shrubs," and trees.

Advances in transportation, navigation, and exploration in the Middle Ages greatly expanded people's lists of observed organisms. In 1555, Swiss naturalist Conrad Gessner published *Historia Animalium,* categorizing thousands of animals into quadrupeds, birds, fish, and snakes. One hundred years later in his *Historia Plantarum*, English naturalist John Ray organized thousands of plants based on visual similarities and differences. In 1735, Swedish naturalist Carolus Linnaeus produced *Systema Naturae,* which categorized thousands of organisms into a hierarchy starting with genus and species and building to higher taxa including two kingdoms.

Several refinements have come to these higher taxa. German biologist Ernst Haeckel organized a "Tree of Life" in 1866. In 1894,

he redrew its branches into three kingdoms. In 1959, American ecologist R. H. Whittaker established a five-kingdom taxonomy. In 1966, German biologist Willi Hennig invented cladistics, which classifies organisms based on their shared, derived traits in order to reflect their evolutionary history. Molecular data obtained by using ribosomal RNA sequences as an evolutionary measure allowed American molecular biologist Carl Woese to propose in 1977 a six-kingdom system that divided the then-existing kingdom Monera into two new kingdoms: Archaebacteria and Eubacteria. In 1990, Woese introduced the three-domain system that is used today.

### Review

1. Describe how prehistoric humans "classified" species.

2. Why has the need for a system of classification grown over the centuries?

3. How do modern classification systems differ from the system of classification used by John Ray?

4. Describe a scientific advancement that enabled Woese to introduce the six-kingdom system.

# SYSTEMATICS

*More than 200 years ago, Linnaeus grouped organisms according to similarities that he could readily see. Modern biologists consider not only visible similarities but also similarities in embryos, chromosomes, proteins, and DNA. In* **systematics,** *the goal is to classify organisms in terms of their natural relationships. This section will discuss some modern methods of systematics.*

### OBJECTIVES

- **Identify** the kinds of evidence that modern biologists use in classifying organisms.
- **Explain** what information a phylogenetic diagram displays.
- **State** the criteria used in cladistic analysis.
- **Describe** how a cladogram is made.
- **Discuss** how proteins and chromosomes are used to classify organisms.
- **Explain** cladistic taxonomy, and identify one conclusion that is in conflict with classical taxonomy.

### VOCABULARY

systematics
phylogenetics
phylogenetic diagram
cladistics
shared character
derived character
clade
cladogram

## PHYLOGENETICS

Biologists today may choose among and sometimes combine several systems of classification. Increasingly, systematic taxonomists agree that an organism's classification should reflect phylogeny. Recall that *phylogeny* is the evolutionary history of a species or a taxon. Thus, modern taxonomists are often involved in **phylogenetics,** the analysis of the evolutionary or ancestral relationships among taxa.

Systematists usually use several types of evidence to hypothesize about phylogenetics. Often, they compare the visible similarities among currently living species or fossils from extinct organisms. Biologists may also compare patterns of embryonic development and the ways in which the embryos of different species express similar genes. Furthermore, they may compare similar chromosomes and macromolecules, such as DNA or RNA, from different species to deduce phylogenetic relationships.

Systematists often represent their hypotheses in the form of a **phylogenetic diagram,** also called a *phylogenetic tree.* This type of diagram looks like a family tree and has a branching pattern that indicates how closely related a subset of taxa are thought to be. As with all hypotheses, phylogenetic diagrams may change whenever new discoveries and investigations cause scientists to revise their hypotheses.

### Evidence of Shared Ancestry

Biologists use fossils as important clues for the timing of evolutionary changes and divergence. The use of fossils in the study of evolutionary relationships is critical, but the fossil record may lack evidence about many kinds of organisms, especially small and soft-bodied organisms, such as worms, fungi, or bacteria. The fossil record can help provide the framework of a phylogenetic diagram, but a systematist would test inferred relationships with additional evidence.

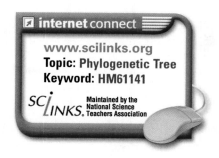

**internet** connect

**www.scilinks.org**
**Topic:** Phylogenetic Tree
**Keyword:** HM61141

SC*LINKS.* Maintained by the National Science Teachers Association

Systematists also compare *homologous* features, items that share a common ancestry. For example, the jaws of pangolins and of dogs are homologous. It is essential to separate homologous features from *analogous* features (features that are similar because they have a similar function rather than a similar lineage). Scales are an example of analogous features. Both pangolins and snakes have scales, but the fossil record shows that scales evolved independently in the two taxa. The greater the number of homologous features shared by two organisms, the more closely related the organisms are.

Embryological evidence also helps establish phylogenetic relationships. For example, a fluid-filled sac called an *amnion* surrounds the embryos of reptiles, birds, and mammals. The embryos of other vertebrates lack an amnion. This shared and homologous embryological feature is used to define *amniotes.* All amniotes are combined into one taxon that includes all reptiles, birds, and mammals but excludes other vertebrates.

# CLADISTICS

In 1966, German biologist Willi Hennig developed **cladistics** (kluh-DIS-tiks), a system of phylogenetic analysis that uses shared and derived characters as the only criteria for grouping taxa. A **shared character** is a feature that all members of a group have in common, such as hair in mammals or feathers in birds. A **derived character** is a feature that evolved only within the group under consideration. For example, feathers are thought to be a derived character for birds. Among living and fossil animals, the only animals that have feathers are birds and a few extinct reptiles that were very similar to birds in other ways. Therefore, it is reasonable to hypothesize that feathers evolved only within the bird lineage and were not inherited from the ancestors that birds share with reptiles.

Cladists assume that organisms that share one or more derived characters probably inherited those characters from a common ancestor. Cladists use the term **clade** for the group of organisms that includes an ancestor plus all of its descendants. Notice that clades do not have category names such as "class" or "phylum." Cladists create phylogenetic diagrams called **cladograms** (KLAD-uh-GRAMZ), such as the one in Figure 17-3.

Because cladists use strict criteria, their taxonomies may differ from those of traditional systematists. For example, traditional systematists grouped crocodiles with turtles, lizards, and snakes in the class Reptilia, but placed birds in their own class, Aves.

**FIGURE 17-3**

Traditional systematists placed crocodiles in the class Reptilia, but placed birds in the class Aves. In contrast, cladistic taxonomists have grouped crocodiles and birds together in a clade named *Archosauria.* Notice that clades do not have category names such as "class" or "phylum."

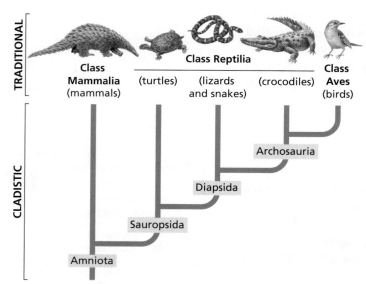

In contrast, cladistic taxonomists have grouped crocodiles and birds together in a clade named *Archosauria*. This grouping reflects the hypothesis that crocodiles and birds share a more recent ancestor than either group shares with any other animals. Archosauria is then grouped with successively less-related clades of animals.

## Constructing a Cladogram

Because cladistic analysis is comparative, the analysis deliberately includes an organism that is only distantly related to the other organisms. This organism is called an *out-group*. The out-group is a starting point for comparisons with the other organisms being evaluated.

To make a cladogram like Figure 17-4, start by making a data table like Table 17-2. Place organisms in a column at the left and their characteristics in a row at the top. Choose an out-group organism. In our example, moss has fewer traits in common with and seems most distantly related to the other groups in the table. So, moss is the choice for an out-group. Score the characters that are lacking in the out-group as a 0, and score the presence of a derived character as a 1. For example, mosses lack seeds, so they receive a 0 for the "seeds" character. Only pines and flowering plants have seeds, so they receive a 1 for that character.

The table now reveals the derived character that is shared by most of the taxa. In this example, that character is vascular tissue—vessels that transport water and sugars. This character is shown at the base of the first branch of the cladogram. The second most common character is seeds. Because ferns lack seeds, they are placed on the second branch of the cladogram. The least common character is flowers. Because pines lack flowers, they are placed on the third branch. Finally, flowering plants are placed on the last branch.

The resulting "tree" is a cladistic hypothesis for the evolutionary relationships among these plants. In addition to considering obvious physical characters, such as seeds and flowers, cladists may consider molecular characters, such as an individual nucleotide in a gene sequence or an amino acid sequence within a protein.

**FIGURE 17-4**

This cladogram groups several major kinds of plants according to their shared, derived characters. The most common character (vascular tissue) is shared by all groups. The least common character (flowers) separates flowering plants from all the other plants.

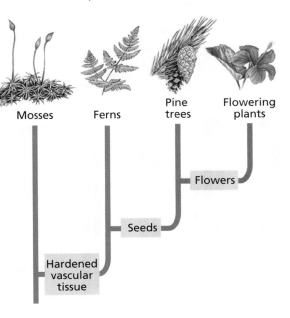

| TABLE 17-2 *Data Table for Cladogram* | | | |
|---|---|---|---|
| | **Characters** | | |
| **Group of organisms** | **Vascular tissue** | **Seeds** | **Flowers** |
| Mosses (out-group) | 0 | 0 | 0 |
| Ferns | 1 | 0 | 0 |
| Pine trees and other conifers | 1 | 1 | 0 |
| Flowering plants | 1 | 1 | 1 |

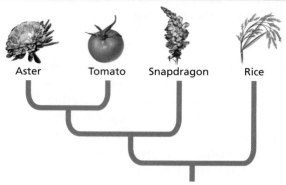

**Amino Acid Sequence of a Petal-Forming Gene in Different Plants**

| | | | | | | | | | | | | | | | | | | | | | | | | | | | | | | | | | | | | | | | | | | | | | | | |
|---|---|---|---|---|---|---|---|---|---|---|---|---|---|---|---|---|---|---|---|---|---|---|---|---|---|---|---|---|---|---|---|---|---|---|---|---|---|---|---|---|---|---|---|---|---|---|
| Aster | M | G | R | G | K | I | E | I | K | K | I | E | N | N | T | N | R | Q | V | T | Y | S | K | R | R | N | G | I | F | K | K | A | H | E | L | T | V | L | C | D | A | K | V | S | L | I |
| Tomato | – | – | – | G | K | I | E | I | K | K | I | E | N | S | T | N | R | Q | V | T | Y | S | K | R | R | N | G | I | F | K | K | R | K | E | L | T | V | L | C | D | A | K | I | S | L | I |
| Snapdragon | M | A | R | G | K | I | Q | I | K | R | I | E | N | Q | T | N | R | Q | V | T | Y | S | K | R | R | N | G | L | F | K | K | A | H | E | L | S | V | L | C | D | A | K | V | S | I | I |
| Rice | M | G | R | G | K | I | E | I | K | R | I | E | N | A | T | N | R | Q | V | T | Y | S | K | R | R | T | G | I | M | K | K | A | R | E | L | T | V | L | C | D | A | Q | V | A | I | I |

(continued)

| M | F | S | N | T | G | K | F | H | E | Y |
|---|---|---|---|---|---|---|---|---|---|---|
| M | L | S | S | T | R | K | Y | H | E | Y |
| M | I | S | S | T | Q | K | L | H | E | Y |
| M | F | S | S | T | G | K | Y | H | E | F |

Aster  Tomato  Snapdragon  Rice

## FIGURE 17-5

This cladogram is based on similar amino acid sequences in a specific protein produced by these plants. The initials M, G, and so on indicate different amino acids. The yellow squares indicate differences within the otherwise-identical sequences.

## FIGURE 17-6

In this example, the karyotype of species A is very similar to that of species B. The diagram compares 4 of species A's chromosomes with 5 of species B's chromosomes. The banding pattern similarities suggest that chromosomes B2 and B3, combined, are homologous to chromosome A2.

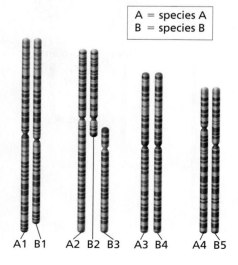

A = species A
B = species B

A1  B1    A2  B2  B3    A3  B4    A4  B5

# Molecular Cladistics

A biologist can count the shared, derived amino acids at each position in a protein and, from the analysis, construct a tree that hypothesizes relationships between various species. On a molecular cladogram, branch lengths are proportional to the number of amino acid changes. Such molecular data are independent of physical similarities or differences. The analysis shown in Figure 17-5 is of the amino acid sequence of a protein involved in flower development.

Biologists have used evolutionary changes in the sequence of macromolecules, such as DNA, RNA, and proteins, as a form of *molecular clock,* a tool for estimating the sequence of past evolutionary events. The molecular clock hypothesis suggests that the greater the differences between a pair of sequences, the longer ago those two sequences diverged from a common ancestor. A researcher who matches a molecular clock carefully with the fossil record can use it to hypothesize when various characteristics arose and when organisms diverged from ancestral groups.

# Chromosomes

Analyzing karyotypes can provide still more information on evolutionary relationships. As Figure 17-6 shows, chromosomes can be stained to reveal a pattern of bands. If two species have the same banding pattern in regions of similar chromosomes, the regions are likely to have been inherited from a single chromosome in the last common ancestor of the two species. Karyotypic data are totally independent of both physical similarities and molecular data.

For example, the chromosomes of two species are shown in Figure 17-6. Several of the chromosomes have similar banding patterns, suggesting that the chromosomes are homologous. In addition, two of species B's chromosomes are similar to parts of one of species A's chromosomes. In such cases, biologists may still hypothesize that all of the chromosomes were inherited from the same ancestor. It is possible that in one of the descendants, one chromosome became two or two chromosomes became one.

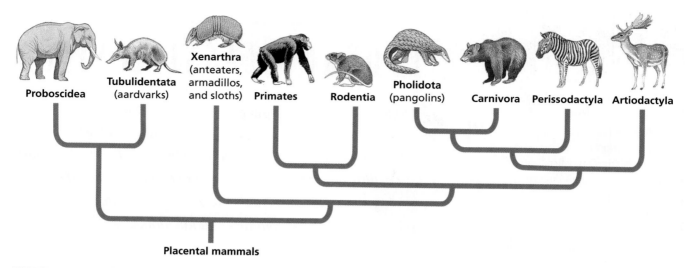

Proboscidea  Tubulidentata (aardvarks)  Xenarthra (anteaters, armadillos, and sloths)  Primates  Rodentia  Pholidota (pangolins)  Carnivora  Perissodactyla  Artiodactyla

Placental mammals

# PUTTING IT ALL TOGETHER

To classify an organism and represent its systematics in an evolutionary context, biologists use many types of information to build and revise phylogenetic models. Systematists will use data about physical features, embryos, genes in the nucleus, mitochondrial DNA, and ribosomal RNA.

Consider the classification of pangolins that is shown in Figure 17-7. African and Asian pangolins share several adaptations with other mammals that eat ants, including African aardvarks and South American anteaters. These adaptations include narrow snouts, strong digging claws, and long, sticky tongues. These shared characteristics, however, are analogous, not homologous. Deeper analysis of other characteristics, such as skeletal structures and nucleotide sequences in several genes, indicate that all three anteating taxa—pangolins, anteaters, and aardvarks—occupy quite different branches on the mammalian phylogenetic tree. Therefore, systematists place pangolins closer to the group that includes dogs and bears than to either aardvarks or anteaters.

**FIGURE 17-7**

This phylogenetic diagram is based on analyses of the DNA of many kinds of mammals. These analyses do not support a systematic grouping of pangolins with either African aardvarks or South American anteaters. Instead, pangolins seem to be most closely related to carnivores, such as bears and dogs. Biologists sometimes revise their classifications in light of such new evidence.

## SECTION 2 REVIEW

1. Identify two types of information that modern taxonomists use to classify organisms.

2. What is systematics, and what kinds of data are used by a systematist?

3. Define the term *phylogenetic diagram.*

4. What is a shared, derived character?

5. Compare cladistic taxonomy with more traditional taxonomy.

6. How can a comparative analysis of the karyotypes of two species provide clues to the degree of relatedness between the species?

**CRITICAL THINKING**

7. **Analyzing Models** Examine the phylogenetic model shown in Figure 17-3, and explain why the Class Reptilia is not a clade.

8. **Making Inferences** Explain how a taxonomist might use embryological evidence in classifying an organism.

9. **Evaluating Concepts** How could a biologist use cladistics to deduce whether the flippers of a sea lion and a whale are homologous or analogous characters?

### OBJECTIVES

- **Describe** the evidence that prompted the invention of the three-domain system of classification.
- **List** the characteristics that distinguish between the domains Bacteria, Archaea, and Eukarya.
- **Describe** the six-kingdom system of classification.
- **Identify** problematic taxa in the six-kingdom system.
- **Explain** why taxonomic systems continue to change.

### VOCABULARY

Bacteria
Archaea
Eukarya
Eubacteria
Archaebacteria
Protista
Fungi
Plantae
Animalia

# MODERN CLASSIFICATION

*Biologists continue to develop taxonomies to organize life's enormous diversity. They regularly revise the many branches of the "tree of life" to reflect current hypotheses of the evolutionary relationships between groups. They have even revised the largest and most fundamental categories of the Linnean-inspired classification system—domains and kingdoms.*

## THE TREE OF LIFE

Looking at the cells of any organism under a microscope, biologists can easily identify one of two fundamental types of cells. On this basis, biologists may divide all life into two large groups. One of these groups consists of *eukaryotes,* or organisms whose cells possess a membrane-enclosed nucleus and many other cell organelles. Eukaryotes include organisms such as pangolins, people, and amoebas. The second group consists of *prokaryotes.* Prokaryotic cells are smaller than eukaryotic cells and have neither a nucleus nor membrane-enclosed organelles. Prokaryotes include bacteria.

### Revising the Tree

Although the differences between eukaryotes and prokaryotes are obvious, systematists cannot assume that all organisms in one of these groups are equally related. A systematist can draw inferences about evolutionary relationships only by identifying homologous features. Because all members of one of these groups have few other physical traits in common, it is difficult to make comparisons between them. However, eukaryotes and prokaryotes do contain homologous macromolecules, such as proteins and RNAs used for storing and translating genetic information. When methods became available to compare such macromolecules, biologists began to use macromolecules in phylogenetic analyses.

Such analyses led molecular microbiologist Carl Woese of the University of Illinois to propose a major revision of the system that had classified Earth's diversity into six kingdoms. In 1977, Woese began comparing ribosomal RNA (rRNA) sequences from many different organisms and then grouping these organisms according to their similarities. All of today's living organisms, even prokaryotes, have ribosomes. Furthermore, the nucleotide sequences of the genes that encode rRNA seem to have changed little throughout most of evolutionary history. Thus, rRNA genes are uniquely useful for studying the most basic evolutionary relationships between Earth's diverse organisms.

# THREE DOMAINS OF LIFE

Phylogenetic analyses of rRNA genes gave scientists new insights about the relationships between major groups and suggested a new "tree of life." Three of the most important insights were as follows:

1. The data are consistent with the hypothesis that all living organisms inherited their rRNA genes from an ancient organism or form of life. Scientists refer to this unknown ancestor as the *last universal common ancestor.*

2. At the broadest level, all living things seem to be related by ancestry to one of three major lineages, or *domains.* The three domains are named *Bacteria, Archaea,* and *Eukarya.* Most of the organisms that we are familiar with, such as plants and animals, belong to just one of the domains—Eukarya. Figure 17-8 shows a phylogenetic diagram for the three domains.

3. The most surprising insights were those related to the domain Archaea. The species in this domain were identified and studied more recently than those in the other two domains. At first, the archaea were classified as bacteria. However, scientists have found that archaea differ greatly from bacteria in many important ways. More recently, scientists hypothesized that modern archaea descended from a unique kind of prokaryotes that existed early in Earth's history.

**Word Roots and Origins**

*domain*

from the Latin *dominium,* meaning "right of ownership"

## Domain Bacteria

The domain **Bacteria** is made up of small, single-celled prokaryotic organisms that usually have a cell wall and reproduce by cellular fission. Each bacterium has a cell wall, a plasma membrane, a cytoplasm that lacks complex organelles, and at least one circular chromosome. Bacteria do not have a membrane-bound DNA and thus lack a true nucleus. Most bacteria are small—many are just 2 µm long. By comparison, human cells can be 6 µm long or more. The oldest known fossils of cells appear to be bacterial cells.

## Domain Archaea

The second domain also consists of prokaryotes and is named **Archaea.** The archaea have distinctive cell membranes and other unique biochemical and genetic properties. Some archaeal species are autotrophic and are able to produce food by chemosynthesis. Some species produce flammable gases, such as methane, as waste products. Many archaeal species inhabit harsh environments, such as sulfurous hot springs, deep-sea thermal vents, salty lakes, wastewater from mining, and the intestines of some animals.

**FIGURE 17-8**

This phylogenetic diagram represents hypotheses of the evolutionary relationships between the major recognized groups of organisms. Notice the alignment of the three domain names (*Bacteria, Archaea,* and *Eukarya*) with three major "branches" of the "tree" of all life. For updates on phylogenetic information, visit **go.hrw.com** and enter the keyword **HM6 Phylo.**

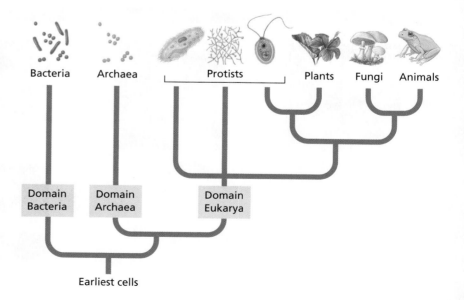

Bacteria   Archaea   Protists   Plants   Fungi   Animals

Domain Bacteria   Domain Archaea   Domain Eukarya

Earliest cells

Because of the unique adaptations of the archaea, scientists think that archaea were among the earliest organisms on Earth. Furthermore, scientists think that archaea and bacteria have co-evolved during Earth's history, meaning that the cells have interacted closely within environments and that the cells could have exchanged nutrients and genetic material. These possibilities, along with biochemical evidence, have led to the *theory of endosymbiosis,* which holds that eukaryotic cells arose when ancient prokaryotic cells began to live together as one cell.

## Domain Eukarya

The most familiar groups of organisms are members of the domain **Eukarya** (yoo-KAR-ee-uh), which consists of eukaryotic organisms. The cells of these organisms are large and have a true nucleus and complex cellular organelles. The domain Eukarya includes plants, animals, fungi, and a variety of single-celled organisms.

# SIX KINGDOMS

The system of three domains generally aligns with the more traditional system of six kingdoms, as represented in Figure 17-9 and summarized in Table 17-3. In the six-kingdom system, the first kingdom aligns with the domain Bacteria, the second kingdom aligns with the domain Archaea, and the remaining four kingdoms align with the domain Eukarya.

## Kingdom Eubacteria

The kingdom **Eubacteria** (YOO-bak-TIR-ee-uh) aligns with the domain Bacteria. The name *Eubacteria* means "true bacteria," distinguishing this group from the archaea, which are no longer considered to be bacteria.

**FIGURE 17-9**

The six-kingdom system of classification can be aligned with the newer system of three domains. However, biologists have proposed adding, subdividing, or replacing some kingdoms. Biologists have also proposed other levels of taxa.

| Domain Bacteria | Domain Archaea | Domain Eukarya |
| --- | --- | --- |

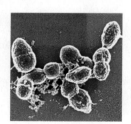

Kingdom Eubacteria

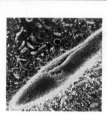

Kingdom Archaebacteria

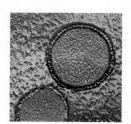

Kingdom Protista

Kingdom Plantae

Kingdom Fungi

Kingdom Animalia

# Kingdom Archaebacteria

The kingdom **Archaebacteria** (AHR-kee-bak-TIR-ee-uh) aligns with the domain Archaea. The name *Archaebacteria* means "ancient bacteria," but archaea are so different from bacteria that many biologists now prefer to use only the name *archaea* for this group.

# Kingdom Protista

One of the four kingdoms of eukaryotes is **Protista** (proh-TIST-uh), whose members are called *protists*. This kingdom has been defined as those eukaryotes that are not plants, animals, or fungi. This definition is troublesome because it defines organisms based on what they are *not* rather than on what they *are*. Most protists are unicellular organisms, but it is difficult to make other generalizations about them. Molecular analyses indicate that many protists are less related to each other than plants are to animals. For all of these reasons, many biologists think that the taxon *Protista* is no longer useful, and several new taxa are being considered.

Common examples of unicellular protists are amoebas and paramecia. Examples of multicellular protists include some kinds of seaweeds and molds. Each of these protists is similar to animals, plants, or fungi in some ways yet different in other ways.

## TABLE 17-3 *Kingdom and Domain Characteristics*

| Taxon | Cell type | Cell surfaces | Body plan | Nutrition |
|---|---|---|---|---|
| Domain Bacteria (aligns with Kingdom Eubacteria) | prokaryotic; lack nucleus and other organelles | cell wall:contains peptidoglycans; cell membrane: contains fatty acids | unicellular | heterotrophic and autotrophic by chemosynthesis or photosynthesis |
| Domain Archaea (aligns with Kingdom Archaebacteria) | prokaryotic; lack nucleus and other organelles | cell wall: lacks peptidoglycan; cell membrane: contains hydrocarbons other than fatty acids | unicellular | heterotrophic and autotrophic by chemosynthesis |
| Domain Eukarya Kingdom Protista | eukaryotic; have nucleus and complex organelles | cell wall: made of cellulose or other materials; cell membrane: contains fatty acids | mostly unicellular; multicellular forms: lack tissue organization | autotrophic by photosynthesis, some heterotrophic by phagocytosis, or both |
| Domain Eukarya Kingdom Fungi | eukaryotic; have nucleus and complex organelles | cell wall: made of chitin; cell membrane: contains fatty acids | unicellular and multicellular | heterotrophic by secreting digestive enzymes into environment |
| Domain Eukarya Kingdom Plantae | eukaryotic; have nucleus and complex organelles | cell wall: made of cellulose; cell membrane: contains fatty acids | multicellular; develop from embryos | autotrophic by photosynthesis |
| Domain Eukarya Kingdom Animalia | eukaryotic; have nucleus and complex organelles | cell wall: none cell membrane: contains fatty acids | multicellular; develop from embryos | heterotrophic by phagocytosis |

## Kingdom Fungi

The second kingdom of eukaryotes is **Fungi** (FUHN-jie). The kingdom Fungi consists of eukaryotic, heterotrophic organisms that are unicellular or multicellular and that gain nutrients in a unique way. Unlike animal cells and some protists, fungi absorb rather than ingest nutrients. The about 70,000 species of fungi include mushrooms, puffballs, rusts, smuts, mildews, and molds.

## Kingdom Plantae

The third kingdom of eukaryotes is **Plantae** (PLAN-tee), which consists of eukaryotic, multicellular plants. Except for a few parasitic species, most plants are autotrophic, use photosynthesis as a source of energy, and develop from embryos. Most plants live on land and include mosses, ferns, conifers, and flowering plants.

## Kingdom Animalia

The fourth kingdom of eukaryotes is **Animalia** (AN-uh-MAH-lee-uh). Animals are eukaryotic, multicellular, and heterotrophic organisms that develop from embryos. Most animals have symmetrical body organization and move around their environment to find and capture food.

## Future Taxonomic Systems

Because taxonomic systems are scientific models, they are subject to change. Since the time of Linnaeus, biologists have proposed, used, evaluated, and modified many classification systems. Modern biologists have proposed alternatives to the six-kingdom and three-domain systems. For example, some biologists have proposed three or more new kingdoms to replace Kingdom Protista. Some use taxonomic categories such as "subkingdom" and "superorder" to adapt the more traditional Linnaean categories to newer systematic models. Some favor pure cladistics over Linnaean categories. Surely, new systems will result from future investigations into the millions of known and unknown species on Earth.

## SECTION 3 REVIEW

1. What kind of evidence supports the classification of all organisms into the three-domain system?

2. Contrast bacteria with archaea.

3. List and briefly describe the kingdoms in the six-kingdom system of classification.

4. What is problematic about the kingdom name *Archaebacteria*?

5. What is problematic about defining the kingdom Protista?

6. Why do protists, fungi, plants, and animals share a single domain in the three-domain system?

### CRITICAL THINKING

7. **Evaluating Viewpoints** Biologists once classified all species of prokaryotes in a single kingdom called *Monera*. Justify their reasoning.

8. **Applying Information** You have discovered a new organism. It is unicellular and has mitochondria, chloroplasts, and a nucleus. To what kingdom does this organism belong? Justify your answer.

9. **Recognizing Differences** Describe the characteristics that differentiate plants from fungi. In what ways are plants and fungi similar?

# CHAPTER HIGHLIGHTS

## SECTION 1 — Biodiversity

- Naturalists have invented several systems for categorizing biodiversity, which is the variety of organisms considered at all levels from populations to ecosystems.

- Naturalists replaced Aristotle's classification system because it did not adequately cover all organisms and because his use of common names was problematic.

- Taxonomy is the science of describing, naming, and classifying organisms.

- Carolus Linnaeus devised a seven-level hierarchical system for classifying organisms according to their form and structure. From the most general to the most specific, the levels are kingdom, phylum, class, order, family, genus, and species. An adaptation of this system is still in use today.

- An important part of Linnaeus's system was assigning each species a two-part scientific name—a genus name, such as *Homo*, and a species identifier, such as *sapiens*.

### Vocabulary

| | | | |
|---|---|---|---|
| biodiversity (p. 337) | domain (p. 339) | order (p. 339) | binomial nomenclature (p. 339) |
| taxonomy (p. 338) | phylum (p. 339) | family (p. 339) | subspecies (p. 339) |
| taxon (p. 338) | division (p. 339) | genus (p. 339) | |
| kingdom (p. 339) | class (p. 339) | species (p. 339) | |

## SECTION 2 — Systematics

- A modern approach to taxonomy is systematics, which analyzes the diversity of organisms in the context of their natural relationships.

- When classifying organisms, scientists consider fossils, homologous features, embryos, chromosomes, and the sequences of proteins and DNA.

- A phylogenetic diagram displays how closely related a subset of taxa are thought to be.

- Homologous features as well as similarities in patterns of embryological development provide information about common ancestry.

- Cladistics uses shared, derived characters as the only criterion for grouping taxa.

- Molecular similarities, such as similar amino acid or nucleotide sequences, as well as chromosome comparisons can help determine common ancestry.

### Vocabulary

| | | | |
|---|---|---|---|
| systematics (p. 341) | phylogenetic diagram (p. 341) | shared character (p. 342) | clade (p. 342) |
| phylogenetics (p. 341) | cladistics (p. 342) | derived character (p. 342) | cladogram (p. 342) |

## SECTION 3 — Modern Classification

- The phylogenetic analysis of rRNA nucleotide sequences led to a new "tree of life" consisting of three domains aligned with six kingdoms.

- The three domains are Bacteria, Archaea, and Eukarya.

- Domain Bacteria aligns with Kingdom Eubacteria, which consists of single-celled prokaryotes that are true bacteria.

- Domain Archaea aligns with Kingdom Archaebacteria, which consists of single-celled prokaryotes that have distinctive cell membranes and cell walls.

- Domain Eukarya includes the kingdoms Protista, Fungi, Plantae, and Animalia. All members of this domain have eukaryotic cells.

### Vocabulary

| | | | |
|---|---|---|---|
| Bacteria (p. 347) | Eubacteria (p. 348) | Protista (p. 349) | Plantae (p. 350) |
| Archaea (p. 347) | Archaebacteria (p. 349) | Fungi (p. 350) | Animalia (p. 350) |
| Eukarya (p. 348) | | | |

## USING VOCABULARY

1. Use each of the following terms in a separate sentence: *biodiversity, binomial nomenclature, species identifier,* and *subspecies.*

2. Explain the relationship between a phylum and a division.

3. Choose the term that does not belong in the following group, and explain why the term does not belong: *homologous, derived character, shared character,* and *analogous.*

4. **Word Roots and Origins** The word *taxonomy* is derived from the Greek words *taxis,* which means "to put in order," and *nomia,* which means "a set of rules or laws." Using this information, explain why the term *taxonomy* is a good name for the process that the term describes.

## UNDERSTANDING KEY CONCEPTS

5. **Explain** the primary difficulty of organizing Earth's biodiversity.

6. **Describe** how Aristotle's and Linnaeus's classification systems for organisms were similar.

7. **Explain** why a consistent naming system for species is important in scientific work.

8. **List** the seven levels of Linnaeus's classification hierarchy from most general to most specific.

9. **Name** the kinds of evidence that systematists use in constructing a phylogenetic tree.

10. **Identify** the system of classification that is based on an analysis of shared, derived characters.

11. **Describe** how amino acid and nucleotide sequences function as a molecular clock.

12. **Summarize** one way that cladistic taxonomy differs from traditional taxonomy.

13. **Name** the three domains and six kingdoms, and indicate the relationships of the two sets of taxa.

14. **Describe** the molecular evidence that led to the three-domain system of classification.

15. **Differentiate** between bacteria and archaea.

16. **Compare** plants and fungi, and describe what they have in common with animals.

17. **CONCEPT MAPPING** Use the following terms to create a concept map that describes how biologists classify a new species: *genus, species, binomial nomenclature, kingdom, homologous structures, taxonomy, derived characters, cladogram,* and *systematics.*

## CRITICAL THINKING

18. **Evaluating Viewpoints** Scientists sometimes disagree about the phylogenetic histories of organisms. Cladistic taxonomists see reptiles in a different light than traditional taxonomists do. Why might scientists disagree with each other about the history of evolution?

19. **Evaluating Models** The evolutionary history of reptiles can be studied by comparing their macromolecules. The degree of difference can be related to the time that has passed since any two species descended from a common ancestor. Would the phylogenetic tree derived from macromolecular comparisons more closely resemble the results of cladistic analysis or the traditional classification?

20. **Evaluating Information** Biologists think that there may be millions of undescribed and unclassified species on Earth. Why might so many species still be undescribed or unclassified today?

21. **Analyzing Concepts** Legs are an example of a shared, derived character in vertebrates. Arthropods, such as lobsters and crickets, also have legs, but their legs are not homologous to the legs of vertebrates. Explain this difference.

22. **Justifying Conclusions** Several years ago, scientists found a living coelacanth, a fish that was thought to have become extinct 65 million years ago. The earliest fossils of coelacanths are about 350 million years old. The appearance of this species has changed little in 350 million years. If you could obtain macromolecules, such as proteins, from a 350 million–year-old fossil coelacanth and compare them with those of a freshly caught coelacanth, what would you expect to find and why?

23. **Interpreting Graphics** A taxonomist has recorded the data below.

### Derived Characters in Plants

| Plants | Seeds | Vascular system |
|---|---|---|
| Horsetails | no | yes |
| Liverworts | no | no |
| Pine trees | yes | yes |

Identify the least common derived character. List the order that the plants in the table would be placed on a cladogram.

# Standardized Test Preparation

**DIRECTIONS:** Choose the letter of the answer choice that best answers the question.

1. Which information is given in a species name?
   A. genus and order
   B. division and genus
   C. genus and species identifier
   D. species identifier and phylum

2. To which level of classification does a group of closely related species of organisms belong?
   F. class
   G. order
   H. genus
   J. kingdom

3. Eukaryotic organisms that have a nucleus and organelles, have a cell wall made of chitin, and secrete digestive enzymes belong to which kingdom?
   A. Fungi
   B. Plantae
   C. Protista
   D. Animalia

**INTERPRETING GRAPHICS:** The cladogram below shows the phylogenetic relationships among four kinds of plants. Use the cladogram to answer the question that follows.

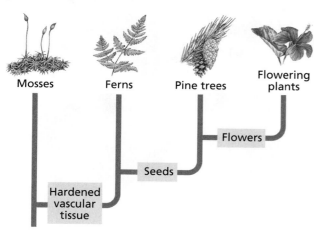

4. On the basis of this cladogram, which plants share the most recent common ancestor?
   F. mosses and ferns
   G. mosses and pine trees
   H. ferns and flowering plants
   J. pine trees and flowering plants

**DIRECTIONS:** Complete the following analogy.

5. class : order :: kingdom :
   A. genus
   B. domain
   C. species
   D. phylum

**INTERPRETING GRAPHICS:** The diagram below represents the eight levels of classification. Use the diagram to answer the question that follows.

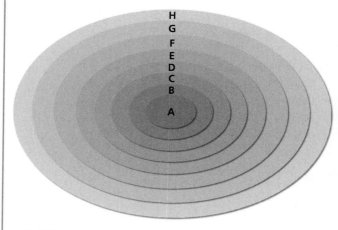

6. Which level of classification represents a species?
   F. A
   G. C
   H. D
   J. G

**SHORT RESPONSE**

Consider the characteristics of members of Kingdom Protista.

Explain why Kingdom Protista includes so many diverse organisms.

**EXTENDED RESPONSE**

To study the biodiversity of a rain forest, researchers sometimes collect species in vast numbers.

*Part A* How would traditional taxonomy aid a researcher who found 955 beetle species in one kind of tropical tree?

*Part B* How could molecular phylogenetics assist that same researcher?

**Test TIP** If time permits, take short mental breaks to improve your concentration during a test.

# Using and Formulating Dichotomous Keys

## OBJECTIVES

■ Use a dichotomous key to identify leaves.
■ Construct a dichotomous identification key.

## PROCESS SKILLS

■ identifying
■ classifying
■ designing
■ interpreting
■ organizing data
■ comparing and contrasting

## MATERIALS

■ pencil
■ paper
■ shoes
■ masking tape
■ marker

## Background

1. Taxonomy is the science of naming, describing, and classifying organisms.
2. Why is classification essential to biology?
3. A dichotomous key uses pairs of contrasting, descriptive statements to lead to the identification of an organism (or other object).
4. The principle behind dichotomous keys—the forced choice—is used in many different situations to narrow the path toward an answer. If you have ever had your eyes examined for corrective lenses, you are familiar with the series of forced choices that end with the choice of the correct lenses for your eyes.
5. Do not confuse a dichotomous key with a cladogram. A cladogram represents evolutionary relationships, whereas a dichotomous key does not.

## PART A  Using a Dichotomous Key

1. Field guides often use dichotomous keys to help you identify organisms. Use the dichotomous key shown here to identify the tree leaves below. Begin with the paired descriptions 1a and 1b, and follow the directions. Proceed through the list of paired descriptions until you identify the leaf in question. In your lab report, write the names of the leaves as you identify them.

(a)

(b)

(c)

(d)

(e)

(f)

## Dichotomous Key for Identifying Common Leaves

**1a.** If the edge of the leaf has no teeth and has no lobes, go to 2 in the key.

**1b.** If the edge of the leaf has teeth or lobes, go to 3 in the key.

**2a.** If the leaf has slightly wavy edges, the plant is a shingle oak.

**2b.** If the leaf has smooth edges, go to 4 in the key.

**3a.** If the leaf edge is toothed, the plant is a Lombardy poplar.

**3b.** If the leaf edge has lobes, go to 5 in the key.

**4a.** If the leaf is heart-shaped with veins branching from the base, the plant is a redbud.

**4b.** If the leaf is not heart-shaped, the plant is a live oak.

**5a.** If the leaf edge has a few large lobes, the plant is an English oak.

**5b.** If the leaf edge has many small lobes, the plant is a chestnut oak.

### PART B  Making a Dichotomous Key

**2.** Gather 10 different single shoes, and use masking tape and a marker to label the soles of the shoes with the owner's name. The labeled shoes should then be placed on a single table in the classroom.

**3.** Form small groups. Discuss the appearance of the shoes. In your lab report, make a table like the one below that lists some of the shoes' general characteristics, such as the type and size. Also list the names of the students who own the shoes. Complete the chart by describing the characteristics of each person's shoe.

**4.** Use the information in your table to make a dichotomous key that can be used to identify the owner of each shoe. Remember that a dichotomous key includes pairs of opposing descriptions. At the end of each description, the key should either identify an object or give directions to go to another specific pair of descriptions. Write your dichotomous key in your lab report.

**5.** After all groups have completed their key, exchange keys with a member of another group. Use the key to identify the owner of each shoe, and then verify the accuracy of your identification by reading the label on the shoe. If the key has led you to an inaccurate identification, return the key so that corrections can be made.

**6.** Clean up your materials before leaving the lab.

### Analysis and Conclusions

**1.** What other characteristics might be used to identify leaves with a dichotomous key?

**2.** Were you able to identify the shoes using another group's key? If not, describe the problems you encountered.

**3.** How was it helpful to list the characteristics of the shoes before making the key?

**4.** Does a dichotomous key begin with general descriptions and then proceed to more specific descriptions, or vice versa? Explain your answer, giving an example from the key you made.

**5.** Are dichotomous keys based on a phylogenetic or morphological approach to classification? Explain your answer.

### Further Inquiry

List characteristics that might be used to identify birds or other animals using a dichotomous key. Compare your list of characteristics with those used in a dichotomous key in a field guide for identifying birds or other animals.

### DISTINGUISHING FEATURES OF A SAMPLE OF SHOES

|   | Left/right | Men's/women's | Laced/slip-on | Color | Size | Owner |
|---|---|---|---|---|---|---|
| 1 | | | | | | |
| 2 | | | | | | |
| 3 | | | | | | |
| 4 | | | | | | |
| 5 | | | | | | |

# ECOLOGY

"We and our fellow vertebrates are largely along for the ride on this planet. If we want to perpetuate the dream that we are in charge of our destiny and that of our planet, it can only be by maintaining biological diversity—not by destroying it. In the end, we impoverish ourselves if we impoverish the biota."

From "Diverse Considerations," by Thomas E. Lovejoy from *Biodiversity*, edited by E. O. Wilson. Copyright © 1988 by the National Academy of Sciences. Reproduced by permission of **National Academy Press**.

References to *Scientific American* project ideas are located throughout this unit.

**internet** connect

National Science Teachers Association *sci*LINKS Internet resources are located throughout this unit.

SCI LINKS Maintained by the National Science Teachers Association

*Coral reef communities are second only to rain forests in diversity.*

*Bears are among the largest terrestrial predators.*

*The biosphere*

*Mimicry helps this mantid hide from both predators and potential prey.*

*Tropical rain forests are richer in species than other areas of Earth are.*

# INTRODUCTION TO ECOLOGY

Ecology is the study of the interactions of organisms with each other and with the nonliving parts of Earth. This image is a view of Earth as seen from space.

**Unit 7—Ecosystem Dynamics**
Topics 1, 4–6

# INTRODUCTION TO ECOLOGY

*Ecology* is the study of the interactions between organisms and the living and nonliving components of their environment. Each of the variety of organisms on Earth depends in some way on other living and nonliving things in its environment. Ecology is a broad science that involves collecting information about organisms and their environments, observing and measuring interactions, looking for patterns, and seeking to explain these patterns.

## SECTION 1

### OBJECTIVES

- **Identify** a key theme in ecology.
- **Describe** an example showing the effects of interdependence upon organisms in their environment.
- **Identify** the importance of models to ecology.
- **State** the five different levels of organization at which ecology can be studied.

### VOCABULARY

ecology
interdependence
ecological model
biosphere
ecosystem
community
population

## INTERDEPENDENCE: A KEY THEME IN ECOLOGY

Although the field of ecology was not named until 1866, ecological information and understanding have always been crucial to humans. Before the development of agriculture, about 10,000–12,000 years ago, our ancestors obtained all of their food by hunting animals and gathering plants, seeds, berries, and nuts. Their survival depended on practical knowledge about the environment. Although most humans today don't survive as hunter-gatherers, they interact with the environment and other organisms every day.

### Organisms and Their Environments

All organisms interact with other organisms in their surroundings and with the nonliving portion of their environment. Their survival depends on these interactions. Ecologists refer to this quality as *interconnectedness* or **interdependence.**

Interdependence is a key theme found throughout ecology. For example, you could not survive without the plants and other photosynthetic organisms that produce oxygen. Your cells need oxygen to release the energy in food, and cells will die if deprived of oxygen for even a few minutes. Conversely, photosynthetic organisms depend on the release of carbon dioxide gas by the cellular respiration of other organisms, such as humans, and geochemical processes, such as volcanic eruptions. Carbon dioxide gas is an essential raw material for making carbohydrates by photosynthesizers.

### Word Roots and Origins

*ecology*

from the Greek *oikos,* meaning "house," and *logos,* meaning "study of"

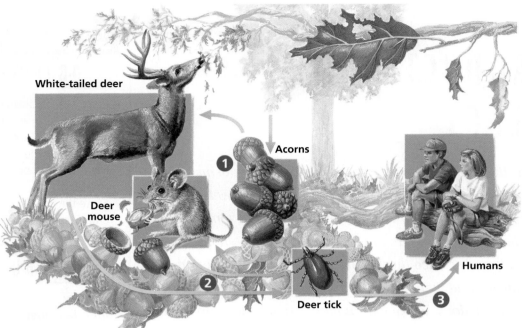

White-tailed deer

Acorns

**1**

Deer mouse

Humans

**2**

Deer tick

**3**

**FIGURE 18-1**

All of the different species shown are interconnected in the forest. **1** An unusually plentiful crop of acorns helps support a large population of deer and mice. **2** The deer and mice help support a large population of ticks. **3** Ticks carry the bacterium that causes Lyme disease. They pass on the disease to humans who visit the forest.

## Effects of Interdependence

A consequence of interdependence is that any change in the environment can spread through the network of interactions and affect organisms that appear far removed from the change. One example is the interrelationships among species in forests in the eastern United States. Through these relationships, as shown in Figure 18-1, acorn production is connected to the spread of Lyme disease, an infection that can damage the human nervous system.

In most years, oak trees produce few or no acorns. Every few years, however, they produce a huge crop of acorns. The large number of acorns supports larger populations of deer and mice, which feed on acorns. Ticks feed on the blood of animals, so the tick population also increases. The increased number of ticks increases the chance that ticks will bite any humans in the forest. The bite of the deer tick can transmit the bacterium that causes Lyme disease to humans. So, in general, after a season of high acorn production, the cases of Lyme disease increase.

# ECOLOGICAL MODELS

Ecology is extremely complex and difficult to study. One way that ecologists deal with this complexity is to use **ecological models** to represent or describe the components of an ecological system. A model may be physical, conceptual, or mathematical. Ecologists construct models to help them understand environmental interactions and to make predictions about possible changes. These predictions can be tested by comparing them with observations from the natural world. Models are widely used to help plan and evaluate solutions to environmental problems. However, an ecological model may be limited in its application, because it cannot always account for the influence of every variable in a real environment.

# LEVELS OF ORGANIZATION

Scientists recognize a hierarchy of different levels of organization within organisms. Each organism is composed of one or more organs. Each organ is composed of tissues, which, in turn, are composed of cells, and so on. Likewise, ecologists recognize a hierarchy of organization in the environment, as illustrated in Figure 18-2.

Each level has unique properties that result from interactions between its components, so a complete study of ecology would look at all levels. But for practical reasons, ecologists often focus their research on one level of organization while recognizing that each level is influenced by processes at other levels.

## The Biosphere

The broadest, most inclusive level of organization is the **biosphere** (BIE-oh-SFIR), the thin volume of Earth and its atmosphere that supports life. All organisms are found within the biosphere. It is about 20 km (13 mi) thick and extends from about 8 to 10 km (5 to 6 mi) above the Earth's surface to the deepest parts of the oceans. In comparison, the Earth's diameter is about 12,700 km (7,900 mi), or more than 600 times the thickness of the biosphere. If Earth were the size of an apple, the biosphere would only be as thick as the apple's skin. Ecologists often describe the biosphere as a thin film of life covering an otherwise lifeless planet. Living things are not distributed evenly throughout the biosphere. Many organisms are found within a few meters of the surface of the land or oceans.

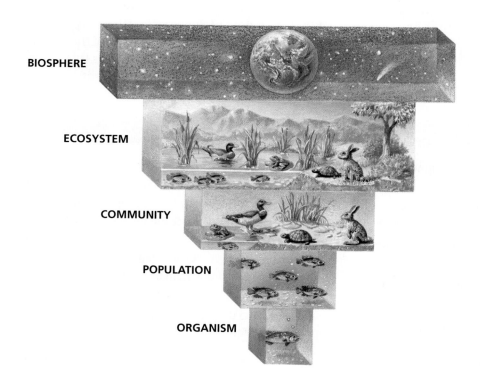

BIOSPHERE

ECOSYSTEM

COMMUNITY

POPULATION

ORGANISM

**FIGURE 18-2**

Ecology has been organized into five levels because of the complexity of the science. This diagram is a model illustrating the hierarchical organization of ecology.

## Ecosystems

The biosphere is composed of smaller units called ecosystems. An **ecosystem** (EK-oh-SIS-tuhm) includes all of the organisms and the non-living environment found in a particular place. Consider a pond ecosystem. It contains a variety of living things, such as fish, turtles, aquatic plants, algae, insects, and bacteria. These organisms interact in ways that affect their survival. For instance, insects and fish eat aquatic plants, and turtles eat fish. The pond ecosystem also includes all the nonliving (physical and chemical) aspects of the pond that influence its inhabitants. The chemical composition of the pond—its pH, its levels of dissolved oxygen and carbon dioxide, and its supply of nitrogen—helps to determine what kinds of organisms live in the pond and how abundant they are. A very important physical factor is the amount of sunlight the pond receives, because sunlight is the ultimate source of energy for the pond's inhabitants.

## Communities, Populations, and Organisms

Whereas an ecosystem contains both living and nonliving components, a community includes only species of organisms. A **community** is all the interacting organisms living in an area. For instance, all the fish, turtles, plants, algae, and bacteria in the pond described above make up a community. Although it is less inclusive than an ecosystem, a community is still very complex, and it may contain thousands of species. Ecologists studying a community often focus on how species interact and how these interactions influence the nature of the community. Remember that the word *community* has a specific meaning in biology that differs from its everyday meaning.

Below the community level of organization is the population level, where the focus is on the members of a single species. A **population** includes all the members of a species that live in one place at one time. An example of a population of flowers is shown in Figure 18-3. The simplest level of organization in ecology is that of the organism. Research at this level concentrates on the adaptations that allow organisms to overcome the challenges of their environment.

## SECTION 1 REVIEW

1. Explain why interdependence is an important theme in ecology.

2. Describe one example of the effects of interdependence upon organisms in their environment.

3. Why are models used so often in the science of ecology?

4. How does a population differ from a community?

5. Define the term *biosphere*.

6. List the five main levels of organization in ecology.

**CRITICAL THINKING**

7. **Predicting Results** Assuming wolves eat deer, how could a disease that kills a large portion of the wolf population affect the mice population in a forest ecosystem?

8. **Analyzing Concepts** Why is the amount of sunlight important to the animals in an ecosystem?

9. **Applying Information** Would bacteria that inhabit a cave deep inside Earth be considered part of the biosphere? Explain.

# ECOLOGY OF ORGANISMS

*The place where an organism lives is its **habitat**. But why does it live there and not elsewhere? What parts of its habitat does it use? The answers to these questions depend on an organism's evolutionary history, its abilities, and its needs.*

## SECTION 2

### OBJECTIVES

- **Compare** abiotic factors with biotic factors, and list two examples of each.
- **Describe** two mechanisms that allow organisms to survive in a changing environment.
- **Explain** the concept of the niche.

### VOCABULARY

habitat
biotic factor
abiotic factor
tolerance curve
acclimation
conformer
regulator
dormancy
migration
niche
generalist
specialist

## ECOSYSTEM COMPONENTS

Ecologists separate the environmental factors that influence an organism into two types. The living components of the environment are called **biotic** (bie-AHT-ik) **factors.** Biotic factors include all of the living things that affect the organism. The nonliving factors, called **abiotic** (AY-bie-AHT-ik) **factors,** are the physical and chemical characteristics of the environment.

### Biotic and Abiotic Factors

Abiotic factors include temperature, humidity, pH, salinity, oxygen concentration, amount of sunlight, availability of nitrogen, and precipitation. The importance of each factor varies from environment to environment. Abiotic and biotic factors are not independent; organisms change their environment and are influenced by those changes. For example, the availability of nitrogen in the soil affects how fast plants can grow, and plants affect nitrogen availability by absorbing nitrogen from the soil.

Abiotic factors are not constant. They vary from place to place and over time, as shown in Figure 18-4. Consider temperature, which is a very important abiotic factor. Temperature varies from hour to hour, from day to day, from season to season, and from place to place. Also important are the small differences in temperature within a habitat, such as the difference between an area in the shade of a tree and an area exposed to direct sunlight.

## ORGANISMS IN A CHANGING ENVIRONMENT

Each organism is able to survive within a limited range of environmental conditions. For example, an organism may be able to function only within a specific range of temperatures. It is possible to determine this range for an organism by measuring how efficiently it performs at different temperatures. A graph of performance versus values of an environmental variable, such as temperature, is called a **tolerance curve.**

**FIGURE 18-4**

These pictures show the same area of forest at different times of the year. On the top, the forest displays spring foliage. On the bottom, the same area is covered with snow in the winter.

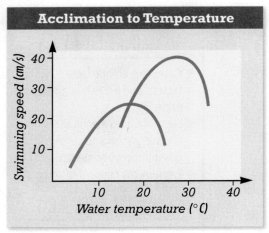

## Acclimation to Temperature

Swimming speed (m/s) vs. Water temperature (°C)

■ Fish raised at 5°C
■ Fish raised at 25°C

**FIGURE 18-5**

Goldfish raised at 25°C are acclimated to higher temperatures, so they have a different tolerance curve than the fish raised at 5°C do.

An organism can survive and function in conditions outside its optimal range, but its performance is greatly reduced. It cannot survive under conditions that fall outside its tolerance limits. An organism's range may be determined by the levels of one or more factors, such as pH, temperature, or salinity.

## Acclimation

Some organisms can adjust their tolerance to abiotic factors through the process of **acclimation** (AK-luh-MAY-shuhn). For example, goldfish raised at different temperatures have somewhat different tolerance curves, as shown in Figure 18-5. Be sure not to confuse *acclimation* with *adaptation*. Acclimation occurs within the lifetime of an individual organism. Adaptation is genetic change in a species or population that occurs from generation to generation over time.

## Control of Internal Conditions

Environments fluctuate in temperature, light, moisture, salinity, and other chemical factors. There are two ways for organisms to deal with some of these changes in their environment. **Conformers** are organisms that do not regulate their internal conditions; they change as their external environment changes. The internal conditions of a conformer remain within the optimal range only as long as environmental conditions remain within that range. In contrast, **regulators** are organisms that use energy to control some of their internal conditions. Regulators can keep an internal condition within the optimal range over a wide variety of environmental conditions.

## Escape from Unsuitable Conditions

Some species can survive unfavorable environmental conditions by escaping from them temporarily. For example, desert animals usually hide underground or in the shade during the hottest part of the day. Many desert species are active at night, when temperatures are much lower. A longer-term strategy is to enter a state of reduced activity, called **dormancy,** during periods of unfavorable conditions, such as winter or drought. Another strategy is to move to a more favorable habitat, called **migration.** An example of migration is the seasonal movements of birds, which spend spring and summer in cooler climates and migrate to warmer climates in the fall.

**www.scilinks.org**
Topic: Niche/Habitats
Keyword: HM61029

**SCiLINKS.** Maintained by the National Science Teachers Association

# THE NICHE

Species do not use or occupy all parts of their habitat at once. The specific role, or way of life, of a species within its environment is its **niche** (NICH). The niche includes the range of conditions that the species can tolerate, the resources it uses, the methods by which it obtains resources, the number of offspring it has, its time of reproduction, and all other interactions with its environment. Parts of a lion's niche are shown in Figure 18-6.

**Generalists** are species with broad niches; they can tolerate a range of conditions and use a variety of resources. An example of a generalist is the Virginia opossum, found across much of the United States. The opossum feeds on almost anything, from eggs and dead animals to fruits and plants. In contrast, species that have narrow niches are called **specialists.** An example is the koala of Australia, which feeds only on the leaves of a few species of eucalyptus trees.

Some species have more than one niche within a lifetime. For example, caterpillars eat the leaves of plants, but as adult butterflies, they feed on nectar.

**Word Roots and Origins**

*niche*

from the Old French *nichier,* meaning "to nest"

**FIGURE 18-6**

Plants and animals are able to share the same habitats because they each have different niches.

---

## SECTION 2 REVIEW

1. Distinguish between biotic and abiotic factors.

2. Explain how migration allows organisms to cope with a changing environment.

3. What does a tolerance curve indicate about an organism?

4. How does an organism's niche differ from its habitat?

5. Give examples of a generalist and a specialist not mentioned in the text above.

**CRITICAL THINKING**

6. **Analyzing Concepts** Why do different species never occupy exactly the same niche?

7. **Applying Information** If some of the resources in a habitat are destroyed, which would be more likely to survive, a generalist species or a specialist species? Explain.

8. **Drawing Conclusions** A small rodent species and a bird species are adapted to cold temperatures. How might each species survive a major temperature increase?

### OBJECTIVES

- **Summarize** the role of producers in an ecosystem.
- **Identify** several kinds of consumers in an ecosystem.
- **Explain** the important role of decomposers in an ecosystem.
- **Compare** the concept of a food chain with that of a food web.
- **Explain** why ecosystems usually contain only a few trophic levels.

### VOCABULARY

producer
chemosynthesis
gross primary productivity
biomass
net primary productivity
consumer
herbivore
carnivore
omnivore
detritivore
decomposer
trophic level
food chain
food web

# ENERGY TRANSFER

*All organisms need energy to carry out essential functions, such as growth, movement, maintenance and repair, and reproduction. In an ecosystem, energy flows from the sun to autotrophs, then to organisms that eat the autotrophs, and then to organisms that feed on other organisms. The amount of energy an ecosystem receives and the amount that is transferred from organism to organism affect the ecosystem's structure.*

## PRODUCERS

Autotrophs, which include plants and some kinds of protists and bacteria, manufacture their own food. Because autotrophs capture energy and use it to make organic molecules, they are called **producers.** Recall that *organic* molecules are molecules that contain carbon.

Most producers are photosynthetic, so they use solar energy to power the production of food. However, some autotrophic bacteria do not use sunlight as an energy source. These bacteria carry out **chemosynthesis** (KEE-moh-SIN-thuh-sis), in which they use energy stored in inorganic molecules to produce carbohydrates. In terrestrial ecosystems, plants are usually the major producers. In aquatic ecosystems, photosynthetic protists and bacteria are usually the major producers.

### Measuring Productivity

**Gross primary productivity** is the rate at which producers in an ecosystem capture the energy of sunlight by producing organic compounds. Photosynthetic producers use energy and carbon dioxide to make sugar, an energy-rich organic molecule. Some of the sugar is used for cellular respiration, some is used for maintenance and repair, and some is used for making new organic material through either growth or reproduction. Ecologists refer to the organic material that has been produced in an ecosystem as **biomass.** Producers add biomass to an ecosystem by making organic molecules.

Only energy stored as biomass is available to other organisms in the ecosystem. Ecologists often measure the rate at which biomass accumulates, called the **net primary productivity.** Net primary productivity is typically expressed in units of energy per unit area per year ($kcal/m^2/y$) or in units of dry organic mass per unit area per year ($g/m^2/y$). Net primary productivity equals gross primary productivity minus the rate of respiration in producers.

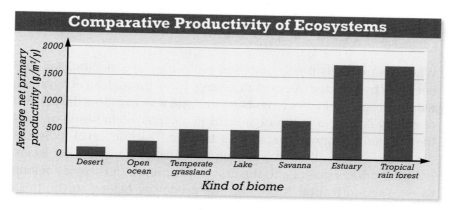

## Comparative Productivity of Ecosystems

(Average net primary productivity (g/m²/y) vs. Kind of biome)

Biomes shown: Desert, Open ocean, Temperate grassland, Lake, Savanna, Estuary, Tropical rain forest

**FIGURE 18-7**

As the histogram shows, the net primary productivity in a tropical rain forest is very similar to the net primary productivity in an estuary. Temperate grasslands and freshwater lakes are also very similar in productivity.

Figure 18-7 shows that net primary productivity can vary greatly between ecosystems. For example, the average net primary productivity in a tropical rain forest is 25 times greater than the rate in a desert of the same size. Although rain forests occupy only about 5 percent of Earth's surface, they account for almost 30 percent of the world's net primary productivity. Variations in three factors—light, temperature, and precipitation—account for most of the variation in productivity among terrestrial ecosystems. An increase in any of these variables usually leads to a productivity increase. In aquatic ecosystems, productivity is usually determined by only two factors: light and the availability of nutrients.

### Word Roots and Origins

**omnivore**

from the Latin *omnis,* meaning "all," and *-vore,* meaning "one who eats"

# CONSUMERS

All animals, most protists, all fungi, and many bacteria are heterotrophs. Unlike autotrophs, heterotrophs cannot manufacture their own food. Instead, they get energy by eating other organisms or organic wastes. Ecologically speaking, heterotrophs are **consumers.** They obtain energy by consuming organic molecules made by other organisms. Consumers can be grouped according to the type of food they eat. **Herbivores** eat producers. An antelope that eats grass is a herbivore. **Carnivores** eat other consumers. Lions, cobras, and praying mantises are examples of carnivores. **Omnivores** eat both producers and consumers. The grizzly bear, whose diet ranges from berries to salmon, is an omnivore.

**Detritivores** (dee-TRIET-uh-VAWRZ) are consumers that feed on the "garbage" of an ecosystem. This waste, or *detritus,* includes organisms that have recently died, fallen leaves, and animal wastes. The vulture shown in Figure 18-8 is a detritivore. Many bacteria and fungi are detritivores that cause decay by breaking down complex molecules into simpler molecules. So, they are specifically called **decomposers.** Some of the molecules released during decay are absorbed by the decomposers, and some are returned to the soil or water. Decomposers make the nutrients that were contained in detritus available again to the autotrophs in the ecosystem. Thus, the process of decomposition recycles chemical nutrients.

**FIGURE 18-8**

This turkey vulture, *Cathartes aura,* is a detritivore that consumes dead animals. Detritivores play the important role of cleaning up dead organisms and aiding decomposition.

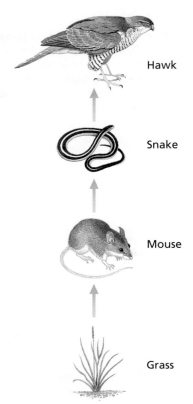

**FIGURE 18-9**

Energy is transferred from one organism to another in a food chain. The food chain shown above begins with a producer, grass, and ends with a carnivore, a hawk.

# ENERGY FLOW

When one organism eats another, molecules are metabolized and energy is transferred. As a result, energy flows through an ecosystem, moving from producers to consumers. One way to follow the pattern of energy flow is to group organisms in an ecosystem based on how they obtain energy. An organism's **trophic** (TRAHF-ik) **level** indicates the organism's position in a sequence of energy transfers. For example, all producers belong to the first trophic level. Herbivores belong to the second trophic level, and the predators belong to the third level. Most terrestrial ecosystems have only three or four trophic levels, whereas marine ecosystems often have more.

## Food Chains and Food Webs

A **food chain** is a single pathway of feeding relationships among organisms in an ecosystem that results in energy transfer. A food chain may begin with grass, which is a primary producer. The chain may continue with a consumer of grass seeds—a meadow mouse. Next, a carnivorous snake may kill and eat the mouse. A hawk then may eat the snake, as shown in Figure 18-9.

The feeding relationships in an ecosystem are usually too complex to be represented by a single food chain. Many consumers eat more than one type of food. In addition, more than one species of consumer may feed on the same organism. Many food chains interlink, and a diagram of the feeding relationships among all the organisms in an ecosystem would resemble a web, as shown in Figure 18-10. For this reason, the interrelated food chains in an ecosystem are called a **food web.**

**FIGURE 18-10**

Because a large carnivore may be at the top of several food chains, it is helpful to show as many feeding relationships as possible in a food-web diagram. Not all organisms are listed in the food web. For example, no decomposers are shown.

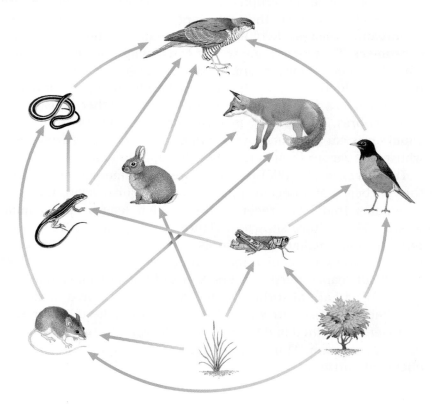

## Energy Transfer

Figure 18-11 represents the amount of energy stored as organic material in each trophic level in an ecosystem. The pyramid shape of the diagram indicates the low percentage of energy transfer from one level to the next. On average, 10 percent of the total energy consumed in one trophic level is incorporated into the organisms in the next.

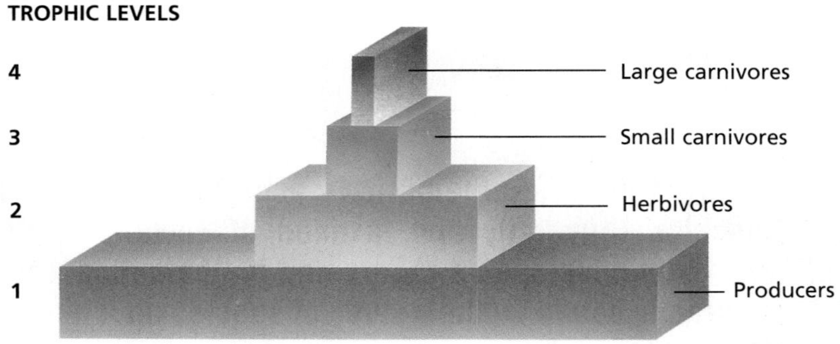

Why is the percentage of energy transfer so low? One reason is that some of the organisms in a trophic level escape being eaten. They eventually die and become food for decomposers, but the energy contained in their bodies does not pass to a higher trophic level. Even when an organism is eaten, some of the molecules in its body will be in a form that the consumer cannot break down and use. For example, a cougar cannot extract energy from the antlers, hooves, and hair of a deer. Also, the energy used by prey for cellular respiration cannot be used by predators to synthesize new biomass. Finally, no transformation or transfer of energy is 100 percent efficient. Every time energy is transformed, such as during the reactions of metabolism, some energy is lost as heat.

## Limitations of Trophic Levels

The low rate of energy transfer between trophic levels explains why ecosystems rarely contain more than a few trophic levels. Because only about 10 percent of the energy available at one trophic level is transferred to the next trophic level, there is not enough energy in the top trophic level to support more levels.

Organisms at the lowest trophic level are usually much more abundant than organisms at the highest level. In Africa, for example, you will see about 1,000 zebras, gazelles, and other herbivores for every lion or leopard you see, and there are far more grasses and shrubs than there are herbivores. Higher trophic levels contain less energy, so, they can support fewer individuals.

**TROPHIC LEVELS**

**FIGURE 18-11**

This diagram represents energy transfer through four trophic levels. The amount of energy transferred from one level to another can vary, so the structure shown can vary. What is always true, however, is that the top level is much smaller than the lowest level. Hence, energy-transfer diagrams are always roughly pyramid shaped.

---

## SECTION 3 REVIEW

1. How do producers and consumers obtain energy?

2. Name five types of consumers.

3. What important role do decomposers play in an ecosystem?

4. How does a food chain differ from a food web?

5. Give two reasons for the low rate of energy transfer within ecosystems.

6. Explain why food chains usually do not exceed three to four levels.

**CRITICAL THINKING**

7. **Predicting Results** Describe the probable effects on an ecosystem if all the plants were to die. What if all the decomposers were to die?

8. **Evaluating Models** A student has modeled a terrestrial ecosystem with seven trophic levels. Is this number reasonable? Explain.

9. **Analyzing Concepts** Explain why the same area can support a greater number of herbivores than carnivores.

# Science in Action

## Testing a Theory of Biogeography

In the 1960s, mathematical ecologist Robert H. MacArthur of Princeton University and taxonomist Edward O. Wilson of Harvard University developed a theory and mathematical model of island biogeography based on their study of species on islands. This model, and others inspired by it, is used to explain patterns of species distribution around the world.

**Robert H. MacArthur**

**Edward O. Wilson**

### HYPOTHESIS: The Number of Species on Any Island Is Constant

Ant biologist Edward O. Wilson (1929–) and mathematical ecologist Robert H. MacArthur (1930–1972) were both interested in community patterns within nature. Shortly after they met, they decided to work together on a study of species on islands.

Wilson noticed that the number of ant species on an island correlate with the size of the island. He also noticed that when a new ant species arrives on an island, one of the species already on the island becomes extinct. However, the total number of ant species remains constant. Wilson and MacArthur hypothesized that islands have a constant number of species. They proposed that the number of species on an island reflects an equilibrium—a balance between the rate at which new species colonize the island and the rate at which established species become extinct.

### METHOD: Construct and Test a Model

MacArthur and Wilson developed a mathematical model to explain their observations. The mathematics of the theory is complex, but the broad outlines center on two observable patterns: (1) large islands have more species than small islands have and (2) remote islands—those located far from the mainland or from a larger island—have fewer species than less remote ones.

MacArthur and Wilson decided to test their model on Krakatau, an island in Indonesia on which a volcano had erupted in 1883, killing most forms of life on the island. The return of plant and animal life to the island had been carefully recorded since Krakatau was first revisited in 1886.

### RESULTS: Species Reached Equilibrium

After examining the records of bird life at Krakatau, they learned that the number of species had climbed to 27 before leveling off.

### CONCLUSION: Prediction Was Close

Using their model, MacArthur and Wilson predicted that at the point of equilibrium, the number of bird species would be about 30. Their prediction had come close.

### Recent Tests of Island Biogeography

More recent studies of islands, such as those in the Sea of Cortez, suggest that many models of island biogeography may be required to explain patterns of species distributions. Researchers have generated alternative models that account for factors such as island history, climate, and species interactions.

*When the volcano that forms the island of Krakatau erupted in the 1880s, it destroyed most life on the island. As life returned, scientists had a unique opportunity to study ecology in action.*

### REVIEW

1. Describe MacArthur and Wilson's model of island biogeography.

2. Summarize the results from testing the model on Krakatau.

3. **Critical Thinking** Suggest how island factors might prevent equilibrium from being reached in MacArthur and Wilson's model.

**internet** connect

**www.scilinks.org**
**Topic:** Island
Biogeography
**Keyword: HM61693**

SCI LINKS. Maintained by the National Science Teachers Association

# ECOSYSTEM RECYCLING

*As energy and matter flow through an ecosystem, matter must be recycled and reused. Substances such as water, carbon, nitrogen, calcium, and phosphorus each pass between the living and nonliving worlds through* **biogeochemical cycles.**

## THE WATER CYCLE

Water is crucial to life. Cells contain 70 to 90 percent water, and water provides the environment in which most of life's chemical reactions occur. The availability of water is one of the key factors that regulate the productivity of terrestrial ecosystems. However, very little of the available water on Earth is trapped within living things at any given time. Bodies of water, such as lakes, rivers, streams, and oceans, contain a substantial percentage of Earth's water. The atmosphere also contains water—in the form of water vapor. In addition, some water is found below ground. Water in the soil or in underground formations of porous rock is known as **groundwater.**

The movement of water between these various reservoirs, known as the **water cycle,** is illustrated in Figure 18-12. Three important processes in the water cycle are evaporation, transpiration, and precipitation.

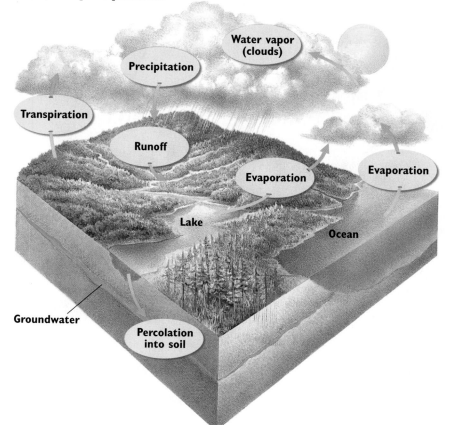

**FIGURE 18-12**

In the water cycle, water falls to Earth's surface as precipitation. Some water reenters the atmosphere by evaporation and transpiration. Some water runs into streams, lakes, rivers, and oceans. Other water seeps through the soil and becomes groundwater. Follow the pathways of the water cycle in the figure.

## Quick Lab

### Modeling Groundwater

**Materials** disposable gloves, lab apron, 3 L plastic bottle (cut in half), small stones (250 mL), dry sod with grass, water, graduated cylinder, 500 mL beaker

**Procedure**

1. Put on your lab apron, goggles, and disposable gloves.
2. Invert the top half of the plastic bottle, and place it inside the bottom half of the bottle to form a column.
3. Place the stones in the bottom of the inverted top half of the bottle. Place a chunk of dry sod with grass on top of the stones.
4. Pour 250 mL of water over the sod, and observe how the water penetrates the soil and moves through the column.
5. When the water is no longer draining, remove the top half of the column, and pour the water from the bottom of the column into a beaker. Measure the volume of liquid in the beaker.

**Analysis** What is the volume of the water that drained through the sod? How much of the water remained in the soil? Where does the water go when applied to a real lawn or crop? What might the fate of fertilizer or pesticides be that are applied to a lawn or crop?

**FIGURE 18-13**

Carbon exists in the atmosphere as carbon dioxide. Cellular respiration, combustion, and decomposition of organic matter are the three major sources of carbon dioxide in the short-term carbon cycle. By burning large amounts of fossil fuels, humans are releasing carbon dioxide from a long-term reservoir and increasing the amount of carbon dioxide in the atmosphere.

Evaporation adds water as vapor to the atmosphere. Heat causes water to evaporate from bodies of water, from the soil, and from the bodies of living things. The process by which water evaporates from the leaves of plants in terrestrial ecosystems is called **transpiration.** Transpiration causes plants to take in water through their roots to replace the water that is being lost through their leaves. Animals also participate in the water cycle. Animals drink water or obtain it from their food. They release this water when they breathe, sweat, or excrete.

Water leaves the atmosphere through precipitation. The amount of water the atmosphere can hold depends on abiotic factors, such as temperature and air pressure. Once the atmosphere becomes saturated with water vapor, precipitation occurs in the form of rain, snow, sleet, hail, or fog.

## THE CARBON CYCLE

Photosynthesis and cellular respiration form the basis of the short-term **carbon cycle,** illustrated in Figure 18-13. In photosynthesis, plants and other autotrophs use carbon dioxide ($CO_2$), along with water and solar energy, to make carbohydrates. Both autotrophs and heterotrophs use oxygen to break down carbohydrates during cellular respiration. The byproducts of cellular respiration are carbon dioxide and water. Decomposers release carbon dioxide into the atmosphere when they break down organic compounds.

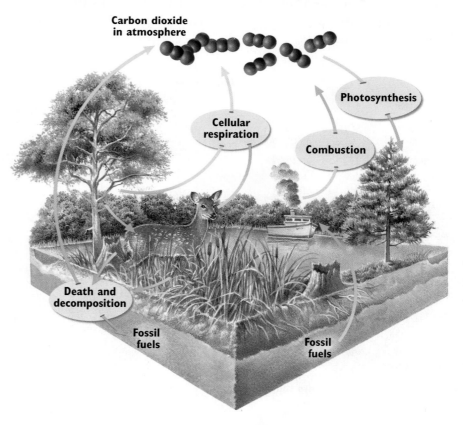

Carbon dioxide in atmosphere

Photosynthesis

Cellular respiration

Combustion

Death and decomposition

Fossil fuels

Fossil fuels

## Human Influences on the Carbon Cycle

In the last 150 years, the concentration of atmospheric carbon dioxide has risen more than 30 percent. Humans contribute to this increase by burning fossil fuels and other organic matter. Our industrial society depends on the energy released by the burning of fossil fuels—coal, oil, and natural gas. Fossil fuels are the remains of organisms that have been transformed by decay, heat, and pressure into energy-rich molecules. Burning releases the energy in these molecules, but it also releases carbon dioxide. When large areas of forest are burned each year to clear land for agriculture, less vegetation remains to absorb carbon dioxide from the atmosphere through photosynthesis.

# NITROGEN CYCLE

All organisms need nitrogen to make proteins and nucleic acids. The complex pathway that nitrogen follows in an ecosystem is called the **nitrogen cycle,** as shown in Figure 18-14. Nitrogen gas, $N_2$, makes up about 78 percent of the atmosphere, so it might seem that it would be readily available for living things. However, most plants can use nitrogen only in the form of nitrate. The process of converting $N_2$ gas to nitrate is called **nitrogen fixation.**

Most organisms rely on **nitrogen-fixing bacteria** to transform nitrogen gas into a usable form. These bacteria live in the soil and inside swellings on the roots of some kinds of plants, such as beans, peas, clover, and alfalfa. These plants supply carbohydrates for the bacteria, and the bacteria produce usable nitrogen for the plant. Additional nitrogen is released into the soil.

**FIGURE 18-14**

This figure shows the cycling of nitrogen within a terrestrial ecosystem. Bacteria are responsible for many of the steps in the nitrogen cycle, including the conversion of atmospheric nitrogen into ammonium. Nitrogen-fixing bacteria live in the soil or in the roots of plants. These bacteria convert nitrogen gas into ammonium. Other bacteria convert the ammonium into nitrates. Plants take up the nitrates produced by the bacteria. Animals get nitrogen by eating plants or other animals.

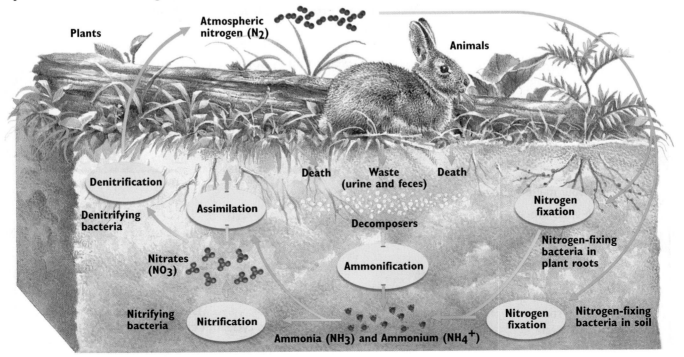

## Recycling Nitrogen

The bodies of dead organisms contain nitrogen, mainly in proteins and nucleic acids. Urine and dung also contain nitrogen. Decomposers break down these materials and release the nitrogen they contain as ammonia, $NH_3$, which in soil becomes ammonium, $NH_4^+$. This process is known as **ammonification.** Through this process, nitrogen is again made available to other organisms.

Soil bacteria take up ammonium and oxidize it into nitrites, $NO_2^-$, and nitrates, $NO_3^-$, in a process called **nitrification.** The erosion of nitrate-rich rocks also releases nitrates into an ecosystem. Plants use nitrates to form amino acids. Nitrogen is returned to the atmosphere through **denitrification.** Denitrification occurs when anaerobic bacteria break down nitrates and release nitrogen gas into the atmosphere. Plants can absorb nitrates from the soil, but animals cannot. Animals obtain nitrogen in the same way they obtain energy—by eating plants and other organisms and then digesting the proteins and nucleic acids.

# PHOSPHORUS CYCLE

Phosphorus is an element that is an essential material needed by animals to form bones, teeth, and parts of molecules, such as DNA and RNA. Plants get the phosphorus they need from soil and water, whereas animals get their phosphorus by eating plants or other animals. The **phosphorus cycle** is the movement of phosphorus from the environment to organisms and then back to the environment. This cycle is slow and does not normally occur in the atmosphere, because phosphorus rarely occurs as a gas.

When rocks erode, small amounts of phosphorus dissolve as phosphate, $PO_4^{3-}$, in soil and water. Plants absorb phosphorus in the soil through their roots. Phosphorus is also added to soil and water when excess phosphorus is excreted in wastes from organisms and when organisms die and decompose. Some phosphorus applied to fields as fertilizer washes off the land into streams and groundwater.

## SECTION 4 REVIEW

1. Identify four major biogeochemical cycles.

2. Through what process does most water vapor enter the atmosphere?

3. Outline the steps of the carbon cycle.

4. Describe the role of decomposers in the nitrogen cycle.

5. Identify the sources of phosphorus in the phosphorus cycle.

**CRITICAL THINKING**

6. **Inferring Relationships** How might the removal of vegetation affect oxygen levels in the atmosphere?

7. **Making Comparisons** Identify the role of bacteria in the carbon, nitrogen, and phosphorus cycles.

8. **Analyzing Concepts** Explain the statement that nutrients cycle, but energy flows.

# CHAPTER HIGHLIGHTS

## SECTION 1  Introduction to Ecology

- Species interact with both other species and their nonliving environment.
- Interdependence is a theme in ecology, and states that one change can affect all species in an ecosystem.
- Ecological models help to explain the environment.
- Ecology is usually organized into five levels: organism, population, community, ecosystem, and biosphere.

**Vocabulary**

ecology (p. 359)
interdependence (p. 359)
ecological model (p. 360)
biosphere (p. 361)
ecosystem (p. 362)
community (p. 362)
population (p. 362)

## SECTION 2  Ecology of Organisms

- Both biotic, or living, factors and abiotic, or nonliving, factors influence organisms. Examples of nonliving things are climate, sunlight, and pH.
- A niche is a way of life, or a role in an ecosystem.
- Some species survive unfavorable environmental conditions by becoming dormant or by migrating.

**Vocabulary**

habitat (p. 363)
biotic factor (p. 363)
abiotic factor (p. 363)
tolerance curve (p. 363)
acclimation (p. 364)
conformer (p. 364)
regulator (p. 364)
dormancy (p. 365)
migration (p. 365)
niche (p. 365)
generalist (p. 365)
specialist (p. 365)

## SECTION 3  Energy Transfer

- Most producers are photosynthetic and make carbohydrates by using energy from the sun.
- Consumers obtain energy by eating other organisms and include herbivores, omnivores, carnivores, detritivores, and decomposers.
- Decomposers feed on dead organisms and wastes, which releases the nutrients back into the environment.
- A single pathway of energy transfer is a food chain. A network showing all paths of energy transfer is a food web.
- Ecosystems contain only a few trophic levels because there is a low rate of energy transfer between each level.

**Vocabulary**

producer (p. 366)
chemosynthesis (p. 366)
gross primary
  productivity (p. 366)
biomass (p. 366)
net primary
  productivity (p. 366)
consumer (p. 367)
herbivore (p. 367)
carnivore (p. 367)
omnivore (p. 367)
detritivore (p. 367)
decomposer (p. 367)
trophic level (p. 368)
food chain (p. 368)
food web (p. 368)

## SECTION 4  Ecosystem Recycling

- Key processes in the water cycle are evaporation, transpiration, and precipitation.
- Photosynthesis and cellular respiration are the two main steps in the carbon cycle.
- Nitrogen-fixing bacteria are important in the nitrogen cycle because they change nitrogen gas into a usable form of nitrogen for plants.
- Phosphorus moves from phosphate deposited in rock, to the soil, to living organisms, and finally to the ocean.

**Vocabulary**

biogeochemical cycle (p. 371)
groundwater (p. 371)
water cycle (p. 371)
transpiration (p. 372)
carbon cycle (p. 372)
nitrogen cycle (p. 373)
nitrogen fixation (p. 373)
nitrogen-fixing
  bacteria (p. 373)
ammonification (p. 374)
nitrification (p. 374)
denitrification (p. 374)
phosphorus cycle (p. 374)

## USING VOCABULARY

1. For each pair of terms, explain how the meanings of the terms differ.
   a. *conformer* and *regulator*
   b. *community* and *ecosystem*
   c. *migration* and *dormancy*
   d. *nitrogen fixation* and *ammonification*

2. Use the following terms in the same sentence: *producer, consumer, herbivore, omnivore, carnivore, detritivore,* and *decomposer*.

3. **Word Roots and Origins** The word *transpiration* is derived from the Latin *trans*, which means "through," and *spirare*, which means "breathe." Using this information, explain why the term *transpiration* is a good name for the process it describes.

## UNDERSTANDING KEY CONCEPTS

4. **Explain** how an understanding of interdependence in ecosystems might be important to public health officials.

5. **Evaluate** how models are valuable to ecologists.

6. **Describe** some limitations of ecological models.

7. **Identify** five levels of organization in ecology.

8. **Propose** two examples of biotic factors and abiotic factors.

9. **Explain** the ecological concept of a niche.

10. **Distinguish** between conformers and regulators in how they deal with environmental change.

11. **Compare** photosynthetic and nonphotosynthetic producers.

12. **Distinguish** between a herbivore, a carnivore, and an omnivore.

13. **State** an example of each of the following: a herbivore, a carnivore, and an omnivore.

14. **Explain** the importance of decomposers in an ecosystem.

15. **Describe** why a food web is a more complete picture of the feeding relationships in an ecosystem than a food chain is.

16. **Identify** the reasons why most ecosystems normally contain only a few trophic levels.

17. **Compare** the transfer of energy with the transfer of nutrients in an ecosystem.

18. **Explain** how plants return water to the atmosphere as part of the water cycle.

19. **Describe** two processes in the carbon cycle.

20. **List** the mutual benefits in the association between nitrogen-fixing bacteria and the plants that they inhabit.

21. **Summarize** the phosphorus cycle.

22. **CONCEPT MAPPING** Use the following terms to create a concept map that shows some of the processes involved in the water cycle: *evaporation, precipitation, transpiration,* and *condensation*.

## CRITICAL THINKING

23. **Interpreting Graphics** Examine the diagram below of a tolerance curve. Briefly describe the conditions in each zone of tolerance and the reactions a species may have to them.

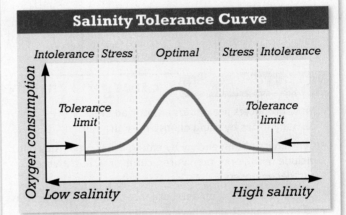

**Salinity Tolerance Curve**

24. **Relating Concepts** Nitrogen, water, phosphorus, and carbon are recycled and reused within an ecosystem, but energy is not. Explain why energy cannot be recycled.

25. **Drawing Conclusions** In the fall, many kinds of songbirds migrate from the United States to Central America or South America. Explain the benefits of migration for songbirds. What are some possible costs of this behavior?

26. **Analyzing Concepts** Ecologists have identified several characteristics that increase the likelihood that a species will become extinct. Specialization is one such characteristic. Explain why a very specialized species is likely to be more vulnerable to extinction.

27. **Making Models** Farmers often grow alfalfa, clover, or bean plants in fields after they have grown a grain crop. Explain this practice in terms of biochemistry.

# Standardized Test Preparation

**DIRECTIONS:** Choose the letter of the answer choice that best answers the question.

1. What are the levels of organization in ecology?
   **A.** cell, tissue, organ, organ system, body
   **B.** organ, organism, population, community
   **C.** organism, population, community, ecosystem, biosphere
   **D.** population, habitat, ecosystem, biogeochemical system, planet

2. What makes up an ecosystem?
   **F.** all the habitat types on Earth
   **G.** all parts of Earth where life exists
   **H.** all members of a species in the same area
   **J.** all the living and nonliving factors in an environment

3. Which of the following are abiotic factors?
   **A.** plants
   **B.** animals
   **C.** sunlight
   **D.** microorganisms

4. How do decomposers benefit an ecosystem?
   **F.** by returning nutrients to the soil
   **G.** by manufacturing energy from sunlight
   **H.** by removing excess nutrients from the soil
   **J.** by removing predators from the ecosystem

5. Which organisms are most critical in the nitrogen cycle?
   **A.** plants
   **B.** nitrates
   **C.** animals
   **D.** bacteria

**INTERPRETING GRAPHICS:** The illustration below represents a trophic pyramid. Use the illustration to answer the question that follows.

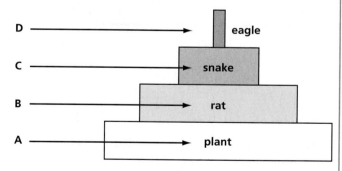

6. What is the term for the kinds of organisms that make up the trophic level labeled C?
   **F.** producers
   **G.** consumers
   **H.** detritivores
   **J.** decomposers

**DIRECTIONS:** Complete the following analogy.

7. bear : omnivore :: vulture :
   **A.** producer
   **B.** herbivore
   **C.** detritivore
   **D.** decomposer

**INTERPRETING GRAPHICS:** The illustration below represents a food chain. Use the illustration to answer the questions that follow.

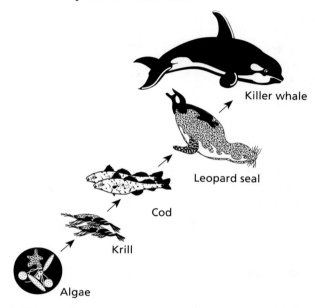

8. What role do the krill have in this food chain?
   **F.** They are producers.
   **G.** They are consumers.
   **H.** They are detritivores.
   **J.** They are decomposers.

## SHORT RESPONSE

Give two reasons why the destruction of tropical rain forests can contribute to an increase in carbon dioxide levels in the atmosphere.

## EXTENDED RESPONSE

Some species are generalized with regard to their niche, and other species are specialized.

*Part A* Compare the niche of a generalist species with one of a specialist species.

*Part B* Predict how two different herbivores can share the same plant resource.

**Test TIP** If you are not sure about the spelling of certain words when answering the short or extended response questions, look at the question itself to see if the same word appears in the question.

# Observing Habitat Selection

## OBJECTIVES

- Assess the effect of light on habitat selection by brine shrimp.

## PROCESS SKILLS

- observing
- measuring
- collecting data
- organizing data
- analyzing data

## MATERIALS

- safety goggles
- marking pen
- clear, flexible plastic tubing (44 cm long)
- 4 test tubes with stoppers
- test-tube rack
- 2 corks to fit tubing
- graduated cylinder
- funnel
- brine shrimp culture
- aluminum foil
- 3 screw clamps
- 1 pipet
- Petri dish
- methyl cellulose
- fluorescent lamp or grow light
- 14 pieces of screen or thin cloth
- calculator

## Background

1. Recall that a species' habitat is a specific area where it lives.
2. A species habitat selection depends on how well the location fits within the species' tolerance range. The more optimal all limiting factors are within a portion of an organism's range, the more likely the organism is to select that area for its habitat.
3. What limiting factors might be involved in habitat selection?
4. What is a niche?

## PART A Setting Up

1. Mark the plastic tubing at 12 cm, 22 cm, and 32 cm from one end so that you will have the tube divided into four sections. Starting at one end, label the sections 1, 2, 3, and 4. Label four test tubes 1, 2, 3, and 4.
2. Place a cork in one end of the tubing. Use a graduated cylinder and a funnel to transfer about 50 mL of brine shrimp culture into the tubing. Cork the open end, and lay the tubing on the desktop.
3. You and your partner will complete either Part B or Part C and then share your results with the other students on your team. **CAUTION You will be working with live animals. Be sure to treat them gently and to follow directions carefully.**

## PART B Control Group

1. Cover the tubing with aluminum foil, and let it remain undisturbed for 30 minutes. While you are waiting, create a data table like Table A, below, in your lab report to record the numbers of shrimp in each section of the tubing.

### TABLE A CONTROL GROUP

| Test tube number | Count 1 | Count 2 | Count 3 | Count 4 | Count 5 | Average number of shrimp in test tube |
|---|---|---|---|---|---|---|
| 1 | | | | | | |
| 2 | | | | | | |
| 3 | | | | | | |
| 4 | | | | | | |

2. After 30 minutes have passed, attach screw clamps to each spot that you marked on the tubing. While your partner holds the corks firmly in place, tighten the middle clamp first, and then tighten the outer clamps.
3. Immediately pour the contents of each section of tubing into the test tube labeled with the corresponding number.

4. ⬥ ⬥ **CAUTION Put on safety goggles before handling methyl cellulose. If you get methyl cellulose in your eyes, immediately flush it out at the eyewash station while calling to your teacher.** Stopper test tube 1, and invert it gently to distribute the shrimp. Use a pipet to draw a 1 mL sample of shrimp culture and transfer the culture to a Petri dish. Add a few drops of methyl cellulose to the Petri dish to slow down the shrimp. Count the live shrimp, and record the count in your lab report.

5. ⬥ Dispose of the shrimp as your teacher directs. Repeat step 4 four more times for a total of five counts from test tube 1.

6. Calculate the average number of shrimp in test tube 1, and record the result in the data table you made in your lab report.

7. Repeat steps 4–6 for the contents of each of the remaining test tubes.

8. ⬥ ⬥ Clean up your materials, and wash your hands before leaving the lab.

9. In your lab report, make a histogram showing the total number of shrimp you counted in each section of tubing.

## PART C Experimental Group

1. Set a fluorescent lamp 20 cm away from the tubing.

2. Cover section 1 of the tubing with eight layers of screen. Place four layers of screen on section 2 and two layers of screen on section 3. Leave section 4 uncovered. Leave this setup in place for 30 minutes. While you are waiting, create a data table in your lab report like Table B, below, to record the numbers of shrimp in each section of the tubing.

### TABLE B EXPERIMENTAL GROUP

| Test tube number | Count 1 | Count 2 | Count 3 | Count 4 | Count 5 | Average number of shrimp in test tube |
|---|---|---|---|---|---|---|
| 1 | | | | | | |
| 2 | | | | | | |
| 3 | | | | | | |
| 4 | | | | | | |

3. After 30 minutes have passed, attach screw clamps to each spot that you marked on the tubing. While your partner holds the corks firmly in place, tighten the middle clamp first, and then tighten the outer clamps.

4. Immediately pour the contents of each section of tubing into the test tube labeled with the corresponding number.

5. ⬥ ⬥ **CAUTION Put on safety goggles before handling methyl cellulose. If you get methyl cellulose in your eyes, immediately flush it out at the eyewash station while calling to your teacher.** Stopper test tube 1, and invert it gently to distribute the shrimp. Use a pipet to draw a 1 mL sample of shrimp culture and transfer the culture to a Petri dish. Add a few drops of methyl cellulose to the Petri dish to slow down the shrimp. Count the live shrimp, and record the count in your lab report.

6. ⬥ Dispose of the shrimp as your teacher directs. Repeat step 5 four more times for a total of five counts from test tube 1.

7. Calculate the average number of shrimp in test tube 1, and record the result in the data table you made in your lab report.

8. Repeat steps 5–7 for the contents of each of the remaining test tubes.

9. ⬥ ⬥ Clean up your materials, and wash your hands before leaving the lab.

10. In your lab report, make a histogram showing the number of shrimp in each section of tubing. Identify each section with the amount of screen.

## Analysis and Conclusions

1. Describe the differences between the histogram of the control group and the histogram of the experimental group.

2. Why was a control (Part B) necessary?

3. How did the brine shrimp react to differences in light? Justify your conclusion.

## Further Inquiry

Design an experiment to test the reaction of brine shrimp to a gradient of heat.

# POPULATIONS

These bottlenose dolphins, *Tursiops truncatus*, are part of a population.

**SECTION 1** *Understanding Populations*

**SECTION 2** *Measuring Populations*

**SECTION 3** *Human Population Growth*

BIOLOGY INTERACTIVE TUTOR

Unit 7—Ecosystem Dynamics
Topic 2

# UNDERSTANDING POPULATIONS

*The human population of the world was about 6.3 billion in 2003, over three times its size in 1900. During this period of rapid human population growth, populations of many other species have decreased dramatically. Will the human population continue to grow? Will populations of other species continue to get smaller? An understanding of populations is crucial to answering these questions.*

## PROPERTIES OF POPULATIONS

A **population** is a group of organisms that belong to the same species and live in a particular place at the same time. All of the bass living in a pond during a certain period of time make up a population because they are isolated in the pond and do not interact with bass living in other ponds. The boundaries of a population may be imposed by a feature of the environment, such as a lake shore, or they can be arbitrarily chosen to simplify a study of the population. The humans shown in Figure 19-1 are part of the population of a city. The properties of populations differ from those of individuals. An individual may be born, it may reproduce, or it may die. A population study focuses on a population as a whole—how many individuals are born, how many die, and so on.

### Population Size

A population's size is the number of individuals that the population contains. Size is a fundamental and important population property but can be difficult to measure directly. If a population is small and composed of immobile organisms, such as plants, its size can be determined simply by counting individuals. Often, though, individuals are too abundant, too widespread, or too mobile to be counted easily, and scientists must estimate the number of individuals in the population.

Suppose that a scientist wants to know how many oak trees live in a 10 km$^2$ patch of forest. Instead of searching the entire patch of forest and counting all the oak trees, the scientist could count the trees in a smaller section of the forest, such as a 1 km$^2$ area. The scientist could then use this value to estimate the population of the larger area.

## SECTION 1

### OBJECTIVES

- **Describe** the main properties that scientists measure when they study populations.
- **Compare** the three general patterns of population dispersion.
- **Identify** the measurements used to describe changing populations.
- **Compare** the three general types of survivorship curves.

### VOCABULARY

**population**
**population density**
**dispersion**
**birth rate**
**death rate**
**life expectancy**
**age structure**
**survivorship curve**

**FIGURE 19-1**

A population can be widely distributed, as Earth's human population is, or confined to a small area, as species of fish in a lake are.

**FIGURE 19-2**

These migrating wildebeests in East Africa are too numerous and mobile to be counted. Scientists must use sampling methods at several locations to monitor changes in the population size of the animals.

**Word Roots and Origins**

*dispersion*

from the Latin *dis-*, meaning "out," and *spargere*, meaning "to scatter"

If the small patch contains 25 oaks, an area 10 times larger would likely contain 10 times as many oak trees. A similar kind of sampling technique might be used to estimate the size of the population shown in Figure 19-2. To use this kind of estimate, the scientist must assume that the distribution of individuals in the entire population is the same as that in the sampled group. Estimates of population size are based on many such assumptions, so all estimates have the potential for error.

## Population Density

**Population density** measures how crowded a population is. This measurement is always expressed as the number of individuals per unit of area or volume. For example, the population density of humans in the United States is about 30 people per square kilometer. Table 19-1 shows the population sizes and densities of humans in several countries in 2003. These estimates are calculated for the total land area. Some areas of a country may be sparsely populated, while other areas are very densely populated.

## Dispersion

A third population property is dispersion (di-SPUHR-zhuhn). **Dispersion** is the spatial distribution of individuals within the population. In a *clumped* distribution, individuals are clustered together. In a *uniform* distribution, individuals are separated by a fairly consistent distance. In a *random* distribution, each individual's location is independent of the locations of other individuals in the population. Figure 19-3 illustrates the three possible patterns of dispersion.

Clumped distributions often occur when resources such as food or living space are clumped. Clumped distributions may also occur because of a species' social behavior, such as when animals gather into herds or flocks. Uniform distributions may result from social behavior in which individuals within the same habitat stay as far away from each other as possible. For example, a bird may locate its nest so as to maximize the distance from the nests of other birds.

| TABLE 19-1 **Population Size and Density of Some Countries** | | |
|---|---|---|
| **Country** | **Population size (in millions)** | **Population density (in individuals/km²)** |
| China | 1,289 | 135 |
| India | 1,069 | 325 |
| United States | 292 | 30 |
| Russia | 146 | 8 |
| Japan | 128 | 337 |
| Mexico | 105 | 54 |
| Kenya | 32 | 54 |
| Australia | 20 | 3 |

(a) RANDOM        (b) UNIFORM        (c) CLUMPED

The social interactions of birds called *gannets,* which are shown in Figure 19-3b, result in a uniform distribution. Each gannet chooses a small nesting area on the coast and defends it from other gannets. In this way, each gannet tries to maximize its distance from all of its neighbors, which causes a uniform distribution of individuals.

Few populations are truly randomly dispersed. Rather, they show degrees of clumping or uniformity. The dispersion pattern of a population sometimes depends on the scale at which the population is observed. The gannets shown in Figure 19-3b are uniformly distributed on a scale of a few meters. However, if the entire island on which the gannets live is observed, the distribution appears clumped because the birds live only near the shore.

**FIGURE 19-3**

The three dispersion patterns are *random* (a), *uniform* (b), and *clumped* (c). However, the observed dispersion of a population sometimes depends on the scale at which the population is observed.

# POPULATION DYNAMICS

All populations are dynamic—they change in size and composition over time. To understand these changes, scientists must know more than the population's size, density, and dispersion. One important measure is the **birth rate,** the number of births occurring in a period of time. In the United States, for example, there are about 4 million births per year. A second important measure is the **death rate,** or *mortality rate,* which is the number of deaths in a period of time. The death rate for the United States is about 2.6 million deaths per year. Another important statistic is **life expectancy,** or how long on average an individual is expected to live. In the United States in 2003, the life expectancy for a man was 74 years, and for a woman it was 80 years.

FIGURE 19-4

These two diagrams show the age structure by gender of two countries. A comparison indicates that Country A has a higher percentage of young people and a lower percentage of elderly people than Country B does.

## Age Structure of Country A and Country B

Country A

Male        Female

Country B

Male        Female

Age

80
60
40
20

7.5  5.0  2.5  0  2.5  5.0  7.5        5.0  2.5  0  2.5  5.0

*Percentage of Population*

## Age Structure

The distribution of individuals among different ages in a population is called **age structure.** Age structures are often presented in graphs, as in Figure 19-4. Many important population processes vary with age. In humans, very old individuals do not reproduce. If human populations have a high percentage of young individuals, they may have a greater potential for rapid growth.

## Patterns of Mortality

The mortality data of different species tend to match one of three curves on a graph, as shown in Figure 19-5. These curves are called **survivorship curves** because they show the probability that members of a population will survive to a certain age. In humans or elephants, for instance, the likelihood of dying is small until late in life, when mortality increases rapidly. This pattern of mortality produces the Type I survivorship curve. For other organisms, such as some species of birds, the probability of dying does not change throughout life, giving a linear, or Type II, survivorship curve. Finally, many organisms are very likely to die when young. If an individual survives this early period, however, it has a good chance of surviving to old age. This type of survivorship curve, called Type III, is characteristic of animals such as oysters and salmon, and of many insects.

**FIGURE 19-5**

Humans have a Type I survivorship curve. Some species of birds have a Type II survivorship curve. Some species of fish are examples of a Type III survivorship.

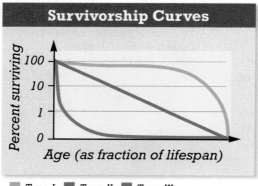

## Survivorship Curves

Percent surviving

100
10
1
0

*Age (as fraction of lifespan)*

■ Type I  ■ Type II  ■ Type III

## SECTION 1 REVIEW

1. Explain how two populations can be the same size but have different densities.

2. Explain how uniform distributions could result from social interactions between individuals.

3. How can the dispersion of one population be described as both uniform and clumped?

4. Explain what *birth rate* and *death rate* mean.

5. In Figure 19-4, which country has a higher percentage of elderly people?

6. Compare the three types of survivorship curves.

**CRITICAL THINKING**

7. **Relating Concepts** Explain why natural selection might favor a high reproduction rate in organisms with Type III survivorship curves.

8. **Analyzing Methods** Explain two difficulties an ecologist might have in counting a population of migratory birds. Develop and explain a method for estimating the size of such a population.

9. **Predicting Patterns** Which pattern of dispersion does the global human population have?

# MEASURING POPULATIONS

*Charles Darwin calculated that a single pair of elephants could increase to a population of 19 million individuals within 750 years. The fact that the world is not overrun with elephants is evidence that some factor or factors restrain the population growth of elephants. In this section you will study how populations grow and what factors limit their growth.*

### OBJECTIVES

- **Identify** the four processes that determine population growth.
- **Compare** the exponential model and the logistic model of population growth.
- **Differentiate** between density-dependent and density-independent regulation of populations.
- **Explain** why small populations are more vulnerable to extinction.

### VOCABULARY

growth rate
immigration
emigration
exponential model
limiting factor
logistic model
carrying capacity
density-independent factor
density-dependent factor
inbreeding

## POPULATION GROWTH RATE

Demographers, scientists who study population dynamics, define the **growth rate** of a population as the amount by which a population's size changes in a given time.

Whether a population grows, shrinks, or remains the same size depends on four processes: birth, death, emigration, and immigration. **Immigration** (IM-uh-GRAY-shuhn) is the movement of individuals into a population, and **emigration** (EM-i-GRAY-shuhn) is the movement of individuals out of the population. Two of these processes—birth and immigration—add individuals to a population, while the other two processes—death and emigration—subtract individuals from the population. For simplicity's sake, demographers usually assume that immigration and emigration are zero when calculating a population's growth rate. By making this assumption, they can describe a population's growth rate in mathematically simple terms.

### Population Size

It is customary for demographers to divide large populations into groups of 1,000 and to present data *per capita,* meaning per individual. Birth rates, death rates, and growth rates for a large population are usually expressed per capita. For example, if there are 52 births and 14 deaths per 1,000 individuals in a large population in one year, the birth rate would be $\frac{52}{1,000}$, or 0.052 births per capita per year. The death rate would be $\frac{14}{1,000}$, or 0.014 deaths per capita per year.

The growth rate can be found by the following simple equation:

$$\text{birth rate} - \text{death rate} = \text{growth rate}$$

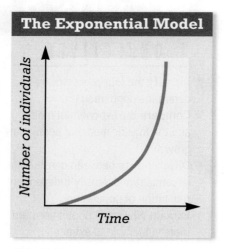

**The Exponential Model**

Number of individuals

Time

**FIGURE 19-6**

The graph of exponential population growth has a characteristic J shape. The exponential model indicates constantly increasing population growth.

**FIGURE 19-7**

The population increase of bacteria in the laboratory produces a characteristic graph of exponential growth. With this kind of graph, the size of the population of bacteria at any future time can be predicted if the culture is provided with unlimited resources, such as food.

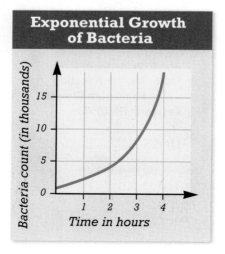

**Exponential Growth of Bacteria**

Bacteria count (in thousands)

15

10

5

0

1    2    3    4

Time in hours

Using the same example, we can calculate the per capita growth rate as follows:

0.052 (births per capita) − 0.014 (deaths per capita)
= 0.038 (growth per capita)

To find the number of new individuals that will be added to the population in a year, simply multiply the per capita growth rate by the number of individuals in the population. If the population in our example numbers 50,000, the population will increase by 1,900 individuals in one year.

$$0.038 \times 50,000 = 1,900$$

If the growth rate is a positive number, the population is increasing. If it is a negative number, the population is shrinking.

# THE EXPONENTIAL MODEL

As long as the birth rate of a population exceeds the death rate, the population size will continue to increase. At a steady, positive per capita growth rate, the population will add a larger number of individuals with each generation. So, a population can increase rapidly with even a small growth rate. A pattern of increase in number due to a steady growth rate is called *exponential growth*. The observation that populations can grow in this pattern is called the **exponential** (EKS-poh-NEN-shuhl) **model** of population growth.

One way to understand the exponential model is to study a graph of population size over time. A graph of exponential growth makes the characteristic J-shaped curve shown in Figure 19-6. With exponential growth, population size grows slowly when it is small, but growth speeds up as individuals join the population. The exponential model leads us to predict that the population size will increase indefinitely and by a greater number with each time period.

## Applying the Exponential Model

A scientific model is useful if it helps to predict or explain patterns that can be observed in reality. Indeed, the exponential model matches observed patterns of growth of real populations, but only under certain conditions and for limited periods of time. For example, a population of microorganisms can grow exponentially if provided with an abundance of food and space and if waste is removed. Figure 19-7 shows the growth of bacteria in a laboratory.

However, the exponential model does not apply to most populations. In natural environments, populations cannot grow indefinitely because the resources they depend on become scarce and harmful wastes accumulate. Any factor, such as space, that restrains the growth of a population is called a **limiting factor.** All populations are ultimately limited by their environment.

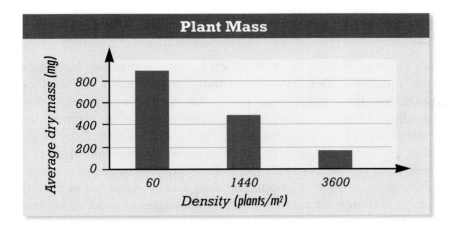

**Plant Mass**

*Average dry mass (mg)* vs *Density (plants/m²)*

FIGURE 19-8

The graph displays the results of an experiment that tested how the growth of a group of plants was affected under three conditions of crowding. Under the condition of least crowding (fewer plants per square meter), the plants were observed to grow larger on average.

As a population grows, competition among individuals for the shrinking supply of resources intensifies, and each individual, on average, obtains a smaller share. Thus, each individual's ability to fight off disease, grow, and reproduce decreases. As a result, the population's birth rate declines and death rate increases. Figure 19-8 shows how increasing population size affected the growth of a plant species in a limited area.

# THE LOGISTIC MODEL

Birth rates and death rates are not constant but vary with population size: birth rates decline and death rates rise as the population grows. The **logistic** (loh-JIS-tik) **model** of population growth builds on the exponential model but accounts for the influence of limiting factors. The logistic model includes a new term, **carrying capacity** (symbolized by $K$), the number of individuals the environment can support over a long period of time.

A graph of logistic growth looks like a stretched-out letter *S*. Examine Figure 19-9. When the population size is small, birth rates are high and death rates are low, and the population grows at very near the exponential rate. But as the population size approaches the carrying capacity, the population growth rate slows because of the falling birth rate and the increasing death rate. When a population size is at its carrying capacity, the birth rate equals the death rate and growth stops. This pattern of growth is known as *logistic growth*.

The logistic model, like the exponential model, contains some assumptions. One such assumption is that the carrying capacity is constant and does not fluctuate with environmental changes. In reality, carrying capacity does fluctuate. It is greater when prey is abundant, for instance, and smaller when prey is scarce. The logistic and exponential models are not universal representations of real populations, but they are an important tool that scientists use to explain population growth and regulation.

FIGURE 19-9

This graph of logistic population growth is typical of populations in new environments. In the first phase, the population shows rapid, nearly exponential growth. In the second phase, the growth rate slows until the carrying capacity, $K$, is reached. In the third phase, the population has become stable, neither increasing nor decreasing in size. Real populations may fit this pattern for some period of time but rarely remain stable.

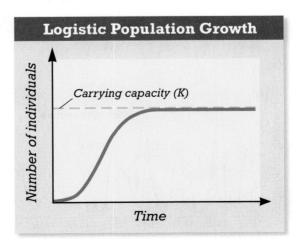

**Logistic Population Growth**

*Number of individuals* vs *Time*

Carrying capacity ($K$)

# POPULATION REGULATION

Two kinds of limiting factors, which control population size, have been identified. **Density-independent factors,** such as weather, floods, and fires, reduce the population by the same proportion, regardless of the population's size. For example, if a forest fire destroys a population of chipmunks, it does not matter if the population of chipmunks is 1 or 100. An unseasonable cold snap is a density-independent factor because its severity and duration are completely independent of population size. **Density-dependent factors** include resource limitations, such as shortages of food or nesting sites, and are triggered by increasing population density. With density-dependent factors, an individual's chance of surviving or reproducing depends on the number of individuals in the same area.

## Population Fluctuations

All populations fluctuate in size. Some population fluctuations are clearly linked to environmental changes. For example, a drought may reduce a population of deer living in a forest. Some population fluctuations are not obviously connected to environmental fluctuations, and explaining their occurrence is much more difficult. For example, consider the population changes shown in Figure 19-10. These cycles of change were first described by Charles S. Elton (1900–1991), one of the pioneers of ecology. Elton obtained more than 70 years of records showing the number of snowshoe hare pelts the Hudson's Bay Company of Canada purchased from trappers. He assumed that the number of pelts purchased in a year indicated the size of the snowshoe hare population. The records showed that the hare population underwent a very regular cycle, with about 10 years between peaks in population size. When Elton examined the records for the number of lynx pelts purchased, he found that the lynx, a medium-sized species of cat that preys on snowshoe hares, also followed a population cycle. The peaks in the lynx population usually occurred near the peaks in the hare population.

Elton thought that each species was the cause of the other's cycle. Thus, when the population of snowshoe hares increased, providing more food for the lynxes, the lynx population also increased. The increased lynx population then ate more hares, so the hare population decreased. With less food, more lynxes starved and the lynx population declined, allowing the hare population to increase and start the cycle over again. However, the observation that the same cycles occur in snowshoe hare populations living on islands without lynxes indicates that this explanation is insufficient. Another possible explanation is that the lynx cycle is dependent on the hare population but the hare cycle is dependent on some other factor.

**FIGURE 19-10**

The hare and the lynx (a) were observed by Elton to have parallel changes in their population cycles. The graph below (b) shows the data recorded by Elton supporting his idea that each animal controlled the other animal's cycle. You can see that the cycles fluctuate together. Because hares show the same population cycles when there are no lynxes present, it is now known that lynxes are not controlling factors in the hares' cycles.

(a)

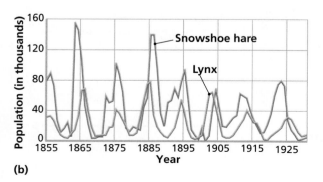

(b)

(a)

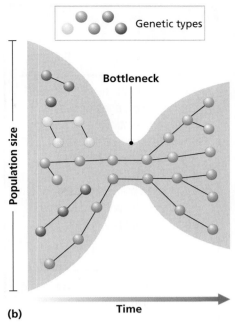

Genetic types

Bottleneck

Population size

Time

(b)

## Perils of Small Populations

The rapidly growing human population has caused extreme reductions in the populations of some other species and subspecies. For example, only about 200 Siberian tigers remain in the wild because of hunting and habitat destruction. Even greater reductions have been experienced by the California condor, which was once found throughout the southwestern United States. In the 1980s, the condor's wild population had been reduced to nine individuals, although recovery efforts have since increased the numbers.

Small populations, such as the cheetahs shown in Figure 19-11a, are particularly vulnerable to extinction. Environmental disturbances, such as storms, fires, floods, or disease outbreaks, can kill off the entire population or leave too few individuals to maintain the population. Also, the members of a small population may be descended from only a few individuals, increasing the likelihood of **inbreeding,** or mating with relatives. Inbreeding in small populations often leads to decreased genetic variability, as shown in Figure 19-11b. Over evolutionary time, populations with low variability are less likely to adapt to changing environmental conditions.

**FIGURE 19-11**

The genetic diversity of cheetahs (a) is so low that biologists think the cheetah population may have been reduced to a very small size in the past. Such a reduction is called a *genetic bottleneck,* illustrated in (b). The diagram shows how the genetic variation in a population can be reduced when the size of that population is reduced.

## SECTION 2 REVIEW

1. Explain the relationship between birth rate, death rate, and growth rate.

2. Explain the pattern described by the exponential model of population growth.

3. According to the logistic model, how do birth and death rates change with population size?

4. List two density-independent factors that could limit population growth.

**CRITICAL THINKING**

5. **Relating Concepts** Explain how inbreeding can threaten the survival of a small population.

6. **Predicting Results** What type of limiting factor is a disease that is transmitted by parasites?

7. **Evaluating Methods** What unknown factors might make it hard to predict the future size of the human population of a country?

### OBJECTIVES

- **Explain** how the development of agriculture changed the pattern of human population growth.
- **Describe** changes in human population size in the past 10,000 years.
- **Compare** observed patterns of population growth in developed and developing countries.

### VOCABULARY

hunter-gatherer lifestyle
agricultural revolution
developed country
developing country
demographic transition

**internet** connect

www.scilinks.org
**Topic:** History of
Population Growth
**Keyword:** HM60746

SCI
LINKS. Maintained by the
National Science
Teachers Association

# HUMAN POPULATION GROWTH

*In the time it takes you to read this chapter, the human population will grow by about 10,000 people. The rapid growth of the human population over the last several centuries is unprecedented in history. What caused this rapid growth? How long can it continue? This section examines these questions.*

## HISTORY OF HUMAN POPULATION GROWTH

From the origin of *Homo sapiens,* more than 500,000 years ago, until about 10,000–12,000 years ago, the human population grew very slowly. During this time, humans lived in small nomadic groups and obtained food by hunting animals and gathering roots, berries, nuts, shellfish, and fruits. This way of life is called the **hunter-gatherer lifestyle.** By studying the few hunter-gatherer societies that exist today, scientists have learned that a low rate of population growth results from small populations and high mortality rates. Population growth is slowed especially when mortality is high among infants and young children, because fewer individuals reach reproductive maturity.

### The Development of Agriculture

The hunter-gatherer lifestyle began to change about 10,000 to 12,000 years ago, when humans began to domesticate animals and cultivate certain plants for food. This dramatic change in lifestyle is called the **agricultural revolution,** and it led to profound changes in every aspect of life. Most important, the practice of agriculture greatly stabilized and increased the available food supply. As a result, the human population began to grow faster. About 10,000 years ago, there were between 2 million and 20 million people on Earth. By about 2,000 years ago, the population had increased to between 170 million and 330 million.

### The Population Explosion

As you can see in Figure 19-12, human population growth continued through the Middle Ages despite some short-term reversals. The outbreak of bubonic plague in 1347–1352 is thought to have killed about 25 percent of the population of Europe.

Human population growth began to accelerate after 1650, primarily because of a sharp decline in death rates. Reasons for this decline in death rates included better sanitation and hygiene, control of disease, increased availability of food, and improved economic conditions. While death rates fell, birth rates remained high, resulting in rapid population growth. The human population was about 500 million in 1650 and had risen to about 1 billion by 1800 and 2 billion by 1930.

Mortality rates fell sharply again in the decades immediately following World War II because of improvements in health and hygiene in the world's poorer countries. Birth rates in these countries remained high, pushing the per capita growth rate to its highest values. It took most of human history for the human population to reach 1 billion, but the population grew from 3 billion to 5 billion in just the 27 years between 1960 and 1987.

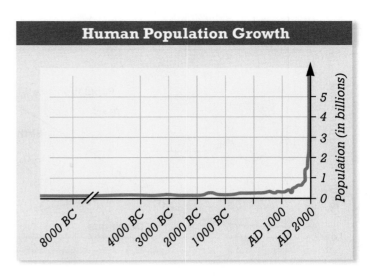

**FIGURE 19-12**

The J shape of the graph is characteristic of exponential growth. Many ecologists agree that the current human population growth rate is not sustainable.

## Population Growth Today

The global growth rate peaked in the late 1960s at about 0.021 per capita. Because birth rates have decreased in many countries, the growth rate has gradually declined slowly to its 2004 level of about 0.012 per capita. This decline has led some people to mistakenly conclude that the population is not increasing. In fact, the number of people that will be added to the world population this year is larger than it was when the growth rate was at its peak. This is simply a function of today's greater population size. For example, in 1970 there were about 3.7 billion people, and the growth rate was about 0.0196. In 1970, therefore, about 3,700,000,000 × 0.0196, or about 73 million people, were added to the world's population. In 1999 there were about 6 billion people and the growth rate was 0.014 per capita, so the number of people added to the population was 6,000,000,000 × 0.014, or 84 million.

Today about 20 percent of the world's population live in **developed countries.** This category includes all of the world's modern, industrialized countries, such as the United States, Japan, Germany, France, the United Kingdom, Australia, Canada, and Russia. On average, people in developed countries are better educated, healthier, and live longer than the rest of the world's population. Population growth rates in developed countries are very low—about 0.003 per capita. The populations of some of these countries, such as Russia, Germany, and Italy, are shrinking because death rates exceed birth rates.

Most people (about 80 percent of the world's population) live in **developing countries,** a category that includes most countries in Asia, Central America, South America, and Africa. In general, these countries are poorer, and their populations are growing faster—at a rate of about 0.015 per capita.

 **Quick Lab**

### Demonstrating Population Doubling

**Materials** pencil, paper, sheet of newspaper

**Procedure**

1. Make a data table. Label the columns "Fold number," "Number of layers," and "Power of 2." Write the numbers 1–10 in the first column.

2. Fold a sheet of newspaper repeatedly in half, as your teacher demonstrates. Fill in your data table after each fold.

**Analysis** If each layer in the paper represented 100 million people and each fold in the paper represented one human generation (about 35 years), how quickly could a starting population of 100 million grow to exceed 6 billion?

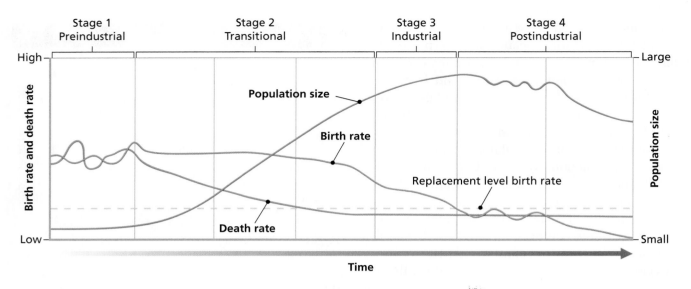

Stage 1
Preindustrial

Stage 2
Transitional

Stage 3
Industrial

Stage 4
Postindustrial

Population size

Birth rate

Replacement level birth rate

Death rate

Birth rate and death rate

High

Low

Large

Population size

Small

Time

**FIGURE 19-13**

The demographic transition model consists of four stages. Note the relative changes in birth rates, death rates, and population size.

# DEMOGRAPHIC TRANSITION

Human populations have undergone rapid growth, yet in some developed countries, populations have stopped growing. The **demographic transition** model shows how these population changes happen. The theory behind the model is that industrial development causes economic and social progress that then affects population growth rates. Figure 19-13 compares general trends in birth rates, death rates, and population sizes during four stages.

In the first stage of the model, the birth rate and the death rate are both at high levels, and the population size is stable. In the second stage, a population explosion occurs. Death rates decline as hygiene, nutrition, and education improve. But birth rates remain high, so the population grows very fast. In the third stage, population growth slows because the birth rate decreases. As the birth rate becomes close to the death rate, the population size stabilizes. In the fourth stage, the birth rate drops below replacement level, so the size of the population begins to decrease. It has taken from one to three generations for the demographic transition to occur in most developed countries.

## Word Roots and Origins

*demographic*

from the Greek *demos,* meaning "the people," and *graphein,* meaning "to write"

## SECTION 3 REVIEW

1. What effect did the agricultural revolution have on the growth of the human population?

2. Explain why mortality rates began to decline rapidly around 1650.

3. Why did population growth rates increase rapidly after World War II?

4. Compare living standards in developing countries with those in developed countries.

5. Summarize the demographic transition model.

**CRITICAL THINKING**

6. **Evaluating Models** Which general model of population growth most closely resembles that seen in Figure 19-13? Explain your answer.

7. **Predicting Results** How might vaccines against diseases affect population growth rates?

8. **Analyzing Data** How is it possible for some countries with low birth rates to have high rates of population growth?

# CHAPTER HIGHLIGHTS

## SECTION 1   Understanding Populations

- Populations can be measured in terms of size, density, dispersion, growth rate, age structure, and survivorship.

- A population's size is the number of individuals that the population contains. Density is a measure of how crowded the population is.

- Dispersion describes the distribution of individuals within the population and may be random, uniform, or clumped.

- A population's age structure indicates the percentage of individuals at each age.

- Populations show three patterns of mortality: Type I (low mortality until late in life), Type II (constant mortality throughout life), and Type III (high mortality early in life followed by low mortality for the remaining life span).

**Vocabulary**

population (p. 381)
population density (p. 382)
dispersion (p. 382)
birth rate (p. 383)
death rate (p. 383)
life expectancy (p. 383)
age structure (p. 384)
survivorship curve (p. 384)

## SECTION 2   Measuring Populations

- The exponential model describes perpetual growth at a steady rate in a population. The model assumes constant birth and death rates and no immigration or emigration.

- In the logistic model, birth rates fall and death rates climb as the population grows. When the carrying capacity is reached, the population becomes stable.

- Population-limiting factors are density-dependent if the effect on each individual depends on the number of other individuals present in the same area.

- Small populations have low genetic diversity and are subject to inbreeding, so they are less likely to adapt to environmental changes.

**Vocabulary**

growth rate (p. 385)
immigration (p. 385)
emigration (p. 385)
exponential model (p. 386)
limiting factor (p. 386)
logistic model (p. 387)
carrying capacity (p. 387)
density-independent factor (p. 388)
density-dependent factor (p. 388)
inbreeding (p. 389)

## SECTION 3   Human Population Growth

- About 10,000 to 12,000 years ago, the development of agriculture increased the growth rate of the human population.

- Around 1650, improvements in hygiene, diet, and economic conditions further accelerated population growth.

- After World War II, the human population grew at the fastest rate in history, largely because of better sanitation and medical care in poorer countries.

- Today, developing countries have faster human population growth and lower standards of living than developed countries do.

**Vocabulary**

hunter-gatherer lifestyle (p. 390)
agricultural revolution (p. 390)
developed country (p. 391)
developing country (p. 391)
demographic transition (p. 392)

# CHAPTER REVIEW

## USING VOCABULARY

1. For each pair of terms, explain how the meanings of the terms differ.
   a. *density* and *dispersion*
   b. *exponential model* and *logistic model*
   c. *density-dependent factor* and *density-independent factor*
   d. *developing country* and *developed country*

2. Use the following terms in the same sentence: *growth rate, birth rate, death rate, immigration,* and *emigration*.

3. Describe what is meant by the term age *structure*.

4. **Word Roots and Origins** The word *population* is derived from the Latin word *populus,* which means "people." Using this information, explain how the term *population* has been adapted to fit its ecological definition.

## UNDERSTANDING KEY CONCEPTS

5. **Describe** how a uniform distribution differs from a random distribution.

6. **Explain** two reasons that a population of turtles in a pond might have a clumped distribution.

7. **Identify** four kinds of measurements used to describe changing populations.

8. **Differentiate** between the three general types of survivorship curves.

9. **Name** the four processes that determine population growth.

10. **Compare** the main assumptions and predictions of the exponential model of population growth with those of the logistic model.

11. **Predict** the possible outcome of placing on a ranch a population of livestock that exceeds the carrying capacity of the ranch.

12. **Determine** if a volcanic eruption would result in density-dependent or density-independent regulation of populations that lived near the volcano.

13. **Explain** three reasons that small populations are particularly vulnerable to extinction.

14. **Summarize** the agricultural revolution's effects on how people obtained food and on human population growth.

15. **Describe** three factors that caused the human population to begin to grow rapidly about 1650.

16. **Identify** the main causes of the decline in death rates following World War II.

17. **Compare** population growth and standards of living in developed and developing countries.

18. **CONCEPT MAPPING** Use the following terms to create a concept map that compares models of population growth: *logistic model, exponential model, density-dependent factors, density-independent factors, limited growth, unlimited growth, disease, drought, food availability,* and *forest fires*.

## CRITICAL THINKING

19. **Analyzing Concepts** Because we humans alter our environment more than other animals do, we can affect the carrying capacity of our environment. How do we increase or decrease the carrying capacity of our local area?

20. **Applying Information** The cause of the population cycle of the snowshoe hare is still a subject of debate. Suggest a hypothesis to explain this cycle, and suggest a way to test it.

21. **Drawing Conclusions** How could disease be a density-dependent factor in a population?

22. **Interpreting Graphics** The population of country X is projected to grow rapidly in the next few decades, while slow growth is projected for country Y. Explain these projections based on the age structure graphs shown below.

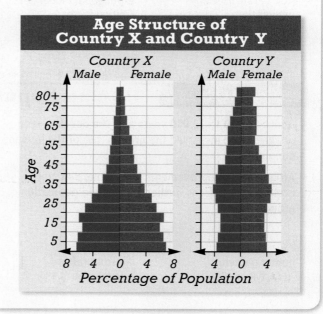

**Age Structure of Country X and Country Y**

# Standardized Test Preparation

**DIRECTIONS:** Choose the letter of the answer choice that best answers the question.

1. Which of the following is a population?
   A. all the fish in a pond
   B. all the birds in New York City
   C. all the members of a family of humans
   D. all the fish of the same species in a lake

2. Which of the following is true in the exponential model of population growth?
   F. Population growth continues indefinitely.
   G. Population growth stops at the carrying capacity.
   H. Population growth increases and then decreases.
   J. The immigration rate falls with increasing population size.

3. Which of the following refers to the population size that can be sustained by an environment over time?
   A. bell curve
   B. allele frequency
   C. carrying capacity
   D. exponential growth

4. Which of the following is a density-dependent factor for a population of deer in a forest?
   F. a drought
   G. a landslide
   H. a period of freezing weather
   J. the number of cougars in the forest

**INTERPRETING GRAPHICS:** The graph below shows the size of a particular population over time. Use the graph to answer the question that follows.

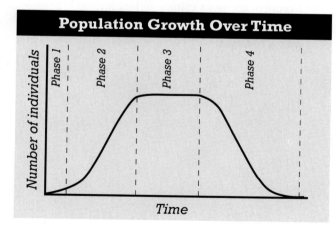

5. In the graph, which time period shows negative growth of the population?
   A. phase 1
   B. phase 2
   C. phase 3
   D. phase 4

**DIRECTIONS:** Complete the following analogy.

6. birth rate : death rate :: immigration :
   F. mortality
   G. migration
   H. emigration
   J. growth rate

**INTERPRETING GRAPHICS:** The graph below shows the growth of a population of fruit flies over time. Use the graph to answer the question that follows.

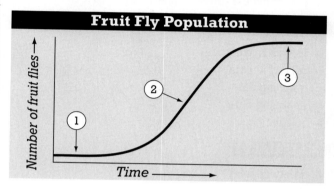

7. At which point would a density-dependent limiting factor have a greater impact on the population?
   A. 1
   B. 2
   C. 3
   D. Both 1 and 3

## SHORT RESPONSE

Study the graph of fruit fly population growth above.

Explain why the population stops increasing after it reaches the point labeled 3 on the curve.

## EXTENDED RESPONSE

Study the graph of fruit fly population growth above. Use the graph to support your answers to the following questions.

*Part A* Name one limiting factor that could affect this population of fruit flies.

*Part B* At which point on the curve would this limiting factor have the greatest effect on the population? Explain your reasoning.

**Test TIP** For a question involving graphs, try to understand the graph by reading the graph's title and the labels on the graph's axes. For graphs that show change in some variable over time, keep in mind that the steepness and direction of a curve indicate the relative rate of change at a given point in time.

# Studying Population Growth

## OBJECTIVES

- Observe the growth and decline of a population of yeast cells.
- Determine the carrying capacity of a yeast culture.

## PROCESS SKILLS

- using a microscope
- collecting data
- graphing data
- analyzing data
- calculating

## MATERIALS

- safety goggles
- lab apron
- yeast cell culture
- 2 1 mL pipets
- 2 test tubes
- 1% methylene blue solution
- ruled microscope slide (2 x 2 mm)
- coverslip
- compound microscope

## Background

1. What is a limiting factor and how does it affect population size?
2. How are the terms population growth, birth rate and death rate all interrelated?

## Procedure

### Counting Yeast Cells

1. **CAUTION Always wear safety goggles and lab apron to protect your eyes and clothing.** Put on safety goggles and lab apron.

   **CAUTION Do not touch or taste any chemicals. Know the location of the emergency shower and eyewash station and know how to use them. Methylene blue will stain your skin and clothing. If you get a chemical on your skin or clothing wash it off at the sink while calling to the teacher. Notify the teacher immediately of any spills. Spills should be cleaned up promptly, according to your teacher's directions. Glassware is fragile. Notify the teacher of broken glass or cuts. Do not clean up broken glass or spills with broken glass unless the teacher tells you to do so.**

2. Transfer 1 mL of yeast culture to a test tube. Add 2 drops of methylene blue to the tube. The methylene blue will remain blue in dead cells but will turn colorless in living cells.

3. Make a wet mount by placing 0.1 mL, or about 1 drop, of the yeast culture and methylene blue mixture on a ruled microscope slide. Cover the slide with a coverslip.

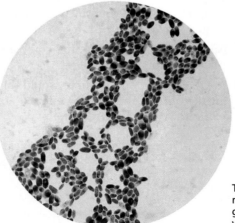

These yeast cells have been stained with methylene blue and magnified with a high-power microscope. Methylene blue gives a deep blue color to dead yeast cells, but live yeast cells will actively remove the stain.

4. Observe the wet mount under the low power of a compound microscope. Notice the squares on the slide. Then switch to the high power. *Note: Adjust the light so that you can clearly see both stained and unstained cells.* Move the slide so that the top left-hand corner of one square is in the center of your field of view. This will be area 1, as shown in the diagram below.

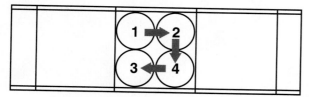

5. Count the live (unstained) cells and the dead (stained) cells in the four corners of a square using the pattern shown in the diagram above. In a data table similar to the one below, record the number of live cells and dead cells that you counted in the entire square.
6. Repeat step 5 until you have counted all 6 squares on the slide.
7. Dispose of solutions and broken glass in the designated waste containers. Do not pour chemicals down the drain or put lab materials in the trash unless your teacher tells you to do so.
8. Clean up you work area and all lab equipment. Return lab equipment to its proper place. Wash your hands thoroughly with soap and water before you leave the lab and after you finish all work.
9. Refer back to your data table. Find the total number of live cells in the 6 squares. Divide this total by 6 to find the average number of live cells per square. Record this number in your data table. Repeat this procedure for the dead cells.
10. Estimate the population of live cells in 1 mL (the amount in the test tube) by multiplying the average number of cells per square by 2,500. Record this number in your data table. Repeat this procedure for dead cells.
11. Repeat steps 1 through 8 each day for 4 more days.

## Analysis and Conclusions

1. Why were several areas and squares counted and then averaged each day?
2. Graph the changes in the numbers of live yeast cells and dead yeast cells over time. Plot the number of cells in 1 mL of yeast culture on the *y*-axis and the time (in hours) on the *x*-axis.
3. What limiting factors probably caused the yeast population to decline?

## Further Inquiry

1. Write a question about population growth that could be explored in another investigation.

| Time (hours) | Number of cells per square | | Population size (cells/mL) |
|---|---|---|---|
| | Squares 1–6 | Average | |
| 0 | | | |
| 24 | | | |
| 48 | | | |
| 72 | | | |
| 96 | | | |

**DATA TABLE**

# COMMUNITY ECOLOGY

A large variety of organisms interact within this coral reef community.

**SECTION 1** *Species Interactions*

**SECTION 2** *Patterns in Communities*

*BIOLOGY* INTERACTIVE TUTOR

**Unit 7—Ecosystem Dynamics**
Topic 3

SCIENTIFIC AMERICAN

For project ideas from
*Scientific American,* visit
go.hrw.com and type in
the keyword **HM6SAD.**

# SPECIES INTERACTIONS

*Just as populations contain interacting members of a single species, communities contain interacting populations of many species. Many species have specific types of interactions with other species. This chapter introduces the five major types of interactions among species: predation, competition, parasitism, mutualism, and commensalism. These categories are based on whether each species causes any benefit or harm to the other species in a given relationship.*

## SECTION 1

### OBJECTIVES

- **Identify** two types of predator adaptations and two types of prey adaptations.
- **Identify** possible causes and results of interspecific competition.
- **Compare** parasitism, mutualism, and commensalism, and give one example of each.

### VOCABULARY

predation
interspecific competition
symbiosis
parasitism
mutualism
commensalism

## PREDATION

In **predation** (pree-DAY-shuhn), an individual of one species, called the *predator,* eats all or part of an individual of another species, called the *prey.* Predation is a powerful force in a community. The relationship between predator and prey influences the size of each population and affects where and how each species lives. Examples of predators include *carnivores*—predators that eat animals—and *herbivores*—predators that eat plants. Many types of organisms can act as predators or prey. All heterotrophs are either predators or parasites or both.

### Predator Adaptations

Natural selection favors the evolution of predator adaptations for finding, capturing, and consuming prey. For example, rattlesnakes have an acute sense of smell and have heat-sensitive pits located below each nostril. These pits enable a rattlesnake to detect warm-bodied prey, even in the dark. Many snakes use venom to disable or kill their prey. A venomous rattlesnake is shown in Figure 20-1.

Other predator adaptations include the sticky webs of spiders, the flesh-cutting teeth of wolves and coyotes, the speed of cheetahs, and the striped pattern of a tiger's coat, which provides camouflage in a grassland habitat. Many herbivores have mouthparts suited to cutting and chewing tough vegetation.

A predator's survival depends on its ability to capture food, but a prey's survival depends on its ability to avoid being captured. Therefore, natural selection also favors adaptations in prey that allow the prey to escape, avoid, or otherwise ward off predators.

**FIGURE 20-1**

A rattlesnake has several adaptations that make it an effective predator.

(a) Green leaf mantid, *Choeradodus rhombicollis*     (b) Amazonian poison frog, *Dendrobates ventrimaculatus*

**FIGURE 20-2**

Coloration is an adaptation in prey as well as predators. In (a), the mantid cannot readily be detected among the leaves. In (b), the frog's bright colors warn other organisms that the frog is toxic if eaten.

## Quick Lab

### Modeling Predation

**Materials** 4.1 m white string, 4 stakes, 40 colored toothpicks, stopwatch or timer, meterstick

**Procedure**

1. Use the stakes and string to mark off a 1 m square in a grassy area.

2. One partner should scatter the toothpicks randomly throughout the square. The other partner will have 1 minute to pick up as many toothpicks as possible, one at a time. This procedure should be repeated until each team has performed five trials.

3. Record your team's results in a data table.

**Analysis** Toothpicks of which colors were picked up most often? Which toothpicks were picked up least often? How do you account for this difference?

## Adaptations in Animal Prey

Animals may avoid being eaten by carnivores in different ways. Some organisms flee when a predator approaches. Others escape detection by hiding or by resembling an inedible object, as shown in Figure 20-2a. Some animals use deceptive markings, such as fake eyes or false heads, to startle a predator. Some animals have chemical defenses. Animals such as the frog shown in Figure 20-2b produce toxins and use bright colors to warn would-be predators of their toxicity.

In *mimicry* (MIM-ik-ree), one species closely resembles another species. For example, the harmless king snake is a mimic of the venomous coral snake, as shown in Figure 20-3. This form of mimicry is called *Batesian mimicry*. Another form of mimicry called *Müllerian mimicry*, exists when two or more dangerous or distasteful species look similar. For example, many kinds of bees and wasps have similar patterns of alternating yellow and black stripes. This kind of mimicry benefits each species involved because predators learn to avoid similar-looking individuals.

## Adaptations in Plant Prey

Plants cannot run away from a predator, but many plants have evolved adaptations that protect them from being eaten. Physical defenses, such as sharp thorns, spines, sticky hairs, and tough leaves, can make plants more difficult to eat. Plants have also evolved a range of chemical defenses that are poisonous, irritating, or bad-tasting. These chemicals are often byproducts of the plants' metabolism and are called *secondary compounds*. Some examples of secondary compounds that provide a defensive function are strychnine (STRIK-nin), which is produced in plants of the genus *Strychnos,* and nicotine, which is produced by the tobacco plant. Poison ivy and poison oak produce an irritating chemical that causes an allergic reaction on some animals' skin.

**(a)** Scarlet king snake, *Lampropeltis triangulum*

**(b)** Eastern coral snake, *Micrurus fulvius*

# COMPETITION

**Interspecific competition** is a type of interaction in which two or more species use the same limited resource. For example, both lions and hyenas compete for prey such as zebras. Likewise, many plant species compete for soil or sunlight. Some species of plants prevent other species from growing nearby by releasing toxins into the soil. If two populations compete for a resource, the result may be a reduction in the number of either species or the elimination of one of the two competitors. More often, one species will be able to use a resource more efficiently than the other. As a result, less of the resource will be available to the other species.

## Competitive Exclusion

Ecologist George F. Gause was one of the first scientists to study competition in the laboratory. In test tubes stocked with a food supply of bacteria, Gause raised several species of paramecia in various combinations. When grown in separate test tubes, *Paramecium caudatum* and *Paramecium aurelia* each thrived. But when the two species were combined, *P. caudatum* always died out because *P. aurelia* was a more efficient predator of bacteria. Ecologists use the principle of *competitive exclusion* to describe situations in which one species is eliminated from a community because of competition for the same limited resource. Competitive exclusion may result when one species uses the limited resource more efficiently than the other species does.

Joseph Connell's study of barnacles along the Scottish coast in the 1960s documented competition in the wild. Connell studied two species, *Semibalanus balanoides* and *Chthamalus stellatus*. These barnacles live in the intertidal zone, the portion of the seashore that is exposed during low tide.

**FIGURE 20-3**

The king snake in (a) may avoid predators because of its mimicry of the color patterns of the coral snake in (b). A closer look reveals the differences: the king snake has a red snout and a black ring separating its red and yellow rings, and the coral snake has a black snout and adjacent red and yellow rings. The ring patterns of other species of coral snakes may differ from the patterns shown in the photo above.

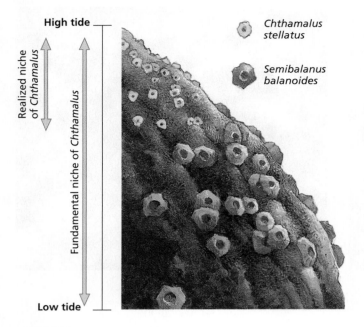

**FIGURE 20-4**

The realized niche of the *Chthamalus* barnacle species is smaller than its fundamental niche because of competition from the *Semibalanus* species. Although *Chthamalus* can survive at all levels of the intertidal zone, it is usually crowded out at the lower level by the faster-growing *Semibalanus*. But *Semibalanus* cannot survive in the upper level, which is left dry for longer periods.

**internet** connect

**www.scilinks.org**
**Topic:** Competition
**Keyword:** HM60326

**SCI**
**LINKS** Maintained by the
National Science
Teachers Association

As Figure 20-4 shows, each species of barnacle occupied a distinct band within the intertidal zone. *Chthamalus* lived higher on the rocks than *Semibalanus* did. Connell demonstrated that this difference was partly due to competition. When a rock covered with *Chthamalus* was transplanted to the lower zone, *Chthamalus* was clearly able to tolerate the conditions in the lower zone. However, *Semibalanus* would soon settle on the rock and eventually crowd out *Chthamalus*. Connell concluded that competition restricted the range of *Chthamalus*. Although *Chthamalus* could survive lower on the rocks, competition from *Semibalanus* prevented it from doing so. Higher on the rocks, *Chthamalus* is free from competition because it can tolerate drying out more than *Semibalanus* can.

## Reduced Niche Size

Recall that a species' *niche* (NICH) is the role that the species plays in its environment. But this role may vary due to interactions with other species. So, ecologists differentiate between the fundamental niche and the realized niche of a species. The *fundamental niche* of a species is the range of conditions that it can potentially tolerate and the range of resources that it can potentially use. Often, predation and competition limit the species' use of these ranges. Thus, the *realized niche* is the part of the niche that the species actually uses, as shown in Figure 20-4.

## Character Displacement

Competition has the potential to be an important influence on the nature of a community. The composition of a community may change as competitors win, lose, or evolve differences that lessen the intensity of competition. Natural selection favors differences between competitors, especially where the niches of the competitors overlap. This evolution of differences in a characteristic due to competition is called *character displacement*. Character displacement is a way of reducing niche overlap.

The beaks of Galápagos Island finches provide an example of character displacement. Many of these closely related finch species eat seeds that come from the small number of plant species on the islands. Furthermore, the size of each bird's beak determines the size of the seeds that the bird can eat. When the average beak size of each species is compared with the average beak size of each of the other species, the greatest difference in beak size is observed between species that share an island. Differences in beak size reduce competition by enabling species that share an island to favor different food sources.

## Resource Partitioning

As Charles Darwin noted, competition is likely to be most intense between similar species that require the same resources. When similar species coexist, each species may avoid competition with others by using a specific part of an available resource. This pattern of resource use is called *resource partitioning*. For example, the pioneering ecologist Robert MacArthur (1930–1972) studied several species of warblers that feed on insects in spruce and fir trees. MacArthur discovered that when more than one species of warbler is foraging within the same tree, each species hunts for insects only in a particular section of the tree. As a result, competition among the species is reduced.

**Word Roots and Origins**

*parasite*

from the Latin word *parasitus,* meaning "one who eats at the table of another"

# SYMBIOSIS

A **symbiosis** (SIM-bie-OH-sis) is a close, long-term relationship between two organisms. Three examples of symbiotic relationships include: parasitism, mutualism, and commensalism. **Parasitism** (PAR-uh-SIET-IZ-UHM) is a relationship in which one individual is harmed while the other individual benefits. **Mutualism** (MYOO-choo-uhl-IZ-uhm) is a relationship in which both organisms derive some benefit. In **commensalism** (kuh-MEN-suhl-IZ-uhm), one organism benefits, but the other organism is neither helped nor harmed.

## Parasitism

Parasitism is similar to predation in that one organism, called the *host,* is harmed and the other organism, called the *parasite,* benefits. However, unlike many forms of predation, parasitism usually does not result in the immediate death of the host. Generally, the parasite feeds on the host for a long time rather than kills it. Parasites such as aphids, lice, leeches, fleas, ticks, and mosquitoes that remain on the outside of their host are called *ectoparasites*. Parasites that live inside the host's body are called *endoparasites*. Familiar endoparasites are heartworms, disease-causing protists, and tapeworms, such as the one shown in Figure 20-5. Natural selection favors adaptations that allow a parasite to exploit its host efficiently. Parasites are usually specialized anatomically and physiologically for a parasitic lifestyle.

Parasites can have a strong negative impact on the health and reproduction of the host. Consequently, hosts have evolved a variety of defenses against parasites. Skin is an important defense that prevents most parasites from entering the body. Tears, saliva, and mucus defend openings through which parasites could pass, such as the eyes, mouth, and nose. Finally, the cells of the immune system may attack parasites that get past these defenses.

**FIGURE 20-5**

Tapeworms are endoparasites that can grow to 20 m or greater in length. Tapeworms are so specialized for a parasitic lifestyle that they do not have a digestive system. They live in the host's small intestine and absorb nutrients directly through their skin. Tapeworms reproduce by producing egg-filled chambers, which are released in their host's feces to be unknowingly picked up by a future host.

**FIGURE 20-6**

Acacia trees in Central America have a mutualistic relationship with certain types of ants. The trees provide food and shelter to the ants, and the ants defend the tree from insect herbivores.

## Mutualism

Mutualism is a relationship in which two species derive some benefit from each other. Some mutualistic relationships are so close that neither species can survive without the other. An example of mutualism, shown in Figure 20-6, involves ants and some species of *Acacia* plants. The ants nest inside the acacia's large thorns and receive food from the acacia. In turn, the ants protect the acacia from herbivores and cut back competing vegetation.

Pollination is one of the most important mutualistic relationships on Earth. Animals such as bees, butterflies, flies, beetles, bats, and birds that carry pollen between flowering plants are called *pollinators*. A flower is a lure for pollinators, which are attracted by the flower's color, pattern, shape, or scent. The plant usually provides food—in the form of nectar or pollen—for its pollinators. As a pollinator feeds in a flower, it picks up a load of pollen, which it may then carry to other flowers of the same species.

## Commensalism

Commensalism is an interaction in which one species benefits and the other species is not affected. Species that scavenge for leftover food items are often considered commensal species. However, a relationship that appears to be commensalism may simply be mutualism in which the mutual benefits are not apparent.

An example of a commensal relationship is the relationship between cattle egrets and Cape buffaloes in Tanzania. The birds feed on small animals such as insects and lizards that are forced out of their hiding places by the movement of the buffaloes through the grass. Occasionally, the cattle egrets also feed on ectoparasites from the hide of the buffaloes, but the buffaloes generally do not benefit from the presence of the egrets.

---

## SECTION 1 REVIEW

1. List the five major kinds of species interactions.

2. Describe one adaptation of a herbivore and one adaptation of a carnivore for obtaining food.

3. Identify two possible results of interspecific competition.

4. What is the competitive exclusion principle?

5. Identify the ways that parasites are similar to predators.

6. In the relationship between cattle egrets and Cape buffaloes, if the egrets regularly removed ticks from the buffaloes, would this relationship still be considered commensal? Explain your answer.

**CRITICAL THINKING**

7. **Analyzing Concepts** Explain how two similar species of birds could nest in the same tree and yet occupy different niches.

8. **Making Comparisons** How does predation on plants differ from predation on animals, in terms of the usual effect on the prey?

9. **Analyzing Concepts** Species A and B have a very similar niche. Species A recently arrived in a location where species B previously lived and carried a disease that killed all members of species B. Is this situation an example of competitive exclusion? Explain your answer.

# PATTERNS IN COMMUNITIES

*The investigation of community properties and interactions is an active area of ecology. Which properties are most significant in structuring a community? What determines the number of species in a community? How do communities recover from disturbance? These questions are central to a study of communities.*

## SECTION 2

### OBJECTIVES

- **Describe** the factors that affect species richness in a community.
- **Explain** how disturbances affect community stability.
- **Distinguish** between types of succession, and explain why succession may not be predictable.

### VOCABULARY

species richness
species evenness
species-area effect
disturbance
stability
ecological succession
primary succession
secondary succession
pioneer species
climax community

## SPECIES RICHNESS

One characteristic of a community is **species richness,** the number of species in the community. A related measure is **species evenness,** which is the relative abundance of each species. These two measures provide slightly different information. Species richness is a simple count of the species in the community. Each species contributes one count to the total regardless of whether the species' population is one or 1 million.

In contrast, species evenness takes into account how common each species is in the community. To calculate the species evenness of a community, ecologists must measure or estimate the population size of all species in the community. In general, ecologists study both species richness and species evenness when they investigate communities.

### Latitude and Species Richness

Species richness varies with latitude (distance from the equator). As a general rule, the closer a community is to the equator, the more species it will contain. Species richness is greatest in the tropical rain forests. For example, entomologists Edward O. Wilson and Terry Erwin identified nearly as many species of ants in a single tree in Peru as can be found in the entire British Isles.

Why do the Tropics contain more species than the temperate zones do? One hypothesis is that temperate habitats, having formed since the last Ice Age, are younger. Therefore, tropical habitats were not disturbed by the ice ages, but habitats closer to the poles were disturbed. Also, the climate is more stable in the Tropics. This stability allows species to specialize to a greater degree than they could in temperate regions, where the climate is more variable.

**internet** connect

www.scilinks.org
**Topic:** Species Interactions and Richness
**Keyword:** HM61435

SCLINKS. Maintained by the National Science Teachers Association

FIGURE 20-7

This species-richness map of North American and Central American birds shows that fewer than 100 species of birds inhabit arctic regions, whereas more than 600 species occupy some tropical regions. This evidence suggests that species richness increases closer to the equator. Equatorial rain forests are biologically the richest habitats on Earth.

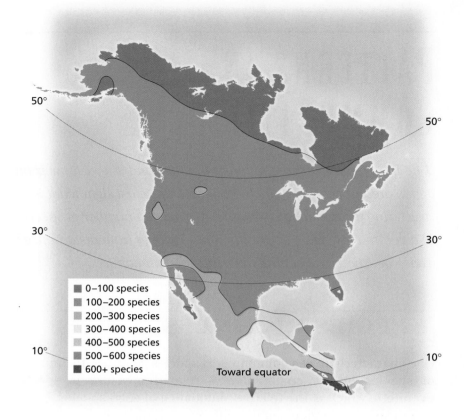

Another hypothesis suggests that because plants can photosynthesize year-round in the Tropics, more energy is available to support more organisms. The high richness of species in the Tropics, as shown in Figure 20-7, is likely the result of several factors.

## Habitat Size and Species Richness

Another pattern of species richness is that larger areas usually contain more species than smaller areas do. This relationship is called the **species-area effect.** The species-area effect is most often applied to islands, where area is clearly limited by geography. In the Caribbean, for example, more species of reptiles and amphibians live on large islands, such as Cuba, than on small islands, such as Redonda, as shown in Figure 20-8. Because all of these islands are close together, differences in species richness cannot be due to differences in latitude. Why does species richness increase as area increases? Larger areas usually contain a greater diversity of habitats and thus can support more species.

The species-area effect has one very important practical consequence: reducing the size of a habitat reduces the number of species that the habitat can support. Today, natural habitats are shrinking rapidly under pressure from the ever-growing human population. About 2 percent of the world's tropical rain forests are destroyed each year, for example. The inevitable result of the destruction of habitats is the extinction of species.

**FIGURE 20-8**

In a 1971 survey, the large islands of Cuba and Hispaniola each had about 100 species of reptiles and amphibians, whereas the small island of Redonda only had about 5 species. In general, species richness increases as available habitat increases. This principle is true for inland forests as well as islands.

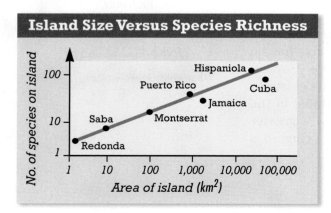

## Species Interactions and Species Richness

Interactions among species sometimes affect species richness. Several studies have demonstrated that predators can prevent competitive exclusion among their prey. In the 1960s, zoologist Robert Paine showed the importance of the sea star *Pisaster ochraceus,* shown in Figure 20-9, in maintaining the species richness of communities on the Washington coast. Paine removed all *Pisaster* individuals from one site and for several years prevented any new *Pisaster* individuals from settling there. This change caused a dramatic shift in the community. The mussel *Mytilus californianus,* which had previously coexisted with several other species, became much more abundant, spread over the habitat, and crowded out other species. The number of other species fell from almost 20 to fewer than 5 within a decade. Evidently, *Mytilus* was the superior competitor for space on the rocks, but its population was normally held in check by predation from *Pisaster.*

**FIGURE 20-9**

Predation by the sea star *Pisaster ochraceus* on the mussel *Mytilus californianus* promoted diversity of mussel species by controlling the *Mytilus* population.

## Community Stability and Species Richness

One of the most important characteristics of a community is how it responds to disturbance. **Disturbances** are events that change communities, remove or destroy organisms from communities, or alter resource availability. Examples of abiotic disturbances are droughts, fires, floods, volcanic eruptions, earthquakes, and storms. Examples of animal disturbances include elephants tearing up trees while feeding and prairie dogs moving soil around while digging their burrows. Human disturbances include bulldozing, clear-cutting, paving, plowing, and mowing land.

Disturbances affect practically all communities at some point. A number of organisms may even depend on a certain type of disturbance in order to survive. For example, the lodgepole pine, shown in Figure 20-10, depends on periodic fires to disperse its seeds. The cones of this tree contain a tough resin seal that is cracked open by intense heat. Disturbances may also create opportunities for species that have not previously occupied a habitat to become established.

**Stability** is the tendency of a community to maintain relatively constant conditions. Stability therefore relates to the community's resistance to disturbances. Ecologists suspect that a community's stability is also related to its species evenness and species richness, because communities that have more species contain more links between species. These links may spread out the effects of the disturbance and lessen disruption of the community. One line of evidence cited in support of this view is the vulnerability of agricultural fields to outbreaks of insect pests, given that these fields usually consist of one species of plants. Further evidence came from a study of grassland plots in the 1980s. Ecologists observed that during a drought, species-rich plots lost a smaller percentage of plant mass than did species-poor plots. The species-rich plots also took less time to recover from the drought.

**FIGURE 20-10**

These young lodgepole pines have started growing after a devastating forest fire. The heat of the fire helped release the pine seeds from their cones, which allowed the seeds to germinate.

# SUCCESSIONAL CHANGES IN COMMUNITIES

During the summer and early fall of 1988, fires burned large areas of Yellowstone National Park. Approximately 320,900 hectares (793,000 acres) were affected. If you visit Yellowstone today, you will find that regrowth is well underway in the burned areas. In time, if no further major disturbances take place, the burned areas of Yellowstone National Park will undergo a series of regrowth stages. The gradual, sequential regrowth of a community of species in an area is called **ecological succession** (EK-uh-LAHJ-i-kuhl suhk-SESH-uhn). You can see early stages of succession in vacant lots, along roads, and even in sidewalks or parking lots where weeds are pushing up through cracks in the concrete. Figure 20-11 shows the successional changes that took place after the eruption of Mount St. Helens in 1980.

Ecologists recognize two types of succession. **Primary succession** is the development of a community in an area that has not supported life previously, such as bare rock, a sand dune, or an island formed by a volcanic eruption. In primary succession, soil is not initially present. **Secondary succession** is the sequential replacement of species that follows disruption of an existing community. The disruption may stem from a natural disturbance, such as a forest fire or a strong storm, or from human activity, such as farming, logging, or mining. Secondary succession occurs where soil is already present.

Any new habitat, whether it is a pond left by heavy rain, a freshly plowed field, or newly exposed bedrock, is an invitation to many species that are adapted to the new conditions. The species of organisms that predominate early in succession are called **pioneer species.** Pioneer species tend to be small, to grow quickly, and to reproduce quickly, so they are well suited for invading and occupying a disturbed habitat. They also may be very good at dispersing their seeds, which enables them to quickly reach disrupted areas.

**FIGURE 20-11**

Successional changes in communities are most apparent after a major disturbance, such as a volcanic eruption. The aftermath of the 1980 Mount St. Helens eruption is shown in (a). The photo in (b) was taken 12 years after the eruption. Many herbaceous plants and young trees had grown up.

**(a)**

**(b)**

(a)

(b)

(c)

## Primary Succession

Primary succession often proceeds very slowly because the soil is too thin or lacks enough minerals to support plant growth. For example, when glaciers last retreated from eastern Canada, about 12,000 years ago, they left a huge stretch of barren bedrock from which all the soil had been scraped. This geologic formation, called the Canadian Shield, was a place where plants and most animals could not live. Repeated freezing and thawing broke this rock into smaller pieces. In time, lichens—mutualistic associations between fungi and either algae or cyanobacteria—colonized the barren rock. Acids in the lichens and mildly acidic rain washed nutrient minerals from the rock. Eventually, the dead organic matter from decayed lichens, along with minerals from the rock, began to form a thin layer of soil in which a few grasslike plants could grow. These plants then died, and their decomposition added more organic material to the soil. Soon, mosses and then larger plants began to grow. Today, much of the Canadian Shield is densely populated with pine, balsam, and spruce trees, whose roots cling to soil that in some areas is still only a few centimeters deep. A similar series of changes has been documented at Glacier Bay, Alaska, shown in Figure 20-12.

## Secondary Succession

Secondary succession occurs where an existing community has been cleared by a disturbance, such as agriculture, but the soil has remained intact. In secondary succession, the original ecosystem returns through a series of well-defined stages. In eastern temperate regions, secondary succession typically begins with weeds, such as annual grasses, mustards, and dandelions, whose seeds may be carried to the site by wind or by animals. If no major disturbance occurs, succession in these regions proceeds with perennial grasses and shrubs, continues with trees such as dogwoods, and eventually results in a deciduous forest community. The complete process takes about 100 years.

**FIGURE 20-12**

Ecologists study the process of primary succession by examining a variety of areas at different successional stages. These photos were taken at different locations at Glacier Bay, Alaska; the changes that occur between the stage shown in (a) and the stage shown in (c) take about 200 years. Shown in (a) is lifeless glacial "till" (pulverized bare rocks) left in the wake of the retreating glacier. Shown in (b) is an early stage of succession in which small plants and shrubs are growing on the site. A mature forest is shown in (c), an end stage of succession.

internet connect

www.scilinks.org
**Topic:** Succession
**Keyword:** HM61475

SCiLINKS. Maintained by the National Science Teachers Association

**FIGURE 20-13**

A recently abandoned agricultural field is being pioneered by weeds. Eventually, taller plants and shrubs will compete with the pioneers. If no further disturbances occur, a forest of pine or cottonwood may follow, succeeded by a hardwood forest. The whole process will take about 100 years.

Human disturbances such as mining, logging, farming, and urban development often start the process of succession. A recently abandoned farm field is shown in Figure 20-13. After areas such as woodlands and prairies are cleared by humans, grasses and weeds often begin to grow, thus beginning the process of secondary succession.

# THE COMPLEXITY OF SUCCESSION

The traditional description of succession is that the community proceeds through a predictable series of stages until it reaches a stable end point, called the **climax community.** The organisms in each stage alter the physical environment in ways that make it less favorable for their own survival but more favorable for the organisms that eventually succeed them. In a sense, each stage paves the way for the next, leading ultimately to the climax community, which remains constant for a long period of time.

When ecologists began to study and document many instances of succession, they found a more complex picture. Some so-called climax communities, for example, are not stable and continue to change. Instead of proceeding inevitably toward the climax community, succession may be regularly "reset" by disturbances. For example, many grasslands give way to forests, but periodic fires prevent the forests from developing. There may be many possible successional pathways in a particular area. The actual path followed may depend on the identities of the species present, the order in which the species arrive, the climate, and many other factors. Ecologists agree that the idea of a single successional pathway ending in a stable climax community is too simple to describe what actually occurs in nature.

## SECTION 2 REVIEW

1. What is the difference between species richness and species evenness?

2. Explain the relationship between species richness and latitude.

3. Identify examples of how animal and human disturbances can affect a community.

4. Explain how species richness can affect community stability.

5. Identify differences between primary and secondary succession.

**CRITICAL THINKING**

6. **Applying Information** Why is the species-area effect important in efforts to conserve species?

7. **Distinguishing Relevant Information** Explain how the example of agricultural fields relates species richness to stability.

8. **Evaluating Viewpoints** Do you agree with the following statement: "Communities are usually in a state of recovery from disturbance"? Consider both animals and plants in your answer.

## SECTION 1   Species Interactions

- Ecologists recognize five major kinds of species interactions in communities: predation, parasitism, competition, mutualism, and commensalism.

- Predation is an interaction in which one organism (the predator) captures and eats another organism (the prey).

- Predators have adaptations to efficiently capture prey, whereas prey species have adaptations to avoid capture. Mimicry is an adaptation in which a species gains an advantage by resembling another species or object.

- Competition may cause competitive exclusion, the elimination of one species in a community. Competition may also drive the evolution of niche differences among competitors.

- In parasitism, one species (the parasite) feeds on, but does not always kill, another species (the host).

- In mutualism, both interacting species benefit.

- In commensalism, one species benefits, and the other is not affected.

**Vocabulary**

predation (p. 399)

interspecific competition (p. 401)

symbiosis (p. 403)
parasitism (p. 403)

mutualism (p.403)
commensalism (p. 403)

## SECTION 2   Patterns in Communities

- Species richness is the number of species in a community. Species evenness is the relative abundance of each species.

- In general, species richness is greatest near the equator, and larger areas support more species. Species interactions such as predation can promote species richness.

- Disturbances can alter a community by eliminating or removing organisms or altering resource availability.

- Species richness may improve a community's stability. Areas of low species richness may be less stable in the event of an ecological disturbance.

- Ecological succession is a change in the species composition of a community over time. Primary succession is the assembly of a community on newly created habitat. Secondary succession is the change in an existing community following a disturbance.

- Primary succession occurs in areas that have been recently exposed to the elements and lack soil. Primary succession typically proceeds from lichens and mosses to a climax community.

- Secondary succession occurs in areas where the original ecosystem has been cleared by a disturbance. Secondary succession typically proceeds from weeds to a climax community.

**Vocabulary**

species richness (p. 405)
species evenness (p. 405)
species-area effect (p. 406)

disturbance (p. 407)
stability (p. 407)
ecological succession (p. 408)

primary succession (p. 408)
secondary succession (p. 408)
pioneer species (p. 408)

climax community (p. 410)

## USING VOCABULARY

1. For each pair of terms, explain how the meanings of the terms differ.
   a. *mutualism* and *commensalism*
   b. *parasitism* and *predation*
   c. *species richness* and *species evenness*
   d. *primary succession* and *secondary succession*
   e. *pioneer species* and *climax community*

2. **Word Roots and Origins** The word *niche* is derived from the Old French word *nichier,* which means "to nest." Using this information, explain why *niche* is a good term for the role of an organism in its environment.

## UNDERSTANDING KEY CONCEPTS

3. **Compare** the five major types of relationships between species by creating a table.

4. **Describe** two evolutionary adaptations that enable organisms to be efficient predators.

5. **Identify** two evolutionary adaptations that enable prey species to avoid being eaten.

6. **Explain** some of the adaptations that may enable a host species to defend itself against parasites.

7. **Describe** the experiments that Gause conducted on competition in paramecia, and explain what the results demonstrated.

8. **State** why, in the study of competition between two species of barnacles, *Semibalanus balanoides* was the superior competitor, yet *Chthamalus stellatus* was not excluded from the community.

9. **Identify** the benefits that certain ants derive from their relationship with *Acacia* plants and the benefits that the plants receive from the ants.

10. **Explain** the possible consequences of habitat loss in terms of the species-area effect.

11. **Describe** how a disturbance could benefit some species in a community.

12. **Summarize** one view on how species richness affects community stability.

13. **State** some reasons why the process of succession may be more complex than once thought.

14. **BIOLOGY INTERACTIVE TUTOR** Write a short report summarizing how artificial ecosystems used in the management and treatment of wastewater and pollutants can demonstrate succession.

15. **CONCEPT MAPPING** Use the following terms to create a concept map that compares the two types of succession: *primary succession, secondary succession, pioneer species, climax community, bare rock, lichens, organic matter, soil, weeds, shrubs,* and *trees.*

## CRITICAL THINKING

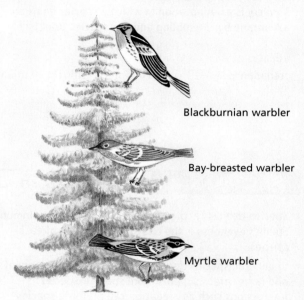

Blackburnian warbler

Bay-breasted warbler

Myrtle warbler

16. **Interpreting Graphics** Examine the figure above. These three warbler species each feed on insects in spruce trees at the same time. However, each species tends to forage in a different area of the tree.
    a. What ecological process is demonstrated by the feeding patterns of these species?
    b. In some areas, there are five species of warblers that feed in spruce trees. Form a hypothesis about the feeding patterns of the other two species.

17. **Analyzing Concepts** Can two species that never come in contact with each other compete for the same resource? Explain your answer.

18. **Analyzing Relationships** Some plants are pollinated by only one pollinator. Explain why this situation might benefit the plant. How could this relationship be a danger to the plant species?

19. **Making Inferences** Explain why measuring the species evenness of a community is usually harder than measuring species richness.

# Standardized Test Preparation

**DIRECTIONS:** Choose the letter of the answer choice that best answers the question or completes the sentence.

1. A certain tropical tree has a fruit that is eaten by only one species of bats. As the bat digests the fruit, the seeds are made ready to sprout. When the bat excretes the wastes of the fruit, it drops seeds in new locations. Which of the following is the correct term for the relationship between the bat and the tree?
   **A.** predation
   **B.** mutualism
   **C.** competition
   **D.** commensalism

2. Which of the following is a parasite?
   **F.** a lion hunting a zebra
   **G.** a deer grazing on grass
   **H.** a tick sucking blood from a dog
   **J.** a snake swallowing a bird's egg

3. Three species of birds forage for insects in the same tree. However, each species tends to forage in different parts of the tree. This pattern of foraging is best explained as an adaptation to which of the following relationships?
   **A.** predation
   **B.** mutualism
   **C.** competition
   **D.** commensalism

**INTERPRETING GRAPHICS:** The map below shows two islands. Use the map to answer the question that follows.

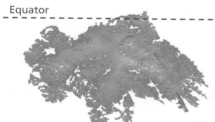

Island A
Area = 150 km2

Equator

Island B
Area = 1,000 km2

4. What can you infer about the number of species on each of these islands?
   **F.** Island A has more species.
   **G.** Island B has more species.
   **H.** Island A and Island B will have the same number of species.
   **J.** Both islands will have fewer species than islands that are located farther north.

**DIRECTIONS:** Complete the following analogy.

5. predator : prey :: herbivore :
   **A.** carnivore
   **B.** plant
   **C.** parasite
   **D.** predation

**INTERPRETING GRAPHICS:** The shading in the graph below indicates the frequency with which a certain bird species obtains prey, by prey size and location. Use the graph to answer the question that follows.

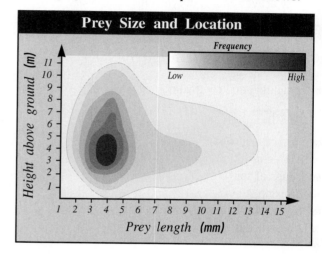

6. Which of the following statements is best supported by this graph?
   **F.** Most often, the bird eats insects.
   **G.** Most often, the bird nests above ground.
   **H.** Most often, the bird finds prey at ground level.
   **J.** Most often, the bird eats prey that is between 3 and 5 mm long.

## SHORT RESPONSE

Some plants produce chemicals that are irritating or poisonous to some animals.

Explain the role of these adaptations in an ecological community.

## EXTENDED RESPONSE

The gradual, sequential change in species in an area is called *ecological succession.*

*Part A* Describe the stages of primary succession.

*Part B* Compare primary succession and secondary succession.

**Test TIP** Carefully read all instructions, questions, and answer options completely before attempting to choose an answer.

# Observing Symbiosis: Root Nodules

## OBJECTIVES

- Examine root nodules in legumes.
- Investigate the differences between a legume (bean) and a nonlegume (radish).
- View active cultures of symbiotic *Rhizobium*.

## PROCESS SKILLS

- recognizing relationships
- hypothesizing
- comparing and contrasting

## MATERIALS

- protective gloves
- 2 three-inch flowerpots
- 2 cups of soil
- 2 mixing sticks
- 1.2 mL (1/4 tsp) of *Rhizobium* bacteria per pot
- 2 bean seeds
- 2 radish seeds
- 2 microscope slides
- 2 coverslips
- 1 prepared slide of a soybean root nodule with symbiotic *Rhizobium* bacteria
- compound light microscope
- stereoscope or magnifying glass
- scalpel

## Background

1. Define *symbiosis*, and give examples.
2. Nitrogen-fixing bacteria and leguminous plants have a symbiotic relationship.
3. *Rhizobium* is a genus of nitrogen-fixing bacteria. *Rhizobium* species exist in soil and in the root nodules of leguminous plants such as soybeans.
4. Green root nodules indicate actively reproducing bacteria that are not fixing nitrogen. Pink nodules indicate bacteria that are actively fixing nitrogen but are not reproducing.
5. The process of nitrogen fixation is the basis of the nitrogen cycle. Only a few kinds of organisms are capable of converting nitrogen gas into a form that is usable by other organisms.

## PART A  Growing the Test Plants

1. Fill two flowerpots with soil. Using a mixing stick, stir approximately 1/4 tsp of the *Rhizobium* mixture into each pot.
2. Plant two bean seeds in one pot, and label the pot "Bean." Plant two radish seeds in the other pot, and label this pot "Radish." Water each pot so that the soil is moist but not saturated.
3. Place the plants where they will receive direct sunlight. Water the soil when necessary to keep the soil moist but not saturated. Do not fertilize the plants.
4. After approximately one week, check to see if both seeds germinated in each pot. If they did, remove the smaller seedling. The plants will be ready to be examined after six to eight weeks. Monitor the plants each day. (Note: The radish seeds will germinate faster than the bean seeds.)
5. Clean up your materials, and wash your hands before leaving the lab.

## PART B  Observing the Roots of Beans

6. Prepare a data table similar to the one below. As you work, record your observations in your data table.
7. **CAUTION Wear disposable gloves while handling plants. Do not rub any plant part or plant juice on your eyes or skin.** Remove the bean plant from the pot by grasping the bottom of the stem and gently pulling the plant out. Be careful not to injure the plant. Carefully remove all dirt from the roots.
8. View the roots of the bean plant under a stereoscope. Compare the appearance of the bean root system with the photograph above. Note the formation of any

### OBSERVATIONS OF ROOT NODULES

| | |
|---|---|
| Color of nodule | |
| Shape of nodule | |
| Number of nodules | |
| Number of pink nodules | |
| Number of green nodules | |

nodules on your bean plant's roots. Draw a root with a nodule in your lab report, and label each structure.

9. **CAUTION Use the scalpel with care. A scalpel is a very sharp instrument. When cutting, make sure that the blade faces away from your body. If you cut yourself, quickly apply direct pressure to the wound, and call for your teacher.** Remove a large nodule from the bean root, and carefully cut the nodule in half with a scalpel. The pink nodules contain active nitrogen-fixing bacteria. The green nodules contain bacteria but cannot fix nitrogen because they are actively reproducing. *Rhizobium* bacteria will begin fixing nitrogen only after they stop reproducing. View the cross section under a stereoscope. Note the arrangement of symbiotic cells within the nodule. Draw and label this arrangement.

## PART C Observing the Roots of Radishes

10. **CAUTION Wear disposable gloves while handling plants. Do not rub any plant part or plant juice on your eyes or skin.** Remove the radish plant from the pot by grasping the bottom of the stem and gently pulling the plant out. Be careful not to injure the plant. Carefully remove all dirt from the roots.

11. Examine the roots of the radish plant under a stereoscope. Compare the radish roots with the roots of the bean plant that you have already examined. Do the roots of the radish plant contain any nodules? Draw the root of the radish plant in your lab report. Label the drawing "Radish."

## PART D Preparing a Wet Mount of *Rhizobium*

12. **CAUTION Handle the slide and coverslip carefully. Glass slides break easily, and the sharp edges can cut you.** Prepare a wet mount by placing part of a pink nodule on a microscope slide, adding a drop of water, and covering the slide with a coverslip.

13. Place the slide on a flat surface. Gently press down on the slide with your thumb. Use enough pressure to squash the nodule. Make sure that the coverslip does not slide.

14. Examine the slide under a microscope. Draw and label your observations in your lab report. Note the power of magnification used.

15. Compare your wet mount preparation with the prepared slide of *Rhizobium* bacteria and the photograph on the right. Cells with active *Rhizobium* bacteria should look like the reddish cells in the photograph at right.

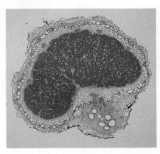

16. Clean up your materials, and wash your hands before leaving the lab.

## Analysis and Conclusions

1. Which plant had the most nodules?
2. How many nodules were found on the radish plants?
3. How do legumes become inoculated with bacteria in nature?
4. What kind of relationship exists between the legume plant and *Rhizobium* bacteria? How does this relationship benefit the legume plant? How does this relationship benefit the bacteria?
5. If you were to try to grow legumes without root nodules to use as experimental controls, why should you plant the seeds in sterile soil?

## Further Inquiry

Perform the experiment by using beans with and without *Rhizobium* bacteria. Count the number of leaves on each plant, and measure the mass of each whole plant as well as the masses of roots, stems, and leaves separately. Predict which part of the plant will differ the most.

# ECOSYSTEMS

Tropical rain forests are the most biologically diverse of all of the biomes on Earth. This scarlet macaw, *Ara macao*, lives in the rain forests of the Americas.

**SECTION 1** *Terrestrial Biomes*

**SECTION 2** *Aquatic Ecosystems*

**Unit 7—Ecosystem Dynamics,** Topic 1

For project ideas from *Scientific American*, visit go.hrw.com and type in the keyword **HM6SAE**.

# TERRESTRIAL BIOMES

*Biomes* (BIE-OHMZ) *are very large climatic regions that contain a number of smaller but related ecosystems within them. A certain biome may exist in more than one location on Earth, but each of those locations has a similar climate and inhabitants with similar adaptations.*

## SECTION 1

### OBJECTIVES

- **Identify** the eight major biomes.
- **Compare** tundra with taiga.
- **Compare** the different kinds of forests.
- **Compare** the different kinds of grasslands.
- **Describe** the adaptations of desert organisms.

### VOCABULARY

biome
tundra
permafrost
tropical forest
canopy
epiphyte
coniferous tree
deciduous tree
temperate deciduous forest
taiga
temperate grassland
savanna
chaparral
desert

## THE MAJOR BIOMES

Biomes are distinguished by the presence of characteristic plants and animals, but they are commonly identified by their dominant plant life. For example, hardwood trees, such as oaks and maples, are the dominant form of plant life in the deciduous forest biome. Most ecologists recognize eight major biomes, shown on the map in Figure 21-1, and several minor biomes. In this section, you will learn about the characteristics of these major biomes: tundra, tropical forest, temperate forest, taiga, temperate grassland, savanna, chaparral, and desert.

Because abiotic factors change over a landscape, biomes seldom have distinct boundaries. As climate varies over the Earth's surface, for example, deserts tend to gradually change into grasslands, tundra into taiga, and so on. Figure 21-1 shows how the major biomes are distributed over the Earth. Because climate varies with elevation, mountains contain a variety of communities and do not belong to any one biome. Table 21-1 describes the major biomes and lists their average annual temperature and rainfall.

**FIGURE 21-1**

The eight biomes cover most of Earth's land surface. Antarctica is not shown because it has no major biomes.

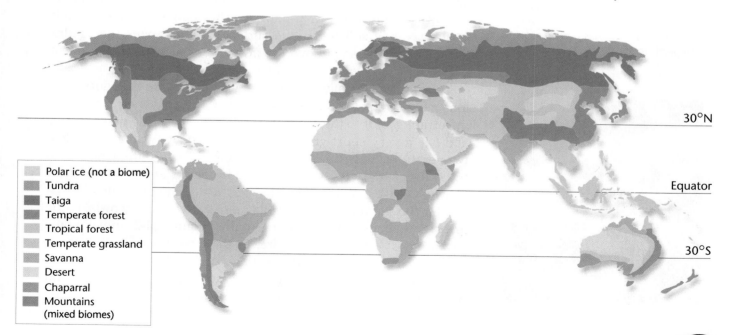

- Polar ice (not a biome)
- Tundra
- Taiga
- Temperate forest
- Tropical forest
- Temperate grassland
- Savanna
- Desert
- Chaparral
- Mountains (mixed biomes)

30°N

Equator

30°S

## TABLE 21-1  Characteristics of the Major Biomes

| Biome | Average yearly temperature range | Average yearly precipitation | Soil | Vegetation |
|-------|----------------------------------|------------------------------|------|------------|
| Tundra | −26°C to 12°C | <25 cm | moist, thin topsoil over permafrost; low in nutrients; slightly acidic | mosses, lichens, grasses, and dwarf woody plants |
| Taiga | −10°C to 14°C | 35–75 cm | low in nutrients; highly acidic | coniferous evergreen trees |
| Temperate forest | 6°C to 28°C | 75–125 cm | moist, moderately thick topsoils; moderate nutrient levels | broad-leaved deciduous trees and shrubs or evergreen coniferous trees |
| Tropical forest | 20°C to 34°C | 200–400 cm | moist, thin topsoil; low in nutrients | broad-leaved evergreen trees and shrubs |
| Temperate grassland | 0°C to 25°C | 25–75 cm | deep layer of topsoil; very rich in nutrients | dense, tall grasses in moist areas; short grasses in drier areas |
| Savanna | 16°C to 34°C | 75–150 cm | dry, thin topsoil; porous; low in nutrients | tall grasses and scattered trees |
| Chaparral | 10°C to 18°C | <25 cm | rocky, thin topsoil; low in nutrients | evergreen shrubs and small trees |
| Desert | 7°C to 38°C | <25 cm | dry, often sandy; low in nutrients | succulent plants and scattered grasses |

# TUNDRA

**FIGURE 21-2**

This herd of caribou lives in the treeless tundra in Canada. The photo shows the tundra in the summer, after the top layer of soil has thawed enough for plants to grow.

The **tundra** (TUHN-druh) is a cold and largely treeless biome that forms a continuous belt across northern North America, Europe, and Asia. It is the largest and northernmost biome, covering about one-fifth of the world's land surface. **Permafrost,** a permanently frozen layer of soil under the surface, characterizes the tundra. Even the surface soil above the permafrost remains frozen for all but about eight weeks of the year.

Trees do not usually grow in the tundra because the winters are long and extremely cold and permafrost prevents their roots from penetrating far into the soil. The tundra receives little precipitation and has a very short growing season of about two months. Cold temperatures slow down decay, so few nutrients are available in the soil. For these reasons, most tundra plants are small and grow slowly. Grasses, sedges, and mosses are common. Animals that inhabit the tundra include caribou, musk oxen, snowy owls, arctic foxes, lemmings, and snowshoe hares. Figure 21-2 shows some caribou in the Canadian tundra. In the brief summer, the upper layers of ice and soil thaw, creating ponds and bogs. Swarms of insects appear, and ducks, geese, cranes, other waterfowl, and predatory birds arrive in great numbers to feed.

# FORESTS

Scientists have classified up to 26 types of forests worldwide. Forest biomes are divided into three main types: tropical, temperate, and boreal forests, or taiga.

## Tropical Forests

**Tropical forests** occur near the equator, in the region between 23.5°N and 23.5°S, known as the *tropics*. This region includes parts of Asia, Africa, South America, and Central America. Stable temperature and abundant rainfall make tropical forests the most productive biome type. Tropical forests have only two seasons—one wet and one dry. *Tropical rain forests* are characterized by long wet seasons and tall trees and plants that grow year-round. *Tropical dry forests* have long dry seasons during which trees lose their leaves.

Competition for light is intense in a tropical rain forest. Most of the plants are trees, and some have evolved to grow as tall as 50 to 60 m (164 to 197 ft). The treetops form a continuous layer, called the **canopy,** which shades the forest floor. Though you may think of the tropical rain forest as an impenetrable jungle, much of the forest floor is relatively free of vegetation because so little sunlight reaches the ground. The very dense growth known as *jungle* is found along riverbanks and in disrupted areas where sunlight can reach the forest floor. Because of the intense competition for sunlight, many small plants live on the branches of tall trees. These plants are called **epiphytes** (EP-uh-FIETS) and include mosses, orchids and bromeliads, such as the one shown in Figure 21-3. Epiphytes use other organisms as support, but they are not parasitic because they make their own food.

Tropical forests have the highest species richness of all the biomes. One hectare of tropical rain forest (about the size of two football fields) may contain as many as 300 species of trees. An area of temperate deciduous forest of the same size, by contrast, would probably contain fewer than 12 species of trees. Animal life is also very diverse in the tropical rain forest. Rain-forest vertebrates include many kinds of monkeys, snakes, lizards, and colorful birds, such as parrots. Insect species are particularly diverse in tropical rain forests. There may be more than 1 million species of tree-dwelling beetles in the tropical rain forest biome alone. Overall, tropical rain forests probably contain about one-half of the world's species.

## Temperate Forests

Temperate forests occur in eastern North America, western and central Europe, and northeastern Asia. This biome is characterized by distinct seasons and a moderate climate. Temperate forests can be characterized by the type of tree that is most common, such as **coniferous trees,** which bear seeds in cones and tend to be evergreen, or **deciduous trees,** which shed their leaves each year.

**FIGURE 21-3**

The tall trees in a rain forest are home to many epiphytic species, such as this bromeliad. The red structure in the middle of the bromeliad shown here is a fruiting structure similar to a pineapple.

**Word Roots and Origins**

*epiphyte*

from the Greek word *epi,* meaning "on" or "upon" and *phyton,* meaning "a plant"

internet connect

www.scilinks.org
Topic: Forests
Keyword: HM60609

SCLINKS. Maintained by the National Science Teachers Association

## Temperate Deciduous Forests

Trees that lose all of their leaves in the fall and regrow them each spring characterize **temperate deciduous forests.** Deciduous forests stretch across eastern North America, much of Europe, and parts of Asia and the Southern Hemisphere. These regions have pronounced seasons, with precipitation unevenly distributed throughout the year. Compared with taiga, discussed below, temperate deciduous forests have warmer winters and longer summers and receive more precipitation. Deciduous trees have broad, thin leaves with a large surface area that permits maximum light absorption. Familiar deciduous trees include the birch, beech, maple, oak, hickory, sycamore, elm, ash, willow, and cottonwood. Bears, wolves, white-tailed deer, foxes, raccoons, and squirrels are typical mammals of the temperate deciduous forests. Large areas of temperate deciduous forest in the United States, Europe, and Asia have been cut for timber or cleared to make way for farms, towns, and cities. Figure 21-4 shows a stand of trees in a temperate deciduous forest.

## Taiga

South of the tundra and north of the temperate regions is the **taiga** (TIE-guh), a forested biome dominated by coniferous trees, such as pines, firs, and spruces. Taiga, also called *boreal forest,* stretches across large areas of northern Europe, Asia, and North America between 50°N and 60°N. During the long winter, snow covers and insulates the ground, protecting tree roots against freezing.

Plants living in the taiga are adapted for long, cold winters; short summers; and nutrient-poor soil. On a coniferous tree, the waxy, needle-shaped leaves remain on the tree all winter long. The shape of the needle is a leaf adaptation that reduces water loss, because the small holes through which the leaves exchange air are partially enclosed in the needle. Typical mammals of this biome include moose, bears, wolves, lynxes, and hares. Animals that are adapted to survive the winter may stay in the taiga year-round, but others migrate to warmer climates in the fall and return in the spring. Many species hibernate six to eight months of the year. Figure 21-5 shows a representative area of taiga.

# GRASSLANDS

Grasslands are, as the name suggests, dominated by a variety of grasses. Grasslands are known by different names in different parts of the world: *prairies* in North America, *steppes* in Asia, *pampas* in South America, and *veldts* in southern Africa.

## Temperate Grasslands

**Temperate grasslands** usually form in the interior of continents, at about the same latitude as temperate deciduous forests. However, rainfall patterns make these areas too dry to support trees. This biome once covered large areas of North America, Asia, Europe, Australia, and South America.

Temperate grasslands have rich, fertile soil. In areas that have remained relatively undisturbed by humans, grasslands support large herds of grazing mammals, such as the North American bison shown in Figure 21-6a. Grass can survive repeated grazing by animals and occasional fires that sweep across the area because the actively growing part of the plant is at or below the ground rather than at the tip of the stem. Because grasslands have such rich soil, much of the world's temperate grassland has been transformed into farmland for growing crops such as wheat and corn. Only fragments of undisturbed prairie remain in the midwestern United States.

## Savanna

**Savannas** (suh-VAN-uhz) are tropical or temperate grasslands that have scattered deciduous trees and shrubs. The savannas of Africa are the best known, but this biome also occurs in South America and Australia. Savannas receive more rainfall than deserts do but less rainfall than tropical or temperate forests do. Alternating wet and dry seasons characterize savannas. Like temperate grasslands, savannas support large numbers of herbivores, such as zebras, wildebeests, giraffes, and gazelles, as Figure 21-6b shows. Large carnivores, such as lions, leopards, and cheetahs, feed on these herbivores.

Because most of the rain falls during the wet season, the plants and animals of the savanna must be able to deal with prolonged periods of drought. Some trees of the savanna shed their leaves during the dry season to conserve water, and the above-ground parts of grasses often die during the dry season and regenerate after a period of rain.

## Chaparral

**Chaparral** (SHAP-uh-RAL) is a biome that is dominated by dense, spiny shrubs and has scattered clumps of coniferous trees, as Figure 21-6c shows. Chaparral is characterized by mild, rainy winters and hot, dry summers with periodic fires. This biome is located in the middle latitudes, about 30° north and 30° south of the equator. Chaparral is found primarily in coastal regions—for example, around the Mediterranean Sea and in southern California.

**FIGURE 21-6**

Temperate grasslands once covered a large portion of the United States and supported huge herds of herbivores, such as bison (a). An area rich in wildlife, the savanna biome supports great herds of large herbivores (b). The chaparral biome supports grasses, shrubs, and clumps of small trees (c).

**(a)** Temperate grassland

**(b)** Savanna

**(c)** Chaparral

# DESERTS

**Deserts** are areas that receive an average of less than 25 cm (9.9 in.) of rainfall per year. Large parts of North Africa, central Australia, southwestern North America, and eastern Asia are desert. Contrary to popular belief, deserts are not hot all the time. So-called cold deserts, such as the Great Basin in the western United States and the Gobi in eastern Asia, are hot in summer but cold in winter. Even in hot deserts, temperatures may fall by as much as 30°C (54°F) at night because the dry air is a poor insulator, allowing the heat that builds up during the day to escape.

Desert vegetation is often sparse and consists mainly of plants that have adapted to the dry climate. The leaves of the creosote bush of the United States and Mexico, for example, have a waxy coating that reduces evaporation. Plants in moist environments normally allow a great deal of water to escape through evaporation and transpiration from *stomata*, tiny openings in their leaves. In contrast, desert plants may have few stomata or may open the stomata only at night. A common type of desert plant is a cactus, such as the saguaro cactus shown in Figure 21-7. It has an expandable body that can store water and leaves that have evolved into sharp spines that protect the plant from herbivores. A single saguaro can hold about 1,000 kg (2,200 lb) of water. The saguaro cactus is found in Arizona, California, and Mexico.

Like desert plants, desert animals must conserve water. Many animals avoid the heat of the day by hiding in small spots of shade or by burrowing into the ground. Others, such as kit foxes and some kinds of lizards and snakes, are active only at night, when loss of water to evaporation is low.

**FIGURE 21-7**

All of the organisms of the desert biome are adapted to endure dry, often hot conditions by conserving energy and water. This saguaro cactus is full of water, which it has stored from the infrequent rains in the desert.

## SECTION 1 REVIEW

1. List at least one animal that lives in each of the eight major biomes.

2. Compare the level of biodiversity in a tropical rain forest with that in a temperate deciduous forest.

3. Why do so few trees grow in the tundra?

4. What other name is used for grasslands in North America?

5. Where in the world could you travel to see savanna? chaparral?

6. Describe three adaptations of desert organisms for water conservation.

**CRITICAL THINKING**

7. **Evaluating Information** For deciduous trees, compare the benefits and possible disadvantages of shedding leaves in the fall.

8. **Comparing Concepts** Discuss the similarities between temperate grassland and savanna.

9. **Comparing Concepts** Discuss the differences between tundra and taiga.

10. **Calculating Information** Summarize the conditions that determine which type of biome is present in a particular location. Provide at least two abiotic factors and one biotic factor.

# AQUATIC ECOSYSTEMS

*As terrestrial organisms, we tend to focus on the other land-dwelling organisms we see around us. But on the geologic time scale, life seems to have originated and existed in the oceans long before it came onto land. Water covers about three-fourths of Earth and is home to a variety of organisms.*

## OCEAN ZONES

The ocean covers about 70 percent of Earth's surface and has an average depth of 3.7 km (2.3 mi). The deepest parts of the ocean are about 11 km (6.8 mi) deep. The water contains about 3 percent salt, mostly sodium chloride, a factor that strongly affects the biology of the organisms that live there.

Another important factor affecting marine organisms is the availability of light. Most of the ocean is cold and dark. This zone, where sunlight cannot penetrate and photosynthesis cannot occur, is called the **aphotic** (ay-FOHT-ik) **zone.** Because water absorbs light, sunlight penetrates only the upper few hundred meters of the ocean. The part of the ocean that receives sunlight is the **photic** (FOHT-ik) **zone.** The depth of the photic zone varies.

Ecologists recognize three zones relative to the ocean's edges, as illustrated in Figure 21-8. The **intertidal zone** is the area of shoreline that is twice daily covered by water during high tide and exposed to air during low tide. Farther out is the **neritic** (nee-RIT-ik) **zone,** which extends from the intertidal zone over the continental shelf and to relatively shallow water depths of about 180 m.

### OBJECTIVES

- **Identify** the major ocean zones.
- **Compare** the aphotic zone with the photic zone.
- **Compare** the neritic zone with the oceanic zone.
- **Describe** estuaries.
- **Compare** eutrophic lakes with oligotrophic lakes.
- **Explain** the significance of gradient in rivers and streams.
- **Describe** freshwater wetlands.

### VOCABULARY

aphotic zone
photic zone
intertidal zone
neritic zone
oceanic zone
pelagic zone
benthic zone
plankton
estuary
eutrophic lake
oligotrophic lake
freshwater wetland

**FIGURE 21-8**

This diagram shows the major ecological zones of the ocean.

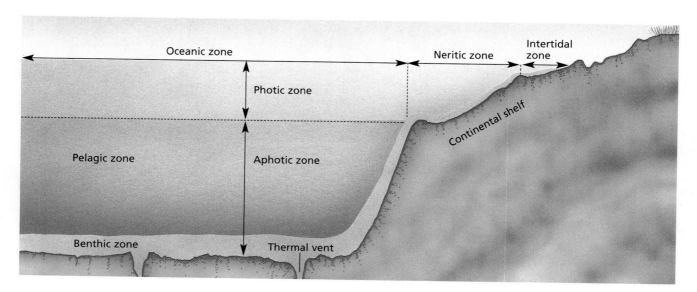

Beyond the continental shelf is the **oceanic zone,** which is the deep water of the open sea. The neritic and oceanic zones are further divided. The open ocean is known as the **pelagic** (pi-LAJ-ik) **zone,** and the ocean bottom is known as the **benthic zone.**

## The Intertidal Zone

Organisms in the intertidal zone are adapted to periodic exposure to air during low tide. Crabs avoid dehydration by burrowing into the sand or mud. Clams, mussels, and oysters retreat into their shells at low tide. Organisms living in the intertidal zone must be able to withstand the force of crashing waves. Sea anemones cling to rocks with a muscular disk, and sea stars use tube feet to adhere to surfaces. Figure 21-9 shows some of the organisms living in the rocky intertidal zone of the California coast.

## The Neritic Zone

The neritic zone is the most productive zone in the ocean, supporting more species and numbers of organisms than any other zone. The water throughout most of the neritic zone is shallow enough for photosynthesis to occur. Strong currents called *upwellings* carry nutrients from the ocean bottom and mix them with nutrients contained in runoff from land. These waters are rich in **plankton,** communities of small organisms that drift with the ocean currents. Plankton is consumed by many larger animals. Numerous fishes, sea turtles, and other animals also live in these waters.

Coral reefs form in the neritic zone of tropical areas. Like tropical rain forests, coral reefs are very productive and rich in species. A coral reef is built by coral animals over a long time period. They construct external skeletons of calcium carbonate. As the animals grow and die, the skeletons accumulate to form the base of a reef, as shown in Figure 21-10. A reef is home to many species of fishes, crustaceans, mollusks, and other animals. Most species of reef-forming coral have a mutualistic relationship with photosynthetic protists, from which they receive food.

**FIGURE 21-9**

The intertidal zone shown here is similar to intertidal zones all over the planet. A sandy beach is part of the intertidal zone, but it is usually distinguished from the rocky intertidal zones and not as rich in species as the rocky intertidal zones are.

**FIGURE 21-10**

Coral reefs, such as the one shown here, are among the most diverse ecosystems on Earth. Coral reefs are extremely sensitive to pollution. Many reefs around the world are threatened, and many have been damaged or destroyed as a result of human activities.

# The Oceanic Zone

The oceanic zone encompasses the deepest parts of the ocean and contains fewer species than the neritic zone does. Even in photic areas, nutrient levels are too low to support as much life. Although the productivity per square meter of open ocean is very low, the total productivity of the oceanic zone is high because the ocean covers such a vast area. About half of the photosynthesis that occurs on Earth takes place in the oceanic zone. The producers of the upper parts of the oceanic zone are microscopic protists, bacteria, plants, and invertebrates in the plankton. Animals include fishes, mammals such as whales, and many large invertebrates.

In the aphotic zone, animals feed primarily on sinking plankton and dead organisms. Organisms living deep in the ocean must cope with near-freezing temperatures and crushing pressure. Deep-sea organisms, such as the squid shown in Figure 21-11, have slow metabolic rates and reduced skeletal systems. Fishes in these depths have large jaws and teeth and expandable stomachs that can accommodate the rare prey that they can catch.

In the 1970s, scientists found diverse communities living near volcanic vents 2,500 m (8,200 ft) below the surface. These vents release water that is rich in minerals and often exceeds 750°C. The producers for this ecosystem are chemosynthetic bacteria that use energy contained in hydrogen sulfide, $H_2S$, from the vents. Unique clams, crabs, and worms feed on these bacteria. Tube worms living near the vents have lost their digestive system over evolutionary time and receive all of their food directly from chemosynthetic bacteria living in their bodies.

## Estuaries

An **estuary** (ES-tyoo-er-ee) occurs where freshwater rivers and streams flow into the sea. Examples of estuary communities include bays, mud flats, mangrove swamp forests, and salt marshes. The shallow water receives plenty of light, and rivers deposit large amounts of mineral nutrients. However, the interaction between fresh water and salt water causes great variation in temperature and salinity. In addition, like the surface of the intertidal zone, the surface of an estuary is partly exposed during low tide. Inhabitants of estuaries are adapted for frequent change. For example, some kinds of mangrove trees have special glands on their leaves that eliminate excess salt water taken up by the roots. Softshell clams lie buried in mud with only their long siphons protruding above the surface. The siphon filters plankton from the salt water at high tide and detects predators at low tide, contracting whenever it senses danger. Figure 21-12 shows an example of an estuary.

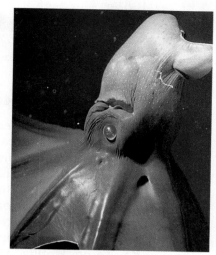

**FIGURE 21-11**

Organisms in the deep ocean have many adaptations to their environment. The squid in the photograph, *Vampyroteuthis* sp., is adapted to eating a large quantity of food at once because prey is hard to find.

**FIGURE 21-12**

Estuaries are almost as rich in species as tropical rain forests are. Estuaries serve as stopovers and nurseries for both terrestrial and marine organisms. Organisms that spend at least part of their lives in estuaries include shrimp, oysters, mullet, redfish, anchovies, striped bass, and other animals that people consume as food.

# RESTORING AN ECOSYSTEM: Molasses Reef

For years, Molasses Reef looked like a colorful carpet of living coral with thousands of tropical fish species darting in and out of the reef, as the photo at the bottom of the page shows. This barrier reef stretches for miles southeast of Key Largo, Florida, and is part of the third-largest reef system in the world.

## Disaster Strikes the Reef

The *Wellwood,* a cargo ship measuring 366 feet long, wrecked on Molasses Reef on August 4, 1984. It took 12 days for tugboats to remove the ship with steel cables, as the photo below shows. This motion crushed large areas of coral. Furthermore, the ship created shade over the coral, starving its symbiotic photosynthesizers for days. As a result, the shaded coral lost its living layer and lost its color, a condition known as *bleaching.* Animals such as fishes and crabs left the area. By the end of summer, one-half of a square mile of Molasses Reef was pulverized, and an additional 6 square miles were damaged.

## Restoration and Stabilization of Molasses Reef

The owners of the *Wellwood* agreed to fund the restoration of Molasses Reef. Soon after the accident, divers put some of the fallen coral back in place. They later transplanted several species of living coral from nearby reef sites. The most extreme repair involved filling large holes and cracks in the reef with concrete and building 22 structures to restore the basic shape of the reef. Each structure weighed more than 3,500 pounds. Ultimately, biologists hoped to restore the appearance of the reef and stabilize the biological community. More than 20 years later, marine biologists are seeing the regrowth of many, but not all, of the original coral species.

## Future Protection of the Florida Keys Reef Ecosystem

People can damage reef systems in other ways as well. More than 3 million people visit the Keys each year, and about 80,000 people live there. The U.S. Coast Guard and the National Oceanic and Atmospheric Administration have ongoing goals for protecting Molasses Reef, which is now part of the Florida Keys National Marine Sanctuary. One goal is to control sewage runoff. Another goal is to educate residents and visitors about damage from boats, divers, fishers, and beachgoers. Programs are underway to protect this unique ecosystem.

## REVIEW

1. What events led to coral reef bleaching at Molasses Reef?
2. Why is education important in protecting Molasses Reef?
3. **Critical Thinking** Do you think boats should be allowed in a marine sanctuary? Explain your answer.

*In the 12 days it took to remove the wrecked* Wellwood *from Molasses Reef, much of the reef community was lost. But efforts to restore the community are beginning to have positive results.*

**internet** connect

www.scilinks.org
**Topic: Coral Reefs**
**Keyword: HM60356**

SC*LINKS.* Maintained by the National Science Teachers Association

# FRESHWATER ZONES

 **Quick Lab**

Low levels of dissolved salts characterize freshwater ecosystems. The salt content of fresh water is about 0.005 percent. Examples of freshwater ecosystems include lakes, ponds, freshwater wetlands, clear mountain streams, and slow, sediment-rich rivers.

## Lakes and Ponds

Ecologists divide lakes and ponds into two categories. **Eutrophic** (yoo-TRAHF-ik) **lakes** are rich in organic matter and vegetation, so the waters are relatively murky. As the number of plants and algae in a lake grows, the number of bacteria feeding on decaying organisms also grows. These bacteria use the oxygen dissolved in the lake's waters. Eventually, the reduced amount of oxygen kills organisms that need oxygen to survive. Lakes naturally become eutrophic over a long period of time.

In contrast, **oligotrophic** (AHL-i-goh-TRAHF-ik) **lakes** contain little organic matter. The water is much clearer, and the bottom is usually sandy or rocky. Fishes inhabit both eutrophic and oligotrophic lakes. Freshwater lakes and ponds support a variety of other animals, including mammals such as the otter and muskrat, birds such as ducks and loons, reptiles such as turtles and snakes, and amphibians such as salamanders and frogs.

## Rivers and Streams

A river or stream is a body of freshwater that flows down a gradient, or slope, toward its mouth, as shown in Figure 21-13. Water flows swiftly down steep gradients, and organisms are adapted to withstand powerful currents. For example, the larvae of caddis flies and the nymphs of mayflies cling to the rocky bottom, and brook trout and other fishes have evolved the strength to swim upstream. Slow-moving rivers and their backwaters are richer in nutrients and therefore support a greater diversity of life. Rooted plants and the fishes that feed on them are adapted to the weaker currents of slow-moving rivers.

## Comparing Organisms in Terrestrial and Aquatic Biomes

**Materials** paper, scissors, magazines, glue

**Procedure** Cut out and collect images of plants, animals, and other organisms from magazines. Sort out the images based on which major biome each organism would live in. Develop a collage of each major biome.

**Analysis** Of the images you collected, which organisms live in terrestrial biomes (specify the type of terrestrial biome)? in aquatic biomes (specify the type)? What types of adaptations do each of the organisms have that allow them to live in the biome?

**FIGURE 21-13**

Streams in mountain areas flow rapidly down steep slopes. These streams usually have rocky bottoms and clear water (a). Rivers that flow slower carry more fine sediment and commonly have muddy bottoms (b).

(a)

(b)

**FIGURE 21-14**

The American alligator, *Alligator mississippiensis,* is the largest reptile in North America. It lives in marshes and swamps in Florida, Louisiana, South Carolina, Georgia, Alabama, and Texas. The alligator is protected by law because of its similarity to the very rare American crocodile.

## Freshwater Wetlands

**Freshwater wetlands** are areas of land that are covered with fresh water for at least part of each year. The two main types of freshwater wetlands are *marshes* and *swamps*. Marshes contain non-woody plants, such as cattails, and swamps are dominated by woody plants, such as trees and shrubs. Another type of freshwater wetland is a *bog,* which is dominated by sphagnum mosses.

Freshwater wetlands are the most productive freshwater ecosystem. They contain a wide variety of birds, fishes, mammals, amphibians, invertebrates, and reptiles. Wetlands in the United States are home to rare, large predators such as the whooping crane, the Florida panther, the American crocodile, and the American alligator, shown in Figure 21-14. Many wetlands are important as stopovers for migratory birds. Wetlands, like estuaries, provide protection for spawning organisms, such as fishes. Wetlands are also important to people economically and environmentally. Wetlands act as filters to clean pollutants out of the water flowing through them and also act as flood control when they absorb large quantities of water that could otherwise flood homes, farms, and businesses.

For many decades, wetlands have been diverted, drained, and filled in. But now, the vital importance of wetlands to the economic and environmental health of many areas is being recognized. In some cases, government agencies and private organizations are working together to protect wetlands and to restore areas that have been damaged. One of the most important wetlands in the world is the Everglades National Park in southern Florida. There is currently a major effort to restore the flow of water through the Everglades, upon which the entire ecosystem depends. The Everglades has been designated a World Heritage Site, an International Biosphere Reserve, and a Wetlands of International Importance.

## SECTION 2 REVIEW

1. Distinguish between the photic and aphotic zones.

2. Describe the intertidal zone, and give examples of organisms living there.

3. Describe the differences between the neritic and oceanic zones in the ocean.

4. What are two sources of nutrients in the neritic zone?

5. What role do chemosynthetic bacteria play in deep-sea volcanic-vent ecosystems?

6. What is the main difference between oligotrophic and eutrophic lakes?

**CRITICAL THINKING**

7. **Applying Information** What could happen to the organisms that live in a fast-moving river if a dam were built on the river?

8. **Evaluating Information** Estuaries serve as breeding sites and nurseries for thousands of species of marine animals. What are the possible advantages and disadvantages to the organisms using estuaries for these purposes?

9. **Drawing Conclusions** Why are freshwater wetlands considered to be economically and environmentally important?

# CHAPTER HIGHLIGHTS

**Terrestrial Biomes**

- The major types of terrestrial ecosystems, known as biomes, are tundra, tropical forest, temperate forest, taiga, temperate grassland, savanna, chaparral, and desert.

- Tundra is a cold biome characterized by permafrost under the surface of the ground.

- Tropical forests receive abundant rainfall and have stable temperatures. They have a greater species richness than any other biome.

- Temperate biomes have four annual seasons. The trees in temperate deciduous forests shed all of their leaves in the fall.

- Taiga is cold but is warmer than tundra and receives more precipitation. Taiga is dominated by coniferous forests.

- Temperate grasslands occur in areas with cold winters and hot summers. They are dominated by grasses and herds of grazing animals.

- Savannas are tropical grasslands with alternating wet and dry seasons. They are dominated by herds of grazing animals.

- Chaparral is found in coastal regions with warm, dry summers and mild winters. It is dominated by dense, spiny shrubs.

- Deserts receive less than 25 cm (9.9 in.) of precipitation per year. Desert inhabitants have adaptations for conserving water.

### Vocabulary
biome (p. 417)
tundra (p. 418)
permafrost (p. 418)
tropical forest (p. 419)
canopy (p. 419)
epiphyte (p. 419)
coniferous tree (p. 419)
deciduous tree (p. 419)
temperate deciduous forest (p. 420)
taiga (p. 420)
temperate grassland (p. 421)
savanna (p. 421)
chaparral (p. 421)
desert (p. 422)

---

**SECTION 2** **Aquatic Ecosystems**

- The photic zone in the ocean receives light, but the aphotic zone does not. Other zones of the ocean are defined based on their relative locations.

- In the intertidal zone, organisms must be able to tolerate drying and pounding by waves.

- The neritic zone receives nutrients from the bottom of the ocean and from land. It is the ocean's richest zone in terms of the number of species and individuals.

- Production in the oceanic zone is limited by a shortage of nutrients.

- Estuaries are very productive areas where rivers and streams flow into the sea.

- Oligotrophic lakes are clear and lacking in nutrients. Eutrophic lakes are rich in nutrients and are often murky.

- Rivers and streams are bodies of water that flow down an elevation gradient within a watershed.

- Freshwater wetlands are areas of land, such as marshes and swamps, that are covered with fresh water for at least part of each year.

### Vocabulary
aphotic zone (p. 423)
photic zone (p. 423)
intertidal zone (p. 423)
neritic zone (p. 423)
oceanic zone (p. 424)
pelagic zone (p. 424)
benthic zone (p. 424)
plankton (p. 424)
estuary (p. 425)
eutrophic lake (p. 427)
oligotrophic lake (p. 427)
freshwater wetland (p. 428)

## USING VOCABULARY

1. For each pairs of terms, explain how the meanings of the terms differ.
   a. *savanna* and *desert*
   b. *tundra* and *taiga*
   c. *photic zone* and *aphotic zone*
   d. *estuary* and *freshwater wetland*

2. For each pair of terms, explain the relationship between the terms.
   a. *tropical rain forest* and *canopy*
   b. *tundra* and *permafrost*
   c. *neritic zone* and *plankton*

3. **Word Roots and Origins** The word *epiphtye* is derived from the Greek *phytos,* which means "plant," and the prefix *epi-,* which means "on top of." Using this information, explain why the term *epiphtye* is a good name for the type of organism than the term describes.

## UNDERSTANDING KEY CONCEPTS

4. **Explain** why tundra soil is poor in nutrients.

5. **Describe** a tropical rain forest.

6. **Explain** how the destruction of tropical rain forests can contribute to an increase in carbon dioxide levels in the atmosphere.

7. **Compare** the dominant vegetation of temperate deciduous forests with that of taiga.

8. **Identify** the adaptive function of the needle-like leaves on a coniferous tree.

9. **Contrast** a temperate grassland with a savanna.

10. **Describe** the typical plants and soil of a desert.

11. **List** the approximate latitudes where the following biomes are mostly located: tropical rain forests, tundra, and chaparral.

12. **Identify** which terrestrial biomes are the most productive.

13. **Identify** the major zones in the oceans.

14. **Identify** which ocean zones are most productive.

15. **Explain** why the oxygen content of eutrophic lakes decreases over time.

16. **Explain** why estuaries are more productive than most other biomes.

17. **Explain** how gradient affects rivers and streams.

18. **BIOLOGY INTERACTIVE TUTOR** **Write** a report summarizing how artificial aquatic ecosystems are used to eliminate pollutants from wastewater. Find out which kinds of modern urban facilities use artificial ecosystems.

19. **CONCEPT MAPPING** Use the following terms to create a concept map that shows how biomes can be classified based on climate: *desert, savanna, tropical rain forest, temperate grassland, temperate deciduous forest, tundra, taiga, climate, arid, cold, temperate, tropical, hot, dry, trees,* and *grass.*

## CRITICAL THINKING

20. **Interpreting Graphics** The rare species of squid in the photo below has several adaptations for living in very deep water. Explain some of the selective pressures that exist at great depths.

21. **Analyzing Information** Which biome occurs in all of the following locations: Spain, Australia, Canada, and the northeastern United States?

22. **Evaluating Information** Which soil is better suited for agricultural use: the soil of a tropical rain forest or the soil of a temperate deciduous forest? Explain your answer.

23. **Inferring Relationships** The organisms found near deep-sea volcanic vents do not use sunlight to get energy. What are possible energy sources for these organisms?

24. **Predicting Results** Would a herd of large herbivores be able to survive for many generations in a desert biome? Explain your answer.

25. **Evaluating Viewpoints** Imagine that a local government is debating whether a large freshwater wetland should be drained and filled in so that a new road can be built or whether the area should be turned into a wildlife refuge. Both of these options will have costs and benefits to the community. Draft some arguments that could be made for each side of the debate.

# Standardized Test Preparation

**DIRECTIONS:** Choose the letter of the answer choice that best answers the question.

1. Why are estuaries more productive than most other biomes?
   A. Estuaries contain vast coniferous forests.
   B. Estuaries have shallow, nutrient-laden water.
   C. Estuaries get more sunlight than other biomes.
   D. The majority of land on Earth is covered by estuaries.

2. Which of the following characterizes the neritic zone of the ocean?
   F. It receives little sunlight.
   G. It supports very few species.
   H. It is exposed to the air by low tide.
   J. It receives nutrients washed from land.

3. Which of the following is true of temperate deciduous forests?
   A. They are found near the equator.
   B. They have the lowest rainfall of any biome.
   C. They undergo seasonal changes in temperature.
   D. They have the highest species richness of any biome.

4. Which of the following best describes the water of all eutrophic lakes?
   F. cold
   G. salty
   H. murky
   J. lifeless

**INTERPRETING GRAPHICS:** The graph below shows the relative temperature, precipitation, and soil nutrient content in a specific biome. Use the graph to answer the question that follows.

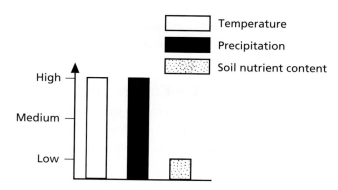

5. Which of the following biomes is best represented by this graph?
   A. tundra
   B. desert
   C. tropical rain forest
   D. temperate grassland

**DIRECTIONS:** Complete the following analogy.

6. grasses : savanna :: coniferous trees :
   F. taiga
   G. tundra
   H. desert
   J. temperate deciduous forest

**INTERPRETING GRAPHICS:** The graph below ranks several types of biomes in terms of their relative productivity. Use the graph to answer the question that follows.

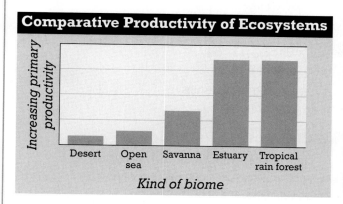

7. If a scientist needed to add a bar representing the temperate grassland biome to this graph, where should the bar be placed?
   A. to the left of desert
   B. between savanna and estuary
   C. between estuary and tropical rain forest
   D. to the right of tropical rain forest

## SHORT RESPONSE

Biomes are very large climatic regions that contain a number of smaller but related ecosystems.

Describe how the major biomes are characterized.

## EXTENDED RESPONSE

Ecologists recognize the following ecological zones in the ocean: *photic, aphotic, intertidal, neritic, oceanic, pelagic,* and *benthic.*

*Part A*  Describe the factors used as a basis for distinguishing the zones.

*Part B*  Relate these factors to the types of organisms that inhabit each zone.

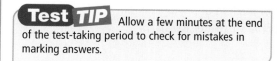

**Test TIP**  Allow a few minutes at the end of the test-taking period to check for mistakes in marking answers.

# Constructing and Comparing Ecosystems

## OBJECTIVES

- Observe the interaction of organisms in a closed ecosystem.
- Compare this ecosystem with others observed in nature.

## PROCESS SKILLS

- observing
- recognizing relationships
- hypothesizing

## MATERIALS

- large glass jar with lid for each ecosystem
- pond water or dechlorinated tap water
- gravel, rocks, and soil
- graph paper
- $8\frac{1}{2} \times 11$ in. acetate sheets
- several colored pens for overhead transparencies

### Ecosystem 1

- pinch of grass seeds
- pinch of clover seeds
- 10 mung-bean seeds
- 3 earthworms
- 4 to 6 isopods (pill bugs or sow bugs)
- 6 mealworms (darkling beetle larvae)
- 6 crickets

### Ecosystem 2

- 5 to 15 strands of aquatic plants
- 1 ounce duckweed
- culture or mixture of phytoplankton
- 1 or 2 ramshorn snails
- 2 to 4 guppies, platys, or comet goldfish

### Ecosystem 3

- small, clear glass container for inner water
- 3 to 7 strands of aquatic plants
- culture or mixture of phytoplankton
- 10 *Daphnia* sp. (water fleas)

- 2 to 4 pond snails (Lymnaeidae family)
- 2 to 4 guppies, platys, or comet goldfish
- pinch of grass seeds
- pinch of clover seeds

## Background

1. How are living things affected by nonliving things in the environment?
2. Relate the theme of interdependence among organisms to ecosystems.
3. How do different types of organisms interact?

## Experiment Setup

1. In this investigation, you will observe organisms in one of three different ecosystems. Look at the organisms listed in the materials list, and choose the ecosystem you would like to observe. Which organisms might be the most numerous? Which organisms might decrease in number? Hypothesize how the organisms will interact.
2. Form a group with classmates who have all chosen the same ecosystem. As a group, prepare the environment in a jar with a chosen substrate. Go to Part A, Part B, or Part C for set-up instructions for your ecosystem.
3. Put lids on the containers, and let the ecosystem remain undisturbed in indirect sunlight for a week. Go to Part D after one week.

### PART A Setting Up Ecosystem 1

1. Place the soil in the bottom of the jar about 4 or 5 in. deep. Clean soil off the inside of the jar.
2. Place rocks in and on top of the soil in a natural-looking arrangement.
3. Moisten the soil carefully. Do not saturate the soil.
4. Plant the seeds according to the package instructions.
5. Clean up your materials, and wash your hands before leaving the lab.

## PART D Observing Your Ecosystem

16. Place the chosen animals in the jar, and loosely replace the lid.
17. Observe the jar for a few minutes daily.
18. Make a chart in your lab report to record the original number of each species in your ecosystem. Record daily any changes you observe.
19. Make a graph for each species in your chart, and plot the number of organisms as a function of time. Place a clear acetate sheet over each graph. Using a pen used for overhead transparencies, trace each graph onto the acetate sheet. Use a different colored pen and a different acetate sheet for each organism.
20. Compare the acetate sheets of two organisms that you hypothesized would interact—a predator and its prey, for example. Hold one sheet on top of the other, and analyze both graphs. Record the results in your lab report.
21. Clean up your materials, and wash your hands before leaving the lab.

## Analysis and Conclusions

1. What happened to the organisms in your ecosystem? How did their population sizes change?
2. What are some possible causes of the change in the populations you observed?
3. Construct a food chain or food web for the ecosystem you observed. Which organisms were producers? Which organisms were consumers?
4. What could you learn if you set up more than one jar in an identical manner?
5. How does your ecosystem resemble a natural ecosystem? How does it differ?
6. How did your observation compare with your hypotheses? If the results differed from what you expected, explain what might have caused the difference.
7. Look at your graphs, and determine what kind of relationship exists between predator and prey populations.
8. How would you modify the ecosystem if you were to repeat this investigation?

## Further Inquiry

Develop an experiment to study the effects of abiotic factors—such as temperature, light, and moisture—on the organisms in the ecosystem you constructed.

## PART B Setting Up Ecosystem 2

6. Place about 2 in. of clean gravel in the bottom of the jar.
7. Gently fill the jar with pond water or dechlorinated tap water until the jar is about three-fourths full.
8. Add the plants and algae to your ecosystem.
9. Clean up your materials, and wash your hands before leaving the lab.

## PART C Setting Up Ecosystem 3

10. Place a small, clear glass container, such as a mayonnaise jar, inside the larger jar and against one side.
11. Carefully place soil in the larger jar about 4 or 5 in. deep, filling around the smaller jar so that you can see through both jars on one side. Do not place any soil on the side where the two jars touch. Clean any soil from the sides of the jar that may obstruct your view.
12. Place some rocks on the soil, and moisten the soil carefully.
13. Place 1 in. of gravel inside the smaller jar, and gently fill with pond water or dechlorinated tap water to the level of the soil.
14. Place the algae and the aquatic plants in the water. Plant the grass seeds and clover seeds in the soil in separate areas of the jar.
15. Clean up your materials, and wash your hands before leaving the lab.

# HUMANS AND THE ENVIRONMENT

This aircraft is leading a flock of whooping cranes in order to teach the birds to migrate between Wisconsin and Florida. The whooping crane, *Grus americana,* is a species that has almost disappeared because of human actions. But scientists and others have made efforts to save this species. Their efforts have included protecting the cranes with laws, preserving the cranes' habitat, breeding the cranes in captivity, and then teaching the cranes to migrate.

**SECTION 1** *An Interconnected Planet*

**SECTION 2** *Environmental Issues*

**SECTION 3** *Environmental Solutions*

*BIOLOGY* INTERACTIVE TUTOR

**Unit 7—Ecosystem Dynamics**
Topics 1–6

# AN INTERCONNECTED PLANET

*The study of the interaction between humans and their own environment is* **environmental science.** *Like all other organisms, humans depend on their environment for food, water, air, shelter, and other resources. Earth and its inhabitants are interconnected in complex ways. However, the ability of humans to understand, manipulate, and possibly damage ecosystems exceeds that of other organisms. Thus, environmental science may be critical to our own survival.*

## EARTH'S LAYERS

One way to understand our unique planet is to think of Earth as a giant sphere made up of layers, or spheres within spheres. Scientists describe three major layers, as Figure 22-1 shows. The **geosphere** is Earth's rock interior that extends from the molten center of the planet's core to the solid surface of its crust. Above the geosphere lies the **hydrosphere,** the portion of Earth that is water, including all oceans, lakes, and rivers. Above the hydrosphere and geosphere floats the **atmosphere,** the mixture of gases that surrounds Earth. Living organisms are known to exist in parts of each of Earth's three main spheres. Thus, scientists also refer to the **biosphere,** meaning the part of Earth where life exists.

### OBJECTIVES

- **Explain** the importance of the study of environmental science.
- **Describe** Earth's major layers.
- **Explain** the natural functions of the ozone layer and greenhouse effect.
- **Summarize** the ways in which biologists measure biodiversity.
- **Discuss** the value of biodiversity.

### VOCABULARY

environmental science
geosphere
hydrosphere
atmosphere
biosphere
ozone layer
greenhouse effect
biodiversity
species diversity
genetic diversity

**FIGURE 22-1**

Layers of air (atmosphere), water (hydrosphere), and rock and soil (geosphere) interact with each other. Living things make up the biosphere, which includes parts of each of these three layers.

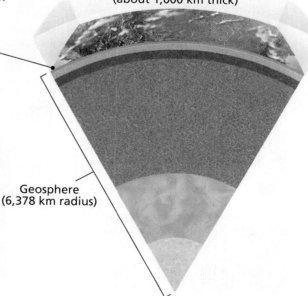

Atmosphere
(about 1,000 km thick)

Hydrosphere 29 km

Biosphere
20 km

9 km

11 km

Geosphere
(6,378 km radius)

## Atmosphere

The atmosphere consists of about 78 percent nitrogen, $N_2$, about 21 percent oxygen, $O_2$, and about 1 percent other gases, including water vapor, $H_2O$, and carbon dioxide, $CO_2$. Atmospheric gases become less dense at greater altitudes. For example, the density (number of molecules per liter) of oxygen at 18,000 ft is half of its density at sea level. While the density of each gas decreases with altitude, the relative proportion of each gas remains about the same. An exception is ozone (OH-zohn), $O_3$, a naturally occurring gas that is vital to life on Earth. The concentration of ozone is greatest in the **ozone layer,** a region that is about 20 km above Earth's surface.

## Climate and Atmosphere

The ozone layer is important because it absorbs most of the sun's ultraviolet radiation before it reaches Earth's surface. Most organisms on Earth depend on this protection because ultraviolet radiation can damage DNA and cause mutations. In contrast, some gases in the atmosphere direct energy toward Earth's surface. Energy from the sun reaches Earth's surface as light but may leave the surface as heat. Some gases in the atmosphere function to radiate this heat back toward Earth's surface. The atmosphere's ability to trap heat in this way is called the **greenhouse effect.** The atmospheric gases that contribute to this effect are sometimes called *greenhouse gases.*

As Figure 22-2 illustrates, Earth can be heated by sunlight in the same way that air in a greenhouse can be. ❶ First, solar energy passes through the atmosphere and strikes Earth's surface. Some of this light is absorbed and converted to heat. ❷ A portion of the heat radiates back through the atmosphere. ❸ Some of the radiated heat escapes into space. ❹ However, some heat is absorbed by gases in the atmosphere and then radiated back to Earth's surface. As a result, Earth's surface is kept warm.

**FIGURE 22-2**

Gases in Earth's atmosphere trap heat near the planet's surface just as the panes of glass on a greenhouse trap heat. Solar energy is trapped near the Earth's surface by greenhouse gases such as carbon dioxide and methane.

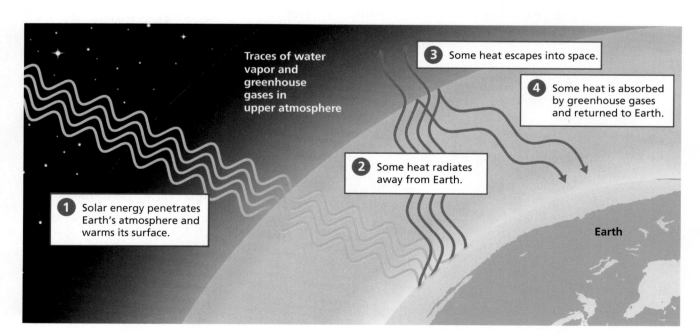

Traces of water vapor and greenhouse gases in upper atmosphere

❸ Some heat escapes into space.

❹ Some heat is absorbed by greenhouse gases and returned to Earth.

❷ Some heat radiates away from Earth.

❶ Solar energy penetrates Earth's atmosphere and warms its surface.

Earth

The concentrations of greenhouse gases, such as $CO_2$ and methane, affect the amount of the sun's heat that is trapped by the atmosphere. $CO_2$ cycles between the atmosphere and living things through the processes of photosynthesis and cellular respiration. Additional $CO_2$ enters the atmosphere when organic matter is burned. Increasingly, humans burn organic matter that is in the form of *fossil fuels,* such as natural gas, coal, and petroleum.

## Hydrosphere

When astronauts in space look at Earth, they see a mostly blue planet because oceans cover about 70 percent of Earth's surface. Water is very important to life on Earth. Especially important is *freshwater,* or water that is not salty and so is suitable for uses such as drinking, bathing, and watering crops. Only about 3 percent of surface water is freshwater, and most of this freshwater is tied up in glaciers at the poles.

## Geosphere

The geosphere exchanges materials with the atmosphere, hydrosphere, and biosphere. Recall that photosynthetic organisms take carbon from the atmosphere and incorporate it into living tissue. After the organisms die, some of the carbon may become coal or oil and thus enter the geosphere. Sulfur, phosphorus, and other elements also cycle between the biosphere and geosphere.

## Biosphere

The biosphere includes all parts of Earth where life exists. The biosphere includes the part of the atmosphere between Earth's surface and approximately 9 km above the surface, most of the hydrosphere, and at least 11 km of the top crust of the geosphere. Scientists occasionally discover life in new places and thus expand the known boundaries of the biosphere. Attempts to replicate an Earth-like system, such as the project shown in Figure 22-3, have shown that Earth's spheres form a complex and delicately balanced system.

### Word Roots and Origins

*biosphere*

From the Greek *bios,* meaning "life," and the Latin *sphaera,* meaning "globe."

**FIGURE 22-3**

With an ambitious project in the Arizona desert called *Biosphere 2,* researchers attempted to build a small, self-contained, Earth-like system that included a biosphere, geosphere, hydrosphere, and atmosphere capable of sustaining human life for long periods. The project encountered many difficulties, showing that Earth's biosphere is not easy to replicate.

# BIODIVERSITY

The term **biodiversity** refers to the variety of forms of life in an area. Biologists study and describe biodiversity in several ways. One measure of biodiversity is **species diversity.** Species diversity, in turn, is reflected by both species richness and species evenness. *Species richness* refers to the number of unique species within an area. This kind of diversity is easiest to notice and is most often what is meant when referring to biodiversity. *Species evenness* refers to the relative number of individuals of each species in an area.

Species evenness is harder to study than species richness but may be more important to understanding ecosystems. Two locations may have the same species richness yet differ in species evenness. For example, suppose that five tree species grow in each of two forests. In one forest, the numbers of each kind of tree are about the same, but in the other forest, one kind of tree far outnumbers the other kinds. A disruption such as a drought would affect the two forests quite differently.

Another measure of biodiversity is **genetic diversity,** or the amount of variation in the genetic material within all members of a population. Genetic diversity is important because it affects a population's ability to adapt in the face of environmental change. Recall that evolution by natural selection acts upon genetic variation within populations. When populations are reduced to small numbers, the amount of genetic variation is reduced for many generations to come. A reduction in a species' genetic variation reduces the likelihood that the species will survive natural selection.

## Measuring Biodiversity

Often, when people think of the importance of other species, they focus on mammals such as pandas, lions, or dolphins. But mammals are a small fraction of biodiversity. Of all of the known species, a huge proportion is made up of insects, as shown in Figure 22-4. We know very little about most of these species.

**FIGURE 22-4**

This diagram represents the relative numbers of species of different categories on Earth. The sizes of the organisms drawn here are proportional to the estimated number of species in each category. There are many more species of insects and plants than there are species of mammals.

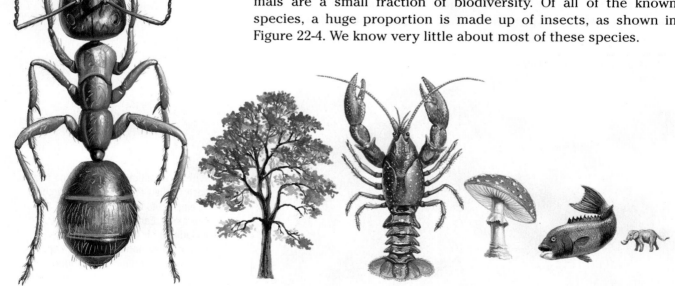

**INSECTS**  **PLANTS**  **CRUSTACEANS**  **FUNGI**  **FISHES**  **MAMMALS**

In terms of species richness only, how much biodiversity exists? Various biologists have made widely different estimates for the number of species on Earth, ranging from 2 million to 100 million species. Yet in about 200 years of cataloging, scientists have named and described about 2 million species.

Because of the frequency and ease with which new species are discovered, scientists acknowledge the likelihood that there are many undescribed species. For example, in recent years, several new species of primates were discovered in Madagascar, and an entirely new order of insects was recognized. In 1982, biologist Terry Erwin announced that his team had studied all of the species of insects in one kind of tree in a tropical rain forest. They counted 1,200 beetle species, 163 of which seemed to inhabit only that one kind of tree.

Our knowledge of smaller organisms and organisms in remote or extreme locations is especially poor. Scientists must use innovative approaches to find and describe these lesser-known organisms. For example, they may build robotic vehicles to explore remote and extreme environments, such as caves, volcanoes, hot springs, and deep sea trenches. It seems that everywhere they look, scientists find new varieties of organisms.

## Valuing Biodiversity

Biodiversity provides important benefits to people. For example, thousands of plant and animal species can serve as food. Trees provide wood for homes and fuel. Many species are sources of medicines and useful chemicals. Undiscovered species may someday supply other benefits. And ecosystems recycle human wastes, including $CO_2$. Writing about such benefits, biologist E. O. Wilson stated, "Biological diversity is the key to the maintenance of the world as we know it."

Some people think that organisms and ecosystems are important for reasons other than their use to humans. These opinions may be based on moral, aesthetic, or religious beliefs that are beyond the scope of biology. People may value biodiversity for multiple reasons.

**Quick Lab**

### Estimating Microscopic Diversity

**Materials** microscope, dissecting scope, 50 mL sample of pond water

**Procedure** Gently stir the pond water. Place one drop of the pond water on a microscope slide. Examine the slide under the dissecting scope and under the microscope at low magnification. Try to find as many different types of organisms as possible. Quickly draw or describe each one. Make a tally of the total number of unique organisms you find.

**Analysis** Compare your total and your descriptions with those of others in your class. How many unique kinds of organisms might there be in the total sample of pond water?

## SECTION 1 REVIEW

1. Explain the importance of the study of environmental science.

2. Name the three major layers between Earth's center and 20 km above Earth's surface.

3. Define the biosphere.

4. How does the greenhouse effect occur?

5. Compare species richness and species evenness.

6. Compare species diversity and genetic diversity.

7. List several reasons to value biodiversity.

**CRITICAL THINKING**

8. **Calculating Information** Compare the density of oxygen in the atmosphere at 36,000 ft above sea level to its density at 18,000 ft above sea level.

9. **Analyzing Models** The amount of greenhouse gases released into the atmosphere by human activities has increased over recent years. Predict a possible result of this trend.

10. **Applying Information** Explain why measuring biodiversity is difficult.

- **Describe** major consequences of air pollution.
- **Relate** air pollution to effects on global climate.
- **Describe** how chemical pollutants may undergo the process of biological magnification.
- **Identify** the primary causes of modern extinctions.
- **Explain** why extinctions and ecosystem disruption are of concern to humans.
- **Relate** human resource use to its impacts on ecosystems.

VOCABULARY

**pollution**
**smog**
**chlorofluorocarbon (CFC)**
**biological magnification**
**acid precipitation**
**extinction**
**keystone species**
**sustainability**

# ENVIRONMENTAL ISSUES

*A*s *the human population increases, so does the human impact on the environment. Humans often cause* **pollution** *by putting substances that cause unintended harm into air, water, or soil. Many human activities disrupt ecosystems.*

## POLLUTION

In many urban areas, the air is visibly polluted with **smog,** water vapor mixed with chemicals that result from human activities. These activities include burning fuels and using chemicals in vehicles, homes, and industries. Smog may contain nitrogen oxides, $NO_x$, sulfur oxides, $SO_x$, organic chemicals, small particles, and ozone, $O_3$. Ozone is produced when nitrogen oxides react with oxygen in air under sunlight. Animals and plants are harmed by respiring the pollutants in smog. Other results of air pollution include ozone thinning, global warming, and acid precipitation.

### Ozone Thinning

Ozone in the lower atmosphere is harmful, but ozone floating 20 km above Earth in a zone called the *stratosphere* shields the planet's surface from harmful ultraviolet radiation, or *UV light.* Unfortunately, several kinds of human-made chemicals contribute to the destruction of the ozone layer. The most important of these are **chlorofluorocarbons** (KLAWR-oh-FLOOR-uh-KAHR-buhnz), or **CFCs.** Gaseous CFCs were once widely used as coolants in refrigerators and air conditioners, as propellants in aerosol spray cans, and in the manufacture of plastic-foam products. After floating up to the stratosphere, CFCs act as catalysts for reactions that break down ozone. Scientists have estimated that a single CFC molecule can help destroy up to 100,000 ozone molecules.

Beginning in the 1980s, scientists discovered thinning areas in the ozone layer over Earth's polar regions, as shown in Figure 22-5, and declining ozone levels elsewhere in the layer. An international study estimated that a 10 percent drop in ozone levels would cause 300,000 new cases of human skin cancer worldwide. UV light also harms plants and photosynthetic algae, so ozone depletion could modify entire ecosystems over time.

Damage to the ozone layer led most countries to stop producing CFCs by 1995. Environmental scientists estimate that it will take the ozone layer 50 to 100 years to recover completely. The effort to protect the ozone layer shows that scientists, the public, and policy makers can work together to solve environmental problems.

**FIGURE 22-5**

An ozone "hole," a region of abnormally low ozone concentration, has formed over Antarctica (pink region in image). This lets more ultraviolet light strike the Earth's surface, where it damages DNA and other molecules of life.

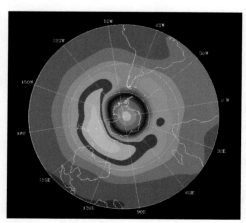

## Global Warming

Scientists have noticed a relationship between average levels of $CO_2$ in the atmosphere and average global temperatures. As $CO_2$ levels have increased, so have temperatures, as shown in Figure 22-6. This pattern, in which two variables change in similar ways, is called a *correlation*. However, a correlation can be difficult to interpret. A correlation could result from a *cause-and-effect relationship,* in which a change in one variable causes a change in another variable. However, a correlation does not necessarily indicate which variable, if any, is the cause. That is, rising $CO_2$ might cause temperature to rise, rising temperature might cause $CO_2$ to rise, or other variables might cause both $CO_2$ and temperature to rise.

Scientists cannot conduct a global experiment to test these hypotheses. However, scientists have strong evidence that $CO_2$ and certain other gases do cause Earth's atmosphere to trap more solar energy. For example, scientists have developed computer models to simulate Earth's climate and predict possible climate changes. Climate models are very complex because they include many factors, such as wind patterns and the effects of oceans on the atmosphere. By varying $CO_2$ levels in climate models, scientists can simulate the possible effects of $CO_2$ on global temperatures. The results of such simulations consistently show that doubling atmospheric $CO_2$ leads to an increase in average global temperatures of 1.0°C to 4.5°C (2°F to 8°F), although the exact temperature change depends on the particular model. Most scientists studying this problem have concluded that increased $CO_2$ levels in the atmosphere cause increases in global temperatures.

The year 2003 was the second-warmest year on record at that time. Average global temperatures were 0.56°C (1.01°F) above the past century's average. The warmest year before 2003 was 1998. An international panel of scientists predicts that temperatures will rise an additional 2°C (4°F) in the next 100 years. This small change could alter rainfall patterns, soil moisture, and sea level around the world. Also, this change could shift agricultural regions and disrupt both terrestrial and aquatic ecosystems. Rising temperatures are already changing biological communities in measurable ways.

## Acid Precipitation

Recall that in the global water cycle, water enters the atmosphere as vapor and returns to Earth's surface in the form of precipitation, such as rain or snow. Some air pollutants combine with water in the atmosphere and form acids. The result is precipitation that is acidic, or **acid precipitation.** Because organisms are adapted to the normal pH range of their environment, increased acidity of soil and water causes disease or death in trees, fish, and other organisms.

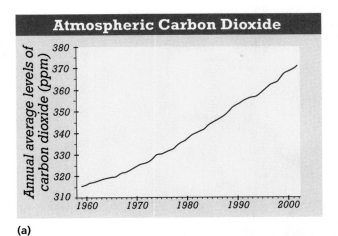

(a)

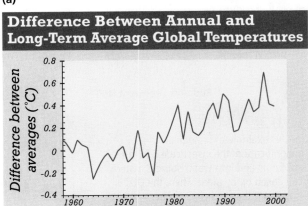

(b)

**FIGURE 22-6**

(a) Atmospheric $CO_2$ concentration has been increasing in recent decades, as measured from the top of Mauna Loa, a large volcano in Hawaii. (b) Average global temperatures have been rising in a similar pattern. The graph shows the difference between recent short-term and past long-term temperature averages.

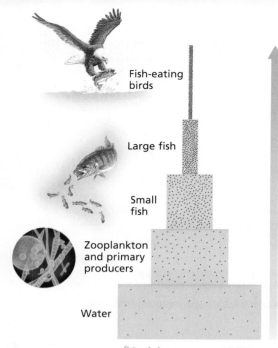

Fish-eating birds

Large fish

Small fish

Zooplankton and primary producers

Water

At the top of the food chain, DDT concentration has increased almost 10 million times.

DDT is stored in primary producers, such as algae.

DDT enters the water through ground water and runoff from land.

Red dots represent DDT.

**FIGURE 22-7**

In this example of biological magnification, the insecticide DDT runs off farms and into water sources, where it is taken up by algae. Then, the DDT passes up the food chain from the algae to zooplankton, to small fish, to bigger fish, and finally to predators such as eagles. DDT accumulates in fatty tissue, and its concentration increases as it moves up the food chain. In predatory birds, DDT can reach levels that cause the production of thin eggshells and leads to the death of offspring. The banning of DDT in the United States may have saved the bald eagle from extinction.

## Land and Water Pollution

Human activities can pollute land and water in several ways. Humans produce and must dispose of waste in the form of sewage and unused materials. Humans produce and use a variety of chemicals in industries, farms, ranches, stores, homes, schools, workshops, and cleaning services. Many of these chemicals are toxic, and some also cause cancer. Some chemicals are not directly harmful but cause damage to ecosystems if they are disposed of improperly or spilled by accident. Some chemicals enter ecosystems and undergo **biological magnification,** a process in which chemicals become more concentrated in an organism the higher on a food chain that organism is, as Figure 22-7 shows. As environmental problems are identified, governments increasingly regulate the manufacture, use, and disposal of chemicals.

# ECOSYSTEM DISRUPTION

The human impacts on air, climate, land, and water described above are happening at the same time. These impacts contribute to *ecosystem disruption,* the destruction or substantial change in the functioning of natural ecosystems. Ecosystem disruption is evident as species—and sometimes entire communities—disappear.

## Extinction

Organisms generally require specific habitats in order to thrive. For example, when whooping cranes are in their winter nesting grounds in Texas, they eat blue crabs. Along their migration routes, they eat various invertebrates in the marshes where they stop to rest. If people drain the marshes for farmland, the crane could experience **extinction,** the death of every member of the species. In fact, whooping cranes are in danger of extinction, or *endangered.* Worldwide, thousands of species have become endangered or extinct as a result of human activities.

One way that species become endangered is when their habitat is destroyed. Habitat destruction occurs as humans convert complex natural ecosystems into simplified systems that do not sustain as many species, such as farmland and urban areas. Since the development of agriculture, people have cut down more than half of the world's forests. Other examples of habitat destruction include damming rivers, draining swamps, surface mining, logging, and clearing land for buildings or roads.

In addition to habitat destruction, the main human causes of the endangerment of species include hunting or harvesting and the transfer of invasive species into new habitats. An increasing number of species are endangered, as Table 22-1 shows. Scientists estimate that perhaps 20 percent of Earth's plant and animal species may become extinct in the next 50 years, a situation called the *biodiversity crisis*. Living species have not been lost at such a high rate since the mass extinction of dinosaurs 65 million years ago. The mass extinction currently underway is unique in that humans are its primary cause.

## Ecosystem Imbalances

No one can predict the results of the loss of millions of species. We do know that some species are critical to the functioning of ecosystems. For example, a species of sea otters, shown in Figure 22-8, once lived in great numbers along the Pacific coast. These otters feed heavily on sea urchins, whereas sea urchins feed on giant kelp (algae) that form the basis of an underwater "forest" community. When people hunted the otters to near-extinction, the sea urchins increased in number and overfed on the kelp. Entire kelp communities began to disappear. Later, biologists reintroduced and helped secure legal protections for the sea otters in some areas, and the kelp recovered. Species such as the sea otter that affect many other species in a community are called **keystone species.** Extinction of keystone species has serious and sometimes unknown effects on ecosystems.

Overusing resources can also unbalance ecosystems. For millennia, the waters off what is now Cape Cod supported huge populations of cod, flounder, haddock and other fish. Until the 1960s, people harvested the fish at about the same rate that the fish reproduced. When newer fishing methods brought in larger harvests, the fish populations decreased rapidly and have not yet recovered. Similar overuse of terrestrial resources has caused the formation of desertlike areas in Africa and the erosion of topsoils in the midwestern United States.

**FIGURE 22-8**

The southern sea otter, *Enhydra lutris nereis,* has the thickest fur of any mammal. Sea otters live in coastal kelp bed communities. They eat sea urchins, other invertebrates, and fish. As people hunted otters to near-extinction in the 1800s and 1900s, the kelp communities where they lived started to disappear.

**TABLE 22-1** *Species Known to Be Threatened or Extinct Worldwide*

| Group of species | Number threatened (all categories of risk) | Number extinct (since ~1800) | Percent of known species that are threatened |
|---|---|---|---|
| Mammals | 1,130 | 78 | 23 |
| Birds | 1,194 | 132 | 12 |
| Reptiles | 293 | 22 | 4 |
| Amphibians | 146 | 7 | 3 |
| Fishes | 750 | 91 | 3 |
| Insects | 553 | 70 | 0.06 |
| Mollusks | 967 | 303 | 1 |
| Other invertebrates | 439 | 8 | 1 |
| Plants | 6,774 | 106 | 2 |

# HUMAN RESOURCE USE

The global human population uses an estimated 10 to 55 percent of Earth's *primary production,* the total energy stored through photosynthesis by terrestrial organisms. People use this resource in the form of fuel and food for both humans and domestic animals. As the human population increases, so does its use of this resource.

Another analysis of human impact on ecosystems is known as an *ecological footprint.* This analysis accounts for people's use of food and natural resources, such as land and water, as well as people's production of wastes and pollution. Ecologists are concerned that the biosphere has a limited capacity to renew or repair itself in the face of these impacts. One group of ecologists and economists calculated that since the 1980s, human demand has exceeded the biosphere's renewal capacity.

Although making such analyses is difficult, it is clear that Earth's capacity to support humans has an upper limit. This problem is a question of sustainability. **Sustainability** means the ability to meet human needs in such a way that a human population can survive indefinitely. To live sustainably, humans must close the gaps between Earth's renewable resources and capacities, our own needs, and the needs of Earth's other living species.

One approach is to develop new technologies for uses such as energy production, transportation, agriculture, housing, and waste disposal. Another approach is to slow or reverse human population growth. A third approach is to reduce our consumption of resources. For example, the U.S. Department of Energy estimates that increasing energy efficiency could cut national energy use by up to 20 percent in a few decades. This kind of change would require government policies as well as private efforts that reduce the use and improve the efficiency of cars, appliances, buildings, factories, and the systems that produce and distribute energy.

## SECTION 2 REVIEW

1. Identify some of the components of smog.
2. Explain how the release of chlorofluorocarbons affects the ozone layer.
3. Explain atmospheric scientists' predictions for global temperatures over the next 100 years.
4. Describe how pesticides, such as DDT, undergo the process of biological magnification.
5. Identify the primary causes of modern species extinctions.
6. Describe the factors considered in an analysis of a person's or population's ecological footprint.

**CRITICAL THINKING**

7. **Applying Information** Choose a species that might be affected by global warming, and predict how that species might be affected.
8. **Calculating Information** The human population doubles every 36 years. If people currently use 25 percent of Earth's primary production, in what year might humans use 100 percent?
9. **Analyzing Models** Sketch a model of your own ecological footprint. Include boxes to represent the resources you use, their original sources, and any activities that affect your environment. Draw arrows to indicate relationships between factors.

# MILESTONES IN Environmental Protection

## Timeline

**1835** Ralph Waldo Emerson writes essay "Nature."

**1865** Frederick Law Olmsted advocates preservation of Yosemite.

**1872** The world's first national park, Yellowstone, is established.

**1892** John Muir founds the Sierra Club.

**1905** U.S. Forest Service is established under Theodore Roosevelt.

**1916** National Park Service is established under Woodrow Wilson.

**1962** Rachel Carson publishes *Silent Spring*.

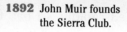
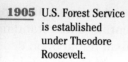

**1967** Congress passes Clean Air Act.

**1968** Paul Ehrlich publishes *The Population Bomb*.

**1970** The Environemntal Protection Agency is established, and the first Earth Day is celebrated.

**2002** The World Summit on Sustainable Development occurs.

---

*Throughout U.S. history, people have demonstrated and written about their concern for the environment. Thousands of citizens have tried to stop pollution, promote public health, and preserve America's natural assets. Prompted largely by a few individuals and events, environmental awareness has increased over the decades.*

In 1835, Ralph Waldo Emerson wrote the essay "Nature" and thus began a tradition of writing about nature. Henry D. Thoreau, Walt Whitman, and others continued this literary tradition. These and other public figures drew attention to the value of ecosystems.

In 1865, landscape architect Frederick Law Olmsted (best known for designing New York's Central Park) submitted a report on preserving Yosemite Valley in California. This was the first justification for public preservation and management of natural areas that was based on the areas' value to humans. Soon after, the U.S. government established Yellowstone National Park and thus began the national park system.

Scottish-born naturalist and writer John Muir advocated for preserving western lands as wilderness. He founded the first major environmental organization, the Sierra Club, in San Francisco in 1892. This group was and continues to be dedicated to the preservation of wilderness and natural areas.

In 1903, President Theodore Roosevelt created the first National Bird Preserve on Pelican Island, Florida. This was the start of the National Wildlife Refuge system. He also established the U.S. Forest Service in 1905. By 1909, the Roosevelt administration had created 42 million acres of national forests and 53 national wildlife refuges. In 1916, the National Park Service was established with 40 national parks and monuments.

In 1962, biologist Rachel Carson published a landmark book, *Silent Spring*. The book warned people about the dangers of the increasing use of toxic pesticides, such as DDT. In 1968, Stanford ecologist Paul Ehrlich warned of the hazards of rapid population growth with his book, *The Population Bomb*. These books contributed to a surge of environmental awareness in the United States.

In 1970, the U.S. Environmental Protection Agency (EPA) was created to enforce new environmental policies, such as the Clean Water Act and Clean Air Act. The first Earth Day was celebrated internationally. The Endangered Species Act became law in 1973.

In 2002, the World Summit on Sustainable Development met in South Africa. Leaders there agreed that the future of human survival will depend on an international commitment to work together to protect Earth's ecosystems.

## Review

1. Describe the role of literature in the environmental movement.

2. **Applying Concepts** What environmental issues affect your life right now?

3. **Conducting Research** Use the Web site below to create a timetable of the history of U.S. environmental laws.

**internet** connect

www.scilinks.org
**Topic: Environmental Law**
**Keyword: HM60527**

SCILINKS. Maintained by the National Science Teachers Association

## OBJECTIVES

- **State** the goals of conservation and restoration biology.
- **Describe** examples of efforts to protect species and their habitats.
- **Summarize** international strategies for protecting entire ecosystems.
- **Discuss** the roles of governments and laws in addressing environmental problems.
- **List** several things that individuals can do to help solve environmental problems.

## VOCABULARY

conservation biology
restoration biology
bioindicator
biodiversity hotspot
ecotourism
urban ecology

# ENVIRONMENTAL SOLUTIONS

*Our planet's air, water, land, and organisms are interconnected. Environmental problems connect across national boundaries, so solutions may require worldwide efforts. Scientists, governmental bodies, and individual citizens must work together to live responsibly within the biosphere.*

## CONSERVATION AND RESTORATION BIOLOGY

As human populations have increased rapidly, so has the human impact on ecosystems. Scientific understanding of these impacts is weak, but is improving. Meanwhile, individuals, such as the students in Figure 22-9, can contribute to scientific understanding and also take responsibility for minimizing human impacts on ecosystems.

In a discipline called **conservation biology,** scientists seek to identify, protect, and manage natural areas that still retain much biodiversity. Where humans have had the largest impacts—agricultural areas, former strip mines, and drained wetlands, for example—biologists must often devise plans to reverse changes and replace missing ecosystem components. In **restoration biology,** scientists deal with extreme cases of ecosystem damage. For example, restoring a grassland community to an area that was strip-mined may involve recontouring the land surface, reintroducing bacteria to the soil, planting grass and shrub seedlings, and using periodic controlled fires to manage the growth of vegetation.

**FIGURE 22-9**

Dwarf wedge mussels are an endangered species in the Aschuelot River of New Hampshire. These high school students from a nearby town are making a census of mussel populations to help save the species from extinction and to monitor water quality in the river.

Even the best scientific efforts may not be able to completely restore an ecological community. But biologists can encourage restoration by applying their understanding of processes such as energy flow, species interactions, and biogeochemical cycling.

## Species and Habitats

One principle that biologists have learned to apply is that species and their habitats are interconnected. Figure 22-9 shows students studying dwarf wedge mussels *(Alasmidonta heterodon)* in the Ashuelot River in New Hampshire. In 1990, government biologists classified this mollusk as an endangered species because its population was declining rapidly. The students looked for clues to explain the decline. The dwarf wedge mussel is a **bioindicator,** a species that is especially sensitive to ecological change. Because the mollusk is harmed by tiny amounts of water pollution, it acts as an early warning signal for environmental problems. Its decline suggested a pollution problem in the Ashuelot River, and the students' research helped to find the source of the pollution.

## Case Study: Saving the Whooping Crane

The whooping crane, or "whooper," is an example of a species that is on the road to recovery, thanks to protective laws, international cooperation, and the efforts of volunteers. Before 1870, about 20,000 whoopers migrated annually between Canada and the Gulf Coast. Then, American settlers began to hunt the birds for their feathers and drain the marshes where birds fed during migrations.

By 1937, only about 15 whoopers remained. Meanwhile, the federal government had begun to regulate the hunting of migratory birds and then established a winter refuge for the cranes in Texas. In 1967, the U.S. Fish and Wildlife Service established a captive breeding program for the cranes, and people learned how to encourage whooper reproduction. For example, Figure 22-10 shows a man imitating a courtship dance with a female crane. This ritual dance prompts female cranes to produce eggs, which can then be fertilized artificially with a male crane's sperm. The resulting offspring may survive in the wild, but may not know how to migrate.

**FIGURE 22-10**

(a) To help save whooping cranes from extinction, conservationists have tried to recreate many aspects of the crane's natural lives, including the courtship dance shown here. (b) Several generations of cranes have been bred and raised in captivity and released into the wild, although with mixed success.

(a)

(b)

At one point, biologists tried placing whooping crane eggs in the nests of wild sandhill cranes in the hopes that the sandhill cranes would raise the whooper chicks and teach them to migrate. The whooper chicks did learn to migrate but did not learn how to court other whoopers for successful mating.

Captive breeding programs now produce about 30 whooping crane chicks each year. To be sure that the chicks learn to live with other whoopers, the people who raise the chicks wear crane costumes or use crane puppets. The young cranes are released into the wild, but they will not migrate on their own. Since 2001, pilots have used small aircraft to lead cranes along their historical 2000-mile migration route. Like many migratory birds, the cranes learn the route after one trip.

The whooping crane case shows that protecting species from extinction is not easy. But it can be done with creative ideas, cooperation, an understanding of each organism's biology, and the efforts of ordinary citizens.

# PROTECTING ECOSYSTEMS

**FIGURE 22-11**

An international group of conservation biologists identified these 25 regions (shaded in green) as *biodiversity hotspots*. These regions contain especially high densities of unique but threatened species.

Ecosystem protection is clearly very important in the long term. But in the short term, economic costs and human freedoms should also be considered. How can society protect ecosystems while protecting individuals' property rights and economic opportunities? One strategy is to focus protection efforts on the regions that currently harbor most of Earth's biodiversity.

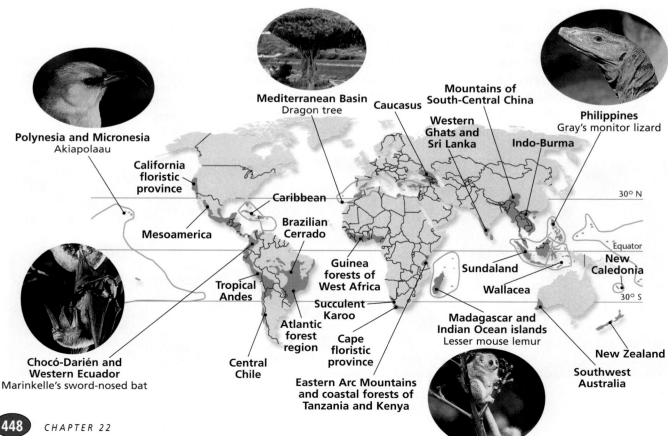

Polynesia and Micronesia
Akiapolaau

California floristic province

Mesoamerica

Caribbean

Brazilian Cerrado

Mediterranean Basin
Dragon tree

Caucasus

Mountains of South-Central China

Western Ghats and Sri Lanka

Indo-Burma

Philippines
Gray's monitor lizard

30° N

Tropical Andes

Guinea forests of West Africa

Succulent Karoo

Atlantic forest region

Cape floristic province

Sundaland

Wallacea

New Caledonia

Equator

30° S

Chocó-Darién and Western Ecuador
Marinkelle's sword-nosed bat

Central Chile

Eastern Arc Mountains and coastal forests of Tanzania and Kenya

Madagascar and Indian Ocean islands
Lesser mouse lemur

New Zealand

Southwest Australia

## Biodiversity Hotspots

In the face of crisis, conservationists look for efficient strategies to protect biodiversity. Many have decided to focus on ecological regions that are richest in unique species and that are most in need of protection. In 2000, an international group identified 25 of these **biodiversity hotspots,** shown in Figure 22-11. These regions contain about 44 percent of all species of vascular plants and 35 percent of all species in four groups of vertebrates. Yet, these regions cover less than 2 percent of the globe. Three of the hotspots include parts of the United States. Internationally, governments and conservation organizations are looking for ways to preserve large enough portions of these hotspots to ensure the survival of a majority of species.

# GOVERNMENTS AND LAWS

Governments and laws can play a critical role in solving environmental problems. In the United States, governments at the local, state, and federal levels have used laws, policies, and public funds to address environmental issues. Government actions include legally protecting endangered species and habitats, setting aside land for public use, cleaning up pollution, regulating destructive activities, conducting scientific studies, and encouraging responsible resource use through education and economic incentives.

However, many environmental problems cannot be solved by a single government or law. Ecosystems cross political boundaries. Whooping cranes migrate between the United States and Canada. Pollutants emitted by factory smokestacks in Ohio can fall as acid rain in New York. Storms in Africa blow dust and microorganisms into Europe and out to sea. Thus, to solve many environmental problems, governments must cooperate with each other.

Internationally, countries regularly meet and make agreements to decrease pollution, protect endangered species, or plan for future human activities. Sometimes, many countries agree and solve problems successfully. For example, an agreement to reduce CFC use worldwide seems to have slowed the thinning of the ozone layer. However, countries have had less success agreeing on ways to decrease the threat of global warming. Most countries agree that they need to decrease the amount of greenhouse gases being added to the atmosphere, but they do not agree on how much responsibility each country should have. With many environmental issues, the interests of countries that are more developed differ from the interests of countries that are less developed.

Many developing countries have little money but large amounts of unique habitat and natural resources. This situation presents the opportunity of a *debt-for-nature swap*. In this exchange, richer countries or private organizations pay some of the debts of a developing country and the developing country takes steps such as preserving undeveloped land or educating its citizens.

### Quick Lab

**Evaluating Environmental Issues in the News**

**Materials** newspapers, magazines, television news broadcasts, or other news sources

**Procedure** Find a news article or watch a news broadcast about a current environmental issue. First, record its title or topic and its date of broadcast or publication. Then, as you read or watch, take notes, and write down your immediate thoughts and questions. Finally, reread your notes, and write any additional thoughts that you have.

**Analysis** Did the report relate to any of the information in this chapter? Did the report present the issue accurately and fairly? Was more than one view of the issue represented? Was scientific information included in the report? Describe how you might have presented the report differently.

# Urban Ecologist

**Job Description** Urban ecologists are scientists who study the relationships between humans, animals, and the cities in which they live. Some urban ecologists manage parks, reserves, or water quality. Urban ecologists can work in universities, government agencies, parks, botanical gardens, and private industry.

### Focus On an Urban Ecologist

"I like big cities and I like the outdoors!" says urban ecologist Charles Nilon. As a boy, Nilon loved to catch frogs and turtles. "Ecology deals with the things that I like to do." Today, Nilon studies urban wildlife ecology and conservation. "The 'wildlife' portion of my job focuses on learning how different kinds of animals live in urban areas. The 'conservation' side studies how to manage the contact—both good and bad—between people and animals," says Nilon. Nilon helps local governments manage park areas to protect key wildlife sites. "I also work with private landowners and developers to help them design subdivisions in ways that will enable wildlife to thrive even when there are lots of houses." Nilon's job is all about finding the right balance.

### Education and Skills

- **High school**—three years of science courses and four years of math courses
- **College**—bachelor of science in biology, including course work in botany, zoology, ecology, and wildlife biology; a master's (M.S.) or doctoral degree (Ph.D.) to conduct research
- **Skills**—strong writing skills, strong social skills, excellent observation skills, patience, and research skills

For more about careers, visit **go.hrw.com** and type in the keyword **HM6 Careers.**

---

**FIGURE 22-12**

Rachel Carson awakened millions of readers to important environmental issues, such as the consequences of using the insecticide DDT.

# PRIVATE EFFORTS AND COOPERATION

Conservationists have encouraged a variety of strategies to help developing countries derive economic benefit from their land's biodiversity. One approach is **ecotourism,** a form of tourism that supports the conservation of ecologically unique areas while bringing economic benefit to local people. In ecotourism, tourists pay for nature guides, food, and lodging in exchange for the opportunity to experience the ecosystem and its unique organisms.

Cooperation between conservation groups, individuals, and governments is crucial in identifying and addressing environmental issues. In the United States, conservation groups such as the Nature Conservancy, Sierra Club, and Ducks Unlimited make efforts to educate people, protect land, and influence the making of laws.

Individuals and the media also play an important role in raising awareness of environmental issues. In 1962, biologist Rachel Carson, shown in Figure 22-12, made millions of people aware of the dangers of pesticides in her book *Silent Spring.* French oceanographer Jacques Cousteau was internationally famous for his books and television programs about the undersea world.

# CONSERVATION CASE STUDY: THE EVERGLADES

The Everglades ecosystem is essentially a wide, shallow, slow-moving river that flows south across much of southern Florida, as shown in Figure 22-13. The area is a swampy patchwork of islands among water that is knee deep in grasses and reeds. The area is home to panthers, alligators, storks, and a wealth of other unique and rare species. The Everglades National Park is one of the largest protected areas in the United States. However, many human interests continue to compete for use of the ecosystem's resources.

Early in the 20th century, the beautiful beaches and pleasant climate of southern Florida attracted land developers. However, most of the land was too wet to build on, and mosquitoes discouraged people from living there. Over time, the developers dug drainage canals to divert water flows toward the ocean and dry out the land. They also planted non-native melaleuca trees because these trees take up large amounts of water from the soil.

At that time, few people could foresee the ecological consequences of these actions. However, journalist Marjory Stoneman Douglas (1890–1998) saw them clearly. She worked to help establish Everglades National Park. In 1947, she wrote a book that described the Everglades ecosystem and explained its importance. Douglas spent a lifetime trying to protect the Everglades.

Still, by the end of the century, half of the area's wetlands had been drained. Ninety percent of the wading birds had disappeared. Because salt concentrations had doubled in Florida Bay, sea grass and shrimp nurseries had died. Fertilizers from agricultural fields flowed along with the water, which poisoned many species and made fish dangerous to eat. Development had diverted so much water that many farmers and homeowners experienced shortages of groundwater. And the melaleuca trees had become an invasive weed.

## FIGURE 22-13

The Everglades ecosystem (a) is a large region with enough natural habitat for large predators, such as the highly endangered Florida panther (b). Little islands called *hummocks* rise above the river and are home to a diversity of organisms, including trees, birds, alligators, snakes, and insects. The Everglades National Park (c) contains only about 20 percent of the ecosystem.

(c)

(a)

(b)

**TABLE 22-2**
*Things You Can Do to Be Environmentally Responsible*

Use cars less by riding a bike, walking, carpooling, or using public transportation instead.

Recycle or reuse packaging and materials such as cans, bottles, boxes, and paper; buy items that have less packaging and that have recyclable packaging.

Use less water by turning off faucets when they are not in use; use water-saving devices and appliances.

Use less energy in your home; look for ways to use less air conditioning or heat; turn off lights and appliances when they are not in use.

Find out the environmental impacts of the products that you buy; ask for environmentally responsible products.

Plant native trees and plants, which provide shade and wildlife habitat and produce $O_2$ while absorbing $CO_2$ from the atmosphere.

Conservationists have since established a 20-year plan for the Everglades ecosystem. The plan includes eliminating some of the drainage canals, restoring the Kissimmee River to its original channel, cutting back stands of melaleuca trees, and purchasing more than 40,000 hectares (100,000 acres) of land surrounding Everglades National Park. This plan is the most ambitious ecosystem restoration project so far attempted in the United States.

# YOUR ROLE IN THE ENVIRONMENT

A new environmental field, called **urban ecology,** is the study of biodiversity in areas that are densely populated by humans. You can be an amateur urban ecologist by learning about your local environment. For example, try to identify five plants that are native to your area, determine their growing seasons, and learn which plants can be used for landscaping homes or businesses. Find out the names of local birds, how the birds survive, and whether any special laws protect them. Learn which crops and livestock are raised locally, and find out how farmers or ranchers obtain water. Identify endangered species in your area, and find out the reasons that they are endangered. Investigate where your garbage goes after it is collected, and learn whether your sanitation department supports recycling. If you want to study further and do more, find out if there are parks, organizations, or projects in your local area that need volunteers to help with conservation efforts.

No one can predict our environment's future, but it is clear that individuals can make a difference in its fate. Thus, it is important for you, as an individual, to understand your role in the environment and to take responsibility for that role. Taking responsibility can involve simple efforts, such as those listed in Table 22-2. In addition, a planet full of undiscovered species, unknown ecological interactions, and unanswered questions awaits your exploration.

## SECTION 3 REVIEW

1. Contrast conservation biology with restoration biology.

2. Give an example of a bioindicator species, and explain its importance.

3. Outline the whooping crane recovery effort.

4. Explain why different governmental bodies must work together to address environmental problems.

5. What is a debt-for-nature swap?

6. Explain the idea of ecotourism.

**CRITICAL THINKING**

7. **Applying Information** What benefits might people living near Everglades National Park gain from efforts to preserve the ecosystem?

8. **Critiquing Arguments** A student argues that we should not worry about the loss of species because extinction is natural. Evaluate this argument.

9. **Conducting Research** Research an area of high biodiversity near you, and summarize your findings.

# CHAPTER HIGHLIGHTS

## SECTION 1    An Interconnected Planet

- Earth's geosphere, hydrosphere, and atmosphere are interconnected in many ways. Life exists in parts of each sphere. Together, these parts make up the biosphere.

- Important parts of the atmosphere are greenhouse gases, which trap heat on Earth, and the ozone layer, which shields Earth from UV radiation.

- A very small portion of the hydrosphere is fresh water, and much of this fresh water is not easily usable.

- Biodiversity refers to the variety of life found in an area and can be measured in different ways, including by species richness, species evenness, and genetic diversity.

- Biodiversity is valued for various reasons.

### Vocabulary

| | | | |
|---|---|---|---|
| environmental science (p. 435) | atmosphere (p. 435) | biosphere (p. 437) | genetic diversity (p. 438) |
| geosphere (p. 435) | ozone layer (p. 436) | biodiversity (p. 438) | |
| hydrosphere (p. 435) | greenhouse effect (p. 436) | species diversity (p. 438) | |

## SECTION 2    Environmental Issues

- Over a short time period, human activities have affected global ecosystems in ways that harm humans and other species. Human impacts range from local pollution to global change in ecosystems.

- Industrial chemicals called chlorofluorocarbons (CFCs) act as catalysts in chemical reactions that break down $O_3$ molecules in the ozone layer. Most countries have banned CFCs, and the ozone layer seems to be recovering.

- The correlation of increasing atmospheric $CO_2$ and rising global temperature suggests a cause-and-effect relationship. Considering several types of evidence, many scientists have concluded that increased $CO_2$ levels have caused warmer surface temperatures on Earth.

- Certain air pollutants cause acid precipitation, which harms or kills many organisms.

- The release of toxic chemicals, such as DDT, into the biosphere can impact ecosystems in many ways, especially when chemicals undergo biological magnification.

- Human impacts on the environment are causing an increasing number of extinctions. Important causes of extinctions are habitat destruction, the transfer of invasive species to new habitats, and overharvesting or hunting. This loss of species has both known and unknown effects on ecosystems.

- Current levels of human resource use are probably not sustainable.

### Vocabulary

| | | | |
|---|---|---|---|
| smog (p. 440) | acid precipitation (p. 441) | extinction (p. 442) | sustainability (p. 444) |
| chlorofluorocarbon (CFC) (p. 440) | biological magnification (p. 442) | keystone species (p. 443) | |

## SECTION 3    Environmental Solutions

- Conservation biologists are concerned with identifying and maintaining ecosystems, while restoration biologists are usually involved with repairing badly damaged ecosystems.

- Populations of many migratory birds, such as the whooping crane, are in decline because of human activities. However, some populations are recovering as a result of legal protection, breeding programs, habitat restoration, and international partnerships.

- International and cooperative efforts to preserve habitat and prevent extinctions include identifying biodiversity hotspots, making debt-for-nature swaps, and promoting ecotourism.

- Environmental problems can be addressed through the combined efforts of governments, scientists, businesses, and individuals.

- The Everglades restoration project is the most ambitious ecosystem-wide restoration project attempted in the United States.

### Vocabulary

| | | |
|---|---|---|
| conservation biology (p. 446) | bioindicator (p. 447) | ecotourism (p. 450) |
| restoration biology (p. 446) | biodiversity hotspot (p. 449) | urban ecology (p. 452) |

## USING VOCABULARY

1. In your own words, write a definition for the term *environmental science*.

2. Use the following terms in the same sentence:
   a. *geosphere, hydrosphere, atmosphere,* and *biosphere*
   b. *biodiversity, species diversity,* and *genetic diversity*

3. For each pair of terms, explain how the meanings of the terms differ.
   a. *keystone species* and *bioindicator*
   b. *conservation biology* and *restoration biology*

4. **Word Roots and Origins** The word *conservation* is derived from the Latin *conservare*, which means "to keep" or "to preserve". Using this information, explain why the term *conservation* is a good name for the act it represents.

## UNDERSTANDING KEY CONCEPTS

5. **Define** the biosphere in relation to Earth's three major layers.

6. **Explain** Earth's greenhouse effect.

7. **Identify** three major consequences of air pollution.

8. **Explain** how the chemical ozone can be both beneficial and harmful to living things.

9. **Explain** why scientists must distinguish between a correlation and a cause-and-effect relationship.

10. **Describe** the biological magnification of DDT.

11. **Identify** the three primary causes of modern extinctions.

12. **Give** examples of several ways that people could value a single species.

13. **Define** an ecological footprint.

14. **Summarize** the efforts to save the whooping crane from extinction.

15. **Identify** three regions of the United States that are parts of biodiversity hotspots.

16. **Justify** the need for a conservation plan for the Everglades ecosystem.

17. **List** four things that individuals could do to reduce their ecological footprint.

18. **BIOLOGY** Write a short report that explains why efficient use of groundwater is important and that summarizes several ways that people can work to reduce the depletion and pollution of groundwater.

19. **CONCEPT MAPPING** Use the following terms to create a concept map that describes two ways in which human activities have an impact on the entire planet: *pollution, atmosphere, carbon dioxide, chlorofluorocarbons, greenhouse effect, ozone layer,* and *climate*.

## CRITICAL THINKING

20. **Analyzing Concepts** What do environmental scientists mean by *interdependence*? Give an example of interdependence from this chapter.

21. **Applying Information** Suggest some species interactions that are likely to be influenced by global warming.

22. **Inferring Relationships** The formation of the ozone layer depended on the presence of oxygen in the atmosphere. Drawing on what you have learned about the history of life, explain how organisms effected and were affected by the ozone layer as it was first forming.

23. **Predicting Patterns** Predict how future human population growth could affect the biosphere.

24. **Evaluating Methods** Humans need clean, fresh water. Environmental scientists think that fresh water may become a limiting factor for human population growth. Explain how you could estimate Earth's carrying capacity for humans based on the availability of fresh water. What information would you need to make this estimate? How might technological advances change your estimate?

25. **Recognizing Relationships** As part of the global treaty to eliminate CFCs, developed countries are contributing to a fund to help developing countries buy CFC substitutes. What benefits do developed countries receive from this investment?

26. **Forming Reasoned Opinions** After considering Table 22-2, what other ideas could you add to the list? Explain your reasoning.

27. **Interpreting Graphics** Using the illustration below, explain the greenhouse effect. In your explanation, refer to the numbered parts.

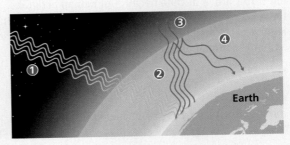

# Standardized Test Preparation

**DIRECTIONS:** Choose the letter of the answer choice that best answers the question.

1. Which of the following is the term for the parts of Earth where water is located?
   - **A.** biosphere
   - **B.** geosphere
   - **C.** atmosphere
   - **D.** hydrosphere

2. What is the term for the natural ability of Earth's atmosphere to trap energy from the sun?
   - **F.** global warming
   - **G.** ozone depletion
   - **H.** greenhouse effect
   - **J.** biological magnification

3. What does Earth's ozone layer shield its inhabitants from?
   - **A.** solar heating
   - **B.** meteor impacts
   - **C.** ozone depletion
   - **D.** ultraviolet radiation

4. Which of the following groups of organisms contains the largest estimated number of species?
   - **F.** birds
   - **G.** plants
   - **H.** insects
   - **J.** mammals

5. What term describes a measure of the number of species in an area?
   - **A.** species richness
   - **B.** species evenness
   - **C.** bioindicator species
   - **D.** biological magnification

**INTERPRETING GRAPHICS:** The graph below shows trends in two global measurements over several decades. Use the graph to answer the question that follows.

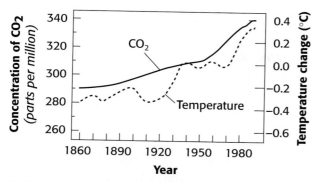

6. What is the term commonly used to describe the trend shown in this graph?
   - **F.** water pollution
   - **G.** global warming
   - **H.** ozone depletion
   - **J.** biodiversity crisis

**DIRECTIONS:** Complete the following analogy.

7. thinning of ozone layer : chlorofluorocarbons :: biological magnification :
   - **A.** pesticides
   - **B.** wastewater
   - **C.** carbon dioxide
   - **D.** greenhouse gases

**INTERPRETING GRAPHICS:** The table below compares the measurements of two environmental factors for the populations of three countries. Use the table to answer the question that follows.

|  | United States | Japan | Indonesia |
|---|---|---|---|
| People per square mile | 78 | 829 | 319 |
| Garbage produced per person per year | 720 kg | 400 kg | 43 kg |

8. Which country produces the greatest amount of garbage per square mile?
   - **F.** Japan
   - **G.** Indonesia
   - **H.** United States
   - **J.** They all produce the same amounts.

## SHORT RESPONSE

The term *biodiversity* can be used in several ways.

Explain two measures of biodiversity.

## EXTENDED RESPONSE

Imagine that your local government has asked for citizen input to plan for the future use of a currently roadless area that is near a body of water. Some citizens would like a new mall to be built there, and some citizens would like the area to be made into a public park.

*Part A* Make a table of the possible problems or benefits that could result from each option.

*Part B* Write a letter to the local government that expresses your opinion about this issue and explains your reasons for that opinion.

**Test TIP** Before choosing an answer to a question, try to answer the question without looking at the answer choices on the test.

# Testing the Effects of Thermal Pollution

## OBJECTIVES

- Model the effects of thermal pollution on living organisms.
- Apply the underlying scientific principles to environmental issues.

## PROCESS SKILLS

- hypothesizing
- experimenting
- observing
- organizing data
- analyzing data

## MATERIALS

- 400 mL beakers, 2
- ice
- hot water
- thermometer
- U-shaped glass tubing, 30 cm long
- 2 corks to fit both ends of the tubing
- 125 mL beaker
- distilled or non-chlorinated water
- culture of paramecia
- hand lens or dissecting scope
- stopwatch or clock
- glass-marking pen or wax pencil

## Background

1. Some power plants use water from rivers as a coolant. After the water is used, it is much hotter than the water in the river.
2. What is a pollutant?
3. How can heat be considered a pollutant?
4. How can power plants release nonharmful water?

## Procedure

1. Discuss the objectives of this investigation with your partners. Develop a hypothesis concerning the effect of temperature on paramecia.

2. Design an experiment using the given materials to test your hypothesis. In your experiment, the paramecia will be contained in the U-shaped tube. One large beaker will be filled with ice, and the other large beaker will be filled with hot water. Other materials that you can use in your experiment are listed in your materials list.

3. In designing your experiment, decide which factor will be an independent variable. Plan how you will vary your independent variable. In your lab report, list your independent variable and your method of varying it.

4. Decide which factor will be the dependent variable in your experiment. Plan how you will measure your dependent variable. In your lab report, list your dependent variable and your method of measuring it.

5. In most experiments, a control is necessary. Plan your control, and describe it in your lab report.

6. Discuss your planned experiment with your teacher. Proceed with your experiment only after you have received your teacher's permission to do so.

7. ⚠ CAUTION **Water hotter than 60°C can scald. Be careful handling hot water, and alert your teacher if you burn yourself.** Fill a 400 mL beaker with ice and water. Make sure that ice remains in the beaker for the entire experiment. Fill another 400 mL beaker with 60°C tap water.

8. In a 125 mL beaker, gently swirl 20 mL of water and 20 mL of a culture of paramecia. Your teacher will provide aged tap water or distilled water for you to use during this step. (Chlorinated water would kill the paramecia.)

9. While your partner holds the test tube steady, carefully pour the paramecia-and-water mixture into the U-shaped tube. Fill the tube completely, leaving just enough room for a cork at each end of the tube. Make sure there are no large air bubbles in the tube. Place a cork at each end of the tube.

10. Create a table similar to the one shown to record your data. For example, the table shown is designed

to record the number of paramecia in three parts of the U-shaped tube over time. Design your data table to fit your own experiment. Remember to allow plenty of space for recording your data.

11. Proceed with your experiment, using the tube, ice water, hot water, and hand lens to observe any response of the paramecia to the environment.

12. As you conduct your experiment, record your results, including the number of paramecia and the time involved, in your data table. Organize your data so that others reading your lab report will be able to understand the results of your experiment.

13.  Clean up your materials and wash your hands before leaving the lab.

## Analysis and Conclusions

1. Did the results of your experiment support your hypothesis? Explain your answer.

2. What effect did heat and cold have on the paramecia in your experiment?

3. What evidence do you have that paramecia preferred one temperature range to another?

4. What are some possible sources of error in your experiment?

5. How might a pollutant cause an increase in the number of organisms? Explain.

6. Judging from your experiment, how do you think other organisms might react to a change in water temperature?

7. How could a power plant change the type of organisms that live in the water where it releases its cooling water?

## Further Inquiry

Develop a hypothesis about the effects of acid rain on paramecia, and design an experiment to test your hypothesis.

| NUMBER OF PARAMECIA | | | | |
|---|---|---|---|---|
| | | Cold end | Hot end | Middle |
| | 0 | | | |
| | 15 | | | |
| Elapsed | 30 | | | |
| time | 45 | | | |
| | 60 | | | |
| | 75 | | | |

# MICROBES, PROTISTS, AND FUNGI

" In the leaves of every forest, in the flowers of every garden, in the waters of every rivulet, there are worlds teeming with life... "

From *Thoughts on Animalcules,* or *A Glimpse of the Invisible World Revealed by the Microscope,* by G. A. Mantell, as quoted in Primo Levi's book *Other People's Trades.*

**Mushrooms, members of the kingdom Fungi, are important decomposers in nature.**

**internet** connect

National Science Teachers Association *sci* LINKS Internet resources are located throughout this unit.

*sci* LINKS. Maintained by the National Science Teachers Association

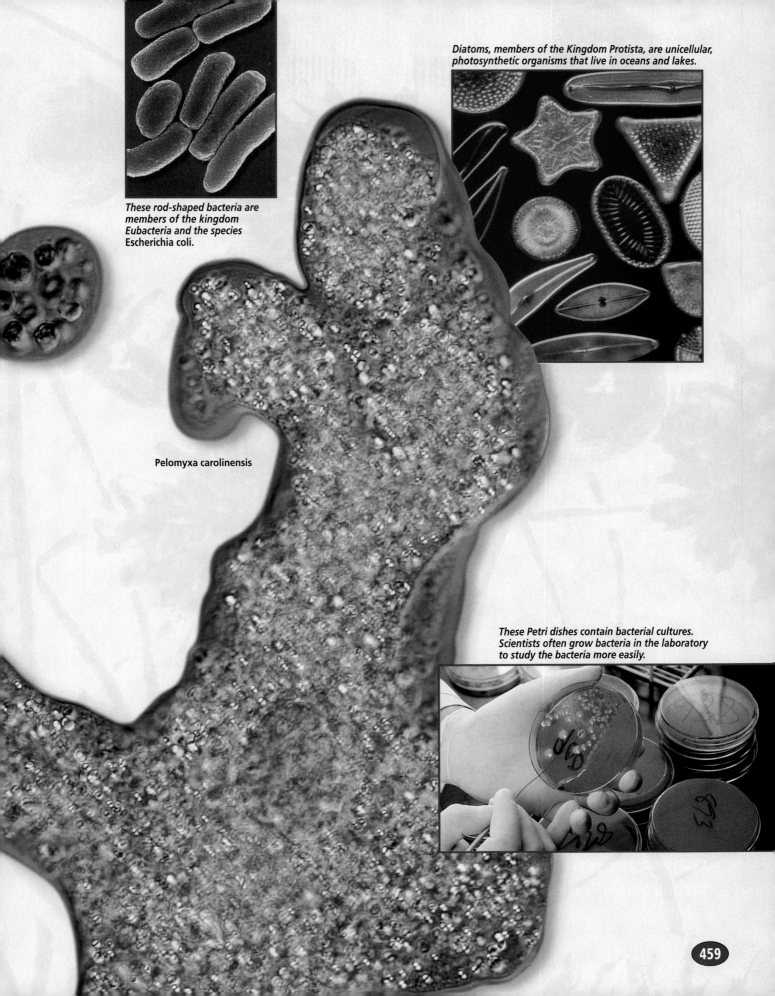

These rod-shaped bacteria are members of the kingdom Eubacteria and the species Escherichia coli.

Diatoms, members of the Kingdom Protista, are unicellular, photosynthetic organisms that live in oceans and lakes.

Pelomyxa carolinensis

These Petri dishes contain bacterial cultures. Scientists often grow bacteria in the laboratory to study the bacteria more easily.

459

# BACTERIA

This is a scanning electron microscope (SEM) image of *Helicobacter pylori* cells on human stomach cells. *H. pylori* causes about 80 percent of peptic ulcers. *H. pylori* bacteria survive the acidic environment of the stomach by secreting an enzyme that neutralizes stomach acids. Irritation is caused by the bacteria burrowing into the lining of the stomach and duodenum.

**SECTION 1** *Prokaryotes*

**SECTION 2** *Biology of Prokaryotes*

**SECTION 3** *Bacteria and Humans*

# PROKARYOTES

*Prokaryotes are the most numerous organisms on Earth. They are found almost everywhere, from the skin of a fingertip to the waters of a thermal geyser to the freezing landscape of the Antarctic. The earliest fossils of prokaryotes, which are about 3.5 billion years old, indicate that prokaryotes lived long before other forms of life evolved.*

## TWO MAJOR DOMAINS: ARCHAEA AND BACTERIA

**Prokaryotes** are single-celled organisms that do not have a membrane-bound nucleus. They live in nearly every environment on Earth. Many live in places where no other organisms can live, such as scalding hot water and inside solid rock. Prokaryotes are a major source of food for many organisms. They also help many organisms, including humans, cattle, and insects, digest food. Prokaryotes also play an important role as decomposers of dead organic matter in the environment.

Even though most prokaryotes are tiny organisms, they differ greatly in their genetic traits, in their sources of energy and nutrients, and in their habitats. Through DNA technology, scientist Carl Woese and his colleagues found in the late 1970s that there are two major branches, or domains, of prokaryotes. One branch, formerly called *Eubacteria* (YOO-bak-TIR-ee-uh), is called *Bacteria*. The other branch is called *Archaea* (ahr-KEE-uh), formerly called *Archaebacteria*. The name *archaea* means "archaic" or "ancient." Most known species of archaea live in extreme environments thought to resemble harsh environments present millions of years ago.

Figure 23-1 shows the phylogenetic relationship between living organisms based on comparisons of ribosomal RNA (rRNA) sequences. The rRNAs are well suited for such studies because they make up part of ribosomes, which are organelles that all organisms have. Also, the structure of rRNA changes very slowly over time. Surprisingly, rRNA analysis has shown that archaea are more closely related to eukaryotes than they are to bacteria. In addition, archaea have some genes that are the same as bacterial genes, but most archaeal genes more closely resemble genes found in eukaryotes. This similarity of genes suggests that archaea and eukarya likely share a more recent common ancestor than eukarya and bacteria do.

## SECTION 1

### OBJECTIVES

- **Explain** the phylogenetic relationships between the domains Archaea, Bacteria, and Eukarya.
- **Identify** three habitats of archaea.
- **Describe** the common methods used to identify bacteria.
- **Identify** five groups of bacteria.
- **Explain** the importance of nitrogen-fixing bacteria for many of Earth's ecosystems.

### VOCABULARY

prokaryote
peptidoglycan
methanogen
halophile
thermoacidophile
bacillus
coccus
spirillum
streptococcus
staphylococcus
Gram-negative bacterium
Gram-positive bacterium
antibiotic

**FIGURE 23-1**

Living organisms have been categorized into three main groups, or domains, based on ribosomal RNA analysis: Bacteria and Archaea, which contain prokaryotic cells, and Eukarya, which contains individual eukaryotic cells and includes humans.

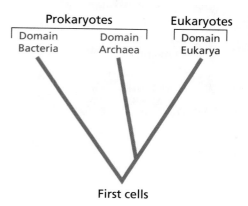

Prokaryotes | Eukaryotes

Domain Bacteria | Domain Archaea | Domain Eukarya

First cells

**FIGURE 23-2**

The fluid gushing from a hydrothermal vent, as this one seen through the window of the miniature submarine *Alvin*, can reach temperatures up to 300°C (572°F). The fluid often contains dissolved sulfides from which thermoacidophilic archaea extract energy. Vents such as this one are called *black smokers* because the vent fluids are dark in color and contain high levels of iron, manganese, and copper.

# DOMAIN ARCHAEA

Archaea are not like bacteria in many ways. Archaea differ in the makeup of their cell walls. They also differ in their membrane lipids and in their genetics and metabolism. For example, archaeal cell walls do not have **peptidoglycan** (PEP-ti-doh-GLIE-KAN), a protein-carbohydrate compound found in bacterial cell walls. Archaeal cell walls have different amino acids than bacterial cell walls do. Archaea also have different types of lipids in their cell membranes. Archaea are like eukaryotic cells in that archaeal genes have introns, portions of DNA that do not code for amino acids and that are transcribed into RNA but are removed before being translated into proteins.

Archaea were first discovered in extreme environments, such as swamps, salt lakes, and hot springs. Until recently, scientists believed that archaea lived only in these extreme environments. However, after finding archael genetic material in samples of surface waters from the North Pacific and Antarctic Oceans, scientists now think that archaea may be more common than they once thought.

## Archaeal Groups

Genetic analysis of archaea has revealed at least three groups of archaea: methanogens, halophiles, and thermoacidophiles.

**Methanogens** (muh-THAN-uh-JENZ) are named for their unique way of getting energy: they convert hydrogen gas and carbon dioxide into methane gas. Oxygen is poisonous to them, so methanogens can live only in anaerobic environments (environments that lack oxygen), such as in deep fresh water, marine mud, swamp mud, and sewage. The methane that bubbles out at sites such as swamps is called *marsh gas*. Methanogens also thrive in the intestinal tracts of organisms such as cows and termites. A cow can belch between 200 and 400 liters of methane per day.

**Halophiles** (HAL-oh-FIELZ) are "salt-loving" archaea that live in environments that have very high salt concentrations, such as the Great Salt Lake and the Dead Sea. High salt concentrations would kill most bacteria but favor the growth of halophiles because halophiles have adapted to live in very salty water.

**Thermoacidophiles** (THUHR-moh-uh-SID-uh-FIELZ) live in very acidic environments that have very high temperatures, such as the hot springs of Yellowstone National Park. Some thermoacidophiles live at temperatures up to 110°C (230°F) and at a pH of less than 2. Thermoacidophiles also live near volcanic vents on land or near hydrothermal vents called *black smokers*. Black smokers are cracks in the ocean floor that leak very hot, dark-colored, acidic water, as shown in Figure 23-2. Scientists have found large communities of worms, clams, crabs, and mussels living near these thermal vents. These communities live at great depths and in total darkness, where photosynthesis cannot take place, so they depend on thermoacidophilic archaea as a primary source of food.

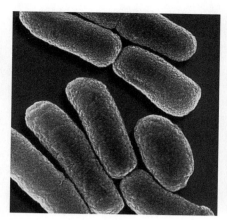

**(a)** Bacillus (rod-shaped)
*Escherichia coli*

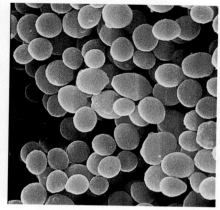

**(b)** Coccus (round-shaped)
*Micrococcus luteus*

**(c)** Spirillum (spiral-shaped)
*Spirillum volutans*

# DOMAIN BACTERIA

Most known prokaryotes are bacteria. They occur in many shapes and sizes and have distinct biochemical and genetic characteristics. Most bacteria have one of three basic shapes, as shown in Figure 23-3. Rod-shaped bacteria are called **bacilli** (buh-SIL-IE). Sphere-shaped bacteria are called **cocci** (KAHK-SIE), and spiral-shaped bacteria are called **spirilla** (spie-RIL-uh). When cocci occur in chains, they are called **streptococci** (STREP-tuh-KAHK-SIE). Grapelike clusters of cocci are called **staphylococci** (STAF-uh-loh-KAHK-SIE).

## Gram Stain

Biologists group most species of bacteria into two categories based on the structure of their cell walls as shown by a laboratory technique called the *Gram stain.* Figure 23-4a shows that Gram-negative bacteria have cell walls that are complex and have relatively small amounts of peptidoglycan. **Gram-negative bacteria** take up the second, red dye of the Gram stain process which makes the cells appear reddish pink under a microscope. Figure 23-4b shows that the walls of Gram-positive bacteria are simpler and have more peptidoglycan. **Gram-positive bacteria** retain the purple dye in their cell walls and appear purple.

**FIGURE 23-3**

The most common bacterial shapes are (a) bacillus, (b) coccus, and (c) spirillum.

**FIGURE 23-4**

After the Gram-staining procedure, a Gram-negative bacterium (a) appears pink because the cells become counterstained by the safranin red stain after being decolorized by an alcohol/acetone wash. Gram-positive cells (b) retain the crystal violet stain and appear purple.

**(a) GRAM-NEGATIVE**

**(b) GRAM-POSITIVE**

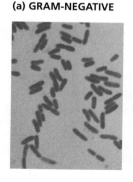

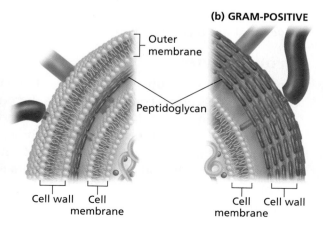

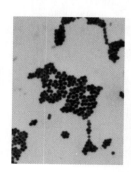

Outer membrane

Peptidoglycan

Cell wall    Cell membrane

Cell membrane    Cell wall

## FIGURE 23-5

Bacteria provide essential nutrients to many organisms. Members of the genus *Rhizobium* live symbiotically within these soybean root nodules. They fix nitrogen from the air into ammonia, a form of nitrogen that both bacteria and plants can use to make molecules such as amino acids, proteins, and nucleic acids.

# IMPORTANT BACTERIAL GROUPS

In addition to classifying bacteria based on their shape and reaction to Gram staining, biologists also classify bacteria by their biochemical properties and evolutionary relationships. Studies of DNA and rRNA similarities have improved biologists' understanding of how bacteria are related to each other. But questions about the flow of genes from one species to another and other issues remain. Prokaryotes can pick up genes from DNA in the environment by transformation. This passing of DNA from one species to another can sometimes confuse true evolutionary relationships. However, most rRNA comparison data support the bacterial lineages that are discussed below.

## Proteobacteria

Proteobacteria make up one of the largest and most diverse groups of bacteria. This group contains several subgroups that have several nutritional needs and includes both aerobic and anaerobic bacteria.

Many proteobacteria live symbiotically with other organisms. For example, the nitrogen-fixing bacteria (genus *Rhizobium*) seen in Figure 23-5 live in nodules inside the roots of legumes. Legumes are plants of the pea and bean family. Legumes also include alfalfa and clover.

Nitrogen-fixing bacteria are important to the success of many ecosystems. Even though almost 80 percent of Earth's atmosphere is made up of nitrogen gas, $N_2$, plants and animals cannot use it directly to make proteins, nucleic acids, and other nitrogen-containing molecules. In a process called *nitrogen fixation,* species of the genus *Rhizobium* convert nitrogen in the atmosphere to ammonia, which plants can use. These species are a major source of soil nitrogen for plants. The huge populations in root nodules can make about 250 kg (114 lb) of fixed nitrogen per hectare (2.5 acres) of alfalfa in a single year. Soil bacteria of the genus *Nitrosomonas,* another genus of proteobacteria, play an important part in the nitrogen cycle. Nitrosomonads form nitrite from ammonia in the soil. Nitrites are then converted into nitrates by other bacteria. Plants also use nitrates as a source of nitrogen.

Some proteobacteria cause diseases in plants and animals. For example, species of the genus *Agrobacterium* cause tumors in plants. Rickettsiae cause diseases such as Rocky Mountain spotted fever in humans. *Helicobacter pylori,* shown in the chapter opener photo, is a bacterium that commonly causes stomach ulcers.

Some species of proteobacteria are enteric bacteria—they live in human and animal intestines. Enteric bacteria such as *Escherichia coli* make vitamin K and help digestive enzymes in the breakdown of foods in the intestines. Some strains of *E. coli* and species of the genus *Salmonella* cause foodborne illnesses either by invading the cells that line the intestines or by making toxins.

## Gram-Positive Bacteria

Most members of this group are Gram-positive, but not all are. Biologists place a few species of Gram-negative bacteria in this group because these species are genetically similar to Gram-positive bacteria. This group is very large and has many members. Members include the streptococcal species that causes strep throat and *Clostridium botulinum*, the bacterium that makes the toxin that causes botulism. Botulinum toxin is used medicinally to treat painful muscle spasms and, more recently, to erase "frown lines" from the face. Lactic acid bacterial species, such as species of the genus *Lactobacilli,* which turn milk sour and make yogurt, are also members of this phylum. Anthrax is caused by the Gram-positive rod *Bacillus anthracis*, shown in Figure 23-6. *B. anthracis* is often linked to its use as a biological weapon.

Actinomycetes (AK-tuh-noh-MIE-SEETS) are Gram-positive bacteria that form branching filaments of colonies. Many species of actinomycetes grow in soil and make **antibiotics,** chemicals that inhibit the growth of or kill other microorganisms. Antibiotics kill neighboring bacteria and fungi that compete for resources. Streptomycin (which is made by species of the genus *Streptomyces*) and tetracycline are examples of antibiotics that are used medicinally. Members of the genus *Mycobacteria,* another genus of actinomycetes, cause tuberculosis and Hansen's disease (leprosy).

internet connect

www.scilinks.org
Topic: Biological Weapons
Keyword: HM61692

SCiLINKS. Maintained by the National Science Teachers Association

**FIGURE 23-6**

Human infection by Gram-positive *Bacillus anthracis* (a) is usually through a cut in the skin (cutaneous anthrax). However, inhaling endospores may result in pulmonary anthrax. If endospores reach the intestine, gastrointestinal anthrax may result. Photo (b) shows the ulcerated lesion, called an *eschar* (ES-KAHR), of cutaneous anthrax on a shoulder.

**(a)**

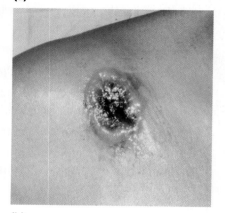

**(b)**

## Cyanobacteria

Cyanobacteria use photosynthesis to get energy from sunlight and make carbohydrates from water and the carbon dioxide in the air. They give off oxygen as a waste product. Certain cyanobacteria, such as those in the genus *Anabaena* shown in Figure 23-7, grow in filaments. Some of the organisms in the genus *Anabaena* form specialized cells called *heterocysts*. Heterocysts have enzymes for fixing atmospheric nitrogen into ammonia, which plants can use. Nitrogen-fixing cyanobacteria have nature's simplest nutritional requirements. They need only light energy, carbon dioxide, nitrogen, water, and some minerals in order to grow.

Cyanobacteria are very numerous and offer a large amount of food to marine and freshwater ecosystems. They were Earth's first oxygen-producing organisms. They are believed to have been responsible for making the oxygen-rich atmosphere in which aerobic (oxygen-using) organisms evolved. Once called *blue-green algae,* cyanobacteria are now known to be bacteria because they lack a membrane-bound nucleus and chloroplasts.

## Spirochetes

Spirochetes (SPIE-roh-KEETS) are Gram-negative, spiral-shaped bacteria. Some are aerobic, and some are anaerobic. They move by means of a corkscrew-like rotation. Spirochetes live freely or as pathogens. The spirochete *Treponema pallidum* causes syphilis, a sexually transmitted infection (STI), and *Borrelia burgdorferi* causes Lyme disease.

## Chlamydia

Gram-negative, coccoid pathogens of the group Chlamydia live only inside animal cells. They depend on the animal cells for protection and nutrients. Unlike the cell walls of other bacteria, the cell walls of chlamydia do not have peptidoglycan. *Chlamydia trachomatis* causes nongonococcal urethritis, or chlamydia, an STI.

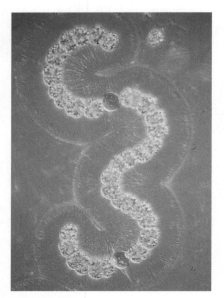

**FIGURE 23-7**

Cyanobacteria, such as this filament of cells of the genus *Anabaena*, play an important role in the carbon cycle because they take up large amounts of carbon from the atmosphere during photosynthesis. The orange cells are the heterocysts in which nitrogen fixation occurs.

## SECTION 1 REVIEW

1. Describe the major ways in which archaea differ from bacteria and eukarya.

2. Name three habitats where archaea live.

3. Explain how a Gram stain helps identify bacteria.

4. Name one organism from each of the five groups of bacteria discussed.

5. Discuss the importance of nitrogen-fixing bacteria.

6. Describe the significance of cyanobacteria in the formation of Earth's atmosphere.

**CRITICAL THINKING**

7. **Applying Information** If Earth suddenly lost its light source but kept the same temperature, what forms of life would most likely remain?

8. **Relating Information** Would you expect to find thermoacidophilic bacteria and enteric bacteria living in the same environment? Explain.

9. **Inferring Relationships** Certain antibiotics kill only Gram-positive bacteria. Why is this information important to consider when treating a patient who has a bacterial infection of unknown cause?

# BIOLOGY OF PROKARYOTES

*A look at prokaryotic cells under a light microscope shows that they are very small. Such a view, however, leaves unexplained the complexity of the cells' internal workings. Here, we will study the structure of prokaryotic cells and the many ways that they gather nutrients and energy and reproduce.*

## SECTION 2

### OBJECTIVES

- **Describe** the internal and external structure of prokaryotic cells.
- **Identify** the need for endospores.
- **Compare** four ways in which prokaryotes get energy and carbon.
- **Identify** the different types of environments in which prokaryotes can live.
- **List** three types of genetic recombination that prokaryotes use.

### VOCABULARY

plasmid
capsule
glycocalyx
pilus
endospore
heterotroph
autotroph
phototroph
chemotroph
obligate anaerobe
facultative anaerobe
obligate aerobe
transformation
conjugation
transduction

## STRUCTURE AND FUNCTION

In general, prokaryotes are made up of a cell wall, a cell membrane, and cytoplasm that has ribosomes, DNA, and small molecules and ions. Recall that prokaryotes do not have membrane-bound organelles. Additional distinctive structures help some bacteria adapt to their own niches.

### Cell Wall

Most members of the domains Bacteria and Archaea have a cell wall. The cell wall gives a cell its shape and protects the cell from toxic substances. The cell walls of many disease-causing bacteria have structures that add to the disease-causing abilities of the organisms. Bacterial cell walls are made of peptidoglycan, not cellulose, which makes up plant cell walls. Archaeal cell walls do not have peptidoglycan; instead, some of them contain *pseudomurein,* a compound made of unusual lipids and amino acids.

### Cell Membrane and Cytoplasm

Just inside the cell wall, prokaryotes have a cell membrane, or *plasma membrane.* Both bacterial and archaeal cell membranes are lipid bilayers that have proteins. However, the lipids and proteins of archaeal cell walls differ from those of bacterial cell walls.

The cell membrane acts as a selective barrier by controlling the molecules that move into and out of the cell. In this way, the cell membrane helps keep the internal environment of the organism stable. The cell membrane is also the place where many important metabolic functions occur. For example, enzymes that catalyze the reactions of cellular respiration are found in the bilayer.

Photosynthetic bacteria have cell membranes whose internal foldings are called *thylakoids* (THIE-luh-KOYDZ). These foldings are much like the stacked membranes of plant chloroplasts. Like thylakoids in plant chloroplasts, bacterial thylakoids have photosynthetic pigments that trap light energy.

### Word Roots and Origins

*pseudomurein*

from the Greek *pseudes,* meaning "false," and the Latin *murus,* meaning "wall"

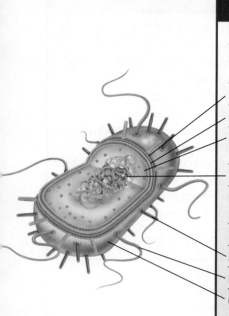

**TABLE 23-1 Structural Characteristics of a Bacterial Cell**

| Structure | Function |
|---|---|
| Capsule | protects the cell and helps the cell attach to other cells and surfaces |
| Cell wall | protects the cell and gives the cell its shape |
| Cell membrane | regulates the types of molecules that move into and out of the cell |
| Cytoplasm | contains DNA, ribosomes, and organic compounds that are needed for life |
| Chromosome | carries genetic information from one generation to the next |
| Plasmid | carries genes that are transferred through genetic recombination; is a small, circular DNA loop |
| Endospore | contains DNA; is a thick-coated, resistant structure |
| Pilus | helps the cell attach to surfaces and other cells during conjugation |
| Flagellum | propels the cell by rotating in a whiplike motion |
| Outer membrane | protects the cell against some antibiotics (present only in Gram-negative bacteria) |

Bacterial cells do not have membrane-bound organelles in their cytoplasm. Instead, the cytoplasm is a semifluid solution that contains ribosomes, DNA, small organic and inorganic molecules, and ions, as shown in Table 23-1.

## DNA

Prokaryotic DNA is a single closed loop of double-stranded DNA attached at one point to the cell membrane. Unlike eukaryotic DNA, prokaryotic DNA is not enclosed in a nucleus. Along with this single main chromosome, some prokaryotes have plasmids. **Plasmids** are small, circular, self-replicating loops of double-stranded DNA. Plasmids are usually not necessary for the cell's growth and reproduction, but some plasmids carry genes that enable the bacterium to cause disease. Other plasmids carry genes that provide the bacterium with resistance to certain antibiotics.

## Capsules and Pili

Many bacteria have an outer covering of polysaccharides called a **capsule.** These sugars bind to the cell wall and protect the cell against drying or harsh chemicals. The capsule also helps protect a pathogenic (disease-causing) bacterium from the host's white blood cells, which could otherwise engulf the bacterium. A capsule made up of a fuzzy coat of sticky sugars is called a **glycocalyx** (GLIE-koh-KAY-liks). This structure allows bacteria to connect to the surface of host cells and tissues.

**Pili** (PIL-ee) (singular, *pilus*) are short, hairlike protein structures on the surface of some bacteria. Pili help bacteria connect to each other and to surfaces, such as those of a host cell. Pili can also serve as a bridge to pass genetic material between bacteria.

## Endospores

Some Gram-positive bacteria can form a thick-coated, resistant structure called an **endospore** when environmental conditions become harsh. The harsh conditions may destroy the original cell, but the endospore containing the cell's DNA can survive. Endospores can resist high temperatures, strong chemicals, radiation, drying, and other environmental extremes. When good conditions return, the endospore gives rise to a normal bacterial cell. Species of the genera *Bacillus* and *Clostridium* can form endospores. Figure 23-8 shows a *C. botulinum* cell with an endospore. The endospores of *C. botulinum* can germinate in improperly sterilized canned foods. The bacteria make a toxin that if eaten can cause the nerve disease *botulism*. While rare, botulism is often fatal if it is not treated promptly.

## Prokaryotic Movement

Many prokaryotes have long flagella that allow the prokaryotes to move toward food sources or away from danger. Movement toward or away from a stimulus is called *taxis* (TAKS-is). In *chemotaxis*, prokaryotes react to chemical stimuli by moving toward food or away from a toxin. Prokaryotic flagella rotate and move the prokaryote in a "run-and-tumble" motion. Prokaryotes can have a single whiplike flagellum or many flagella.

Some bacteria do not have flagella but can move by other means. Species of the genus *Myxobacteria*, for example, form a layer of slime. Wavelike contractions of the outer membrane move the organisms through the slime. Some spiral-shaped bacteria move by a corkscrew-like rotation. Filaments inside the organism's cell walls contract and cause the bacterium to turn and move ahead.

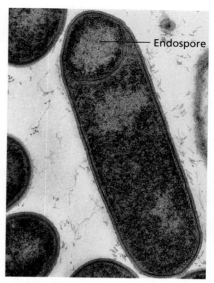

**FIGURE 23-8**

Unfavorable conditions can cause some bacteria, such as the Gram-positive rod *Clostridium botulinum*, to form endospores. After forming the endospore, the bacterial cell disintegrates, and the endospore containing the cell's DNA is released. Endospores can survive in harsh environments for a long time.

# NUTRITION AND METABOLISM

Prokaryotes have two chief nutritional needs: a source of carbon to build the organic molecules of their cells and a source of energy. They have many ways of getting both carbon and energy from the environment. Organisms that get their carbon from other organisms are called **heterotrophs. Autotrophs** are organisms that get their carbon directly from the inorganic molecule carbon dioxide, $CO_2$. Organisms that get energy from light are called **phototrophs. Chemotrophs** get energy from chemicals taken from the environment. Table 23-2 shows how these ways of getting nutrients can be used to divide prokaryotes into four nutritional groups.

| TABLE 23-2 *Major Bacterial Nutritional Modes* | |
|---|---|
| **Nutritional mode** | **Energy and carbon source** |
| **Heterotroph** | |
| Photoheterotroph | uses light energy but gets its carbon from other organisms |
| Chemoheterotroph | obtains both energy and carbon from other organisms |
| **Autotroph** | |
| Photoautotroph | uses light energy and gets carbon from $CO_2$ |
| Chemoautotroph | extracts energy from inorganic compounds and uses $CO_2$ as a carbon source |

Prokaryotes that have different pigments live at different temperatures in a Yellowstone hot spring. Some are photoautotrophs, some are chemoautotrophs, and others are chemoheterotrophs.

**FIGURE 23-10**

*Thermus aquaticus* cells form a long, stringy mass in the outflow channel of a hot spring. *T. aquaticus* was first isolated from a hot spring in Yellowstone by Thomas D. Brock. Later, the heat-tolerant enzyme *Taq* polymerase was isolated from *T. aquaticus*. Biotechnologists now routinely use *Taq* polymerase to rapidly replicate pieces of DNA in the polymerase chain reaction (PCR).

Most prokaryotes that we have studied so far are photoautotrophs (FOHT-oh-AWT-oh-TROHFS) and chemoheterotrophs (KEE-moh-HET-uhr-oh-TROHFS). Prokaryotes such as cyanobacteria that gather sunlight for photosynthesis are photoautotrophs. Photoautotrophs harvest energy with light-trapping compounds similar to those of plants. Chemoautotrophs, a group of autotrophs, oxidize inorganic compounds to get energy. For example, members of the genus *Nitrosomonas* oxidize ammonia, $NH_3$, forming nitrite, $NO_2$, and use the released energy. Methanogens living in a cow's digestive tract make methane gas from inorganic molecules. Pathogenic (disease-causing) bacteria are chemoheterotrophs. Figure 23-9 shows an environment in which various prokaryotes that have different kinds of nutritional needs live close together.

# PROKARYOTIC HABITATS

Prokaryotes live in certain habitats based on their biochemical abilities. Many bacteria are **obligate anaerobes** (AHB-luh-git AN-uhr-OHBS), organisms that cannot live where molecular oxygen, $O_2$, is present. The obligate anaerobe *Clostridium tetani* causes the nerve disease *tetanus*. **Facultative anaerobes** (FAK-uhl-TAYT-iv AN-uhr-OHBS) can live with or without oxygen. *Escherichia coli*, which is common in the human digestive tract, is a facultative anaerobe. Prokaryotes that need oxygen to live are called **obligate aerobes.** The obligate aerobe *Mycobacterium tuberculosis* causes the disease tuberculosis (TB).

Prokaryotes have varying temperature requirements for growth. Psychrophilic (SIE-kroh-FIL-ik) (cold-loving) prokaryotes grow well at 0°C to 20°C (32°F to 68°F). Their cellular enzymes and cell membranes work well at cold temperatures. Some prokaryotes of the Antarctic survive very cold temperatures by living just under the surfaces of rocks. The weak sunlight warms the rocks just enough so that the psychrophiles have a slow-growing life cycle.

Prokaryotes that grow best at temperatures between 20°C (68°F) and 40°C (104°F) are called *mesophiles*. Humans are also classified as mesophiles. Prokaryotes that grow at very hot temperatures—between 45°C (113°F) and 110°C (230°F)—are called *thermophiles* (THUHR-moh-FIELZ). Thermophilic species have evolved proteins that resist being destroyed by heat. The development of biotechnology owes much to the purification of the heat-stable, DNA-replicating enzyme *Taq* polymerase from the thermophile *Thermus aquaticus*, shown in Figure 23-10. *T. aquaticus* was first isolated from a hot spring in Yellowstone National Park.

Most bacterial species grow best at a pH of 6.5 to 7.5 (7.0 is neutral). However, certain species, such as those that make yogurt and sour cream from milk, favor acidic environments that have a pH of 6.0 or lower. Acid-loving prokaryotes are called *acidophiles*.

# REPRODUCTION AND RECOMBINATION

Prokaryotes usually reproduce by binary fission, which is a form of asexual reproduction. During binary fission, shown in Figure 23-11, the DNA replicates and the two daughter DNA molecules are pulled to opposite ends of the cell. Finally, the cell membrane pinches in two to form two identical daughter cells.

Prokaryotes can exchange pieces of DNA that can be added to the cell's DNA without reproduction. This process is called *recombination*. Prokaryotes can get DNA from other prokaryotes in three ways: transformation, bacterial conjugation, and transduction. **Transformation** occurs when a prokaryote takes in DNA from its outside environment. **Conjugation** is the process by which two prokaryotes bind together and one cell transfers DNA to the other cell through a structure called a *sex pilus*. In **transduction,** a virus obtains a small part of DNA from a host prokaryote. The virus then copies itself inside the host, and new copies of the prokaryotic DNA are made with the viral DNA. After the new viruses have been released, they carry the prokaryotic gene to the next prokaroyote.

Understanding these methods of bacterial genetic exchange is of great importance to our understanding of genetics. Transformation provided the evidence that DNA is the genetic material of cells. Investigations on the process of conjugation gave scientists key information about the mechanisms of genetic recombination common to all organisms. Transformation is used every day in thousands of labs to transfer bits of human and other DNAs into bacterial cells to identify and isolate certain genes. The sequencing of the human genome, one of the greatest feats in history, relied on recombining human genes into artificial plasmids and artificial chromosomes called *bacterial artificial chromosomes* (BACs). The BACs and plasmids were then inserted into bacterial cells by transformation. The results of such studies are being used to develop a better understanding of human health and to find improved treatment for disease.

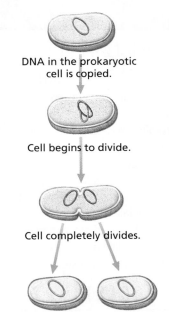

DNA in the prokaryotic cell is copied.

Cell begins to divide.

Cell completely divides.

Two identical daughter cells result.

**FIGURE 23-11**

Most prokaryotes reproduce by binary fission, in which two identical cells are produced from one cell.

## SECTION 2 REVIEW

1. List the functions of six structures of a prokaryotic cell.

2. Describe three ways in which prokaryotes move.

3. Identify how the oxygen requirements of a prokaryote can affect the types of environments in which it can live.

4. How do autotrophs and heterotrophs differ?

5. List and summarize the three methods of prokaryotic recombination.

**CRITICAL THINKING**

6. **Relating Concepts** What eukaryotic organelle is functionally similar to the prokaryotic cell membrane and its infoldings?

7. **Applying Information** Why is improperly sterilized canned food an ideal environment for the obligate anaerobe *Clostridium botulinum*?

8. **Analyzing Information** Identify why recombination is not a form of reproduction.

- **Describe** the ways in which bacteria can cause disease in humans.
- **Explain** how a bacterial population can develop resistance to antibiotics.
- **Identify** reasons for recent increases in the numbers of certain bacterial infectious diseases.
- **Identify** ways of preventing a foodborne illness at home.
- **List** four industrial uses of bacteria.

### VOCABULARY

pathology
exotoxin
endotoxin
antibiotic resistance
zoonosis
bioremediation

# BACTERIA AND HUMANS

*Bacteria are probably best known for the diseases that they cause in humans. However, most bacteria that live on human skin are harmless, and other bacteria are used biotechnologically, as in the production of yogurt. Still other bacteria that live in soil change atmospheric nitrogen into ammonia and nitrites, which plants use for growth.*

## BACTERIA AND HEALTH

The scientific study of disease is called **pathology** (puh-THAHL-uh-jee), and bacteria and other organisms that cause disease are called *pathogens*. Table 23-3 summarizes several bacterial diseases. Some bacteria cause disease by making certain poisons called *toxins* (TAHKS-ins). **Exotoxins** (EKS-oh-TAHK-sins) are toxic substances that bacteria secrete into their environment. Some Gram-positive bacteria secrete protein exotoxins. For example, *Clostridium tetani* secretes an exotoxin that causes tetanus in humans. **Endotoxins** are toxic substances made of lipids and carbohydrates associated with the outer membrane of Gram-negative bacteria, such as *E. coli*. Endotoxins are not released until the cell dies. After they are released, endotoxins can cause fever, body aches, diarrhea, hemorrhage, and weakness.

## TABLE 23-3 *Bacterial Diseases*

| Disease | Bacterium | Areas affected by illness | Mode of transmission |
|---|---|---|---|
| Anthrax | *Bacillus anthracis* | lungs, skin, or intestines | airborne spores; may be picked up from environmental surfaces |
| Botulism | *Clostridium botulinum* | nerves | improperly preserved foods |
| Cholera | *Vibrio cholerae* | intestine | feces-contaminated water |
| Dental caries (tooth decay) | *Streptococcus mutans, S. sanguis,* and *S. salivarius* | teeth and gums | dense collections of bacteria normally found in the mouth |
| Gonorrhea | *Neisseria gonorrhoeae* | urethra, fallopian tubes, and epididymis | person-to-person transmission by sexual contact |
| Lyme disease | *Borrelia burgdorferi* | skin, joints, and heart | tick bite |
| *Salmonella* food poisoning | species of the genus *Salmonella,* such as *S. typhimurium* | intestine | feces-contaminated water and food |
| Tetanus | *Clostridium tetani* | nerve cells at synapses | soil-contaminated skin wounds |
| Staph infection | *Staphylococcus aureus* | skin, soft tissue, lungs, and blood | direct contact of skin wounds with *S. aureus* |

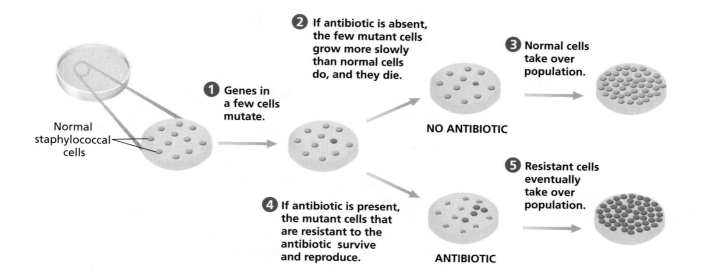

**②** If antibiotic is absent, the few mutant cells grow more slowly than normal cells do, and they die.

**①** Genes in a few cells mutate.

**③** Normal cells take over population.

**NO ANTIBIOTIC**

Normal staphylococcal cells

**④** If antibiotic is present, the mutant cells that are resistant to the antibiotic survive and reproduce.

**⑤** Resistant cells eventually take over population.

**ANTIBIOTIC**

Bacteria also cause disease by destroying body tissues. As bacteria stick to body cells, they secrete digestive enzymes that break down tissue for its nutritional value, which allows further bacterial invasion. For example, some species of the genus *Streptococcus* make a blood clot-dissolving enzyme that allows bacteria to spread easily from tissue to tissue.

## Antibiotics and Antibiotic Resistance

Antibiotics affect bacteria by interfering with certain cellular activities. Penicillin (PEN-i-SIL-in), for example, blocks the ability to build new cell wall material, while tetracycline (TE-truh-SIE-klin) blocks protein synthesis. Antibiotics are made naturally by some fungi and bacteria, and they kill neighboring bacteria or fungi that compete for resources. Scientists have worked to improve the effectiveness of these and other chemicals. Antibiotics that can kill more than one kind of organism are called *broad-spectrum antibiotics.*

A big worry for modern medicine is **antibiotic resistance,** the evolution of populations of pathogenic bacteria that antibiotics are unable to kill. Antibiotic resistance may develop in a population of bacteria in several ways. In one case, mutations in bacterial DNA give a bacterium resistance to antibiotics. A cell with such a mutation has a selective advantage when antibiotics are present. Mutant bacteria multiply and take over the population and thus stop the antibiotic's curing power. Figure 23-12 shows how resistance can evolve in a population of bacteria.

Unfortunately, antibiotics have been misused by doctors who overprescribe them and patients who do not finish their course of prescribed antibiotics. Many resistance genes are now present on plasmids called *R-plasmids*, which can pass easily between many bacteria by transformation. R-plasmids can carry resistance genes to many antibiotics. In this way, they give the bacterium *multiple resistances* to antibiotics. Many diseases that were once easy to treat with antibiotics, such as TB and staphylococcal infections, are now becoming more difficult to treat because of multiple resistances.

**FIGURE 23-12**

**①** Individual bacteria in a large population may have mutated genes that give the bacteria resistance to an antibiotic. **②** If the antibiotic is absent, these resistant cells usually grow very slowly. **③** The nonmutated cells eventually take over the population. **④** If the antibiotic is present, however, it kills off the normal cells and leaves the mutant, antibiotic-resistant cells. **⑤** The mutant cells continue to grow and to take over the population. Antibiotics provide a selective advantage to antibiotic-resistant bacteria in this way.

**☑ internet** connect

www.scilinks.org
**Topic:** Antibiotic
        Resistance
**Keyword:** HM60081

*SCLINKS.* Maintained by the National Science Teachers Association

## Emerging Infectious Diseases Caused by Bacteria

Physicians and scientists have become worried by emerging infectious diseases. Diseases such as TB, which is caused by species of the genus *Mycobacteria,* and staphylococcal post-surgical infections, which are caused by *Staphylococcus aureus,* are becoming more difficult to treat because of the increased numbers of antibiotic-resistant bacteria. Other diseases, such Lyme disease, are becoming more common than they were in the past. Lyme disease is caused by the bacterium *Borrelia burgdorferi.* If a tick infected with the bacterium bites a person, the bacterium can enter the person's bloodstream and cause flulike symptoms, arthritis, and sometimes heart inflammation.

Most emerging diseases develop when infectious agents, such as bacteria, pass from wild animals to humans. A disease that can pass from animals to humans is called a **zoonosis** (ZO-uh-NOH-sis). One reason for the emergence of Lyme disease is the flow of human populations into previously untouched natural areas. As people move into these areas, the chance of contact with infected ticks increases. The increase in global travel has also added to the spread of new and difficult-to-treat infectious diseases around the world.

## Food Hygiene and Bacteria

Foodborne illnesses can be a major public health hazard, especially if an outbreak happens in a place such as a restaurant, where food is served to large numbers of people. However, the improper preparation, handling, or storage of food at home may cause most cases of foodborne illness in the United States. Many illnesses, such as campylobacteriosis (caused by *Campylobacter jejuni*), are relatively mild. Usual symptoms are nausea, vomiting, and intestinal cramps that last less than a week. However, certain foodborne pathogens, such as the *E. coli* O157:H7 strain, can cause serious illness and complications such as kidney damage in children and older adults. *E. coli* O157:H7–related illness is usually due to eating undercooked, contaminated hamburger meat.

Many foodborne illnesses can be avoided by selecting, storing, cooking, and handling food properly. For example, choose only fresh, clean foods, and wash raw fruit and vegetables well in clean water before eating them. Wash hands, kitchen towels, and kitchen utensils often in hot, soapy water to avoid cross-contamination during food preparation. Also, avoid cross-contamination of raw and cooked foods by keeping these foods separated during preparation and storage. Always refrigerate raw foods (including eggs) and deli meats at 4°C (39°F). Cook foods, especially meats, thoroughly and heat them to recommended temperatures to kill possible pathogens. Also, refrigerate leftovers promptly, and then reheat them thoroughly before eating them. Wash your hands well with soap and water for 10 to 15 seconds. Always wash your hands after using the bathroom, changing a diaper, handling animals, working outdoors, and coughing or sneezing into your hands.

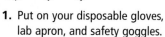

### Quick Lab

**Modeling the Spread of Disease**

**Materials** disposable gloves, lab apron, and safety goggles; clear plastic cup with liquid

**Procedure**

1. Put on your disposable gloves, lab apron, and safety goggles.

2. Obtain a cup of liquid from your teacher.

3. Pour the contents of your cup into a classmate's cup. Have the classmate pour the liquid back into your cup. Repeat this step with two other classmates. Do not touch anyone else's hands.

4. Predict the number of classmates that have been "exposed" to the "disease." Your teacher will test the liquid in each student's cup to see who has caught the "disease." Count the number of "infected" students.

**Analysis** How did the actual results compare with your prediction? Was direct contact needed?

# MILESTONES IN Treating Bacterial Diseases

## Timeline

**1677** Anton van Leeuwenhoek first observes living bacteria.

**1861** Louis Pasteur invents sterilization.

**1876** Joseph Lister uses sterile surgical techniques.

**1876** Robert Koch proves *Bacillus anthracis* causes anthrax.

**1910** Paul Ehrlich invents Salversan, a drug for syphilis.

**1928** Alexander Fleming discovers antibiotic effects of penicillium mold.

**1939** Howard Florey and Ernst Chain isolate penicillin and create first antibiotic drug.

**1950s** Faster antibiotic development and successful prevention and treatment of disease occur.

**1980** Molecular techniques aid the study of pathogens.

**Present** Development of antibiotic resistance spurs more research into antibiotic treatment.

*Most pharmacies today carry many antibiotics for treating bacterial diseases, yet until World War II, no such medicines existed. Not until the 19th century was it discovered that bacteria could cause disease. Much of modern medicine rests on the pioneering work of the researchers discussed here.*

In 1677, Dutch tradesman Anton van Leeuwenhoek first observed bacteria. His hand-held microscopes magnified objects much better than other microscopes of his day did. In the sticky plaque of his own teeth, he observed "many little living animalcules, very prettily a moving."

In 1850, Hungarian physician Ignaz Semmelweis instructed his medical students to wash their hands between seeing patients. This first simple antiseptic procedure spared thousands of new mothers from deadly puerperal (pyoo-UHR-puhr-uhl), or child-bed, fever.

In 1861, French chemist Louis Pasteur proved that germs did not grow by spontaneous generation. He also showed that heating broth can kill bacteria and sterilize the broth. By sterilizing his hands, surgical instruments, and his patient's incisions with carbolic acid, British surgeon Joseph Lister applied Pasteur's ideas. This action greatly reduced the loss of life from infection.

In 1876, Robert Koch, a German physician, was the first to prove the link between a bacterium and a disease. He isolated *Bacillus anthracis* from a sick animal and established the bacterium's role in the disease anthrax. Within 20 years, Koch and colleagues across Europe and the United States had discovered the causal agents for dozens of infectious diseases.

The growing knowledge of bacteria and disease in the late 1800s encouraged researchers to look for safer antibacterial drugs, because heavy metals such as mercury often harmed the patient.

In 1910, German physician Paul Erlich developed the compound Salversan, which sucessfully treated syphilis. In 1928, British microscopist Alexander Fleming accidentally discovered the antibacterial effect of penicillium mold, which was to become the source of penicillin, the first mass-produced antibiotic.

During the last half of the 20th century, many new antibiotics were created. More recently, molecular techniques have opened a new era of medical research for the treatment of bacterial diseases. Computer programs are now commonly used to design more-effective antibiotics and vaccines. This advancement is especially important because of the increasing numbers of bacteria that are not affected by traditional antibiotics, such as penicillin and streptomycin.

## Review

1. Identify two conclusions drawn from Louis Pasteur's 1861 experiment.

2. **Critical Thinking** Is hand washing still an important way to prevent the spread of disease? Explain.

3. **Critical Thinking** It was once believed that poisonous vapors called *miasmas* caused disease. Why do you think this belief existed?

internet connect

**www.scilinks.org**
**Topic: Germ Theory of Disease**
**Keyword: HM61691**

SCiLINKS. Maintained by the National Science Teachers Association

(a)

(b)

**FIGURE 23-13**

Bacteria are important in many industries. *Bacillus thuringiensis,* or Bt, is commonly sold as an organic pesticide to kill pests, such as the corn earworm caterpillar in (a). After an oil spill, cleanup crews spray fertilizer, which encourages the growth of naturally occurring prokaryotes to break down the oily sludge (b).

# BACTERIA IN INDUSTRY

Bacteria are used to make and process many common foods and important chemicals. By fermenting the lactose in milk, bacteria make sour-milk products such as buttermilk, sour cream, and yogurt. Bacteria are also used to make cheeses such as mozzarella, ricotta, cheddar, and Roquefort. Fermented foods, such as sauerkraut, pickles, kimchi, coffee, and soy sauce, are products of bacterial fermentation. Bacteria are also grown in huge fermenters to make certain chemicals, such as acetone, acetic acid, enzymes, antibiotics, and insulin. They help break down organic waste in sewage and recycle carbon and nitrogen. Mining engineers also use bacteria in mining minerals and recovering petroleum.

Heat-loving prokaryotes are a major source of heat-resistant enzymes for biomedicine and industry. The heat-tolerant enzyme *Taq* polymerase allows biotechnologists to copy pieces of DNA rapidly, while other enzymes from thermophilic archaea, when added to laundry detergent, help dissolve stains.

Bacteria can cause diseases in crops and farm animals, but certain species are also useful for agriculture. *Bacillus thuringiensis,* or Bt, makes tiny crystals of protein that act as an endotoxin for certain plant pests, such as the corn earworm caterpillar shown in Figure 23-13a. After the insect feeds on a plant with Bt, the Bt crystals break down the insect's gut and kill the insect. Geneticists have inserted the gene that encodes the Bt toxic protein into the genome of some corn strains, so the corn now kills insects directly.

Biologists have also learned to harness bacteria to recycle compounds in a process called **bioremediation,** which uses bacteria to break down pollutants. After an oil spill, as shown in Figure 23-13b, bioremediation workers can spray contaminated beaches with nitrogen- and phosphorus-containing fertilizers. These nutrients, along with the oil along the shoreline, aid the growth of naturally occurring prokaryotes that can break down the petroleum and use it as an energy source.

## SECTION 3 REVIEW

1. Describe two ways that bacteria can cause disease.

2. Describe the function of antibiotics in nature.

3. Explain how antibiotic resistance can evolve in bacteria.

4. Identify the main problem associated with antibiotic resistance.

5. List ways to avoid a foodborne illness.

6. Explain how bioremediation works to clean up environmental pollution.

**CRITICAL THINKING**

7. **Analyzing Concepts** How does the development of antibiotic resistance in a population of bacteria support the theory of evolution through natural selection?

8. **Applying Information** Why would a pickle processor carry out the preparation of pickles in anaerobic conditions?

9. **Drawing Conclusions** A student said that one should never allow bacteria near any foods. Explain whether this conclusion is appropriate.

## SECTION 1 — Prokaryotes

- Prokaryotes are single-celled organisms that do not have a membrane surrounding their DNA. Prokaryotes occupy two domains of life: Archaea and Bacteria.

- Members of the domain Archaea contain certain genes more similar to eukarya, which include plants, animals, and fungi, than to the genes of bacteria.

- The domain Archaea includes methanogens, which produce methane gas and live in anaerobic environments; extreme halophiles, which live in very salty environments; and thermoacidophiles, which live in extremely acidic, hot environments.

- Gram staining distinguishes between Gram-positive and Gram-negative bacteria. Bacteria also occur in several variations of three shapes: rods, spheres, and spirals.

- The domain Bacteria is classified into five groups: Proteobacteria, Gram-positive bacteria, Cyanobacteria, Spirochetes, and Chlamydia.

- Nitrogen-fixing bacteria fix nitrogen gas from the air into a form that both prokaryotes and plants can use.

### Vocabulary

prokaryote (p. 461)
peptidoglycan (p. 462)
methanogen (p. 462)
halophile (p. 462)

thermoacidophile (p. 462)
bacillus (p. 463)
coccus (p. 463)
spirillum (p. 463)

streptococcus (p. 463)
staphlyococcus (p. 463)
Gram-negative bacterium (p. 463)

Gram-positive bacterium (p. 463)
antibiotic (p. 465)

## SECTION 2 — Biology of Prokaryotes

- The major structures of a prokaryotic cell include a cell wall, a cell membrane, cytoplasm, a capsule, pili, endospores, ribosomes, and sometimes structures for movement, called *flagella*.

- Endospores are thick-coated, resistant cells that some Gram-positive bacteria form when conditions become unfavorable. Endospores can survive high temperatures, strong chemicals, drying, and radiation and can survive for long periods of time.

- Prokaryotes obtain nutrients either from the nonliving environment or by utilizing the products or bodies of living organisms. Heterotrophs obtain carbon from other organisms. Autotrophs obtain their carbon from $CO_2$.

- Different prokaryotic species live in different environments. Temperature requirements range from 0°C to 110°C. Most prokaryotic species grow best at a neutral pH.

- Genetic recombination in bacteria can occur through transformation, conjugation, and transduction.

### Vocabulary

plasmid (p. 468)
capsule (p. 468)
glycocalyx (p. 468)
pilus (p. 468)

endospore (p. 469)
heterotroph (p. 469)
autotroph (p. 469)
phototroph (p. 469)

chemotroph (p. 469)
obligate anaerobe (p. 470)
facultative anaerobe (p. 470)
obligate aerobe (p. 470)

transformation (p. 471)
conjugation (p. 471)
transduction (p. 471)

## SECTION 3 — Bacteria and Humans

- Human diseases may result from toxins produced by bacteria or from the destruction of body tissues.

- A mutation in the DNA of a single bacterium can confer resistance to an antibiotic. Cells with the mutant gene have a selective advantage when the antibiotic is present. Mutant cells take over the population when the normal cells die.

- The number of certain bacterial diseases has increased because of the increase in the number of antibiotic-resistant bacteria, the movement of people into previously untouched areas, and global travel.

- Foodborne illnesses can be avoided by selecting, storing, cooking, and handling food properly. Frequent hand washing in hot, soapy water is also very important.

- Many species of bacteria are used to produce and process different foods, to produce industrial chemicals, to mine for minerals, to produce insecticides, and to clean up chemical and oil spills.

### Vocabulary

pathology (p. 472)
exotoxin (p. 472)

endotoxin (p. 472)
antibiotic resistance (p. 473)

zoonosis (p. 474)
bioremediation (p. 476)

## USING KEY TERMS

1. For each pair of terms, explain how the meanings of the terms differ.
   a. *halophile* and *thermoacidophile*
   b. *phototroph* and *chemotroph*
   c. *transduction* and *conjugation*

2. Explain the relationship between antibiotics and antibiotic resistance.

3. **Word Roots and Origins** The term *autotroph* comes from the Greek *autos,* meaning "self," and *trophikos,* meaning "food." Using this information, explain why the term *autotroph* is a good name for cyanobacteria.

## UNDERSTANDING CONCEPTS

4. **Identify** the method that scientists have used to investigate how eukaryotes, bacteria, and archaea are related.

5. **List** one distinguishing characteristic of each of the three main groups of archaea.

6. **List** three common methods that are used to identify bacteria.

7. **State** reasons that cyanobacteria are considered the most self-sufficient organisms in nature.

8. **Identify** a nitrogen-fixing bacterium commonly found in the root nodules of legumes.

9. **Name** one bacterium that produces an antibiotic that is used in medicine.

10. **Label** the parts of the bacterium below.

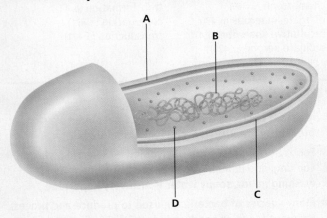

11. **Summarize** how chemoautotrophs get carbon and energy from their environment.

12. **Name** the term used to describe bacteria that can live in the presence or absence of oxygen.

13. **Describe** one way that bacteria can exchange genetic information.

14. **List** four diseases caused by bacteria and the organs that the diseases affect.

15. **Summarize** how antibiotic resistance can develop in a bacterial population.

16. **Relate** three things that you can do to prevent foodborne illness in your home.

17. **Identify** the metabolic process that bacteria use to make food products such as pickles, coffee, and sauerkraut.

18. **CONCEPT MAPPING** Create a concept map that identifes the three main cell shapes of bacteria and describes the nutritional modes of bacteria. Include the following terms in your concept map: *prokaryotes, bacilli, cocci, spirilla, chemotrophic, heterotrophic, endotoxin, exotoxin, Gram-negative,* and *Gram-positive.*

## CRITICAL THINKING

19. **Applying Information** Scientists have only recently discovered fossilized prokaryotes. Explain why these fossils may have taken so long to discover.

20. **Predicting Results** *Clostridium perfringens,* the soil-dwelling bacterium that causes gas gangrene, is an obligate anaerobe. Using this information, predict which would be more likely to become infected with *C. perfringens:* a deep puncture wound or a surface cut. Explain the reason for your inference.

21. **Recognizing Relationships** Penicillin works by interfering with the ability of bacteria to polymerize the peptidoglycan cell wall. Given this fact, explain why Gram-positive bacteria are more susceptible to the effects of penicillin than Gram-negative bacteria are.

22. **Analyzing Graphics** Examine the photograph below, which shows bacteria that have been treated with a Gram stain. Would you hypothesize that these bacteria produce endotoxins? Explain your answer.

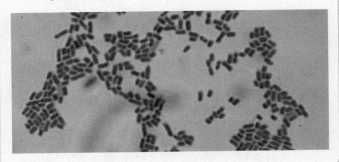

# Standardized Test Preparation

**DIRECTIONS:** Choose the letter of the answer choice that best answers the question.

1. How do bacteria produce yogurt from milk?
   A. by conjugation
   B. by fermentation
   C. by nitrogen fixation
   D. by aerobic respiration

2. What are rod-shaped bacteria called?
   F. cocci
   G. bacilli
   H. spirilla
   J. halophiles

3. What are thermoacidophiles?
   A. bacteria
   B. archaea
   C. spirochetes
   D. cyanobacteria

4. Genetic recombination in bacteria can occur during which process?
   F. conjugation
   G. binary fission
   H. heterocyst formation
   J. endospore production

**INTERPRETING GRAPHICS:** The table below lists the response of a bacterium to several antibiotics. A score of 0 means not sensitive, and sensitivity increases as the score increases. Use the table to answer the questions that follow.

| Antibiotic | Sensitivity |
| --- | --- |
| Ampicillin | 3 |
| Bacitracin | 0 |
| Cephalosporin | 0 |
| Penicillin | 0 |
| Rifampin | 0 |
| Streptomycin | 3 |
| Tetracycline | 2 |

5. Which of the following antibiotics killed the bacteria most effectively?
   A. penicillin
   B. bacitracin
   C. tetracycline
   D. streptomycin

6. Which of the following antibiotics had no effect on the bacterium?
   F. ampicillin
   G. tetracycline
   H. streptomycin
   J. cephalosporin

**DIRECTIONS:** Complete the following analogy.

7. obligate aerobe : oxygen :: obligate anaerobe :
   A. low pH
   B. absence of oxygen
   C. presence of methane
   D. high salt concentration

**INTERPRETING GRAPHICS:** The image below shows different shapes in bacteria. Use the image to answer the questions that follow.

Organism A          Organism B          Organism C

8. What shape is represented by organism C?
   F. coccus
   G. bacillus
   H. spirillum
   J. filamentous

9. You would expect the members of the bacterial genus *Bacillus* to be what type of shape?
   A. rod shaped
   B. spiral shaped
   C. square shaped
   D. sphere shaped

## SHORT RESPONSE

The Gram stain is used to distinguish bacteria based on a certain physiological difference between the bacteria.

Describe the color of Gram-positive and Gram-negative bacteria when they are treated with the Gram stain.

## EXTENDED RESPONSE

Species of the symbiotic bacterial genus *Rhizobium* live within the root nodules of legumes, such as soybeans and peanuts. Some farmers take advantage of the nitrogen-fixing abilities of these species when they rotate their crops every few years and grow legumes instead of their normal food crops.

*Part A* Define *nitrogen fixation*.

*Part B* Explain the benefits of crop rotation on the soil.

**Test TIP** When asked to complete an analogy, focus on the completed pair of terms provided. Identify the relationship that exists between the two terms; then, find the answer choice that has the same relationship with the third term provided.

# Culturing Bacteria

## OBJECTIVES

- Test common surfaces for the presence of bacteria.
- Learn a simple procedure for culturing bacteria.

## PROCESS SKILLS

- observing
- hypothesizing
- experimenting
- collecting data
- analyzing data

## MATERIALS

- Petri dish with nutrient agar
- glass-marking pen
- 4 sterile cotton swabs
- distilled water
- tape
- protective gloves

### Background

1. Culturing bacteria involves growing microorganisms in a nutrient medium that is favorable for growth.
2. What are favorable conditions for the growth of most bacteria?
3. List some places in your school where bacteria are likely growing.

### PART A  Setting Up the Experiment

1. Make a hypothesis about places in your school that would be likely to contain bacteria or that have conditions under which bacteria grow best. Make a list of three places where you will test for the presence of bacteria. Do not choose places outside your laboratory without your teacher's permission.

2. **CAUTION  Put on a lab apron and disposable gloves.** Obtain a Petri dish with nutrient agar from your teacher. Divide your Petri dish into four equal quadrants by writing on the outer bottom surface of the dish with the marking pen. Label the quadrants 1, 2, 3, and 4, as shown in the photograph at left. Also label the bottom of the dish with your group name or number. Do not mark on the top of the Petri dish because it will rotate with respect to the agar.

3. Use quadrant 1 as a control. Take a sterile cotton swab, and moisten it with distilled water. Be careful not to touch the cotton swab to any other surfaces, including your fingers. Remove the cover to the Petri dish, and rub the cotton swab across the nutrient agar in quadrant 1. Be careful not to tear the surface of the agar. Replace the cover immediately.

4. Take another sterile cotton swab, and moisten it with distilled water. Swipe the moistened swab across a surface that you have decided to test for the presence of bacteria. Be careful not to touch the cotton swab to any other surface. Touching the swab to other surfaces could contaminate the swab with bacteria other than the bacteria from your selected surface.

5. Remove the cover to the Petri dish, and rub the cotton swab across the nutrient agar in quadrant 2. This process transfers bacteria from the surface you have sampled to the nutrient agar in the Petri dish. Replace the cover immediately.

6. Using a clean cotton swab each time, repeat steps 4–5 for quadrants 3 and 4. Be sure to note in your lab report the areas that you swipe for each quadrant.

7. After you have swiped a sample in each quadrant of the Petri dish, seal the Petri dish with tape. CAUTION **Do not open the Petri dish again. Treat the contents of the Petri dish as you would any other pathogens.**

8. Place the Petri dish in a warm place with the cover side down for 24 hours or in an incubator at 37°C overnight.

9. Dispose of the cotton swabs and gloves according to your teacher's directions.

10. Clean up your lab materials and wash your hands before leaving the lab.

## PART B  Collecting Data

11. In your lab report, create a data table similar to the model shown below. Allow plenty of space to record your observations for each quadrant swabbed.

12. Check the Petri dish daily for bacterial growth until you no longer find new bacterial colonies (about seven days). Bacterial colonies tend to look shiny and wet, whereas fungal colonies tend to look dry and fuzzy. Record your observations in your data table. What is enabling you to see bacteria? What does each colony represent?

13. Discard your Petri dish as directed by your teacher.

## Analysis and Conclusions

1. On which surfaces did you find the most bacteria? the fewest bacteria? Did your results conform to your expectations? Explain.

2. Compare the colonies of bacteria that grew in each quadrant. What can you tell about the bacteria from the kinds of colonies the bacteria produced?

3. What are some possible sources of error in the procedure you followed?

4. Combine the data obtained by the entire class. Which surfaces yielded the most bacteria?

5. Which of the surfaces that you sampled would you prefer to use as a food-preparation area? Explain your choice.

6. Would the amount of surface area that you sampled with your swab affect the number of colonies that grew on your dish? Explain your answer.

7. Can you tell by looking at the colonies on the dish if they would cause disease? Why or why not?

8. What test described in this chapter could you use to partially identify your bacteria? What characteristics of the bacteria could you learn from this test?

## Further Inquiry

Design an experiment to test the effects of one variable, such as temperature or the presence of antibacterial soap, on the growth of bacteria. What would you use as a control in your experiment?

| PRESENCE OF BACTERIA ON COMMON SURFACES | | | | | | | |
|---|---|---|---|---|---|---|---|
| Surface swabbed | Day 1 | Day 2 | Day 3 | Day 4 | Day 5 | Day 6 | Day 7 |
| | | | | | | | |
| | | | | | | | |
| | | | | | | | |
| | | | | | | | |

# CHAPTER 24

# VIRUSES

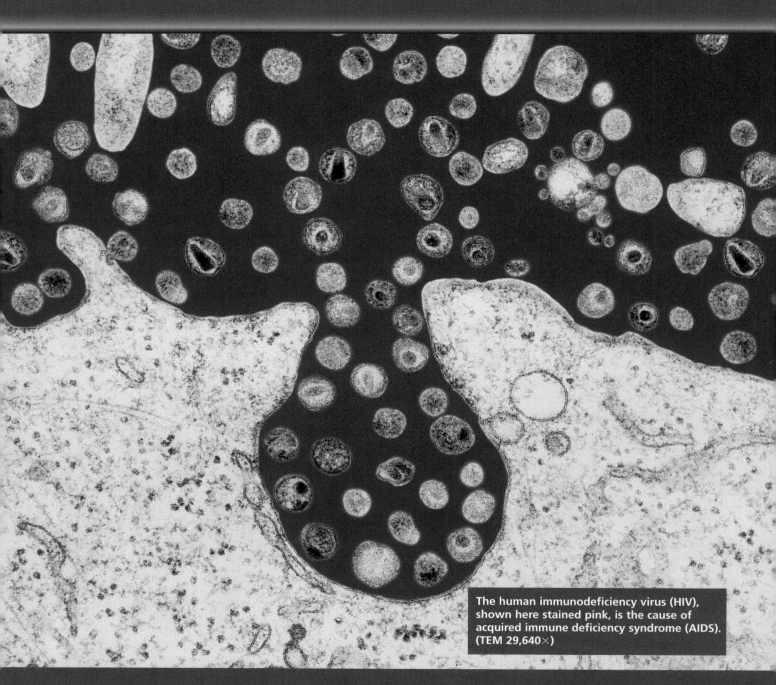

The human immunodeficiency virus (HIV), shown here stained pink, is the cause of acquired immune deficiency syndrome (AIDS). (TEM 29,640×)

**SECTION 1** *Viral Structure and Replication*

**SECTION 2** *Viral Diseases*

# VIRAL STRUCTURE AND REPLICATION

*In 2003, some people in China started showing symptoms of a new illness. These symptoms were similar to those of pneumonia. The condition was highly infectious. Soon, scientists found that the disease was caused by a virus. They called the disease* severe acute respiratory syndrome, *or SARS.*

## SECTION 1

### OBJECTIVES

- **Summarize** the discovery of viruses.
- **Describe** why viruses are not considered living organisms.
- **Describe** the basic structure of viruses.
- **Compare** the lytic and lysogenic cycles of virus replication.
- **Summarize** the origin of viruses.

### VOCABULARY

virus
capsid
envelope
provirus
retrovirus
reverse transcriptase
bacteriophage
lytic cycle
virulent
lysis
lysogenic cycle
temperate virus
prophage

## DISCOVERY OF VIRUSES

A **virus** is a nonliving particle made up of nucleic acid and a protein coat or nucleic acid and a lipid-protein (lipoprotein) coat. Even though viruses are not living organisms, they are of interest to biologists because they cause many diseases in living organisms and they are useful tools for genetic research.

Scientists began studying viruses in the late 1800s after they found that a factor smaller than bacteria could cause disease. At that time, scientists did not have the technology to see viruses. But they wanted to know if viruses were very small cells or simply nonliving groups of molecules.

In 1935, Wendell Stanley crystallized the tobacco mosaic virus (TMV). TMV is a virus that infects plants, such as tobacco and tomato plants. The disease causes plants to wither and develop mosaic-like spots on their leaves, as shown in Figure 24-1. Scientists concluded that an infective agent that could be crystallized was unlikely to be made up of cells.

## CHARACTERISTICS OF VIRUSES

Viruses are not alive because they lack some of the key characteristics of living organisms. For example, viruses do not have cytoplasm or organelles. They cannot carry out cellular functions such as metabolism and homeostasis. They do not grow as cells do by dividing in two. Even though viruses do have genetic material, or a genome—either DNA or RNA—they cannot reproduce outside their host cell. They must enter a living cell and use the host cell's ribosomes, ATP, enzymes, and other molecules to reproduce.

**FIGURE 24-1**

Tobacco mosaic virus (TMV) was the first virus that was crystallized. When TMV infects a plant, it causes small mosaic-like (patchy) blotches on the leaves, as shown in this infected tobacco plant.

Magnification: 1,250,000×          Magnification: 135,000×          Magnification: 202,500×

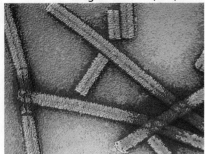

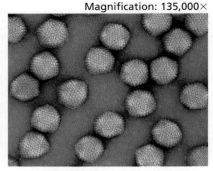

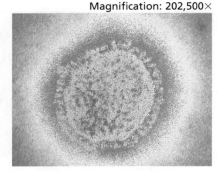

**(a) Tobacco mosaic virus (helical)**          **(b) Adenovirus (polyhedral)**          **(c) Influenza (enveloped)**

**FIGURE 24-2**

Viruses have a variety of sizes and shapes. (a) The tobacco mosaic virus is about 18 nm in diameter and has a helical shape. (b) The adenoviruses are about 80–110 nm in diameter and have the shape of an icosahedron. (c) The spherical influenza viruses are between 50–120 nm in diameter.

## Quick Lab

**Calculating Nanometers**

**Materials** meterstick with millimeter marks, paper, scissors, tape, pencil

**Procedure** Cut the paper into strips. Tape the strips together to form one strip that is 2 m long, and label 1 m, 20 cm, 2 cm, and 2 mm.

**Analysis**

1. Write an equation at the 1 m mark and at the end of the strip that shows the relationship between the length of the paper in meters and nanometers.

2. Write equations beside the 2 cm and the 20 cm marks to show the relationship of centimeters to nanometers.

3. Write an equation by the 2 mm mark to show its relationship to nanometers.

## Viral Size and Structure

Viruses are some of the smallest particles that are able to cause disease. But they vary in size and shape, as shown in Figure 24-2. The shape of a virus is the result of its genome and the protein coat that covers the genome. A protein coat, or **capsid** (KAP-sid), is the only layer surrounding some viruses. The capsid of some viruses, such as TMV, forms a *helix*, shown in Figure 24-2a. The rabies and measles viruses are also helical viruses. As shown in Figure 24-2b, the adenovirus capsid has the shape of an *icosahedron* (IE-koh-suh-HEE-druhn), a shape with 20 triangular faces and 12 corners. Other viruses with this shape include those that cause herpes simplex, chickenpox, and polio. The influenza virus, shown in Figure 24-2c, is spherical in shape.

Some viruses have a bilipid membrane called an **envelope** that surrounds the capsid. The envelope is formed from either the nuclear membrane or the cell membrane of the host cell as the viral capsid buds from the host cell. Proteins in the envelope, such as those of the influenza virus shown in Figure 24-2c, help new viruses recognize host cells. Enveloped viruses include the chickenpox virus (varicola virus) and human immunodeficiency virus (HIV), which causes acquired immunodeficiency syndrome (AIDS).

## Classification of Viruses

Viruses can be classified by whether they have RNA or DNA as their genome and whether their genome is single stranded or double stranded and linear or circular. Viruses are also classified based on the nature of their capsid and on the presence or absence of an envelope. Table 24-1 describes some viruses that affect human health. For example, the virus that causes severe acute respiratory syndrome (SARS) is a *coronavirus*. *Corona* is the Latin word for "crown." The SARS virus has single-stranded, linear RNA and an envelope with lollipop-shaped proteins that make the envelope look like a crown.

## TABLE 24-1 Some Important Viruses That Infect Humans

| Viral group | Genetic material | Envelope | Shape and structure | Examples of diseases |
| --- | --- | --- | --- | --- |
| Papovaviruses | DNA, circular, ds | no | icosahedral | warts, cervical cancer |
| Adenoviruses | DNA, linear, ds | no | icosahedral | respiratory infections |
| Herpesviruses | DNA, linear, ds | yes | icosahedral | cold sores, genital sores |
| Poxviruses | DNA, linear, ds | yes | brick-shaped, enveloped | smallpox, cowpox |
| Parvoviruses | DNA, linear, ss | no | icosahedral | roseola, fifth disease |
| Picornaviruses | RNA, linear, ss | no | icosahedral | polio, hepatitis, colds |
| Orthomyxoviruses | RNA, linear, ss | yes | oval or filamentous | influenza A, B, and C |
| Rhabdoviruses | RNA, linear, ss | yes | helical | rabies |
| Retroviruses | RNA, linear, ss | yes | spherical | AIDS, leukemia |
| Coronaviruses | RNA, linear, ss | yes | helical, surrounded by lollipop-shaped proteins | upper respiratory infections, SARS |

# VIRAL REPLICATION

Outside the host cell, a virus is a lifeless particle with no control over its movements. It is spread by air, in water, in food, or by body fluids. Viruses infect both prokaryotes and eukaryotes.

Viruses first need to recognize a host cell before they can infect it. An enveloped virus can do so by a "lock-and-key" fit between certain envelope proteins and specific receptor molecules on the host cell. A viral infection begins when a virus enters the host cell. The viral genome takes over the metabolic machinery of the cell and makes new viruses. Viruses are *obligate intracellular parasites*—they replicate only by using host cell enzymes and organelles to make more viruses. DNA and RNA viruses differ in the way they replicate.

## Replication in DNA Viruses

When the DNA of some DNA viruses enters a host cell, it makes mRNA, which is the template for making proteins during protein synthesis. The DNA of other DNA viruses inserts into the host cell's chromosome. This inserted viral DNA is known as a **provirus.** The host cell's enzymes then transcribe the provirus into mRNA and translate this RNA into viral proteins. DNA viruses also use the host cell's enzymes to make new viral DNA. The replicated viral DNA and proteins assemble to make new viral particles.

## Replication in RNA Viruses

The genome of some RNA viruses enters host cells and serves directly as mRNA, which is translated into new viral proteins immediately after infection. The genome of other RNA viruses is first transcribed and thus serves as both a template for the synthesis of mRNA and as a template for the synthesis of more copies of the viral genome.

**Word Roots and Origins**

*retrovirus*

from the first two letters of the two words *reverse transcriptase* combined with the word *virus*

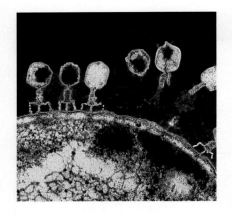

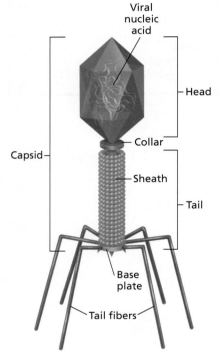

Viral nucleic acid

Head

Capsid

Collar

Sheath

Tail

Base plate

Tail fibers

**FIGURE 24-3**

This TEM and diagram show the structural complexity of a T phage. Scientists named the seven T phages—T1, T2, T3, T4, T5, T6, and T7—to match the order in which they were discovered. (TEM 138,600×)

**Word Roots and Origins**

*lysis*

from the Greek *lysis,* meaning "loosening" or "dissolving"

Some RNA viruses, called **retroviruses** (RE-troh-VIE-ruhs-uhz), contain the enzyme *reverse transcriptase* (tran-SKRIP-tays) in addition to RNA. **Reverse transcriptase** uses RNA as a template to make DNA, which then inserts into the host cell's genome. Reverse transcriptase reverses the normal process of transcription, in which DNA serves as a template for producing RNA. The host cell's enzymes transcribe the virus DNA, and cell ribosomes translate the RNA into proteins that become part of the new viruses. Human immunodeficiency virus (HIV) is a retrovirus.

## Replication in Viruses That Infect Prokaryotes

Scientists have gained a better understanding of virus replication by studying **bacteriophages** (bak-TIR-ee-uh-FAYJ-uhz), viruses that infect bacteria. Bacteriophages, or phages, have complex capsids, shown in Figure 24-3. Phage capsids are made up of a hexagonal head filled with DNA. Attached to the head is a protein tail with one or more tail fibers. The tail fibers attach the virus to a cell. The tail helps the virus inject its genome into the host cell. The most commonly studied bacteriophages, T phages, infect *Escherichia coli,* a bacterium found in the digestive tract of many animals and humans. The TEM in Figure 24-3 shows an *E. coli* cell infected with many T phages. Research led to the discovery that many phages and other viruses can reproduce by one or both of two different processes: the lytic cycle or the lysogenic cycle.

## Lytic Cycle

During the **lytic cycle,** a virus, such as a T4 phage, invades a host cell, produces new viruses, and ruptures (lyses) the host cell when releasing newly formed viruses. Viruses that reproduce only by the lytic cycle are called **virulent.** T phages are virulent viruses. Virulent viruses destroy the cells that they infect.

During the lytic cycle, a phage first attaches its tail fibers to specific receptor molecules on the cell surface of a susceptible bacterium, as shown in step ❶ of Figure 24-4. Recall that viruses cannot efficiently infect cells that do not have the specific protein receptors for that virus. The phage then injects its DNA into the cell but leaves its protein-containing head and tail outside the host cell. In step ❷, the ends of the viral DNA attach to each other, forming a circle. The viral DNA remains separate from the host cell's DNA. In step ❸, virulent viruses continue the lytic cycle. The viral DNA takes control of the host's protein-synthesis pathway, and the viral genome is copied. Enzymes transcribe mRNA from the viral DNA. Host ribosomes translate the mRNA into viral proteins, and enzymes replicate the viral DNA. In step ❹, head proteins bind to the newly made phage genomes. Heads containing DNA bind to tails, and tails assemble into tail fibers. Finally, the phage enzyme called *lysozyme* digests the cell wall, and up to 200 new phage particles burst from the bacterial cell in a process called **lysis** (LIE-sis), shown in step ❺.

# Lysogenic Cycle

A lytic cycle directly bursts an infected cell, but an infection cycle called a **lysogenic** (LIE-soh-JEN-ik) **cycle** allows viruses to hide in their host cell for days, months, or years. A virus whose replication includes the lysogenic cycle is called a **temperate virus.**

As shown in step ❶ of Figure 24-4, temperate phages, such as phage lambda (λ), enter bacteria in the same way that virulent phages do. In a lysogenic cycle, however, the phage DNA that enters the bacterial cell integrates into the host cell's chromosome, shown in step ❻. Phage DNA that is integrated into a specific site of the host cell's chromosome is called a **prophage** (PROH-fayj). In step ❼, the prophage is replicated when the host bacterium replicates its own DNA. Each daughter cell is therefore infected with a prophage. In this way, a single infected cell can give rise to a large population of infected cells. In step ❽, the prophage can exit the bacterial chromosome and enter the lytic cycle. Radiation or certain chemicals can cause the phage DNA to leave the bacterial chromosome. Phage particles are replicated and assembled and are released as the host cell lyses.

**FIGURE 24-4**

After entering the host cell, the DNA of a temperate virus can immediately start the production of new viruses in the lytic cycle. Alternatively, it can insert itself into the bacterial DNA in the lysogenic cycle. During lysogenic growth, the prophage does not harm the host cell.

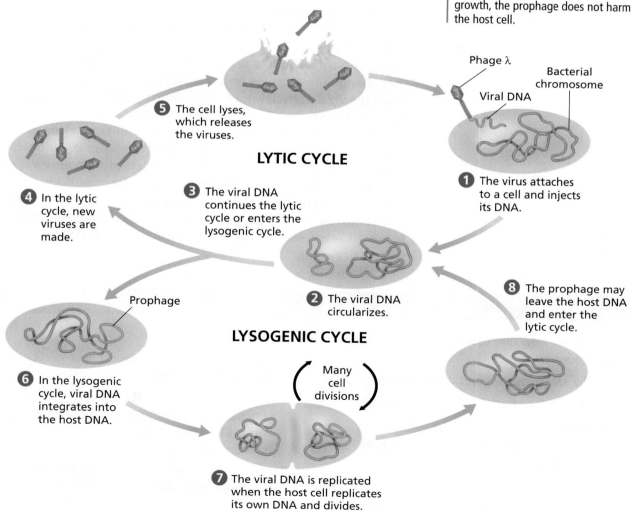

**LYTIC CYCLE**

**LYSOGENIC CYCLE**

❺ The cell lyses, which releases the viruses.

Phage λ
Bacterial chromosome
Viral DNA

❶ The virus attaches to a cell and injects its DNA.

❹ In the lytic cycle, new viruses are made.

❸ The viral DNA continues the lytic cycle or enters the lysogenic cycle.

Prophage

❷ The viral DNA circularizes.

❽ The prophage may leave the host DNA and enter the lytic cycle.

❻ In the lysogenic cycle, viral DNA integrates into the host DNA.

Many cell divisions

❼ The viral DNA is replicated when the host cell replicates its own DNA and divides.

## Viruses: Tools for Biotechnology

The virus life cycle makes viruses important research tools. A researcher can replace large pieces of the DNA of a phage with DNA of particular interest, such as the human gene for cystic fibrosis. The researcher can then insert this recombinant DNA into empty phage heads and allow these viruses to infect bacteria. As the virus grows over and over through the lytic cycle, the number of copies of the foreign gene increases until millions of copies are available for study. Bacteriophages have also been invaluable tools for medical research.

# THE ORIGIN OF VIRUSES

Because viruses need host cells for replication, most scientists reason that viruses evolved from early cells. One hypothesis is that the first viruses were probably naked pieces of nucleic acid that could travel from one cell to another. The viruses entered cells through damaged cell membranes. Over time, genes evolved that coded for protective protein coats as well as special proteins that bind to target cells, allowing viruses to invade healthy cells.

An example of evolution by natural selection can be seen in the influenza virus. The immune system usually destroys most influenza viruses, but a few viruses may have genetic mutations that change the proteins on their surfaces. These genetic changes make the viral particles unrecognizable to the immune system, and the mutated viruses then take over the viral population.

Viruses that mutate quickly, such as influenza virus and HIV, make it difficult for the immune system to recognize and destroy them. Rapid mutation also makes it difficult to develop vaccines that prevent these viral infections over long periods of time. Therefore, each year, makers of influenza vaccine try to produce a specific "flu shot" that targets the strain of influenza virus that is most likely to infect the greatest number of people during that influenza season.

## SECTION 1 REVIEW

1. Describe how the tobacco mosaic virus was discovered.

2. Why are viruses not considered living organisms?

3. Describe the structure of a bacteriophage.

4. Compare the lytic and lysogenic cycles.

5. Discuss how the earliest viruses may have originated.

**CRITICAL THINKING**

6. **Applying Information** Viruses have genetic material, but they are not alive. Explain.

7. **Drawing Conclusions** The assembly of new viral particles can sometimes take place in the host cell's nucleus. However, such assembly does not occur with phage particles. Why not?

8. **Evaluating Information** Evaluate the following statement: Antibiotics will cure a cold.

# VIRAL DISEASES

*In recent years, several viral diseases, such as SARS, have appeared and spread quickly. Where do viral diseases such as these come from? How do these viral diseases spread, and how are they prevented and treated?*

## VECTORS OF VIRAL DISEASE

Because viruses are lifeless particles, their spread depends on other agents. A **vector** is an intermediate host that transfers a pathogen or a parasite to another organism. Vectors of viral diseases include humans, animals, mosquitoes, ticks, and fleas. The West Nile virus, a virus that causes fever and headache and, in very rare cases, coma and paralysis, infects mainly birds, such as crows and jays. If a mosquito bites a bird infected with West Nile virus and then bites a human, the virus can be spread. Mosquitoes can transmit several other viruses, such as the yellow fever virus.

## HUMAN VIRAL DISEASES

Viruses cause many diseases in humans, such as flu, chickenpox, measles, polio, and viral hepatitis. Viral infections can affect various human organs, including the brain, liver, heart, lungs, and skin.

### Chickenpox and Shingles

Chickenpox and shingles are caused by the same varicella-zoster herpesvirus. The virus multiplies in the lungs and travels to blood vessels in the skin. The symptoms of chickenpox include fever and skin rash. The virus is spread through direct contact with the skin rash and through the air. After recovery, a person has lifelong resistance to reinfection. The virus, however, can sometimes stay in nerve cells as a provirus. The virus can later cause a disease called *shingles*. The shingles rash, shown in Figure 24-5, can shed new chickenpox viruses and infect susceptible children and adults.

### Viral Hepatitis

*Hepatitis* (HEP-uh-TIET-is), or inflammation of the liver, can be caused by at least five viruses. Hepatitis A and hepatitis E can be spread by fecally contaminated food and water. Hepatitis B, C, and D are spread by sexual contact, by contact with infected blood and serum, and by the use of contaminated needles. Symptoms of hepatitis can include fever, nausea, jaundice, and liver failure.

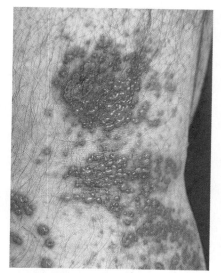

**FIGURE 24-5**

The painful shingles rash, caused by a herpes virus, is limited to an area of the skin innervated by a particular nerve branch, for example, on the side of the chest.

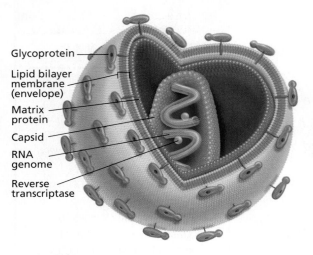

Glycoprotein

Lipid bilayer
membrane
(envelope)

Matrix
protein

Capsid

RNA
genome

Reverse
transcriptase

**FIGURE 24-6**

Human immunodeficiency virus (HIV)
contains two identical RNA molecules
and two molecules of reverse
transcriptase, which makes double-
stranded DNA from the RNA.

## Acquired Immune Deficiency Syndrome (AIDS)

The human immunodeficiency virus (HIV) causes AIDS. HIV gradually destroys an infected person's immune system. HIV is spread by sexual contact; by contact with infected body fluids, such as blood, semen, or vaginal fluids; and from mother to fetus. Glycoproteins on the surface of HIV, shown in Figure 24-6, bind to specific receptor proteins found on *macrophages,* which are immune system cells.

Figure 24-7 summarizes how HIV infects macrophages. First, the virus attaches to the CD4 and CCR5 receptors on the cell surface. To enter the cell, the HIV glycoprotein must bind to both CD4 and the CCR5 coreceptor. Then, the viral envelope fuses with the cell membrane and releases the capsid into the host cell. The enclosed capsid enters the cell cytoplasm, where viral RNA and the enzyme reverse transcriptase are released. Reverse transcriptase uses the viral RNA as a template for making a double-stranded DNA version of the viral genome. The HIV DNA enters the cell's nucleus and inserts itself into the DNA of the host's chromosome, becoming a provirus. Cellular enzymes transcribe and then translate the HIV genes into viral proteins. Then, some of the HIV particles assemble. Finally, the cell membrane pinches off and forms a viral envelope as the newly made HIV particles separate from the cell. Viral replication of HIV results in many mutations. Eventually, the virus recognizes other coreceptors, such as those found on helper T cells. In helper T cells, the HIV particles are released by lysis.

**FIGURE 24-7**

The human immunodeficiency virus (HIV)
infects certain cells of the immune
system. In step ❶, HIV attaches to
receptors on the cell surface. In step ❷,
the capsid is released into the host cell.
In steps ❸ and ❹, the viral RNA is
copied into double-stranded DNA. As
shown in step ❺, the viral DNA inserts
into the host cell's DNA. In step ❻, viral
proteins are made. Then, in step ❼, HIV
particles assemble. In step ❽, newly
made HIV particles pinch off from the
cell membrane. In some immune cells,
HIV particles are released by lysis, shown
in step ❾.

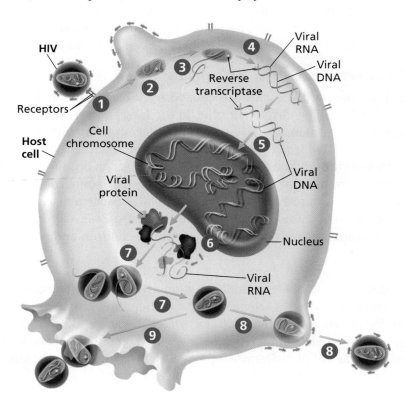

Researchers working on a cure for AIDS are studying the HIV life cycle for weak points to target with new therapies. Because normal human cells do not make reverse transcriptase, this enzyme provided the first target for a chemical therapy. For example, the drug *azidothymidine* (uh-ZIE-doh-THIE-muh-DEEN) (AZT) inhibits the ability of reverse transcriptase to make a DNA copy of the viral RNA. Another class of drugs, called **protease inhibitors,** blocks the synthesis of new viral capsids. Combinations of protease inhibitors and AZT have been shown to be helpful in slowing the progression of HIV infection to full-blown AIDS.

internet connect

www.scilinks.org
Topic: AIDS Virus
Keyword: HM60028

SCiLINKS. Maintained by the National Science Teachers Association

### Viruses and Cancer

Cancer results when cells divide at an uncontrolled rate and form a tumor that invades surrounding tissue. Some viruses contain viral **oncogenes,** genes that cause cancer by blocking the normal controls on cell reproduction. Other viruses cause cancer because the viral DNA inserts itself into a host's chromosome near a **proto-oncogene,** which usually controls cell growth. The proto-oncogene is converted to an oncogene. Human papillomavirus (HPV) can cause cervical cancer, and hepatitis B virus can cause liver cancer. Other viruses, such as human T-lymphotrophic virus (HTLV), can cause leukemia, and Epstein-Barr virus (EBV) can cause Burkitt's lymphoma, a malignant tumor of the jaw.

# EMERGING VIRAL DISEASES

**Emerging diseases** are illnesses caused by new or reappearing infectious agents that typically exist in animal populations—often in isolated habitats—and can infect humans who interact with these animals. For example, some animals living in tropical forests of central Africa most likely harbor Ebola virus. Researchers think that as people clear these forests for agriculture or housing, the people become exposed to infected animals. The Ebola virus is one of many viruses known to cause *hemorrhagic fever,* an often fatal syndrome characterized by fever, vomiting, internal bleeding, and circulatory system collapse. Hantavirus, which is harbored by deer mice and other rodents, caused a fatal outbreak of pneumonia in the southwestern United States in 1993. The SARS virus may have transferred to humans from civet cats.

Both wild and domestic animals can harbor viruses that can be transmitted to people. Close interaction of animals with humans, as shown in Figure 24-8, can lead to the transfer of many diseases. Such diseases are of great concern to public health agencies worldwide. Vaccines are expensive to develop and often difficult to distribute, especially in underdeveloped countries. The cost of public health education to help people understand how they can prevent outbreaks of disease is also high. In addition, laws banning the sale of certain animals as pets or for food can be difficult to enforce.

**FIGURE 24-8**

Avian, or bird, flu is an emerging viral disease. The close interaction of people and poultry on farms and in markets, such as this one in Hong Kong, contributes to the transfer of viruses from birds to humans.

# PREVENTION AND TREATMENT

Healthcare providers and public health officials prevent and treat viral diseases through vaccination, vector control, and drug therapy. So far, the first two measures have been the most successful.

## Vaccinations

A vaccine is a solution that contains a harmless version of a virus, bacterium, or a toxin that causes an immune response when introduced to the body. Vaccination is a highly effective way to prevent viral infection. Viral vaccines can be made from inactivated viruses, attenuated viruses, or parts of the viral coat. An **inactivated virus** is not able to replicate in a host. An **attenuated virus** is a weakened form of the virus that cannot cause disease. In general, attenuated viruses provide greater protection from disease. Vaccines against measles, mumps, rubella, polio, hepatitis A and B, and chickenpox have greatly reduced the incidence of these diseases. The genetic diversity of HIV makes the development of an AIDS vaccine a difficult task. Educating people about HIV transmission is currently the best approach to slowing the spread of AIDS.

Smallpox once killed 40 percent of the people it infected, leaving survivors scarred and often blind. The smallpox virus is a DNA virus that is spread by nasal droplets from sneezing or coughing. Symptoms include fever, headache, backache, and development of a lumpy skin rash, shown in Figure 24-9. The World Health Organization (WHO) began a smallpox eradication program in 1967 through vaccination and the quarantine of sick people. The last naturally acquired smallpox case occurred in Somalia in 1977. In 1980, WHO declared that smallpox had been eradicated in nature.

## Vector Control

An important part of preventing viral disease is the control of animal vectors. Mosquito-control programs eradicated yellow fever in the United States. Rabies vaccinations keep pets free of infection and also protect humans. Wildlife officials set out meat that contains rabies vaccine to control rabies in coyotes and wolves.

## Drug Therapy

Several kinds of antiviral drugs interfere with viral nucleic acid synthesis. Unfortunately, the number of antiviral drugs is small compared to that of drugs that treat bacterial, fungal, and parasitic infections. Because viruses use host cells in their life cycles, it is difficult to design a drug that blocks the virus but doesn't harm cells. The drug *acyclovir* (ay-SIE-kloh-VIR) blocks the DNA polymerase of herpes viruses and chickenpox virus. Such drugs do not destroy a given virus but allow time for the body to build up an immune response to the virus.

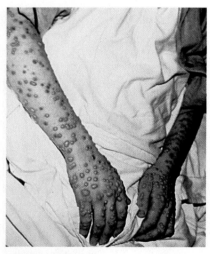

**FIGURE 24-9**

The smallpox virus causes painful lesions that cover the face, shoulders, and chest and, in late stages, the arms and legs. These lesions can leave disfiguring scars, can cause blindness, and may result in death due to hemorrhaging.

# MARINE VIRUSES: What Is Their Role?

In the early 1990s, marine biologists discovered something startling: every milliliter of sea water contains millions of virus particles. Prokaryotic marine organisms, such as cyanobacteria, and eukaryotic protist producers form the base of nearly all marine food chains. These tiny organisms, or *phytoplankton,* fix most of Earth's carbon and release most of its oxygen annually. The discovery of so many virus particles in sea water raised immediate questions: Do the viruses infect the phytoplankton and keep their numbers in check? How do viruses affect food chains and carbon and oxygen cycles? How must biologists factor marine viruses into their models for ocean ecosystems? Do any of these viruses pose a health risk to humans?

## The Role of Marine Viruses

Since the 1990s, scientists have learned more about marine viruses. For example, Lita Proctor of the University of California at Los Angeles carried out pioneering studies on marine viruses.

Using electron microscopy, Proctor discovered that many marine viruses live on or in host cells and float freely only after their cellular hosts die.

Marine ecologist Curtis Suttle and his colleagues at the University of British Columbia identified specific types of marine viruses and their activities. Suttle used antibodies labeled with a fluorescent dye to identify particular viruses and their host cells. Suttle discovered that many types of marine viruses infect cells in phytoplankton and stop photosynthesis. He tried removing specific types of viruses to protect their hosts. However, Suttle found that the rest of the phytoplankton in the water sample stopped growing! Apparently, the other organisms depended on the nutrients released when the viruses killed their hosts.

Suttle also found that viral infection seems to be a constant occurrence in phytoplankton—about 20 percent of the organisms are killed by viruses at any given time.

Suttle's studies helped show that marine viruses are an important part of the carbon cycle and other ecological interactions.

## The Search for Marine Viruses That Infect Humans

Researchers have used the tools of molecular genetics to search the waters around many coastal cities for viruses known to cause human disease. Sewage dumped into the oceans contains many kinds of pathogenic viruses. So far, poliovirus, hepatitis A, and possibly HIV have been found in sea water. However, scientists are unsure whether these submerged viruses can infect swimmers.

Marine viruses are clearly important, but the study of them is in its infancy. At this point, researchers can culture only about 2 percent of phytoplankton, so the study of marine viruses is hampered in this very basic way.

## REVIEW

1. What is phytoplankton?
2. Identify two effects of viral infection on phytoplankton.
3. **Critical Thinking** Why were marine viruses not discovered until the early 1990s?

*Fluorescent dyes allow scientists to see viruses in marine waters. The small dots in the photo are viruses; the larger, brighter dots are bacteria.*

**internet** connect

www.scilinks.org
**Topic:** Carbon Cycle
**Keyword:** HM60216

SCiLINKS. Maintained by the National Science Teachers Association

# VIROIDS AND PRIONS

Even simpler than viruses is a group of disease-causing agents called viroids. **Viroids** (VIE-roydz) are the smallest known particles that are able to replicate. A viroid is made up of a short, circular, single strand of RNA that does not have a capsid. Viroids infect plants. These naked RNA molecules can disrupt plant-cell metabolism and damage entire crops. Economically important plants affected by viroids include coconuts, potatoes, and oranges.

In late December 2003, the U.S. Department of Agriculture diagnosed a single cow in Washington State with bovine spongiform encephalopathy (BSE), commonly known as *mad cow disease*. BSE is a degenerative brain disease that results in muscle paralysis, wasting, and death. A cow with BSE is shown in Figure 24-10. Research suggests that mad cow disease is caused by prions (PRIE-AHNZ). **Prions** are infectious protein particles that do not have a genome. They are abnormal forms of a natural brain protein that appear to convert normal brain proteins into prion particles. Scientists hypothesize that the prions then clump together inside cells and cause cell death.

Prions appear to cause a number of other degenerative brain diseases, including scrapie in sheep and Creutzfeldt-Jakob (KROYTZ-felt-YAH-kohb) disease (CJD) and kuru in humans. The BSE epidemic in the United Kingdom in the early 1990s was most likely caused by the feeding of scrapie-contaminated meat and bone meal to cattle. Scientific evidence indicates that BSE has been transmitted to humans, causing a variant form of CJD (vCJD). This evidence comes from studies that followed the unusually high numbers of young people in the United Kingdom that developed this rare disease in the late 1990s. Eating BSE-contaminated beef and beef products was the probable cause of vCJD in these cases. Measures to protect the food supply are the best safeguards. However, the overall risk to human health from BSE is very low.

**FIGURE 24-10**

This cow, which is unable to stand and walk, is showing signs of mad cow disease, a disease caused by prions.

## SECTION 2 REVIEW

1. Give an example of a vector of a viral disease and the disease it transmits.

2. Identify four viral diseases of humans.

3. What is the relationship between viruses and cancer?

4. Explain how human actions have contributed to the increase of emerging viral diseases.

5. What are three ways to fight viruses?

6. Compare viroids, prions, and viruses.

**CRITICAL THINKING**

7. **Applying Information** Consider how emerging viruses develop. Would you consider emerging viruses to be new viruses? Explain.

8. **Evaluating Conclusions** Explain why microbiologists oppose the use of antibiotics in patients with viral infections.

9. **Applying Information** Once inside the body, HIV's surface glycoproteins can mutate to recognize a new type of cell receptor. How does this mutation aid the virus in its life cycle?

# CHAPTER HIGHLIGHTS

## SECTION 1 — Viral Structure and Replication

- Researchers in the late 1800s discovered that something smaller than bacteria could cause disease.

- Wendell Stanley demonstrated that viruses were not cells when he crystallized TMV, the virus that causes tobacco mosaic disease in tobacco and tomato plants.

- Viruses are nonliving particles containing DNA or RNA and are surrounded by a protein coat called a capsid. Some viruses also have an envelope that is derived from a host cell's nuclear membrane or cell membrane.

- Viruses do not have all of the characteristics of life and are therefore not considered to be living.

- Viruses can be classified based on whether they have RNA or DNA, whether the RNA or DNA is single or double stranded and circular or linear, by capsid shape, and whether or not they have an envelope.

- DNA viruses can enter host cells and directly produce RNA, or they can insert into a host's chromosome, where they are transcribed to RNA along with the host's DNA.

- The RNA genome of some RNA viruses can be directly translated to make viral proteins. Others use reverse transcriptase and RNA as a template to make DNA, which is then used to produce viral RNA and proteins.

- Bacteriophages can follow a lytic cycle (making new viral particles immediately) or a lysogenic cycle (becoming part of the host genome and making new particles later).

- Viruses are important tools for biotechnology.

- Most scientists think viruses originated from fragments of host-cell nucleic-acid material.

### Vocabulary

virus (p. 483)
capsid (p. 484)
envelope (p. 484)
provirus (p. 485)

retrovirus (p. 486)
reverse transcriptase (p. 486)
bacteriophage (p. 486)

lytic cycle (p. 486)
virulent (p. 486)
lysis (p. 486)
lysogenic cycle (p. 487)

temperate virus (p. 487)
prophage (p. 487)

## SECTION 2 — Viral Diseases

- Vectors of viral diseases include humans, animals, and insects.

- Viruses cause many human diseases, including the common cold, flu, hepatitis, rabies, chickenpox, certain types of cancer, and AIDS.

- Some viruses contain oncogenes that can cause cancer, while other viruses convert proto-oncogenes to oncogenes.

- The human immunodeficiency virus (HIV) is an RNA virus spread by sexual contact, by contact with infected body fluids, and from mother to fetus. HIV targets macrophages and thus damages the body's immune system in the disease called acquired immunodeficiency syndrome (AIDS).

- Emerging viruses usually infect animals isolated in nature but can jump to humans when contact occurs in the environment.

- Vaccines have helped to greatly reduce certain viral diseases. Control efforts, including killing mosquitoes and other vectors and quarantining ill patients, have helped reduce the spread of certain viral diseases.

- Antibiotics are ineffective against viral diseases. Viral drugs, such as acyclovir, block specific steps in viral replication.

- Viroids are short, circular, single strands of RNA lacking a capsid that infect plant cells.

- Prions are infectious particles containing protein but no nucleic acids. Prions cause mad cow disease and similar degenerative brain diseases.

### Vocabulary

vector (p. 489)
protease inhibitor (p. 491)
oncogene (p. 491)

proto-oncogene (p. 491)
emerging disease (p. 491)

inactivated virus (p. 492)
attenuated virus (p. 492)

viroid (p. 494)
prion (p. 494)

## USING VOCABULARY

1. For each pair of terms, explain how the meanings of the terms differ.
   a. *virus* and *viroid*
   b. *oncogene* and *proto-oncogene*
   c. *capsid* and *envelope*
   d. *provirus* and *vector*

2. Use the following terms in the same sentence: *virus, lytic cycle, lysogenic cycle,* and *bacteriophage.*

3. Use each of the following terms in a separate sentence: *prion, prophage, temperate virus,* and *bacteriophage.*

4. **Word Roots and Origins** The word *virus* is derived from the Greek *ios,* which means "poison." Using this information, explain why the term *virus* is a good name for these particles.

## UNDERSTANDING KEY CONCEPTS

5. **Summarize** how the structure of viruses was discovered by Wendell Stanley.

6. **Discuss** why viruses are not considered living organisms.

7. **Describe** three different shapes viruses can have.

8. **Compare** replication in DNA viruses to replication in RNA viruses.

9. **Differentiate** the lytic cycle of viral replication from the lysogenic cycle of viral replication in bacteriophages.

10. **Summarize** how viruses are thought to have originated.

11. **Describe** four diseases caused by viruses that occur in humans.

12. **Name** three vectors of viral diseases that can spread viruses to humans.

13. **Discuss** the role of viruses and oncogenes in the onset of cancer.

14. **Describe** the structure of HIV.

15. **Explain** the activity of reverse transcriptase in the replication cycle of the human immuno-deficiency virus (HIV).

16. **Summarize** how emerging diseases can occur.

17. **Discuss** three methods humans use to control the spread of viral diseases.

18. **Describe** how viruses, viroids, and prions differ from one another.

19. **CONCEPT MAPPING** Use the following terms to create a concept map that describes the lytic cycle: *viruses, virulent, phage, injects, DNA, replicates, assemble, protein,* and *lyse.*

## CRITICAL THINKING

20. **Evaluating Information** The drug azidothymidine (AZT) works by blocking the enzyme reverse transcriptase. Explain how AZT can help patients infected with HIV.

21. **Applying Information** Shingles is a disease caused by the same herpesvirus that causes chickenpox. How do you account for the fact that shingles often appears years after the initial chickenpox attack?

22. **Applying Current Research** Based on your knowledge of HIV structure and replication, describe one way to interrupt the replication of HIV.

23. **Applying Information** How does the increase of resistance to antiviral drugs in HIV relate to the theory of evolution by natural selection?

24. **Applying Information** Tobacco mosaic virus does not infect humans, but humans can transmit TMV from infected plants to healthy plants. What role do humans play in this mode of transmission?

25. **Making Real-Life Connections** For viral diseases without known cures, such as AIDS, certain types of hepatitis, and Ebola, identify ways in which the incidence of such diseases can be reduced.

26. **Interpreting Graphics** Look at the graph below. Discuss how the sharp jump in the number of viruses outside the cell corresponds to the phases of the lytic cycle.

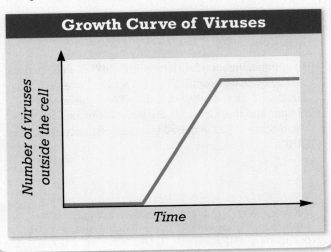

**Growth Curve of Viruses**

*Number of viruses outside the cell*

*Time*

# Standardized Test Preparation

**DIRECTIONS:** Choose the letter of the answer choice that best answers the question.

1. What are viruses made of?
   - **A.** enzymes and fats
   - **B.** carbohydrates and ATP
   - **C.** protein and nucleic acids
   - **D.** mitochondria and lysosomes

2. How do viroids differ from viruses?
   - **F.** Viroids are larger in size.
   - **G.** Viroids do not have a capsid.
   - **H.** Viroids do not have nucleic acids.
   - **J.** Viroids can cause disease in plants.

3. During which of the following processes does a phage kill its host?
   - **A.** conjugation
   - **B.** transcription
   - **C.** the lytic cycle
   - **D.** the lysogenic cycle

4. Which of the following is one reason why viruses are not considered living organisms?
   - **F.** Viruses are able to grow.
   - **G.** Viruses do not metabolize.
   - **H.** Viruses can reproduce by splitting.
   - **J.** Viruses are too small to be easily observed.

**INTERPRETING GRAPHICS:** Study the figure below to answer the following questions.

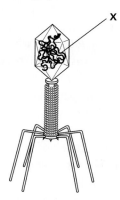

5. Which of the following does the diagram represent?
   - **A.** a virus
   - **B.** a prion
   - **C.** a viroid
   - **D.** a bacterium

6. To which of the following is label X pointing?
   - **F.** envelope
   - **G.** nucleic acid
   - **H.** protein coat
   - **J.** cell membrane

**DIRECTIONS:** Complete the following analogy.

7. skin : person :: capsid :
   - **A.** virus
   - **B.** insect
   - **C.** fungus
   - **D.** bacterium

**INTERPRETING GRAPHICS:** The figure below represents the human immunodeficiency virus. Use the figure to answer the question that follows.

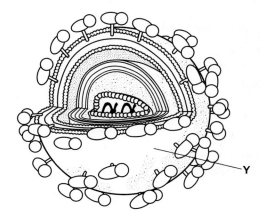

8. The structure labeled Y represents which of the following?
   - **F.** capsid
   - **G.** envelope
   - **H.** RNA genome
   - **J.** reverse transcriptase

## SHORT RESPONSE

Reverse transcriptase is an enzyme that catalyzes the synthesis of DNA from RNA.

Explain why retroviruses must have reverse transcriptase to replicate.

## EXTENDED RESPONSE

Viruses share several characteristics of living organisms. However, viruses are not considered to be living.

*Part A* Compare the characteristics viruses share with living organisms to the characteristics they do not share with living organisms.

*Part B* Would you anticipate more or fewer emerging viral diseases to appear in the future? Explain.

**Test TIP** When using a diagram to answer questions, carefully study each part of the figure as well as any lines or labels used to indicate parts of the figure.

# Infecting Plants with Tobacco Mosaic Virus

## OBJECTIVES

■ Study the effect of cigarette tobacco on leaves of tobacco plants.

## PROCESS SKILLS

■ observing
■ comparing and contrasting
■ experimenting

## MATERIALS

■ lab apron
■ protective gloves
■ safety goggles
■ 2 tobacco or tomato plants
■ glass-marking pencil
■ tobacco from several brands of cigarettes
■ mortar and pestle
■ 10 mL 0.1 M dibasic potassium phosphate solution
■ 100 mL beaker
■ cotton swabs
■ 400 grit carborundum powder

## Background

1. The tobacco mosaic virus, TMV, infects tobacco as well as other plants.
2. Plants that are infected with TMV have lesions and yellow patches on their leaves.

3. In what form do viruses exist outside host cells?
4. The tobacco mosaic virus is an RNA virus with rod-shaped capsids and proteins arranged in a spiral.
5. Plants damaged by wind, low temperatures, injury, or insects are more susceptible to plant viruses than healthy plants are.
6. Plant viruses are transmitted by insects, gardening tools, inheritance from the parent, and sexual reproduction.
7. In this investigation, you will test whether tobacco from cigarettes can infect tobacco plants with TMV.

## PART A  Setting Up the Experiment

1. Put on a lab apron, gloves, and goggles before beginning this investigation.
2. Obtain two tobacco plants that have not been infected with TMV. Label one of the plants "control plant." Label the other plant "experimental plant."
3. **CAUTION Use poisonous chemicals with extreme caution. Keep your hands away from your face when handling plants or chemical mixtures.** Place pinches of tobacco from different brands of cigarettes into a mortar. Add 5 mL of dibasic potassium phosphate solution, and grind the mixture with a pestle as shown in the figure at left.
4. Pour the mixture into a labeled beaker. This mixture can be used to test whether cigarette tobacco can infect plants with TMV.
5. Wash your hands and all laboratory equipment used in the previous steps with soap and water to avoid the accidental spread of the virus.
6. Moisten a sterile cotton swab with the mixture, and sprinkle a small amount of carborundum powder onto the moistened swab. Apply the mixture to two leaves on the "experimental" plant by swabbing the surface of the leaves several times. Why do you think swabbing the leaves with carborundum powder might facilitate infection?

7. Moisten a clean swab with dibasic potassium phosphate solution, and sprinkle a small amount of carborundum powder onto the moistened swab. This swab should *not* come into contact with the mixture of cigarette tobacco. Swab over the surface of two leaves on the control plant several times.

8. Do not allow the control plants to touch the experimental plants. Keep both plants away from other plants that may be in your investigation area, such as houseplants or garden plants. Wash your hands after handling each plant to avoid the accidental spread of TMV.

9. Treat both plants in precisely the same manner. The only difference between the two plants should be the experimental factor—exposure to cigarette tobacco. Both plants should receive the same amount of light and water.

10. Clean up your materials according to your teacher's instructions and wash your hands before leaving the lab.

11. In your lab report, create a data table similar to the model shown below. Allow plenty of space to record your observations of each plant.

12. Check the control and experimental plants each day for one week. Record your observations of each plant in your lab report. Wash your hands after handling each plant to prevent contaminating your results.

## Analysis and Conclusions

1. What differences, if any, did you detect in the two plants after one week?

2. Did the plants exposed to cigarette tobacco become infected with the tobacco mosaic virus?

3. Why do you think it was necessary to use tobacco from different brands of cigarettes?

4. What are some of the possible sources of error in the experiment?

5. Greenhouse operators generally do not allow smoking in their greenhouses. Aside from health and safety issues, how might your results support this practice?

## Further Inquiry

The tobacco mosaic virus is capable of infecting different species of plants. Design an experiment to determine which of several types of plants are susceptible to the virus.

| | OBSERVATIONS OF TOBACCO PLANTS | |
|---|---|---|
| Day | Control plant | Experimental plant |
| 1 | | |
| 2 | | |
| 3 | | |
| 4 | | |
| 5 | | |
| 6 | | |
| 7 | | |

# PROTISTS

The single-celled organisms shown here are protists from the genus *Stentor*, named after a Greek announcer who had a very loud voice. These trumpet-shaped cells are highly complex and adapted for capturing and consuming prey.

# CHARACTERISTICS OF PROTISTS

*P*rotists are a diverse collection of eukaryotic organisms, such as protozoa, algae, slime molds, and water molds. Protists are sometimes described as animal-like, plantlike, or funguslike. However, these organisms lack the cellular differentiation found in animals, plants, and fungi.

## SECTION 1

### OBJECTIVES

- **Define** *protist*.
- **Describe** a hypothesis for the origin of eukaryotic cells.
- **Explain** how protists are classified.
- **Describe** the two major ways by which protists obtain energy.
- **List** three structures protists use for movement.
- **Describe** how protists reproduce.

### VOCABULARY

protist
binary fission
multiple fission
conjugation

## A DIVERSE GROUP OF EUKARYOTES

Single-celled or simple multicellular eukaryotic organisms that generally do not fit in any other kingdom are called **protists.** Most protists are microscopic, but a few protists, such as some algae, are several meters in length. Protists are defined by exclusion—most protists are eukaryotic organisms that cannot be classified as fungi, plants, or animals. As a result, protists are the most diverse group of eukaryotes. Protists have varying body plans, types of movement, and means of obtaining food. Protists are made up of eukaryotic cells, each containing a nucleus and other organelles. Most living protists contain mitochondria. Some protists, such as *Euglena* shown in Figure 25-1, also contain chloroplasts.

### The First Eukaryotes

Protists emerged early in the history of domain Eukarya. Some of the oldest eukaryotic cells were protists. Protists emerged as much as 2 billion years ago.

By analyzing genetic information in the nucleus, mitochondria, and chloroplasts of protists, scientists have found strong evidence that the first protists arose from prokaryotic cells. Nuclear genes in protists and in other eukaryotes resemble archaeal and bacterial genes. Additionally, the genetic information found in the mitochondria and chloroplasts of protists and other eukaryotes is similar to genetic information found in bacteria and cyanobacteria. Because of these genetic similarities, scientists hypothesize that protists and other eukaryotes arose from ancient prokaryotes that lived in *endosymbiosis*. In endosymbiosis, an organism lives inside a larger organism. Scientists think that mitochondria and chloroplasts arose from ancient prokaryotes that lived inside larger prokaryotes. Over time, the endosymbiotic prokaryotes became organelles within eukaryotic protists.

**FIGURE 25-1**

Most *Euglena* are unicellular, contain chloroplasts, move about, and sometimes consume other organisms. Because *Euglena* have both plantlike and animal-like characteristics, they cannot be classified in the plant or animal kingdoms. So, they are classified as protists.

# CLASSIFICATION

Often, protists are classified by the characteristics that resemble those of fungi, plants, and animals. For example, the reproduction of some protists resembles the reproduction of fungi. Other protists capture light energy for photosynthesis, as plants do. Some protists move and consume other organisms, as animals do.

The great diversity among protist species makes them difficult to classify. Protists have traditionally been classified in kingdom Protista. Because of ongoing molecular analyses, many scientists now hypothesize that kingdom Protista should be divided into several kingdoms. Scientists are still revising the classification of protists.

# CHARACTERISTICS

Table 25-1 summarizes the characteristics of several protist phyla. There are few general characteristics of protists, but they can be characterized by body plan, means of obtaining food, and motility.

## TABLE 25-1  *Characteristics of Various Protist Phyla*

| Phylum | Common name | Body plan | Motility | Nutrition type | Representative genera |
|---|---|---|---|---|---|
| Protozoa | protozoa, sarcodines, mycetozoans | unicellular | pseudopodia | heterotrophic, some parasitic | *Amoeba, Entamoeba, Radiolaria* |
| Ciliophora | ciliates | unicellular | cilia | heterotrophic, some parasitic | *Paramecium, Balantidium, Stentor* |
| Sarcomastigophora | mastigophorans | unicellular | flagella | heterotrophic, some parasitic | *Trypanosoma, Leishmania* |
| Apicomplexa | apicomplexans | unicellular | none in adult | heterotrophic, parasitic | *Plasmodium, Toxoplasma* |
| Chlorophyta | green algae | unicellular, colonial, multicellular | some with flagella | autotrophic | *Spirogyra, Volvox, Chlamydomonas, Protococcus* |
| Bacillariophyta | diatoms | unicellular, colonial | mostly no flagella | autotrophic | *Cocconeis, Bacillaria* |
| Dinoflagellata | dinoflagellates | unicellular | flagella | autotrophic, some heterotrophic | *Noctiluca, Ceratium* |
| Euglenophyta | euglenoids | unicellular | flagella | autotrophic, some heterotrophic | *Euglena* |
| Dictyostelida | cellular slime molds | unicellular, multicellular | pseudopodia | heterotrophic | *Dictyostelium* |
| Oomycota | water molds | unicellular, multicellular | some with flagella | heterotrophic, some parasitic | *Phytophthora* |

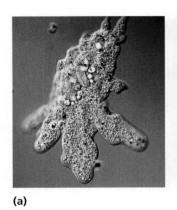
(a)

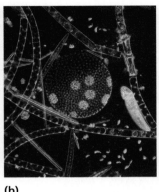
(b)

(c)

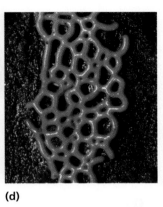
(d)

## Unicellular and Multicellular

As shown in Figure 25-2, protists come in a wide variety of body plans. Most protists are unicellular, such as the amoeba shown in Figure 25-2a. Some protists, such as the *Volvox* in Figure 25-2b, form colonies in which several cells are joined into a larger body. Some of these colonies have a division of labor; certain cells specialize in reproduction, and other cells specialize in obtaining energy.

A few protists, such as the brown algae in Figure 25-2c and the pretzel slime mold in Figure 25-2d, form large multicellular bodies. Some brown algae may grow to more than 60 m in length. These marine giants have specialized regions for reproduction, photosynthesis, and attachment to the ocean floor. However, these regions lack the cellular differentiation found in true tissues and organs.

## Nutrition

Protists obtain energy in a number of ways. Many protists are *autotrophs,* organisms that can make their own food molecules. These protists make food in much the same way that plants do. The protists absorb energy from sunlight with the aid of specialized light-absorbing pigments. Protists often utilize chlorophyll, as plants do, but they may use additional pigments. The protists use the captured light energy, water molecules, and carbon dioxide molecules to make carbohydrates.

Some protists are *heterotrophs,* organisms that must get their food by eating other organisms or their byproducts and remains. Some heterotrophic protists engulf smaller protists and digest them. Other heterotrophic protists obtain energy in the same way that fungi do. These protists secrete digestive enzymes into the environment. The enzymes break down cells or bits of food into small molecules that the protists can absorb and use.

## Motility

Most protists are able to move at some time during their life cycles. Some protists move with the aid of long, whiplike structures called *flagella* (singular, *flagellum*). Other protists move with the aid of *cilia* (singular, *cilium*), which are shorter than flagella and often form rows. Finally, some protists, such as amoebas, move by temporarily extending structures called *pseudopodia* (singular, *pseudopodium*).

FIGURE 25-2

Protists have a variety of body plans. (a) The single-celled *Amoeba proteus* constantly changes its body shape. (b) Cells from *Volvox,* a colonial protist, have coordinated activity. (c) Brown algae, such as this kelp (*Macrocystis pyrifera*), are multicellular giants among protists. (d) This pretzel slime mold (*Hemitrichia serpula*) reproduces similarly to fungi.

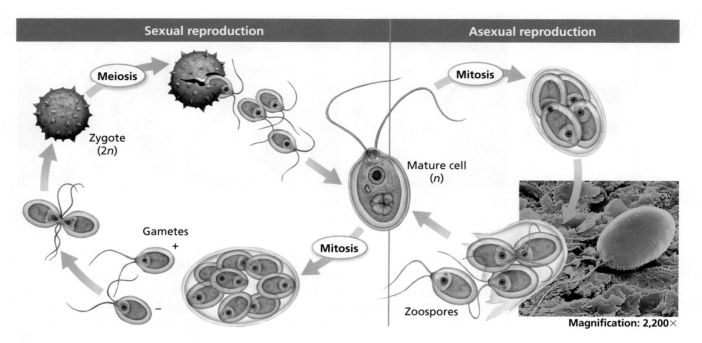

| Sexual reproduction | Asexual reproduction |

Meiosis

Zygote
(2n)

Gametes
+

−

Mitosis

Mitosis

Mature cell
(n)

Zoospores

**Magnification: 2,200×**

**FIGURE 25-3**

Algae of the genus *Chlamydomonas* are unicellular green algae that undergo both asexual and sexual reproduction. For many protist producers, the type of reproduction alternates by generation. For example, a parent may reproduce asexually, but its offspring may reproduce sexually. For other protists, sexual reproduction occurs only when environmental conditions are stressful.

# REPRODUCTION

Many protists reproduce asexually. During **binary fission,** a single protist cell divides into two cells. Some protists reproduce by **multiple fission,** a form of cell division that produces more than two offspring. Both types of fission produce offspring that are genetically identical to the parent cell.

One way by which many protists reproduce sexually is conjugation. During **conjugation,** two individuals join and exchange genetic material stored in a small second nucleus. Then, the cells divide to produce four offspring. The offspring are genetically different from the parent cells. As shown in Figure 25-3, many protists can reproduce both asexually and sexually.

## SECTION 1 REVIEW

1. What is the definition of *protist*?

2. What is a hypothesis for how eukaryotic cells arose?

3. How are protists often classified?

4. Describe unicellular and multicellular protists.

5. What are two ways by which protists obtain energy?

6. How do protists move?

7. Describe how some protists reproduce both asexually and sexually.

**CRITICAL THINKING**

8. **Applying Information** Why might scientists argue that protists should be classified in several kingdoms rather than in one kingdom?

9. **Relating Concepts** Compare binary fission and conjugation.

10. **Calculating Information** Make a bar graph comparing the volumes of the following: a protist (cone shaped, 500 μm long, 200 μm in diameter); a human white blood cell (sphere shaped, 10 μm in diameter); and a bacterial cell (cylinder shaped, 2 μm long, 0.8 μm in diameter).

# Science in Action

## How Did Eukaryotic Cells Evolve?

The idea that cellular organelles were originally separate organisms was first proposed in the early 1900s. The few scientists who later became aware of this hypothesis thought that it was preposterous. In the 1960s, Lynn Margulis thought that the idea should be reexamined. Her research led her to form a theory that shook the foundations of the biological community.

**Lynn Margulis**

### HYPOTHESIS: Cellular Organelles Were the Result of Endosymbiosis

Endosymbiosis is a relationship in which one organism lives inside another. Lynn Margulis, an American biologist, thought that endosymbiosis led to the evolution of eukaryotic cells. Margulis proposed that mitochondria and chloroplasts, the cell's energy-producing organelles, were initially separate organisms that had become integral parts of larger cells.

Margulis hypothesized that the first cells with chloroplasts probably came about when a host organism ingested photosynthetic bacteria. A few of these bacteria were not digested. These unlikely partnerships provided something for everyone: The guest gave the host a source of food, while the host protected the guest. Margulis also surmised that mitochondria arose in a similar way.

### METHODS: Use Electron Microscopy to Observe Organelles and Cells

Margulis took advantage of advances in electron microscopy and molecular biology to obtain evidence in support of her hypothesis. Working with her graduate research advisor, Hans Ris, Margulis used high-powered electron microscopy to carefully observe and compare mitochondria, chloroplasts, eukaryotic cells, and prokaryotic cells. In addition, she looked for the presence of DNA in the chloroplasts of *Euglena gracilis* by using radioactively labeled nucleotides.

### RESULTS: Organelles Are Similar to Bacteria

Margulis found that bacteria and organelles show many similarities. Like prokaryotes, mitochondria and chloroplasts have circular DNA. These organelles also have their own ribosomes, which are the same size as those found in prokaryotes but smaller than those found in the cytoplasm of eukaryotes. Both mitochondria and chloroplasts are found enclosed in membranes as though they were captured in a vacuole of a larger cell. Also, mitochondria and chloroplasts divide by fission, as bacteria do.

An endosymbiotic relationship was witnessed by Kwang Jeon at the University of Tennessee.

One day, Jeon noticed that bacteria had infected his amoebas and that a few of the amoebas did not die. Their new partners replicated along with the hosts. Generations later, these amoebas are thriving; yet the formerly separate organisms are totally dependent upon one another. If the invader is removed from the host, both die.

### CONCLUSION: Organelles Arose Through Endosymbiosis

Today, endosymbiosis is the accepted explanation for how eukaryotes arose. Additional support for Margulis's theory comes from examining modern organisms that contain intracellular symbiotic bacteria and photosynthetic protists. For example, sea slugs incorporate chloroplasts into some of their cells, which provides a source of energy for the sea slugs when other food is scarce.

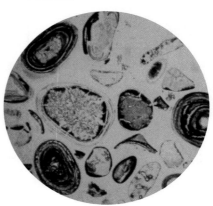

*Endosymbiosis led to the formation of eukaryotic cells. Multicellular eukaryotes, such as these fossil algae, arose around 2 billion years ago.*

### REVIEW

1. Restate the endosymbiosis hypothesis in your own words.

2. In what ways do prokaryotes resemble chloroplasts and mitochondria?

3. **Critical Thinking** Why must modern plants be the result of at least two separate endosymbiotic events?

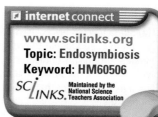

internet connect

www.scilinks.org
Topic: Endosymbiosis
Keyword: HM60506

SCiLINKS. Maintained by the National Science Teachers Association

## OBJECTIVES

- **Discuss** the key characteristics of Protozoa, Ciliophora, Sarcomastigophora, and Apicomplexa.
- **Describe** how protozoa use pseudopodia to move and to capture food.
- **Explain** how ciliates move and reproduce.
- **Describe** how mastigophorans move and capture food.
- **Describe** the role of apicomplexans in disease.

## VOCABULARY

pseudopodium
amoeboid movement
test
cilium
pellicle
oral groove
mouth pore
gullet
anal pore
contractile vacuole
macronucleus
micronucleus
flagellum

# ANIMAL-LIKE PROTISTS

*Protists aren't animals. However, four major groups of protists move and obtain food in animal-like ways. Having animal-like characteristics would seem to suggest that animal-like protists are closely related to animals in an evolutionary sense, but animal-like protists and animals are not closely related.*

## PHYLUM PROTOZOA

Most animal-like protists are heterotrophs that move about capturing and consuming prey. Animal-like protists are sometimes called *protozoa*. Protozoa are single-celled protists that can move independently without cilia or flagella. Biologists group more than 40,000 species of protozoa in the phylum Protozoa, which includes the subphyla Sarcodina (SAHR-kuh-DIE-nuh) and Mycetozoa (mie-SEET-uh-ZOH-uh). Of these species, about three-quarters are identified only by fossil remains. Figure 25-4 shows two examples of protozoans.

A key characteristic of most protozoa is the formation of pseudopodia (SOO-doh-POH-dee-uh). **Pseudopodia** are large, rounded cytoplasmic extensions that function both in movement and feeding. A pseudopodium forms when the cytoplasm flows forward to create a blunt, armlike extension. Simultaneously, other pseudopodia retract, and the cytoplasm flows in the direction of the new pseudopodium, causing the cell to move. This type of locomotion is called **amoeboid movement.** Amoeboid movement is a form of *cytoplasmic streaming,* the internal flowing of a cell's cytoplasm.

Protozoa actively prey on smaller cells, such as bacteria and smaller protists, and food particles. A sarcodine feeds by surrounding the food with pseudopodia and trapping the food in a vesicle. The sarcodine releases enzymes to digest the food trapped inside the vesicle. Figure 25-4a shows a sarcodine, an amoeba, using pseudopodia to capture food.

**FIGURE 25-4**

(a) Some sarcodines, such as amoebas, send out pseudopodia that engulf smaller organisms (indicated by the yellow circle). (b) Some mycetozoans, such as radiolarians, have distinctive glassy shells.

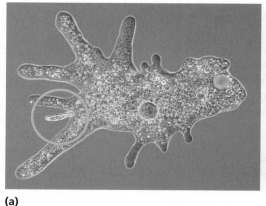
(a)

(b)

## Protozoan Diversity

Sarcodines include hundreds of species that inhabit freshwater environments, marine environments, and soil. The cell membranes of some sarcodines, such as amoebas, are exposed directly to the environment. Other sarcodines are covered with a protective **test,** or shell. For example, *foraminifera* (fuh-RAM-uh-NIF-uhr-uh) are found primarily in oceans and are covered with intricate tests of calcium carbonate. The shells of ancient foraminifera accumulated at the ocean bottom where, after millions of years, they became limestone. The tests of a group of mycetozoans, the *radiolarians* (RAY-dee-oh-LER-ee-uhnz), contain silicon dioxide. Radiolarians often have radially arranged spines. Both foraminiferans and radiolarians have slender pseudopodia that extend through tiny openings in the test.

Although most amoebas live freely, some species live in human intestines and may cause disease. One such amoeba, *Entamoeba histolytica,* enters the body through contaminated food and water. It releases enzymes that attack the lining of the large intestine and cause ulcers. A sometimes fatal disease called *amebiasis* may result, causing acute abdominal pain.

# PHYLUM CILIOPHORA

The nearly 8,000 species that make up the phylum Ciliophora (SIL-ee-AHF-uh-ruh) share one key feature: they have cilia. **Cilia** are short, hairlike cytoplasmic projections that line the cell membrane. Cilia make it possible for these protists to move. Members of the genus *Paramecium,* shown in Figure 25-5, are among the most thoroughly studied ciliates. Paramecia are found in ponds and slow-moving streams that contain plants and decaying organic matter. A paramecium has cilia arranged in rows across its cell membrane. The cilia beat in waves, moving the cell through the water. Ciliates often feed on bacteria, algae, and other small organisms in their marine and freshwater habitats.

**FIGURE 25-5**

Like other ciliates, paramecia move by using hundreds of short projections called *cilia.* Paramecia have a large macronucleus, which controls many cell functions, and one or more micronuclei, which are involved in reproduction. The oral groove, mouth pore, and gullet collect food into vacuoles.

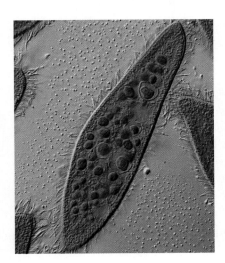

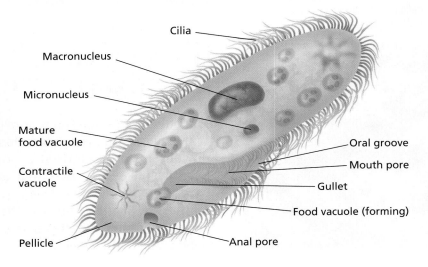

## Characteristics

Ciliates have the most elaborate organelles of any protist. A clear, elastic layer of protein, called a **pellicle,** surrounds the cell membrane. The pellicle has a funnel-like depression called an **oral groove.** Cilia lining the oral groove create currents that sweep food down the groove to the **mouth pore.** The mouth pore opens into a **gullet,** which forms food vacuoles that move throughout the cytoplasm. Enzymes in the vacuoles digest food into small organic molecules that enter the cytoplasm. Undigested materials move to the **anal pore,** which contracts and expels them. Ciliates also have **contractile vacuoles,** saclike organelles that expand to collect excess water and contract to squeeze the water out of the cell.

Ciliates have two types of nuclei. The large **macronucleus** contains multiple copies of DNA that direct the cell's metabolism and development. The smaller **micronucleus** participates in the exchange of genetic material during conjugation.

## Reproduction

Asexual reproduction in ciliates occurs by binary fission. In this process, the micronucleus divides by mitosis. The macronucleus, which has up to 500 times more DNA than the micronucleus, simply elongates and splits in half. One half goes to each new cell.

Sexual reproduction in ciliates involves conjugation. During conjugation, two cells join, and their macronuclei disintegrate. Each diploid micronucleus then undergoes meiosis, producing four haploid micronuclei. In each cell, all but one micronucleus disintegrates. The remaining micronucleus divides by mitosis, producing two identical haploid micronuclei. The two cells then exchange one micronucleus. The two micronuclei in each cell then fuse to form one diploid micronucleus. The two cells separate, and a macronucleus forms in each cell from products of mitotic divisions of the micronucleus. Although the cells exchange genetic material during conjugation, they produce no new cells. After conjugation, the two cells divide, forming four offspring.

**Word Roots and Origins**

*macronucleus*

from the Greek *makros,* meaning "long," and the Latin *nucleus,* meaning "nut" or "kernel"

**FIGURE 25-6**

Flagella are a key characteristic of mastigophorans, such as these trypanosomes (*Trypanosoma* sp.), shown with red blood cells. Trypanosome flagella are structurally similar to the tails of human sperm.

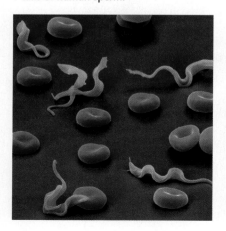

# PHYLUM SARCOMASTIGOPHORA

The phylum Sarcomastigophora (SAR-koh-mas-ti-GAHF-uh-ruh) includes 1,500 species and the subphylum Mastigophora. Members of this phylum are characterized by one or more flagella. **Flagella** are long, whiplike structures that are made up of microtubules and used for movement. Flagella can be seen in Figure 25-6. The rapid motion of flagella moves the protist through water. Many mastigophorans are free-living species that inhabit lakes and ponds, where they feed on smaller organisms.

Some mastigophorans are parasites, including many in the genus *Trypanosoma.* Trypanosomes live in the blood of fish, amphibians, reptiles, birds, and mammals and are carried from host to host by bloodsucking insects. Two species of *Trypanosoma* cause sleeping sickness. The tsetse fly, which lives only in Africa, transmits these parasites. The disease is characterized by increasing fever, lethargy, mental deterioration, and coma.

# PHYLUM APICOMPLEXA

The phylum Apicomplexa (AY-PI-kuhm-PLEKS-uh) includes at least 4,000 species that have adult forms with no means of locomotion. Many apicomplexans were once known as *sporozoans* (SPOH-ruh-ZOH-uhnz). All apicomplexan species are animal parasites.

Apicomplexans have complex life cycles involving both asexual and sexual reproduction. The reproduction of apicomplexans often results in *sporozoites,* infectious cells that are protected by resistant coats. Apicomplexan sporozoites are characterized by an *apical complex,* or a group of organelles specialized for entering host cells and tissues. Because of their complex life cycles, many apicomplexans require two or more different hosts to complete their life cycle. For example, *Plasmodium,* the parasite that causes malaria, needs both mosquitoes and humans to complete its life cycle.

As apicomplexans inhabit a host's cells and tissues, the apicomplexans absorb nutrients and destroy host cells. Apicomplexans may have killed more people than any other group of pathogens on Earth. Each year, millions of people die as a result of *Plasmodium* infection. Another apicomplexan, *Toxoplasma gondii,* causes few symptoms in healthy adult humans but can be dangerous to developing fetuses and newborn babies. *Cryptosporidium,* which is shown in Figure 25-7, is often transmitted by contaminated drinking water or contact with the feces of infected animals.

**FIGURE 25-7**

*Cryptosporidium* (stained purple) is a genus of apicomplexans that cause diarrhea, abdominal pain, and vomiting. They sometimes spread to humans through the feces of infected animals, such as cats.

---

## SECTION 2 REVIEW

1. Describe the key characteristics of each phylum of animal-like protists.

2. How are pseudopodia used for movement and the capture of food?

3. Describe reproduction in Ciliophora.

4. How do protozoa, ciliates, and mastigophorans move?

5. What is the role of apicomplexans in disease?

6. List five protists that cause disease, and briefly describe each disease.

**CRITICAL THINKING**

7. **Applying Information** How might controlling mosquito populations prevent the spread of malaria? Explain your answer.

8. **Making Inferences** Apicomplexans lack a means of locomotion. How does this relate to the fact that apicomplexans are parasites?

9. **Analyzing Information** A scientist found an animal-like protist that lacks cilia or flagella and does not form spores. To which phylum does the protist most likely belong? Explain.

## OBJECTIVES

- **Describe** four main body forms of algae.
- **List** the common name for each of the seven phyla of plantlike protists.
- **Explain** how green algae and plants are similar.
- **Describe** four phyla of funguslike protists.
- **Compare** plasmodial slime molds, cellular slime molds, and water molds.

## VOCABULARY

alga
gametangium
phytoplankton
thallus
accessory pigment
diatom
shell
bioluminescence
red tide
euglenoid
fruiting body
water mold
plasmodial slime mold
cellular slime mold

# PLANTLIKE AND FUNGUSLIKE PROTISTS

*Algae are plantlike protists that vary in size from tiny unicellular organisms to multicellular giants that reach 60 m in length. Although many funguslike protists are called* molds, *they do not fit in kingdom Fungi. Funguslike protists include slime molds and water molds.*

## CHARACTERISTICS OF ALGAE

Many plantlike protists are known as algae. Unlike animal-like protists, which are heterotrophic, **algae** (singular, *alga*) are autotrophic protists. Algae have chloroplasts and produce their own carbohydrates by photosynthesis, as plants do. Older classification systems placed algae in kingdom Plantae. However, algae lack tissue differentiation and thus have no true roots, stems, or leaves. The reproductive structures of algae also differ from those of plants. Algae form gametes in single-celled gamete chambers called **gametangia** (GAM-uh-TAN-jee-uh). By contrast, plants form gametes in multicellular gametangia.

Despite their diversity, algae share several features. Algae have the photosynthetic pigment chlorophyll *a*. Most algae are aquatic and have flagella at some point in their life cycle. Algal cells often contain *pyrenoids* (pie-REE-NOYDZ), structures associated with algal chloroplasts that synthesize and store starch.

Algae have four basic body forms. *Unicellular algae* consist of a single cell. Most unicellular algae are free-living aquatic organisms and together are known as **phytoplankton.** Phytoplankton form the base of nearly all marine and freshwater food chains. *Colonial algae,* such as *Volvox,* consist of groups of individual cells acting in a coordinated manner. Some of the cells may become specialized, allowing for a division of labor. *Filamentous algae,* such as *Spirogyra,* are multicellular algae that are slender, rod shaped, and composed of cells joined end to end. Some filamentous algae have structures that anchor the organism to the ocean bottom. *Multicellular algae,* such as the kelp shown in Figure 25-8, are usually large and complex and often appear plantlike. Many large multicellular algae are also known as *seaweeds.* The plantlike body portion of a seaweed is called a **thallus** (THAL-uhs), and its cells are usually haploid.

**FIGURE 25-8**

Multicellular algae, such as kelp, often have air bladders, which help the algae float upright underwater or in mats on the ocean surface.

## TABLE 25-2  Phyla of Plantlike Protists

| Phylum | Body form | Photosynthetic pigments | Form of food storage | Cell-wall composition |
|---|---|---|---|---|
| Chlorophyta (green algae) | unicellular, colonial, filamentous, multicellular | chlorophylls *a* and *b*, carotenoids | starch | polysaccharides, cellulose |
| Phaeophyta (brown algae) | multicellular | chlorophylls *a* and *c*, carotenoids, fucoxanthin | laminarin (a polysaccharide) | cellulose with alginic acid |
| Rhodophyta (red algae) | multicellular | chlorophyll *a*, phycobilins, carotenoids | starch | cellulose or pectin, many with calcium carbonate |
| Bacillariophyta (diatoms) | unicellular, colonial | chlorophylls *a* and *c*, carotenoids, fucoxanthin, some with none | laminarin, leucosin (an oil) | pectin, many with silicon dioxide |
| Dinoflagellata (dinoflagellates) | unicellular | chlorophylls *a* and *c*, carotenoids, xanthophyll, some with none | starch | cellulose |
| Chrysophyta (golden algae) | unicellular, colonial | chlorophylls *a* and *c*, carotenoids, fucoxanthin, xanthophyll, some with none | laminarin, leucosin | cellulose |
| Euglenophyta (euglenoids) | unicellular | chlorophylls *a* and *b*, carotenoids, many with none | paramylon (a starch) | no cell wall, protein-rich pellicle |

# PLANTLIKE PROTISTS

Plantlike protists are classified into seven phyla based on type of pigments, form of food storage, and cell-wall composition. The characteristics of the seven phyla are summarized in Table 25-2.

## Phylum Chlorophyta (Green Algae)

The phylum Chlorophyta (klaw-RAHF-uh-tuh) contains more than 17,000 identified species of protists called *green algae*. Green algae have an amazing number of body forms, ranging from single cells and colonies to filamentous and multicellular forms.

Green algae share several characteristics with plants. Both green algae and plants have chlorophylls *a* and *b*. They both have carotenoids, which are **accessory pigments** that capture light energy and transfer it to chlorophyll *a*. Green algae and plants store food as starch and have cell walls made up of cellulose. The similarities between green algae and plants suggest that they may have had a common ancestor or that ancient green algae gave rise to land plants.

Most species of green algae are aquatic. Some species, such as the *Protococcus* shown in Figure 25-9, inhabit moist terrestrial environments, such as soil and tree trunks. Some green algae live as symbiotic partners with invertebrates, such as corals. Other green algae live with fungi as a part of organisms called *lichens*.

**FIGURE 25-9**

Many green algae, such as *Protococcus*, inhabit moist environments on land, such as the shady, often north-facing sides of tree trunks.

**FIGURE 25-10**

Giant kelp *(Macrocystis pyrifera)* forms kelp gardens along the Pacific coast and provides habitat for a rich variety of life, including crustaceans, fishes, sharks, and sea otters.

## Phylum Phaeophyta (Brown Algae)

The phylum Phaeophyta (fee-AHF-uh-tuh) contains approximately 1,500 species of multicellular organisms called *brown algae*. Brown algae contain chlorophylls *a* and *c* and fucoxanthin (FYOO-koh-ZAN-thin), an accessory pigment that gives the algae their characteristic brown color. Brown algae store food as laminarin, a carbohydrate whose glucose units are linked differently than those in starch.

Brown algae are mostly marine organisms, and they include plantlike seaweeds and kelps. They are most common along rocky coasts where ocean water is cool. A few species of brown algae, such as *Sargassum,* can be found far offshore, where they form dense, floating mats.

Some of the largest algae known are classified in the phylum Phaeophyta. The large brown alga shown in Figure 25-10 is *Macrocystis pyrifera,* a giant kelp that thrives in intertidal zones and reaches 60 m in length. The thallus is anchored to the ocean bottom by a rootlike *holdfast.* The stemlike portion of the alga is called the *stipe.* And the leaflike region, modified to capture sunlight for photosynthesis, is the *blade.*

**Word Roots and Origins**

*stipe*

from the Latin *stipes,* meaning "log" or "trunk of a tree"

## Phylum Rhodophyta (Red Algae)

The 4,000 species in the phylum Rhodophyta (roh-DAHF-uh-tuh) are known as *red algae.* Red algae contain chlorophyll *a* and accessory pigments called *phycobilins.* Phycobilins play an important role in absorbing light for photosynthesis. These pigments can absorb the wavelengths of light that penetrate deep into the water. As a result, phycobilins allow red algae to live at depths where algae lacking these pigments cannot survive. Some species of red algae have been found at depths of nearly 270 m, which is about three times deeper than organisms from any other algal phyla have been found.

A few species of red algae live in fresh water or on land, but most red algae are marine seaweeds. Despite their common name, not all red algae are reddish in appearance. The depth at which red algae live determines the amount of phycobilins they have. The *Corallina* alga shown in Figure 25-11 displays typical red algae pigmentation and body shape.

**FIGURE 25-11**

Red algae, such as this *Corallina* species, are smaller than most brown algae, but members of both phyla are often referred to as *seaweeds.*

## Phylum Bacillariophyta (Diatoms)

The phylum Bacillariophyta (BAS-uh-ler-ee-AHF-uh-tuh) contains as many as 100,000 species of unicellular protists called **diatoms.** Diatoms have cell walls, or **shells,** consisting of two pieces that fit together like a box and lid. Each half is called a *valve,* and the shells contain silicon dioxide. There are two basic types of diatoms. *Centric diatoms* have circular or triangular shells and are most abundant in marine environments. *Pennate diatoms* have rectangular shells and are most abundant in freshwater environments. Diatoms are an abundant component of phytoplankton and important producers in freshwater and marine food webs. In addition, diatoms release atmospheric oxygen.

## Phylum Dinoflagellata (Dinoflagellates)

More than 2,000 species of organisms called *dinoflagellates* make up the phylum Dinoflagellata (DIE-noh-FLAJ-uh-LAH-tuh). Dinoflagellates, such as those shown in Figure 25-12, are small, usually unicellular organisms bearing two flagella of unequal length. The flagella are oriented perpendicular to each other. Dinoflagellates have cell walls made of cellulose plates that look like armor when seen under a microscope.

Most dinoflagellates are photosynthetic autotrophs, but a few species are colorless and heterotrophic. Photosynthetic dinoflagellates usually have a yellowish green to brown color due to large amounts of carotenoids, as well as chlorophylls *a* and *c*.

Some species of dinoflagellates, such as those in genus *Noctiluca*, can produce **bioluminescence,** the production of light by means of a chemical reaction in an organism. Other species produce toxins and red pigments. When the populations of these species explode, they turn the water brownish red, resulting in a phenomenon known as **red tide.** Red tides are fairly common in the Gulf of Mexico. Red tide toxins can kill large numbers of fish. When shellfish, such as oysters, feed on red tide dinoflagellates, they also consume the toxins, which are dangerous to humans who eat the shellfish.

## Phylum Chrysophyta (Golden Algae)

The phylum Chrysophyta (kruh-SAHF-uh-tuh) contains about 1,000 species of *golden algae*. Most golden algae live in fresh water, but a few species are found in marine environments. Golden algae cells form highly resistant cysts that enable them to survive beneath the frozen surfaces of lakes during winter and dry lake beds during summer. Two flagella of unequal length are located at one end of each cell.

Most golden algae appear yellow or brown because of the presence of carotenoids. Golden algae also have chlorophylls *a* and *c* and store much of their surplus energy as oil. Golden algae likely played a role in the formation of petroleum deposits.

## Phylum Euglenophyta (Euglenoids)

The phylum Euglenophyta (YOO-gluh-NAHF-uh-tuh) contains about 1,000 species of flagellated unicellular algae called **euglenoids.** Euglenoids are both plantlike and animal-like. Many are autotrophic, like plants, but they lack a cell wall and are highly motile, like animals. Euglenoids contain chlorophylls *a* and *b* and carotenoids. Most euglenoids live in fresh water, but a few occupy moist environments, such as soil or the digestive tracts of certain animals.

*Euglena*, shown in Figure 25-13, are abundant in fresh water, especially water polluted by excess nutrients. *Euglena* lack a cell wall, so they are flexible and can change their shape. *Euglena* have an elastic, transparent pellicle made of protein just beneath their cell membrane. Eyespots help *Euglena* sense their environment. Euglena also have a contractile vacuole that expels excess water. Although usually photosynthetic, *Euglena* raised in the dark do not form chloroplasts and become heterotrophs.

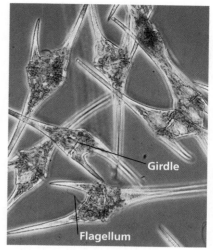

**FIGURE 25-12**

Flagella spin dinoflagellates, such as these members of genus *Ceratium*, through the water like tops. Only one of the two flagella is clearly visible in this picture. The second flagellum lies in the girdle at the middle of the organism. (450×)

Girdle

Flagellum

**FIGURE 25-13**

Members of the genus *Euglena* contain chloroplasts like a plant but move around like an animal. *Euglena* are common in ponds. They are propelled by a long flagellum. An eyespot guides them toward light.

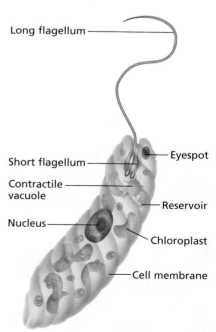

Long flagellum

Short flagellum

Contractile vacuole

Nucleus

Eyespot

Reservoir

Chloroplast

Cell membrane

Slime molds often grow on decomposing organic matter, such as rotting logs. Slime molds consume small organisms and organic matter.

# FUNGUSLIKE PROTISTS

Biologists recognize two groups of funguslike protists: slime molds and water molds. Slime molds are typically found on moist, decaying matter. They appear as glistening white, yellow, or red masses of slime, as shown in Figure 25-14. Slime molds have life cycles in which they spend part of their lives in a mobile, amoeba-like feeding form, consuming organic matter and bacteria much as protozoa do. However, these protists have a stationary reproductive stage in which they produce a funguslike, spore-bearing structure called a **fruiting body,** shown in Figure 25-15. A **water mold** is a funguslike protist composed of branching filaments of cells. Water molds are found mainly in bodies of fresh water but sometimes live in soil or as parasites.

## Phylum Myxomycota (Plasmodial Slime Molds)

The phylum Myxomycota (MIKS-oh-mie-KOH-tuh) includes about 700 species of **plasmodial slime molds.** During the feeding stage of its life cycle, a plasmodial slime mold is a mass of cytoplasm, called a *plasmodium,* that may be as large as several square meters. Each plasmodium is multinucleate, containing many diploid nuclei that are not separated by cell walls. As the plasmodium creeps along the forest floor by cytoplasmic streaming, it consumes decaying leaves and other debris by phagocytosis.

When food or water is scarce, the plasmodium begins to reproduce. It forms stalked fruiting bodies in which haploid spores are produced by meiosis. Spores are resistant to harsh conditions. Under favorable conditions, spores crack open and give rise to haploid reproductive cells. Two such cells fuse, and their nuclei combine to form a diploid nucleus. Repeated mitotic divisions follow, but the cells do not undergo cytokinesis. The lack of cytokinesis results in the multinucleated plasmodium.

## Phylum Dictyostelida (Cellular Slime Mold)

The phylum Dictyostelida (dik-TEE-oh-STEL-uh-duh) includes about 65 species of cellular slime molds. **Cellular slime molds** live as individual haploid cells that move about like amoebas. Each cell moves as an independent organism, creeping over the ground or swimming in fresh water and ingesting food.

When food or water becomes scarce, the cells release a chemical that attracts nearby cells, causing them to gather by the thousands into a dense structure called a *pseudoplasmodium.* A pseudoplasmodium is a coordinated colony of individual cells that resembles a slug and leaves a slimy trail as it crawls. Although the cells move as one unit, each cell retains its membrane and identity. Eventually, the pseudoplasmodium settles and forms fruiting bodies in which haploid spores develop. When a fruiting body breaks open, the spores are dispersed. Each spore may grow into an individual amoeboid cell, thus completing the life cycle.

Both plasmodial slime molds and cellular slime molds produce fruiting bodies that resemble those of fungi.

FIGURE 25-16

Some parasitic water molds attack aquatic organisms, such as fish, forming long filaments that eventually harm the fish.

## Phylum Oomycota (Water Molds)

The phylum Oomycota (OH-mie-KOH-tuh) includes a number of organisms that are parasitic. For example, some oomycotes affect fish, as shown in Figure 25-16. Oomycotes reproduce asexually and sexually. During asexual reproduction, they produce flagellated zoospores. Zoospores germinate into threadlike cells. Some zoospores form a *zoosporangium,* which produces new zoospores. During sexual reproduction, water mold cells develop egg-containing and sperm-containing structures. Fertilization tubes grow between the two types of structures, enabling sperm to fertilize eggs, which forms diploid zygotes. A zygote grows into a new mass of filaments, which can again reproduce asexually or sexually.

## Phylum Chytridiomycota (Water Molds)

Members of phylum Chytridiomycota (kie-TRID-ee-oh-mie-KOH-tuh), or the *chytrids* (KIE-tridz), are primarily aquatic protists characterized by gametes and zoospores with a single, posterior flagellum. Most chytrids are unicellular and parasitic.

Chytrids share many characteristics with fungi. They have similar means of obtaining nutrients, cell walls made of the same type of material, filamentous bodies, and similar enzymes and biochemical pathways. Because of these similarities, many biologists classify chytrids as fungi. Other biologists hypothesize that chytrids are a link between protists and fungi.

 **Quick Lab**

### Comparing Funguslike Protists

**Materials** paper and pencil

**Procedure** Create a chart that compares the phyla of funguslike protists. Include descriptions of cellular structure, locomotion, and means of reproduction.

**Analysis** Which funguslike protists are haploid? Which are diploid? Which funguslike protists reproduce sexually? Which reproduce asexually?

## SECTION 3 REVIEW

1. What are four body forms of algae?

2. List seven phyla of plantlike protists.

3. Why do biologists theorize that ancient green algae gave rise to plants?

4. How are brown algae different from green and red algae?

5. What are the main characteristics of slime molds and water molds?

6. Compare plasmodial slime molds and cellular slime molds.

**CRITICAL THINKING**

7. **Applying Information** *Pseudo* means "false." Why do biologists call the migrating structure of a cellular slime mold a *pseudoplasmodium*?

8. **Identifying Relationships** Assume that chytrids are a link between protists and fungi, and draw a phylogenetic tree reflecting this information.

9. **Applying Information** An organism contains chlorophylls *a* and *c* and carotenoids, and it is unicellular. To which phylum does it belong? Explain your answer.

## OBJECTIVES

- **State** four environmental roles of protists.
- **Describe** algal blooms and red tides and their impact.
- **State** an important role for protists in research.
- **List** a use of protists as food and three uses of protist byproducts.
- **Describe** four protist-caused diseases.

## VOCABULARY

algal bloom
chemotaxis
alginate
carrageenan
agar
diatomaceous earth
malaria
sporozoite
merozoite
gametocyte
giardiasis
cryptosporidiosis
trichomoniasis

internet connect
www.scilinks.org
**Topic:** Protists
**Keyword:** HM61245

SC<sup>i</sup>LINKS. Maintained by the National Science Teachers Association

# PROTISTS AND HUMANS

*A casual glance out the window usually will not include a sighting of protists, except perhaps for some green algae growing on a tree trunk or some slime collected at a pond's edge. Protists have a profound impact on human lives through their modification of the environment, their use in research and industry, and the harm they may cause to human health.*

## PROTISTS IN THE ENVIRONMENT

Protists are seldom apparent to the naked eye, but they play important roles in the environment. They produce large amounts of oxygen, form the foundation of food webs, recycle materials, and play a role in several symbiotic relationships.

Along with plants and photosynthetic bacteria, protists produce large quantities of atmospheric oxygen. Nearly every organism on Earth relies on this oxygen for *cellular respiration,* the process in which oxygen is used to obtain energy from organic molecules.

Photosynthetic protists are also critical components of marine and freshwater food webs. Photosynthetic protists produce carbohydrates. Larger protists and other aquatic organisms feed on these carbon-rich protists. For example, diatoms support large schools of anchovy, which sea lions eat before they, themselves, become the prey of orcas.

Protists play an important role in the carbon cycle. Photosynthetic protists use carbon dioxide and water from the environment to make carbohydrates, which are taken up by other living things or used by the protists for cellular processes. When protists use the carbohydrates, they release carbon dioxide and water back into the environment. Some protists, such as slime molds, are decomposers that aid in the cycling of other nutrients as well.

Protists form several important symbiotic relationships. For example, protists living in symbiosis with corals give the corals both their color and much of their carbon supply. Symbiosis between algae and fungi forms lichens. When lichens grow on newly exposed rocks, their secretions break down the rock. This process creates new soil that can support the growth of plants. Finally, protists found in the guts of some animals help the animals digest cellulose. For example, *Trichonympha* is one of the protists that help termites digest cellulose.

## Ecology of Protists

Temperature and the availability of light and nutrients influence the growth of algal populations. Algae grow in the *photic zone,* the portion of a body of water through which light penetrates. Nitrate and phosphate availability usually limits algal growth rates. In the open ocean, the availability of iron ions may limit algal growth.

High water temperatures and nutrient concentrations can cause **algal blooms,** a vast increase in the concentration of diatoms and other photosynthetic protists. Algal blooms often occur during spring in bays and estuaries and frequently harm these environments. During an algal bloom, large numbers of dying protists sink to the bottom, where they decompose. Bacterial decomposers use up oxygen, which fish, crustaceans, and other sea life need to survive. Dropping oxygen levels can cause these larger species to die off.

Dinoflagellate blooms cause red tides, shown in Figure 25-17. Toxins produced by dinoflagellate blooms concentrate as they move up the food chain. These toxins can sicken or kill humans and other organisms that consume clams, oysters, or krill that have fed on the red tide dinoflagellates.

**FIGURE 25-17**

Because red tides produce dangerous toxins, people in some areas are often advised not to eat shellfish during the summer months, the time when red tides are most likely to happen.

# PROTISTS IN RESEARCH

Research on protists has helped biologists understand a number of fundamental cellular functions, such as cell movement. For example, individual cells of the cellular slime mold *Dictyostelium discoidum* move toward a source of AMP, a precursor to the energy-storage molecule ATP. These cells crawl using amoeboid movement, shown in Figure 25-18.

Researchers are interested in learning how *Dictyostelium* cells can recognize AMP and crawl toward it, a process called **chemotaxis.** The researchers think that human leukocytes, or white blood cells, also perform chemotaxis as they crawl toward sites of infection. Biologists studying chemotaxis in human leukocytes have found the same proteins and cell movement seen in *Dictyostelium* cells. This discovery has improved the understanding of how leukocytes protect against disease. Some scientists believe this knowledge may help improve the treatment of diseases, such as cancers.

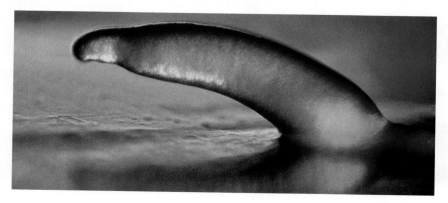

**FIGURE 25-18**

*Dictyostelium* uses amoeboid movement to reach a source of AMP. Understanding how *Dictyostelium* cells move improves the understanding of how human leukocytes move.

# PROTISTS IN INDUSTRY

Humans make daily use of protists and their byproducts. Humans eat protists directly and use them as food additives, as fertilizers, and in cosmetics and medicines.

Scientists from the United States Department of Agriculture are conducting field studies with the protist *Edhazardia aedis* to test its effectiveness as a control agent for disease-carrying mosquitoes. The chemical DDT was used previously, but it was banned in the 1970s after it was discovered to be harmful to bird populations. *E. aedis,* which was discovered in Argentina, infects mosquito larvae in the water and kills them. Scientists think that this protist will prevent disease while causing no environmental damage.

## Protists as Food

For thousands of years, humans have been collecting seaweeds for food. People in Japan began cultivating seaweeds for food nearly 300 years ago. Today, about 10 percent of the Japanese diet is seaweeds. Among the most popular of these seaweeds is *nori,* a red alga from the genus *Porphyra.* Nori is used in soups, salads, and sushi, shown in Figure 25-19. More than half a million tons of nori are harvested each year. *Porphyra* has also been used for hundreds of years by people in Great Britain and is known there as *laverbread. Kombu,* made from kelps of the genus *Laminaria,* is another staple in Asian diets. More than 10 million tons of these kelps are harvested annually.

## Protist Byproducts

The cell walls of most brown algae, especially large kelps, contain alginic acid. Alginic acid is a source of a commercially important polysaccharide called **alginate.** Alginate is used in cosmetics and various drugs and as a stabilizer in ice cream and salad dressings. Alginate is also used in textiles, water-soluble medical dressings for burns, and inks.

Certain species of red algae have cell walls that are coated with a sticky substance called **carrageenan** (KAR-uh-GEEN-uhn). Carrageenan is a polysaccharide that is used to control the texture of many commercial and food products. It is used in the production of cosmetics, gelatin capsules, and some types of cheese.

**FIGURE 25-19**

Sushi, a traditional food in Asian countries, has become more popular in the United States. The seaweeds used in sushi are high in protein, vitamins, and minerals.

**Agar** is another polysaccharide that comes from the cell walls of red algae. Agar is commonly used in scientific research. It is the gel-forming base used for culturing microbes, such as bacteria. Agar is also widely used by the food industry in canned foods and bakery items.

Diatoms are quite abundant in aquatic ecosystems. As diatoms die, their shells sink and accumulate in large numbers at the bottom of lakes and oceans, forming a layer of material called **diatomaceous** (DIE-uh-tuh-MAY-shuhs) **earth.** This slightly abrasive material is a component of many commercial products, such as detergents, paint removers, and toothpaste. Diatomaceous earth is also used in filters, and some people use it as a natural insecticide.

# PROTISTS AND HEALTH

Many protists are parasites. Table 25-3 summarizes the effects of three protist parasites.

## Malaria

Apicomplexans from the genus *Plasmodium* cause **malaria,** which is characterized by severe chills, headache, fever, and fatigue. Each year, nearly 3 million people die from malaria. The four species of *Plasmodium* that infect humans all have life cycles involving an *Anopheles* mosquito. When an infected *Anopheles* mosquito bites a person, *Plasmodium* cells called **sporozoites** enter the bloodstream and infect the liver. New cells called **merozoites** emerge from the liver and infect red blood cells. At regular intervals, merozoites burst from red blood cells and release toxins, causing malarial symptoms. Without treatment, merozoites may remain in the liver for years, causing recurrent disease.

Some merozoites in the blood develop into the sexual forms of the parasite, **gametocytes.** When an *Anopheles* mosquito bites an infected person, the mosquito ingests these gametocytes. The gametocytes form gametes, which combine to form zygotes that develop into more sporozoites. When the insect bites another person, the life cycle begins again. Figure 25-20 shows the life cycle of *Plasmodium*.

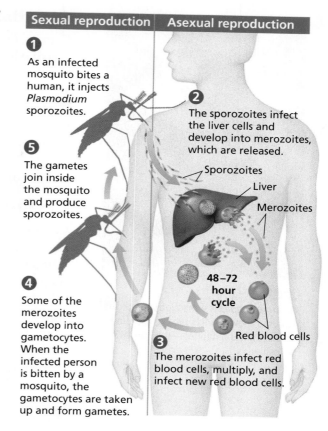

**Sexual reproduction** | **Asexual reproduction**

**1** As an infected mosquito bites a human, it injects *Plasmodium* sporozoites.

**2** The sporozoites infect the liver cells and develop into merozoites, which are released.

Sporozoites
Liver
Merozoites

**5** The gametes join inside the mosquito and produce sporozoites.

48–72 hour cycle

**4** Some of the merozoites develop into gametocytes. When the infected person is bitten by a mosquito, the gametocytes are taken up and form gametes.

**3** The merozoites infect red blood cells, multiply, and infect new red blood cells.

Red blood cells

**FIGURE 25-20**

The life cycle of the malaria-causing *Plasmodium* requires two hosts.

## TABLE 25-3 Examples of Disease-Causing Protists

| Disease | Pathogen (Phylum) | Symptoms | Spread by | Precautions |
|---------|-------------------|----------|-----------|-------------|
| Amebiasis | *Entamoeba histolytica* (Protozoa) | severe diarrhea, fever, and gastrointestinal tract hemorrhage | contaminated water or food | *E. histolytica* is common in developing countries. Drink bottled, boiled, or filter-purified water. Peel fresh fruit, and avoid unpasteurized dairy products. |
| Sleeping sickness | *Trypanosoma* sp. (Sarcomastigophora) | swollen lymph nodes, severe headaches, fever, fatigue, and coma | tsetse flies | Tsetse flies are found only in Africa. Wear protective clothing, such as long pants and long-sleeved shirts. Use insect repellent, and avoid open vehicles and bushes. |
| Leishmaniasis | *Leishmania donovani* (Sarcomastigophora) | skin sores, swollen glands, fever, and swollen spleen and liver | sand flies | Sand flies are found mostly in tropical and subtropical regions. Stay indoors during the day, when sand flies are most active. Wear protective clothing, and use insect repellents. |

**FIGURE 25-21**

*Giardia lamblia* is a mastigophoran. The *Giardia* shown in this picture are shown in their natural habitat—the human intestine.

## Giardiasis

*Giardia lamblia,* shown in Figure 25-21, causes an illness called **giardiasis** (JEE-ahr-DIE-uh-sis). Giardiasis is characterized by severe diarrhea and intestinal cramps. Cattle, beavers, and several other animals carry the parasite and contaminate water with their feces. Hikers and other people who are likely to drink this contaminated water are susceptible to giardiasis. Thousands of cases occur annually in the United States. The disease usually is not fatal, and drugs aid recovery. Drinking bottled, boiled, or filtered water prevents giardiasis.

## Cryptosporidiosis

**Cryptosporidiosis** (KRIP-toh-spawr-I-dee-OH-sis) is characterized by diarrhea and is most often caused by *Cryptosporidium parvum,* an apicomplexan that lives on the surface of cells lining the small intestine. A stage called the *oocyst* (OH-sist) can pass in feces from infected animals to humans. An outer shell protects the parasite outside the body, allowing it to survive for long periods and making it resistant to chlorine disinfectants. Cryptosporidiosis is usually not fatal, but it can be dangerous for people with immune disorders. Washing hands thoroughly after coming in contact with feces and avoiding untreated water can prevent cryptosporidiosis.

## Trichomoniasis

The mastigophoran *Trichomonas vaginalis* is responsible for **trichomoniasis** (TRIK-oh-moh-NIE-uh-sis), a sexually transmitted disease. The parasite does not survive well outside the body, so it is mainly spread by sexual contact. Trichomoniasis is one of the most common sexually transmitted diseases.

Many people do not have symptoms when infected with trichomoniasis. However, women are more likely to have symptoms of trichomoniasis than men are. Symptoms include discolored discharge, genital itching, and the urge to urinate. Abstinence from sexual intercourse prevents trichomoniasis.

## SECTION 4 REVIEW

1. Outline three environmental roles of protist producers.

2. What are three examples of protist symbioses?

3. Why do researchers use slime molds to study chemotaxis?

4. How are protists used for food?

5. Identify three protist byproducts and how people use them.

6. Describe four protist-caused diseases, and name the organisms that cause the diseases.

**CRITICAL THINKING**

7. **Applying Information** What basic precautions can decrease exposure to protist diseases?

8. **Making Predictions** Some scientists hypothesize that global warming will increase mosquito populations. Predict what might happen to rates of malaria as a result.

9. **Calculating Information** If 500 million people contract malaria annually and 6.5 billion people live on Earth, what fraction of the human population becomes infected with malaria annually?

# CHAPTER HIGHLIGHTS

Characteristics of Protists

- Protists are unicellular or simple multicellular eukaryotic organisms that are not plants, fungi, or animals. Protists are classified by the characteristics that make them funguslike, plantlike, or animal-like.
- Evidence suggests that the first protists arose from endosymbiotic prokaryotes.

- Many protists are autotrophs. Other protists are heterotrophs. Protists use flagella, cilia, or pseudopodia for locomotion.
- Protists reproduce either asexually, sexually, or both. They reproduce asexually by binary fission or multiple fission. They often reproduce sexually by conjugation.

**Vocabulary**

protist (p. 501)     binary fission (p. 504)     multiple fission (p. 504)     conjugation (p. 504)

SECTION 2    Animal-like Protists

- Animal-like protists include the phyla Protozoa, Ciliophora, Sarcomastigophora, and Apicomplexa. For locomotion, protozoa use pseudopodia, ciliates use cilia, and sarcomastigophorans use flagella.

- Ciliates reproduce asexually by binary fission and sexually by conjugation.
- Apicomplexans lack locomotion, so they are parasites.

**Vocabulary**

pseudopodium (p. 506)     pellicle (p. 508)     gullet (p. 508)     macronucleus (p. 508)
amoeboid movement (p. 506)     oral groove (p. 508)     anal pore (p. 508)     micronucleus (p. 508)
test (p. 507)     mouth pore (p. 508)     contractile vacuole (p. 508)     flagellum (p. 508)
cilium (p. 507)

SECTION 3    Plantlike and Funguslike Protists

- Algae can be unicellular, colonial, filamentous, or multicellular. Seven phyla of plantlike protists are Chlorophyta, Phaeophyta, Rhodophyta, Bacillariophyta, Dinoflagellata, Chrysophyta, and Euglenophyta.
- Green algae and plants have the same pigments, store food as starch, and have cell walls made of cellulose.

- Slime molds are found on decaying matter and spend part of their lives as mobile feeding forms and the other part as stationary reproductive forms.
- Plasmodial slime molds are multinucleate, and cellular slime molds live as individual haploid cells. Water molds are composed of branching filaments.

**Vocabulary**

alga (p. 510)     accessory pigment (p. 511)     red tide (p. 513)     plasmodial slime mold
gametangium (p. 510)     diatom (p. 512)     euglenoid (p. 513)     (p. 514)
phytoplankton (p. 510)     shell (p. 512)     fruiting body (p. 514)     cellular slime mold (p. 514)
thallus (p. 510)     bioluminescence (p. 513)     water mold (p. 514)

SECTION 4    Protists and Humans

- Protists produce large amounts of oxygen, form the foundation of food webs, recycle materials, and play a role in several symbiotic relationships.
- Algal blooms can lead to the depletion of oxygen in water. Red tides produce harmful toxins.

- Protists can help scientists understand the movement of leukocytes, provide food, and provide important byproducts, such as alginate, carrageenan, and agar.
- Parasitic protists cause malaria, giardiasis, cryptosporidiosis, and trichomoniasis in humans.

**Vocabulary**

algal bloom (p. 517)     agar (p. 518)     sporozoite (p. 519)     giardiasis (p. 520)
chemotaxis (p. 517)     diatomaceous earth (p. 518)     merozoite (p. 519)     cryptosporidiosis (p. 520)
alginate (p. 518)     malaria (p. 519)     gametocyte (p. 519)     trichomoniasis (p. 520)
carrageenan (p. 518)

## USING VOCABULARY

1. **Choose** the term that does not belong in the following group, and explain why it does not belong: *binary fission, macronucleus, multiple fission,* and *conjugation.*

2. For each pair of terms, explain the relationship between the terms.
   a. *pseudopodia* and *amoeboid movement*
   b. *macronucleus* and *micronucleus*
   c. *algae* and *thallus*
   d. *sporozoites* and *merozoites*

3. Use each of the following terms in a separate sentence: *algal bloom, red tide, fruiting body,* and *pellicle.*

4. **Word Roots and Origins** The word *diatom* comes from the Greek word *diatomos,* which means "cut in half." Using this information, explain how *diatom* is an appropriate term for the organisms it describes.

## UNDERSTANDING KEY CONCEPTS

5. **Define** *protist.*

6. **Describe** a hypothesis for the origin of eukaryotic cells.

7. **State** the way in which protists are generally classified.

8. **Compare** two ways by which protists obtain food and three ways by which they move.

9. **List** three ways by which protists reproduce.

10. **Differentiate** between Protozoa, Ciliophora, Sarcomastigophora, and Apicomplexa.

11. **Explain** how protozoa use pseudopodia to move and capture food.

12. **Relate** how ciliates reproduce.

13. **Compare** movement in sarcodines, ciliates, and mastigophorans.

14. **Identify** the relationship between apicomplexans and disease.

15. **List** four body forms of algae.

16. **State** the common name for each of the seven phyla of plantlike protists.

17. **Compare** green algae and plants.

18. **Summarize** the main characteristics of the four phyla of funguslike protists.

19. **Describe** plasmodial slime molds and cellular slime molds.

20. **Describe** four roles of protists in the environment.

21. **Describe** algal blooms and red tides.

22. **Name** an important role for protists in research.

23. **List** four uses of protists and protist byproducts.

24. **Summarize** the characteristics of four protist-caused diseases.

25. **CONCEPT MAPPING** Use the following terms to create a concept map that describes the characteristics of animal-like protists: *Protozoa, amoeboid movement, pseudopodia, Ciliophora, flagella, Sarcomastigophora, cilia, cytoplasmic streaming, test, pellicle, parasites,* and *Apicomplexa.*

## CRITICAL THINKING

26. **Relating Concepts** Health officials advise that people should not eat shellfish from certain areas during the summer months. Explain the reason for this warning.

27. **Analyzing Data** Scientists are trying to develop a vaccine against malaria. Because malaria has several life stages, scientists must decide which life stage should be the target of the vaccine. Some scientists are trying to develop a vaccine against gametocytes as a way of controlling malaria. If they are successful in developing this vaccine, how will it help people living in areas where malaria regularly occurs? Explain your answer.

28. **Making Comparisons** How is the movement of *Dictyostelium* toward AMP similar to the movement of leukocytes? How is it different? Based on this information, is *Dictyostelium* a good model for leukocytes? Justify your answer.

29. **Interpreting Graphics** A scientist found two different euglenoids. The scientist concluded that specimen a is exclusively heterotrophic but specimen b is not. Examine the images of the specimens below, and determine if the scientist is correct in his or her conclusions.

 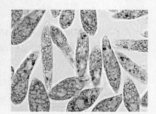

(a)          (b)

# Standardized Test Preparation

**DIRECTIONS:** Choose the letter of the answer choice that best answers the question.

1. Most scientists believe that protists evolved from which of the following?
   A. fungi
   B. plants
   C. euglenoids
   D. prokaryotes

2. Protist habitats are often characterized by the presence of which of the following?
   F. soil
   G. algae
   H. blood
   J. moisture

3. Flagella are characteristic of members of which phylum?
   A. Protozoa
   B. Ciliophora
   C. Apicomplexa
   D. Sarcomastigophora

**INTERPRETING GRAPHICS:** The table below shows cases of amebiasis and malaria in the United States between 1986 and 1994. Use the table to answer the questions that follow.

### Protist-Caused Diseases in the United States, 1986–1994

| Year | Number of cases | |
| --- | --- | --- |
| | Amebiasis | Malaria |
| 1986 | 3,532 | 1,123 |
| 1988 | 2,860 | 1,099 |
| 1990 | 3,328 | 1,292 |
| 1992 | 2,942 | 1,087 |
| 1994 | 2,983 | 1,229 |

4. How many people had malaria in 1992?
   F. 1,087
   G. 1,229
   H. 1,292
   J. 2,942

5. How did the number of cases of amebiasis change between 1986 and 1994?
   A. The number of cases increased.
   B. The number of cases decreased.
   C. The number of cases stayed the same.
   D. The number of cases increased, then decreased.

**DIRECTIONS:** Complete the following analogy.

6. Bacillariophyta : autotrophs :: Apicomplexa :
   F. cilia
   G. flagella
   H. parasites
   J. plasmodium

**INTERPRETING GRAPHICS:** The graph below shows the cycle of fever in a malaria patient. Use the graph to answer the question that follows.

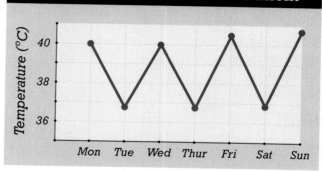

7. In this patient, how often does the cycle of fever repeat?
   A. every 12 h
   B. every 24 h
   C. every 48 h
   D. every 96 h

## SHORT RESPONSE

*Anopheles* mosquitoes require water to breed.

What would happen to malaria cases during a dry season and during a wet season?

## EXTENDED RESPONSE

A scientist wants to examine the effect of fertilizer on algal blooms. In the laboratory, the scientist adds increasing amounts of fertilizer to three samples of pond water and adds no fertilizer to a fourth sample of pond water.

*Part A* Which samples will show increased algal growth? Explain your answer.

*Part B* How can the scientist apply his or her laboratory results to a natural ecosystem? Compare the scientist's experiment to a natural ecosystem, such as a pond.

**Test TIP** For a question involving experimental data, determine the constants, variables, and control **before** answering the question.

# Classifying Green Algae

## OBJECTIVES

- Observe live specimens of green algae.
- Compare unicellular, colonial, filamentous, and multicellular green algae.
- Classify genera of colonial green algae.

## PROCESS SKILLS

- observing
- comparing and contrasting
- classifying
- inferring

## MATERIALS

- culture of *Chlamydomonas*
- colonial green algae culture (*Chlamydomonas, Eudorina, Gonium, Pandorina, Volvox,* and *Hydrodictyon*)
- culture of *Spirogyra*
- 3 depression slides
- 3 coverslips
- 3 medicine droppers
- compound light microscope

## Background

1. Distinguish between the terms *protozoa* and *algae*.
2. Green algae are either unicellular, colonial, filamentous, or multicellular.
3. Explain why green plants are thought to have evolved from green algae.

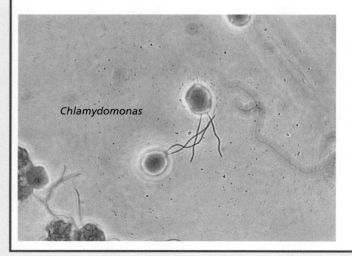

Chlamydomonas

4. List characteristics of green algae. Include ways that algae differ from plants.
5. How do green algae differ from other algae?

## PART A  Observing Unicellular Green Algae

1. Make a table similar to the one below in your lab report. Allow substantial space in your data table for labeled sketches of the different kinds of green algae you will view in this investigation. Use your data table to record your observations of each kind of green algae that you view.
2. ⚠ CAUTION  **Slides break easily. Use caution when handling them.** Prepare a wet mount of the *Chlamydomonas* culture by placing a drop of the culture on a microscope slide with a medicine dropper and placing a coverslip on top of the specimen.

| OBSERVATIONS OF GREEN ALGAE | | |
|---|---|---|
| Genus | Sketch of organism | Type of green algae (unicellular, colonial, filamentous, or multicellular) |
| | | |
| | | |
| | | |
| | | |
| | | |
| | | |
| | | |
| | | |

3. Examine the slide of *Chlamydomonas,* first under low power and then under high power.
4. In your lab report, make a sketch of *Chlamydomonas.* Label the cell wall, flagella, nucleus, and chloroplasts if they are visible.

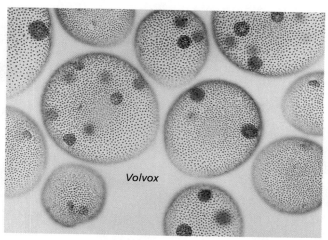
*Volvox*

## PART B Observing and Identifying Colonial Green Algae

5. **CAUTION** **Slides break easily. Use caution when handling them.** Prepare a wet mount of the colonial green algae culture using a clean medicine dropper, a clean microscope slide, and a clean coverslip.
6. Examine the slide of mixed colonial green algae under low power, switching to the high-power setting as needed for clarity. Some of the organisms on your slide should resemble the photograph of *Volvox* above. How many different kinds of colonial green algae can you find?
7. In your data table, draw each type of colonial green algae you observe. How are these algae different in appearance from *Chlamydomonas*?
8. Use the dichotomous key, above right, to identify each type of colonial green algae. Choose an alga, and start at 1. Decide which choice best describes the alga. If the alga is not identified, go to the next number and make the next decision. Continue until you identify the alga. Then, label your drawing of the alga.

## PART C Observing Filamentous Green Algae

9. **CAUTION** **Slides break easily. Use caution when handling them.** Prepare a wet mount of

### DICHOTOMOUS KEY FOR COLONIAL GREEN ALGAE

| 1a | single cells | *Chlamydomonas* |
|----|------------------------------|------------------|
| 1b | colony of cells | go to 2 |
| 2a | flattened or netlike colony | go to 3 |
| 2b | round colony | go to 4 |
| 3a | netlike colony | *Hydrodictyon* |
| 3b | flattened colony | *Gonium* |
| 4a | more than 100 cells in colony | *Volvox* |
| 4b | fewer than 100 cells in colony | go to 5 |
| 5a | cells close together | *Pandorina* |
| 5b | cells apart from each other | *Eudorina* |

the *Spirogyra* culture using a clean medicine dropper, a clean microscope slide, and a clean coverslip.
10. Examine *Spirogyra* under low power. Switch to the high-power setting if you need more magnification to see the specimen clearly. How does *Spirogyra* differ in appearance from the other kinds of algae you have observed in this investigation?
11. In your data table, make a sketch of *Spirogyra.* Label the filaments and the individual cells in your drawing. Also, label the spiral-shaped chloroplasts if they are visible.
12. Clean up your lab materials, and wash your hands before leaving the lab.

## Analysis and Conclusions

1. What characteristics did all of the algae you viewed have in common?
2. Describe examples of specialization in the different kinds of algae you viewed. In which types of algae do some cells depend on others?
3. What differences did you observe between small and large colonies of algae?
4. Which specializations in algae are characteristic of green plants?

## Further Inquiry

How might you search for evidence of evolutionary relationships among algae and between algae and green plants?

Some fungi—such as the fungus *Amanita muscaria,* commonly known as *fly agaric*—are important mutualists in nature. Other fungi are important decomposers of dead organic matter. Although beautiful, *A. muscaria* is poisonous if eaten.

**SECTION 1** *Overview of Fungi*

**SECTION 2** *Classification of Fungi*

**SECTION 3** *Fungi and Humans*

# OVERVIEW OF FUNGI

*F*ungi are in their own kingdom—kingdom Fungi. They differ from other organisms in many ways, including structure, method of reproduction, and methods of obtaining nutrients.

## SECTION 1

### OBJECTIVES

- **List** the characteristics of fungi.
- **Describe** how fungi obtain nutrients.
- **Distinguish** between hyphae and a mycelium.
- **Compare** the ways fungi reproduce.
- **Describe** one hypothesis about the origin of fungi.

### VOCABULARY

mold
yeast
mycology
hypha
chitin
mycelium
septum
coenocyte
dimorphism
sporangiophore
sporangium
sporangiospore
conidium
conidiophore
fragmentation
budding

## CHARACTERISTICS

Fungi are eukaryotic, nonphotosynthetic organisms, and most are multicellular heterotrophs. Most fungi are microscopic molds or yeasts. **Molds,** such as the fungi that grow on bread and oranges, are tangled masses of filaments of cells. **Yeasts** are unicellular fungi whose colonies resemble those of bacteria. Yeasts are best known as the microorganisms that make bread rise. The study of fungi is called **mycology** (mie-KAHL-uh-jee).

### Obtaining Nutrients

Fungi get their nutrients by absorbing organic molecules from their environment. Fungi also secrete enzymes into their food and then absorb the digested nutrients through their cell walls. Like animals, fungi store energy in the form of glycogen. Most fungi are *saprophytic*—that is, they live on organic compounds that they absorb from dead organisms in the environment. This characteristic makes fungi a very important recycler of organic material in nature.

### Structure of Fungi

Filaments of fungi are called **hyphae** (HIE-fee) (singular, *hypha*). The cell walls of hyphae contain **chitin** (KIE-tin), a polysaccharide that also makes up the exoskeleton of insects, crustaceans, and other arthropods. The presence of chitin distinguishes cell walls of fungi from those of plants, which have cellulose but no chitin.

A mat of hyphae that forms the body of a fungus is a **mycelium** (mie-SEE-lee-uhm). In some species, the cells that make up hyphae are divided by cross sections called **septa** (SEP-tuh) (singular, *septum*). Hyphae whose cells are divided by septa are called *septate hyphae.*

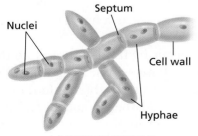

**(a) SEPTATE HYPHAE**

Nuclei
Septum
Cell wall
Hyphae

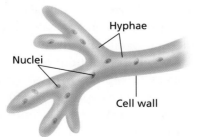

**(b) COENOCYTIC HYPHAE**

Hyphae
Nuclei
Cell wall

**FIGURE 26-1**

The hyphae of some fungi have separating walls called *septa* (a). The hyphae of other fungi do not have septa and are called *coenocytic hyphae* (b).

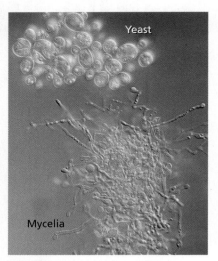

Yeast

Mycelia

**FIGURE 26-2**

This light micrograph shows the dimorphic fungus *Paracoccidioides brasiliensis* as it changes from its unicellular yeast form at 37°C (98.6°F) to a mycelial form at 25°C (77°F).

**FIGURE 26-3**

Fungi reproduce asexually in many ways. Yeasts, such as *Saccharomyces cerevisiae*, form buds that eventually pinch off to produce new cells.

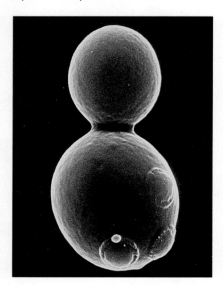

Fungal species that have hyphae lacking septa are called **coenocytes** (SEE-noh-SIETS). The general structures of septate and nonseptate hyphae are shown in Figure 26-1. Hyphae increase in length by cellular growth and division at the tip. As the hyphae grow, the size of the mycelium increases. When hyphae encounter organic matter, such as a tree trunk or dead animal, they secrete digestive enzymes and then absorb the digested nutrients. Fungi range in size from the microscopic yeast to the largest single organism in the world. Fungi of the genus *Armillaria,* or honey mushrooms, can occupy an area of up to 800 hectares (3.1 mi²).

Several species of fungi can change form in response to changes in their environment. For example, *Histoplasma capsulatum,* which causes a severe disease in humans that can resemble tuberculosis, normally grows as a mycelium in soil. However, when it invades a human, the increased temperature and available nutrients cause the fungus to grow unicellularly as a yeast. This ability to exist in two different forms, demonstrated in Figure 26-2, is called **dimorphism** (die-MAWR-FIZ-uhm).

# REPRODUCTION

Most fungi reproduce both sexually and asexually. Unlike most eukaryotes, most fungi are haploid throughout most of their life cycle.

## Asexual Reproduction

Asexually, fungi produce thousands of genetically identical haploid spores, usually on modified cells of the hyphae. When these spores are placed in favorable environmental conditions, they germinate and grow new hyphae, each of which can form a mycelium and produce thousands of new asexual spores.

A variety of asexual spores are formed by different fungi. For example, **sporangiophores** (spoh-RAN-jee-oh-FAWHRZ) are specialized hyphae that look like upright stalks. On top of a sporangiophore is a sac called a **sporangium** (spoh-RAN-jee-UHM). Inside each sporangium, spores called **sporangiospores** (spoh-RAN-jee-oh-SPOHRZ) are made. *Rhizopus,* the black mycelial fungus that is commonly found growing on bread, is a sporangiospore-forming fungus.

Other fungi form spores called **conidia** (koh-NID-ee-uh) (singular, *conidium*), which are formed without the protection of a sac. Conidia are formed on top of a stalklike structure called a **conidiophore** (koh-NID-ee-uh-FAWHR). *Penicillium,* which is used to produce penicillin and certain types of cheeses, is a fungus that reproduces asexually by means of conidia.

Asexual reproduction may also occur by **fragmentation.** In this process, a septate hypha dries and shatters, releasing individual cells that act as spores. The fungus that causes athlete's foot reproduces this way. Yeasts reproduce by a process called budding, shown in Figure 26-3. **Budding** is an asexual process in which part of a yeast cell pinches itself off to produce a small offspring cell.

## TABLE 26-1 Three Phyla of Fungi

| Phylum and number of species | Structure | Asexual reproduction | Sexual reproduction (where identified) | Examples |
|---|---|---|---|---|
| Zygomycota 600 species | coenocytic hyphae | spores from sporangia | conjugation results in zygospores | *Mucor, Rhizopus* |
| Basidiomycota 25,000 species | septate hyphae | rare (conidia in a few species) | basidia produce basidiospores | *Puccinia, Ustilago* (mushrooms) |
| Ascomycota 60,000 species | septate or unicellular hyphae | conidia, budding | asci produce ascospores | yeasts, morels, *Penicillium* species |

## Sexual Reproduction

Many, but not all, species of fungi are also able to reproduce sexually. Fungi are neither male nor female. Instead, they occur in mating types that are sometimes called *minus* and *plus*. When two different mating types of the same species encounter one another, the hyphae of one mating type fuse with the hyphae of the opposite mating type. These fused hyphae give rise to a specialized structure, which produces and scatters genetically diverse spores.

The ability of some fungi to reproduce both sexually and asexually provides an adaptive advantage. When the environment is favorable, rapid asexual reproduction can ensure an increased spread of the species. During environmental stress, sexual reproduction can ensure genetic diversity, increasing the likelihood that offspring will be better adapted to the new environmental conditions.

### Eco Connection

**Fungi in the Food Chain**

The northern spotted owl depends indirectly on a forest fungus for its survival. The owls prey on northern flying squirrels, and the squirrels depend on truffles for the bulk of their diet. Truffles are the sexual reproductive structure of some fungal species.

## EVOLUTION

The first fungi were probably unicellular organisms that might have clung together after mitosis. Biologists hypothesize that fungi colonized land at about the same time that early plants did. They reason that fungi, like other eukaryotes, arose from endosymbiotic prokaryotes. According to the fossil record, fungi first appeared about 460 million years ago. Three phyla of modern fungi are listed in Table 26-1.

internet connect

**www.scilinks.org**
**Topic:** Fungi
**Keyword:** HM60628

SCI LINKS. Maintained by the National Science Teachers Association

---

## SECTION 1 REVIEW

1. Name three characteristics found in all fungi.

2. Describe how fungi obtain nutrients.

3. What is the difference between hyphae and a mycelium?

4. Identify three forms of asexual reproduction in fungi.

5. Describe one hypothesis about the origin of fungi.

**CRITICAL THINKING**

6. **Analyzing Concepts** How does being saprophytic make fungi important recyclers in nature?

7. **Making Inferences** Explain how fungi could have adapted to living on land *before* plants did.

8. **Evaluating Information** How can both sexual and asexual reproduction have an adaptive advantage over just asexual reproduction?

OBJECTIVES

● **List** characteristics that distinguish three phyla of fungi.
● **Compare** the life cycles of zygomycetes, basidomycetes, and ascomycetes.
● **Distinguish** between mycorrhizae and lichens.
● **Explain** the importance of mycorrhizae and lichens to the environment.

VOCABULARY

rhizoid
stolon
gametangium
zygosporangium
basidium
basidiocarp
basidiospore
ascogonium
antheridium
ascocarp
ascus
ascospore
mycorrhiza
lichen

# CLASSIFICATION OF FUNGI

*F*ungi are classified in three phyla. Traditionally, fungi have been classified according to their structure and form of sexual reproduction. Though no longer the sole bases of classification, these characteristics are still useful in identifying fungi.

## PHYLUM ZYGOMYCOTA

Most species in the phylum Zygomycota (ZIE-goh-mie-KOH-tuh) are terrestrial organisms found primarily in soil that is rich in organic matter. The hyphae of zygomycetes are coenocytic. *Rhizopus stolonifer,* the common bread fungus shown in Figure 26-4, is a zygomycete. The hyphae that anchor the mold to the surface of the bread and that penetrate the bread's surface are called **rhizoids** (RIE-ZOYDZ). Digestive enzymes produced by rhizoids break down the bread to release nutrients. Other hyphae, called **stolons** (STOH-LAHNZ), grow across the surface of the bread.

Sexual reproduction in zygomycetes is called *conjugation.* Conjugation in fungi occurs when the hyphae of two compatible mating types (parents) meet. Short branches form on the hyphae of both types and grow outward until they touch each other. A septum forms near the tip of each branch, and a cell called a gametangium develops. A **gametangium** (GAM-uh-TAN-jee-uhm) is a sexual reproductive structure that contains a nucleus of a mating type. The nucleus within each parent's gametangium divides several times. When the gametangia fuse, the nuclei mix and form into pairs, each pair containing a nucleus from each mating type.

**FIGURE 26-4**

During sexual reproduction zygomycetes produce gametangia. The nuclei from both mating types fuse and eventually produce genetically diverse spores.

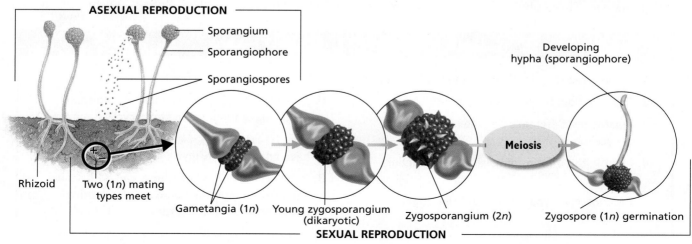

ASEXUAL REPRODUCTION

Sporangium
Sporangiophore
Sporangiospores

Developing hypha (sporangiophore)

**Meiosis**

Rhizoid

Two (1*n*) mating types meet

Gametangia (1*n*)

Young zygosporangium (dikaryotic)

Zygosporangium (2*n*)

Zygospore (1*n*) germination

SEXUAL REPRODUCTION

Fused gametangia form a structure called a **zygosporangium** (ZIE-goh-spoh-RAN-jee-uhm), which contains many diploid nuclei. The zygosporangium then forms a thick wall and becomes dormant. Germination depends on environmental conditions. A sporangiophore grows from the diploid zygosporangium and produces a sporangium, which releases numerous haploid spores.

# PHYLUM BASIDIOMYCOTA

Basidiomycetes (buh-SID-ee-oh-MIE-SEETS) are often called *club fungi* because during sexual reproduction, they produce small, clublike reproductive structures called **basidia** (buh-SID-ee-uh) (singular, *basidium*). Sexual reproduction in basidiomycetes is shown in Figure 26-5. The spore-bearing structure of basidiomycetes is an aboveground structure called the **basidiocarp** (buh-SID-ee-oh-KAHRP). Mushrooms are basidiocarps. The basidiocarp consists of a stem called a *stalk* and a flattened structure known as a *cap*. On the underside of the cap are rows of *gills* that radiate out from the center. As shown in step ❶, each gill is lined with thousands of dikaryotic (die-KAR-ee-AHT-ik) basidia. Dikaryotic cells contain two nuclei. Step ❷ shows that in each basidium, two nuclei fuse to form a zygote (2*n*). In step ❸, the zygote undergoes meiosis to form four haploid nuclei. These develop into four **basidiospores** (buh-SID-ee-oh-SPAWRZ), which are released into the air. As shown in step ❹, under favorable environmental conditions, basidiospores germinate to produce haploid mycelia that grow underground. In steps ❺ and ❻, when compatible mating types encounter one another, their hyphae fuse and form a basidiocarp, which emerges aboveground.

## Quick Lab

### Dissecting a Mushroom

**Materials** mushroom, scalpel, hand lens, slides, coverslips, water, microscope

**Procedure**
1. Before beginning, tell your teacher if you are allergic to fungi. Cut the cap of a mushroom lengthwise.
2. Examine the mushroom with a hand lens. Draw and write down your observations.
3. Make a wet mount of the hyphae. Use a microscope to observe the cell structure of the hyphae.

**Analysis** What structures did you observe with the hand lens? with the microscope? What is the function of each structure?

**FIGURE 26-5**

Basidiomycetes usually reproduce sexually by means of a fruiting body, also called a *mushroom*.

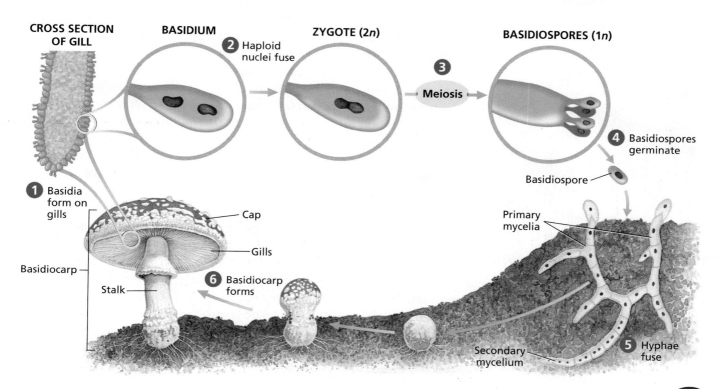

CROSS SECTION OF GILL

BASIDIUM

❷ Haploid nuclei fuse

ZYGOTE (2*n*)

❸ Meiosis

BASIDIOSPORES (1*n*)

❹ Basidiospores germinate

Basidiospore

❶ Basidia form on gills

Cap

Gills

Basidiocarp

Stalk

❻ Basidiocarp forms

Primary mycelia

Secondary mycelium

❺ Hyphae fuse

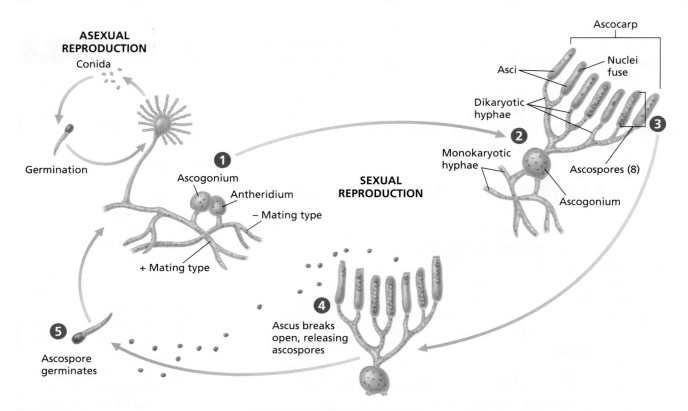

**ASEXUAL REPRODUCTION**

Conida

Germination

① Ascogonium

Antheridium

– Mating type

+ Mating type

**SEXUAL REPRODUCTION**

Ascocarp

Asci

Nuclei fuse

Dikaryotic hyphae

② 

③

Monokaryotic hyphae

Ascospores (8)

Ascogonium

④ Ascus breaks open, releasing ascospores

⑤ Ascospore germinates

**FIGURE 26-6**

① Compatible mating types form special structures that fuse to form an ascogonium. ② From the ascogonium, dikaryotic hyphae grow and intertwine with monokaryotic hyphae to form an ascocarp. ③ The tips of the dikaryotic hyphae form asci inside, and ascospores form. ④ When the ascus ruptures, it releases the ascospores, which then germinate, ⑤, to form new monokaryotic hyphae.

**FIGURE 26-7**

These ascocarps of the ascomycete *Sarcoscypha coccinea,* commonly known as the *scarlet cup fungus,* are the structures from which ascospores are released during sexual reproduction.

# PHYLUM ASCOMYCOTA

Ascomycetes (AS-koh-MIE-seets) are distinguished by the presence of saclike compartments where sexually produced spores form. Ascomycetes, also called *sac fungi,* live parasitically and in various habitats, including salt water, fresh water, and land.

Sexual reproduction in the ascomycetes begins when the hyphae of two different haploid mating types form male and female haploid gametangia. The female gametangium is called an **ascogonium** (AS-koh-GOH-nee-uhm), and the male gametangium is called an **antheridium** (AN-thuhr-ID-ee-uhm), as shown in Figure 26-6. As the ascogonium and antheridium approach one another, a tube forms between them, and the nuclei from the antheridium cross the tube and enter the ascogonium. Dikaryotic hyphae grow out of the ascogonium and intertwine with the monokaryotic hyphae of the original fungi (parents) to form a visible cuplike structure called the **ascocarp** (AS-koh-KAHRP). Cells that contain one nucleus are called *monokaryotic* (mahn-oh-KAR-ee-AHT-ik). An example of an ascocarp is shown in Figure 26-7.

Within the ascocarp, sacs called **asci** (AS-KIE) (singular, *ascus*) develop at the tips of the dikaryotic hyphae. Within the asci, the haploid nuclei fuse. The resulting zygotes undergo meiosis once and divide again by mitosis to form eight haploid nuclei. The nuclei form walls and become **ascospores** (AS-koh-SPAWRZ). When an ascospore is released and germinates, a new haploid hypha emerges.

Many yeasts, such as *Saccharomyces cerevisiae,* are ascomycetes. *S. cerevisiae* makes bread rise, ferments grapes to make wine and grain to make beer, and is an important research organism.

## Deuteromycota

Fungi that do not have a sexual stage are classified in a group called *fungi imperfecti,* or deuteromycota. Continuing phylogenetic analyses have led some mycologists to place these fungi in the three established phyla. Most species of fungi that were formerly classified as fungi imperfecti can now be classified in the phylum Ascomycota. However, some biologists disagree with this reclassification.

**Word Roots and Origins**

*mycorrhiza*

from the Greek *mykes,* meaning "fungus," and *rhiza,* meaning "root"

# MYCORRHIZAE AND LICHENS

A **mycorrhiza** (MIE-koh-RIE-zuh) is a symbiotic structure formed by a fungus and plant roots. More than 80 percent of vascular plants contain such fungi on their roots. The fungus absorbs and concentrates nitrogen, phosphate, and other ions for delivery to the plant root and increases surface area of the plant's root system. In turn, the fungus receives sugars that the plant makes during photosynthesis. All three fungal phyla form mycorrhizae. These mycorrhizal relationships appear to have coevolved with plants.

**Lichens** (LIE-kuhnz) represent symbiotic relationships between a fungus and a photosynthetic partner (usually a cyanobacterium or green alga). Most fungi in lichens are ascomycetes. The photosynthesizer makes sugars for the fungus, and the fungus provides moisture, shelter, and anchorage for the photosynthesizer. The fungus produces acids that decompose rocks, making minerals available to the lichen. The chemical decomposition of rocks by lichens contributes to the production of soil.

Lichens are identified according to their distribution and structure. *Crustose lichens* grow as a layer on the surface of rocks and trees. *Fruticose lichens* are shrublike, and some grow up to 1.5 m (5 ft) in length. *Foliose lichens* live on flat surfaces, where they form matlike growths with tangled bodies. One example of a lichen is shown in Figure 26-8.

**FIGURE 26-8**

Lichens are grouped according to their type of body. For example, this red lichen is a crustose lichen that grows on rocks.

## SECTION 2 REVIEW

1. Compare and contrast the basidiocarp with the ascocarp.

2. What is the difference between a rhizoid and a stolon?

3. Describe the Ascomycota life cycle.

4. What are mycorrhizae and lichens?

5. How are mycorrhizae and lichens important to the environment?

**CRITICAL THINKING**

6. **Recognizing Differences** What is the difference between a dikaryotic fungal cell and a diploid fungal zygote?

7. **Predicting Results** If the mycorrhizae in a forest were to suddenly die off, what would probably happen to plants in the forest?

8. **Evaluating Information** What is the importance of conjugation for fungi?

OBJECTIVES

- **Describe** three ways that fungi cause disease in humans.
- **List** three ways that fungi contribute to good health.
- **Provide** examples of fungi's industrial importance.
- **List** three types of food that fungi provide.

VOCABULARY

aflatoxin

internet connect

www.scilinks.org
**Topic:** Yeast and Molds
**Keyword:** HM61678

*sci*LINKS. Maintained by the National Science Teachers Association

**FIGURE 26-9**

Ringworm is a fungal infection of the skin. The dried skin that falls off a lesion is contaminated with fungal spores. These spores can infect other people and spread the infection.

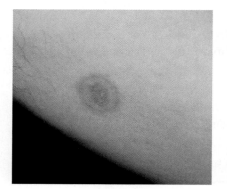

# FUNGI AND HUMANS

*Fungi are important to humans. Some fungi cause devastating human and plant diseases, while others serve as important food sources for humans. Fungi are also used to produce chemicals, fuels, and pharmaceutical compounds.*

## HUMAN FUNGAL DISEASES

Certain fungi can attack the tissues of living plants and animals and cause disease. Fungal disease is a major concern for humans because fungi attack not only us but also our food sources, making fungi competitors with humans for nutrients.

Mold spores can cause mild to serious allergies in some people. Mold spores can become airborne and may then be inhaled, triggering an allergic reaction. Sniffling, sneezing, and respiratory distress are symptoms of an allergic reaction. Some fungi can also infect and poison humans. Table 26-2 lists some human fungal diseases.

### Common Fungal Infections

Fungi may infect the skin, hair, nails, and tissues of the body. For example, fungi on the skin can cause ringworm. Ringworm, as shown in Figure 26-9, can occur almost anywhere on the skin. Athlete's foot, another form of ringworm, occurs on the foot and between the toes.

Another fungal pathogen is *Candida albicans.* This yeast is commonly found in the mouth, intestine, and, in women, in the vaginal tract. Generally, *C. albicans* exists in balance with other microorganisms, such as bacteria that live in and on the body. However, if the normal balance of microorganisms changes, such as when some antibiotics are used or when pregnancy or illness occurs, *C. albicans* can flourish and cause a disease called *candidiasis,* commonly known as a *yeast infection.*

### Other Fungal Illnesses

Serious fungal diseases that involve the internal organs are often caused by dimorphic fungi such as *Histoplasma capsulatum, Paracoccidiodes brasiliensis, Coccidioides immitis,* and *Blastomyces dermatitidis.* If the spores of these fungi are inhaled, they can cause severe respiratory illness and spread to other organs, sometimes resulting in death. They grow as a mold in soil, but at human body temperature (37°C or 98.6°F), they become unicellular. *H. capsulatum* often grows as a mold in the feces of birds and can become airborne and inhaled when feces dry out. In some people, the mold causes *histoplasmosis,* which is characterized by fever and respiratory problems that resemble those of tuberculosis.

### TABLE 26-2 Some Common Human Fungal Diseases

| Disease | Symptoms | Fungus/Phylum | Route of transmission |
|---|---|---|---|
| Athlete's foot | fluid-filled blisters, scaly skin, itching | species of the genus *Trichophyton* or species of the genus *Epidermophyton* (Ascomycota) | contact with skin lesions or contaminated floors |
| Ringworm | ring-shaped skin lesions | *Microsporum, Trichophyton* (Ascomycota) | contact with skin lesions, contaminated floors, or contaminated objects |
| Candidiasis (yeast infection) | burning sensation, itching, thick discharge | *Candida* (Ascomycota) | poorly controlled diabetes; antibiotic treatments increase susceptibility |
| Tinea cruris (jock itch) | intense itching, ring-shaped lesions | *Microsporum, Trichophyton* (Ascomycota) | contact with skin lesions, contaminated floors, or contaminated objects |
| Histoplasmosis | fever, chills, headache, body aches, chest pains, nonproductive cough | *Histoplasma capsulatum* (Ascomycota) | inhalation of airborne conidia |

Sometimes, humans accidentally eat poisonous mushrooms. For example, many species from genus *Amanita* resemble edible mushrooms. However, they contain extremely dangerous toxins that can quickly destroy a person's liver. Figure 26-10 shows an *Amanita* mushroom. Poisonous mushrooms cause varying symptoms when eaten, including upset stomach, vomiting, or diarrhea. Some species can cause death.

Other fungal toxins include the **aflatoxins** (AF-luh-*tahks*-ins), poisons produced by some species of *Aspergillus*. Aflatoxins can cause liver cancer. Fungi that make aflatoxin can contaminate corn, peanuts, cottonseed, and tree nuts.

**FIGURE 26-10**

Poisonous mushrooms, such as this *Amanita virosa* (death angel) harm people when they are mistaken for edible mushrooms.

# FUNGI IN INDUSTRY

Fungi produce many products used in nonfood industries. Several fungal species are used in the production of important medicines. For example, species of the genus *Penicillium* produce the antibiotic penicillin, and species of the genus *Cephalosporium* produce cephalosporin antibiotics. Species of the genus *Rhizopus* cause chemical transformations of specific chemicals to make cortisone, an anti-inflammatory drug used to treat skin rashes and reduce joint swelling.

The yeast *Saccharomyces cerevisiae* is an important tool in genetic engineering. For example, the vaccine for hepatitis B was developed by inserting hepatitis B genes into yeast plasmids. The yeast uses the inserted viral genes to produce viral proteins that are used as vaccines. Yeast is also used to produce ethanol, a main ingredient in the automobile fuel gasohol.

**FIGURE 26-11**

Morels and truffles are prized for their delicate flavor. Truffles (top) grow in association with oak trees. Morels (bottom) grow wild in the Americas and are usually found in the spring.

**TABLE 26-3** *Food Products and Fungi*

| Type of food | Fungus |
|---|---|
| Cheeses: blue, brie, Camembert, Gorgonzola, Roquefort | species of the genus *Penicillium* |
| Beer, wine | *Saccharomyces carlsbergensis*, *Saccharomyces cerevisiae* |
| Soy products: miso (Japanese), soy sauce, tempeh (Indonesian), tofu (Japanese) | *Aspergillus oryzae*, species of the genus *Rhizopus*, species of the genus *Mucor* |
| Nutritional yeast | species of the genus *Saccharomyces* |
| Breads | *Saccharomyces cerevisiae* |

## Fungi and Food Industries

Many fungi are valuable food sources for humans. Yeast, such as species of the genus *Saccharomyces,* is an important nutritional supplement because it contains vitamins, minerals, and other nutrients. Species of the genus *Agaricus* (white button), shiitake, and portabella mushrooms are often found in grocery stores in the United States. People also prize the taste of other fungi, such as truffles and morels, which are pictured in Figure 26-11. Truffles and morels are ascocarps found near the roots of trees. Table 26-3 summarizes some of the uses of fungi in food.

Fungi can also cause damage to foods. Many fungi are important plant pathogens that attack grain or fruit. For example, wheat rust is a basidiomycete that attacks wheat grains. Other fungi can attack crops such as corn, beans, onions, squashes, and tomatoes.

Fungi also produce several chemical compounds that are important to the food-processing industry, such as citric and gluconic acids. Citric acid is used in soft drinks and candies. *Ashbya gossypii* is a producer of vitamin $B_2$, an important nutritional supplement.

## SECTION 3 REVIEW

1. Identify three ways in which fungi can cause disease in humans.

2. How are fungi used to promote health?

3. Name three nonfood substances that are produced by fungi.

4. List three types of foods that are derived from fungi.

**CRITICAL THINKING**

5. **Relating Concepts** How might upsetting the balance of microorganisms in the body cause a yeast infection?

6. **Applying Information** Why might it be better to rely on fungi to produce citric acid instead of the older method of extracting the acid from lemons?

7. **Comparing Concepts** How do lichens help the process of biological succession?

# CHAPTER HIGHLIGHTS

Overview of Fungi

- Fungi are eukaryotic, nonphotosynthetic organisms that can be unicellular or multicellular in form.
- Fungi are among the most important decomposers of organic matter. Fungi obtain nutrients by secreting enzymes and absorbing simple organic molecules from their environment.
- Fungi are made up of short filaments called hyphae. Mats of hyphae are called mycelium. Some species have partitions called septa in their hyphae, making individual cells. Fungal cell walls contain chitin rather than cellulose, which is found in plant cell walls.
- Most fungi reproduce both asexually and sexually.
- Fungi evolved about 460 million years ago. Fungi probably evolved from prokaryotes and then adapted to various terrestrial environments.

### Vocabulary

| | | | |
|---|---|---|---|
| mold (p. 527) | chitin (p. 527) | dimorphism (p. 528) | conidium (p. 528) |
| yeast (p. 527) | mycelium (p. 527) | sporangiophore (p. 528) | conidiophore (p. 528) |
| mycology (p. 527) | septum (p. 527) | sporangium (p. 528) | fragmentation (p. 528) |
| hypha (p. 527) | coenocyte (p. 528) | sporangiospore (p. 528) | budding (p. 528) |

Classification of Fungi

- The phylum Zygomycota is coenocytic (their hyphae lack septa). Asexual sporangiospores form within sacs called sporangia. Sexual reproduction results in zygospores.
- The phylum Basidiomycota includes mushrooms. Mushrooms are sexual reproductive structures called *basidiocarps*. Basidiocarps produce basidia, on which basidiospores form.
- Most fungi are in the phylum Ascomycota, or sac fungi. Hyphae form a cup-shaped ascocarp, in which ascospores form.
- Yeast are unicellular Ascomycota. They reproduce asexually by budding. Yeast are used in brewing, baking, and genetic engineering.
- Mycorrhizae are symbiotic structures that form between plant roots and a fungus. The fungus provides certain ions and other nutrients to the plant and, in turn, the fungus gets sugars from the plant.
- Lichens represent symbiotic relationships between fungi and photosynthetic organisms, such as cyanobacteria or green algae.

### Vocabulary

| | | | |
|---|---|---|---|
| rhizoid (p. 530) | basidium (p. 531) | antheridium (p. 532) | mycorrhiza (p. 533) |
| stolon (p. 530) | basidiocarp (p. 531) | ascocarp (p. 532) | lichen (p. 533) |
| gametangium (p. 530) | basidiospore (p. 531) | ascus (p. 532) | |
| zygosporangium (p. 531) | ascogonium (p. 532) | ascospore (p. 532) | |

Fungi and Humans

- Fungi can cause disease in humans when humans inhale airborne spores, when they eat food contaminated by toxic fungi, when toxic fungi come in contact with skin, or when they accidentally eat poisonous mushrooms.
- Pathogenic fungi that cause serious disease include *Histoplasma capsulatum, Blastomyces dermatitidis,* and *Coccidioides immitis. H. capsulatum* is associated with bird feces.
- Various fungi are used in the production of vitamin $B_2$, cortisone, penicillin and other antibiotics, and some genetically engineered drugs.
- Fungi are used in the production of familiar foods such as cheeses, bread, beer, wines, and soy products.

### Vocabulary

aflatoxin (p. 535)

# CHAPTER REVIEW

## USING VOCABULARY

1. For each pair of terms, explain how the meanings of the terms differ.
   a. *hypha* and *mycelium*
   b. *septate hyphae* and *coenocytic hyphae*
   c. *basidiocarp* and *ascocarp*
   d. *mycorrhiza* and *mycelium*

2. Choose the term that does not belong in the following group, and explain why it does not belong: *hypha, mycelium,* and *lichen.*

3. Use each of the following terms in a separate sentence: *mold, yeast, chitin,* and *rhizoid.*

4. **Word Roots and Origins** The word *gametangium* comes from two Greek words: *gamete,* meaning "spouse," and *angeion,* meaning "case" or "capsule." Using this information, explain why *gametangium* is a suitable term for what happens when two different mating types of fungal filaments meet.

## UNDERSTANDING KEY CONCEPTS

5. **State** how fungi and plants differ from each other.

6. **Explain** how hyphae provide nutrients for a fungus.

7. **Name** the structure that makes up the body of a fungus.

8. **List** three methods of asexual reproduction in fungi.

9. **Summarize** one hypothesis about the origin of fungi.

10. **Define** *dimorphism* and give an example of a fungus that is dimorphic.

11. **Name** an example of each of the three phyla of modern fungi.

12. **Describe** why some fungi are called *club fungi.*

13. **Differentiate** between a root and a rhizoid.

14. **Differentiate** between a gametangium and a zygosporangium.

15. **Summarize** the similarities between a mycorrhiza and a lichen.

16. **Explain** how mycorrhizae are of importance to both plants and fungi.

17. **Relate** how a fungus in bird feces can be potentially dangerous to humans.

18. **List** three ways in which fungi are beneficial to the health of humans.

19. **Identify** a chemical compound used in candies and soft drinks that is produced by certain fungi.

20. **Give** two examples of foods that are produced with the use of fungi.

21. **CONCEPT MAPPING** Use the following terms to create a concept map that shows the sequence of events in the formation of an ascocarp and that begins with a germinating ascospore: *ascocarp, ascogonium, asci, tube, ascospores, meiosis, antheridium,* and *mitosis.*

## CRITICAL THINKING

22. **Interpreting Graphics** A winemaker experimenting with three different strains of yeast charts the number of viable yeast remaining in the wine as the grapes ferment. The three strains were grown in separate containers, at the same temperature, and with the same type of grape. Give reasons why strain C survived longer than strains A and B.

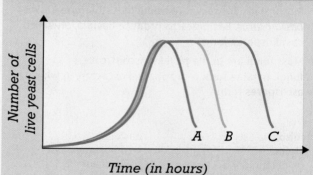

**Growth of Three Strains of Yeast**

*Number of live yeast cells* (vertical axis)

*A   B   C*

*Time (in hours)* (horizontal axis)

23. **Critiquing Relationships** Comment on the validity of this statement: The relationship mycorrhizae have with trees is an example of mutualism.

24. **Relating Concepts** What adaptive advantage does dimorphism give a fungus?

25. **Analyzing Concepts** What advantages might a fungal spore have over a seed?

26. **Applying Information** A folk remedy for the treatment of an infected wound calls for a piece of moistened, moldy bread to be placed on the wound. How might this practice help a wound to heal?

# Standardized Test Preparation

**DIRECTIONS:** Choose the letter of the answer choice that best answers the question.

1. What are fungi that feed on decaying organic matter called?
   A. parasites
   B. mutualists
   C. symbionts
   D. saprophytes

2. Lichens represent a symbiotic association between a fungus and which other type of organism?
   F. an alga
   G. a plant
   H. a mold
   J. a rhizoid

3. In a mycorrhiza, a fungus lives in a symbiotic relationship with which of the following?
   A. a virus
   B. a plant
   C. a bacterium
   D. a slime mold

**INTERPRETING GRAPHICS:** The diagram below shows the fruiting bodies of a type of fungus. Use the diagram to answer the questions that follow.

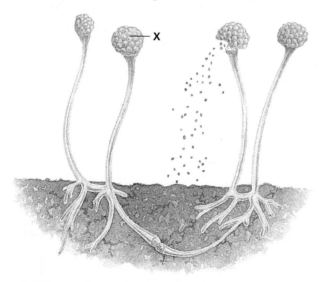

4. What is the structure labeled *X* called?
   F. a hypha
   G. a zygote
   H. a sporangium
   J. a sporangiospore

5. To what phylum does the fungus in the diagram above belong?
   A. Ascomycota
   B. Zygomycota
   C. Basidiomycota
   D. fungi imperfecti

**DIRECTIONS:** Complete the following analogy.

6. septa : septum :: asci :
   F. ascus
   G. ascocarp
   H. ascospore
   J. ascogonium

**INTERPRETING GRAPHICS:** The diagram below shows the typical structure of a member of the phylum Basidiomycota. Use the diagram below to answer the question that follows.

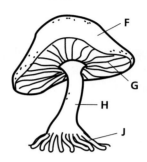

7. Which structure is responsible for meeting the food requirements of the organism shown?
   A. F
   B. G
   C. H
   D. J

## SHORT RESPONSE

Fungi are important decomposers that break down organic matter.

Explain how fungi contribute to nutrient recycling in the environment.

## EXTENDED RESPONSE

Fungi are major competitors with humans for food.

*Part A* Explain what needs humans and fungi have in common.

*Part B* Explain why fungi could easily win the battle for nutrients.

**Test TIP** When studying for a test on fungi life cycles, organize the information into a table. It will be easier to recall information from isolated parts of the table when you have to answer a question.

# Exploring the Growth of Fungi on Food

## OBJECTIVES

- Recognize fungal growth on food.
- Identify environmental conditions that favor the growth of fungi on food.

## PROCESS SKILLS

- designing an experiment
- collecting data
- analyzing results
- hypothesizing
- organizing data

## MATERIALS

- safety goggles
- lab apron
- disposable gloves
- 2 sterile Petri dishes with nutrient medium (such as potato dextrose agar)
- 2 sterile Petri dishes with nutrient medium and propionic acid
- fungal samples
- stereomicroscope
- toothpicks
- wax pencil
- masking tape

## Background

1. How do multicellular fungi, such as molds, obtain nutrients?
2. How do multicellular fungi reproduce and grow?
3. What ecological role do fungi fulfill?
4. How might a fungus growing on food harm someone who eats it?

### PART A  Experimental Setup

1. **CAUTION  Tell your teacher if you have any allergies to fungi. Put on safety goggles, a lab apron, and disposable gloves.** Obtain four sterile Petri dishes, two with nutrient medium and two with nutrient medium plus propionic acid. Label the dishes for the presence or absence of propionic acid.
2. Examine the fungal samples through a dissecting microscope. Select a dense growth of a fungus from which you will take samples.
3. Use a toothpick to scoop up a small sample of the fungus you have selected. In the two Petri dishes without propionic acid, gently touch the sample to the medium in four places. Raise the lids of the dishes as little as possible while doing this. Do the same for the two Petri dishes with propionic acid, using a clean toothpick and another small sample of the same fungus. Dispose of the toothpicks according to the teacher's instructions.
4. Place a piece of masking tape on opposite sides of each dish to hold the lid and bottom together. Label each Petri dish with your name.
5. Design an experiment to determine which of two opposite environmental conditions is better for fungal growth. Some possible combinations are warm/cold, light/dark, and moist/dry. Label one of the dishes that contain propionic acid with one of the two environmental conditions you selected. Label the other dish with the other condition. Do the same for the two dishes that do not contain propionic acid. Then, incubate all four dishes under the appropriate conditions.

## FUNGAL GROWTH IN DIFFERENT ENVIRONMENTS

| Dish | Environmental condition | Propionic acid? | Source of fungus | Growth |
|------|------------------------|-----------------|------------------|--------|
| 1 | | | | |
| 2 | | | | |
| 3 | | | | |
| 4 | | | | |

**6.** Create a data table similar to the model above to record your experimental observations for your lab report. For example, the table above is designed to record any growth that may occur under two different environmental conditions (warm/cold, sunlight/dark, moist/dry), the source of the fungus, and if propionic acid is present. Design your data table to fit your own experiment. Remember to allow plenty of space to record your observations. Be sure to label your Petri dishes with the appropriate environmental conditions and with the date on which the experiment began.

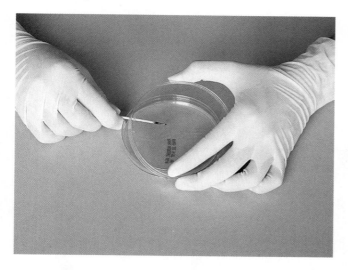

**PART B** **Comparing Amounts of Growth**

**7.** After one week, examine each dish under the stereomicroscope without opening the dish.

**8.** Record your observations in your data table in your lab report.

**9.** Examine the fungi in other groups' dishes, especially fungi grown under different environmental conditions.

**10.** Add your observations of those dishes to your lab report.

**11.** Clean up your materials, and wash your hands before leaving the lab. Dispose of all materials according to instructions provided by your teacher.

### Analysis and Conclusions

**1.** Besides the environmental conditions you chose, what additional factor was tested in your experiment?

**2.** What steps were taken in your experiment to avoid contamination of the plates?

**3.** How would contamination of the plates affect the results of your experiment? What are the possible sources of contamination of your experiment?

**4.** What does extensive fungal growth on a plate indicate? What does lack of fungal growth on a plate indicate?

**5.** What effect does propionic acid have on fungal growth? How do you know?

**6.** Why do you think propionic acid is added to foods?

**7.** Which environmental conditions favor fungal growth? Which inhibit it?

**8.** Compare the results for the different kinds of fungi grown. Did fungi from certain food sources grow more rapidly than others?

**9.** Based on your conclusions, under what conditions would you keep a nonsterile food product if you wanted to prevent it from becoming moldy?

**10.** Has this lab changed your attitude toward food storage? If so, how?

### Further Inquiry

Design an experiment that determines which kinds of foods best support fungal growth and whether the presence of chemicals inhibits fungal growth.

# PLANTS

66 *The day passed delightfully. Delight itself, however, is a weak term to express the feelings of a naturalist who, for the first time, has wandered by himself in a Brazilian forest. The elegance of the grasses, the novelty of the parasitical plants, the beauty of the flowers, the glossy green of the foliage, but above all the general luxuriance of the vegetation, filled me with admiration.* 99

Charles Darwin, *Voyage of the* Beagle, *1839*

References to *Scientific American* project ideas are located throughout this unit.

**internet** connect

National Science Teachers Association *sci* LINKS Internet resources are located throughout this unit.

SCI LINKS. **Maintained by the National Science Teachers Association**

*These autumn leaves show bright colors because they have lost most of their chlorophyll.*

Rafflesia arnoldii *has the largest known flowers.*
*Although they are large and beautiful, these*
*flowers emit the smell of rotting meat, which*
*attracts flies as pollinators.*

**Strawberry plants have above-ground stems that are able to form new plants.**

*This cotton boll developed from the ovary of a flower of a cotton plant.*

*Orchid cactus*

# THE IMPORTANCE OF PLANTS

Rice fields, often called paddies, thrive in regions with abundant rainfall. Rice is a prime food source for more than 60 percent of the world's population. About 90 percent of the world's rice is grown in Asia, primarily in China and India.

**SECTION 1** *Plants and People*

**SECTION 2** *Plants and the Environment*

# PLANTS AND PEOPLE

*P*lants are essential to our survival because they produce virtually all our food. We eat plants either directly, in the form of fruits, vegetables, and grains, or indirectly, by eating animals that consume plants. Plants also provide medicines, clothing, paper, cosmetics, and many other products. Plants play a major role in the continuous cycling of the Earth's water, oxygen, carbon dioxide, and mineral nutrients. The study of plants is called **botany** *(BAHT-nee).*

### OBJECTIVES

- **Summarize** the history of plant cultivation.
- **Identify** the categories of food crops.
- **Explain** how humans have increased food production in the world.
- **Describe** non-food uses of plants.

### VOCABULARY

botany
agriculture
cultivar
cereal
root crop
legume
fruit
vegetable
nut
spice
herb
quinine
fertilizer
pesticide
aspirin
gasohol

## PLANT CULTIVATION

Of the more than 350,000 plant species, people use at least 10,000 species for food. Incredibly, fewer than 20 plant species provide more than 90 percent of our food supply. The cultivation of plants for food probably began about 11,000 years ago in the Middle East. Wheat, barley, lentils, and peas were the first domesticated food crops. Growing plants and raising animals for human use is called **agriculture** (AG-ri-KUHL-chuhr). People propagated, or reproduced, individual plants that had valuable characteristics, such as plants that produced the largest or tastiest fruits.

In the 11,000 years that humans have been cultivating plants, we have changed many of the plants so much that they could not grow and survive without us. For example, the wild wheat stalk, as shown in Figure 27-1, breaks easily in the wind, an adaptation that increases the dispersal of its seeds. But early farmers used seeds from plants with stalks that did not break easily for replanting. When these plants were grown, the seeds could be harvested before they fell from the plant. This form of selection—with people acting as selecting agents—has resulted in high-quality food plants.

You have probably eaten Thompson Seedless grapes, McIntosh apples, or Valencia oranges. They are just three examples of several hundred thousand different cultivars. The word *cultivar* is a contraction of the two terms *cultivated* and *variety.* **Cultivars** (KUHL-ti-VAHRZ) are selected by people, and they have at least one distinguishing characteristic that sets them apart from other members of their species. The famous Japanese flowering cherry trees in Washington, D.C., Yoshino cherries, are another example of a cultivar.

**FIGURE 27-1**

Wheat is one of the world's most important food crops. It is used to make breads, crackers, macaroni, and spaghetti.

### Making a Plant-Based Menu

**Materials** paper, pencil

**Procedures**

1. Prepare a written lunch menu that consists only of plant-derived foods. Be careful to design a fully nutritional meal. Then, write a description of a lunch setting that is also completely derived from plants, including utensils and furniture.

2. Share your menu and lunch-setting description with your classmates.

**Analysis** Was it difficult or easy to devise a lunch that includes only plant-based items? Write down any interesting or unusual plant choices or purposes for them that you and your classmates included.

# FOOD CROPS

Food crops are usually classified partly by use and partly by family. The classification system in Table 27-1 is not like the taxonomic classification used by scientists because most categories contain species that are not closely related. Also, many crops fit into more than one category. For example, corn is a cereal, but it can also be classified as an oil crop, a sweetener, a vegetable, and a beverage.

## Cereals

**Cereals** are grasses that contain grains. Grains are the edible, dry fruits of a cereal. Over half of the world's cultivated land is devoted to cereal crops, such as rice, wheat, corn, oats, sorghum, rye, and millet. Worldwide, cereals provide about 50 percent of the calories in the average human diet. In addition, much of the harvested grain is used for animal feed, so it is indirectly consumed by people as meat, poultry, eggs, and dairy products.

Wheat and corn are produced in the largest amounts. Wheat grows well in moderate to cold climates, including parts of the United States, Russia, and Canada. The United States is the leading producer of corn, also called maize. Rice is different from other cereals because it grows best in shallow water. Rice thrives in areas with warm temperatures.

### TABLE 27-1 *Food Crops*

| Category | Example plants |
| --- | --- |
| Cereals | rice, wheat, corn, oats, sorghum, rye, barley, millet |
| Root crops | potato, cassava, sweet potato, yam, taro |
| Legumes | soybean, peanut, bean, pea, alfalfa, lentils |
| Fruits | apple, peach, banana, grape, orange, blueberry, pineapple, cherry, mango, pear |
| Nuts | walnut, cashew, pecan, coconut, almond, macadamia, filbert, pistachio |
| Vegetables | spinach, cabbage, sweet corn, pea, turnip, asparagus, tomato, artichoke, zucchini |
| Forages | cereals, legumes, grasses |
| Oils | cottonseed, rapeseed, palm, sesame, soybean, corn, safflower, sunflower |
| Beverages | coffee, tea, cola, cacao, fruit juice, grape (wine), corn (whiskey), barley and hops (beer) |
| Sweeteners | sugar cane, sugar beet, sugar maple, corn |
| Spices | pepper, cinnamon, vanilla, paprika, cloves, saffron, nutmeg, ginger, allspice |
| Herbs | rosemary, thyme, sage, dill, basil, oregano, mint |
| Flavorings | cacao (chocolate), coconut, carob, licorice, quinine |
| Colorings | red beet, anatto, turmeric, saffron, carrot |
| Additives | guar, locust bean, citrus (pectin), gum arabic, chicle tree |
| Garnishes | sesame, caraway, and poppy seeds; parsley; pimento |
| Snacks | popcorn, sunflower seeds, pumpkin seeds |

## Root Crops

**Root crops** are roots or underground stems that are rich in carbohydrates. In many parts of the world, root crops substitute for cereals in providing the major part of the diet. However, diets of root crops or cereals alone are usually low in some important amino acids. To correct this deficiency, people must eat other foods, such as legumes or animal protein.

Root crops include beets, carrots, radishes, rutabagas, turnips, and sweet potatoes. Other kinds of potatoes and yams are actually *tubers* (modified underground stems) but are considered root crops because they grow underground. You may have eaten tapioca pudding, which comes from cassava, a root crop grown in the Tropics and shown in Figure 27-2.

## Legumes

**Legumes** are members of the pea family and bear seeds in pods. Soybean, shown in Figure 27-3, is the most important legume crop because it is produced in the largest amount and has many important uses. Soybean is used to make vegetable oil, soy milk, soy sauce, tofu, and margarine. Alfalfa and clover are legumes used mainly as feed for livestock. Legumes are important in agriculture because they improve the nitrogen content of soil. Recall that some bacteria form a symbiotic relationship with many legumes and convert atmospheric nitrogen into a form that plants can use.

## Fruits, Vegetables, and Nuts

Many "vegetables" we know, such as tomatoes, green beans, and squash, are actually botanically classified as fruits. A **fruit** is the part of a flowering plant that usually contains seeds. Foods derived from the leaves, stems, seeds, and roots of nonwoody plants are often called **vegetables.** Fruits and vegetables are excellent sources of many important vitamins and minerals, making them essential parts of a healthy diet. A **nut** is a dry, hard fruit that does not split open to release its seed. Nuts include almonds, walnuts, pecans, and hazelnuts. Peanuts are commonly considered to be nuts but are actually classified as legumes. Nuts and legumes are higher in protein than other plant foods.

## Spices, Herbs, and Flavorings

Other food crops add variety and pleasure to our diet by flavoring our water, beverages, and food. More than half the population ingests caffeine through drinking coffee, tea, and cola drinks. Both **spices** and **herbs** are used to add taste to food. In general, spices come from plant parts other than the leaf and are tropical. Herbs usually come from leaves and usually can be grown in a home garden. Flavorings, such as chocolate and coconut, are not usually considered spices or herbs and are therefore placed in a separate category. Another flavor, quinine, is used to make tonic water. **Quinine** comes from the bark of the cinchona tree and is used to treat malaria.

**FIGURE 27-2**

An important root crop in the Tropics is cassava, which has thick roots that are eaten like potatoes. The starch-filled roots of cassava can be 30–120 cm (1–4 ft) long.

**FIGURE 27-3**

Soybean is an important legume crop grown in the midwestern and southern parts of the United States. The soybean plant is covered with short, fine fibers and is usually 60–120 cm (2–4 ft) tall. It is an inexpensive and useful source of protein.

Many people are making their own fertilizer through a technique called *composting.* Compost is a type of organic fertilizer that is made from decayed plant matter. Compost improves the texture of soil and provides inorganic nutrients that plants need.

It's easy to start your own compost pile. Collect dead plant matter, such as grass clippings, leaves, coffee grounds, or sawdust. Make a pile by alternating layers of plant matter with a thin layer of soil or manure. Sprinkle water on the pile to speed the process of decay. After the compost has been allowed to decay for about six months, it should be ready for use in your garden.

### Word Roots and Origins

*pesticide*

contains the suffix *-cide,* from the Latin *cida,* meaning "cut down" or "kill"

## Food Production

For decades, experts have been predicting widespread food shortages due to the continuing increase in the world population. However, massive food shortages have not occurred mainly because of increased use of irrigation, fertilizers, and pesticides. Improvements in cultivars; farm machinery; food preservation techniques; and methods of controlling diseases, weeds, and pests have also helped improve food production. **Fertilizers** supply plants with essential mineral nutrients like nitrogen and phosphorus. **Pesticides** are chemicals that kill undesirable organisms that harm crops, such as some insects.

People have made many trade-offs to support an adequate food supply. The negative consequences include massive soil erosion, depletion of fossil fuel and water supplies, pollution, and destruction of wild populations of plants and animals as more land is cultivated.

# NONFOOD USES OF PLANTS

In addition to providing us with food, plants provide us with thousands of other essential products. It is hard to imagine how we could live without plants, given the variety of products that contain substances from plants.

## Medicines

The ancient Greeks treated headaches with the bark of the white willow tree, which contains the chemical salicin. This use gave scientists the idea to test the chemical acetylsalicylic (uh-SEET-uhl-SAL-uh-SIL-ik) acid. The willow is in the genus *Salix,* hence the names *salicin* and *salicylic.* Acetylsalicylic acid is **aspirin,** the world's most widely used medicine. Besides pain relief, aspirin is used to thin blood and thereby prevent heart attacks and strokes. Plants were our first medicines, and early plant biologists, like Linnaeus, were often doctors.

### TABLE 27-2  *Plants in Medicine*

| Plant | Genus name | Drug | Use |
| --- | --- | --- | --- |
| Cinchona | *Cinchona* | quinine | treat malaria and certain disorders of heart rhythm |
| Foxglove | *Digitalis* | digitalis | treat heart disease, help regulate heart rate |
| Yam | *Dioscorea* | cortisone | treat inflammation and allergies |
| White willow | *Salix* | acetylsalicylic acid (aspirin) | relieve pain, prevent heart attacks and strokes |
| Yew | *Taxus* | taxol | treat ovarian cancer, breast cancer, and some types of lung cancer |

(a)

(b)

Many modern medicines either still come from plants or were originally obtained from plants and are now synthesized in the laboratory. Table 27-2 lists examples of plants that are used in medicine. Two of these plants, yew and foxglove, are shown in Figure 27-4. Scientists are currently evaluating thousands of plant species that may have medicinal properties. One of the reasons scientists are very concerned about the destruction of rain forests is because many rain-forest plant species have yet to be researched. In addition to medicines, plants provide many other products, which are summarized on the next page in Table 27-3.

Your local health-food store carries a wide range of plant products that claim to prevent disease or improve health. These substances are not regulated by the Food and Drug Administration (FDA). Consumers should remember that the effectiveness and safety of herbal remedies have not been confirmed by the rigorous scientific testing that new medicines must undergo before receiving FDA approval. The FDA, pharmaceutical companies, and health-care providers are working together to investigate the claims of those who market these remedies.

## Clothing and Fabric Dyes

Figure 27-5 shows cotton, which is used to make most of our clothing. Some clothing is woven with linen, which is made from the flax plant. Artificial fabrics, like rayon, arnel, and cellulose acetate, are made from processed wood fibers. Leather is made from animal hides, but it is usually treated with tannin, a chemical obtained from many tree species. Tannin makes leather stronger and prevents it from rotting.

Prior to the mid-1800s, fabrics were dyed with natural plant dyes. Today most clothing is colored with dyes manufactured from coal, which is formed from the remains of ancient plants.

**FIGURE 27-4**

(a) Taxol, originally derived from the bark of the Pacific yew, is a recently discovered cancer drug. This evergreen tree or shrub produces seeds that look like berries. (b) Foxglove is the source of digitalis, which is used in the treatment of heart disease. The beautiful flowers grow in a cluster.

**FIGURE 27-5**

Cotton, the world's most widely used source of clothing, consists of fibers attached to the seed.

## TABLE 27-3 *Nonfood Uses of Plants*

| Use | Example plants |
|---|---|
| Brooms/brushes | broomcorn, palms, coconut |
| Building materials | trees, bamboo, reeds, palms, grasses |
| Carpets/mats | jute, coconut (coir), cotton, trees |
| Clothing | cotton, flax (linen), ramie, pineapple, trees (rayon and arnel) |
| Cosmetics | corn, avocado, carrot, almond, cacao, soybean, macadamia, aloe |
| Fabric dyes | indigo (blue), madder (red), onion (yellow), black walnut (brown), peach (green), maple (pink) |
| Fuels | trees, bamboo, water hyacinth, grain alcohol, vegetable oils, gopher plant |
| Furniture | redwood, oak, rattan, teak, willow (wicker), rushes |
| Hair dyes | henna, rhubarb, chamomile, black walnut |
| Incense | frankincense, myrrh, cinnamon |
| Inks | soybean, flax (linseed oil), tung-oil tree |
| Leather | black wattle, quebracho, Spanish chestnut (tannin) |
| Lipstick | jojoba, castor bean, carnauba palm, soybean, coconut |
| Medicines and remedies | foxglove (digitalis), cinchona (quinine), yew (taxol), opium poppy (morphine and codeine), yam (cortisone), aloe, ipecac, ginseng, ginkgo, guarana, purple coneflower, kudzu, saw palmetto |
| Miscellaneous | cork oak (cork), incense cedar (pencil shafts), trees (disposable baby diapers and cellulose acetate plastic), kapok (life preserver stuffing), rosary pea (bead necklaces), water hyacinth (water purification), lignum vitae (submarine engine bearings) |
| Musical instruments | ebony (black piano keys), maple (violins), reed (woodwind reeds), African blackwood (woodwinds) |
| Ornamentals | shade trees, shrubs, lawns, cut flowers, Christmas trees, houseplants |
| Paints | flax (linseed oil), tung-oil tree, soybean, pine (turpentine) |
| Paper/cardboard | trees, cotton, flax, hemp, bamboo, papyrus |
| Perfumes | rose, orange, lavender, orchids, sandalwood, lilac, jasmine, lily of the valley, pine |
| Pesticides/repellents | tobacco (nicotine sulfate), derris (rotenone), chrysanthemum (pyrethrum), citronella, garlic, citrus |
| Rope | hemp, agave (sisal) |
| Rubber | rubber tree, guayule |
| Shampoo | palm oil, coconut, jojoba, aloe, trees, herbs, fruits |
| Soaps | coconut, palm oil, cacao, lavender, herbs, fruits |
| Sports equipment | balata (golf balls), persimmon (golf club heads), ash (baseball bats), ebony and ash (pool cues) |
| Toothpaste | mint, wheat, palm oil, coconut |
| Tourist attractions | redwoods, giant sequoias, saguaro cactuses, fall foliage, Holland tulips |
| Waxes | carnauba palm, cauassu, candelilla, bayberry |

**FIGURE 27-6**

Coal is a dark-colored, organic rock. Complex chemical and physical changes produced coal from the remains of plants that grew in prehistoric swamps millions of years ago.

## Fuels

Most of the energy we use for heat, electricity, and machine fuel comes from fossil fuels—coal, oil, and natural gas. Figure 27-6 shows a coal deposit being uncovered by an earth-moving machine. Fossil fuels are composed of stored photosynthetic energy from millions of years ago. In developing nations, much of the fuel comes from wood or other plant materials. For example, grains can be fermented into alcohol and mixed with gasoline to make gasohol. **Gasohol,** which is made of about 10 percent alcohol, is an alternative fuel for automobiles.

internet connect
www.scilinks.org
**Topic:** Fossil Fuels
**Keyword:** HM60614
SCiLINKS. Maintained by the National Science Teachers Association

# Careers
## in BIOLOGY

# Ethnobotanist

**Job Description** Ethnobotanists are scientists who study the ways in which people make use of plants, whether for food, medicine, or other purposes. Ethnobotanists are often involved in the collection of plants, the conservation of endangered species, and the research of traditional plant medicines.

**Focus On an Ethnobotanist**
Ethnobotanist Paul Cox travels to remote places to look for plants that can help cure diseases. He seeks the advice of native healers in his search. For example, Cox traveled to the Pacific island of Samoa in 1984 to meet a 78-year-old healer named Epenesa. She was able to identify more than 200 medicinal plants, and she had an accurate understanding of human anatomy. Epenesa gave Cox

samples of her medicines, which he brought back to the United States for study. American researchers studying her remedies discovered antiviral and anti-inflammatory compounds. Many other plant substances, obtained by ethnobotanists with the assistance of native healers, are being studied in laboratories for their healing properties. Many of the practitioners of traditional medicine are elderly. When they die, generations of medical knowledge often die with them. The need for Cox and other ethnobotanists to record the ancient wisdom of native healers is urgent.

**Education and Skills**
• **High school**—three years of science courses and four years of math courses.

• **College**—bachelor of science (B.S.) in biology, including course work in botany, chemistry, and anthropology, followed by a doctoral degree (Ph.D.) in botany, chemistry, anthropology, or linguistics, plus field and lab experience.

• **Skills**—patience, ability to learn new languages, self-motivation, respect for other cultures, and field survival skills.

For more about careers, visit **go.hrw.com** and type in the keyword **HM6 Careers**.

## Other Uses of Plants

Ornamental trees, shrubs, and other plants outside our homes do much more than provide beauty. Besides their decorative function, they improve the environment by preventing soil erosion, reducing noise, providing habitats for wild animals, acting as windbreaks, providing shade, and moderating temperatures, which, in turn, reduces home heating and cooling costs. Scientists have also found that ornamental plants improve our mental well-being. Gardening has long been a popular hobby in the United States, and it is an important form of exercise for millions of people.

Many plants have become major tourist attractions, such as the California redwoods shown in Figure 27-7. Another popular American tourist attraction is the Petrified Forest National Park in Arizona. The park features large areas of fossilized trees. And many yearly festivals, including the Tournament of Roses in California every New Year's Day and the Cherry Festival in Michigan each May, are held around the United States to celebrate plants. In addition, many people visit the forests of the northeastern United States every fall to view the spectacular changing leaf colors.

Plants are essential to our survival because they produce virtually all of our food, and they enhance our lives in many ways. Growing cut flowers is now a multibillion-dollar-a-year industry, and it is only a small part of the huge business of growing and using plants.

Plants can also provide the inspiration to develop innovative products. The cocklebur plant provided the idea for hook and loop fasteners when the hooked fruit was caught in the inventor's clothing. Plants have made our lives better in numerous ways, and they undoubtedly will continue to do so in the future.

**FIGURE 27-7**

The California redwood trees are a majestic sight. Redwoods usually grow 60–84 m (200–275 ft) high. The bark is very thick, making the trees resistant to fires.

## SECTION 1 REVIEW

1. Define the term *agriculture*.

2. Distinguish between the food crops known as *cereals, root crops, legumes, fruits,* and *vegetables*.

3. List three activities that humans have conducted to increase production of food crops, thus avoiding predicted food shortages.

4. List four personal grooming products that are manufactured using ingredients from plants.

**CRITICAL THINKING**

5. **Applying Information** How might transferring specific genes from legumes into rice plants help reduce malnutrition?

6. **Analyzing Information** How might farmers use legumes to reduce their use of fertilizers?

7. **Relating Concepts** Swiss physician Paracelsus (1493–1541) stated that the difference between a poison and a remedy is the dose. Explain how this statement might apply to the investigation of herbal remedies.

# MILESTONES IN Using Plants for Medicine

*Today, one-quarter of all prescription drugs contain a useful plant ingredient. More than 100 prescription drugs are made from plants. When did the relationship between plants, people, and medicine begin?*

## Timeline

**4000 BC** Sumerian clay tablets list plant remedies.

**1500 BC** Egyptian scroll lists 850 plant remedies.

**1000 BC** The *Pen Tsao* lists 375 botanicals, including opium and ephedra.

**300 BC** Theophrastus writes *Historia Plantarum.*

**100 AD** Dioscorides mentions white willow tree in *de Materia Medica.*

**1658** Cinchona bark is advertised for sale in England.

**1899** Aspirin, a buffered form of salicin, is introduced.

**1957** Extracts from the rosy periwinkle are found to cure childhood leukemia.

**1993** Taxol, derived from the Pacific yew, is approved by the FDA as an anticancer drug.

Throughout human history, people have used and passed down information about plants that can ease pain, infections, and physical maladies. About 4000 BC, Sumerian healers engraved cuneiform characters for various medicinal plants onto clay tablets. These may have been the first *herbals,* or lists of healing plants. A 70-foot-long Egyptian scroll dated to 1500 BC recorded 850 plant remedies, including garlic, for preventing illness.

An Indian poem from this same era, called the *Rig Veda,* describes many plant remedies, including snakeroot (*Rauvolfia serpentina*) for snakebite. Modern researchers discovered that snakeroot contains the compound reserpine, which lowers blood pressure. A Chinese herbal from 1000 BC, the *Pen Tsao,* lists 375 botanicals, including opium and ephedra, that are still used as painkillers and stimulants.

Around 300 BC, Aristotle described various herbal remedies, and his student Theophrastus wrote the text *Historia Plantarum.* In 100 AD, the Roman scholar Dioscorides wrote *de Materia Medica,* in which he mentions white willow, later found to be a source of aspirin. Both books were still in use in the Middle Ages. At least one herbal written in 1250 AD includes foxglove (*Digitalis purpurea*), the source of a heart stimulant.

The modern era of medicinal plants began with the use of quinine for treating malaria. Peruvian Indians had long recognized the value of the cinchona tree for treating feverish patients. Bark from this tree was first advertised for sale in England in 1658. However, it wasn't until 1820 that quinine was isolated from the bark of the cinchona tree by French chemists.

The development of aspirin presents a similar story. Extracts from the white willow tree had been known from the time of the ancient Greeks to ease pain. However, the pain-relieving substance, salicin, wasn't isolated until 1829. Because salicin causes stomach problems, more research was required for the development of a buffered derivative, aspirin, which was offered to the public in 1899.

During the 1950s, drug companies began to seek medicinal plants all over the world. In 1957, scientists discovered that extracts from the Madagascar rosy periwinkle are effective against childhood leukemia. Deaths from childhood leukemia have since dropped by 80 percent. Taxol, derived from the Pacific yew and approved for medical use in 1993, is an effective treatment against ovarian cancer. So far, however, only a small percentage of the world's plants have been tested for useful medicines such as these.

## Review

1. Name two medicinal plants used in ancient times and today.
2. **Critical Thinking** Why is it important to preserve the medicinal knowledge of indigenous cultures?
3. **Critical Thinking** How might the destruction of rain forests impact the future of medicine?

### OBJECTIVES

- **Summarize** the contributions of plants to the environment.
- **Describe** the ways that plants interact with other organisms.
- **Explain** how some plants can cause harm.

### VOCABULARY

plant ecology
weed
hay fever

# PLANTS AND THE ENVIRONMENT

*Based solely on weight, algae and photosynthetic bacteria are dominant organisms in the oceans, and plants are dominant on land. Photosynthetic plants are called producers because they make food for other living things. Organisms that eat other organisms, like animals, are called consumers and depend on plants for a source of organic compounds.*

## PLANT ECOLOGY

The study of the interactions between plants and the environment is called **plant ecology.** The most important interaction involves the ability of plants to capture solar energy through photosynthesis. In photosynthesis, plants absorb carbon dioxide from the air, produce sugar and starch, and break apart water, releasing oxygen into the air. Consumers, like the one shown in Figure 27-8, use sugar and oxygen in cellular respiration and produce carbon dioxide and water. Organic compounds from plants provide consumers with energy, cellular "building blocks," and essential compounds such as vitamins and fiber.

Plants also provide organisms with inorganic nutrients. Plant roots are very efficient at mining the soil for inorganic nutrients, such as nitrogen, phosphorus, potassium, iron, and magnesium. Plants use these inorganic nutrients for metabolism and to make organic compounds. Consumers ingest these organic compounds and incorporate the inorganic nutrients into their own bodies.

**FIGURE 27-8**

About half of the world's species of plants and animals live in tropical rain forests. One of the reasons scientists are very concerned about the destruction of rain forests is because many plant species have yet to be researched.

Eventually, these same inorganic nutrients are returned to the soil when the consumer's waste material or dead body is decomposed by bacteria and fungi. Plants thus play a major role in the continuous cycling of the Earth's water, oxygen, carbon dioxide, and inorganic nutrients.

Plants are also responsible for the formation and maintenance of soil. Roots bind soil particles together, leaves reduce the soil-eroding impact of wind and rain, and dead plant parts add organic matter to the soil.

## Plant-Animal Interactions

Plants interact with animals in many fascinating ways. Many flowering plants attract pollinators, animals that carry pollen from one plant to another. Usually the pollinator gets a reward for its efforts in the form of food from nectar. The size, shape, color, and odor of many flowers make them attractive to their pollinators. For example, Figure 27-9 shows that in some orchid species, the flowers have evolved to look and smell like the female of their wasp or bee pollinators. A male wasp or bee lands on a flower believing he has located a mate. The pollen he touches sticks to his body and is transferred to the next orchid he visits. In this case, the flower lures the pollinator with the promise of a mate, but fools the insect into picking up pollen without receiving a reward.

## Plant-Microbe Interactions

Two important aspects of plant ecology are plant interactions with fungi and with bacteria. Plant-microbe interactions may be harmful to plants, as in the case of fungal and bacterial diseases. Diseases often cause major crop losses. However, bacteria and fungi also form important beneficial relationships with plants.

The majority of plant species form *mycorrhizae,* which are symbiotic relationships between fungi and the roots of a plant. A mycorrhizal fungus penetrates a root, often changing the root structure. However, the fungus does not harm the root. Instead, it greatly increases the root's ability to absorb water and other inorganic nutrients, such as phosphorus and potassium. In return, the root supplies the fungus with energy.

The roots of many plant species also form beneficial associations with bacteria. Some bacteria can take nitrogen gas from the air and "fix" it, or convert it to a form that plants can use. Plants of the legume family, such as peas, beans, and peanuts, commonly host bacteria that fix nitrogen.

## Plant-Human Interactions

We protect and care for many plants that provide us with food, clothing, shelter, medicine, and many other products. However, humans have drastically changed natural plant populations by introducing foreign plant species, diseases, and animals. Introduced plants, such as the water hyacinth shown in Figure 27-10, kudzu, crabgrass, and dandelion have become widespread weeds.

**FIGURE 27-9**

Some orchid species have evolved to resemble their wasp or bee pollinators.

**FIGURE 27-10**

The water hyacinth has become a weed that clogs waterways in the southeastern United States.

**Weeds** are undesirable plants that often crowd out crop plants or native plant species. For example, water hyacinths float on lakes and rivers, growing so fast and dense that they impede boats and shade underwater plants. The introduction of a fungal disease, chestnut blight, in 1904 virtually wiped out the American chestnut as a dominant forest tree in the eastern United States. Government inspectors now carefully screen plant materials entering the country to prevent the introduction of plant pests and diseases that native plants have no resistance against.

**FIGURE 27-11**

Giant ragweed, which can grow to more than 4 m (13 ft.) tall, produces massive amounts of pollen that is a major cause of hay fever. The small, dull flowers indicate that it is wind-pollinated.

# HARMFUL PLANTS

Despite the many benefits plants provide, some plants can also cause harm. Many deaths are caused by addictive plant products, such as tobacco, cocaine, opium, and alcohol. Some plant species are harmful when eaten or touched. Poison ivy and poison oak give an itchy rash to millions of Americans each year. Children are often poisoned, though usually not fatally, when they eat the leaves or colorful berries of house or garden plants. Despite widespread reports to the contrary, the popular Christmas plant poinsettia is not deadly, but its sap may cause skin irritation. However, holly berries and parts of mistletoe are poisonous.

Tens of millions of people suffer from pollen allergies, one cause of hay fever. **Hay fever** is an allergic reaction that results in sneezing, a runny nose, and watering eyes. Pollen allergies occur at three seasons. In early spring, deciduous trees, such as oak, ash, birch, and sycamore release pollen. In late spring or early summer, it is mainly wild and pasture grasses that cause allergy problems. Of the cereal crops, only rye pollen seems to be an important cause of allergies. In late summer and fall, the highly allergenic pollen of ragweeds, shown in Figure 27-11, affects many people. Contrary to popular belief, large, colorful flowers do not cause hay fever. Pollen that causes allergies comes from small, drab flowers that are wind-pollinated.

## SECTION 2 REVIEW

1. What is the name for the study of the interactions that occur between plants and the environment?

2. How do plants play a role in the continuous recycling of many of the Earth's inorganic nutrients?

3. How do plants benefit from their interactions with animals?

4. List three ways that some plants can cause harm to people.

**CRITICAL THINKING**

5. **Recognizing Differences** Purple loosestrife, a weed that can dominate American wetlands, does not cause problems in its native Europe and Asia. Explain a possible reason for this.

6. **Relating Concepts** Explain the adaptive benefits for plants that have evolved to look like insects.

7. **Recognizing Relationships** Considering how pollination occurs, why do you think hay fever is caused by pollen from grasses and trees?

## SECTION 1 — Plants and People

- The study of plants is called botany. The practical applications of botany are evident in agriculture, which is the raising of crops and livestock for food or other uses.

- Humans have cultivated plants for approximately 11,000 years and have changed, by selection, many plant species so much that these plants can no longer survive in the wild.

- Food crops can be classified in many ways, including by their use and by their taxonomic classification.

- The major part of the human diet is provided by a few cereal crops in the grass family, especially corn, wheat, and rice.

- Everyday definitions of fruits and vegetables are different from botanical definitions. Many common vegetables, such as green beans, tomatoes, squash, and pumpkins, are actually fruits. Botanically speaking, a fruit is the part of a flowering plant that usually contains seeds.

- Plants provide many important medicines, such as digitalis, quinine, morphine, and anti-cancer drugs.

- Several factors have increased food production, including the use of fertilizers and pesticides. As land is cultivated to produce an adequate food supply, the health of the environment is compromised by soil erosion, depleted water supplies, and pollution.

- Plants provide thousands of nonfood products, including clothing, fabric dye, lumber, paper, cosmetics, fuel, cork, rubber, turpentine, and pesticides.

- Ornamental plants improve the human environment in many important ways: they provide shade, minimize soil erosion, reduce noise, and lower home energy costs.

### Vocabulary

| | | | |
|---|---|---|---|
| botany (p. 545) | root crop (p. 547) | nut (p. 547) | fertilizer (p. 548) |
| agriculture (p. 545) | legume (p. 547) | spice (p. 547) | pesticide (p. 548) |
| cultivar (p. 545) | fruit (p. 547) | herb (p. 547) | aspirin (p. 548) |
| cereal (p. 546) | vegetable (p. 547) | quinine (p. 547) | gasohol (p. 551) |

## SECTION 2 — Plants and the Environment

- Plant ecology is the study of the interactions between plants and the environment.

- Plants play a major role in recycling the Earth's water, oxygen, carbon dioxide, and inorganic nutrients.

- Plants provide animals with inorganic nutrients as well as organic nutrients.

- Most plant roots are penetrated by beneficial mycorrhizal fungi, which greatly increase the roots' ability to absorb inorganic nutrients.

- Most nitrogen in living organisms must first be fixed by bacteria, which may live in association with plant roots, especially the roots of legumes.

- Plants associate with animals in many mutually beneficial ways. For example, plants provide food to animals that protect them or carry their pollen.

- People have affected wild plant populations negatively by introducing foreign species of plants, animals, and disease organisms.

- Plants can cause harm in several ways. Many deaths are caused by addictive plant products. Some plant species are poisonous when eaten or touched. And millions of people suffer from allergies to pollen.

### Vocabulary

| | | |
|---|---|---|
| plant ecology (p. 554) | weed (p. 556) | hay fever (p. 556) |

## USING VOCABULARY

1. For each pair of terms, explain the relationship between the terms.
   a. *botany* and *agriculture*
   b. *fertilizer* and *pesticide*
   c. *fruit* and *vegetable*
   d. *aspirin* and *quinine*

2. Choose the term that does not belong in the following group, and explain why it does not belong: *legume, nut,* and *root crop.*

3. Use the following terms in the same sentence: *gasohol, plant ecology,* and *cereal.*

4. **Word Roots and Origins** The word *herb* is derived from the Latin *herba,* which means "grass." Using this information, explain why the term *herb* is a good name for the plants that the term describes.

## UNDERSTANDING KEY CONCEPTS

5. **Describe** how people have acted as selecting agents in the evolution of food plants.

6. **Distinguish** between a fruit and a vegetable.

7. **State** two negative impacts of modern agricultural methods.

8. **List** three nonfood, nonmedicinal uses of plants.

9. **Name** three types of plants that provide fiber used in clothing.

10. **List** five medicines that are derived from plants.

11. **Describe** how ornamental trees improve the environment.

12. **Identify** one inorganic plant nutrient, and describe the role of plants in recycling this nutrient.

13. **Explain** how plants and microbes interact in mutually beneficial ways.

14. **Explain** why plant materials entering the country are screened by government inspectors.

15. **Name** three addictive plant products.

16. **CONCEPT MAPPING** Use the following terms to create a concept map that illustrates plant ecology: *humans, pollination, plants, animals, hay fever, mycorrhizae, bees* and *microbes.*

## CRITICAL THINKING

17. **Predicting Results** If all animals disappeared from the Earth, what would the positive and negative effects be on plants?

18. **Analyzing Information** During the rainy season in the Brazilian rain forest, the rivers flood the land. Many fish from these rivers then swim among the land plants and eat their fruit. How might this intermingling of fish and plants help the plants?

19. **Analyzing Concepts** Suppose a friend asks you why corn, which he or she considers to be a vegetable, is listed as a cereal crop in the encyclopedia. To answer this question, write a paragraph that explains why corn is a cereal crop, agriculturally, and why corn is a fruit, botanically. Identify other examples of foods that are classified as vegetables or grains but also are fruits.

20. **Relating Concepts** How did artificial selection by humans play a role in the origin of agricultural crops? How is artificial selection similar to natural selection?

21. **Interpreting Graphics** Many athletes consume carbohydrates before a competition to increase their endurance. The table below shows a variety of legumes and grains that can be purchased at a grocery store. Compare their prices and nutritional composition. Determine which food is the least expensive source of carbohydrates.

## Common Legumes and Grains

| Food | Package size | Price | Serving (g) | Calories | Total fat (g) | Total carbohydrate (g) | Total protein (g) |
|------|-------------|-------|-------------|----------|---------------|------------------------|-------------------|
| Navy beans | 454 g | .69 | 45 | 80 | 0 | 23 | 8 |
| Rice | 907 g | .79 | 45 | 150 | 0 | 35 | 3 |
| Barley | 454 g | .49 | 45 | 100 | 0 | 24 | 3 |
| Soybeans | 454 g | .89 | 45 | 170 | 8 | 14 | 15 |
| Spaghetti | 907 g | .79 | 45 | 200 | 1 | 34 | 6 |

# Standardized Test Preparation

**DIRECTIONS:** Choose the letter of the answer choice that best answers the question.

1. Early farmers selected wheat plants that had which of the following characteristics?
   A. fewest grains
   B. largest seed pods
   C. easily dispersed seeds
   D. stalks not easily broken in the wind

2. Which plants are the major source of food for the world today?
   F. spices
   G. cereals
   H. legumes
   J. root crops

3. Which of the following is an inorganic nutrient recycled by plants?
   A. sugar
   B. starch
   C. cellulose
   D. phosphorus

**INTERPRETING GRAPHICS:** The illustration below shows four types of food plants. Use the illustration to answer the question that follows.

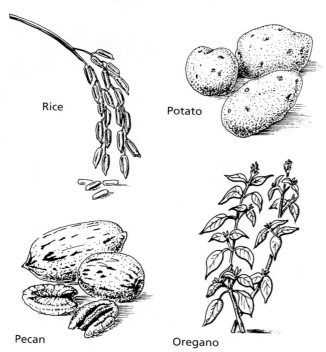

Rice

Potato

Pecan

Oregano

4. Plants classified as root crops have edible underground structures. Which of the food plants shown above is a root crop?
   F. rice
   G. pecan
   H. potato
   J. oregano

**DIRECTIONS:** Complete the following analogy.

5. vegetable : root crop :: grain :
   A. herb
   B. spice
   C. cereal
   D. quinine

**INTERPRETING GRAPHICS:** The illustration below shows how plants might be grown together. Use the illustration to answer the question that follows.

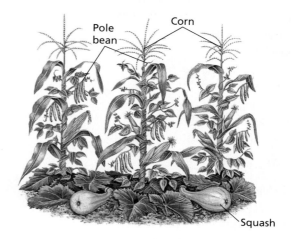

Pole bean

Corn

Squash

6. How does this arrangement help these plants?
   F. The squash can use the corn as a support.
   G. The beans grow apart from the squash and corn.
   H. The corn covers the ground and reduces erosion.
   J. Beans, which are legumes, will provide nitrogen fertilizer for the corn and squash.

## SHORT RESPONSE

Look again at the illustration above.

Explain the advantage to the human diet of growing and eating these food crops together.

## EXTENDED RESPONSE

Plants have been cultivated for at least 11,000 years.

*Part A* Identify 5 plants people use for food and 5 plants people use for other purposes.

*Part B* How has human cultivation changed some plants?

**Test TIP** For a question that uses a word you don't know, try to determine the meaning of the word by breaking it down into smaller parts and inferring the meaning of these parts.

# Comparing Soil-Grown Plants with Hydroponic Plants

## OBJECTIVES

- Compare hydroponic plant-cultivation techniques with conventional plant-cultivation techniques.
- Observe the germination of wheat seeds over a two-week period.

## PROCESS SKILLS

- analyzing data
- measuring
- comparing and contrasting

## MATERIALS

- 2 clear plastic cups
- plastic-foam floater with 6 holes in it
- 50 mL of potting soil
- cheesecloth (must be large enough to cover the plastic-foam floater)
- 12 wheat seeds
- 50 mL of complete nutrient solution
- plastic dropper
- labeling tape
- marking pen
- 50 mL graduated cylinder
- metric ruler

## Background

1. Hydroponic cultivation is a technique for growing plants in a solution that contains all of the inorganic nutrients the plant needs. Plants that are grown hydroponically do not require soil.
2. The beginning of growth in a seed is called *germination.*

## PART A  Day 1

1. Using the marking pen and the labeling tape, label one clear plastic cup "Soil Cultivated," and label the other plastic cup "Hydroponically Cultivated."
2. Fill the cup labeled "Soil Cultivated" halfway with moist potting soil. Place six wheat seeds on the surface of the soil; use the distance between the holes in the foam floater as a guide to determine the spacing of the wheat seeds. (Do not place the floater on the soil.)
3. Press the seeds into the soil until they are approximately 0.5 cm below the surface. Cover the seeds with soil, and press down firmly.
4. Water the seeds with 10 mL of distilled water.
5. Add 50 mL of complete nutrient solution to the cup labeled "Hydroponically Cultivated," and place the plastic-foam floater on the surface of the solution, as shown in the figure below.

6. Place the cheesecloth on top of the floater, as illustrated in the figure. Press lightly at the location of the holes in the floater to moisten the cheesecloth.

7. Place the remaining six wheat seeds on top of the cheesecloth in the cup labeled "Hydroponically Cultivated." Position the seeds so that each one lies in an indentation formed by the cheesecloth in a hole in the floater. Press each seed lightly into the hole until the seed coat is moistened.
8. Place both cups in a warm, dry location. Water the soil-cultivated seeds as needed, monitoring the amount of water added. Aerate the roots of the hydroponic plants every day by using a clean plastic dropper to blow air into the nutrient solution.
9. In your lab report, prepare data tables similar to Table A and Table B. Write your observations of the seeds in your data tables.
10. Clean up your lab materials and wash your hands before leaving the lab.

| TABLE A  OBSERVATIONS OF SOIL-GROWN PLANTS | | |
| --- | --- | --- |
| Day | Appearance of seedlings | Average height (mm) |
| 1 | | |
| 2 | | |
| 3 | | |
| 4 | | |
| 5 | | |
| 6 | | |
| 7 | | |
| 8 | | |
| 9 | | |
| 10 | | |
| 11 | | |
| 12 | | |
| 13 | | |
| 14 | | |

| TABLE B  OBSERVATIONS OF HYDROPONICALLY GROWN SEEDS | | |
| --- | --- | --- |
| Day | Appearance of seedlings | Average height (mm) |
| 1 | | |
| 2 | | |
| 3 | | |
| 4 | | |
| 5 | | |
| 6 | | |
| 7 | | |
| 8 | | |
| 9 | | |
| 10 | | |
| 11 | | |
| 12 | | |
| 13 | | |
| 14 | | |

## PART B  Days 2–14

11. Compare the contents of each cup every day for two weeks, and record the appearance of the wheat seedlings in your data tables. If you are unable to observe your seedlings over the weekend, be sure to note in your data table that no observations were made on those days.

12. Each time that you observe the seedlings after they have begun to grow, measure their height and record the average height of the seedlings in each cup in your data tables. To find the average height for one cup, add the heights of each seedling in the cup together and divide by the number of seedlings (6).

13. After the seeds in the cup containing nutrient solution have germinated and formed roots, allow an air pocket to form between the floater and the surface of the nutrient solution. A portion of the roots should still be submerged in the nutrient solution. The air pocket allows the roots of the seeds to absorb the oxygen necessary for metabolic processes while continuing to absorb nutrients from the nutrient solution. Continue to observe and record the progress of the seedlings in each cup on a daily basis.

14. Clean up your lab materials and wash your hands before leaving the lab.

## Analysis and Conclusions

1. Based on the data you recorded, which seeds germinated more quickly? Which seeds attained the greatest height?

2. Compare your results with those of your classmates. Were the results the same for each group of students?

3. You planted six seeds in each cup. Why do you think the lab had you do this instead of having you plant a single seed in each cup? Why is the use of more than one sample important?

4. How could hydroponic growing techniques be useful to countries that have either a growing season that is too short to grow a variety of crops or soil that does not support most agricultural crops?

## Further Inquiry

The nutrient solution you used in this investigation should have provided all of the inorganic nutrients that the wheat seeds needed for proper growth. How could you determine exactly which inorganic nutrients a plant requires by using hydroponic cultivation?

# CHAPTER 28 PLANT EVOLUTION AND CLASSIFICATION

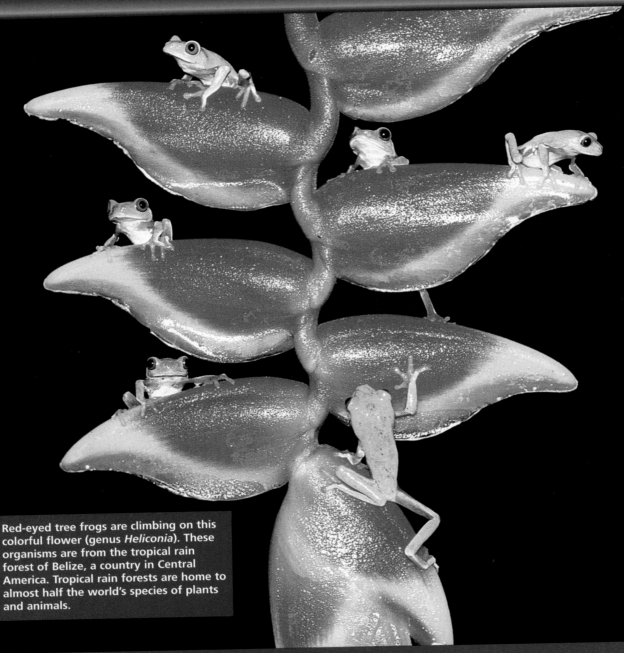

Red-eyed tree frogs are climbing on this colorful flower (genus *Heliconia*). These organisms are from the tropical rain forest of Belize, a country in Central America. Tropical rain forests are home to almost half the world's species of plants and animals.

**SECTION 1** *Overview of Plants*

**SECTION 2** *Nonvascular Plants*

**SECTION 3** *Vascular Plants*

# OVERVIEW OF PLANTS

*Plants dominate the land and many bodies of water. Plants exhibit tremendous diversity. Some plants are less than 1 mm (0.04 in.) in width, and some plants grow to more than 100 m (328 ft) in height. The 12 phyla, or divisions, of kingdom Plantae include more than 270,000 species. Some plants complete their life cycle in a few weeks, but others may live nearly 5,000 years.*

## OBJECTIVES

- **Name** three adaptations plants have made to life on land.
- **Summarize** the classification of plants.
- **Describe** alternation of generations.

## VOCABULARY

cuticle
spore
seed
vascular tissue
xylem
phloem
nonvascular plant
vascular plant
seed plant
gymnosperm
angiosperm
sporophyte
gametophyte
alternation of generations

## ADAPTING TO LAND

Although life had flourished in the oceans for more than 3 billion years, no organisms lived on land until about 475 million years ago, when a layer of ozone formed. The ozone protected organisms from the sun's ultraviolet radiation. Eventually, small club-shaped plants began to grow in the mud at the water's edge. Three adaptations allowed plants to thrive on land: the ability to prevent water loss, the ability to reproduce in the absence of water, and the ability to absorb and transport nutrients.

### Preventing Water Loss

The move to land offered plants distinct advantages, including more exposure to sunlight for photosynthesis, increased carbon dioxide levels, and a greater supply of inorganic nutrients. However, the land environment also presented challenges. Plants on land are susceptible to drying out through evaporation.

The **cuticle** (KYOOT-i-kuhl), a waxy protective covering on plant surfaces that prevents water loss, was one early adaptation to life on land. Although it protects a plant by keeping water in the plant, the cuticle also keeps out carbon dioxide. Plants that had small openings in their surfaces, called *stomata,* were able to survive. Stomata allow the exchange of carbon dioxide and oxygen.

### Reproducing by Spores and Seeds

Successful land plants also developed structures that helped protect reproductive cells from drying out. A **spore** is a haploid reproductive cell surrounded by a hard outer wall. Spores allowed the widespread dispersal of plant species. Eventually, most plants developed seeds. A **seed** is an embryo surrounded by a protective coat. Some seeds also contain *endosperm,* a tissue that provides nourishment for the developing plant. Figure 28-1 shows the unusual adaptation of the sugar maple tree for seed dispersal. Seeds are more effective at dispersal than spores are.

**FIGURE 28-1**

The seeds of a sugar maple tree are found inside a winged fruit. Wind can carry the winged fruit away from the tree, thus helping the seeds to disperse away from the parent plant.

## Absorbing and Transporting Materials

Aquatic plants take nutrients from the water around them. On land, most plants absorb nutrients from the soil with their roots. Although the first plants had no roots, fossils show that fungi lived on or within the underground parts of many early plants.

Certain species of plants evolved a type of tissue known as **vascular** (VAS-kyuh-luhr) **tissue,** which transports water and dissolved substances from one part of the plant to another. Two types of specialized tissue make up vascular tissue. **Xylem** (ZIE-luhm) carries absorbed water and inorganic nutrients in one direction, from the roots to the stems and leaves. **Phloem** (FLOH-EM) carries organic compounds, such as carbohydrates, and some inorganic nutrients in any direction, depending on the plant's needs. In addition to transporting absorbed materials, vascular tissue also helps support the plant, which is an important function for land plants.

# CLASSIFYING PLANTS

Study the classification of plants in Table 28-1. The 12 phyla of plants, formerly referred to as divisions, can be divided into two groups based on the presence of vascular tissue. The three phyla of **nonvascular plants** have neither true vascular tissue nor true roots, stems, or leaves. The nine phyla of **vascular plants** have vascular tissue and true roots, stems, and leaves.

### TABLE 28-1 *The 12 Phyla of the Plant Kingdom*

| Type of plant | Phylum | Common name | Approximate number of existing species |
|---|---|---|---|
| **Nonvascular** | Bryophyta | mosses | 10,000 |
| | Hepatophyta | liverworts | 8,000 |
| | Anthocerophyta | hornworts | 100 |
| **Vascular, seedless** | Psilophyta | whisk ferns | 10–13 |
| | Lycophyta | club mosses | 1,000 |
| | Sphenophyta | horsetails | 15 |
| | Pteridophyta | ferns | 12,000 |
| **Vascular, seed** Gymnosperms | Cycadophyta | cycads | 100 |
| | Ginkgophyta | ginkgoes | 1 |
| | Coniferophyta | conifers | 550 |
| | Gnetophyta | gnetophytes | 70 |
| Angiosperms | Anthophyta | flowering plants | 240,000 |
| | class Monocotyledones | monocots | 70,000 |
| | class Dicotyledones | dicots | 170,000 |

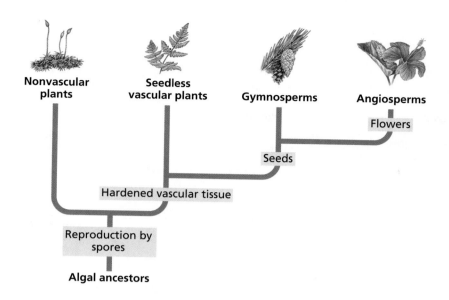

**FIGURE 28-2**

This phylogenetic diagram represents a hypothesis for the evolutionary relationships between plants and green algae. The earliest plants were nonvascular. These plants evolved into more-complex forms of plants, the vascular plants. For updates on phylogenetic diagrams, visit **go.hrw.com.** Enter the keyword **HM6 Phylo.**

Nonvascular plants

Seedless vascular plants

Gymnosperms

Angiosperms

Flowers

Seeds

Hardened vascular tissue

Reproduction by spores

Algal ancestors

Notice in Table 28-1 that vascular plants can be further divided into two groups, seedless plants and seed plants. Seedless plants include the phylum of ferns and three phyla made up of plants closely associated with ferns. **Seed plants**—plants that produce seeds for reproduction—include four phyla of gymnosperms (JIM-noh-SPUHRMZ) and one phylum of angiosperms (AN-jee-oh-SPUHRMZ). **Gymnosperms,** which include pine trees, are seed plants that produce seeds that are not enclosed in fruits. **Angiosperms,** also known as flowering plants, are seed plants that produce seeds within a protective fruit. Examples are apple and orange trees.

### The Fossil Record of Plants

Figure 28-2 shows the possible origin of major plant groups. Much of what is now known about plant phylogeny comes from the fossil record. The fossil record is incomplete, but scientists hypothesize that plants evolved from algal ancestors. The strongest evidence lies in the similarities between modern green algae and plants. Both have the same photosynthetic pigments—chlorophylls *a* and *b*, both store energy as starch, and both have cell walls made of cellulose.

# ALTERNATING LIFE CYCLES

All plants have a life cycle that involves two phases, which are named for the type of reproductive cells they produce. Recall that cells having two sets of chromosomes are referred to as *diploid,* and cells having only one set of chromosomes are referred to as *haploid.* The first phase of a plant's life cycle consists of a diploid ($2n$) **sporophyte** (SPOH-ruh-FIET) plant that produces spores. The second phase consists of a haploid ($1n$) **gametophyte** (guh-MEET-uh-FIET) plant that produces eggs and sperm. A life cycle that alternates between the gametophyte phase and sporophyte phase is called **alternation of generations.**

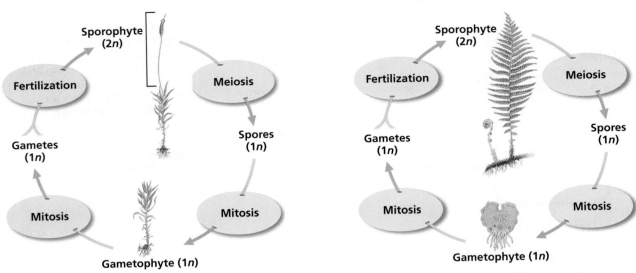

**(a) NONVASCULAR PLANT LIFE CYCLE**

Sporophyte (2n)

Fertilization

Meiosis

Gametes (1n)

Spores (1n)

Mitosis

Mitosis

Gametophyte (1n)

**(b) VASCULAR PLANT LIFE CYCLE**

Sporophyte (2n)

Fertilization

Meiosis

Gametes (1n)

Spores (1n)

Mitosis

Mitosis

Gametophyte (1n)

**FIGURE 28-3**

In the life cycle of a plant, there is an alternation of the haploid gametophyte generation and the diploid sporophyte generation. (a) The life cycle of a nonvascular plant, such as a moss, is characterized by a long, thin sporophyte growing up from the top of the more prominent gametophyte. (b) The life cycle of a vascular plant, such as a fern, is characterized by a large sporophyte and a very small gametophyte.

Figure 28-3 shows the life cycles of a nonvascular plant and a vascular plant. In alternation of generations, the gametophyte (1n) undergoes mitosis to form gametes—eggs and sperm. Once an egg is fertilized by a sperm and produces a zygote, the plant begins the diploid phase of its life cycle. The zygote divides by mitosis to form a sporophyte plant. The sporophyte (2n) produces cells that undergo meiosis to form haploid spores. These spores are released by most seedless plants but are retained by seed plants. The life cycle begins again when spores divide by mitosis to form new gametophytes.

In nonvascular plants, the gametophyte is the dominant phase. In contrast, the sporophyte is the dominant phase of vascular plants. Oak trees are large sporophytes that dominate some landscapes. In seedless vascular plants, the gametophyte is usually a separate small organism quite different from the sporophyte. In seed plants, the gametophyte is a very small parasite of the sporophyte. For example, gametophytes of flowering plants are microscopic parts of their flowers that are not photosynthetic.

## SECTION 1 REVIEW

1. How does the cuticle represent an adaptive advantage for early land plants?

2. Compare the structure of a spore with that of a seed.

3. What is the main difference between the nine phyla of vascular plants and the three phyla of nonvascular plants?

4. Explain how alternation of generations between the gametophyte phase and the sporophyte phase differs in vascular plants and nonvascular plants.

**CRITICAL THINKING**

5. **Justifying Conclusions** Why are vascular plants more successful than nonvascular plants as land plants?

6. **Inferring Relationships** How have a vascular system and a dominant sporophyte contributed to the success of plants on land?

7. **Organizing Information** For each of the following pairs, identify the most recently evolved characteristic: spore/seed; vascular tissue/no vascular tissue; and cuticle/no cuticle.

# NONVASCULAR PLANTS

*The three phyla of nonvascular plants are collectively called* **bryophytes.** *Botanists have identified about 16,600 species of bryophytes. They lack vascular tissue and do not form true roots, stems, and leaves. These plants usually grow on land near streams and rivers.*

## SECTION 2

### OBJECTIVES

- **Identify** the characteristics of bryophytes.
- **Describe** plants in the phylum Bryophyta.
- **Describe** plants in the phylum Hepatophyta.
- **Describe** plants in the phylum Anthocerophyta.

### VOCABULARY

bryophyte
liverwort
hornwort

## CHARACTERISTICS OF BRYOPHYTES

Bryophytes are the most primitive type of plants. Overall, their characteristics are more like those of plants than of algae. Bryophytes are mostly terrestrial and have an alternation-of-generations life cycle. Bryophytes are seedless, and they produce spores. Because they do not have vascular tissue, they are very small, usually 1–2 cm (0.4–0.8 in.) in height.

Bryophytes need water to reproduce sexually because the sperm must swim through water to an egg. In dry areas, bryophytes can reproduce sexually only when adequate moisture is available. The asexual production of haploid spores does not require water.

## PHYLUM BRYOPHYTA

Almost every land environment is home to at least one species of moss in the phylum Bryophyta (brie-AHF-uh-tuh). The thick green carpets of moss on shady forest floors actually consist of thousands of moss gametophytes. Each gametophyte is attached to the soil by rootlike structures called *rhizoids* (RIE-ZOYDZ). Unlike roots, rhizoids do not have vascular tissue. But rhizoids do function like roots by anchoring the moss and by absorbing water and inorganic nutrients.

Moss gametophytes are usually less than 3 cm (1.2 in.) tall. The moss sporophyte grows up from the top of the gametophyte, as shown in Figure 28-4. Gametophytes may be male, may be female, or may contain both male and female reproductive parts.

Mosses are called *pioneer plants* because they are often the first species to inhabit a barren area. Mosses gradually accumulate inorganic and organic matter on rock surfaces, creating a layer of soil in which other plants can grow. In areas devastated by fire, volcanic action, or human activity, pioneering mosses can help trigger the development of new biological communities. They also help prevent soil erosion by covering the soil surface and absorbing water.

**FIGURE 28-4**

Moss sporophytes (thin, brown stalks) depend on the gametophytes (green, "mossy" parts) to which they are attached, because sporophytes do not undergo photosynthesis.

FIGURE 28-5

A peat farmer cuts blocks of peat, produced from moss of the genus *Sphagnum,* to heat his farmhouse in County Clare, Ireland.

*Peat moss* (of the genus *Sphagnum*) is a major component of bogs in northern parts of the world. Peat moss produces an acid that slows down decomposition in the swamplike bogs. Compression and chemical breakdown in peat bogs produces *peat,* which consists of partially decomposed plant matter. In many northern European and Asian countries, peat is mined and dried for use as fuel, as shown in Figure 28-5. Dried peat moss is widely used to enhance the water-retaining ability of potting and gardening soils. Dried peat moss is also used by florists to pack bulbs and flowers for shipping.

## Word Roots and Origins

### liverwort

from the familiar *liver* (body organ) and the Old English *wort,* meaning "herb"

# PHYLUM HEPATOPHYTA

Phylum Hepatophyta (HEP-uh-TAHF-uh-tuh) includes the **liverworts,** unusual-looking plants that grow in moist, shady areas. Most liverworts have thin, transparent leaflike structures arranged along a stemlike axis, as shown on the left side of Figure 28-6. Some liverworts have a *thalloid* (THAL-oyd) form—that is, a flat body with distinguishable upper and lower surfaces, as shown on the right side of Figure 28-6. All liverworts lie close to the ground. This adaptation allows them to absorb water readily. In some species, the gametophyte is topped by an umbrella-shaped structure that holds the reproductive cells.

**FIGURE 28-6**

A leafy liverwort (a) has two rows of leaflike structures growing on a stem. A thalloid liverwort (b) has very flat, thin lobes.

(a)

(b)

**FIGURE 28-7**

Hornworts grow in warm, moist habitats, such as along roads or near streams.

# PHYLUM ANTHOCEROPHYTA

Phylum Anthocerophyta (AN-thoh-suh-RAHF-uh-tuh) includes the **hornworts,** which also grow in moist, shaded areas. The name "hornwort" refers to the long, thin, hornlike sporophytes that grow out from the top of the plant, as shown in Figure 28-7. When the sporophytes are not present, hornworts look very similar to thalloid liverworts. Hornworts do not have a stem or leaves; the gametophyte of a hornwort is anchored to the ground by rhizoids. Hornworts share an unusual characteristic with algae: Each cell usually has a single large chloroplast rather than numerous small chloroplasts.

The sporophytes of hornworts are different from the sporophytes of mosses and liverworts in that they are green and carry out photosynthesis. The sporophytes continue to grow throughout the plant's life. They also are covered with a cuticle and have stomata. Tubelike cells at the center of the sporophytes resemble cells of vascular tissue and may transport materials in these plants. These characteristics indicate that the hornworts are closely related to vascular plants.

## SECTION 2 REVIEW

1. List two characteristics shared by all nonvascular plants.

2. Describe the role that mosses play in the early development of biological communities.

3. Explain why liverworts lie close to the ground.

4. Describe how the sporophytes of hornworts differ from the sporophytes of mosses or liverworts.

**CRITICAL THINKING**

5. **Making Comparisons** What advantage do gametophytes that are either male or female have over gametophytes with both male and female structures?

6. **Evaluating Information** Why can't mosses grow as large as maple or oak trees?

7. **Applying Information** How is a moss's ability to absorb water advantageous?

- **Describe** the adaptive advantages that vascular plants have over nonvascular plants.
- **Summarize** the characteristics of the four phyla of seedless vascular plants.
- **State** the major differences between gymnosperms and angiosperms.
- **Determine** why angiosperms have been so successful.
- **Compare** monocots and dicots.

## VOCABULARY

strobilus
rhizome
fiddlehead
frond
germinate
seedling
cone
deciduous
ovary
cotyledon
monocot
dicot
vein
parallel venation
net venation

# VASCULAR PLANTS

*Vascular plants contain specialized conducting tissues (xylem and phloem) that transport water and dissolved substances from one part of the plant to another. Vascular plants can grow larger and live in more environments than nonvascular plants. The strong stems of vascular plants allow the plants to grow tall, enabling them to rise above other plants and receive more sunlight than shorter plants do.*

## SEEDLESS VASCULAR PLANTS

Seedless vascular plants dominated the Earth until about 200 million years ago. Characteristics of the four phyla of seedless vascular plants are summarized in Table 28-2. The first three phyla are called *fern allies,* while members of the last phylum are *ferns.* Spores are the mobile sexual reproductive parts of all seedless plants.

### Phylum Psilophyta

The phylum Psilophyta (sie-LAHF-uh-tuh) is represented by whisk ferns, illustrated in Figure 28-8. Despite their name, whisk ferns are not ferns at all. They have no roots or leaves and produce spores on the ends of short branches. These features suggest that whisk ferns resemble early land plants. Some species of the phylum Psilophyta are *epiphytes,* which means they grow on other plants. But they are not parasites because they do not harm their host plant.

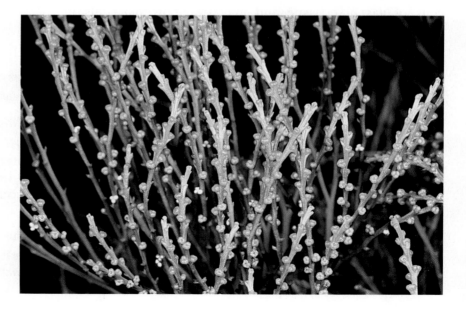

**FIGURE 28-8**

The whisk fern produces spores at the ends of branched stem tips. These plants are found in tropical and subtropical regions.

## TABLE 28-2  Seedless Vascular Plants

| Example plant | Phylum | Features | Size | Location |
|---|---|---|---|---|
| Whisk ferns | Psilophyta | • produce reproductive structures on the ends of forked branches<br>• no roots or leaves | • about 30 cm (1 ft) tall | • tropical and temperate regions, as far north as South Carolina |
| Club mosses | Lycophyta | • evergreens that produce spores in cones<br>• have roots | • about 5 cm (2 in.) tall | • tropical and temperate regions, on forest floors, in swamps, or as epiphytes |
| Horsetails | Sphenophyta | • jointed stems<br>• outer cells of stems contain silica, the major component of sand | • about 60–90 cm (2–3 ft) tall | • tropical and temperate regions, usually in moist soil |
| Ferns | Pteridophyta | • leaves<br>• most have an underground stem<br>• most produce spores on the underside of their leaves | • range from less than 1 cm (0.4 in.) to 25 m (82 ft) tall | • all climates, on forest floors, as epiphytes, some in full sun, some aquatic |

## Phylum Lycophyta

The phylum Lycophyta (lie-KAHF-uh-tuh) contains the club mosses, an example of which is shown in Figure 28-9. Because they look like miniature pine trees, club mosses are also called ground pines. They produce a **strobilus** (stroh-BIE-luhs), or cone, which is a cluster of sporangia-bearing modified leaves. Club mosses were once widely collected as Christmas decorations.

Another member of phylum Lycophyta is a spike moss called *Selaginella lepidophylla,* native to the American Southwest. *Selaginella* turns brown and curls up in a ball during drought. However, when moistened, the plant uncurls and turns green again after a few hours.

🔲 internet connect

www.scilinks.org
**Topic: Vascular Plants**
**Keyword: HM61595**

SCI LINKS. Maintained by the National Science Teachers Association

**FIGURE 28-9**

The club mosses, sometimes known as ground pines, are members of the phylum Lycophyta. The tips of the aerial stems contain conelike structures.

## Phylum Sphenophyta

The phylum Sphenophyta (sfee-NAHF-uh-tuh) includes horsetails of the genus *Equisetum*. Horsetails have jointed photosynthetic stems that contain silica, with scalelike leaves at each joint. The vertical stems of horsetails, which grow from a rhizome, are hollow and have joints. Spores form in cones located at the tips of stems.

American pioneers used horsetails to scrub pots and pans; hence, they are frequently called *scouring rushes*. As you can see in Figure 28-10, the shoots are often highly branched and remind some people of a horsetail.

## Phylum Pteridophyta

Ferns probably originated over 350 million years ago. Ferns belong to the phylum Pteridophyta (tuhr-uh-DAHF-uh-tuh) and represent a diverse group. Some are floating plants that are less than 1 cm (0.4 in.) across. Ferns also grow above the Arctic Circle and in desert regions. The largest living ferns are tree ferns, shown in Figure 28-11. These ferns can reach 25 m (82 ft) in height, and some have leaves 5 m (16 ft) long. Tree ferns live in tropical and subtropical areas.

Most ferns have an underground stem called a **rhizome** (RIE-ZOHM). The fibrous rhizomes of a few species of ferns are used as a growing medium for orchids. The tightly coiled new leaves of ferns are called **fiddleheads.** The young fiddleheads of some species are eaten by humans as a vegetable. Fiddleheads uncoil and develop into mature leaves called **fronds.**

**FIGURE 28-10**

This horsetail, of the genus *Equisetum*, has hollow, jointed stems that contain silica. About 300 million years ago, some species of the genus *Equisetum* were large trees, growing with large club moss trees and ferns in steaming swamps. Over millions of years, the trees and other plants died, became buried, and turned into coal.

**FIGURE 28-11**

Tree ferns, such as the *Dicksonia antarctica* shown here, look like palm trees but are actually the largest living ferns. Sometimes, epiphytic ferns grow on the trunk of tree ferns.

# VASCULAR SEED PLANTS

The mobile sexual reproductive part of seed plants is the multicellular seed. Seeds are an evolutionary success story. Plants with seeds have a greater chance of reproductive success than seedless plants. Inside the tough, protective outer coat of a seed is an embryo and a nutrient supply. When conditions are too hot or too cold, or too wet or too dry, the seed remains inactive. When conditions favor growth, the seed sprouts, or **germinates**—that is, the embryo begins to grow into a young plant, called a **seedling.**

There are two main groups of seed-bearing vascular plants, gymnosperms and angiosperms. The four phyla of gymnosperms produce naked seeds, which means the seeds are not enclosed and protected in fruits. Most gymnosperms are evergreen and bear their seeds in cones. A **cone** is a reproductive structure composed of hard scales. The seeds lie open on the surface of the scales. The one phylum of angiosperms produces seeds that are enclosed and protected in fruits. Angiosperms are commonly referred to as flowering plants. Cones serve some of the same functions for gymnosperms that flowers serve for angiosperms.

## Phylum Cycadophyta

*Cycads* (SIE-KADZ), such as the one shown in Figure 28-12, are gymnosperms of the phylum Cycadophyta (sie-kad-AHF-uh-tuh). Although cycads flourished during the age of the dinosaurs, only about 100 species survive today. Most are native to the Tropics and grow slowly. Some cycads live for almost a thousand years. Many are endangered because of habitat loss, overcollection, and their slow growth. Most cycads have fernlike, leathery leaves at the top of a short, thick trunk. Cycad plants are either male or female, and they bear large cones. Cycads are mostly used as ornamental plants.

## Phylum Ginkgophyta

Like cycads, ginkgoes (GING-kohz) flourished during the time of the dinosaurs. The only species existing today is *Ginkgo biloba,* which is native to China. It is called a living fossil because it closely resembles fossil ginkgoes that are 125 million years old. The ginkgo tree has fan-shaped leaves that fall from the tree at the end of each growing season—an unusual characteristic for a gymnosperm. Trees that lose their leaves at the end of the growing season, like the ginkgo, are called **deciduous.** Most gymnosperms are evergreens and retain their leaves year-round.

Ginkgoes are tolerant of air pollution, making them good plants for urban settings. Ginkgo seeds are considered a delicacy in China and Japan. Notice the plum-shaped, fleshy seeds on the ginkgo shown in Figure 28-13. They are often mistakenly called berries or fruits.

## Phylum Coniferophyta

The conifers (KAHN-uh-fuhrz), which are gymnosperms of the phylum Coniferophyta (kahn-uh-fuhr-AHF-uh-tuh), include pine, cedar, redwood, fir, spruce, juniper, cypress, and bald cypress trees. They are important sources of wood, paper, turpentine, ornamental plants, and Christmas trees. Juniper seeds can be used to flavor food. Amber is yellow or brownish yellow fossilized resin that once flowed from ancient conifers. Prehistoric insects are often preserved in amber.

**FIGURE 28-12**

The cycad is a gymnosperm that looks like a palm or fern. Cycads can sometimes grow to 18 m (60 ft) in height.

  **Quick Lab**

### Examining Ferns

**Materials** disposable gloves, lab apron, potted fern, hand lens, water

**Procedure**

1. Put on your disposable gloves and lab apron.
2. Choose a frond of the fern, and examine its underside for the structures that contain spores.
3. Wash the soil from the underground structures. Examine the fern's horizontal stems and rhizome.

**Analysis** How do ferns differ from nonvascular plants? What enables ferns to surpass nonvascular plants in height and size? From what part of the fern do the fronds grow?

**FIGURE 28-13**

The ginkgo, *Ginkgo biloba,* has large seeds and unusual fan-shaped leaves. This gymnosperm tree can reach heights of 24 m (80 ft).

**(a)** Fir needles and cones

**(b)** Pine needles and cones

**(c)** Yew needles and seeds

**FIGURE 28-14**

The needles and cones of conifers come in many shapes and sizes. (a) The fir tree displays its female cones. Its needle-shaped leaves grow evenly all around the branch. (b) The pine tree shows its small male and larger female cones. Some pines reach heights of 60 m (200 ft). (c) The seed of the yew tree is surrounded by a red covering that looks like a berry. Its leaves are flat, pointed needles that are dark green on top and pale green underneath.

Conifers are woody plants, and most have needle or scalelike leaves, as shown in Figure 28-14. A conifer usually bears both male and female cones. Small male cones typically grow in clusters. Male cones release clouds of dustlike pollen, and then the cones fall from the branches. The pollen falls or blows into the larger female cones, where the egg cells are attached to the scales of the cone. After pollination, the female cone closes up tightly. This protects the developing seeds, which mature after one or two years. The mature seeds are released when the female cone opens.

Redwoods and giant sequoia trees provide a majestic forest setting along the West Coast of the United States. These conifers are the Earth's tallest and most massive living organisms. The tallest living coastal redwood, *Sequoia sempervirens,* is about 110 m (360 ft) tall, the height of a 30-story building. The most massive tree is a giant sequoia, *Sequoiadendron giganteum,* estimated to weigh 5,600 megagrams (6,200 tons).

## Phylum Gnetophyta

Gnetophytes (NEE-tuh-FIETS), an odd group of cone-bearing gymnosperms, have vascular systems that more closely resemble those of angiosperms. As Figure 28-15 shows, *Ephedra* (ih-FED-ruh) is a genus of desert shrubs with jointed stems that look like horsetails. It is the source of the drug *ephedrine,* which can be used as a decongestant.

**FIGURE 28-15**

*Ephedra viridis,* called Mormon tea, grows on the rim of the Grand Canyon. This highly branched shrub has small, scalelike leaves. It is the source of the drug ephedrine and can be brewed to make a tea.

Figure 28-16 shows the unique *Welwitschia mirabilis* plant. The plant's stem is only a few centimeters tall but can grow to 1 m (3.3 ft) in diameter. Two leaves elongate from their base on the stem and then become tattered and split lengthwise by the wind. A mature leaf may be nearly 1 m (3.3 ft) wide and 3 m (10 ft) long. *Welwitschia* grows in the Namib Desert of southwestern Africa. The Namib Desert lies near the Atlantic Ocean, so a thick night fog often rolls in over the desert. *Welwitschia* apparently gets most of its water from the dew that condenses from the fog.

## Phylum Anthophyta

Anthophyta (an-THAHF-uh-tuh), the largest phylum of plants, includes over 240,000 species of flowering plants. Angiosperms, or the flowering plants, are seed plants characterized by the presence of a flower and fruit. Botanists define a *fruit* as a ripened ovary that surrounds the seeds of angiosperms. The **ovary** is the female part of the flower that encloses the egg(s).

Angiosperms grow in many forms and occupy diverse habitats. Some are herbaceous plants with showy flowers, such as violets and impatiens. Others, such as rose bushes, are shrubs. Some angiosperms are vines, such as grape plants. Oak, aspen, and birch trees are all flowering plants that have woody stems, although you may never have noticed their small flowers. Grasses are also angiosperms, but you must look closely to see their small, highly modified flowers. The world's largest flower, which can grow to 1 m (3.3 ft) in diameter, is shown in Figure 28-17.

**FIGURE 28-16**

*Welwitschia mirabilis* has a short, wide stem and twisting leaves. The female plants of this unusual gymnosperm bear large seed cones that are reddish in color.

# THE EVOLUTION OF ANGIOSPERMS

Angiosperms first appeared in the fossil record about 135 million years ago. By about 90 million years ago, angiosperms had probably begun to outnumber gymnosperms. Several factors probably led to the success of this new kind of plant. In many angiosperms, seeds germinate and produce mature plants, which in turn produce new seeds, all in one growing season. This is a tremendous advantage over gymnosperms, which often take 10 or more years to reach maturity and produce seeds. Also, the fruits of flowering plants protect seeds and aid in their dispersal. Angiosperms also have a more efficient vascular system and are more likely to be associated with mycorrhizae than gymnosperms are. Angiosperms also may gain an advantage by using animal pollination rather than the less-efficient wind pollination method used by gymnosperms. However, wind pollination is used by many successful angiosperms, including many deciduous trees. Finally, angiosperms are more diverse than gymnosperms, so they occupy more niches, such as in aquatic, epiphytic, and parasitic environments.

**FIGURE 28-17**

The stinking-corpse lily, *Rafflesia arnoldii*, has the world's largest flowers but no leaves or stems. The flowers can be male or female, and they are pollinated by flies. The plant lacks chlorophyll and is parasitic on a woody vine native to Southeast Asia.

## TABLE 28-3  Comparing Monocots and Dicots

| Plant type | Embryos | Leaves | Stems | Flower parts | Examples |
|---|---|---|---|---|---|
| Monocots | One cotyledon | Parallel venation | Scattered vascular bundles | Usually occur in threes | lilies, irises, orchids, palms, tulips, bananas, pineapples, onions, bamboo, coconut, grasses (including wheat, corn, rice, and oats) |
| Dicots | Two cotyledons | Net venation | Radially arranged vascular bundles | Usually occur in fours or fives | beans, lettuce, oaks, maples, elms, roses, carnations, cactuses, most broad-leaved forest trees |

# MONOCOTS AND DICOTS

**internet** connect

www.scilinks.org
Topic: Monocots/Dicots
Keyword: HM60989

SC*LINKS.* Maintained by the National Science Teachers Association

The flowering plants are divided into Monocotyledones (monocots) and Dicotyledones (dicots). The primary feature that distinguishes these two classes is the number of **cotyledons** (KAHT-uh-LEED′nz), or seed leaves, in a plant embryo. **Monocots** (MAHN-oh-KAHTS) usually have one cotyledon, while **dicots** (DIE-KAHTS) typically have two. By comparison, gymnosperms usually have two or more cotyledons.

Several characteristics can be used to identify monocots and dicots, as shown in Table 28-3. For example, most mature monocot leaves have several main **veins,** or bundles of vascular tissue, running parallel to each other. This vein arrangement is called **parallel venation.** Most dicots have one or more nonparallel veins that branch repeatedly, forming a network. This vein arrangement is called **net venation.** More than one characteristic should be used to determine whether a species is a monocot or a dicot.

## SECTION 3 REVIEW

1. Identify the reproductive advantages seed plants have over seedless vascular plants and nonvascular plants.

2. Name the reproductive characteristic that all seedless vascular plants share.

3. Describe the main differences between gymnosperms and angiosperms.

4. Explain why angiosperms have been more successful than gymnosperms.

5. List three characteristics that distinguish monocots from dicots.

### CRITICAL THINKING

6. Making Comparisons Compare the vascular tissue of vascular plants with the circulatory system of vertebrate animals.

7. Analyzing Information Explain how the evolutionary advancements present in both seed plants and seedless vascular plants benefit land plants.

8. Inferring Relationships Conifers, which typically have needles or scalelike leaves, are the dominant plants in areas with cold winter climates. Identify the adaptive advantage of having narrow or small leaves.

## Overview of Plants

- Three adaptations have allowed plants to be successful on land: a cuticle to prevent water loss, spores and seeds to protect reproductive cells, and special tissues for absorbing and transporting materials within the plant.

- The 12 phyla of plants are divided into two groups based on the presence of vascular tissue. The three phyla of nonvascular plants have neither true vascular tissue nor roots, stems, or leaves. Most members of the nine phyla of vascular plants have vascular tissue and true roots, stems, and leaves.

- Vascular plants can be further divided into two groups, seedless plants and seed plants. Seed plants include four phyla of gymnosperms and one phylum of angiosperms.

- All plants have a life cycle known as alternation of generations. In alternation of generations, a haploid gametophyte produces gametes. Gametes unite and give rise to a diploid sporophyte. Through meiosis, the sporophyte produces haploid spores, which develop into gametophytes.

**Vocabulary**

cuticle (p. 563)
spore (p. 563)
seed (p. 563)
vascular tissue (p. 564)

xylem (p. 564)
phloem (p. 564)
nonvascular plant (p. 564)
vascular plant (p. 564)

seed plant (p. 565)
gymnosperm (p. 565)
angiosperm (p. 565)
sporophyte (p. 565)

gametophyte (p. 565)
alternation of generations (p. 565)

## Nonvascular Plants

- The three phyla of nonvascular plants are collectively called bryophytes. These plants do not have true roots, stems, or leaves. They are very small and are usually found in moist areas.

- Bryophytes in the phylum Bryophyta are mosses. Mosses are attached to the soil by structures called rhizoids. Peat moss is a moss that has many uses.

- Bryophytes in the phylum Hepatophyta are liverworts. Liverworts lie close to the ground, which allows them to absorb water readily.

- Bryophytes in the phylum Anthocerophyta are hornworts. Hornworts do not have a stem or leaves. Hornworts have long, thin, hornlike sporophytes that grow out of the top of the plant.

**Vocabulary**

bryophyte (p. 567)          liverwort (p. 568)          hornwort (p. 569)

## Vascular Plants

- Vascular plants have several adaptive advantages over nonvascular plants, including specialized conducting tissues, the ability to grow large and live in many environments, and strong stems that allow them to grow tall and receive more sunlight.

- Seedless vascular plants include the four phyla Psilophyta, Lycophyta, Sphenophyta, and Pteridophyta. Seedless vascular plants include ferns and fernlike plants. Ferns are the dominant phylum of seedless plants. Most ferns have a rhizome, an underground stem.

- There are two main groups of seed-bearing vascular plants, gymnosperms and angiosperms. Gymnosperms are characterized by naked seeds and no flowers. Angiosperms have flowers and seeds enclosed by a fruit.

- Angiosperms have been successful for many reasons, including the production of fruit that protects seeds, quick germination, and an efficient vascular system.

- Dicots are distinguished from monocots on the basis of several characteristics: cotyledon number, leaf venation, arrangement of stem vascular tissue, and number of flower parts.

**Vocabulary**

strobilus (p. 571)
rhizome (p. 572)
fiddlehead (p. 572)
frond (p. 572)

germinate (p. 572)
seedling (p. 572)
cone (p. 572)
deciduous (p. 573)

ovary (p. 575)
cotyledon (p. 576)
monocot (p. 576)
dicot (p. 576)

vein (p. 576)
parallel venation (p. 576)
net venation (p. 576)

## USING VOCABULARY

1. For each pair of terms, explain the relationship between the terms.
   a. *seed* and *spore*
   b. *vascular plant* and *nonvascular plant*
   c. *phloem* and *xylem*

2. Choose the term that does not belong in the following group, and explain why it does not belong: *cuticle, spore, seed,* and *strobilus.*

3. For each pair of terms, explain how the meanings of the terms differ.
   a. *gymnosperm* and *angiosperm*
   b. *gametophyte* and *sporophyte*
   c. *monocot* and *dicot*

4. Use the following terms in the same sentence: *cotyledon, germinate,* and *seedling.*

5. **Word Roots and Origins** The word *deciduous* is derived from the Latin *de,* which means "down," and *cadere,* which means "to fall." Using this information, explain why the term *deciduous* is a good name for the plants that this term describes.

## UNDERSTANDING KEY CONCEPTS

6. **Summarize** how plants are adapted to living successfully on land.

7. **Name** two basic differences between nonvascular plants and vascular plants.

8. **Describe** how alternation of generations in nonvascular plants differs from that in vascular plants.

9. **Explain** why bryophytes are the most primitive type of plant.

10. **Describe** why plants in the phylum Bryophyta are sometimes called pioneer plants.

11. **Differentiate** between leafy liverworts and thalloid liverworts.

12. **State** the characteristic that hornworts do not share with other bryophytes.

13. **Explain** how specialized conducting tissues give vascular plants an adaptive advantage over nonvascular plants.

14. **Relate** how ferns and fern allies are able to reproduce without seeds.

15. **Differentiate** between a cone and a fruit.

16. **Explain** how the diversity of angiosperms has helped them be more successful than gymnosperms.

17. **State** the primary basis used for classifying angiosperms.

18. **CONCEPT MAPPING** Use the following terms to create a concept map that describes the possible evolutionary relationships of plants: *angiosperm, cone, flower, dicot, gymnosperm, monocot, ovary,* and *seed plant.*

## CRITICAL THINKING

19. **Analyzing Information** Fossil trees are easier to find than fossils of small plants. Give two possible explanations.

20. **Interpreting Graphics** Look at the plants in the photo below. Do you think the cuticles of these plants are thicker on the upper surface of the leaf or on the lower surface? Explain.

21. **Organizing Information** Copy the chart below into your notebook. Indicate with a check mark (✓) which groups of plants have vascular tissue. Also, indicate which groups of plants have a dominant sporophyte as part of their life cycle.

### Plant Evolution

| Phylum | Has vascular tissue | Has dominant sporophyte |
|---|---|---|
| Anthophyta | | |
| Bryophyta | | |
| Coniferophyta | | |
| Hepatophyta | | |
| Pteridophyta | | |

# Standardized Test Preparation

**DIRECTIONS:** Choose the letter of the answer choice that best answers the question.

1. Which of the following plants are bryophytes?
   A. ferns and cycads
   B. conifers and ginkgoes
   C. hornworts and liverworts
   D. horsetails and club mosses

2. In which way do mosses help start new biological communities?
   F. forming new soil
   G. producing spores
   H. detecting air pollution
   J. slowing decomposition

3. True roots, stems, and leaves are characteristics of which types of plants?
   A. all plants
   B. only seed plants
   C. only angiosperms
   D. all vascular plants

4. Which of the following is a vascular seed plant?
   F. ferns
   G. cycads
   H. horsetails
   J. club mosses

**INTERPRETING GRAPHICS:** The diagram below shows a plant life cycle. Use the diagram to answer the question that follows.

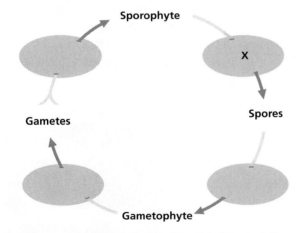

5. Which process occurs at *X* in this life cycle?
   A. mitosis
   B. meiosis
   C. alternation
   D. fertilization

6. Which of the following phrases describes monocots?
   F. bear seeds in cones
   G. have parallel venation
   H. do not produce flowers
   J. have vascular bundles arranged in a circle

**DIRECTIONS:** Complete the following analogy.

7. bryophyte : spore :: angiosperm :
   A. seed
   B. cone
   C. ovary
   D. cuticle

**INTERPRETING GRAPHICS:** The phylogenetic diagram below shows a possible evolutionary relationship between plants and algae. Use the diagram to answer the question that follows.

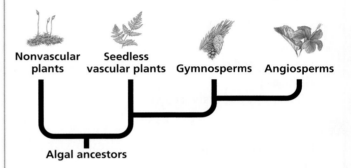

8. According to this diagram, which plants have evolved most recently?
   F. angiosperms
   G. gymnosperms
   H. nonvascular plants
   J. seedless vascular plants

## SHORT RESPONSE

The plant kingdom is very diverse, from small non-vascular plants to large flowering vascular plants.

Explain why some plants have been more successful on land than other plants have been.

## EXTENDED RESPONSE

All plants have a life cycle that alternates between haploid and diploid phases.

*Part A* Name the two phases of a plant life cycle and describe how they differ from each other.

*Part B* Describe the life cycle of one nonvascular plant and one vascular plant, including the relative sizes of the different forms and other characteristics.

**Test TIP** For questions involving life cycles, draw as much of the life cycle as you can remember. Looking at such a model may help you understand the question better and determine the answer.

# Observing Plant Diversity

## OBJECTIVES

- Compare similarities and differences among phyla of living plants.
- Relate structural adaptations to the evolution of plants.

## PROCESS SKILLS

- observing
- comparing and contrasting
- classifying
- relating structure and function

## MATERIALS

- live and preserved specimens representing four plant phyla
- stereomicroscope or hand lens
- compound light microscope
- prepared slides of male and female gametophytes of mosses and ferns

## Background

1. How do plants you commonly see compare with their ancestors, the green algae?
2. What are the differences between nonvascular plants and vascular plants? How do these differences relate to the size of a plant?
3. What is alternation of generations? Is it found in all plants?
4. Do all plants produce spores? Do all plants produce seeds? What are the advantages of producing seeds?
5. What do you think was the evolutionary pressure that resulted in colorful flowers?

## Procedure

1. **CAUTION  Put on protective gloves. Keep your hands away from your face while handling plants.** You will travel to four stations to observe plants from four phyla. Record the answers to the questions in your lab report.

### STATION 1  Mosses

2. Use a stereomicroscope or a hand lens to examine the samples of mosses, which are bryophytes. Which part of the moss is the gametophyte? Which part of the moss is the sporophyte? Make a sketch of your observations in your lab report. In your drawing, label the gametophyte and sporophyte portions of the moss plant and indicate whether each is haploid or diploid.
3. Use a compound microscope to look at the prepared slides of male and female gametophytes. What kinds of reproductive cells are produced in each of these structures? Draw the cells in your lab report.
4. Do mosses have roots? How do mosses obtain water and nutrients from the soil?

### STATION 2  Ferns

5. Look at the examples of ferns at this station. The fern leaf is called a frond. Use the hand lens to examine the fronds.
   a. How does water travel throughout a fern? List observations supporting your answer.
   b. Make a drawing of the fern plant in your lab report.

c. Indicate whether the leafy green frond in your drawing is haploid or diploid.

d. Search the underside of the fern fronds for evidence of reproductive structures. Make a drawing of your findings in your lab report. What kind of reproductive cells are produced by these structures?

6. Examine the examples of fern gametophytes.

a. Locate and identify the reproductive organs found on the gametophytes. In your lab report, sketch and label these organs and identify the reproductive cells produced by each.

b. Are the gametophytes haploid or diploid?

7. In what ways are ferns like bryophytes? In what ways are they different?

## STATION 3  Conifers

8. The gymnosperms most familiar to us are conifers. Look at the samples of conifers at this station.

a. When you look at the limb of a pine tree, which portion (gametophyte or sporophyte) of the plant life cycle are you seeing?

b. In what part of the conifer would you find reproductive structures?

9. Name an evolutionary advancement found in gymnosperms but lacking in ferns.

## STATION 4  Angiosperms

10. Draw one of the representative angiosperms at this station in your lab report. Label the representative angiosperm as a monocot or a dicot, and list at least two characteristics you used to identify it.

11. Name an evolutionary development that is present in both gymnosperms and angiosperms but absent in bryophytes and ferns.

12. How do the seeds of angiosperms differ from those of gymnosperms?

13. Examine the fruits found at this station. How have fruits benefited angiosperms?

14. 🧤 🚿  Clean up your materials and wash your hands before leaving the lab.

## Analysis and Conclusions

1. In bryophytes, how do the sperm travel from the male gametophyte to the female gametophyte?

2. In angiosperms, how do the sperm get to the part of the flower containing the egg?

3. Which portion of the plant life cycle is dominant in bryophytes? Which portion is dominant in ferns, gymnosperms, and angiosperms?

4. What is a seed? Why is the seed a helpful adaptation for terrestrial plants?

5. Why are gymnosperms referred to as *naked* seed plants?

6. Which group of plants is the most successful and diverse today? What are some adaptations found among members of this group?

## Further Inquiry

1. Find out how the geographic distribution of the phyla of living plants relates to their structures.

2. Research the deforestation of tropical rain forests. How are the different groups of plants affected by deforestation?

# PLANT STRUCTURE AND FUNCTION

Montezuma baldcypress trees, *Taxodium mucronatum*, line the banks of the Rio Cuchujaqui in the southern region of the Mexican state of Sonora. The tangled surface roots allow the trees to take advantage of surface water from floods. Some of the trees have taproots that reach very deep into the aquifer below to help them survive the dry seasons.

SCIENTIFIC AMERICAN

For project ideas from *Scientific American*, visit go.hrw.com and type in the keyword **HM6SAF**.

# PLANT CELLS AND TISSUES

*Plants have adapted to a range of environments over the course of their evolution. As plants grow, their cells become specialized for particular functions. The tissue patterns vary in each plant's roots, stems, and leaves. They also vary depending on the plant's stage of growth and taxonomic group. This chapter examines the structure and function of roots, stems, and leaves.*

## PLANT CELLS

All organisms are composed of cells. Recall that plant cells have unique structures, including a central vacuole, plastids, and a cell wall that surrounds the cell membrane. These common features are found in three basic types of plant cells—parenchyma, collenchyma, and sclerenchyma—which are shown in Figure 29-1. Small changes in the structure of these plant cells help make different functions possible. The three types of plant cells are arranged differently in roots, stems, and leaves.

**Parenchyma** (puh-REN-kuh-muh) cells are usually loosely packed cube-shaped or elongated cells with a large central vacuole and thin, flexible cell walls. Parenchyma cells are involved in metabolic functions, including photosynthesis, storage of water and nutrients, and healing. These cells usually form the bulk of nonwoody plants (plants with flexible, green stems). The fleshy parts of most fruit are made up mostly of parenchyma cells.

The cell walls of **collenchyma** (koh-LEN-kuh-muh) cells are thicker than those of parenchyma cells. Collenchyma cell walls are also irregular in shape. The thicker walls provide support for the plant.

## SECTION 1

### OBJECTIVES

- **Describe** the three basic types of plant cells.
- **Compare** the three plant tissue systems.
- **Describe** the type of growth that occurs in each of the three main types of meristems.
- **Differentiate** between primary and secondary growth.

### VOCABULARY

parenchyma
collenchyma
sclerenchyma
epidermis
cuticle
tracheid
pit
vessel element
vessel
sieve tube member
sieve tube
sieve plate
companion cell
meristem
apical meristem
lateral meristem
vascular cambium
cork cambium

**FIGURE 29-1**

Plants are composed of three basic types of cells: (a) parenchyma, (b) collenchyma, and (c) sclerenchyma.

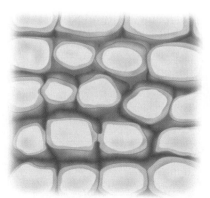

**(a) PARENCHYMA**

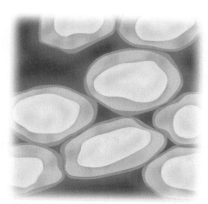

**(b) COLLENCHYMA**

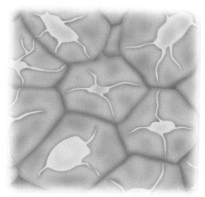

**(c) SCLERENCHYMA**

Collenchyma cells are usually grouped in strands. They are specialized for supporting regions of the plant that are still lengthening. Celery stalks contain a great amount of collenchyma cells.

**Sclerenchyma** (skluh-REN-kuh-muh) cells have thick, even, rigid cell walls. They support and strengthen the plant in areas where growth is no longer occurring. This type of cell is usually dead at maturity, providing a frame to support the plant. The hardness of the shells around nuts is due to the presence of sclerenchyma cells.

# PLANT TISSUE SYSTEMS

Cells that work together to perform a specific function form a *tissue*. Tissues are arranged into systems in plants, including the *dermal system, ground system,* and *vascular system,* which are summarized in Table 29-1. These systems are further organized into the three major plant organs—the roots, stems, and leaves. The organization of each organ reflects adaptations to the environment.

## Dermal Tissue System

The *dermal tissue system* forms the outside covering of plants. In young plants, it consists of the **epidermis** (EP-uh-DUHR-muhs), the outer layer made of parenchyma cells. The outer epidermal wall is often covered by a waxy layer called the **cuticle,** which prevents water loss. Some epidermal cells of the roots develop hairlike extensions that increase water absorption. Openings in the leaf and stem epidermis are called *stomata.* Stomata regulate the passage of gases and moisture into and out of the plant. In woody stems and roots, the epidermis is replaced by dead cork cells.

**TABLE 29-1** *Characteristics of Plant Tissue Systems*

| Tissue system | Type of cells | Location | Function in roots | Function in stems | Function in leaves |
|---|---|---|---|---|---|
| **Dermal tissue system** | flat, living parenchyma (epidermal cells) in nonwoody parts; flat, dead parenchyma (cork cells) in woody parts | outermost layer(s) of cells | absorption, protection | gas exchange, protection | gas exchange, protection |
| **Ground tissue system** | mostly parenchyma, usually with some collenchyma and fewer sclerenchyma | between dermal and vascular in nonwoody plant parts | support, storage | support, storage | photosynthesis |
| **Vascular tissue system** | elongated sclerenchyma cells, with some parenchyma | tubes throughout plant | transport, support | transport, support | transport, support |

## Ground Tissue System

Dermal tissue surrounds the *ground tissue system,* which consists of all three types of plant cells. Ground tissue functions in storage, metabolism, and support. Parenchyma cells are the most common type of cell found in ground tissue. Nonwoody roots, stems, and leaves are made up primarily of ground tissue. Cactus stems have large amounts of parenchyma cells for storing water in dry environments. Plants that grow in waterlogged soil often have parenchyma with large air spaces that allow air to reach the roots. Nonwoody plants that must be flexible to withstand wind have large amounts of collenchyma cells. Sclerenchyma cells are found where hardness is an advantage, such as in the seed coats of hard seeds and in the spines of cactuses.

## Vascular Tissue System

Ground tissue surrounds the *vascular tissue system,* which functions in transport and support. Recall that the term *vascular tissue* refers to both xylem and phloem. Xylem tissue conducts water and mineral nutrients primarily from roots upward in the plant. Xylem tissue also provides structural support for the plant. Phloem tissue conducts organic compounds and some mineral nutrients throughout the plant. Unlike xylem, phloem is alive at maturity.

In angiosperms, xylem has two major components—tracheids and vessel elements. Both are dead cells at maturity. Look at Figure 29-2a. A **tracheid** (TRAY-kee-id) is a long, thick-walled sclerenchyma cell with tapering ends. Water moves from one tracheid to another through **pits,** which are thin, porous areas of the cell wall. A **vessel element,** shown in Figure 29-2b, is a sclerenchyma cell that has either large holes in the top and bottom walls or no end walls at all. Vessel elements are stacked to form long tubes called **vessels.** Water moves more easily in vessels than in tracheids. The xylem of most seedless vascular plants and most gymnosperms contains only tracheids, which are considered a primitive type of xylem cell. The vessel elements in angiosperms probably evolved from tracheids. Xylem also contains parenchyma cells.

The conducting parenchyma cell of angiosperm phloem is called a **sieve tube member.** Look at Figure 29-2c. Sieve tube members are stacked to form long **sieve tubes.** Compounds move from cell to cell through end walls called **sieve plates.** Each sieve tube member lies next to a **companion cell,** a specialized parenchyma cell that assists in transport. Phloem also usually contains sclerenchyma cells called *fibers.* Commercially important hemp, flax, and jute fibers are phloem fibers.

Vascular tissue systems are adapted to different environmental conditions. For example, xylem forms the wood of trees, providing the plants with strength while conducting water and mineral nutrients. In aquatic plants, such as duckweed, xylem is not necessary for support or water transport and may be nearly absent from the mature plant.

**FIGURE 29-2**

(a) Tracheids are long and thin, and they contain pits in their cell walls. (b) Vessel elements are shorter and wider than tracheids. Both tracheids and vessel elements transport water. (c) Sieve tube members are long and tubular, and they contain pores in their cell walls. Sugar is transported through sieve tube members.

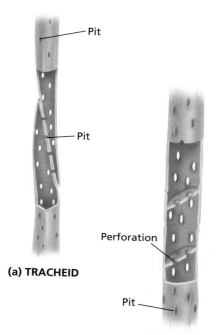

Pit

Pit

Perforation

**(a) TRACHEID**

Pit

**(b) VESSEL ELEMENT**

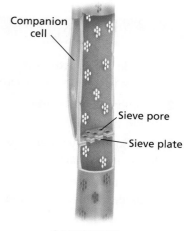

Companion cell

Sieve pore

Sieve plate

**(c) SIEVE TUBE MEMBER**

**TABLE 29-2  Types of Meristems**

| Type | Location | Growth function |
|------|----------|-----------------|
| Apical meristem | tips of stems and roots | increase length at tips |
| Intercalary meristem | between the tip and base of stems and leaves | increase length between nodes |
| Lateral meristem | sides of stems and roots | increase diameter |

# PLANT GROWTH

Plant growth originates mainly in **meristems** (MER-i-STEMZ), regions where cells continuously divide. Look at Table 29-2. Most plants grow in length through **apical** (AP-i-kuhl) **meristems** located at the tips of stems and roots. Some monocots grow in length through *intercalary* (in-TUHR-kah-ler-ee) *meristems* located above the bases of leaves and stems. Intercalary meristems allow grass leaves to quickly regrow after being grazed or mowed.

Gymnosperms and most dicots also have **lateral meristems,** which allow stems and roots to increase in diameter. Lateral meristems are located near the outside of stems and roots. There are two types of lateral meristems. The **vascular cambium,** located between the xylem and phloem, produces additional vascular tissues. The **cork cambium,** located outside the phloem, produces cork. *Cork* cells replace the epidermis in woody stems and roots. Cork cells are dead cells that provide protection and prevent water loss.

You have probably noticed that trees grow taller and wider over time. Growth in length is called *primary growth* and is produced by apical and intercalary meristems. Growth in diameter is called *secondary growth* and is produced by the lateral meristems.

## SECTION 1 REVIEW

1. How do the structures of parenchyma cells, collenchyma cells, and sclerenchyma cells differ?

2. Describe the structures of the three major plant tissue systems.

3. What kind of meristems do monocots and dicots have in common?

4. Distinguish between primary growth and secondary growth in a tree.

**CRITICAL THINKING**

5. **Making Comparisons** What vertebrate animal structures have cells that carry out functions similiar to those of sclerenchyma?

6. **Applying Information** Describe some factors that may influence the transport of water through xylem tissue.

7. **Analyzing Information** Describe how the plant kingdom would be different if plant growth only occurred in lateral meristems.

# ROOTS

*Plants have three kinds of organs—roots, stems, and leaves. A plant's root system includes the structures that typically grow underground. Roots are important because they anchor the plant in the soil. They also absorb and transport water and mineral nutrients. The storage of water and organic compounds is provided by roots.*

## TYPES OF ROOTS

When a seed sprouts, it produces a primary root. If this first root becomes the largest root, it is called a **taproot,** as illustrated in Figure 29-3a. Many plants, like carrots and certain trees, have taproots. Contrary to what you might think, even taproots rarely penetrate the ground more than a meter or two. A few species, such as cottonwoods, do have some roots that grow 50 m (164 ft) deep to tap into underground water supplies.

In some plants, the primary root does not become large. Instead, numerous small roots develop and branch to produce a **fibrous root system,** like that shown in Figure 29-3b. Many monocots, such as grasses, have fibrous root systems. Fibrous roots of monocots often develop from the base of the stem rather than from other roots.

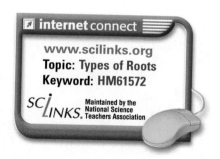

internet connect

www.scilinks.org
**Topic: Types of Roots**
**Keyword: HM61572**

SCILINKS. Maintained by the National Science Teachers Association

(a) **TAPROOT**

(b) **FIBROUS ROOT SYSTEM**

**FIGURE 29-3**

Plants can have either a taproot or a fibrous root system. (a) Many dicots, including the radish, have a large central taproot with small lateral roots. (b) Most monocots, including grasses, have a highly branched fibrous root system.

FIGURE 29-4

Some plants grow adventitious roots from above-ground parts, including stems and leaves. (a) Corn plants grow prop roots at their base to provide additional stability. (b) This orchid grows *aerial roots*, which absorb water and mineral nutrients from the surface of the tree and from the air.

(a)

(b)

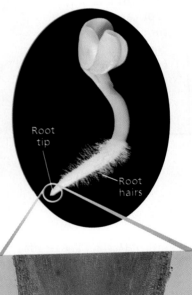

Root tip

Root hairs

Apical meristem

Root cap

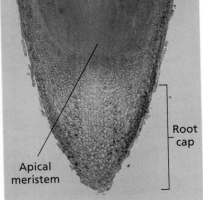

FIGURE 29-5

The root tip of this seedling has many root hairs, which increase surface area and help the plant absorb water and mineral nutrients from the soil. The root cap protects the apical meristem of a root tip.

Specialized roots that grow from uncommon places, such as stems and leaves, are called **adventitious roots.** Figure 29-4a shows the prop roots of corn, which help keep the plant's stems upright. The aerial roots of an epiphytic orchid, shown in Figure 29-4b, obtain water and mineral nutrients from the air. Aerial roots on the stems of ivy and other vines enable them to climb walls and trees.

# ROOT STRUCTURES

Root structures are adapted for several functions. Study Figure 29-5. Notice that the root tip is covered by a protective **root cap,** which covers the apical meristem. The root cap produces a slimy substance that functions like lubricating oil, allowing the root to move more easily through the soil as it grows. Cells that are crushed or knocked off the root cap as the root moves through the soil are replaced by new cells produced in the apical meristem, where cells are continuously dividing.

**Root hairs,** which are extensions of epidermal cells, increase the surface area of the root and thus increase the plant's ability to absorb water and minerals from the soil. Root hairs are shown in Figure 29-5. Most roots form symbiotic relationships with fungi to form a *mycorrhiza.* The threadlike hyphae of a mycorrhiza also increase the surface area for absorption. The spreading, usually highly branched root system increases the amount of soil that the plant can "mine" for water and mineral nutrients and aids in anchoring the plant. The large amount of root parenchyma usually functions in storage and general metabolism. Roots are dependent on stems and leaves for their energy, so they must store starch to use as an energy source during periods of little or no photosynthesis, such as winter.

# Primary Growth in Roots

Roots increase in length through cell division, elongation, and maturation in the apical meristem in the root tip (shown in Figure 29-5 on the previous page). Dermal tissue matures to form the epidermis, which is the outermost boundary of the root. Ground tissue in roots matures into two different, specialized regions: the cortex and the endodermis. The **cortex** is located just inside the epidermis, as you can see below in Figure 29-6. This largest region of the primary root is made of loosely packed parenchyma cells.

The innermost boundary of the cortex is the **endodermis** (EN-doh-DUHR-mis), also shown in Figure 29-6. Endodermal cell walls contain a narrow band of a waterproof substance that stops the movement of water beyond the endodermal cells. To enter farther into the root than the endodermis, water and dissolved substances must pass through a selectively permeable membrane. Once past this membrane, dissolved substances can move from cell to cell via small channels in cell walls that interconnect the cytoplasm of adjoining cells, including those of the endodermis. The endodermis thus controls the flow of dissolved substances into the vascular tissue of the root. The endodermis also prevents dissolved substances from backing into the cortex.

Vascular tissue in roots matures into the innermost core of the root. In most dicots and gymnosperms, xylem makes up the central core of the root, as shown in Figure 29-6a. Dicot root xylem usually forms an X-shaped structure with pockets of phloem between the xylem lobes. In monocots, the center of the root usually contains a pith of parenchyma cells, as Figure 29-6b shows. Monocot root xylem occurs in many patches that circle the pith. Small areas of phloem occur between the xylem patches.

**FIGURE 29-6**

(a) This cross section of a dicot root shows the arrangement of vascular tissue and ground tissue. Note how the xylem tissue forms an "X." The cortex and the endodermis, which are composed of ground tissue, surround the vascular tissue. (b) This cross section of a monocot root shows a prominent endodermis, the innermost boundary of the cortex. The center of the root, called the *pith,* is made up of parenchyma cells.

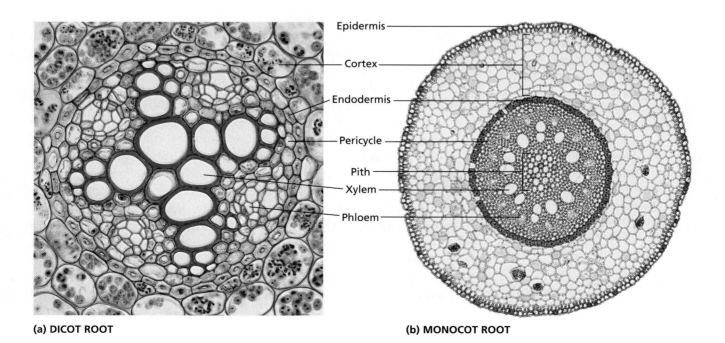

Epidermis
Cortex
Endodermis
Pericycle
Pith
Xylem
Phloem

**(a) DICOT ROOT**

**(b) MONOCOT ROOT**

FIGURE 29-7

The vascular tissues of a primary root are surrounded by the pericycle, a tissue that produces lateral roots. The pericycle is also shown in Figure 29-6 on the previous page.

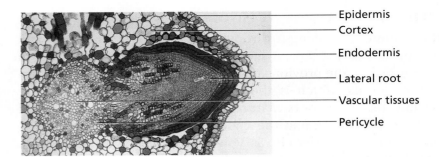

- Epidermis
- Cortex
- Endodermis
- Lateral root
- Vascular tissues
- Pericycle

The outermost layer or layers of the central vascular tissues is termed the **pericycle** (PER-i-SIE-kuhl). Lateral roots are formed by the division of pericycle cells. The developing lateral root connects its vascular tissues and endodermis to those of the parent root. Figure 29-7 shows how a lateral root grows out through the parent root's endodermis and cortex, finally emerging from the epidermis.

## Secondary Growth in Roots

Dicot and gymnosperm roots often experience secondary growth. Secondary growth begins when a pericycle and other cells form a vascular cambium between primary xylem and primary phloem. The vascular cambium produces secondary xylem toward the inside of the root and secondary phloem toward the outside. The expansion of the vascular tissues in the center of the root crushes all the tissues external to the phloem, including the endodermis, cortex, and epidermis. A cork cambium develops in the pericycle, replacing the crushed cells with cork.

# ROOT FUNCTIONS

Besides anchoring a plant in the soil, roots serve two other primary functions. First, they absorb water and a variety of minerals or mineral nutrients that are dissolved in water in the soil. Roots are selective about which minerals they absorb. Roots absorb some minerals and exclude others. Table 29-3 on the next page lists the 13 minerals that are essential for all plants. They are absorbed mainly as ions. Carbon, hydrogen, and oxygen are not listed because they are absorbed as water and carbon dioxide.

Plant cells use some minerals, such as nitrogen and potassium, in large amounts. These elements are called **macronutrients** and usually are required in amounts greater than 1,000 mg/kg of dry matter. Plant cells use other minerals, such as manganese, in smaller amounts. These are called **micronutrients** and usually are required in amounts less than 100 mg/kg of dry matter.

Adequate amounts of all 13 mineral nutrients in Table 29-3 are required for normal growth. Plants with deficiencies show characteristic symptoms and reduced growth. Severe mineral deficiencies can kill a plant. Excess amounts of some essential mineral nutrients also can be toxic to a plant.

## Quick Lab

### Observing Roots

**Materials** wilted radish seedlings, hand lens, Petri dish, water, pipet

**Procedure**

1. Place the wilted radish seedlings in a Petri dish. Observe them with the hand lens. Record your observations.

2. Using a pipet, cover only the roots with water. Observe the seedlings with the hand lens every 5 minutes for 15 minutes. Record each of your observations.

3. Use the hand lens to observe the roots. Draw and label what you see through the lens.

**Analysis** What happened to the wilted seedlings when you put them in water? How can you explain what happened? Describe two functions of a root.

## TABLE 29-3  *Essential Mineral Nutrients in Plants*

**Macronutrients**

| Element | Absorbed as | Role in plants |
|---|---|---|
| Nitrogen | $NO_3^-$, $NH_4^+$ | part of proteins, nucleic acids, chlorophyll, ATP |
| Phosphorus | $H_2PO_4^-$ | part of nucleic acids, ATP, phospholipids, coenzymes |
| Potassium | $K^+$ | required for stomatal opening and closing, enzyme cofactor |
| Calcium | $Ca^{2+}$ | part of cell walls and cell membranes |
| Magnesium | $Mg^{2+}$ | part of chlorophyll |
| Sulfur | $SO_4^{2-}$ | part of proteins |

**Micronutrients**

| Element | Absorbed as | Role in plants |
|---|---|---|
| Iron | $Fe^{2+}$ | part of molecules in electron transport |
| Manganese | $Mn^{2+}$ | required by many enzymes |
| Boron | $B(OH)_3$ | thought to be involved in carbohydrate transport |
| Chlorine | $Cl^-$ | required to split water in photosynthesis |
| Zinc | $Zn^{2+}$ | essential part of many enzymes |
| Copper | $Cu^{2+}$ | essential part of many enzymes |
| Molybdenum | $MoO_4^{2-}$ | required for nitrogen metabolism |

Some roots also store carbohydrates or water. Phloem tissue carries sugars made in leaves to roots. Sugars that roots do not immediately use for energy or building blocks are stored. In roots, these carbohydrates are usually converted to starch and stored in parenchyma cells. You are probably familiar with the storage roots of carrots, turnips, and sweet potatoes. The roots of some species in the pumpkin family store large amounts of water, which helps the plants survive during dry periods.

## SECTION 2 REVIEW

1. What are the differences between a taproot, a fibrous root system, and an adventitious root?

2. Explain how root hairs increase the ability of a plant to absorb water from the soil the plant grows in.

3. State one function of a root cap.

4. What is the difference between primary growth and secondary growth in roots?

5. What are the major functions performed by the root systems of plants?

**CRITICAL THINKING**

6. **Analyzing Information** Why might a taproot be an advantage to some plants, whereas a fibrous root system might be an advantage to others?

7. **Applying Information** How are the roots of most plants adapted to perform the major root functions?

8. **Relating Concepts** Suggest an environmental condition in which the regulation of water movement by endodermal cells might help ensure a plant's survival.

### OBJECTIVES

- **Explain** why stems differ in shape and growth.
- **Describe** the structure of stems.
- **Distinguish** between primary growth and secondary growth in stems.
- **Discuss** the three main functions of stems.

### VOCABULARY

node
internode
bud
bud scale
pith
wood
heartwood
sapwood
bark
springwood
summerwood
annual ring
source
sink
translocation
pressure-flow hypothesis
transpiration
cohesion-tension theory

# STEMS

*In contrast to roots, which are mainly adapted for absorption and anchoring, stems are usually adapted to support leaves. Whatever their sizes and shapes, stems also function in transporting materials and providing storage.*

## TYPES OF STEMS

A typical stem grows upright and is either woody or nonwoody. The many different forms of stems seen in nature, including those shown in Figure 29-8, represent adaptations to the environment. Strawberry *stolons* grow along the soil surface and produce new plants. Stems such as the edible white potato tuber are modified for storing energy as starch. Cactuses have green fleshy stems that both store water and carry on all the plant's photosynthesis. Stems of the black locust and the honeylocust develop sharp thorns that can protect the plant from animals.

**(a) STRAWBERRY (STOLONS)**

**FIGURE 29-8**

Stems provide a supporting framework for leaves. Some plants produce stems that are modified for other functions. (a) A strawberry plant has stolons, which are horizontal, above-ground stems that form new plants. (b) The potato plant has tubers, which are enlarged, short, underground stems used for storing starch. (c) A cactus is called a *succulent* because of its fleshy, water-storing stems.

**(b) POTATO (TUBERS)**

**(c) CACTUS (FLESHY STEMS)**

# STEM STRUCTURES

Stems have a more complex structure than roots, yet they are similar in many ways. Did you know that a sign nailed 2 m (about 7 ft) high on a tree will remain 2 m high, even though the tree may grow much taller? That is because most stems, like roots, grow in length only at their tips, where apical meristems produce new primary tissues. Stems, like roots, grow in circumference through lateral meristems.

Stems have several features that roots lack, as Figure 29-9 shows. Each leaf is attached to the stem at a location called a **node.** The spaces between nodes are called **internodes.** At the point of attachment of each leaf, the stem bears a lateral bud. A **bud** is capable of developing into a new *shoot system* (the above-ground part of a plant, consisting of stems and leaves). A bud contains an apical meristem and is enclosed by specialized leaves called **bud scales.** The tip of each stem usually has a terminal bud.

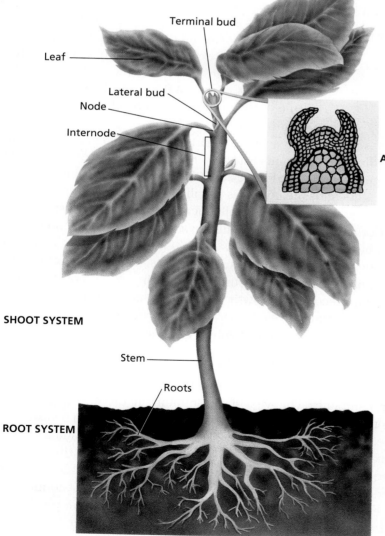

**FIGURE 29-9**

Apical meristems, responsible for the primary elongation of the plant body, are found in the shoot system and root system. Each leaf is attached to the stem at a node. The space between nodes, called the *internode,* is much larger in the older part of the stem.

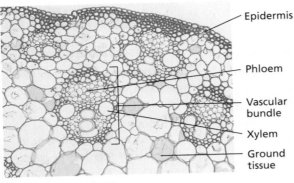

Epidermis

Phloem

Vascular bundle

Xylem

Ground tissue

**(a) MONOCOT STEM**

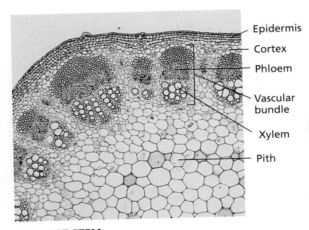

Epidermis

Cortex

Phloem

Vascular bundle

Xylem

Pith

**(b) DICOT STEM**

**FIGURE 29-10**

Primary growth in stems produces dermal, ground, and vascular tissues. (a) The cross section of a herbaceous stem of corn, a monocot, shows the vascular bundles scattered throughout the ground tissue. (b) In the sunflower, a dicot, the vascular tissues appear as a single ring of bundles between the cortex and the pith. Notice that the cortex lies just inside the epidermis, as it does in the root.

In some plants that live in cold winter environments, the terminal bud opens and the bud scales fall off when growth resumes in the spring. The bud scales leave scars on the stem surface. Trees and shrubs often are identified in winter by stem characteristics.

Root tips usually have a protective layer, the root cap. The stem apical meristem is protected by bud scales only when the stem is not growing. A surface bud forms very close to the stem tip with one or more buds at each node. In contrast, lateral roots originate farther back from the root tip and form deep inside the root at no particular location along the root axis.

## Primary Growth in Stems

As in roots, apical meristems of stems give rise to the dermal, ground, and vascular tissues. Locate each of these tissues in Figure 29-10. The dermal tissue is represented by the epidermis, or the outer layer of the stem. Its main functions are to protect the plant and to reduce the loss of water to the atmosphere while still allowing gas exchange through stomata.

In gymnosperm and dicot stems, ground tissue usually forms a cortex and a pith. The cortex frequently contains flexible collenchyma cells. The **pith** is located in the center of the stem. The ground tissue of monocot stems is usually not clearly separated into pith and cortex.

Vascular tissue formed near the apical meristem occurs in bundles—long strands that are embedded in the cortex. Look at the vascular bundles in Figure 29-10. Each bundle contains xylem tissue and phloem tissue. Xylem is usually located toward the inside of the stem, while phloem is usually located toward the outside.

Compare the arrangement of vascular bundles in monocots and dicots. Monocot stem vascular bundles are usually scattered throughout the ground tissue. Stem vascular bundles of dicots and gymnosperms usually occur in a single ring. Most monocots have little or no secondary growth, and they retain the primary growth pattern their entire lives. However, in many dicots and gymnosperms, the primary tissues are eventually replaced by secondary tissues.

## Secondary Growth in Stems

Stems increase in thickness due to the division of cells in the vascular cambium. The vascular cambium in dicot and gymnosperm stems first arises between the xylem and phloem in a vascular bundle. Eventually, the vascular cambium forms a boundary. The vascular cambium produces secondary xylem to the inside and secondary phloem to the outside. It usually produces much more secondary xylem than it does secondary phloem. Secondary xylem is called **wood.** Occasionally, the vascular cambium produces new cambium cells, which increase the stem's diameter.

Older portions of the xylem eventually stop transporting water. They often become darker than the newer xylem due to the accumulation of resins and other organic compounds produced by the few live cells remaining in the xylem. This darker wood in the center of a tree is called **heartwood,** as shown in Figure 29-11a. The functional, often lighter-colored wood nearer the outside of the trunk is **sapwood.** In a large-diameter tree, the heartwood keeps getting wider while the sapwood remains about the same thickness.

The phloem produced near the outside of the stem is part of the bark. **Bark** is the protective outside covering of woody plants. It consists of cork, cork cambium, and phloem. The cork cambium produces cork near the outside. However, cork cells are dead at maturity and cannot elongate, so the cork ruptures as the stem continues to expand in diameter. This results in the bark pattern of some trees, such as oaks and maples, appearing rough or irregular in texture.

During spring, if water is plentiful, the vascular cambium can form new xylem with cells that are wide and thin walled. This wood is called **springwood,** as shown in Figure 29-11b. In summer, when water is limited, the vascular cambium produces **summerwood,** which has smaller cells with thicker walls. In a stem cross section, the abrupt change between small summerwood cells and the following year's large springwood cells produces an **annual ring.** The circles that look like rings on a target in Figure 29-11a are the annual rings of the stem. Because one ring is usually formed each year, you can estimate the age of the stem by counting its annual rings. Annual rings also form in dicot and gymnosperm roots, but they are often less pronounced because the root environment is more uniform. Annual rings often do not occur in tropical trees because of their uniform year-round environment.

**FIGURE 29-11**

(a) Wood consists of secondary xylem. The dark-colored wood is called *heartwood,* and the light-colored wood is called *sapwood.* Bark is the outside protective covering of woody plants. (b) You can see the annual rings produced by alternating springwood cells and summerwood cells. The abundant water of the spring season helps expand the cell walls of springwood cells.

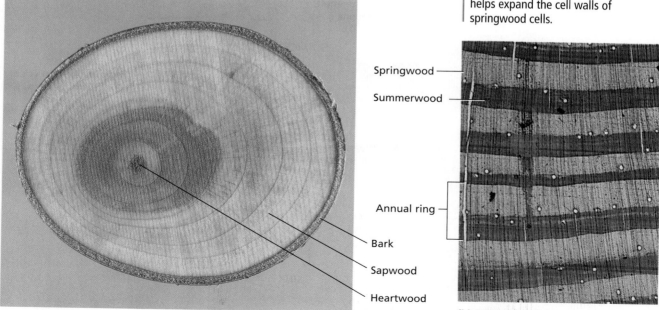

Springwood

Summerwood

Annual ring

Bark

Sapwood

Heartwood

**(a) HEARTWOOD AND SAPWOOD**

**(b) SPRINGWOOD AND SUMMERWOOD**

# STEM FUNCTIONS

Stems function in the transportation of nutrients and water, the storage of nutrients, and the support of leaves. Sugars, some plant hormones, and other organic compounds are transported in the phloem. The movement of sugars occurs from where the sugars are made or have been stored, called a **source.** The place where they will be stored or used is called a **sink.** Botanists use the term **translocation** to refer to the movement of sugars through the plant. For example, most of the time, sugars move from the leaves to the roots, to the shoot apical meristems, and to the developing flowers or fruits. Sugars may be newly made in photosynthetic cells or may have been stored as starch in roots or other stems.

Movement of sugars in the phloem is explained by the **pressure-flow hypothesis,** which states that sugars are actively transported into sieve tubes. Look at Figure 29-12. As sugars enter the sieve tubes, water is also transported in by osmosis. Thus, a positive pressure builds up at the source end of the sieve tube. This is the pressure part of the pressure-flow hypothesis.

At the sink end of the sieve tube, this process is reversed. Sugars are actively transported out, water leaves the sieve tube by osmosis, and pressure is reduced at the sink. The difference in pressure causes water to flow from source to sink. This water is also carrying dissolved substances with it. Transport in the phloem can occur in different directions at different times.

**PRESSURE-FLOW HYPOTHESIS**

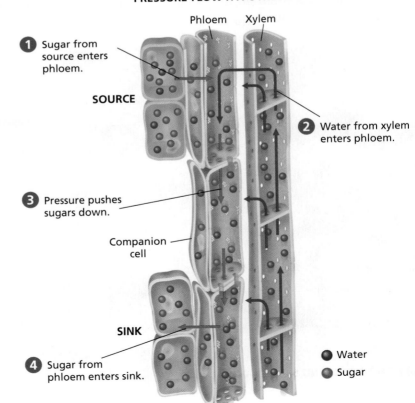

**FIGURE 29-12**

❶ Sugars from a source enter the sieve tubes of the phloem. ❷ Water moves from the xylem to the phloem by osmosis. ❸ The water creates pressure that moves the sugars down the phloem. ❹ The sugars exit the phloem and enter the sink, where they will be used or stored.

## Transport of Water

The transport of water and mineral nutrients occurs in the xylem of all plant organs, but it occurs over the greatest distances in the stems of tall trees. During the day, water is constantly evaporating from the plant, mainly through leaf stomata. This water loss is called **transpiration** (TRAN-spuh-RAY-shuhn). The large amount of water lost from the plant is a result of the plant's need to obtain carbon dioxide from the air through the stomata. Exactly how do huge trees, like redwoods, move water and mineral nutrients up their 100 m tall trunks?

According to the **cohesion-tension theory,** water is pulled up the stem xylem by the strong attraction of water molecules to each other, a property of water called *cohesion*. The movement also depends on the rigid xylem walls and the strong attraction of water molecules to the xylem wall, which is called *adhesion*. The thin, continuous columns of water extend from the leaves through the stems and into the roots. As water evaporates from the leaf, the water column is subject to great tension. However, the water column does not break because of cohesion, and it does not pull away from the xylem walls because of adhesion. The only other possibility is for it to be pulled upward. The pull at the top of the tree extends all the way to the bottom of the column. As water is pulled up the xylem, more water enters the roots from the soil.

## Storing Water and Nutrients

With abundant parenchyma cells in the cortex, plant stems are adapted for storage in most species. In some species, storage is a major function. Cactus stems are specialized for storing water. The roots of a cactus are found close to the soil surface, enabling them to absorb rainwater quickly and transport it to the cactus's fleshy stem. The edible white potato is an underground stem that is specialized for storing starch. The "eyes" of white potatoes are buds that have the ability to develop into new shoots.

### Word Roots and Origins

**transpiration**

from the Latin *trans,* meaning "across," and *spirare,* meaning "to breathe"

internet connect

www.scilinks.org
**Topic: Transpiration**
**Keyword: HM61552**

SC*i*LINKS. Maintained by the National Science Teachers Association

---

## SECTION 3 REVIEW

1. Explain why a plant species might develop thorny stems in response to its environment.

2. Describe the similarities of the apical meristems of roots to the apical meristems of stems.

3. Compare primary growth in monocots with primary growth in dicots.

4. Describe how summerwood and springwood form annual rings.

5. Describe how water is transported through xylem tissue.

**CRITICAL THINKING**

6. **Analyzing Information** Some squirrels damage trees by stripping off portions of the bark. Why might a squirrel eat bark?

7. **Evaluating Differences** What adaptive advantages might the dead cells of the xylem tissue provide over transporting cells that are alive?

8. **Inferring Relationships** The transport cells of the phloem tissue are connected end to end, and sugars flow through them. What inferences can you make about the contents of these cells?

# Science in Action

## Do Wild Animals Self-Medicate?

**Many plants have chemical compounds that defend the plants against herbivores. Such compounds are the active ingredients in many familiar medicines. With so many plants in existence, how do scientists know which ones to test for possible medical benefit? Michael Huffman studies animal feeding behavior for clues.**

**Dr. Michael Huffman**

### HYPOTHESIS: Chimpanzees Eat Some Plants for Medicinal Purposes

Researchers studying chimpanzees in Africa have noted that chimps have an unusual feeding habit when they are ill. Before eating the shoots of the plant *Vernonia amygdalina*, chimps carefully remove the outer bark and leaves to chew on the exposed pith, the spongy material found in some vascular plants. The chimps extract juice from the pith, which the researchers found odd because the juice is extremely bitter. Even though the plant is available year-round, chimps rarely eat it. Based on his observations and those of other scientists, Michael A. Huffman, a researcher at the Primate Research Institute in Japan, wanted to find out whether chimps are self-medicating by eating these plants.

### METHODS: Observe Behavior, Collect Samples, and Test Plants

Huffman began by collecting chimpanzee fecal samples at Mahale, Tanzania. He also made detailed observations of as many individual chimps as possible. The fecal samples were from chimps seen eating *V. amygdalina* during times of apparent illness. Huffman collaborated with other scientists already studying chemicals found in *V. amygdalina*.

### RESULTS: Chimps Recover; Fecal Samples Contain Parasites; Plant Analysis Reveals Antiparasitic Compounds

Huffman and his colleagues found that within 24 hours after eating *V. amygdalina*, chimps regain their appetites, have reduced numbers of parasites, and recover from constipation or diarrhea. Scientists working with Huffman showed that the pith of *V. amygdalina* contains several bioactive chemicals. Tests revealed that these chemicals are effective against many different parasites. For example, vernonioside B1 and vernoniol B1 were shown to suppress movement and egg laying in *Schistosoma japonicum*, a parasitic worm. Scientists also found that chemicals from the pith are effective against drug-resistant malarial parasites.

### CONCLUSIONS: Chimpanzees Self-Medicate by Eating Plants with Beneficial Chemical Compounds

Interestingly, a more toxic compound, vernodalin, was found in the leaves. The pith of the plant instead contained large amounts of vernonioside B1. This same pattern was later verified in analyses of other *V. amygdalina* specimens collected at various locations in Mahale during different seasons. Huffman and his colleagues think that because chimps discard the bark and leaves and just eat the pith, the chimps have learned that certain parts of the plant are harmful and certain parts are beneficial.

Additional research has revealed that *V. amygdalina* has been part of Tanzanian folk medicine for years. The WaTongwe people of this area use *V. amygdalina* for stomachaches and parasitic infections. Other African tribes use *V. amygdalina* to treat ailments in their livestock, which suggests agricultural applications for other countries.

*An adult male chimp with a nematode infection chews on the pith of* Vernonia amygdalina.

### REVIEW

1. What observations led Huffman to propose his hypothesis?

2. Can chimpanzees learn from experience? Explain your reasoning.

3. **Critical Thinking** Why was it important for Huffman to work with other scientists?

# LEAVES

*Most leaves are thin and flat, an adaptation that helps them capture sunlight for photosynthesis. Although this structure may be typical, it is certainly not universal. Like roots and stems, leaves are extremely variable. This variability represents adaptations to environmental conditions.*

## TYPES OF LEAVES

Look at the leaves in Figure 29-13a. The coiled structure is a **tendril,** a modified leaf found in many vines, such as peas and pumpkins. It wraps around objects and supports the climbing vine. In some species, like grape, tendrils are specialized stems.

An unusual leaf modification occurs in carnivorous plants such as the pitcher plant, shown in Figure 29-13b. In carnivorous plants, leaves function as food traps. These plants grow in soil that is poor in several mineral nutrients, especially nitrogen. The plant receives substantial amounts of mineral nutrients when it traps and digests insects and other small animals.

Leaves, or parts of leaves, are often modified into spines that protect the plant from being eaten by animals, as shown in Figure 29-13c. Because spines are small and nonphotosynthetic, they greatly reduce transpiration in desert species such as cactuses.

## SECTION 4

### OBJECTIVES

- **Describe** adaptations of leaves.
- **Identify** the difference between a simple leaf, a compound leaf, and a doubly compound leaf.
- **Describe** the tissues that make up the internal structure of a leaf.
- **Describe** the major functions of leaves.

### VOCABULARY

tendril
blade
petiole
simple leaf
compound leaf
leaflet
mesophyll
palisade mesophyll
spongy mesophyll
vein
venation
parallel venation
net venation
guard cell

**FIGURE 29-13**

Many plant species have developed leaf adaptations. (a) The pea plant has tendrils that climb. (b) The pitcher plant has tubular leaves that trap insects. (c) The barberry has spines that may protect against herbivores.

**(a) TENDRIL**

**(b) TUBULAR LEAF**

**(c) SPINES**

**(a) SIMPLE LEAF**

**(b) COMPOUND LEAF**

**(c) DOUBLY COMPOUND LEAF**

**FIGURE 29-14**

(a) A sugar-maple leaf is called a simple leaf because it has only one blade. (b) A white clover leaf is called a compound leaf because the leaf blade is divided into distinct leaflets. (c) The honeylocust has a doubly compound leaf because each leaflet is subdivided into smaller leaflets.

# LEAF STRUCTURES

Leaves come in a wide variety of shapes and sizes and are an important feature used for plant identification. Leaves can be round, straplike, needlelike, or heart-shaped. The broad, flat portion of a leaf, called the **blade,** is the site of most photosynthesis. The blade is usually attached to the stem by a stalklike **petiole.** The maple leaf shown in Figure 29-14a is a **simple leaf;** it has a single blade. In **compound leaves,** such as the white clover in Figure 29-14b, the blade is divided into **leaflets.** In some species, the leaflets themselves are divided. The result is a doubly compound leaf, such as that of the honeylocust shown in Figure 29-14c.

Leaves consist of three tissue systems. The dermal tissue system is represented by the epidermis. In most leaves the epidermis is a single layer of cells coated with a nearly impermeable cuticle. Water, oxygen, and carbon dioxide enter and exit the leaf through stomata in the epidermis. Epidermal hairs are often present and usually function to protect the leaf from insects and intense light.

The number of stomata per unit area of leaf varies by species. For example, submerged leaves of aquatic plants have few or no stomata. Corn leaves have up to 10,000 stomata per square centimeter on both upper and lower surfaces. Scarlet oak has over 100,000 stomata per square centimeter on the lower leaf surface and none on the upper surface. Regardless of their exact distribution, stomata are needed to regulate gas exchange.

In most plants, photosynthesis occurs in the leaf **mesophyll** (MEZ-oh-FIL), a ground tissue composed of chloroplast-rich parenchyma cells. In most plants, the mesophyll is organized into two layers, which are shown in Figure 29-15 on the next page. The **palisade mesophyll** layer occurs directly beneath the upper epidermis and is the site of most photosynthesis. Palisade cells are columnar and appear to be packed tightly together in one or two layers. However, there are air spaces between the long side walls of palisade cells. Beneath the palisade layer is the **spongy mesophyll.** It usually consists of irregularly shaped cells surrounded by large air spaces, which allow oxygen, carbon dioxide, and water to diffuse into and out of the leaf.

The vascular tissue system of leaves consists of vascular bundles called **veins.** Veins are continuous with the vascular tissue of the stem and the petiole, and they lie embedded in the mesophyll. Veins branch repeatedly so that each cell is usually less than 1 mm (0.04 in.) from a vein.

**Venation** is the arrangement of veins in a leaf. Leaves of most monocots, such as grasses, have **parallel venation,** meaning that several main veins are roughly parallel to each other. The main veins are connected by small, inconspicuous veins. Leaves of most dicots, such as sycamores, have **net venation,** meaning that the main vein or veins repeatedly branch to form a conspicuous network of smaller veins.

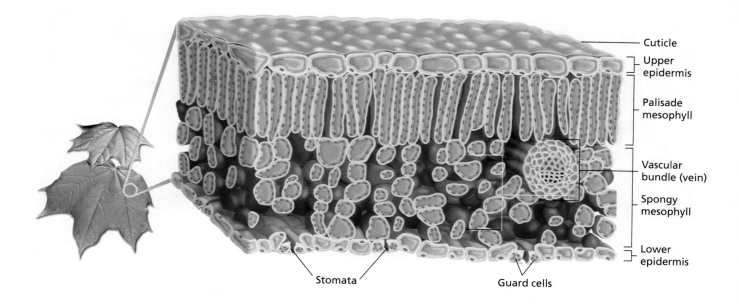

Cuticle
Upper epidermis
Palisade mesophyll
Vascular bundle (vein)
Spongy mesophyll
Lower epidermis
Stomata
Guard cells

# LEAF FUNCTIONS

Leaves are the primary site of photosynthesis in most plants. Mesophyll cells in leaves use light energy, carbon dioxide, and water to make sugars. Light energy also is used by mesophyll cells to synthesize amino acids and a variety of other organic molecules. Sugars made in a leaf can be used by the leaf as an energy source or as building blocks for cells. They also may be transported to other parts of the plant, where they are either stored or used for energy or building blocks.

A major limitation to plant photosynthesis is insufficient water due to transpiration. For example, up to 98 percent of the water that is absorbed by a corn plant's roots is lost through transpiration. However, transpiration may benefit the plant by cooling it and by speeding the transport of mineral nutrients through the xylem.

## Modifications for Capturing Light

Leaves absorb light, which, in turn, provides the energy for photosynthesis. The leaves of some plant species have adapted to their environment to maximize light interception. On the same tree, leaves that develop in full sun are thicker, have a smaller area per leaf, and have more chloroplasts per unit area. Shade-leaf chloroplasts are arranged so that shading of one chloroplast by another is minimized, while sun-leaf chloroplasts are not.

In dry environments, plants often receive more light than they can use. Structures have evolved in these plants that reduce the amount of light absorbed. For example, many desert plants have evolved dense coatings of hairs that reduce light absorption. The cut window plant shown in Figure 29-16 protects itself from its dry environment by growing underground. Only its leaf tips protrude above the soil to gather light for photosynthesis.

**FIGURE 29-15**

Cells from all three tissue systems are represented in a leaf. The epidermis is part of the dermal system, and the vascular bundle (vein) is part of the vascular system. The mesophyll is ground tissue made of parenchyma cells, and it generally contains chloroplasts.

**FIGURE 29-16**

The cut window plant (*Haworthia truncata*) has flat-topped leaves that look as if they have been cut. The transparent leaf tips are sacs that diffuse sunlight before channeling it to the plant's buried leaves.

(a) MONOCOT LEAF

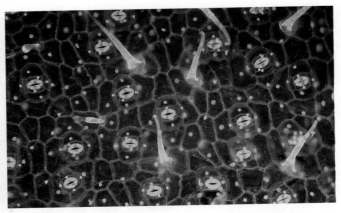

(b) DICOT LEAF

**FIGURE 29-17**

These micrographs of monocot and dicot leaves show how the arrangement of stomata in each is different. (a) In the corn leaf, the stomata are in a parallel arrangement, which is typical of monocots. (b) In the potato leaf, the stomata are in a random arrangement, which is typical of dicots.

## Gas Exchange

Plants must balance their need to open their stomata to receive carbon dioxide and release oxygen with their need to close their stomata to prevent water loss through transpiration. A stoma is bordered by two kidney-shaped guard cells. **Guard cells,** shown in Figure 29-15 on the previous page, are modified cells on the leaf epidermis that regulate gas and water exchange. Figure 29-17 shows how the stomata are arranged differently in monocots and dicots.

The stomata of most plants open during the day and close at night. The opening and closing of a stoma is regulated by the amount of water in its guard cells. When epidermal cells of leaves pump potassium ions ($K^+$) into guard cells, water moves into the guard cells by osmosis. This influx of water makes the guard cells swell, which causes them to bow apart and form a pore. During darkness, potassium ions are pumped out of the guard cells. Water then leaves the guard cells by osmosis. This causes the guard cells to shrink slightly and the pore to close.

Stomata also close if water is scarce. The closing of stomata greatly reduces further water loss and may help the plant survive until the next rain. However, stomata closure virtually shuts down photosynthesis by cutting off the supply of carbon dioxide.

## SECTION 4 REVIEW

1. Describe three adaptations found in different types of leaves.

2. What is the difference between a simple leaf, a compound leaf, and a doubly compound leaf?

3. Describe the basic function of each of the three leaf tissues.

4. Explain the function of the guard cells in regulating the opening and closing of stomata on a leaf's surface.

**CRITICAL THINKING**

5. **Evaluating Information** Why might it be an advantage for a plant to have most of its stomata on the underside of a horizontal leaf?

6. **Inferring Relationships** Why do plants grown in greenhouses in winter rarely grow as fast as the same type of plant grown outside in the summer, even if the temperatures are the same?

7. **Predicting Results** Suppose a plant had a mutation that produced defective potassium ion pumps. What might happen to this plant?

# CHAPTER HIGHLIGHTS

**Plant Cells and Tissues**

- Parenchyma, collenchyma, and sclerenchyma are basic plant cell types.
- The three types of plant tissue systems are dermal, ground, and vascular.

- Plant growth occurs in the apical, intercalary, and lateral meristems.
- Primary growth occurs mainly in the apical meristems. Secondary growth occurs in the lateral meristems.

**Vocabulary**

parenchyma (p. 583)
collenchyma (p. 583)
sclerenchyma (p. 584)
epidermis (p. 584)
cuticle (p. 584)

tracheid (p. 585)
pit (p. 585)
vessel element (p. 585)
vessel (p. 585)
sieve tube member (p. 585)

sieve tube (p. 585)
sieve plate (p. 585)
companion cell (p. 585)
meristem (p. 586)
apical meristem (p. 586)

lateral meristem (p. 586)
vascular cambium (p. 586)
cork cambium (p. 586)

---

**Roots**

- A taproot is a large primary root. A fibrous root system has many small branching roots. Adventitious roots are specialized roots that grow from uncommon places.
- Roots are made up of root caps, apical meristems, and root hairs.

- Primary growth in roots occurs at the root tip. Secondary growth occurs when a vascular cambium forms between primary xylem and primary phloem.
- Roots anchor the plant and store and absorb water and mineral nutrients from the soil.

**Vocabulary**

taproot (p. 587)
fibrous root system (p. 587)

adventitious root (p. 588)
root cap (p. 588)
root hair (p. 588)

cortex (p. 589)
endodermis (p. 589)
pericycle (p. 590)

macronutrient (p. 590)
micronutrient (p. 590)

---

**Stems**

- Stem shape and growth are adaptations to the environment.
- Both nonwoody and woody stems contain xylem and phloem.

- Most monocot stems have only primary growth. Dicot stems often produce abundant secondary growth.
- Stems support leaves and transport and store nutrients and water.

**Vocabulary**

node (p. 593)
internode (p. 593)
bud (p. 593)
bud scale (p. 593)
pith (p. 594)

wood (p. 594)
heartwood (p. 595)
sapwood (p. 595)
bark (p. 595)
springwood (p. 595)

summerwood (p. 595)
annual ring (p. 595)
source (p. 596)
sink (p. 596)
translocation (p. 596)

pressure-flow
   hypothesis (p. 596)
transpiration (p. 597)
cohesion-tension
   theory (p. 597)

---

**Leaves**

- The variability in leaf structures represents adaptations to environmental conditions. Leaves may be simple, compound, or doubly compound.

- Photosynthesis occurs mostly in the mesophyll.
- Some leaves are modified to maximize light interception. Gas exchange is controlled by stomata.

**Vocabulary**

tendril (p. 599)
blade (p. 600)
petiole (p. 600)
simple leaf (p. 600)

compound leaf (p. 600)
leaflet (p. 600)
mesophyll (p. 600)
palisade mesophyll (p. 600)

spongy mesophyll (p. 600)
vein (p. 600)
venation (p. 600)
parallel venation (p. 600)

net venation (p. 600)
guard cell (p. 602)

## USING VOCABULARY

1. For each pair of terms, explain the relationship between the terms.
   a. *taproot* and *fibrous root*
   b. *sieve tube member* and *vessel element*
   c. *transpiration* and *translocation*

2. Use the following terms in the same sentence: *parenchyma, collenchyma,* and *sclerenchyma.*

3. For each pair of terms, explain how the meanings of the terms differ.
   a. *apical meristem* and *lateral meristem*
   b. *simple leaf* and *compound leaf*
   c. *root hair* and *root cap*

4. **Word Roots and Origins** The word *mesophyll* is derived from the Latin *meso,* which means "middle," and the Greek *phyllon,* which means "leaf." Using this information, explain why the term *mesophyll* is a good name for the part of the leaf that the term describes.

## UNDERSTANDING KEY CONCEPTS

5. **Compare** the structure and function of parenchyma, collenchyma, and sclerenchyma cells.

6. **Compare** the functions of the three plant tissue systems.

7. **Differentiate** the type of growth that occurs in each of the three kinds of meristems.

8. **Explain** the difference between primary growth and secondary growth.

9. **Name** two types of adventitious roots.

10. **Sequence** the structures of a root that a water molecule would pass through as it enters and then moves through a plant.

11. **Relate** what causes a plant stem or root to grow in diameter.

12. **Name** two familiar examples of carbohydrate storage in roots.

13. **Explain** why stems vary in shape and growth patterns.

14. **Distinguish** the structure of a root from the structure of a stem.

15. **Explain** how annual rings form in a woody plant.

16. **Differentiate** between the mechanisms of water and sugar transport in a plant.

17. **Explain** why all leaves do not look alike.

18. **Describe** the structure of a doubly compound leaf.

19. **Name** the type of plant tissue that makes up the mesophyll.

20. **Identify** a leaf adaptation for maximizing light interception.

21. **CONCEPT MAPPING** Use the following terms to create a concept map that illustrates the structures and functions of one type of plant tissue: *phloem, vessel, sieve tube member, tracheid, vascular tissue, vessel element, carbohydrates,* and *xylem.*

## CRITICAL THINKING

22. **Applying Information** When transplanting a plant, it is important to not remove any more soil than necessary from around the root system. From your knowledge of the function of roots and root hairs, why do you think this is so important?

23. **Analyzing Data** Suppose you examine a tree stump and notice that the annual rings are thinner and closer together 50 rings in from the edge. What would you conclude about the climate in the area 50 years ago?

24. **Applying Information** Why would an agricultural practice that eliminated transpirational water loss be disadvantageous for plants?

25. **Evaluating Differences** Would you expect water absorption in a plant to be greater in parts of roots that have undergone secondary growth or in parts that have not? Explain your reasoning.

26. **Interpreting Graphics** What causes a knot in a board, like the one shown in the photo below?

# Standardized Test Preparation

**DIRECTIONS:** Choose the letter of the answer choice that best answers the question.

1. Which of the following are the main function of collenchyma and sclerenchyma?
   A. storage
   B. support
   C. transport
   D. photosynthesis

2. Most monocots do not have which of the following?
   F. xylem
   G. phloem
   H. primary growth
   J. secondary growth

3. Which of the following structures is found in stems but not in roots?
   A. node
   B. cortex
   C. epidermis
   D. vascular tissue

4. The movement of water through a plant is driven by the loss of water vapor from which structure?
   F. buds
   G. nodes
   H. leaves
   J. root hairs

**INTERPRETING GRAPHICS:** The illustration below shows a cross section of a monocot root. Use the illustration to answer the question that follows.

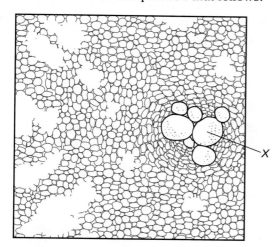

5. What is the structure marked with an *X*?
   A. xylem
   B. cortex
   C. phloem
   D. endodermis

**DIRECTIONS:** Complete the following analogy.

6. Mesophyll : photosynthesis :: sapwood :
   F. storage
   G. sugar transport
   H. water transport
   J. production of new cells

**INTERPRETING GRAPHICS:** The illustration below shows a leaf. Use the illustration to answer the question that follows.

7. What type of leaf is shown?
   A. tendril
   B. simple
   C. compound
   D. doubly compound

### SHORT RESPONSE

The primary function of leaves is to carry out photosynthesis.

Explain how a leaf's structure is an adaptation that allows intake of carbon dioxide with minimal water loss.

### EXTENDED RESPONSE

A stem contains tissues that transport water along with dissolved minerals and sugars.

*Part A* Identify the cells that transport water, and describe how water moves through a plant.

*Part B* Identify the cells that transport sugar, and describe how sugars move through a plant.

**Test TIP** For the short- or extended-response questions, be sure to write in complete sentences. When you have finished writing your answer, be sure to proofread for spelling, grammar, and punctuation errors.

# Observing Roots, Stems, and Leaves

## OBJECTIVES

- Observe the tissues and structures that make up roots, stems, and leaves.
- Explain how roots, stems, and leaves are adapted for the functions they perform.

## PROCESS SKILLS

- observing
- identifying
- relating structure and function

## MATERIALS

- prepared slides of the following tissues:
  - *Allium* root tip longitudinal section
  - *Syringa* leaf cross section
  - *Ranunculus* root cross section
  - *Ranunculus* stem cross section
  - *Zea mays* stem cross section
- compound light microscope

## Background

1. Which plant tissues are responsible for the absorption of water and mineral nutrients?
2. How is sugar, which is produced in the leaf, moved to other parts of the plant?
3. How are woody and nonwoody stems different, and how are they alike?
4. What tissues are continuous in the root, stem, and leaf?
5. How does the leaf conserve water?

## PART A   Roots

1. **CAUTION Glass slides may break and cut you.** Observe the prepared slide of the *Allium* root tip under low power. Locate the root cap and the root tip meristematic cells. You may look at the photograph in the chapter for help. Note the long root hairs in the area above the root tip.
2. In your lab report, draw the root tip that you observe, and label the root cap, meristem, and root hairs in your drawings.

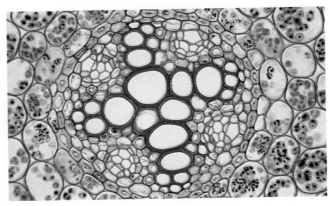

**Ranunculus *root (275×)—a dicot***

3. Change slides to the root cross section of the dicot *Ranunculus.* This slide should look similar to the photograph above. The inner core is the vascular tissue, which is surrounded by the endodermis. This area is involved in the transport of water, mineral nutrients, and organic compounds. Look for the X-shaped xylem and the smaller phloem cells surrounding the xylem.
4. In your lab report, draw what you see, and identify the xylem tissue and the phloem tissue in your drawing.
5. Locate the cortex, where starch is stored, which surrounds the vascular cylinder. Outside the cortex, find the epidermal cells and their root hairs. Draw a one-quarter section of the root tissues. Label all the tissues in your lab report.

## PART B   Stems

6. Observe a prepared slide of the stem of *Zea mays,* a monocot, and find the epidermis and the photosynthetic layer. It should look like the top photograph on the next page. In the center, look for the vascular bundles made up of xylem and phloem. Draw a diagram showing the location of the vascular bundles and the epidermis layer as they appear when viewed under low power.
7. Switch to high power, and observe a vascular bundle. Draw the vascular bundle, and label the tissues.
8. Observe a cross section of *Ranunculus,* a nonwoody dicot stem. Compare your slide with the photograph

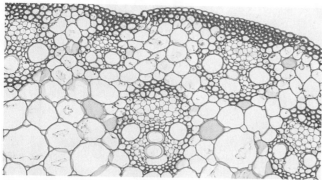

Zea mays *stem (130×)—a monocot*

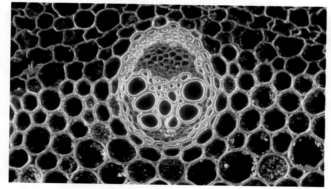

Ranunculus *stem (151×)—a dicot*

of *Ranunculus* shown above. Look for the epidermis and cortex layers. Notice that in a dicot, the stem is more complex than the root. Note the arrangement of the vascular bundles. In your lab report, draw what you observe. Label the epidermis, cortex, and individual vascular bundles.

9. Focus on a vascular bundle under high power. Draw and label a diagram of a vascular bundle in your lab report.

**PART C** Leaves

10. Observe a prepared slide of a lilac leaf, *Syringa,* shown below, under low power, and find the lower epidermis.

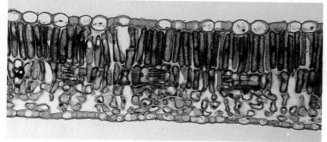

Syringa *leaf (530×)*

11. Identify the stomata on the lower epidermis of the lilac leaf. Find the guard cells that open and close a particular stoma. Locate an open stoma and a closed stoma. Draw and label diagrams of the stomata and the guard cells in your lab report.

12. Look at the center part of the cross section. Note the spongy texture of the mesophyll layer. Locate a vein containing xylem and phloem. Now identify the palisade layer, the upper epidermis, and finally the clear, continuous, noncellular layer on top. This layer is called the *cuticle.* Draw and label a diagram of your observations in your lab report.

13. Clean up your materials before leaving the lab.

## Analysis and Conclusions

1. In the dicot root that you observed, where are phloem and xylem located?
2. Where are the xylem and phloem found in the nonwoody stem that you observed?
3. How are the vascular bundles different in the monocot and dicot stems that you observed?
4. How are the root cap cells different from the root tip meristematic cells?
5. What is the function of the root hairs?
6. How do the arrangements of xylem and phloem differ in roots, stems, and leaves?
7. What is the function of a stoma?
8. What is the function of the air space in the mesophyll of the leaf?
9. Which leaf structures help to conserve water?
10. Which tissues of the leaf are continuous with the stem and root tissues? How is this functional?
11. Look at the various tissues found in your drawings of roots, stems, and leaves. Classify each tissue as either dermal tissue, ground tissue, or vascular tissue.

## Further Inquiry

The parts of a flower are actually modified stems and leaves. Design—but do not carry out—a procedure for dissecting a flower. Include a diagram of the parts of the flower to be viewed. Use references from the library to determine which kinds of flowers are best for dissection.

# PLANT REPRODUCTION

Two pollen grains (yellow) have been deposited on the stigma of a goose-grass *(Galium aparine)* flower. A pollen tube can be seen growing from the pollen grain on the right. The pollen tube provides a path for sperm to travel from the pollen grain to the egg so that fertilization may occur.

**SECTION 1** *Plant Life Cycles*

**SECTION 2** *Sexual Reproduction in Flowering Plants*

**SECTION 3** *Dispersal and Propagation*

SCIENTIFIC AMERICAN

For project ideas from *Scientific American*, visit go.hrw.com and type in the keyword **HM6SAG**.

# PLANT LIFE CYCLES

*A life cycle includes all of the stages of an organism's growth and development. Recall that a plant's life cycle involves two alternating multicellular stages—a diploid (2n) sporophyte stage and a haploid (1n) gametophyte stage. This type of life cycle is called* alternation of generations. *Also recall that the size of gametophytes and sporophytes varies among the plant groups.*

## THE LIFE CYCLE OF MOSSES

The dominant form of a moss is a clump of green gametophytes. Look at the moss life cycle illustrated in Figure 30-1. Moss gametophytes produce gametes in two types of reproductive structures—antheridia and archegonia. An **antheridium** (AN-thuhr-ID-ee-uhm) is a male reproductive structure that produces hundreds of flagellated sperm by mitosis. An **archegonium** (AWR-kuh-GOH-nee-uhm) is a female reproductive structure that produces a single egg by mitosis. During moist periods, sperm break out of the antheridia and swim to the archegonia. One sperm fertilizes the egg at the base of an archegonium, forming a diploid zygote. Through repeated mitotic divisions, the zygote forms an embryo and develops into a sporophyte.

**FIGURE 30-1**

The life cycle of mosses alternates between clumps of gametophytes (the dominant generation) and a sporophyte that consists of a spore capsule on a bare stalk.

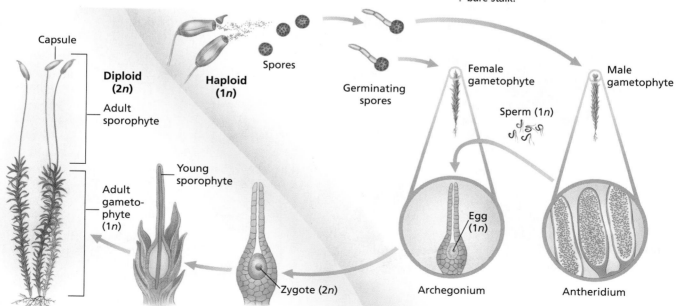

Capsule

**Diploid (2n)**

Adult sporophyte

Adult gametophyte (1n)

Young sporophyte

Zygote (2n)

**Haploid (1n)**

Spores

Germinating spores

Female gametophyte

Sperm (1n)

Male gametophyte

Egg (1n)

Archegonium

Antheridium

A moss sporophyte begins as a thin stalk that grows from the tip of a gametophyte. The sporophyte remains attached to the gametophyte and depends on it for nourishment. Soon, cells at the tip of a stalk form a sporangium, called the *capsule*. Cells in the capsule undergo meiosis to form haploid spores, which are all the same. The production of one type of spore is called **homospory** (hoh-MAHS-puh-ree). Therefore, the life cycle of mosses is called *homosporous* (hoh-MAHS-puh-ruhs) *alternation of generations*. When the spores are mature, the capsule splits open, and the spores are carried away by the wind. Spores that land in favorable environments may germinate and grow into new gametophytes.

# THE LIFE CYCLE OF FERNS

The life cycle of a typical fern, shown in Figure 30-2, is similar to the moss life cycle. Like mosses, most ferns are homosporous. And as in mosses, the fern sporophyte grows from the gametophyte. But in the fern life cycle, the sporophyte, not the gametophyte, is the dominant generation. Fern gametophytes are tiny (about 10 mm, or 0.5 in., in diameter), flat plants that are anchored to the soil by rhizoids. Both antheridia and archegonia may form on the lower surface of a fern gametophyte. When water is present, sperm released by antheridia swim to archegonia. One sperm fuses with the egg in an archegonium, forming a zygote, which is the first cell of a new sporophyte.

The zygote grows into an embryo and then into a young fern sporophyte through mitotic cell division. Once the sporophyte can survive on its own, the gametophyte will die. A mature fern sporophyte usually has compound leaves that are known as *fronds*.

**FIGURE 30-2**

The life cycle of most ferns alternates between a large sporophyte (the dominant generation) and a small gametophyte. Both the egg and sperm may be produced on the same gametophyte.

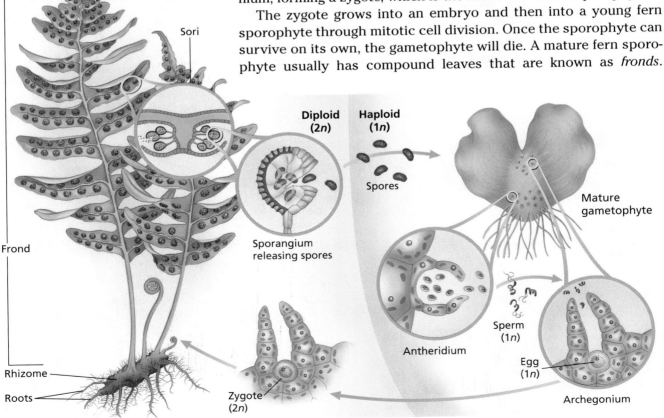

Sori

Diploid
(2n)

Haploid
(1n)

Spores

Mature gametophyte

Sporangium releasing spores

Frond

Sperm
(1n)

Antheridium

Egg
(1n)

Archegonium

Rhizome

Roots

Zygote
(2n)

Adult sporophyte

Fronds grow from an underground stem, or rhizome. In most ferns, certain cells on the underside of the fronds develop into sporangia. In many ferns, the sporangia are clustered together. A cluster of sporangia is called a **sorus** (SOH-ruhs), plural, *sori* (SOH-ree). Cells inside a sporangium undergo meiosis, forming haploid spores. At maturity, the sporangium opens and the spores are catapulted 1 cm (0.4 in.) or more and are then carried away by air currents. When the spores land, they may grow into new gametophytes.

**Word Roots and Origins**

*sorus*

from the Greek *soros*, meaning "heap"

# THE LIFE CYCLE OF GYMNOSPERMS

Unlike mosses and most ferns, gymnosperms produce two types of spores—male **microspores** and female **megaspores.** Microspores grow into male gametophytes, while megaspores grow into female gametophytes. The production of different types of spores is called **heterospory** (HET-uhr-AHS-puh-ree). Thus, the gymnosperm life cycle is called *heterosporous* (HET-uhr-AHS-puh-ruhs) *alternation of generations.* All seed plants, spike mosses, quillworts, and a few fern species have heterospory. The microspores of heterosporous plants produce male gametophytes that stay attached to the much larger sporophyte and develop into pollen. Pollen can be transported through the air to female gametophytes. Sexual reproduction in seed plants therefore can take place independent of seasonal rains or other periods of moisture. Figure 30-3 shows the life cycle of a conifer, the most common kind of gymnosperm.

**FIGURE 30-3**

The life cycle of a gymnosperm alternates between a large sporophyte (the dominant generation), which produces two types of spores in cones, and microscopic gametophytes, which produce gametes. Female gametophytes produce eggs, and male gametophytes produce sperm.

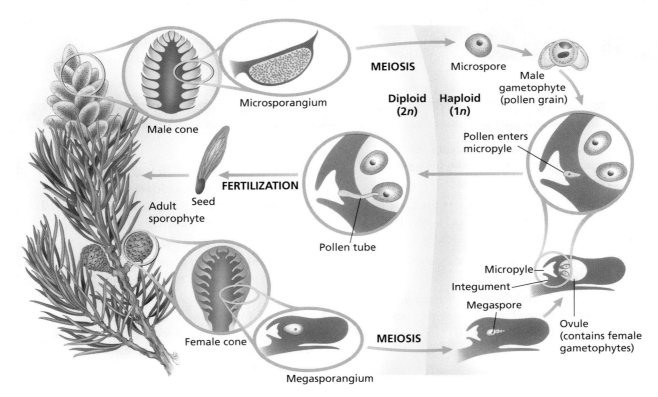

In the pine (a conifer), sexual reproduction takes more than two years. During the first summer, a mature pine tree produces separate female and male cones. The female cones produce *megasporangia,* while the male cones produce *microsporangia.* The following spring, cells in all sporangia undergo meiosis and divide to produce haploid spores. These spores never leave the parent to develop independently. *Megasporangia* produce megaspores, which develop into *megagametophytes,* or female gametophytes. A thick layer of cells called an **integument** (in-TEG-yoo-muhnt) surrounds each megasporangium. The integument has a small opening called the **micropyle** (MIE-kroh-PIEL). Together, a megasporangium and its integument form a structure called an **ovule** (AHV-yool). Two ovules develop on each scale of a female cone. *Microsporangia* produce microspores, which develop into *microgametophytes,* or male gametophytes. A **pollen grain** is a microgametophyte of a seed plant.

The male cones of a pine release huge numbers of pollen grains, as seen in Figure 30-4. Pine pollen travels on the wind, and only a few grains may land on a female cone. The pollen grains drift between the cone scales until they reach the ovules. The transfer of pollen to ovules is called **pollination.** A drop of fluid at the micropyle captures the pollen grain. As the fluid dries, the pollen grain is drawn into the micropyle. After pollination, the female gametophyte within the ovule produces archegonia and eggs.

After pollination, the pollen grain begins to grow a **pollen tube,** a slender extension of the pollen grain that enables sperm to reach an egg. Unlike the sperm of seedless plants, pine sperm do not have flagella and they do not swim to an egg. The pollen tube takes about a year to reach an egg only a few millimeters away. During this time, two sperm develop in the pollen tube. When the pollen tube reaches an archegonium, one sperm unites with an egg to form a zygote. The other sperm and the pollen tube die. Over the next few months, the zygote develops into an embryo as the ovule matures into a seed.

**FIGURE 30-4**

The male cones (pollen cones) of pines produce millions of pollen grains. The male cones then die. Wind-pollinated species typically produce large amounts of pollen. Large numbers of pollen grains increase the odds that female cones (seed cones) will be pollinated.

## SECTION 1 REVIEW

1. Distinguish between an antheridium and an archegonium in mosses, including their structures and functions.

2. List three differences between the life cycle of a typical fern and the life cycle of a pine tree (a gymnosperm).

3. Explain why a pine tree (a gymnosperm) has two different types of cones.

4. What is the difference between homosporous alternation of generations and heterosporous alternation of generations?

**CRITICAL THINKING**

5. **Evaluating Differences** How do the differences in the environments in which mosses and gymnosperms live relate to the differences in sexual reproduction in these plants?

6. **Forming Reasoned Opinions** How might the presence of a haploid generation (the gametophyte) in plants serve as a "filter" for natural selection?

7. **Making Comparisons** Compare male and female gametophytes of mosses with those of gymnosperms in terms of their resistance to harsh environmental conditions.

# SEXUAL REPRODUCTION IN FLOWERING PLANTS

*Many flowers have bright colors, attractive shapes, and pleasing aromas. These adaptations help ensure successful sexual reproduction by attracting animals that will transfer pollen. But some flowers are not colorful, large, or fragrant. Such flowers rely on wind or water for the transfer of pollen.*

## PARTS OF A FLOWER

Recall that early land plants lacked leaves and roots and consisted of only stems. Leaves evolved from branches of stems. Botanists consider flowers to be highly specialized branches and the parts of a flower to be specialized leaves. These specialized leaves form on the swollen tip of a floral "branch" or **receptacle.**

Flower parts are usually found in four concentric whorls, or rings, as shown in Figure 30-5. **Sepals** (SEE-puhlz) make up the outer whorl. They protect the other parts of a developing flower before it opens. **Petals** make up the next whorl. Most animal-pollinated flowers have brightly colored petals. The petals and sepals of wind-pollinated plants are usually small or absent.

The two innermost whorls of flower parts contain the reproductive structures. The male reproductive structures are **stamens** (STAY-muhnz), each of which consists of an anther and a filament. An **anther** contains microsporangia, which produce microspores that develop into pollen grains. A stalklike **filament** supports an anther. The innermost whorl contains the female reproductive structures, which are called **carpels** (KAHR-puhlz).

### OBJECTIVES

- **Identify** the four main flower parts, and state the function of each.
- **Describe** gametophyte formation in flowering plants.
- **Relate** flower structure to methods of pollination.
- **Describe** fertilization in flowering plants.

### VOCABULARY

receptacle
sepal
petal
stamen
anther
filament
carpel
pistil
ovary
style
stigma
embryo sac
polar nuclei
tube cell
generative cell
nectar
double fertilization

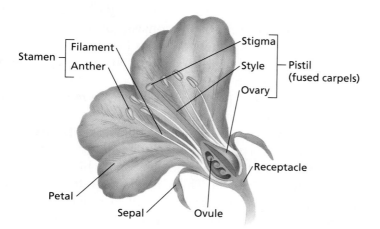

**FIGURE 30-5**

This diagram shows a complete flower that has all four whorls of flower parts—sepals, petals, stamens, and carpels. Most species of flowering plants have flowers that have both stamens and carpels.

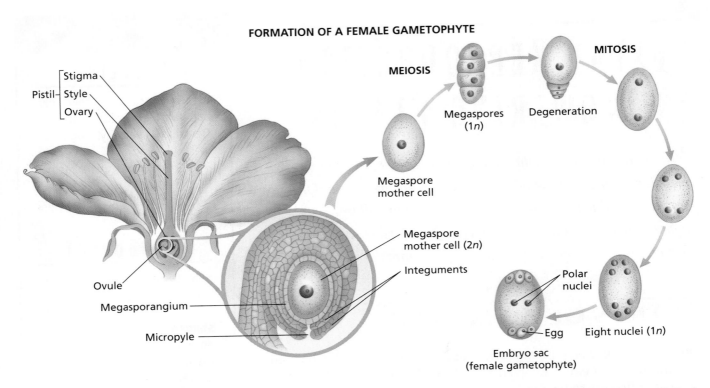

**FORMATION OF A FEMALE GAMETOPHYTE**

MEIOSIS

MITOSIS

Megaspores (1n)

Degeneration

Megaspore mother cell

Pistil — Stigma, Style, Ovary

Stigma

Style

Ovary

Ovule

Megasporangium

Micropyle

Megaspore mother cell (2n)

Integuments

Polar nuclei

Egg

Eight nuclei (1n)

Embryo sac (female gametophyte)

**FIGURE 30-6**

A cross section of an immature ovule from a flower reveals a single large cell, a megaspore mother cell. This cell undergoes meiosis and produces four megaspores. One of the megaspores undergoes a series of mitotic divisions that results in the formation of an embryo sac (a female gametophyte).

One or more carpels fused together make up the structure called a **pistil** (also shown in Figure 30-6). The enlarged base of a pistil is called the **ovary.** A **style,** which is usually stalklike, rises from the ovary. The tip of the style is called the **stigma.** Generally, a stigma is sticky or has hairs, enabling it to trap pollen grains.

# GAMETOPHYTE FORMATION

In angiosperms, gametophytes develop within the reproductive structures of flowers. **Embryo sacs,** which are the female gametophytes in angiosperms, form within the ovary of the pistil. Pollen grains, the male gametophytes, form within the anthers of the stamens.

## Embryo Sac Formation

In flowering plants, ovules form in the ovary of a pistil. As Figure 30-6 shows, an angiosperm ovule consists of a megasporangium surrounded by two integuments. These two integuments do not completely enclose the megasporangium. At one end of the ovule is the micropyle, through which a pollen tube can enter.

An ovule contains a large diploid cell called a *megaspore mother cell.* A megaspore mother cell undergoes meiosis and produces four haploid megaspores. In many species of flowering plants, only one megaspore enlarges. The other three degenerate. The remaining megaspore undergoes three mitotic divisions, which produce a cell that has eight haploid nuclei. These nuclei migrate to certain locations within the cell. The nuclei are initially arranged in two groups of four, with one group of nuclei at each end of the cell.

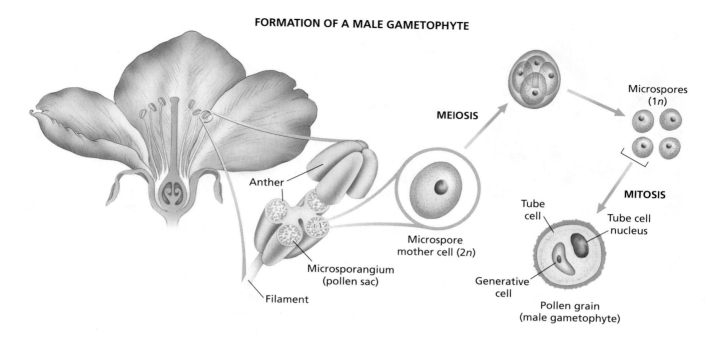

## FORMATION OF A MALE GAMETOPHYTE

**MEIOSIS**

Microspores (1*n*)

**MITOSIS**

Anther

Microsporangium (pollen sac)

Filament

Microspore mother cell (2*n*)

Tube cell

Tube cell nucleus

Generative cell

Pollen grain (male gametophyte)

One nucleus from each group migrates to the center of the cell. These two nuclei are called **polar nuclei** because they came from the ends, or poles, of the cell. Cell walls then form around each of the remaining six nuclei. One of the three cells that are nearest to the micropyle enlarges and becomes the egg. The two cells on either side of the egg will later help attract the pollen tube toward the egg. The function of the three cells at the other end of the cell is unclear. These five non-egg cells will eventually die after fertilization occurs.

The resulting structure, which usually contains eight nuclei and seven cells (the egg, the five non-egg cells, and the large central cell enclosing these cells), is the embryo sac. The embryo sac is the mature female gametophyte, or megagametophyte. The embryo sac is another feature that is seen in angiosperms but is not seen in gymnosperms. The surrounding integuments and the embryo sac now form a mature ovule, which may eventually develop into a seed.

### Pollen Grain Formation

An anther contains four microsporangia, or *pollen sacs,* as shown in Figure 30-7. Initially, the pollen sacs contain many diploid cells. These diploid cells are called *microspore mother cells.* Each of these microspore mother cells undergoes meiosis and produces four haploid microspores. A microspore undergoes mitosis and produces two haploid cells, but these cells do not separate. A thick wall then develops around the microspore. The resulting two-celled structure is a pollen grain, which is the male gametophyte, or microgametophyte. The larger of the two cells is the **tube cell,** from which the pollen tube will form. The **generative cell,** which is enclosed in the tube cell, will divide by mitosis to form two sperm.

**FIGURE 30-7**

A cross section of an anther of a flower reveals four pollen sacs (microsporangia). Microspore mother cells within the microsporangia undergo meiosis and produce microspores. Each microspore then develops into a two-celled pollen grain (a male gametophyte).

# POLLINATION

Before a sperm can fertilize the egg contained in an embryo sac, pollination must occur. In flowering plants, pollination occurs when pollen grains are transferred from an anther to a stigma. Pollination that involves just one flower, flowers on the same plant, or flowers from two genetically identical plants is called *self-pollination*. In contrast, pollination that involves two genetically different plants is called *cross-pollination*.

The pollination of flowering plants occurs in several ways. Flower structure promotes self-pollination in plants, such as peas and beans, that have flowers with petals that completely enclose both the male and female flower parts. Some aquatic plants, such as sea grasses, have pollen that is dispersed by water. Many plants, such as oak trees and grasses, release their pollen into the air. The flowers of such wind-pollinated angiosperms are small and lack showy petals and sepals. Successful wind pollination depends on four conditions: the release of large amounts of pollen, the ample circulation of air to carry pollen, the relative proximity of other plants for the pollen to be transferred to, and dry weather to ensure that pollen is not washed from the air by rain.

Most plants that have colorful or fragrant flowers are pollinated by animals. Bright petals and distinctive odors attract animals that feed on pollen and **nectar,** a nourishing solution of sugars. Animal pollinators include bats, bees, beetles, moths, butterflies, mosquitoes, monkeys, and hummingbirds. When these animals gather nectar, pollen sticks to their bodies. As they collect more nectar, the animals deposit some of the pollen on other flowers. For example, as the hummingbird in Figure 30-8 collects nectar from a flower, pollen from the anthers is deposited on the hummingbird's beak and head. When the hummingbird moves on to another flower, the pollen may be transferred to the stigma of the second flower.

# FERTILIZATION

Fertilization, the union of haploid gametes resulting in a diploid zygote, may follow pollination, as shown in Figure 30-9. For fertilization to occur in angiosperms, a pollen grain must land on a stigma and then absorb moisture. The pollen grain will then germinate. Germination occurs when the nucleus of the tube cell causes the tube cell to form a pollen tube that grows through the stigma and style toward the ovary. The pollen tube grows to an ovule within the ovary and enters the ovule through the micropyle. After the pollen tube penetrates the embryo sac, two sperm (produced from the mitotic division of the generative cell in the pollen grain) can travel through the pollen tube and reach the egg. Unlike a gymnosperm's pollen tubes, an angiosperm's pollen tubes usually reach an egg a day or two after pollination.

## POLLINATION AND FERTILIZATION IN FLOWERING PLANTS

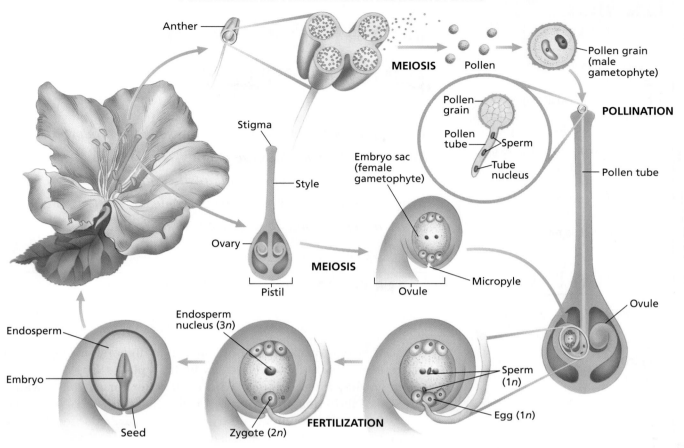

One of the two sperm fuses with the egg, forming a diploid zygote. The zygote eventually develops into an embryo. The second sperm fuses with the two polar nuclei, producing a triploid ($3n$) nucleus. This nucleus then develops into tissue called *endosperm*. The endosperm provides nourishment for the embryo. Kernels of corn are mostly endosperm. In many plants, however, the endosperm is absorbed by the embryos as the seeds mature. This process of two cell fusions, which is called **double fertilization**, is unique to angiosperms.

**FIGURE 30-9**

In a process called *double fertilization,* one sperm fuses with an egg, forming a zygote. Another sperm fuses with two polar nuclei, forming an endosperm.

## SECTION 2 REVIEW

1. Draw a generalized flower and show the four types of flower parts in relation to each other. Be sure to label each structure.

2. Name the male and female gametophytes in flowering plants.

3. How do the flowers of wind-pollinated plants differ from the flowers of animal-pollinated plants?

4. Why is fertilization in flowering plants called *double fertilization?*

**CRITICAL THINKING**

5. **Interpreting Graphics**  What type of pollination is shown in the illustration above?

6. **Distinguishing Relevant Information**  The vast majority of the known species of plants are angiosperms. What are some characteristics of this group of plants that help explain their evolutionary success?

7. **Making Comparisons**  How is meiosis in flowering plants like meiosis in humans?

### OBJECTIVES

- **Describe** adaptations for fruit and seed dispersal.
- **Name** the three major categories of fruits.
- **Compare** the structure and germination of different types of seeds.
- **Recognize** the advantages and disadvantages of asexual reproduction.
- **Describe** human methods of plant propagation.

### VOCABULARY

propagation
seed coat
plumule
epicotyl
hypocotyl
radicle
hilum
dormancy
clone
vegetative reproduction
cutting
layering
grafting
tissue culture

# DISPERSAL AND PROPAGATION

*F*ruits and seeds normally result from sexual reproduction in flowering plants. Fruits are adapted for dispersing, or distributing, seeds. Seeds are adapted for the dispersal and **propagation** (production of new individuals) of plants. Many plants also propagate through asexual reproduction.

## DISPERSAL OF FRUITS AND SEEDS

Recall that one property of populations is dispersion, the spatial distribution of individuals. If individual plants are too close together, they must compete with each other for available water, nutrients, and sunlight. One reason for the success of the seed plants is the development of structures that are adapted for dispersing offspring—fruits and seeds.

Fruits and seeds are dispersed by animals, wind, water, forcible discharge, and gravity. You may have walked through a field and unwittingly collected burrs, or stickers, on your shoes or socks. These burrs are fruits, and you helped disperse them. The smell, bright color, or flavor of many fruits attract animals. When animals eat such fruits, the seeds are transported to new locations and often pass unharmed through the animals' digestive systems.

Fruits and seeds dispersed by wind or water are adapted for those methods of dispersal. Orchids have tiny, dustlike seeds that can easily be carried by a slight breeze. Figure 30-10 shows an example of seeds adapted for wind dispersal. Many plants that grow near water produce fruits and seeds that contain air chambers, which allow them to float. Coconuts, for example, may float thousands of kilometers on ocean currents.

The most dramatic method of seed dispersal occurs in plants that forcibly discharge their seeds from their fruits. The tropical sandbox tree, which has fruits that hurl seeds up to 100 m (328 ft), appears to hold the distance record.

Although gymnosperms do not produce fruits, their cones may help protect seeds and aid in seed dispersal. Female pine cones close after pollination and open again only when the seeds are mature. Pine seeds may be dispersed when gravity causes cones to drop and roll away from the parent tree. Pine seeds have "wings" that aid in wind dispersal.

**FIGURE 30-10**

Milkweed seeds have "parachutes" that help them drift with the wind.

# TYPES OF FRUITS

Botanists define a *fruit* as a mature ovary. Many different types of fruits have evolved among the flowering plants. Figure 30-11 shows examples of some of these fruit types. Fertilization usually initiates the development of fruits. Fruits protect seeds, aid in their dispersal, and often delay their sprouting. Fruits are classified mainly on the basis of two characteristics: how many pistils or flowers form the fruit, and whether the fruit is dry or fleshy. Table 30-1 presents a classification system for fruits. Notice that fruits with common names that include "nut" or "berry" may not be actual nuts or berries. For example, a peanut is actually a legume, not a nut. You may have heard the fleshy seeds of ginkgo, juniper, and yew trees referred to as berries. These names are misleading because ginkgo, juniper, and yew trees are gymnosperms, which do not form fruits.

**FIGURE 30-11**

A pea pod is a simple fruit. A raspberry is an aggregate fruit. A pineapple is a multiple fruit.

## TABLE 30-1   *Fruit Classification*

| Major categories and types of fruits | Examples |
|---|---|
| **Simple fruit**—formed from one pistil of a single flower | |
| **A.** Dry at maturity | |
|    **1.** Usually splits open | |
|       **a. Legume**—splits along two sides to form two halves | pea, peanut, black locust |
|       **b. Follicle**—splits along one side | milkweed, columbine |
|       **c. Capsule**—splits in a variety of other ways | poppy, tulip |
|    **2.** Usually does not split open | |
|       **a. Grain**—thin ovary wall fused to seed coat | corn, wheat |
|       **b. Nut**—thick, woody ovary wall not fused to single seed | oak, chestnut |
|       **c. Achene**—thin ovary wall not fused to single seed | sunflower, dandelion |
|       **d. Samara**—like an achene but with a thin, flat wing | ash, elm, maple |
| **B.** Fleshy at maturity and usually not opening | |
|    **1.** Usually contains only one seed | |
|       **a. Drupe**—stony inner layer around the seed | cherry, coconut, pecan |
|    **2.** Usually contains many seeds | |
|       **a. Pome**—core with seeds surrounded by papery ovary walls; outer part formed from sepals | apple, pear |
|       **b. Typical berry**—thin skin | grape, tomato, banana |
|       **c. Pepo**—berry with a thick, hard rind | watermelon, cucumber |
|       **d. Hesperidium**—berry with leathery, easily removed skin | orange, grapefruit, lemon |
| **Aggregate fruit**—formed from several pistils of a single flower | |
| **A.** Dry at maturity | tulip tree, magnolia |
| **B.** Fleshy at maturity | raspberry, strawberry |
| **Multiple fruit**—formed from several flowers growing together | |
| **A.** Dry at maturity | sweetgum, sycamore |
| **B.** Fleshy at maturity | pineapple, fig |

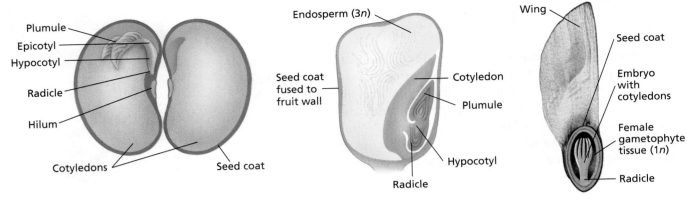

Plumule
Epicotyl
Hypocotyl
Radicle
Hilum
Cotyledons
Seed coat

**(a) BEAN SEED (DICOT)**

Endosperm (3n)
Seed coat fused to fruit wall
Cotyledon
Plumule
Hypocotyl
Radicle

**(b) CORN KERNEL (MONOCOT)**

Wing
Seed coat
Embryo with cotyledons
Female gametophyte tissue (1n)
Radicle

**(c) PINE SEED (GYMNOSPERM)**

**FIGURE 30-12**

(a) A bean seed has two cotyledons and no endosperm. (b) A corn kernel contains a single seed, which has one cotyledon and endosperm. (c) A pine seed has cotyledons and tissue from the female gametophyte.

## Quick Lab

### Predicting Seed Dispersal

**Materials** five different fruits, balance or scale

**Procedure**

1. Create a data table that has at least five rows. Your table should have six columns with the following headings: "Fruit name," "Fruit type" (from Table 30-1), "Dry/fleshy," "Seed mass in grams," "Whole fruit mass in grams," and "Dispersal method."

2. Examine your fruits, and fill in your data table. Discuss with your group how characteristics of fruits and seeds might relate to dispersal methods.

**Analysis** Form a hypothesis about a dispersal method for one of the fruits you have examined. Describe how you might test your hypothesis.

# STRUCTURE OF SEEDS

A *seed* is a plant embryo surrounded by a protective coat called the **seed coat.** The structure of seeds differs among the major groups of seed plants—angiosperms, which include monocots and dicots, and gymnosperms. To understand some of the differences, examine the seeds shown in Figure 30-12.

Look at the bean seed in Figure 30-12a, which has been opened to reveal the structures inside. Most of the interior of a bean seed is filled by two large, fleshy cotyledons (seed leaves), which are part of the embryo. Recall that dicots have two cotyledons in their embryos. Therefore, beans are dicots. A mature bean seed has no endosperm. The endosperm was absorbed by the fleshy cotyledons.

Between the two cotyledons of a bean seed are the parts that make up the rest of the embryo. The shoot tip, along with any embryonic leaves, is called the **plumule** (PLOO-MYOOL). The **epicotyl** (EP-I-KAHT-uhl) extends from the plumule to the attachment point of the cotyledons. The **hypocotyl** (HIE-poh-KAHT-uhl) extends from the attachment point of the cotyledons to the radicle. The **radicle** is the embryonic root. Along the concave edge of the seed, beneath the radicle, is the **hilum** (HIE-luhm), which is a scar that marks where the seed was attached to the ovary wall.

Now examine the corn kernel in Figure 30-12b. Technically, a corn kernel is a fruit, but the seed occupies almost the entire kernel. The wall of the fruit is very thin and is fused to the seed coat. A single umbrella-shaped cotyledon is pressed close to the endosperm. The cotyledon of a monocot seed does not store nutrients, as bean cotyledons do. Instead, it absorbs nutrients from the endosperm and transfers them to the embryo.

Finally, look at the pine seed in Figure 30-12c. A pine seed contains a sporophyte embryo that has needle-like cotyledons. The embryo is surrounded by tissue of the female gametophyte. Like the triploid endosperm of angiosperm seeds, the haploid tissue of the female gametophyte functions as a source of nourishment for the embryo.

# SEED GERMINATION

Many plants are easily grown from seeds. Although its embryo is alive, a seed will not germinate, or sprout, until it is exposed to certain environmental conditions, The delay of germination often assures the survival of a plant. For example, if seeds that mature in the fall were to sprout immediately, the young plants could be killed by cold weather. Similarly, if a plant's seeds were to sprout all at once and all of the new plants died before producing seeds, the species could become extinct. Many seeds will not germinate even when exposed to conditions ideal for germination. Such seeds exhibit **dormancy,** which is a state of reduced metabolism in which growth and development do not occur. The longevity of dormant seeds is often remarkable. A botanist once germinated lotus seeds that were almost 1,000 years old.

## Conditions Needed for Germination

Environmental factors, such as water, oxygen, and temperature, can trigger seed germination. Most mature seeds are very dry and must absorb water to germinate. Water softens the seed coat and activates enzymes that convert starch in the cotyledons or endosperm into simple sugars, which provide energy for the embryo to grow. As the embryo begins to grow, the softened seed coat cracks open. This enables the oxygen needed for cellular respiration to reach the embryo. Many small seeds need light for germination. This adaptation prevents the seeds from sprouting if they are buried too deeply in the soil. In addition, some seeds germinate only if exposed to temperatures within a certain range.

Some seeds germinate only after being exposed to extreme conditions. For example, animals often swallow the seeds of fruits they eat, as shown in Figure 30-13. Acids in the digestive system wear away the hard seed coat. The seeds may germinate after passing through the digestive systems of these animals. As an added bonus, the seed is deposited with a bit of natural fertilizer.

**FIGURE 30-13**

Many animals eat apples or other fruits. The seeds are swallowed and are exposed to acids as they pass through the animal's digestive system. The acids wear away the seed coat. Once the seed is on the ground, water and oxygen can enter the seed and enable the growing embryo to break out.

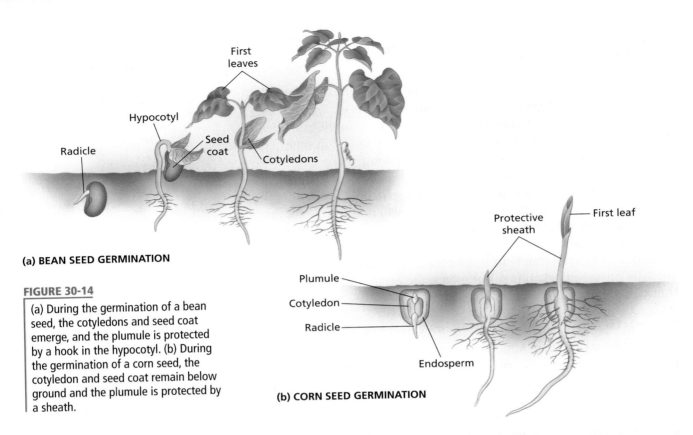

First leaves

Hypocotyl

Seed coat

Radicle

Cotyledons

**(a) BEAN SEED GERMINATION**

Protective sheath

First leaf

Plumule

Cotyledon

Radicle

Endosperm

**(b) CORN SEED GERMINATION**

**FIGURE 30-14**

(a) During the germination of a bean seed, the cotyledons and seed coat emerge, and the plumule is protected by a hook in the hypocotyl. (b) During the germination of a corn seed, the cotyledon and seed coat remain below ground and the plumule is protected by a sheath.

🖥 **internet** connect

**www.scilinks.org**
**Topic:** Seed Germination
**Keyword:** HM61366

SC*LINKS* Maintained by the National Science Teachers Association

Other seeds, including apple seeds, must be exposed to near-freezing temperatures for several weeks before they sprout. This temperature requirement prevents the seeds from germinating in the fall and thus ensures that the seedlings will not be killed by the cold temperatures of winter. The cold temperatures cause chemical changes within the seed. These changes enable the embryo to grow.

## Process of Germination

Figure 30-14 compares germination in corn and bean seeds. The first visible sign of seed germination is the emergence of the radicle. In beans, the entire root system develops from the radicle. In corn, most of the root system develops from the lower part of the radicle. Soon after the radicle breaks the seed coat, the shoot begins to grow.

In some seeds, such as bean seeds (Figure 30-14a), the hypocotyl curves and becomes hook-shaped. Once the hook breaks through the soil, the hypocotyl straightens. This straightening pulls the cotyledons and the embryonic leaves into the air. The embryonic leaves unfold, synthesize chlorophyll, and begin photosynthesis. After their stored nutrients are used up, the shrunken bean cotyledons fall off.

In contrast, the cotyledon of the corn seed (Figure 30-14b) remains underground and transfers nutrients from the endosperm to the growing embryo. Unlike the bean shoot, the corn cotyledon remains below ground. The corn plumule is protected by a sheath that pushes through the soil. Once the sheath has broken through the soil surface, the plumule grows up through the sheath and the first leaf unfolds.

# ASEXUAL REPRODUCTION

Recall that asexual reproduction is the production of an individual without the union of gametes. Elaborate technology has recently yielded some success in the asexual reproduction of mammals to create **clones,** or exact duplicates of organisms. But people who create clones of themselves are still the subjects of science fiction movies and books. However, asexual reproduction to create clones is common in the plant kingdom.

Asexual reproduction can be an advantage to individuals that are well-adapted to their environment. Many new individuals can be produced in a short time, which enables the clones to spread rapidly and fill available space. A disadvantage of asexual reproduction is the lack of genetic variation among the offspring. All of the offspring are genetically identical. Thus, the clones have the same tolerance to an environment and are attacked by the same diseases and pests. Many of our plant cultivars are clones.

In nature, plants reproduce asexually in many ways, including the development of spores and vegetative reproduction. **Vegetative reproduction** is asexual reproduction involving vegetative (nonreproductive) parts of a plant, such as leaves, stems, or roots. Many structures specialized for vegetative reproduction have evolved in plants. Table 30-2 lists some of these structures. One example of vegetative reproduction is shown in Figure 30-15.

**FIGURE 30-15**

New plants are vegetatively reproduced from the stolons (runners) of an airplane plant, also called a *spider plant.*

# PROPAGATION OF PLANTS BY HUMANS

People often use vegetative structures to propagate plants. Many species of plants are vegetatively propagated by humans from the structures described in Table 30-2. People have also developed several methods of propagating plants from other vegetative parts, such as roots and even tissue samples. These methods include layering, grafting, and using cuttings and tissue cultures.

## TABLE 30-2  *Plant Structures Adapted for Vegetative Reproduction*

| Name | Description | Examples |
| --- | --- | --- |
| Stolon (runner) | horizontal, aboveground stem that produces leaves and roots at its nodes; a new plant can grow from each node | strawberry, airplane (spider) plant, Boston fern |
| Rhizome | horizontal, belowground stem that produces leaves and roots at its nodes; a new plant can grow from each node | ferns, horsetails, iris, ginger, sugar cane |
| Bulb | very short, underground monocot stem with thick, fleshy leaves adapted for storage; bulbs divide naturally to produce new plants | tulip, daffodil, onion, garlic, hyacinth |
| Tuber | underground, swollen, fleshy stem specialized for storage; the buds on a tuber can grow into new plants | potato, caladium, Jerusalem artichoke |

## Cuttings

In some plants, roots will form on a cut piece of a stem, or shoots will form on a piece of a root. Pieces of stems and roots that are cut from a plant and used to grow new plants are called **cuttings.** Plants such as African violets can be grown from leaf cuttings, which will form both roots and shoots. Cuttings are widely used to propagate houseplants, ornamental trees and shrubs, and some fruit crops.

## Layering

In some species, such as raspberries, roots form on stems where they make contact with the soil. People often stake branch tips to the soil or cover the bases of stems with soil to propagate such plants. The process of causing roots to form on a stem is called **layering.** Air layering, wounding a stem and placing moist peat moss around the wound, is another common form of layering.

## Grafting

**Grafting** is the joining of two or more plant parts to form a single plant. In grafting, a bud or small stem of one plant is attached to the roots or stems of a second plant. The vascular cambium of both parts must be aligned for a graft to be successful. Grafting enables the desirable characteristics of two cultivars to be combined. Grafting is used to propagate virtually all commercial fruit and nut trees and many ornamental trees and shrubs.

## Tissue Culture

Figure 30-16 shows plants grown by **tissue culture,** the production of new plants from pieces of tissue placed on a sterile nutrient medium. Unlike most animal cells, plant cells contain functional copies of all the genes needed to produce a new plant. Thus, it is possible for a whole plant to regrow from a single cell. Millions of identical plants can be grown from a small amount of tissue. Tissue culture is used in the commercial production of orchids, houseplants, cut flowers, fruit plants, and ornamental trees, shrubs, and nonwoody plants.

**FIGURE 30-16**

Tissue culture can be used to grow round-leaved sundews, *Drosera rotundifolia*. The jelly in the Petri dish is a sterile soil substitute that contains needed nutrients.

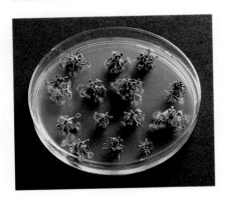

---

## SECTION 3 REVIEW

1. Name three common methods of fruit and seed dispersal.

2. Name one fruit from each of the three major categories of fruit.

3. How do the structure and germination of a bean seed and a corn seed differ from each other?

4. Compare asexual reproduction with sexual reproduction.

5. Make a table that compares structures and methods for propagation of plants by humans.

**CRITICAL THINKING**

6. **Justifying Conclusions** How might seed dormancy be an evolutionary advantage?

7. **Applying Information** Many fruits are green until they are mature. How might this be an advantage in terms of seed dispersal by animals?

8. **Evaluating Information** Instructions on packets of large seeds state that they should be planted deeply. Instructions on packets of small seeds state that they should be planted shallowly. Why are these instructions different?

# CHAPTER HIGHLIGHTS

## SECTION 1 — Plant Life Cycles

- Plants have a life cycle called *alternation of generations*, in which a multicellular haploid gametophyte stage alternates with a multicellular diploid sporophyte stage.

- In the moss life cycle, a spore develops into a leafy green gametophyte that produces eggs in archegonia and flagellated sperm in antheridia. A moss sporophyte grows from a fertilized egg.

- In the fern life cycle, a spore develops into a small, flat gametophyte that produces eggs in archegonia and flagellated sperm in antheridia. A fern sporophyte grows from a fertilized egg.

- In the gymnosperm life cycle, a large sporophyte produces two types of spores, and microscopic gametophytes produce gametes. Nonflagellated sperm reach an ovule through a pollen tube.

- Mosses and most ferns are homosporous (produce only one type of spore). All seed plants as well as a few other species are heterosporous (produce male microspores and female megaspores).

### Vocabulary

antheridium (p. 609)
archegonium (p. 609)
homospory (p. 610)
sorus (p. 611)

microspore (p. 611)
megaspore (p. 611)
heterospory (p. 611)

integument (p. 612)
micropyle (p. 612)
ovule (p. 612)

pollen grain (p. 612)
pollination (p. 612)
pollen tube (p. 612)

## SECTION 2 — Sexual Reproduction in Flowering Plants

- Flowers are reproductive structures. Most flowers consist of four parts—protective sepals, colorful petals, pollen-producing stamens, and egg-containing carpels.

- An immature ovule contains a megaspore mother cell that undergoes meiosis and produces four megaspores. One of the megaspores divides by mitosis to form an embryo sac.

- Pollen grains form in stamens. Microspore mother cells in pollen sacs undergo meiosis and produce microspores, each of which develops into a pollen grain.

- Many flowering plants have flowers adapted for animal pollination or for wind pollination.

- In double fertilization, one sperm combines with the egg to form a zygote. A second sperm combines with two polar nuclei to form the endosperm.

### Vocabulary

receptacle (p. 613)
sepal (p. 613)
petal (p. 613)
stamen (p. 613)
anther (p. 613)

filament (p. 613)
carpel (p. 613)
pistil (p. 613)
ovary (p. 613)

style (p. 613)
stigma (p. 613)
embryo sac (p. 614)
polar nuclei (p. 615)

tube cell (p. 615)
generative cell (p. 615)
nectar (p. 616)
double fertilization (p. 617)

## SECTION 3 — Dispersal and Propagation

- Fruits and seeds are dispersed by animals, wind, water, forcible discharge, and gravity. Many fruits and seeds are adapted for a particular type of dispersal.

- The three major categories of fruits are simple, aggregate, and multiple.

- The structure of seeds differs among the major groups of seed plants. Seeds need water, oxygen, suitable temperatures, and sometimes light to germinate. Delayed germination often assures the survival of a plant.

- Asexual reproduction enables plants to spread rapidly in a favorable environment but can result in a lack of genetic variation among offspring.

- Human methods of plant propagation include using cuttings, layering, grafting, and tissue culture.

### Vocabulary

propagation (p. 618)
seed coat (p. 620)
plumule (p. 620)
epicotyl (p. 620)

hypocotyl (p. 620)
radicle (p. 620)
hilum (p. 620)
dormancy (p. 621)

clone (p. 623)
vegetative
  reproduction (p. 623)
cutting (p. 624)

layering (p. 624)
grafting (p. 624)
tissue culture (p. 624)

## USING VOCABULARY

1. For each pair of terms, explain how the meanings of the terms differ.
   a. *microspore* and *megaspore*
   b. *pollination* and *double fertilization*
   c. *sepal* and *petal*

2. For each pair of terms, explain the relationship between the terms.
   a. *homospory* and *heterospory*
   b. *polar nuclei* and *embryo sac*
   c. *integument* and *micropyle*

3. Use the following terms in the same sentence: *dormancy, plumule, radicle,* and *seed coat.*

4. **Word Roots and Origins** The word *carpel* is derived from the Greek word *karpos,* which means "fruit." Using this information, explain why the term *carpel* is a good name for the structure that the term describes.

## UNDERSTANDING KEY CONCEPTS

5. **Name** the sexual reproductive structures in a moss life cycle, and describe the function of each.

6. **Identify** the dominant stage in the life cycle of a fern.

7. **Summarize** the adaptation that allows gymnosperms to sexually reproduce in the absence of environmental moisture.

8. **Explain** how heterospory can be an advantage over homospory.

9. **Describe** the roles of the parts of a flower that do not participate directly in reproduction.

10. **Describe** the roles of the parts of a flower that do participate directly in reproduction.

11. **Distinguish** between embryo sac formation and pollen grain formation.

12. **Draw** a diagram showing the events and plant structures involved in angiosperm pollination.

13. **Distinguish** the process of fertilization in gymnosperms from the process of fertilization in flowering plants.

14. **Identify** one example of a plant structure that is an adaptation for fruit or seed dispersal.

15. **Describe** the two characteristics used for classifying fruits.

16. **Explain** the advantage of the hypocotyl hook that the embryos of some seeds form as the plant emerges after germination.

17. **Explain** why asexual reproduction can be an advantage for plants that are well-adapted to their environment.

18. **Compare** two methods of plant propagation used by humans.

19. **CONCEPT MAPPING** Use the following terms to create a concept map that describes male reproductive structures in flowering plants: *anther, generative cell, microspore mother cell, stamen, microspore, pollen grain,* and *tube cell.*

## CRITICAL THINKING

20. **Recognizing Relationships** In many flowers with both stamens and pistils, the stigma is located well above the anthers. What might be the value of such an arrangement?

21. **Analyzing Information** Following the self-pollination of some plants, the pollen tubes die before reaching ovules. What is the significance of this event?

22. **Justifying Conclusions** If you were to discover a new type of rose, would you use vegetative parts or seeds to propagate the rose and produce large numbers of identical plants? Justify your answer.

23. **Interpreting Graphics** In the photograph below, the houseplant on the left shows a *Sansevieria trifasciata,* which has yellow-edged leaves. A section of the leaf, or a leaf cutting, can be used to produce new plants. However, as shown on the right side of the photograph, only shoots with all-green leaves and no yellow edges will form. How do you explain this?

# Standardized Test Preparation

**DIRECTIONS:** Choose the letter of the answer choice that best answers the question.

1. The production of a single type of spore is a characteristic of the life cycles of which kinds of plants?
   **A.** mosses and most ferns
   **B.** most ferns and gymnosperms
   **C.** mosses and most gymnosperms
   **D.** mosses, most ferns, and gymnosperms

2. Why is sexual reproduction in gymnosperms and other seed plants independent of seasonal rains?
   **F.** These plants grow only near streams and rivers.
   **G.** Pollinators or wind carry the sperm to the eggs.
   **H.** Fertilization occurs inside structures within the spores.
   **J.** Fertilization always involves eggs and sperm of the same plant.

**INTERPRETING GRAPHICS:** The illustration below shows the four concentric whorls of a typical flower. Use this illustration to answer the question that follows.

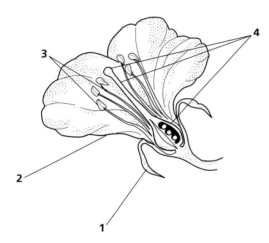

3. In which whorl are the male reproductive structures found?
   **A.** *1*
   **B.** *2*
   **C.** *3*
   **D.** *4*

4. Pollination in flowering plants is said to take place when which of the following occurs?
   **F.** when insects ingest nectar
   **G.** when pollen lands on a stigma
   **H.** when a sperm fuses with an egg
   **J.** when a spore leaves a sporangium

**DIRECTIONS:** Complete the following analogy.

5. Generative cell : pollen grain :: egg cell :
   **A.** ovary
   **B.** carpel
   **C.** receptacle
   **D.** embryo sac

**INTERPRETING GRAPHICS:** The illustration below shows the structure of a corn kernel, which is a monocot seed. Use this illustration to answer the question that follows.

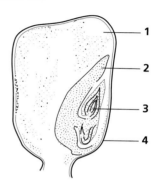

6. Which structure of the corn kernel is the endosperm, the source of nutrients?
   **F.** *1*
   **G.** *2*
   **H.** *3*
   **J.** *4*

## SHORT RESPONSE

A seed will not germinate until it is exposed to certain environmental conditions.

List two environmental factors that influence seed germination, and describe the mechanisms by which they trigger the germination process.

## EXTENDED RESPONSE

Double fertilization is unique to angiosperms.

*Part A* What cells participate in double fertilization, and what products do they form?

*Part B* What are the evolutionary advancements seen only in angiosperms, and what advantages do they confer?

**Test TIP** If you are not sure about the spelling of certain words when answering the short- or extended-response questions, look at the question to see if the same word appears in the question.

# EXPLORATION LAB

# Comparing Seed Structure and Seedling Development

## OBJECTIVES

- Observe the structures of dicot and monocot seeds.
- Compare the structure of dicot and monocot embryos.
- Compare the development of dicot and monocot seedlings.

## PROCESS SKILLS

- relating structure to function
- comparing and contrasting
- identifying
- collecting data

## MATERIALS

- 1 pea seed soaked overnight
- 6 bean seeds soaked overnight
- 6 corn kernels soaked overnight
- stereomicroscope
- scalpel
- Lugol's iodine solution in dropper bottle
- paper towels
- 2 rubber bands
- 2 150 mL beakers
- glass-marking pen
- metric ruler
- microscope slide and cover slip
- medicine dropper
- compound light microscope

## Background

1. What are the parts of a seed?
2. In what ways are seeds like their parent plant?
3. How do monocotyledons and dicotyledons differ?
4. What changes occur as a seed germinates?

## PART A  Seed Structure

1. Obtain one each of the following seeds—pea, bean, and corn.
2. Remove the seed coats of the pea and bean seeds. Open the seeds, and locate the two cotyledons in each seed.

3. Using the stereomicroscope, examine the embryos of the pea seed and the bean seed.
4. In your lab report, draw the pea and bean embryos and label all of the parts that you can identify.
5. **CAUTION  Put on a lab apron, safety goggles, and gloves. In this lab, you will be working with a chemical that may irritate your skin or stain your skin and clothing. If you get a chemical on your skin or clothing, wash it off at the sink while calling to your teacher. If you get a chemical in your eyes, immediately flush it out at the eyewash station while calling to your teacher. Use the scalpel carefully to avoid injury.** Examine a corn kernel, and find a small, oval, light-colored area that shows through the seed coat. Use the scalpel to cut the kernel in half along the length of this area. Place a drop of iodine solution on the cut surface.
6. Use the stereomicroscope to examine the corn embryo. In your lab report, sketch the embryo and label all the parts that you can identify.

## PART B  Seedling Development

7. Set five corn kernels on a folded paper towel. Roll up the paper towel, and put a rubber band around the roll. Stand the roll in a beaker with 1 cm of water in the bottom. The paper towel will soak up water and moisten the corn. Keep water at the bottom of the beaker, but do not allow the corn kernels to be covered by the water.

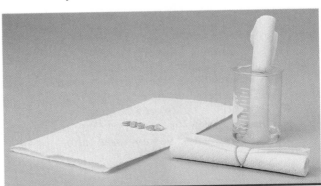

8. Repeat step 7 with five bean seeds.

9. After three days, unroll the paper towels and examine the corn and bean seedlings. Use a glass-marking pen to mark the roots and shoots of the developing seedlings. Starting at the seed of the corn and at the cotyledon node of the bean, make a mark every 0.5 cm along the root of each seedling. And again starting at the seed of the corn and at the cotyledon node of the bean, make a mark every 0.5 cm along the stem of each seedling. Measure the distance from the last mark on the root to the root tip of each seedling. Also measure the distance from the last mark on the stem to the shoot tip of each seedling. Record these data in your lab report.

10. Draw a corn seedling and a bean seedling in your lab report. Using a fresh paper towel, roll up the seeds, place the rolls in the beakers, and add fresh water to the beakers.

11. Make a data table similar to the one shown below in your lab notebook. Expand your table by adding columns under each "Roots" and "Stems" head to account for every section of the roots and stems of your seedlings.

12. After two days, reexamine the seedlings. Measure the distance between the marks, and record the data in your data table.

13. **CAUTION Use the scalpel carefully to avoid injury.** Using the scalpel, make a cut about 2 cm from the tip of the root of a bean seedling. Place the root tip on a microscope slide and add a drop of water. Place a cover slip over the root tip. Using a compound light microscope on low power, observe the root tip. In your lab report, draw the root tip.

14. Clean up your materials and wash your hands before leaving the lab.

## Analysis and Conclusions

1. What protects the tips of corn shoots as they push through the soil? What protects the bean shoots?

2. What types of leaves first appear on the bean seedling?

3. What substance does the black color in the corn kernel indicate? Why might you expect to find this substance in the seed?

4. Examine the data you recorded for steps 9 and 12. Has the distance between the marks changed? If so, where has it changed?

5. What parts of the embryo were observed in all seeds on the third day?

6. How does the structure and development of the corn kernel differ from the structure and development of the pea and bean seeds?

7. What was the source of nutrients for each seed embryo? What is your evidence?

8. Describe the growth in the seedlings you observed.

9. Corn and beans are often cited as representative examples of monocots and dicots, respectively. Relate the seed structure of each to the terms *monocotyledon* and *dicotyledon*.

## Further Inquiry

Design an experiment to find out how monocots and dicots compare in general plant growth and in the structure of their leaves and flowers.

### CORN AND BEAN SEEDLING GROWTH AFTER TWO DAYS

| | Corn seedlings | | | | Bean seedlings | | | |
| | Roots | | Stems | | Roots | | Stems | |
| Seedling | Seed to first mark | Root tip to last mark | Seed to first mark | Shoot tip to last mark | Seed to first mark | Root tip to last mark | Seed to first mark | Shoot tip to last mark |
|---|---|---|---|---|---|---|---|---|
| 1 | | | | | | | | |
| 2 | | | | | | | | |
| 3 | | | | | | | | |
| 4 | | | | | | | | |
| 5 | | | | | | | | |

# PLANT RESPONSES

Venus' flytrap *(Dionaea muscipula),* a carnivorous plant, has leaves that are hinged in the middle. In response to an insect landing on an open leaf, the leaf can snap shut in less than a second. Glands on the leaf's surface then secrete enzymes that digest the insect, providing the plant with nutrients it does not get from the poor soil in which it grows.

**SECTION 1**  *Plant Hormones*

**SECTION 2**  *Plant Movements*

**SECTION 3**  *Seasonal Responses*

SCIENTIFIC AMERICAN

For project ideas from *Scientific American,* visit go.hrw.com and type in the keyword **HM6SAH**.

# PLANT HORMONES

*The growth and development of a plant are influenced by genetic factors, external environmental factors, and chemicals. Plants respond to chemicals that occur naturally inside plants and to synthetic chemicals.*

## SECTION 1

### OBJECTIVES

- **List** the actions of the five major types of plant hormones.
- **Describe** agricultural or gardening applications for each of the five major types of plant hormones.
- **Discuss** how growth retardants are used commercially.

### VOCABULARY

plant hormone
growth regulator
auxin
indoleacetic acid
naphthalene acetic acid
apical dominance
2,4-D
Agent Orange
gibberellin
ethylene
ethephon
abscission
cytokinin
abscisic acid
growth retardant

## GROUPS OF HORMONES

**Plant hormones** are chemical messengers that affect a plant's ability to respond to its environment. Hormones are organic compounds that are effective at very low concentrations; they may be made in one part of the plant and transported to another part. They interact with specific target tissues to cause physiological responses, such as growth or fruit ripening. Each response may be the result of two or more hormones acting together.

Because hormones stimulate or inhibit plant growth, many botanists also refer to them as plant **growth regulators.** Many hormones can be synthesized in the laboratory, which increases the quantity of hormones available for commercial applications. Botanists recognize at least five major groups of hormones: auxins, gibberellins, ethylene, cytokinins, and abscisic acid. These groups of hormones are examined in Table 31-1 on the next page.

## AUXINS

**Auxins** (AWK-suhnz) are hormones involved in plant-cell elongation, shoot and bud growth, and rooting. A well-known natural auxin is **indoleacetic** (IN-DOHL-uh-SEET-ik) **acid,** or IAA. Developing seeds produce IAA, which stimulates the development of fleshy structures such as fruit. An experiment with strawberries, shown in Figure 31-1, provides one form of experimental evidence about the role of IAA in plants. The removal of the seed-containing parts from a strawberry prevents the fleshy structure from enlarging. However, if IAA is then applied, the strawberry enlarges normally.

(a) (b) (c)

**FIGURE 31-1**

(a) Strawberry plants normally produce a fleshy, heart-shaped "berry." The "berry" is not truly a fruit—it is a swollen flower receptacle. The yellowish "seeds" covering the "berry" are truly complete fruits, each containing a seed. (b) If the "seeds" are removed from a young "berry," it does not enlarge. (c) But if the "berry" is then treated with IAA, it grows normally.

## TABLE 31-1 Five Groups of Plant Hormones

| Plant hormone | Actions | Features | Examples |
|---|---|---|---|
| Auxins | • promote cell growth<br>• promote root formation on stem and leaf cuttings<br>• promote shoot and bud growth<br>• promote setting of fruits<br>• prevent dropping of fruit | • produced in growing regions of plant (shoot tips, young leaves, developing seeds)<br>• important role in tropisms | • indoleacetic acid, IAA (natural)<br>• indolebutyric acid, IBA (natural and synthetic)<br>• naphthalene acetic acid, NAA (synthetic)<br>• herbicides 2,4-D and Agent Orange (synthetic) |
| Gibberellins (GA) | • promote elongation growth<br>• promote germination and seedling growth<br>• increase size of fruit<br>• overcome bud dormancy<br>• substitute for long-day or vernalization requirements for flowering | • produced in young shoots and immature seeds<br>• more than 100 naturally occurring types | • gibberellic acid, $GA_3$ (natural) |
| Ethylene | • promotes ripening of fruit<br>• promotes flowering in mangoes and pineapples<br>• promotes abscission | • produced in fruits, flowers, leaves, and roots<br>• colorless gas | • ethephon (synthetic) breaks down and releases ethylene (natural) |
| Cytokinins | • promote cell division<br>• promote lateral bud growth in dicots | • produced in developing roots, fruits, and seeds<br>• auxin-to-cytokinin ratio is important | • zeatin (natural)<br>• kinetin (synthetic)<br>• benzyladenine (synthetic) |
| Abscisic acid (ABA) | • promotes stomatal closure<br>• promotes dormancy<br>• inhibits other hormones<br>• blocks growth | • produced in leaves<br>• expensive to synthesize | • ABA (natural or synthetic) |

Indoleacetic acid is produced in actively growing shoot tips and developing seeds, and it is involved in elongation. Before a cell can elongate, the cell wall must become less rigid so that it can expand. Indoleacetic acid triggers an increase in the plasticity, or stretchability, of cell walls, which allows elongation to occur.

### Synthetic Auxins

Auxins have a variety of possible effects, so they are used for several purposes in gardening, commercial agriculture, and scientific research. Chemists have synthesized several inexpensive compounds similar in structure to IAA. Synthetic auxins, such as **naphthalene** (NAF-thuh-LEEN) **acetic** (uh-SEET-ik) **acid,** or NAA, are used to promote root formation on stem and leaf cuttings, as shown in Figure 31-2 on the next page. Such vegetative propagation of genetically identical plants is useful in agriculture and in laboratory research.

**FIGURE 31-2**

(a) This stem cutting from a coleus plant, *Coleus hybridus,* is growing roots in pure water. (b) This coleus stem cutting has been treated with a synthetic auxin—naphthalene acetic acid (NAA). Roots form more rapidly when the stem is treated with NAA. Both cuttings were taken at the same time.

(a)  (b)

When NAA is sprayed on young fruits of apple and olive trees, some of the fruits drop off so that the remaining fruits grow larger. When NAA is sprayed directly on some other fruits—such as pears and citrus fruits—several weeks before they are ready to be picked, NAA prevents the fruits from dropping off the trees before they are mature. The fact that auxins can have opposite effects—they cause fruit to drop or prevent fruit from dropping—illustrates an important point: The effects of a hormone on a plant often depend on the stage of the plant's development.

Naphthalene acetic acid is used to prevent the undesirable sprouting of stems from the base of ornamental trees. Recall that stems contain a lateral bud at the base of each leaf. In many stems, these buds fail to sprout as long as the plant's shoot tip is intact. The inhibition of lateral buds by the presence of a shoot tip is called **apical dominance.** If the shoot tip is removed, the lateral buds begin to grow. If IAA or NAA is applied to the cut tip of the stem, the lateral buds remain dormant. NAA is used commercially to prevent buds from sprouting on potato tubers during storage.

Another important synthetic auxin is **2,4-D,** which is a weed-killer. At certain concentrations, it kills dicots, such as dandelions, without injuring monocots, such as lawn grasses and cereal crops. Given our dependence on cereals for food, 2,4-D has been important to agriculture. **Agent Orange,** a mixture of 2,4-D and another auxin, was used to defoliate jungles in the Vietnam War. A nonauxin contaminant in Agent Orange is thought to have caused health problems in many people who were exposed to it.

# GIBBERELLINS

In the 1920s, scientists in Japan discovered that a substance produced by fungi of the genus *Gibberella* caused fungus-infected rice plants to grow abnormally tall. This type of hormone, named **gibberellin** (JIB-uh-REL-uhn), was later found to be produced in small quantities by plants themselves.

FIGURE 31-3

These bird's nest ferns, *Asplendium nidus,* are the same age. The fern in (b), however, has been treated with gibberellin, which stimulates the leaves to grow larger.

(a)                                              (b)

Gibberellins have many effects on a plant, but they primarily stimulate elongation growth. Spraying some plants with gibberellins may cause them to grow larger than normal, as shown in Figure 31-3.

Like auxins, gibberellins are hormones that have important commercial applications. Many seedless grapes, such as those shown in Figure 31-4, are sprayed with gibberellins to increase the size of the fruit. Beer makers use gibberellins to increase the alcohol content of beer by increasing the amount of starch converted to sugar in the brewing process. Gibberellins are also used to treat seeds, because they break seed dormancy and promote uniform germination.

**FIGURE 31-4**

Almost all of the raisins produced in California are made from Thompson Seedless grapes. Normal Thompson Seedless grapes are smaller than those treated with a gibberellin hormone. The grapes on the left were treated with a gibberellin. As you can see, the addition of a gibberellin to grapes stimulates the grapes to grow larger.

# ETHYLENE

The hormone **ethylene** (ETH-uh-LEEN) plays a role in the ripening of fruits. Unlike other plant hormones, ethylene is a gas at room temperature. Ethylene gas diffuses easily through the air from one plant to another. The saying "One bad apple spoils the barrel" has its basis in ethylene gas. One rotting apple will produce ethylene gas, which stimulates nearby apples to ripen and then spoil.

In commercial use, ethylene is usually applied in a solution of **ethephon** (ETH-uh-fohn), a synthetic chemical that breaks down to release ethylene gas. It is used to ripen bananas, honeydew melons, and tomatoes. Oranges, lemons, and grapefruits often remain green when they are ripe. Although the green fruit may taste good, consumers will not usually buy them. The application of ethylene to green citrus fruits causes desirable citrus colors, such as yellow and orange, to develop.

In some plant species, ethylene promotes **abscission,** the detachment of leaves, flowers, or fruits. Growers can use mechanical tree shakers to harvest cherries and other crops if the fruit is sprayed with ethylene before harvest. Leaf abscission can be an adaptive advantage. Dead, damaged, or infected leaves drop off rather than shading healthy leaves or spreading disease. The plant can minimize water loss in winter, when water in the environment is often frozen.

# CYTOKININS

Cytokinins (SIE-toh-KIE-ninz) promote cell division in plants. They are produced in the developing shoots, roots, fruits, and seeds of a plant. Cytokinins are very important in the culturing of plant tissues in the laboratory. A high ratio of auxins to cytokinins in a tissue-culture medium stimulates root formation. A low ratio promotes shoot formation. Cytokinins are also used to promote lateral bud growth of flower crops.

# ABSCISIC ACID

Abscisic (ab-SIS-ik) **acid,** or ABA, generally inhibits other hormones, such as IAA. It was originally thought to promote abscission, hence its name. Botanists now think that ethylene is the main abscission hormone. Abscisic acid helps to bring about dormancy in a plant's buds and maintains dormancy in its seeds. Abscisic acid causes a plant's stomata to close in response to drought. Water-stressed leaves produce large amounts of ABA. It is too costly to synthesize ABA for agricultural use.

# OTHER GROWTH REGULATORS

Many growth regulators are used on ornamental plants. These substances do not fit into the five classes of hormones. For example, utility companies in some areas may apply **growth retardants,** chemicals that prevent plant growth, to trees to prevent the trees from interfering with utility lines. It is sometimes less expensive to apply these chemicals than to repeatedly prune the trees. Scientists are still searching for a hormone to retard the growth of lawn grass so that it does not have to be mowed so often.

## SECTION 1 REVIEW

1. List the five major types of plant hormones.
2. Which plant hormones generally have stimulatory effects, and which generally have inhibitory effects?
3. What are important commercial uses of auxins, gibberellins, and ethylene?
4. Explain why growth retardants are useful in maintaining ornamental plants.

**CRITICAL THINKING**

5. **Analyzing Methods** How might a grower use auxin and cytokinin to grow large plants quickly from pieces of stem tissue?
6. **Applying Information** Why is it adaptive for some plants to grow a fleshy fruit even when each seed has its own food source?
7. **Relating Concepts** How might gibberellins cause an embryo to end its dormancy?

## OBJECTIVES

- **List** the environmental stimuli to which plants respond for each type of tropism.
- **Explain** the current hypotheses regarding auxins and their function in phototropism and gravitropism.
- **Describe** two types of nastic movements, and explain how they help a plant survive.

## VOCABULARY

tropism
phototropism
solar tracking
thigmotropism
gravitropism
chemotropism
nastic movement
thigmonastic movement
nyctinastic movement

# PLANT MOVEMENTS

*Plants appear immobile because they are rooted in place. However, time-lapse photography reveals that parts of plants frequently move. Most plants move too slowly for us to notice. Plants move in response to several environmental stimuli, such as light, gravity, and mechanical disturbances. Tropisms are growth responses that occur slowly, while nastic movements happen more quickly.*

## TROPISMS

A **tropism** (TROH-piz-uhm) is a response in which a plant grows either toward or away from an environmental stimulus. Growth toward an environmental stimulus is called a *positive* tropism, and growth away from a stimulus is called a *negative* tropism. Each kind of tropism is named for its stimulus. For example, plant growth in response to light coming from one direction is called **phototropism.** Thus, in Figure 31-5, the shoot tips of a plant that grow toward the light source are positively phototropic. Types of tropisms are summarized in Table 31-2.

### Phototropism

Phototropism is illustrated by the appearance of the sprouts in Figure 31-5. Scientists have observed that light causes the hormone auxin to move to the shaded side of the shoot. The auxin is thought to cause the cells on the shaded side to elongate more than the cells on the lighted side. As a result, the shoot grows toward the light and exhibits positive phototropism.

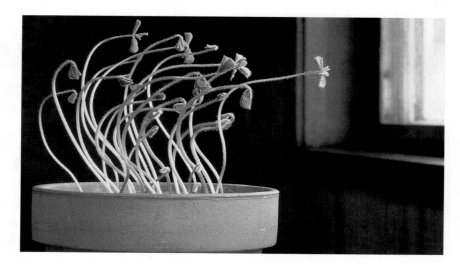

**FIGURE 31-5**

The way these new sprouts of the flowering shamrock, *Oxalis rubra,* grow toward a light is an example of positive phototropism. The hormone auxin stimulates the cells on the shaded side of the plant stem to elongate.

**TABLE 31-2** *Various Plant Tropisms*

| Tropism | Stimulus | Positive example |
|---------|----------|------------------|
| Phototropism | light | plant grows toward light |
| Thigmotropism | contact with object | vine twines around a tree |
| Gravitropism | gravity | roots grow downward |
| Chemotropism | chemical | pollen tube grows toward ovule |

**Quick Lab**

### Visualizing Phototropism

**Materials** 2 in. pots (2) containing potting soil, 4 bean seeds, cardboard box

**Procedure**

1. Plant two bean seeds in each pot. Label each pot for your group. Place one pot in a window or under a plant light.

2. Cut a rectangular window in the box, and place the box over the second pot so that the window faces the light. Place the box in a different location from the open pot. Keep both pots moist for several days.

3. Remove the box 2–3 days after the seedlings have emerged from the soil. Compare the seedlings grown in the light with the ones grown in the box. Sketch your observations.

**Analysis** How are the seedlings different? How do you account for the difference? Describe or draw what you think the cells inside the curved part of the stem look like.

In some plant stems, phototropism is not caused by auxin movement. In these instances, light may cause the production of a growth inhibitor on the lighted side. Negative phototropism is sometimes seen in vines that climb on flat walls where coiling tendrils have nothing to coil around. These vines have stem tips that grow away from light, toward the wall. This growth brings adventitious roots or adhesive discs in contact with the wall on which they can cling.

**Solar tracking,** also called *heliotropism,* is the motion of leaves or flowers as they follow the sun's movement across the sky, as shown in Figure 31-6. By continuously facing toward a moving light source, the plant maximizes the light available for photosynthesis. These movements are not actually a tropism but a related kind of movement.

### Thigmotropism

**Thigmotropism** is a plant's growth response to touching a solid object. Tendrils and stems of vines, such as morning glories, coil when they touch an object. Thigmotropism allows some vines to climb other plants or objects, increasing the vine's chance of intercepting light for photosynthesis. It is thought that ethylene and a type of auxin are involved in this response.

**Word Roots and Origins**

***thigmotropism***

from the Greek *thiga,* meaning "touch," and *tropos,* meaning "turning"

**FIGURE 31-6**

These sunflower plants face the sun as it sets in the evening. In the morning, the plants face the sun as it rises, then they follow it as it moves across the sky. This movement is called *solar tracking.*

## Gravitropism

**Gravitropism** is a plant's growth response to gravity. A root usually grows downward and a stem usually grows upward—that is, roots are positively gravitropic and stems are negatively gravitropic.

Like phototropism, gravitropism appears to be at least partly regulated by auxins. One hypothesis proposes that when a seedling is placed horizontally, auxins accumulate along the lower sides of both the root and the stem. This concentration of auxins stimulates cell elongation along the lower side of the stem, and the stem grows upward. A similar concentration of auxins inhibits cell elongation in the lower side of the root, and the root grows downward, as shown in Figure 31-7.

## Chemotropism

Plant growth that occurs in response to a chemical is called **chemotropism.** An example is the growth of a pollen tube after a flower is pollinated. The pollen tube grows out from the pollen grain and down through the stigma and style to the ovule, in the direction of increasing concentrations of chemicals produced by the ovule.

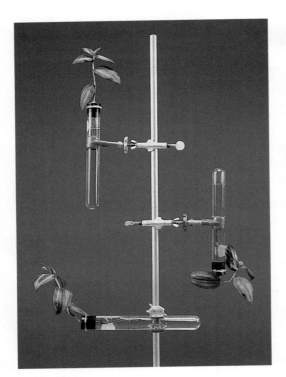

**FIGURE 31-7**

This photograph was taken seven days after cuttings of the inch plant, *Zebrina pendula,* were placed in growing tubes in different orientations. Notice that the two lower cuttings have started to grow upward. The upward growth of the lower cuttings is caused by the plants' response to gravity and is called *negative gravitropism.* When the roots turn and begin to grow in a downward direction, the growth is called *positive gravitropism.*

# NASTIC MOVEMENTS

Plant movements that occur in response to environmental stimuli but that are independent of the direction of stimuli are called **nastic movements.** These movements are regulated by changes in the water pressure against the cell wall *(turgor pressure)* of certain plant cells.

## Thigmonastic Movements

**Thigmonastic** (THIG-mah-nas-tik) **movements** are nastic movements that occur in response to touching a plant. Many thigmonastic movements are rapid, such as the closing of the leaf trap of a Venus' flytrap around an insect. Figure 31-8 shows how the leaves of a sensitive plant fold within a few seconds after being touched.

**FIGURE 31-8**

(a) *Mimosa pudica,* also called the *sensitive plant,* is a small shrub that has leaflets. (b) When a leaflet is touched, it folds together. This rapid movement is a thigmonastic movement.

(a)

(b)

(a)

(b)

This movement is caused by the rapid loss of turgor pressure in certain cells, a process similar to that which occurs in guard cells. Physical stimulation of the plant leaf causes potassium ions to be pumped out of the cells at the base of leaflets and petioles. Water then moves out of the cells by osmosis. As the cells shrink, the plant's leaves move.

The folding of a plant's leaves in response to touch is thought to discourage insect feeding. In addition, thigmonastic movements may help prevent water loss in plants. When the wind blows on a plant, the rate of transpiration is increased. So if the leaves of a plant fold in response to the "touch" of the wind, water loss is reduced. This could be an important adaptive advantage to a plant.

## Nyctinastic Movements

**Nyctinastic** (NIK-tuh-NAS-tik) **movements** are responses to the daily cycle of light and dark. These movements involve the same type of osmotic mechanism as thigmonastic movements, but the changes in turgor pressure are more gradual. Nyctinastic movements occur in many plants, including bean plants, honeylocust trees, and silk trees. The prayer plant, shown in Figure 31-9, gets its name from the fact that its leaf blades are vertical at night, resembling praying hands. During the day, its leaf blades are horizontal. The botanist Linnaeus planted many plant species with nyctinastic movements in a big circle to make a "flower clock." The nyctinastic movements of each species occurred at a specific time of day.

**FIGURE 31-9**

A common houseplant is the prayer plant, *Maranta leuconeura*. (a) During the day, the leaf blades of the prayer plant are oriented horizontally in response to light. (b) During the night, the leaf blades are oriented vertically. This movement is called a *nyctinastic movement*.

internet connect

www.scilinks.org
**Topic: Nastic Movements**
**Keyword: HM61012**

SCI
LINKS. Maintained by the
National Science
Teachers Association

## SECTION 2 REVIEW

1. Give an example of each of the four types of tropisms.

2. What role is auxin thought to play in the growth of plants in response to light and gravity?

3. What adaptive advantages might thigmonastic movements provide a plant?

4. Explain how a tropism and a nastic movement differ.

**CRITICAL THINKING**

5. **Evaluating Information** Why is it adaptive for plant cells to respond to stimuli received from the environment?

6. **Predicting Results** Would you expect a plant that had its shoot tip removed to exhibit phototropism? Why or why not?

7. **Inferring Relationships** Why aren't nastic movements regulated by hormones?

OBJECTIVES

- **Define** photoperiodism.
- **Describe** the role of critical night length in flowering.
- **Explain** the process of vernalization.
- **Explain** changing fall colors in leaves.

VOCABULARY

photoperiodism
critical night length
short-day plant
long-day plant
day-neutral plant
phytochrome
vernalization
biennial
bolting
fall color

# SEASONAL RESPONSES

*In nontropical areas, plant responses are strongly influenced by seasonal changes. For example, many trees shed their leaves in the fall, and most plants flower only at certain times of the year. How do plants "sense" seasonal changes? Although temperature is involved in some cases, plants mark the seasons primarily by sensing changes in night length.*

## PHOTOPERIODISM

A plant's response to changes in the length of days and nights is called **photoperiodism.** Photoperiodism affects many plant processes, including the formation of storage organs and bud dormancy. However, the most-studied photoperiodic process is flowering. Some plants require a particular night length to flower. In other species, a particular night length merely makes the plant flower sooner than it otherwise would.

### Day Length and Night Length

Researchers have found that the important factor in flowering is the amount of darkness, or night length, that a plant receives. Many plant species have specific requirement for darkness, called the **critical night length.** Although scientists now know that night length, and not day length, regulates flowering, the terms *short-day plant* and *long-day plant* are still used. A **short-day plant** flowers when the days are short and the nights are longer than a certain length. Conversely, a **long-day plant** flowers when the days are long and the nights are shorter than a certain length.

Plants can be divided into three groups, depending on their response to the photoperiod, which acts as a season indicator. The three groups of plants are summarized in Table 31-3. The largest group, made up of **day-neutral plants** (DNPs), is not affected by day length. Plants that are DNPs for flowering include tomatoes, dandelions, roses, corn, cotton, and beans.

### TABLE 31-3 *Flowering Photoperiodism*

| Type of plant | Conditions needed for flowering | Seasons of flowering |
|---|---|---|
| Day-neutral plant (DNP) | not affected by day-night cycle | spring to fall |
| Short-day plant (SDP) | short days (long nights) | spring, fall |
| Long-day plant (LDP) | long days (short nights) | summer |

Short-day plants (SDPs) flower in the spring or fall, when the day length is short. For example, ragweed flowers when the days are shorter than 14 hours, and poinsettias flower when the days are shorter than 12 hours. Chrysanthemums, goldenrods, strawberries, tulips, and soybeans are typically SDPs for flowering.

Long-day plants (LDPs) flower when days are long, usually in summer. For example, wheat flowers only when the days are longer than about 10 hours. Radishes, asters, irises, spinach, and beets are typically LDPs for flowering.

## Adjusting the Flowering Cycles of Plants

Examine Figure 31-10, which compares the flowering of a poinsettia (an SDP) with that of an iris (LDP). With an 8-hour night, the LDP flowers but the SDP does not. With a 16-hour night, the SDP flowers and the LDP does not. However, if a 16-hour night is interrupted in the middle by one hour of light, the LDP flowers and the SDP does not. This response shows that the length of uninterrupted darkness is the important factor. Even though there is a daily total of 15 hours of darkness, the SDP does not flower because of that one hour of light. Flower growers who want to obtain winter flowering of LDPs simply expose them to a low level of incandescent light in the middle of the night. Summer flowering of SDPs is obtained by covering the plants in the late afternoon with an opaque cloth so that the SDPs receive enough darkness.

## Regulation by Phytochrome

Plants monitor changes in day length with a bluish, light-sensitive pigment called **phytochrome** (FIET-uh-KROHM). Phytochrome exists in two forms, based on the wavelength of the light that it absorbs. The form that absorbs red rays is called $P_r$, and the form that absorbs far red (infrared) rays is called $P_{fr}$. Daylight converts $P_r$ to $P_{fr}$. In the dark, $P_{fr}$ is converted to $P_r$. Phytochrome plays a role in bud dormancy and seed germination as well as in flowering.

**FIGURE 31-10**

The figure compares a short-day plant (SDP) with a long-day plant (LDP) in three variations of night length. The SDP has a critical night length of 14 hours. The LDP has a critical night length of 10 hours.

**LENGTH OF EXPOSURE**

**PLANT RESPONSE**

A | 16 hours light | 8 hours dark

B | 8 hours light | 16 hours dark

C | 8 hours light | 7.5 hours dark | 7.5 hours dark

SDP     LDP

# VERNALIZATION

**Vernalization** is a low-temperature stimulation of flowering. Vernalization is important for fall-sown grain crops, such as winter wheat, barley, and rye. Farmers often take advantage of vernalization to grow and harvest their crops before a summer drought sets in. For example, wheat seeds are sown in the fall and survive the winter as small seedlings. Exposure to cold winter temperatures causes the plants to flower in early spring, and an early crop is produced. If the same wheat is sown in the spring, it will take about two months longer to produce a crop. Thus, cold temperatures are not absolutely required for many grain crops, but they do quicken flowering.

A **biennial** plant is a plant that usually lives for only two years, producing flowers and seeds during the second year. Biennial plants, such as carrots, beets, celery, and foxglove, survive their first winter as large roots with small plants above ground. In the spring, their flowering stem elongates rapidly, a process called **bolting.** Most biennials must undergo vernalization before they flower during the second year. They then die after flowering. Treating a biennial with gibberellin is sometimes used as a substitute for cold temperatures.

**FIGURE 31-11**

The colors of the carotenoids are visible in these autumn leaves, which have lost most of their chlorophyll.

# FALL COLORS

Some trees are noted for their spectacular fall colors, as shown in Figure 31-11. The changing **fall colors** are caused mainly by a photoperiodic response. As nights become longer in the fall, leaves stop producing chlorophyll. As the green pigment degrades, other leaf pigments—the carotenoids (kuh-RAHT′n-OYDZ)—become visible. Carotenoids include the orange carotenes and the yellow xanthophylls (ZAN-thuh-filz). The carotenoids were always in the leaf but were hidden by the chlorophyll. Another group of leaf pigments, the anthocyanins (AN-thoh-SIE-uh-ninz), produce red and purplish red colors in cool, sunny weather.

## SECTION 3 REVIEW

1. State the name of a plant's response to changes in the length of days and nights.

2. How do flower growers get short-day plants, such as chrysanthemums, to flower at any time of year?

3. In what ways do farmers use the process of vernalization to their benefit?

4. Explain the process by which tree leaves change color in the fall.

**CRITICAL THINKING**

5. **Analyzing Concepts** Why might the term *nyctoperiodism* be a better term for describing the process known as *photoperiodism*?

6. **Recognizing Relationships** Explain how the floral business might be affected if the flowering cycle could not be altered artificially.

7. **Evaluating Results** Many plants will flower if just a single leaf is exposed to the appropriate night length. How can you explain this finding?

## Plant Hormones

- Plant hormones are formed in many plant parts and regulate many aspects of growth and development. There are five major groups of plant hormones: auxins, gibberellins, ethylene, cytokinins, and abscisic acid.

- Hormonal responses often have adaptive advantages.

- Synthetic auxins are used for killing weeds, stimulating root formation, and stimulating or preventing fruit drop.

- Gibberellins are used to increase the size of fruit, to stimulate seed germination, and to brew beer.

- Ethylene is used to ripen fruit and promote abscission.

- Cytokinins are used to culture plant tissues in the lab and to promote lateral bud growth of flower crops.

- Abscisic acid promotes dormancy in plant buds, maintains dormancy in seeds, and causes stomata to close.

- Growth retardants are widely used to reduce plant height.

### Vocabulary

| | | | |
|---|---|---|---|
| plant hormone (p. 631) | naphthalene acetic acid (p. 632) | Agent Orange (p. 633) | abscission (p. 634) |
| growth regulator (p. 631) | apical dominance (p. 633) | gibberellin (p. 633) | cytokinin (p. 635) |
| auxin (p. 631) | 2,4-D (p. 633) | ethylene (p. 634) | abscisic acid (p. 635) |
| indoleacetic acid (p. 631) | | ethephon (p. 634) | growth retardant (p. 635) |

## Plant Movements

- Tropisms and nastic movements are plant responses to environmental stimuli. Tropisms occur slowly; nastic movements happen more quickly.

- A tropism is a response in which a plant grows either toward or away from an environmental stimulus. Tropisms can occur in response to light, touch, gravity, and chemicals.

- Phototropism is thought to occur in some plants when auxin moves to the shaded side of a plant and causes cells there to elongate more than the cells on the lighted side.

- Gravitropism is thought to occur when auxin accumulates on the lower sides of a horizontal root and stem. This accumulation causes cell elongation on the lower side of the stem and inhibits cell elongation on the lower side of the root.

- Nastic movements are responses to environmental stimuli but are independent of the direction of the stimuli. Thigmonastic movements occur in response to touch, and nyctinastic movements occur in response to the daily cycle of light and dark.

### Vocabulary

| | | | |
|---|---|---|---|
| tropism (p. 636) | thigmotropism (p. 637) | nastic movement (p. 638) | nyctinastic movement (p. 639) |
| phototropism (p. 636) | gravitropism (p. 638) | thigmonastic movement (p. 638) | |
| solar tracking (p. 637) | chemotropism (p. 638) | | |

## Seasonal Responses

- Photoperiodism is a plant's response to changes in the length of days and nights.

- Plants fit in one of three photoperiodic classes for flowering: day-neutral, short-day, and long-day plants. Short-day and long-day plants have a specific requirement for darkness, called the *critical night length.*

- Vernalization is the promotion of flowering by cold temperatures. Farmers often plant wheat seeds in the fall so that the seedlings can be exposed to winter temperatures and will flower before summer droughts begin.

- Changing fall colors in tree leaves are due to chlorophyll degradation, which reveals other pigments already present.

### Vocabulary

| | | | |
|---|---|---|---|
| photoperiodism (p. 640) | long-day plant (p. 640) | vernalization (p. 642) | fall color (p. 642) |
| critical night length (p. 640) | day-neutral plant (p. 640) | biennial (p. 642) | |
| short-day plant (p. 640) | phytochrome (p. 641) | bolting (p. 642) | |

## USING VOCABULARY

1. For each pair of terms, explain how the meanings of the terms differ.
   a. *auxin* and *gibberellin*
   b. *apical dominance* and *abscission*
   c. *tropism* and *nastic movement*
   d. *short-day plant* and *long-day plant*

2. Use the following terms in the same sentence: *thigmotropism, gravitropism,* and *chemotropism.*

3. For each pair of terms, explain the relationship between the terms.
   a. *vernalization* and *biennial*
   b. *abscisic acid* and *abscission*
   c. *short-day plant* and *critical night length*

4. **Word Roots and Origins** The word *auxin* is derived from the Greek *auxein,* which means "to increase." Using this information, explain why the term *auxin* is a good name for the plant hormone that the term identifies.

## UNDERSTANDING KEY CONCEPTS

5. **Summarize** the observed actions of each of the five types of plant hormones.

6. **Identify** an adaptive advantage of abscisic acid production.

7. **Describe** three ways in which a home gardener might use auxin.

8. **Discuss** the commercial use of gibberellins.

9. **Describe** how a fruit grower might use ethylene on crops.

10. **Compare** the functions of cytokinins and abscisic acid.

11. **Describe** how growth retardants are used on plants.

12. **Identify** the type of plant movement that is a growth response.

13. **Identify** the environmental stimulus involved in each of the plant tropisms.

14. **Explain** how auxins are thought to cause plant growth in response to gravity.

15. **Summarize** the adaptive advantages of the two types of nastic movements.

16. **Define** photoperiodism.

17. **Explain** how critical night length applies to photoperiodism.

18. **Describe** how a biennial plant lives, and explain why vernalization is important in its life cycle.

19. **Name** the type of pigment that becomes visible in a leaf when chlorophyll begins to degrade.

20. **CONCEPT MAPPING** Use the following terms to create a concept map that shows the major effects of some plant hormones: *apical dominance, auxin, cytokinin, gibberellin, gravitropism, plant hormone, phototropism,* and *thigmotropism.*

## CRITICAL THINKING

21. **Predicting Results** Suppose you placed a green banana in each of several plastic bags, placed a ripe pear in half of the bags, and then sealed all of the bags. Which group of bananas do you think would ripen sooner? Justify your answer.

22. **Evaluating Results** Suppose that a friend who lives in North Dakota gives you a cutting from a flowering plant that you admired when you saw it growing in your friend's yard. You plant the cutting at your home in Georgia. The plant grows but does not produce flowers. Based on your knowledge of plant responses, what might be preventing the plant from flowering?

23. **Inferring Relationships** The growth of most deciduous trees in the northern United States and Canada, where winters are severe, is regulated strictly by photoperiodism. That is, temperature plays no part in the regulation of their yearly growing cycle. Explain why this is ecologically significant.

24. **Interpreting Graphics** Suppose you notice that your neighbor has a perfect yard but that some of the plants in your yard have distorted leaves, like those in the photo shown below. What likely caused the leaves' unusual appearance?

# Standardized Test Preparation

**DIRECTIONS:** Choose the letter of the answer choice that best answers the question.

1. Which of the following is the name for the process in which flowering is stimulated by exposure of plants to cold?
   A. dormancy
   B. vernalization
   C. thigmotropism
   D. photoperiodism

2. Which of the following is a result of abscission?
   F. Leaves fall off stems.
   G. Cuttings are produced.
   H. Plants sense night length.
   J. Abscisic acid is produced.

3. Which of the following describes the relationship between nastic movements and a stimulus?
   A. Nastic movements occur without a stimulus.
   B. Nastic movements occur toward a stimulus.
   C. Nastic movements occur away from a stimulus.
   D. Nastic movements occur independently of the direction of a stimulus.

4. What is the response of a plant to the length of days and nights called?
   F. gravitropism
   G. phototropism
   H. photoperiodism
   J. thigmotropism

**INTERPRETING GRAPHICS:** The illustration below shows a growing seedling. Use the illustration to answer the question that follows.

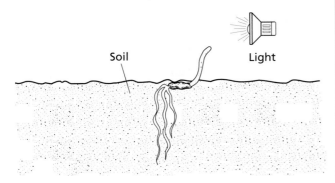

5. Which of the following statements about this seedling is true?
   A. The seedling is exhibiting abscission.
   B. The shoot is exhibiting positive phototropism.
   C. The roots are exhibiting negative gravitropism.
   D. The seedling is exhibiting negative thigmotropism.

**DIRECTIONS:** Complete the following analogy.

6. cell elongation : gibberellins :: cell division :
   F. auxins
   G. ethylene
   H. cytokinins
   J. abscisic acid

**INTERPRETING GRAPHICS:** The diagrams below represent three different growing conditions. Use the diagrams to answer the question that follows.

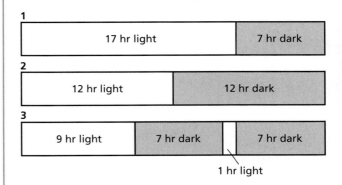

7. In which of the conditions will a long-day plant with a critical night length of 8 hours flower?
   A. 1
   B. 2
   C. 1 and 3
   D. 2 and 3

## SHORT RESPONSE

The Venus' flytrap obtains nutrients by closing its leaves around insects and then digesting the insects.

Explain why a thigmonastic movement is a more useful plant response than a thigmotropic response would be in this situation.

## EXTENDED RESPONSE

Reproduction is essential for survival of flowering plant species.

*Part A* Identify two plant hormones that have roles in flowering, fruiting, and/or seed or fruit dispersal, and describe these roles.

*Part B* Identify the important environmental signals for flowering, and describe how these signals affect flowering.

> **Test TIP** For a question about a structure or phenomenon that has a complex name, write down the name and review its meaning before answering the question.

# Testing the Effect of a Gibberellin on Plant Growth

## OBJECTIVES

- Study the effect of a gibberellin on the growth of bean seedlings.

## PROCESS SKILLS

- observing
- hypothesizing
- measuring
- comparing and contrasting
- collecting data
- organizing data

## MATERIALS

- safety goggles
- lab apron
- disposable gloves
- 2 flowerpots, 20 cm or larger
- marking pen
- labeling tape
- potting-soil mixture
- 10 bean seedlings, at least 3 cm tall
- centimeter ruler
- cotton swabs
- gibberellic acid solution (contains a gibberellin)
- water

## Background

1. Gibberellins are found in all parts of plants but are most concentrated in immature seeds. Gibberellins are only one of many kinds of hormones that affect plant functions.
2. What is the major effect of gibberellins on plant tissues?

## PART A  Testing a Hypothesis

1. Discuss the objective of this investigation with your lab partners. You will apply gibberellic acid solution to the leaves and shoot tips of one group of bean seedlings, and you will apply only water to an identical group of bean seedlings. Develop a hypothesis about the effect of gibberellic acid solution on bean seedlings. Record your hypothesis in your lab report.

2. **CAUTION** **Wear safety goggles, a lab apron, and disposable gloves at all times during this investigation.**
3. Obtain two flowerpots, and label them A and B. Also write your initials on the flowerpots.
4. Fill each flowerpot with potting-soil mixture. The pots should be filled to the same level.
5. **CAUTION** **Keep the seeds, which may have been treated with a fungicide, away from your skin.** Plant five bean seedlings in each flowerpot, spacing them evenly around the edge. Each seedling's roots should be at least 1 cm below the soil surface.
6. Measure the height of each plant in pot A to the nearest millimeter. Measure from the soil surface to the shoot tip. In your lab report, record your measurements in a data table similar to the table on the facing page.
7. Average the height of the five seedlings. In your lab report, record your average measurement under "Initial height" in your data table.
8. Repeat steps 6 and 7 using the plants in pot B.
9. Wet a cotton swab with water. Rub the water over the leaves and shoot tips of each seedling in pot A.
10. **CAUTION** **Gibberellic acid is an irritant. If you get gibberellic acid solution on your skin or clothing, rinse it off at the sink while calling to your teacher. If you get gibberellic acid solution in your eyes, flush it out immediately at an eyewash station while calling to your teacher.** Wet a clean cotton swab with gibberellic acid solution. Apply the solution to the seedlings in pot B by rubbing the cotton swab on the leaves and shoot tips.
11. Place both flowerpots in a window or other area where they are likely to get light. Ensure that each seedling will receive the same amount of water, sunlight, darkness, and air circulation for the next 10 days.
12. Clean up your materials, and wash your hands before leaving the lab.

## PART B Observing the Results

13. Each day over the next 10 days, measure the height of each seedling. Average the height of the seedlings in each flowerpot, and record the average height in your data tables.

14. Calculate the average change in height for each day. For example, the average change in height during the second day is equal to the average height on day 2 minus the average height on day 1.

15. If you are unable to make measurements over the weekend, simply record in your data table the number of days that elapsed since the last measurement was taken. To calculate the average change in height for the days when measurements were not taken, you will need to divide the amount of change by the number of days that have elapsed since your last measurement.

16. At the end of 10 days, clean up your materials according to your teacher's instructions.

## Analysis and Conclusions

1. Use the data you have recorded to calculate the percentage increase—between your first measurement and your last measurement—in the average height of the two groups of plants.

2. Use your data to make a line graph of height as a function of time. Label the *x*-axis of your graph *Time,* and measure time in days. Label the *y*-axis *Height,* and measure height in millimeters.

3. Do your data support your hypothesis? Explain why or why not.

4. What differences, other than height, did you detect in the bean seedlings?

5. What were some of the possible sources of error in this experiment?

6. How might a knowledge of plant regulatory chemicals be of use to farmers and other plant growers?

## Further Inquiry

Design an experiment to determine whether gibberellic acid accelerates the germination of bean seeds.

### FLOWERPOT A: *EFFECTS OF WATER ON BEAN SEEDLINGS*

| Day | Height (mm) | Total change in height (mm) |
|---|---|---|
| Initial | | |
| 1 | | |
| 2 | | |
| 3 | | |
| 4 | | |
| 5 | | |
| 6 | | |
| 7 | | |
| 8 | | |
| 9 | | |
| 10 | | |

### FLOWERPOT B: *EFFECTS OF GIBBERELLIC ACID ON BEAN SEEDLINGS*

| Day | Height (mm) | Total change in height (mm) |
|---|---|---|
| Initial | | |
| 1 | | |
| 2 | | |
| 3 | | |
| 4 | | |
| 5 | | |
| 6 | | |
| 7 | | |
| 8 | | |
| 9 | | |
| 10 | | |

# INVERTEBRATES

66 *It has taken biologists some 230 years to identify and describe three quarters of a million insects; if there are indeed at least thirty million, as Erwin (Terry Erwin, The Smithsonian Institution) estimates, then, working as they have in the past, insect taxonomists have ten thousand years of employment ahead of them.* 99

From "Endless Forms Most Beautiful," from *The Sixth Extinction: Patterns of Life and the Future of Humankind* by Richard Leakey and Roger Lewin. Published by Doubleday, a division of Random House, Inc., New York, 1995.

SCIENTIFIC AMERICAN

References to *Scientific American* project ideas are located throughout this unit.

internet connect

National Science Teachers Association *sci*LINKS Internet resources are located throughout this unit.

*sci*LINKS. Maintained by the National Science Teachers Association

**This Sally lightfoot crab lives on bare volcanic rock on the Galápagos Islands.**

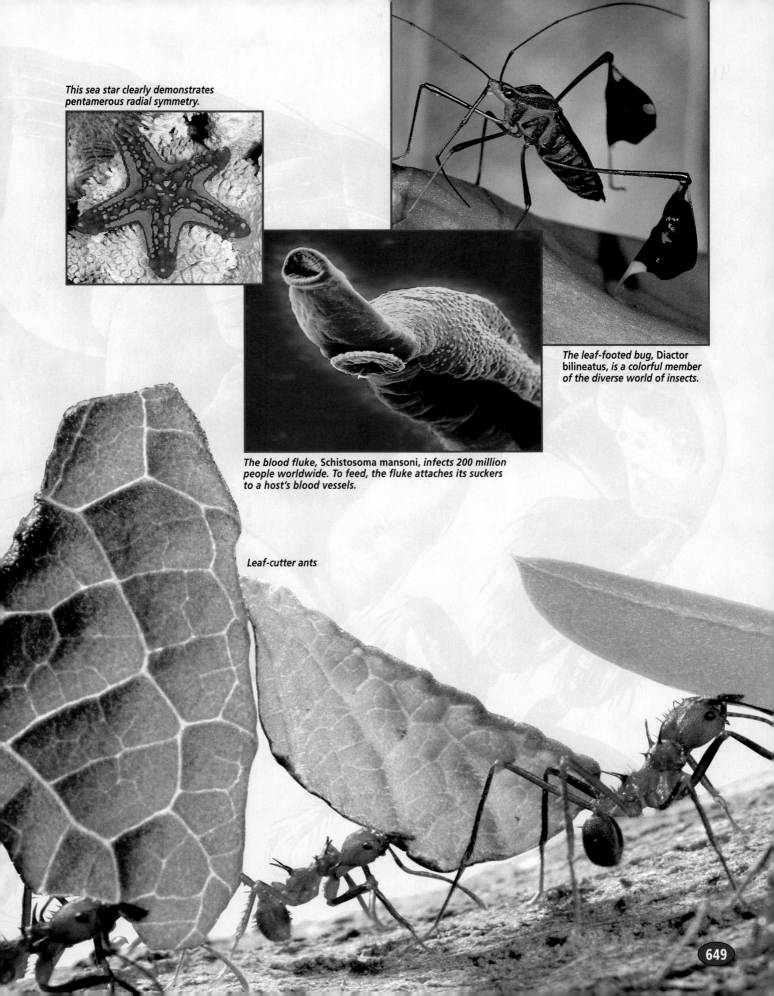

This sea star clearly demonstrates pentamerous radial symmetry.

The blood fluke, Schistosoma mansoni, *infects 200 million people worldwide. To feed, the fluke attaches its suckers to a host's blood vessels.*

The leaf-footed bug, Diactor bilineatus, *is a colorful member of the diverse world of insects.*

Leaf-cutter ants

# INTRODUCTION TO ANIMALS

The diversity of animal life is staggering. Animals have adapted to Earth's lushest environments and to its harshest environments. This Sally Lightfoot crab, *Grapsus grapsus,* lives on the bare volcanic rock of the geologically young Galápagos Islands.

**SECTION 1** *The Nature of Animals*

**SECTION 2** *Invertebrates and Vertebrates*

**SECTION 3** *Fertilization and Development*

# THE NATURE OF ANIMALS

*If you are asked to name an animal, you might respond with the name of a familiar large-bodied animal, such as a horse, a shark, or an eagle. But the kingdom Animalia is much more diverse than many people realize.*

## CHARACTERISTICS

**Animals** are multicellular heterotrophic organisms that lack cell walls. Some animals, called **vertebrates,** have a backbone. Other animals, called **invertebrates,** do not have a backbone. Invertebrates account for more than 95 percent of all animal species alive today. Most members of the animal kingdom share other important characteristics, including sexual reproduction and movement.

### Multicellular Organization

The bodies of animals are multicellular. Some animals contain large numbers of cells. For example, some scientists estimate that the body of an adult human contains 50 trillion to 100 trillion cells. Unlike the cells of unicellular organisms, the cells of multicellular organisms do not lead independent lives. Each cell depends on the presence and functioning of other cells.

In all but the simplest animal phyla, there is a division of labor among cells. **Specialization** is the evolutionary adaptation of a cell for a particular function. Just as a general contractor makes use of carpenters, electricians, and plumbers to build a house, a multicellular organism makes use of specialized cells to perform particular functions, such as digesting food, removing wastes, or reproducing.

A *tissue* is a group of similar cells that perform a common function. Most animal bodies are composed of combinations of different kinds of tissues. The formation of tissue from many individual cells is made possible by *cell junctions,* connections between cells that hold the cells together as a unit. The members of most animal phyla have *organs,* body structures that are composed of more than one type of tissue and that are specialized for a certain function.

Without multicellularity, the enormous variety found in the animal kingdom would not exist. The size of unicellular organisms is limited. Moreover, all of their functions, such as reproduction and digestion, must be handled within a single cell. Multicellularity and cell specialization have enabled organisms to evolve and adapt to many environments.

### OBJECTIVES

- **Identify** four important characteristics of animals.
- **List** two kinds of tissues found only in animals.
- **Explain** how the first animals may have evolved from unicellular organisms.
- **Identify** four features found only in chordates.
- **Identify** two functions of the body cavity.
- **List** the structural features that taxonomists use to classify animals.

### VOCABULARY

animal
vertebrate
invertebrate
specialization
ingestion
zygote
differentiation
chordate
notochord
dorsal nerve cord
pharyngeal pouch
symmetry
radial symmetry
dorsal
ventral
anterior
posterior
bilateral symmetry
cephalization
germ layer

**internet** connect

www.scilinks.org
**Topic: Multicellular Organisms**
**Keyword: HM61002**

SC*LINKS.* Maintained by the National Science Teachers Association

## Heterotrophy

Plants and some unicellular organisms are autotrophic. They make food using simple molecules from their environment and an energy source, such as the sun. Animals, on the other hand, are heterotrophic. They must obtain complex organic molecules from other sources. Most animals accomplish this by ingestion. During **ingestion,** an animal takes in organic material or food, usually in the form of other living things. Digestion then occurs within the animal's body, and carbohydrates, lipids, amino acids, and other organic molecules are extracted from the material or cells the animal has ingested.

## Sexual Reproduction and Development

Most animals can reproduce sexually, and some can also reproduce asexually. In sexual reproduction, two haploid gametes fuse. The **zygote,** the diploid cell that results from the fusion of the gametes, then undergoes repeated mitotic divisions. Mitotic division of a cell produces two identical offspring cells. How does an adult animal, with its many different organs, tissues, and cell types, arise from a single cell? In the process called *development,* the enlarging mass of dividing cells undergoes differentiation. During **differentiation** (DIF-uhr-EN-shee-AY-shuhn), cells become specialized and therefore different from each other. For example, some cells may become blood cells, and others may become bone cells. The process of differentiation is the path to cell specialization.

## Movement

Although some animals, such as barnacles, spend most of their lives attached to a surface, most animals move about in their environment. The ability to move results from the interrelationship of two types of tissue found only in animals: nervous tissue and muscle tissue. Nervous tissue allows an animal to detect stimuli in its environment and within its own body. Cells of nervous tissue, called *neurons,* conduct electrical signals throughout an animal's body. Multiple neurons work together to take in information, transmit and process it, and initiate an appropriate response. Often, this response involves muscle tissue, which can contract and exert a force to move specific parts of the animal's body. The bat shown in Figure 32-1 continuously processes information about its position in space and the position of its prey. It can adjust its muscular responses so rapidly that it can intercept insects in flight.

**FIGURE 32-1**

Capturing fast-moving prey requires exquisitely timed coordination between the nervous tissue and muscle tissue in the body of this heart-nosed bat, *Cardioderma cor.*

# ORIGIN AND CLASSIFICATION

The first animals probably arose in the sea. The structural characteristics of invertebrates suggest that they were the first multicellular animals and that they evolved from protists. Because protists are both heterotrophic and eukaryotic, scientists have inferred that multicellular invertebrates may have developed from colonies of loosely connected, flagellated protists, such as the one shown in Figure 32-2.

What path did cell specialization take in these early organisms? Colonial protists may have lost their flagella over the course of evolution as individual cells in the colony grew more specialized. They may have been similar to modern colonial protists that do show some degree of cell specialization, such as some species of algae. In these species, the gametes are distinct from nonreproductive cells. A similar division of labor in early colonial protists may have been the first step toward multicellularity.

Scientists often use a type of branching diagram called a *phylogenetic diagram,* such as the one in Figure 32-3, to show how animals are related through evolution. Taxonomists have grouped animals into several phyla (singular, *phylum*) by comparing animals' fossils, body symmetry, patterns of embryo development, and ribosomal RNA (rRNA) and other macromolecules. Taxonomy is an ever-changing branch of science; therefore, it should not be surprising that the actual number and names of animal phyla continue to change and be debated. Many taxonomists recognize 30 or more different animal phyla, though some phyla contain a very small number of species.

**FIGURE 32-2**

The first animals may have evolved from colonial protists similar to the one shown in this drawing.

**FIGURE 32-3**

This phylogenetic diagram represents a hypothesis for the relationship among members of the animal kingdom based on rRNA analysis. Notice on the diagram the locations of similarities in body tissues, body symmetry, and embryo development. For updates on phylogenetic information, visit **go.hrw.com.** Enter the keyword **HM6 Phylo.**

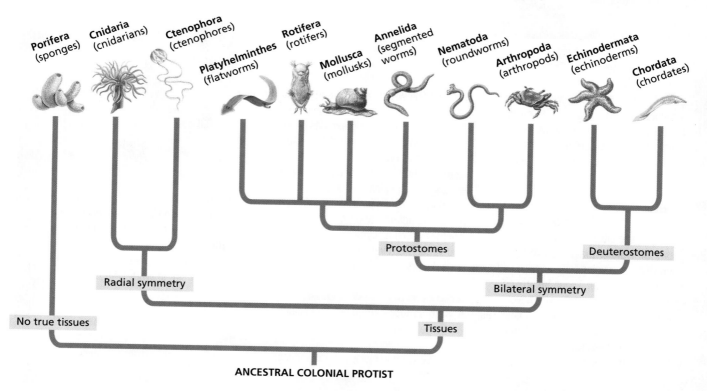

**FIGURE 32-4**

The palm spider, *Nephila* sp., is an arthropod, with a segmented body and body parts specialized for trapping, killing, and eating its prey.

internet connect

www.scilinks.org
**Topic: Vertebrates**
**Keyword: HM61602**

SCLINKS. Maintained by the National Science Teachers Association

## Invertebrates

Invertebrate body plans range from the absence of body symmetry and true tissues, as is found in sponges, to bilateral symmetry and specialized body parts found in arthropods, such as the spider shown in Figure 32-4. Invertebrates do not have a backbone. Invertebrates make up the greatest number of animal species.

## Chordates

The name **chordate** (KAWR-DAYT) refers to animals with a **notochord,** a firm, flexible rod of tissue located in the dorsal part of the body. At some stage in development, all chordates have a notochord, a dorsal nerve cord, pharyngeal pouches, and a postanal tail. The **dorsal nerve cord** is a hollow tube above the notochord. **Pharyngeal** (fuh-RIN-jee-uhl) **pouches** are small outpockets of the anterior digestive tract. The postanal tail consists of muscle tissue and lies behind the posterior opening of the digestive tract. A few chordates retain their early chordate characteristics all their lives. In most vertebrates, a subphylum of the chordates, the dorsal nerve cord develops into the brain and the spinal cord, and the notochord is replaced by the backbone. In aquatic vertebrates, the pharyngeal pouches have evolved into gills for breathing.

Although vertebrates are only one small subphylum of animals, they merit discussion from a human perspective. Humans are vertebrates, and the ecology of humans includes extensive interaction with other vertebrate species.

## Careers in BIOLOGY

# Veterinarian

**Job Description** Veterinarians are doctors who are trained to protect the health of animals, such as pets and livestock. Some veterinarians also protect animals and people from the diseases that they each carry.

**Focus on a Veterinarian**
Dr. Jack Walther grew up on a ranch, so animals were always part of his life. Today, Dr. Walther practices two days each week in a veterinary practice with another veterinarian. When he arrives each day, animal patients who have experienced overnight injuries or illnesses are already waiting. Dr. Walther handles these emergencies. He also sees patients with appointments for vaccinations,

surgical follow-ups, exams, and other routine needs. Dr. Walther emphasizes that a veterinarian's role extends beyond just treating the family pet. "Vets also work to conserve animal resources; for example, they help study and preserve endangered species in Africa." Veterinarians are also at the forefront in protecting animals and people against diseases, such as Lyme disease and West Nile virus. "As a vet, you help not only the animal world, but also humanity."

**Education and Skills**
- **High school**—three years of science courses and four years of math courses
- **College**—bachelor of science including course work in biology, mathematics,

chemistry, and physics; four years of additional schooling to earn doctor of veterinary medicine (D.V.M.) degree
- **Skills**—self-motivation, curiosity, patience, ability to work independently, ability to work with animals

For more about careers, visit **go.hrw.com** and type in the keyword **HM6 Careers**.

**(a) NO SYMMETRY**   **(b) RADIAL SYMMETRY**   **(c) BILATERAL SYMMETRY**

# BODY STRUCTURE

Animal bodies range from those that lack true tissues and an organized body shape to those that have very organized tissues and a consistent body shape.

## Patterns of Symmetry

A *body plan* describes an animal's shape, symmetry, and internal organization. **Symmetry** is a body arrangement in which parts that lie on opposite sides of an axis are identical. An animal's body plan results from the animal's pattern of development. Sponges have the simplest body plan of all animals. Sponges, as shown in Figure 32-5a, are *asymmetrical*—they do not display symmetry. Animals that have a top and bottom side, but no front, back, right, or left end, display **radial symmetry**—a body plan in which the parts are organized in a circle around an axis. Cnidarians, such as the sea anemone in Figure 32-5b, are radially symmetrical.

Most animals have a **dorsal** (back) and **ventral** (abdomen) side, an **anterior** (toward the head) and **posterior** (toward the tail) end, and a right and left side, as shown by the squirrel in Figure 32-5c. Such animals have two similar halves on either side of a central plane and are said to display **bilateral symmetry.** Bilaterally symmetrical animals tend to exhibit **cephalization** (SEF-uh-li-ZAY-shuhn)—the concentration of sensory and brain structures in the anterior end of the animal. As a cephalized animal moves through its environment, the anterior end precedes the rest of the body, sensing the environment.

## Germ Layers

**Germ layers** are tissue layers in the embryos of all animals except sponges, which have no true tissues. The embryos of cnidarians and ctenophores have two germ layers. All other animals have three germ layers. Every organ and tissue arises from a germ layer.

**FIGURE 32-5**

(a) The sponge lacks a consistent pattern of structure. (b) The sea anemone, an aquatic animal, displays radial symmetry. (c) The squirrel displays bilateral symmetry and cephalization.

**Word Roots and Origins**

*cephalization*

from the Greek word *kephale,* meaning "head"

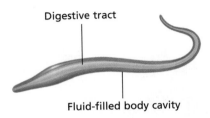

Digestive tract

Fluid-filled body cavity

**FIGURE 32-6**

The body of a roundworm is held erect by its fluid-filled body cavity, which is firm but flexible, like a balloon filled with water.

## Body Cavities

Most animals have some type of body cavity, a fluid-filled space that forms between the digestive tract and the outer wall of the body during development. Some animals, such as flatworms, have three germ layers but have a solid body. These animals lack a body cavity.

In the roundworm shown in Figure 32-6, the body cavity aids in movement by providing a firm, fluid-filled structure against which muscles can contract. The body cavity also allows some degree of movement of the exterior of the body with respect to the internal organs, resulting in more freedom of movement for the animal. Finally, the fluid in the body cavity acts as a reservoir and medium of transport for nutrients and wastes, which diffuse into and out of the animal's body cells.

## Body Structure and Relatedness

Biologists use similarities in body plans and patterns of development to help them classify animals and hypothesize about the evolutionary history of animals. Biologists use information from extant (living) species and extinct species to develop phylogenetic diagrams, such as the one shown in Figure 32-3. Animal phyla shown on the same branch of the phylogenetic diagram, such as flatworms and rotifers, are thought to be related to each other more closely than they are to other animals and are characterized by similarities in morphology and rRNA sequences. Conversely, animals shown in different parts of the diagram are thought to be more distantly related.

- Multicellularity and a limited degree of cell specialization characterize the sponges. Sponges have no organized body shape and no true tissues.
- True tissues in two layers are found in the cnidarians and the ctenophores.
- True tissues in three layers and bilateral symmetry characterize all of the other animal phyla.

## SECTION 1 REVIEW

1. What are the four characteristics common to most animals?

2. Identify how nervous tissue and muscle tissue are interrelated.

3. Summarize how unicellular organisms may have given rise to the first animals.

4. What are the features that all vertebrates share at some point in their development?

5. Identify the body-symmetry type that includes both an anterior end and a posterior end.

6. Name three body features that taxonomists use to help develop phylogenetic trees.

**CRITICAL THINKING**

7. **Recognizing Relationships** Animals such as sponges lack nervous tissue and muscle tissue. What does this tell you about sponges?

8. **Relating Concepts** In 1994, Western scientists first observed the Vietnamese saola, a hoofed mammal. The saola was shown to be related to wild cattle and buffalo. How do you think scientists identified the saola's closest relatives?

9. **Evaluating Information** How is cephalization advantageous to an animal in finding food?

# INVERTEBRATES AND VERTEBRATES

*Comparative anatomy, the study of the structure of animal bodies, is one of the oldest disciplines in biology. Some modern scientists work to establish the relationships between different animals, while others try to establish the relationships between the form and function of morphological features of animals and the role of these features in animal ecology.*

## OBJECTIVES

- **Compare** symmetry, segmentation, and body support in invertebrates and vertebrates.
- **Describe** the differences in the respiratory and circulatory systems of invertebrates and vertebrates.
- **Compare** the digestive, excretory, and nervous systems of invertebrates and vertebrates.
- **Contrast** reproduction and development in invertebrates and vertebrates.

## VOCABULARY

segmentation
exoskeleton
gill
open circulatory system
closed circulatory system
hermaphrodite
larva
endoskeleton
vertebra
integument
lung
kidney

## INVERTEBRATE CHARACTERISTICS

Although it may be difficult for us to see many similarities between a clam and an octopus, they are classified in the same phylum. Adult invertebrates show a tremendous amount of morphological diversity.

### Symmetry

Most invertebrates display radial or bilateral symmetry. The radial symmetry of a jellyfish, which drifts rather than swims, allows the animal to receive stimuli from all directions. Most invertebrates have bilateral symmetry, which is an adaptation to a more motile lifestyle. Bilateral symmetry allows for cephalization, which is present in varying degrees in different animals. Some bilaterally symmetric invertebrates, such as the sea hare shown in Figure 32-7, are not highly cephalized. Members of *Aplysia* do not have a true brain and are capable of only basic responses to the environment. Other invertebrates, such as squids and octopuses, are highly cephalized and have a distinct head and a nervous system dominated by a well-organized brain.

### Segmentation

**Segmentation** in animals refers to a body composed of a series of repeating similar units. Segmentation is seen in its simplest form in the earthworm, an annelid in which each unit of the body is very similar to the next one. Within the phylum Arthropoda, however, segments may look different and have different functions. In the arthropod shown in Figure 32-8 on the next page, fusion of the anterior segments has resulted in a large structure that includes the animal's head and chest regions.

**FIGURE 32-7**

The California sea hare, *Aplysia californica,* is a shell-less mollusk that has a simple nervous system.

**FIGURE 32-8**

In animals such as this crayfish, *Procambarus* sp., segments are fused, producing larger structures. The head and chest structure in this crayfish results from the fusion of several segments. Segments may also give rise to other structures, such as limbs. The crayfish's exoskeleton is also clearly visible.

## Support of the Body

Invertebrate bodies have diverse means of support. Sponges have a simple skeleton that supports their soft tissue; the dried, brown, irregularly shaped "natural sponge" found in stores is this skeleton. The bodies of some other invertebrates, such as roundworms, are supported by the pressure of their fluid-filled body cavity.

An **exoskeleton** is a rigid outer covering that protects the soft tissues of many animals, including arthropods, such as crustaceans, which include crayfish, shown in Figure 32-8. An exoskeleton limits the size and may impede the movement of the organism. Also, an exoskeleton does not grow and must be shed and replaced as the animal grows.

## Respiratory and Circulatory Systems

Animals produce carbon dioxide, $CO_2$, as a byproduct of metabolism. Therefore, carbon dioxide in the blood must be exchanged with oxygen, $O_2$, from the environment. This process, called *gas exchange,* occurs most efficiently across a moist membrane. In the simplest aquatic invertebrates, gas exchange occurs directly across the body covering. Aquatic arthropods and mollusks, however, have **gills,** organs that consist of blood vessels surrounded by a membrane and are specialized for gas exchange in water.

In most animals, the circulatory system moves blood or a similar fluid through the body to transport oxygen and nutrients to cells. At the same time, carbon dioxide and wastes are transported away from the cells. Sponges and cnidarians have no circulatory system, so nutrients and gases are exchanged directly with the environment by diffusion across cell membranes. Arthropods and some mollusks have an **open circulatory system,** in which circulatory fluid is pumped by the heart through vessels and into the body cavity and is then returned to the vessels. Annelids and other mollusks have a closed circulatory system. In a **closed circulatory system,** blood is pumped by a heart and circulates through the body in vessels that form a closed loop. The exchange of gases, nutrients, and wastes occurs between body cells and very small blood vessels that lie near each cell.

## Digestive and Excretory Systems

In sponges, digestion occurs within individual cells. In cnidarians, a central chamber with one opening serves as the digestive system. Most other invertebrates, however, have a digestive tract, or *gut,* running through their body. In these animals, food is broken down in the gut, and the nutrients are absorbed by specialized cells that line the gut.

In simple aquatic invertebrates, wastes are excreted as dissolved ammonia, $NH_3$. In terrestrial invertebrates, specialized excretory structures filter ammonia and other wastes from the body cavity. The ammonia is then converted to less toxic substances, and water is reabsorbed by the animal before the waste is excreted.

## Nervous System

The extraordinary degree of diversity among invertebrates is reflected in their nervous systems. Sponges have no neurons, although individual cells can react to environmental stimuli in much the same way that protozoa can. Neurons evolved in cnidarians, which have a very simple, loosely connected nervous system. Within a single invertebrate phylum, Mollusca, we can trace a stepwise progression of cephalization and the evolution of the brain.

The mollusks have very diverse nervous systems. Recall the sea hare, shown in Figure 32-7. Although its head is not well defined and its nervous system can perform only simple information processing, the sea hare can learn to contract a part of its body in response to certain stimuli. Contrast this simple behavior with that of a highly cephalized mollusk, such as the octopus. The octopus shows very complex decision-making behavior, and it can build a shelter from debris it finds on the ocean floor.

## Reproduction and Development

Invertebrates are capable of some form of sexual reproduction, and many can also reproduce asexually. Some invertebrates, such as earthworms, are hermaphrodites. A **hermaphrodite** (huhr-MAF-roh-DIET) is an organism that produces both male and female gametes, allowing a single individual to function as both a male and a female.

Invertebrates may undergo indirect or direct development. Animals that undergo *indirect development* have an intermediate larval stage, as is shown in Figure 32-9. A **larva** (plural, *larvae*) is a free-living, immature form of an organism that is morphologically different from the adult. Larvae often exploit different habitats and food sources than adult organisms do. As a result, organisms in each stage are more likely to survive. Many insects, which constitute a class of arthropods, have indirect development.

In contrast, in *direct development,* the young animal is born or hatched with the same appearance and way of life it will have as an adult; no larval stage occurs. Most invertebrates undergo indirect development. A few, such as grasshoppers, undergo direct development.

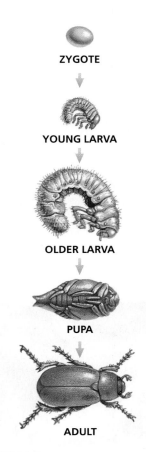

**ZYGOTE**

**YOUNG LARVA**

**OLDER LARVA**

**PUPA**

**ADULT**

**FIGURE 32-9**

Animals with indirect development, such as this beetle, have an intermediate, larval stage. A larva is an immature form that exhibits physical traits that are different from those of the adult form.

# VERTEBRATE CHARACTERISTICS

Vertebrates are chordates that have a backbone. Classes of vertebrates include fishes, amphibians, reptiles, birds, and mammals. All vertebrate classes except fishes spend part or all of their life on land. Many characteristics of terrestrial vertebrates are adaptations to life on land and fall into two broad categories: support of the body and conservation of water.

## Segmentation and Support of the Body

Although it is not immediately apparent, vertebrates are segmented animals. Segmentation is evident in the ribs and the **vertebrae** (vuhr-tuh-bree), the repeating bony units of the backbone. As terrestrial vertebrates evolved from aquatic vertebrates, their limbs and associated muscles evolved to give the animals better support and greater mobility. For example, the legs of amphibians, the first land vertebrates to evolve, are positioned to the side of the body, as shown in Figure 32-10a. However, the legs of mammals, such as the deer shown in Figure 32-10b, are positioned directly beneath the body, allowing the animal to move faster and with a longer stride. Humans show an extreme version of this trait: we are bipedal, and our head is positioned directly over our body.

Vertebrates have an **endoskeleton,** an internal skeleton made of bone and cartilage, which includes the backbone. The endoskeleton grows as the animal grows.

## Body Coverings

The outer covering of an animal is called the **integument** (in-TEG-yoo-muhnt). Although the integuments of fishes and most amphibians are adapted only to moist environments, the integuments of most terrestrial vertebrates are adapted to the dry conditions of a terrestrial environment. All animal bodies are composed of water-filled cells, and if the water content of the cells is reduced appreciably, the animal will die. Thus, the outer covering of terrestrial vertebrates, such as reptiles, birds, and mammals, is largely watertight. Integuments also serve other purposes. The moist skin of an amphibian functions as a respiratory organ for the exchange of gases. The scales of a reptile help protect it from predators. The feathers of birds and the fur of mammals efficiently insulate the body.

## Respiratory and Circulatory Systems

Gas exchange occurs in the gills of aquatic vertebrates, including fishes and larval amphibians, but these gills do not function out of water. **Lungs** are organs for gas exchange composed of moist, membranous surfaces deep inside the animal's body. Lungs evolved in terrestrial vertebrates.

Vertebrates have a closed circulatory system with a multichambered heart. In some vertebrates, the multichambered heart separates oxygenated and deoxygenated blood, improving the efficiency of the circulatory system over that found in other vertebrates and many invertebrates.

## Digestive and Excretory Systems

Digestion occurs in the gut, which runs from the mouth, at the anterior end, to the anus, at the posterior end. In many vertebrates, the gut is very long and folded, which helps increase the surface area over which nutrients can be absorbed. The human digestive tract is about 7 m (23 ft) long.

(a)

(b)

**FIGURE 32-10**

(a) The legs of amphibians, such as this tree frog, *Agalychnis saltator,* are sharply bent and positioned away from the body. (b) The legs of terrestrial mammals, such as this deer, *Odocoileus virginianus,* are straighter than those of amphibians, providing greater mobility and speed.

Both vertebrates and invertebrates must deal with the very toxic ammonia their bodies produce. Most vertebrates must expel wastes while conserving water. Like invertebrates, most vertebrates convert ammonia to less toxic substances. In most vertebrates, organs called **kidneys** filter wastes from the blood while regulating water levels in the body.

## Nervous System

Vertebrates have highly organized brains, and the control of specific functions occurs in specific centers in the brain. The structure and function of the nervous system vary among vertebrate classes. For example, much of a fish's brain processes sensory information. Fishes have limited neural circuitry devoted to decision making. A fish's responses to stimuli in its environment are rigid, that is, they vary little from situation to situation and from fish to fish.

Other animals, such as dogs, display complex and flexible behavior. Much of the tissue in the dog's brain is given over to decision making, and its brain is large with respect to body size.

## Reproduction and Development

In most fish and amphibian species, eggs and sperm are released directly into the water, where fertilization takes place. In reptiles, birds, and mammals, the egg and sperm unite within the body of the female, increasing the likelihood that an egg will be fertilized.

The fertilized eggs of many fishes, amphibians, reptiles, and birds develop outside the body. A developing embryo is nourished by the egg yolk and protected by jellylike layers or a shell. The zygotes of some fishes, amphibians, and reptiles remain inside the body of the female, nourished by the yolk until they hatch. In contrast, most mammals give birth to live offspring. Embryos of placental mammals develop in the female's body, nourished by the mother's blood supply until the young are born. With the exception of amphibians and some fishes, vertebrates undergo direct development. So, the young and the adults can share the same resources—an advantage if those resources are plentiful.

## SECTION 2 REVIEW

1. Identify the primary function for the body covering of terrestrial animals.

2. Compare the structure of exoskeletons and endoskeletons.

3. Compare a closed circulatory system to an open circulatory system.

4. Compare the nervous systems of vertebrates and invertebrates.

5. Describe briefly invertebrate and vertebrate development.

**CRITICAL THINKING**

6. **Inferring Relationships** How might the segmented bodies of arthropods help them survive?

7. **Recognizing Relationships** How is the structure of the nervous system related to an animal's behavior?

8. **Comparing Concepts** Compare the advantages and disadvantages of the two types of development (direct and indirect development).

# MILESTONES IN Developmental Biology

## Timeline

**1817** Christian Pander identifies germ layers.

**1828** Karl Ernst von Baer discovers mammalian eggs and the fate of neural folds and opposes preformation.

**1875** Oscar Hertwig observes fertilization.

**1883** August Weismann publishes germ plasm theory.

**1924** Spemann and Mangold discover the neural organizer.

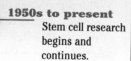

**1950s to present** Stem cell research begins and continues.

**1969** Lewis Wolpert studies pattern formation and positional information in embryos.

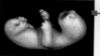

**1983** Researchers discover homeotic genes.

**1996** Scottish researchers clone Dolly the sheep from a mammary cell.

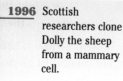

**Present** Researchers find stem cells in many types of adult tissues.

*People have known only since the the 1800s that eggs and sperm unite at fertilization. In a little more than a century, researchers have come to understand a great deal about how one cell divides repeatedly to form a mass of cells and how a complex multicellular organism develops from that mass of dividing cells. As in many areas of biology, the speed and sophistication of research in developmental biology has been remarkable.*

Until the 19th century, biologists believed that embryos grew from very small versions of complete organisms. In 1817, a Russian naturalist named Christian Pander observed developing chicks and described the three embryonic layers now called *ectoderm, mesoderm,* and *endoderm.* In 1828, Karl Ernst von Baer published a paper in which he concluded that the neural fold of an animal embryo gives rise to the animal's nervous system and notochord.

In 1875, German embryologist Oscar Hertwig first observed the union of the nuclei of male and female gametes at fertilization. Soon after, in 1883, another German biologist, August Weismann, laid out his germ plasm theory. This theory states that the body has germ cells, which pass along hereditary traits, and somatic cells, which do not pass along traits to new generations.

In 1924, German embryologists Hans Spemann and Hilde Mangold studied how cells "know" when to divide and what to do in a growing embryo. They hypothesized that one group of cells might "organize" the rest of the cells. Spemann and Mangold discovered that cells that were transplanted from the blastopore region of a blastula to another region of the blastula caused a new nervous system to form. Today, scientists are still searching for the signal these "organizer cells" give. Part of that search has been the study of pattern formation, or how cells respond to signals and form cells and tissues that have particular functions.

In 1969, Lewis Wolpert proposed that morphogens, or pattern-directing substances, diffuse through a body region—a limb bud, for example—and cause fingers or toes to form in a certain order.

In 1983, researchers discovered genes called *homeotic genes* that help control where limbs, such as the legs or antennae, grow on a fruit fly embryo.

Another recent line of research centers on stem cells. Stem cells are undifferentiated cells that are found in embryos and adult tissues and that can give rise to new cells. Researchers have recently discovered that adult stem cells exist in many more types of tissues than were once thought possible. A related line of research led to the birth of Dolly in 1996, the first mammal to be cloned from an adult somatic cell.

## Review

1. What does the germ plasm theory state?
2. **Critical Thinking** Why are "organizer cells" important to the growing embryo.
3. **Critical Thinking** How does the production of genetic clones affect the germ plasm theory?

# FERTILIZATION AND DEVELOPMENT

*Development of a multicellular animal from an egg cell is a truly remarkable process. Each cell in an animal has the same set of genes that are used to build the animal, yet animals have many different kinds of cells. From the fertilized egg come large numbers of cells—trillions in humans—that consistently give rise to structural features of the animal body.*

## FERTILIZATION AND EARLY DEVELOPMENT

In animals, **fertilization** is the union of female and male gametes to form a zygote. Fertilization results in the combination of the haploid sets of chromosomes from two individuals into a single diploid zygote.

### Gametes

In most animal species, the sperm cell, shown in Figure 32-11, is specialized for movement—it is very streamlined and small. The head of the sperm contains chromosomes, and the tail of the sperm is composed of a long flagellum.

The egg, also shown in Figure 32-11, is typically large because it has a large store of cytoplasm and yolk. The size of an egg produced by a given species seems to depend on how long the food supply in the yolk must last. For aquatic animals in which the embryo begins to feed itself early, eggs are small, and there is little yolk. In sharp contrast, the embryos of birds must live on the yolk until they hatch. In these eggs, the yolk volume is very large.

### Fertilization

At the start of fertilization, the sperm's cell membrane fuses with the egg's cell membrane, and the nucleus of the sperm enters the cytoplasm of the egg. The fusion of the cell membranes of the egg and sperm causes an electrical change in the egg membrane that blocks entry to the egg by other sperm cells. The sperm nucleus merges with the egg nucleus to form the diploid nucleus of the zygote. Once a zygote is formed, replication of DNA begins, and the first cell division soon follows.

**FIGURE 32-11**

The small, flagellated sperm is adapted for motility and speed. It must seek out and fertilize the much larger, yolk-filled egg.

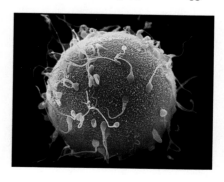

## Cleavage and Blastula Formation

The series of cell divisions that occurs immediately following fertilization is termed **cleavage.** Figure 32-12, steps ❶, ❷, and ❸ show that as cleavage progresses, the number of cells increases, from 2 to 4, then to 8, and so on. During cleavage, mitotic divisions rapidly increase the number of cells, but the cells do not grow in size. Thus, cleavage yields smaller and smaller individual cells. Cleavage increases the surface area–to-volume ratio of each cell, which enhances gas exchange and other environmental interactions.

In most species, cleavage produces a raspberry-shaped mass of 16 to 64 cells, as shown in step ❹. As the number of dividing cells further increases, the mass becomes a hollow ball of cells called a **blastula,** shown in step ❺. The central cavity of a blastula is called the *blastocoel* (BLAS-toe-SEEL).

## Gastrulation and Organogenesis

At the start of the next stage of development, shown in Figure 32-13, an area of the blastula begins to collapse inward. As shown in steps ❶ and ❷, reorganization of the cells of the hollow blastula begins with the inward movement of cells at one end of the blastula. This process, called **gastrulation,** transforms the blastula into a multilayered embryo, called the **gastrula,** shown in step ❸. Gastrulation is marked by changes in the shape of cells and the way the cells interact with each other.

As the inward folding continues, the now cup-shaped embryo enlarges, and a deep cavity, called the **archenteron,** or primitive gut, develops. The open end of the archenteron is called the **blastopore.** Forming the outer layer of the gastrula is the outer germ layer, the **ectoderm,** shown in blue in step ❸. The inner germ layer, the **endoderm,** is shown in yellow. In most phyla, the gastrula does not remain a two-layer structure. As development progresses, a third layer, the **mesoderm,** forms between the endoderm and the ectoderm.

Each of the germ layers formed during gastrulation develops into certain organs in a process called *organogenesis.* The endoderm forms the lining of the urinary system, the reproductive system, and most of the digestive tract; it also forms the pancreas, liver, lungs, and gills. The ectoderm forms the outer layer of skin, hair, nails, and the nervous system. The mesoderm forms many body parts, including the skeleton, muscles, the inner layer of skin, the circulatory system, and the lining of the body cavity.

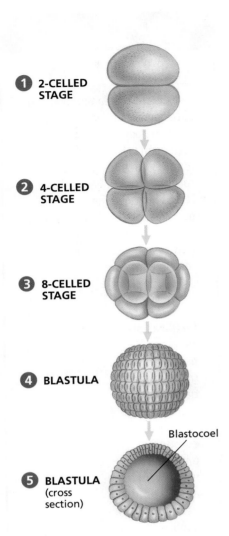

❶ **2-CELLED STAGE**

❷ **4-CELLED STAGE**

❸ **8-CELLED STAGE**

❹ **BLASTULA**

Blastocoel

❺ **BLASTULA** (cross section)

**FIGURE 32-12**

During cleavage, the zygote divides repeatedly without undergoing cell growth, producing a many-celled hollow blastula.

**FIGURE 32-13**

Echinoderms, such as the sea urchin, undergo the gastrulation process shown here. The blastula reorganizes and forms the cup-shaped gastrula. Other phyla have somewhat different patterns of gastrulation.

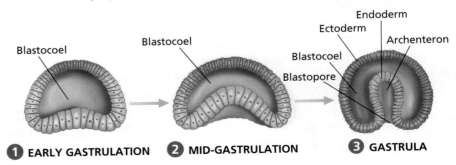

Blastocoel

Blastocoel

Endoderm

Ectoderm

Archenteron

Blastocoel

Blastopore

❶ **EARLY GASTRULATION**    ❷ **MID-GASTRULATION**    ❸ **GASTRULA**

# PATTERNS OF DEVELOPMENT

The distinct patterns of cleavage and formation of body-plan features found in different animal phyla are clues to the phylogenetic history of the organisms.

## Types of Body Cavities

Animals, such as flatworms, that do not have a body cavity are called **acoelomates** (uh-SEE-luh-MAYTS). The interior of the animal is solid, as shown in Figure 32-14a. The endodermic gut, shown in yellow, and the outer covering of the animal, shown in blue, are connected by the solid tissue of the mesoderm.

However, most animal phyla have body cavities that separate their digestive tract from the outer body wall. Within this group, there are differences in how the body cavity develops. In some phyla, including rotifers and roundworms, the mesoderm lines the interior of the coelom but does not surround the exterior of the endodermic gut. A cavity that is not completely lined by mesoderm is called a **pseudocoelom** (SOO-doh-SEE-luhm), which means "false body cavity." Roundworms have pseudocoeloms such as the one shown in Figure 32-14b and are thus called *pseudocoelomates*. In pseudocoelomates, mesoderm lines the fluid-filled body cavity, and the endodermic gut is suspended in this fluid.

A cavity completely lined by mesoderm is called a **coelom** (SEE-luhm), as shown in Figure 32-14c. Animals that have coeloms are called *coelomates* (SEE-luh-MAYTS). In coelomates, mesoderm lines the body cavity and surrounds and supports the endodermic gut. The mesoderm also forms the tissues of attachment for the organs located in the coelom, such as the liver and the lungs. Mollusks, annelids, arthropods, chordates, and echinoderms are coelomates.

## Cleavage and Blastopore Fate

Recall from Figure 32-3 that echinoderms and chordates share a branch of the phylogenetic diagram of animals; and mollusks, annelids, and arthropods share another branch. There are two distinct patterns of development in animals with a coelom. In the embryos of mollusks, arthropods, and annelids, the blastopore develops into a mouth, and a second opening forms at the other end of the archenteron, forming an anus. These organisms are called **protostomes** (PROHT-oh-STOHMZ), which means "first mouth."

Many protostomes undergo *spiral cleavage,* in which the cells divide in a spiral arrangement. In the embryos of echinoderms and chordates, the blastopore develops into an anus, and a second opening at the other end of the archenteron becomes the mouth. These organisms are called **deuterostomes** (DOOT-uhr-oh-STOHMZ), which means "second mouth." Most deuterostomes undergo *radial cleavage,* in which the cell divisions are parallel to or at right angles to the axis from one pole of the blastula to the other.

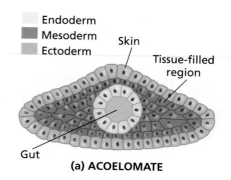

Endoderm
Mesoderm
Ectoderm

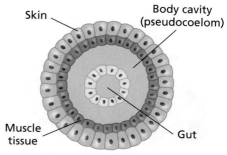

Skin
Tissue-filled region
Gut

**(a) ACOELOMATE**

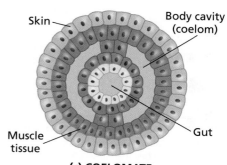

Skin
Body cavity (pseudocoelom)
Muscle tissue
Gut

**(b) PSEUDOCOELOMATE**

Skin
Body cavity (coelom)
Muscle tissue
Gut

**(c) COELOMATE**

**FIGURE 32-14**

In three-layered acoelomates (a), the endodermic gut is surrounded by a solid layer of mesoderm. In pseudocoelomates (b), the endodermic gut is suspended in a fluid-filled cavity that is surrounded by mesoderm. In coelomates (c), the endodermic gut is surrounded by and suspended by mesoderm, which also surrounds the coelom, or body cavity.

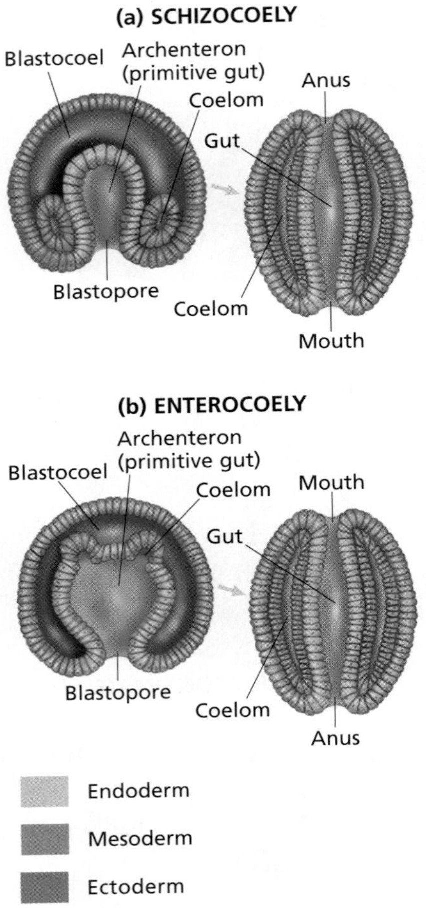

**(a) SCHIZOCOELY**

Blastocoel

Archenteron (primitive gut)

Anus

Coelom

Gut

Blastopore

Coelom

Mouth

**(b) ENTEROCOELY**

Archenteron (primitive gut)

Blastocoel

Coelom

Mouth

Gut

Blastopore

Coelom

Anus

Endoderm

Mesoderm

Ectoderm

**FIGURE 32-15**

In protostomes, the coelom arises in a process called schizocoely (a), and the blastopore becomes the mouth. In deuterostomes, the coelom arises by enterocoely (b), and the blastopore becomes the anus.

Protostomes and deuterostomes also differ in how early the cells of the embryo specialize. If the cells of some protostome embryos are separated at the four-cell stage of development, each cell will develop into only one-fourth of a complete embryo, and the developing organism will die. Thus, the path of each cell is fixed early in the development of the protostome in a pattern called *determinate cleavage*.

In contrast, if the cells of most four-celled deuterostome embryos are separated, each cell will embark on its own path to become a separate organism. This type of development is called *indeterminate cleavage*. Indeterminate cleavage is responsible for the development of identical twins in humans.

## Coelom Formation

The way in which the coelom forms in many protostomes differs from the way it forms in many deuterostomes. Figure 32-15a shows coelom formation in protostomes. Cells located at the junction of the endoderm and ectoderm (at the rim of the cup-shaped embryo) move toward the interior of the gastrula. Rapid division of these cells (shown in pink) in the blastocoel forms the mesoderm. The mesoderm then spreads and splits to form the coelom. This process of coelom formation is called **schizocoely** (SKIZ-oh-SEEL-ee), or "split body cavity."

Figure 32-15b shows coelom formation in deuterostomes. The mesoderm forms when the cells lining the dorsal, or top, part of the archenteron begin dividing rapidly. These rapidly dividing cells (shown in pink) form pouches that become mesoderm. The coelom develops within the mesodermal pouches. This process of coelom formation is called **enterocoely** (EN-tuhr-oh-SEEL-ee), which means "gut body cavity." During both enterocoely and schizocoely, mesodermal cells spread out to completely line the coelom, and the blastocoel disappears. Thus, in both protostomes and deuterostomes, mesoderm lines the interior of the outer body wall and surrounds the gut.

## SECTION 3 REVIEW

1. Beginning with fertilization, list the steps of development through mesodermal formation.

2. Name the three germ layers and two body parts that arise from each layer.

3. Compare the development of protostomes and deuterostomes.

4. Identify how the mesoderm is formed in schizocoely, and differentiate it from the process in enterocoely.

5. Identify the type of cleavage that can give rise to identical human twins.

**CRITICAL THINKING**

6. **Inferring Relationships** Which adaptive advantage is associated with indeterminate cleavage?

7. **Recognizing Relationships** What is the relationship between endoderm formation and coelom formation in echinoderms?

8. **Predicting Patterns** While exploring a tide pool, you find a periwinkle, which is a marine snail. Which kind of development does a periwinkle have? Explain.

# CHAPTER HIGHLIGHTS

SECTION 1 The Nature of Animals

- Animals are either invertebrates—lack a backbone—or vertebrates—have a backbone.
- Animals are multicellular organisms that lack cell walls and are heterotrophic. Most animals reproduce sexually and can move.
- Movement and response to the environment are governed by an animal's nervous and muscle tissues.
- The first animals may have evolved from colonial protists.

- At some stage of their lives, chordates have a notochord, dorsal nerve cord, postanal tail, and pharyngeal pouches.
- Most animals have tissues and radial or bilateral symmetry. Bilateral symmetry is associated with cephalization. Most animals have a body cavity that aids movement and the transport of nutrients and wastes.
- Animals are classified by degree of cell specialization, number of tissue layers, type of symmetry, and most recently, by sequencing of rRNA.

**Vocabulary**

animal (p. 651)
vertebrate (p. 651)
invertebrate (p. 651)
specialization (p. 651)
ingestion (p. 652)

zygote (p. 652)
differentiation (p. 652)
chordate (p. 654)
notochord (p. 654)
dorsal nerve cord (p. 654)

pharyngeal pouch (p. 654)
symmetry (p. 655)
radial symmetry (p. 655)
dorsal (p. 655)
ventral (p. 655)

anterior (p. 655)
posterior (p. 655)
bilateral symmetry (p. 655)
cephalization (p. 655)
germ layer (p. 655)

SECTION 2 Invertebrates and Vertebrates

- Symmetry, segmentation, and type of skeleton are related to the lifestyle of an animal.
- Invertebrates include morphologically diverse phyla, the members of which are mostly radially or bilaterally symmetrical.
- In an open circulatory system, circulatory fluid is pumped by the heart through vessels and into the body cavity and is then returned to the vessels.

- In a closed circulatory system, blood is pumped by a heart and circulates throughout the body in tubelike vessels that form a closed loop.
- Vertebrates have highly organized brains in which specific functions occur in specific centers of the brain. The larger the decision-making portion of the brain is, the more complex and flexible the behavior of the animal.
- Most animals reproduce sexually. Fertilization and development may be external or internal.

**Vocabulary**

segmentation (p. 657)
exoskeleton (p. 658)
gill (p. 658)

open circulatory
   system (p. 658)
closed circulatory
   system (p. 658)

hermaphrodite (p. 659)
larva (p. 659)
endoskeleton (p. 660)
vertebra (p. 660)

integument (p. 660)
lung (p. 660)
kidney (p. 661)

SECTION 3 Fertilization and Development

- Development includes cleavage, blastula formation, gastrulation, and organogenesis. The germ layers include ectoderm, endoderm, and mesoderm.
- Ectoderm forms, among other things, the outer layer of skin; endoderm forms many internal organs; and mesoderm forms the skeleton and muscles.

- Acoelomates are animals without a body cavity. Pseudocoelomates are animals whose body cavity is not completely lined by mesoderm. Coelomates have a body cavity completely lined by mesoderm.
- Protostomes have spiral cleavage and schizocoely. Deuterostomes have radial cleavage and enterocoely.

**Vocabulary**

fertilization (p. 663)
cleavage (p. 664)
blastula (p. 664)
gastrulation (p. 664)
gastrula (p. 664)

archenteron (p. 664)
blastopore (p. 664)
ectoderm (p. 664)
endoderm (p. 664)
mesoderm (p. 664)

acoelomate (p. 665)
pseudocoelom (p. 665)
coelom (p. 665)
protostome (p. 665)
deuterostome (p. 665)

schizocoely (p. 666)
enterocoely (p. 666)

## USING VOCABULARY

1. For each pair of terms, explain how the meanings of the terms differ.
   a. *radial symmetry* and *bilateral symmetry*
   b. *open circulatory system* and *closed circulatory system*
   c. *vertebrate* and *invertebrate*
   d. *spiral cleavage* and *radial cleavage*

2. Explain the relationship between cell specialization and differentiation.

3. Choose the term that does not belong in the following group, and explain why it does not belong: *notochord, cephalization, dorsal nerve cord,* and *radial symmetry.*

4. **Word Roots and Origins** The word *blastopore* comes from the Greek *blastos,* which means "bud," and *poros,* which means "passage." Using this information, explain why the term *blastopore* is a good name for the structure it describes.

## UNDERSTANDING KEY CONCEPTS

5. **Describe** each of the four characteristics that define animals.

6. **Explain** how neural tissue and muscle tissue work together in an animal's body to allow the animal to respond to its environment.

7. **Describe** the probable changes that early colonial flagellates underwent as they evolved into the first animals.

8. **List** the four features common to all chordates at some time in their life. What has happened to two of these features in an adult human?

9. **Summarize** what happened to the position of the body with respect to the legs as vertebrates adapted to life on land.

10. **Explain** how having a body cavity aids movement.

11. **Infer** the relationship between two phyla that are represented on the same branch of a phylogenetic tree. Which features are used to determine the relationship?

12. **Identify** the most probable type of movement that an organism with bilateral symmetry would exhibit.

13. **Contrast** segmentation in invertebrates with segmentation in vertebrates.

14. **Sequence** the development of the nervous system from cnidarians to mammals.

15. **Identify** the structure that the archenteron becomes in a developing animal.

16. **Name** two body parts formed by each of the following: endoderm, mesoderm, and ectoderm.

17. **Identify** how a closed circulatory system differs from an open circulatory system.

18. **Compare** schizocoely with enterocoely.

19. **CONCEPT MAPPING** Use the following terms to create a concept map that shows development from blastula to coelom formation in a deuterostome: *blastula, gastrula, archenteron, blastopore, anus, mouth, germ layers, ectoderm, endoderm, mesoderm,* and *coelom.*

## CRITICAL THINKING

20. **Recognizing Relationships** Considering that an endoskeleton can support more weight than an exoskeleton, would a large-bodied animal with an exoskeleton be more likely to live in the water or on land? Explain.

21. **Recognizing Relationships** On mammals and birds, the head is positioned higher with respect to the body than it is on amphibians and reptiles. Why might it be helpful to have a head positioned over the body?

22. **Interpreting Graphics** Observe the animal pictured below, and answer the following questions.
   a. Which kind of symmetry does the animal display?
   b. Is this animal cephalized?
   c. How many germ layers does this animal have?
   d. How many openings does this animal's digestive system have?
   e. Does this animal have neurons?

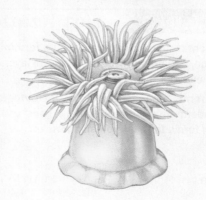

# Standardized Test Preparation

**DIRECTIONS:** Choose the letter of the answer choice that best answers the question.

1. What is the name for the process that leads to cell specialization in multicellular organisms?
   A. evolution
   B. fertilization
   C. differentiation
   D. asexual reproduction

2. What process takes place as a zygote begins to divide after fertilization?
   F. meiosis
   G. cleavage
   H. gastrulation
   J. organogenesis

3. Which animals do not have true tissues?
   A. sponges
   B. chordates
   C. cnidarians
   D. ctenophores

4. What are the basic tissue types in an embryo called?
   F. coeloms
   G. germ layers
   H. notochords
   J. pharyngeal pouches

**INTERPRETING GRAPHICS:** The diagrams below illustrate a certain type of body-cavity development. Study the diagrams to answer the questions that follow.

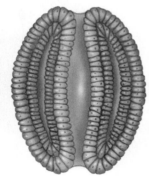

5. The diagrams represent the development of which of the following animals?
   A. fish
   B. sponge
   C. octopus
   D. cnidarian

6. With which of the following is the process illustrated above associated?
   F. acoelomates
   G. deuterostomes
   H. spiral cleavage
   J. indeterminate cleavage

**DIRECTIONS:** Complete the following analogy.

7. Ectoderm : skin :: mesoderm :
   A. lungs
   B. nerves
   C. vertebrae
   D. intestines

**INTERPRETING GRAPHICS:** The diagrams below illustrate different organisms. Study the images to answer the question that follows.

Sponge          Beetle          Jellyfish

8. Which of the organisms has radial symmetry?
   F. beetle
   G. sponge
   H. jellyfish
   J. both the beetle and the sponge

## SHORT RESPONSE

Ctenophores and cnidarians are considered closely related to one another. Chordates and echinoderms are also considered closely related to one another.

Explain how it was determined that cnidarians are less closely related to chordates and echinoderms than they are to ctenophores.

## EXTENDED RESPONSE

Three types of body-cavity organization exist in animals—acoelomate, pseudocoelomate, and coelomate.

*Part A* Explain how acoelomates and pseudo-coelomates differ from coelomates.

*Part B* Explain how the lining of the body cavity develops in coelomates.

**Test TIP** If you find particular questions difficult, put a light pencil mark beside them and keep working. (Do not write in this book.) As you answer later questions, you may find information that helps you answer the difficult questions.

# Dissecting a Sheep's Heart

## OBJECTIVES

- Describe the appearance of the external and internal structures of a sheep's heart.
- Name the structures and functions of a sheep's heart.

## PROCESS SKILLS

- observing structures
- identifying
- demonstrating

## MATERIALS

- sheep's heart
- dissecting tray
- blunt metal probe
- scissors
- scalpel
- tweezers

## Background

1. The heart has a left and a right side. It has two upper chambers, the left and right atria, and two lower chambers, the left and right ventricles. Why do multiple chambers result in a more efficient heart?
2. Blood enters the heart from the body through the superior or inferior vena cava. The blood then enters the right atrium and flows through valves into the right ventricle. Blood flows from the right ventricle through the pulmonary artery to the lungs. What process occurs in the lungs?
3. Oxygenated blood flows from the lungs through the pulmonary veins to the left atrium. Then, it flows through valves into the thick-walled left ventricle. Blood flows from the left ventricle through the large aorta to the rest of the body.

## Procedure

1. In this lab, you will observe the external structure of a sheep's four-chambered heart and dissect the heart to study its internal structure.
2. Put on safety goggles, gloves, and a lab apron.

3. Place a sheep's heart in a dissecting tray. Turn the heart so that the ventral surface is facing you, as shown in the diagram below. Use the diagram of the ventral view to locate the left and right atria, the left and right ventricles, the aorta, the superior and inferior vena cava, and the pulmonary arteries. Turn the heart over. Use the diagram of the dorsal view to locate once again the structures just named, as well as the pulmonary veins.
4. Use a blunt metal probe to explore the blood vessels that lead into and out of the chambers of the heart.
5. Locate a diagonal deposit of fat along the lower two-thirds of the heart. This serves as a guideline to mark the wall between the two ventricles. Use this fatty deposit to guide your incision into the heart.

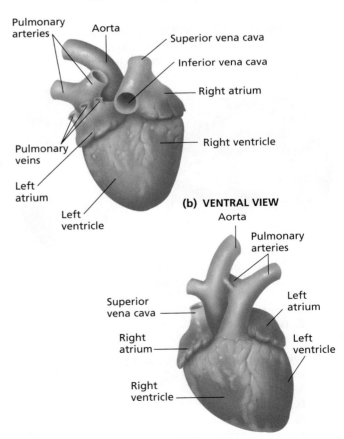

**(a) DORSAL VIEW**

Pulmonary arteries
Aorta
Superior vena cava
Inferior vena cava
Right atrium
Right ventricle
Pulmonary veins
Left atrium
Left ventricle

**(b) VENTRAL VIEW**

Aorta
Pulmonary arteries
Left atrium
Superior vena cava
Left ventricle
Right atrium
Right ventricle

6. Follow the cutting diagram below very carefully to study the anatomy of the right side of the heart.

7. 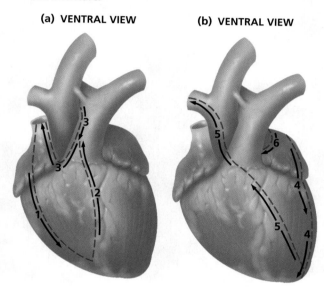 Again, turn the heart with the ventral surface facing you and the apex pointing downward. Use scissors to cut along line 1. **CAUTION Always cut in a direction away from your face and body.** Cut just deep enough to go through the atrial wall. Continue the cut into the right ventricle. With a probe, push open the heart at the cut, and examine the internal structure.

**(a) VENTRAL VIEW**       **(b) VENTRAL VIEW**

8. Cut along line 2, and extend the cut upward toward the pulmonary artery. Cut just deep enough to go through the ventricle wall. Complete the cut on line 3. Cut downward along the pulmonary artery, around through the wall of the right atrium, and upward along the right superior vena cava.

9. With tweezers, carefully lift the resulting flap to expose the structures underneath.

10. Follow the cutting diagram above very carefully to study the anatomy of the *left* side of the heart.

11. Start to cut on line 4 at the top of the left atrium, and continue into the left ventricle. Cut just deep enough to go through the ventricle wall.

12. Cut on line 5 across the middle of the left ventricle into the aorta. Leave a small margin between this cut

and the cut previously made for line 2. Begin to cut on line 6 on the left atrium where cut 4 began. Extend this cut around and through the pulmonary artery upward on the aorta to the right of cut 5.

13. With tweezers, carefully lift up the resulting flap to expose the structure underneath.

14. Observe the thick septum dividing the left and right ventricles. Also, note the greater thickness of the walls of the left ventricle.

15. Locate the tricuspid valve between the right atrium and ventricle. Locate the mitral valve between the left atrium and ventricles. Observe that the valves are connected by fibers to the inner surface of the ventricle. Use a probe to explore the openings in the valves.

16. With a scalpel, cut across a section of the aorta and a section of the vena cava. Compare the thickness of their walls.

17. Dispose of your materials according to the directions from your teacher.

18. Clean up your work area, and wash your hands before leaving the lab.

## Analysis and Conclusions

1. Trace the path of blood from the right atrium to the aorta.

2. Pulmonary circulation carries blood between the heart and the lungs. Systemic circulation carries blood to the rest of the body. In which chambers of the heart does pulmonary circulation begin and end? In which chambers does systemic circulation begin and end?

3. What is the function of the septum separating the left and right ventricles?

4. What is the function of the mitral and tricuspid valves?

5. Why are the walls of the left ventricle thicker than the walls of the right ventricle?

## Further Inquiry

The heartbeat originates in a small bundle of tissue in the right atrium. This bundle is the sinoatrial, or S-A, node. Read about the S-A node. What does it do? Why is the S-A node known as the pacemaker?

# CHAPTER 33

# SPONGES, CNIDARIANS, AND CTENOPHORES

Delicate polyps of Monet's tube coral, *Dendrophyllia gracilis*, extend from a hard skeleton.

SECTION 1 *Porifera*

SECTION 2 *Cnidaria and Ctenophora*

# PORIFERA

*Invertebrates are animals that do not have backbones. Invertebrates include more than a million species. About 97 percent of all known animal species are invertebrates, among the simplest of which are sponges.*

## BODY PLAN OF SPONGES

**Sponges** are aquatic animals that make up the phylum Porifera (pohr-IF-uhr-uh). These simple organisms clearly represent the transition from unicellular to multicellular life. Because sponges are heterotrophic, multicellular organisms that do not have cell walls, they are classified as animals. Sponges have no gastrula stage, exhibit less cell specialization than most other animals, and have no true tissues or organs.

But sponges do have a key property of all animal cells—cell recognition. A living sponge can be passed through a fine mesh, which separates the sponge into individual cells. These separated cells will then regroup to form a new sponge. There are about 5,000 named species of sponges. About 150 species live in fresh water, while the rest are marine.

Sponges are so unlike other animals that early biologists thought that sponges were plants. Most sponges do resemble plants in some ways. For example, adult sponges are **sessile** (SEHS-il), which means that they attach themselves firmly to a surface and do not move. Sponges grow in many shapes, sizes, and colors and often look like mossy mats, cactuses, or blobs of fungus. Sponges can be as small as 1 cm (0.4 in.) in length or as large as 2 m (6.6 ft) in diameter.

The basic body plan of a sponge consists of two layers of cells separated by a jellylike substance called *mesohyl* (MEHZ-oh-hil). In the simplest sponges, the body wall forms a hollow cylinder that is closed at the bottom and open at the top. The interior of the cylinder is lined with flagellated cells called **choanocytes** (koh-AN-oh-siets), or collar cells. By beating their flagella, choanocytes draw water into the sponge through numerous pores, called **ostia** (AHS-tee-uh) (singular, *ostium*), that penetrate the body wall. In fact, the name *Porifera* comes from a Latin word meaning "pore-bearer." The water that is pumped into the interior of the sponge leaves through the **osculum** (AHS-kyoo-luhm), the opening at the top of the sponge that you can see in Figure 33-1 on the next page.

A sponge would collapse without some type of supporting structure. In some sponges, support is provided by a simple skeleton made of a network of tough, flexible protein fibers called **spongin** (SPUHN-jin). Other sponges have skeletons consisting of **spicules**.

## SECTION 1

### OBJECTIVES

- **Describe** the basic body plan of a sponge.
- **Describe** the process of filter feeding in sponges.
- **Contrast** the processes of sexual and asexual reproduction in sponges.

### VOCABULARY

sponge
sessile
choanocyte
ostium
osculum
spongin
spicule
filter feeding
amoebocyte
gemmule
regeneration
hermaphrodite

**internet** connect

www.scilinks.org
**Topic:** Sponges
**Keyword:** HM61443

*SciLINKS.* Maintained by the National Science Teachers Association

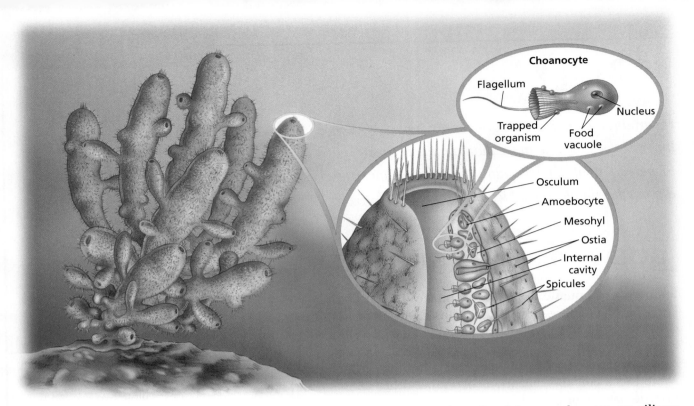

**Choanocyte**

Flagellum

Nucleus

Trapped organism

Food vacuole

Osculum

Amoebocyte

Mesohyl

Ostia

Internal cavity

Spicules

**FIGURE 33-1**

The body of a sponge is a hollow cylinder. Water is drawn into the cylinder through many small pores (ostia) in the sponge's body and exits through the osculum, the opening at the top of the sponge.

**Word Roots and Origins**

*amoebocyte*

from the Greek *amoibe*, meaning "change," and *kytos*, meaning "cavity"

Spicules are tiny, hard particles of calcium carbonate or silicon dioxide that are often shaped like spikes. Calcium carbonate is one of the compounds that give bones and teeth their hardness, and silicon dioxide is the major component of glass and quartz. Still other sponges have a combination of spongin and spicules.

# FEEDING AND DIGESTION IN SPONGES

Because they are sessile, sponges cannot pursue food. Instead, most sponges feed by sieving food out of the water. The flagella of the choanocytes beat, drawing water through the ostia. The choanocytes trap plankton and other tiny organisms in their small, hairlike projections. This feeding method is called **filter feeding.** Other food of filter-feeding sponges includes bits of organic matter. However, scientists have discovered a sponge species that uses movable filaments covered with hooked spicules to snare small shrimp. The shrimp are then absorbed into the sponge's body.

The food that a sponge collects is engulfed and digested by the choanocytes. Nutrients pass from the choanocytes to cells that crawl about within the body wall and deliver the nutrients to the rest of the body. Scientists call these crawling cells **amoebocytes** (uh-MEE-buh-siets) because the cells resemble amoebas. Locate the amoebocytes in Figure 33-1. Carbon dioxide and other wastes produced by the sponge's cells diffuse into the water that passes through the sponge. The water carries these wastes as it flows out through the osculum, thus removing the wastes from the sponge.

# REPRODUCTION IN SPONGES

Sponges can reproduce asexually by forming small buds that break off and live separately. The sponge shown in Figure 33-1 has many buds. During droughts or cold weather, some fresh-water sponges produce internal buds called **gemmules** (JEM-yoolz). Each gemmule is a food-filled ball of amoebocytes surrounded by a protective coat made of organic material and spicules. Gemmules can survive harsh conditions that may kill adult sponges. When conditions improve, sponge cells emerge from the gemmules and grow into new sponges. Sponges also have remarkable powers of **regeneration,** the regrowth of missing cells, tissues, or organs. A very small piece of a sponge can regenerate a complete new sponge.

Sponges can also reproduce sexually. As you can see in Figure 33-2, sperm released into the water from one sponge enter the pores of a second sponge. Choanocytes in the sec-ond sponge engulf the sperm and transfer them to amoebo-cytes. Amoebocytes carry the sperm to an egg located in the mesohyl. After the egg is fertilized, it develops into a larva. A *larva* is an immature stage of an animal that is usu-ally very different in form from the adult. Flagella on the larva's surface enable the larva to leave its parent sponge. Eventually, the larva settles and attaches to an object. Its cells then reorganize to form an adult sponge.

Some species of sponges have separate sexes, but in most species, each individual is a hermaphrodite (her-MAF-roh-diet). **Hermaphrodites** produce both eggs and sperm. Self-fertilization rarely happens in hermaphroditic species. Instead, the sperm of one individual usually fertilize the eggs of another individual. Because each hermaphrodite produces eggs, the chances of fertil-ization are greater than in species in which only females produce eggs. Hermaphroditism is common in invertebrates that are ses-sile, that move slowly, or that live in low-density populations.

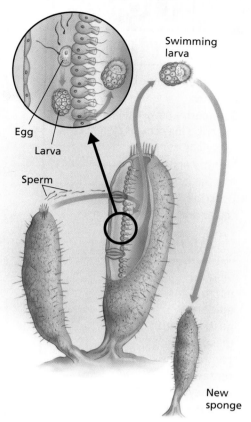

**FIGURE 33-2**

Sponges can reproduce asexually and sexually. In sexual reproduction, the union of an egg and sperm ultimately results in a swimming larva that escapes from the parent sponge and grows into a new individual.

---

## SECTION 1 REVIEW

1. Compare the structure of spongin with the structure of spicules.

2. Describe two different ways in which sponges feed.

3. How do gemmules help some freshwater sponges survive unfavorable conditions?

4. What role do amoebocytes play in the sexual reproduction of sponges?

**CRITICAL THINKING**

5. **Analyzing Concepts** How is it possible for a population of sponges, which are sessile animals, to disperse?

6. **Applying Information** Consider the properties of a natural bath sponge that is made of spon-gin. How is a spongin skeleton adaptive?

7. **Relating Concepts** Why are sponges not con-sidered to be predators?

- **Describe** the basic body plan of a cnidarian.
- **Summarize** how cnidarians feed.
- **Describe** the nervous system of cnidarians.
- **Identify** and give examples of the four classes of cnidarians.
- **Describe** the common characteristics of ctenophores.

## VOCABULARY

medusa
polyp
epidermis
gastrodermis
mesoglea
gastrovascular cavity
tentacle
cnidocyte
nematocyst
nerve net
planula
coral reef
colloblast
apical organ
bioluminescence

# CNIDARIA AND CTENOPHORA

*Cnidaria (nie-DER-ee-uh) and Ctenophora (tee-NAHF-uhr-uh) are two phyla of radially symmetrical invertebrates. The animals in these phyla are more complex than the sponges. Their cells are organized into tissues, and they have a few simple organs. All members of the phyla Cnidaria and Ctenophora are aquatic, and most live in the ocean.*

## BODY PLAN OF CNIDARIANS

Tiny freshwater hydra, stinging jellyfish, and flowerlike coral all belong to the phylum Cnidaria. Animals in this phylum are called *cnidarians.* As you can see in Figure 33-3, the body of a cnidarian may be either bell-shaped or vase-shaped. The bell-shaped **medusa** (me-DOO-suh) is specialized for swimming. In contrast, the vase-shaped form, called a **polyp** (PAHL-ip), is specialized for a sessile existence.

Figure 33-3 also shows that all cnidarians have bodies constructed of two cell layers—an outer **epidermis** and an inner **gastrodermis.** Between these layers is a jellylike material known as **mesoglea** (mez-uh-GLEE-uh). In the center of the body is a hollow gut called the **gastrovascular cavity,** which has a single opening, or mouth. Surrounding the mouth are numerous flexible extensions called **tentacles.**

**FIGURE 33-3**

The contrasting forms of medusae and polyps result from different arrangements of the same body parts. Medusa forms are free-floating and jellylike. Jellyfish are medusae. Polyp forms, such as hydras and sea anemones, are usually attached to a rock or some other object.

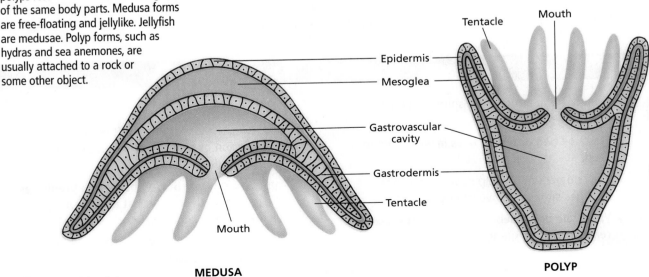

MEDUSA

POLYP

# FEEDING AND DEFENSE IN CNIDARIANS

One of the distinguishing features of cnidarians is the presence of cnidocytes (NIE-duh-siets), which give the phylum its name. **Cnidocytes** are specialized cells used for defense and capturing prey. Figure 33-4 shows a type of cnidocyte organelle called a **nematocyst** (nuh-MAT-uh-sist), which has a long filament coiled up inside it. In some cnidarians, the cnidocytes are concentrated in the epidermis, especially on the tentacles. When an object brushes against the "trigger" on a cnidocyte, the nematocyst inside it suddenly pushes the filament out of the cell with great force. Some nematocysts have filaments with sharp tips and spines that puncture the object and inject poison. Others have filaments that adhere to the object by wrapping around it.

The relationship between structure and function is clearly seen in the way cnidarians feed. The tentacles capture small animals with their nematocysts and paralyze them with the poison they inject. The tentacles then push the prey into the gastrovascular cavity through the mouth. After enzymes inside the gastrovascular cavity break up the prey, cells lining the cavity absorb the nutrients. Undigested food and waste are expelled through the mouth.

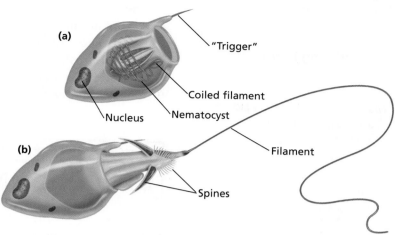

**FIGURE 33-4**

(a) The nematocyst inside this cnidocyte contains a coiled filament. (b) When something touches the "trigger," the nematocyst suddenly ejects the filament.

# NERVOUS SYSTEM IN CNIDARIANS

Nervous responses in cnidarians are controlled by a diffuse web of interconnected nerve cells called a **nerve net.** In many cnidarians, like the polyp shown in Figure 33-5, the nerve net is distributed uniformly throughout the entire body. There is no brain or similar structure that controls the rest of the nerve net. But in the medusa form of some cnidarians, such as jellyfish, some of the nerve cells are clustered in rings around the edge of the bell-shaped body.

The nerve net enables cnidarians to respond to specific stimuli in their environment. For example, when cells in the epidermis are touched, they relay a signal to nerve cells. The nerve cells, in turn, transmit a signal via the nerve net to contractile cells, which can cause the animal to withdraw from the stimulus. In cnidarians with the simplest nerve nets, a stimulus anywhere on the body causes signals to be sent through the nerve net in all directions. These signals bring about a contraction of the entire body.

**FIGURE 33-5**

The interconnected nerve cells in the nerve net of this cnidarian (a hydra), coordinate the animal's responses to its environment.

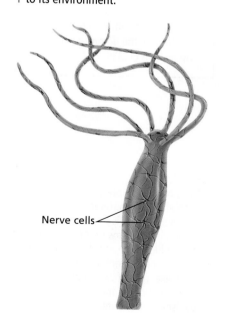

The nerve net also coordinates the complex activities of the body that are necessary for feeding and traveling through the environment. The movements by which the tentacles bring prey to the mouth and push it into the gastrovascular cavity are controlled by the nerve net, as are the rhythmic contractions of the body that propel swimming medusae through the water.

# CLASSIFICATION OF CNIDARIANS

Scientists recognize four classes of cnidarians—Hydrozoa, Cubozoa, Scyphozoa, and Anthozoa. The members of these classes are known as hydrozoans, cubozoans, scyphozoans, and anthozoans, respectively. Some species of hydrozoans live only as polyps, some live only as medusae, some alternate between these two forms, and some live as mixed colonies of polyps and medusae. Cubozoans and scyphozoans spend most of their lives as medusae, while anthozoans live only as polyps.

## Class Hydrozoa

The class Hydrozoa includes about 3,700 species, most of which live as colonial organisms in the oceans. Examples of colonial hydrozoans are species of the genus *Obelia*. As Figure 33-6a illustrates, one such species has many polyps attached to branched stalks. Some of the polyps function in gathering food, while others are responsible for reproduction.

The hydrozoan shown in Figure 33-6b, the Portuguese man-of-war (genus *Physalia*), exists as a colony of medusae and polyps. Its gas-filled float, which can measure as much as 30 cm (1 ft) across, keeps the colony at the surface of the ocean. The polyps in the colony are specialized for feeding, digestion, or sexual reproduction. Tentacles up to 20 m (65 ft) long dangle from the feeding polyps and carry large numbers of cnidocytes. The Portuguese man-of-war preys mostly on small fish, but its cnidocytes contain a neurotoxin (nerve poison) that can be painful and even fatal to humans.

**FIGURE 33-6**

These organisms are two examples of colonial hydrozoans. (a) This colony of the genus *Obelia* is made up of polyps, although organisms of the genus *Obelia* can produce medusae that reproduce sexually. (b) The tentacles of this Portugese man-of war, genus *Physalia*, have both polyps and medusae that have specialized functions.

(a)

(b)

One hydrozoan that has been extensively studied is the hydra. Hydras are not typical hydrozoans because they exist only as polyps, they are not colonial, and they live in fresh water. Hydras range from 1 to 4 cm (0.4 to 1.6 in.) in length. Most hydras are white or brown, but some, like the one shown in Figure 33-7, appear green because of the algae that live symbiotically inside cells of their gastrodermis. Hydras can be found in quiet ponds, lakes, and streams. They attach themselves to rocks or water plants by means of a sticky secretion produced by cells at the hydra's base.

A hydra can leave one place of attachment and move to another. This can happen when the base secretes bubbles of gas, which cause the hydra to float upside down on the surface of the water. Hydras can also move by tumbling. This movement occurs when the tentacles and the mouth end bend over and touch the surface to which the hydra was attached while the base pulls free.

During warm weather, hydras generally reproduce asexually. Small buds, such as the one you can see in Figure 33-8, develop on the outside of the hydra's body. These buds grow their own tentacles and then separate from the body and begin living independently.

Sexual reproduction usually occurs in the fall, when low temperatures trigger the development of eggs and sperm. The eggs are produced by meiosis along the body wall in swellings called *ovaries*. Motile sperm are formed by meiosis in similar swellings called *testes*. In some species, eggs and sperm are produced in the same hermaphroditic individual, as indicated in Figure 33-8. In other species, the individuals are either male or female. In either case, sperm are released into the water, and those that reach ovaries can fertilize egg cells. Each fertilized egg then divides and grows into an embryo. A hard covering protects the embryo through the winter, and in the spring the embryo hatches and develops into a new hydra.

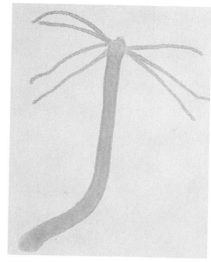

**FIGURE 33-7**

The green color of this hydra, *Chlorohydra viridissima*, comes from the algae that live inside the hydra's cells. (LM 30×)

internet connect

www.scilinks.org
Topic: Hydra
Keyword: HM60774

SCLINKS. Maintained by the National Science Teachers Association

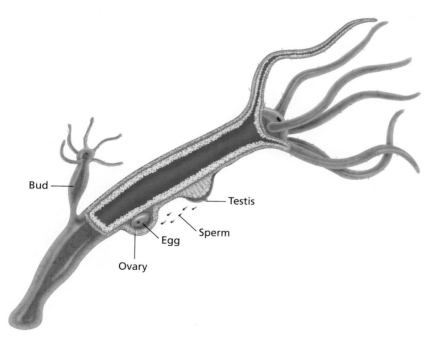

Bud

Testis

Sperm

Egg

Ovary

**FIGURE 33-8**

Hydras can reproduce either asexually, by forming buds, or sexually, by producing sperm that fertilize eggs.

## Class Cubozoa

The cubozoans, or box jellies, were once classified in the class Schyphozoa. As their name implies, cubozoans have cube-shaped medusae. Their polyp stage is inconspicuous and has never been observed in some species. Most box jellies are only a few centimeters in height, although some reach 25 cm (10 in.) tall. A tentacle or group of tentacles is found at each corner of the "box." The cnidocytes of some species, such as the sea wasp, can inflict severe pain and even death among humans. The sea wasp lives in the ocean along the tropical northern coast of Australia.

## Class Scyphozoa

The name *Scyphozoa* (sie-foh-ZOH-uh) means "cup animals," which describes the medusa, the dominant form of the life cycle of this class. There are more than 200 species of scyphozoans, known commonly as jellyfish. The cups of the medusae range from 2 cm (0.8 in.) to 4 m (13 ft) across, and some species have tentacles that are several meters long. Pulsating motions of the cup propel the jellyfish through the water. Like the Portuguese man-of-war, some jellyfish carry poisonous nematocysts that can cause severe pain and even death in humans.

The common jellyfish, genus *Aurelia,* is a scyphozoan whose life cycle includes both medusa and polyp forms. As you can see in Figure 33-9, step ❶, adult medusae release sperm and eggs into the water, where fertilization occurs. The resulting zygote divides many times to form a blastula, as shown in step ❷. In step ❸, the blastula then develops into a ciliated larva called a **planula** (PLAN-yuh-luh). In step ❹, the planula attaches to the ocean bottom. The planula becomes a polyp by developing a mouth and tentacles at the unattached end as shown in step ❺. As the polyp grows, shown in step ❻, it forms a stack of medusae. Finally, as shown in step ❼, the medusae detach and develop into free-swimming jellyfish.

**FIGURE 33-9**

The common jellyfish, genus *Aurelia,* reproduces when sperm from an adult male medusa fertilize eggs from an adult female medusa. Each fertilized egg produces a blastula, which develops into larva known as a planula. The planula forms a polyp, which produces more medusae.

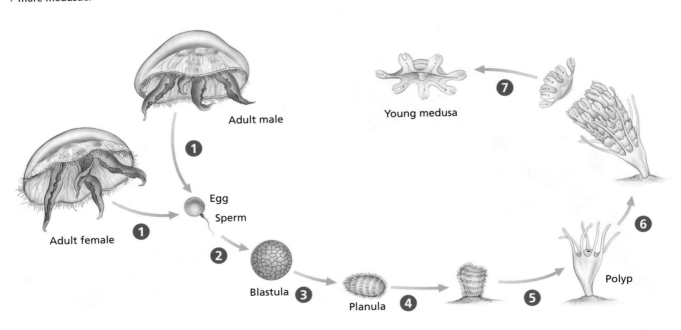

Adult male

Young medusa

❼

❶

Egg

Sperm

❶

Adult female

❻

❷

Polyp

Blastula ❸

Planula ❹

❺

## Class Anthozoa

The name *Anthozoa* means "flower animals," which is a fitting description for the approximately 6,100 marine species in this class. Two examples of anthozoans are sea anemones and corals, which are shown in Figure 33-10.

Sea anemones are polyps commonly found in coastal areas, where they attach themselves to rocks and other submerged objects. Anemones feed on fishes and other animals that swim within reach of their tentacles. However, some anemones in the Pacific Ocean have a symbiotic relationship with the clownfish, as Figure 33-11 demonstrates. The two animals share food and protect each other from predators. The movements of the clownfish also help prevent sediments from burying the anemone. The clownfish produces a slimy mucus that prevents the anemone from firing its nematocysts when the clownfish touches the anemone's tentacles.

Corals are small polyps that usually live in colonies. Each polyp cements its calcium carbonate skeleton to the skeletons of adjoining polyps in the colony. When the polyps die, their hardened skeletons remain, serving as the foundation for new polyps. Over thousands of years, these polyps build up large, rocklike formations known as **coral reefs.** Only the top layer of the reef contains the living polyps. Coral reefs provide food and shelter for an enormous and colorful variety of fishes and invertebrates.

Nearly all coral reefs are restricted to a band of ocean within 30 degrees north or south of the equator. Most form at shallow depths in warm, clear waters. These conditions are necessary in order for photosynthesis to be carried out by the algae that live symbiotically inside coral cells. These corals depend on the algae to provide oxygen and to speed up the accumulation of calcium from the sea water. The algae in turn depend on the corals to supply vital nutrients.

(a)

(b)

**FIGURE 33-10**

Anthozoans, including this crimson anemone, *Cribrinopsis fernaldi* (a), and this golden cup coral, genus *Tubastraea* (b), live as polyps along ocean coasts.

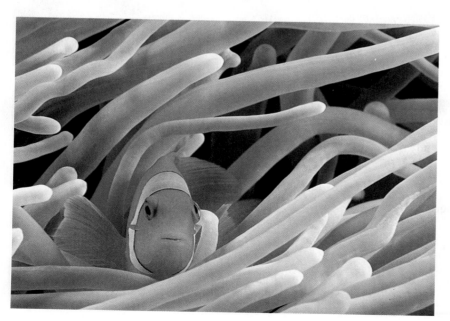

**FIGURE 33-11**

The clownfish, *Amphiprion ocellaris,* lives symbiotically among the tentacles of sea anemones. The anemone's stinging tentacles protect the clownfish from predators. The clownfish, in turn, drives away other fish that try to feed on the anemone.

# PHYLUM CTENOPHORA

The phylum Ctenophora includes about 100 species of marine animals known as *ctenophores.* A typical ctenophore is shown in Figure 33-12. *Ctenophora* means "comb holder" and refers to the eight comblike rows of cilia that run along the outside of the animal. Ctenophores resemble jellyfish and are often called *comb jellies.*

Ctenophores differ from jellyfish and other cnidarians in several ways. Rather than pulsating like jellyfish, they move through the water by beating their cilia. They are the largest organisms to move in this fashion. Also, ctenophores do not have cnidocytes. Instead, many have cells called **colloblasts,** which secrete a sticky substance that binds to their prey. Colloblasts are usually located on two tentacles. Ctenophores also have a sensory structure called an **apical organ** at one end of their body. This organ enables ctenophores to sense their orientation in the water. Nerves running from the apical organ coordinate the beating of the cilia. Most ctenophores are hermaphroditic.

One of the most striking features of ctenophores is their **bioluminescence** (BIE-oh-loo-muh-NES-ens), or production of light by means of a chemical reaction. Bioluminescent ctenophores often occur in large swarms near the surface of the ocean, which creates a spectacular display at night.

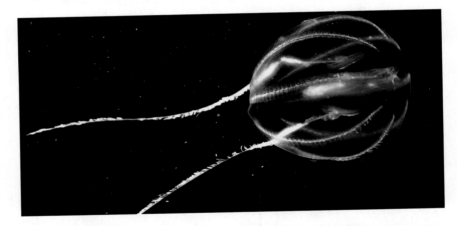

**FIGURE 33-12**

A ctenophore, *Pleurobrachia pileus,* moves through the water by beating its cilia, trailing its two long tentacles behind it.

## SECTION 2 REVIEW

1. What are three characteristics that all cnidarians have in common?

2. Describe how cnidarians feed.

3. What is the name given to the nervous system of a cnidarian?

4. Describe one organism from each of the four cnidarian classes.

5. Describe three characteristics of ctenophores.

**CRITICAL THINKING**

6. **Analyzing Concepts** What might be the advantage of having a life cycle consisting of both medusae and polyps instead of only polyps?

7. **Inferring Relationships** Explain how having nerve cells clustered around the edge of its bell is advantageous to a medusa.

8. **Making Comparisons** Compare the movement of cnidarians with the movement of ctenophores.

# CHAPTER HIGHLIGHTS

## Porifera

- The phylum Porifera is made up of sponges, sessile invertebrates that have no true tissues or organs. The simplest types of sponges are shaped like hollow cylinders.

- The body wall of a sponge is composed of two layers of cells that are separated by a jellylike substance called *mesohyl.* The body is supported by a skeleton made of spongin, spicules, or both.

- Choanocytes which line the inside of a sponge beat their flagella, thus drawing a current of water into the sponge through pores (ostia) in the body wall. Water leaves through the osculum, an opening at the top of the sponge.

- Sponges feed by filtering small organisms and organic matter out of the water that passes through their body. Nutrients are distributed through the body by amoebocytes, cells which crawl about within the body wall.

- Sponges can reproduce asexually, through budding or regeneration, and sexually, through the joining of egg and sperm. Most sponges are hermaphroditic, meaning that a single animal can produce both eggs and sperm.

### Vocabulary

| | | | |
|---|---|---|---|
| sponge (p. 673) | ostium (p. 673) | spicule (p. 673) | gemmule (p. 675) |
| sessile (p. 673) | osculum (p. 673) | filter feeding (p. 674) | regeneration (p. 675) |
| choanocyte (p. 673) | spongin (p. 673) | amoebocyte (p. 674) | hermaphrodite (p. 675) |

## Cnidaria and Ctenophora

- Animals in the phylum Cnidaria can be either sessile polyps or swimming medusae. Some cnidarians alternate between polyp and medusa stages during their life cycles.

- The body of a cnidarian consists of two cell layers—an outer epidermis and an inner gastrodermis—separated by a jellylike mesoglea.

- Cnidarians have cells called *cnidocytes,* which contain organelles known as *nematocysts.* When a cnidocyte is stimulated, its nematocyst ejects a filament that can paralyze or ensnare prey.

- The cnidarian nervous system is a diffuse web of interconnected nerve cells called a *nerve net.*

- The four classes of cnidarians are Hydrozoa (which includes animals such as the hydra), Cubozoa (box jellies), Scyphozoa (jellyfish), and Anthozoa (which includes sea anemones and corals).

- Hydrozoans may live as polyps, medusae, or mixed colonies of polyps and medusae. Cubozoans and scyphozoans spend most of their lives as medusae. Anthozoans live only as polyps.

- Animals in the phylum Ctenophora move through the water by beating the cilia that occur in eight rows on the outside of a ctenophore's body.

- Ctenophores capture prey with a sticky substance secreted by cells called *colloblasts,* which are usually located on a pair of tentacles.

- An apical organ at one end of the body enables ctenophores to sense their orientation in the water. Most ctenophores are hermaphroditic, and many are bioluminescent.

### Vocabulary

| | | | |
|---|---|---|---|
| medusa (p. 676) | mesoglea (p. 676) | nematocyst (p. 677) | colloblast (p. 682) |
| polyp (p. 676) | gastrovascular cavity (p. 676) | nerve net (p. 677) | apical organ (p. 682) |
| epidermis (p. 676) | tentacle (p. 676) | planula (p. 680) | bioluminescence (p. 682) |
| gastrodermis (p. 676) | cnidocyte (p. 677) | coral reef (p. 681) | |

## USING VOCABULARY

1. For each pair of terms, explain how the meanings of the terms differ.
   a. *spongin* and *spicule*
   b. *medusa* and *polyp*
   c. *epidermis* and *gastrodermis*
   d. *cnidocyte* and *nematocyst*
   e. *gemmule* and *planula*

2. Explain the relationship between choanocytes and filter feeding.

3. Use each of the following terms in a separate sentence: *colloblast, apical organ,* and *bioluminescence.*

4. **Word Roots and Origins** The name *Porifera* is derived from the Latin *porus,* meaning "channel," and *ferre,* meaning "to bear." Explain why *Porifera* is a good name for the sponge phylum.

## UNDERSTANDING KEY CONCEPTS

5. **Identify** three ways that sponges represent the transition from unicellular to multicellular life.

6. **Describe** why sponges are classified as animals.

7. **Outline** the path of water through a sponge, and explain what causes water to flow through a sponge.

8. **Explain** how a sponge's usual method of feeding is suited to its sessile lifestyle.

9. **State** the role of gemmules in the life cycles of sponges.

10. **Summarize** the process of sexual reproduction in sponges.

11. **Compare** the two types of body structures that cnidarians have.

12. **Describe** how a cnidarian captures and ingests its prey.

13. **Identify** the specialization that is found among the individuals that make up a Portuguese man-of-war.

14. **Name** the benefits a sea anemone obtains from its symbiotic relationship with a clownfish. What benefit does the clownfish obtain from this relationship?

15. **Explain** why coral reefs are limited to warm, shallow environments.

16. **Compare** ctenophores and cnidarians. Include at least two differences.

17. **CONCEPT MAPPING** Use the following terms to create a concept map that sequences sexual reproduction in a typical scyphozoan: *adult male, medusa, blastula, adult female, sperm, polyp, planula,* and *egg.*

## CRITICAL THINKING

18. **Applying Information** A single species of sponges may assume various appearances, depending on substrate, availability of space, and the velocity and temperature of water currents. How might these factors make the classification of sponges confusing? What features besides outward appearance can biologists use to classify sponges and eliminate some of this confusion?

19. **Analyzing Information** Sponge larvae have flagella on the outside of their bodies, while adult sponges have flagella lining their internal cavity. How is this structural difference related to functional differences between the larval and adult stages of sponges?

20. **Analyzing Patterns** Hydras generally reproduce asexually during warm weather and sexually in cooler weather. Based on what you have learned about the hydra embryo, what is the advantage of reproducing sexually when the weather turns cool?

21. **Predicting Results** What would happen to a coral reef if pollution or sediment caused the water around the reef to become less clear? Explain your answer.

22. **Interpreting Graphics** The pie chart below shows the relative numbers of hydrozoans, scyphozoans, and anthozoans. Which segment of the chart represents scyphozoans? How do you know?

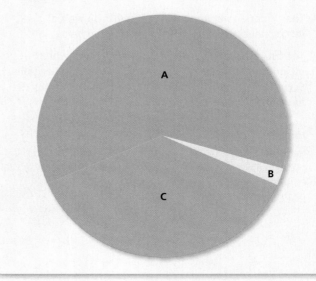

# Standardized Test Preparation

**DIRECTIONS:** Choose the letter of the answer choice that best answers the question.

**1.** Why are spongin and spicules important to a sponge?
   **A.** They digest food.
   **B.** They remove wastes.
   **C.** They provide support.
   **D.** They produce offspring.

**2.** Which of the following structures are involved in both feeding and sexual reproduction in sponges?
   **F.** spicules and gemmules
   **G.** amoebocytes and spongin
   **H.** gemmules and choanocytes
   **J.** choanocytes and amoebocytes

**3.** Which of the following is *not* a characteristic of cnidarians?
   **A.** tentacles
   **B.** choanocytes
   **C.** nematocysts
   **D.** gastrovascular cavity

**4.** What do colloblasts do?
   **F.** They produce light.
   **G.** They secrete a sticky substance.
   **H.** They draw water through sponges.
   **J.** They form medusae that live in colonies.

**INTERPRETING GRAPHICS:** The diagram below illustrates a hydra. Study the diagram to answer the questions that follow.

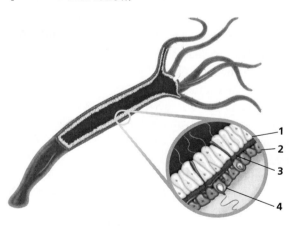

**5.** Identify the substance found at point 3.
   **A.** osculum
   **B.** mesoglea
   **C.** gastrodermis
   **D.** gastrovascular cavity

**6.** Which structure is involved in defense?
   **F.** 1
   **G.** 2
   **H.** 3
   **J.** 4

**DIRECTIONS:** Complete the following analogy.

**7.** Sponge : osculum :: hydra :
   **A.** mouth
   **B.** tentacle
   **C.** nerve net
   **D.** nematocyst

**INTERPRETING GRAPHICS:** The diagram below illustrates a medusa. Study the diagram to answer the question that follows.

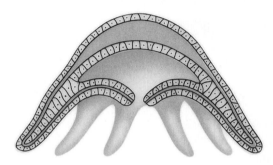

**8.** In which class is this body form dominant?
   **F.** Cnidaria
   **G.** Hydrozoa
   **H.** Anthozoa
   **J.** Scyphozoa

## SHORT RESPONSE

Cnidarians have two tissue layers, which is an important evolutionary advancement.

Describe the tissue layers and general body structure of a typical cnidarian.

## EXTENDED RESPONSE

Sponges reproduce asexually in a number of ways.

*Part A* Describe three forms of asexual reproduction in sponges.

*Part B* Explain how reproducing asexually is advantageous to sponges.

**Test TIP** You can sometimes figure out an answer to a question before you look at the answer choices. After you answer the question in your mind, compare your answer with the answer choices. Choose the answer that most closely matches your own answer.

# Observing Hydra Behavior

## OBJECTIVES

- Observe live specimens of hydra.
- Determine how hydras respond to different stimuli.
- Determine how hydras capture and feed on prey.

## PROCESS SKILLS

- observing
- relating structure to function

## MATERIALS

- silicone culture gum
- microscope slide
- hydra culture
- 2 medicine droppers
- compound microscope
- methylene blue solution
- vinegar
- stereomicroscope
- filter paper cut into pennant shapes
- forceps
- concentrated beef broth
- culture of *Daphnia pulex* or *Daphnia magna*

## Background

1. How do animals respond to stimuli in their environment?
2. What is a hydra?

3. What characteristics do hydras share with other cnidarians?
4. How does a sessile animal, such as a hydra, obtain food?
5. What is a nematocyst?

**PART A** Close-up Examination of a Hydra

1. △ **CAUTION** **Slides break easily. Use care when handling them.** Using a long piece of silicone culture gum, make a circular "well" on a microscope slide, as shown in the illustration below.

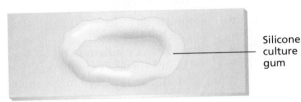

Silicone culture gum

2. △ **CAUTION** **You will be working with a live animal. Be sure to treat it gently and to follow directions carefully.** With a medicine dropper, gently transfer a hydra from the culture dish to the well on the slide, making sure the hydra is in water. The hydra should be transferred quickly; otherwise, it may attach itself to the medicine dropper. Allow the hydra to settle. As you go through the following steps, add water to the slide periodically to replace water that has evaporated, and keep the hydra wet.

3. Examine the hydra under the low-power setting of a compound microscope. Add a drop of methylene blue solution to the well containing the hydra to make the tentacles more visible. Identify and draw the hydra's body stalk, mouth, and tentacles in your lab report.

4. In your lab report, make a data table like the one shown on the next page. As you complete the following steps, record your observations in your data table.

5. As you continue to observe the hydra at low power, add a drop of vinegar to the well. Record what happens to the bumps on the tentacles. These bumps are cnidocytes.

**6.** Transfer the hydra to the culture dish labeled "Used hydras." Rinse the well on your microscope slide with water to remove all traces of methylene blue and vinegar.

### PART B Feeding Behavior

**7.** Hydras eat small invertebrates, such as daphnia. With a medicine dropper, gently transfer another hydra to the well on your slide. Then transfer live daphnia to the well in the same manner.

**8.** Observe the hydra carefully with the high-power setting of the stereomicroscope. Watch for threadlike nematocysts shooting out from the hydra. Some nematocysts release a poison that paralyzes prey. If the hydra does not respond after a few minutes, obtain another hydra from the culture dish and repeat this procedure.

**9.** Observe the way the hydra captures and ingests daphnia, and record your observations in your data table. Record how long it takes for a hydra to ingest a daphnia.

**10.** Transfer the hydra to the culture dish labeled "Used hydras." Rinse the well on your microscope slide with water to remove the daphnia.

### PART C Response to Stimuli

**11.** Transfer another hydra to the well on your slide, and examine it with the high-power setting of the stereomicroscope. Using forceps, move the long tip of a pennant-shaped piece of filter paper near the hydra's tentacles. Be careful not to touch the hydra with the filter paper. Observe the hydra's response to the filter paper, and record your observations in your data table.

**12.** Now observe how the hydra responds to a chemical stimulus. Dip the same piece of filter paper in beef broth, and repeat the procedure in step 11. Again, be careful not to touch the hydra. Record the hydra's response to the beef broth in your data table.

**13.** Finally, investigate how the hydra responds to touch. Using the long tip of a clean pennant-shaped piece of filter paper, touch the hydra's tentacles, mouth, and body stalk. **CAUTION Touch the hydra gently.** Record your observations in your data table.

**14.** Transfer the hydra to the culture dish labeled "Used hydras." Clean up your materials and wash your hands before leaving the lab.

## Analysis and Conclusions

**1.** Is vinegar a normal part of a hydra's diet? Why do you think vinegar is used in this step?

**2.** Based on your observations, how do you think a hydra behaves when it is threatened in its natural habitat?

**3.** Describe a hydra's feeding behavior.

**4.** What happens to food that has not been digested by a hydra?

**5.** What was the purpose of using the clean filter paper in step 11?

**6.** Did the hydra show a feeding response or a defensive response to the beef broth? Explain.

**7.** How is a hydra adapted to a sessile lifestyle?

**8.** How is the feeding method of a hydra different from that of a sponge?

**9.** Do you think the hydra's response is triggered by water vibrations, by chemicals that daphnia releases, or by daphnia touching the hydra?

## Further Inquiry

Design an experiment to determine how hydras respond to other stimuli, such as light.

### OBSERVATIONS OF HYDRA BEHAVIOR

| Behavior | Observations |
|---|---|
| Response to vinegar | |
| Feeding behavior | |
| Response to filter paper | |
| Response to beef broth on filter paper | |
| Response to touch with filter paper | |

# CHAPTER 34
# FLATWORMS, ROUNDWORMS, AND ROTIFERS

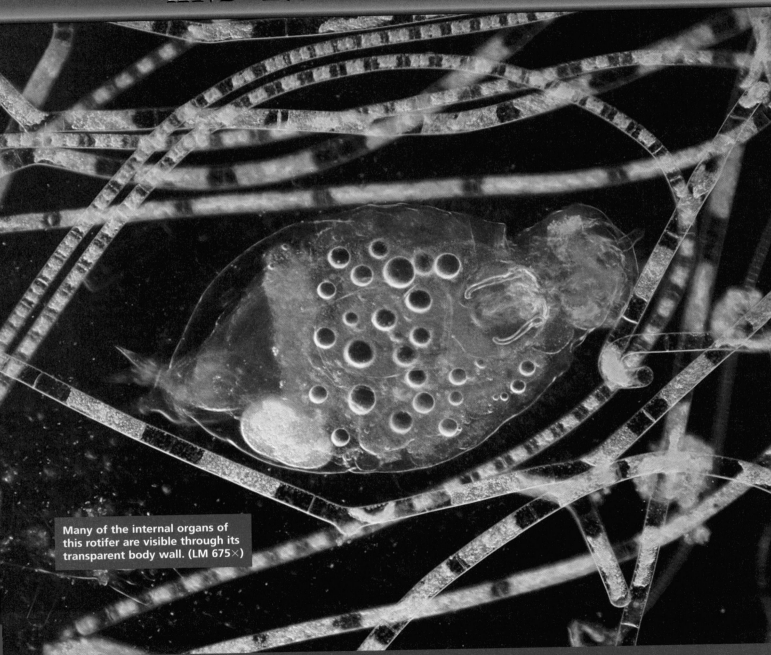

Many of the internal organs of this rotifer are visible through its transparent body wall. (LM 675×)

**SECTION 1** *Platyhelminthes*

**SECTION 2** *Nematoda and Rotifera*

# PLATYHELMINTHES

*T*he phylum Platyhelminthes *(PLAT-ee-hel-MINTH-eez) includes organisms called* flatworms. *Their bodies develop from three germ layers and are more complex than those of sponges, cnidarians, and ctenophores. Flatworms have bilaterally symmetrical bodies, with dorsal and ventral surfaces, right and left sides, and anterior and posterior ends.*

## SECTION 1

### OBJECTIVES

- **Summarize** the distinguishing characteristics of flatworms.
- **Describe** the anatomy of a planarian.
- **Compare** free-living and parasitic flatworms.
- **Diagram** the life cycle of a fluke.
- **Describe** the life cycle of a tapeworm.

### VOCABULARY

pharynx
flame cell
cerebral ganglion
eyespot
fluke
tegument
primary host
intermediate host
schistosomiasis
scolex
proglottid
cyst

## STRUCTURE AND FUNCTION OF FLATWORMS

Flatworms are the simplest animals with bilateral symmetry. The tissues in bilaterally symmetrical animals develop from three germ layers: ectoderm, mesoderm, and endoderm. In flatworms, the three germ layers are pressed against one another to form a solid body. Because flatworms do not have a hollow body cavity between the endoderm and the mesoderm, they are acoelomates.

The acoelomate body plan gives flatworms the thin, dorsoventrally flattened bodies for which they are named. This body shape ensures that no cell in a flatworm is very far from the animal's external environment. Thus, the cells can exchange oxygen and carbon dioxide directly with the environment through diffusion, allowing flatworms to survive without a circulatory system or respiratory system. Like cnidarians, most flatworms have a gastrovascular cavity, which is a gut with a single opening, and a mouth. Food is taken in and digested in the gastrovascular cavity, and any undigested material is eliminated through the same opening. Most of the sensory organs and nerve cells of flatworms, such as the marine species shown in Figure 34-1, are located at the anterior end of the body. This characteristic is known as *cephalization.*

The classification of Platyhelminthes has undergone many recent changes. Currently, the more than 20,000 species of flatworms are divided into four classes: Turbellaria, Trematoda, Monogenea, and Cestoda. Trematodes, monogeneans, and cestodes (SES-tohdz) live as parasites on or inside other animals. Almost all turbellarians are nonparasitic, free-living organisms found in marine and freshwater habitats and in moist terrestrial environments. Parasitic flatworms probably evolved from free-living organisms. As parasites evolved, some organs that were advantageous to free-living became modified for parasitism, while other organs were lost entirely.

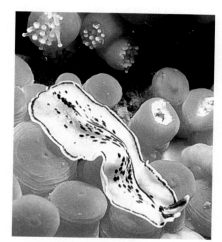

**FIGURE 34-1**

Many of the sensory organs in this marine flatworm, of the genus *Eurylepta,* are concentrated in the two tentacles at the anterior end of its body. This characteristic is an example of cephalization.

# CLASS TURBELLARIA

The majority of the approximately 4,500 species in the class Turbellaria live in the ocean. However, the most familiar turbellarian is the freshwater planarian *Dugesia,* shown in Figure 34-2. Planarians have a spade-shaped anterior end and a tapered posterior end. They move through the water by swimming with a wavelike motion of their body. Over solid surfaces, planarians glide on a layer of mucus that they secrete, propelled by the cilia that cover their bodies.

## Digestion and Excretion in Planarians

Planarians feed by scavenging for bits of decaying plant or animal matter. They also prey on smaller organisms, such as protozoa. Food is ingested through a muscular tube called the **pharynx** (FAR-eenks), which the planarian extends from the middle of its body. As Figure 34-2a indicates, the pharynx leads to the highly branched gastrovascular cavity. Cells lining the cavity secrete digestive enzymes and absorb nutrients and small pieces of food. The nutrients then diffuse to other body cells.

Organisms that live in fresh water must deal with the water that constantly enters their bodies by osmosis. Planarians eliminate excess water through a network of excretory tubules that run the length of the body. Figure 34-2b shows that each tubule is connected to several **flame cells,** which are so named because they enclose tufts of beating cilia that resemble flickering candle flames. The beating of cilia in the flame cells draws in the excess water. The water is then transported through the tubules and excreted from numerous pores scattered over the body surface.

**FIGURE 34-2**

The organ systems of a planarian allow it to maintain its free-living existence. (a) The digestive system consists of the pharynx and gastrovascular cavity, which has many branches. (b) In the excretory system, flame cells collect excess water, which travels through excretory tubules to pores on the surface of the body. (c) The nervous system is a ladderlike arrangement of nerves with two cerebral ganglia at the anterior end. (d) Since planarians are hermaphrodites, their reproductive system includes both testes and ovaries.

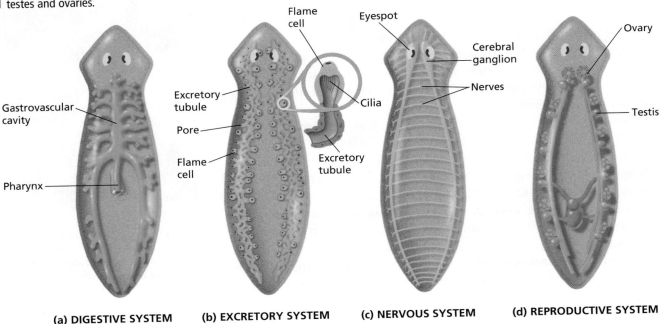

(a) DIGESTIVE SYSTEM  (b) EXCRETORY SYSTEM  (c) NERVOUS SYSTEM  (d) REPRODUCTIVE SYSTEM

## Neural Control in Planarians

The planarian nervous system is more complex than the nerve net of cnidarians, as Figure 34-2c illustrates. Two clusters of nerve cells at the anterior end, the **cerebral ganglia** (suh-REE-bruhl GAN-glee-uh), serve as a simple brain. They receive information from sensory cells and transmit signals to the muscles along a ladderlike arrangement of nerves. A planarian's nervous system gives it the ability to learn. For example, a planarian normally moves away from light, but it can be trained to remain still when illuminated.

Planarians sense the intensity and direction of light with two cup-shaped **eyespots** located near the cerebral ganglia. You can see the eyespots in Figure 34-2c. Other sensory cells respond to touch, water currents, and chemicals in the environment. These cells are distributed over the body, but most are concentrated at the anterior end.

## Reproduction in Planarians

Because planarians are free-living and motile, they can encounter and mate with other individuals of the same species. As shown in Figure 34-2d, planarians are hermaphrodites—they have both male sex organs (testes) and female sex organs (ovaries). When two planarians reproduce sexually, they simultaneously fertilize each other. Their eggs are laid in protective capsules that stick to rocks or debris and hatch in two to three weeks.

Planarians also reproduce asexually, generally during the summer. During asexual reproduction, the body constricts just behind the pharynx. While the posterior part of the worm is attached to a solid surface, the anterior part moves forward until the worm splits in two. This type of asexual reproduction is known as *fission*. The two halves then regenerate their missing parts to produce two complete planaria. During regeneration, each part of the planarian retains information about its original orientation in the body. If a piece is cut from the middle of a planarian, the anterior end of the piece will always regenerate a head and the posterior end of the piece will regenerate a tail.

# CLASSES TREMATODA AND MONOGENEA

The classes Trematoda and Monogenea consist of parasitic **flukes,** leaf-shaped flatworms that parasitize many kinds of animals, including humans. Some flukes are endoparasites that live in the blood, intestines, lungs, liver, or other organs. Others are ectoparasites that live on the external surface of aquatic hosts, such as fish and frogs. Trematodes tend to parasitize a wide range of hosts, whereas monogeneans are mostly ectoparasites of fish and other aquatic animals.

internet connect

www.scilinks.org
**Topic:** Flukes
**Keyword:** HM60587

SC*LINKS*. Maintained by the National Science Teachers Association

## Structure of Flukes

A fluke clings to the tissues of its host by an anterior sucker and a ventral sucker, which are shown in Figure 34-3. The anterior sucker surrounds the fluke's mouth, which draws the host's body fluids into the gastrovascular cavity. A fluke's nervous system is similar to a planarian's, but flukes have no eyespots and their other sensory structures are very simple. The external surface of a fluke is covered by a layer called the **tegument.** The outer zone of the tegument consists of a layer of proteins and carbohydrates that makes the fluke resistant to the defenses of the host's immune system. The tegument also protects the fluke against the enzymes secreted by the host's digestive tract.

## Reproduction and Life Cycle of Flukes

Most flukes have highly developed reproductive systems and are hermaphroditic. Fertilized eggs are stored in a fluke's uterus, which is a long, coiled tube, until they are ready to be released. Each fluke may release tens of thousands of eggs at a time.

Flukes have complicated life cycles that involve more than one host species. A good example is provided by the trematode blood flukes of the genus *Schistosoma,* as shown in Figure 34-4. Adult schistosomes live inside human blood vessels. Therefore, a human is the schistosome's **primary host,** the host from which the adult parasite gets its nourishment and in which sexual reproduction occurs. Unlike most flukes, schistosomes have separate sexes. Eggs produced by the female are fertilized by the male. In step ❶, some of the fertilized eggs make their way to the host's intestine or bladder and are excreted with the feces or urine. Human feces and urine often pollute freshwater supplies in regions with poor sewage control. In step ❷, the eggs that enter fresh water develop into ciliated larvae that swim. In step ❸, if the larvae encounter a snail of a particular species, such as one of genus *Oncomelania,* within a few hours, they burrow into the snail's tissues and begin to reproduce asexually. The snail serves as the schistosome's **intermediate host,** the host from which the larvae derive their nourishment. ❹ Eventually, the larvae develop tails and escape from the snail. ❺ These tailed larvae swim through the water. If they find the bare skin of a human, they penetrate the skin, enter a blood vessel, and develop into adults. The cycle then begins again. Exposure to the larvae can happen when humans swim, bathe, wash clothes, or work in fresh water that contains the larvae.

**FIGURE 34-3**

Suckers on this blood fluke, *Schistosoma mansoni,* attach the fluke to the blood vessels of its host. (SEM 550×)

**FIGURE 34-4**

In the life cycle of schistosomes, fertilized eggs are released into the host's blood vessels. The eggs pass out of the primary host in feces or urine. In water, the eggs develop into ciliated larvae. The larvae burrow into certain species of snails, which serve as intermediate hosts. The larvae develop tails, escape from the snail, and swim about. The tailed larvae bore through the exposed skin of a person and settle in his or her blood vessels. There, the larvae develop into adults, and the cycle repeats.

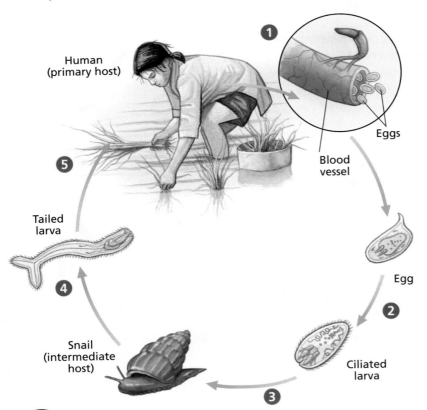

Human (primary host)

Blood vessel

Eggs

Egg

Tailed larva

Snail (intermediate host)

Ciliated larva

Not all schistosome eggs leave the human body, however. Many are carried by the blood to the lungs, intestines, bladder, and liver, where they may block blood vessels and cause irritation, bleeding, and tissue decay. The eggs may also penetrate the walls of veins and the small intestine or urinary bladder, where they can cause much tissue damage and bleeding. The resulting disease, called **schistosomiasis** (SHIS-tuh-soh-MIE-uh-suhs), can be fatal. It affects about 200 million people worldwide, mostly in Asia, Africa, and South America.

Other kinds of flukes cause less-serious diseases in humans. For example, a small brown fluke common in freshwater lakes of North America is responsible for swimmer's itch, a condition characterized by minor skin irritation and swelling.

**Word Roots and Origins**

*schistosomiasis*

from the Greek *schizein,* meaning "to cleave or split," and *soma,* meaning "body," and *iasis,* meaning "process or condition"

# CLASS CESTODA

About 5,000 species of tapeworms make up the class Cestoda. Tapeworms can live in the intestines of almost all vertebrates. Humans may harbor any of seven different species. Tapeworms enter their host when the host eats raw or undercooked food containing eggs or larvae. A tapeworm infection may cause digestive problems, weight loss, lack of energy, and anemia, which is a decrease in the number of red cells in the blood.

## Structure of Tapeworms

Like flukes, tapeworms are surrounded by a tegument that protects them from their host's defenses. As Figure 34-5 shows, at the anterior end of a tapeworm is a knob-shaped organ called the **scolex** (SKOH-leks), which has hooks and suckers that enable the worm to attach to its host. A short neck connects the scolex with a long series of body sections called **proglottids** (proh-GLAHT-idz). As a tapeworm grows, it adds proglottids just behind the neck, pushing the older proglottids toward the rear. A single tapeworm may have 2,000 proglottids and exceed 10 m (33 ft) in length.

The excretory system and nervous system of a tapeworm are similar to those of other flatworms. However, tapeworms lack eyespots and other light-sensitive structures, and they have no mouth, gastrovascular cavity, or other digestive organs. They absorb nutrients directly from the host's digestive tract through their tegument. The tegument is highly folded, which increases the surface area available for absorption.

**FIGURE 34-5**

A tapeworm grows by adding proglottids behind its scolex. Each proglottid contains both male and female reproductive organs.

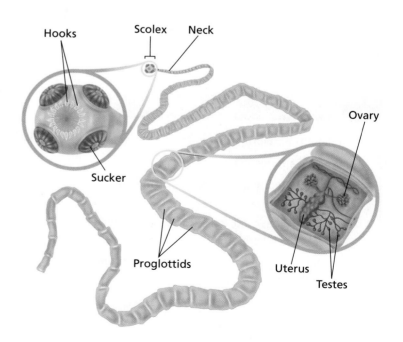

Hooks · Scolex · Neck · Sucker · Proglottids · Ovary · Uterus · Testes

## Reproduction and Life Cycle of Tapeworms

Nearly all tapeworms are hermaphrodites. You can see in Figure 34-5 that each proglottid contains both male and female reproductive organs, but little else. As the proglottids move to the rear of the tapeworm, they grow, mature, and begin producing eggs. The oldest proglottids are almost completely filled with 100,000 or more eggs. Eggs in one proglottid are usually fertilized by sperm from a different proglottid, either in the same individual or a different individual if the host has more than one tapeworm.

The life cycle of the beef tapeworm, *Taenia saginatus,* is illustrated in Figure 34-6. Like the blood fluke, the beef tapeworm has two hosts. The primary host is a human. In the human intestine, mature proglottids break off from the adult and are eliminated with the host's feces. If the feces are deposited on the ground, the proglottids crawl out of the feces and onto nearby vegetation. The eggs they release may remain alive for several months before the vegetation is eaten by a cow, the intermediate host. Inside the cow, the eggs develop into larvae that burrow through the cow's intestine and enter the bloodstream. The larvae then make their way to muscle tissue and form **cysts,** or dormant larvae surrounded by protective coverings. Humans become infected when they eat beef that has not been cooked well enough to kill the worms inside the cysts. Once a cyst enters the human intestine, the cyst wall dissolves and releases the worm. The worm then attaches to the intestinal wall and develops into an adult, beginning the cycle again.

Another tapeworm that infects humans is the pork tapeworm, *Taenia solium.* Its life cycle is similar to that of the beef tapeworm, except that a pig serves as the intermediate host.

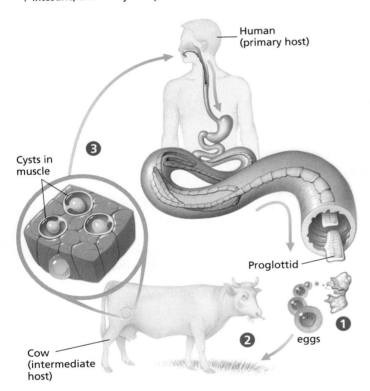

**FIGURE 34-6**

Adult beef tapeworms live in the intestines of humans, their primary hosts. ❶ Proglottids pass out of the primary host in feces, crawl onto vegetation, and release the tapeworm eggs. ❷ A cow, the intermediate host, ingests the eggs when it eats the vegetation. The eggs hatch into larvae that form cysts in the cow's muscles. ❸ When a person eats undercooked beef, the larvae in the beef develop into adult tapeworms in the person's intestine, and the cycle repeats.

Human (primary host)

Cysts in muscle

❸

Proglottid

Cow (intermediate host)

❷ eggs

❶

---

## SECTION 1 REVIEW

1. Why are flatworms called acoelomates?

2. What is a flame cell?

3. Describe two ways in which a planarian shows cephalization.

4. Summarize how the schistosome blood fluke affects the human body.

5. Explain why tapeworms can survive without a digestive system.

**CRITICAL THINKING**

6. **Recognizing Relationships** Why is it an adaptive advantage that a parasite not kill its host?

7. **Analyzing Concepts** How is asexual reproduction advantageous to a free-living flatworm?

8. **Applying Concepts** Considering the life cycle of the schistosome blood fluke, recommend an effective way of controlling the spread of schistosomiasis.

# NEMATODA AND ROTIFERA

*Members of the phyla Nematoda (nee-muh-TOHD-uh) and Rotifera (roh-TIF-uhr-uh) have bilaterally symmetrical bodies that contain a fluid-filled space. This space holds the internal organs and serves as a storage area for eggs and sperm. It also supports the body and provides a structure against which the muscles can contract.*

## SECTION 2

### OBJECTIVES

- **Describe** the body plan of a nematode.
- **Outline** the relationships between humans and parasitic roundworms.
- **Describe** the anatomy of a rotifer.

### VOCABULARY

roundworm
cuticle
hookworm
trichinosis
pinworm
filarial worm
elephantiasis
rotifer
mastax
cloaca
parthenogenesis

## PHYLUM NEMATODA

The phylum Nematoda is made up of **roundworms,** worms with long, slender bodies that taper at both ends. Roundworms are among several phyla of animals known as *pseudocoelomates.* Pseudocoelomates are so named because they have a pseudo-coelom, which is a hollow, fluid-filled cavity that is lined by mesoderm on the outside and endoderm on the inside.

Roundworms range in length from less than 1 mm to 120 cm (4 ft). In contrast to cnidarians, ctenophores, and flatworms, which have a gastrovascular cavity with a single opening, roundworms have a digestive tract with two openings. Food enters the digestive tract through the mouth at the anterior end, and undigested material is eliminated from the anus (AY-nuhs) at the posterior end. A digestive tract represents a significant advancement over a gastrovascular cavity because food moves through the tract in only one direction. This allows different parts of the tract to be specialized for carrying out different functions, such as enzymatic digestion and absorption of nutrients. Most roundworms have separate sexes and are covered by a protective, noncellular layer called the **cuticle** (KYOO-ti-kuhl).

About 15,000 species of roundworms are known, but biologists estimate that there may be 500,000 or more species. The vast majority of roundworm species are free-living on land, in salt water, and in fresh water. One free-living roundworm, *Caenorhabditis elegans,* is a favorite organism of scientists studying developmental biology. However, more than 150 species of roundworms are parasites of plants and animals. These parasitic species damage plant crops and can harm livestock, pets, and humans. Humans are host to about 50 roundworm species. As you read about these roundworms, notice their adaptations for parasitism.

## Eco Connection

### Roundworms for Your Garden—Just Add Water

Some garden supply companies now sell kits containing millions of microscopic roundworms. When released, these roundworms seek out and kill hundreds of varieties of insect pests, fleas, and ticks. Other types of soil-dwelling roundworms consume bacteria and fungi that attack plants. These roundworms are also known as *beneficial nematodes.*

However, not all roundworms are good for plants. Some species parasitize the roots of plants. Effective pest control with roundworms requires a knowledge of which species are harmful and which are beneficial.

## Ascaris

*Ascaris* (AS-kuh-ris) is a genus of roundworm parasites that live in the intestines of pigs, horses, and humans. Ascarids feed on the food that passes through the intestines of their host. As Figure 34-7 shows, they can become so numerous that they completely block the host's intestines if left untreated. The adult female can reach lengths of up to 30 cm (1 ft). The smaller male has a hooked posterior end that holds the female during mating.

One ascarid female can produce up to 200,000 eggs every day. The fertilized eggs leave the host's body in feces. If they are not exposed to sunlight or high temperatures, they can remain alive in the soil for years. Ascarid eggs enter the body of another host when the host ingests contaminated food or water. The eggs develop into larvae in the intestines. The larvae bore their way into the bloodstream and are carried to the lungs and throat, where they develop further. They are coughed up, swallowed, and returned to the intestines, where they mature and mate, completing the life cycle. If the infection is severe, larvae in the lungs can block air passages and cause bleeding from small blood vessels.

## Hookworms

**Hookworms** are another group of intestinal parasites. As you can see in Figure 34-8, a hookworm's mouth has cutting plates that clamp onto the intestinal wall. Hookworms feed on their host's blood. Because they remove much more blood than they need for food, a heavy hookworm infection can cause anemia. Hookworm infections in children can result in slowed mental and physical development.

Like ascarids, hookworms release their eggs in the host's feces. The eggs produce larvae in warm, damp soil, and the larvae enter new hosts by boring through the host's feet. They then travel through the blood to the lungs and throat. Swallowing takes them to the intestines, where they develop into adults. Hookworms infect about one billion people worldwide. Most infections occur in tropical and subtropical regions.

**FIGURE 34-7**

This pig intestine is completely blocked by roundworms of the genus *Ascaris*.

**internet** connect

www.scilinks.org
**Topic: Hookworms**
**Keyword: HM60757**

SC*LINKS*. Maintained by the National Science Teachers Association

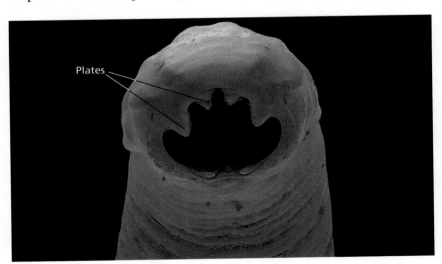

Plates

**FIGURE 34-8**

This SEM shows the hookworm *Ancyclostoma duodenale,* which uses its plates to cut into the host's intestine, releasing blood on which the hookworm feeds.

## Trichinella

Roundworms of the genus *Trichinella* infect humans and a variety of other mammals, including pigs. Adult trichina worms live embedded in the walls of the host's intestine. They produce larvae that travel through the bloodstream to the muscles, where they form cysts. Figure 34-9 shows several such cysts. People become infected when they eat undercooked meat—usually pork—that is contaminated with cysts. After they are eaten, the cysts release the larvae, which burrow into the intestinal wall and mature into adults. Trichina infections are responsible for the disease **trichinosis** (TRIK-i-NOH-sis), which causes muscle pain and stiffness. It can even cause death if large numbers of cysts form in the heart muscle. However, trichinosis is now rare in the United States. Farmers no longer feed raw meat to hogs, and meatpackers generally freeze pork, which kills the worms. Thoroughly cooking pork also prevents trichinosis.

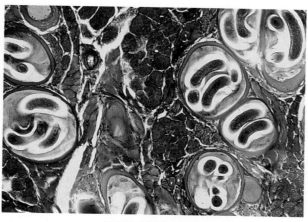

**FIGURE 34-9**

Larvae of the trichina roundworm coil up inside cysts in their hosts' muscle tissue. The cysts are stained blue in this light micrograph (100×).

## Other Parasitic Roundworms

The most common roundworm parasite of humans in the United States is the **pinworm**, *Enterobius*. School-age children have the highest infection rate, which in some areas is as many as 50 percent of children. Despite their high rate of infection, pinworms do not cause any serious disease. Adult pinworms are 5–10 mm (0.2–0.4 in.) in length and resemble white threads. They live and mate in the lower portion of the intestine. At night, the females migrate out of the intestine and lay eggs on the skin around the anus. When an infected person scratches during sleep, the eggs are picked up by the person's hands and spread to anything the person touches. Eggs that are ingested hatch in the intestine, where the worms develop into adults.

**Filarial** (fuh-LAR-ee-uhl) **worms** are disease-causing roundworms that infect over 250 million people in tropical countries. The most dangerous filarial worms live in the lymphatic system, a part of the circulatory system that collects excess fluid around cells and returns it to the blood. The adult worms can be as long as 100 mm (4 in.). The larvae they produce enter the blood and are picked up by mosquitoes that draw blood from an infected person. The larvae develop into an infective stage inside the mosquitoes and are injected into the blood of another person when the mosquitoes feed again. Inside the new host, the larvae complete their development and settle in the lymphatic system. When they are present in large numbers, filarial worms can block the lymphatic vessels, causing fluid to accumulate in the limbs. In severe cases, the limbs become extremely swollen and skin hardens and thickens, a condition known as **elephantiasis** (EL-uh-fuhn-TIE-uh-sis). Another type of filarial worm infects dogs and cats. Large numbers of *Toxocara canis* or *T. cati* live in the heart and large arteries of the lungs and are responsible for heartworm disease.

 **Quick Lab**

### Comparing Flatworms and Roundworms

**Materials** living planarian, preserved specimens of tapeworms, male and female ascarids, hand lens or stereomicroscope

**Procedure** Examine specimens of tapeworms, ascarids, and the living planarian. Try to locate the following structures on each worm: anterior end, posterior end, mouth, eyespot, hooks, suckers, and anus. Draw each worm and label each of the features you located.

### Analysis

1. List the features found on the posterior and anterior end of each worm.
2. Which worm has a separate mouth and an anus?
3. Which worm "absorbs" digested nutrients?
4. Which worm has a digestive tract?

FIGURE 34-10

Cilia surrounding the mouth of a rotifer sweep food into the animal's digestive tract.

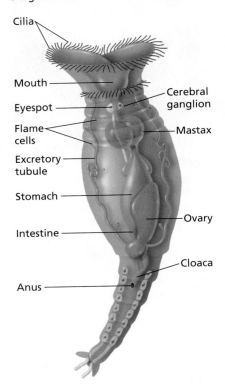

- Cilia
- Mouth
- Eyespot
- Flame cells
- Excretory tubule
- Stomach
- Intestine
- Anus
- Cerebral ganglion
- Mastax
- Ovary
- Cloaca

# PHYLUM ROTIFERA

Another group of pseudocoelomates are the approximately 1,750 species in the phylum Rotifera. Members of this phylum are called **rotifers.** Most rotifers are transparent, free-living animals that live in fresh water, although some live in salt water and damp soil. They typically range in length from 100 to 500 $\mu$m, with males being much smaller than females. Many rotifers can survive without water for long periods, during which they dry up and look like grains of sand. When wet conditions return, they absorb water and resume their activities. Although rotifers are tiny, they are truly multicellular and have specialized organ systems.

As Figure 34-10 illustrates, rotifers have a crown of cilia surrounding their mouth. Under a microscope, the crown with its beating cilia looks like a pair of rotating wheels. Rotifers use their cilia to sweep food—algae, bacteria, and protozoa—into their digestive tract. As shown in Figure 34-10, food moves from the mouth to the **mastax,** a muscular organ that breaks the food into smaller particles. The food is further digested in the stomach, and the nutrients are absorbed in the intestine. Indigestible material passes from the intestine to the **cloaca** (kloh-AY-kuh), a common chamber into which the digestive, reproductive, and excretory systems empty. Like planarians, rotifers use flame cells and excretory tubules to collect excess water in the body. The excess water, along with wastes from the intestine and eggs from the ovaries of females, leaves the cloaca through the anus. Rotifers exhibit cephalization, with a pair of cerebral ganglia and, in some species, two eyespots at the anterior end of the body.

Rotifer reproduction is unusual because some species of rotifers reproduce by parthenogenesis. In the process of **parthenogenesis** (PAHR-thuh-NOH-JEN-uh-sis), unfertilized eggs develop into adult females. Other species produce two types of eggs. Eggs of one type develop into small males that produce sperm. The sperm fertilizes eggs of the other type, which then form tough-coated zygotes that can survive poor conditions.

## SECTION 2 REVIEW

1. Identify two features of roundworms and rotifers that flatworms do not have.

2. How are the roundworms of the genus *Ascaris* transmitted from one host to another?

3. Describe one parasitic adaptation of a roundworm.

4. What is the function of the cilia found on the anterior end of a rotifer?

**CRITICAL THINKING**

5. **Inferring Relationships** How are parasites able to recognize their hosts?

6. **Applying Concepts** Based on what you have learned about the life cycle of roundworms, recommend a method of preventing the transmission of parasitic roundworms.

7. **Analyzing Graphics** Study Figure 34-10. Suggest a function of the projections at the posterior end of the rotifer.

# CHAPTER HIGHLIGHTS

## Platyhelminthes

- The phylum Platyhelminthes is made up of flatworms, the simplest animals that have bilateral symmetry. Flatworms have three germ layers and are acoelomates.

- Most flatworms have a gut with a single opening, called a gastrovascular cavity. These cephalized animals also have excretory, nervous, and reproductive systems.

- The class Turbellaria consists mostly of nonparasitic flatworms, including the freshwater planarian. Planarians are sexually reproducing hermaphrodites that can also reproduce asexually by splitting in two and regenerating the missing parts.

- The classes Trematoda and Monogenea consist of parasitic flukes. Fluke life cycles include two types of hosts: a primary host, from which the adults derive their nourishment, and an intermediate host, from which the larvae derive their nourishment.

- The class Cestoda consists of parasitic tapeworms. Tapeworms do not have a digestive system, so they absorb nutrients through their body surface. Tapeworms have a series of body sections called proglottids, each of which contains reproductive structures. Tapeworm life cycles involve primary and intermediate hosts.

### Vocabulary

pharynx (p. 690)
flame cell (p. 690)
cerebral ganglion (p. 691)
eyespot (p. 691)
fluke (p. 691)
tegument (p. 692)
primary host (p. 692)
intermediate host (p. 692)
schistosomiasis (p. 693)
scolex (p. 693)
proglottid (p. 693)
cyst (p. 694)

## Nematoda and Rotifera

- The phylum Nematoda consists of roundworms. Most roundworms are free-living, but some are parasites of plants and animals.

- Nematodes are pseudocoelomates. They have a hollow, fluid-filled cavity called a pseudocoelom between the mesoderm and the endoderm. They also have a digestive tract with an anterior mouth and posterior anus.

- Ascarid worms infect people who consume food or water containing eggs of the genus *Ascaris*. The eggs develop into larvae that migrate through the body and mature in the intestines.

- Hookworm larvae in the soil burrow through a person's feet. The larvae migrate through the body and mature in the intestines.

- Trichina worms infect people who consume undercooked meat containing cysts of the genus *Trichinella*. The cysts release larvae that burrow into the intestinal wall and develop into adults.

- Pinworms live in the lower intestine and lay eggs on the skin around the anus. After being transmitted by the hands to other objects, the eggs may be ingested. They then hatch in the intestine, where the worms mature.

- Filarial worms include species that live in the human lymphatic system. Their larvae are transmitted between hosts by mosquitoes.

- Rotifers are pseudocoelomates, and most rotifers are free-living in fresh water. The cilia surrounding a rotifer's mouth sweeps food into its digestive tract.

### Vocabulary

roundworm (p. 695)
cuticle (p. 695)
hookworm (p. 696)
trichinosis (p. 697)
pinworm (p. 697)
filarial worm (p. 697)
elephantiasis (p. 697)
rotifer (p. 698)
mastax (p. 698)
cloaca (p. 698)
parthenogenesis (p. 698)

## USING VOCABULARY

1. For each pair of terms, explain how the meanings of the terms differ.
   a. *tegument* and *cuticle*
   b. *primary host* and *intermediate host*
   c. *schistosomiasis* and *trichinosis*
   d. *anus* and *cloaca*
   e. *scolex* and *mastax*

2. Choose the term that does not belong in the following group, and explain why it does not belong: *eyespot*, *flame cell*, *gastrovascular cavity*, and *proglottid*.

3. Explain the relationship between *proglottid* and *cyst*.

4. **Word Roots and Origins** The word part *roti-* means "wheel," and the suffix *-fera* means "bearer." Using this information, explain why *Rotifera* is a good name for the phylum of organisms it describes.

## UNDERSTANDING KEY CONCEPTS

5. **Explain** how a flatworm can survive without a circulatory system or a respiratory system.

6. **Describe** the nervous system of a planarian.

7. **Summarize** reproduction in planarians.

8. **Sequence** the following steps in the schistosome life cycle in the correct order, beginning with the first step after sexual reproduction.
   a. Tailed larvae swim through the water.
   b. Ciliated larvae swim through the water.
   c. Larvae penetrate the skin of a human.
   d. Larvae reproduce asexually in the intermediate host.
   e. Larvae burrow into a snail.
   f. Larvae enter a blood vessel and develop into adults.
   g. Fertilized eggs leave the primary host in the feces or urine.

9. **Compare** a primary host to an intermediate host.

10. **Identify** some adaptations of flukes to a parasitic way of life.

11. **Explain** how tapeworms are specialized for a parasitic way of life.

12. **Relate** how a person can avoid becoming infected by a beef tapeworm.

13. **Compare** the body plan of a nematode to that of a flatworm.

14. **Name** some features shared by roundworms and rotifers.

15. **Describe** feeding and digestion in a rotifer.

16. **CONCEPT MAPPING** Use the following terms to create a concept map that shows the major characteristics of the phylum Nematoda: *roundworms, pseudocoelomates, digestive tract, cuticle, free-living, water, parasites, separate sexes,* and *eggs.*

## CRITICAL THINKING

17. **Applying Information** The Aswan High Dam across the Nile River in Egypt was completed in 1970. The dam was built to increase the supply of irrigation water, control major flooding, and provide a source of hydroelectric power. Since the dam was built, however, there has been an increase in the incidence of schistosomiasis in the region. Why do you think this has happened?

18. **Distinguishing Relevant Information** A person infected with a tapeworm may show symptoms such as tiredness, loss of weight, and anemia, which could indicate any number of diseases. How might a doctor be certain that the symptoms are caused by a tapeworm?

19. **Recognizing Relationships** Hookworm infections are extremely common in China, where rice is grown in paddies that are periodically flooded. Considering what you know about how hookworms invade the human body, why do you think hookworm infections are so common in this part of the world?

20. **Analyzing Patterns** Some rotifers can survive being dried out for as long as four years. When they are placed in water again, they revive. For what kind of environment might this characteristic be adaptive?

21. **Interpreting Graphics** Identify the animal in the photograph below. Give reasons for your choice.

# Standardized Test Preparation

**DIRECTIONS:** Choose the letter that best answers the question.

1. What does a planarian use its pharynx for?
   **A.** feeding
   **B.** movement
   **C.** reproduction
   **D.** to respond to light

2. Where do blood flukes of the genus *Schistosoma* reproduce asexually?
   **F.** in water
   **G.** inside a snail
   **H.** inside a cow's intestine
   **J.** inside a human's blood vessels

3. What does a tapeworm use its scolex for?
   **A.** to reproduce
   **B.** to attach itself to its host
   **C.** to eliminate excess water
   **D.** to force food into its mouth

4. Which of the following is true of most rotifers?
   **F.** They are parasitic.
   **G.** They live in the soil.
   **H.** They feed with the help of cilia.
   **J.** They have a gastrovascular cavity.

**INTERPRETING GRAPHICS:** The figure below shows the internal structure of a planarian of the genus *Dugesia*. Use the figure to answer the questions that follow.

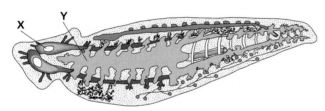

5. What type of animal is shown in the figure?
   **A.** flatworm
   **B.** tapeworm
   **C.** roundworm
   **D.** rotifer

6. What is the structure labeled *X*?
   **F.** the brain
   **G.** the mouth
   **H.** an eyespot
   **J.** a nerve cord

7. What is the structure labeled *Y*?
   **A.** the mouth
   **B.** a flame cell
   **C.** an eyespot
   **D.** the gastrovascular cavity

**DIRECTIONS:** Complete the following analogy.

8. fluke : schistosomiasis :: filarial worm :
   **F.** trichinosis
   **G.** elephantiasis
   **H.** encysted meat
   **J.** swimmer's itch

**INTERPRETING GRAPHICS:** The figure below shows the internal structure of a rotifer. Use the figure to answer the question that follows.

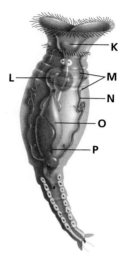

9. Which structures are involved in excretion?
   **A.** K and L
   **B.** L and O
   **C.** M and N
   **D.** M and P

## SHORT RESPONSE

Planarians and rotifers eliminate water through a network of excretory structures that run the length of the body.

Explain why the excretory structures in planarians and rotifers are called flame cells.

## EXTENDED RESPONSE

Parasitic flatworms have life cycles that include primary and intermediate hosts.

*Part A* Distinguish between primary and intermediate hosts in flatworms.

*Part B* Sequence the life cycle of a beef tapeworm. Identify the primary and intermediate hosts.

**Test TIP** Take the time to read each question completely on a standardized test, including all the answer choices. Consider each possible choice before determining which answer is correct.

# Observing Flatworm Responses to Stimuli

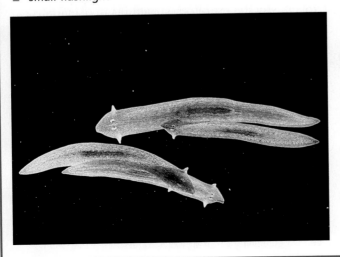

## Background

1. What are some characteristics of the phylum Platyhelminthes?
2. *Dugesia,* a planarian, is a nonparasitic flatworm belonging to the class Turbellaria. What are some characteristics of this class?
3. What is meant by cephalization, and why is it an important evolutionary advance?
4. What structures does a planarian have that enable it to sense light? Where are these structures located?

### PART A  Observing a Flatworm

1. **CAUTION  You will be working with a live animal. Be sure to treat it gently and to follow directions carefully.** Use a medicine dropper to transfer one flatworm to a small culture dish. Gently cover the flatworm with water from the culture jar. Why should you use water from the culture jar instead of tap water?
2. Examine the flatworm under the low-power setting of the stereomicroscope. Notice the shape of its body. What kind of symmetry does it have? What structural features demonstrate this symmetry? Does the flatworm appear to have a distinct head and tail? How can you tell?
3. Observe how the flatworm moves. Look at the surface of the flatworm under high power. Can you see any structures that could account for its movement?

### PART B  Response to Touch

4. In your lab report, make a data table like the one shown. Predict the behavior you think will occur to each type of stimulus. As you complete the following steps, record your observations of the flatworm in your data table.
5. **CAUTION  Touch the flatworm gently.** Using a blunt probe, gently touch the posterior end of the flatworm. Notice its response. Now gently touch its anterior end. How does the response compare? What can you conclude from your observations?

## PART C  Feeding Behavior

6. Place a tiny piece of raw liver in the culture dish. Observe the flatworm for several minutes and describe its feeding response in your data table. Why is it important to use flatworms that have not been recently fed?

7. After several minutes, use the probe to gently turn the flatworm over. What do you observe? If you have time, watch as the flatworm eats the liver. Where do you think the undigested waste will come out?

## PART D  Response to Gravity

8. With a wax pencil, draw a line around the middle of a test tube.

9. Fill the test tube almost full with water from the culture jar. Then use a medicine dropper to transfer one flatworm to the test tube. Seal the test tube with a stopper.

10. Hold the test tube horizontally and move it slowly back and forth until the flatworm is centered on the line you drew.

11. To test whether the flatworm can sense gravity, place the test tube vertically in the test-tube rack. Which way should the flatworm move to show a positive response to gravity? Observe the flatworm for several minutes. Use a stopwatch to measure the amount of time the flatworm spends above the line and below the line. Record the times in your data table.

## PART E  Response to Light

12. Check the lighting in the room. The light must be low and even during this part of the investigation.

13. Using a piece of aluminum foil, make a cover that is big enough to fit over the bottom half of the test tube

you used in Part D. Set the cover aside. Place the test tube horizontally on a white sheet of paper. Make sure the test tube is level. Why is it important for the test tube to be level in this experiment?

14. Position the flashlight so that it will shine directly on the test tube, but do not turn it on.

15. Wait for the flatworm to move to the center line. Then gently place the foil cover over the bottom half of the test tube, and turn the flashlight on. Which way should the flatworm move to show a positive response to light? Observe the movements of the flatworm. Use the stopwatch to measure the amount of time the flatworm spends in each half of the test tube. Record the times in your data table.

16. Return the flatworm to the culture jar. Then clean up your materials, and wash your hands before leaving the lab.

## Analysis and Conclusions

1. What evidence does the flatworm show of cephalization?

2. The flatworm has an incomplete digestive system and no circulatory system. How do you think a flatworm's food gets to the cells after it is digested?

3. How does the flatworm respond to gravity? Is the response positive or negative?

4. How does the flatworm respond to light? Is the response positive or negative?

5. Are the flatworm's anterior and posterior ends equally sensitive to light?

## Further Inquiry

Design an experiment to study the responses of flatworms to other stimuli, such as vibrations or sound.

### OBSERVATIONS OF FLATWORM BEHAVIOR

| Behavior | Predictions | Observations |
|---|---|---|
| Response to touch with blunt probe | | |
| Feeding behavior | | |
| Response to gravity | | |
| Response to light | | |

# MOLLUSKS AND ANNELIDS

This Caribbean reef octopus, *Octopus briareus*, is an active predator with a complex brain.

**SECTION 1** *Mollusca*

**SECTION 2** *Annelida*

# MOLLUSCA

*Despite their very different appearances, invertebrates such as clams, snails, slugs, and octopuses belong to the same phylum, Mollusca (muh-LUHS-kuh). Members of this phylum are called mollusks, a name that comes from the Latin molluscus, which means "soft." Although some mollusks have soft bodies, most have a hard shell that protects them.*

## CHARACTERISTICS OF MOLLUSKS

The phylum Mollusca is a diverse group of more than 112,000 species. Among animals, only the phylum Arthropoda has more species. Some mollusks are sedentary filter feeders, while others are fast-moving predators with complex nervous systems.

Mollusks are among several phyla of animals known as *coelomates*. Coelomates are so named because they have a true coelom, a hollow, fluid-filled cavity that is completely surrounded by mesoderm. Coelomates differ from pseudocoelomates, such as roundworms, which have a body cavity lined by mesoderm on the outside and endoderm on the inside.

A coelom has several advantages over a pseudocoelom. With a coelom, the muscles of the body wall are separated from those of the gut. Therefore, the body wall muscles can contract without hindering the movement of food through the gut. A coelom also provides a space where the circulatory system can transport blood without interference from other internal organs. The coelomate body plan is shared by annelids, which are discussed in the second half of this chapter, and by three other major phyla of animals: arthropods, echinoderms, and chordates, which include humans.

Another feature that is shared by most aquatic mollusks and annelids is a larval stage of development called a **trochophore** (TRAHK-oh-FAWR), illustrated in Figure 35-1. In some species, the trochophore hatches from the egg case and exists as a free-swimming larva. Cilia on the surface of a free-swimming trochophore propel the larva through the water and draw food into its mouth. As free-swimming trochophores are carried by ocean currents and tides, they contribute to the dispersal of their species. The presence of a trochophore in mollusks and annelids suggests that these two groups of animals may have evolved from a common ancestor.

**FIGURE 35-1**

A trochophore is a larva that develops from the fertilized egg of most mollusks and annelids. Cilia at both ends and in the middle propel free-swimming trochophores through the water.

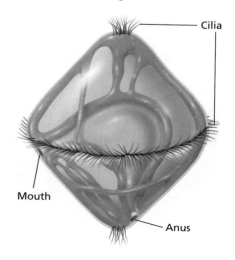

Cilia

Mouth

Anus

FIGURE 35-2

In the basic body plan of a mollusk, the body is divided into the head-foot and the visceral mass, which contains the internal organs. Covering the visceral mass is the mantle, which secretes the shell.

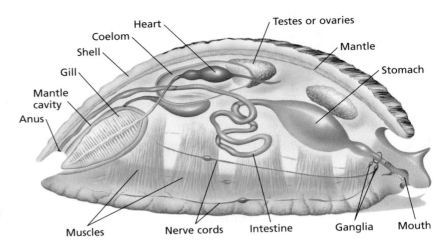

Visceral mass

Head-foot

FIGURE 35-3

Inside the mouth (a), many mollusks have a radula, a band of tissue covered with teeth that can scrape food from other surfaces. The SEM in (b) shows the sharp edges of these teeth (600×).

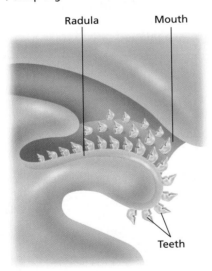

(a)

(b)

# BODY PLAN OF MOLLUSKS

Figure 35-2 shows that the body of a mollusk is generally divided into two main regions: the head-foot and the visceral mass. As its name suggests, the head-foot consists of the head, which contains the mouth and a variety of sensory structures, and the foot, a large, muscular organ usually used for locomotion. Above the head-foot is the **visceral** (VIS-uhr-uhl) **mass,** which contains the heart and the organs of digestion, excretion, and reproduction. As shown in Figure 35-2, the coelom is limited to a space around the heart. Covering the visceral mass is a layer of epidermis called the **mantle.**

In most mollusks, the mantle secretes one or more hard shells containing calcium carbonate. Although shells protect the soft bodies of mollusks from predators, they also reduce the surface area available for gas exchange. This disadvantage is offset by another structural adaptation: gills. Gills provide a large surface area that is in contact with a rich supply of blood. In this way, gills are specialized for the exchange of gases. Figure 35-2 also shows that the delicate gills of mollusks are protected within the **mantle cavity,** a space between the mantle and the visceral mass.

Unlike many coelomates, mollusks do not have segmented bodies. Like flatworms and roundworms, most mollusks are bilaterally symmetrical. This symmetry is apparent in the nervous system, which consists of paired clusters of nerve cells called **ganglia.** The ganglia are situated in the head-foot and visceral mass and are connected by two pairs of long nerve cords. Nerve cells in the ganglia control the muscles involved in locomotion and feeding and process sensory information from specialized cells that respond to light, touch, and chemicals in the environment.

The main feeding adaptation of many mollusks is the **radula** (RAJ-u-luh). As Figure 35-3 shows, in most species the radula is a flexible, tonguelike strip of tissue covered with tough, abrasive teeth that point backward. Through evolution, the radula has become adapted for a variety of functions in different mollusks.

**TABLE 35-1 Features of Three Classes of Mollusks**

| Class | External shell | Head | Radula | Locomotion |
|---|---|---|---|---|
| Gastropoda | one (most species) | yes | yes | crawling (most) |
| Bivalvia | two | no | no | sessile (most) |
| Cephalopoda | none (most species) | yes | yes | rapid swimming |

Terrestrial snails use the radula to cut through the leaves of garden plants, while aquatic snails use it to scrape up algae or to drill holes in the shells of other mollusks. The cone shell has a harpoon-shaped radula with which it captures fish and injects venom.

Most biologists use structural differences to divide mollusks into seven classes. Three of these classes are discussed below: class Gastropoda (gas-TRAHP-uh-duh), class Bivalvia (bie-VALV-ee-uh), and class Cephalopoda (SEF-uh-LAHP-uh-duh). Table 35-1 summarizes the major features of these three classes.

**Word Roots and Origins**

*gastropod*

from the Greek *gaster,* meaning "stomach," and *pous,* meaning "foot"

# CLASS GASTROPODA

The largest and most diverse class of mollusks is Gastropoda, whose members are called **gastropods** (GAS-troh-PAHDZ). Most of the 40,000 species of gastropods, including snails, abalones, and conchs, have a single shell. Others, such as slugs and nudibranchs, have no shell at all.

Gastropods undergo a process called *torsion* during larval development. During torsion, the visceral mass twists around 180 degrees in relation to the head. This twisting brings the mantle cavity, gills, and anus to the front of the animal, as shown in Figure 35-4. Because of torsion, a gastropod can withdraw its head into its mantle cavity when threatened. Coiling of the shell is unrelated to torsion.

Wavelike muscular contractions of the foot move gastropods smoothly over surfaces. You can see these contractions if you look closely at the underside of a snail or slug as it crawls across a windowpane or the side of an aquarium.

Gastropods have an open circulatory system, meaning that the circulatory fluid, called **hemolymph,** does not remain entirely within vessels. Instead, it is collected from the gills or lungs, pumped through the heart, and released directly into spaces in the tissues. These fluid-filled spaces compose what is known as a **hemocoel** (HEE-moh-SEEL), or blood cavity. From the hemocoel, the hemolymph returns via the gills or lungs to the heart.

**FIGURE 35-4**

In a gastropod, such as this snail, the mantle cavity, anus, and gills are near the head as a result of torsion during development.

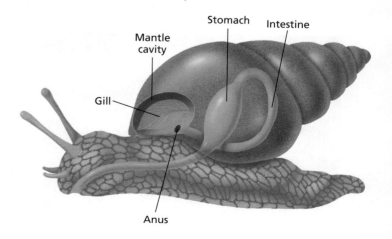

Stomach

Intestine

Mantle cavity

Gill

Anus

**FIGURE 35-5**

The extensions on the back of this horned nudibranch, *Hermissenda crassicornia*, provide a large surface area for gas exchange.

## Snails

Snails are gastropods that live on land, in fresh water, and in the ocean. Two eyes at the end of delicate tentacles on the head help most snails locate food. If danger arises, the tentacles retract into the head. Aquatic snails respire through gills in the mantle cavity. In land snails, the mantle cavity acts as a modified lung that exchanges oxygen and carbon dioxide with the air. The thin membrane lining the mantle cavity must be kept moist to allow gases to diffuse through it. For this reason, land snails are most active when the air has a high moisture content. Snails survive dry periods by becoming inactive and retreating into their shells. They seal the opening to their shell with a mucous plug, which keeps them from drying out.

## Other Gastropods

Slugs are terrestrial gastropods that look like snails without shells. Like land snails, slugs respire through the lining of their mantle cavity. They avoid drying out by hiding in moist, shady places by day and feeding at night.

Nudibranchs (NOO-di-BRANGKS), such as the one in Figure 35-5, are marine gastropods that lack shells. *Nudibranch* means "naked gill," which refers to the fact that gas exchange occurs across the entire body surface of these animals. The surface of most nudibranchs is covered with numerous ruffles or delicate, fingerlike extensions that increase the total area available for gas exchange.

Some gastropods show unusual adaptations of the foot. In pteropods, or "sea butterflies," for example, the foot is modified into a winglike flap that is used for swimming rather than crawling.

Gastropods show great diversity in their reproduction. Many species have separate sexes, but hermaphrodites are common among aquatic and terrestrial gastropods.

**FIGURE 35-6**

The two valves that make up the hinged shell of a bivalve can separate, allowing water to circulate through the animal. Some bivalves, such as this scallop, of the genus *Argopecten*, have a row of eyes near the outer margin of each valve.

# CLASS BIVALVIA

Members of the class Bivalvia include aquatic mollusks, such as clams, oysters, and scallops. These mollusks are called **bivalves** because, as Figure 35-6 shows, their shell is divided into two halves, or valves, connected by a hinge. A bivalve can close its shell by contracting the powerful adductor muscles that are attached to the inside surface of each valve. When the adductor muscles relax, the valves open.

Each valve consists of three layers that are secreted by the mantle. The thin outer layer protects the shell against acidic conditions in the water. The thick middle layer of calcium carbonate strengthens the shell. The smooth, shiny inner layer protects the animal's soft body.

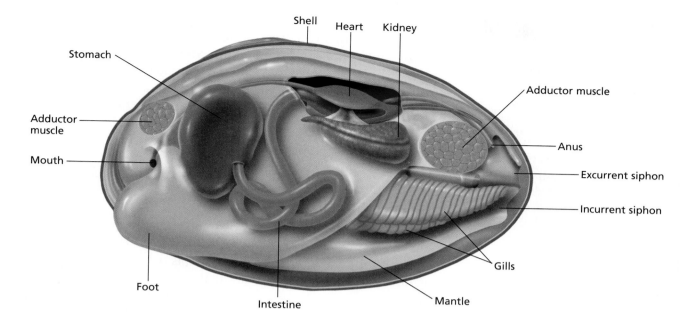

Stomach

Adductor muscle

Mouth

Foot

Intestine

Shell   Heart   Kidney

Adductor muscle

Anus

Excurrent siphon

Incurrent siphon

Gills

Mantle

In contrast with gastropods, which move about in search of food, most bivalves are sessile. Some species extend their muscular foot into the sand and fill the foot with hemolymph to form a hatchet-shaped anchor. The muscles of the foot then contract, pulling the animal down into the sand. As an adaptation for a sessile existence, bivalves usually are filter feeders. They are the only mollusks without a radula.

Bivalves lack a distinct head. Their nervous system consists of three pairs of ganglia: one pair near the mouth, another pair in the digestive system, and the third pair in the foot. The ganglia are connected by nerve cords. Nerve cells in the ganglia receive information from sensory cells in the edge of the mantle that respond to touch or to chemicals in the water. Some bivalves also have a row of small eyes along each mantle edge. Stimuli detected by these sensory structures can trigger nerve impulses that cause the foot to withdraw and the shell to close.

## Clams

Clams are bivalves that live buried in mud or sand. The mantle cavity of a clam is sealed except for a pair of hollow, fleshy tubes called *siphons,* which you can see in Figure 35-7. Cilia beating on the gills set up a current of water that enters through the **incurrent siphon** and leaves through the **excurrent siphon.** As the water circulates inside the clam, the gills filter small organisms and organic debris from the water. The filtered material becomes trapped on the gills in a sticky mucus that moves in a continuous stream toward the mouth. Water passing over the gills also exchanges oxygen and carbon dioxide with the hemolymph.

Most species of clams have separate sexes. Marine clams reproduce by shedding sperm and eggs into the water, and fertilization occurs externally. The fertilized egg becomes a trochophore that eventually settles to the bottom and develops into an adult.

**FIGURE 35-7**

In this illustration, one valve has been omitted to show a clam's anatomy. The internal structure of a clam is typical of most bivalves.

### Describing a Mollusk

**Materials** 2–3 bivalve shells, colored pencils, paper

**Procedure**
1. Using colored pencils, draw a bivalve shell on a sheet of paper.
2. Use Figure 35-7 to help you locate and label the adductor muscle scars, the mantle cavity, and the hinge area on the bivalve.

**Analysis** Describe the shell of the bivalve, including its color, its ridges, the appearance and texture of the mantle, and the location of the hinge area.

In some clam species, adults may weigh 200 kg (440 lb) and be more than 1 m (3.3 ft) across. In most freshwater clams, eggs are fertilized internally by sperm that enter through the incurrent siphon. The larvae that develop are discharged into the water through the excurrent siphon. If they contact a passing fish, they may live as parasites on its gills or skin for several weeks before settling to the bottom.

## Other Bivalves

Oysters are bivalves that become permanently attached to a hard surface early in their development. Some are grown commercially as food or as sources of cultured pearls. Scallops can move through the water by repeatedly opening their valves and snapping them shut. This motion expels bursts of water, creating a form of jet propulsion. The teredo, or shipworm, is one of the few bivalves that does not filter-feed. Instead, it bores into driftwood or ship timbers and ingests the particles that are produced by the drilling. The wood cellulose is broken down by symbiotic bacteria that live in the shipworm's intestine.

# CLASS CEPHALOPODA

Members of the class Cephalopoda include octopuses, squids, cuttlefishes, and chambered nautiluses. These marine mollusks are called **cephalopods** (SEF-uh-loh-PAHDZ), a term that means "head-foot." Cephalopods are specialized for a free-swimming, predatory existence. Extending from the head is a circle of tentacles, as you can see in Figure 35-8. The tentacles' powerful suction cups allow cephalopods to grasp objects and capture prey. Cephalopods kill and eat their prey with the help of a pair of jaws that resemble a parrot's beak.

The nervous system is more advanced in cephalopods than in any other group of mollusks. The cephalopod brain, which is the largest of any invertebrate brain, is divided into several lobes and contains millions of nerve cells. Octopuses, for example, can learn to perform tasks and discriminate between objects on the basis of their shape or texture. The sensory systems of cephalopods are also well developed. Most cephalopods have complex eyes that form images. The tentacles contain numerous cells that sense chemicals in the water.

Cephalopods have a closed circulatory system. Closed circulatory systems transport fluid more rapidly than open circulatory systems do. Thus, nutrients, oxygen, and carbon dioxide are carried quickly through the body of these highly active animals. Cephalopods also have separate sexes. The male uses a specialized tentacle to transfer packets of sperm from his mantle cavity to the mantle cavity of the female, where fertilization occurs. The female lays a mass of fertilized eggs and guards the eggs until they hatch. Unlike other mollusks, cephalopods develop from an egg into a juvenile without becoming a trochophore.

**FIGURE 35-8**

Most of the body of cephalopods is made up of a large head attached to tentacles. The tentacles of cephalopods, such as this cuttlefish, *Sepia latimanus*, surround their mouth. The streamlined body of many cephalopods enables them to swim rapidly in pursuit of prey.

Many cephalopods can release a dark fluid into the water to temporarily distract predators. They also have pigment cells called *chromatophores* (kroh-MAT-uh-FAWHRZ), which are located in the outer layer of the mantle. Chromatophores can produce a sudden change in the color of a cephalopod, allowing the animal to blend in with its surroundings.

## Squids

Squids are cephalopods with ten tentacles. The longest two tentacles are used for capturing prey, and the other eight tentacles force the prey into the squid's mouth. The muscular mantle propels the squid swiftly through the water by pumping jets of water through an excurrent siphon. Most squids grow to about 30 cm (1 ft) in length, but a few species can be much longer. The giant squid, *Architeuthis,* may reach a length of 18 m (about 60 ft) and a weight of more than 900 kg (about 1 ton). *Architeuthis* is the world's largest known invertebrate.

internet connect

www.scilinks.org
**Topic:** Squids
**Keyword:** HM61446

*SCiLINKS.* Maintained by the National Science Teachers Association

## Octopuses

Octopuses have eight tentacles and share many characteristics with squids, including their methods of escaping from predators. Instead of using jet propulsion to chase prey, however, octopuses are more likely to crawl along the ocean bottom with their tentacles or lie in wait in caves and rock crevices. Octopuses average 1 m (3.3 ft) or less in length, although the giant Pacific octopus may grow to a length of 9 m (about 30 ft).

## Chambered Nautiluses

Squids and cuttlefish have small internal shells. The chambered nautilus, shown in Figure 35-9, is the only existing cephalopod that has retained its external shell. The nautilus shell is coiled and divided into a series of gas-filled chambers separated by partitions. The soft body of the nautilus is confined to the outermost chamber. As the nautilus grows, it moves forward in its shell, makes a new partition, and fills the chamber behind the partition with gas. The gas makes the nautilus buoyant.

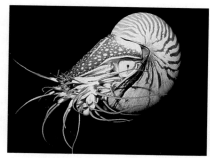

**FIGURE 35-9**

Although cephalopods evolved from shelled ancestors, the chambered nautilus is the only living cephalopod species with an external shell.

---

## SECTION 1 REVIEW

1. What is one advantage of a true coelom over a pseudocoelom?

2. In which phyla of animals is the larval trochophore stage found?

3. For what purpose is a radula used?

4. Why are land snails more active when the air around them is moist?

5. Compare the circulatory systems of each of the three major classes of mollusks.

**CRITICAL THINKING**

6. **Analyzing Concepts** Suggest why an open circulatory system is sufficient to meet the needs of a gastropod.

7. **Making Comparisons** Compare the adaptations of clams and squids and relate them to lifestyle.

8. **Inferring Relationships** Which features of bivalves indicate that they are bilaterally symmetrical?

# LEECHES: New Uses for an Old Remedy

**W**hy are leeches called *bloodsuckers*? Do they really suck blood? Yes, they do, and their role as bloodsuckers could help save your life.

For centuries, leeches were used in medical practice. In the second century C.E., the Greek physician Galen described the use of leeches in removing blood from patients in a procedure called *bloodletting*. An excess of blood in the body was believed to be responsible for a variety of illnesses, from headaches and fevers to heart disease. Physicians used the leeches to remove this "bad blood" from a patient's body.

Bloodletting was common in Europe through the early 1800s. During the late 19th century, however, medical science discredited the idea that excess blood causes disease, and bloodletting fell out of favor.

### Uses in Microsurgery

Leeches are making a comeback in medicine, although with new purposes. One of these purposes is to increase the success rate of surgical operations to reattach severed limbs, fingers, ears, or toes. Such operations involve microsurgery, a process in which surgeons reconnect tendons, blood vessels, and nerves by using tiny instruments and powerful microscopes. However, in some microsurgery, physicians cannot reconnect tiny, delicate blood vessels. As a result, circulation in the reattached limb, finger, or toe is impaired.

The tissues may become congested with blood. If congestion occurs, the tissues of the reattached part will not heal and will eventually die.

One solution to this congestion problem is to place leeches on the reattached body part. Once attached to the wound site, the leeches begin to suck out the accumulated blood, relieving congestion and allowing the tissues to remain healthy until the veins can grow back. At about $10 each, leeches are a relatively inexpensive treatment for a serious problem.

### Uses as Anticoagulants

Leeches have medical uses that go beyond their ability to remove blood. Scientists have known since the 1800s that leech saliva contains a powerful anticoagulant, a substance that inhibits blood clotting. The leech's anticoagulant, called *hirudin,* can cause four hours or more of steady bleeding.

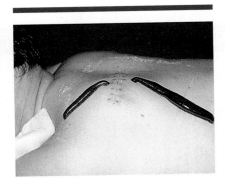

*Leeches have been applied to this patient's sutures across his upper back to reduce blood congestion. Each leech can remove up to 5 mL of blood.*

The steady bleeding helps prevent blood from clotting so the leech can feed freely.

### New Applications

Today, hirudin is made through genetic engineering, without the aid of leeches. It has proven useful in the treatment of some heart patients, particularly those who have had heart attacks, who suffer from angina, or who have undergone angioplasty, a procedure to open blocked arteries. One research study even indicated that hirudin may be effective against the spread of cancer.

The amazing uses that have been found for a substance in leech saliva are encouraging to medical researchers, who continue to explore how knowledge of invertebrate organisms can be beneficially combined with medical technology.

### REVIEW

1. Outline how leeches help surgeons in microsurgery.
2. Identify three potential new applications of hirudin.
3. **Critical Thinking** Why is hirudin now made by genetic engineering instead of being taken directly from leeches?

# ANNELIDA

*Colorful feather-duster worms, common earthworms, and bloodsucking leeches are all members of the phylum Annelida (uh-NEL-i-duh). An animal in this phylum is called an* annelid *(AN-uh-LID), a term that means "little rings." The name refers to the many body segments that make an annelid look as if it is composed of a series of rings.*

## CHARACTERISTICS OF ANNELIDS

The phylum Annelida consists of about 15,000 species of bilaterally symmetrical, segmented worms. Segmentation is the most distinctive feature of annelids. Like mollusks, annelids have a true coelom, but the coelom in annelids is divided into separate compartments by partitions. Division of the coelom represents an evolutionary advance over the earliest wormlike coelomates. In an undivided coelom, the force of muscle contraction in one part of the body is transmitted to other parts by the fluid in the coelom. A segmented coelom enables different parts of the body to contract or expand independently. In addition, duplication of some of the organ systems in each segment provides a form of insurance against injury. If one segment becomes disabled, the others can still function.

Most annelids have external bristles called **setae** (SEET-ee) (singular, *seta*), and some have fleshy protrusions called **parapodia** (PAR-uh-POH-dee-uh) (singular, *parapodium*). Both of these structures are visible in Figure 35-10. The number of setae and the presence or absence of parapodia provide the basis for dividing annelids into three classes: Oligochaeta (AHL-uh-goh-KEET-uh), Polychaeta (PAHL-i-KEE-tuh), and Hirudinea (HIR-yoo-DIN-ee-uh). All organ systems are well developed in most members of each class.

## CLASS OLIGOCHAETA

Annelids of the class Oligochaeta generally live in the soil or in fresh water and have no parapodia. *Oligochaeta* means "few bristles," and as the name suggests, these annelids have a few setae on each segment. The most familiar member of the class Oligochaeta is the earthworm. As you read about the earthworm, look for adaptations that enable this animal to lead a burrowing life.

## SECTION 2

### OBJECTIVES

- **Identify** the structures that provide the basis for dividing annelids into three classes.
- **List** the advantages of body segmentation.
- **Describe** the structural adaptations of earthworms.
- **Compare** the three classes of annelids.

### VOCABULARY

seta
parapodium
crop
gizzard
typhlosole
aortic arch
nephridium
clitellum
seminal receptacle
chitin

**FIGURE 35-10**

Numerous setae help this bearded fireworm, *Hermodice carunculata*, move through its environment. The setae extend from fleshy flaps called *parapodia*. Also known as bristle worms, bearded fireworms are members of the class Polychaeta.

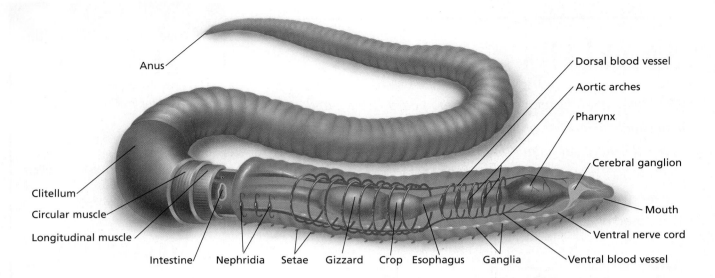

Anus

Dorsal blood vessel

Aortic arches

Pharynx

Cerebral ganglion

Mouth

Clitellum

Circular muscle

Longitudinal muscle

Ventral nerve cord

Ventral blood vessel

Intestine   Nephridia   Setae   Gizzard   Crop   Esophagus   Ganglia

**FIGURE 35-11**

The segmentation of annelids, such as this earthworm, is visible both externally and internally. Some of the internal structures, such as ganglia and nephridia, are repeated in each segment.

## Structure and Movement

An earthworm's body is divided into more than 100 segments, most of which are virtually identical. Figure 35-11 shows that circular and longitudinal muscles line the interior body wall of an earthworm. To move, the worm anchors some of the middle segments by their setae and contracts the circular muscles in front of those segments. Contraction of the circular muscles increases the pressure of the coelomic fluid in those segments. This increased pressure elongates the animal and pushes the anterior end forward. Setae in the anterior segments then grip the ground as the longitudinal muscles contract, pulling the posterior segments forward. This method of locomotion in earthworms is an example of the kind of movement made possible by segmentation.

## Feeding and Digestion

Earthworms ingest soil as they burrow through it. Soil is sucked into the mouth by the muscular pharynx. The soil then passes through a tube called the *esophagus* (ee-SAHF-uh-guhs) to a temporary storage area known as the **crop.** From the crop, the soil moves to a thick, muscular part of the gut called the **gizzard.** Find these parts of the digestive tract in Figure 35-11. The gizzard grinds the soil, releasing and breaking up organic matter. As the soil passes through the long intestine, digested organic compounds and nutrients in the soil are absorbed by the blood. An infolding of the intestinal wall called the **typhlosole** (TIF-luh-SOHL) increases the surface area available for digestion and absorption. Undigested material is eliminated from the earthworm's body through the anus.

Earthworms play an important role in maintaining the fertility of soil. By decomposing dead leaves and other organic materials, earthworms help release nutrients into the soil. The burrows made by earthworms allow air to penetrate into the soil, bringing oxygen to plant roots and soil microorganisms. Earthworms also loosen the soil, making it easier for roots to grow and for water to seep into the soil.

## Circulation

A closed circulatory system transports oxygen, carbon dioxide, nutrients, and wastes through the body of an earthworm. The blood travels toward the posterior end through a ventral blood vessel and then returns to the anterior end through a dorsal blood vessel. As you can see in Figure 35-11, five pairs of muscular tubes, the **aortic** (ay-AWR-tik) **arches,** link the dorsal and ventral blood vessels near the anterior end of the worm. Contractions of the dorsal blood vessel and the aortic arches force blood through the circulatory system.

## Respiration and Excretion

Oxygen and carbon dioxide diffuse directly through the skin, which contains many small blood vessels. This exchange of gases can take place only if the skin is moist. Therefore, earthworms avoid dry ground and extreme heat. Secretions of mucus and the presence of a thin cuticle also help keep an earthworm's skin moist.

Earthworms eliminate cellular wastes and excess water through excretory tubules called **nephridia** (nee-FRID-ee-uh), some of which are shown in Figure 35-11. Each segment, except the first three and the last one, contains a pair of nephridia. As coelomic fluid passes through the nephridia, some of the water is reabsorbed by blood vessels. The remaining fluid and the wastes dissolved in it are released from the body through pores on the ventral surface.

## Neural Control

The nervous system of an earthworm consists of a chain of ganglia connected by a ventral nerve cord. Most body segments contain a single ganglion. Nerves branching from each ganglion carry impulses to the muscles and from the sensory cells in that segment. In the most anterior segments, several ganglia are fused to form the cerebral ganglia, or brain, as you can see in Figure 35-11. One of the main functions of the cerebral ganglia is to process information from sensory structures that respond to light, touch, chemicals, moisture, temperature, and vibrations. Although these sensory structures are found in all segments, they are concentrated at the anterior end.

## Reproduction

Earthworms are hermaphrodites, but an individual worm cannot fertilize its own eggs. Mating occurs when two earthworms press their ventral surfaces together with their anterior ends pointing in opposite directions. The worms are held together by their setae and by a film of mucus secreted by each worm's **clitellum** (klie-TEL-uhm). The clitellum, also shown in Figure 35-11, is a thickened section of the body. Each earthworm injects sperm into the mucus. The sperm from each worm move through the mucus to the **seminal receptacle** of the other, where the sperm are stored. The worms then separate. After several days, the clitellum of each worm secretes a tube of mucus and a tough carbohydrate known as **chitin** (KIE-tin).

**Word Roots and Origins**

*nephridium*

from the Greek *nephros,* meaning "kidney," and *idion,* meaning "small"

As this tube slides forward, it picks up the worm's eggs and the stored sperm from the other worm. Fertilization occurs inside the tube, which closes up to form a protective case. The young worms develop inside the case for 2–3 weeks before hatching.

# CLASSES POLYCHAETA AND HIRUDINEA

About two-thirds of all annelids are members of the class Polychaeta. *Polychaeta* means "many bristles," which refers to the numerous setae that help polychaetes move. The setae project from parapodia, some of which function in gas exchange. Polychaetes differ from other annelids in that they have antennae and specialized mouthparts. They are also the only annelids that have a trochophore stage. Most polychaetes live in marine habitats. Some are free-swimming predators that use their strong jaws to feed on small animals. Others feed on sediment as they burrow through it or use their tentacles to scour the ocean bottom for food.

Hirudinea is the smallest class of annelids, consisting of about 500 species of leeches. Most leeches live in calm bodies of fresh water, but some species live among moist vegetation on land. Leeches have no setae or parapodia. At each end of a leech's body is a sucker that can attach to surfaces. By attaching the anterior sucker and then pulling the rest of the body forward, leeches can crawl along solid objects. Aquatic leeches can also swim with an undulating movement of their body. Many leeches are carnivores that prey on small invertebrates, but some species, including the one shown in Figure 35-12, are parasites that suck blood from other animals. After attaching themselves to the skin of their host, parasitic leeches secrete an anaesthetic that prevents the host from feeling their presence. They also secrete a substance that prevents blood from clotting. If undisturbed, a leech can ingest 10 times its own weight in blood.

**FIGURE 35-12**

The leech *Haemadipsa* sp. is a parasite that sucks blood from animals, including humans. Other leeches are free-living carnivores.

## SECTION 2 REVIEW

1. What are the advantages of a segmented body?

2. How are an earthworm's circular and longitudinal muscles used in locomotion?

3. How does an earthworm exchange oxygen and carbon dioxide with its environment?

4. How do polychaetes differ from earthworms?

5. Describe how some leeches are adapted to a parasitic lifestyle.

**CRITICAL THINKING**

6. **Analyzing Patterns** In earthworms, blood flows in opposite directions in the dorsal and ventral vessels. How is this helpful to the animal?

7. **Applying Information** Why do you see so many earthworms after a long rainy period?

8. **Recognizing Differences** How is the form of parasitism shown in some leeches different from that of a tapeworm or a liver fluke?

# CHAPTER HIGHLIGHTS

Mollusca

- Mollusks and annelids have true coeloms. Most aquatic mollusks and annelids develop from a trochophore.

- A mollusk's body is divided into the head-foot and the visceral mass, which contains the internal organs. Most mollusks have at least one shell, which is secreted by a layer of epidermis called the mantle. Aquatic mollusks have gills through which gas exchange takes place.

- The main feeding adaptation of most mollusks is the radula, a tonguelike structure that is modified in different species for scraping, drilling, or harpooning.

- Gastropods undergo torsion—the visceral mass twists during larval development. Snails and most other gastropods have a single shell, while some gastropods, such as slugs and nudibranchs, lack shells. Gastropods move by means of wavelike, muscular contractions of the foot and have an open circulatory system.

- Bivalves have a shell that is divided into two valves, which can be pulled together by contracting powerful adductor muscles. Bivalves lack a distinct head and have no radula. Most are sessile and filter food from the water. In clams, water enters through an incurrent siphon and exits through an excurrent siphon. Food is strained from the water as it passes through the gills.

- Cephalopods, including octopuses and squids, are free-swimming, predatory mollusks with numerous tentacles. They have an advanced nervous system with a large brain and well-developed sensory organs. Cephalopods have a closed circulatory system and do not pass through a trochophore stage during development.

### Vocabulary

trochophore (p. 705)
visceral mass (p. 706)
mantle (p. 706)
mantle cavity (p. 706)

ganglion (p. 706)
radula (p. 706)
gastropod (p. 707)
hemolymph (p. 707)

hemocoel (p. 707)
bivalve (p. 708)
incurrent siphon (p. 709)
excurrent siphon (p. 709)

cephalopod (p. 710)

Annelida

- Annelids have a true coelom and a body that is divided into many segments. Most annelids have external bristles called *setae,* and some have fleshy protrusions called *parapodia.*

- The number of setae and the presence or absence of parapodia provide the basis for dividing annelids into three classes: Oligochaeta, Polychaeta, and Hirudinea.

- Segmentation enables the different parts of the body to carry out various functions independently. It also protects the organism in case of injury because uninjured segments can continue to function.

- Members of the class Oligochaeta generally live in the soil or in fresh water. They have no parapodia and relatively few setae.

- The most familiar member of the class Oligochaeta is the earthworm, which feeds on organic matter as it burrows through the soil. Earthworms have a closed circulatory system. They exchange gases through their skin and eliminate cellular wastes and excess water through excretory tubules called *nephridia.*

- Polychaetes have numerous setae that project from parapodia. They also have antennae and specialized mouthparts, and they pass through a trochophore stage during their development. Most polychaetes live in the ocean.

- Members of the class Hirudinea, leeches live in fresh water or on land. They have no setae or parapodia. Many leeches are carnivores that prey on small invertebrates, but some are bloodsucking parasites.

### Vocabulary

seta (p. 713)
parapodium (p. 713)
crop (p. 714)

gizzard (p. 714)
typhlosole (p. 714)
aortic arch (p. 715)

nephridium (p. 715)
clitellum (p. 715)
seminal receptacle (p. 715)

chitin (p. 715)

# CHAPTER REVIEW

## USING VOCABULARY

1. For each pair of terms, explain how the meanings of the terms differ.
   a. *crop* and *gizzard*
   b. *gastropod* and *cephalopod*
   c. *setae* and *parapodia*
   d. *clitellum* and *seminal receptacle*
   e. *incurrent siphon* and *excurrent siphon*

2. Explain the relationship between *hemolymph* and *hemocoel*.

3. Choose the term that does not belong in the following group, and explain why it does not belong: *incurrent siphon, excurrent siphon, trochophore,* and *crop*.

4. **Word Roots and Origins** The word *chitin* is derived from the Greek *chiton,* meaning "tunic." Using this information, explain why the term *chitin* is a good name to describe this compound.

## UNDERSTANDING KEY CONCEPTS

5. **Identify** the functions performed by the cilia on a free-swimming trochophore.

6. **List** the main parts in the basic body plan of a mollusk.

7. **Describe** the main feeding adaptation of mollusks.

8. **Identify** whether or not each of the following mollusks has a shell: nudibranch, clam, snail, and slug.

9. **Compare** the body structure of a cephalopod to that of a gastropod.

10. **Distinguish** between polychaetes and other annelids. Which characteristics set polychaetes apart?

11. **Explain** how segmentation aids movement in earthworms.

12. **Summarize** why earthworms require a moist environment to survive.

13. **Describe** the organization of an earthworm's nervous system.

14. **Identify** a typical environment in which one member of each of the three classes of annelids may be found.

15. **Summarize** the characteristics shared by mollusks and annelids.

16. **CONCEPT MAPPING** Use the following terms to create a concept map that shows the major characteristics of the phylum Annelida: *annelids, segmented worms, coelomates, setae, parapodia, Oligochaeta, Polychaeta, Hirudinea, earthworm, bearded fireworm,* and *leech.*

## CRITICAL THINKING

17. **Applying Information** If a grain of sand or other irritant gets inside the shell of a bivalve, the mantle coats the irritant with the material that lines the inner layer of the shell. Many layers of this material form a pearl. However, making a pearl consumes resources that an oyster could use for other purposes, such as strengthening its shell. Of what advantage is it to an oyster to make a pearl?

18. **Inferring Relationships** Clams reproduce by releasing sperm and eggs into the water. How might this process affect the reproductive success of these mollusks? Would you expect clams to release many sperm and eggs or only a few?

19. **Making Comparisons** Clams are aquatic, and earthworms are terrestrial. Nevertheless, the feeding methods of clams and earthworms are somewhat similar. Explain how they are similar.

20. **Interpreting Graphics** The graph below plots the movement of the anterior end of an earthworm over time. Was the anterior end moving or stationary during the periods represented by the horizontal sections of the graph? Which of the earthworm's sets of muscles were contracting during the periods represented by the horizontal sections? Explain.

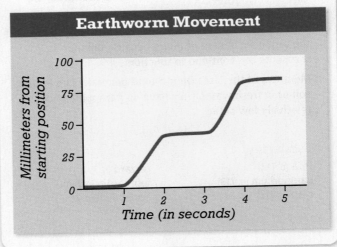

**Earthworm Movement**

*Millimeters from starting position* (y-axis: 0, 25, 50, 75, 100)

*Time (in seconds)* (x-axis: 1, 2, 3, 4, 5)

# Standardized Test Preparation

**DIRECTIONS:** Choose the letter of the answer choice that best answers the question.

1. Why do terrestrial snails and slugs need an environment with a high moisture content?
   A. to avoid drying out
   B. to see and hear better
   C. to swim more efficiently
   D. to avoid being eaten by birds

2. Which of the following are the only mollusks with a closed circulatory system?
   F. snails
   G. bivalves
   H. gastropods
   J. cephalopods

3. Annelids are divided into three classes based partly on the number of which of the following?
   A. setae
   B. segments
   C. nephridia
   D. aortic arches

4. Parapodia are a distinguishing characteristic of which class of annelids?
   F. Bivalvia
   G. Hirudinea
   H. Polychaeta
   J. Oligochaeta

**INTERPRETING GRAPHICS:** The diagram below shows the internal structure of a bivalve. Use the diagram to answer the questions that follow.

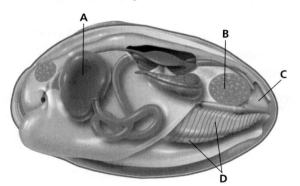

5. Which of the structures is involved in respiration and feeding?
   A. A
   B. B
   C. C
   D. D

6. What is structure B?
   F. a gill
   G. a siphon
   H. the mantle
   J. an adductor muscle

**DIRECTIONS:** Complete the following analogy.

7. Nephridium : excretion :: clitellum :
   A. digestion
   B. circulation
   C. respiration
   D. reproduction

**INTERPRETING GRAPHICS:** The diagram below shows the mouth structure of a class of organisms. Use the diagram to answer the question that follows.

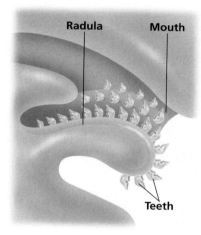

8. In which class of organisms is the mouth structure shown above most likely to be found?
   F. bivalves
   G. hirudines
   H. gastropods
   J. polychaetes

## SHORT RESPONSE

During larval development, gastropods undergo a process called *torsion.*

Describe the outcome of torsion.

## EXTENDED RESPONSE

Earthworms have three main structural features that enable movement.

*Part A* Describe these features.

*Part B* Explain how they work together to enable movement.

> **Test TIP** In tests, analogies compare pairs of items, such as *kitten : cat :: puppy : ?* Before looking at the possible answers, identify how the first pair of terms is related. For example, since a kitten is a young cat, the relationship is baby : adult, so the correct answer would be *puppy : dog.*

# Testing Earthworm Behavior

### OBJECTIVES

- Observe a live earthworm.
- Test how an earthworm responds to light, moisture, and ammonia.
- Test the effect of temperature on heart rate.

### PROCESS SKILLS

- observing
- hypothesizing
- experimenting
- collecting data
- analyzing data

### MATERIALS

- safety goggles
- live earthworm
- shallow pan
- paper towels
- medicine dropper
- hand lens
- black paper or piece of cardboard
- fluorescent lamp
- 2 cotton swabs
- 3% aqueous ammonia solution
- 15 cm Petri dish
- thermometer
- stopwatch or clock with second hand
- 2 plastic tubs for water baths
- warm tap water
- ice cubes

### Background

1. How does an earthworm benefit from cephalization?
2. Describe how gases enter and exit an earthworm's body.

### PART A  Observing an Earthworm

1. **CAUTION You will be working with a live animal. Be sure to treat it gently and to follow directions carefully.** Place a moist paper towel in a pan, and place an earthworm on the paper towel. **CAUTION Rinse the earthworm frequently with water from a medicine dropper to prevent the worm from drying out.**

2. Observe the behavior of the earthworm for a few minutes. Identify the earthworm's anterior and posterior ends by watching it move in the pan. As the worm crawls around in the pan, it will lead with its anterior end.

3. Locate the earthworm's clitellum. Is the clitellum closer to the anterior end or the posterior end? What is the function of the clitellum?

4. Identify the earthworm's dorsal and ventral surfaces by gently rolling the worm over. The dorsal surface will be on top after the worm rights itself.

5. Pick up the earthworm, and feel its skin with your fingers. One surface of the earthworm should feel slightly rougher than the other. The roughness is due to the hairlike setae that project from the earthworm's skin. On which surface are the setae located? Use a hand lens to examine the setae up close.

6. Return the earthworm to the pan, and use the hand lens to find a thick purple line running along the dorsal surface of the worm. This line is the dorsal blood vessel. Does the earthworm have an open or a closed circulatory system?

7. Draw a picture of the earthworm, and label its anterior and posterior ends, dorsal and ventral surfaces, clitellum, setae, and dorsal blood vessel.

### PART B  Earthworm Responses to Stimuli

8. In this part of the laboratory investigation, you will test the earthworm's responses to three different stimuli. With your lab partners, develop three separate hypotheses that describe an earthworm's responses to light, moisture, and a base. In your lab report, make a data table like the one on the next page.

9. To test the earthworm's response to light, cover half of the pan with black paper or cardboard. Check the lighting in the room. The light must be low and even during this test. Position the fluorescent lamp over the uncovered portion of the pan. Place the earthworm in the center of the pan, and observe its movements. Record your observations in your data table.

## OBSERVATIONS OF EARTHWORM BEHAVIOR

| Behavior | Observations |
|---|---|
| Response to light | |
| Response to moisture | |
| Response to water on a swab | |
| Response to ammonia | |

10. To test the earthworm's response to moisture, turn off the fluorescent lamp, move it away from the pan, and remove the paper covering half of the pan. Place a piece of dry paper towel on one side of the pan and a piece of wet paper towel on the other side of the pan. Lay the earthworm across the two paper towels. Observe the earthworm's response to the two environments, and record your observations in your data table.

11. To test the earthworm's response to ammonia, make sure the paper towels on both sides of the pan are wet. Moisten a cotton swab with water. Hold the cotton swab first near the earthworm's anterior end and then near its posterior end. Do not touch the earthworm with the swab. Record your observations in your data table.

12. **CAUTION Wear safety goggles at all times during the following procedure. If you get ammonia on your skin or clothing, wash it off at the sink while calling to your teacher. If you get ammonia in your eyes, immediately flush it out at the eyewash station while calling to your teacher.** Moisten a different cotton swab with ammonia solution, and repeat step 11. Do not touch the earthworm with the swab or the ammonia solution. Record your observations in your data table.

### PART C  Effect of Temperature on Heart Rate

13. In this part of the laboratory investigation, you will examine how an earthworm's heart rate changes as its body temperature changes. Add enough tap water to a Petri dish to barely cover the bottom of the dish. Place an earthworm in the dish.

14. Using a hand lens, look for rhythmic contractions of the dorsal blood vessel. Each contraction represents a single heartbeat. Calculate the worm's heart rate by counting the number of contractions that occur in exactly one minute. This is easiest to do if one person counts contractions while another person watches a stopwatch or clock.

15. **CAUTION Glassware is fragile. Notify the teacher of broken glass or cuts. Do not clean up broken glass or spills involving broken glass unless the teacher tells you to do so.** Place a thermometer next to the worm in the Petri dish, and measure the temperature. Record the worm's heart rate and the temperature in a table on the chalkboard.

16. Float the Petri dish containing the worm on top of either a warm-water bath or a cold-water bath. Place the thermometer next to the worm in the Petri dish, and watch the temperature until it reaches either 30°C (for the warm-water bath) or 10°C (for the cold-water bath).

17. Remove the Petri dish from the water bath, and immediately begin counting heartbeats for exactly one minute. After one minute, measure the temperature in the dish again. Calculate the average temperature to the nearest degree. Record the worm's heart rate and the average temperature in the table on the chalkboard.

18. Using data from the whole class, graph heart rate as a function of temperature. Draw the best-fit curve through the points.

19. Return the earthworm to the container from which you obtained it. Clean up your materials, and wash your hands before leaving the lab.

### Analysis and Conclusions

1. State whether your hypotheses in Part B were supported by your observations. Explain.
2. What is the adaptive advantage of the earthworm's responses to light and moisture?
3. List variables that, if not controlled, might have affected the results in Part B.
4. Describe the relationship between the earthworm's heart rate and temperature as shown by your graph.

### Further Inquiry

Design an experiment to determine which colors of light an earthworm is sensitive to or which areas on an earthworm are sensitive to light.

# ARTHROPODS

The jointed appendages and hard exoskeleton of this red reef lobster, *Enoplometopus occidentalis*, are characteristic of arthropods.

**SECTION 1** *Phylum Arthropoda*

**SECTION 2** *Subphylum Crustacea*

**SECTION 3** *Subphyla Chelicerata and Myriapoda*

# PHYLUM ARTHROPODA

*Two-thirds of all animal species belong to the phylum Arthropoda (ahr-THRAHP-uh-duh). This phylum contains a variety of bilaterally symmetrical coelomates, including lobsters, crabs, spiders, and insects. These animals have adapted to almost every environment on Earth.*

## SECTION 1

### OBJECTIVES

- **Describe** the distinguishing characteristics of arthropods.
- **Explain** the process of molting in an arthropod.
- **List** the five major subphyla of the phylum Arthropoda.

### VOCABULARY

**arthropod**
**appendage**
**chitin**
**compound eye**
**molting**
**trilobite**
**tagma**
**mandible**
**chelicera**

## CHARACTERISTICS OF ARTHROPODS

The members of the phylum Arthropoda are called **arthropods** (AHR-thruh-PAHDS). Like annelids, arthropods are segmented animals. In arthropods, however, the body segments bear jointed extensions called **appendages,** such as legs and antennae. In fact, *arthropod* means "jointed foot."

Another distinguishing feature of arthropods is their exoskeleton, which provides protection and support. As Figure 36-1 shows, the arthropod exoskeleton is made up of three layers that are secreted by the epidermis, which lies just beneath the layers. The waxy outer layer is composed of a mixture of protein and lipid. It repels water and helps keep terrestrial arthropods from drying out. The middle layer, which provides the primary protection, is made mainly of protein and **chitin,** a tough polysaccharide. In some arthropods, the middle layer is hardened by the addition of calcium carbonate. The inner layer also contains protein and chitin, but its flexibility at the joints allows arthropods to move freely. Muscles that attach to the inner layer on either side of the joints move the body segments.

Arthropods show a high degree of cephalization. Recall that *cephalization* is the concentration of sensory and brain structures at the anterior end. A variety of segmented appendages around the mouth serve as sensors and food handlers. Most arthropods have segmented antennae that are specialized for detecting chemicals. Most arthropods also have **compound eyes**—eyes made of many individual light detectors, each with its own lens. In addition, many arthropods have simpler structures that sense light intensity. These sensory structures on the head send nerve impulses to the brain, which coordinates the animal's actions. As in annelids, impulses travel from the brain along a ventral nerve cord, which links ganglia in the other segments of the body.

All arthropods have open circulatory systems. Recall that in an open circulatory system, the heart pumps circulatory fluid through vessels that empty into spaces in the body.

**FIGURE 36-1**

The arthropod exoskeleton consists of three layers that cover the epidermis. Wax in the outer layer is secreted by wax glands. Sensory hairs projecting from the exoskeleton allow arthropods to respond to vibrations and chemicals in their environment.

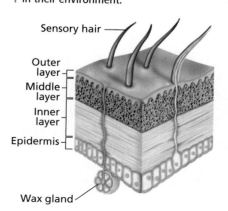

Sensory hair

Outer layer
Middle layer
Inner layer

Epidermis

Wax gland

**FIGURE 36-2**

This green cicada, *Tibicen superbus,* is in the process of molting. The outer layer of its old exoskeleton appears brown.

## Molting

A rigid exoskeleton limits the size to which an arthropod can grow. So, each arthropod periodically sheds its exoskeleton and makes a new one in the process of **molting.** An anthropod goes through many cycles of molting during its life. Figure 36-2 shows an insect in the process of molting.

A cycle of molting begins as the tissues of an arthropod gradually swell. When the pressure inside the exoskeleton is very strong, a hormone that triggers molting is produced. In response to this hormone, the cells of the epidermis secrete enzymes that digest the inner layer of the exoskeleton. At the same time, the epidermis begins to make a new exoskeleton by using the digested material. Eventually, the outer layer of the old exoskeleton loosens, breaks apart, and is shed. The new exoskeleton, which is flexible at first, stretches to fit the enlarged animal.

The new exoskeleton takes a few hours to a few days to become as hard as the one that it replaced. During this time, the animal is vulnerable to predators and, if the arthropod is terrestrial, to desiccation. For these reasons, arthropods usually stay in hiding from the time that they begin to molt until their new exoskeleton has hardened. The "soft-shelled crabs" sold in some restaurants are crabs that have been caught immediately after molting.

## EVOLUTION AND CLASSIFICATION

Animals having arthropod characteristics first appeared about 545 million years ago. Because all arthropods have a true coelom, an exoskeleton, and jointed appendages, biologists infer that all arthropods evolved from a common ancestor. However, biologists are still uncertain about the order in which subgroups of arthropods evolved and the exact relationships between the subgroups. The phylogenetic diagram in Figure 36-3 shows possible evolutionary relationships between the highly diverse arthropod subgroups.

The similar characteristics of many modern subgroups of arthropods may be the result of convergent evolution. For example, ancient and extinct arthropods, such as **trilobites,** had many body segments and one pair of appendages on each segment. However, most living arthropod species have some segments that lack appendages and some segments that are fused into a larger structure called a **tagma** (plural, *tagmata*). The tagmata tend to be specialized for functions such as feeding, locomotion, and reproduction.

Arthropods are usually divided into five subphyla on the basis of differences in development and in the structure of appendages, such as mouthparts. The two major types of mouthparts are **mandibles,** which are jawlike, and **chelicerae** (singular, *chelicera*), which are pincerlike. The five main subphyla are Trilobita, Crustacea, Chelicerata, Myriapoda, and Hexapoda, as Figure 36-3 shows.

**Word Roots and Origins**

*chelicera*

from the Greek *chele,* meaning "claw," and *keras,* meaning "horn"

**FIGURE 36-3**

This phylogenetic diagram shows hypotheses of the evolutionary relationships between the highly diverse arthropod subgroups. Dashed lines indicate relationships that are poorly understood or that are heavily debated. For updates on phylogenetic information, visit **go.hrw.com** and enter the keyword **HM6 Phylo**.

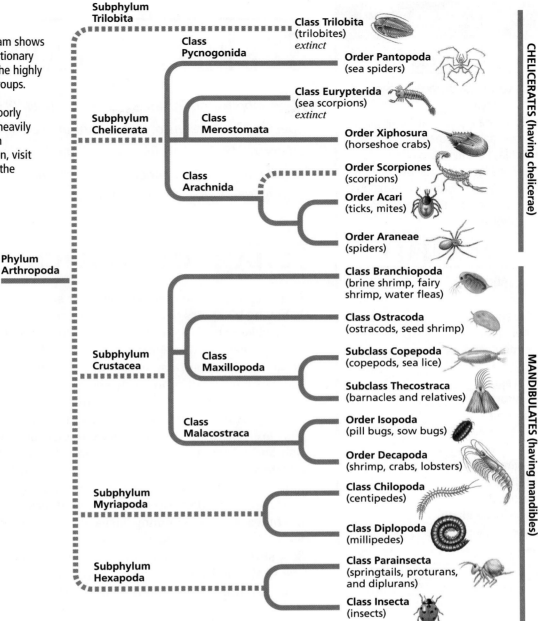

Subphylum Trilobita — Class Trilobita (trilobites) *extinct*

Subphylum Chelicerata — Class Pycnogonida — Order Pantopoda (sea spiders)

Class Merostomata — Class Eurypterida (sea scorpions) *extinct*; Order Xiphosura (horseshoe crabs)

Class Arachnida — Order Scorpiones (scorpions); Order Acari (ticks, mites); Order Araneae (spiders)

CHELICERATES (having chelicerae)

Phylum Arthropoda

Subphylum Crustacea — Class Branchiopoda (brine shrimp, fairy shrimp, water fleas)

Class Maxillopoda — Class Ostracoda (ostracods, seed shrimp); Subclass Copepoda (copepods, sea lice); Subclass Thecostraca (barnacles and relatives)

Class Malacostraca — Order Isopoda (pill bugs, sow bugs); Order Decapoda (shrimp, crabs, lobsters)

Subphylum Myriapoda — Class Chilopoda (centipedes); Class Diplopoda (millipedes)

Subphylum Hexapoda — Class Parainsecta (springtails, proturans, and diplurans); Class Insecta (insects)

MANDIBULATES (having mandibles)

---

## SECTION 1 REVIEW

1. What characteristics do all arthropods share?

2. What is the main function of each layer of an arthropod's exoskeleton?

3. What is a compound eye?

4. What is molting?

5. Identify the difference between chelicerae and mandibles.

6. Identify examples of organisms in each of the five main subphyla of arthropods.

**CRITICAL THINKING**

7. **Inferring Relationships** What is the adaptive advantage of having a layered exoskeleton?

8. **Analyzing Concepts** After its old exoskeleton has been shed but before the new one has hardened, an aquatic arthropod absorbs water and swells. How is this behavior adaptive?

9. **Interpreting Graphics** Study Figure 36-3. Are pill bugs more closely related to centipedes or to barnacles? Explain your answer.

## OBJECTIVES

- **Describe** the characteristics of crustaceans.
- **Compare** aquatic crustaceans with terrestrial crustaceans.
- **Explain** the functions of the appendages on a crayfish.
- **Summarize** digestion, respiration, circulation, excretion, and neural control in crayfish.

## VOCABULARY

nauplius
cirrus
isopod
decapod
cephalothorax
thorax
carapace
abdomen
antenna
antennule
cheliped
swimmeret
telson
uropod
digestive gland
green gland

# SUBPHYLUM CRUSTACEA

*The subphylum Crustacea contains about 38,000 known species. Crustaceans are abundant in oceans, lakes, and rivers, and a few species live on land. Some crustaceans are sessile, while others move by walking on legs, swimming with paddle-like appendages, or drifting with the currents.*

## CHARACTERISTICS

Crustaceans are so diverse that their single defining characteristic is having two pairs of antennae. Also, most crustaceans have a pair of jawlike, chewing mouthparts called *mandibles*. In most crustaceans, each body segment has a pair of appendages, and at least some of those appendages are branched. Although some crustaceans have 60 or more body segments, most crustaceans have 16 to 20 segments, which are fused into several tagmata.

Some small crustaceans, such as pill bugs, respire through the thin areas of their exoskeleton. Larger crustaceans, such as crayfish and lobsters, use gills to respire. The exoskeletons of aquatic crustaceans, such as lobsters, often contain large amounts of calcium carbonate and thus are extremely hard.

During the development of many crustaceans, the embryo becomes a free-swimming larva called a **nauplius** (NAH-plee-uhs), which looks quite different from an adult of the species. As Figure 36-4 shows, a nauplius has three pairs of appendages and a single eye in the middle of its head. Through a series of molts, the nauplius eventually takes on the adult form.

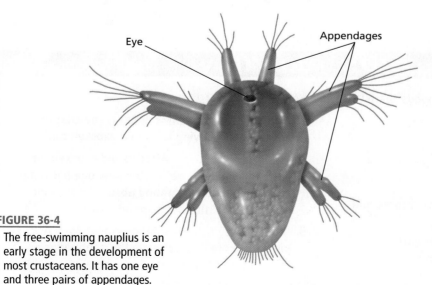

Eye

Appendages

**FIGURE 36-4**

The free-swimming nauplius is an early stage in the development of most crustaceans. It has one eye and three pairs of appendages.

## DIVERSITY OF CRUSTACEANS

Crustaceans exist in a range of sizes, but most are small. For example, copepods (KOH-puh-PAHDZ), as shown in Figure 36-5a, are no larger than the comma in this sentence. At the other end of the size spectrum is the Japanese spider crab, shown in Figure 36-5b. With a leg span of 4 m (13 ft), this crab is the largest living arthropod.

**(a)** Copepod, *Cyclops* sp.

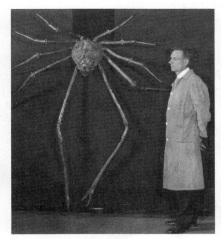

**(b)** Japanese spider crab, *Macrocheira kaempferi*

**(c)** Goose barnacle, *Lepas anatifera*

## Aquatic Crustaceans

Copepods are extremely abundant in marine environments and may be the most abundant animals in the world. Copepods are an important part of the ocean's *plankton,* the collection of small organisms that drift or swim weakly near the surface of the water.

In freshwater environments, on the other hand, much of the plankton is composed of crustaceans known as *water fleas,* which are about the size of copepods. A common type of water flea is a member of the genus *Daphnia.*

Barnacles, such as the one shown in Figure 36-5c, are marine crustaceans that are sessile as adults. Free-swimming barnacle larvae attach themselves to rocks, piers, boats, sea turtles, whales, and just about any other surface. They then develop a shell composed of calcium carbonate plates that completely encloses the body in most species. Their swimming appendages develop into six pairs of long legs called **cirri** (SIR-IE) (singular, *cirrus*). The cirri extend through openings in the shell, sweeping small organisms and food particles from the water and directing them to the mouth.

## Terrestrial Crustaceans

Sow bugs and pill bugs are terrestrial members of a group of crustaceans called **isopods.** Terrestrial isopods lack adaptations for conserving water, such as a waxy cuticle, and can lose water quickly through their exoskeleton. Therefore, they live only in moist environments, such as under leaves and rocks, in crevices around garden beds, and in the spaces between house foundations and sidewalks. In addition, pill bugs are capable of rolling into a ball when disturbed or threatened with desiccation, as shown in Figure 36-6. Sow bugs and pill bugs generally feed on decaying vegetation, but they may also eat garden bulbs, vegetables, and fruits that lie on or in the soil.

**FIGURE 36-5**

Crustaceans include tiny species, such as the copepod (a), as well as giant species, such as the Japanese spider crab (b). Some aquatic species, such as barnacles (c), attach themselves to submerged marine surfaces.

**FIGURE 36-6**

Pill bugs are isopod terrestrial crustaceans that are often found in moist environments with decaying vegetation. Pill bugs and sow bugs look similar, but only pill bugs roll up when disturbed.

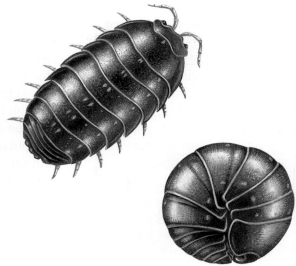

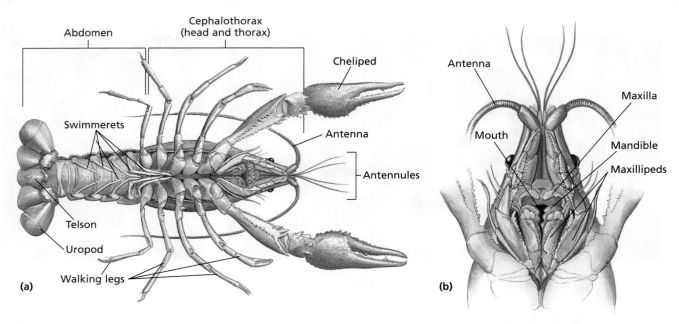

Abdomen

Cephalothorax (head and thorax)

Cheliped

Swimmerets

Antenna

Antennules

Telson

Uropod

Walking legs

(a)

Antenna

Maxilla

Mouth

Mandible

Maxillipeds

(b)

**FIGURE 36-7**

(a) Each of the 20 body segments of a crayfish has a pair of appendages, as seen in this ventral view. (b) Some of the appendages of the anterior cephalothorax are visible in this closer ventral view.

| TABLE 36-1 *Crayfish Appendages* | |
|---|---|
| **Appendage** | **Function** |
| Antennule | touch, taste, and balance |
| Antenna | touch and taste |
| Mandible | chewing food |
| Maxilla | manipulating food and drawing water currents over gills |
| Maxilliped | touch, taste, and manipulating food |
| Cheliped | capturing food and defense |
| Walking leg | locomotion over solid surfaces |
| Swimmeret | creating water currents and transferring sperm (males) |

# THE CRAYFISH

The crayfish is a freshwater crustacean that is well studied because of its size and abundance. Crayfish are structurally similar to lobsters, which are marine crustaceans. Crayfish, lobsters, crabs, and shrimp are **decapods** (DEK-uh-PAHDZ), or members of the order Decapoda. *Decapoda* means "10 feet," a name used because these crustaceans have five pairs of legs that are used for locomotion.

## External Structure

The crayfish's external structure is shown in Figure 36-7. The body is divided into two major sections: the abdomen and the cephalothorax (SEF-uh-loh-THAWR-AKS). The **cephalothorax** consists of two tagmata: the head, which has five segments, and the **thorax,** which has eight segments and lies behind the head. The dorsal exoskeleton over the cephalothorax is a single, tough covering known as the **carapace** (KAR-uh-PAYS). The **abdomen,** the tagma behind the cephalothorax, is divided into six segments.

A pair of appendages is attached to each segment of the crayfish. Several pairs have specialized functions, as summarized in Table 36-1. The two pairs of **antennae** include the branched **antennules,** which serve as feelers sensitive to touch, taste, and balance. The long antennae are also feelers that respond to touch and taste. Crayfish use a pair of *mandibles* to chew food and use two pairs of *maxillae* (maks-IL-ee) and three pairs of *maxillipeds* (maks-IL-i-PEDS) to manipulate food. The posterior pair of maxillae also function in respiration, and the maxillipeds are sensitive to touch and taste. The most anterior pair of walking legs, the **chelipeds** (KEE-luh-PEDS), end in large pincers used for capturing food and for defense. The other four pairs of walking legs carry the crayfish over solid surfaces; two of these pairs end in small pincers that can grasp small objects. The **swimmerets,** which are attached to the five anterior abdominal segments, create water currents and function in reproduction.

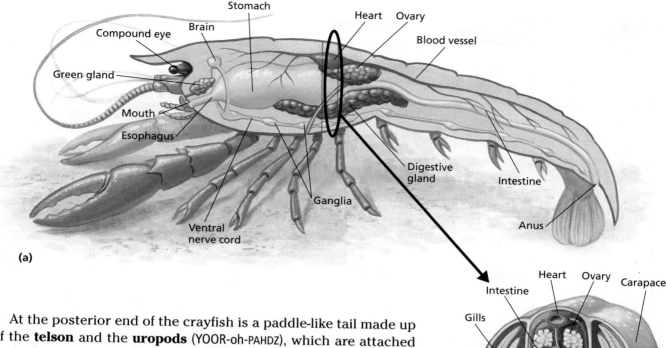

**(a)**

At the posterior end of the crayfish is a paddle-like tail made up of the **telson** and the **uropods** (YOOR-oh-PAHDZ), which are attached to the sixth abdominal segment. Powerful abdominal muscles can propel the animal rapidly backward in a movement referred to as a *tail flip.*

## Digestion

The major parts of the digestive tract of a crayfish are shown in Figure 36-8a. Food passes through the esophagus to the stomach, where teeth made of chitin and calcium carbonate grind the food into a fine paste. After the paste is mixed with enzymes secreted by a **digestive gland** near the stomach, it enters the intestine for further digestion and absorption. Waste leaves through the anus.

## Respiration

Like most crustaceans, crayfish have featherlike gills for respiration. Figure 36-8b shows that the gills extend from the base of each walking leg into a chamber under the carapace. As a crayfish walks, its legs circulate water across its gills. Feathery branches on the posterior pair of maxillae also help direct water over the gills. Each gill is covered by an extension of the exoskeleton that is thin enough to permit gases to diffuse across the gill surface.

## Circulation

The main components of the crayfish's open circulatory system are shown in Figures 36-8a and 36-8b. In this system, the dorsal heart pumps a circulatory fluid called *hemolymph* into several large vessels that carry the fluid to different regions of the body. The fluid leaves the vessels and enters spaces within the body, where it bathes the various tissues. It then passes through the gills, where it exchanges carbon dioxide with oxygen in the water. From the gills, the fluid returns to the dorsal part of the crayfish and enters the heart.

**(b)**

**FIGURE 36-8**

The major internal organs of a crayfish are seen in this cutaway side view (a) and cross section through the heart region (b).

internet connect

www.scilinks.org
**Topic: Crustaceans**
**Keyword: HM60368**

SC*LINKS.* Maintained by the National Science Teachers Association

## Quick Lab

### Observing Crayfish Behavior

**Materials** crayfish in container with water, tapping instrument

**Procedure**

   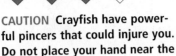

**CAUTION** Crayfish have powerful pincers that could injure you. Do not place your hand near the crayfish.

1. Gently tap the anterior (head) end of the crayfish, and record your observations.
2. Tap the posterior (tail) end of the crayfish, and record your observations.

**Analysis** Describe each behavioral response you observed when you tapped the crayfish. How does each behavior aid the animal in its survival?

## Excretion

As freshwater organisms, crayfish live in a hypotonic environment. Remember that a *hypotonic environment* is one in which the concentration of solute molecules is lower than that in the organism's cells. Therefore, water constantly enters the tissues of a crayfish by osmosis. This excess water, along with wastes, is eliminated by excretory organs called **green glands,** which are visible in Figure 36-8a. The dilute fluid collected by the green glands leaves the body through a pore at the base of the antennae.

## Neural Control

The nervous system of the crayfish is illustrated in Figure 36-8a. It is typical of arthropods and is similar to the nervous system of annelids. The crayfish brain consists of a pair of ganglia above the esophagus that receive nerve impulses from the eyes, antennules, and antennae.

Two bundles of nerve fibers extend from the brain and pass around either side of the esophagus to a ganglion that controls the mandibles, maxillae, and maxillipeds. The ventral nerve cord runs posteriorly from this ganglion, connecting a series of ganglia that control the appendages and muscles in the segments of the thorax and abdomen.

## Sensory Organs

Crayfish sense vibrations and chemicals in the water with thousands of small sensory hairs that project from the exoskeleton. Sensory hairs are visible in Figure 36-1. These sensory hairs are distributed over the entire body, but they are especially concentrated on the antennules, antennae, mouthparts, chelipeds, and telson.

The compound eyes of a crayfish are set on two short, movable stalks. Each eye has thousands of light-sensitive units, each with its own lens. At the base of the antennules are organs that can detect the animal's orientation with respect to gravity.

## SECTION 2 REVIEW

1. What characteristics are shared by most or all crustaceans?
2. What is the important role of copepods in marine ecosystems?
3. What are the functions of the mandibles and the chelipeds on a crayfish?
4. What structural adaptations of crayfish promote effective respiration in water?
5. Describe the type of circulation found in a crayfish.

**CRITICAL THINKING**

6. **Inferring Relationships** Why are the largest crustaceans found only in aquatic environments?
7. **Applying Information** Barnacles spend most of their adult life attached to a marine surface. What structural adaptations for this lifestyle do barnacles have?
8. **Inferring Relationships** What is the adaptive advantage of having two pairs of antennae?
9. **Predicting Results** What problem would a crayfish have if it were born without a green gland?

# SUBPHYLA CHELICERATA AND MYRIAPODA

*Unlike crustaceans, nearly all members of the subphyla Chelicerata, Myriapoda, and Hexapoda are terrestrial.*

## SECTION 3

### OBJECTIVES

- **List** the characteristics of arachnids, as represented by a spider.
- **Explain** the adaptations that spiders have for a predatory life on land.
- **Identify** the unique characteristics of scorpions, mites, and ticks.
- **Compare** the characteristics of millipedes and centipedes.

### VOCABULARY

arachnid
pedipalp
spinneret
book lung
trachea
spiracle
Malpighian tubule

## SUBPHYLUM CHELICERATA

The subphylum Chelicerata, made up of *chelicerates,* includes spiders, scorpions, mites, sea spiders, and horseshoe crabs. Chelicerates lack antennae and typically have six pairs of appendages. The first pair of appendages, the *chelicerae,* are modified into pincers or fangs. The major group in Chelicerata is class Arachnida (uh-RAK-ni-duh), which has more than 70,000 species.

### Class Arachnida

Members of the class Arachnida, called **arachnids,** include spiders, scorpions, mites, and ticks. Like crayfish, arachnids have a body that is divided into a cephalothorax and an abdomen. The cephalothorax usually bears six pairs of jointed appendages: one pair of chelicerae; one pair of **pedipalps,** which aid in holding food and chewing; and four pairs of walking legs.

### Anatomy of a Spider

Spiders range in length from less than 0.5 mm long to as long as 9 cm (3.5 in.) long in some tropical tarantula species. As Figure 36-9 shows, the body of a spider is very narrow between the cephalothorax and the abdomen.

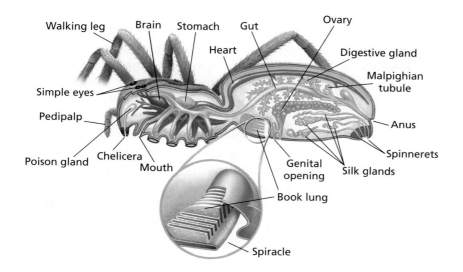

**FIGURE 36-9**

The major internal organs of a female spider are shown in this cutaway side view. The inset shows a closer view of a book lung, one of the spider's adaptations to life on land.

**Word Roots and Origins**

*spiracle*

from the Latin *spiraculum,*
meaning "air hole"

**FIGURE 36-10**

The black widow, *Latrodectus mactans*
(a), and the brown recluse, *Loxosceles
reclusa* (b), are the only two spiders
in the United States whose venom
is dangerous to humans. Note the
red hourglass-shaped spot on the
abdomen of the female black widow
and the dark violin-shaped marking on
the cephalothorax of the brown recluse.

(a)

(b)

The chelicerae of spiders are modified as fangs and are used to inject venom into prey. The venom is produced by poison glands in the cephalothorax and flows through ducts in the chelicerae to the tips of the fangs. Most spiders have eight simple eyes at the anterior end of the cephalothorax. Each simple eye has a single lens.

On the tip of the abdomen of many spiders are three pairs of organs called **spinnerets,** which are visible in Figure 36-9. Each spinneret is composed of hundreds of microscopic tubes that connect to silk glands in the abdomen. A protein-containing fluid produced in the silk glands hardens into threads as it is secreted from the spinnerets. Spiders use their silk threads to spin webs, build nests, and protect eggs. In some species, spider silk also aids in dispersing spiders from one habitat to another. Young spiders move to new habitats when the wind pulls them through the air by their threads.

The nervous, digestive, and circulatory systems of spiders are similar to those of crustaceans. Because spiders are terrestrial, however, their respiratory system is quite different. In some spiders, respiration occurs in **book lungs,** paired sacs in the abdomen with many parallel folds that resemble the pages of a book. The folds in a book lung provide a large surface area for gas exchange. Other spiders have a system of tubes called **tracheae** (TRAY-kee-ee) that carry air directly to the tissues from openings in the exoskeleton known as **spiracles.** Some spiders have both book lungs and tracheae.

The excretory system of spiders is also modified for life on land. The main excretory organs, called **Malpighian** (mal-PIG-ee-uhn) **tubules,** are hollow projections of the digestive tract that collect body fluids and wastes and carry them to the intestine. After most of the water is reabsorbed, the wastes leave the body in a nearly solid form with the feces. Thus, the Malpighian tubules help spiders conserve water in terrestrial environments.

## Life of a Spider

Spiders feed mainly on insects, although some can catch fish, frogs, and even birds. Different species of spiders are adapted to capture their prey in different ways. Some chase after prey, some hide beneath trapdoors waiting for prey to approach, and some snare prey in webs spun from silk. When an insect becomes trapped in the sticky web, the spider emerges from its hiding place near the edge of the web and paralyzes the insect with its venom. Many spiders also immobilize their prey by wrapping them in silk. They can then consume the body fluids of the prey at a later time.

Spider venom is usually harmless to humans, and most spiders bite only when threatened. There are, however, two kinds of spiders in the United States whose bites can be dangerous to humans. They are the black widow and the brown recluse, shown in Figure 36-10. The female black widow has a bright red or orange mark shaped like an hourglass on the ventral surface of its abdomen. The venom attacks the nervous system.

The brown recluse has a violin-shaped mark on the dorsal surface of its cephalothorax. Therefore, it is sometimes called the "violin spider." The venom of the brown recluse kills and digests the tissues surrounding the bite.

A male spider is usually smaller than a female of the same species. When the male is mature, he transfers sperm to special sacs in the tips of his pedipalps. The sperm are then placed in the seminal receptacle of the female during mating. As soon as mating has occurred, the male darts away. If he is not quick enough, he may be eaten by the female. Eggs are fertilized as they pass out of the female into a silken case that she has spun. The female may carry the egg case with her or attach it to a web or plant. The young spiders hatch in about two weeks and undergo their first molt before leaving the case.

**FIGURE 36-11**

Scorpions, such as *Paruroctonus mesaensis,* have pincerlike pedipalps and a venomous stinger at the end of their segmented abdomen.

## Scorpions

Scorpions, such as the one shown in Figure 36-11, differ from spiders in two ways. Scorpions have large, pincerlike pedipalps, which they hold in a forward position. They also have a segmented abdomen with a large stinger on the last segment, which can be curled over the body. Scorpions usually hide during the day and hunt at night, mostly for insects and spiders. They seize prey with their pedipalps and inject venom into the prey with their stinger. Only a few species of scorpions have venom that can be fatal to humans. Most scorpions live in tropical or semitropical areas, but some are found in dry temperate or desert regions.

## Mites and Ticks

Mites and ticks are the most abundant and most specialized arachnids. About 30,000 species have been identified, but the actual number of species may be much larger than that. Unlike spiders and scorpions, mites and ticks have a completely fused cephalothorax and abdomen, with no sign of separation between them.

Most mites are less than a millimeter in length, and some are small enough to live on particles of dust. They can be found in freshwater, marine, and terrestrial habitats. Many mites are entirely free living, while others are parasites during at least part of their life cycle. Spider mites parasitize fruit trees and many other agricultural crops by sucking the fluid from their leaves. The larvae of harvest mites—also known as chiggers—attach themselves to the skin of vertebrates, including humans. They break the skin with their chelicerae and feed on blood, causing swelling and itching. Other species of mites live on the bodies of chickens, dogs, cattle, humans, and other animals, where they feed on sloughing skin, hair, and feathers.

Ticks, such as the one shown in Figure 36-12, are parasites that feed on their hosts by piercing the flesh and sucking on the blood. Many species of ticks carry bacteria and other microorganisms in their guts that may cause diseases in the host. While the tick feeds, the microorganisms are transmitted to the new host. Rocky Mountain spotted fever and Lyme disease are transmitted in this way. Ticks range in length from a few millimeters to 3 cm (about 1 in.).

**FIGURE 36-12**

The lone star tick, *Amblyomma americanum,* is an arachnid that parasitizes humans and other mammals.

(a) Millipede, *Narceus americanus*

(b) Giant centipede, *Scolopendra sp.*

**FIGURE 36-13**

(a) Millipedes have a rounded body and two pairs of legs on each body segment except the last two. (b) Centipedes have a flattened body and one pair of legs on each body segment except the first and the last two.

# SUBPHYLUM MYRIAPODA

The subphylum Myriapoda (MIR-ee-AHP-uh-duh), includes the class Diplopoda (duh-PLAH-puh-duh), which consists of millipedes, and the class Chilopoda (KIE-LAHP-uh-duh), which consists of centipedes. *Myriapoda* means "many feet," and is so named because myriapods have many body segments, most of which have one or two pairs of legs each. Unlike crustaceans, myriapods have one pair of unbranched antennae. They are terrestrial but lack a waxy exoskeleton. They avoid drying out by living in damp areas.

## Class Diplopoda

Millipedes are members of the class Diplopoda. Most millipedes have two pairs of legs on each body segment except the last two. Millipedes may have up to 100 body segments and thus 200 pair of legs. The legs are well adapted for burrowing through humus and soil, but because the legs are short, millipedes move slowly. As Figure 36-13a shows, the bodies of millipedes are rounded.

Millipedes have short antennae and two groups of simple eyes on their head. They have poor vision but a good sense of smell. Millipedes use their maxillae and mandibles to chew on plants or decaying plant matter in the soil.

## Class Chilopoda

Centipedes are members of the class Chilopoda. Centipedes may have as few as 15 or as many as 175 pairs of legs. In tropical regions centipedes reach lengths of 30 cm (12 in.). Their bodies are more flattened than those of millipedes, and their legs are longer relative to their body, as Figure 36-13b shows. Each body segment behind the head, except the first segment and the last two segments, has one pair of jointed legs. The appendages on the first segment are modified into a pair of poison claws. Long antennae and two clusters of simple eyes are located on the head. Centipedes can move quickly in search of earthworms, insects, and other prey. They kill the prey with their poison claws and use their mandibles and maxillae to tear it apart. Most centipedes are not harmful to humans.

## SECTION 3 REVIEW

1. List the major characteristics of arachnids.

2. Describe the functions of pedipalps.

3. Describe three ways in which spiders are adapted for catching prey.

4. Name two ways in which scorpions differ from spiders.

5. How do mites and ticks differ?

6. How do millipedes and centipedes differ?

**CRITICAL THINKING**

7. **Making Comparisons** Compare the excretory system of a spider with that of a crayfish.

8. **Inferring Relationships** How might spiders benefit humans?

9. **Applying Information** A cubic meter of soil may contain thousands of millipedes. What role might millipedes serve in an ecosystem?

# CHAPTER HIGHLIGHTS

## Phylum Arthropoda

- Arthropods are segmented animals that have jointed appendages, an exoskeleton, a high degree of cephalization, a ventral nerve cord, and an open circulatory system.

- To grow, an arthropod must shed its exoskeleton periodically in a process called molting.

- The five major subphyla of Arthropoda are Trilobita, Crustacea, Chelicerata, Myriapoda, and Hexapoda. The subphylum Trilobita consists of extinct animals called trilobites.

**Vocabulary**

arthropod (p. 723)
appendage (p. 723)
chitin (p. 723)

compound eye (p. 723)
molting (p. 724)

trilobite (p. 724)
tagma (p. 724)

mandible (p. 724)
chelicera (p. 724)

## SECTION 2 — Subphylum Crustacea

- Crustaceans, members of the subphylum Crustacea, have two pairs of antennae. Most crustaceans have a pair of chewing mouthparts called mandibles and one pair of branched appendages on each body segment. The exoskeletons of many crustaceans contain large amounts of calcium carbonate.

- Crustaceans include shrimps, lobsters, crabs, crayfish, barnacles, isopods, copepods, and water fleas. Most crustaceans are aquatic, use gills to respire, and have a larval stage called a nauplius.

- The body of a crayfish is divided into a cephalothorax and an abdomen. The appendages on each body segment are specialized for sensing, feeding, respiration, locomotion, or reproduction.

- Crayfish have a digestive gland that is near the stomach and that secretes enzymes for digestion. Walking circulates water across the gills for respiration. The circulatory system is open. Green glands assist in excretion of excess water that enters the body by osmosis.

**Vocabulary**

nauplius (p. 726)
cirrus (p. 727)
isopod (p. 727)
decapod (p. 728)

cephalothorax (p. 728)
thorax (p. 728)
carapace (p. 728)
abdomen (p. 728)

antenna (p. 728)
antennule (p. 728)
cheliped (p. 728)
swimmeret (p. 729)

telson (p. 729)
uropod (p. 729)
digestive gland (p. 729)
green gland (p. 730)

## SECTION 3 — Subphyla Chelicerata and Myriapoda

- Members of the subphylum Chelicerata lack antennae and have pincerlike mouthparts called chelicerae.

- Arachnids include spiders, scorpions, mites, and ticks. Their bodies are divided into a cephalothorax and an abdomen, and they usually have six pairs of jointed appendages: one pair of chelicerae, one pair of pedipalps, and four pairs of walking legs.

- Spiders have eight simple eyes and chelicerae modified as fangs. Spiders produce silk threads that are used for several functions. Spiders are terrestrial; they respire by means of book lungs, tracheae, or both. Malpighian tubules function to excrete wastes while conserving water.

- Scorpions have large, pincerlike pedipalps and a stinger on the last segment of the abdomen.

- Mites and ticks have a completely fused cephalothorax and abdomen. Many species are parasitic, and some spread diseases that affect humans.

- Members of the subphylum Myriapoda have antennae, mandibles, and unbranched appendages.

- Millipedes have rounded bodies and two pairs of jointed legs on each body segment except the last two segments. Centipedes have flattened bodies and one pair of jointed legs on each body segment except the first segment and the last two segments.

**Vocabulary**

arachnid (p. 731)
pedipalp (p. 731)

spinneret (p. 732)
book lung (p. 732)

trachea (p. 732)
spiracle (p. 732)

Malpighian tubule (p. 732)

## USING VOCABULARY

1. For each pair of terms, explain how the meanings of the terms differ.
   a. *mandible* and *chelicera*
   b. *isopod* and *decapod*
   c. *cephalothorax* and *abdomen*
   d. *antennae* and *antennules*
   e. *cheliped* and *telson*
   f. *book lung* and *trachea*

2. Explain the relationship between the cephalothorax and the thorax.

3. Choose the term that does not belong in the following group, and explain why it does not belong: *book lung, trachea, spiracle,* and *green gland.*

4. **Word Roots and Origins** The word *tagma* is derived from the Greek *tassein,* which means "to arrange." Using this information, explain why the term *tagma* is a good name for the structure that the term describes.

## UNDERSTANDING KEY CONCEPTS

5. **Describe** the key characteristics of arthropods.

6. **Explain** how arthropods molt.

7. **List** the five subphyla of arthropods.

8. **Summarize** the major characteristics of crustaceans.

9. **Explain** how a barnacle feeds.

10. **Summarize** the function of the major appendages of a crayfish.

11. **Describe** excretion in a crayfish.

12. **Compare** respiration in crayfish and spiders.

13. **Identify** the main characteristics of the members of subphylum Chelicerata.

14. **Compare** the appendages on the cephalothorax of a spider with those of a scorpion.

15. **List** three predatory behaviors of spiders.

16. **Identify** a distinguishing characteristic of mites.

17. **Explain** how parasitic ticks spread diseases.

18. **Identify** the main characteristics of the members of subphylum Myriapoda.

19. **Compare** the characteristics of millipedes and centipedes.

20. **Summarize** how myriapods avoid desiccation in terrestrial environments.

21. **CONCEPT MAPPING** Use the following terms to create a concept map that sequences the process of molting in an arthropod: *exoskeleton, enzymes, inner layer, hormone, molting,* and *epidermis.*

## CRITICAL THINKING

22. **Interpreting Graphics** Identify structures A through F in the diagram below.

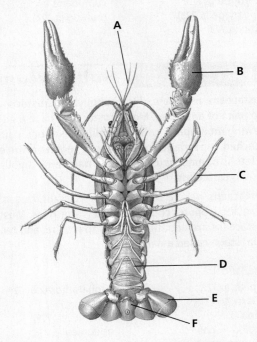

23. **Applying Information** Arthropods first lived on land about 400 million years ago. They have survived several time periods in which other phyla became extinct. What characteristics might have enabled arthropods to survive and adapt?

24. **Relating Concepts** A water flea of the genus *Daphnia* eats algae. How might this organism acquire its food?

25. **Inferring Relationships** Barnacles are sessile crustaceans. What adaptation enables them to compete with motile organisms for food? What adaptation protects them from predators?

26. **Recognizing Relationships** The cephalothorax of a crayfish is covered by the carapace, a fused plate of exoskeleton. What are some advantages and disadvantages of this fused structure?

27. **Analyzing Patterns** Crayfish have a high concentration of sensory hairs on the telson. What might be the advantage of having so many sensory structures at the posterior end?

# Standardized Test Preparation

**DIRECTIONS:** Choose the letter of the answer choice that best answers the question.

1. What do all arthropods have in common?
   A. spiracles
   B. antennae
   C. a cephalothorax
   D. jointed appendages

2. What is the chitin-containing structure that protects and supports the body of an arthropod?
   F. a tagma
   G. a chelicera
   H. an appendage
   J. an exoskeleton

3. Which of the following statements about compound eyes is true?
   A. Compound eyes have a single lens.
   B. Compound eyes are located on the abdomen of scorpions.
   C. Compound eyes are found in all arthropods except crayfish.
   D. Compound eyes are composed of many individual light detectors.

4. What are the major respiratory organs of crayfish?
   F. gills
   G. lungs
   H. tracheae
   J. book lungs

5. How do mites and ticks differ from spiders?
   A. Mites and ticks have mandibles.
   B. Mites and ticks have two pairs of antennae.
   C. Mites and ticks have a unique respiratory system.
   D. Mites and ticks have a fused cephalothorax and abdomen.

**INTERPRETING GRAPHICS:** The illustration below shows four animals. Use the illustration to answer the question that follows.

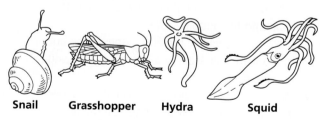

Snail     Grasshopper     Hydra     Squid

6. Which animal has a chitinous exoskeleton?
   F. snail
   G. grasshopper
   H. hydra
   J. squid

**DIRECTIONS:** Complete the following analogy.

7. mandible : crayfish :: chelicera :
   A. pill bug
   B. scorpion
   C. barnacle
   D. millipede

**INTERPRETING GRAPHICS:** The graph below shows data about molting and two causes of mortality in crabs. Use the graph to answer the questions that follow.

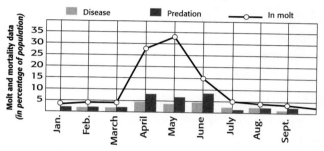

8. During which months are you most likely to find crabs in molt?
   F. January through March
   G. April through June
   H. July through September
   J. September through January

9. What is the relationship between molting and mortality?
   A. Molting increases mortality.
   B. Molting decreases mortality.
   C. Molting has no effect on mortality.
   D. Molting and mortality occur at different times of the year.

## SHORT RESPONSE

Some arthropods are terrestrial and some are aquatic.

Give examples and describe the distinguishing characteristics of each type of arthropod.

## EXTENDED RESPONSE

All arthropods undergo many cycles of molting throughout their lifetime.

*Part A* Describe the process of molting in arthropods.

*Part B* Explain how the anatomical structure of an arthropod relates to the function of molting.

**Test TIP** For questions involving graphs, be sure to study the graph's title, axes, and labels carefully before choosing a final answer.

# Investigating Pill Bug Behavior

## OBJECTIVES

- Review characteristics of the phylum Arthropoda and the subphylum Crustacea.
- Observe the external anatomy of a living terrestrial isopod.
- Investigate the behavior of terrestrial isopods.

## PROCESS SKILLS

- observing
- hypothesizing
- experimenting

## MATERIALS

- 5 live pill bugs for each pair of students
- 1 plastic medicine dropper
- water
- potato
- 3 sheets of filter paper cut to fit a Petri dish
- Petri dish with cover
- aluminum foil
- bright lamp or flashlight
- 4 fabrics of different texture
- cellophane tape
- scissors

## Background

1. What are the major characteristics of arthropods and crustaceans?
2. Where would you expect to find pill bugs?
3. How are pill bugs different from most other crustaceans?

## PART A  Response to Light

1. Put several drops of water on a piece of filter paper until the paper becomes slightly moist. Place the filter paper in the bottom of a Petri dish. Cover half the bottom of the Petri dish with aluminum foil.
2. Check the lighting in the room. The light must be low and even during this part of the investigation.
3. ⚠ CAUTION **You will be working with live animals. Be sure to treat them gently and to follow directions carefully.** Place five pill bugs in the center of the filter paper. Shine a lamp directly over the Petri dish so that half the filter paper is brightly illuminated and the other half is in darkness, shaded by the foil.
4. Based on your knowledge of the natural habitat of pill bugs, can you predict where they will go? Make a data table like the one shown, and record your prediction as well as the actual responses of the pill bugs.

## PART B  Response to Moisture

5. ⚠ CAUTION **Sharp or pointed objects can cause injury. Handle scissors carefully.** Cut a piece of filter paper in half. Moisten one of the halves with water and place it in the bottom of a Petri dish. Make sure that drops of water do not leak onto the bottom of the dish.
6. Place the dry half of the filter paper in the bottom of the Petri dish, leaving a 2 mm gap between it and the damp filter paper.
7. Place five pill bugs along the boundary between the wet and dry areas. Place the top on the dish.
8. To which side do you predict the pill bugs will move? Write your prediction in your data table. Observe the pill bugs for 3 to 5 minutes, and record your observations in your data table. Do your observations agree with your predictions?

## PART C  Response to Food

9. Again dampen a piece of filter paper and place it in the bottom of a Petri dish. Next place a thin slice of potato near the edge of the dish.
10. Place five pill bugs in the Petri dish opposite the potato slice, and place the lid on the dish.
11. Where do you predict the pill bugs will go? Write your prediction in your data table. Observe the pill bugs for 3 to 5 minutes, and record your observations in your data table. Do your observations agree with your predictions?

## PART D  Response to Surface Texture

12. Trace the outline of the bottom of a Petri dish on one of the fabrics. Cut the circle out of the fabric and fold it in half. Then cut along the fold to produce two half-circles.
13. Repeat step 12 using the other three fabrics. You should now have eight half-circles.
14. Tape together two half-circles, each of a different fabric. Place the full circle in the bottom of a Petri dish, tape side down, as shown in the figure below.
15. On a sheet of paper, draw the fabric circle and label the two types of fabric that make up the circle.

16. Place a pill bug in the center of the circle and observe its movements. One student should keep track of the amount of time the animal spends on each fabric. On the drawing that was made in step 15, the other student should draw the path the pill bug travels in the circle. After 5 minutes, stop your observations and record the amount of time the pill bug spent on each fabric.
17. Repeat steps 14–16 for two other pairs of fabrics.
18. ♦ ♦ **Return the pill bugs to their container. Clean up your materials and wash your hands before leaving the lab.**

## Analysis and Conclusions

1. In Part A, why was the entire filter paper moistened?
2. In Part B, why was there a slight separation between the wet and dry halves of the filter paper?
3. In Part C, why was the entire filter paper moistened?
4. In Part D, which fabric did the pill bugs prefer? Describe the texture of that fabric.
5. How do the responses of pill bugs to light, moisture, and food in these experiments reflect adaptations to their natural surroundings?
6. How is being able to detect surface texture a good adaptation for pill bugs in their natural habitat?

## Further Inquiry

1. Design an experiment to investigate the response of pill bugs to temperature. Think carefully about how you will construct your apparatus. Seek approval from your teacher before you actually conduct this experiment. How do you think the pill bugs will respond?
2. Design an experiment to investigate whether pill bugs have preferences for certain types of food.

### OBSERVATIONS OF PILL-BUG BEHAVIOR

| Stimulus | Prediction | Observation |
|---|---|---|
| Light | | |
| Moisture | | |
| Food | | |

The leaf-footed bug, *Diactor bilineatus,* is a colorful member of the extremely diverse world of insects.

**SECTION 1** *The Insect World*

**SECTION 2** *Insect Behavior*

SCIENTIFIC
AMERICAN

For project ideas from *Scientific American,* visit go.hrw.com and type in the keyword **HM6SAJ**.

# THE INSECT WORLD

*Insects have thrived for more than 400 million years, since long before the rise and fall of the dinosaurs. The story of insects is one of great biological success through evolution and adaptation. Today, insects account for more than half of all animal species on Earth.*

### OBJECTIVES

- **Relate** the major characteristics of insects to insects' biological success.
- **List** both harmful and beneficial effects of insects on human society.
- **Describe** the external structure and organ systems of a grasshopper.
- **Compare** incomplete and complete metamorphosis in insects.
- **Describe** defensive adaptations in insects.

### VOCABULARY

entomology
labrum
labium
tympanum
ovipositor
metamorphosis
incomplete metamorphosis
nymph
complete metamorphosis
pupa

## CHARACTERISTICS AND CLASSIFICATION OF INSECTS

Many of the adaptations that have made insects successful are characteristics they share with other arthropods, such as a segmented body, jointed appendages, and an exoskeleton. Insects belong to the class Insecta in the subphylum Hexapoda (hek-SAP-uh-duh), which also includes three minor orders that are not considered true insects.

The body of an insect is divided into three tagmata: the head, thorax, and abdomen. Like myriapods, insects have mandibles and one pair of antennae on their head, and the antennae and other appendages are unbranched. The thorax has three pairs of jointed legs and, in many species, one or two pairs of wings. The abdomen is composed of 9 to 11 segments, and in adults it has neither wings nor legs.

Most insects are small. Among the smallest is a parasitic wasp, which is only 0.14 mm (0.005 in.) in length. Some insects are much larger. For example, the African Goliath beetle reaches 10 cm (4 in.) in length, and the atlas moth has a wingspan of more than 25 cm (10 in.). These two giants of the insect world are shown in Figure 37-1.

**FIGURE 37-1**

The African goliath beetle (a) and Atlas moth (b) are among Earth's largest insects.

**(a)** African goliath beetle, *Goliathus goliatus*

**(b)** Atlas moth, *Attacus atlas*

# Entomologist

**Job Description** Entomologists are scientists who study insects and other terrestrial arthropods. Studying insects can be exciting because insects make up more than half of all animal species. Some entomologists research the classification, distribution, or physiology of insects. Some work in medicine and agriculture to reduce insect pests that spread disease or to use beneficial insects to control harmful pests. Entomologists may work in universities, museums, private companies, or government agencies.

**Focus on an Entomologist**
"You look for beauty in the small," says entomologist and professor Genaro López. López and his students are performing field surveys of pseudoscorpions. "My students can be world experts if they continue to study them for another year or two!" notes López. López enjoys telling stories about scorpions, butterflies, dragonflies, and other insects, to capture his biology students' attention. López specialized in entomology for several reasons. "I wanted to study an entire animal—and, I wanted to be outdoors," says López. He also likes studying insects because they play roles that are important to humans.

**Education and Skills**
- **High school**—three years of science courses and four years of math courses.
- **College**—bachelor of science (B.S.) in biology, including course work in ecology, botany, and zoology; for research, a master's degree (M.S.) or doctoral degree (Ph.D.) is needed.
- **Skills**—attention to detail, self-motivation, curiosity, patience, ability to work independently, fitness, and survival skills.

For more about careers, visit **go.hrw.com** and type in the keyword **HM6 Careers.**

The study of insects and other terrestrial arthropods is called **entomology** (ENT-uh-MAHL-uh-jee), and the scientists who engage in it are known as *entomologists*. Entomologists classify insects into more than 25 orders based on characteristics such as the structure of mouthparts, number of wings, and type of development. Several of the more common insect orders are listed in Table 37-1.

## The Success of Insects

Insects live almost everywhere in the world except in salt water. Entomologists have described and classified nearly 1 million insect species, or more species than exist in all other animal groups combined. In terms of their widespread distribution and great abundance, insects are very successful.

One of the most important factors responsible for the remarkable success of insects is their ability to fly, which enables them to escape from predators and disperse rapidly into new environments. Like other arthropods, insects also benefit from having a light but sturdy exoskeleton and jointed appendages that perform a variety of functions. In addition, most insects are small, so several species can inhabit different local environments within an area without competing with one another for food or other resources. Finally, insects generally have very short life spans and produce large numbers of eggs. Therefore, natural selection can occur more quickly in insects than in organisms that take longer to reach maturity.

## TABLE 37-1  Common Insect Orders

| Order (meaning of order name) | Approximate number of species | Examples | Type of metamorphosis | Characteristics | Significance to humans |
|---|---|---|---|---|---|
| Hemiptera ("half wing") | 55,000 | true bugs | incomplete | two pairs of wings during part of life; piercing, sucking mouthparts | damage crops and garden plants; transmit disease |
| Homoptera ("like wing") | 20,000 | aphids mealy bugs cicadas | incomplete | membranous wings held like roof over body (some species wingless); piercing, sucking mouthparts | damage crops, garden plants, and young trees |
| Isoptera ("equal wing") | 2,000 | termites | incomplete | at times, two pairs of membranous wings; chewing mouthparts | decompose wood in buildings; recycle resources in forests |
| Odonata ("toothed") | 5,000 | dragonflies damselflies | incomplete | two pairs of long, narrow, membranous wings; chewing mouthparts | destroy harmful insects; nymphs serve as food for freshwater fish |
| Orthoptera ("straight wing") | 30,000 | grasshoppers crickets katydids | incomplete | two pairs of straight wings; chewing mouthparts | damage crops, garden plants, and stored foods |
| Coleoptera ("sheathed wing") | 400,000 | weevils ladybugs beetles | complete | hard forewings, membranous hind wings; chewing mouthparts | destroy crops; damage trees; prey on other insects |
| Diptera ("two wing") | 120,000 | mosquitoes flies gnats | complete | one pair of wings (hind pair reduced to knobs); sucking, piercing, or lapping mouthparts | carry diseases; destroy crops; pollinate flowers; act as decomposers |
| Hymenoptera ("membrane wing") | 100,000 | bees wasps ants | complete | two pairs of membranous wings (some species wingless); biting, sucking or lapping mouthparts; some species social | pollinate flowers; make honey; destroy harmful insects; may sting |
| Lepidoptera ("scaled wing") | 140,000 | butterflies moths | complete | large, scaled wings; chewing mouthparts in larvae, siphoning mouthparts in adults | pollinate flowers; larvae and pupae produce silk; larvae damage clothing and crops |

FIGURE 37-2

Some insects are harmful to humans, but most are beneficial. (a) Termites, such as *Reticulitermes flavipes,* can destroy a building by feeding on the wood. (b) The blister beetle, *Lytta fulvipennis,* cross-fertilizes plants by spreading pollen from flower to flower as it searches for nectar. Insects serve important roles in many agricultural systems.

(a)  (b)

## Insects and People

Because insects are so abundant, it is not surprising that they affect our lives in many ways. Some insects, such as grasshoppers, boll weevils, and corn earworms, compete with humans for food by eating crops. In fact, nearly every crop plant has some insect pest. Other insects spread diseases by biting humans or domesticated animals. For example, some fleas may transmit the bacteria that cause plague; some female mosquitoes may transmit the protists that cause malaria; and the tsetse fly may transmit the protists that cause African sleeping sickness. Termites, shown in Figure 37-2a, attack the wood in buildings, and some moths consume wool clothing and carpets.

Despite the problems some insects cause, it would be a serious mistake to think that the world would be better off without any insects. Insects play vital roles in almost all terrestrial and freshwater environments. They serve as food for numerous species of fish, birds, and other animals. Many kinds of insects, such as the beetle shown in Figure 37-2b, are essential for the cross-pollination of plants. It is estimated that insects pollinate 40 percent of the world's flowering plants, including many of those cultivated as food for humans and livestock. Insects also manufacture a number of commercially valuable products, including honey, wax, silk, and shellac. We tend to think of termites as destructive pests because of their effects on buildings, but by feeding on decaying wood, they also help recycle nutrients needed to maintain a healthy forest. Other insects recycle the nutrients contained in animal carcasses.

## THE GRASSHOPPER

In this section, the grasshopper will be used to demonstrate some of the details of insect structure and function. As you read, remember that these details are not shared by all insects. The diversity of the insect world is so great that no typical insect exists.

## External Structure

The major features of an adult grasshopper's external structure are illustrated in Figure 37-3. The body of a grasshopper clearly shows three tagmata. The most anterior tagma, the head, bears the mouthparts. It also has a pair of unbranched antennae as well as simple and compound eyes.

The middle tagma, the thorax, is divided into three parts: the prothorax, mesothorax, and metathorax. The *prothorax* attaches to the head and bears the first pair of walking legs. The *mesothorax* bears the forewings and the second pair of walking legs. The *metathorax* attaches to the abdomen and bears the hindwings and the large jumping legs. The muscles inside the jumping legs store energy when the legs are flexed. Release of this energy causes the legs to extend suddenly, launching the grasshopper into the air and away from danger. A flexible joint at the base of each leg provides the legs with great freedom of motion. Spines and hooks on the legs enable the grasshopper to cling to branches and blades of grass.

The leathery forewings cover and protect the membranous hindwings when the grasshopper isn't flying. Although the forewings help the grasshopper glide during flight, the hindwings actually propel it through the air. The wings are powered by muscles attached to the inside of the exoskeleton in the thorax. Note that insect wings develop as outgrowths of the thorax and are composed of exoskeleton material. Thus, they are not homologous to bird and bat wings, which develop from limb buds.

The segments in the most posterior tagma, the abdomen, are composed of upper and lower plates that are joined by a tough but flexible sheet of exoskeleton. The same flexible sheet also connects the segments to one another. The exoskeleton is covered by a waxy cuticle that is secreted by the cells of the epidermis. The rigid exoskeleton supports the grasshopper's body, and the cuticle retards the loss of body water. Both structures are adaptations for a terrestrial life.

**FIGURE 37-3**

The external anatomy of a grasshopper shows features that are characteristic of most insects: a body consisting of a head, thorax, and abdomen; a pair of unbranched antennae; three pairs of jointed legs; and two pairs of wings.

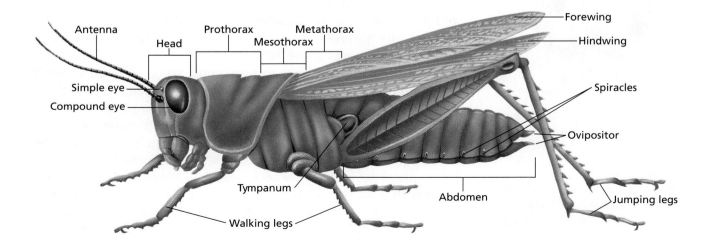

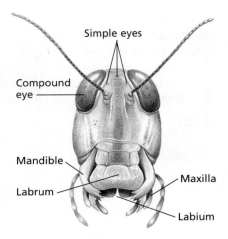

Simple eyes

Compound eye

Mandible

Labrum

Maxilla

Labium

**(a) GRASSHOPPER MOUTHPARTS**

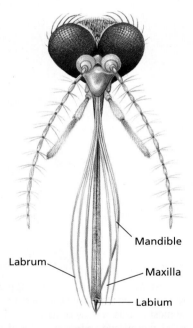

Mandible

Labrum

Maxilla

Labium

**(b) MOSQUITO MOUTHPARTS**

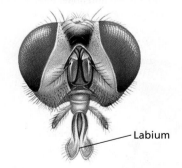

Labium

**(c) HOUSEFLY MOUTHPARTS**

**FIGURE 37-4**

Insect mouthparts are adapted for different functions in different species. Mouthparts are used for biting and chewing in grasshoppers (a), piercing and sucking in mosquitoes (b), and sponging and lapping in houseflies (c).

# Feeding and Digestion

Grasshoppers feed on plants. The mouthparts of grasshoppers, shown in Figure 37-4a, are modified for cutting and chewing leaves and blades of grass. The **labrum** and **labium** are mouthparts that function like upper and lower lips, respectively. They hold the food in position so that the sharp-edged *mandibles* can tear off edible bits. Behind the mandibles are the *maxillae,* which also help hold and cut the food. Recall that all anthropods have mandibles and maxillae.

The mouthparts of other insects are specialized for the types of food they eat, as you can see in Figures 37-4b and 37-4c. For example, mosquitoes have long, thin mouthparts that fit together to form a needle-like tube, which the females use to pierce the skin of other animals and suck up blood. The mouthparts of many flies, in contrast, are soft, spongelike lobes that soak up fruit juices and other liquids.

The digestive tract of a grasshopper is shown in Figure 37-5. Food enters the mouth, is moistened by saliva from the *salivary* (SAL-uh-VER-ee) *glands* and then passes through the esophagus and into the *crop* for temporary storage. From the crop, food passes into the *gizzard,* where sharp, chitinous plates shred it. The shredded mass then enters a portion of the digestive tract called the *midgut.* There, the food is broken down by enzymes secreted by the *gastric ceca* (GAS-trik SEE-kuh), which are pockets that branch from the digestive tract. Nutrients are absorbed into the coelom through the *midgut.* Undigested matter enters the posterior section of the digestive tract, the *hindgut,* and leaves the body through the *anus.*

# Circulation, Respiration, and Excretion

Nutrients and other materials are transported through the body of a grasshopper by an open circulatory system that is similar to that of the crayfish. Hemolymph flows through a large dorsal vessel called the *aorta* (ay-OHR-tuh), which is shown in Figure 37-5. The muscular heart, which is located in the abdomen and thorax, pumps the hemolymph forward through the aorta and into the part of the coelom nearest the head. The hemolymph then percolates through the coelom toward the abdomen and reenters the heart through small pores along its length.

Most animals transport oxygen and carbon dioxide through their circulatory system. However, insects exchange these gases with the environment through a complex network of air tubes called *trachea.* Trachea also serve this purpose in some spiders. In grasshoppers, air enters the tracheae through spiracles on the sides of the thorax and abdomen, as seen in Figures 37-3 and 37-5. The ends of the tracheae branch near the cells of the body and are filled with fluid. Oxygen diffuses into the cells from this fluid while carbon dioxide diffuses in the reverse direction. Air can be pumped in and out of the tracheae by the movements of the abdomen and wings.

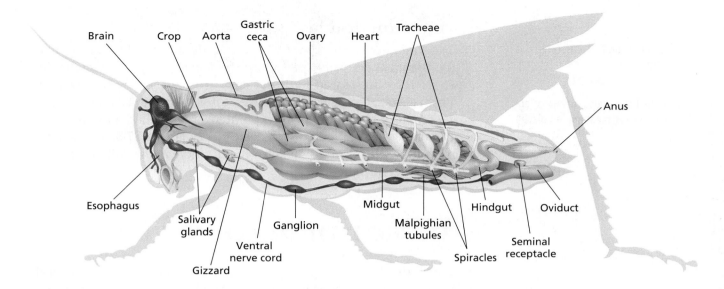

Brain　Crop　Aorta　Gastric ceca　Ovary　Heart　Tracheae

Anus

Esophagus

Salivary glands　Ganglion　Ventral nerve cord　Gizzard

Midgut　Malpighian tubules　Hindgut　Oviduct　Spiracles　Seminal receptacle

Like spiders, insects have excretory organs called *Malpighian tubules* that collect water and cellular wastes from the hemolymph. As Figure 37-5 shows, the Malpighian tubules are attached to the digestive tract between the midgut and the hindgut. In insects that live in dry environments, the Malpighian tubules return most of the water to the hemolymph, producing a very concentrated mixture of wastes that is deposited in the hindgut and leaves the body with the feces. This is another method by which insects are adapted for life on land.

**FIGURE 37-5**

The major internal organs of a female grasshopper are seen in this cutaway side view.

## Neural Control

The grasshopper's central nervous system consists of a brain and a ventral nerve cord with ganglia located in each body segment. Nerves extend from the brain to the antennae, eyes, and other organs of the head. The antennae contain sensory structures that respond to touch and smell. The three simple eyes are arranged in a row just above the base of the antennae. The simple eyes function to sense the intensity of light. Two bulging compound eyes, which are composed of hundreds of individual light detectors and lenses, provide a wide field of view. In addition to sensing light intensity, the compound eyes can detect movement and form images.

Other nerves extend from the ganglia to the muscles and sensory structures in the thorax and abdomen. One such structure is a sound-sensing organ called the **tympanum** (TIM-puh-nuhm). The tympanum is a large, oval membrane that covers an air-filled cavity on each side of the first abdominal segment. Sounds cause the tympanum to vibrate, and the vibrations are detected by nerve cells that line the cavity. Tympana are also found in many other insects that use sound in communication, such as crickets and cicadas. In addition, sensory hairs that are similar to those of a crayfish are distributed over an insect's body. At the base of each hair is a nerve cell that is activated if the hair is touched or moved by vibration.

**Word Roots and Origins**

*tympanum*

from the Latin *tympanum*, meaning "drum"

## Reproduction

Grasshoppers have separate sexes, as do all insects. During mating, the male deposits sperm into the female's seminal receptacle, where they are stored until the eggs are released by the ovaries. After release, the eggs are fertilized internally. The last segment of the female's abdomen forms a pointed organ called an **ovipositor** (OH-vuh-PAHZ-uht-uhr), which you can see in Figure 37-3. The female grasshopper uses her ovipositor to dig a hole in the soil, where she lays the fertilized eggs.

# INSECT DEVELOPMENT

After hatching from the egg, a young insect must undergo several molts before it reaches its adult size and becomes sexually mature. Silverfish and a few other insects go through the molting process without changing body form. The majority of insects undergo some type of change in form as they develop into adults. This phenomenon of developmental change in form is called **metamorphosis** (MET-uh-MOHR-fuh-suhs). There are two main kinds of metamorphosis in insects: incomplete and complete.

### Incomplete Metamorphosis

In **incomplete metamorphosis,** illustrated in Figure 37-6, a nymph hatches from an egg and gradually develops into an adult. A **nymph** is an immature form of an insect that looks somewhat like the adult, but it is smaller, and its wings and reproductive organs are undeveloped. The nymph molts several times. With each molt, the wings become larger and more fully formed. The final molt transforms the nymph into an adult that can reproduce and, in most species, fly. Insects that undergo incomplete metamorphosis include grasshoppers, mayflies, dragonflies, and termites. Several other examples are listed in Table 37-1.

### Complete Metamorphosis

In **complete metamorphosis,** an insect undergoes two stages of development between the egg and the adult. In both of those stages, the insect looks substantially different from its adult form. Figure 37-7 illustrates complete metamorphosis in the monarch butterfly. A wormlike larva, commonly called a *caterpillar,* hatches from the egg. Insect larvae may or may not have legs on the thorax and may or may not have leglike appendages on the abdomen. The larva eats almost constantly, growing large on a diet composed mostly of leaves. Thus, it is the larval stage of most insects that causes the most damage to plants.

**FIGURE 37-6**

In incomplete metamorphosis, shown here in a grasshopper, a nymph hatches from an egg and molts several times before becoming an adult. Nymphs resemble adults but are not sexually mature and lack functional wings.

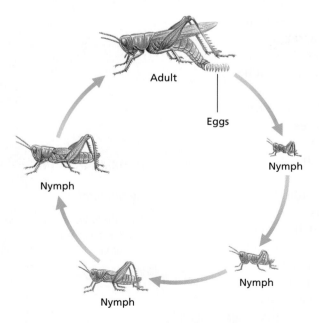

Adult

Eggs

Nymph

Nymph

Nymph

Nymph

**INCOMPLETE METAMORPHOSIS**

The monarch larva molts several times as it grows. In the last larval stage, it develops bands of black, white, and yellow along its body. It continues to feed, but soon finds a sheltered spot and hangs upside down. Its body becomes shorter and thicker. Its exoskeleton then splits down the dorsal side and falls off, revealing a green pupa. A **pupa** (PYOO-puh), also called a *chrysalis* (KRIS-uh-luhs), is a stage of development in which an insect changes from a larva to an adult. The pupa of butterflies is enclosed in a protective case. Moth pupae are enclosed in a case called a *cocoon*. Inside the pupa, the larval tissues break down, and groups of cells called imaginal disks develop into the wings and other tissues of the adult. When metamorphosis is complete, the pupa molts into a sexually mature, winged butterfly. Most insects go through complete metamorphosis. Table 37-1 lists several examples besides butterflies and moths, such as beetles, mosquitoes, and bees.

## Importance of Metamorphosis

In a life cycle based on complete metamorphosis, the larval and adult stages often fulfill different functions, live in different habitats, and eat different foods. Therefore, the larvae and adults do not compete for space and food. For example, mosquito larvae live in fresh water and feed by filtering small food particles out of the water. When they become adults, the mosquitoes leave the water and feed on plant sap or the blood of terrestrial animals.

Metamorphosis also enhances insect survival by helping insects survive harsh weather. For instance, most butterflies and moths spend the winter as pupae encased in chrysalises or cocoons, which are often buried in the soil.

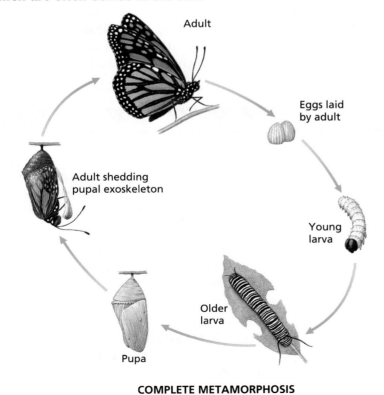

Adult

Eggs laid by adult

Adult shedding pupal exoskeleton

Young larva

Older larva

Pupa

**COMPLETE METAMORPHOSIS**

**FIGURE 37-7**

In complete metamorphosis, shown here in the monarch butterfly, a larva hatches from an egg and goes through several molts before becoming a pupa, which then develops into an adult. Neither the larva nor the pupa resembles the adult.

# INSECT DEFENSE

FIGURE 37-8

Batesian mimicry is shown by the harmless syrphid fly of the genus *Arctophila* (a), which looks very similar to the stinging bumblebee of the genus *Bombus* (b).

**(a)**

**(b)**

Insects have many defensive adaptations that increase their chances for survival. Some adaptations provide a passive defense. One form of passive defense that is frequently observed in insects is camouflage. Camouflage enhances survival by making it difficult for predators to recognize an insect. Insects often resemble parts of the plants on which they feed or hunt for food. For example, many varieties of stick insects and mantises look so much like twigs or leaves that they are easy to overlook unless they move.

Insects that are poisonous or taste bad as a defense often have bold, bright color patterns that make them clearly recognizable and warn predators away. This type of coloration is known as *warning coloration*. In some cases, several dangerous or poisonous species have similar warning coloration. For example, many species of stinging bees and wasps display a pattern of black and yellow stripes. This adaptation, in which one dangerous species mimics the warning coloration of another, is called *Müllerian* (myoo-LER-ee-uhn) *mimicry*. Figure 37-8 shows that the black and yellow stripes of bees and wasps are found in some species of flies, which lack stingers and are harmless. Mimicry of this type, in which a harmless species mimics the warning coloration of a dangerous species, is called *Batesian* (BAYTZ-ee-uhn) *mimicry*. Both Müllerian and Batesian mimicry discourage predators from preying on similarly marked species.

Other defensive adaptations of insects are more aggressive, such as the venomous stingers of female bees and wasps. One of the most elaborate adaptations is that of the bombardier beetle, which defends itself by spraying a stream of a noxious chemical. The beetle can even rotate an opening on its abdomen to aim the spray at an attacker.

## SECTION 1 REVIEW

1. What are some major characteristics of the class Insecta that have contributed to the biological success of insects?

2. List two ways that insects are harmful to society and two ways that they are beneficial.

3. State the function of each of the following parts of an insect: labrum, tympanum, and ovipositor.

4. What are the differences between incomplete and complete metamorphosis?

5. Describe two types of mimicry in insects.

**CRITICAL THINKING**

6. **Inferring Relationships** What is the adaptive advantage of having a tracheal system rather than respiring through the skin?

7. **Analyzing Concepts** Metamorphosis is part of the process of growth and maturation of insects. What kind of internal mechanism likely controls metamorphosis?

8. **Recognizing Differences** The monarch butterfly and the viceroy butterfly have similar markings, and birds do not eat either type. Monarchs are distasteful to birds, but viceroys are not. What type of defensive adaptation is being described?

# INSECT BEHAVIOR

*One reason for the success of insects is their ability to engage in complex behaviors. This ability is made possible by insects' jointed appendages, elaborate sense organs, and relatively complex brains. Insects are capable of interpreting sensory information to escape from predators, find food and mates, and communicate with one another.*

## COMMUNICATION

Insects communicate in many different ways. Many insects use pheromones, sound, and light to communicate.

One of the most common forms of communication among insects is chemical communication involving pheromones. A **pheromone** (FER-uh-MOHN) is a chemical released by an animal that affects the behavior or development of other members of the same species through the sense of smell or taste. Pheromones play a major role in the behavior patterns of many insects. For example, you may have noticed ants, like those in Figure 37-9, marching along a tightly defined route on the ground. The ants are following a trail of pheromones left by the ants that preceded them. Such trails are often laid down by ants that have found a source of food as they make their way back to the nest. As other ants follow the trail, they too deposit pheromones, so the trail becomes stronger as more ants travel along it.

Pheromones are also used for other purposes. For example, honeybees use pheromones to identify their own hives and to recruit other members of the hive in attacking animals that threaten the hive. Some insects secrete pheromones to attract mates. The female silkworm moth, for example, can attract males from several kilometers away by secreting less than 0.01 µg of a pheromone. Sensory hairs on the large antennae of a male moth make it exquisitely sensitive to the pheromone.

Many insects communicate through sound. Male crickets produce chirping sounds by rubbing a scraper located on one forewing against a vein on the other forewing. They make these sounds to attract females and to warn other males away from their territories. Each cricket species produces several calls that differ from those of other cricket species. In fact, because many species look similar, entomologists often use a cricket's calls rather than its appearance to identify its species.

### OBJECTIVES

- **Identify** three ways that insects communicate, and give an example of each.
- **Describe** the social organization of honeybees.
- **Explain** how honeybees communicate information about the location of food.

### VOCABULARY

pheromone
social insect
innate behavior
worker bee
queen bee
drone
royal jelly
queen factor
altruistic behavior
kin selection

**FIGURE 37-9**

These leaf-cutter ants, *Atta colombica,* are following a pheromone trail as they carry sections of leaves to their underground nest.

Mosquitoes communicate through sound, too. Males that are ready to mate fly directly to the buzzing sounds produced by females. A male senses the buzzing by means of sensory hairs on his antennae that vibrate only at the frequency produced by females of the same species.

Insects may also communicate by generating flashes of light. Fireflies, for example, use light to find mates. Males emit flashes in flight, and females flash back in response. Each species of firefly has its own pattern of flashes, which helps males find females of the same species.

# BEHAVIOR IN HONEYBEES

Some insects, such as certain species of bees, wasps, ants, and termites, live in complex colonies. In these colonies, some individuals gather food, others protect the colony, and others reproduce. Insects that live in such colonies are called **social insects.** The division of labor among social insects creates great interdependence and a heightened need for communication. This section will look at the behavioral adaptations of one well-studied species of social insect, the honeybee. As you read about the complex behaviors of honeybees, keep in mind that these behaviors are neither taught nor learned. Instead, they are genetically determined. Genetically determined behavior is called **innate behavior.**

A honeybee colony consists of three distinct types of individuals, which are illustrated in Figure 37-10: worker bees, the queen bee, and drones. **Worker bees** are nonreproductive females that make up the vast majority of the hive population, which may reach more than 80,000. The workers perform all the duties of the hive except reproduction. The **queen bee** is the only reproductive female in the hive, and her only function is to reproduce. **Drones** are males that develop from unfertilized eggs. Their only function is to deliver sperm to the queen. Their mouthparts are too short to obtain nectar from flowers, so the workers must feed them. The number of drones in the hive may reach a few hundred during the summer, but when the honey supply begins to run low, the workers kill the drones and clear them from the hive.

## Worker Bees

Worker bees perform many functions during their lifetime, which lasts about six weeks. After making the transition from pupa to adult, workers feed honey and pollen to the queen, drones, and larvae. During this stage, the workers are called *nurse bees.* They secrete **royal jelly,** a high-protein substance that they feed to the queen and youngest larvae. After about a week, worker bees stop secreting royal jelly and begin to secrete wax, which they use to build and repair the honeycomb. During this stage, they may also clean and guard the hive and fan their wings to circulate air through the hive.

**FIGURE 37-10**

In a honeybee colony, worker bees perform the work of the hive, while drones and the queen are involved exclusively with reproduction.

Worker bee

Drone

Queen bee

The workers spend the last weeks of their life gathering nectar and pollen. A number of structural adaptations aid them in this work. Their mouthparts are specialized for lapping up nectar, and their legs have structures that serve to collect and transport pollen from flowers.

The workers do not use their ovipositors for egg laying. Instead, their ovipositors are modified into barbed stingers that the workers use to protect the hive. When a worker bee stings an animal, the stinger and attached venom sac are left behind in the victim as the bee flies away. The worker, having lost part of its body and much of its hemolymph, dies a day or two later. Wasps also have stingers that are modified ovipositors. Unlike honeybees, they can sting many times because their stinger is not barbed.

## The Queen Bee

The queen bee develops from an egg identical to the eggs that develop into the workers. Queen bees develop only when selected larvae are fed a continuous diet of royal jelly throughout their larval development. As a queen matures, she secretes a pheromone called the **queen factor** that prevents other female larvae from developing into queens.

The queen's role is to reproduce. Within a few days after she completes metamorphosis and emerges as an adult, she flies out of the hive and mates in the air with one or more drones. During mating, millions of sperm are deposited in the queen's seminal receptacle, where they will remain for the five or more years of her life. Although the queen mates only once, she may lay thousands of eggs each year.

When the hive becomes overcrowded, the queen leaves the hive. As she leaves, she secretes a swarming pheromone that induces about half of the workers in the hive to follow her and form a swarm. Eventually the swarm finds another location for a new hive. Meanwhile, in the old hive, the remaining workers begin feeding royal jelly to other larvae. When a new queen emerges, she produces the queen factor, and in response, the workers destroy the other developing queens. The new queen departs on a mating flight, and the cycle begins again.

## The Dances of the Bees

When honeybees leave the hive and find a source of pollen and nectar, how do they communicate the location of this food source to other workers in the hive? An Austrian biologist, Karl von Frisch (1886–1982), spent 25 years answering this question. His careful experimentation earned him a Nobel Prize in 1973.

To study bees, von Frisch built a glass-walled hive and placed feeding stations stocked with sweetened water near the hive. He noted that "scout bees" returning from the feeding stations would perform a series of dancelike movements in the hive. The scout bee would circle first to the right and then to the left, a behavior that von Frisch called the *round dance*.

## Quick Lab

### Interpreting Nonverbal Communication

**Materials** pencil, paper, wrapped candy pieces

**Procedure**
1. Choose one member of your group to play the part of the "scout" bee. The others in the group will be the "worker" bees.
2. Your teacher will secretly tell the scout bee where a "food source" (piece of candy) is located. The scout bee will develop a method of nonverbal communication to let the worker bees know where the food is hidden. The scout bee may not point to the food. Use Figure 37-11 for ideas on how to develop your method of communication.
3. When the food has been located, the scout will hide another piece of food and select a new scout. The new scout will develop a different way to tell the group where the food is located. Repeat the procedure until everyone in your group has been a scout.

**Analysis**
1. How effective were each of your scout's methods for showing the location of the food?
2. Did the worker bees improve their ability to find the food after several trials?
3. List and describe some types of nonverbal communication that humans use.

**(a) ROUND DANCE**

**(b) WAGGLE DANCE**

**FIGURE 37-11**

Honeybees use two types of dances to convey information about food sources. (a) The round dance indicates that a food source is nearby. (b) The waggle dance indicates the direction of food and the food's distance from the hive.

A round dance pattern is shown in Figure 37-11a. After many observations, von Frisch concluded that the round dance told other worker bees that a food source was near the hive, but it did not inform them of the exact location of the food.

Von Frisch also observed that when the food source was far from the hive, the scout bees would perform another type of dance on a vertical surface inside the hive. He called this dance the *waggle dance* because the scout bees waggled their abdomens from side to side. As you can see in Figure 37-11b, the pattern of the waggle dance is like a figure eight. The scout bee makes a circle in one direction, then a straight run while waggling her abdomen, and then another circle in the opposite direction from the first. The direction of food is indicated by the angle of the straight run on the vertical surface. Straight up, for example, indicates a direction toward the sun. The distance to the food source is indicated by the duration of the dance and the number of waggles on each run.

## Altruistic Behavior

When worker bees sting an intruder to defend the colony, they cause their own deaths. This behavior is an example of **altruistic** (AL-troo-IS-tik) **behavior,** which is the aiding of other individuals at one's own risk or expense. The stinging of honeybees is an innate behavior. You might think that the genes directing this behavior would eventually be eliminated from the population, since dead bees can't reproduce. However, this does not happen.

Genetics explains why evolution has selected for altruistic behavior in honeybees. Worker bees are nonreproductive. Therefore, they cannot pass on their own genes by reproducing. However, they can pass on some of their genes by helping a closely related individual reproduce. By defending the colony, a worker bee increases the chances that the queen bee will survive. If the queen survives, she will produce more workers who will share many of the same genes. Thus, by behaving altruistically, a worker can cause more of her genes to be propagated in the population. This mechanism of propagating one's own genes by helping a closely related individual reproduce is called **kin selection.**

## SECTION 2 REVIEW

1. Name three ways that insects communicate, and give an example of each way.

2. What determines whether a fertilized honeybee egg will develop into a worker or a queen?

3. How do honeybees behave when their hive is overcrowded?

4. How do honeybees convey information about the direction and distance of a food source that is far from the hive?

**CRITICAL THINKING**

5. **Evaluating Methods** How could you experiment to show that an insect is responding to pheromones and not visual cues?

6. **Recognizing Relationships** What is the adaptive advantage of innate behavior?

7. **Analyzing Current Research** Queen bees sometimes mate with drones from other hives. How might this behavior benefit the colony?

# CHAPTER HIGHLIGHTS

## The Insect World

- The insect body is divided into three tagmata. The head has mandibles and one pair of unbranched antennae; the thorax has three pairs of jointed legs and, in many species, one or two pairs of wings; and the abdomen has 9 to 11 segments but neither wings nor legs in adults.

- Insects live in almost every terrestrial and freshwater environment. Factors responsible for their success include their ability to fly, exoskeleton, jointed appendages, small size, and short life span.

- Insects negatively affect humans by competing for food, transmitting diseases, and destroying buildings and other manufactured products. However, insects are also beneficial. They serve as food for other animals, pollinate flowers, make valuable products such as honey, and recycle nutrients.

- The mouthparts of insects are often specialized for tearing and cutting solid food or for sucking or soaking up liquid food.

- Insects have an open circulatory system that transports nutrients through the body. Gas exchange occurs by means of air-filled tracheae that reach deep into the body. Malpighian tubules remove cellular wastes from the hemolymph while conserving water.

- Insect sensory structures include simple and compound eyes, sound-sensing tympana in some species, and sensory hairs on the antennae and other body parts.

- Most insects go through metamorphosis. In incomplete metamorphosis, a nymph hatches from an egg and resembles the adult but has undeveloped reproductive organs and no wings. The nymph molts several times to become an adult.

- In complete metamorphosis, a wormlike larva hatches from an egg and molts several times before becoming a pupa. The pupa molts to produce the adult, which resembles neither the larva nor the pupa.

- Insects can defend themselves by stinging, using camouflage, or releasing noxious chemicals. Insects that are dangerous or taste bad often have warning coloration that makes them recognizable to predators. The warning coloration of a dangerous species may be mimicked by harmless species.

### Vocabulary

entomology (p. 742)
labrum (p. 746)
labium (p. 746)

tympanum (p. 747)
ovipositor (p. 748)
metamorphosis (p. 748)

incomplete metamorphosis (p. 748)
nymph (p. 748)

complete metamorphosis (p. 748)
pupa (p. 749)

## Insect Behavior

- Insects communicate by releasing pheromones and by producing sounds and flashes of light.

- Honeybees live in complex colonies consisting mostly of nonreproductive female workers that perform all duties except reproduction. Reproduction in each colony is the exclusive function of one queen and a few hundred male drones.

- Honeybees communicate the direction and distance to food sources by performing dances inside the hive.

- In defending the colony, worker bees show altruistic behavior toward their close relatives in the colony. By doing so, they increase the propagation of their own genes.

### Vocabulary

pheromone (p. 751)
social insect (p. 752)
innate behavior (p. 752)

worker bee (p. 752)
queen bee (p. 752)
drone (p. 752)

royal jelly (p. 752)
queen factor (p. 753)
altruistic behavior (p. 754)

kin selection (p. 754)

## USING VOCABULARY

1. For each pair of terms, explain how the meanings of the terms differ.
   a. *mesothorax* and *metathorax*
   b. *labrum* and *labium*
   c. *nymph* and *pupa*
   d. *worker bee* and *queen bee*
   e. *royal jelly* and *queen factor*

2. Explain the relationship between altruistic behavior and kin selection.

3. Choose the term that does not belong in the following group, and explain why it does not belong: *egg, larva, pupa,* and *nymph*.

4. **Word Roots and Origins** The word *gastric* is derived from the Greek *gaster,* which means "stomach." The word *cecum* is from the Latin *caecus,* which means "blind." Using this information, explain why the term *gastric cecum* is a good name for the structure that the term describes.

## UNDERSTANDING KEY CONCEPTS

5. **Identify** three characteristics that entomologists use to divide insects into orders.

6. **State** how the small size of insects has contributed to the biological success of insects.

7. **Explain** why insect wings are not homologous to the wings of birds and bats.

8. **Describe** the function of spiracles in insects.

9. **Define** *tympanum,* and identify where it is located on a grasshopper.

10. **Explain** the function of warning coloration.

11. **Describe** how crickets produce sounds, and explain the functions of these sounds.

12. **Define** *innate behavior,* and give an example.

13. **List** the three types of individuals that make up a honeybee society.

14. **Compare** the round dance with the waggle dance of honeybees.

15. **Explain** how altruistic behavior may have been selected in honeybees.

16. **CONCEPT MAPPING** Use the following terms to create a concept map that sequences the stages of complete metamorphosis: *older larva, pupal exoskeleton, eggs, pupa, adult,* and *young larva.*

## CRITICAL THINKING

17. **Relating Structure and Function** Insects and crustaceans both belong to the phylum Arthropoda and share many characteristics. Recall that the largest crustacean, the Japanese spider crab, has a leg span of 4 m. In contrast, the largest insects, such as the atlas moth, have a wingspan of only about 25 cm. Identify some possible reasons that the largest crustaceans are so much bigger than the largest insects.

18. **Applying Information** What characteristics may have helped insects survive the major climatic changes that led to the extinction of the dinosaurs and many other species about 65 million years ago?

19. **Interpreting Graphics** The graph below shows changes in size of two insect populations over a six-year period. One population is considered a pest, and the other is considered a beneficial species. At year 4, a pesticide is applied. Describe the relationship between the two species before year 4. How did the populations change after the application of the pesticide? Propose an explanation for the changes that occurred in the two populations after the use of pesticides.

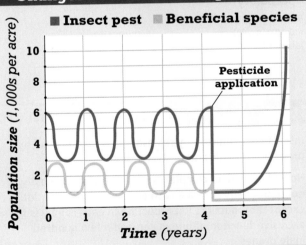

**Changes in Two Insect Populations**

■ **Insect pest**   ■ **Beneficial species**

Pesticide application

Population size (1,000s per acre)

Time (years)

20. **Relating Concepts** Recall that squids and other cephalopods have a closed circulatory system, which supports their active lifestyle by circulating blood quickly through their bodies. Many insects, such as dragonflies and bees, are also very active, but all insects have an open circulatory system. How can insects maintain active lifestyles while having an open circulatory system?

# Standardized Test Preparation

**DIRECTIONS:** Choose the letter of the answer choice that best answers the question.

1. What are an insect's legs and wings attached to?
   **A.** head
   **B.** thorax
   **C.** labrum
   **D.** abdomen

2. What are the mouthparts of a grasshopper specialized for?
   **F.** sucking fluids
   **G.** lapping up liquids
   **H.** cutting and tearing fibers
   **J.** filtering food out of muddy water

3. What is the term for the immature form of an insect that undergoes incomplete metamorphosis?
   **A.** adult
   **B.** pupa
   **C.** infant
   **D.** nymph

**INTERPRETING GRAPHICS:** The illustration below shows the life cycle of a butterfly. Use the illustration to answer the questions that follow.

**Life Cycle of a Butterfly**

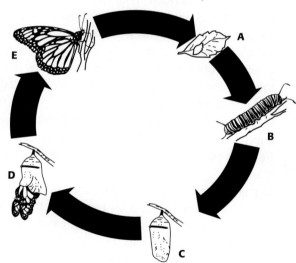

4. What kind of life cycle is shown?
   **F.** direct development
   **G.** seasonal development
   **H.** complete metamorphosis
   **J.** incomplete metamorphosis

5. What is the term for the developmental stage labeled *C*?
   **A.** pupa
   **B.** larva
   **C.** nymph
   **D.** caterpillar

**DIRECTIONS:** Complete the following analogy.

6. queen factor : queen bee :: royal jelly :
   **F.** drone
   **G.** worker
   **H.** queen bee
   **J.** pheromone

**INTERPRETING GRAPHICS:** The diagram below shows the external structure of a grasshopper. Use the diagram to answer the questions that follow.

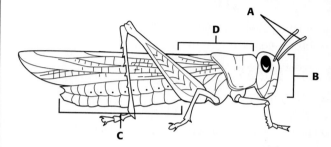

7. What is the term for the structure(s) labeled *D*?
   **A.** thorax
   **B.** labrum
   **C.** abdomen
   **D.** antennae

8. Which of the following structures is part of the structure labeled *B*?
   **F.** ovipositor
   **G.** mandibles
   **H.** tympanum
   **J.** malpighian tubules

## SHORT RESPONSE

Defensive adaptations in insects increase the chances of insects' survival.

Distinguish between passive defenses and aggressive defenses, and give two examples of each.

## EXTENDED RESPONSE

Farmers often try to limit the number of insects on crops by applying chemical insecticides to the crops. Sometimes, an insecticide that had previously been effective no longer affects certain types of insects.

*Part A* Why do farmers try to control insects?

*Part B* How can the effect of insecticides on certain insect populations change?

**Test TIP** For a question about an illustration that has labels, read the labels carefully and then check that the answer you choose matches your interpretation of the labels.

# Observing Grasshopper Anatomy

## OBJECTIVES

- Examine the external and internal anatomy of a grasshopper.
- Infer function from observation of structures.

## PROCESS SKILLS

- relating structure and function
- observing

## MATERIALS

- safety goggles
- gloves
- preserved grasshopper (1 for each student)
- dissection tray
- forceps
- fine dissection scissors, with pointed blades
- hand lens or dissecting microscope
- blunt probe
- sharp probe
- dissection pins

## Background

1. List the distinguishing characteristics of insects.
2. In this lab, you will dissect a grasshopper to observe its external and internal structure. To which order of insects do grasshoppers belong?
3. What characteristics of the grasshopper place it into this order?

### PART A Observing the External Anatomy of the Grasshopper

1. CAUTION **Wear safety goggles and gloves during this lab. Keep your hands away from your eyes and face when working with preserved specimens.** Using forceps, hold a preserved grasshopper under running water to gently but thoroughly remove excess preservative. Then place the grasshopper in a dissection tray.

2. Use a hand lens to observe the grasshopper's parts. While referring to Figure 37-3, identify the head, thorax, and abdomen. Note how the thorax and abdomen are divided into segments.

3. Use forceps to spread out and examine both pairs of wings. Notice that the forewings are narrow and the hindwings are wide. Observe how the hindwings fold fanlike against the body.

4. Observe the legs. Grasp one of each pair of legs and notice how the legs are divided into segments. Gently bend the legs to observe their normal range of motion.

5. Examine the 11 segments of the abdomen. On abdominal segment 1, find the tympanum. Then, along each side of abdominal segments 1–8, locate the spiracles, which look like small dots. Gently touch the abdomen with a blunt probe to find the flexible membrane that connects the segments to one another.

6. While referring to Figure 37-4a, examine the grasshopper's head. Find the two antennae, two compound eyes, and three simple eyes. Use a sharp probe to push apart the mouthparts. Locate and identify the mandibles, maxillae, labium, and labrum. Note that each maxilla has a segmented feeler called a palpus and that the labium has two palpi.

## PART B Observing the Internal Anatomy of the Grasshopper

7. ⚠ CAUTION **Dissecting instruments can cut you. Always cut in a direction away from your face and body.** Using scissors, snip off the grasshopper's legs, wings, and antennae at their bases. Pin the body to the dissection tray. Then use the scissors to make a shallow cut just above the spiracles through the exoskeleton along both sides of the thorax and abdomen.

8. As you remove the exoskeleton, look at its underside, where the heart and aorta may be attached. Also look for muscles attached to the inside of the exoskeleton. Find and remove any fatty tissue (which your teacher can help you identify) that may hide other organs.

9. If your grasshopper is a female, look for its ovaries, which may contain elongated eggs. Refer to Figure 37-5 to see what the ovaries look like. If your grasshopper is a male, examine the ovaries and eggs in the female grasshopper of another student. Remove the ovaries and eggs (if present) from one side of the abdomen to uncover the digestive tract.

10. Make a table in your lab report like the one shown. As you observe each of the structures listed in the table, fill in the function of that structure.

11. Referring to Figure 37-5, look for the organs of the digestive tract: esophagus, crop, gizzard, midgut, hindgut, and anus. Find the salivary glands and the gastric ceca, which are also parts of the digestive system.

12. On the surface of the midgut and hindgut, look for the Malpighian tubules, which are tiny tubes that connect to the digestive tract.

13. Locate and identify the brain, ventral nerve cord, and ganglia.

14. Carefully cut away and remove the organs of the digestive system to expose some parts of the respiratory system. Referring to Figure 37-5, locate and identify tracheae that run along the dorsal and ventral parts of the body, as well as other tracheae that connect them. The larger tracheae lead to spiracles in the abdomen. Look also for swollen tracheae, called air sacs, which increase the volume of air drawn into the abdomen when the grasshopper breathes.

15. ⚠ ⚠ Dispose of your specimen according to the directions from your teacher. Then clean up your materials and wash your hands before leaving the lab.

### FUNCTION OF GRASSHOPPER STRUCTURES

| Structure | Function |
|---|---|
| Esophagus | |
| Crop | |
| Gizzard | |
| Midgut | |
| Hindgut | |
| Salivary glands | |
| Gastric ceca | |
| Malpighian tubules | |
| Tracheae | |
| Spiracles | |

## Analysis and Conclusions

1. How do you think the membrane between segments helps the grasshopper in its movements?
2. How does the function of the stiff, leathery forewings differ from that of the more delicate hindwings?
3. Trace the path of food through the grasshopper's digestive tract.
4. To what system do the Malpighian tubules belong?
5. Why is the circulatory system of the grasshopper described as an open circulatory system?
6. Compared with invertebrates such as flatworms and earthworms, grasshoppers are highly responsive to environmental stimuli. What are some structural adaptations of the grasshopper that make this responsiveness possible?

## Further Inquiry

1. Prepare an illustrated chart that compares and contrasts the characteristics of grasshoppers, beetles (order Coleoptera), and butterflies (order Lepidoptera). What trait of each kind of insect is reflected in the name of its order? Include other traits in your chart.
2. The fruit fly of the genus *Drosophila* is an insect that, unlike the grasshopper, undergoes complete metamorphosis. Research the life cycles of the grasshopper and the fruit fly, and make a chart that compares and contrasts their life cycles.

# ECHINODERMS AND INVERTEBRATE CHORDATES

This blue sea star, *Linckia laevigata*, shows the pentaradial symmetry of most echinoderms.

**SECTION 1** *Echinoderms*

**SECTION 2** *Invertebrate Chordates*

# ECHINODERMS

*The phylum Echinodermata (ee-KIE-noh-duhr-MAH-tuh) is a group of invertebrates that includes sea stars, sand dollars, sea urchins, and sea cucumbers. The members of this phylum, called **echinoderms**, inhabit marine environments ranging from shallow coastal waters to ocean trenches more than 10,000 m deep. They vary in diameter from 1 cm to 1 m and often are brilliantly colored.*

### OBJECTIVES

- **Discuss** four distinguishing characteristics of echinoderms.
- **Describe** representative species from each of the five classes of echinoderms.
- **Describe** the water-vascular system and other major body systems of echinoderms.
- **Compare** sexual and asexual reproduction in sea stars.

### VOCABULARY

echinoderm
ossicle
water-vascular system
tube foot
test
pedicellaria
madreporite
stone canal
ring canal
radial canal
ampulla
cardiac stomach
pyloric stomach
bipinnaria

## CHARACTERISTICS

Echinoderms are radially symmetrical animals. Like cnidarians and ctenophores, which are also radially symmetrical, echinoderms have no head or any other sign of cephalization. Unlike cnidarians and ctenophores, however, adult echinoderms develop from bilaterally symmetrical larvae. A few examples of echinoderm larvae are illustrated in Figure 38-1. This feature of development indicates that echinoderms probably evolved from bilaterally symmetrical ancestors.

The fossil record of echinoderms dates back to the Cambrian period, more than 500 million years ago. Early echinoderms from this period appear to have been sessile, and biologists believe these animals evolved radial symmetry as an adaptation to a sessile existence. Echinoderms later evolved the ability to move from place to place. Today, the vast majority of echinoderm species can move by crawling slowly along the ocean bottom, and only about 80 species are sessile.

Echinoderms are deuterostomes, which makes them different from the other invertebrates you have studied so far. Recall that *deuterostomes* are coelomates whose embryos have radial cleavage.

**FIGURE 38-1**

Notice the bilateral symmetry in these echinoderm larvae. The larvae develop into radially symmetrical adults.

**SEA STAR LARVA**
(bipinnaria)

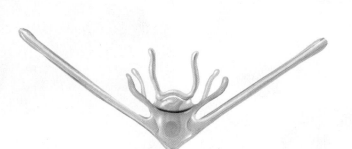

**BRITTLE STAR LARVA**

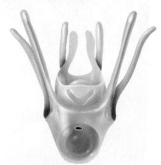

**SEA URCHIN LARVA**

Also, in deuterostomes, the anus forms from the blastopore, and the mesoderm arises from outpockets of the endoderm. Because they develop as deuterostomes, echinoderms are more closely related to chordates than they are to other invertebrates. Chordates are also deuterostomes and are discussed in the second part of this chapter.

Echinoderms have four major characteristics that are not shared by any other phylum. (1) Most echinoderms have a type of radial symmetry called *pentaradial symmetry,* in which the body parts extend from the center along five spokes. (2) They have an endoskeleton composed of calcium carbonate plates known as **ossicles.** The ossicles may be attached to spines or spicules that protrude through the skin. The name *echinoderm* means "spiny skin." (3) They have a **water-vascular system,** which is a network of water-filled canals inside their body. (4) They have many small, movable extensions of the water-vascular system called **tube feet,** which aid in movement, feeding, respiration, and excretion. The water-vascular system and tube feet will be discussed in more detail.

# CLASSIFICATION

Taxonomists divide the 7,000 species of echinoderms into six classes, five of which will be described here: Crinoidea (kri-NOYD-ee-uh), Ophiuroidea (OH-fee-yoor-OYD-ee-uh), Echinoidea (EK-uh-NOYD-ee-uh), Holothuroidea (HOH-loh-thuh-ROYD-ee-uh), and Asteroidea (AS-tuh-ROYD-ee-uh).

## Class Crinoidea

Members of the class Crinoidea, called *crinoids* (KRI-NOYDZ), include the sea lilies and feather stars, which are shown in Figure 38-2. The name *crinoid* means "lily-like." Sea lilies most closely resemble the fossils of ancestral echinoderms from the Cambrian period. They are sessile as adults, remaining attached to rocks or the sea bottom by means of a long stalk. Feather stars, in contrast, can swim or crawl as adults, although they may stay in one place for long periods.

**FIGURE 38-2**

This sea lily, *Cenocrinus* (a), and these feather stars, *Oxycomanthus bennetti* (b), are members of the class Crinoidea. Notice their adaptations for filter feeding.

(a)

(b)

In both types of crinoids, five arms extend from the body and branch to form many more arms—up to 200 in some feather star species. Mucus-covered tube feet located on each arm filter small organisms from the water. The tube feet also serve as a respiratory surface across which crinoids exchange oxygen and carbon dioxide with the water. Cilia on the arms transport trapped food to the crinoid's mouth at the base of the arms. The mouth faces up in crinoids, but in most other echinoderms the mouth faces downward.

## Class Ophiuroidea

The 2,000 species of basket stars and brittle stars make up the largest echinoderm class, Ophiuroidea, which means "snake-tail." Members of this class are distinguished by their long, narrow arms, which allow them to move more quickly than other echinoderms. As you can see in Figure 38-3, the thin, flexible arms of basket stars branch repeatedly to form numerous coils that look like tentacles. Brittle stars, so named because parts of their arms break off easily, can regenerate missing parts.

Basket stars and brittle stars live primarily on the bottom of the ocean, often beneath stones or in the crevices and holes of coral reefs. They are so numerous in some locations that they cover the sea floor. Some species feed by raking in food with their arms or gathering it from the ocean bottom with their tube feet. Others trap suspended particles with their tube feet or with mucous strands located between their spines.

## Class Echinoidea

The class Echinoidea consists of about 900 species of sea urchins and sand dollars. *Echinoidea* means "spinelike," a description that applies especially well to many of the sea urchins, such as the ones shown in Figure 38-4. In both sea urchins and sand dollars, the internal organs are enclosed within a fused, rigid endoskeleton called a **test.**

The spherical sea urchins are well adapted to life on hard sea bottoms. They move by means of their tube feet and feed by scraping algae from hard surfaces with the five teeth that surround their mouth. The teeth and the muscles that move them are part of a complex jawlike mechanism called *Aristotle's lantern.* The spines that protrude from the test may be short and flat, long and thin, or wedge shaped, depending on the species. In some sea urchins, the spines are barbed, and in others, they are hollow and contain a venom that is dangerous to predators as well as swimmers.

Sand dollars live along seacoasts. As their name implies, they are usually found in sandy areas and have the flat, round shape of a silver dollar. Their shape is an adaptation for shallow burrowing. The short spines on a sand dollar are used in locomotion and burrowing, and they help clean the surface of the body. Sand dollars use their tube feet to capture food that settles on or passes over their body.

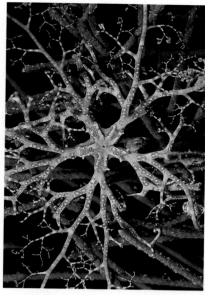

**FIGURE 38-3**

This basket star, *Astrophyton muricatum,* has long, flexible arms with many coiled branches.

internet connect

www.scilinks.org
**Topic:** Echinoidea
**Keyword:** HM60459

SC*i*LINKS. Maintained by the National Science Teachers Association

**FIGURE 38-4**

The long, sharp spines that cover these sea urchins, *Strongylocentrotus,* provide protection against most predators.

FIGURE 38-5

Tentacles around the mouth of this sea cucumber collect food and bring it to the animal's mouth. Five rows of tube feet that run along the body are evidence of the sea cucumber's pentaradial symmetry.

## Class Holothuroidea

Sea cucumbers belong to the class Holothuroidea. Most of these armless echinoderms live on the sea bottom, where they crawl or burrow into soft sediment by using their tube feet. The ossicles that make up their endoskeleton are very small and are not connected to each other, so their bodies are soft. Modified tube feet form a fringe of tentacles around the mouth. When these tentacles are extended, as shown in Figure 38-5, the animals resemble the polyp form of some cnidarians. This resemblance explains the name of this class, which means "water polyp." A sea cucumber uses its tentacles to sweep up sediment and water. It then stuffs its tentacles into its mouth and cleans the food off them.

## Class Asteroidea

The sea stars, or starfish, belong to the class Asteroidea, which means "starlike." Sea stars live in coastal waters all over the world. They exist in a variety of colors and shapes, two of which are shown in Figure 38-6. Sea stars are economically important because they prey on oysters, clams, and other organisms that humans use as food.

**FIGURE 38-6**

Sea stars are found on rocky coastlines worldwide. One of the more colorful varieties is the African sea star, *Protoreaster linckii* (a). The sunflower star, *Pycnopodia helianthoides* (b), can have up to two dozen arms.

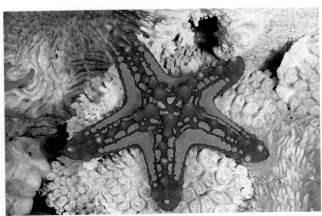

(a)

(b)

# STRUCTURE AND FUNCTION OF ECHINODERMS

The sea star will be used to demonstrate some of the details of echinoderm structure and function. As you read about how echinoderms carry out life functions, consider how they differ from the other groups of invertebrates you have studied.

## External Structure

As you can see in Figure 38-7, the body of a sea star is composed of several arms that extend from a central region. Sea stars typically have five arms, but in some species, such as the one shown in Figure 38-6b, there may be as many as 24. Two rows of tube feet run along the underside of each arm. The body is often flattened.

In echinoderms, the side of the body where the mouth is located is referred to as the *oral surface*. The side of the body that is opposite from the mouth is called the *aboral* (A-BOHR-uhl) *surface*. In sea stars, the oral surface is on the underside of the body.

The body of a sea star is usually covered with short spines that give the animal a rough texture. Surrounding each spine in many sea stars are numerous tiny pincers called **pedicellariae** (PED-uh-suh-LAR-ee-ee), which are shown in Figure 38-7. Pedicellariae help keep the body surface free of foreign objects, including algae and small animals that might grow on the sea star or damage its soft tissues. Pedicellariae are found in sea stars and some sea urchins.

**FIGURE 38-7**

Sea stars have a number of structural features that are unique to the phylum Echinodermata. Their pentaradial symmetry is indicated by their five arms, each of which contains a division of their internal organ systems. The water-vascular system consists of a network of canals connected to hundreds of tube feet. The inset shows that the sea star's exterior is dotted with short spines, pincerlike pedicellariae, and skin gills.

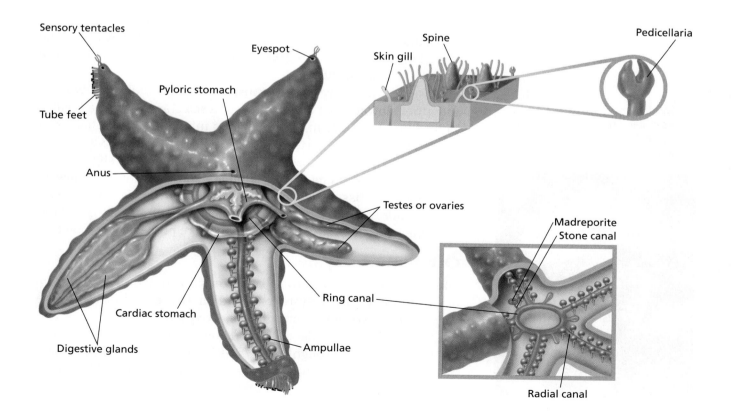

Sensory tentacles · Eyespot · Spine · Pedicellaria · Skin gill · Pyloric stomach · Tube feet · Anus · Testes or ovaries · Madreporite · Stone canal · Cardiac stomach · Ring canal · Digestive glands · Ampullae · Radial canal

## Water-Vascular System

The water-vascular system is a network of water-filled canals that are connected to the tube feet. Use Figure 38-7 to follow the path of water through the water-vascular system. Water enters the system through small pores in the **madreporite** (MA-druh-PAWR-IET), a sieve-like plate on the aboral surface. Water then passes down the **stone canal,** a tube that connects the madreporite to the **ring canal,** which encircles the mouth. Another tube, the **radial canal,** extends from the ring canal to the end of each arm. The radial canals carry water to the hundreds of hollow tube feet. Valves prevent water from flowing back into the radial canals from the tube feet.

The upper end of each tube foot is expanded to form a bulblike sac called an **ampulla** (am-PUHL-uh). Contraction of muscles surrounding the ampullae forces water into the tube feet, causing them to extend. Contraction of muscles lining the tube feet forces water back into the ampullae and shortens the tube feet. In this way, the sea star uses water pressure to extend and withdraw its tube feet. In many species, small muscles raise the center of each tube foot's disklike end, creating suction when the tube feet are pressed against a surface. These coordinated muscular contractions enable sea stars to climb slippery rocks and capture prey.

## Feeding and Digestion

The sea star's mouth is connected by a short esophagus to the **cardiac stomach,** which the sea star can turn inside out through its mouth when it feeds. The cardiac stomach transfers food to the **pyloric stomach,** which connects to a pair of digestive glands in each arm. The cardiac stomach, pyloric stomach, and digestive glands break down food with the help of the enzymes they secrete. Nutrients are absorbed into the coelom through the walls of the digestive glands, and undigested material is expelled through the anus on the aboral surface.

Most sea stars are carnivorous, feeding on mollusks, worms, and other slow-moving animals. When a sea star captures a bivalve mollusk, such as a clam, it attaches its tube feet to both halves of the clamshell and exerts a steady pull, as Figure 38-8 shows. Eventually, the clam's muscles tire, and the shell opens slightly. The sea star then inserts its cardiac stomach into the clam and digests the clam's soft tissues while they are still in the shell. The sea star then withdraws the stomach, containing the partially digested food, back into its body, where the digestive process is completed.

## Other Body Systems

Like other echinoderms, the sea star has no circulatory, excretory, or respiratory organ systems. Fluid in the coelom bathes the organs and distributes nutrients and oxygen. Gas exchange and waste excretion take place by diffusion through the thin walls of the tube feet and through the *skin gills,* hollow tubes that project from the coelom lining to the exterior. You can see the skin gills in the inset in Figure 38-7, on the previous page.

**Word Roots and Origins**

*ampulla*

form the Latin *ampulla,* meaning "flask"

**FIGURE 38-8**

This sea star, *Asterias rubens,* is prying open the shell of a clam to feed on the clam's soft tissues.

Because echinoderms have no head, they also have no brain. The nervous system consists mainly of a *nerve ring* that circles the mouth and a *radial nerve* that runs from the nerve ring along each arm. The nerve ring and radial nerves coordinate the movements of the tube feet. If the radial nerve in one arm is cut, the tube feet in that arm lose coordination. If the nerve ring is cut, the tube feet in all arms become uncoordinated, and the sea star cannot move.

Sea stars also have a nerve net near the body surface that controls the movements of the spines, pedicellariae, and skin gills. The end of each arm has an eyespot that responds to light and several tentacles that respond to touch. The tube feet also respond to touch, and other touch-sensitive and chemical-sensitive cells are scattered over the surface of the sea star's body.

## Reproduction and Development

Most sea star species have separate sexes, as do most other echinoderms. Each arm of the sea star contains a pair of ovaries or testes. Females produce up to 200 million eggs in one year. Fertilization occurs externally, when the eggs and sperm are shed into the water. Each fertilized egg develops into a bilaterally symmetrical, free-swimming larva called a **bipinnaria** (BIE-pin-AR-ee-uh). After about two months, the larva settles to the bottom, and begins metamorphosis into a pentaradially symmetrical adult.

Echinoderms have remarkable powers of regeneration. Sea stars can regenerate arms from the central region of their body, even if they lose all of their arms. The process of regeneration is very slow, taking as long as a year. Sea stars use their regenerative ability as a defensive mechanism, automatically shedding an arm at its base when the arm is captured by a predator. As you can see in Figure 38-9, some sea stars can even regenerate a complete, new individual from a detached arm, as long as the arm is attached to a portion of the central region. Certain species reproduce asexually when the body splits through the central region. The two parts that are formed then regenerate the missing structures.

**FIGURE 38-9**

As long as a sea star retains part of its central region, it can regenerate any arms it loses. The sea star shown here, a member of the genus *Echinaster,* is regenerating five new arms.

---

## SECTION 1 REVIEW

1. What are the characteristics that distinguish Echinodermata from other phyla?

2. Give the common names of members of each of the five classes of echinoderms.

3. How does a sea star extend and withdraw its tube feet?

4. Describe how sea stars are able to reproduce asexually.

**CRITICAL THINKING**

5. **Making Comparisons** Compare development in sea urchins with development in mollusks.

6. **Inferring Relationships** How would a sea star's ability to feed be affected by losing the water in its water-vascular system?

7. **Analyzing Concepts** Sea stars release millions of eggs during reproduction. How is this method of reproduction adaptive?

### OBJECTIVES

- **List** the major characteristics of chordates.
- **Describe** the evolution and classification of invertebrate chordates.
- **Describe** the structure of lancelets.
- **Describe** the structure of tunicates.

### VOCABULARY

atriopore

# INVERTEBRATE CHORDATES

*The phylum Chordata (kawr-DAY-tuh) includes all of the vertebrates, or animals with backbones. It also includes two groups of invertebrates—animals that lack backbones.*

## CHARACTERISTICS

All animals with a backbone are vertebrates, and they make up one of the subphyla in the phylum Chordata, whose members are called *chordates.* Chordates are so named because they have a *notochord,* a stiff but flexible rod of cells that runs the length of the body near the dorsal surface. Figure 38-10 illustrates the notochord. The stiffness of the notochord provides a resistance against which the body muscles can exert force when they contract. The flexibility of the notochord allows the body to bend from side to side as well as up and down.

Some kinds of chordates retain the notochord throughout their life. In most vertebrates, however, the notochord is present in embryos but becomes greatly reduced when the vertebral column, or backbone, develops. In adult mammals, the notochord persists only as small patches of tissue between the bones of the vertebral column.

Recall that in addition to having a notochord, all chordates have the following three characteristics during some stage of their life: (1) a dorsal nerve cord, (2) pharyngeal pouches, and (3) a postanal tail. These characteristics are also illustrated in Figure 38-10. Unlike the ventral nerve cords of invertebrates such as annelids and arthropods, the dorsal nerve cord of a chordate is a hollow tube.

**internet** connect

www.scilinks.org

**Topic:** Chordates
**Keyword:** HM60285

SC*i*LINKS. Maintained by the National Science Teachers Association

**FIGURE 38-10**

All chordates have a notochord, a dorsal nerve cord, pharyngeal pouches, and a postanal tail during at least some stage of their life.

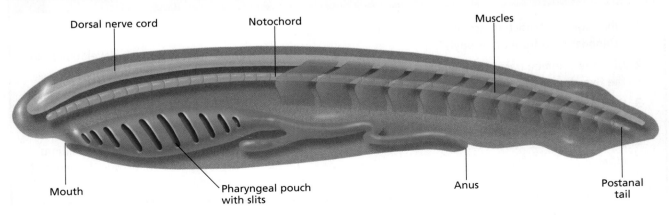

Dorsal nerve cord     Notochord     Muscles

Mouth     Pharyngeal pouch with slits     Anus     Postanal tail

In vertebrates, the anterior end of the nerve cord enlarges during development to form the brain, and the posterior end forms the spinal cord. The brain receives information from a variety of complex sensory organs, many of which are concentrated at the anterior end of the body.

The pharyngeal pouches are outpockets in the pharynx, the portion of the digestive tract between the mouth and the esophagus. In aquatic chordates, the pharyngeal pouches have slits and evolved first into filter-feeding structures and later into gill chambers. In terrestrial chordates, the pouches evolved into a variety of structures, including the jaws and inner ear.

The notochord extends into the postanal tail, and muscles in the tail can cause it to bend. The postanal tail provides much of the propulsion in many aquatic chordates. Invertebrates in other phyla lack this form of propulsion, and the anus, if present, is located at the end of the body.

# EVOLUTION AND CLASSIFICATION

Like echinoderms, chordates are deuterostomes. This similarity provides evidence that echinoderms and chordates likely evolved from a common ancestor. The phylum Chordata is divided into three subphyla: Vertebrata, Cephalochordata (SEF-uh-loh-kawr-DAY-tuh), and Urochordata (YOOR-uh-kawr-DAY-tuh). Members of the subphylum Vertebrata, the vertebrates, constitute more than 95 percent of all chordate species. Members of the other two subphyla live only in the ocean. They are the closest living relatives of the early animals from which all chordates evolved.

## Subphylum Cephalochordata

The subphylum Cephalochordata contains about two dozen species of blade-shaped animals known as *lancelets*. Figure 38-11 shows that lancelets look much like the idealized chordate drawn in Figure 38-10. They retain their notochord, dorsal nerve cord, pharyngeal pouches, and postanal tail throughout their life.

 **Quick Lab**

### Modeling Chordate Characteristics

**Materials** several colors of clay, toothpicks, masking tape

**Procedure** Build clay models of a lancelet and an adult tunicate by using different colors of clay for the structures shown in Figures 38-11 and 38-12. Make flags using masking tape attached to toothpicks, and use them to identify any of the four major characteristics of chordates that are found in your models.

**Analysis** Which of the major characteristics of chordates are found in the lancelet? the adult tunicate? Which of the four characteristics is shared by both? Why is the tunicate classified as a chordate despite the fact that it has only three of the four chordate characteristics?

**FIGURE 38-11**

(a) The lancelet *Branchiostoma lanceolatum* lives with most of its body buried in the sand. (b) Even as adults, lancelets clearly show all four chordate characteristics.

(a)

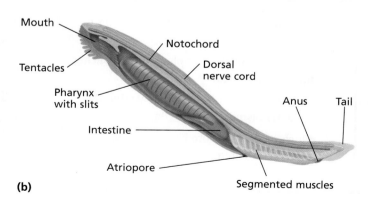

(b)

Mouth
Tentacles
Pharynx with slits
Intestine
Atriopore
Notochord
Dorsal nerve cord
Anus
Tail
Segmented muscles

(a)

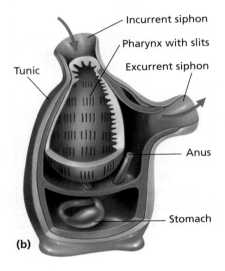

Incurrent siphon

Pharynx with slits

Tunic

Excurrent siphon

Anus

Stomach

(b)

**FIGURE 38-12**

Most adult tunicates, such as *Polycarpa aurata* (a), are sessile filter feeders. A drawing of a tunicate's internal structure (b) shows its enlarged pharynx with slits, the only chordate characteristic retained by adult tunicates.

Lancelets live in warm, shallow waters. They wriggle backward into the sand with a muscular tail. Only their anterior end protrudes from the sand. Lancelets have cilia that draw water into the pharynx through the mouth. Food particles in the water are trapped as the water passes through the slits in the pharynx. The food enters the intestine to be digested. The water leaves the body through an opening called the **atriopore** (AY-tree-oh-POHR).

Lancelets can swim weakly, powered by the coordinated contraction of muscles that run the length of their body. If you look closely at Figure 38-11, you can see that these muscles are arranged as a series of repeating segments. Body segmentation is another common feature of chordates. Recall that annelids and arthropods also have segmented bodies. However, animals in those phyla probably evolved body segmentation independently of chordates.

## Subphylum Urochordata

The 2,000 species in the subphylum Urochordata are commonly called *tunicates* because their bodies are covered by a tough covering, or tunic. Tunicates are also called *sea squirts* because they squirt out a stream of water when touched. As adults, most tunicates are sessile, barrel-shaped animals that live on the sea bottom. They may be solitary or colonial.

Figure 38-12 shows that tunicates are adapted for filter feeding. Propelled by the beating of cilia, water enters the body through an incurrent siphon, passes through slits in the pharynx, and exits through an excurrent siphon. Food that is filtered by the pharynx moves into the stomach. Undigested material leaves via the anus, which empties into the excurrent siphon.

Tunicates are hermaphrodites. Sperm and eggs are released through the excurrent siphon into the surrounding water, where fertilization occurs.

Adult tunicates bear little resemblance to the idealized chordate shown in Figure 38-10. Although they do have a pouchlike pharynx with slits, they have no notochord, dorsal nerve cord, or postanal tail. Larval tunicates, however, possess all four chordate characteristics, but they lose most of them during metamorphosis.

## SECTION 2 REVIEW

1. What are the four major characteristics of chordates?

2. What is the function of pharyngeal pouches in aquatic chordates?

3. What evidence of body segmentation do lancelets display?

4. Which of the chordate characteristics do tunicates retain as adults?

**CRITICAL THINKING**

5. **Making Comparisons** Compare the function of pharyngeal gill slits with that of gills in a crayfish.

6. **Inferring Relationships** How is burrowing backward, with the head out, adaptive in lancelets?

7. **Relating Concepts** In tunicates, the anus empties into the excurrent siphon. What is the advantage of this anatomical arrangement?

# CHAPTER HIGHLIGHTS

Echinoderms

- Most echinoderms develop from free-swimming, bilaterally symmetrical larvae into bottom-dwelling adults with pentaradial symmetry. The larval stage is evidence that echinoderms may have evolved from bilaterally symmetrical ancestors.

- Echinoderms have an endoskeleton made of ossicles and a water-vascular system, which includes many movable extensions called tube feet.

- The class Crinoidea includes sea lilies and feather stars, which are filter feeders that catch small organisms with their mucus-covered tube feet.

- The class Ophiuroidea consists of basket stars and brittle stars, fast-moving echinoderms with long, flexible arms.

- The class Echinoidea includes sea urchins and sand dollars, whose internal organs are enclosed inside a rigid endoskeleton called a test. Many sea urchins have long spines.

- The class Holothuroidea is made of sea cucumbers, armless echinoderms with soft bodies.

- The class Asteroidea consists of sea stars, which have from 5 to 24 arms. Two rows of tube feet run along the underside of each arm.

- The water-vascular system of a sea star consists of a network of canals that connect to bulblike ampullae. Contraction of muscles surrounding the ampullae extends the tube feet, and contraction of muscles lining the tube feet makes the tube feet retract.

- Sea stars can turn one of their stomachs inside out through their mouth to feed on prey they have captured. After the food is partially digested outside the body, it is brought inside, where digestion is completed.

- Sea stars lack circulatory, excretory, and respiratory organ systems, and they have no head or brain. They use skin gills for gas exchange and waste excretion.

- Most sea stars have separate sexes, and fertilization is external. Sea stars can also reproduce asexually by regeneration.

### Vocabulary

| | | | |
|---|---|---|---|
| echinoderm (p. 761) | tube foot (p. 762) | stone canal (p. 766) | cardiac stomach (p. 766) |
| ossicle (p. 762) | test (p. 763) | ring canal (p. 766) | pyloric stomach (p. 766) |
| water-vascular system (p. 762) | pedicellaria (p. 765) | radial canal (p. 766) | bipinnaria (p. 767) |
| | madreporite (p. 766) | ampulla (p. 766) | |

Invertebrate Chordates

- Chordates have a notochord, a stiff but flexible rod that runs the length of the body. In one group of chordates, the vertebrates, the notochord is largely replaced by the vertebral column, or backbone.

- Other common characteristics of chordates are a dorsal nerve cord, pharyngeal pouches, and a postanal tail. These characteristics are not present at all life stages in all chordates.

- Like echinoderms, chordates are deuterostomes, which suggests that echinoderms and chordates evolved from a common ancestor.

- Lancelets are animals in the subphylum Cephalochordata. These blade-shaped animals live partially buried in the sand, but they can swim from place to place. They retain all of the major chordate characteristics throughout their life.

- Tunicates are animals in the subphylum Urochordata. Tunicate larvae have all of the major chordate characteristics, but they lose most of them when they develop into adults. Most tunicate adults are sessile.

### Vocabulary
atriopore (p. 770)

# CHAPTER REVIEW

## USING VOCABULARY

1. For each pair of terms, explain how the meanings of the terms differ.
   a. *ossicle* and *test*
   b. *tube foot* and *pedicellaria*
   c. *stone canal* and *ring canal*
   d. *madreporite* and *atriopore*

2. Explain the relationship between the *cardiac stomach* and the *pyloric stomach* in sea stars.

3. Choose the term that does not belong in the following group, and explain why it does not belong: *tube foot, bipinnaria, radial canal,* and *ampulla*.

4. **Word Roots and Origins** The word *pyloric* is derived from the Greek *pyloros,* which means "gatekeeper." Using this information, explain why the term *pyloric stomach* is a good name for the structure that the term describes.

## UNDERSTANDING KEY CONCEPTS

5. **Explain** why echinoderms are thought to have evolved from bilaterally symmetrical ancestors.

6. **Identify** the functions for which echinoderms use their tube feet.

7. **Compare** feeding in crinoids and basket stars.

8. **Compare** the ways that sea urchins and sand dollars are adapted to their environment.

9. **Describe** how the sea cucumber transports food to its mouth.

10. **Explain** why sea stars are of economic importance.

11. **Summarize** the process of feeding and digestion in the sea star.

12. **Compare** sexual and asexual reproduction in sea stars.

13. **Summarize** how pharyngeal pouches have become modified through evolution in aquatic chordates and in terrestrial chordates.

14. **Interpret** the significance of the notochord and the postanal tail to aquatic chordates, such as the lancelet.

15. **Explain** why members of the subphylum Urochordata are called tunicates.

16. **CONCEPT MAPPING** Use the following terms to create a concept map that sequences the path of water through the water-vascular system of a sea star: *water, radial canal, madreporite, ring canal, tube foot,* and *stone canal*.

## CRITICAL THINKING

17. **Forming Reasoned Opinions** Scientists have found many echinoderm fossils from the Cambrian period, but they have found few fossils of other species from this period. What might explain the large number of fossilized echinoderms?

18. **Analyzing Concepts** Sea lilies and sea cucumbers are mostly sessile animals as adults. Their larvae, however, can swim. What adaptive advantage do swimming larvae provide?

19. **Inferring Relationships** Basket stars are active at night. During the day, basket stars curl up their arms and become a compact mass. What are possible explanations for this behavior?

20. **Interpreting Graphics** Identify the structures labeled "A–F" in the diagram below.

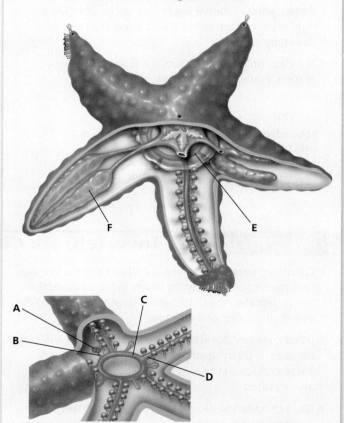

21. **Applying Information** Commercial oyster farmers usually want to prevent sea stars from feeding in the oyster beds. In the past, the farmers would control the sea stars by chopping the sea stars in half and throwing them back into the water. Was this a good way to protect the oysters from predation by the sea stars? Why or why not? If not, describe a better method.

# Standardized Test Preparation

**DIRECTIONS:** Choose the letter of the answer choice that best answers the question.

1. In a sea star, gas exchange and excretion of wastes take place by diffusion through which of the following structures?
   A. pharynx
   B. skin gills
   C. atriopore
   D. radial canals

2. Which of the following types of symmetry is characteristic of echinoderms?
   F. biradial
   G. bilateral
   H. pentaradial
   J. pentalateral

3. Which of the following classes of echinoderms most closely resembles the fossils of ancient echinoderms?
   A. Crinoidea
   B. Asteroidea
   C. Echinoidea
   D. Holothuroidea

4. Which of the following is found in adult tunicates, or sea squirts?
   F. eyespot
   G. notochord
   H. spinal cord
   J. pharynx with slits

**INTERPRETING GRAPHICS:** The illustration below shows a sea star and a sand dollar. Use the illustration to answer the question that follows.

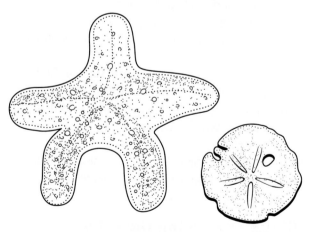

5. To which phylum do these animals belong?
   A. Chordata
   B. Vertebrata
   C. Arthropoda
   D. Echinodermata

**DIRECTIONS:** Complete the following analogy.

6. Cardiac stomach : digestion :: atriopore :
   F. excretion
   G. respiration
   H. circulation
   J. reproduction

**INTERPRETING GRAPHICS:** The diagram below shows a lancelet. Use the diagram to answer the question that follows.

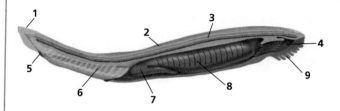

7. Which four structures are the main distinguishing characteristics of chordates?
   A. *1, 2, 3, 4*
   B. *1, 2, 3, 8*
   C. *2, 3, 4, 6*
   D. *2, 3, 4, 9*

## SHORT RESPONSE

Echinoderms and chordates are believed to have evolved from a common ancestor.

Describe the evidence that supports this view.

## EXTENDED RESPONSE

The fossil record of echinoderms dates to the Cambrian period, more than 500 million years ago. Scientists have observed many well-preserved echinoderm species from this period.

*Part A* Based on the fossil evidence, which characteristics did the earliest adult echinoderms have, in terms of symmetry and ability to move?

*Part B* Based on your answer to Part A, describe the evolution of echinoderms.

**Test TIP** If you are unsure of the answers to particular questions, put a mark beside them (on your answer sheet or test booklet), and go on to other questions. If you have time, go back and reconsider the questions you skipped. (Do not write in this book.)

# Comparing Echinoderms

## OBJECTIVES

- Compare the structure of two types of echinoderms.
- Infer function from the observation of structures.

## PROCESS SKILLS

- using dissection instruments and techniques
- observing

## MATERIALS

- preserved sea star
- preserved sea urchin
- sea urchin test
- dissection tray
- fine dissection scissors with pointed blades
- hand lens or dissecting microscope
- forceps
- blunt probe
- sharp probe
- dissection pins
- gloves (optional)
- 100 mL beaker
- household bleach
- Petri dish

## Background

1. List the major characteristics of echinoderms.
2. Which feature of echinoderms gives their phylum its name?
3. To which classes of echinoderms do sea stars and sea urchins belong?
4. What is pentaradial symmetry?

## PART A Observing the External Anatomy of a Sea Star

1. CAUTION **Put on safety goggles, gloves, and a lab apron.** Using forceps, hold a preserved sea star under running water to gently but thoroughly remove excess preservative. Then, place the sea star in a dissection tray.
2. What evidence can you find that indicates that the sea star has pentaradial symmetry?
3. Make a table in your lab report like the one shown on the next page. As you observe each of the structures listed in the table, fill in the function of that structure.
4. While referring to Figure 38-7, find the madreporite on the aboral surface of your sea star. Record the madreporite's position and appearance.
5. Use a hand lens to examine the sea star's spines. Describe their size and shape. Are they distributed in any recognizable pattern on the surface of the sea star? Are they covered by tissue or exposed? Are they movable or fixed?
6. Are pedicellariae present? What is their location and arrangement? Draw one as it appears under the hand lens or dissecting microscope.
7. Use the dissecting microscope to look for small skin gills. If any are present, describe their location and structure.
8. Now, examine the sea star's oral surface. Find the mouth, and describe its location and structure. Use forceps or a probe to gently move aside any soft tissues. What structures are found around the mouth?
9. Locate the tube feet. Describe their distribution. Using a dissecting microscope, observe and then draw a single tube foot.

## PART B Observing the Internal Anatomy of a Sea Star

10. Using scissors and forceps, carefully cut the body wall away from the aboral surface of one of the sea star's arms. Start near the end of the arm, and work toward the center. The internal

organs may stick to the inside of the body wall, so use a sharp probe to gently separate them from the body wall as you cut. Be careful not to damage the madreporite.

11. While referring to Figure 38-7, find the digestive glands in the arm you have opened. Describe their appearance. If you have dissected carefully, you should be able to find a short, branched tube that connects the digestive glands to the pyloric stomach. If you cannot find the digestive glands or this tube, repeat step 10 on one of the other arms, and look for them there.

12. Cut the tube that connects the digestive glands to the pyloric stomach, and move the digestive glands out of the arm. Look for the testes or ovaries. If your specimen is an immature animal, these organs may be small and difficult to find.

13. Locate the two rows of ampullae that run the length of the arm. What is the relationship between the ampullae and the tube feet, which you observed on the oral surface?

14. Carefully remove the body wall from the aboral surface of the central region of the sea star. Try to avoid damaging the underlying structures. Locate the pyloric stomach and the cardiac stomach. How does a sea star use its cardiac stomach during feeding?

15. Remove the stomachs, and find the canals of the water-vascular system: stone canal, ring canal, and radial canals. In which direction does water move through these canals?

16. ⚠ **CAUTION** **Bleach is a highly corrosive agent. If you get it on your skin or clothing, wash it off at the sink while calling to your teacher. If you get it in your eyes, immediately flush it out at the eyewash station while calling to your teacher.** Cut a 1 cm cross section out of the middle of one of the arms. Using forceps, transfer the section to a small beaker containing enough bleach to cover it. The bleach will eat away the soft tissues, exposing the endoskeleton.

17. After about 10–15 minutes, use the forceps to carefully transfer the endoskeleton to a Petri dish containing tap water. Observe the endoskeleton under a dissecting microscope. Can you find individual ossicles?

## FUNCTION OF SEA STAR STRUCTURES

| Structure | Function |
|---|---|
| Madreporite | |
| Pedicellaria | |
| Skin gill | |
| Tube foot | |
| Digestive gland | |
| Ampulla | |
| Ossicle | |

### PART C  Observing the Anatomy of a Sea Urchin

18. Using forceps, hold a preserved sea urchin under running water to remove excess preservative. Then, place the sea star in a dissection tray. What evidence can you find that indicates that the sea urchin has pentaradial symmetry?

19. Observe the sea urchin's spines. Answer the same questions for the sea urchin's spines that you answered for the sea star's spines in step 5.

20. Examine the sea urchin's oral surface. Find the mouth, and use a sharp probe to explore the structures around the mouth. How does the sea urchin's mouth differ from the sea star's?

21. Examine the sea urchin test. What might be the function of the rows of small pores on the test? What might be the function of the small bumps on the test?

22. ⚠⚠ Dispose of the specimens according to the directions from your teacher. Then, clean up your materials, and wash your hands before leaving the lab.

## Analysis and Conclusions

1. Which features are shared by sea stars and sea urchins?

2. What are some of the structural differences between sea stars and sea urchins?

## Further Inquiry

Observe how living sea stars move in a saltwater aquarium. Add some live mussels, and observe the feeding behavior of the sea stars.

# VERTEBRATES

> ❝ *Nature discloses the secrets of her past with the greatest reluctance. We paleontologists weave our tales from fossil fragments poorly preserved in incomplete sequences of sedimentary rocks. Most fossil mammals are known only from teeth—the hardest substance in our bodies— and a few scattered bones.* ❞

From "History of the Vertebrate Brain," from *Ever Since Darwin: Reflections in Natural History,* by Stephen Jay Gould. Copyright © 1973, 1974, 1975, 1976, 1977 by the American Museum of Natural History. Reproduced by permission of **W. W. Norton & Company, Inc.**

References to *Scientific American* project ideas are located throughout this unit.

**internet** connect

National Science Teachers Association *sci*LINKS Internet resources are located throughout this unit.

*sci*LINKS. Maintained by the National Science Teachers Association

Opossums are the only North American marsupial mammals.

This blue-spotted stingray, *Taeniura lymna, is one of* about 100 species of stingrays that belong in the class Chondrichthyes.

These colorful rainbow lorikeets, also known as brush-tongued parrots, can be found in eastern Australia, where they feed on eucalyptus flowers.

Antlers, such as those on this caribou, are bony outgrowths that are shed each winter.

Flap-necked chameleon, Chamaeleo delipis

# FISHES

The whale shark lives in a saltwater environment, for which it has special organs and biochemical adaptations. The whale shark is the largest fish, growing up to 46 feet long. Notice the size of the whale shark compared to the diver above.

**SECTION 1** *Introduction to Vertebrates*

**SECTION 2** *Jawless and Cartilaginous Fishes*

**SECTION 3** *Bony Fishes*

# INTRODUCTION TO VERTEBRATES

## OBJECTIVES

- **Identify** the distinguishing characteristics of vertebrates.
- **List** an example for each of the nine classes of vertebrates.
- **Describe** the characteristics of the early vertebrates.
- **Explain** the importance of jaws and paired fins for fishes.

## VOCABULARY

vertebrae
cranium
gill arches

*Although the vertebrates are not the most diverse or numerous group of animals, they are the most familiar to us. Vertebrates are an important part of our diet, and many are pets.*

## CHARACTERISTICS

Members of the subphylum Vertebrata, within the phylum Chordata (kawr-DAY-tuh) have, at some stage of life, a notochord (a rod-shaped supporting axis below the nerve cord), a dorsal hollow nerve cord, pharyngeal pouches (paired structures in the throat region), and a post-anal tail (a tail that extends beyond the anus). Vertebrates have three characteristics that distinguish them from other chordates. First, vertebrates have **vertebrae** (singular, *vertebra*), bones or cartilage that surround the dorsal nerve cord and form the spine. Second, vertebrates have a **cranium,** or skull, that protects the brain. Third, all vertebrates have an endoskeleton (an internal skeleton) composed of bone or cartilage.

### Vertebrate Classes

Today, there are about 45,000 species of vertebrates. They occupy all but the most extreme terrestrial habitats. The nine classes of vertebrates are summarized below.

- **Hagfishes** (class Myxini)—These fishes have elongated, eel-like bodies. They lack jaws, paired fins, and bone. The notochord remains throughout life. Hagfishes do not have vertebrae. Many scientists do not consider them vertebrates. They are included with vertebrates because they do have a cranium and an endoskeleton.

- **Lampreys** (class Cephalaspidomorphi)—Lampreys lack jaws, paired fins and bone, and retain a notochord throughout life. However, unlike hagfishes, lampreys have a primitive vertebral column composed of cartilage that surrounds the notochord.

- **Sharks, Rays, Skates, and Ratfishes** (class Chondrichthyes)—These predatory fishes have jaws and paired fins. Their skeleton is made of cartilage, not bone, and many have skin covered by a unique kind of scale.

- **Ray-finned Fishes** (class Actinopterygii)—Most familiar fishes are ray-finned fishes. All have jaws and paired fins, most have a skeleton composed of bone. These fish have fins supported by rays of bone that fan out from a central bony axis.

**Word Roots and Origins**

*vertebra*

from the Latin *vertebra*, meaning "a joint"

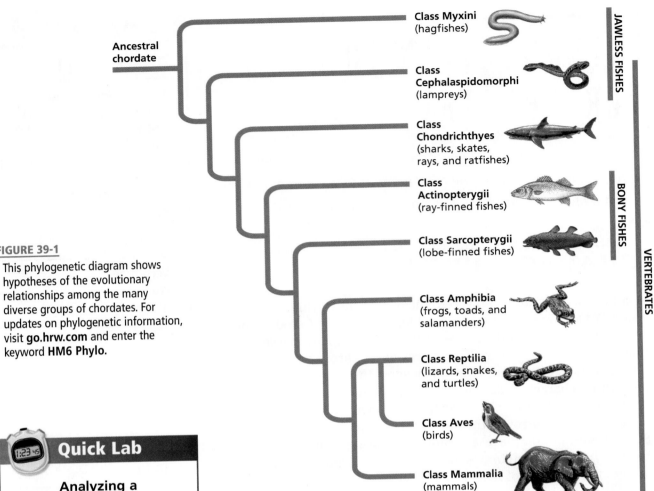

**FIGURE 39-1**

This phylogenetic diagram shows hypotheses of the evolutionary relationships among the many diverse groups of chordates. For updates on phylogenetic information, visit **go.hrw.com** and enter the keyword **HM6 Phylo.**

## Quick Lab

### Analyzing a Phylogenetic Tree

**Materials**  paper, pencil

**Procedure**

1. Draw the phylogenetic tree shown on this page on your paper.

2. Using the information on pp. 779 and 780, determine the key characteristics that distinguish each vertebrate group. Indicate these evolutionary changes on the branches of the tree to make a diagram of the relationship that exists among vertebrates. Begin at the bottom of the tree with the key characteristics that distinguish vertebrates from other chordates.

**Analysis**  Which characteristics are shared by all vertebrates? Which key characteristic separates the classes Chondrichthyes and Actinopterygii? Which adaptations led to the divergence of mammals?

- **Lobe-finned Fishes** (class Sarcopterygii)—These fishes have fins that are supported by a main axis of bone. There are two living groups of lobe-finned fishes: lungfishes and the coelacanth. Extinct lobe-finned fishes are thought to be the ancestors of amphibians.

- **Amphibians** (class Amphibia)—About 4,880 species of frogs, toads, and salamanders belong to this group. Their skin is thin and is permeable to gases and water. Most species lay their eggs in water and pass through an aquatic larval stage.

- **Reptiles** (class Reptilia)—This group includes turtles, crocodiles, alligators, lizards, and snakes. The skin of reptiles is dry and scaly. The eggs of reptiles protect the embryo from drying out and can be laid on land. There are about 8,000 species.

- **Birds** (class Aves)—Birds are characterized by adaptations that enable flight, including feathers, hollow bones, and a unique respiratory system. There are over 10,000 species.

- **Mammals** (class Mammalia)—Humans, cats, mice, and horses are among the members of this group. All mammals have hair and nurse their young with milk. There are about 4,400 species.

Figure 39-1 shows the relationships among the nine classes of living vertebrates.

# VERTEBRATE EVOLUTION

Most biologists think that vertebrates originated about 560 million years ago, shortly after the first chordates appear in the fossil record. The oldest known vertebrate fossils are those of tadpole-like jawless fishes. They appear in the fossil record about 560 million years ago. Figure 39-2 shows an artist's reconstruction of one of these fishes. Jawless fishes were the only vertebrates for more than 50 million years. The survivors became the ancestors of today's jawless fishes.

## Origin of Jaws and Paired Fins

Almost 450 million years ago, the first fishes with jaws and paired fins appeared. Paired fins increased fishes' stability and maneuverability, and jaws allowed them to seize and manipulate prey. Jaws are thought to have evolved from the first pair of **gill arches,** the skeletal elements that support the pharynx. Figure 39-3 shows three possible stages in this transformation. Modern fishes—the sharks and rays and the bony fishes—make their first appearance in the fossil record about 400 million years ago.

**FIGURE 39-2**

Early jawless fishes, such as this *Pharyngolepis*, lacked paired fins and probably fed on small invertebrates. Most species of early jawless fishes were less than 15 cm (6 in.) in length.

**FIGURE 39-3**

Jaws are thought to have developed from the anterior gill arches of early jawless fishes. These figures represent hypothesized stages of evolution.

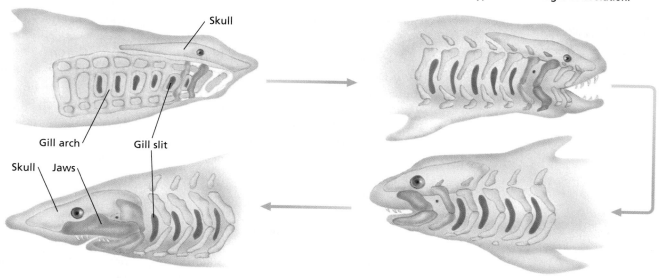

Skull

Gill arch    Gill slit

Skull    Jaws

---

## SECTION 1 REVIEW

1. List three distinguishing characteristics of vertebrates.

2. List the nine classes of vertebrates, using both their scientific and common names.

3. State the characteristics of early jawless fishes.

4. Identify the advantages for fish of having jaws and paired fins over not having these structures.

**CRITICAL THINKING**

5. **Analyzing Information** Why is it important to use unique characteristics to classify animals?

6. **Applying Information** Explain why early jawless fishes might have been awkward swimmers.

7. **Recognizing Relationships** Explain why scientists think that vertebrates evolved from chordates in the sea.

OBJECTIVES

- **Identify** three characteristics that make fishes well suited to aquatic life.
- **Describe** three sensory systems in fishes.
- **Evaluate** the similarities between jawless fishes and early vertebrates.
- **Identify** two characteristics of cartilaginous fishes.
- **Contrast** reproduction in lampreys with reproduction in cartilaginous fishes.

VOCABULARY

chemoreception
lateral line
external fertilization
cartilage
placoid scale
internal fertilization

# JAWLESS AND CARTILAGINOUS FISHES

*The term fish generally refers to three distinct groups of living vertebrates: jawless fishes; cartilaginous fishes; and bony fishes. Fishes are the most numerous and widespread of all vertebrates.*

## FISH ADAPTATIONS

The body plan of a fish makes it well suited to live in water. A streamlined shape and a muscular tail enable most fishes to move rapidly through the water. Paired fins allow fishes to maneuver right or left, up or down, and backward or forward. Unpaired fins on the back and belly increase stability. In addition, most fishes secrete a mucus that reduces friction as they swim, and that helps protect them from infections.

Most of the tissues in a fish's body are denser than water. By controlling the amount of gas in their bodies, many fishes can regulate their vertical position in the water. Some fishes also store lipids, which are less dense than water and therefore add buoyancy.

Fishes need to absorb oxygen and rid themselves of carbon dioxide. However, scales on fishes limit diffusion through the skin. Instead, most exchanges between water and blood take place across the membranes of gills—the internal respiratory organs of fishes.

### Homeostasis

The concentration of solutes in a fish's body usually differs from the concentration of solutes in the water in which the fish swims. The body of a freshwater fish is *hypertonic*. It has a higher concentration of solutes than the surrounding water does, so the fish tends to gain water and lose ions, such as sodium and chloride ions, through diffusion. Most saltwater fishes are *hypotonic;* they contain lower concentrations of solutes than their surroundings do. Thus, saltwater fishes tend to lose water and gain ions.

Like all organisms, fishes must also rid themselves of the waste products produced by metabolism. The kidneys and gills play important roles in maintaining homeostasis in the tissues and in getting rid of metabolic wastes. The kidneys filter the blood and help regulate the concentration of ions in the body. The gills release wastes, such as carbon dioxide and ammonia, and either absorb or release ions, depending on whether the fish lives in fresh water or in salt water.

## Sensory Functions

Fishes have a variety of organs that allow them to sense the world around them. Fish can sense light, chemicals, and sound. Some can also sense electrical and magnetic fields. Fish eyes are similar to eyes of land vertebrates. Many bony fishes have color vision, but most cartilaginous fishes do not.

**Chemoreception** is the ability to detect chemicals in the environment. Chemoreception includes the senses of smell and taste. Most fish have one or two nostrils, which lead to sensory cells located in olfactory sacs on both sides of the head. Sharks and salmon are examples of fish with a well-developed sense of smell. Fishes have taste buds located in their mouths. They may also have taste buds on their lips, fins, and skin and on whisker-like organs near their mouths called *barbels*.

Fishes have a unique organ called the **lateral line,** which allows them to sense vibration in the water. The lateral line is made of a system of small canals in the skin. The canals are lined with cells that are sensitive to vibration. Fishes also perceive sound waves with their inner ears, which contain a fluid-filled set of canals that contain sensory cells similar to those in the lateral line canals.

Cartilaginous fishes also have sense organs called the *ampullae of Lorenzini* that can detect weak electrical fields, such as those given off by muscles when they contract. This system has been shown to help them locate prey.

**Word Roots and Origins**

*agnatha*

from the Greek *gnathus,* meaning "jaws," and *a,* meaning "without"

# JAWLESS FISHES

The only existing jawless fishes are the 80 species of hagfishes and lampreys. These fish were formerly grouped together in the class Agnatha. They are now divided into two classes: Myxini (hagfishes) and Cephalaspidomorphi (lampreys). Their skin has neither plates nor scales. Hagfishes and lampreys have an eel-like body, a cartilaginous skeleton, and unpaired fins. The notochord remains throughout life. Hagfishes live only in the oceans. Many lampreys live permanently in fresh water, and all lamprey species reproduce in fresh water.

## Hagfishes

Hagfishes, shown in Figure 39-4, are bottom dwellers in cold marine waters. Hagfishes are unique in that they do not have vertebrae. Hagfishes are also unique because they are *isotonic,* which means that their body fluids have nearly the same ion concentration as sea water. They feed on small invertebrates or on dead and dying fish. Because the hagfish lacks jaws, it cannot bite, but within its mouth are two movable plates and a rough tonguelike structure that it uses to pinch off chunks of flesh. Hagfishes often burrow into the body of a dead fish through the gills, skin, or anus. Once inside, they eat the internal organs.

**FIGURE 39-4**

Hagfishes are modern jawless fishes. Hagfishes lack paired fins, which allows them to burrow into the bodies of the dead fish on which they feed.

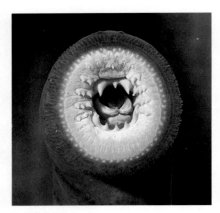

**FIGURE 39-5**

A lamprey's mouth is adapted for latching onto prey and feeding on body fluids of other fishes.

## Lampreys

About half the species of lampreys are free-living (non-parasitic). The other half are parasites as adults and feed on the blood and body fluids of other fishes. Once a suitable host is located, a lamprey uses its disk-shaped mouth, shown in Figure 39-5, to attach to the host. Then, it scrapes a hole in the host with its rough tongue and secretes a chemical that keeps the host's blood from clotting. After feeding, the lamprey drops off. The host may recover, bleed to death, or die from an infection.

Some lamprey species spend most of their adult lives in the ocean. Others live in rivers or lakes and never enter salt water. All lampreys breed in fresh water. Fertilization occurs outside the body of either parent, a process known as **external fertilization.** The eggs hatch into larvae that resemble an amphioxus, an invertebrate chordate. The larvae eventually transform into adults.

# CARTILAGINOUS FISHES

Sharks, skates, and rays belong to the class Chondrichthyes. Because the fishes in this class have skeletons composed of cartilage, they are also called *cartilaginous fishes.* **Cartilage** is a flexible, lightweight material made of cells surrounded by tough fibers of protein. Sharks, skates, rays, and ratfishes differ from lampreys and hagfishes in that they have movable jaws, skeletons, and paired fins. Almost all of the approximately 800 species of sharks, skates, rays, and ratfishes live in salt water. All species are carnivores, and some are scavengers. The skin of cartilaginous fishes is covered with **placoid** (PLAK-OYD) **scales**—small, toothlike spines that feel like sandpaper. Placoid scales, shown in Figure 39-6, probably reduce turbulence of the water flow and thus increase swimming efficiency.

**FIGURE 39-6**

These teethlike placoid scales are found on the skin of cartilaginous fishes. What advantage might they give a shark in swimming?

### Sharks

Sharks have smooth, torpedo-shaped bodies that reduce turbulence when swimming. This shape is called a *fusiform* body shape. Figure 39-7 shows the smooth, fusiform body of a shark.

The largest sharks, the whale shark (up to 18 m, or 59 ft, long) and the basking shark (up to 15 m, or 49 ft, long), feed on plankton, floating plants and animals. Like other filter-feeding fishes, the whale and basking sharks filter the water with slender projections on the inner surface of the gills, called *gill rakers.*

The mouth of a typical shark has 6 to 20 rows of teeth that point inward. When a tooth in one of the front rows breaks or wears down, a replacement moves forward to take its place. One shark may use more than 20,000 teeth over its lifetime. The structure of each species' teeth is adapted to that species' feeding habits. Sharks that feed primarily on large fish or mammals have big, triangular teeth with sawlike edges that hook and tear flesh.

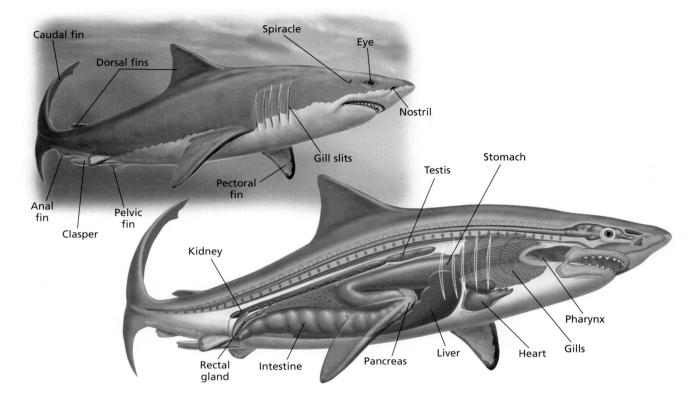

Caudal fin · Dorsal fins · Spiracle · Eye · Nostril · Gill slits · Pectoral fin · Pelvic fin · Clasper · Anal fin

Testis · Stomach · Kidney · Pharynx · Gills · Heart · Liver · Pancreas · Intestine · Rectal gland

## Rays and Skates

Rays and skates have flattened bodies with paired winglike pectoral fins and, in some species, whiplike tails. Rays have diamond- or disk-shaped bodies, but most skates have triangular bodies. Most rays and skates are less than 1 m (3.3 ft) long. Rays and skates are primarily bottom dwellers. Their flat shape and coloration camouflage them against the floor of their habitat. Most rays and skates feed on mollusks and crustaceans. Figure 39-8 shows an example of a ray.

## Ratfishes

There are about 25 species of strange-looking, mostly deep-water cartilaginous fishes that are grouped separately because of their unique features. The ratfishes, or *chimaeras,* have gill slits covered by a flap of skin. Some have a long, ratlike tail. They feed on crustaceans and mollusks.

## Adaptations of Cartilaginous Fishes

In cartilaginous fishes, gas exchange occurs in the gills, which lie behind the head. Efficient gas exchange requires a continuous flow of water across the gills. Some fast-swimming sharks are able to push water through their mouth, over their gills, and out of their gill slits by swimming. However, most cartilaginous fishes pump water over their gills by expanding and contracting their mouth cavity and pharynx. When lying on the bottom, rays and skates cannot bring in water through their mouth, which is located on the ventral surface of their body; instead, they draw water in through their spiracles, which are two large openings on the top of the head, just behind the eyes.

**FIGURE 39-7**

A fusiform body shape allows sharks to slip through the water with little resistance. The dorsal fins provide stability. The pectoral fins provide lift similar to the way airplane wings function in the air. The shark's internal anatomy includes organs for digestion, reproduction, and maintaining homeostasis.

**FIGURE 39-8**

This blue-spotted stingray, *Taeniura lymna,* is an example of a bottom dweller. This stingray was photographed in the Red Sea near Egypt.

## Quick Lab

### Modeling a Shark Adaptation

**Materials** 8 cm dialysis tubing, 8 cm length of string (2), 100 mL salt solution (5 percent), 250 mL beaker, 10 mL distilled water, scale, graduated cylinder

**Procedure**

1. Tightly tie one end of the dialysis tubing with string. Place 10 mL of distilled water inside the dialysis tubing, and tie the other end of the tube tightly with string.

2. Record the initial weight of the filled tube.

3. Add the filled dialysis tubing to a beaker filled with 100 mL of salt solution.

4. After 10 minutes, remove the tubing from the beaker, blot the outside, and reweigh it. Record your observations.

**Analysis** Explain the reason for the change in the weight of the tube, if any. Are sharks likely to lose or gain ions? What physical structures of a shark play a key role in maintaining ionic homeostasis in sharks?

Instead of releasing ammonia, cartilaginous fishes use energy to convert ammonia into a compound called *urea,* which is much less toxic. Sharks retain large amounts of urea in their blood and tissues, thus raising the concentration of solutes in their body to at least the same level as that found in sea water. Because the concentration of sodium and chloride in the body of a shark is less than the concentration found in sea water, these ions still diffuse into the body across the gills and are absorbed with food. The *rectal gland,* located in the posterior portion of the intestine, removes excess sodium and chloride ions from the blood and releases them into the rectum for elimination. Sharks that periodically migrate to fresh water excrete sodium, chloride, and urea along with any excess water that enters their bodies.

Cartilaginous fishes maintain their position in the water in two ways. First, because the caudal and pectoral fins generate lift, or upward force, as a fish swims, it can remain at the same level in the water, counteracting the tendency to sink, as long as it keeps moving. Second, many cartilaginous fishes store large amounts of low-density lipids, usually in the liver. A shark's lipid-filled liver may account for 25 percent of its mass. Lipids give these sharks buoyancy by reducing the overall density of the body.

## Reproduction in Cartilaginous Fishes

Cartilaginous fishes differ from jawless fishes in that fertilization occurs inside the body of the female. This type of fertilization is called **internal fertilization.** During mating, the male transfers sperm into the female's body using modified pelvic fins called *claspers.* In a few species of sharks and rays, the females lay large yolky eggs right after fertilization. The young develop within the egg, are nourished by the yolk, and hatch as miniature versions of the adults. The eggs of many species develop in the female's body, and the young are born live. In some of these species, the mother nourishes the developing sharks while they are in her body. No cartilaginous fishes provide parental care for their young after birth or hatching.

## SECTION 2 REVIEW

1. Identify each characteristic of fishes that makes them well suited to aquatic life.

2. Describe two unique sensory systems that can be found in fishes.

3. Contrast the feeding behavior of hagfish to the feeding behavior of lampreys.

4. List three characteristics that distinguish cartilaginous fishes from living jawless fishes.

5. Identify the advantages of internal fertilization versus external fertilization.

**CRITICAL THINKING**

6. **Forming a Hypothesis** A student takes fish A from a saltwater tank and fish B from a freshwater tank. The student returns each fish to the wrong aquarium, and the next day both fish are dead. Form a hypothesis that explains why.

7. **Evaluating Differences** Organisms that use external fertilization usually produce more eggs at one time than organisms that use internal fertilization. What might explain this difference?

8. **Inferring Relationships** Explain why all scales point toward a fish's tail.

# BONY FISHES

*Of the 25,000 known species of fishes, about 95 percent are bony fishes, formerly grouped in the class Osteichthyes. Bony fishes account for most of the vertebrates living in fresh water and in salt water. In this section, you will study some of the adaptations of this group.*

## SECTION 3

### OBJECTIVES

- **List** three characteristics of bony fishes.
- **Distinguish** between lobe-finned fishes and ray-finned fishes.
- **Describe** three key features of bony fishes' external anatomy.
- **Summarize** the major body systems in bony fishes.
- **Describe** the function of the swim bladder.
- **Discuss** reproduction in bony fishes.

### VOCABULARY

swim bladder
lobe-finned fish
ray-finned fish
operculum
countercurrent flow
optic tectum
spawning

## CHARACTERISTICS

The bony fishes are characterized by three key features:
- **Bone**—This material is typically harder and heavier than cartilage. The skeletons of most bony fishes contain bone.
- **Lungs or swim bladder**—Early bony fishes had *lungs*, internal respiratory organs in which gas is exchanged between the air and blood. Only a few species of bony fishes have lungs today. Most bony fishes have a **swim bladder**, a gas-filled sac that is used to control buoyancy. The swim bladder is thought to have evolved from the lungs of the early bony fishes.
- **Scales**—The body of a bony fish is usually covered with scales. Scales protect the fish and reduce friction when swimming.

There are two main groups of bony fishes. These are the lobe-finned fishes and the ray-finned fishes.

### Characteristics of Lobe-Finned Fishes

The **lobe-finned fishes** have fleshy fins that are supported by a series of bones. Two groups of lobe-finned fishes exist today, six species of lungfishes and one species of coelacanth. Lungfishes, shown in Figure 39-9a, exchange gases through both lungs and gills. They live in shallow tropical ponds that periodically dry up. The coelacanth, shown in Figure 39-9b, lives deep in the ocean and was thought to be extinct until 1938. Extinct lobe-finned fishes are ancestors of amphibians.

**FIGURE 39-9**

Lobe-finned fishes have fleshy fins that are supported by a series of bones. Lungfishes (a) have the ability to gulp air into lungs as an oxygen source. Coelacanths (b) have muscular fins with stout bones.

(a)

(b)

## Characteristics of Ray-Finned Fishes

**Ray-finned fishes** do not have fins with a central bony axis—they have fins that are supported by long, segmented, flexible bony elements called *rays*. Rays probably evolved from scales. Ray-finned fishes are diverse in appearance, behavior, and habitat. Ray-finned fishes include most familiar fishes, such as, yellow perch, trout, salmon, guppies, bass, herring, goldfish, and eels.

# EXTERNAL ANATOMY

Figure 39-10 shows the external anatomy of a yellow perch, a bony fish common in freshwater lakes of the eastern United States and Canada. The yellow perch, like all bony fishes, has distinct head, trunk, and tail regions. On each side of the head is the **operculum** (oh-PUHR-kyoo-LUHM), a hard plate that opens at the rear and covers and protects the gills.

## Fins

The fins of the yellow perch are adapted for swimming and navigating through the water. The caudal fin extends from the tail. It moves from side to side and amplifies the swimming motion of the body. Two dorsal fins, one anterior and one posterior, and a ventral anal fin help keep the fish upright and moving in a straight line. The fish uses paired pelvic fins and pectoral fins to navigate, stop, move up and down, and even back up. The pelvic fins also orient the body when the fish is at rest. The fins are supported by either rays or spines. Rays are bony yet flexible, while spines are bony and rigid.

## Skin

The skin of the yellow perch is covered with scales. Scales are thin, round disks of a bonelike material that grow from pockets in the skin. As Figure 39-10 shows, scales overlap like roof shingles. They all point toward the tail to minimize friction as the fish swims. Scales grow throughout the life of the fish, adjusting their growth pattern to the food supply. The scales grow quickly when food is abundant and slowly when it is scarce.

**Word Roots and Origins**

*operculum*

from the Latin *operculum,* meaning "cover"

**FIGURE 39-10**

The external features of the yellow perch, *Perca flavescens,* are representative of bony fishes. Note the growth rings on the scales shown in the inset. They indicate the fish's approximate age.

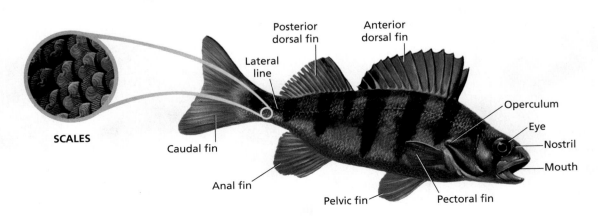

SCALES

Posterior dorsal fin

Anterior dorsal fin

Lateral line

Operculum

Eye

Nostril

Mouth

Caudal fin

Anal fin

Pelvic fin

Pectoral fin

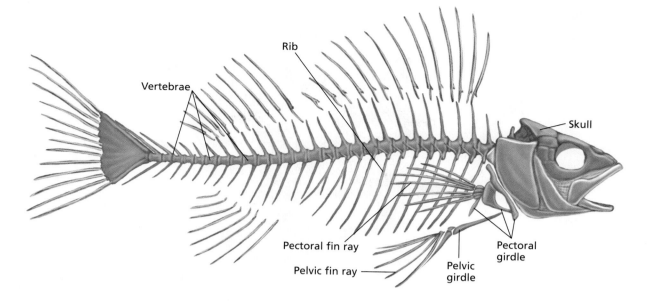

Vertebrae

Rib

Skull

Pectoral fin ray

Pectoral girdle

Pelvic fin ray

Pelvic girdle

# INTERNAL ANATOMY

The major parts of a fish's skeleton, shown in Figure 39-11, are the skull, spinal column, pectoral girdle, pelvic girdle, and ribs. The spinal column is made up of many bones, called vertebrae, with cartilage pads between each. The spinal column also partly encloses and protects the spinal cord. The *pectoral girdle* supports the pectoral fins, and the *pelvic girdle* supports the pelvic fins. In a human skeleton, the pectoral girdle is the shoulder and its supporting bones, and the pelvic girdle is the hips. A fish's skull is composed of a large number of bones (far more than are in the human skull) and is capable of a wide range of movements. Note the pectoral fin rays and pelvic fin rays that are key characteristics of ray-finned fishes.

## Digestive System

Bony fishes have diverse diets but commonly are carnivores. The jaws of predatory fishes are lined with many sharp teeth that point inward to keep prey from escaping. Strong muscles operate the jaws, which are hinged to allow the mouth to open wide.

Figure 39-12 on the next page shows the internal anatomy of a bony fish. Food passes from the mouth into the pharynx, or throat cavity, and then moves through the *esophagus* to the stomach. The *stomach* secretes acid and digestive enzymes that begin to break down food. From the stomach, food passes into the *intestine,* where digestion is completed and nutrients are absorbed.

The *liver,* located near the stomach, secretes *bile,* which helps break down fats. The *gallbladder* stores bile and releases it into the intestine. The *pancreas,* also located near the stomach, releases digestive enzymes into the intestine. The lining of the intestine is covered with fingerlike extensions called villi that increase the surface area for absorption of digested foods. Undigested material is then eliminated through the *anus.*

**FIGURE 39-11**

The skeleton of *Perca flavescens* is similar to that of other bony fishes. The general structure of the vertebrae, rib cage, and fins is found in many fishes.

internet connect

www.scilinks.org

**Topic: Anatomy of a Bony Fish**

**Keyword: HM60065**

SCiLINKS. Maintained by the National Science Teachers Association

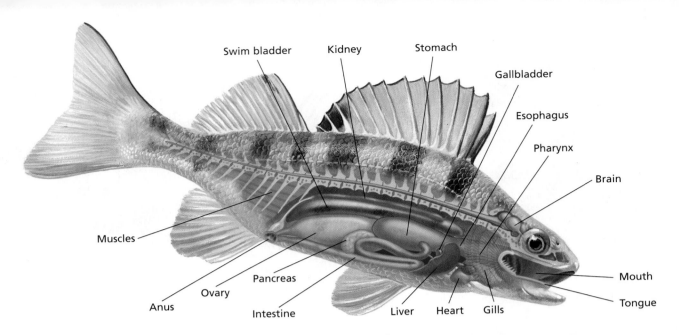

Swim bladder Kidney Stomach
Gallbladder
Esophagus
Pharynx
Brain
Muscles
Mouth
Pancreas Tongue
Ovary
Anus Intestine Liver Heart Gills

**FIGURE 39-12**

The internal anatomy of a bony fish, such as this perch, is a model for the arrangement of organs in all vertebrate descendants of fish. Food passes first from the mouth through the esophagus, then to the stomach and intestines. Finally, undigested waste is eliminated through the anus. Digestion of protein occurs in the stomach, and absorption of nutrients occurs in the intestine.

**FIGURE 39-13**

A fish's heart is a series of two chambers that act in sequence to move blood through the body, transporting oxygen to the cells and wastes to organs for elimination. Note the thickness of the muscle in the ventricle.

## Circulatory System

The circulatory system of a fish delivers oxygen and nutrients to the cells of the body. It also transports wastes produced by metabolism—carbon dioxide and ammonia—to the gills and kidneys for elimination. The circulatory system consists of a heart, blood vessels, and blood. The heart pumps blood through *arteries* to small, thin-walled vessels, called *capillaries,* in the gills. There the blood picks up oxygen and releases carbon dioxide. From the gills, the blood then travels to the body tissues, where nutrients and wastes are exchanged. The blood returns to the heart through *veins.*

The heart of a bony fish has two chambers in a row, as you can see in Figure 39-13. Deoxygenated blood from the body empties into a collecting chamber called the *sinus venosus.* Next, blood moves into the larger *atrium.* Contraction of the atrium speeds up the blood and drives it into the muscular *ventricle,* the main pumping chamber of the heart. Contraction of the ventricle provides most of the force that drives the blood through the circulatory system. The *conus arteriosus* is a thickened, muscular part of the main artery leaving the heart. It has an elastic wall and usually contains valves to prevent blood from flowing back into the ventricle. The conus arteriosus smooths the flow of blood from the heart to the gills.

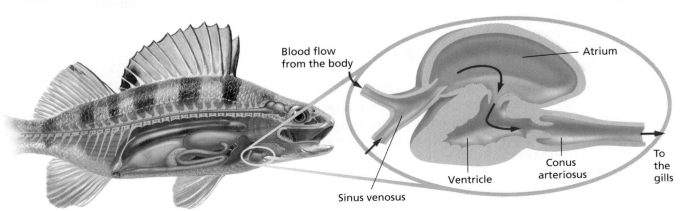

Blood flow from the body
Atrium

To the gills

Ventricle Conus arteriosus

Sinus venosus

## Respiratory and Excretory Systems

The large surface area of a fish's gills allows for rapid gas exchange. Gills are supported by four sets of curved bones on each side of the fish's head. Each gill has a double row of thin projections, called *gill filaments*. In most bony fishes, water is taken into the mouth and pumped over the gills, where it flows across the gill filaments before exiting behind the operculum. As you can see in Figure 39-14, water flows across the gill filaments in a direction opposite to blood flow. This arrangement is known as **countercurrent flow.** Countercurrent flow causes more oxygen to diffuse into the blood than would be possible if blood and water flowed in the same direction.

A fish's kidneys filter dissolved chemical wastes from the blood. The resulting solution, called *urine*, contains ammonia, ions such as sodium and chloride, and water. Urine is carried from the kidneys through a system of ducts to the *urinary bladder*, where it is stored and later expelled. By varying the amount of water and salts in the urine, the kidneys help regulate the water and ion balance in fresh and saltwater fishes.

As blood flows through the gill filaments, ammonia generated by metabolism diffuses from the blood into the water passing over the gills and is removed from the body. The gills also regulate the concentration of ions in the body. Recall that saltwater fishes have lower ion concentrations than sea water has. Therefore, they lose water through osmosis and gain ions, such as sodium and chloride ions. Saltwater fishes make up for this water loss by excreting small amounts of concentrated urine and by drinking sea water, but this increases their internal concentration of sodium and chloride ions. Both kinds of ions are actively transported out through the gills. Freshwater fishes tend to gain water and lose ions. They respond by producing large amounts of dilute urine and actively transporting sodium and chloride ions in through the gills.

## Swim Bladder

Most bony fishes have a swim bladder. This thin-walled sac in the abdominal cavity contains a mixture of oxygen, carbon dioxide, and nitrogen obtained from the bloodstream. Fish adjust their overall density by regulating the amount of gas in the swim bladder, enabling them to move up or down in the water.

Swim bladders evolved from balloonlike lungs, which ancestral bony fishes may have used to supplement the oxygen absorbed by the gills. In some fishes, the swim bladder is known to amplify sound by vibrating and transmitting sound to the inner ear.

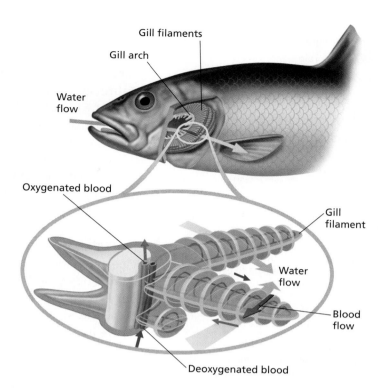

Gill filaments
Gill arch
Water flow
Oxygenated blood
Gill filament
Water flow
Blood flow
Deoxygenated blood

**FIGURE 39-14**

The gills are located directly behind the head and interior to the operculum. The gill filaments provide the organism with a large surface area, thus enabling gas exchange to occur quickly.

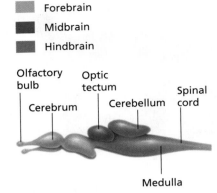

■ Forebrain
■ Midbrain
■ Hindbrain

Olfactory bulb | Optic tectum | Spinal cord
Cerebrum | Cerebellum
Medulla

**FIGURE 39-15**

The fish brain, like the shark brain, has a well-developed medulla to coordinate muscle control.

**FIGURE 39-16**

This male ringtailed cardinal fish, *Apogon aureus,* is carrying fertilized eggs in its mouth. This behavior lowers losses of eggs to predators and contributes to the success of the species.

## Nervous System

The nervous system of a bony fish includes the brain, spinal cord, nerves, and various sensory organs. The fish brain is illustrated in Figure 39-15. The most anterior part of the brain, the forebrain, contains the olfactory bulbs, which process information on smell. The forebrain also includes the *cerebrum,* which has areas that integrate information from other parts of the brain. Behind the forebrain lies the midbrain, which is dominated by the **optic tectum.** The optic tectum receives and processes information from the fish's visual, auditory, and lateral-line systems.

The most posterior division of the brain is the hindbrain, which contains the *cerebellum* (SER-uh-BEL-uhm) and the *medulla oblongata* (mi-DUL-uh AHB-lahng-GAHT-uh). The cerebellum helps coordinate muscles, movement, and balance. The medulla oblongata helps control some body functions and acts as a relay station for stimuli from sensory receptors throughout the fish's body. From the medulla oblongata, the spinal cord extends the length of the body and carries nerve impulses to and from the brain.

## REPRODUCTION

Eggs are produced by ovaries in the female, and sperm are produced by the testes in the male. Eggs and sperm are released through an opening behind the anus. Fertilization in most species takes place externally. Mortality among the eggs and young fishes is often very high. Many species of fishes lay large numbers of eggs, which ensures that at least a few individuals survive to become adult fish.

Some bony fishes bear live young. Using a modified anal fin, the male inserts sperm into the female, and fertilization is internal. The female carries the eggs in her body until the young are born. Other species care for the eggs as shown in Figure 39-16.

The reproductive, or **spawning,** behavior of bony fishes varies widely. Some species build crude nests from plants, sticks, and shells. Many species migrate to warm, protected shallow water to spawn.

## SECTION 3 REVIEW

1. List three key features that characterize bony fishes.

2. Contrast ray-finned and lobe-finned fishes.

3. Describe the external anatomy of a bony fish.

4. Identify the organs of four internal organ systems found in fishes.

5. Name two functions of the swim bladder.

6. Describe two methods of reproduction that can be found in bony fishes.

**CRITICAL THINKING**

7. **Applying Information** Which is the most muscular chamber of the fish heart? Explain why.

8. **Forming a Hypothesis** Bottom-dwelling fish often lack a swim bladder. Explain why lack of a swim bladder is an adaptive advantage.

9. **Recognizing Relationships** Explain how countercurrent flow allows the diffusion of more oxygen into the blood than would be possible if blood and water flowed in the same direction.

# CHAPTER HIGHLIGHTS

Introduction to Vertebrates

- Vertebrates are chordates and have a hollow dorsal nerve cord, notochord, pharyngeal pouches, and a post-anal tail at some stage of life.

- The characteristics that distinguish vertebrates from other chordates are vertebrae, a cranium, and an endoskeleton.

- Vertebrates are classified into nine classes: hagfish (class Myxini); lampreys (class Cephalaspidomorphi); sharks and rays (class Chondrichthyes); lobe-finned fishes (class Sarcopterygii); ray-finned fishes (class Actinopterygii); amphibians (class Amphibia); reptiles (class Reptilia); birds (class Aves); and mammals (class Mammalia).

- Early vertebrates were jawless fishes, which had bony scales, cartilaginous skeletons, and no paired fins.

- Paired fins increased stability and maneuverability in fishes; jaws allowed fish to seize and manipulate prey.

### Vocabulary
vertebrae (p. 779)          cranium (p. 779)          gill arches (p. 781)

---

**SECTION 2** Jawless and Cartilaginous Fishes

- Fishes have streamlined bodies, paired fins, and secrete mucus that reduces friction when swimming. The fish body plan makes them well suited to aquatic life.

- Fishes have a variety of organs that allow them to sense their environment. Fish can see, smell, and taste the world around them. They can also sense vibration, and some can sense electrical fields.

- Like early vertebrates, living agnathans lack jaws and paired fins and retain a notochord throughout life.

- Lampreys and hagfish are two types of jawless fishes that are alive today. Hagfishes burrow into and eat dead fish. Parasitic lampreys attach themselves to their host with their disc-shaped mouths and feed on the host's blood.

- Cartilaginous fishes have internal skeletons made of cartilage, and their skin is covered with placoid scales.

- Jawless fishes reproduce by external fertilization (fertilization occurs outside of the body of either parent). Most cartilaginous fishes reproduce by internal fertilization (the male inserts sperm into the female's body, and the young develop in an egg inside the female).

### Vocabulary
chemoreception (p. 783)          external fertilization (p. 784)          placoid scale (p. 784)
lateral line (p. 783)            cartilage (p. 784)                        internal fertilization (p. 786)

---

**SECTION 3** Bony Fishes

- Bony fishes are characterized by three key features: scales on the body, lungs or a swim bladder, and bone in the skeleton.

- Lobe-finned fishes have fleshy fins with a central bony axis, while ray finned fishes have non-fleshy fins supported by long flexible bones called rays.

- The external anatomy of a bony fish has several distinct characteristics—an operculum, fins, and scales.

- A fish's heart has two chambers that work together to move blood through the body.

- Water flows over fishes gills in a direction opposite to blood flow. Oxygen diffuses from the water into the blood very efficiently as a result of this process, which is called *countercurrent flow.*

- Fish adjust their overall density by regulating the amount of gas in the swim bladder, enabling them to move up or down in the water.

- Unlike cartilaginous fishes, most bony fishes reproduce by external fertilization in a process called *spawning.*

### Vocabulary
swim bladder (p. 787)          ray-finned fish (p. 787)          countercurrent flow (p. 791)          spawning (p. 792)
lobe-finned fish (p. 787)      operculum (p. 788)                optic tectum (p. 792)

# CHAPTER REVIEW

## USING VOCABULARY

1. For each pair of terms, explain how the meanings of the terms differ.
   a. *atrium* and *ventricle*
   b. *caudal fin* and *anal fin*
   c. *internal fertilization* and *external fertilization*
   d. *operculum* and *gill*

2. Use the following key terms in the same sentence: *cerebrum, optic tectum, cerebellum,* and *medulla oblongata.*

3. Explain the relationship between olfactory bulbs and lateral line system.

4. **Word Roots and Origins** The word *Actinopterygii* comes from the Greek *actinos,* meaning "ray," and *pteryx,* meaning "wing" or "fin." Using this information, explain why *Actinopterygii* is a good name for these fish.

## UNDERSTANDING KEY CONCEPTS

5. **List** the characteristics that would be found in a typical vertebrate.

6. **Identify** the class of vertebrates to which each of the following organisms belong: goldfish, sand sharks, pigeons, dogs, Pacific lamprey, bullfrog.

7. **Name** the characteristics that distinguish early vertebrates from modern vertebrates.

8. **Describe** two major changes in fish anatomy over millions of years.

9. **Evaluate** the relationship between fishes' body form and function in an aquatic environment.

10. **Identify** the structures that are involved in sensory systems in fishes.

11. **Name** one characteristic of early chordates that distinguishes hagfishes from lampreys.

12. **Describe** the key characteristics that distinguish cartilaginous fishes.

13. **Contrast** the reproductive strategy of lampreys with the reproductive strategy of sharks.

14. **Identify** the characteristics that distinguish bony fishes from cartilaginous fishes.

15. **Explain** the differences between the two main groups of bony fishes.

16. **State** how the caudal, dorsal, pectoral, and pelvic fins function in helping fish swim.

17. **Explain** how the heart and gills function in fish.

18. **Propose** a possible explanation for the evolution of primitive lungs into swim bladders.

19. **Compare** the advantages and disadvantages of internal fertilization and spawning.

20. **CONCEPT MAPPING** Use the following terms to create a concept map that describes the characteristics of jawless, cartilaginous, and bony fishes: *bony fishes, gills, cartilage, operculum,* and *countercurrent flow.*

## CRITICAL THINKING

21. **Applying Information** Sometimes fish develop a swim bladder disorder when they are overfed and food displaces the swim bladder. How might displacement of the swim bladder by food impair the function of this organ?

22. **Analyzing Research** A famous study showed that a shark could locate and capture a stationary fish buried in the sand at the bottom of its tank. When the fish was enclosed in electrical insulation and then buried, however, the shark could not locate it. From this information can you conclude that the shark is using only its electrical sense to locate the buried fish?

23. **Recognizing Relationships** Cod fishes lay eggs near the surface of the water. In contrast, the male largemouth bass scoops out a nest in a river bottom and waits for a female to deposit her eggs. What hypothesis would you make regarding the relative number of cod and bass eggs?

24. **Analyzing Graphics** Study the chart below, which shows the excreted ion concentration of a fish as it travels from one body of water to another. Is the fish traveling from fresh water to salt water or salt water to fresh water?

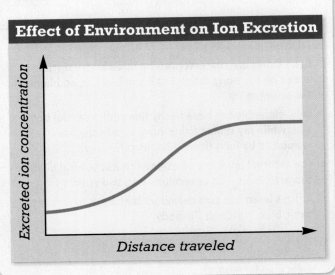

**Effect of Environment on Ion Excretion**

Excreted ion concentration (vertical axis)

Distance traveled (horizontal axis)

# Standardized Test Preparation

**DIRECTIONS:** Choose the letter of the answer choice that best answers the question.

1. Which of the following is true of sharks and rays?
   **A.** They have lungs.
   **B.** They have placoid scales.
   **C.** Most species live in fresh water.
   **D.** They do not have a lateral line system.

2. Which of the following is not involved in controlling buoyancy?
   **F.** a fat-filled liver
   **G.** the rectal gland
   **H.** the swim bladder
   **J.** continuous swimming

3. What is the function of the lateral line system?
   **A.** initiates migration
   **B.** detects vibrations
   **C.** acts as camouflage
   **D.** keeps fish moving in a straight line

4. What do sharks use claspers for?
   **F.** startle other fish
   **G.** increase maneuverability
   **H.** transfer sperm while mating
   **J.** hold on to prey while feeding

**INTERPRETING GRAPHICS:** The table below shows the salinity of fresh water, salt water, and the body fluids of fish. Use the table to answer the questions that follow.

## Salinity of Water and Fish Body Fluids

|                  | Salinity of fresh water | Salinity of salt water | Salinity of body fluids |
|------------------|-------------------------|------------------------|-------------------------|
| Freshwater fish  | <0.1%                   | —                      | 0.8 – 1%                |
| Saltwater fish   | —                       | 3.5%                   | 0.8 – 1.4%              |

5. What tendency do freshwater fish have in a freshwater environment?
   **A.** lose water and salts
   **B.** take on water and salts
   **C.** take on water and lose salts
   **D.** lose water and take on salts

6. What tendency do saltwater fish have in a saltwater environment?
   **F.** lose water and salts
   **G.** take on water and salts
   **H.** lose water and take on salts
   **J.** take on water and lose salts

**DIRECTIONS:** Complete the following analogy.

7. Hagfish : Myxini :: Sharks :
   **A.** Aves
   **B.** Agnatha
   **C.** Mammalia
   **D.** Chondrichthyes

**INTERPRETING GRAPHICS:** The figure below shows the external anatomy of a bony fish. Use the figure to answer the following question.

8. Which of the fins shown on the fish are dorsal fins?
   **F.** 1 & 2
   **G.** 2 & 4
   **H.** 5 & 6
   **J.** 5 & 4

## SHORT RESPONSE

Countercurrent flow enhances the diffusion of oxygen from the water into the bloodstream of fishes.

Explain the meaning of countercurrent flow in gills.

## EXTENDED RESPONSE

Humans have a four chambered heart with two ventricles. One ventricle pumps blood to the lungs and the other pumps blood that returns from the lungs to the body.

*Part A* Compare the structure and blood flow of the fish heart to the human heart.

*Part B* Which heart is able to pump blood more forcefully around the body? Why?

**Test TIP** For a question involving experimental data, determine the constants, variables, and control **before** answering the questions.

# Observing Structure and Behavior in Fishes

## OBJECTIVES

- Observe body shapes, camouflage, and feeding behavior in various species of fish.
- Relate observed adaptations to the survival of each species.

## PROCESS SKILLS

- making observations
- collecting data
- identifying and recognizing patterns
- interpreting data
- predicting
- analyzing results
- drawing conclusions

## MATERIALS

- clipboard and paper or notebook
- live fish in an aquarium tank
- pencil or pen

## Background

1. Identify the three major categories of modern fish.
2. State some key characteristics of bony fish.
3. Define an adaptation.
4. How are fish adapted to life in water?

## PART A Observing Body Shapes

1. CAUTION **To avoid injuring live fish do not touch or frighten them.** Find a tank that contains several types of tropical fish.
2. Identify the species of fish in the tank. In Table 1, record the common and scientific names of the species.
3. Describe the shape of the fish's body. In Table 1, record your description.
4. Observe the activity of the fish. How does it spend most of its time? In Table 1, record your observations.
5. Repeat steps 2–4 with another species of fish.

## PART B Observing Body Color and Patterns

6. Find three examples of fish that use body colors, markings, or postures to blend with their surroundings.
7. For each species, record its common and scientific names in Table 2, and describe the type of camouflage it uses.

### TABLE 1 *BODY SHAPES AND ACTIVITY*

| Species | Body shape | Activity |
|---------|------------|----------|
|         |            |          |
|         |            |          |
|         |            |          |

## TABLE 2 *CAMOUFLAGE*

| Species | Type of camouflage |
|---------|--------------------|
|         |                    |
|         |                    |

**PART C** Observing Feeding Behaviors

8. Find three examples of fish that use different methods for feeding.
9. For each species, record its common and scientific names in Table 3, and describe its feeding method.

### Analysis and Conclusions

1. How are the body shapes of the fishes you observed related to the types of activities that those fishes engage in?
2. What structural adaptations are associated with the different feeding behaviors that you observed?
3. How does camouflage help fish to survive in the cases where you observed it?
4. Would you expect camouflage to be more important for fish that live in shallow water or for those that live in very deep water? Explain your reasoning.

### Further Inquiry

Design an experiment about fish behavior using fish sold at a local pet store and materials available in your classroom. Report the results of your experiment in an oral presentation.

## TABLE 3 *FEEDING BEHAVIOR*

| Species | Type of feeding behavior |
|---------|--------------------------|
|         |                          |
|         |                          |

Amphibians are thought to have been the first vertebrates on land. Many amphibians, such as this southern leopard frog *(Rana pipiens)*, still live part or all of their life in water.

**SECTION 1** *Origin and Evolution of Amphibians*

**SECTION 2** *Characteristics of Amphibians*

**SECTION 3** *Reproduction in Amphibians*

# ORIGIN AND EVOLUTION OF AMPHIBIANS

## OBJECTIVES

- **Describe** three preadaptations involved in the transition from aquatic to terrestrial life.
- **Describe** two similarities between amphibians and lobe-finned fishes.
- **List** five characteristics of living amphibians.
- **Name** the three orders of living amphibians, and give an example of each.

## VOCABULARY

preadaptation
tadpole

*About 360 million years ago, amphibians became the first vertebrates to live on land. The name* amphibian *comes from the Greek words meaning "double" and "life" and reflects the fact that many amphibians spend part of their life on land and part in water.*

## ADAPTATION TO LAND

The first amphibians to spend a significant part of their life on land most likely evolved from lobe-finned fishes. Lobe-finned fishes had several preadaptations that allowed them to transition to life on land. **Preadaptations** are adaptations in an ancestral group that allow a shift to new functions which are later favored by natural selection.

Lobe-finned fishes ancestral to amphibians had a bone structure within their fins that worked as legs that could walk on land. Ancient lobe-finned fishes also had modified pouches in their digestive tracts, which evolved into the lungs of lungfish and swim bladders in most modern fishes. Some groups of ancient lobe-finned fishes also had internal nostrils that functioned in air breathing. In lobe-finned fishes ancestral to amphibians, these structures worked as a means of breathing on land.

Early amphibians required more oxygen than their fish ancestors. Because gravity makes movement on land more difficult than movement in water, early amphibians were likely to have had a higher metabolism than their fish ancestors. As a result, efficient hearts were an important adaptation that allowed oxygen to be delivered to the body more efficiently.

### Characteristics of Early Amphibians

Amphibians and lobe-finned fishes share many anatomical similarities, including features of the skull and vertebral column. Also, the bones in the fin of a lobe-finned fish are similar in shape and position to the bones in the limb of an amphibian. Figure 40-1 shows a sarcopterygian (sar-KOP-te-RIJ-ee-uhn), an extinct lobe-finned fish that is thought to be closely related to amphibians. This fish probably lived in shallow water and used its sturdy pelvic and pectoral fins to move along the bottom and to support its body while resting.

**FIGURE 40-1**

Early lobe-finned fishes, such as this sarcopterygian, are thought to be ancestors of the first land vertebrates.

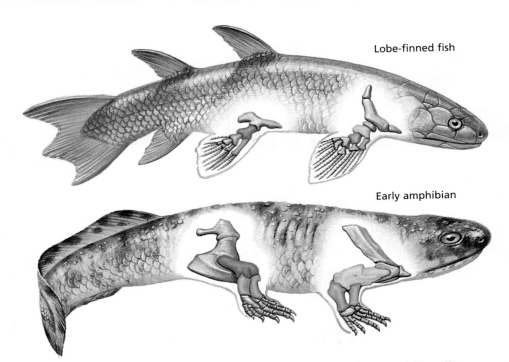

Lobe-finned fish

Early amphibian

## Quick Lab

### Comparing Fish and Amphibian Skin

**Materials** disposable gloves, lab apron, safety goggles, paper, colored pencils, living or preserved specimens of a fish and a frog

**Procedure**

1. Put on your disposable gloves, lab apron, and safety goggles.

2. Handle living animals gently. Touch and examine the skin of the specimens provided by your teacher. Record your observations.

3. When you are finished with your observations, remove your disposable gloves, lab apron, and safety goggles. Wash your hands with soap and water.

**Analysis** Why can a frog use its skin as a respiratory membrane, while a fish cannot? What behaviors in amphibians enable them to maintain moist skin?

The oldest known amphibian fossils date from about 360 million years ago. All of the early amphibians had four strong limbs, which developed from the fins of their fish ancestors, as shown in Figure 40-2. The forelimbs of amphibians (and all other terrestrial vertebrates) are homologous to the pectoral fins of fishes, and the hind limbs are homologous to the pelvic fins. The early amphibians also breathed air with lungs. Lungs arose early in the history of fishes and are found in the descendants of these early fishes—including terrestrial vertebrates.

Although the early amphibians showed several adaptations for life on land, such as sense organs for detecting airborne scents and sounds, they probably spent most of their time in the water. For example, some of the first amphibians had a large tail fin and lateral-line canals on their head. Their teeth were large and sharp, indicating a diet of fish, not insects. In addition, some of the early amphibians appear to have had gills like those of fishes.

## Diversification of Amphibians

During the late Devonian period and the Carboniferous period (359 million to 299 million years ago), amphibians split into two main evolutionary lines. One line included the ancestors of modern amphibians, and the other line included the ancestors of reptiles. Amphibians have been a diverse, widespread, and abundant group since this early diversification.

Today there are about 4,500 species of amphibians, belonging to three orders. The largest order, with more than 3,900 species, is Anura, which includes the frogs and toads. The order Caudata contains about 400 species of salamanders. And the third order, Gymnophiona, consists of about 160 species of caecilians, which are legless tropical amphibians. Figure 40-3 on the following page shows hypotheses for the phylogenetic relationships between these three groups.

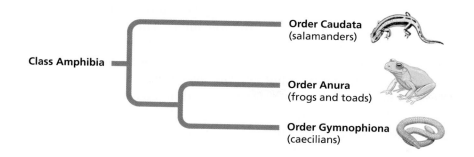

Class Amphibia
Order Caudata (salamanders)
Order Anura (frogs and toads)
Order Gymnophiona (caecilians)

**FIGURE 40-3**

This phylogenetic diagram shows hypotheses of the evolutionary relationship among modern amphibian orders. For updates on phylogenetic information, visit **go.hrw.com** and enter the keyword **HM6 Phylo.**

# MODERN AMPHIBIANS

Modern amphibians are a very diverse group, but they do share several key characteristics:

- Most change from an aquatic larval stage to a terrestrial adult form. This transformation is called *metamorphosis.*
- Most have moist, thin skin with no scales.
- Feet, if present, lack claws and often are webbed.
- Most use gills, lungs, and skin in respiration.
- Eggs lack multicellular membranes or shells. They are usually laid in water or in moist places and are usually fertilized externally.

## Order Anura

Anurans (frogs and toads) are found worldwide except in polar climates and a few isolated oceanic islands. They live in a variety of habitats, from deserts and tundra to tropical rain forests. Many anurans spend at least part of their life in water, and some species are permanently aquatic. Many other species live and reproduce on land. Figure 40-4 shows two examples of anurans. The term *toad* is commonly used for any anuran that has rough, bumpy skin, as seen in Figure 40-4a. The term *frog* commonly refers to anurans having smooth, moist skin, such as in Figure 40-4b. These terms are general descriptions, however, and do not refer to any formal groups of anurans.

**FIGURE 40-4**

Anurans include toads and frogs such as the plains spadefoot toad (a), *Scaphiopus bombifrons,* which can be found throughout the United States, and the White's tree frog (b), *Litoria caerulea,* which is common in Australia.

(a)

(b)

Anurans are characterized by a body adapted for jumping. Long, muscular legs provide power for the jump. The anuran body is compact, with a short, rigid spine and strong forelimbs that help absorb the shock of landing. The word *anuran* means "tailless" and reflects the fact that no adult anuran has a tail.

Adult anurans are carnivores that feed on any animal they can capture. Some frogs have a sticky tongue that can be extended to catch prey. Many species of anurans return to water to reproduce. In nearly all species, eggs are fertilized externally. The fertilized eggs hatch into swimming, tailed larvae called **tadpoles.**

## Order Caudata

Salamanders have elongated bodies, long tails, and moist skin. Except for a few aquatic species, they have four limbs. The smallest salamanders are only a few centimeters long, while the largest reach lengths of 1.5 m (4.5 ft). Like anurans, salamander species range from fully aquatic to permanently terrestrial. Terrestrial salamanders usually live in moist places, such as under logs and stones. Larval and adult salamanders are carnivores. They are active mainly at night. Figure 40-5 shows two representative salamanders.

Most salamander species live in North America and Central America. There are very few species in Africa and South America, several species are found in Asia and in Europe, and there are no species found in Australia. With more than 300 species, the lungless salamanders (family Plethodontidae) are the largest group of salamanders. As their name suggests, these salamanders lack lungs. They absorb oxygen and release carbon dioxide through their skin.

Like most anurans, many salamanders lay their eggs in water, and the eggs hatch into swimming larval forms. Other species can reproduce in moist land environments. Eggs laid on land usually hatch into miniature adult salamanders and do not pass through a free-living larval stage. Most salamander species have a type of internal fertilization by which females pick up sperm packets deposited by males. In some terrestrial species, the female stays with the eggs until they hatch, which can take up to several weeks.

**FIGURE 40-5**

The flatwoods salamander (a), *Ambystoma cingulatum,* and the spotted salamander (b), *Ambystoma maculatum,* are members of the order Caudata. *A. cingulatum,* which lives only in Florida, is an endangered species; *A. maculatum* can be found from eastern Canada to eastern Texas.

(a)

(b)

(a)

(b)

## Order Gymnophiona

The common name used to refer to members of the order Gymnophiona is caecilian (see-SIL-yuhn). Caecilians are a highly specialized group of legless amphibians that resemble small snakes, as you can see in Figure 40-6. Caecilians live in tropical areas of Asia, Africa, and South America. Caecilians average about 30 cm (12 in.) in length, but some species reach lengths of 1.5 m (4.5 ft). Because they have very small eyes that are located beneath the skin or even under bone, caecilians often are blind.

Caecilians are rarely seen, and little is known about their ecology and behavior. Most species burrow in the soil, but some species are aquatic. All species have teeth in their jawbones that enable them to catch and consume prey. They eat worms and other invertebrates, which they detect by means of a chemosensory tentacle located on the side of their head. All species are thought to have internal fertilization. Some species lay eggs, which the female guards until they hatch. In a few species, the young are born alive. These caecilians provide nutrition to their developing embryos. The young use their jaws and teeth to scrape secretions, called "uterine milk," from the walls of the female's reproductive tract.

**FIGURE 40-6**

Caecilians, such as *Ichthyophis kohtaoensis* (a) and *Caecilia nigricans* (b), are primarily carnivores. They are burrowing amphibians that are usually blind, and a few species have scales embedded in their skin.

## SECTION 1 REVIEW

1. Describe three adaptations that allowed early sarcopterygians to move onto land.

2. Identify two characteristics that amphibians share with modern lobe-finned fishes.

3. Name five key characteristics that are common to modern amphibians.

4. Differentiate each of the three living orders of amphibians.

### CRITICAL THINKING

5. **Applying Information** Early amphibian fossils do not indicate the presence of lungs. Why do scientists think that early amphibians had lungs?

6. **Forming Reasoned Opinions** Is the lack of legs a primitive characteristic for amphibians or a later amphibian adaptation? Support your answer.

7. **Analyzing Information** Why do modern amphibians not have a lateral line?

## OBJECTIVES

- **Relate** the structure of amphibian skin to the types of habitats in which amphibians can survive.
- **Identify** three adaptations for life on land shown by the skeleton of a frog.
- **Sequence** the flow of blood through an amphibian's heart.
- **Describe** how a frog fills its lungs with air.
- **Describe** the digestive and excretory systems of amphibians.
- **Discuss** an amphibian's nervous system.

## VOCABULARY

mucous gland
pulmonary circulation
systemic circulation
pulmonary respiration
cutaneous respiration
duodenum
ileum
mesentery
vent
nictitating membrane
tympanic membrane
columella

# CHARACTERISTICS OF AMPHIBIANS

*As you have already seen, terrestrial vertebrates face challenges that are far different from those faced by aquatic vertebrates. In this section, you will learn about some of the ways amphibians meet the challenges of living on land.*

## SKIN

The skin of an amphibian serves two important functions—respiration and protection. The skin is moist and permeable to gases and water, allowing rapid diffusion of oxygen, carbon dioxide, and water. Numerous **mucous glands** supply a lubricant that keeps the skin moist in air. This mucus is what makes a frog feel slimy. The skin also contains glands that secrete foul-tasting or poisonous substances that provide protection from predators.

However, the same features that allow efficient respiration also make amphibians vulnerable to dehydration, the loss of body water. Therefore, amphibians live mainly in wet or moist areas on land. Many species are active at night, when loss of water through evaporation is reduced. Although some species of frogs and toads survive in deserts, they spend most of their life in moist burrows deep in the soil. Only after heavy rains do these amphibians come to the surface to feed and reproduce.

Amphibians are affected by pollution. Chemicals present in water can be absorbed by amphibian skin. As a result, amphibians can serve as indicators of the health of an ecosystem.

## SKELETON

While water supports the body of an aquatic vertebrate against the force of gravity, terrestrial vertebrates must rely on the support of their strong internal skeleton. The vertebrae of the spine interlock and form a rigid structure that can bear the weight of the body. Strong limbs support the body during walking or standing. The forelimbs attach to the pectoral girdle (the shoulder and supporting bones), while the hind limbs attach to the pelvic girdle (the "hips"). The pectoral and pelvic girdles transfer the body's weight to the limbs. The cervical vertebra at the anterior end of the spine allows neck movement.

The frog skeleton in Figure 40-7 shows several specializations for jumping and landing. In frogs, the bones of the lower forelimb are fused into a single bone, the radio-ulna. The bones of the lower hind limb are fused into the tibiofibula. Frogs have few vertebrae, and the vertebrae at the posterior end of the spine are fused into a single bone called the urostyle. The pectoral girdle has thick bones that are braced to absorb the impact of landing.

# CIRCULATORY SYSTEM

The circulatory system of an amphibian is divided into two separate loops. The **pulmonary circulation** carries deoxygenated blood from the heart to the lungs and back to the heart. The **systemic circulation** carries oxygenated blood from the heart to the body and back to the heart.

The three-chambered heart of an amphibian reflects the division of the circulatory system into pulmonary and systemic circulation. Deoxygenated blood from the body first enters the right side of the heart, as shown in step ❶ of Figure 40-8. Blood moves into the right atrium. In step ❷, oxygenated blood from the lungs enters the left atrium. In step ❸, contraction of the atria forces the deoxygenated and oxygenated blood into the single ventricle, the main pumping chamber of the heart. Although the ventricle is not divided, its spongy interior surface and the coordinated contractions of the atria keep the oxygenated and deoxygenated blood from mixing. In step ❹, ventricular contraction expels both kinds of blood into the conus arteriosus, which directs deoxygenated blood to the lungs and oxygenated blood to the body.

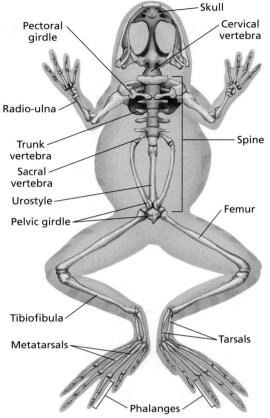

**FIGURE 40-7**

The skeleton of the frog has adapted to absorb shocks when the frog jumps and lands.

Skull
Pectoral girdle
Cervical vertebra
Radio-ulna
Trunk vertebra
Sacral vertebra
Urostyle
Pelvic girdle
Spine
Femur
Tibiofibula
Metatarsals
Tarsals
Phalanges

**FIGURE 40-8**

Amphibians have a three chambered heart that pumps blood to the lungs and throughout the body.

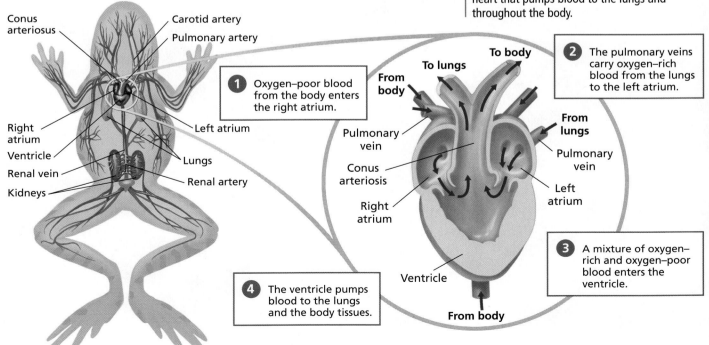

Conus arteriosus
Carotid artery
Pulmonary artery
Right atrium
Ventricle
Renal vein
Kidneys
Left atrium
Lungs
Renal artery

❶ Oxygen–poor blood from the body enters the right atrium.

❷ The pulmonary veins carry oxygen–rich blood from the lungs to the left atrium.

❸ A mixture of oxygen–rich and oxygen–poor blood enters the ventricle.

❹ The ventricle pumps blood to the lungs and the body tissues.

To body
To lungs
From body
From lungs
Pulmonary vein
Conus arteriosis
Right atrium
Pulmonary vein
Left atrium
Ventricle
From body

All other terrestrial vertebrates also have a "double-loop" circulatory pattern. This pattern of circulation provides a significant advantage over the "single-loop" circulation of a fish—faster blood flow to the body. In a fish, the blood loses some of its force as it passes through the narrow capillaries of the gills, and blood flow slows as a result. The lungs of an amphibian also contain narrow capillaries that slow blood flow. But after passing through the capillaries of the lung, blood returns to the heart to be pumped a second time before circulating to the body.

# RESPIRATION

Larval amphibians respire, or exchange carbon dioxide and oxygen, through their gills and skin. Most adult amphibians lose their gills during metamorphosis, but they can respire in two ways: through the lungs and through the skin. Respiration through the lungs is called **pulmonary respiration.** Amphibians ventilate their lungs with a unique mechanism that pumps air into the lungs; this is called *positive-pressure breathing*. For example, a frog breathes by changing the volume and pressure of air in its mouth while either opening or closing its nostrils, as shown in Figure 40-9. Both inhalation and exhalation involve a two-step process during which the floor of the frog's mouth is raised and lowered. The frog controls the direction of air flow by opening or closing its nostrils. Because amphibians have a small surface area in the lungs for gas exchange, respiration through the skin, or **cutaneous respiration,** is very important to most aquatic and terrestrial amphibians.

**FIGURE 40-9**

Frogs breathe by creating pressure that forces air into their lungs. ❶ When the floor of the frog's mouth drops, air capacity increases in the frog's mouth, and air rushes in. ❷ When the nostril is closed and the mouth floor rises, the air is forced into the lungs of the frog. ❸ The mouth floor lowers and air is forced out of the lungs. ❹ Then the nostril opens and the mouth floor rises again, forcing air out the nostril.

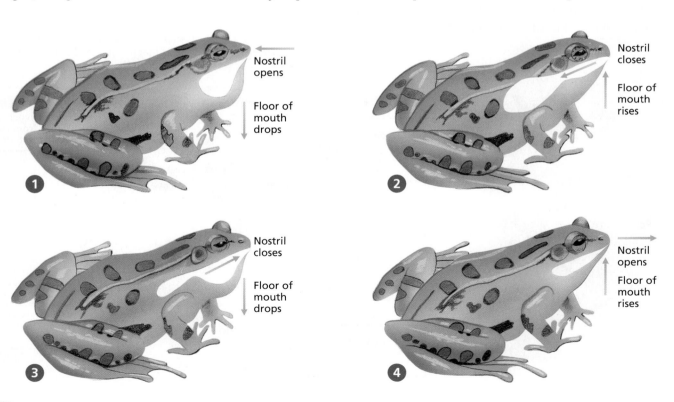

Nostril opens

Floor of mouth drops

Nostril closes

Floor of mouth rises

Nostril closes

Floor of mouth drops

Nostril opens

Floor of mouth rises

# DIGESTIVE SYSTEM

All adult amphibians are carnivorous. Because most amphibians are small, insects and other arthropods are their most commonly consumed prey. Larger amphibians sometimes eat mice, snakes, fish, other amphibians, and even sometimes birds. Many amphibian larvae, such as those of frogs, are herbivorous, feeding on algae, bacteria, or plants. The larvae of some species, such as those of salamanders, are carnivorous, and some feed on the larvae of other species.

The amphibian digestive system includes the pharynx, esophagus, stomach, liver, gallbladder, small intestine, large intestine, and cloaca. Figure 40-10 shows a ventral view of the digestive system of a frog.

The elastic esophagus and stomach allow an amphibian to swallow large amounts of food. Once food reaches the stomach, tiny glands in the stomach walls secrete gastric juices that help break down, or digest, the food. A muscle called the pyloric sphincter at the lower end of the stomach relaxes, which allows digested food to move into the small intestine. The upper portion of the small intestine is called the **duodenum** (DOO-oh-DEE-nuhm). The coiled middle portion of the small intestine is the **ileum** (IL-ee-uhm). A membrane resembling plastic wrap, called the **mesentery,** holds the small intestine in place. Inside the small intestine, digestion is completed and the released nutrients pass through capillary walls into the bloodstream, which carries them to all parts of the body.

The lower end of the small intestine leads into the large intestine. Here indigestible wastes are collected and pushed by muscle action into a cavity called the *cloaca* (kloh-AY-kuh). Waste from the kidneys and urinary bladder, as well as either eggs or sperm from the gonads, also passes into the cloaca. Waste materials exit the body through the **vent.**

## Accessory Glands

Other glands and organs aid in the digestion process. The liver produces bile, which is stored in the gallbladder. Bile helps break down fat into tiny globules that can be further digested and absorbed. A gland called the pancreas, located near the stomach, secretes enzymes that enter the small intestine and help break down food into products that can be absorbed by the blood.

**FIGURE 40-10**

The frog digestive system is shown in ventral view. Notice how the short small intestine is an adaptation for a carnivorous diet.

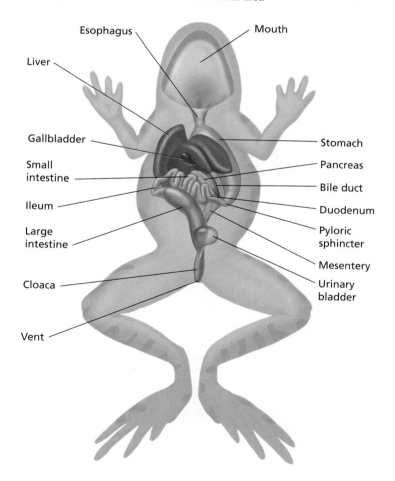

Esophagus

Mouth

Liver

Gallbladder

Stomach

Small intestine

Pancreas

Ileum

Bile duct

Large intestine

Duodenum

Pyloric sphincter

Cloaca

Mesentery

Vent

Urinary bladder

# EXCRETORY SYSTEM

The kidneys are the primary excretory organs. One kidney lies on either side of the spine against the dorsal body wall. The kidneys filter nitrogenous wastes from the blood. These wastes, flushed from the body with water, are known as urine. Urine flows from the kidneys to the cloaca through tiny tubes called urinary ducts. From the cloaca, it flows into the urinary bladder, which branches from the ventral wall of the cloaca. For many terrestrial amphibians, the urinary bladder serves as a water-storage organ. During dry periods, water can be reabsorbed from the urine in the bladder.

Like the larvae of fishes, most amphibian larvae excrete the nitrogen-containing wastes as ammonia. Because ammonia is very toxic, it must be removed from the body quickly or diluted with large amounts of water in the urine. To conserve water, adult amphibians transform ammonia into urea, a less-toxic substance that can be excreted without using as much water. Although this transformation uses energy, it helps save water. During metamorphosis, larval amphibians change from excreting ammonia to excreting urea.

**FIGURE 40-11**

This diagram shows the frog's nervous system in ventral view. The brain of the frog is sufficiently developed to cope with both land and water environments.

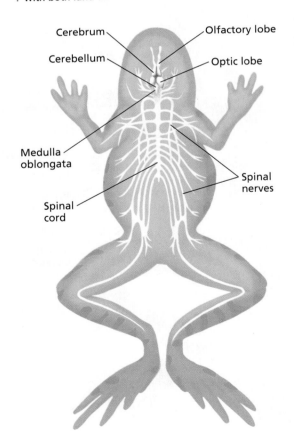

Cerebrum

Cerebellum

Olfactory lobe

Optic lobe

Medulla oblongata

Spinal cord

Spinal nerves

# NERVOUS SYSTEM

Use the diagram in Figure 40-11 to find the main components of the amphibian nervous system. An amphibian's brain is about the same size as that of a fish of similar size. The olfactory lobes, which are the center of the sense of smell, are larger in amphibians than in fish, and they lie at the anterior end of the brain. Behind the olfactory lobes are the long lobes of the cerebrum, the area of the brain that integrates behavior and is responsible for learning.

The optic lobes, which process information from the eyes, lie behind the cerebrum. The cerebellum, a small band of tissue that lies at a right angle to the long axis of the brain, is the center of muscular coordination and is not as well developed in amphibians as it is in other tetrapods. The medulla oblongata lies at the back of the brain and joins the spinal cord. It controls some organ functions, such as heart rate and respiration rate.

There is continuous communication among most areas of the brain. Ten pairs of cranial nerves extend directly from the brain. The spinal cord conducts signals from all parts of the body to the brain and from the brain back to the body. Encased in protective bony vertebrae, the spinal cord extends down the back. As in fishes, the spinal nerves branch from the spinal cord to various parts of the body.

**FIGURE 40-12**

Frogs have a well-developed sense of sight, which is necessary for locating prey and avoiding predators. Frogs also have good hearing. Note the tympanic membrane (the circle below and to the left of the eye), which transmits sound to the inner ear.

## Sense Organs

Some sense organs work as well in air as in water, but others do not. For example, the lateral line system, used by fishes to detect disturbances in the water, works only in water. Thus, while larval amphibians have a lateral line, it is usually lost during metamorphosis. Only a few species of aquatic amphibians have a lateral line as adults.

The senses of sight, smell, and hearing are well developed in most amphibians. Visual information is often important in hunting and in avoiding predators. The eyes are covered by a transparent, movable membrane called a **nictitating** (nik-ti-tayt-eeng) **membrane.**

Sound is detected by the inner ear, which is embedded within the skull. Sounds are transmitted to this organ by the **tympanic** (tim-PAN-ik) **membrane,** or eardrum, and the **columella** (CAHL-yoo-mel-uh), a small bone that extends between the tympanic membrane and the inner ear. Sounds first strike the tympanic membrane, which is usually located on the side of the head, just behind the eye as shown in Figure 40-12. Vibrations of the tympanic membrane cause small movements in the columella that are transmitted to the fluid-filled inner ear. In the inner ear, the sound vibrations are converted to nervous impulses by sensitive hair cells. These impulses are transmitted to the brain through a nerve.

**Word Roots and Origins**

*nictitating*

from the Latin *nictare,* meaning "to wink"

## SECTION 2 REVIEW

1. Identify an advantage and a disadvantage to the permeability of amphibian skin.

2. Explain three ways in which a frog's skeleton is adapted for jumping.

3. Identify the relationship between the structure of a frog's heart and "double-loop" circulation.

4. Explain how a frog uses positive pressure to move air into and out of its lungs.

5. What feature do the digestive and excretory systems in frogs have in common?

**CRITICAL THINKING**

6. **Applying Information** Which are the two largest features of an amphibian's brain? Why do you think these lobes are the largest?

7. **Making Comparisons** Which sense organ of a terrestrial amphibian resembles the fish's lateral line in function? Explain your answer.

8. **Recognizing Relationships** Why are the skeletal bones in a frog's shoulders thicker than the bones in a frog's pelvic girdle?

- **Explain** how a male frog attracts a female of the same species.
- **Discuss** the reproductive system of a frog.
- **Describe** the life cycle of a frog.
- **Describe** the changes that occur during metamorphosis in frogs.
- **Identify** two examples of parental care in amphibians.

### VOCABULARY

amplexus

# REPRODUCTION IN AMPHIBIANS

*One of the biggest differences between aquatic and terrestrial life-forms is their method of reproduction. Most amphibians depend on water for reproduction. They lay their eggs in water and spend the early part of their lives as aquatic larvae.*

## COURTSHIP AND FERTILIZATION

In the first warm days of spring in the temperate zones, frogs emerge from hibernation. They migrate in great numbers to ponds and slow-moving streams. Males call to attract females of their own species and to warn off other males, as shown in Figure 40-13. Each species has its own mating call. The frog's croak is produced by air that is driven back and forth between the mouth and the lungs, vibrating the vocal folds. Male frogs have vocal sacs that amplify their calls. The female responds only to the call from a male of the same species.

When a female approaches, the male frog climbs onto her back. He grasps her firmly in an embrace called **amplexus** (am-PLEKS-uhs). The male clings to the female until she lays her eggs. When the female finally releases her eggs into the water, the male frog discharges his sperm over them, and direct external fertilization takes place. The frogs then separate and resume their solitary lives. Courtship behavior and fertilization often differ between species.

### Reproductive System

The reproductive system of the male frog includes two bean-shaped testes located near the kidneys. During the breeding season, sperm cells develop in the testes and pass through tubes to the kidneys and urinary ducts. During mating, sperm leave the body through the cloacal opening. In female frogs, a pair of large, lobed ovaries containing thousands of tiny immature eggs lie near the kidneys. During the breeding season, the eggs enlarge, mature, and burst through the thin ovarian walls into the body cavity. Cilia move the eggs forward into the funnel-like openings of the oviducts. As the eggs pass down the oviducts, they are coated with a protective jellylike material. The eggs exit by the cloaca to the external environment, where they are fertilized.

**FIGURE 40-13**

Most frogs that sing are males. Their songs attract females and warn off males of the same species.

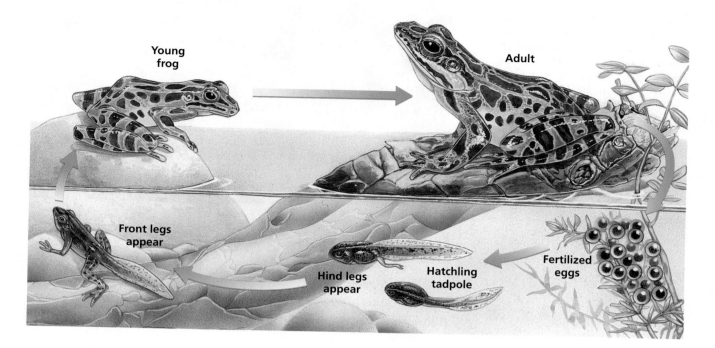

Young frog

Adult

Front legs appear

Hind legs appear

Hatchling tadpole

Fertilized eggs

# LIFE CYCLE

Within a few days of fertilization, the eggs hatch into tadpoles. A newly hatched tadpole lives off yolk stored in its body. It gradually grows larger and develops three pairs of gills. Eventually, the tadpole's mouth opens, allowing it to feed. The tadpole grows and slowly changes from an aquatic larva into an adult. This process of change is called *metamorphosis*. Legs grow from the body, and the tail and gills disappear. The mouth broadens, developing teeth and jaws, and the lungs become functional.

Biologists have long studied the process of metamorphosis and regeneration to learn what controls such dramatic physical changes. A hormone called *thyroxine* is produced by the thyroid gland and circulates throughout the bloodstream to stimulate metamorphosis.

The life cycles of many amphibians are similar to that of the frog shown in Figure 40-14. But there are a variety of alternative reproductive patterns among amphibians. For example, many amphibians do not lay their eggs in water. They select a moist place on land, such as under a rock, inside a rotting log, or in a tree. One or both parents may even construct a nest for the eggs. A number of frog species make a nest of mucus, whipping it into a froth by kicking their hind legs. And not all amphibians undergo metamorphosis. Some salamanders, such as the axolotl in Figure 40-15, remain in the larval stage for their entire life. The axolotl's thyroid does not produce thyroxine. Other amphibians bypass the free-living larval stage and hatch from the egg as a small version of the adult.

**FIGURE 40-14**

The life cycle of a frog begins with mating. When the eggs hatch, a tadpole is released. One of the first developments of metamorphosis is the growth of hind legs. When the tadpole completes metamorphosis, a small adult emerges from the water onto the land.

**FIGURE 40-15**

The axolotl does not produce thyroxine, and as a result, does not undergo metamorphosis. It retains its gills and lives a completely aquatic life.

FIGURE 40-16

*Rhinoderma darwinii* male frogs exhibit parental care by holding the maturing eggs and larvae in their vocal sacs. This frog has already released his offspring, whose tails are still visible. Not all frogs express parental care in this way, and some frogs express no parental behavior at all.

# PARENTAL CARE

Parental care is common among amphibians. Eggs and larvae are vulnerable to predators, but parental care helps increase the likelihood that some offspring will survive. Most often, one parent (often the male) remains with the eggs, guarding them from predators and keeping them moist until they hatch. The male Darwin's frog *(Rhinoderma darwinii)* of Chile takes the eggs into his vocal sacs, where they hatch and eventually undergo metamorphosis. The young frogs climb out of the vocal sacs and emerge from the male's mouth, as shown in Figure 40-16.

Female gastric-brooding frogs of Australia swallow their eggs, which hatch and mature in the stomach. The eggs and tadpoles are not digested because the stomach stops producing acid and digestive enzymes until the young pass through metamorphosis and are released. Two species of gastric-brooding frogs are known, but both appear to have become extinct within the last two decades. Females of some species of frogs, such as *Eleutherodactylus,* sit on their eggs until they hatch, not to provide warmth but to prevent the eggs from desiccating. The female normally lays the eggs in the leaves of trees or bushes, where they may dry up.

## SECTION 3 REVIEW

1. Identify two functions of the male frog's call.

2. Sequence the stages of a frog's life cycle.

3. Identify the features that are lost and the features that are gained during metamorphosis in frogs.

4. Name the hormone responsible for stimulating tadpoles to undergo metamorphosis.

5. Describe two strategies that have been found in frogs for protecting eggs and developing young.

**CRITICAL THINKING**

6. **Applying Information** Why is standing water not always necessary for frog reproduction?

7. **Recognizing Relationships** How do you think the number of eggs produced by amphibians relates to the amount of parental care invested?

8. **Justifying Conclusions** Would you expect an amphibian that bypasses the larval stage to produce more or less thyroxine? Explain.

# CHAPTER HIGHLIGHTS

## SECTION 1    Origin and Evolution of Amphibians

- Preadaptations are inherited traits used for new functions for which the traits are later selected.

- Fleshy fins with strong bone structure, nostrils, and lungs were preadaptations that allowed the transition from aquatic to terrestrial life.

- Early amphibians had lungs and four legs. Like lobe-finned fish, they were predominantly aquatic, they had a lateral line and a fishlike tail fin, similar skull and vertebral column, similar limb bones, and some had gills.

- Modern amphibians share several characteristics. Most change from aquatic larvae to terrestrial adult. Most have moist thin skin, with no scales. Feet, if present, lack claws and are often webbed. Most use gills, lungs, and skin in respiration. Most lay eggs that lack multicellular membranes or shells.

- Modern amphibians are divided into three orders: Anura (frogs and toads), Caudata (salamanders), and Gymnophiona (caecilians).

### Vocabulary

preadaptation (p. 799)          tadpole (p. 802)

## SECTION 2    Characteristics of Amphibians

- Adult amphibians respire through their lungs and skin. Mucous glands produce slimy mucus that helps retain moisture.

- The skeleton of an amphibian supports the body against the pull of gravity. In addition, the spine interlocks to provide rigid structure, strong limbs support the body, and the pectoral and pelvic girdle transfer body weight to the limbs.

- The amphibian pulmonary circuit carries blood between the heart and lungs. The systemic circuit carries blood to the body and returns blood to the heart.

- The heart of an amphibian consists of two atria and one ventricle. The right atrium receives blood from the body, pumps blood to the ventricle, and then pumps blood to the lungs. The left atrium receives blood from the lungs, pumps blood to the ventricle, and then to the body.

- Amphibians pump air into their lungs by raising and lowering the floor of their mouth cavity while closing and opening their nostrils.

- In an amphibian, food passes through the mouth, esophagus, stomach, small intestine, large intestine, and cloaca. The kidneys remove wastes from the blood. Adult amphibians eliminate nitrogenous wastes as urea.

- The brain of a frog has large optic lobes that process visual information, large olfactory lobes that control the sense of smell, a cerebrum that integrates behavior and controls learning, a cerebellum that coordinates movement, and a medulla oblongata that controls the heart and respiration rate. Fish have brains of similar size, but with smaller olfactory lobes.

### Vocabulary

mucous gland (p. 804)
pulmonary
   circulation (p. 805)
systemic circulation (p. 805)

pulmonary
   respiration (p. 806)
cutaneous
   respiration (p. 806)

duodenum (p. 807)
ileum (p. 807)
mesentery (p. 807)
vent (p. 807)

nictitating
   membrane (p. 809)
tympanic membrane (p. 809)
columella (p. 809)

## SECTION 3    Reproduction in Amphibians

- Male frogs call to attract females of the same species.

- The male frog grasps the female in an embrace called amplexus and fertilizes her eggs as they are released.

- A life cycle is the stages through which an organism passes from fertilization to reproductive maturity. Most amphibians lay their eggs in water, and have an aquatic larval stage and a terrestrial adult stage.

- The hormone thyroxine triggers metamorphosis. During metamorphosis, the tadpole loses its tail and gills and grows legs and lungs.

- Many amphibians show parental care by guarding their eggs and keeping their eggs moist. Some take their eggs into their body to develop.

### Vocabulary

amplexus (p. 810)

## USING VOCABULARY

1. For each pair of terms, explain how the meanings of the terms differ.
   a. *systemic circulation* and *pulmonary circulation*
   b. *amplexus* and *metamorphosis*
   c. *pulmonary respiration* and *cutaneous respiration*

2. Use the following key terms in the same sentence: *duodenum, mesentery* and *ileum*.

3. Explain the relationship between preadaptation and adaptation.

4. **Word Roots and Origins** The word *columella* comes from the Latin *columna,* which means "pillar." Using this information, list two characteristics of this amphibian ear bone.

## UNDERSTANDING KEY CONCEPTS

5. **Discuss** the preadaptiations important in the evolution of amphibians.

6. **Identify** two characteristics that indicate that amphibians are descendants of ancient lobe-finned fish.

7. **Name** five major characteristics of amphibians.

8. **Identify** the order to which each of the following belong: frogs, salamanders, caecilians.

9. **Explain** how some species of frogs survive in desert environments even though they do not have watertight skin.

10. **Relate** the adaptations in the amphibian skeleton to the change in gravity with life on land.

11. **Outline** the route of blood flow through the body of a frog, beginning with the right atrium.

12. **Determine** the next step for air within the oral cavity of a frog when it closes its nostrils and raises the mouth floor.

13. **Trace** the digestive process as food passes through a frog's digestive system.

14. **Explain** how an amphibian's nervous system is similar to that of a bony fish.

15. **Explain** how male frogs attract the attention of female frogs during mating season.

16. **Describe** the reproductive system of a frog.

17. **Discuss** the life cycle of a frog.

18. **Contrast** the physical characteristics of a larval frog to those of an adult frog.

19. **Describe** two different examples of parental care found in frogs.

20. **CONCEPT MAPPING** Use the following terms to create a concept map that shows the methods of respiration in frogs: *frogs, skin, mouth floor, body wall muscles, nostrils, lungs, air pressure, oral cavity, environment.*

## CRITICAL THINKING

21. **Inferring Relationships** Charles Darwin noticed that frogs and toads are often absent from oceanic islands, such as the Galápagos Islands, even though they may be found on the nearby mainland. Darwin conducted some experiments that showed that frogs' eggs cannot tolerate exposure to salt water. What hypothesis do you think Darwin was trying to test?

22. **Recognizing Relationships** In the brains of amphibians, the largest parts are the olfactory lobes and the optic lobes, the centers of smell and sight. This is very important to amphibians in hunting prey and avoiding predators. Why else is the capacity for hearing important?

23. **Recognizing Relationships** The female gastric-brooding frogs of Australia did not produce stomach acid or digestive enzymes while brooding their young in their stomachs until the tadpoles completed metamorphosis and left. If the mother frog did not eat during this period, from where did she get her energy?

24. **Analyzing Graphics** When tadpoles undergo metamorphosis, their bodies begin to produce an enzyme that converts ammonia into urea. The time that a tadpole takes to produce this enzyme varies among species. In the graph below, the rate of enzyme production is shown for a species that inhabits a desert-like environment and a species that inhabits a forest environment. Which curve represents which frog? Explain.

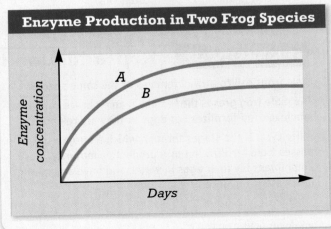

**Enzyme Production in Two Frog Species**

*Enzyme concentration*

*A*

*B*

*Days*

# Standardized Test Preparation

**DIRECTIONS:** Choose the letter that best answers the question or completes the sentence.

1. The forelimbs of vertebrates evolved from which structures in lobe-finned fishes?
   A. anal fin
   B. pelvic fins
   C. pectoral fins
   D. pectoral girdle

2. Amphibians must lay eggs in water primarily for what reason?
   F. The eggs are not laid in nests.
   G. The eggs need oxygen from water.
   H. The eggs need protection from predators.
   J. The eggs do not have multicellular membranes and a shell.

3. Metamorphosis must take place before amphibians are able to do what?
   A. swim
   B. live on land
   C. respire with gills
   D. feed themselves

**INTERPRETING GRAPHICS:** The figure below shows a longitudinal section, dorsal view, of a frog heart. Use the figure below to answer question 4.

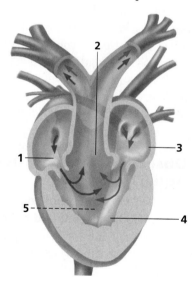

4. Identify the source of blood flow in the section of the heart labeled 1.
   F. the body
   G. the aorta
   H. the lungs
   J. both lungs and body

**DIRECTIONS:** Complete the following analogy.

5. Anura : frogs :: Gymnophiona :
   A. toads
   B. newts
   C. caecilians
   D. salamanders

**INTERPRETING GRAPHICS:** The figure below shows an artist's rendering of *Ichthyostega*. Use the figure to answer the question that follows.

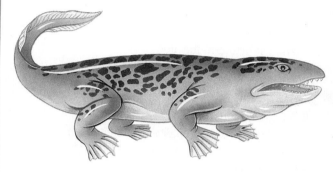

6. *Ichthyostega* is an early amphibian. Which of the following characteristics is most likely to help it live on land?
   F. fishlike tail
   G. seven-toed feet
   H. four strong limbs
   J. lateral-line canals on the head

## SHORT RESPONSE

Modern amphibians are a diverse group, but they do have some common characteristics.

Describe five key characteristics shared by modern amphibians.

## EXTENDED RESPONSE

Frogs breathe by a positive pressure system.

*Part A* Describe how frogs move air into their lungs. Which part of inhaling is "positive pressure?"

*Part B* Describe how frogs move air out of their lungs and into the atmosphere.

**Test TIP** Be sure to read all of the answer choices carefully. Do not assume that the first correct answer is the only one.

# Observing Live Frogs

## OBJECTIVES

- Observe the behavior of a frog.
- Explain how a frog is adapted to life on land and in water.

## PROCESS SKILLS

- observing
- relating structure to function
- recognizing relationships

## MATERIALS

- live frog in a terrarium
- aquarium half-filled with dechlorinated water
- live insects (crickets or mealworms)
- 600 mL beaker

## Background

1. What does *amphibious* mean?
2. Describe how amphibians live part of their life on land and part in water.
3. What are some major characteristics of amphibians?

### PART A Observing the Frog in a Terrarium

1. Observe a live frog in a terrarium. Closely examine the external features of the frog. Make a drawing of the frog in your lab report. Label the eyes, nostrils, tympanic membranes, front legs, and hind legs. The tympanic membrane, or eardrum, is a disc-like membrane behind each eye.
2. In your lab report, make a table similar to the one on the facing page to note all your observations of the frog in this investigation.
3. Watch the frog's movements as it breathes. Record your observations in your data table.
4. Look closely at the frog's eyes, and note their location. Examine the upper and lower eyelids as well as a third transparent eyelid called a *nictitating membrane*. The upper and lower eyelids do not move. The nictitating membrane moves upward over the eye. This eyelid protects the eye when the frog is underwater and keeps the eye moist when the frog is on land.
5. Study the frog's legs. Note in your data table the difference between the front and hind legs.
6. Place a live insect, such as a cricket or a mealworm, in the terrarium. Observe how the frog reacts.
7. Gently tap the side of the terrarium farthest from the frog, and observe the frog's response.

### PART B Observing the Frog in an Aquarium

8. **CAUTION** **You will be working with a live animal. Handle it gently and follow instructions carefully.** Frogs are slippery. Do not allow the frog to injure itself by jumping from the lab bench to the floor. Place a 600 mL beaker in the terrarium. Carefully pick up the frog and examine its skin. How does it feel? The skin of a frog acts as a respiratory organ, exchanging oxygen and carbon dioxide with the air or water. A frog also takes in and loses water through its skin.
9. Place the frog in the beaker. Cover the beaker with your hand, and carry it to a freshwater aquarium. Tilt the beaker and gently submerge it beneath the surface of the water until the frog swims out of the beaker.

## OBSERVATIONS OF A LIVE FROG

| Characteristic | Observation |
|---|---|
| Breathing | |
| Eyes | |
| Legs | |
| Response to food | |
| Response to noise | |
| Skin texture | |
| Swimming behavior | |
| Skin coloration | |

10. Watch the frog float and swim in the aquarium. How does the frog use its legs to swim? Notice the position of the frog's head.

11. As the frog swims, bend down and look up into the aquarium so that you can see the underside of the frog. Then look down on the frog from above. Compare the color on the dorsal and ventral sides of the frog. When you are finished observing the frog, your teacher will remove the frog from the aquarium.

12. Record your observations of the frog's skin texture, swimming behavior, and skin coloration in your data table.

13.  Clean up your materials and wash your hands before leaving the lab.

### Analysis and Conclusions

1. From the position of the frog's eyes, what can you infer about the frog's field of vision?

2. How does the position of the frog's eyes benefit the frog while it is swimming?

3. How does a frog hear?

4. How can a frog take in oxygen while it is swimming in water?

5. Why must a frog keep its skin moist while it is on land?

6. How are the hind legs of a frog adapted for life on land and in water?

7. What adaptive advantage do frogs have in showing different coloration on their dorsal and ventral sides?

8. What features provide evidence that an adult frog has an aquatic life and a terrestrial life?

9. What adaptations does the frog display in order to eat? What senses are involved in catching prey?

10. What movement does the frog make in order to breathe?

### Further Inquiry

Observe other types of amphibians, or do research to find out how they are adapted to life on land and in water. How do the adaptations of other types of amphibians compare with those of the frog you observed in this investigation?

A marine iguana, *Amblyrhynchus cristatus*, of the Galápagos Islands warms itself by basking on a rock. These are the only marine lizards in the world, and they feed exclusively on seaweed.

**SECTION 1** *Origin and Evolution of Reptiles*

**SECTION 2** *Characteristics of Reptiles*

**SECTION 3** *Modern Reptiles*

# ORIGIN AND EVOLUTION OF REPTILES

SECTION 1

*T*he reptiles (class Reptilia) are one of the largest groups of terrestrial vertebrates. This chapter will discuss the diversity of reptiles and some of the characteristics that make the reptiles a successful group.

## OBJECTIVES

- **Summarize** the factors that led to the rise of reptiles as the dominant land vertebrates.
- **Identify** three factors that contributed to the success of dinosaurs.
- **Compare** two hypotheses to explain the extinction of the dinosaurs.
- **Identify** examples of the four modern orders of reptiles.
- **Describe** three characteristics of modern reptiles that make them well adapted to life on land.

## VOCABULARY

dinosaur
asteroid impact hypothesis
amniotic egg
amnion
yolk sac
allantois
chorion
albumen
keratin

## HISTORY OF REPTILES

From studies of fossils and comparative anatomy, biologists infer that reptiles arose from amphibians. The oldest known fossils of reptiles were found in deposits from the early Carboniferous period (359 million to 299 million years ago). The earliest reptiles were small, four-legged vertebrates that resembled lizards and had teeth adapted for eating insects. The abundance of insects at the time may have been one reason the early reptiles flourished. By the Permian period (299 million to 251 million years ago) reptiles had become the dominant land vertebrates.

By the end of the Permian nearly all of the continents had joined to form the supercontinent *Pangaea* (pan-JEE-uh), shown in Figure 41-1. The interior of Pangaea had a dryer climate than the coastal regions. Reptiles were suited to dry climates and were highly successful. The end of the Permian period (and of the Paleozoic era) is marked by a mass extinction during which a large number of species became extinct. The cause of this extinction is still debated. Reptiles that survived diversified to take over the ecological roles of the extinct species. The Mesozoic era (251 million to 66 million years ago) is often called the Age of Reptiles because nearly all of the large vertebrates during that time were reptiles.

## EVOLUTION OF DINOSAURS

Beginning about 235 million years ago, **dinosaurs,** a group of extinct reptiles, dominated life on land for roughly 150 million years. They evolved from *thecodonts,* an extinct group of crocodile-like reptiles. Dinosaurs include a wide variety of reptiles that were adapted to very different environments. One factor that affected dinosaur evolution was the movement of the continents. Early in the Mesozoic era, Pangaea started to break apart. The climates of the separate landmasses changed. Some species of dinosaurs could not adapt and became extinct, while new kinds flourished.

**FIGURE 41-1**

When dinosaurs first appeared, all of Earth's landmasses were joined in a single supercontinent called *Pangaea,* shown above.

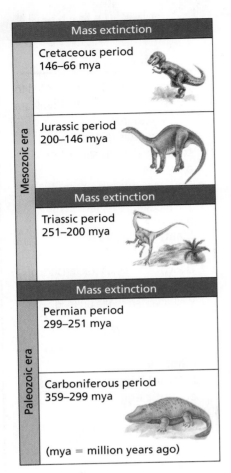

| | Mass extinction |
|---|---|
| **Mesozoic era** | Cretaceous period 146–66 mya |
| | Jurassic period 200–146 mya |
| | Mass extinction |
| | Triassic period 251–200 mya |
| | Mass extinction |
| **Paleozoic era** | Permian period 299–251 mya |
| | Carboniferous period 359–299 mya |

(mya = million years ago)

**FIGURE 41-2**

The evolution of reptiles has been marked by three mass extinction events. For more information about the geologic time scale, see the Appendix at the back of this textbook.

## Triassic Dinosaurs

The oldest known dinosaur fossils are in rocks from the early Triassic period, about 235 million years ago. By the end of the Triassic, small, carnivorous dinosaurs, were very common and had largely replaced the thecodonts.

There are at least three reasons why dinosaurs were so successful. First, legs positioned directly under the body provided good support for the dinosaur's body weight, enabling dinosaurs to be faster and more agile runners than the thecodonts. Second, dinosaurs were well adapted to the dry conditions found in Pangaea during the late Triassic period. Finally, at the end of the Triassic period, another mass extinction wiped out about 80% of living species, including the thecodonts and the last of the large amphibians. Recent research suggests that asteroid impacts in what are now Canada, France, the Ukraine, and Minnesota occurred almost simultaneously and contributed to this mass extinction event. This event marked the end of the Triassic period, outlined in Figure 41-2. Reduction in competition for resources may have allowed dinosaurs to flourish.

## Jurassic and Cretaceous Dinosaurs

The Jurassic period, graphed in Figure 41-2, is considered the golden age of dinosaurs because of the variety and abundance of dinosaurs that lived during this time. They included the largest land animals of all time, the sauropods (SAWR-uh-PAHDZ), shown in Figure 41-3a.

By the late Jurassic period, a new type of dinosaur had evolved. The carnivorous theropods (THER-uh-PAHDZ), shown in Figure 41-3c stood on two powerful legs and had short arms. Their large heads were equipped with sharp teeth, and each foot had sickle-shaped claws used for ripping open prey. Theropods preyed on the large herbivorous dinosaurs and were the dominant terrestrial predators until the end of the Cretaceous (kruh-TAY-shus) period.

**FIGURE 41-3**

Sauropods (a) were herbivores. Some herbivores, like triceratops (b), had armor to defend themselves against carnivorous (meat-eating) dinosaurs like the theropods (c).

(a)

(b)

(c)

## Dinosaur Diversity

Dinosaurs were not limited to terrestrial habitats. Some Mesozoic reptiles called *pterosaurs* (TER-uh-SAWRS), shown in Figure 41-4a, evolved the ability to fly. Several other groups of reptiles, including the ichthyosaurs (IK-thee-uh-SAWRS) and plesiosaurs, lived in the oceans. Ichthyosaurs, illustrated in Figure 41-4b, were sleek aquatic reptiles that resembled modern bottlenose dolphins. Plesiosaurs had long, flexible necks and compact bodies.

# EXTINCTION OF DINOSAURS

**FIGURE 41-4**

(a) Pterosaurs ranged in size from the smallest, which were only the size of sparrows, to the largest, which were about the size of a small airplane, with wingspans of 12 m (about 39 ft).
(b) Like dolphins, ichthyosaurs were probably fast swimmers and fed on fish.

Although the fossil record provides many clues about what dinosaurs were like, paleontologists who study dinosaurs still have many unanswered questions. For example, why did the dinosaurs and many other species become extinct 66 million years ago, at the end of the Cretaceous period?

## Asteroid Impact Hypothesis

Until recently, most scientists thought that a single catastrophic event was responsible for the mass extinction of dinosaurs. The **asteroid impact hypothesis** suggests that a huge asteroid hit Earth and formed a crater on the Yucatán Peninsula in southern Mexico. The impact sent so much dust into the atmosphere that the amount of sunlight reaching the Earth's surface was greatly reduced. The reduced sunlight caused severe climatic changes that led to the mass extinction. The asteroid impact hypothesis is supported by the fact that sediments from the end of the Cretaceous period contain unusually high concentrations of iridium. Iridium is a metal that is very rare in the Earth's crust but more abundant in asteroids and other meteroids. According to this hypothesis, the dinosaurs would have become extinct very quickly.

## Multiple Impact Hypothesis

Another hypothesis, called the *multiple impact hypothesis,* proposes that asteroid impacts began before the mass extinction took place. Along with other unfavorable environmental conditions, multiple asteroid impacts, including the impact on the Yucatán peninsula, led to a decline in numbers of organisms among species. In 2004, paleontologist Gerta Keller and her colleagues provided evidence to support this hypothesis. Results of their research suggest that conditions hostile to dinosaur survival were spread over many years. It is likely that these reptiles were not wiped out by a single asteroid impact.

# SUCCESS OF REPTILES

Representatives of the four modern orders of reptiles—Chelonia (turtles and tortoises), Squamata (lizards and snakes), Rhynchocephalia (tuataras), and Crocodilia (crocodiles, alligators, caimans)—survived the mass extinction of the Cretaceous period. These four orders of reptiles have diversified to more than 6,000 species. Reptiles successfully occupy a variety of terrestrial and aquatic habitats on all continents except Antarctica. Figure 41-5 is a phylogenetic diagram that shows hypotheses for the relationship among reptiles, birds, and mammals.

## Modern Reptiles

The turtles have the most ancient origins and have changed very little in structure since before the time of the dinosaurs. Tuataras belong to a small group of lizard-like reptiles. The vast majority of living reptiles belong to the group snakes and lizards. The fourth line of living reptiles includes the crocodiles and their relatives. Crocodilians have changed very little in more than 200 million years. Like dinosaurs, crocodilians are descendants of the thecodonts.

In some ways, such as the structure of their heart, crocodilians resemble birds far more than they resemble other living reptiles. And crocodilians are the only living reptiles that care for their young. What does this mean in terms of their relationships to other vertebrate species? Today, many biologists think that birds are direct descendants of the dinosaurs.

**FIGURE 41-5**

This phylogenetic diagram represents hypotheses for the relationship among reptiles, birds, and mammals. For updates on phylogenetic information, visit **go.hrw.com.** Type in the keyword **HM6 Phylo.**

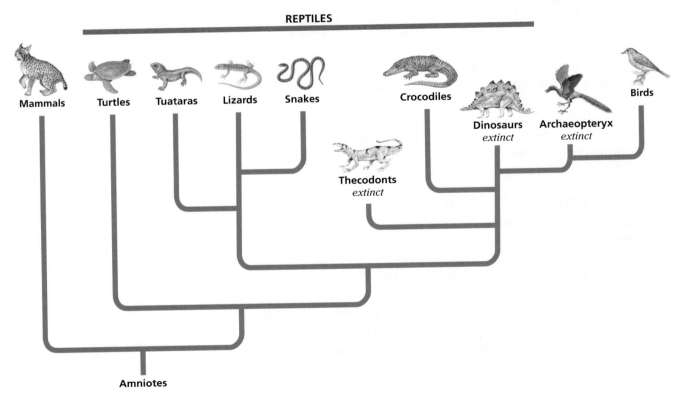

## The Amniotic Egg

Although amphibians were the first vertebrates to successfully invade land, they did not make a full transition to terrestrial life. They still require water in their environment to reproduce. Reptiles are considered the first fully terrestrial vertebrates because they do not need to reproduce in water, as most amphibians do. Reptiles produce **amniotic eggs,** which encase the embryo in a secure, self-contained aquatic environment. Amniotic eggs provide more protection for the developing embryo than do the jellylike eggs of amphibians.

Figure 41-6 shows the internal structure of the amniotic egg, including its four specialized membranes: the amnion, yolk sac, allantois, and chorion. The egg is named for the **amnion** (AM-nee-uhn), the thin membrane enclosing the fluid in which the embryo floats. The **yolk sac** encloses the yolk, a fat-rich food supply for the developing embryo. The **allantois** (uh-LAN-toh-is) stores the nitrogenous wastes produced by the embryo. Its blood vessels, which lie near the porous shell, function in the exchange of oxygen and carbon dioxide gases. The **chorion** (KAWR-ee-AHN) surrounds all the other membranes and helps protect the developing embryo. Protein and water needed by the embryo are contained in the **albumen** (al-BYOO-muhn). You are familiar with albumen as the egg white in a chicken's egg. In most reptiles, the leathery outer shell provides protection from physical damage, limits the evaporation of water from the egg, and allows diffusion of oxygen and carbon dioxide.

The amniotic egg first evolved in reptiles, but it also occurs in mammals and birds. The presence of this feature is strong evidence that reptiles, birds, and mammals evolved from a common ancestor. The eggs of some reptiles and nearly all mammals lack shells, and the embryo develops within the mother's body.

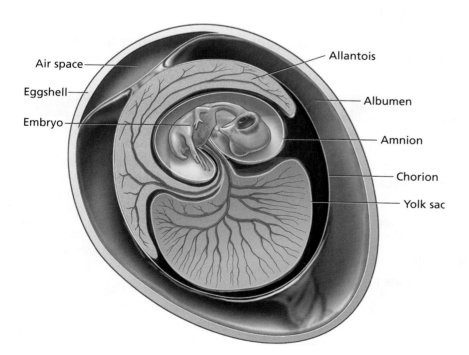

Air space
Eggshell
Embryo
Allantois
Albumen
Amnion
Chorion
Yolk sac

**FIGURE 41-6**

Amniotic eggs have four major membranes. The tough but porous shell provides protection while allowing the exchange of oxygen and carbon dioxide. The amniotic eggs of reptiles and birds (shown here) are very much alike internally.

FIGURE 41-7

The skin of this spiny lizard, *Sceloporus poinsetti,* protects it from the rugged terrestrial environment and from water loss.

## Watertight Skin

Because amphibians exchange gases through their skin, the skin must be moist and thin enough to allow rapid diffusion. A drawback of this kind of skin is that amphibians face the loss of body water through evaporation. Reptiles, such as the lizard shown in Figure 41-7, are covered by a thick, dry, scaly skin that prevents water loss. This scaly covering develops as surface cells fill with **keratin,** the same protein that forms your fingernails and hair. Lipids and proteins in the skin help make the skin watertight. The tough skin of a reptile not only helps conserve body water but also protects the animal against infections and injuries.

## Respiration and Excretion

Modern reptiles have developed efficient respiratory and excretory systems that help them conserve water. All reptiles have lungs for gas exchange. All of the tissues involved in gas exchange are located inside the body, where they can be kept moist in even the driest environments. The excretory system of reptiles also helps them conserve body water. Land-dwelling reptiles excrete nitrogenous wastes in the form of uric acid which requires little water for dilution. Reptiles lose small amounts of water in their urine.

## SECTION 1 REVIEW

1. Explain the role of climate in the success of early reptiles.

2. Compare and contrast characteristics of Triassic and Jurassic dinosaurs.

3. Explain the importance of iridium found in sediments from the end of the Cretaceous period.

4. Summarize the two asteroid impact hypotheses.

5. Describe three characteristics that contribute to the success of reptiles on land.

**CRITICAL THINKING**

6. **Analyzing Information** Why might dinosaurs have survived the asteroid impact at the end of the Triassic period but not one at the end of the Cretaceous?

7. **Relating Concepts** Dinosaurs are now thought to have been warmblooded. How does this support the theory about their relationship to birds?

8. **Inferring Relationships** In what ways are the adaptations of reptiles to land similar to the adaptations of plants to land?

# CHARACTERISTICS OF REPTILES

*Reptiles live in many different habitats and show a great deal of diversity in size and shape. Think of the differences between a snake and a turtle or between a lizard and a crocodile. This section discusses some of the anatomical, physiological, and behavioral characteristics of reptiles.*

## CIRCULATORY SYSTEM

The circulatory system of a reptile, like those of all terrestrial vertebrates, is composed of two loops. The pulmonary loop carries deoxygenated blood from the heart to the lungs and returns oxygenated blood to the heart. The systemic loop transports oxygenated blood to the tissues of the body, where oxygen and nutrients are unloaded and where carbon dioxide and wastes are picked up, and returns deoxygenated blood to the heart.

### Heart Structure and Function

In lizards, snakes, tuataras, and turtles, the heart has two atria and a single ventricle partially divided by a wall of tissue called a **septum.** In crocodiles, there are two atria and two separate ventricles. The sinus venosus and the conus arteriosus, which are major accessory structures to the heart of a fish, are much smaller in reptiles. The sinus venosus is absent in some species. When it is present, it collects blood from the body and channels it into the right atrium. The conus arteriosus forms the base of the three large arteries exiting from the reptilian heart.

Because the ventricle is not completely divided (except in crocodiles), it might seem that deoxygenated and oxygenated blood would mix. However, very little blood mixing occurs when a reptile is active. Deoxygenated and oxygenated blood are kept separate during contraction of the heart by the actions of the heart valves and the movement of the septum and ventricular walls.

Pumping blood through lungs requires energy. Under some conditions, it is advantageous for a reptile to divert blood away from the lungs to conserve energy. For example, an inactive reptile needs so little oxygen that it may go a long time without breathing. Similarly, aquatic reptiles do not breathe while they are underwater. Under these conditions, the heart pumps blood to the body while reducing circulation through the lungs.

### SECTION 2

#### OBJECTIVES

- **Identify** advantages associated with the structure of a reptile's heart.
- **Describe** the respiratory system of reptiles.
- **Describe** four methods reptiles use to sense their environment.
- **Explain** how reptiles regulate their body temperature.
- **Compare** oviparity, ovoviviparity, and viviparity as reproductive strategies.

#### VOCABULARY

septum
alveolus
Jacobson's organ
thermoregulation
ectotherm
endotherm
oviparity
ovoviviparity
viviparity
placenta

**internet** connect

www.scilinks.org
**Topic: Reptiles**
**Keyword: HM61299**

SCI LINKS. Maintained by the National Science Teachers Association

**FIGURE 41-8**

The turtle's heart, shown in cross section, has a partially divided ventricle, unlike an amphibian's three-chambered heart or a crocodile's four-chambered heart. Because the flow of blood through a turtle's heart is asynchronous, deoxygenated blood and oxygenated blood pass through the upper part of the ventricle at different times and so mix very little.

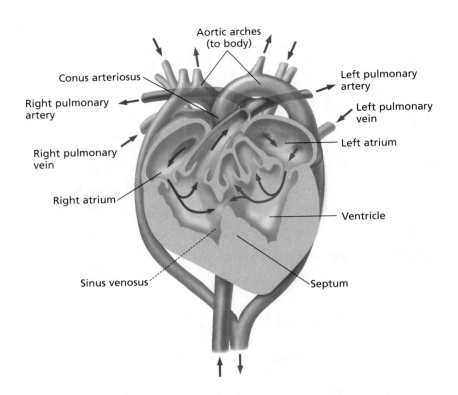

By constricting the pulmonary arteries, a reptile's blood flow through the heart can be redirected to send some deoxygenated blood back to the body instead of to the lungs. Bypassing the lungs may help a reptile raise its body temperature quickly—warm blood from the skin can be directed to the organs deep within the body. During periods of activity, almost all deoxygenated blood is directed to the lungs to meet the muscles' demand for oxygen. The reptilian heart has a degree of circulatory flexibility that the hearts of birds and mammals do not. Instead of being a handicap, this flexibility is actually well suited to reptilian physiology and activity patterns. Figure 41-8 shows a schematic diagram of the heart of a turtle.

# RESPIRATORY SYSTEM

The lungs of reptiles are large, and they are often divided internally into several chambers. The lining of the lungs may be folded into numerous small sacs called **alveoli.** Alveoli greatly increase the internal surface area of the lungs, thus increasing the amount of oxygen that can be absorbed. In most snakes, only the right lung actively functions. It is elongated and may be half as long as the body. The left lung is either reduced to a small nonfunctional sac or absent entirely.

A reptile fills its lungs by expanding its rib cage. This expansion reduces the pressure within the thorax and draws air into the lungs. When the ribs return to their resting position, pressure within the thorax increases, and air is forced out of the lungs. Similar movements help humans to breathe.

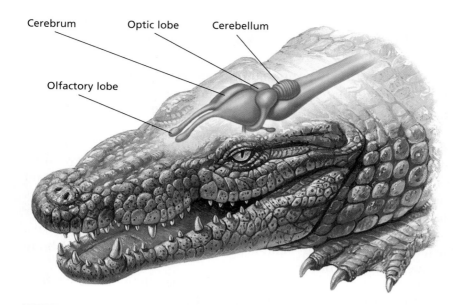

Cerebrum    Optic lobe    Cerebellum

Olfactory lobe

**FIGURE 41-9**

The crocodile's sense of smell is very important for its survival. The olfactory lobe of the reptile's brain, where the sense of smell is located, is highly developed.

# NERVOUS SYSTEM

The brain of a reptile is about the same size as that of an amphibian of the same size. However, the reptilian cerebrum is much larger. This region of the brain is involved in controlling and integrating behavior. Because vision is an important sense for most reptiles, the optic lobes, which receive input from the eyes, are large. Figure 41-9 shows the structure of a crocodile's brain.

Most reptiles rely on their sense of sight to detect predators and prey. The eyes of reptiles are usually large, and many species have keen vision. Hearing is also an important sense. As in amphibians, sound waves first strike the tympanum, or eardrum, and are transmitted to the inner ear through the movements of a small bone called the *columella*. The inner ear contains the receptors for sound. Snakes lack a tympanum and are sensitive only to low-frequency sounds. They are able to detect ground vibrations, which are transmitted to the columella by the bones of the jaw.

**Jacobson's organ** is a specialized sense organ located in the roof of the mouth of reptiles. Jacobson's organ is sensitive to odors. Like the snake shown in Figure 41-10, reptiles use their tongue to collect small particles from the environment. These particles are transferred to the Jacobson's organ when the tongue is drawn back into the mouth. Jacobson's organ is found in all reptiles except crocodiles and most turtles, but it is highly developed in lizards and snakes.

Pit vipers, such as rattlesnakes, copperheads, and water moccasins, are able to detect the heat given off by warm-bodied prey, such as mammals and birds. These snakes have one heat-sensitive pit below each eye, as shown in Figure 41-10. Input from these pits allows a snake to determine the direction of and distance to a warm object.

**FIGURE 41-10**

Some snakes have reduced senses of sight and hearing. They compensate with a sensitive forked tongue that is an organ of touch and smell. As the tongue darts in and out of the mouth, it picks up particles that are taken into the Jacobson's organ inside the snake's mouth, where even extremely low concentrations of odors can be detected.

# THERMOREGULATION

The control of body temperature is known as **thermoregulation.** Vertebrates regulate their body temperature in two different ways. An **ectotherm** warms its body by absorbing heat from its surroundings. Reptiles, fishes, and amphibians are ectotherms. **Endotherms,** such as mammals and birds, have a rapid metabolism, which generates heat needed to warm the body. Most endotherms have insulation, such as hair, feathers, or fat, to retain heat. The body temperatures of many aquatic ectotherms, such as fishes and amphibians, remain close to the temperature of their surroundings. Terrestrial ectotherms, such as lizards and snakes, usually keep their body temperatures about the same as the body temperatures of endotherms.

Most reptiles live in warm climates and regulate their body temperature by controlling how much heat they absorb. For example, when a lizard emerges from its nest after a cool night, its body temperature is low and must be raised before it can become active. The lizard warms itself by basking in the sun, as shown in Figure 41-11a. The lizard's warm blood is diverted from the skin to the interior of the body. As the graph in Figure 41-11b shows, a lizard can maintain its body temperature within a narrow range despite variations in air temperature. The lizard uses a variety of behaviors to accomplish this.

## Advantages and Limitations of Ectothermy

Because their metabolism is very slow, ectotherms require very little energy and need only about one-tenth as much food as an endotherm of the same size. Ectotherms cannot live in very cold climates, and they can survive temperate climates only by becoming dormant during the coldest months. Furthermore, ectotherms can run or swim at maximum speed only for short periods of time. Ectothermic metabolism cannot provide enough energy for sustained exertion.

**FIGURE 41-11**

(a) A lizard regulates its body temperature throughout the day, basking in the sun to warm and seeking shade to prevent overheating. If its body temperature rises too high, the lizard may pant to accelerate heat loss (b). The graph shows an early-morning increase in the lizard's body temperature. The body temperature fluctuates only slightly during the remainder of the day, despite wide fluctuations in ground temperature.

(a)

(b)

**Temperature Regulation of a Lizard**

Ground surface temperature (full sun)

Body temperature of lizard

Temperature (°C)

Time of day

# REPRODUCTION AND PARENTAL CARE

There are three patterns of reproduction among reptiles. The differences between these three patterns lie in how long the eggs remain within the female and in how she provides them with nutrition.

In **oviparity,** the female's reproductive tract encloses each egg in a tough protective shell. The female then deposits the eggs in a favorable place in the environment. Oviparity is characteristic of most reptiles, all birds, and three species of mammals.

One way to protect delicate eggs is to retain the eggs within the female's body for a time. This strategy, seen in some reptiles including American pit vipers, is called **ovoviviparity.** The eggs may be laid shortly before hatching, or they may hatch within the female's body. The eggs absorb water and oxygen from the female, but they receive no nutrition other than the yolk.

In **viviparity,** a shell does not form around the egg, and the young are retained within the female's body until they are mature enough to be born. Nutrients and oxygen are transferred from mother to embryo through a structure called the **placenta.** The placenta forms from the membranes within the egg, and it brings blood vessels from the embryo near the vessels of the mother. Viviparity is the reproductive pattern shown by most mammals, but it is also found in a few species of lizards and snakes.

Many reptiles provide no care for their eggs or young. However, some species of lizards and snakes guard and warm the eggs until they hatch. Crocodiles and alligators provide the greatest amount of parental care. A female crocodilian, for example, builds a nest for her eggs. She remains nearby while the eggs incubate, guarding against nest-robbing predators. After the young hatch, she breaks open the nest and carries the hatchlings to the water in her mouth, as shown in Figure 41-12. The mother crocodile may protect her young for a year or more.

### Word Roots and Origins

*ovoviviparous*

from the Latin *ovum,* meaning "egg," *vivus,* meaning "alive," and *parere,* meaning "to bring forth"

**FIGURE 41-12**

Reptiles generally do not provide care for their young, but the hatchlings are usually able to fend for themselves as soon as they emerge from the shell. Crocodiles and alligators, however, care for their young for up to two years. The female crocodile in the photograph is transporting her baby in her mouth.

## SECTION 2 REVIEW

1. Describe how the heart of a turtle differs from the heart of a crocodile.

2. Describe how reptiles inhale and exhale.

3. Identify two sense organs reptiles and amphibians share and two sense organs that are unique to reptiles.

4. Compare thermoregulation in animals that are endothermic versus thermoregulation in animals that are ectothermic.

5. Contrast oviparity with viviparity.

**CRITICAL THINKING**

6. **Applying Information** Which of the patterns of reproduction in reptiles best serves to protect the eggs from predators? Explain.

7. **Making Comparisons** Both crocodiles and turtles are ectothermic. Why do you think crocodile hearts are different from turtle hearts?

8. **Justifying Conclusions** Would change in body temperature over the course of a day prove that an animal is an ectotherm? Why or why not?

## OBJECTIVES

- **Compare** the anatomy of turtles with that of other reptiles.
- **Describe** the structure that allows crocodilians to swallow prey under water.
- **Explain** three antipredator defenses of lizards.
- **Describe** two ways snakes subdue their prey.
- **Identify** two reasons that tuataras are rarely seen.

## VOCABULARY

carapace
plastron
autotomy
constrictor
elapid
viper

# MODERN REPTILES

*Modern reptiles are classified into four orders: Chelonia, Crocodilia, Squamata, and Rhynchocephalia. As different as two species of reptile—such as a turtle and a snake—appear to be, all species of modern reptiles share the following characteristics: an amniotic egg; internal fertilization of eggs; dry, scaly skin; respiration through lungs; and ectothermic metabolism.*

## ORDER CHELONIA

The order Chelonia consists of about 250 species of turtles and tortoises. The term *tortoise* is generally reserved for the terrestrial members of the order, such as the Galápagos tortoise shown in Figure 41-13a. *Turtle* usually refers to chelonians that live in water, such as the green sea turtle shown in Figure 41-13b.

The earliest known turtle fossils, which are more than 200 million years old, show that ancient chelonians differed little from today's turtles and tortoises. This evolutionary stability may be the result of the continuous benefit of the basic turtle design—a body covered by a shell. The shell consists of fused bony plates. The **carapace** is the top, or dorsal, part of the shell, and the **plastron** is the lower, or ventral, portion. In most species, the vertebrae and ribs are fused to the inner surface of the carapace. Because the ribs are fused to the carapace, the pelvic and pectoral girdles lie within the ribs instead of outside the ribs, as they do in all other terrestrial vertebrates. Unlike other reptiles, turtles have a sharp beak instead of teeth.

**FIGURE 41-13**

(a) The Galápagos tortoise, *Geochelone gigantops,* is protected from predators by its high domed carapace. (b) The green sea turtle, *Chelonia mydas,* is streamlined for life in the sea.

(a)

(b)

Turtles and tortoises live in a variety of habitats. Some species are permanently aquatic, some are permanently terrestrial, and some spend time both on land and in the water. The differing demands of these habitats are reflected in the shells and limbs of turtles. For example, water-dwelling turtles usually have a streamlined, disk-shaped shell that permits rapid turning in water, and their feet are webbed for swimming. The limbs of marine turtles, which spend their entire lives in the ocean, have evolved into flippers for swimming and maneuvering. Many tortoises have a domed carapace into which they can retract their head, legs, and tail as a means of protection from predators. Their limbs are sturdy and covered with thick scales.

### Reproduction

All turtles and tortoises lay eggs. The female selects an appropriate site on land, scoops out a hole with her hind limbs, deposits the eggs, and covers the nest. She provides no further care for the eggs or the hatchlings. Marine turtles often migrate long distances to lay their eggs on the same beach where they hatched. For example, Atlantic green sea turtles travel from their feeding grounds off the coast of Brazil to Ascension Island in the South Atlantic—a distance of more than 2,000 km (1,242 mi). These turtles probably rely on several environmental cues, possibly even the Earth's magnetic field and the direction of currents, to find this tiny island.

# ORDER CROCODILIA

The living reptiles most closely related to the dinosaurs are the crocodilians, order Crocodilia. This group is composed of about 21 species of large, heavy-bodied, aquatic reptiles. In addition to crocodiles and alligators, the order includes the caimans and the gavial. Figure 41-14 shows some examples of crocodilians.

Crocodilians live in many tropical and subtropical regions of the world. Alligators live in China and the southern United States. Caimans are native to Central America and South America, and they have been introduced into Florida.

**FIGURE 41-14**

(a) Crocodiles, such as genus *Crocodylus,* are found in Africa, Asia, Australia, and the Americas. (b) The gavial, *Gavialis gangeticus,* is a crocodilian with an extremely long and slender snout adapted for seizing and eating fish. Gavials live only in India and Burma.

(a)

(b)

All crocodilians are carnivorous. They feed on fish and turtles and on land animals that come to the water to feed or drink. Crocodilians capture their prey by lying in wait until an animal approaches and then attacking swiftly. A crocodilian can see and breathe while lying quietly submerged in water. A valve at the back of the throat prevents water from entering the air passage when a crocodilian feeds underwater.

# ORDER SQUAMATA

The order Squamata consists of about 5,500 species of lizards and snakes. A distinguishing characteristic of this order is an upper jaw that is loosely joined to the skull. Squamates are the most structurally diverse of the living reptiles, and they are found worldwide.

## Lizards

There are about 3,000 species of living lizards. Common lizards include iguanas, chameleons, and geckos. Lizards live on every continent except Antarctica. Figure 41-15 shows some examples of lizards. Most lizards prey on insects or on other small animals. A few of the larger species, such as the chuckwalla and desert iguana of the southwestern United States, feed on plants. The Komodo dragon feeds on prey as large as goats and deer. Only two species of lizards are venomous. They are the Gila monster of the southwestern United States and northern Mexico and the related beaded lizard of southern Mexico.

Most lizards rely on agility, speed, and camouflage to elude predators. If threatened by a predator, some lizards have the ability to detach their tail. This ability is called **autotomy.** The tail continues to twitch and squirm after it detaches, drawing the predator's attention while the lizard escapes. The lizard grows a new tail in several weeks to several months, depending on the species.

Most lizards are small, measuring less than 30 cm (12 in.) in length. The largest lizards belong to the monitor family (Varanidae). Like snakes, monitors have deeply forked tongues that pick up airborne particles and transfer them to the Jacobson's organ in the roof of the mouth.

**FIGURE 41-15**

(a) The largest of all monitors is the Komodo dragon, *Varanus komodoensis,* of Indonesia. The Komodo dragon can grow to 3 m long (10 ft). (b) A colorful gecko of the genus *Phelsuma* has specialized structures on the pads of its fingers and toes that allow it to cling to almost any surface.

(a)

(b)

(a)

(b)

## Snakes

There are about 2,500 species of snakes, and like lizards, they are distributed worldwide. Figure 41-16 shows some examples of snakes. The most obvious characteristic of snakes is the lack of legs, which affects all other aspects of their biology. What was the selective pressure that caused snakes to evolve leglessness? One possibility is that the ancestors of snakes were terrestrial but lived in thick vegetation, where legs were a hindrance to rapid movement.

The graceful movements of snakes are made possible by their unique anatomy. A snake has a backbone of 100 to 400 vertebrae, and a pair of ribs is attached to each vertebra. These bones provide the framework for thousands of muscles. The muscles manipulate not only the skeleton but also the snake's skin, causing the overlapping scales to extend and contract, propelling the snake.

## Capturing and Consuming Prey

A snake may just seize and swallow its prey. However, many snakes employ one of two methods for killing: constriction or injection of venom. Snakes that are **constrictors** wrap their bodies around prey. A constrictor suffocates its prey by gradually increasing the tension in its coils, squeezing a little tighter each time the prey breathes out. This technique is used both by large snakes, such as boas, pythons, and anacondas, and by smaller snakes, such as gopher snakes and king snakes.

Some snakes inject their prey with a toxic venom in one of three different ways. The snakes with fangs in the back of the mouth, such as the boomslang and twig snakes of Africa, bite the prey and use grooved teeth in the back of the mouth to guide the venom into the puncture. Cobras, kraits, and coral snakes are elapids. **Elapid** snakes inject poisons through two small, fixed fangs in the front of the mouth. **Vipers** inject venom through large, mobile fangs in the front of the mouth. Rattlesnakes, copperheads, and water moccasins are examples of vipers. When a viper strikes, these hinged fangs swing forward from the roof of the mouth and inject venom more deeply than can the fangs of elapids.

**FIGURE 41-16**

(a) The Gaboon viper, *Bitis gabonica*, injects a toxic venom to kill its prey before it begins the process of swallowing. (b) The boa constrictor, *Constrictor constrictor*, suffocates its prey.

 **Quick Lab**

### Modeling Snake Swallowing

**Materials** rubber tubing, small marble

**Procedure** Find a way to get the marble into the middle of the rubber tubing.

**Analysis** How is this model similar to the feeding mechanism of a snake? If you used a marble that was larger than the opening of the tubing, what problems would you encounter? Why is the size of larger prey not a problem for snakes?

**FIGURE 41-17**

This series of photographs shows a snake, *Dasypeltis scabra,* swallowing a bird's egg. Prey is often larger than the diameter of the snake's head, so the process of swallowing can take an hour or more.

Once killed, the prey must be swallowed whole because a snake's curved, needlelike teeth are not suited for cutting or chewing. Several features of a snake's skull enable it to swallow an animal larger in diameter than its head, as shown in Figure 41-17. The upper and lower jaws are loosely hinged, move independently, and can open to an angle of 130 degrees. In addition, a snake's lower jaw, palate, and parts of its skull are joined by a flexible, elastic ligament that allows the snake's head to stretch around its prey.

**FIGURE 41-18**

Unlike most reptiles, the endangered tuataras, such as the one shown, are most active at low temperatures.

# ORDER RHYNCHOCEPHALIA

The order Rhynchocephalia (RING-koe-suh-FAY-lee-uh) is an ancient one that contains only the tuataras of the genus *Sphenodon.* Tuataras inhabit only a few small islands of New Zealand. The Maoris of New Zealand named the tuataras for the conspicuous spiny crest that runs down the animal's back, seen in Figure 41-18. The word *tuatara* means "spiny crest". Tuataras grow to about 60 cm (24 in.) in length. They usually hide in a burrow during the day and feed on insects, worms, and other small animals at night.

Since arriving in New Zealand about 1,000 years ago, humans have radically changed the landscape and introduced predators such as rats and cats, which feed on tuataras and their eggs. As a result, tuataras have disappeared from most of their original range.

## SECTION 3 REVIEW

1. Compare the characteristics of aquatic turtles to the characteristics of land tortoises.

2. Identify characteristics of crocodilians that allow them to feed efficiently in water.

3. Identify three strategies employed by lizards to avoid predators.

4. Describe two methods snakes use for killing prey.

5. Explain why tuataras are rarely seen in the wild.

**CRITICAL THINKING**

6. **Making Comparisons** Compare the costs versus the benefits of autotomy for lizards.

7. **Inferring Relationships** Why do you think turtles migrate long distances to lay eggs on the same shore on which they hatched?

8. **Applying Information** Why do you think snakes have many more vertebrae than any other group of reptiles does?

# CHAPTER HIGHLIGHTS

## SECTION 1  Origin and Evolution of Reptiles

- An abundance of food, a dry climate, and a mass extinction of other species led to the dominance of reptiles. The Mesozoic era is often called the age of reptiles.

- Several factors contributed to the success of dinosaurs. Legs positioned under their bodies made dinosaurs faster and more agile than other reptiles. Dinosaurs were well adapted to dry conditions. At the end of the Triassic period, a mass extinction reduced competition and allowed dinosaurs to flourish.

- Dinosaurs became extinct about 65 million years ago. Evidence suggests that environmental conditions over many years endangered dinosaur survival, and either a single asteroid impact or multiple asteroid impacts might have triggered a mass extinction event.

- There are four modern orders of reptiles: Chelonia (turtles and tortoises), Crocodilia (alligators and crocodiles), Squamata (lizards and snakes), and Rhynchocephalia (tuataras).

- Three characteristics that contribute to the success of reptiles on land are the amniotic egg, watertight skin, and efficient respiration and excretion.

### Vocabulary

dinosaur (p. 819)
asteroid impact
  hypothesis (p. 821)

amniotic egg (p. 823)
amnion (p. 823)
yolk sac (p. 823)

allantois (p. 823)
chorion (p. 823)
albumen (p. 823)

keratin (p. 824)

## SECTION 2  Characteristics of Reptiles

- Most reptiles have a three-chambered heart, but crocodiles have a four-chambered heart. Reptiles can divert blood from the lungs to conserve energy and warm their bodies.

- Reptiles inflate their lungs by expanding the ribs, which lowers air pressure in the chest cavity and draws in air. When the ribs relax, air is forced out.

- A reptile's brain is about the same size as the brain of an amphibian but has a much larger cerebrum. A reptile's senses include sight, hearing, smell, and heat detection.

- All living reptiles are ectotherms. Ectotherms warm their bodies mainly by absorbing heat from their surroundings.

- Many reptiles lay shelled eggs, which is called oviparity. Some species retain shelled eggs inside the female's body, which is ovoviviparity. Other species have eggs with placentas rather than shells, which develop within the female's body. This is viviparity.

- Of the reptiles, crocodiles and alligators provide the greatest amount of parental care.

### Vocabulary

septum (p. 825)
alveolus (p. 826)
Jacobson's organ (p. 827)

thermoregulation (p. 828)
ectotherm (p. 828)
endotherm (p. 828)

oviparity (p. 829)
ovoviviparity (p. 829)
viviparity (p. 829)

placenta (p. 829)

## SECTION 3  Modern Reptiles

- The order Chelonia, which includes turtles and tortoises, have a shell composed of bony plates. The vertebrae and ribs are fused to the interior surface of the shell.

- Members of the order Crocodilia are large aquatic or semiaquatic carnivores. They include crocodiles, alligators, caimans, and gavials. A valve in the oral cavity of crocodilians covers the esophagus and windpipe while the mouth is submerged. This allows crocodilians to capture and swallow prey underwater.

- The order Squamata consists of lizards and snakes. Most lizards rely on speed, agility, and camouflage to elude predators. Some can detach their tail to distract predators.

- Some snakes kill their prey by constriction. Others kill their prey by injecting venom.

- The order Rhynchocephalia contains only the tuataras. Tuataras hide in burrows during the day and feed at night. The arrival of humans and new predators in New Zealand has reduced the number of tuataras.

### Vocabulary

carapace (p. 830)
plastron (p. 830)

autotomy (p. 832)
constrictor (p. 833)

elapid (p. 833)
viper (p. 833)

# CHAPTER REVIEW

## USING VOCABULARY

1. Choose the term that does not belong in the following group, and explain why it does not belong: *elapids, vipers, constrictors,* and *dinosaurs.*

2. Explain the relationship between amnion and chorion.

3. Use each of the following terms in a separate sentence: *oviparity, ovoviviparity,* and *viviparity.*

4. **Word Roots and Origins** The word *ectotherm* comes from the Greek word *ecto,* meaning "outside" and *therm,* meaning "heat". The word *endotherm* comes from the Greek word *endo,* meaning "within" and *therm,* meaning "heat". Explain why each term is a good name for the biological process that the term describes.

## UNDERSTANDING KEY CONCEPTS

5. **Summarize** the events that led to the rise of reptiles during the Permian period.

6. **Identify** three factors that contributed to the success of dinosaurs during the Triassic period.

7. **Explain** why scientists advocate the asteroid impact hypothesis for dinosaur extinction.

8. **Name** one example of each of the four modern orders of reptiles.

9. **Explain** how the evolution of the amniotic egg is an adaptation to life on land.

10. **Explain** how the respiratory and excretory systems in reptiles show adaptations for life on land.

11. **Contrast** a turtle's heart and a crocodile's heart.

12. **Describe** how the structure of a turtle's heart allows for flexibility in blood circulation.

13. **Identify** the advantage of alveoli in respiration.

14. **Describe** two senses other than vision and hearing that reptiles use to find prey.

15. **Identify** the major benefit of ectothermy.

16. **Compare** the reproductive strategies of oviparity, ovoviviparity, and viviparity.

17. **Describe** the features that make turtles unique among reptiles.

18. **Explain** how crocodilians swallow prey underwater.

19. **Explain** the purpose of a lizard's ability to lose its tail and grow a new one.

20. **List** three ways in which snakes can inject venom into their prey.

21. **Identify** the reason populations of tuataras have decreased in the last 1,000 years.

22. **CONCEPT MAPPING** Use the following terms to create a concept map that relates various adaptations of reptiles to life on land: *reptiles, water loss, amniotic eggs, keratin, scales, watertight,* and *skin.*

## CRITICAL THINKING

23. **Analyzing Information** If birds did not evolve from the pterosaurs, what can you conclude about the evolution of the ability to fly?

24. **Analyzing Concepts** Why is it advantageous for a snake to kill its prey, either through constriction or venom, before trying to eat the prey?

25. **Recognizing Relationships** The skin of a basking lizard is usually dark. As the lizard warms, the skin lightens. Suggest a functional explanation for this change. (Hint: Consider how this change might affect the lizard's absorption of heat.)

26. **Analyzing Data** Fossil evidence collected in Alaska suggests that some dinosaurs were year-round residents of areas subject to freezing temperatures and long periods of darkness. Does this evidence of arctic dinosaurs support or contradict the hypothesis that the extinction of dinosaurs was due to the intense cold produced by a cloud of debris in the atmosphere? Explain your answer.

27. **Relating Concepts** Some viviparous snakes and lizards live in cold climates. Why might viviparity be advantageous in such environments?

28. **Interpreting Graphics** The following diagram shows five parts of the amniotic egg, indicated by the letters A, B, C, D, and E. Name and identify the function of each part.

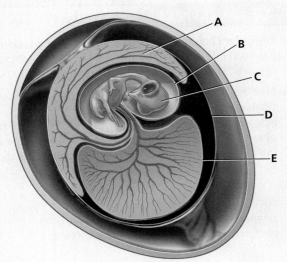

**DIRECTIONS:** Choose the letter of the answer choice that best answers the question.

1. Which is an adaptation that made reptiles the dominant species in the Mesozoic era?
   A. They were endotherms.
   B. They could live in Antarctica.
   C. They were all large predators.
   D. They were well adapted to dry areas.

2. What are the two basic parts of a turtle's shell?
   F. septum and amnion
   G. chorion and allantois
   H. keratin and columella
   J. carapace and plastron

3. What is the purpose of a lizard's ability to lose its tail and grow a new one?
   A. to capture prey
   B. to hide from predators
   C. to escape from predators
   D. to reduce its need for food

4. Long legless bodies may have arisen as an adaptation that helped snakes do what?
   F. catch prey
   G. swallow large animals
   H. absorb oxygen through their skin
   J. burrow and move through thick vegetation

**INTERPRETING GRAPHICS:** The graph below shows changes in air temperature and changes in the body temperature of a lizard. Use the graph below to answer the question that follows.

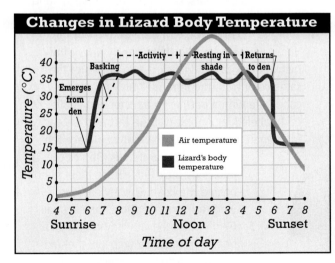

5. In order for the lizard to raise its internal temperature it must do which of the following?
   A. rest in the shade
   B. bask in sunshine
   C. increase its internal temperature through activity
   D. decrease its internal temperature through activity

**DIRECTIONS:** Complete the following analogy.

6. Ectotherm : reptiles :: endotherm :
   F. fishes
   G. insects
   H. mammals
   J. amphibians

**INTERPRETING GRAPHICS:** The illustration below shows a cross section of a turtle's heart. Use the illustration to answer the question that follows.

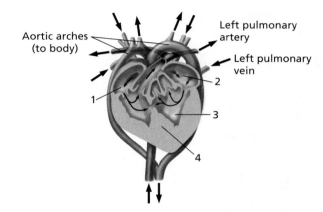

7. Which feature of a turtle's heart structure is different from that of a crocodile?
   A. 1
   B. 2
   C. 3
   D. 4

**SHORT RESPONSE**

A reptile can redirect blood flow through the heart to send some deoxygenated blood back to the body instead of to the lungs.

What is the advantage to the lizard of redirecting blood flow in this manner?

**EXTENDED RESPONSE**

There are three patterns of reproduction among reptiles. They differ in how long eggs remain in the female and how the developing young are provided with nutrition.

*Part A* With these differences in mind, compare oviparity, ovoviviparity, and viviparity.

*Part B* In which pattern of reproduction is a placenta present? Explain the function of the placenta.

**Test TIP** When analyzing a graph, pay attention to its title. It should tell you what the graph is about and provide a context for the data.

# Observing Color Adaptation in Anoles

## OBJECTIVES

- Observe live anoles.
- Test whether background color stimulates color change in anoles.

## PROCESS SKILLS

- observing
- hypothesizing
- experimenting
- organizing data
- analyzing data

## MATERIALS

- glass-marking pencil
- 2 large clear jars with wide mouths and lids with air holes
- 2 live anoles
- 6 shades each of brown and green construction paper, ranging from light to dark (2 swatches of each shade)

## Background

1. Anoles include 250–300 species of lizards in the genus *Anolis.*
2. Anoles can change color, ranging from brown to green, and are sometimes mottled.

3. Anoles live in shrubs, grasses, and trees. Describe some ways in which the ability to change color might be an advantage to anoles.
4. Light level, temperature, and other factors, such as whether the anole is frightened or whether it has eaten recently, can affect color. When anoles are frightened, they usually turn a dark grey or brown and are unlikely to respond to other stimuli.
5. Anoles can change color within a few minutes.

## Procedure

1. Observe the anoles in two terraria, and discuss the purpose of this investigation with your partners. Develop a hypothesis that describes a relationship between anole skin color and background color. Write your hypothesis in your lab report.
2. Obtain swatches of construction paper in at least six different shades of green and brown. You will need two swatches of paper in each color.
3. Obtain two clear jars. Label one jar "Anole 1," and label the other jar "Anole 2."
4. ⚠ **CAUTION  You will be working with live animals. Handle them gently and follow instructions carefully.** Select two anoles of the same color from the terraria. Plan your actions and cooperate with a partner to transfer one anole into each labeled jar. Anoles will run fast and are easily frightened. Carefully pick them up and place the animals in separate jars. Do not pick up anoles by their tails. Grasp them gently behind the head. Quickly and carefully place a lid with air holes on each jar.
5. Gently place the jar with Anole 1 on a swatch of construction paper that most closely matches the anole's color. Try not to jostle the anole in the jar, and move the jar as little and as gently as possible. Repeat this procedure for Anole 2. Both anoles should closely match the color of the swatch.

6. When you have obtained and matched two anoles to closely matching colors, label the back of the pieces of paper "Initial Color of Anole 1" and "Initial Color of Anole 2," respectively. Replace the swatches underneath the jars after you have labeled them. The anoles should stay in their respective jars until the end of this investigation.

7. Using the given setup and the remaining swatches of colored construction paper, devise a control experiment to test whether background color stimulates color change in the anole.

8. In your lab report, list the independent variable and the dependent variables that you intend to use in your experiment. Describe how you will vary the independent variable and how you will measure changes in your dependent variable.

9. In your lab report, describe the control you will use in your experiment.

10. Create a data table similar to the one below to record your experimental observations for your lab report. For example, the table below is designed to record any change in anole skin color on four different background colors and the time it took for each change to take place. Design your data table to fit your own experiment. Remember to allow plenty of space to write your observations.

11. Have your experiment approved by your teacher before conducting it. As you conduct your experiment, be sure to record all of your data and observations in your lab report.

12. Attach your color swatches to your lab report, or include a color-coded key so that others reading your report will be able to understand how you measured initial color and color changes in your anoles. Be sure the color that most closely represents the initial color of both anoles is clearly indicated in your lab report.

13. Clean up your materials and wash your hands before leaving the lab.

## Analysis and Conclusions

1. What effect, if any, did changes in the independent variable have on the dependent variable in your experiment?

2. Do your data support your hypothesis? Explain.

3. Can you think of any sources of error in your experiment?

4. Was your experiment a controlled experiment? If yes, describe your control and why you think a control is necessary for your experiment.

5. Were there any uncontrolled variables in your experiment, such as loud noises, bright light, or sudden movements, that could have affected your experiment? Describe how you might be able to improve your methods.

## Further Inquiry

Design an experiment that tests the effects of temperature on anole skin color.

### DATA TABLE   OBSERVING ANOLES

|  | Color 1 | | Color 2 | | Color 3 | | Color 4 | |
|---|---|---|---|---|---|---|---|---|
|  | Change | Time | Change | Time | Change | Time | Change | Time |
| Anole 1 | | | | | | | | |
| Anole 2 | | | | | | | | |

# BIRDS

Young birds, such as this owl, depend on their parents for food and protection.

**SCIENTIFIC AMERICAN**

For project ideas from *Scientific American,* visit go.hrw.com and type in the keyword **HM6SAK.**

# ORIGIN AND EVOLUTION OF BIRDS

*Birds belong to the class Aves, which, with nearly 10,000 species, is the largest class of terrestrial vertebrates. Birds are also the most recently evolved group of vertebrates, having appeared only about 150 million years ago. Among living vertebrates, only birds and bats can fly. The bodies of most birds are well adapted to flight.*

## SECTION 1

### OBJECTIVES

- **Identify** and describe seven major characteristics of birds.
- **List** three similarities between birds and dinosaurs.
- **Describe** the characteristics of *Archaeopteryx*.
- **Summarize** the two main hypotheses for the evolution of flight.

### VOCABULARY

furcula

## CHARACTERISTICS

Although there are many kinds of birds, birds are so distinctive that it is difficult to mistake one for any other kind of vertebrate. All birds—even those that cannot fly—share the seven important characteristics described below.

- **Feathers**—Feathers are unique to birds, and all birds have them. Like hair, feathers are composed mainly of the versatile protein keratin. Feathers are essential for flight, and they insulate a bird's body against heat loss.
- **Wings**—A bird's forelimbs are modified into a pair of wings. Feathers cover most of the surface area of the wing.
- **Lightweight, rigid skeleton**—The skeleton of a bird reflects the requirements of flight. Many of the bones are thin-walled and hollow, making them lighter than the bones of nonflying animals. Air sacs from the respiratory system penetrate some of the bones. Because many bones are fused, the skeleton is rigid and can resist the forces produced by the strong flight muscles.
- **Endothermic metabolism**—A bird's rapid metabolism supplies the energy needed for flight. Birds maintain a high body temperature of 40–41°C (104–106°F). The body temperature of humans, by contrast, is about 37°C, or 98.6°F.
- **Unique respiratory system**—A rapid metabolism requires an abundant supply of oxygen, and birds have the most efficient respiratory system of any terrestrial vertebrates. The lungs are connected to several sets of air sacs, an arrangement that ensures that oxygen-rich air is always in the lungs.
- **Beak**—No modern bird has teeth, but the jaws are covered by a tough, horny sheath called a *beak*.
- **Oviparity**—All birds lay amniotic eggs encased in a hard, calcium-containing shell. In most species, the eggs are incubated in a nest by one or both parents.

FIGURE 42-1

This phylogenetic diagram represents a hypothesis for the relationship among birds, reptiles, mammals, and some extinct relatives of birds. For updates on phylogenetic information, visit **go.hrw.com**. Enter the keyword **HM6 Phylo.**

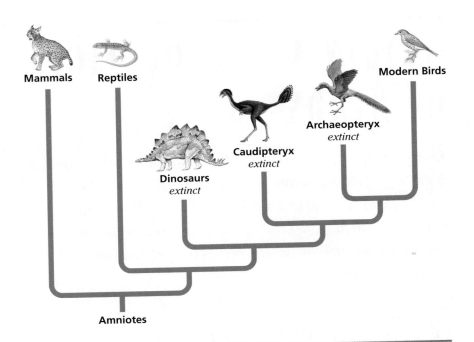

# EVOLUTION

There are many similarities between birds and some dinosaurs, such as *Caudipteryx* show in Figure 42-1. Three of these similarities include a flexible S-shaped neck, a unique ankle joint, and hollow bones. Birds are thought to have evolved from small, fast-running carnivorous dinosaurs during the Jurassic period (200–146 million years ago). Figure 42-1 shows the likely relationships between birds and other terrestrial vertebrates.

The oldest known bird fossils are classified in the genus *Archaeopteryx* and date from the late Jurassic period, about 150 million years ago. In the fossil in Figure 42-2a, the shapes of feathers are clearly visible. Feathers covered *Archaeopteryx's* forelimbs, forming wings, and covered its body and tail as well. Like modern birds, *Archaeopteryx* had hollow bones and a **furcula** (FUHR-kyoo-luh), the fused pair of collarbones commonly called a *wishbone*. The furcula plays an important role in flight by helping to stabilize the shoulder joint. Based on such similarities with modern birds, scientists think that *Archaeopteryx* could fly. However, *Archaeopteryx* also had several characteristics of its dinosaur ancestors, including teeth, claws on its forelimbs, and a long, bony tail. Figure 42-2b shows an artist's conception of what an *Archaeopteryx* might have looked like.

## Origin of Flight

The evolution of a flying animal from nonflying ancestors entails many changes in anatomy, physiology, and behavior. According to one hypothesis, the ancestors of birds were tree dwellers that ran along branches and occasionally jumped between branches and trees. Wings that allowed these animals to glide evolved. Once gliding was possible, the ability to fly by flapping the wings evolved.

**Word Roots and Origins**

*archaeopteryx*

from the Greek *archaios,* meaning "ancient," and *pteryx,* meaning "wing"

(a)

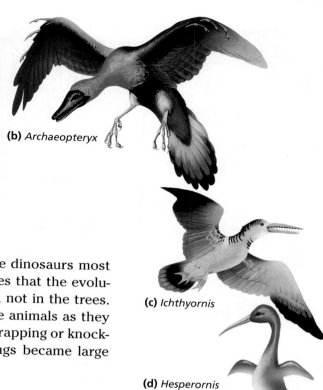

**(b)** *Archaeopteryx*

**(c)** *Ichthyornis*

**(d)** *Hesperornis*

Another hypothesis draws on the fact that the dinosaurs most closely related to birds were terrestrial and states that the evolution of birds must have occurred on the ground, not in the trees. Wings may have originally served to stabilize the animals as they leapt after prey. Or they may have been used for trapping or knocking down insect prey. Over generations, the wings became large enough to allow the animal to become airborne.

## Evolution After *Archaeopteryx*

A number of recent discoveries show that by the early Cretaceous period (146–66 million years ago), birds had begun diversifying. *Sinornis,* a 140-million-year-old specimen discovered in China in 1987, had some key features of modern birds, including a shortened, fused tail and a wrist joint that allowed the wings to be folded against the body. The diversification of birds continued throughout the Cretaceous period. Figures 42-2c and 42-2d show two birds from the late Cretaceous period.

Only two of the modern orders of birds had appeared by the end of the Cretaceous period. Birds survived the global catastrophe that is thought to have wiped out the dinosaurs, and then underwent a dramatic and rapid evolutionary radiation. By about 40 million years ago, most of the modern orders of birds had originated.

**FIGURE 42-2**

In this fossil of *Archaeopteryx* (a), one can find characteristics of both birds and dinosaurs. These artist's renderings of three extinct birds are based on fossil evidence. *Archaeopteryx* (b) is the oldest bird; it still had claws on its wings. *Ichthyornis* (c) had strongly developed wings and was about 21–26 cm (8–10 in.) in length. *Hesperornis* (d) was considered flightless, but its well-developed legs made it a strong swimmer.

## SECTION 1 REVIEW

1. List two unique features of a bird's skeleton.

2. What are two functions of feathers?

3. Identify the characteristics that birds have in common with dinosaurs.

4. Describe two characteristics shared by *Archaeopteryx* and modern birds.

5. Name two differences between *Archaeopteryx* and modern birds.

6. Summarize the two major hypotheses for the evolution of flight.

**CRITICAL THINKING**

7. **Forming Hypotheses** Modern birds lack teeth. Form a hypothesis to explain how birds might have evolved to lack teeth.

8. **Evaluating Hypotheses** After studying the fossil of *Archaeopteryx,* evaluate the two hypotheses for the evolution of flight. Identify strengths and weaknesses of each.

9. **Applying Information** Identify three adaptations that help birds satisfy their high need for oxygen.

### OBJECTIVES

- **Describe** the structure of a contour feather.
- **Identify** two modifications for flight seen in a bird's skeletal system.
- **Contrast** the function of the gizzard with that of the crop.
- **Trace** the movement of air through the respiratory system of a bird.
- **Explain** the differences between altricial and precocial young.

### VOCABULARY

feather
follicle
shaft
vane
barb
barbule
preen gland
sternum
pygostyle
crop
proventriculus
gizzard
vas deferens
oviduct
brood patch
precocial
altricial
ornithologist

# CHARACTERISTICS OF BIRDS

*A number of unique anatomical, physiological, and behavioral adaptations enable birds to meet the aerodynamic requirements of flight. Natural selection has favored a lightweight body and powerful wing muscles that give birds their strength.*

## FEATHERS

**Feathers** are modified scales that serve two primary functions: providing lift for flight and conserving body heat. Soft, fluffy *down feathers* cover the body of very young birds and provide an insulating undercoat in adults. *Contour feathers* give adult birds their streamlined shape and provide coloration and additional insulation. *Flight feathers* are specialized contour feathers on the wings and tail. Birds also have dust-filtering bristles near their nostrils.

The structure of a feather combines maximum strength with minimum weight. Feathers develop from tiny pits in the skin called **follicles.** A **shaft** emerges from the follicle, and two **vanes,** pictured in Figure 42-3a, develop on opposite sides of the shaft. At maturity, each vane has many branches, called **barbs.** The barbs, in turn, have many projections, called **barbules,** equipped with microscopic hooks, as shown in Figure 42-3b. The hooks interlock and give the feather its sturdy but flexible shape. Feathers are made of keratin, an insoluble protein that is highly resistant to decomposition. Keratin is also the protein that makes up fingernails, claws, hair, and scales in animals.

Feathers need care. In a process called *preening,* birds use their beaks to rub their feathers with oil secreted by a **preen gland,** located at the base of the tail. Birds periodically *molt,* or shed and regrow their feathers. Birds living in temperate climates usually replace their flight feathers during the late summer.

**FIGURE 42-3**

Bird feathers, such as this contour feather (a), usually have a shaft, with two vanes growing out either side of the shaft. The vanes (b) consist of barbs and barbules that interlock by means of hooks.

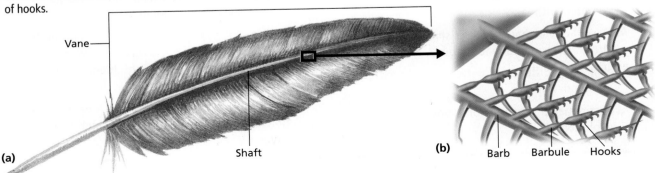

(a) Vane — Shaft

(b) Barb — Barbule — Hooks

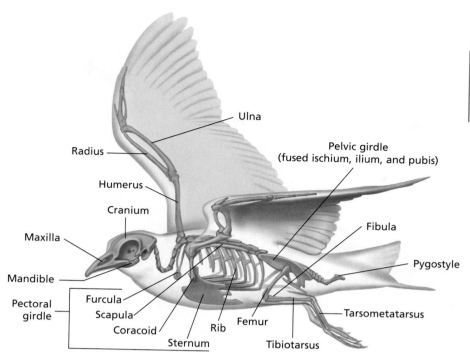

Ulna

Radius

Pelvic girdle
(fused ischium, ilium, and pubis)

Humerus

Cranium

Maxilla

Fibula

Mandible

Pygostyle

Pectoral girdle

Furcula

Scapula

Tarsometatarsus

Coracoid

Rib

Femur

Sternum

Tibiotarsus

**FIGURE 42-4**

The avian skeleton is well adapted for flight. The bones are air filled, making them light but strong. The skeleton is arranged in such a way that it supports the large muscles necessary for flight.

# SKELETON AND MUSCLES

The avian skeleton combines lightness with strength. The bones are thin and hollow. Many bones are fused, so the skeleton is more rigid than the skeleton of a reptile or mammal. The rigid skeleton provides stability during flight. Note in Figure 42-4 that the bones of the trunk and hip vertebrae and the pectoral and pelvic girdles are highly fused. Along with the furcula, the large, keel-shaped **sternum,** or breastbone, is an attachment point for flight muscles. The humerus, ulna, and radius, along with the pectoral girdle and the sternum, support the wing. The **pygostyle** (PIEG-uh-stiel), the fused terminal vertebrae of the spine, supports the tail feathers. The tail provides additional lift and aids in steering and braking.

Flight involves a series of complex wing movements, each one using a different set of muscles. On the downstroke, the wings cut forward and downward through the air. During upstroke, they move upward and backward. These movements are made possible by large, powerful flight muscles in the breast and wings. In some birds, flight muscles account for up to 50 percent of the body weight.

## Quick Lab

### Comparing Wing Structures

**Materials** pictures of different kinds of birds, ruler

**Procedure** Examine each sheet of birds and their wings. Compare the structure and shape of the wings. Measure the wingspan relative to the bird's body length. Record your observations.

**Analysis** Predict the type of habitat in which each bird lives. How does the shape of the wing relate to the bird's niche? Explain why the type of wings each bird has might make the bird unsuccessful if it were introduced into a much different environment.

# METABOLISM

Birds are endothermic; that is, they generate heat to warm the body internally. Rapid breathing and digestion of large quantities of food support the high metabolic rate necessary to generate this heat. Birds, unlike reptiles, cannot go for long periods without eating. To help conserve body heat, birds may fluff out their feathers. Aquatic birds have a thin layer of fat that provides additional insulation.

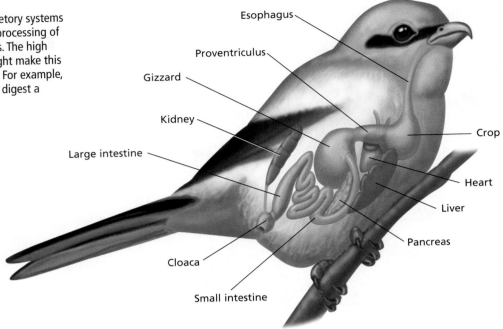

Esophagus

Proventriculus

Gizzard

Kidney

Large intestine

Cloaca

Small intestine

Crop

Heart

Liver

Pancreas

## Digestive and Excretory Systems

The high amount of energy required to fly and regulate body heat is obtained by a quick and efficient digestive system, as illustrated in Figure 42-5. Because birds do not have teeth, they are not able to chew their food. Instead, food passes from the mouth cavity straight to the esophagus. An enlargement of the esophagus called the **crop** stores and moistens food. Food then passes to the two-part stomach. In the first chamber, the **proventriculus** (PROH-ven-TRIK-yoo-luhs), acid and digestive enzymes begin breaking down the food. Food then passes to the **gizzard,** the muscular portion of the stomach, which kneads and crushes the food. The gizzard often contains small stones that the bird has swallowed. These aid in the grinding process. Thus, the gizzard performs a function similar to that of teeth and jaws. Seed-eating birds usually have a larger crop and gizzard—relative to body size—than meat-eating birds do.

From the stomach, food passes into the small intestine. There, bile from the liver and enzymes from the pancreas and intestine further break down the food. The nutrients are then absorbed into the bird's bloodstream. Passage of food through the digestive system of a bird is usually very rapid. For instance, a thrush can eat blackberries, digest them, and excrete the seeds 45 minutes later.

The avian excretory system is efficient and lightweight. Unlike other vertebrates, most birds do not store liquid waste in a urinary bladder. The two kidneys filter a nitrogenous waste called *uric acid* from the blood. Concentrated uric acid travels through ducts called *ureters* to the cloaca, where it mixes with feces and is then excreted. This system is adaptive for flight because birds do not need to carry much water in their bodies.

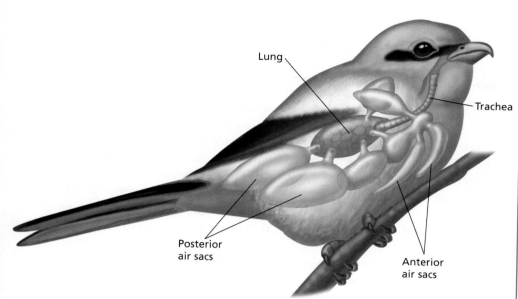

Lung

Trachea

Posterior
air sacs

Anterior
air sacs

## Respiratory System

The high metabolic rate of birds requires large amounts of oxygen. Yet some birds migrate thousands of miles at altitudes as high as 7,000 m (23,000 ft), where air pressure is very low. So, birds have an elaborate and highly efficient respiratory system. Air enters the bird's body through paired nostrils located near the base of the beak. The air passes down the trachea and enters the two primary bronchi. From the bronchi, some of the air moves to the lungs. However, about 75 percent of the air bypasses the lungs and flows directly to posterior air sacs, shown in Figure 42-6. In most birds, nine sacs extend from the lungs and occupy a large portion of the bird's chest and abdominal cavity. These sacs also extend into some of the long bones. Thus, the air sacs not only function in respiration but also greatly reduce the bird's density.

Gas exchange does not occur in the air sacs. Their function is to store and redirect air. When the bird exhales, the oxygen-poor air from its lungs is forced into the anterior air sacs, and the oxygen-rich air in the posterior air sacs is forced into the lungs. This way, the bird has oxygenated air in its lungs during both inhalation and exhalation.

## Circulatory System

The avian circulatory system has characteristics that are similar to those of either reptiles or mammals or both. Like crocodiles and mammals, birds have a four-chambered heart with two separate ventricles. Deoxygenated blood is always kept separate from oxygenated blood. In comparison with most other vertebrates, most birds have a rapid heartbeat. A hummingbird's heart beats about 600 times a minute. An active chickadee's heart beats 1,000 times a minute. In contrast, the heart of the larger, less active ostrich averages 70 beats per minute, or about the same rate as a human heart. Avian red blood cells have nuclei.

## Nervous System and Sense Organs

Relative to their body size, birds have large brains. The most highly developed areas of the bird's brain are those that control flight-related functions, such as the cerebellum, which coordinates movement. The cerebrum is also large. It controls complex behavior patterns, such as navigation, mating, nest building, and caring for the young. The large optic lobes receive and interpret visual stimuli.

Keen vision is necessary for taking off, landing, spotting landmarks, hunting, and feeding. Most birds have strong, color vision that aids them in finding food. In most species, the eyes are large and are located near the sides of the head, giving the bird a wide field of vision. Birds that have eyes located near the front of the head have better binocular vision, meaning they can perceive depth in the area where the visual fields of the two eyes overlap.

Hearing is important to songbirds and to nocturnal species, such as owls, which rely on sounds to help them locate their prey. Though birds lack external ears, owls have feathers around their ear openings that direct sound into the ear. The sense of smell is also strong in many birds.

## REPRODUCTION

In the male bird, sperm is produced in two testes that lie anterior to the kidneys. Sperm passes through small tubes called **vasa deferentia** (singular, *vas deferens*) into the male's cloaca. During mating, the male presses his cloaca to the female's cloaca and releases sperm. Most females have a single ovary located on the left side of the body. The ovary releases eggs into a long funnel-shaped **oviduct,** where the eggs are fertilized by sperm. Fertilized eggs move down the oviduct, where they are encased in a protective covering and a shell. The egg passes out of the oviduct and into the cloaca. From the cloaca, it is expelled from the bird.

### Nest Building and Parental Care

Birds usually lay their eggs in a nest. Nests hold the eggs, conceal young birds from predators, provide shelter from the elements, and sometimes serve to attract a mate. Most birds build nests in sheltered, well-hidden spots—ranging from holes in the ground to treetops. Woodpeckers, for example, nest in a hole they have drilled in a tree. Orioles suspend their nests from branches, well beyond the reach of predators. And barn swallows build a saucer of mud on the beam of a building. Birds construct their nests from almost any available material. Twigs, bark, grasses, feathers, and mud are common materials used.

One or both parents warm, or *incubate,* the eggs by sitting on them and covering them with a thickened, featherless patch of skin on the abdomen called a **brood patch.** Once the eggs hatch, the young usually receive extensive parental care.

## Eco Connection

### DDT and Bird Eggs

DDT is a pesticide that was widely used on crops until the 1970s. DDT was banned in several countries because of the harm it was causing to birds. DDT causes some birds to produce thin egg shells, decreasing survival rates of the birds' offspring. The result was a significant drop in the populations of several species of raptors and pelicans. The thinning of the eggs was so significant that even the weight of an incubating parent could crush the eggs. With the banning of DDT in the United States, populations of the affected birds have increased.

Birds have two general patterns of rearing young. Some birds lay many eggs and incubate them for long periods. These birds hatch **precocial** (pree-KOH-shuhl) young, which can walk, swim, and feed themselves as soon as they hatch. Ducks, quail, chickens, and other ground-nesting species produce precocial offspring. Other birds lay only a few eggs that hatch quickly and produce **altricial** (al-TRISH-uhl) young, which are blind, naked, and helpless, as shown in Figure 42-7. These young depend on both parents for several weeks. The young of woodpeckers, hawks, pigeons, parrots, warblers, and many aquatic birds are altricial.

# MIGRATION

Each year, thousands of bird species exploit the spring and summer food resources of temperate regions. Then, when temperatures drop and the food supply dwindles, they travel to warmer climates. The seasonal movement of animals from one habitat to another habitat is called *migration*. Many of the birds that nest in the United States and Canada during the spring and summer fly south in the fall to spend the winter in Mexico, Central America, the Caribbean, or South America.

How do birds manage to navigate thousands of kilometers across varied terrains and return to the same places each year? **Ornithologists**—biologists who study birds—have learned that birds rely on a variety of cues to help them navigate. Some species monitor the position of the stars or the sun. Others rely on topographical landmarks, such as mountains. The Earth's magnetic field, changes in air pressure due to altitude, and low-frequency sounds may also provide information to migrating birds.

Many species migrate thousands of kilometers and must rely on their fat reserves in order to complete the journey. To prepare for their migration, some birds, such as blackpoll warblers, eat so much food before their journey that their weight nearly doubles.

**FIGURE 42-7**
This yellow warbler cares for its young by feeding and protecting them.

## SECTION 2 REVIEW

1. Distinguish between vanes, barbs, and barbules.

2. What is the function of the keel-shaped sternum?

3. In what way does the gizzard compensate for the lack of teeth in birds?

4. What are the functions of the anterior and posterior air sacs?

5. Contrast altricial and precocial young.

6. Identify the cues birds use to help them navigate during a migration.

**CRITICAL THINKING**

7. **Analyzing Information** Why do you think the brood patch is featherless?

8. **Applying Information** Ground-nesting birds often produce precocial young. How might this improve the odds of survival for the young?

9. **Forming Reasoned Opinions** Some biologists have proposed that birds and reptiles should be grouped in the same class of vertebrates. Do you agree? Support your answer.

# MIGRATING BIRDS IN DANGER:
## Conservation Issues and Strategies

Since Europeans first settled in the Americas, more than half of the Western hemisphere's wetlands have been destroyed. Today, in spite of regulations, wetland destruction continues.

### Crucial Roadside Park

More than 40 North American shorebird species—such as sandpipers, plovers, and curlews—breed in the Arctic and migrate to wintering sites in Central and South America. To complete these long-distance flights, shorebirds must accumulate large fuel reserves. The birds prepare for their journeys at a few food-rich staging areas, which are usually wetlands. In some cases, between 50 and 80 percent of the entire population of a species may visit a single site. The loss of such a staging area could devastate a population of shorebirds.

Studies show that the numbers of shorebirds are declining worldwide. In order to preserve and protect these valuable species, researchers must first determine shorebird populations and map their migratory routes.

### Technology to the Rescue

Today, the work of preserving shorebirds has been greatly advanced through the use of computer technology. One group that uses computers in this work is the International Shorebird Survey (ISS). The ISS was established in 1974 and consists of both volunteers and professional researchers. The volunteers record information on populations, habitat characteristics, weather conditions, and human activity. Researchers use computer programs to identify relationships among these variables. Complex methods of analysis have revealed much about the migratory habits of shorebirds—their velocity, altitude, flight path, and gathering sites, for example. Computer analyses have also helped researchers identify significant trends, such as a 70 to 80 percent drop in the population of sanderlings.

### Sanctuary Without Borders

Another organization that works to protect shorebirds is the Western Hemisphere Shorebird Reserve Network (WHSRN). The WHSRN has identified more than 90 sites where significant numbers of shorebirds breed, feed, and rest. The organization has proposed that these sites be recognized internationally as a single, vast wildlife reserve whose boundaries are, in effect, defined by the migrating birds.

Because most of the staging sites for shorebirds are wetlands, humans must develop a strategy for the conservation of these sites. The hemispheric wildlife reserve is one example of such a strategy.

*Delaware Bay, located between Delaware and New Jersey, is a staging site for shorebirds that migrate between South America and the Arctic. As much as 80 percent of the population of red knots (shown here) feeds and rests at this site.*

## REVIEW

1. What are some threats to shorebirds posed by humans?
2. How is technology aiding the conservation of shorebirds?
3. **Critical Thinking** How do the migration behaviors of shorebirds make them especially vulnerable to habitat loss?

# CLASSIFICATION

*Birds are the most widespread terrestrial vertebrates. Their ability to navigate over long distances and their many adaptations for flight enable them to migrate to and inhabit virtually any environment. Their anatomical diversity reflects the diversity of places they inhabit.*

## DIVERSITY

By looking closely at a bird's beak and feet, you can infer many things about where it lives and how it feeds. Hawks and eagles have powerful beaks and clawed talons that help them capture and tear apart their prey. Swifts have a tiny beak that opens wide like a catcher's mitt and snares insects in midair. Because swifts spend most of their lives in flight, their feet are small and adapted for infrequent perching. The feet of flightless birds, on the other hand, are modified for walking and running. Some examples of the variety of bird beaks and feet are shown in Figure 42-8.

### OBJECTIVES

- **Describe** the relationship between beak shape and diet in birds.
- **List** 10 major orders of living birds, and name an example of each order.
- **Describe** the function of the syrinx.

### VOCABULARY

syrinx
crop milk

**internet** connect

www.scilinks.org
**Topic:** Classification of Birds
**Keyword:** HM60297

SCILINKS. Maintained by the National Science Teachers Association

(a)

(b)

(c)

(d)

**FIGURE 42-8**

This cardinal (a), *Cardinalis cardinalis,* has a short, strong beak for cracking seeds and feet that enable it to perch on small tree branches. This kestrel (b), *Falco sparverius,* has a beak that enables it to tear flesh and talons that enable it to grip and kill prey. This calliope hummingbird (c), *Stellula calliope,* has a long, thin beak that enables it to extract nectar from flowers. This northern shoveler (d), *Anas clypeata,* has a flat beak that enables it to shovel mud while searching for food.

**FIGURE 42-9**

This mute swan, *Cygnus olor,* is able to take off from water and fly at very high speeds despite its great weight. Weighing up to 23 kg (50 lb), mute swans are the heaviest flying birds. Swans are monogamous, meaning they mate for life. While the female incubates the eggs, the male helps guard the nest.

**FIGURE 42-10**

The parrot pictured below is a lesser sulfur-crested cockatoo, *Cacatua sulphurea.* Parrots range in length from 8 cm (3 in.) to over 91 cm (3 ft). The earliest fossils of parrots indicate that they have existed as a group for at least 20 million years. Like most parrots, these cockatoos nest in holes in trees, and they usually lay only two eggs per year. Because of human activities, many species have become extinct or endangered.

Most taxonomists divide about 10,000 species of living birds into 23 orders. Taxonomists have traditionally used morphological evidence from beaks, feet, plumage, bone structure, and musculature to classify birds. Technological advances in the analysis of blood proteins, chromosomes, and DNA have also been used more recently. Despite the introduction of these new methods, the relationships among the 23 orders of birds are still not well resolved. Ten of the most familiar orders of living birds are described below.

## Order Anseriformes

Swans, geese, and ducks—commonly called *waterfowl*—belong to this order of 160 species. Found worldwide, members of this order are usually aquatic and have webbed feet for paddling and swimming. Waterfowl feed on a variety of aquatic and terrestrial foods, ranging from small invertebrates and fish to grass. The bill is typically flattened. The young are precocial, and parental care is usually provided by the female. A mute swan is shown in Figure 42-9.

## Order Strigiformes

This order includes the owls, the nocturnal counterparts to the raptors. Owls are predators that have a sharp, curved beak and sharp talons or claws. As shown in the chapter opener photo, owls also have large, forward-facing eyes that provide improved vision at night. Owls rely on their keen sense of hearing to help locate prey in the dark. There are about 180 species of owls, and they are found throughout the world.

## Order Apodiformes

Hummingbirds and swifts belong to this order. All of the roughly 430 species are small, fast-flying, nimble birds with tiny feet. Swifts pursue insects and capture them in flight. Hummingbirds eat some insects but also feed on nectar, which they lap up with a very long tongue. The long, narrow bill of a hummingbird can reach deep into a flower to locate nectar. Swifts have a worldwide distribution, but hummingbirds live only in the Western Hemisphere.

## Order Psittaciformes

This order includes the parrots and their relatives, the parakeets, macaws, cockatoos, and cockatiels. Most of the roughly 360 species in this order live in the tropics. Parrots are characterized by a strong, hooked beak that is often used for opening seeds or slicing fruits. Their upper mandible is hinged on the skull and movable. Unlike most birds, parrots have two toes that point forward and two toes that point toward the rear, an adaptation for perching and climbing. They are vocal birds, and many species gather in large, noisy flocks. Parrots have long been prized as pets because of their colorful plumage and intelligence and because some species can be taught to mimic human speech. However, habitat destruction and excessive collecting for the pet trade now threaten many parrot species with extinction. Figure 42-10 shows a cockatoo.

## Order Piciformes

This diverse group of tree-dwelling birds contains woodpeckers, honeyguides, and toucans. All members of this order nest in tree cavities. Like parrots, they have two forward-pointing toes and two that point to the rear. There are about 350 species found throughout the world except in Australia. The diversity of foods consumed by these birds is reflected in the diversity of their bills. Woodpeckers, which drill holes into trees to capture insects, have strong, sharp, chisel-like bills. Toucans feed mainly on fruit, which they pluck with a long bill, as shown in Figure 42-11.

## Order Passeriformes

This large order contains about 5,900 species—more than half the total number of bird species—and includes most of the familiar North American birds. Robins, warblers, blue jays, and wrens are just some of the birds belonging to this group.

Passerines are sometimes called *perching birds*. In most birds, three toes point forward and one points backward. Passerines, too, have this arrangement of toes, but the rear toe is enlarged and particularly flexible to provide a better grip on branches. Passerines feed on a variety of foods, including nectar, seeds, fruit, and insects.

Many passerines are called *songbirds* because the males produce long, elaborate, and melodious songs. Male birds sing to warn away other males and to attract females. The song is produced in the structure known as the **syrinx** (SIR-ingks), which is located at the base of the bird's trachea. By regulating the flow of air through the syrinx, birds can generate songs of great range and complexity.

## Order Columbiformes

This globally distributed group contains about 320 species of pigeons and doves. Figure 42-12 shows a mourning dove. These birds usually are plump-breasted and have relatively small heads; short necks, legs, and beaks; and short, slender bills. Most feed on fruit or grain.

The crop, which in most other birds is used to store food, secretes a nutritious milklike fluid called **crop milk.** Both sexes produce crop milk to feed their young. Columbiform birds usually lay a clutch of two eggs, which hatch after a two-week incubation period. The young usually leave the nest two weeks after hatching. Another member of this order is the now-extinct dodo of Mauritius, an island in the Indian Ocean.

## Order Ciconiiformes

The order Ciconiiformes is highly diverse, and has a worldwide distribution. This order includes about 1040 species of herons, storks, ibises, egrets, raptors, and penguins. Many have a long, flexible neck, long legs, and a long bill. Many are wading birds, and they feed on fish, frogs, and other small prey in shallow water. Many species of Ciconiiformes are diurnal (daytime) hunters with keen vision. Vultures, however, feed on dead animals and use their sense of smell to detect the odor of decomposing flesh.

**FIGURE 42-11**

Toucans, such as this keel-billed toucan, *Ramphastos sulfuratus,* mate once per year, usually laying two to four eggs. The male and female toucans take turns sitting on the eggs. The eggs usually hatch after about 15 days of incubation.

**FIGURE 42-12**

The adult mourning dove, *Zenaida macroura,* stands about 30 cm (12 in.) tall and nests in trees or bushes. Mourning doves breed throughout North America. They winter as far south as Panama.

**FIGURE 42-13**

The great blue heron, *Ardea herodias,* uses its spearlike beak to stab fish, frogs, and other prey. Young herons must be taught how to hunt. Scientists have learned that young herons often miss their intended prey and must also learn what is and is not food.

**Word Roots and Origins**

*syrinx*

from the Greek *syrinx,* meaning "reed" or "pipe"

Raptors have a sharp, curved beak and sharp talons and include ospreys, hawks, falcons, vultures, and eagles. About 310 species of raptors are distributed throughout the world. Some members of this order grow to be quite large. Figure 42-13 shows a great blue heron, a large species that is in North America. The marabou stork of Australia, for example, can be more than 1.5 m (59 in.) in height.

Penguins are a unique group of flightless marine birds. All 17 species live in the Southern Hemisphere. The penguin's wedge-shaped wings have been modified into flippers, and the feet are webbed. Underwater, penguins flap their flippers to propel themselves forward—they "fly" through the water. Most penguins have a thick coat of insulating feathers and a layer of fat beneath the skin, enabling them to live in polar conditions. They maintain this fat layer by consuming large quantities of fish and krill.

## Order Galliformes

Members of this group, which includes turkeys, pheasants, chickens, grouse, and quails, are commonly called *fowl.* These terrestrial birds are usually plump-bodied and may have limited flying ability. Grains form a large part of the diet of many fowl, and all species have a large, strong gizzard. Some are also an important part of the human diet. The young are precocial. There are about 220 species distributed worldwide.

## Order Struthioniformes

Some of the world's largest birds belong to this order. They include ostriches, rheas, emus, and cassowaries. Ostriches are native to Africa and can attain a height of nearly 3 m and weigh 150 kg. Ostriches cannot fly, but they are specialized as high-speed runners. Propelled by their long, strong legs, ostriches can reach speeds of 55 km per hour. Each large foot has only two toes. Reduction in the number of toes is common in running animals.

Rheas are a South American version of the ostrich. Emus are the second largest of the world's birds, originally found in Australia. Cassowaries, from New Guinea, are the most colorful of this order, with black bodies and blue heads.

## SECTION 3 REVIEW

1. Explain how a bird's beak and feet can provide information about the bird's lifestyle.

2. Identify the order to which each of the following birds belongs: dove, robin, goose, and penguin.

3. Identify similarities and differences between raptors and owls.

4. Identify the function of the syrinx.

5. Describe the source and function of crop milk.

**CRITICAL THINKING**

6. **Recognizing Relationships** Penguins have a large, keel-shaped sternum, but ostriches do not. Provide an explanation for this difference.

7. **Analyzing Information** Why can birds inhabit more diverse environments than reptiles can?

8. **Applying Information** Why might crops and gizzards be less common in carnivorous birds than in seed-eating birds?

## SECTION 1    Origin and Evolution of Birds

- Seven major characteristics of birds are feathers; wings; a lightweight, rigid flight skeleton; a respiratory system involving air sacs; endothermy; a beak instead of teeth; and oviparity.

- Three similarities between birds and dinosaurs include an S-shaped neck, a unique ankle joint, and hollow bones.

- *Archaeopteryx* had feathers covering its body, tail, and forelimbs. It had hollow bones and a fused collar bone, called a furcula.

- There are two hypotheses for the origin of flight in birds. One hypothesis is that flight evolved in tree-dwellers. The second hypothesis is that flight evolved in ground-dwellers.

### Vocabulary
furcula (p. 842)

## SECTION 2    Characteristics of Birds

- Contour feathers are made of a central shaft composed of two vanes with branches, called barbs, that are connected by interlocking hooked barbules.

- Two modifications to the bird skeletal system include an enlarged sternum and hollow bones.

- The crop stores food. The two parts of the stomach are the proventriculus and the gizzard, which crushes food.

- The lungs of a bird are connected to several air sacs that store and move air but do not participate in gas exchange.

- Birds lack a urinary bladder and excrete their nitrogenous waste as uric acid mixed with feces.

- The cerebellum, cerebrum, and optic lobes of the bird brain are large.

- All birds lay hard-shelled eggs. Precocial young are active as soon as they hatch. Altricial young are born helpless and require parental care for several weeks.

- Many birds migrate using a variety of environmental cues to guide their migration.

### Vocabulary

feather (p. 844)
follicle (p. 844)
shaft (p. 844)
vane (p. 844)
barb (p. 844)

barbule (p. 844)
preen gland (p. 844)
sternum (p. 845)
pygostyle (p. 845)
crop (p. 846)

proventriculus (p. 846)
gizzard (p. 846)
vas deferens (p. 848)
oviduct (p. 848)
brood patch (p. 848)

precocial (p. 849)
altricial (p. 849)
ornithologist (p. 849)

## SECTION 3    Classification

- The feet and beak of a bird reflect its way of life.

- There are currently 23 commonly recognized orders of living birds, but technological advances add to our knowledge of relationships among animals, and taxonomy is subject to change with new information.

- Ducks, geese, and swans belong to the order Anseriformes.

- Owls are nocturnal hunters and belong to the order Strigiformes.

- Swifts and hummingbirds belong to the order Apodiformes.

- Parrots and relatives belong to the order Psittaciformes.

- Woodpeckers and toucans belong to the order Piciformes.

- Perching birds and songbirds belong to the order Passeriformes. Passeriformes have a structure called the syrinx, which they use to produce songs.

- Pigeons and doves belong to the order Columbiformes.

- Raptors, long-legged water birds, and penguins belong to the order Ciconiiformes.

- Chickens and turkeys belong to the order Galliformes.

- Large birds such as the ostrich belong to the order Struthioniformes.

### Vocabulary
syrinx (p. 853)      crop milk (p. 853)

# CHAPTER REVIEW

## USING VOCABULARY

1. For each pair of terms, explain how the meanings of the terms differ.
   a. *furcula* and *sternum*
   b. *flight feathers* and *contour feathers*
   c. *crop* and *gizzard*
   d. *altricial* and *precocial*

2. Explain the relationship between vas deferentia, oviducts, and cloaca.

3. Use the following key terms in the same sentence: *shaft, follicle, vane, barb, barbule, preening,* and *preen gland.*

4. **Word Roots and Origins** The word *precocial* is derived from the Latin prefix *pre-*, which means "before," and the term *coquere,* which means "to mature." Using this information, explain why the term *precocial* is a good word for the type of young birds it describes.

## UNDERSTANDING KEY CONCEPTS

5. **List** the seven defining characteristics of birds.

6. **Identify** characteristics that *Archaeopteryx* shared with its dinosaur ancestors.

7. **Summarize** the evidence indicating that *Archaeopteryx* could fly.

8. **Compare** two possible explanations for the evolution of flight.

9. **Contrast** the function of down feathers with that of contour feathers.

10. **Explain** how a bird's skeleton maximizes strength for flight while minimizing weight.

11. **Describe** the functions of two of the organs in a bird's digestive system.

12. **Name** the structure that grinds food, aided by stones that a bird swallows.

13. **Describe** the role that air sacs play in increasing respiratory efficiency in birds.

14. **Summarize** the differences between newly hatched ducks and newly hatched pigeons.

15. **List** several cues that birds might use to guide their movements when migrating long distances.

16. **Explain** the relationship between beak and feet shapes and the lifestyles of raptors, seed-eating birds, and flightless birds.

17. **Identify** the order to which each of the following birds belongs: ducks, owls, hummingbirds, parrots.

18. **Name** the characteristic that is unique to song-producing members of the order Passeriformes.

19. **Explain** how some members of the order Columbiformes are similar to mammals.

20. **CONCEPT MAPPING** Use the following terms to create a concept map that describes the adaptations of birds for flight: *contour feathers, flight feathers, sternum, keel, pygostyle, hollow, urinary bladder,* and *air sacs.*

## CRITICAL THINKING

21. **Analyzing Concepts** The right and left sides of a bird's heart are completely separated. Thus, the oxygenated blood is never mixed with the deoxygenated blood. Why is this complete separation in the heart necessary?

22. **Interpreting Graphics** Look at the diagram below of a bird's skeleton. Identify the following structures: pelvic girdle, furcula, sternum, femur, humerus, ulna, and tibiotarsus.

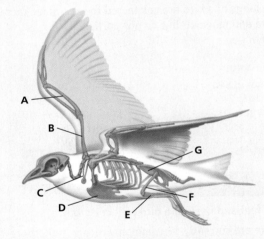

23. **Applying Information** Why is binocular vision important to some birds?

24. **Inferring Relationships** Cowbirds lay their eggs in the nests of other birds. The young cowbirds hatch slightly earlier than the other birds do, and the cowbird hatchlings are slightly larger. Why might these characteristics be advantageous for the young cowbirds?

25. **Making Comparisons** Although many species of temperate-zone birds migrate to the tropics to escape winter, some species remain behind. What benefits might these birds gain from not migrating?

26. **Justifying Conclusions** In terms of evolutionary adaptations, explain why the young of some birds, such as ducks and quail, are precocial.

# Standardized Test Preparation

**DIRECTIONS:** Choose the letter of the answer choice that best answers the question.

1. Which of the following characteristics of *Archaeopteryx* is not shared by modern birds?
   A. tail
   B. teeth
   C. furcula
   D. feathers

2. Which of the following characteristics do birds share with dinosaurs?
   F. crop
   G. lack of teeth
   H. presence of feathers
   J. structure of the ankle joint

3. What is the function of the preen gland?
   A. to produce digestive enzymes
   B. to control salt balance in the body
   C. to release scents that help attract mates
   D. to produce an oily substance used to condition the feathers

4. Which bone supports the tail feathers?
   F. ulna
   G. furcula
   H. pygostyle
   J. pelvic girdle

**INTERPRETING GRAPHICS:** The graph below shows the effect of varying clutch size on the number of surviving offspring in one bird species. Use the graph to answer the question that follows.

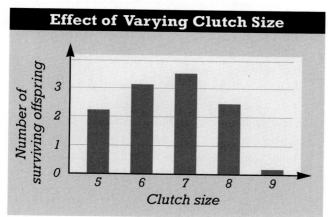

**Effect of Varying Clutch Size**

*Number of surviving offspring* vs *Clutch size*

5. Based on these data, which of the following statements is true for this species?
   A. The optimal number of eggs in a clutch is seven.
   B. The greater the clutch size is, the greater the number of surviving offspring.
   C. Nests with five eggs produced the fewest number of surviving offspring.
   D. More offspring died in nests containing eight eggs than in nests containing nine eggs.

**DIRECTIONS:** Complete the following analogy.

6. crop milk : crop :: song :
   F. syrinx
   G. trachea
   H. proventriculus
   J. anterior air sacs

**INTERPRETING GRAPHICS:** The diagram below shows the digestive system of a bird. Use the diagram to answer the question that follows.

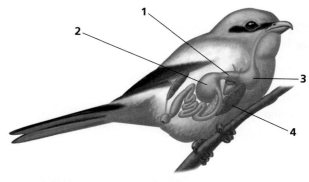

7. Which digestive structure grinds food, aided by stones swallowed by the bird?
   A. 1
   B. 2
   C. 3
   D. 4

## SHORT RESPONSE

Each type of feather on a bird serves a specific purpose.

What are the functions of contour feathers and down feathers in birds?

## EXTENDED RESPONSE

Imagine that a museum display of bird skeletons became mixed up, and all of the labels were lost.

*Part A* How could you separate the skeletons of flightless birds from those of birds that fly?

*Part B* How could you tell which birds flew rapidly and which birds could soar?

**Test TIP** When a question refers to a graph, study the data plotted on the graph to determine any trends before you try to answer the question.

# Comparing Feather Structure and Function

## OBJECTIVES

- Observe a flight feather, a contour feather, and a down feather.
- Compare the structure and function of different kinds of feathers.

## PROCESS SKILLS

- observing
- relating structure to function
- comparing and contrasting

## MATERIALS

- 1 quill feather (large flight feather from wing or tail)
- 1 contour feather
- 1 down feather
- unlined paper
- prepared slide of a contour feather
- compound light microscope
- prepared slide of a down feather

*Quill feather, a large flight feather*

## Background

1. List several distinguishing characteristics of birds.
2. How do birds differ from other vertebrates?
3. What are the functions of feathers?

## Procedure

1. In your lab report, make a table like the one on the next page. Record your observations of each kind of feather in your data table.
2. Examine a quill feather. Hold the base of the central shaft with one hand, and gently bend the tip of the feather with your other hand. Be careful not to break the feather. Next, hold the shaft, and wave the feather in the air. Record your observations concerning the structure of the quill feather. Relate your observations to the feather's possible function. Describe the function of the feather under "Function of feather" in your data table.

3. Examine the vane of the feather. Does the vane appear to be a solid structure? Include a description of the quill feather's vane structure under "Structure of feather" in your data table.
4. Make a drawing of the quill feather. Label the shaft, vanes, and barbs. Compare your feather with the figure above.
5. Examine a contour feather. Make a sketch of the contour feather in your data table. Label the shaft, vanes, and barbs on your sketch. Does the feather resemble the one in the figure on the next page?
6. Describe the structure of the contour feather under "Structure of feather" in your data table.
7. Examine a prepared slide of a contour feather under low power. Note the smaller barbs, called *barbules,* extending from each of the barbs.
8. How might you observe the region between the barbs? Locate the tiny hooks at the end of each barbule. Note the arrangement of the hooks on adjacent barbs. Why do you think the hooks are so small? Make a separate, labeled drawing of the hooks in your lab report.
9. Examine the down feather, and sketch it in your data table. How does your down feather compare with the figure on the next page?
10. Describe the structure of the down feather in your data table. Do you notice a difference in the structure of the contour and down feathers?

## COMPARISON OF FEATHERS

| Type of feather | Sketch of feather | Structure of feather | Function of feather |
|---|---|---|---|
| Quill feather | | | |
| Contour feather | | | |
| Down feather | | | |

Contour feather

Down feather

**11.** Examine the prepared slide of the down feather under low power. Locate the barbs and barbules. Switch your microscope to high power, and make a separate, labeled drawing of the down feather in your lab report. Does it resemble the one in the figure above?

**12.** Clean up your materials, and wash your hands before leaving the lab.

## Analysis and Conclusions

1. What is the function of the shaft? What is the function of the vanes and barbs?
2. How do hooks increase the strength and air resistance of a feather?
3. How is the structure of the quill feather related to its function of aiding flight?
4. Based on your observations, why might down feathers be more effective at keeping a bird warm than the other two feather types you observed?
5. Based on your observations, how do you expect to see these feathers arranged on a bird? Explain how position of the feather affects the function of the feather.
6. What evolutionary pressure(s) would have caused the evolution of these different types of feathers?

## Further Inquiry

Each of the feather types you have examined has a specific structure and function. Review your observations, and try to think of features that account for the efficiency of the three types of feathers.

# MAMMALS

These young opossums depend on their mother's body to supply milk, a nourishing fluid from her mammary glands. The production of milk is one of the key characteristics of mammals.

# ORIGIN AND EVOLUTION OF MAMMALS

*Mammals (class Mammalia) are a highly diverse group. The opossums on the previous page are mammals. What makes them recognizable as mammals? What traits do they share with more than 4,000 other mammalian species?*

## MAJOR CHARACTERISTICS

All mammals, such as the lions shown in Figure 43-1, have the following six major characteristics:

- **Endothermy**—Mammals, like birds, regulate body heat internally through metabolism and externally through insulation. A mammal's body temperature stays high and nearly constant because of adjustments in metabolic rate and regulation of heat loss through the body surface. This manner of controlling body temperature is called **endothermy.**
- **Hair**—All mammals have some hair. Most mammals are covered with a thick coat of hair, which insulates the body against heat loss. Hair is made of filaments of the protein keratin.
- **Completely divided heart**—Mammals have a four-chambered heart whose two ventricles are completely separated by a muscular wall. This division keeps deoxygenated blood from mixing with oxygenated blood and allows efficient pumping of blood through the circulatory system.
- **Milk**—Female mammals produce milk to feed their offspring. Milk is a nutritious fluid that contains fats, protein, and sugars. Milk is produced by **mammary glands,** which are modified sweat glands located on the thorax or abdomen.
- **Single jawbone**—A mammal's lower jaw is made up of a single bone. By comparison, a reptile's lower jaw is made up of several bones. Mammalian fossils are often identified by the jawbone.
- **Specialized teeth**—Mammals have various types of teeth modified for different functions. Teeth at the front of the jaw bite, cut, or hold prey. Teeth along the sides of the jaw crush, grind, or slice. By comparison, most reptiles' teeth are uniformly sharp and cone-like throughout the mouth.

### OBJECTIVES

- **Describe** the major characteristics of mammals.
- **Compare** the characteristics of early synapsids, early therapsids, and modern mammals.
- **Relate** the adaptive radiation of mammals to the history of dinosaurs.
- **Differentiate** between monotremes, marsupials, and placental mammals.

### VOCABULARY

endothermy
mammary gland
synapsid
therapsid
monotreme
oviparous
marsupial
viviparous
placental mammal
placenta

**FIGURE 43-1**

Lions have the six key characteristics of mammals.

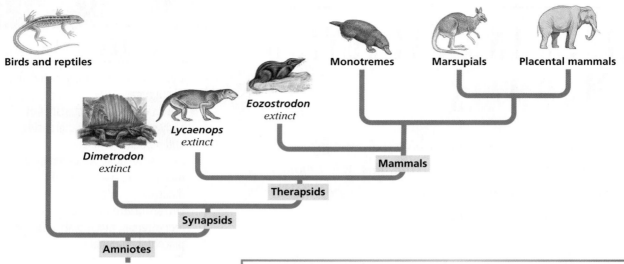

**Birds and reptiles**

*Dimetrodon*
extinct

*Lycaenops*
extinct

*Eozostrodon*
extinct

**Monotremes**

**Marsupials**

**Placental mammals**

**Mammals**

**Therapsids**

**Synapsids**

**Amniotes**

**FIGURE 43-2**

This phylogenetic diagram reflects hypotheses about the evolutionary relationships among mammals and other vertebrates. Mammals are thought to have descended from four-legged, land-dwelling vertebrates known as *therapsids,* which are sometimes referred to as *mammal-like reptiles.*

**FIGURE 43-3**

This synapsid had a sail-like structure on its back. Scientists think that this structure was filled with blood vessels that may have helped regulate the animal's body temperature. This illustration was made based on information from the fossil record.

*Dimetrodon* sp.

# ANCESTORS OF MAMMALS

Scientists think that the ancestors of all mammals appeared more than 300 million years ago. Around that time, amniotes seem to have split into two groups. One group gave rise to dinosaurs, birds, and modern reptiles. The other group, known as **synapsids,** gave rise to mammals and their extinct relatives, as shown in Figure 43-2. Paleontologists recognize early synapsids by the structure of their skull, which has a single opening in a bone just behind the eye socket. This same type of skull is found in all later synapsids, including mammals, although often in a modified form.

The first synapsids were small and looked like modern lizards. By the early Permian period (272 million to 298 million years ago), various large synapsids had appeared. Some reached 4 m (13 ft) in length and weighed more than 200 kg (440 lb). Figure 43-3 shows an illustration of a carnivorous synapsid of the genus *Dimetrodon* (die-MET-ruh-DON). Unlike most other reptiles, which have uniformly shaped teeth, these early synapsids had specialized teeth—long bladelike front teeth and smaller back teeth.

## Therapsids

A subset of synapsids, called **therapsids,** appeared later in the Permian period and gave rise to mammals. Therapsids were the most abundant terrestrial vertebrates during the late Permian period. They survived through the Triassic period (251 million to 203 million years ago) and into the Jurassic period (203 million to 144 million years ago).

A rich fossil record of transitional forms between therapsids and mammals exists. By studying these fossils, scientists can trace the anatomical changes that occurred during this transition and infer additional physiological, ecological, and behavioral changes. Several features we associate with mammals evolved first among early therapsids. For example, like the limbs of many early therapsids, mammals' limbs are directly beneath the body. Evidence suggests that some early therapsids were endothermic and may have had hair.

## Early Mammals

Both the first mammals and the first dinosaurs appeared during the Triassic period. So, dinosaurs coexisted with mammals for more than 150 million years. Figure 43-4 shows a hypothesized image of an early mammal. Early mammals were about the size of mice. Fossil skulls with large eye sockets suggest that these mammals were active at night. Also, their teeth were adapted for feeding on insects. Hiding by day and specializing on insects allowed the mammals to avoid threats from dinosaurs or competition with them. Similarities in the mammary tissues of several kinds of mammals suggest that milk production had evolved by the end of the Triassic.

**FIGURE 43-4**

The earliest mammals, such as this species of the genus *Eozostrodon,* had to compete with the larger, dominant dinosaurs. These early mammals were active at night, when dinosaurs were probably less active.

# DIVERSIFICATION OF MAMMALS

Dinosaurs dominated most terrestrial habitats while populations of small mammals continued to evolve. By the middle of the Cretaceous period, about 100 million years ago, three different kinds of mammals had appeared. Modern mammals belong to one of these three groups. The first group is made up of **monotremes.** They are **oviparous,** meaning that they lay eggs. The second group is made up of **marsupials.** They are **viviparous,** which means that they give birth to live young. In marsupials, the young develop within a pouch on the mother's body for some time after birth. The third group is made up of **placental mammals.** They are also viviparous, but in this group, the fetus typically develops within the mother's reproductive system for a longer time than it does in marsupials. Also, in this group, the developing fetus receives nourishment through a blood-rich structure called the **placenta.**

Many scientists think that some sort of natural disaster changed Earth's climate and forced the dinosaurs into extinction about 65 million years ago, at the end of the Cretaceous period. This change opened up many new habitats and resources to mammals. So, mammals took over many of the ecological roles that dinosaurs previously had. Today, nearly all large terrestrial animals are mammals.

**internet** connect

**www.scilinks.org**
**Topic:** Mammals
**Keyword:** HM60906

SC*LINKS.* Maintained by the National Science Teachers Association

## SECTION 1 REVIEW

1. What is the function of hair in mammals?

2. Identify two differences between the skull of a mammal and the skull of a reptile.

3. Compare the characteristics of early synapsids, early therapsids, and modern mammals.

4. Differentiate between monotremes, marsupials, and placental mammals.

**CRITICAL THINKING**

5. **Analyzing Theories** Describe a possible species that would be a transitional form between therapsids and mammals.

6. **Examining Evidence** What factors limit biologists' knowledge of early mammals?

7. **Making Comparisons** Which trait(s) do monotremes share with reptiles?

## OBJECTIVES

- **Explain** the advantage of endothermy in mammals.
- **Identify** features of the mammalian respiratory and circulatory systems that help sustain a rapid metabolism.
- **Describe** mammalian adaptations for obtaining food.
- **Compare** the nervous system of mammals to that of other groups of animals.
- **Differentiate** among the patterns of development in monotremes, marsupials, and placental mammals.

## VOCABULARY

diaphragm
incisor
canine
premolar
molar
baleen
rumen
cecum
echolocation

# CHARACTERISTICS OF MAMMALS

*Mammals live in many different kinds of habitats and climates all over the world. Several adaptations enable mammals to live in such diverse environments.*

## ENDOTHERMY

All animals produce heat internally when they metabolize, or produce energy from food. Mammals are *endotherms,* meaning they conserve and regulate this body heat. Most other animals, such as insects and lizards, are *ectotherms,* animals that are heated or cooled by their surroundings. Endothermy allows mammals to live in cold climates yet remain active. Moreover, the type of metabolism needed for endothermy also provides energy to perform strenuous activities for extended periods, such as migrating long distances.

Mammalian organ systems are uniquely adapted for endothermy. Figure 43-5 shows the internal anatomy of a mammal. Because of its faster metabolism, a mammal uses more oxygen and food than does a reptile of the same size. So, mammals have unique circulatory and digestive systems. Also, the body temperature of a mammal is often above that of its environment, so heat constantly escapes through the animal's skin and breath. The energy used to heat a mammal's body would be wasted without adaptations such as body insulation. Often, mammals that live in very cold climates have heavy coats of fur and, or thick layers of fat, called *blubber.*

**FIGURE 43-5**

The organs and organ systems of modern mammals have a high demand for energy. The mammalian heart efficiently pumps oxygenated blood throughout the body, delivering nutrients that fuel the high-energy requirements of endothermy.

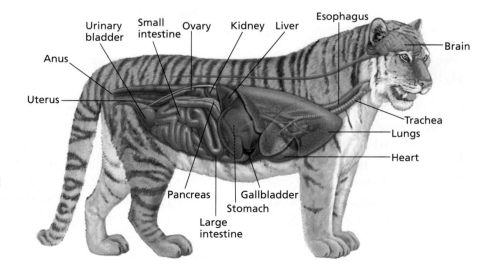

Labels: Urinary bladder, Small intestine, Ovary, Kidney, Liver, Esophagus, Brain, Anus, Uterus, Trachea, Lungs, Heart, Pancreas, Gallbladder, Stomach, Large intestine

## Circulatory System

The structure of the mammalian heart allows efficient pumping of blood throughout the body, as shown in Figure 43-6. The mammalian heart has two atria and two ventricles. A *septum,* or wall of tissue, completely separates the ventricles. The septum prevents oxygenated and deoxygenated blood from mixing. Recall that in the hearts of lizards and turtles, an incomplete septum allows the oxygen-rich blood and oxygen-poor blood to mix when the animal is inactive. The complete septum is an adaptation that allows mammals' bodies to transport oxygen more efficiently.

## Respiratory System

A mammal's respiratory system is adapted for efficient gas exchange. The lungs are large and contain millions of *alveoli,* the small sacs in which gas exchange occurs. As a result, mammalian lungs have a much larger surface area available for gas exchange than reptilian lungs do.

Mammals breathe using two mechanisms: one they share with some reptiles and one that is unique. Lizards and snakes inhale by using their rib-cage muscles to expand the thoracic cavity, the body cavity that holds the lungs. Mammals inherited this breathing mechanism but use it mostly under conditions of strenuous activity. The second mammalian breathing mechanism uses a sheet of muscle below the rib cage called the **diaphragm.** Contraction of the diaphragm enlarges the thorax and thus expands the thoracic cavity. At rest, mammals breathe primarily with the diaphragm.

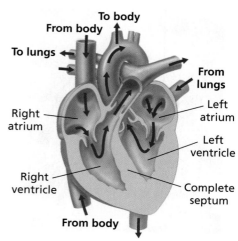

**FIGURE 43-6**

The red arrows show the path of oxygenated blood through the heart, and the blue arrows show the path of deoxygenated blood. Notice that the ventricles are completely separated by a septum. As a result, the blood pumped to the body contains a higher percentage of oxygen than a reptile's or fish's pumping heart can circulate.

# FEEDING AND DIGESTION

For most mammals, the breakdown of food begins with chewing. Other vertebrates simply swallow their food whole or in large pieces. Chewing speeds up digestion by breaking food into small pieces that provide a large surface area for attack by enzymes. Variations in the size and shape of teeth among different mammalian species reflect differences in diet. Chisel-like **incisors** cut. Pointed **canines** grip, puncture, and tear. **Premolars** shear, shred, cut, or grind. **Molars** grind, crush, or cut. For example, predatory carnivores, such as the bear in Figure 43-7, have a set of teeth specialized for gripping, holding, tearing, and crushing food. Mammalian carnivores are recognizable by their sharp incisors and long canines.

Baleen whales, such as the blue whale, lack teeth. Instead, they have **baleen,** thin plates of keratin that hang from the skin of the upper jaw like a curtain. As a baleen whale swims, it gulps water, then closes its mouth, and pushes the water out through the baleen. Shrimp and other invertebrates get trapped behind the baleen and then are swallowed.

**FIGURE 43-7**

Carnivores, such as this bear, have large, sharp incisor and canine teeth that can cut and tear flesh. Bears and many other carnivores also have strong, crushing molars.

## Special Adaptations for Digesting Plants

Meat is simple to digest, so most carnivores have short, simple digestive systems. Plants, however, can be difficult to digest because plants contain *cellulose,* a polymer of the sugar glucose. Animals do not produce enzymes that can break down cellulose. However, the long digestive tracts of herbivorous mammals, such as the zebra shown in Figure 43-8, contain microorganisms that can break down cellulose.

In some herbivorous mammals, the structure that is called a *stomach* is actually made up of four chambers. One of these chambers is the true stomach. Another chamber, known as the **rumen** (ROO-muhn), contains symbiotic microorganisms. Plant material that has been chewed and swallowed enters the rumen, where microorganisms begin to break the cellulose into smaller molecules that can be absorbed into the animal's bloodstream. The material is partly digested in the rumen, then regurgitated, chewed again, and swallowed again. The animal may regurgitate and swallow the same food several times. Mammals that have a rumen are called *ruminants* and include cows, sheep, goats, giraffes, and deer.

In horses, zebras, rodents, rabbits, and elephants, microorganisms that live in the cecum (SEE-kuhm) complete digestion of the food. The **cecum** is a large sac that branches from the small intestine and acts as a fermentation chamber. Food passes through the stomach and small intestine before entering the cecum. Mammals with a cecum do not chew cud.

**FIGURE 43-8**

Many herbivores, such as this zebra, have flat teeth that can efficiently grind grasses, grains, or leaves. Herbivores also have digestive systems that harbor symbiotic microbes that help digest plant materials.

# NERVOUS SYSTEM

A mammal's brain is about 15 times heavier than the brain of a similarly sized fish, amphibian, or reptile. Of all animals, humans have one of the highest ratios of brain size to body size. Whales, dolphins, and some primates also have high ratios. These differences are due mostly to the size of the cerebrum. The *cerebrum* is the outer region of the brain and the largest part of the brain in mammals. The cerebrum's surface is usually folded and fissured, which greatly increases its surface area without increasing its volume. The cerebrum evaluates input from the sense organs, controls movement, initiates and regulates behavior, and functions in memory and learning.

As with other terrestrial vertebrates, a mammal's survival depends on five major senses: vision, hearing, smell, touch, and taste. The importance of each sense depends on the mammal's environment. For example, most bats, which are active at night, rely largely on sound rather than vision for navigating and finding food. Using a process called **echolocation** (EK-oh-loh-KAY-shuhn), these bats emit high-frequency sound waves, which bounce off objects, including potential prey. The bat then analyzes the returning echoes to determine the size, distance, direction, and speed of the objects.

# DEVELOPMENT

In all living mammals, milk from the mother's mammary glands nourishes newborns. However, the pattern of development of the offspring differs from group to group.

## Monotremes

A female monotreme typically lays one or two large eggs encased in thin, leathery shells and then incubates them. Her body heat keeps the eggs warm. The yolk nourishes the developing embryo within the egg. At hatching, a monotreme is very small and only partially developed. Its mother protects it and feeds it milk from her mammary glands until it is ready to survive on its own.

## Marsupials

In marsupials, such as opossums and kangaroos, embryos develop for just a short period within the mother's uterus and then emerge from the uterus and crawl into the mother's pouch, a skin-lined pocket on her abdomen. The newborn offspring of a kangaroo at this stage is only 2 to 3 cm (1 in.) long. In the mother's pouch, the newborn attaches to a nipple to feed. The newborn's development and growth then continue inside the pouch for several months.

## Placental Mammals

Placental mammals, such as the horse in Figure 43-9, give birth to well-developed young after a long period of development inside the uterus. During this period, the placenta provides nourishment and oxygen to the developing offspring. The placenta begins to form shortly after fertilization, when the fertilized egg attaches to the lining of the uterus. Extensions from the *chorion,* the outer membrane of the embryo, grow into the lining of the uterus. Blood vessels from the uterus surround these extensions. Nutrients and oxygen diffuse from the mother's blood into the blood of the offspring, and carbon dioxide and other wastes diffuse from the offspring into the mother's blood. After birth, infants feed on milk for several weeks or months.

**FIGURE 43-9**

Placental mammals, such as horses, carry their developing fetuses for a long time and give birth to infants that are relatively large and well developed, but still need parental care.

### Word Roots and Origins

*placenta*

from the Greek *plakos,* meaning "flat object" or "flat cake"

## SECTION 2 REVIEW

1. A mammal eats about 10 times as much food as a lizard of the same size. Explain this difference.

2. Compare a mammalian heart to a reptilian heart.

3. Describe the function of a rumen.

4. Compare a mammalian brain to a reptilian brain.

5. Compare the developmental patterns of monotremes, marsupials, and placental mammals.

### CRITICAL THINKING

6. **Analyzing Information** What is the advantage of large ears to a bat that is active at night?

7. **Applying Concepts** What ecological relationship does a cow have with the bacteria in its rumen?

8. **Recognizing Relationships** Propose a functional reason why endothermy is associated with an enlarged cerebrum.

- **Identify** an example from each of the 12 major orders of mammals.
- **Distinguish** between monotremes, marsupials, and placental mammals.
- **Compare** the characteristics of artiodactyls and perissodactyls.
- **Compare** the adaptations for aquatic life in cetaceans, pinnipeds, and sirenians.

**VOCABULARY**

pinniped
ungulate

# DIVERSITY OF MAMMALS

*M*ammals can be found in a diverse range of habitats, including the open ocean, underground, and mountaintops. Each mammalian species is uniquely adapted for its particular way of life.

## MAMMALIAN ORDERS

Mammals are commonly classified into a single order of monotremes, 7 orders of marsupials, and about 18 orders of placental mammals. Possible evolutionary relationships between the mammalian orders are shown in Figure 43-10.

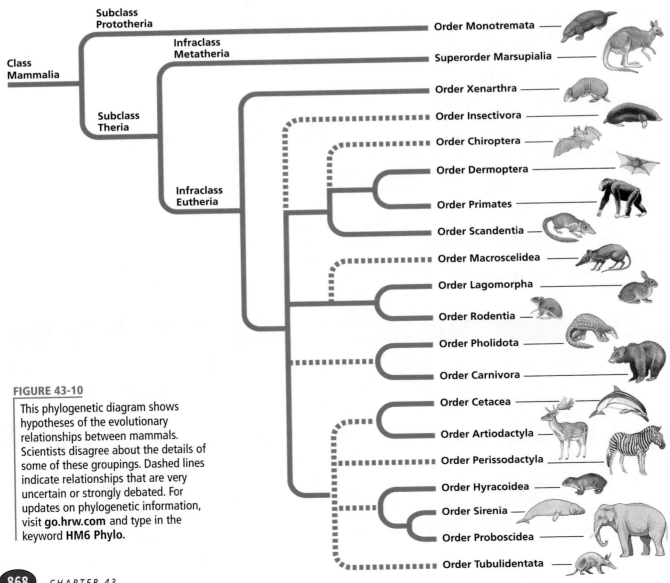

**FIGURE 43-10**

This phylogenetic diagram shows hypotheses of the evolutionary relationships between mammals. Scientists disagree about the details of some of these groupings. Dashed lines indicate relationships that are very uncertain or strongly debated. For updates on phylogenetic information, visit **go.hrw.com** and type in the keyword **HM6 Phylo**.

**(a)** Duckbill platypus, *Ornithorhynchus anatinus*

**(b)** Short-beaked echidna, *Tachyglossus aculeatus*

# MONOTREMES

The order Monotremata (MAHN-oh-truh-MAHT-uh), the *monotremes,* is the only order in the subclass Prototheria. Because monotremes lay eggs, biologists consider this order to be very ancient, meaning that monotremes existed before other kinds of mammals did. Just three species exist today: the platypus and two echidna species.

The duckbill platypus, shown in Figure 43-11a, is adapted to life around rivers or streams in Australia. It has waterproof fur, webbed feet, and a flattened tail that aids in swimming. It uses its wide, flat, leathery bill to find worms, crayfish, and other invertebrates in soft mud. The female platypus digs a den in a riverbank to lay her eggs and curls around the eggs to protect and warm them. The babies lick milk from mammary glands on the mother's abdomen.

The two echidna species live in dry woodlands or deserts in Australia and New Guinea. As shown in Figure 43-11b, they have protective spines, a long snout, and a sticky tongue used to feed on ants and other insects (though they are unrelated to other mammal anteaters). Echidnas incubate their eggs in a pouch on the belly.

**FIGURE 43-11**

Two of the three species of the order Monotremata are shown here: the duckbill platypus (a) and an echidna that is also called a *spiny anteater* (b).

# MARSUPIALS

The marsupials had previously been classified in one order, Marsupialia (mahr-SOO-pee-AY-lee-uh), but are now divided into at least seven orders within the super order Marsupialia. The majority of about 280 species of marsupials live in Australia, but some live in New Guinea and the Americas. The Virginia opossum is the only marsupial native to the United States.

Scientists think that marsupials began to evolve in isolation when Australia and New Guinea drifted away from the other continents more than 40 million years ago. At that time, placental mammals were rare in the Australian region, so marsupials evolved to take advantage of many ecological opportunities. Marsupials were once common in South America as well but were displaced by placental mammals that migrated in from the north.

# PLACENTAL MAMMALS

Nearly 95 percent of all mammalian species are placental mammals, making up the infraclass Eutheria of the subclass Theria. They are classified into about 20 orders.

## Order Xenarthra

The order Xenarthra (zuh-NAHR-thruh) includes about 30 living species of anteaters, armadillos, and sloths living in southern North America, Central America, and South America. Biologists think that, based on fossil and molecular evidence, Xenarthra evolved as a unique lineage in what is now South America. The name *xenarthra* means "strange joints" and refers to the unique structure of the lumbar vertebrae of members of this order.

This order was once named Edentata (EE-den-TAH-duh), meaning "toothless," because many members of this order do not have prominent teeth. Anteaters completely lack teeth. Armadillos and sloths have peglike teeth that lack enamel. Most edentates feed on insects, which they capture with a long, sticky tongue. With their powerful front paws and large, sharp claws, they rip open anthills and termite nests. Armadillos supplement their insect diet with small reptiles, frogs, mollusks, and scavenged meat. Sloths, on the other hand, are herbivores; their continuously growing teeth are adapted to grinding plants.

## Order Lagomorpha

The order Lagomorpha (LAG-uh-MAWR-fuh), members of which are called *lagomorphs*, includes about 70 species of rabbits, hares, and pikas. A pika (PIE-kuh) is shown in Figure 43-12a. Lagomorphs are native to many continents. They differ from rodents in that lagomorphs have a double row of upper incisors, with two large front teeth backed by two smaller ones. The teeth of lagomorphs continue to grow throughout their lifetime. Such teeth are an adaptation to a herbivorous diet.

## Order Rodentia

Related to Lagomorpha is the order Rodentia (roh-DEN-chuh), members of which are called *rodents*. Rodentia is the largest mammalian order, which includes more than 1,800 species, or about 40 percent of all placental mammals. Rodents flourish on every continent except Antarctica and are adapted to a wide range of habitats. They tend to produce many young in each litter. Squirrels, marmots, chipmunks, gophers, muskrats, mice, and rats are rodents. The porcupine in Figure 43-12b is also a rodent.

A rodent's teeth consist of a few molars or premolars and two pairs of incisors that continue to grow as long as the rodent lives. The sharp incisors are an adaptation to gnaw on seeds, twigs, roots, and bark. As a rodent gnaws, the back surface of the tooth wears away faster than the front surface, maintaining the tooth's edge.

**FIGURE 43-12**

The North American pika (a) is a lagomorph, related to rabbits and hares. The North American porcupine (b), a rodent, ranges from Canada to northern Mexico.

**(a)** North American pika, *Ochotona princeps*

**(b)** North American porcupine, *Erethizon dorsatum*

## Order Primates

The order Primates is made up of 235 living species, including lemurs, tarsiers, lorises, monkeys, gibbons, apes, and humans. Most primates are omnivores and have teeth suited for a varied diet. Primates have brains that have a relatively large cortex, which make possible the complex behaviors characteristic of this group.

A wide range of body sizes and adaptations allow primates to live in a variety of terrains. The smallest known primate, the pygmy mouse lemur, weighs only about 30 g and was discovered in 2000 in Madagascar, where it lives mostly in trees. In contrast, the largest primate, the mountain gorilla, can weigh 140–180 kg (300–400 lb) and lives on the ground in dense African mountain forests.

Most primates have forward-facing eyes, a feature that enables depth perception. Many primates are active at night and have large eyes adapted for night vision. All primates have grasping hands and, with the exception of humans, grasping feet. Some primates also have a grasping tail. Many primates live in trees, where grasping feet, hands, and tails are essential adaptations. In humans, grasping hands serve many purposes.

## Order Chiroptera

The only mammals that truly fly, the bats, make up the order Chiroptera (kie-RAHP-tuh-ruh). There are more than 900 species of bats, and they live throughout the world, except in polar environments. A bat's wing is a modified front limb with a membrane of skin that stretches between extremely long finger bones to the hind limb, as shown in Figure 43-13a. A bat's wingspan can measure up to 1.5 m (4.5 ft). The bat's clawed thumb sticks out from the top edge of the wing. Bats use their thumbs for walking, climbing, and grasping.

Most bats have small eyes and large ears and navigate by echolocation. Most bats are active at night and feed on insects. However, some tropical bats are active in the day and feed on fruit or flower nectar. These bats locate food by using their large eyes and keen sense of smell. A few species of bats feed on meat or blood.

## Order Insectivora

The order Insectivora (in-sek-TIV-uh-ruh) includes about 390 species of shrews, hedgehogs, and moles living in North America, Africa, and Europe. Figure 43-13b shows a shrew. Most members of this order are *insectivores,* which means "animals that eat insects." However, not all insectivores are members of the order Insectivora. Furthermore, some Insectivora eat meat.

Scientists disagree about whether to include certain families of mammals in this order. For example, a family of mammals called *colugos,* which are commonly called *flying lemurs,* was once placed in Insectivora. This family is now usually classified as another order, Dermoptera. The Insectivora are usually small animals with a high metabolic rate. Most have long, pointed noses that enable them to probe in the soil for insects, worms, and other invertebrates. Their sharp teeth are adapted for grasping and piercing prey.

**FIGURE 43-13**

(a) Bats, in the order Chiroptera, are the only mammals that truly fly. The physics of the bat's wing in flight gives the bat more lift in relation to its body weight than most birds have. Thus, bats can remain airborne at slower speeds than birds can. (b) Shrews, in the order Insectivora, must eat more than twice their own body weight daily to fuel their high metabolic rate.

**(a)** Peter's epauletted fruit bat, *Epomophorus crypturus*

**(b)** Least shrew, *Cryptotis barua*

**FIGURE 43-14**

This caribou (a) is an artiodactyl. Artiodactyls are native to all continents except Australia and Antarctica. Although this tapir (b) looks like a pig (Order Artiodactyla), it is a perissodactyl. The similarity to a pig is an example of convergent evolution.

**(a)** Caribou, *Rangifer tarandus*

**(b)** Baird's tapir, *Tapirus bairdi*

## Order Carnivora

The 274 living species of the order Carnivora (kahr-NIV-uh-ruh) are distributed worldwide. Most members of this order are called *carnivores,* which means "animals that eat meat." Dogs, cats, raccoons, bears, hyenas, otters, seals, and sea lions are some well-known carnivores. Most are skilled hunters with strong senses of sight and smell. Other adaptations of carnivores include strong jaws, long canine teeth, and clawed toes to seize and hold prey. Many terrestrial carnivores have skeletal adaptations, such as long limbs, to run quickly.

Aquatic carnivores, known as **pinnipeds,** include the sea lions, seals, and walruses. They are efficient at swimming, with streamlined bodies and four limbs adapted as flippers. Although pinnipeds spend much of their time in the sea feeding, they return to land to sleep and to give birth. They are generally larger than land carnivores, and their large size helps them maintain body temperature. Most pinnipeds can dive to depths of 400 m (1,313 ft) and remain underwater for up to five minutes, but some can remain submerged for as long as one hour. Some scientists once placed pinnipeds in their own order—Pinnipedia.

## Order Artiodactyla

Mammals with hoofs are **ungulates** (UHNG-yoo-lits). Two main groups of ungulates are characterized by their foot structure and by the presence of either a rumen or a cecum.

Ungulates with an even number of toes are *artiodactyls,* in the order Artiodactyla (AHRD-ee-oh-DAK-tuh-luh). This order includes about 210 species of deer, cattle, giraffes, pigs, and camels. Artiodactyls are native to every continent except Antarctica and Australia. Figure 43-14a shows a common artiodactyl, a caribou. Most artiodactyls can run quickly to escape predators.

Most artiodactyls are herbivores, although pigs are omnivores. Their molars are usually large and flat, for grinding plant material. Most artiodactyls are ruminants, or animals that have a rumen.

## Order Perissodactyla

Ungulates with an odd number of toes are *perissodactyls,* in the order Perissodactyla (PUH-ris-oh-DAK-tuh-luh). This order includes about 17 living species, such as horses, zebras, rhinoceroses, and tapirs. Most species are native to Africa and Asia. However, some species of tapirs, such as the one in Figure 43-14b, live in Central and South America. Perissodactyls have a cecum.

## Order Cetacea

Closely related to Artiodactyla is the order Cetacea (see-TAY-shuh), members of which are called *cetaceans.* Cetaceans include about 90 species of whales, dolphins, and porpoises worldwide. The orca in Figure 43-15a is an example. Cetaceans have fish-shaped bodies with forelimbs modified as flippers. They lack hind limbs and have broad, flat tails that help propel them through the water.

**(a)** Killer whale, *Orcinus orca*

**(b)** Manatee, *Trichechus manatus*

**FIGURE 43-15**

This orca (a), a cetacean, looks very different from most artiodactyls, but scientists think cetaceans are closely related to artiodactyls. These manatees, or sea cows (b), belong to one of four species of Sirenians. Sirenia may share recent ancestry with Proboscidea.

Cetaceans are totally aquatic but evolved from land-dwelling mammals. They breathe through modified nostrils called *blowholes*. Adult cetaceans lack hair except for a few bristles on the snout. A thick layer of blubber below the skin provides insulation. Cetaceans use echolocation to navigate, communicate, and find prey.

Two subgroups of cetaceans are the toothed whales and baleen whales. Toothed whales include sperm whales, narwhals, dolphins, porpoises, and orcas. Toothed whales can have up to 100 teeth. They prey on fish, squid, seals, and other whales. Baleen whales, such as blue whales, lack teeth and filter food from the water with the baleen attached to the roof of the mouth.

## Order Sirenia

Four species of manatees and dugongs (DOO-gawngz) make up the order Sirenia (sie-REE-nee-uh), commonly called the *sirenians*. These large torpedo-shaped herbivores live in tropical seas, estuaries, and rivers. Their front limbs are flippers modified for swimming. Like whales (order Cetacea), sirenians lack hind limbs and have a flattened tail for propulsion. Although manatees and dugongs look like whales, they are more closely related to elephants. The similarities between whales and sirenians came about through convergent evolution. Figure 43-15b shows the only sirenian found in North America, the manatee.

## Quick Lab

### Comparing Gestation Periods

**Materials**  paper, pencil

**Procedure**

1. Make a table of gestation periods for different mammals. Make three columns labeled "Mammal," "Gestation period," and "Offspring per pregnancy."

2. Fill in your table with the following data:

Bat, 210 days, 1 offspring
Gerbil, 19–21 days, 4–7 offspring
Horse, 332–342 days, 1 offspring
Monkey, 226–232 days, 1 offspring
Rabbit, 31 days, 3–6 offspring
Squirrel, 44 days, 3 offspring
Whale, 420–430 days, 1 offspring
Wolf, 63 days, 4–5 offspring

**Analysis**  Make a graph that relates gestation length and the number of offspring per pregnancy. Then, propose a hypothesis to explain this relationship.

## TABLE 43-1 *Minor Orders of Mammals*

| Order | Description | Examples |
|---|---|---|
| Macroscelidea | ground-dwelling insectivores with long, flexible snouts; 15 species found only in Africa | elephant shrews (not true shrews) |
| Pholidota | insectivores with protective scales composed of fused hair; resemble reptiles; found in Africa and southern Asia | pangolins or scaly anteaters (not true anteaters) |
| Tubulidentata | nearly hairless insectivores with piglike bodies and long snouts; found in southern Africa | aardvarks |
| Scandentia | squirrel-like omnivores that live on ground and in trees; feed on fruit and small animals; found in tropical Asia | tree shrews (not true shrews) |
| Dermoptera | only two species exist; glide in air using a thin membrane stretched between their limbs; found only in parts of Asia | colugos or flying lemurs (not true lemurs) |
| Hyracoidea | small rabbitlike herbivores; 7 species found mostly in Africa | hyrax |

## Order Proboscidea

Members of the order Proboscidea (PROH-buh-SID-ee-uh) have a nose that is modified into a long, boneless trunk, or *proboscis*. The only living species of this order are the Asian elephant and the African elephant, which is the largest living land mammal. Mammoths and mastodons are extinct members of this order. The African elephant can reach 6,000 kg (13,200 lb). To sustain such a large body, an elephant feeds on plants for up to 18 hours a day. The trunk allows an elephant to gather water or gather leaves from high branches. Modified incisors, called *tusks,* efficiently dig up roots and strip bark from branches. Large, jagged molars at the back of the jaw can grow up to 30 cm (1 ft) long and grind plant material.

Elephants have long gestation periods. A calf takes 20 to 22 months to develop. Female elephants can continue to give birth until the age of 70, and elephants can live to be 80 years old.

## Other Orders of Placental Mammals

The 12 orders just described include most of the familiar placental mammals. The 6 remaining orders contain just 1 percent of the mammalian species and are summarized in Table 43-1.

internet connect

www.scilinks.org
**Topic: Placental Mammals**
**Keyword: HM61150**

SCiLINKS. Maintained by the National Science Teachers Association

## SECTION 3 REVIEW

1. Give an example of each from the major orders of mammals.

2. Which continent is a natural home of both monotremes and marsupials?

3. What is unusual about the incisors of rodents?

4. Compare artiodactyls to perissodactyls.

5. Compare manatees to toothed whales.

**CRITICAL THINKING**

6. **Inferring Relationships** Give an adaptive reason why the pouch of the marsupial mole, a burrowing animal, opens toward the rear of its body.

7. **Applying Information** Why is *flying lemurs* a poor name for members of the order Dermoptera?

8. **Making Comparisons** Cetaceans live in cold ocean waters yet lack fur. Explain this.

# PRIMATES AND HUMAN ORIGINS

*To understand human origins, one must understand the relationships of humans to other primates.*

### OBJECTIVES

- **Identify** traits that distinguish primates from other mammals.
- **Describe** fossil evidence relating humans to primate ancestors.
- **Compare** hypotheses concerning hominid evolution.

### VOCABULARY

prehensile appendage
anthropoid primate
opposable thumb
great ape
bipedalism
hominid
australopithecine
human

## PRIMATE CHARACTERISTICS

Some people speak of primates as the "highest" mammalian order. However, as Figure 43-16 shows, many primate characteristics are generalized rather than specialized and are similar to features possessed by ancestral mammals. Primate limbs, for example, are most similar to the limbs of the earliest mammals.

Many primate traits are adaptations for living in groups in trees. Examples include strong three-dimensional vision and **prehensile appendages,** or hands, feet, and tails that can grasp. The primate brain, with its large cerebrum, is able to interpret complex visual information and keep track of subtle shifts in social organization.

**FIGURE 43-16**

Primate characteristics are mostly adaptations for a social life in the trees.

**Large brain parts relative to size**
Primate brains support complex skills, such as using hands, interpreting visual information, interacting socially, and caring for offspring.

**Acute color vision**
Forward-facing eyes allow binocular vision, depth perception, and skilled movement in three-dimensional space.

**Generalist teeth**
The variety of teeth permits herbivorous and omnivorous diets.

**Communication**
Facial and vocal structure enables broad range of expressions and sounds.

**Infant care**
Infants require prolonged care; reduced litter size permits greater mobility and attention to each young; there is usually one pair of mammary glands on the chest.

**Manual dexterity**
Opposable thumbs can touch other four fingers; fingers can grip or manipulate objects; flattened nails protect finger pads.

**Social organization**
Many primates live in social groups with complex behaviors among members.

**Characteristic skeletal structure**
Primates can sit upright, cling to trees, or hang from branches; major bones of limbs are like those of earliest mammals, with one upper and two lower bones.

## Anthropoids

The primate lineages that evolved the earliest include lemurs, lorises, and tarsiers. These groups are sometimes referred to as *prosimians.* The gibbon in Figure 43-17 is one of the **anthropoid primates,** a group that also includes New World monkeys, Old World monkeys, apes, and humans. Anthropoid adaptations include rotating shoulder and elbow joints and an **opposable thumb,** which can touch the other fingers. Anthropoids can hold and manipulate objects precisely, as when a chimpanzee peels a banana or when a student holds a pencil. Nonhuman anthropoids also have grasping feet with an opposable big toe.

Humans, apes, and Old World monkeys have a similar *dental formula,* or number and arrangement of teeth. Each half of the upper and lower mouth includes two incisors, one canine, two premolars, and three molars, as shown in Figure 43-18. Compared to other primates, anthropoids have a more complex brain structure and a larger brain relative to body size.

Orangutans, gorillas, chimpanzees, bonobos, and humans make up the **great apes.** Chimpanzee and human DNA is so similar that humans are thought to be more closely related to chimpanzees than to any other living primates. DNA and fossil evidence suggests that humans and chimpanzees share a common ancestor that lived about 6 million years ago. Humans, however, did not descend from chimpanzees. Rather, modern apes and humans both descended from an ancestral apelike species.

## Modern Humans

Among living mammals, only we humans, *Homo sapiens,* have the trait of **bipedalism** (bie-PED'l-IZ-uhm), the tendency to walk upright on two legs. The human skeleton is adapted for bipedalism in several ways, as shown in Figure 43-18.

**FIGURE 43-17**

Anthropoids such as this white-handed gibbon, *Hylobates lar,* have rotating shoulder and elbow joints. This adaptation enables anthropoids to swing by their arms through trees.

**FIGURE 43-18**

Humans have certain physical traits that differ markedly from those of the chimpanzee, a modern ape: the jaw, pelvis, spine, feet, and toes.

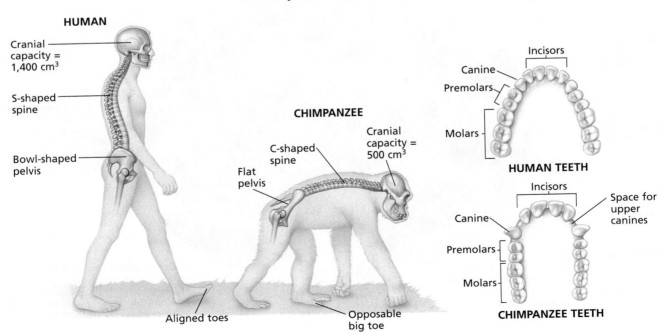

HUMAN

Cranial capacity = 1,400 cm$^3$

S-shaped spine

Bowl-shaped pelvis

Aligned toes

CHIMPANZEE

C-shaped spine

Cranial capacity = 500 cm$^3$

Flat pelvis

Opposable big toe

Incisors

Canine

Premolars

Molars

HUMAN TEETH

Incisors

Canine

Space for upper canines

Premolars

Molars

CHIMPANZEE TEETH

The bowl-shaped human pelvis supports internal organs during upright walking. The human spine curves in an S shape that allows for upright posture. Human toes are aligned with each other and are much shorter than ape toes. Because humans are the only primates that have this foot structure, the shape of the human foot is likely an adaptation for bipedalism.

The larger brain and smaller jaw in modern humans result in a flatter face than that found in apes. The modern human brain has an average size of about 1,400 cm$^3$ and the chimpanzee, about 400 cm$^3$. Among other unique structures, the human brain has extensive areas that function in the production and understanding of speech. Apes have similar areas of their brains that function in communication, and apes can learn to mimic certain forms of human sign language. Apes living in the wild, however, do not use the complexity of signals found in human language.

### Hominids

**Hominids** include humans and extinct humanlike anthropoid species. Bipedalism is the distinguishing characteristic of this group. All other living anthropoid primates are *quadrupedal,* meaning they tend to walk on all four limbs. Apelike ancestors of the first hominids were probably also quadrupedal. How long ago did the first bipedal hominid evolve? And did human traits such as upright walking and a larger brain evolve together or at different times? Fossil evidence has provided some clues to the answers.

# FOSSIL HOMINIDS

Paleontologists and anthropologists (scientists who study humans) have unearthed sufficient fossil evidence to conclude that a variety of humanlike species lived on Earth within the past 10 million years. However, scientists continue to investigate and debate hypotheses about the evolutionary relationships among all known hominids. Even the species name of some fossils is a matter of debate.

One important fossil discovery was made in 1974 in the Afar Valley region of Africa by Donald Johanson and colleagues. The 3.2 million–year-old fossilized skeleton, shown in Figure 43-19, was of an anthropoid primate with the brain size of a chimpanzee. But the skeletal structure clearly showed that this organism was bipedal.

### Australopithecines

Johanson and colleagues gave the new fossil the species name *Australopithecus afarensis* and the nickname "Lucy." Additional fossils of the same species have been discovered in other parts of Africa and date from about 2.5 million to 4 million years ago. A number of fossil organisms similar to Lucy have been classified as species of the genus *Australopithecus* within the subfamily of **australopithecines** (AW-struh-loh-PITH-uh-SEENZ), which may include other genera.

**Word Roots and Origins**

*anthropoid*

from the Greek *anthropos,* meaning "man," and *eidos,* meaning "shape"

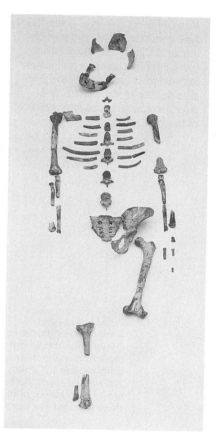

**FIGURE 43-19**

The original fossil find of *Australopithecus afarensis* consisted of a partial skeleton. The team of investigators who discovered it nicknamed the fossil "Lucy."

# MANY HOMINID SPECIES

Paleontologists continue to find new hominid fossils. Although the exact classification of some fossils is strongly debated, it is clear that human evolution did not proceed as a single lineage of increasingly humanlike forms. Rather, several hominid forms arose, thrived, and became extinct over the past 7 million years, as shown in Figure 43-20. Furthermore, different species of hominids may have coexisted in time and possibly interacted.

In 1995, Mary Leakey and colleagues at the National Museums of Kenya announced the finding of a new hominid species, *Australopithecus anamensis*, that predated *A. afarensis* (Lucy's species) by about 300,000 years. Like Lucy's species, this species was also similar to a chimpanzee but probably bipedal. A possible descendant of Lucy's species was *A. africanus*, which lived about 2.3 to 3 million years ago. It was taller and heavier than Lucy's species and had a slightly larger brain capacity (430 to 550 cm³).

Three more-recent species, *A. aethiopicus, A. robustus,* and *A. boisei,* date from about 2.6 million to 1 million years ago. The physical characteristics of these later species suggest that they were a different lineage from *A. afarensis.* For example, they had heavier skulls, larger molars, and generally thicker bodies than Lucy's species did. Their brain capacity ranged from 450 to 600 cm³. Some scientists call these later hominids *robust australopithecines,* and some scientists place them in the genus *Paranthropus* instead of in the genus Australopithecus.

**FIGURE 43-20**

Many different species of hominids may have coexisted in time and possibly interacted during the past 7 million years. Scientists continue to find new hominid fossils and debate the exact classification of some fossils. This diagram represents one interpretation of the fossil record.

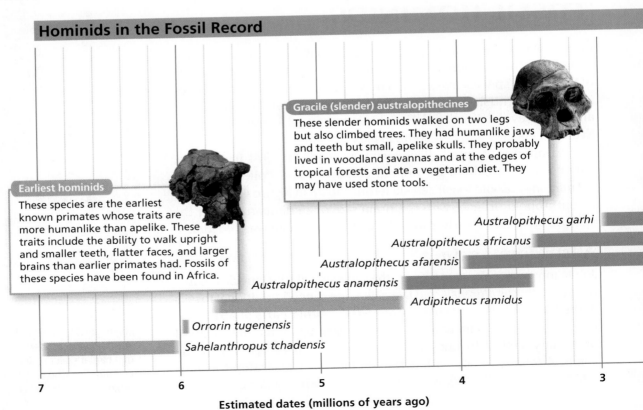

## Hominids in the Fossil Record

**Gracile (slender) australopithecines**

These slender hominids walked on two legs but also climbed trees. They had humanlike jaws and teeth but small, apelike skulls. They probably lived in woodland savannas and at the edges of tropical forests and ate a vegetarian diet. They may have used stone tools.

**Earliest hominids**

These species are the earliest known primates whose traits are more humanlike than apelike. These traits include the ability to walk upright and smaller teeth, flatter faces, and larger brains than earlier primates had. Fossils of these species have been found in Africa.

*Australopithecus garhi*

*Australopithecus africanus*

*Australopithecus afarensis*

*Australopithecus anamensis*

*Ardipithecus ramidus*

*Orrorin tugenensis*

*Sahelanthropus tchadensis*

| 7 | 6 | 5 | 4 | 3 |

**Estimated dates (millions of years ago)**

# HUMANS

Sometime after the appearance of the australopithecines, new hominids appeared that are classified in the genus *Homo*. Extinct and living members of this genus are called **humans.** Many fossil humans have physical structures that are transitions between those of australopithecines and of modern humans.

## *Homo habilis* and *Homo erectus*

In the early 1960s, scientists in East Africa found a hominid skull whose brain capacity was much larger than the brain capacity of Lucy's species but whose body was not much taller than Lucy's body. Importantly, the new fossils were found along with stone tools. Scientists named the new species *Homo habilis*, the "handy human." Fossils of *H. habilis* are between 1.6 million and 2.5 million years old and have a brain capacity of 590 to 690 cm$^3$.

Later species, *Homo erectus* (meaning "upright human"), had a brain capacity of 800 to 1,250 cm$^3$, or about two-thirds that of a modern human. *H. erectus* had a thicker skull, larger brow ridges, a lower forehead, and larger, protruding teeth than modern humans have. Some individuals were as tall as modern humans. Because *H. erectus* fossils have been found on several continents, scientists think that this hominid was the first to travel out of Africa. Charred animal bones indicate that *H. erectus* hunted and cooked its food.

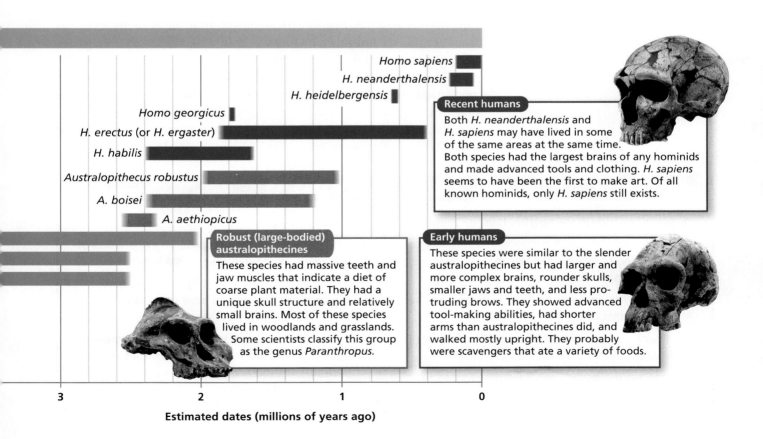

Homo sapiens
H. neanderthalensis
H. heidelbergensis
Homo georgicus
H. erectus (or H. ergaster)
H. habilis
Australopithecus robustus
A. boisei
A. aethiopicus

**Recent humans**

Both *H. neanderthalensis* and *H. sapiens* may have lived in some of the same areas at the same time. Both species had the largest brains of any hominids and made advanced tools and clothing. *H. sapiens* seems to have been the first to make art. Of all known hominids, only *H. sapiens* still exists.

**Robust (large-bodied) australopithecines**

These species had massive teeth and jaw muscles that indicate a diet of coarse plant material. They had a unique skull structure and relatively small brains. Most of these species lived in woodlands and grasslands. Some scientists classify this group as the genus *Paranthropus*.

**Early humans**

These species were similar to the slender australopithecines but had larger and more complex brains, rounder skulls, smaller jaws and teeth, and less protruding brows. They showed advanced tool-making abilities, had shorter arms than australopithecines did, and walked mostly upright. They probably were scavengers that ate a variety of foods.

3　　　　　2　　　　　1　　　　　0

**Estimated dates (millions of years ago)**

## Homo sapiens and Homo neanderthalensis

Neanderthals, a distinctive type of human, lived in Europe and Asia from about 230,000 to 30,000 years ago. They had heavy bones, thick brows, protruding jaws, and brains of about the same size as the brains of modern humans. They lived in caves and made stone scraper tools. The reason for their extinction is an ongoing scientific question. This species had once been classified as a subspecies of *Homo sapiens* but is now mainly classified as *H. neanderthalensis.* Neanderthals may have interacted with *H. sapiens* in some places.

The first humans classified as *H. sapiens* appeared in Africa about 160,000 years ago. The first discovery of *H. sapiens* fossils was in Cro-Magnon cave in France, so some members of *H. sapiens* are referred to as *Cro-Magnons* (KROH-man-YAWNS). Other fossils are known from several continents. The earliest members of *H. sapiens* differed only slightly from modern humans. Their average brain and body size were about the same as modern human's.

As hominid fossils are discovered and studied, scientists revise the classification of some hominid species and debate hypotheses about the possible evolutionary relationship between these species. The ancestry of *H. sapiens* is one such topic of debate.

## Modern Humans

How did modern humans come to occupy the entire globe? In one hypothesis, local populations of *H. erectus* gave rise to local populations of *H. sapiens* all over the world. According to this *multiregional hypothesis,* interbreeding among populations was sufficient to keep all of humanity as a single species. In contrast, the *recent-African-origin hypothesis* suggests that *H. sapiens* evolved from *H. erectus* uniquely in Africa about 100,000 to 200,000 years ago, then migrated out of Africa, and populated the globe. An analysis of mitochondrial DNA from people around the world suggests that humans did arise in Africa. It is possible that humans migrated out of Africa more than once. Also, interbreeding among populations around the world would have been possible during and after these migrations.

## SECTION 4 REVIEW

1. Identify which characteristics humans share with primates and which are unique to humans.

2. What kind of evidence shows that chimpanzees are the closest living relatives of humans?

3. Identify several traits that differ among the variety of hominids known from fossils.

4. Describe how members of *Homo habilis* differ from australopithecines.

5. Contrast the multiregional hypothesis and the recent-African-origin hypothesis.

**CRITICAL THINKING**

6. **Analyzing Processes** Propose an explanation of the adaptive value of bipedalism in hominids.

7. **Analyzing Models** Using Figure 43-20, name the hominids that would have coexisted 2 million, 1 million, and 50,000 years ago.

8. **Calculating Information** From the information about hominid brain size and fossil ages in this section, construct a graph of how hominid brain sizes changed with time.

# CHAPTER HIGHLIGHTS

## SECTION 1 — Origin and Evolution of Mammals

- Six key characteristics of mammals are endothermy, a fully divided heart, hair, milk production by females, a single jawbone, and a diversity of complex teeth.

- Mammals belong to an ancient group of animals called *synapsids*. Synapsids have a skull with one opening in a bone behind the eye socket.

- Mammals are probably descended from a subgroup of early synapsids called *therapsids*. Therapsids had legs that were positioned beneath their body and had complex teeth.

- Small mammals first appeared in the Triassic period. Mammals underwent adaptive radiation after the Cretaceous mass extinction of dinosaurs.

### Vocabulary

endothermy (p. 861)
mammary gland (p. 861)
synapsid (p. 862)
therapsid (p. 862)
monotreme (p. 863)
oviparous (p. 863)
marsupial (p. 863)
viviparous (p. 863)
placental mammal (p. 863)
placenta (p. 863)

## SECTION 2 — Characteristics of Mammals

- Mammals are endothermic. Endothermy enables mammals to occupy a range of habitats and sustain strenuous activity. Endothermy requires large amounts of food and oxygen.

- Mammals have a heart with two atria and two ventricles and have large lungs with a large internal surface area.

- Mammals, unlike most vertebrates, chew their food. Mammal teeth include incisors, canines, premolars, and molars.

- Some mammals digest cellulose with the aid of microorganisms. These mammals have either a rumen or a cecum that contains the symbiotic microorganisms.

- Monotremes lay eggs. Marsupials give birth to young that continue development in the mother's pouch. Placental mammals typically develop young within the uterus for longer periods than marsupials do before giving birth.

### Vocabulary

diaphragm (p. 865)
incisor (p. 865)
canine (p. 865)
premolar (p. 865)
molar (p. 865)
baleen (p. 865)
rumen (p. 866)
cecum (p. 866)
echolocation (p. 866)

## SECTION 3 — Diversity of Mammals

- There are at least 26 living orders of mammals. The most ancient orders are Monotremata and seven orders of marsupials. The remaining orders are placental mammals.

- The major placental mammal orders are Xenarthra, Lagomorpha, Rodentia, Primates, Chiroptera, Insectivora, Carnivora, Artiodactyla, Cetacea, Perissodactyla, Sirenia, and Proboscidea.

### Vocabulary

pinniped (p. 872)
ungulate (p. 872)

## SECTION 4 — Primates and Human Origins

- Most primates share several characteristics, including generalized teeth; dental formula; three-dimensional vision; large brains; and grasping hands, feet, and tails.

- Of all living primates, only humans are bipedal. Bipedalism is the defining characteristic of hominids.

- Paleontologists have found many hominid fossils, including a variety of now-extinct australopithecines and humans.

- The multiregional and recent-African-origin hypotheses seek to explain how humans came to occupy the entire globe.

### Vocabulary

prehensile appendage (p. 875)
anthropoid primate (p. 876)
opposable thumb (p.876)
great ape (p. 876)
bipedalism (p. 876)
hominid (p. 877)
australopithecine (p. 877)
human (p. 879)

## USING VOCABULARY

1. For each pair of terms, explain how the meanings of the terms differ.
   a. *viviparous* and *oviparous*
   b. *septum* and *diaphragm*
   c. *canine* and *molar*
   d. *rumen* and *cecum*
   e. *placenta* and *charion*
   f. *anthropoid primate* and *hominid*

2. Use the following terms in the same sentence: *mammals, synapsids, therapsids,* and *endothermy.*

3. **Word Roots and Origins** The word *incisor* is derived from the Latin *incidere,* which means "to cut into." Using this information, explain why the term *incisor* is a good name for the type of tooth that the term describes.

## UNDERSTANDING KEY CONCEPTS

4. **Identify** six key characteristics of mammals.

5. **Relate** the characteristics of therapsids and synapsids to those of mammals.

6. **Relate** the evolution of mammals to the mass extinction of Cretaceous reptiles.

7. **Compare** the costs and benefits of endothermy for mammals.

8. **Explain** how the structure of the mammalian heart supports endothermy.

9. **Describe** the important adaptations of the teeth of mammals.

10. **Compare** the teeth of rodents to those of lagomorphs.

11. **Describe** two mammalian adaptations for digesting plants.

12. **Identify** the part of the brain that is relatively larger in mammals than in other animal groups.

13. **Describe** the distinguishing characteristic of placental mammals.

14. **Give** an example of an animal from each of the 12 orders of placental mammals.

15. **Compare** the characteristics of artiodactyls and perissodactyls.

16. **Compare** sirenians, pinnipeds, and cetaceans.

17. **Describe** the distinguishing characteristics of primates.

18. **Compare** fossil australopithecines with fossil humans.

19. **CONCEPT MAPPING** Use the following terms to create a concept map that compares the process of reproduction in different animal groups: *reptiles, monotremes, marsupials, placental mammals, oviparous, viviparous,* and *placenta.*

## CRITICAL THINKING

20. **Relating Structure and Function** Mammalian species that live in very cold environments are usually larger than species of the same genus that live in warmer climates. Propose an explanation for this. (Hint: Consider the effect that increasing size has on volume and surface area.)

21. **Analyzing Processes** Some kinds of mice give birth about 21 days after mating. Why might this characteristic make mice ideal laboratory animals for experiments dealing with mammalian development and heredity?

22. **Forming Hypotheses** Sloths are arboreal xenarthrans that spend most of their lives hanging upside down from tree branches as they feed in tropical forests. Most sloths have green algae growing in tiny pits in their hair. What advantage might each species gain from this relationship?

23. **Applying Concepts** In recent years, surgeons have tried transplanting baboon and pig hearts into humans. Explain why surgeons tried these hearts rather than a large turtle's heart.

24. **Analyzing Results** In a famous study conducted 200 years ago, the Italian scientist Lazzaro Spallanzani showed that a blinded bat could still fly and capture insects. However, a bat whose ears had been plugged with wax could neither fly nor hunt. Explain these results.

25. **Interpreting Graphics** Study the two skulls below. Which is more like a mammal skull? Justify your answer.

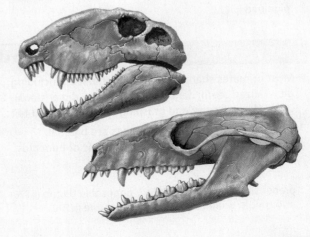

# Standardized Test Preparation

**DIRECTIONS:** Choose the letter of the answer choice that best answers the question.

1. Which of the following structures is found in all modern mammals and birds?
   A. hair
   B. skull with teeth
   C. lungs with air sacs
   D. heart with four chambers

2. What is the function of a mammalian diaphragm?
   F. enables efficient breathing
   G. provides nourishment for young
   H. carries the young inside the uterus
   J. keeps oxygenated blood separate in heart

3. Which of these animals is a marsupial?
   A. lion
   B. echidna
   C. opossum
   D. duckbill platypus

4. Which of these animals is a monotreme?
   F. zebra
   G. opossum
   H. kangaroo
   J. duckbill platypus

5. Which of the following structures is found in cats but not in opossums?
   A. hair
   B. uterus
   C. placenta
   D. mammary gland

**INTERPRETING GRAPHICS:** The illustration below shows the skulls of two different mammals. Use the illustration to answer the question that follows.

A                                    B

6. What can be inferred about these mammals?
   F. Mammal A has more fat than mammal B.
   G. Mammal A has more hair than mammal B.
   H. Mammal A eats more meat than mammal B.
   J. Mammal A eats more grass than mammal B.

**DIRECTIONS:** Complete the following analogy.

7. hair : insulation :: milk :
   A. armor
   B. circulation
   C. endothermy
   D. nourishment

**INTERPRETING GRAPHICS:** The illustration below shows the skulls of two different mammals. Use the illustration to answer the question that follows.

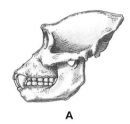

A                                    B

8. Which of the following accurately describes the differences between these skulls?
   F. Skull A has more teeth than skull B does.
   G. Skull A has more brain capacity than skull B does.
   H. Skull A is the skull of a primate, and skull B is not the skull of a primate.
   J. Skull A is the skull of an ape, and skull B is the skull of a human.

## SHORT RESPONSE

Mammals and birds are endothermic vertebrates.

Describe the functional costs and benefits of endothermy.

## EXTENDED RESPONSE

Scientists classify amniotes from 300 million years ago into two major groups: the diapsids and the synapsids. A unique subset of synapsids from 245 million years ago is made up of therapsids. Modern mammals are grouped into the monotremes, the marsupials, and the placental mammals.

*Part A* Describe modern scientific hypotheses about the evolutionary relationships among these groups of amniotes.

*Part B* Describe the kinds of evidence that scientists examine to test these hypotheses.

**Test TIP** For questions requiring an extended response, make an outline listing the key points of your response before you begin writing.

# Examining Mammalian Characteristics

## OBJECTIVES

- Observe examples of mammals.
- Examine the distinguishing characteristics of mammals.

## PROCESS SKILLS

- observing
- inferring

## MATERIALS

- hand lens or stereomicroscope
- microscope slide of mammalian skin
- compound light microscope
- mirror
- selection of vertebrate skulls (some mammalian, some nonmammalian)
- field guide to mammals

## Background

1. List the distinguishing characteristics of mammals.
2. Define the term *endothermy*.
3. Mammalian skin is characterized by cutaneous glands, such as sebaceous glands and sweat glands, that develop as ingrowths from the epidermis into the dermis.

## PART A Mammalian Hair and Skin

1. Use a hand lens to examine several areas of your skin that appear to be hairless. Record your observations in your lab report.
2. Compare the amount of hair on humans with the amount on other mammals that you have seen or read about. What role does hair or fur play in endothermy? What other roles does hair (or whiskers) play in mammals?
3. Examine a slide of mammalian skin under low power. Notice the glands in the skin.
4. Identify the sebaceous glands and the sweat glands in the skin. Sweat glands are found only in mammals, but some mammals do not have them or have few of them. What mechanism for cooling might these other animals have? Which other glands are unique to mammals?

## PART B Mammalian Reproduction

5. Look at the photographs of mammals on this page. Which characteristics do these animals share?
6. Name the two orders of mammals represented in the photographs on this page.

### PART C  Mammalian Mouth and Teeth

7. Use a mirror to look in your mouth, and identify the four kinds of mammalian teeth. Count how many of each you have on one side of your lower jaw.

8. Look at the skulls of several mammals. Identify the four kinds of teeth in each skull, and count them as you counted your own. How are the four types of teeth different from yours?

9. Look at the skulls of several nonmammalian vertebrates. Describe the teeth in each one, and compare them with mammalian teeth.

10. Breathe through your nose with your mouth closed. Do you feel a flow of air into your mouth? You have a hard palate (the roof of your mouth) that separates your mouth from your nose.

11. Look again at the different skulls. In which vertebrates do you see a hard palate? What is an advantage of having a hard palate?

12. Compare the jaws of the mammalian skulls with those of the nonmammalian skulls. Notice how the upper jawbone and the lower jawbone connect in each skull. Is there a similarity in the mammalian jaws that distinguishes them from the nonmammalian jaws? Explain.

13. Create a data table, similar to the model below, to record your observations for your lab report. For example, the table below is designed to record observations of differences that you will find among the animal skulls. Remember to allow plenty of space to record your observations.

### PART D  Vertebrate Diversity

14. Use a field guide to find out more about the following mammalian orders: Cetacea, Xenarthra, Pholidota, and Chiroptera. Answer the following questions about these mammals in your lab report:
   a. Cetaceans, such as whales and dolphins, are marine mammals. Cetaceans are hairless except for a few bristles. Why are cetaceans classified as mammals?
   b. Some mammals—including some members of Xenarthra (anteaters and armadillos) and Pholidota (pangolins)—lack teeth. Which characteristics do these animals share with other mammals?
   c. Like many birds, chiropterans (bats) have wings, fly, and are endotherms. Which characteristics distinguish these mammals from birds?

### Analysis and Conclusions

1. List the characteristics that distinguish mammals from other vertebrates.

2. List several characteristics you observed that most mammals share.

3. Birds are also endotherms. Which structure in birds serves the same function as hair in mammals? Explain.

4. Compare the data you collected on the teeth from different animal skulls with the diet of each of those animals. How does the type of teeth that it has help with the particular diet that each animal has?

### Further Inquiry

Find out how mammalian brains are different from the brains of other vertebrates. What adaptive advantage might these differences provide mammals?

| OBSERVATIONS OF ANIMAL SKULLS | | | | | | | |
|---|---|---|---|---|---|---|---|
| Animal | Mammal? | Number of incisors | Number of canines | Number of premolars | Number of molars | Hard palate? | Jaw |
| | | | | | | | |
| | | | | | | | |
| | | | | | | | |

# CHAPTER 44 ANIMAL BEHAVIOR

Ducklings learn to follow their mother soon after hatching, an instinctive behavior called imprinting.

**SECTION 1** *Development of Behavior*

**SECTION 2** *Types of Animal Behavior*

**Unit 7—Ecosystem Dynamics**
Topic 2

For project ideas from *Scientific American*, visit go.hrw.com and type in the keyword **HM6SAM**.

# DEVELOPMENT OF BEHAVIOR

*A snake plays dead. A mouse presses a lever. A chimpanzee gathers termites on a stick. This section discusses how these and other behaviors are developed.*

## SECTION 1

### OBJECTIVES

- **Identify** four questions asked by biologists who study behavior.
- **Describe** an example of an innate behavior.
- **Compare** four types of learned behavior.
- **Explain** how learning and genes can interact to affect behavior.

### VOCABULARY

ethologist
behavior
innate behavior
fixed action pattern
learning
habituation
operant conditioning
classical conditioning
reasoning
imprinting
sensitive period

## THE STUDY OF BEHAVIOR

Leaf-cutter ants cut sections of leaves with their sharp mouthparts and head back to the nest with their load of leaf bits. In the nest, other individuals tend and harvest the fungi that grow on the leaves as food for the colony. **Ethologists** (ee-THAHL-uh-JISTS), biologists who study behavior, seek to learn about such varied behaviors. **Behavior** is an action or series of actions performed by an organism, usually in response to a stimulus. In order to learn about behavior, ethologists ask questions about how and why a behavior occurs. For example, how do ants find their way to food and back to the colony? Why do ants share leaves with other colony members?

When considering an animal's behavior, ethologists ask four main questions: (1) What causes the behavior? What are the mechanisms that respond to stimuli? (2) What is the role of genes in the behavior; and how does it develop during an individual's lifetime? (3) What is the behavior's evolutionary history? (4) How does the behavior affect the organism's survival and reproduction?

### Genes and Behavior

When studying behavior, ethologists often ask how much of an animal's behavior is determined by genetics and how much of the behavior is based on the unique developmental environment of the animal? Ethologists have studied bees to learn more about the role of genes in behavior. Some adult bees can detect which young in the hive have bacterial infections. These adult "hygienic" bees pull the diseased young from their cells and throw them out of the nest, as in Figure 44-1. In contrast, "nonhygienic" adult bees ignore diseased young.

American and Australian biologists mated hygienic queen bees to nonhygienic males and studied the inheritance pattern of this trait. They found that certain genes with set inheritance patterns control young-removal behaviors. This study showed that genes can underlie animal behavior. The triggers for the behavior, however, come from the environment. In this case, diseased young present in the hive trigger the removal behavior.

**FIGURE 44-1**

"Hygienic" bees carry diseased or dead young from the hive. Studies have shown that this behavior is highly heritable.

**FIGURE 44-2**

A male lion who has taken over a pride will often kill cubs fathered by rival males.

## Natural Selection and Behavior

Ethologists have hypothesized that animals usually behave in ways that promote their survival and offspring production. Because genes control some behaviors, natural selection can affect genetic variation that involves behavioral genes. Lions present a good example of this principle. The males living in a particular pride (family group) father all of the cubs. Eventually new males come along and force out the previous males. After the new males take over, they often kill cubs fathered by the previous males, as shown in Figure 44-2.

Observing this, ethologists wondered how natural selection could favor killing young of the same species? Further observation revealed that females will not breed with males as long as those females are caring for young. If the infants die, however, the female will mate again. By killing the existing offspring, the new male is likely to produce more offspring than males who do not kill cubs. Ethologists hypothesize that natural selection has favored genes that cause male lions to kill cubs that are not their offspring. It is important to remember that this behavior is instinctive. It is neither conscious nor deliberately aimed at other males or their offspring.

# INNATE BEHAVIOR

**Innate behaviors,** more commonly called instincts, are inherited actions that are performed effectively the first time without being taught. An orb spider, for example, builds her web the same way every time. There is very little variation in what she does, and all her female offspring will build their webs in a similar manner without being taught.

## Fixed Action Pattern

A **fixed action pattern** is a rigid innate behavior that all members of a species perform the same way each time they perform it. Figure 44-3 shows an Eastern hognose snake displaying a fixed action pattern in response to a predator. The snake spreads its jaws, hisses, and rolls on its back when threatened. Individuals that perform this behavior are less likely to get eaten and more likely to reproduce than individuals that do not perform this behavior.

Fixed action patterns continue from start to finish without modification once an environmental stimulus triggers them. However, there are still factors that influence whether an animal will perform this behavior or not. For example, Greylag geese retrieve eggs that have rolled out of the nest the same way every time. They will also retrieve other objects that are similar in shape or size to an egg. However, only mother geese retrieve eggs that have rolled out of the nest, and they only perform this behavior between the time of egg laying and hatching.

**FIGURE 44-3**

This Eastern hognose snake *(Heterodon platyrhinos)* is "playing dead." The snake spreads its jaw, hisses, and rolls on its back.

# LEARNED BEHAVIOR

Some aspects of behavior are influenced by genes, but to what degree can behaviors be modified by experience? Learned behaviors are actions that change with experience. **Learning** is the modification of a behavior based on experience. Learning can influence the expression of behaviors that are innate and also behaviors that are not innate. The study of learned behavior is central to much of ethology, and learning types can vary from simple to complex.

## Habituation

The simplest type of learning, **habituation** (huh-bi-choo-AY-shuhn), occurs when an animal learns to ignore a frequent, harmless stimulus. For example, when an object passes overhead, a young gull chick tries to hide. As the chick grows older, and as parents, other common birds, or falling leaves pass over the chick's head without consequence, the youngster learns not to react. When a predatory bird flies over, however, the gull stops feeding to hide. Because the passing of a predator's shape is rare, the chicks never habituate to it. Habituation in gulls saves energy and allows feeding, yet preserves defenses for the rare emergency.

## Operant Conditioning

A more complex type of learning occurs by trial and error. A dog, for example, learns to associate a cat's hiss and arched back with a painful scratch on the nose. When trial-and-error learning occurs under highly controlled conditions, it is called **operant** (AH-puhr-uhnt) **conditioning.** An animal associates some action or operation (the "operant") with a punishment or reward.

American psychologist B. F. Skinner investigated operant conditioning by placing a rat in a box with a lever, such as the one shown in Figure 44-4. As the rat explored the box, the rat eventually pressed the lever, which delivered a food pellet. After several accidental pressings, the rat learned to press the lever deliberately for food. Skinner thought that nearly any behavior could be "conditioned," or trained.

Further research by others, however, showed that although rats can easily learn to press a lever to receive food, they have trouble learning to press a lever to avoid electric shocks to their feet. Rats can learn quite quickly to avoid such foot shocks by jumping. Yet, it's much harder for them to learn to jump to get a food reward. These seeming contradictions do make sense: Rats in nature get food by manipulating objects with their hands, not their feet. Like all animals, rats most easily learn those things that are related to natural skills for survival and reproduction.

## Quick Lab

### Recognizing Learned Behavior

**Materials** small wads of paper towel (one moist; one dry), T maze made of five pieces of cardboard taped in a T shape inside a cardboard box, sow bug, blunt probe

**Procedure**

1. Place the moist paper in the left side of the T. Place the dry paper wad on the right side.

2. Place the sow bug at the bottom of the T. If it does not start to crawl, gently prod it with a blunt probe. Observe what the sow bug does when it reaches the T section.

3. Retrieve the sow bug. Perform as many trials as time allows. Record the results of each trial.

**Analysis** Summarize the sow bug's behavior. Determine if the sow bug modified its behavior through learning. Use evidence to support your answer.

**FIGURE 44-4**

A rat placed in the "Skinner box" shown here will learn to press a lever to obtain food. This behavior is an example of operant conditioning.

## Classical Conditioning

Famed Russian biologist Ivan Pavlov studied another complex type of learning and published his results in 1903. Pavlov observed that dogs salivate at the sight and smell of meat. Was this response learned? To find out, he presented meat to a group of dogs. At the same time that the dogs received the meat, Pavlov would ring a bell. The dogs learned to associate the bell with a meat reward and eventually would salivate in response to the bell tone.

This kind of learning is called **classical conditioning.** The animal learns to associate a response with a predictive stimulus. The animal responds (salivation) after the natural stimulus (the meat) and learns to associate the natural stimulus with the predictive stimulus (the bell). This type of conditioning differs from operant conditioning in which the animal learns to respond (pushing the lever) *before* the reward appears (the food pellet).

Classical conditioning occurs in nature as well as in artificial conditions. For example, a crow learns to associate the sight of shiny, broken eggshells on the beach with the presence of newly hatched gull chicks and swoops down for a tasty meal. Advertising agencies capitalize on classical conditioning in humans by associating their product with positive imagery. They associate a certain car brand with financial success, or a certain cola with healthy good looks, all to trigger the desired response: purchase of their product.

## Problem-Solving and Reasoning

A more complex type of learning is called *problem-solving learning.* Figure 44-5 shows an example of problem solving in which a chimpanzee uses a tool to get termites out of a nest. This behavior may be learned from watching a parent, may be a result of trial-and-error, or a combination of several learning mechanisms.

One type of problem-solving, **reasoning,** involves the ability to solve a problem not previously encountered by the individual in a way that is not dictated by instinct. For example, if a chimpanzee enters a room with boxes scattered on the floor and sees a bunch of bananas tied to the ceiling, the animal will arrange the boxes to form a platform in order to retrieve the bananas.

In another example, researchers placed a jar containing a fish in a tank with an octopus. The octopus used its arms to unscrew the lid, removed the fish, and then discarded the jar and lid. This type of behavior cannot be considered instinctive, because boxes and jars are not in the evolutionary history of these species. The behavior occurred without trial-and-error, as if the animal used reasoning to develop an insight into how to solve the problem.

**FIGURE 44-5**

A chimpanzee will look for a stick and use it as a tool to retrieve termites from the nest for food.

# GENES, LEARNING, AND BEHAVIOR

Biologists have learned from studying bees and other organisms that genes can influence behavior. Some scientists have argued that most behaviors are genetically programmed because different individuals in the same species act in the same ways. Other scientists assert that behaviors are shaped by an animal's experiences. Most ethologists today have come to agree that animal behavior, especially complex behavior such as that seen in primates, is affected both by genes and by experience.

## Imprinting

One class of behavior that is determined by both genes and learning is called imprinting. **Imprinting** is a form of learning in which a young animal forms permanent associations with its environment. The most common imprinting occurs when new-born animals learn to identify a mother figure. Nobel Prize-winning ethologist Konrad Lorenz studied how geese come to identify their mothers and follow them to ponds to feed. Lorenz found that goslings follow the first large object they see moving away from the nest. The goslings would follow wagons, boxes, balloons, and even Lorenz himself, as seen in Figure 44-6.

Another example is found in sea turtles. Sea turtles imprint on characteristics of the beach where they hatch. Years later they are able to find their way back to the same beach to breed.

Imprinting occurs during a specific phase in an animal's development, called a **sensitive period.** During this time, certain types of learning take place that are later very difficult to change. For example, it is much easier for young children to learn multiple languages. This is much more difficult later in life. Scientists hypothesize that this change in the ability to learn as young animals mature is related to genes that control processes of development.

**FIGURE 44-6**

These young geese are following Nobel Prize winner Konrad Lorenz. Lorenz cared for the goslings the first day or so after they hatched, and the goslings imprinted on him.

---

## SECTION 1 REVIEW

1. What are four questions that an ethologist might ask when studying behavior?

2. How is it possible for natural selection to affect an innate behavior?

3. Describe four types of learned behavior.

4. Explain the difference between the learning styles involved with Skinner's box and Pavlov's dogs.

5. Why is imprinting an example of interaction between learned and innate behavior?

**CRITICAL THINKING**

6. **Applying Information** If you trained bears for a stage show, which principles of behavior would you use?

7. **Forming Reasoned Opinions** A 6'10" man has a 5-year-old son. When the son goes through a doorway, he lowers his head as the father does. Do you think this behavior is likely to be learned or innate? Why?

8. **Justifying Conclusions** What do you think is the adaptive value of imprinting? Explain.

# Science in Action

## Does Sonar Cause Whale Strandings?

Every year, thousands of whales and dolphins strand themselves on beaches and often die. Scientists think that the whales may strand themselves individually or in groups for a variety of reasons. In recent years, beaked whales, which are not usually known for this behavior, have been beaching themselves with alarming frequency. Are human actions related to this increase?

**Kenneth Balcomb**

### HYPOTHESIS: Sonar Causes Whale Beachings

The ocean is filled with sounds generated during human activities: shipping, fishing, oil drilling, oceanography research, and military operations. The U.S. Navy, for instance, uses a sonar system to detect submarine movements. The blasts of low frequency sound used by the military are so loud they can travel hundreds of miles at decibel levels equivalent to the sound of jet engines.

In March of 2000, 16 whales beached themselves on the Bahamas within 24 hours of a Naval sonar test. Six died. Kenneth Balcomb heads the Bahamas Marine Mammal Survey research station. Balcomb was aware of several past incidents in which mass strandings occurred around the time of naval maneuvers. It was unknown whether these events were connected. The closeness and timing of the Naval testing in the Bahamas seemed to suggest a sound-related stranding. Balcomb and co-researchers hypothesized that the loud sonar damaged the whales' hearing and in some way led to the beachings.

### METHODS: Autopsy Whales and Analyze Tissue

Balcomb quickly removed the heads of two dead whales, froze the 200-pound specimens, and had them flown to the Woods Hole Oceanographic Institute in Massachusetts. There, he and others performed CT scans and microanalysis of inner ear and brain tissues.

*Scientists are currently studying why whales are beaching themselves at increasing rates. Members of the Marine Animal Rescue Society are performing an autopsy on this beached whale.*

### RESULTS: Tissues Show Signs of Damage

The whales that were examined all showed similar lesions, including internal bleeding, known as hemorrhaging, in the acoustic regions of the cranium and mandible and in tissues next to airspaces around the ear bones. One specimen that was examined by ultra high-resolution computerized tomography showed a brain hemorrhage. In addition, dissection of this same specimen showed lung hemorrhage and laryngeal hemorrhage.

### CONCLUSION: Evidence Supports Sonar-Induced Tissue Damage and Death

Based on the results of specimen examination, the National Marine Fisheries Service and the Navy came to the same conclusion: the injuries were all consistent with an intense acoustic or pressure event.

In September of 2002, 14 more whales stranded themselves in the Canary Islands following military maneuvers by NATO using sonar. Paul Jepson of the Zoological Society of London and colleagues found that the whales suffered tissue and organ damage similar to that found in the whales beached in the Bahamas.

In June 2003, a federal judge-magistrate in San Francisco ruled that the Navy must limit its plans for low-frequency sonar exercises. The Navy is currently working to establish those limits.

### REVIEW

1. What evidence supports Balcomb's hypothesis?

2. Evaluate the conclusion reached by Balcomb. Is it a valid conclusion? Explain your reasoning.

3. **Critical Thinking** Are there situations in which the use of sonar by the military is justified? Explain.

internet connect

www.scilinks.org
**Topic: Communication in the Animal Kingdom**
**Keyword: HM60320**

SCiLINKS. Maintained by the National Science Teachers Association

# TYPES OF ANIMAL BEHAVIOR

*Animals all need to obtain food, find places to live, protect themselves, attract mates, reproduce, and care for young. This section discusses types of behaviors that help animals accomplish these actions.*

## FEEDING BEHAVIOR

Most animals spend the majority of their waking hours searching for, catching, or eating their food. How do they balance the energy they expend versus the energy they gain? One possible explanation is described by the **optimality hypothesis,** the idea that animals tend to behave in a way that maximizes food gathering while minimizing effort and exposure to predators.

For example, researchers have watched crows choose a large whelk (a snail-like mollusk) fly with it to a height of about 5 m (16 ft), and then drop it onto a rock. If the shell breaks, the crow eats the whelk. If the shell fails to break, the crow picks it up and drops it again. The optimality hypothesis would predict that dropping a whelk a second time is more likely to provide a meal than is searching for another large whelk. Experiments confirm that crow behavior optimizes nutrition versus effort expended.

## COMPETITIVE BEHAVIOR

Each species needs a place to live that provides shelter from bad weather, adequate food and water, and access to mates. Because such resources are limited, competition is often the result. Competition between animals of the same species can be seen in several types of behavior.

### Aggressive Behavior

Physical conflict or threatening behavior between animals is called **aggressive behavior.** This type of behavior includes displays and contests of strength that determine which individual is larger or stronger. The male impalas in Figure 44-7 display aggressive behavior when competing for mates. Most often, these contests result in one animal "surrendering" to the other. Usually, the larger or healthier male wins, and both leave unhurt.

### OBJECTIVES

- **Discuss** the optimality hypothesis and feeding behavior.
- **List** three types of competitive behavior.
- **Describe** three different types of reproductive behavior.
- **Name** five kinds of communication.
- **Identify** costs and benefits of social behavior.
- **Describe** four types of cyclic behavior.

### VOCABULARY

optimality hypothesis
aggressive behavior
territory
dominance hierarchy
courtship
communication
aposematic coloration
mimicry
pheromone
social behavior
circadian rhythm
hibernation
migration

**FIGURE 44-7**

Male impalas defend their territories against intrusion by other males.

## Territorial Behavior

One way to ensure that an animal is able to obtain sufficient resources for itself, its mate, and its offspring is for the animal to select and establish a territory. A **territory** is an area that an animal or a group of animals occupies and defends from other members of the same species. An animal establishes a territory in many ways, including marking the boundaries with urine or visual cues, and claiming an area with vocal signals. Territorial animals will threaten or attack intruders.

The male bowerbird shown in Figure 44-8 has established a small territory which includes his nest and the area around it. He has marked the territory by building and decorating a bower and will defend it from other males. Animals may be territorial under certain circumstances. For example, the bowerbird only builds and defends his territory during breeding season. Natural selection can reinforce territorial behavior. When animals space themselves out, they do not compete for the same resources. This behavior increases the likelihood that the young of territorial animals will survive and inherit traits that promote territoriality.

## Dominance Hierarchies

Competition can lead to a clear ranking of individuals within the group, from most dominant to most subordinate. This type of ranking, called a **dominance hierarchy** (HIE-rahr-kee), reduces the need for competition and aggressive behavior as subordinates learn to submit to avoid conflict. One example of a dominance hierarchy is that formed by chickens. The dominant chicken can peck all other chickens. The most subordinate chicken gets pecked by all other chickens in the group. It is from this behavior in chickens that the term "pecking order" is derived.

**FIGURE 44-8**

Male bowerbirds *(Amblyornis inornatus)* build elaborate nests of various shapes and with different decorations. Females choose a mate based on his bower-building abilities.

# REPRODUCTIVE BEHAVIOR

Elaborate behaviors have evolved around the process of reproduction in many animals. These behaviors often differ between males and females. Differences generally center around attracting or competing for a mate. Reproductive behaviors may help animals recognize members of the same species, or members of the opposite sex. They may also be indicators of good health.

## Sexual Selection

Animals generally choose mates based on certain traits or behaviors. This tendency creates a process called *sexual selection*. Traits or behaviors that increase an individual's ability to acquire a mate will appear with increased frequency in a population. The female bowerbird in Figure 44-8 chose this male based on his ability to build and decorate an attractive bower. His offspring will probably build bowers in a similar way.

Another means of attracting a mate involves certain behaviors, called **courtship.** In some species, courtship can include a complex series of behaviors called *rituals.* Courtship rituals are instinctive behaviors that are performed the same way by all members of a population and that may help animals identify receptive mates of the same species. Most courtship rituals consist of specific signals and responses that indicate willingness to mate.

## Mating Systems

Mating systems increase the likelihood that young will survive. Male polygamy (more than one female), monogamy, and female polygamy (more than one male) are reproductive strategies that are determined primarily by the amount and type of parental care required by the young. Monogamy is favored in situations in which there are advantages to both parents raising the young. In birds, for example, it would be difficult for one parent to protect the nest and the hatchlings while also providing enough food for the young. This type of situation may explain why birds tend to be monogamous.

## Parental Behavior

Parental investment is the time and energy an individual must spend to produce and nurture offspring. The benefit of parental care is that it increases the likelihood that young will survive to adulthood. The costs are that parental care can generally only be provided for a small number of young because of the large energy investment by the parent. Usually, females invest more in parental care than males do. In mammals like the whales in Figure 44-9, the female carries the young within her body during development, and after birth the young must nurse. In some species, the male provides the majority of parental investment. Male seahorses, for example, carry the eggs until they hatch.

**Word Roots and Origins**

*monogamy*

from the Greek *mono,* meaning "one," and *gamus,* meaning "marriage"

**FIGURE 44-9**

Whales provide extensive parental care for their young. Baby mammals are often born rather helpless and learn about their environments from parents.

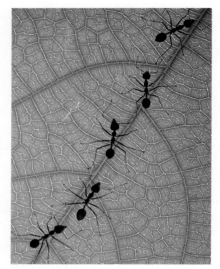

**FIGURE 44-10**

Ants use chemical communication in the form of a pheromone trail, which other ants will follow. The ants above are following a trail on a leaf.

**FIGURE 44-11**

The blurred image in the center of the hive is a bee vigorously performing a waggle dance. Her sisters are receiving information about the direction and distance of a food source in part by touch communication.

# COMMUNICATION

Ant pheromones, bird songs, whale song; these behaviors are all examples of **communication,** signals produced by one animal that result in some type of response in another. There are many ways animals can communicate, including sight, sound, chemicals, touch, and possibly even language.

## Sight and Sound

Species living in open environments often use visual signals to provide rapid communication. Behavioral displays communicate within and between species. Bright colors often serve as a warning that an animal is poisonous. This is called **aposematic** (A-poh-suh-MA-tic) **coloration.** After several encounters, predators learn to associate this color or pattern with a bad experience. Some animals gain protection by looking like a dangerous animal. This strategy is called **mimicry.**

Nocturnal animals, and animals in habitats with restricted visibility, often use sound to communicate. Bullfrogs and crickets, for example, use sound to attract a mate. Elephants communicate at a frequency that is too low for humans to hear.

## Chemicals

Chemical communication can convey information over greater distance and time than can communication by sight or sound. Some animals release chemicals called **pheromones** (FER-uh-mohns) that cause individuals of the same species to react in a predictable way. For example, ants leave a pheromone trail that other individuals can follow, as shown in Figure 44-10. Female moths release a pheromone that attracts a male of her species from miles away.

## Touch

Species that inhabit dark hives or dens often communicate by touch in addition to using sound or chemicals. Honeybees use a display that includes sight, touch, and sound, shown in Figure 44-11, to communicate the direction and distance to a food source.

## Language

Most scientists have regarded language as a uniquely human behavior. In order for communication to be considered language, there are certain criteria that must be met. Among these are *phonemes* (sounds that can be combined to form words), *productivity* (many combinations of phonemes to produce different meanings), and *grammar* (rules for combining words that affect the meaning). Most animal communication lacks at least one of the characteristics of true language. Although animals do not use language systems for communication in the wild, it is possible that they can learn to use them. Research on language is being done with gorillas, chimpanzees, bonobos, parrots, dogs, and dolphins.

# SOCIAL BEHAVIOR

**Social behavior** can be defined as any kind of interaction between two or more animals, usually of the same species. Some species, like the bonobos in Figure 44-12, spend the majority of their lives in social groups.

## Social Groups

Social groups have evolved in the animal kingdom because there are benefits to living in a group. These benefits can include protection from predators and more success in foraging. For example, fish on the outer edges of a school assume most of the danger of predation. The fish swimming on the edges shift constantly, so most individuals are not exposed to danger for a long time. Lions hunting cooperatively can bring down large prey much more efficiently than lions hunting alone.

There are also disadvantages to living in a social group. For example, there is often increased competition for food, mates, and other resources. The risk of spreading disease is also higher within a social group than it would be among a population of nonsocial animals. One species that exemplifies both the benefits and disadvantages of social groups is the blue-gill sunfish. During mating season, blue-gills nest close together. The larger number of individuals helps provide protection against predators. However, disadvantages include competition during courtship, theft of eggs by nonbreeding males, and possibly transmission of disease.

## Altruism

Occasionally, one member of a social group acts in a way that benefits other members of the group while putting the individual at a disadvantage. This type of behavior is called *altruism* (AL-troo-ism). One example of altruism can be seen in the ground squirrel found in North America. These animals live in large colonies. If one member of the colony sees a predator, it will give a high-pitched alarm call, as shown in Figure 44-13. This call warns other members of the colony to hide while putting the animal that calls at risk.

Another example of altruism occurs in animal societies in which the workers are sterile. Bees, ants, termites, and naked mole rats are all examples of animals that live in this type of society. Usually, members of a society are related to each other and share a large proportion of their genes. Therefore, helping a relative survive increases the chance that the genes an individual shares with that relative will be passed to the next generation. This type of natural selection is called *kin selection*.

**FIGURE 44-12**

Bonobos are a species of ape closely related to chimpanzees. Bonobos have a highly complex and unusually peaceful social system.

**FIGURE 44-13**

A ground squirrel gives a piercing warning call that signals the presence of a predator.

# CYCLIC BEHAVIOR

Animals display a variety of cyclic behaviors that are synchronized with changes in their environment. These behaviors generally develop as a result of temperature changes, variations in availability of food, or likelihood of predation.

## Biological Rhythms

During the day, gorillas are busy foraging but during the night, they rest. A daily biological cycle is called a **circadian** (suhr-KAY-dee-uhn) **rhythm.** Predators have evolved biological rhythms in response to the activity of their prey. For example, mice are active at night, and as a result, owls are also active at night.

Many marine animals that live along the shore have biological cycles related to the tides. Tidal cycles are also called *lunar cycles* because the tide is determined by the phases of the moon. For example, fiddler crabs on the eastern coast of the United States emerge from their burrows at every low tide (twice every 24 hours).

There are also annual biological cycles. Some animals go into a period of inactivity and lowered body temperature during the winter when food is scarce. This type of behavior is called **hibernation.** Some hibernating animals, such as ground squirrels, drop their body temperature to a few degrees above freezing and do not wake for weeks at a time.

## Migratory Behavior

**Migration** is a periodic group movement that is characteristic of a population or species. There are many types of migration. The monarch butterflies, shown in Figure 44-14, migrate hundreds of miles each year to winter in Mexico. Salmon migrate from their ocean habitat into streams to breed, then back to the ocean. Migration is exhausting and risky yet it allows animals to find habitats with plentiful seasonal foods and provides nesting sites safe from predators.

**FIGURE 44-14**

Monarch butterflies migrate hundreds of miles to spend their winters in central Mexico.

## SECTION 2 REVIEW

1. Summarize the optimality hypothesis.

2. Give an example of three types of competitive behavior seen in animals.

3. How can sexual selection affect reproductive behaviors?

4. Describe an example of four types of communication used by animals.

5. Identify advantages and disadvantages of living in a social group.

6. Describe four types of cyclic behavior.

**CRITICAL THINKING**

7. **Applying Information** Male widowbirds have very long tails. What might be some advantages and disadvantages of having long tails?

8. **Forming Hypotheses** If a species of squirrel eats only soft acorns, what would the optimality hypothesis predict about the energy required to open hard acorns?

9. **Analyzing Information** How does defending a territory benefit an animal when aggressive competition may cause physical injury?

# CHAPTER HIGHLIGHTS

SECTION 1 Development of Behavior

- Behavior is an action or series of actions performed by an animal in response to a stimulus.

- Ethologists seek to learn the cause, genetic development, evolutionary history, and reproductive advantage of a behavior.

- Innate behaviors are instinctive behaviors that do not vary despite an animal's environment or experience. A fixed action pattern (FAP) is an example of an innate behavior.

- Learned behavior is a behavior that is based on experience.

- The four types of learned behavior are habituation, operant conditioning, classical conditioning, and problem solving.

- In some cases, such as with imprinting, genes and learning can interact to affect behavior.

### Vocabulary

ethologist (p. 887)
behavior (p. 887)
innate behavior (p. 888)

fixed action pattern (p. 888)
learning (p. 889)
habituation (p. 889)

operant conditioning (p. 889)
classical conditioning (p. 890)
reasoning (p. 890)

imprinting (p. 891)
sensitive period (p. 891)

SECTION 2 Types of Animal Behavior

- According to the optimality hypothesis, animals tend to maximize food gathering while minimizing effort and exposure to predators.

- Three types of competitive behavior include aggressive behavior, territorial behavior, and formation of dominance hierarchies.

- Sexual selection happens when certain mates are chosen over others based on a certain trait or set of traits.

- Animals show variation in mating systems and parental care, based on the amount of care the young require at birth.

- Five forms of communication are visual, sound, chemical, touch, and language.

- The benefits of social behavior include predator protection and successful foraging. The costs of social behavior include increased competition and risk of spreading disease.

- Some behaviors occur in synchrony with cyclical changes in the environment. These cyclic behaviors include circadian rhythms, lunar cycles, hibernation, and migration.

### Vocabulary

optimality hypothesis (p. 893)
aggressive behavior (p. 893)
territory (p. 894)
dominance hierarchy (p. 894)

courtship (p. 895)
communication (p. 896)
aposematic coloration (p. 896)
mimicry (p. 896)

pheromone (p. 896)
social behavior (p. 897)
circadian rhythm (p. 898)
hibernation (p. 898)

migration (p. 898)

## USING VOCABULARY

1. For each pair of terms, explain how the meanings of the terms differ.
   a. *innate behavior* and *learned behavior*
   b. *classical conditioning* and *operant conditioning*
   c. *hibernation* and *migration*

2. Explain the relationship between *competitive behavior* and *dominance hierarchy*.

3. Use the following terms in the same sentence: *social behavior*, *altruism*, and *kin selection*.

4. **Word Roots and Origins** The word *ethology* comes from the Greek *etho*, which means "habit" and the suffix *ology* which means "the study of." Using this information, explain why the term *ethology* is a good name for the study of behavior.

## UNDERSTANDING KEY CONCEPTS

5. **Identify** four questions an ethologist would ask when studying a behavior.

6. **Explain** whether nest building in bowerbirds is innate or learned.

7. **Name** the behavior a mother goose is displaying when she rolls a baseball back to her nest.

8. **List** examples of each of the four types of learning.

9. **Describe** the learning experiment involving rats and Skinner's box.

10. **Describe** the experiments of Konrad Lorenz.

11. **Explain** the reason a dog tied to a tree would probably wrap the rope around the trunk while a chimpanzee would not.

12. **Identify** how genes and learning are involved in imprinting.

13. **State** the hypothesis that explains why a cheetah quits chasing prey after 100 yards.

14. **Describe** three types of competitive behavior.

15. **Compare** the costs versus the benefits of territoriality for impalas.

16. **Name** the type of selection that would result in peacocks with larger tails.

17. **Explain** the relationship between parental care and the type of mating system found in a species.

18. **Identify** an example for each of the four different types of communication found in animals.

19. **Identify** the types of communication that are displayed during a waggle dance.

20. **Relate** the costs and benefits of social behavior to life in a prairie dog colony.

21. **Explain** the biological reason for each of the four types of cyclic behaviors.

22. **Describe** the biological cycle that explains jet lag in people who travel across time zones.

23. **CONCEPT MAPPING** Use the following terms to create a concept map that describes animal behavior: *behavior, stimulus, innate behavior, fixed action pattern, learned behavior, conditioning, reasoning, imprinting,* and *sexual selection*.

## CRITICAL THINKING

24. **Analyzing Information** Imagine that a mutation resulted in an animal that could not experience habituation. Explain the effect on the individual and how natural selection might act on this mutation.

25. **Forming Reasoned Opinions** A friend insists that animals can only communicate with members of their own species. Is this true? Explain and support your opinion.

26. **Critiquing a Scientific Explanation** Biologists cut the tails of male widowbirds and found that they mated with only half as many females as males with uncut tails. Should the scientists conclude that female widowbirds prefer long tails? Why or why not?

27. **Recognizing Relationships** In many bird species, the male is more brightly colored than the female. Explain how natural selection and sexual selection might result in these characteristics.

28. **Interpreting Graphics** Identify the type of behavior displayed in the following image. Explain how natural selection might play a role in developing this behavior.

# Standardized Test Preparation

**DIRECTIONS:** Choose the letter of the answer choice that best answers the question.

1. An orb spider builds her web in exactly the same way every time. This is an example of what type of behavior?
   A. random behavior
   B. learned behavior
   C. abnormal behavior
   D. fixed action pattern behavior

2. What type of learning can only occur during a specific period early in an animal's life?
   F. reasoning
   G. assuming
   H. imprinting
   J. conditioning

3. A male lion kills all the young cubs of rival males. The genes of which of the following would be favored by this behavior?
   A. the pride
   B. the female
   C. the male lion
   D. the male lion's siblings

4. Which of the following represents classical conditioning?
   F. rats feeding in Skinner boxes
   G. a dog salivating at the sound of a bell
   H. a male bullfrog croaking loudly in a pond
   J. a primate giving a warning signal to troop members

**INTERPRETING GRAPHICS:** The photo below shows ants following a pheromone trail. Use the photo to answer the questions that follow.

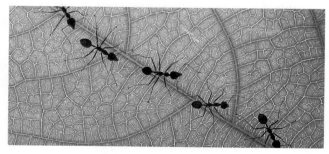

5. The behavior of the ants is most likely to be what type of behavior?
   A. innate
   B. learned
   C. habituation
   D. classical conditioning

6. What type of communication are the ants using?
   F. visual communication
   G. sound communication
   H. communication by touch
   J. chemical communication

**DIRECTIONS:** Complete the following analogy.

7. aggression : competitive behavior :: altruism :
   A. conditioning
   B. social behavior
   C. parental behavior
   D. fixed action pattern behavior

**INTERPRETING GRAPHICS:** The photo below shows Konrad Lorenz with goslings that imprinted on him. Use the photo to answer the question that follows.

8. What is the most likely advantage to the behavior illustrated above?
   F. Goslings who follow buckets are more successful in finding food.
   G. Adult wild geese that associate with humans reproduce more successfully.
   H. Traveling in single file is the most successful way for geese to avoid predators.
   J. Goslings who follow their mother are more likely to find food and safety from predators.

## SHORT RESPONSE

A male lion entering a pride kills all the young cubs.

What are the benefits of the male's behavior?

## EXTENDED RESPONSE

You have been hired to invent a humane method for fighting household ants. Use the behavior pictured in Questions 5–6 to accomplish this job and explain your invention.

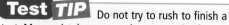

**Test TIP** Do not try to rush to finish a test. Many mistakes are made as a result of carelessness.

# Studying Nonverbal Communication

## OBJECTIVES

- Recognize that posture is a type of nonverbal communication.
- Observe how human posture changes during a conversation.
- Determine the relationship of gender to the postural changes that occur during a conversation.

## PROCESS SKILLS

- observing
- analyzing
- graphing
- collecting data

## MATERIALS

- paper
- pencil
- stopwatch or clock with a second hand

## Background

People communicate nonverbally with their **posture,** or body position. The position of the body while standing is called the **stance.** In an **equal stance,** the body weight is supported equally by both legs. In an **unequal stance,** more weight is supported by one leg than by the other. In this lab, you will observe and analyze how stance changes during conversations between pairs of people who are standing.

1. Write a definition for each boldface term in the paragraph above.
2. Make a data table similar to the one on the next page. The sample data entered in row 1 show how to enter data. Do not copy these data.
3. Based on the objectives for this lab, write a question you would like to explore about nonverbal communication.

## PART A  Observing Behavior

1. Work in a group of two or three to observe conversations between pairs of people. Each conversation must last between 45 seconds and 5 minutes. One person in your group should be the timekeeper and the other group members should record data. Be sure that your subjects are unaware they are being observed.
2. Observe at least three conversations. Record the genders of the two participants in each conversation and the gender of the one person whose posture you observe. Be sure that the timekeeper accurately clocks the passage of each 15-second interval.
3. For each 15-second interval, record all of the changes in stance by the person you are observing. For example, note every time your subject shifts from an equal stance to an unequal stance, or vice versa.

To record the stance simply, you may write *E* to identify an equal stance and *U* to identify an unequal stance.

**4.** If the subject assumes an unequal stance, also record the number of weight shifts from one foot to the other. Indicate a weight shift simply by writing *W.*

**5.** When a conversation ends, write down whether the pair departed together or separately. To record this, write *T* to indicate departing together, or *S* to indicate departing separately.

**6.** After you have completed each observation, tally the total number of weight shifts within each 15-second block. **IMPORTANT!** Retain data only for conversations that last 45 seconds. If a conversation ends before you have collected data for 45 seconds, observe another conversation.

### PART B Analyzing Behavior

**7.** After all observations have been completed, combine the data from all of the groups in your class. Analyze the data, without regard to gender.
  **a.** Determine the most common stance during the first 15 seconds of a conversation, the middle 15 seconds, and the last 15 seconds. Make a bar graph to summarize the class data.
  **b.** Find the average number of weight shifts in the beginning, middle, and end intervals. Make a bar graph to summarize the class data.

**8.** Repeat step 7, but analyze the data according to gender this time.

**9.** Compile the data and make bar graphs for each of the following: males talking with a male, males talking with a female, females talking with a male, and females talking with a female. Compare these graphs with the ones you made in step 7.

### Analysis and Conclusions

**1.** Which stance was used most often during a conversation?

**2.** Based on your observations, which behavior most often signals that a conversation is about to end: stance change or weight shift?

**3.** Do males and females differ in their departure signals? If so, describe the differences you observed. Justify your conclusion.

**4.** What do you think might be an adaptive significance of a departure signal?

**5.** What other behaviors did you observe that were forms of nonverbal communication? Propose a reason for each type of behavior. Justify your answer.

### Further Inquiry

Write a new question about animal behavior. Propose an experiment that you could use to answer your question. Identify the animal that you think would be best for your study and justify your reason for choosing it.

### TABLE 1 *OBSERVING NONVERBAL COMMUNICATION*

| Pairs | Gender | | 15-s intervals | | |
| | Involved | Observed | 15 s | 30 s | 45 s |
|---|---|---|---|---|---|
| 1 | F, M | M | U, W | E | E |
| 2 | | | | | |
| 3 | | | | | |

# HUMAN BIOLOGY

References to *Scientific American* project ideas are located throughout this unit.

🖱 **internet** connect 

National Science Teachers Association *sci*LINKS Internet resources are located throughout this unit.

*sci*LINKS. Maintained by the National Science Teachers Association

**66** *The human body is marvelous. It can move freely, act deliberately, and survive under the most variable conditions. Its construction is complex and its requirements many.* **99**

From "Exploring Man," from *Behold Man: A Photographic Journey of Discovery Inside the Body,* by Lennart Nilsson in collaboration with Jan Lindberg. English translation copyright © 1974 by Albert Bonniers, Förlag, Stockholm. Reprinted by permission of *Little, Brown and Company.*

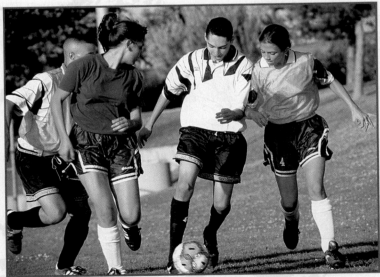

*Near-perfect coordination of the many organ systems enables humans to play soccer and carry out daily activities.*

At six weeks old, this developing human embryo (right) weighs less than 1 g. By eight weeks, all of the major organ systems will be recognizable.

This X ray of a child's hand (below) reveals the hand's many bones.

This researcher, like other scientists around the world, spends many hours in the lab each day searching for safe drugs that can be used to treat human ailments.

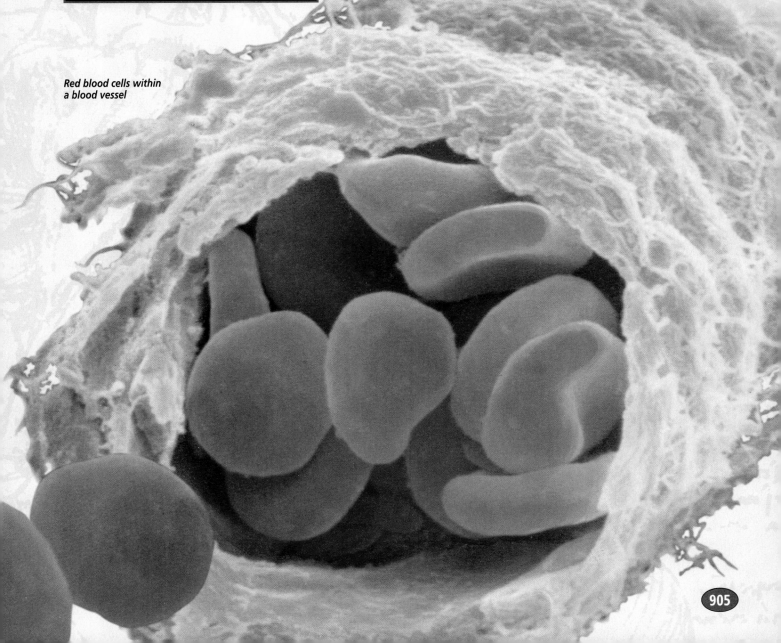

Red blood cells within a blood vessel

# CHAPTER 45

# SKELETAL, MUSCULAR, AND INTEGUMENTARY SYSTEMS

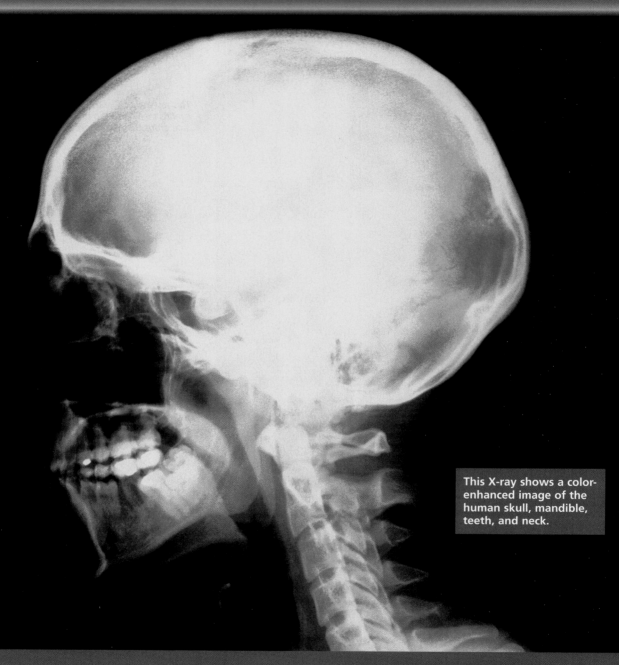

This X-ray shows a color-enhanced image of the human skull, mandible, teeth, and neck.

# THE HUMAN BODY PLAN

*The human body begins to take shape during the earliest stages of embryonic development. While the embryo is a tiny ball of dividing cells, it begins forming the tissues and organs that compose the human body. By the end of its third week, the human embryo has bilateral symmetry and is developing vertebrate characteristics that will support an upright body position.*

## OBJECTIVES

- **Describe** four types of tissues that make up the human body.
- **Explain** how tissues, organs, and organ systems are organized.
- **Summarize** the functions of the primary organ systems in the human body.
- **Identify** the five human body cavities and the organs that each contains.

## VOCABULARY

muscle tissue
skeletal muscle
smooth muscle
cardiac muscle
nervous tissue
neurons
epithelial tissue
connective tissue
matrix
organ
cranial cavity
spinal cavity
diaphragm
thoracic cavity
abdominal cavity
pelvic cavity

## BODY TISSUES

A tissue is a collection of cells that are similar in structure and that work together to perform a particular function. The human body has four main types of tissues: muscle, nervous, epithelial, and connective.

### Muscle Tissue

**Muscle tissue** is composed of cells that can contract. Every function that muscle tissue performs—from creating a facial expression to keeping the eyes in focus—is carried out by groups of muscle cells that contract in a coordinated fashion. The human body has three types of muscle tissue: skeletal, smooth, and cardiac. **Skeletal muscle** moves the bones in your trunk, limbs, and face. **Smooth muscle** handles body functions that you cannot control consciously, such as the movement of food through your digestive system. **Cardiac muscle,** found in your heart, pumps blood through your body. Figure 45-1a, on the following page, shows an illustration of cells of skeletal muscle tissue.

### Nervous Tissue

**Nervous tissue** contains cells that receive and transmit messages in the form of electrical impulses. These cells, called **neurons** (NOO-rahnz), are specialized to send and receive messages throughout the body. Nervous tissue makes up your brain, spinal cord, and nerves. It is also found in parts of sensory organs, such as the retina in your eye. Some nervous tissue senses changes in the internal and external environment. Other nervous tissue interprets the meaning of sensory information. Still other types of nervous tissue cause the body to move in response to sensory information. Coordination of voluntary and involuntary activities and regulation of some body processes are also accomplished by nervous tissue. Figure 45-1b, on the following page, shows an illustration of cells of nervous tissue.

**internet** connect

www.scilinks.org
**Topic:** Tissues
**Keyword:** HM61529

SCLINKS. Maintained by the National Science Teachers Association

**(a) MUSCLE TISSUE**

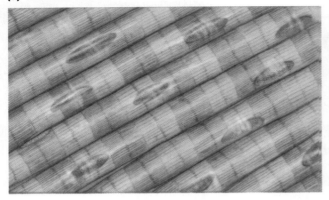

**(b) NERVOUS TISSUE**

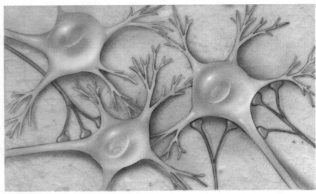

**(c) EPITHELIAL TISSUE (top layer of cells)**

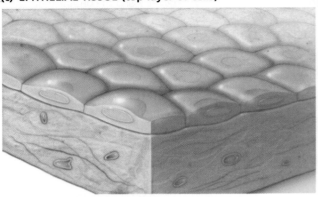

**(d) CONNECTIVE TISSUE**

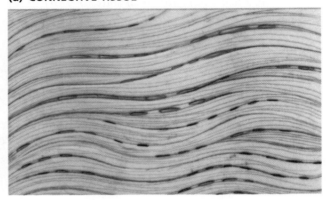

**FIGURE 45-1**

These four drawings show representative cells of the four main types of tissues in the human body: (a) muscle tissue, (b) nervous tissue, (c) epithelial tissue, and (d) connective tissue.

## Epithelial Tissue

**Epithelial** (ep-uh-THEE-lee-uhl) **tissue** consists of layers of cells that line or cover all internal and external body surfaces. Each epithelial layer is formed from cells that are tightly bound together, often providing a protective barrier for these surfaces. Epithelial tissue is found in various thicknesses and arrangements, depending on where it is located. For example, the epithelial tissue that lines blood vessels is a single layer of flattened cells through which substances can easily pass. But the epithelial tissue that lines the trachea consists of a layer of cilia-bearing cells and mucus-secreting cells that act together to trap inhaled particles. The most easily observed epithelial tissue, the body's outer layer of skin, consists of sheets of dead, flattened cells that cover and protect the underlying living layer of skin. Figure 45-1c shows an illustration of cells of epithelial tissue.

## Connective Tissue

**Connective tissue** binds, supports, and protects structures in the body. Connective tissues are the most abundant and diverse of the four types of tissue, and include bone, cartilage, tendons, fat, and blood. These tissues are characterized by cells that are embedded in large amounts of an intercellular substance called **matrix.** Matrix can be solid, semisolid, or liquid. Bone cells are surrounded by a hard, crystalline matrix containing calcium. The cells in cartilage, tendons, and fat are surrounded by a semisolid fibrous matrix. Blood cells are suspended in a liquid matrix. Figure 45-1d shows an illustration of cells of connective tissue.

# ORGANS AND ORGAN SYSTEMS

An **organ** consists of various tissues that work together to carry out a specific function. The stomach, a saclike organ in which food is mixed with digestive enzymes, is composed of the four types of tissues. A single organ, such as the stomach, usually does not function in isolation. Rather, groups of organs interact in an organ system. For example, in the digestive system, the stomach, small intestine, liver, and pancreas all work together to break down food into molecules the body can use for energy. Table 45-1 lists the body's organ systems and names their major structures and functions. As you study the table, think about the ways in which the different organ systems work together to function in an efficient, integrated manner.

### TABLE 45-1 *Summary of Organ Systems*

| System | Major structures | Functions |
|---|---|---|
| Skeletal | bones | provides structure; supports and protects internal organs |
| Muscular | muscles (skeletal, cardiac, and smooth) | provides structure; supports and moves trunk and limbs; moves substances through body |
| Integumentary | skin, hair, nails | protects against pathogens; helps regulate body temperature |
| Cardiovascular | heart, blood vessels, blood | transports nutrients and wastes to and from all body tissues |
| Respiratory | air passages, lungs | carries air into and out of lungs, where gases (oxygen and carbon dioxide) are exchanged |
| Immune | lymph nodes and vessels, white blood cells | provides protection against infection and disease |
| Digestive | mouth, esophagus, stomach, liver, pancreas, small and large intestines | stores and breaks down food; absorbs nutrients; eliminates waste |
| Excretory | kidneys, ureters, bladder, urethra, skin, lungs | eliminates waste; maintains water and chemical balance |
| Nervous | brain, spinal cord, nerves, sense organs, receptors | controls and coordinates body movements and senses; controls consciousness and creativity; helps monitor and maintain other body systems |
| Endocrine | glands (such as adrenal, thyroid, pituitary, and pancreas); hypothalamus and specialized cells in the brain, heart, stomach, and other organs | maintains homeostasis; regulates metabolism, water and mineral balance, growth, behavior, development, and reproduction |
| Reproductive | ovaries, uterus, mammary glands (in females), testes (in males) | produces eggs and milk in females, sperm in males, and offspring after fertilization |

## Integration of Organ Systems

An even higher level of organization is the integration of organ systems. Each organ system has organs associated with it according to the organ's primary function. However, the boundaries are not always well defined. For example, nearly all of the juices produced by the pancreas are designed to aid in digestion. But because the pancreas produces vitally important hormones, it is also considered a component of the endocrine system. Each organ system carries out its own specific function, but for the organism to survive, the organ systems must work together. For example, nutrients from the digestive system are distributed by the cardiovascular system. The efficiency of the cardiovascular system depends on nutrients from the digestive system and oxygen from the respiratory system.

# BODY CAVITIES

Many organs and organ systems in the human body are housed in compartments called body cavities. These cavities protect internal organs from injuries and permit organs such as the lungs to expand and contract while remaining securely supported. As shown in Figure 45-2, the human body has five main body cavities. Each cavity contains one or more organs. The **cranial cavity** contains the brain. The **spinal cavity** surrounds the spinal cord.

The two main cavities in the trunk of the human body are separated by a wall of muscle called the **diaphragm** (DIE-uh-FRAM). The upper compartment, or **thoracic** (thoh-RAS-ik) **cavity,** contains the heart, the esophagus, and the organs of the respiratory system. The lower compartment, or **abdominal** (ab-DAHM-uh-nuhl) **cavity,** contains organs of the digestive system. The **pelvic cavity** contains the organs of the reproductive and excretory systems.

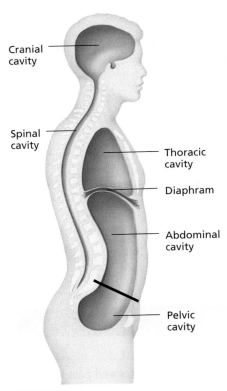

**FIGURE 45-2**

The human body has five main cavities that house and protect delicate internal organs.

Cranial cavity

Spinal cavity

Thoracic cavity

Diaphram

Abdominal cavity

Pelvic cavity

## SECTION 1 REVIEW

1. Name the four types of tissues in the human body, and give an example of each.

2. Explain the difference between muscle tissue and nervous tissue.

3. How are tissues, organs, and organ systems organized in the body?

4. How do the organ systems function together in the human body?

5. Give an example of interaction between the endocrine system and another organ system.

6. Identify the organs each body cavity contains.

**CRITICAL THINKING**

7. **Applying Information** Describe how the skeletal, muscular, nervous, respiratory, and circulatory systems function in a person swimming in a pool.

8. **Analyzing Concepts** Explain how the function of the body's organs might be affected if the body were not divided into cavities?

9. **Forming Reasoned Opinions** The body cavity that protects the brain is encased in bone. Why do you think the abdominal cavity is not encased in bone?

# SKELETAL SYSTEM

*The adult human body consists of approximately 206 bones, which are organized into an internal framework called the* **skeleton.** *The variation in size and shape among the bones that make up the skeleton reflects their different roles in the body.*

## THE SKELETON

As shown in Figure 45-3, the human skeleton is composed of two parts—the axial skeleton and the appendicular (AP-uhn-DIK-yuh-luhr) skeleton. The bones of the skull, ribs, spine, and sternum form the **axial skeleton.** The bones of the arms and legs, along with the scapula, clavicle, and pelvis, make up the **appendicular skeleton.**

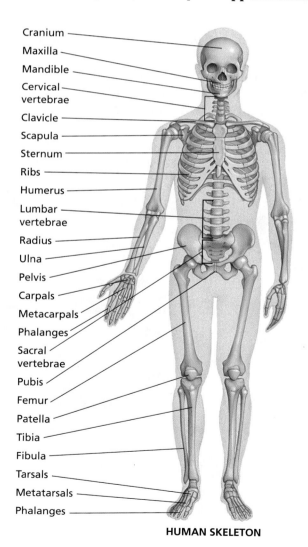

Cranium
Maxilla
Mandible
Cervical vertebrae
Clavicle
Scapula
Sternum
Ribs
Humerus
Lumbar vertebrae
Radius
Ulna
Pelvis
Carpals
Metacarpals
Phalanges
Sacral vertebrae
Pubis
Femur
Patella
Tibia
Fibula
Tarsals
Metatarsals
Phalanges

**HUMAN SKELETON**

## SECTION 2

### OBJECTIVES

- **Distinguish** between the axial skeleton and the appendicular skeleton.
- **Explain** the function and structure of bones.
- **Summarize** how bones develop and elongate.
- **List** three types of joints, and give an example of each.
- **Describe** a common disorder that affects the skeletal system.

### VOCABULARY

skeleton
axial skeleton
appendicular skeleton
periosteum
compact bone
Haversian canal
osteocyte
spongy bone
bone marrow
fracture
ossification
epiphyseal plate
joint
fixed joint
semimovable joint
movable joint
ligament
synovial fluid
rheumatoid arthritis
osteoarthritis

**FIGURE 45-3**

The skeleton is the framework that supports and protects the body. The bones of the axial skeleton are colored purple. The bones of the appendicular skeleton are colored yellow.

# BONE FUNCTION AND STRUCTURE

The bones that make up the skeleton function in a variety of ways. Bones provide a rigid framework against which muscles can pull, give shape and structure to the body, and support and protect delicate internal organs. Notice, for example, that the ribs curve to form a cage that contains the heart and lungs. Similarly, bones in the skull form the cranium, a dome-shaped case that protects the brain. Bones also store minerals, such as calcium and phosphorus, which play vital roles in important metabolic processes. In addition, the internal portion of many bones produces red blood cells, platelets, and white blood cells.

Despite their number and size, bones make up less than 20 percent of the body's mass. The reason for their having relatively little mass can be better understood by looking at bone structure. Bones are not dry, rigid structures, as they may appear in a museum exhibit. They are moist, living tissues.

## Long Bone Structure

As shown in Figure 45-4, a long bone consists of a porous central cavity surrounded by a ring of dense material. The bone's surface is covered by a tough membrane called the **periosteum** (PER-ee-AHS-tee-uhm). This membrane contains a network of blood vessels, which supply nutrients, and nerves, which signal pain.

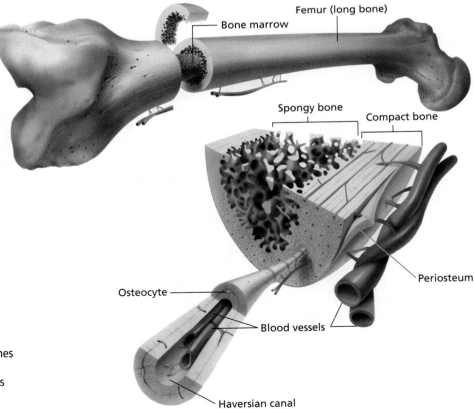

Femur (long bone)

Bone marrow

Spongy bone

Compact bone

Osteocyte

Periosteum

Blood vessels

Haversian canal

**FIGURE 45-4**

Long bones, found in the limbs of the body, are hollow and cylindrical. The outer shell of hard compact bone consists of closely packed rings of minerals and protein fibers. Narrow canals running through these rings contain blood vessels and nerves. Spongy bone is found in small flat bones and in the ends of long bones. The central shaft of the long bone contains marrow and blood vessels.

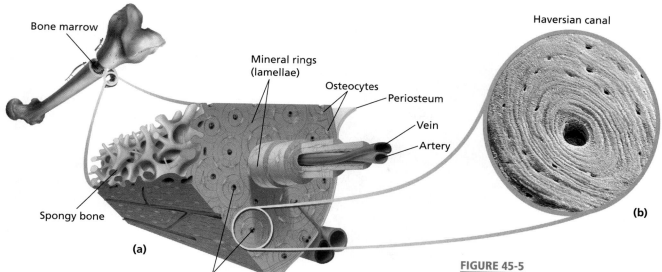

Bone marrow

Mineral rings (lamellae)

Osteocytes

Periosteum

Vein

Artery

Haversian canal

Spongy bone

**(a)**

**(b)**

Haversian canals

**FIGURE 45-5**

The cross section in (a) shows the internal structure of compact bone. A micrograph of a Haversian canal (380×) surrounded by lamellae in compact bone is shown in (b).

Under the periosteum is a hard material called **compact bone.** A thick layer of compact bone enables the shaft of the long bone to endure the large amount of stress it receives during activities such as jumping. In the cross section shown in Figure 45-5a, notice that compact bone is composed of cylinders of mineral crystals and protein fibers called *lamellae.* In the center of each cylinder is a narrow channel called a **Haversian** (huh-VER-shuhn) **canal,** as shown in Figure 45-5b. Blood vessels run through interconnected Haversian canals, creating a network that carries nourishment to the living bone tissue. Several layers of protein fibers wrap around each Haversian canal. Embedded within the gaps between the protein layers are bone cells called **osteocytes** (AHS-tee-uh-SIETS).

Beneath some compact bone is a network of connective tissue called **spongy bone.** Although its name suggests that it is soft, this tissue is hard and strong. As shown in Figure 45-4, spongy bone has a latticework structure that consists of bony spikes arranged along points of pressure or stress, making bones both light and strong.

## Bone Marrow

Many bones also contain a soft tissue called **bone marrow,** which can be either red or yellow. Red bone marrow—found in spongy bone, the ends of long bones, ribs, vertebrae, the sternum, and the pelvis—produces red blood cells, platelets, and white blood cells. Yellow bone marrow fills the shafts of long bones. It consists mostly of fat cells and serves as an energy reserve. It can also be converted to red bone marrow and produce blood cells when severe blood loss occurs.

## Injury and Repair

Despite their strength, bones will crack or even break if they are subjected to extreme loads, sudden impacts, or stresses from unusual directions. The crack or break is referred to as a **fracture.** If circulation is maintained and the periosteum survives, healing will occur even if the damage to the bone is severe.

## Eco Connection

### Bones of Lead

Millions of Americans have been exposed to lead in the environment. Following exposure to lead, the kidneys excrete most of the metal. But 7 to 10 percent of the remaining lead in the body is stored in bone and can stay there for a lifetime. The rapid bone uptake of lead acts as a detoxifying mechanism. But lead may not be permanently locked in bone. As people age, bone degeneration may occur, releasing lead into the bloodstream. Even very small concentrations of lead in the bloodstream can cause damage to kidneys, and high blood pressure.

The United States has outlawed the addition of lead to gasoline, water pipes, and paint. As a result, people who are now under age 25 may not accumulate as much lead in their bones as people from earlier generations.

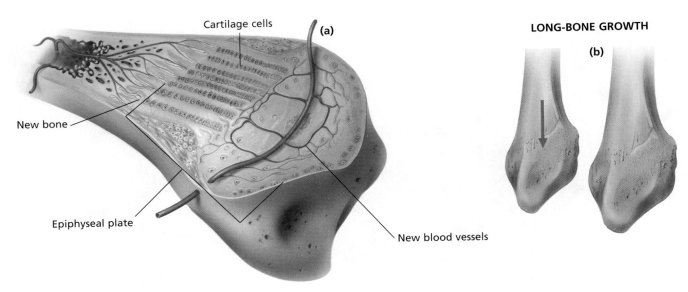

Cartilage cells

**(a)**

New bone

Epiphyseal plate

New blood vessels

**LONG-BONE GROWTH**

**(b)**

**FIGURE 45-6**

The epiphyseal plate, found at the ends of immature long bones, such as the fibula shown above, is the site of bone elongation. This region is rich with cartilage cells, which divide, enlarge, and push older cells toward the middle of the bone shaft. As older cells move back, they are replaced by new bone cells, forming new regions of bone. A long bone (a) will grow in length, circumference, and density in this manner, as shown in (b).

# BONE DEVELOPMENT

Most bones develop from cartilage, a tough but flexible connective tissue. In the second month of fetal development, much of the skeleton is made of cartilage. During the third month, osteocytes begin to develop and release minerals that lodge in the spaces between the cartilage cells, turning the cartilage to bone. The process by which cartilage is slowly replaced by bone as a result of the deposition of minerals is called **ossification** (AHS-uh-fuh-KAY-shuhn). Most fetal cartilage is eventually replaced by bone. However, some cartilage remains, lending flexibility to the areas between bones, at the end of the nose, in the outer ear, and along the inside of the trachea.

A few bones, such as some parts of the skull, develop directly into hard bone without forming cartilage first. In these cases, the osteocytes are initially scattered randomly throughout the embryonic connective tissue but soon fuse into layers and become flat plates of bone. In the skull, suture lines can be seen where the plates of bone meet.

## Bone Elongation

Bones continue to develop after a person's birth. Between early childhood and late adolescence, bone cells gradually replace the cartilage in long bones of limbs, such as the arms and legs. Bone elongation takes place near the ends of long bones in an area known as the **epiphyseal** (EP-uh-FIZ-ee-uhl) **plate.** As shown in Figure 45-6a, the epiphyseal plate is composed of cartilage cells that divide and form columns, pushing older cells toward the middle of the bone. As these older cells die, they are replaced by new bone cells. Growth continues, as shown in Figure 45-6b, until bone has replaced all the cartilage in the epiphyseal plate. At this point, bones no longer elongate and a person has usually reached full height. The epiphyseal plates then become *epiphyseal lines.*

# JOINTS

The place where two bones meet is known as a **joint.** Three major kinds of joints are found in the human body—fixed, semimovable, and movable. Examples of these joints are shown in Figure 45-7.

## Fixed Joints

**Fixed joints** prevent movement. They are found in the skull, where they securely connect the bony plates and permit no movement of those bones. A small amount of connective tissue in a fixed joint helps absorb impact to prevent the bones from breaking.

## Semimovable Joints

**Semimovable joints** permit limited movement. For example, semimovable joints hold the bones of the vertebral column in place and allow the body to bend and twist. The vertebrae of the spine are separated by disks of cartilaginous tissue. These tough, springy disks compress and absorb shocks that could damage the fragile spinal cord. Semimovable joints are also found in the rib cage, where long strands of cartilage connect the upper ten pairs of ribs to the sternum, allowing the chest to expand during breathing.

## Movable Joints

All other joints in the body are **movable joints.** These joints enable the body to perform a wide range of movements and activities. Movable joints include hinge, ball-and-socket, pivot, saddle, and gliding joints. An example of a *hinge joint* is found in the elbow, which allows you to move your forearm upward and downward, like a hinged door. An example of a *ball-and-socket joint* is the shoulder joint, which enables you to move your arm up, down, forward, and backward, as well as to rotate it in a complete circle. The joint formed by the top two vertebrae of your spine is an example of a *pivot joint*; it allows you to turn your head from side to side, as when shaking your head "no." The *saddle joint*, found at the base of each thumb, allows you to rotate your thumbs and helps you grasp objects with your hand. Finally, *gliding joints* allow bones to slide over one another. Examples are the joints between the small bones of your foot, which allow your foot to flex when you walk.

## Joint Structure

Joints, such as the knee, are often subjected to a great deal of pressure and stress, but their structure is well suited to meet these demands. As in all movable joints, the parts of the bones that come in contact with each other are covered with cartilage, which protects the bones' surface from friction. Tough bands of connective tissue, called **ligaments,** hold the bones of the joint in place. The surfaces of the joints that are subjected to a great deal of pressure are lined with tissue that secretes a lubricating substance called **synovial** (sih-NOH-vee-uhl) **fluid.** Synovial fluid helps protect the ends of bones from damage by friction.

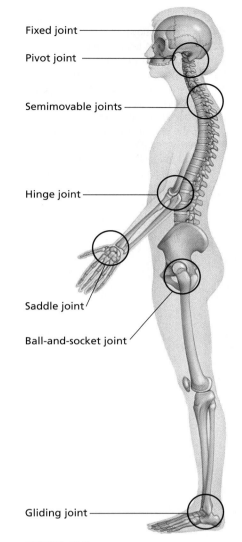

Fixed joint
Pivot joint
Semimovable joints
Hinge joint
Saddle joint
Ball-and-socket joint
Gliding joint

**FIGURE 45-7**

In addition to fixed joints and semimovable joints, the human body has five types of movable joints: pivot, hinge, saddle, ball-and-socket, and gliding.

FIGURE 45-8

The knee is a movable joint formed by the ends of the femur, the tibia, and the patella. Many cordlike ligaments stabilize the joint, especially during movement. Pads of cartilage protect the ends of bones and act as shock absorbers. Like many joints in the body, the knee is a synovial joint. It contains membranes that secrete synovial fluid, which lubricates and nourishes the tissues inside the joint.

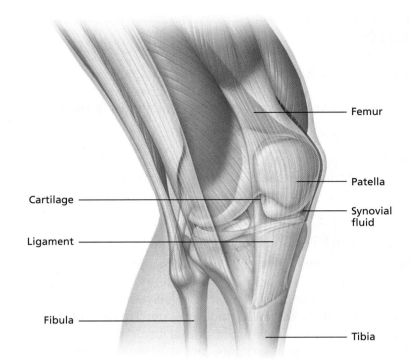

Femur

Patella

Synovial fluid

Cartilage

Ligament

Fibula

Tibia

Sometimes these protective structures are not enough to prevent a joint from becoming injured. Of all the joints in the body, the knee joint is the most susceptible to injury because it carries the body's weight and relies on many ligaments for stability. Damage to the knee joint can cause swelling in the compartment that contains the synovial fluid. Figure 45-8 shows the internal structures of the knee joint.

The term *arthritis* is used to describe disorders that cause painful, swollen joints. There are two forms of arthritis that affect joints. **Rheumatoid arthritis** develops when the immune system begins to attack body tissues. The joints become inflamed, swollen, stiff, and deformed. **Osteoarthritis** is a degenerative joint disease in which the cartilage covering the surface of bone becomes thinner and rougher. As a result, bone surfaces rub against each other, which is sensed by the nerves in the periosteum, and causes severe discomfort.

## SECTION 2 REVIEW

1. List the major parts of the axial skeleton and the major parts of the appendicular skeleton.

2. Name five functions of bones.

3. Illustrate the structure of a long bone.

4. When does the ossification of most of the bones in the body begin and end?

5. Describe the function of the three major types of joints, and give an example of each.

6. Differentiate between the two types of arthritis.

**CRITICAL THINKING**

7. **Applying Information** What is the advantage of a cartilaginous skeleton during prenatal development?

8. **Analyzing Information** Which type of arthritis is not related to age?

9. **Relating Concepts** How are the structures of cartilage and bone related to the function each performs in the body?

# MUSCULAR SYSTEM

*Muscles make up the bulk of the body and account for about one-third of its weight. Their ability to contract and relax not only enables the body to move, but also provides the force that pushes substances, such as blood and food, through the body.*

## MUSCLE TYPES

A muscle is an organ that can contract in a coordinated fashion and includes muscle tissue, blood vessels, nerves, and connective tissue. Some of the major muscles of the human body are shown in Figure 45-9. Recall that the human body has three types of muscle tissues: skeletal, smooth, and cardiac.

Skeletal muscle is responsible for moving parts of the body, such as the limbs, trunk, and face. Skeletal muscle tissue is made up of elongated cells called **muscle fibers.** Each muscle fiber contains many nuclei and is crossed by light and dark stripes, called **striations,** as shown on the following page in Figure 45-10a. Skeletal muscle fibers are grouped into dense bundles called **fascicles.** A group of fascicles are bound together by connective tissue to form a muscle. Because their contractions can usually be consciously controlled, skeletal muscles are described as **voluntary muscles.**

## SECTION 3

### OBJECTIVES

- **Distinguish** between the three types of muscle tissues.
- **Describe** the structure of skeletal muscle fibers.
- **Explain** how skeletal muscles contract.
- **Describe** how muscles move bones.
- **Explain** the process in which a muscle becomes fatigued.

### VOCABULARY

muscle fiber
striation
fascicle
voluntary muscle
involuntary muscle
myofibril
myosin
actin
Z line
sarcomere
tendon
origin
insertion
flexor
extensor
muscle fatigue
oxygen debt

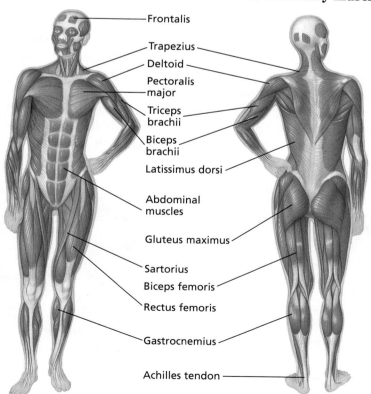

Frontalis
Trapezius
Deltoid
Pectoralis major
Triceps brachii
Biceps brachii
Latissimus dorsi
Abdominal muscles
Gluteus maximus
Sartorius
Biceps femoris
Rectus femoris
Gastrocnemius
Achilles tendon

**FIGURE 45-9**

Skeletal muscle tissue is shown in these diagrams of some of the major muscles in the human body.

## Certified Athletic Trainer

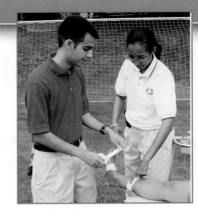

**Job Description** A certified athletic trainer (ATC) is a highly educated and skilled professional who specializes in athletic health care. Certified athletic trainers must have a bachelor's degree, usually in athletic training, health, physical education, or exercise science. In addition, an ATC must pass a certification exam. The job includes the prevention, identification, evaluation, treatment, referral, and rehabilitation of sports-related injuries.

### Focus on Certified Athletic Trainer
In high school, Veronica Ampey was interested in science, medicine, rehabilitation, and community service. Today, she has found a career that brings together all of these interests and her love for sports. "I like the fact that I am not tied to a desk," says Ampey. "I get paid to watch athletes practice and compete."

Ampey works as an ATC at a small high school in Washington, D.C. Ampey says "The bonus is using my education and experience to address incidents when they occur. Additionally, there is a great deal of satisfaction in seeing someone you've worked with return to full athletic participation."

### Education and Skills
- **High School**—at least three years of science courses and four years of math courses.
- **College**—bachelor's degree from a college with an accredited athletic training curriculum, including course work in biology; a master's degree for some jobs; and certification.
- **Skills**—patience, good organizational skills, and ability to work as a member of a team.

For more about careers, visit **go.hrw.com** and type in the keyword **HM6 Careers.**

---

**FIGURE 45-10**

These light micrographs show the three types of muscle tissue. Skeletal muscle tissue (a) has a striped appearance when viewed under a microscope (430×). Smooth muscle tissue (b) is found in the digestive tract, the uterus, the bladder, and the blood vessels (400×). Cardiac muscle tissue (c) is found only in the heart (270×).

Smooth muscle forms the walls of the stomach, intestines, blood vessels, and other internal organs. Individual smooth muscle cells are spindle-shaped, have a single nucleus, and interlace to form sheets, as shown in Figure 45-10b. Notice that smooth muscle lacks the striations found in skeletal muscle tissue. Smooth muscle fibers are surrounded by connective tissue, but the connective tissue does not unite to form tendons as it does in skeletal muscles. Because most of its movements cannot be consciously controlled, smooth muscle is referred to as **involuntary muscle.**

Cardiac muscle, shown in Figure 45-10c, makes up the walls of the heart. Cardiac muscle shares some characteristics with both skeletal muscle and smooth muscle. As with skeletal muscle, cardiac muscle tissue is striated; as with smooth muscle, it is involuntary and each cell has one nucleus.

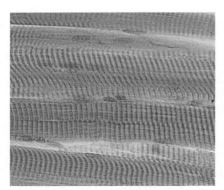

**(a) SKELETAL MUSCLE TISSUE**

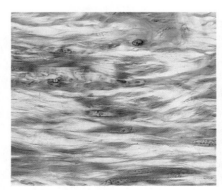

**(b) SMOOTH MUSCLE TISSUE**

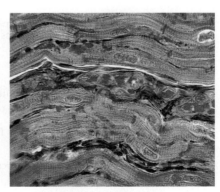

**(c) CARDIAC MUSCLE TISSUE**

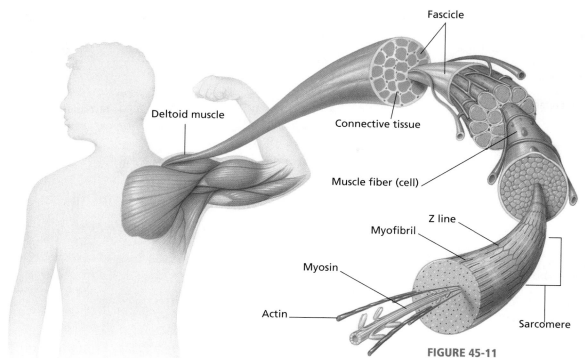

Fascicle

Deltoid muscle

Connective tissue

Muscle fiber (cell)

Z line

Myofibril

Myosin

Actin

Sarcomere

**FIGURE 45-11**

Skeletal muscles consist of densely packed groups of elongated cells, called fascicles, that are held together by connective tissue. Muscle fibers consist of protein filaments called myofibrils. Two types of filaments are found in muscle fibers—actin and myosin. The complementary structures of actin and myosin interact to contract and relax muscles.

# MUSCLE STRUCTURE

A skeletal muscle fiber is a single, multinucleated muscle cell. A skeletal muscle may be made up of hundreds or even thousands of muscle fibers, depending on the muscle's size. Although muscle fibers make up most of the muscle tissue, a large amount of connective tissue, blood vessels and nerves are also present. Like all body cells, muscle cells are soft and easy to injure. Connective tissue covers and supports each muscle fiber and reinforces the muscle as a whole.

The health of a muscle depends on a sufficient nerve and blood supply. Each skeletal muscle fiber has a nerve ending that controls its activity. Active muscles use a lot of energy and therefore require a continuous supply of oxygen and nutrients, which are supplied by arteries. Muscles produce large amounts of metabolic waste that must be removed through veins.

A skeletal muscle fiber, such as the one shown in Figure 45-11, contains bundles of threadlike structures called **myofibrils** (MIE-oh-FIE-bruhlz). Each myofibril is made up of two types of protein filaments—thick ones and thin ones. Thick filaments are made of the protein **myosin** (MIE-uh-suhn), and thin filaments are made of the protein **actin.** Myosin and actin filaments are arranged to form an overlapping pattern, which gives striated muscle tissue its striped appearance. Thin actin filaments are anchored at their endpoints to a structure called the **Z line.** The region from one Z line to the next is called a **sarcomere** (SAHR-kuh-MIR).

**FIGURE 45-12**

In a relaxed muscle, the actin and myosin filaments overlap. During a muscle contraction, the filaments slide past each other and the zone of overlap increases. As a result, the length of the sarcomere shortens.

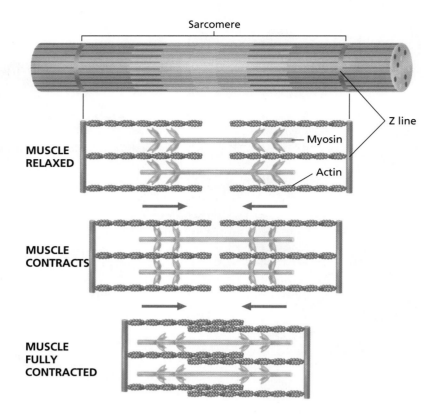

Sarcomere

Z line

Myosin

Actin

**MUSCLE RELAXED**

**MUSCLE CONTRACTS**

**MUSCLE FULLY CONTRACTED**

## Quick Lab

### Testing Muscle Stamina and Strength

**Materials** bathroom scale, notepad, pencil

**Procedure**

1. Create a chart that coompares the strength of pectoral muscles at four different time intervals, each 1 minute apart.

2. Press the scale between the palms of your hands. Have your partner record the amount of pressure applied by your pectoral muscles.

3. Set the scale down and press your hands together in front of you for 1 minute. Press the scale between your hands again and have your partner record the pressure.

4. Repeat steps 2 and 3 two more times. Then repeat the experiment with your partner pressing the scale while you record the pressure.

**Analysis** What trends did you notice, if any, in the amount of pressure recorded? What might be a reason for this trend?

# MUSCULAR CONTRACTION

The sarcomere is the functional unit of muscle contraction. When a muscle contracts, myosin filaments and actin filaments interact to shorten the sarcomere. Myosin filaments have extensions shaped like oval "heads." Actin filaments look like a twisted strand of beads. When a nerve impulse stimulates a muscle to contract, the myosin filaments' heads attach to points between the beads of the actin filaments. The myosin heads then bend inward, pulling the actin with them. The myosin heads then let go, bend back into their original position, attach to a new point on the actin filament, and pull again. This action shortens the sarcomere. The synchronized shortening of sarcomeres along the length of a muscle fiber causes the whole fiber, and hence the muscle, to contract. Figure 45-12 shows a sarcomere's structures.

Muscle contraction requires energy, which is supplied by ATP. This energy is used to detach the myosin heads from the actin filaments. Because myosin heads must attach and detach a number of times during a single muscle contraction, muscle cells must have a continuous supply of ATP. Without ATP, the myosin would remain attached to the actin, keeping a muscle permanently contracted.

Muscle contraction is an all-or-none response—either the fibers contract or they remain relaxed. How, then, are you able to contract your muscles tightly enough to lift a dumbbell or gently enough to lift a pen? The force of a muscle contraction is determined by the number of muscle fibers that are stimulated. As more fibers are activated, the force of the contraction increases.

# MUSCULAR MOVEMENT OF BONES

Generally, skeletal muscles are attached to one end of a bone, stretch across a joint, and are fastened to a point on another bone. Muscles are attached to the outer membrane of bone, the periosteum, either directly or by a tough fibrous cord of connective tissue called a **tendon.** For example, as shown in Figure 45-13, one end of the large biceps muscle in the arm is connected by tendons to the radius in the forearm, while the other end of the muscle is connected to the scapula in the shoulder. When the biceps muscle contracts, the forearm flexes upward while the scapula remains stationary. The point where the muscle attaches to the stationary bone—in this case, the scapula—is called the **origin.** The point where the muscle attaches to the moving bone—in this case the radius—is called the **insertion.**

Most skeletal muscles are arranged in opposing pairs. One muscle in a pair moves a limb in one direction; the other muscle moves it in the opposite direction. Muscles move bones by pulling them, not by pushing them. For example, when the biceps muscle contracts, the elbow bends. The biceps muscle is known as a **flexor,** a muscle that bends a joint. Contraction of the triceps muscle in the upper arm straightens the limb. The triceps muscle is an example of an **extensor,** a muscle that straightens a joint. To bring about a smooth movement, one muscle in a pair must contract while the opposing muscle relaxes.

**FIGURE 45-13**

Skeletal muscles, such as the biceps and triceps muscles in the upper arm, are connected to bones by tendons. (a) When the biceps muscle contracts, the elbow bends. (b) When the triceps muscle contracts, the elbow straightens.

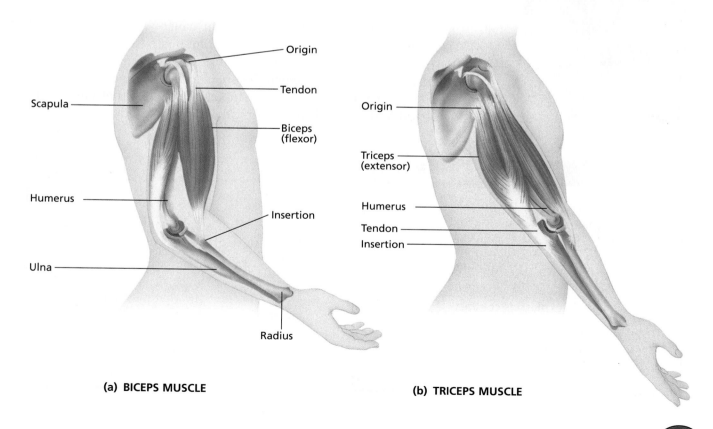

**(a) BICEPS MUSCLE**

**(b) TRICEPS MUSCLE**

# MUSCLE FATIGUE

Muscle cells store glycogen, which is used as a source of energy when the blood cannot deliver adequate amounts of glucose. The breakdown of glycogen releases large amounts of energy, but sometimes even those reserves are used up. During prolonged and vigorous exertion, fat molecules are utilized for energy. Fat molecules contain a greater concentration of potential energy than any other molecule in the body. When energy availability fails to keep pace with its use, muscle fatigue sets in and controlled muscle activity ceases, even though the muscle may still receive nerve stimulation to move. **Muscle fatigue** is the physiological inability of a muscle to contract. Muscle fatigue is a result of a relative depletion of ATP. When ATP is absent, a state of continuous contraction occurs. An example of depletion of ATP is when a marathon runner collapses during a race, suffering from severe muscle cramps.

## Oxygen Debt

Oxygen is used during cellular respiration in the synthesis of ATP. Large amounts of oxygen are needed to maintain the rate of maximum ATP production required to sustain strenuous exercise. However, after several minutes of heavy exertion, the circulatory system and the respiratory system are not able to bring in enough oxygen to meet the demands of energy production. Oxygen levels in the body become depleted. This temporary lack of oxygen availability is called **oxygen debt.** Oxygen debt leads to an accumulation of lactic acid as metabolic waste in the muscle fibers. The presence of lactic acid produces the soreness you may experience after prolonged exercise. Oxygen debt causes a person to spend time in rapid, deep breathing after strenuous exercise, as the athletes shown in Figure 45-14 are doing. The oxygen debt is repaid quickly as additional oxygen becomes available, but muscle soreness may persist until all of the metabolic wastes that have accumulated in the muscle fibers are carried away or converted.

**FIGURE 45-14**

These athletes are in the process of repaying their oxygen debts. Oxygen debt occurs frequently after strenuous, sustained exertion.

## SECTION 3 REVIEW

1. Compare the three main types of muscle tissues found in the body.

2. Why is smooth muscle referred to as involuntary muscle?

3. Why do skeletal muscle fibers appear striated?

4. How do skeletal muscles contract?

5. How do muscles work together to move bones?

6. Contrast the functions of flexors and extensors.

7. What causes muscles to become fatigued?

**CRITICAL THINKING**

8. **Analyzing Information** Rigor mortis is a condition in which all of the body muscles become rigid shortly after a person dies. Why does rigor mortis develop?

9. **Applying Information** What causes muscle cramping after vigorous exercise or repeated movement?

10. **Applying Information** Why do you think the heart muscle never suffers from fatigue?

# Looking Inside the Human Body

In 1895, the development of X-ray equipment provided physicians a way to look at images of dense tissue in the body, such as bones. Modern imaging techniques rely on computers.

### Computerized Tomography

Computerized tomography (CT) uses a focused beam of low-dose X-rays to obtain cross-sectional images of structures in the body. Tomography is the technique used to take images of a specific "slice" or plane of tissue. Computerized tomography can differentiate tissues of various densities.

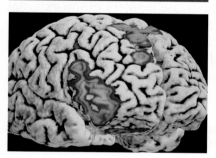

**(a)**

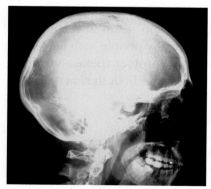

**(b)**

*(a) A three dimensional PET scan shows the surface detail and cellular activity of the brain. (b) This X-ray shows the bones of the skull, mandible, and neck.*

### Positrons and Brain Imaging

Still newer imaging technology is positron emission technology, or PET. Positrons are positively charged particles with the same mass as electrons that result from the disintegration of radioisotopes. Michael M. TerPogossian and his colleagues at Johns Hopkins suggested using short-lived radioisotopes in medical research. They developed scanners to detect the positrons released by radioisotopes that had been injected into a patient's bloodstream. As technology improved, biomedical engineers redesigned scanning equipment to create three-dimensional images from the positron emissions. Positron emission technology is used to map areas of the brain that are involved in memory, sensation, perception, speech, and information processing. In addition, positron emission technology provides clues about the causes of psychiatric disorders, such as depression.

### Holographic Imaging

A new holographic imaging system combines images obtained by computerized tomography or magnetic resonance scanners and displays an accurate three-dimensional image of anatomical structures. Magnetic resonance imaging (MRI) creates images of soft tissues. MRI uses radio waves emitted by the nuclei of hydrogen atoms that are activated by a magnetic scanner. A holograph is a method of photography that uses laser light to produce a three-dimensional image. The transparent but solid looking image floats in front of the holographic film and can be studied from all sides.

### Holograms in Medicine

Physicians can make surgical plans by studying the true appearance of a patient's organs, such as the three dimensional PET scan that highlights the verbal center in the brain (a). Compare the three dimensional PET scan with the X-ray of the same part of the body (b). The X-ray may not be as helpful as the three dimensional PET scan when a physician must diagnose an illness or injury of the brain.

### REVIEW

1. How do X-rays differ from PET scans?
2. How might a holograph be more useful than a PET scan?
3. **Justifying Conclusions** If a surgeon had to remove a piece of metal lodged in a patient's skull, which type of imaging would you choose? Support your answer, and give reasons why you did not choose the other imaging techniques.

**internet** connect

www.scilinks.org
**Topic:** Holography
**Keyword:** HM60752

SCILINKS. Maintained by the National Science Teachers Association

923

## OBJECTIVES

- **Describe** the functions of the skin.
- **Distinguish** between the two layers that form the skin.
- **Identify** two types of glands found in the skin, and describe their functions.
- **Describe** the structure of nails.
- **Describe** the structure of hair.

## VOCABULARY

epidermis
keratin
melanin
dermis
exocrine gland
sweat gland
oil gland
sebum

# INTEGUMENTARY SYSTEM

*The integumentary system, consisting of the skin, hair, and nails, acts as a barrier to protect the body from the outside world. It also functions to retain body fluids, protect against disease, eliminate waste products, and regulate body temperature.*

## SKIN

The skin is one of the human body's largest organs. Subjected to a lifetime of wear and tear, the layers of skin are capable of repairing themselves. Skin contains sensory receptors that monitor the external environment, and mechanisms that rid the body of wastes. The skin is composed of two layers—the epidermis and the dermis.

### Epidermis

The **epidermis,** or outer layer of skin, is composed of many sheets of flattened, scaly epithelial cells. Its top layers are made of mostly dead cells. These cells are exposed to the dangers of the external environment. Scraped or rubbed away on a daily basis, they are replaced by new cells made in the rapidly dividing lower layers. The cells of the epidermis are filled with a protein called **keratin,** which gives skin its rough, leathery texture and its waterproof quality.

There is a great variety in skin color among humans. The color of skin is mainly determined by a brown pigment called **melanin** (MEL-uh-nin), which is produced by cells in the lower layers of the epidermis. Melanin absorbs harmful ultraviolet radiation. The amount of melanin produced in skin depends on two factors: heredity and the length of time the skin is exposed to ultraviolet radiation. Increased amounts of melanin are produced in a person's skin in response to ultraviolet radiation. All people, but especially people with light skin, need to minimize exposure to the sun and protect themselves from its ultraviolet radiation, which can damage the DNA in skin cells and lead to deadly forms of skin cancer.

### Dermis

The **dermis,** the inner layer of skin, is composed of living cells and specialized structures, such as sensory neurons, blood vessels, muscle fibers, hair follicles, and glands. Sensory neurons make it possible for you to sense many kinds of conditions and signals from the environment, such as heat and pressure. Blood vessels provide nourishment to the living cells and help regulate body temperature.

## Word Roots and Origins

**Epidermis**

from the Greek *epi,* meaning "on" or "upon," and *derma,* meaning "skin"

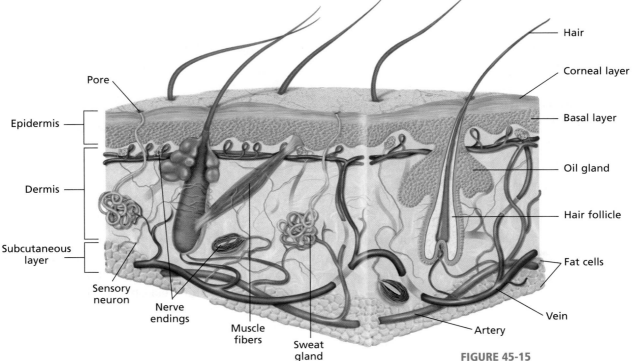

Pore

Epidermis

Dermis

Subcutaneous layer

Sensory neuron

Nerve endings

Muscle fibers

Sweat gland

Hair

Corneal layer

Basal layer

Oil gland

Hair follicle

Fat cells

Vein

Artery

**FIGURE 45-15**

Skin is composed of two layers: the epidermis and the dermis. The top of the epidermis consists of dead, flattened cells that are shed and replaced every day. The dermis contains specialized structures that protect the body from infectious diseases, regulate body temperature, sense the environment, and secrete oil, sweat, and some wastes.

Tiny muscle fibers attached to hair follicles contract and pull hair upright when you are cold or afraid, producing what are commonly called goose bumps. Glands produce sweat, which helps cool your body, and oil, which helps soften your skin. A layer of fat cells lies below the dermis. These cells act as energy reserves; add a protective, shock-absorbing layer; and insulate the body against heat loss. Study the structures of the skin in Figure 45-15.

## Glands

The skin contains **exocrine glands,** glands that release secretions through ducts. The main exocrine glands of the skin are the sweat glands and the oil glands.

The skin functions as an excretory organ by releasing excess water, salts, and urea through the **sweat glands.** By releasing excess water, the skin also helps regulate body temperature. When the body's temperature rises, circulation increases, and the skin becomes warm and flushed, as shown in Figure 45-16. The sweat glands then release more sweat. As the water in sweat evaporates, the skin is cooled.

**Oil glands,** found in large numbers on the face and scalp, secrete the fatty substance **sebum.** Oil glands are usually connected by tiny ducts to hair follicles. Sebum coats the surface of the skin and the shafts of hairs, preventing excess water loss and softening the skin and hair. Sebum is also mildly toxic to some bacteria. The production of sebum is controlled by hormones. During adolescence, high levels of sex hormones increase the activity of the oil glands. If the ducts of oil glands become clogged with excessive amounts of sebum, dead cells, and bacteria, the skin disorder *acne* can result.

**FIGURE 45-16**

Skin acts as a temperature-controlling device. It contains millions of sweat glands that secrete microscopic droplets of water. The water droplets help cool the body when its temperature rises, such as after a rigorous workout.

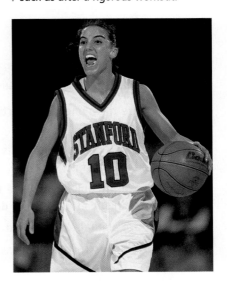

FIGURE 45-17

This illustration of the structure of a fingernail shows that the nail root, from which the nail is constantly regenerated, is protected well beneath the surface of the finger, next to the bone of the fingertip.

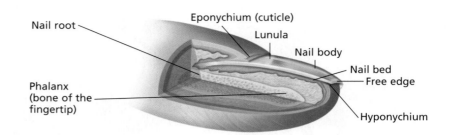

Nail root

Eponychium (cuticle)

Lunula

Nail body

Nail bed

Free edge

Phalanx (bone of the fingertip)

Hyponychium

# NAILS

Nails, which protect the ends of the fingers and toes, form from nail roots under skin folds at the base and sides of the nail. As new cells form, the nail grows longer. Like hair, nails are composed primarily of keratin. The nail body is about 0.5 mm (0.02 in.) thick. Nails grow at about 1 mm (0.04 in.) per week. Nails rest on a bed of tissue filled with blood vessels, giving the nails a pinkish color. The structure of a fingernail can be seen in Figure 45-17.

Changes in the shape, structure, and appearance of the nails may be an indicator of a disease somewhere in the body. They may turn yellow in patients with chronic respiratory disorders, or they may grow concave in certain blood disorders.

# HAIR

Hair, which protects and insulates the body, is produced by a cluster of cells at the base of deep dermal pits called *hair follicles*. The hair shaft is composed of dead, keratin-filled cells that overlap like roof shingles. Oil glands associated with hair follicles prevent hair from drying out. Most individual hairs grow for several years and then fall out.

Hair color is the result of the presence of the pigment melanin in the hair shaft. Black, brown, and yellow variants of melanin combine to determine an individual's hair color. Hair color is influenced by hereditary factors.

## SECTION 4 REVIEW

1. What are the names and functions of the two layers of skin?

2. Identify the reason the dermis is considered the living layer of skin.

3. What are the functions of the two types of exocrine glands found in the dermis?

4. Illustrate and label the structure of a fingernail.

5. Describe the structure of hair.

**CRITICAL THINKING**

6. **Relating Concepts** Why can sunbathing be considered dangerous?

7. **Analyzing Information** A third-degree burn may be surrounded by painful areas of second- and first- degree burns. However, a third-degree burn is often painless. Why?

8. **Recognizing Relationships** How might muscles in the dermis benefit mammals in cold weather?

# CHAPTER HIGHLIGHTS

## SECTION 1   The Human Body Plan

- The human body has four main types of tissue: muscle, nervous, epithelial, and connective.

- A tissue is a collection of cells, an organ is a collection of tissues, and an organ system is a collection of organs.

- Some of the primary organ systems in the body include the integumentary, nervous, and cardiovascular systems.

- Many organs are located in the body's five main cavities: abdominal, cranial, spinal, thoracic, and pelvic.

**Vocabulary**

muscle tissue (p. 907)
skeletal muscle (p. 907)
smooth muscle (p. 907)
cardiac muscle (p. 907)

nervous tissue (p. 907)
neurons (p. 907)
epithelial tissue (p. 908)
connective tissue (p. 908)

matrix (p. 908)
organ (p. 909)
cranial cavity (p. 910)
spinal cavity (p. 910)

diaphragm (p. 910)
thoracic cavity (p. 910)
abdominal cavity (p. 910)
pelvic cavity (p. 910)

## SECTION 2   Skeletal System

- The human skeleton is composed of the axial skeleton (skull, ribs, spine, and sternum) and the appendicular skeleton (arms and legs, scapula, clavicle, and pelvis).

- Bones support muscles, give structure to the body, protect organs, store minerals, and make blood cells.

- Bones are made up of minerals, protein fibers, and cells.

- Most bones develop from cartilage through a process called *ossification*.

- The human body has three types of joints: fixed joints, semimovable joints, and movable joints. The joints can be affected by a disease called arthritis.

**Vocabulary**

skeleton (p. 911)
axial skeleton (p. 911)
appendicular skeleton (p. 911)
periosteum (p. 912)
compact bone (p. 913)

Haversian canal (p. 913)
osteocyte (p. 913)
spongy bone (p. 913)
bone marrow (p. 913)
fracture (p. 913)

ossification (p. 914)
epiphyseal plate (p. 914)
joint (p. 915)
fixed joint (p. 915)
semimovable joint (p. 915)

movable joint (p. 915)
ligament (p. 915)
synovial fluid (p. 915)
rheumatoid arthritis (p. 916)
osteoarthritis (p. 916)

## SECTION 3   Muscular System

- The human body has three types of muscle tissues: skeletal, smooth, and cardiac.

- Skeletal muscles consist of groups of fibers. Muscle fibers contain myofibrils made up of protein filaments.

- During a muscle contraction, myosin and actin filaments interact to shorten the length of a sarcomere.

- Most skeletal muscles are arranged in opposing pairs.

**Vocabulary**

muscle fiber (p. 917)
striation (p. 917)
voluntary muscle (p. 917)
involuntary muscle (p. 918)

myofibril (p. 919)
myosin (p. 919)
actin (p. 919)
Z line (p. 919)

sarcomere (p. 919)
tendon (p. 921)
origin (p. 921)
insertion (p. 921)

flexor (p. 921)
extensor (p. 921)
muscle fatigue (p. 922)
oxygen debt (p. 922)

## SECTION 4   Integumentary System

- Skin, hair, and nails act as barriers that protect the body from the environment.

- Skin is composed of two layers, which are the epidermis and the dermis.

- Hair and nails are composed of the protein keratin; they grow from a root of rapidly dividing cells.

- Sweat glands produce sweat, which cools the body. Oil glands secrete sebum, which softens the skin.

**Vocabulary**

epidermis (p. 924)
keratin (p. 924)

melanin (p. 924)
dermis (p. 924)

exocrine gland (p. 925)
sweat gland (p. 925)

oil gland (p. 925)
sebum (p. 925)

## USING VOCABULARY

1. Choose the term that does not belong in the following group, and explain why it does not belong: *saddle joint, pivot joint, fixed joint,* and *hinge joint,* and *ball-and-socket joint.*

2. Distinguish between *compact bone* and *spongy bone.*

3. Use the following key terms in the same sentence: *actin, muscle fiber, myofibrils,* and *myosin.*

4. **Word Roots and Origins** The word *epidermis* is derived from the Greek *derma,* which means "skin." The prefix *epi* means "on." Using this information, explain why the term *epidermis* is a good name for the anatomical structure it describes.

## UNDERSTANDING KEY CONCEPTS

5. **Define** epithelial tissue.

6. **Explain** the relationship between cells, tissues, organs, and organ systems.

7. **Summarize** the functions of the primary organ systems in the human body.

8. **Describe** the organs that can be found in the abdominal cavity.

9. **List** all of the bones in the axial skeleton.

10. **Identify** the five functions of the skeletal system.

11. **Explain** the role the Haversian canals play in compact bone.

12. **Define** red bone marrow. Where is it produced, and what is its function?

13. **Summarize** how bones develop and elongate.

14. **State** three types of joints, and give examples of each type.

15. **Describe** the cause and symptoms of the disease rheumatoid arthritis.

16. **Explain** the difference between skeletal muscle, smooth muscle, and cardiac muscle.

17. **Describe** the components of a sarcomere.

18. **Illustrate** how a skeletal muscle contracts.

19. **Explain** how muscles move bones.

20. **Name** the functions of tendons and ligaments.

21. **List** four functions of the skin.

22. **Identify** the difference between the epidermis and the dermis.

23. **Define** melanin. What is its role in the body?

24. **Explain** the similarities and differences between nails and hair.

25. **Identify** the substance that prevents the hair and skin from drying out, and the gland where this substance is produced.

26. **CONCEPT MAPPING** Use the following terms to create a concept map that illustrates the body's four levels of structural organization: *muscle tissue, connective tisue, epithelial tissue, nervous tissue, organ,* and *organ system.*

## CRITICAL THINKING

27. **Inferring Relationships** Young thoroughbred horses that are raced too early in life have an increased risk of breaking the bones in their legs. What can you infer about the process of ossification in horses?

28. **Evaluating Information** During a normal birth, a baby passes through the mother's pelvis. A woman's pelvis has a larger diameter and is more oval-shaped than a man's pelvis. In addition, a newborn's skull bones are not completely ossified. How are these skeletal properties advantageous to the birthing process?

29. **Analyzing Concepts** Oil glands secrete an oily substance that helps keep the skin soft and flexible. They also secrete fatty acids, which help kill bacteria. How can the function of oil glands be affected if you wash your skin too frequently?

30. **Interpreting Graphics** Examine the drawing of epithelial cells below. The flat epithelial cells of the skin overlap each other much like shingles on a roof do. How does this arrangement enable these cells to perform their protective function?

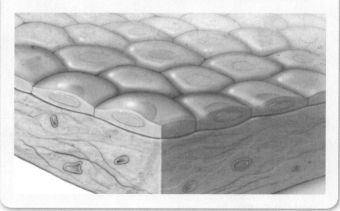

# Standardized Test Preparation

**DIRECTIONS:** Choose the letter that best answers the question or completes the sentence.

1. The thoracic cavity contains which organs?
   - **A.** brain
   - **B.** spine
   - **C.** organs of the digestive system
   - **D.** organs of the respiratory system

2. The cells of connective tissue are embedded in what substance?
   - **F.** matrix
   - **G.** keratin
   - **H.** marrow
   - **J.** synovial fluid

3. The periosteum is a membrane that does which of the following?
   - **A.** covers the bone
   - **B.** contains marrow
   - **C.** produces red blood cells
   - **D.** increases the length of long bones

4. Which of the following is true about the dermis?
   - **F.** It is the top layer of skin.
   - **G.** It contains cardiac muscle.
   - **H.** It is made up of dead cells.
   - **J.** It contains nerves and blood vessels.

**INTERPRETING GRAPHICS:** The graph below shows the relationship between skin type, UV index, and sun burns. Use the table to answer the question that follows.

### Relationship of UV Index and Sunburns

| UV index | Minutes before Skin Type 1 burns | Minutes before Skin Type 4 burns |
|---|---|---|
| 0–2 | 30 | > 120 |
| 3 | 20 | 90 |
| 5 | 12 | 60 |
| 7 | 8.5 | 40 |
| 9 | 7 | 33 |

5. Which of the following statements about skin type 1 is true?
   - **A.** Skin type 4 will never sunburn.
   - **B.** Skin type 1 will always burn in less than 20 minutes.
   - **C.** Skin type 1 is less sensitive to UV exposure than skin type 4 is.
   - **D.** Skin type 1 is more sensitive to UV exposure than skin type 4 is.

**DIRECTIONS:** Complete the following analogy.

6. nerve : neuron :: bone :
   - **F.** marrow
   - **G.** skeleton
   - **H.** osteocyte
   - **J.** Haversian canal

**INTERPRETING GRAPHICS:** The figure below shows a sarcomere and an enlargement of actin and myosin filaments. Use the figure to answer the question that follows.

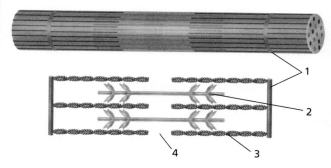

7. Which part of the sarcomere represents the Z line?
   - **A.** feature 1
   - **B.** feature 2
   - **C.** feature 3
   - **D.** feature 4

## SHORT RESPONSE

Red bone marrow inside spongy bone produces red blood cells, which are specialized cells used to carry oxygen throughout the body.

How are red blood cells transported around the body?

## EXTENDED RESPONSE

A single layer of smooth muscle encircles the walls of blood vessels. The walls of the stomach and small intestine have a layer of circular smooth muscle and a layer of longitudinal smooth muscle.

*Part A* How does the muscle arrangement of blood vessels reflect the function of this structure?

*Part B* How does the muscle arrangement of the stomach and small intestine reflect the function of these structures?

**Test TIP** For a question involving experimental data, determine the constants, variables, and control **before** answering the questions.

# Dehydrating and Demineralizing Bone

## OBJECTIVES

- Determine the amount of water and minerals in bone.
- Identify structures in bone cells.

## PROCESS SKILLS

- observing
- identifying
- calculating

## MATERIALS

- balance
- beaker, 250 mL
- beakers, 500 mL (2)
- bones (2)
- bone slides, prepared
- drying oven
- gauze, circular piece
- glass plate or parafilm
- hot pad
- hydrochloric acid, 1 M (300 mL)
- lens paper
- marker, permanent
- microscope, compound
- pencil, wax
- plastic bag, resealable
- specimen tag
- tongs

## Background

1. Dehydration is the process of removing the water from a substance.
2. Demineralization is the process of removing the minerals from a substance.

### PART A Dehydrating a Bone

1. In your lab report, prepare a data table similar to Table A.
2. Put on safety goggles, a lab apron, and gloves. Wear this protective gear during all parts of this investigation.

### TABLE A *DEHYDRATION OF BONE*

| Mass before drying | Mass after drying | Percentage of bone mass lost |
|---|---|---|
|  |  |  |
|  |  |  |

3. Obtain a bone from your teacher. Test the flexibility of the bone by trying to bend and twist it.
4. Place the bone on a balance. Measure the mass of the bone to the nearest 0.1 g, and record it in your data table. Then, use a permanent marker to write the initials of each member of your group on a specimen tag, and tie the tag to the bone.
5. Place the bone in a drying oven at 100°C for 30 minutes. While the bone is in the oven, complete Part C.
6. **CAUTION Do not touch hot objects with your bare hands. Use insulated gloves and tongs as appropriate.** Using tongs, remove the bone from the oven and place it on a heat-resistant pad to cool for 10 minutes.
7. Use tongs to place the cooled bone on the balance. Measure the mass of the bone to the nearest 0.1 g, and record it in your data table.
8. Use the equation below to calculate the percentage of the bone's mass that was lost during heating.

Percentage mass lost =

$$\frac{\text{mass before heating} - \text{mass after heating}}{\text{mass before heating}} \times 100$$

### PART B Demineralizing a Bone

9. In your lab report, prepare a data table similar to Table B.
10. Obtain a second bone from your teacher. Test the flexibility of the bone by trying to bend and twist it.

## TABLE B  DEMINERALIZATION OF A BONE

| Mass before demineralizing | Mass after demineralizing and drying | Percentage of bone mass lost |
|---|---|---|
|  |  |  |
|  |  |  |

11. Place the bone on a balance. Measure the mass of the bone, and record it in your data table.

12. **CAUTION Glassware is fragile. Notify your teacher promptly of any broken glass or cuts. Do not clean up broken glass or spills unless your teacher tells you to do so.** Using a wax pencil, label a 500 mL beaker "1 M HCl." Also label the beaker with the initials of all group members. Place a piece of gauze in the bottom of the beaker.

13. **CAUTION If you get an acid on your skin or clothing, wash it off at the sink immediately while calling to your teacher.** Place the bone on top of the gauze in the beaker, and add enough 1 M HCl to cover the bone. Use a glass plate or parafilm to cover the beaker.

14. Place the beaker under a fume hood, and allow the bone to soak in the acid until it softens and becomes spongy. This should take 5 to 7 days. Periodically use tongs to test the hardness of the bone. *Note: Do not touch the bone with your fingers while it is soaking in acid. Rinse the tongs with water thoroughly each time you finish testing the bone.*

15. When the bone becomes spongy, use tongs to carefully remove it from the beaker, and rinse it under running water for two minutes.

16. After the bone has been thoroughly rinsed, test the bone for hardness by twisting and bending it with your fingers. *Note: Be sure you are wearing gloves.*

17. Then, use a permanent marker to write the initials of each member of your group on a specimen tag, and tie the tag to the bone. Place the bone in a drying oven at 100°C for 30 minutes.

18. **CAUTION Do not touch hot objects with your bare hands. Use insulated gloves and tongs as appropriate.** Using tongs, remove the bone from the oven and place it on a heat-resistant pad. Allow the bone to cool for 10 minutes.

19. Use tongs to place the cooled bone on the balance. Measure the mass of the bone to the nearest 0.1 g, and record the measurement in your data table.

20. Use the equation below to calculate the percentage of the bone's mass that was lost through demineralization and dehydration.

Percentage of mass lost =

$$\frac{\text{mass before demineralizing} - \text{mass after demineralizing and drying}}{\text{mass before demineralizing}} \times 100$$

### PART C  Observing Prepared Slides of Bone

21. **CAUTION Do not use electrical equipment near water or with wet hands or clothing.** Using a compound light microscope, focus on a prepared slide of bone by using low power, and then switch to high power. Locate a Haversian canal, the darkly stained circle in the center of a set of lamellae. Find the darkly stained osteocytes between the lamellae.

22. In your lab report, draw and label the following bone structures: Haversian canal, lamella, and osteocyte.

## Analysis and Conclusions

1. What effect did water loss have on the bone? What effect did mineral loss have on the bone?

2. Why did you have to dehydrate the bone before measuring its mass in Part B?

3. What percentage of bone is water? What percentage of bone is made of minerals?

4. If you were to prepare a slide using the dehydrated and demineralized bone, what do you think the bone would look like?

5. What happened when the demineralized bone was dried? Why do you think this happened?

6. If a person's diet lacked calcium, how could this affect his or her bones?

## Further Inquiry

Research the differences in the amount and distribution of different bone types from various parts of the human skeleton.

# CIRCULATORY AND RESPIRATORY SYSTEMS

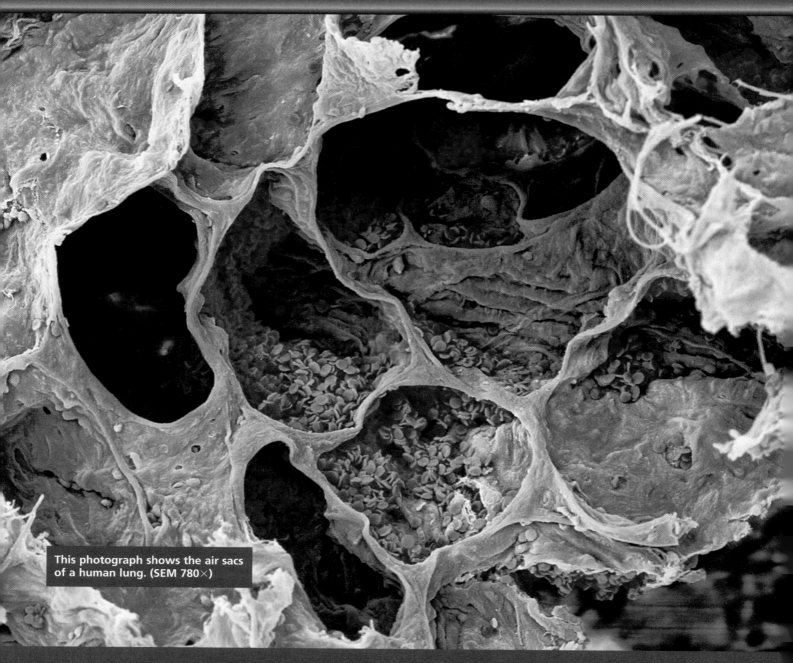

This photograph shows the air sacs of a human lung. (SEM 780×)

# THE CIRCULATORY SYSTEM

*Most of the cells in the human body are not in direct contact with the external environment. The circulatory system acts as a transport service for these cells. Two fluids move through the circulatory system: blood and lymph.*

## THE HEART

The blood, heart, and blood vessels form the **cardiovascular system.** The lymph, lymph nodes, and lymph vessels form the **lymphatic system.** The cardiovascular system and lymphatic system collectively make up the *circulatory system.* The circulatory system transports nutrients, hormones, and gases; gets rid of wastes; and helps maintain a constant body temperature.

The central organ of the cardiovascular system is the heart, the muscular organ that pumps blood through a network of blood vessels. The heart beats more than 2.5 billion times in an average life span. Yet this organ is slightly larger than a fist. The heart lies within the thoracic (chest) cavity, behind the sternum (breastbone) and between the two lungs. A tough, saclike membrane called the *pericardium* surrounds the heart and secretes a fluid that reduces friction as the heart beats.

Notice in Figure 46-1 that a *septum* (wall) vertically divides the heart into two sides. The right side pumps blood to the lungs, and the left side pumps blood to the other parts of the body. Each side of the heart is divided into an upper and lower chamber. Each upper chamber is called an **atrium,** and each lower chamber is called a **ventricle.**

## SECTION 1

### OBJECTIVES

- **Describe** the structure and function of the human heart.
- **Trace** the flow of blood through the heart and body.
- **Distinguish** between arteries, veins, and capillaries in terms of their structure and function.
- **Distinguish** between pulmonary circulation and systemic circulation.
- **Summarize** the functions of the lymphatic system.

### VOCABULARY

cardiovascular system
lymphatic system
atrium
ventricle
valve
aorta
sinoatrial node
atrioventricular node
pulse
artery
blood pressure
hypertension
capillary
vein
pulmonary circulation
systemic circulation
atherosclerosis
lymph

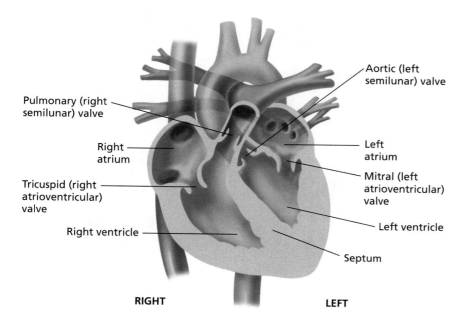

Pulmonary (right semilunar) valve

Right atrium

Tricuspid (right atrioventricular) valve

Right ventricle

Aortic (left semilunar) valve

Left atrium

Mitral (left atrioventricular) valve

Left ventricle

Septum

**RIGHT**          **LEFT**

**FIGURE 46-1**

The septum prevents mixing of blood from the two sides of the heart, and the valves ensure that blood flows in only one direction.

**Valves** are flaps of tissue that open in only one direction. The *atrioventricular* (AY-tree-oh-ven-TRIH-kyuh-luhr) *valve* (AV valve) on the right side of the heart is called the *tricuspid valve*. The *mitral valve*, also called the *bicuspid valve*, is on the left. As the ventricles pump, blood pressure closes the AV valves to prevent blood from flowing backward into the atria. From the ventricles, blood is pumped out of the heart into large vessels. A *semilunar* (SEM-ee-LOON-uhr) *valve* (SL valve) separates the ventricles from these large vessels on each side of the heart. The SL valve on the right side is known as the *pulmonary valve*, and the SL valve on the left side is known as the *aortic valve*. The SL valves prevent blood from flowing back into the ventricles when the heart relaxes.

## Circulation in the Heart

Refer to Figure 46-2 to trace the path of the blood as it circulates through the heart. Blood returning to the heart from parts of the body other than the lungs has a high concentration of carbon dioxide and a low concentration of oxygen. ❶ Deoxygenated ($O_2$-poor) blood enters the right atrium. ❷ The right atrium sends deoxygenated blood into the right ventricle. ❸ The muscles of the right ventricle contract and force the blood into the pulmonary arteries. ❹ The pulmonary artery sends the blood to the lungs. In the lungs, the carbon dioxide diffuses out of the blood, and oxygen diffuses into the blood. ❺ The oxygenated blood returns to the left atrium of the heart. Notice in Figure 46-2 that the flow of blood on the left side of the heart is illustrated with a red arrow representing oxygenated blood, which has a bright red color.

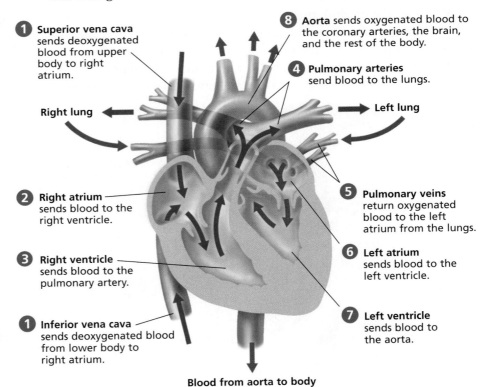

**1 Superior vena cava** sends deoxygenated blood from upper body to right atrium.

**8 Aorta** sends oxygenated blood to the coronary arteries, the brain, and the rest of the body.

**4 Pulmonary arteries** send blood to the lungs.

**Right lung**

**Left lung**

**2 Right atrium** sends blood to the right ventricle.

**5 Pulmonary veins** return oxygenated blood to the left atrium from the lungs.

**3 Right ventricle** sends blood to the pulmonary artery.

**6 Left atrium** sends blood to the left ventricle.

**1 Inferior vena cava** sends deoxygenated blood from lower body to right atrium.

**7 Left ventricle** sends blood to the aorta.

**Blood from aorta to body**

**FIGURE 46-2**

Trace the path of blood through the heart. Notice that illustrations of a heart are drawn as if the heart were in a person facing you. That is, the left side of the heart is shown on the right as you face the heart, and the right side of the heart is on the left as you face the heart.

**⑥** The oxygenated blood is then pumped into the left ventricle. **⑦** Contraction of the muscular walls of the left ventricle forces the blood into a large blood vessel called the **aorta.** **⑧** From the aorta, blood is transported to all parts of the body. The left ventricle is the thickest chamber of the heart because it has to do the most work to pump blood to all parts of the body.

Deoxygenated blood is commonly represented with the color blue. However, it is a misconception that deoxygenated blood is blue. When oxygen is attached to hemoglobin, the blood is bright red. Without oxygen, blood is dark red. The dark red blood in veins appears blue when it shows through the vein walls and skin.

## Control of the Heartbeat

The heart consists of muscle cells that contract in waves. When the first group of cells are stimulated, they in turn stimulate neighboring cells. Those cells then stimulate more cells. This chain reaction continues until all the cells contract. The wave of activity spreads in such a way that the atria and the ventricles contract in a steady rhythm. The first group of heart-muscle cells that get stimulated lie in an area of the heart known as the sinoatrial node, shown in Figure 46-3.

The **sinoatrial** (SIEN-oh-AY-tree-uhl) **(SA) node** is a group of specialized heart-muscle cells located in the right atrium. These muscle cells spontaneously initiate their own electrical impulse and contract. The SA node is often called the *pacemaker* because it regulates the rate of contraction of the entire heart. The electrical impulse initiated by the SA node subsequently reaches another special area of the heart, known as the **atrioventricular (AV) node.** The AV node is located in the septum between the atria, as shown in Figure 46-3. The AV node relays the electrical impulse to the muscle cells that make up the ventricles. As a result, the ventricles contract a fraction of a second after the atria, completing one full heartbeat. In an average adult at rest, the heart beats about 70 times each minute.

A heartbeat has two phases. Phase one, called *systole* (SIS-tohl), occurs when the ventricles contract, closing the AV valves and opening the SL valves to pump blood into the two major vessels that exit the heart. Phase two, called *diastole* (DIE-a-stohl), occurs when the ventricles relax, allowing the back pressure of the blood to close the SL valves and opening the AV valves. The closing of these two heart valves results in the characteristic *lub dup* sound we call a heartbeat. If one of the valves fails to close properly, some blood may flow backward, creating a different sound, which is known as a heart murmur.

A person's **pulse** is a series of pressure waves within an artery caused by the contractions of the left ventricle. When the ventricle contracts, blood surges through the arteries, and the elastic walls in the vessels expand and stretch. The most common site for taking a pulse is at a radial artery, on the thumb side of each wrist. The average pulse rate ranges from 70 to 90 beats per minute for adults.

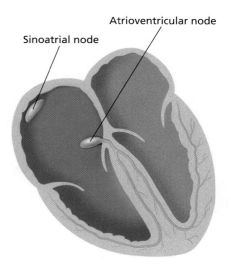

Sinoatrial node  Atrioventricular node

**FIGURE 46-3**

Two areas of specialized tissue, known as nodes, control the heartbeat. A person whose SA node is defective can have an operation to implant an artificial pacemaker. An artificial pacemaker can also help a defective AV node.

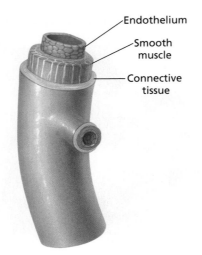

Endothelium

Smooth muscle

Connective tissue

**Artery**
(carries blood away from the heart)

**FIGURE 46-4**

Notice the thick muscular layer of an artery. The layers of the artery wall are separated by elastic tissue. This tissue provides strength, preventing systolic pressure from bursting the artery.

**FIGURE 46-5**

The diameter of a capillary is so small that red blood cells must move single file through these vessels, as shown in this photograph (1,200×). All exchange of nutrients and waste between blood and cells occurs across the thin walls of the capillaries.

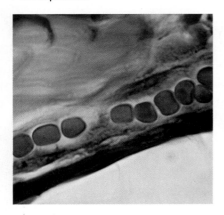

# BLOOD VESSELS

The circulatory system is known as a closed system because the blood is contained within either the heart or the blood vessels at all times. This type of system differs from an open system, in which blood leaves the vessels and circulates within tissues throughout the organism's body. The blood vessels that are part of the closed circulatory system of humans form a vast network to help keep the blood flowing in one direction.

## Arteries and Blood Pressure

The large, muscular vessels that carry blood away from the heart are called **arteries.** As shown in Figure 46-4, the thick walls of the arteries have three layers: an inner endothelial layer, a middle layer of smooth muscle, and an outer layer of connective tissue. This structure gives arteries a combination of strength and elasticity, which allows them to stretch as pressurized blood enters from the heart. You can feel this stretching of arteries—it is your pulse.

Contraction of the heart moves the blood through the arteries with great force. The force that blood exerts against the inside walls of a blood vessel is known as **blood pressure.** Blood pressure is highest in the two main arteries that leave the heart. It is usually measured in the artery that supplies blood to the arm. To measure blood pressure, a trained person inflates a cuff that is placed around a patient's arm, temporarily stopping the flow of blood through the artery. Connected to the cuff is a gauge containing a column of mercury (Hg) that rises as the pressure in the cuff increases. The trained person then releases the air in the cuff slowly while listening to the artery with a stethoscope and watching the column of mercury. The first sounds of blood passing through the artery indicates the *systolic pressure*, or the pressure of the blood when the ventricles contract. In a normal adult, the systolic pressure is about 120 mm of Hg for males and 110 mm of Hg for females. Continuing to release the air in the cuff, the trained person next listens for the disappearance of sound, which indicates a steady flow of blood through the artery in the arm. This indicates the *diastolic pressure*. In a normal adult, the diastolic pressure is about 80 mm of Hg for males and 70 mm of Hg for females.

High blood pressure, or **hypertension,** is a leading cause of death in many countries. Blood pressure that is higher than normal places a strain on the walls of the arteries and increases the chance that a vessel will burst.

## Capillaries and Veins

Recall that when the left ventricle contracts, it forces blood into the aorta, the body's largest artery. From the aorta, blood travels through a network of smaller arteries, which in turn divide and form even smaller vessels, called *arterioles*. The arterioles branch into a network of tiny vessels, called **capillaries.** A capillary is shown in Figure 46-5.

The network formed by capillaries is so extensive that all of the approximately 100 trillion cells in the body lie within about 125 µm of a capillary. This close association between capillaries and cells allows for rapid exchange of materials. Capillary walls are only one cell thick; gases and nutrients can diffuse through these thin walls. Wherever the concentration of oxygen or nutrients is higher in the blood than in the surrounding cells, the substance diffuses from the blood into the cells. Wherever the concentrations of carbon dioxide and wastes are higher in the cells than in the blood, these substances diffuse from the cells into the blood.

Blood flows through capillaries that merge to form larger vessels called *venules* (VEN-yoolz). Several venules in turn unite to form a **vein,** a large blood vessel that carries blood to the heart. Veins returning deoxygenated blood from the lower parts of the body merge to form the *inferior vena cava.* Veins returning deoxygenated blood from the upper parts of the body merge to form the *superior vena cava.* Refer back to Figure 46-2, and locate the inferior vena cava and the superior vena cava.

As you can see in Figure 46-6, although the walls of the veins are composed of three layers, like those of the arteries, they are thinner and less muscular. By the time blood reaches the veins, it is under much less pressure than it was in the arteries. With less pressure being exerted in the veins, the blood could flow backward and disrupt the pattern of circulation. To prevent that, valves in the veins help keep the blood flowing in one direction. Many veins pass through skeletal muscle. When these muscles contract, they are able to squeeze the blood through the veins. When these muscles relax, the valves can close, thus preventing the blood from flowing backward. Figure 46-6 shows the structure of a valve in a vein.

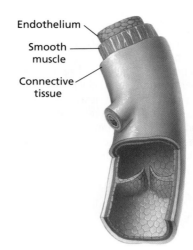

**Vein**
(returns blood to the heart)

**FIGURE 46-6**

Like an artery, a vein has three layers: the outer layer of connective tissue, the middle layer of smooth muscle, and the inner layer of endothelial tissue.

# PATTERNS OF CIRCULATION

The English scientist William Harvey (1578–1657) first showed that the heart and the blood vessels form one continuous, closed system of circulation, as shown in Figure 46-7. He also reasoned that this system consists of two primary subsystems: **pulmonary circulation,** in which the blood travels between the heart and lungs, and **systemic circulation,** in which the blood travels between the heart and all other body tissues.

## Pulmonary Circulation

Deoxygenated blood returning from all parts of the body except the lungs enters the right atrium, where it is then pumped into the right ventricle. When the right ventricle contracts, the deoxygenated blood is sent through the pulmonary artery to the lungs. The pulmonary artery is the only artery that carries deoxygenated blood. The pulmonary artery branches into two smaller arteries, with one artery going to each lung. These arteries branch into arterioles and then into capillaries in the lungs.

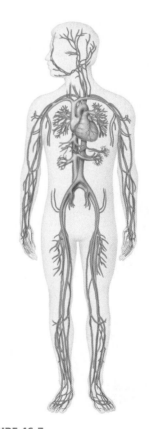

**FIGURE 46-7**

The cardiovascular system transports materials throughout the body and distributes heat.

FIGURE 46-8

The pulmonary circulation between the heart and the lungs involves the pulmonary arteries and the pulmonary veins. Deoxygenated blood flows from the right side of the heart to the lungs. Oxygenated blood is returned to the left side of the heart from the lungs. This is the opposite of systemic and coronary blood flow, in which oxygen-rich blood flows from the heart and oxygen-poor blood is returned to the heart.

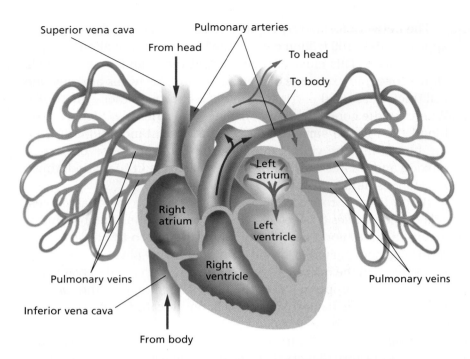

FIGURE 46-9

Notice three subsystems of systemic circulation. Other subsystems transport blood between the heart and the head, arms, and other organs.

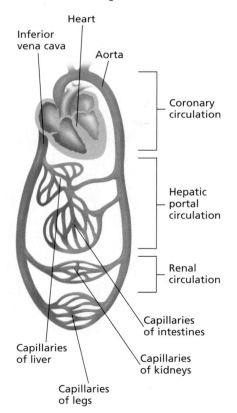

In the lungs, carbon dioxide diffuses out of the capillaries and oxygen diffuses into the capillaries. The oxygenated blood then flows into venules, which merge into the *pulmonary veins* that lead to the left atrium of the heart. From the left atrium, blood is pumped into the left ventricle and then to the body through the aorta. In Figure 46-8, trace the path blood takes as it passes through pulmonary circulation.

## Systemic Circulation

Systemic circulation is the movement of blood between the heart and all parts of the body except the lungs. Trace the path blood follows in systemic circulation in Figure 46-9. Notice that oxygenated blood is pumped out of the left ventricle and into the aorta. From the aorta, blood flows into other subsystems of systemic circulation.

*Coronary circulation* is the subsystem of systemic circulation that supplies blood to the heart itself. If blood flow in the *coronary arteries,* which supply blood to the heart, is reduced or cut off, muscle cells will die. This can happen when an artery is blocked by a blood clot or by **atherosclerosis** (ATH-uhr-oh-skler-OH-sis), a disease characterized by the buildup of fatty materials on the interior walls of the coronary arteries. Either type of blockage can lead to a *heart attack*.

*Hepatic portal circulation* is a subsystem of systemic circulation. Nutrients are picked up by capillaries in the small intestine and are transported by the blood to the liver. Excess nutrients are stored in the liver for future needs. The liver receives oxygenated blood from a large artery that branches from the aorta.

*Renal circulation*, another subsystem of systemic circulation, supplies blood to the kidneys. Nearly one-fourth of the blood that is pumped into the aorta by the left ventricle flows to the kidneys. The kidneys filter waste from the blood.

# LYMPHATIC SYSTEM

In addition to the cardiovascular system, the circulatory system also includes the lymphatic system. One function of the lymphatic system is to return fluids that have collected in the tissues to the bloodstream. Fluids diffuse through the capillary walls just as oxygen and nutrients do. Some of these fluids pass into cells, some return to the capillaries, and some remain in the intercellular spaces.

Excess fluid in the tissues moves into the tiny vessels of the lymphatic system; this fluid is called **lymph.** Lymph vessels merge to form larger vessels. The lymph vessels are similar in structure to capillaries, and the larger lymph vessels are similar in structure to veins. However, an important difference exists between blood vessels and lymph vessels. Blood vessels form a complete circuit so that blood passes from the heart to all parts of the body and then back again to the heart. In contrast, lymph vessels form a one-way system that returns fluids collected in the tissues back to the bloodstream. In addition, the lymphatic system has no pump. Like the blood in veins, lymph must be moved through the vessels by the squeezing of skeletal muscles. Like veins, the larger lymph vessels have valves to prevent the fluid from moving backward.

Notice in Figure 46-10 that lymph vessels form a vast network that extends throughout the body. The lymph that travels in these vessels is a transparent yellowish fluid, much like the liquid part of the blood. As the lymph travels through these vessels on its way to the heart, it passes through small organs known as lymph nodes. Notice in Figure 46-10 that lymph nodes are like beads on a string. These nodes filter the lymph as it passes, trapping foreign particles, microorganisms, and other tissue debris. Lymph nodes also store *lymphocytes*, white blood cells that are specialized to fight disease. When a person has an infection, the nodes may become inflamed, swollen, and tender because of the increased number of lymphocytes.

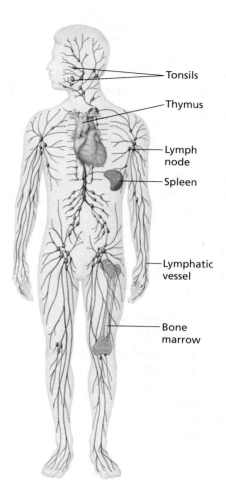

**FIGURE 46-10**

Like the cardiovascular system, the lymphatic system forms a vast network. Concentrated in certain regions of this network are lymph nodes that contain some of the disease-fighting cells of the immune system.

## SECTION 1 REVIEW

1. Describe the structure of the heart.

2. Outline the path that blood follows through the heart and body, starting at the superior vena cava.

3. Describe the process by which the heartbeat is regulated.

4. How are the structures of arteries, veins, and capillaries related to their function?

5. Compare oxygenation levels in pulmonary circulation and systemic circulation.

6. Explain how the lymphatic system works with the cardiovascular system.

**CRITICAL THINKING**

7. **Analyzing Information** Some babies are born with a hole in the septum between the two atria. Based on what you know about blood flow through the heart, explain why this condition would be harmful to the baby.

8. **Forming Reasoned Opinions** In which blood vessels would you expect to find the lowest average blood pressure? Explain your answer.

9. **Applying Information** A man's arm is cut by a piece of glass. Blood comes out of the wound in rapid spurts. Which type of vessel was cut?

### OBJECTIVES

- **List** the components of blood.
- **Distinguish** between red blood cells, white blood cells, and platelets in terms of their structure and function.
- **Summarize** the process of blood clotting.
- **Explain** what determines the compatibility of blood types for transfusion.

### VOCABULARY

plasma
red blood cell (erythrocyte)
hemoglobin
white blood cell (leukocyte)
phagocyte
antibody
platelet
fibrin
blood type
antigen
Rh factor

# BLOOD

*Blood is a liquid connective tissue. The two main functions of the blood are to transport nutrients and oxygen to the cells and to carry carbon dioxide and other waste materials away from the cells. Blood also transfers heat to the body surface and plays a major role in defending the body against disease.*

## COMPOSITION OF BLOOD

Blood is composed of a liquid medium and blood solids (formed elements). Formed elements include red blood cells, white blood cells, and platelets. The liquid makes up about 55 percent of the blood, and formed elements make up the remaining 45 percent. A healthy adult has about 4 to 5 L of blood in his or her body.

### Plasma

**Plasma,** the liquid medium, is a sticky, straw-colored fluid that is about 90 percent water and includes metabolites, nutrients, wastes, salts, and proteins. Cells receive nourishment from dissolved substances carried in the plasma. These substances, which may include vitamins, minerals, amino acids, and glucose, are absorbed from the digestive system and transported to the cells. Plasma also carries hormones and brings wastes from the cells to the kidneys or the lungs to be removed from the body.

A variety of proteins are carried in the plasma. The plasma proteins have various functions. Some of the proteins in the plasma are essential for the formation of blood clots. Another protein, called albumin, plays an important role in the regulation of osmotic pressure between plasma and blood cells and between plasma and tissues. Other proteins, called antibodies, help the body fight disease.

### Red Blood Cells

**Red blood cells,** or **erythrocytes** (uh-RITH-ruh-siets), shown in Figure 46-11, transport oxygen to cells in all parts of the body. Red blood cells are formed in the red marrow of bones. Immature red blood cells synthesize large amounts of an iron-containing protein called **hemoglobin.** Hemoglobin is the molecule that actually transports oxygen and, to a lesser degree, carbon dioxide. During the formation of a red blood cell, its cell nucleus and organelles disintegrate. The mature red blood cell is little more than a membrane containing hemoglobin.

**FIGURE 46-11**

Notice that a mature red blood cell (RBC) is disk-shaped and is concave on both sides. A red blood cell is little more than a cell membrane filled with hemoglobin. How is this structure related to its function?

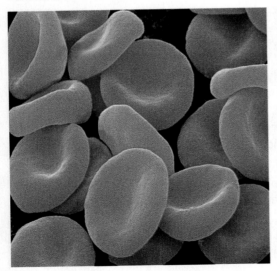

Because red blood cells lack nuclei, they cannot divide and they have a limited survival period, usually 120 to 130 days. Of the more than 30 trillion red blood cells circulating throughout the body at one time, 2 million disintegrate every second. To replace them, new ones form at the same rate in the red marrow of bones. Some parts of the disintegrated red blood cells are recycled. For example, the iron portion of the hemoglobin molecule is carried in the blood to the marrow, where it is reused in new red blood cells.

## White Blood Cells

**White blood cells,** or **leukocytes** (LOO-kuh-siets), help defend the body against disease. They are formed in the red marrow, but some must travel to lymph nodes, tonsils, the thymus, or the spleen to mature. White blood cells are larger than red blood cells and significantly less plentiful. Each cubic millimeter of blood normally contains about 4 million red blood cells and 7,000 white blood cells. White blood cells can squeeze their way through openings in the walls of blood vessels and into the intercellular fluid. In that way, white blood cells can reach the site of infection and help destroy invading microorganisms.

Notice in Figure 46-12 that a white blood cell has a very different structure from that of a red blood cell. For instance, a white blood cell may be irregularly shaped and may have a rough outer surface. There are other differences between red blood cells and white blood cells as well. In contrast with the short-lived red blood cells, white blood cells may function for years. And while there is only one type of red blood cell, there are several types of white blood cells.

The white blood cell shown in Figure 46-12 is the type of white blood cell known as a **phagocyte** (FA-guh-siet). Phagocytes are cells that engulf invading microorganisms. Locate the microorganisms that are being engulfed by the phagocyte in Figure 46-12. Another type of white blood cell produces **antibodies.** Antibodies are proteins that help destroy substances, such as bacteria and viruses, that enter the body and can cause disease. When a person has an infection, the number of white blood cells can double.

### Word Roots and Origins

*leukocyte*

from the Greek *leuco*, meaning "white," and *cyte*, meaning "cell"

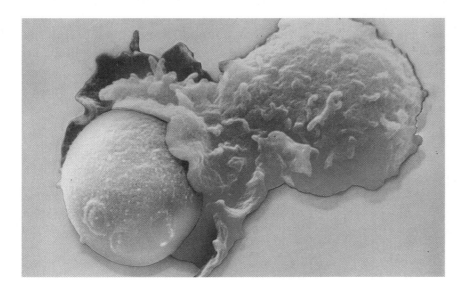

**FIGURE 46-12**

Some white blood cells, like the phagocyte shown in blue, engulf and destroy invading microorganisms.

FIGURE 46-13

Inactive platelets, such as the yellow object shown in (a), derive their name from the fact that they look like little plates. Platelets are colorless and contain chemicals that are involved in the clotting process. (b) The platelets change shape during the clotting process. When activated, the platelets settle and spread on the substrate.

(a)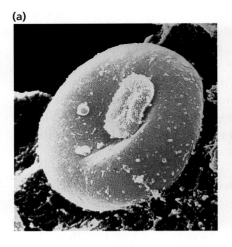

(b)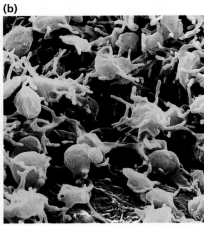

## Eco Connection

### Vampire Bats Help Save Stroke Victims

Vampire bats have an anticoagulant in their saliva that prevents blood clotting when it flows from a wound. In 1995, this enzyme was isolated and named *Draculin.*

Researchers have developed a clot-dissolving agent called *Desmodus rotundus salivary plasminogen activator* (DSPA), which is based on the salivary enzyme Draculin. DSPA targets and destroys fibrin. The current treatment must be given within three hours of the onset of a stroke (a sudden loss of consciousness or paralysis that occurs when the blood flow to the brain is interrupted). Otherwise, brain-cell death and brain damage may occur. According to research, DSPA could be a safe treatment for longer periods of time and appears to have no detrimental effect on brain cells.

## Platelets

**Platelets** are essential to the formation of a blood clot. A blood clot is a mass of interwoven fibers and blood cells that prevents excess loss of blood from a wound. Platelets are not whole cells. They are fragments of very large cells that were formed in the bone marrow. As you can see in Figure 46-13a, platelets get their name from their platelike structure. Platelets lack a nucleus and have a life span of 7 to 12 days. A cubic micrometer of blood may contain as many as half a million platelets.

When a blood vessel tears or rips, platelets congregate at the damaged site, sticking together and forming a small plug. The vessel constricts, slowing blood flow to the area. Then, special clotting factors are released from the platelets and the damaged tissue. These factors begin a series of chemical reactions that occur at the site of the bleeding. The last step in this series brings about the production of a protein called **fibrin.** Fibrin molecules consist of long, sticky chains. As you can see in Figure 46-14, these chains form a net that traps red blood cells, and the mass of fibrin and red blood cells hardens into a clot, or scab.

Hemophilia is a disorder caused by the absence of one or more of the proteins required for blood clotting. When a person with hemophilia is injured, bleeding continues for much longer than it would in a person without hemophilia. Large cuts or internal injuries can be life threatening. Today, people with hemophilia are treated with injections of the missing clotting factors.

**FIGURE 46-14**

The release of enzymes from platelets at the site of a damaged blood vessel initiates a "clotting cascade."

Stimulus

Blood vessel damage → Platelets release clotting protein (enzyme) → Clotting reaction occurs → Fibrin net forms, trapping blood cells and platelets → Blood clot

Result

# BLOOD TYPES

**Blood type** is determined by the type of antigen present on the surface of the red blood cells. An **antigen** is a substance that stimulates an immune response. Antigens that are normally present in a person's body provoke no response. However, when foreign antigens enter the body, cells respond by producing antibodies. In fact, the word *antigen* is an abbreviation for "antibody-generating substance."

In the early 1900s, Karl Landsteiner used blood taken from his laboratory workers and made observations similar to those you see in Figure 46-15. He noticed that mixing blood samples from two people sometimes resulted in the cells clumping together, or *agglutinating*. When samples of two different blood types are mixed together, reactions occur between the antigens on the red blood cells and the antibodies in the plasma, causing the cells to agglutinate. When samples of the same blood type are mixed, no reaction occurs, and the blood cells do not agglutinate.

Landsteiner's observations led to the classification of human blood by blood types. Three of the most important human antigens are called A, B, and Rh. The A-B-O system of blood typing, described below, is based on the A and B antigens.

## A-B-O System

The A-B-O system is a means of classifying blood by the antigens located on the surface of the red blood cells and the antibodies circulating in the plasma. As shown in Table 46-1, an individual's red blood cells may carry an A antigen, a B antigen, both A and B antigens, or no antigen at all. These antigen patterns are called blood types A, B, AB, and O, respectively.

Notice in Table 46-1 that an individual with type A blood also has anti-B antibodies against type B blood. If type B blood is given to a recipient with type A blood, the recipient's anti-B antibodies will react with the B antigens on the donated red blood cells and the blood will agglutinate. In addition, the donor's type B blood has anti-A antibodies. Their presence will compound the antigen-antibody reaction. The result will be agglutinated blood that will block the flow of blood through the vessels. For this reason, transfusion recipients must receive blood that is compatible with their own.

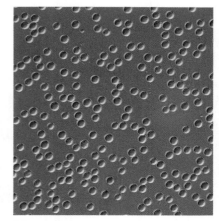

**(a)**

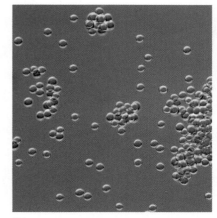

**(b)**

**FIGURE 46-15**

Notice that there is no agglutination of red blood cells in the slide in (a), where blood samples from two people with the same blood type were mixed. Compare this with the slide in (b), where blood samples from two people with different blood types were mixed.

| TABLE 46-1 | *Blood Types, Antigens, and Antibodies* | | | |
|---|---|---|---|---|
| **Blood types** | **Antigen on the red blood cells** | **Antibodies in the plasma** | **Can get blood from** | **Can give blood to** |
| A | A | anti-B | O, A | A, AB |
| B | B | anti-A | O, B | B, AB |
| AB | A and B | none | A, B, AB, O | AB |
| O | none | anti-A, anti-B | O | A, B, AB, O |

People who have type AB blood are *universal recipients*. They can receive A, B, AB, or O blood because they do not have anti-A or anti-B antibodies. People who have type O blood are *universal donors*. They can donate blood to people who have A, B, AB, or O blood because the blood cells of people who have type O blood do not have A or B antigens.

## Rh System

An antigen that is sometimes present on the surface of red blood cells is the **Rh factor,** named after the rhesus monkey in which it was first discovered. Eighty-five percent of the United States' population is Rh-positive ($Rh^+$), meaning that Rh antigens are present. People who do not have Rh antigens are called Rh-negative ($Rh^-$).

If an $Rh^-$ person receives a transfusion of blood that has $Rh^+$ antigens, antibodies may react with the antigen and agglutination will occur. The most serious problem with Rh incompatibility occurs during pregnancy. If the mother is $Rh^-$ and the father is $Rh^+$, the child may inherit the dominant $Rh^+$ allele from the father. During delivery, a small amount of the fetus's $Rh^+$ blood may reach the mother's bloodstream. If this happens, the mother will develop antibodies to the Rh factor. If a second $Rh^+$ child is conceived later, the mother's antibodies can cross the placenta and attack the blood of the fetus. This condition is called *erythroblastosis fetalis*. The fetus may die as a result of this condition, or if the child is born alive, he or she may need an immediate transfusion of $Rh^+$ blood.

To prevent this condition, an $Rh^-$ mother of an $Rh^+$ child can be given antibodies to destroy any $Rh^+$ cells that have entered her bloodstream from the fetus. The mother is, in effect, immunized against the Rh antigen before her immune system has a chance to develop its own antibodies. The antibody treatment prevents Rh sensitization in $Rh^-$ women only if their bodies have not already produced Rh antibodies. If an $Rh^-$ mother has not yet been sensitized, she receives the antibody treatment in the 28th week of pregnancy and again immediately after delivery.

## SECTION 2 REVIEW

1. Identify the four main components of blood.

2. Explain how the structure of red blood cells, white blood cells, and platelets relates to the function of these cells.

3. Identify the stages and structures involved in the clotting process.

4. What factors determine the compatibility of blood types for transfusion?

5. Which blood types, in terms of the A-B-O and Rh antigens, can be donated to somebody with type $AB^-$ blood?

**CRITICAL THINKING**

6. **Analyzing Information** Hemophilia is a disorder in which there is a failure in one of the steps of clot formation. What might be some advantages and disadvantages of this disorder?

7. **Evaluating Results** A patient's blood has an elevated count of leukocytes. What does this most likely indicate?

8. **Relating Concepts** Explain why a pregnant woman should know her blood type and the blood type of her baby's father.

# MILESTONES
## IN Blood Transfusions

*Every three seconds someone needs a blood transfusion—blood, plasma, or saline is introduced into the body. Blood and blood products are used to treat accident and burn victims, cancer patients, and patients undergoing surgeries and medical treatments. The development of safe blood transfusion techniques was an important achievement in modern medicine.*

## Timeline

**1628** William Harvey describes the circulation of blood.

**1667** Jean-Baptiste Denis successfully transfuses blood from a lamb to a human.

**1818** First human-to-human blood transfusion.

**1901** Karl Landsteiner determined three of four blood types (A, B, and O).

**1914** Blood is stored for the first time.

**1937** Bernard Fantus formed the first blood bank.

**1939** Charles Drew set up collection centers for blood to fill World War II needs.

**1950** Carl Walter and W.P. Murphy, Jr. introduced the plastic bag to collect blood.

**1985** Blood is screened for HIV and other diseases.

In 1665, Richard Lower, an English physician, transferred blood between two dogs. Jean-Baptiste Denis, a French physician and astrologer, transfused blood from a lamb to a human in 1667. The first successful human-to-human blood transfusions were performed in 1818 by James Blundell, a British physician, but these were followed by many failures.

In 1901, Austrian-born American physiologist Karl Landsteiner determined the first three blood types—A, B, and O—and that incompatible types will clot. This discovery explained why the outcome of transfusions had been so unpredictable in the past. For his work, Landsteiner received the Nobel Prize in medicine or physiology in 1930.

During World War I, scientists began to study how to preserve and transport blood for wounded soldiers. They found that the addition of sodium citrate prevented clotting, making the storage of blood possible for the first time.

In 1937, Bernard Fantus, a physician, established the first nonprofit blood bank at Cook County Hospital in Chicago. The next year, Charles Drew, a medical doctor, found that blood plasma (the liquid component of blood) could substitute for whole blood in emergency situations.

Germany's attack on France in 1940 created a great need for blood. Based on Drew's findings, the United States began to provide liquid plasma and whole blood for France. Working with the National Research Council and the American Red Cross, Drew set up blood collection centers.

Early in the 1980s, some transfused blood was found to carry the human immunodeficiency virus (HIV), the virus that causes acquired immune deficiency syndrome (AIDS). Since 1985, careful screening for HIV, hepatitis, and other diseases has almost entirely removed the risk of receiving contaminated blood.

Today, many people bank their own blood for later use in surgery. Blood can also be collected during surgery and returned to the patient later. The AIDS epidemic has triggered a race to create artificial blood. Several companies have begun testing blood substitutes from chemically treated animal blood and outdated human blood.

## Review

1. What type of patients can benefit from blood transfusions?

2. **Critical Thinking** How might safe blood transfusion techniques affect you?

3. **Critical Thinking** Use the Web site below to research the latest progress on creating artificial blood. Write a short report to describe your findings.

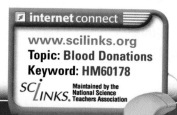

**internet** connect

**www.scilinks.org**
**Topic:** Blood Donations
**Keyword:** HM60178

SCILINKS. Maintained by the National Science Teachers Association

## OBJECTIVES

- **Differentiate** external respiration from internal respiration.
- **Trace** the path of air from the atmosphere to the bloodstream.
- **Describe** how gases are exchanged in the lungs and transported in the bloodstream.
- **Summarize** the skeletal and muscular changes that occur during breathing.
- **Describe** how the rate of breathing is controlled.

## VOCABULARY

respiratory system
external respiration
internal respiration
lung
pharynx
epiglottis
trachea
larynx
bronchus
bronchiole
alveolus
inspiration
diaphragm
expiration

# THE RESPIRATORY SYSTEM

*T*he blood transports oxygen from the lungs to cells and carries carbon dioxide from the cells to the lungs. It is the function of the **respiratory system** to exchange gases with the cardiovascular system.

## RESPIRATION

The respiratory system involves both external respiration and internal respiration. **External respiration** is the exchange of gases between the atmosphere and the blood. **Internal respiration** is the exchange of gases between the blood and the cells of the body. Once oxygen is in the cells, the cells use it to break down glucose and make ATP by the process of aerobic respiration. Without oxygen, the body could not obtain enough energy from food to survive. Excess carbon dioxide produced as a waste product of aerobic respiration is toxic to cells and is removed from the cells by internal respiration.

## THE LUNGS

The **lungs** are the site of gas exchange between the atmosphere and the blood. Notice in Figure 46-16 that the right lung has three divisions, or lobes. It is slightly heavier than the two-lobed left lung. The lungs are located inside the *thoracic cavity*, bounded by the rib cage and the diaphragm. Lining the entire cavity and covering the lungs are *pleura*, membranes that secrete a slippery fluid that decreases friction from the movement of the lungs during breathing.

### The Path of Air

Refer to Figure 46-16 to trace the path air follows from the atmosphere to the capillaries in the lungs. External respiration begins at the mouth and at the nose. Air filters through the small hairs of the nose and passes into the nasal cavity, located above the roof of the mouth. In the nasal cavity, mucous membranes warm and moisten the air, which helps prevent damage to the delicate tissues that form the respiratory system. The walls of the nasal cavity are also lined with cilia. These cilia trap particles that are inhaled and are eventually swept into the throat, where they are swallowed.

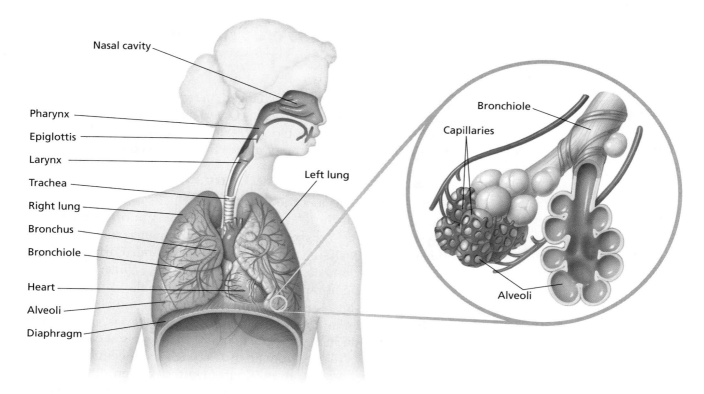

The moistened, filtered air then moves into the throat, or **pharynx** (FER-inks), a tube at the back of the nasal cavities and the mouth. The pharynx contains passageways for both food and air. When food is swallowed, a flap of cartilage, called the **epiglottis**, presses down and covers the opening to the air passage. When air is being taken in, the epiglottis is in an upright position, allowing air to pass into a cartilaginous tube called the windpipe, or **trachea** (TRAY-kee-uh). The trachea is about 10 to 12 cm long and has walls lined with ciliated cells that trap inhaled particles. The cilia sweep the particles and mucus away from the lungs toward the throat.

At the upper end of the trachea is the voicebox, or **larynx** (LER-inks). Sounds are produced when air is forced past two ligaments—the *vocal cords*—that stretch across the larynx. The pitch and volume of the sound produced varies with the amount of tension on the vocal cords and on the amount of air being forced past them.

The trachea then branches into two **bronchi** (BRAHN-kie) (singular, bronchus), each of which leads to a lung. The walls of the bronchi consist of smooth muscle and cartilage and are lined with cilia and mucus. Within the lungs, the bronchi branch into smaller and smaller tubes. The smallest of these tubes are known as **bronchioles,** which are also lined with cilia and mucus. Eventually the bronchioles end in clusters of tiny air sacs called **alveoli** (al-VEE-oh-LIE) (singular, alveolus). A network of capillaries surrounds each alveolus, as you can see in the detailed view shown in Figure 46-16. All exchange of gases in the lungs occurs in the alveoli. To facilitate this exchange, the surface area of the lungs is enormous. A healthy lung contains nearly 300 million alveoli and has a total surface area of about 70 m²—about 40 times the surface area of the skin.

**FIGURE 46-16**

Trace the passage of air from the atmosphere to the lungs. Oxygen in the air finally reaches the alveoli, the functional units of the respiratory system. All exchange of gases between the respiratory system and the cardiovascular system occurs in the alveoli.

# GAS EXCHANGE AND TRANSPORT

In the lungs, gases are exchanged between the alveoli and the blood in the capillaries. Oxygen ($O_2$) to be transported throughout the body moves into the bloodstream, and carbon dioxide ($CO_2$) to be eliminated from the body moves into the alveoli.

## Gas Exchange in the Lungs

Figure 46-17 illustrates the direction in which oxygen and carbon dioxide move in the alveoli. When air moves into the lungs, the oxygen in the air crosses the thin alveolar membranes as well as the capillary walls and dissolves in the blood. Carbon dioxide moves in the opposite direction, crossing the capillary walls and thin alveolar membranes and entering the alveoli.

Air moving into the alveoli is rich in oxygen and contains little carbon dioxide. In contrast, blood in the capillaries surrounding the alveoli is low in oxygen and contains high levels of carbon dioxide. Substances diffuse from an area of higher concentration to an area of lower concentration. Consequently, oxygen diffuses from the alveoli into the blood, and carbon dioxide diffuses from the blood into the alveoli. The enormous surface area of the alveoli increases the rate of diffusion of these two gases.

## Transport of Oxygen

When oxygen diffuses into the blood, only a small amount remains dissolved in the plasma. Most of the oxygen—95 to 98 percent—moves into the red blood cells, where it combines with hemoglobin, an iron-containing protein. Each hemoglobin molecule contains four iron atoms. Each iron atom can bind to one oxygen molecule. Thus, one hemoglobin molecule can carry up to four molecules of oxygen. There are about 250 million hemoglobin molecules in each red blood cell. When oxygenated blood reaches body tissues, the oxygen concentration is higher in the blood than in the body tissues. Thus, oxygen is released from hemoglobin and diffuses out of the capillaries and into surrounding cells.

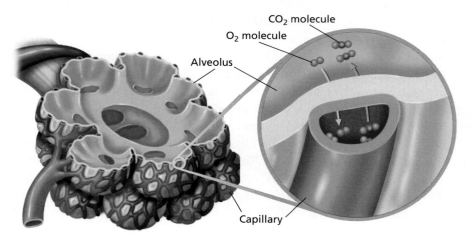

**FIGURE 46-17**

Because of concentration gradients, oxygen and carbon dioxide diffuse across the alveoli and capillary walls.

## Transport of Carbon Dioxide

Because the concentration of carbon dioxide ($CO_2$) is higher in the cells, it diffuses out of the cells and into the blood. Only about 7 percent of the carbon dioxide dissolves in the plasma. Approximately 23 percent binds to hemoglobin. The remaining 70 percent is carried in the blood as bicarbonate ions ($HCO_3^-$). As shown in the equation below, $CO_2$ reacts with water in the plasma to form carbonic acid ($H_2CO_3$). In turn, the carbonic acid disassociates into bicarbonate ions and hydrogen ions ($H^+$):

$$H_2O + CO_2 \rightleftharpoons H_2CO_3 \rightleftharpoons HCO_3^- + H^+$$

Thus, most of the $CO_2$ travels in the blood as bicarbonate ions. When the blood reaches the lungs, the reactions are reversed:

$$HCO_3^- + H^+ \rightleftharpoons H_2CO_3 \rightleftharpoons H_2O + CO_2$$

Bicarbonate ions combine with hydrogen ions to form carbonic acid, which in turn forms carbon dioxide and water. The carbon dioxide diffuses out of the capillaries into the alveoli and is exhaled into the atmosphere.

# MECHANISM OF BREATHING

Breathing is the process of moving air into and out of the lungs. **Inspiration,** shown in Figure 46-18, is the process of taking air into the lungs. When you take a deep breath, your chest expands as muscles contract to move the ribs up and outward. At the same time, your **diaphragm,** a large skeletal muscle that separates the thoracic cavity from the abdominal cavity, flattens and pushes down on the abdomen. Muscles in the abdominal wall in turn relax. This action provides room for the flattened diaphragm.

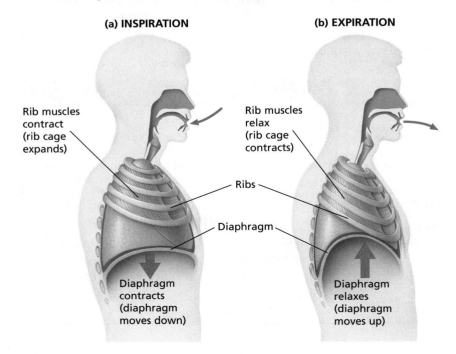

**(a) INSPIRATION**

Rib muscles contract (rib cage expands)

Diaphragm contracts (diaphragm moves down)

**(b) EXPIRATION**

Rib muscles relax (rib cage contracts)

Ribs

Diaphragm

Diaphragm relaxes (diaphragm moves up)

**FIGURE 46-18**

The diaphragm, a large skeletal muscle that separates the thoracic cavity from the abdominal cavity, and the muscles between the ribs control the movement of the thoracic cavity during breathing. If these muscles were paralyzed, then inspiration and expiration would not occur.

**Word Roots and Origins**

*expiration*

from the Latin *expir,* which means "to breathe out"

When the diaphragm flattens and the ribs are lifted up and out, the volume of the lungs increases. An increased volume reduces the air pressure within the lungs. At this point, the air pressure inside the lungs is lower than the air pressure outside the body. As a result, air from the atmosphere moves into the lungs.

During **expiration,** the process of releasing air from the lungs, the reverse movements take place, as shown in Figure 46-18. As the diaphragm and rib muscles relax, the elastic tissues of the lungs recoil, deflating the lungs. The volume of the lungs decreases. Because the volume is smaller, the air pressure inside the cavity becomes greater than the air pressure outside the body. This pressure difference forces air out of the lungs until the pressures are again equal.

## Regulation of Breathing

The rate at which oxygen is used depends on the activity of the cells. The greater their activity, the more oxygen they need and the faster the body needs to breathe. The slower their activity, the slower the body needs to breathe. Both rate and depth of breathing change in order to provide oxygen and eliminate carbon dioxide.

The rate of breathing is controlled by the brain and brain stem, which monitors the concentration of carbon dioxide in the blood. As activity increases, high levels of carbon dioxide in the blood stimulate nerve cells in the brain. The brain stem in turn stimulates the diaphragm to increase the breathing rate and depth. When the carbon dioxide concentration in the blood returns to lower levels, the sensors in the brain send a message to the respiratory muscles to return to a slower breathing rate. All this is controlled subconsciously by control centers in the brain. However, a person can temporarily override the respiratory control system at any time, holding his or her breath until losing consciousness. Then the brain stem takes control, and normal breathing resumes. This mechanism allows humans to swim underwater for short periods and to sleep without concern for breathing.

## SECTION 3 REVIEW

1. How does internal respiration differ from external respiration?

2. Outline the path of oxygen from the atmosphere to the bloodstream.

3. Explain the process of gas exchange in the lungs.

4. Differentiate between oxygen transport and carbon dioxide transport in the bloodstream.

5. Sequence the skeletal and muscular changes that take place when a person inhales.

6. What factors regulate the rate of breathing?

**CRITICAL THINKING**

7. **Relating Concepts** Predict the effect that increasing altitude would have on blood-oxygen saturation.

8. **Applying Information** Why does a single-celled organism not need a respiratory system?

9. **Predicting Results** Normally, arterial blood is about 98 percent saturated with oxygen. What are two conditions that could result in lower oxygen saturation?

- The human circulatory system is made up of the cardiovascular system and the lymphatic system.
- The heart is a muscular organ that pumps blood through an intricate network of blood vessels.
- Blood flows from the body into the heart, which then pumps blood to the lungs. After oxygenation, blood returns to the heart, which pumps blood to the rest of the body.

- Arteries carry blood away from the heart. Materials are exchanged at the capillaries. Veins contain valves and carry blood back to the heart.
- In pulmonary circulation, blood travels between the heart and lungs. In systemic circulation, blood travels between the heart and all other body tissues.
- The lymphatic system returns lymph, fluid that has collected in the tissues, to the bloodstream.

### Vocabulary

cardiovascular system (p. 933)
lymphatic system (p. 933)
atrium (p. 933)
ventricle (p. 933)
valve (p. 934)

aorta (p. 935)
sinoatrial node (p. 935)
atrioventricular node (p. 935)
pulse (p. 935)
artery (p. 936)

blood pressure (p. 936)
hypertension (p. 936)
capillary (p. 936)
vein (p. 937)
pulmonary circulation (p. 937)

systemic circulation (p. 937)
atherosclerosis (p. 938)
lymph (p. 939)

- Blood is composed of plasma (water, metabolites, wastes, salts, and proteins), red blood cells, white blood cells, and platelets.
- Red blood cells transport oxygen. White blood cells help defend the body against disease. Platelets are essential to the formation of a blood clot.

- Blood clotting occurs when platelets release a clotting protein, which causes a clotting reaction to occur. A fibrin net forms, trapping blood cells and platelets.
- Human blood can be grouped into four types—A, B, AB, and O—based on proteins on the surface of red blood cells. Another antigen called *Rh factor*, is sometimes present on red blood cells.

### Vocabulary

plasma (p. 940)
red blood cell (erythrocyte) (p. 940)
hemoglobin (p. 940)

white blood cell (leukocyte) (p. 941)
phagocyte (p. 941)
antibody (p. 941)

platelet (p. 942)
fibrin (p. 942)
blood type (p. 943)

antigen (p. 943)
Rh factor (p. 943)

- External respiration is the exchange of gases between the atmosphere and the blood. Internal respiration is the exchange of gases between the blood and the cells of the body.
- The lungs are the site of gas exchange between the atmosphere and the blood.
- Air enters through the mouth or nose, passes through the pharynx, larynx, trachea, bronchi and bronchioles and into alveoli. A network of capillaries surrounds each alveolus. All exchange of gases in the lungs occurs at the alveoli.

- Most oxygen is carried attached to hemoglobin. Some carbon dioxide is carried bound to hemoglobin. A small amount is dissolved in plasma. Most carbon dioxide is carried as bicarbonate ions.
- During inspiration, the diaphragm and rib muscles contract, the thoracic cavity expands, and air is pulled into the lungs. During expiration, the diaphragm and rib muscles relax, the thoracic cavity contracts, and air is forced out of the lungs.
- The rate of breathing is controlled by nerve centers in the brain that monitor the level of carbon dioxide in the blood.

### Vocabulary

respiratory system (p. 946)
external respiration (p. 946)
internal respiration (p. 946)
lung (p. 946)

pharynx (p. 947)
epiglottis (p. 947)
trachea (p. 947)
larynx (p. 947)

bronchus (p. 947)
bronchiole (p. 947)
alveolus (p. 947)
inspiration (p. 949)

diaphragm (p. 949)
expiration (p. 950)

## USING VOCABULARY

1. Distinguish between *systolic pressure* and *diastolic pressure*.

2. Choose the term that does not belong in the following group: *erythrocyte, hemoglobin, leukocyte,* and *platelet.* Explain why it does not belong.

3. For each pair of terms, explain the relationship between the terms.
   a. *atrioventricular valve* and *semilunar valve*
   b. *artery* and *vein*
   c. *expiration* and *inspiration*

4. **Word Roots and Origins** The word *phagocyte* is derived from the Greek word *phagein,* which means "to eat." The suffix *cyte* means "cell." Using this information, explain why the term *phagocyte* is a good name for the biological process that the term describes.

## UNDERSTANDING KEY CONCEPTS

5. **Identify** the parts of the human heart, and describe the function of each part.

6. **Outline** the route that blood takes through the heart, lungs, and body.

7. **Relate** the structure of arteries, veins, and capillaries to the function of each.

8. **Compare** the pulmonary arteries and the aorta.

9. **Compare** the pulmonary veins and the inferior vena cava.

10. **Summarize** the roles of the lymphatic system.

11. **Discuss** the function of each of the components of blood.

12. **Identify** the structure that red blood cells lack that limits their life span.

13. **Describe** three differences between white blood cells and red blood cells.

14. **Sequence** the process of blood-clot formation that occurs after a vessel is injured.

15. **Explain** the A-B-O blood-typing system.

16. **Identify** the role of the Rh factor in determining blood compatibility for transfusion.

17. **Compare** external respiration with internal respiration.

18. **Sequence** the path oxygen travels from the environment into the blood.

19. **Compare** the transport and exchange of oxygen and carbon dioxide.

20. **Describe** the movement of the diaphragm and the rib muscles during inspiration and expiration.

21. **Name** the factor that stimulates the brain stem to increase the breathing rate.

22. **CONCEPT MAPPING** Use the following terms to create a concept map that shows the relationship between the cardiovascular, lymphatic, and respiratory systems: *artery, capillary, vein, lymphatic system, pulmonary circulation, systemic circulation, atrium, ventricle, aorta,* and *vena cava.*

## CRITICAL THINKING

23. **Inferring Relationships** A person with anemia can have too few red blood cells or low hemoglobin levels. The most common symptom is a lack of energy. Why would anemia cause this symptom?

24. **Applying Information** Explain how the lymphatic system moves lymph through the body without the aid of a pumping organ like that of the cardiovascular system.

25. **Analyzing Concepts** One function of the cardiovascular system is to help maintain a uniform body temperature. Explain how the constant circulation of blood throughout the body can accomplish this task.

26. **Interpreting Graphics** Copy the blood-type table below on a sheet of paper. Fill in the missing information for each type.

| TABLE 1 *Blood Type* | | | | |
|---|---|---|---|---|
| Blood type | Antigen on the red blood cell | Antibodies in plasma | Can receive blood from | Can donate blood to |
| A | | B | O, A | A, AB |
| B | B | | O, B | B, AB |
| AB | A, B | Neither A nor B | O, A, B, AB | |
| O | Neither A nor B | A, B | | O, A, B, AB |

27. **Calculating Data** Calculate the number of times a person's heart will beat if the person lives 75 years. Assume that the average heart beats 70 times per minute.

28. **Recognizing Relationships** Assuming that the heart of an overweight person beats an additional 10 times per minute, explain why being overweight can put additional strain on the heart.

# Standardized Test Preparation

**DIRECTIONS:** Choose the letter of the answer choice that best answers the question.

1. In what direction does blood move during ventricular systole?
   **A.** from the atria to the veins
   **B.** from the ventricles to the atria
   **C.** from the atria to the ventricles
   **D.** from the ventricles to the arteries

2. What is the function of the lymphatic system?
   **F.** It opens two-way vessels.
   **G.** It helps the body fight infections.
   **H.** It interacts with the respiratory system.
   **J.** It transports intercellular fluid away from the heart.

3. Fibrin is a protein that does which of the following?
   **A.** transports oxygen
   **B.** helps form a blood clot
   **C.** destroys invading microorganisms
   **D.** stimulates the production of antibodies

**INTERPRETING GRAPHICS:** The graph below shows how systolic pressure is affected by salt intake. Use the graph to answer the question that follows.

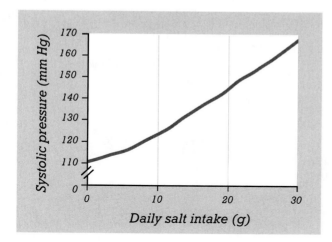

4. What is the relationship between salt intake and blood pressure?
   **F.** As salt intake increases, blood pressure increases.
   **G.** As salt intake increases, blood pressure decreases.
   **H.** Salt intake of 20 g per day results in stable blood pressure.
   **J.** Salt intake of 30 g per day results in stable blood pressure.

**DIRECTIONS:** Complete the following analogy.

5. superior vena cava : deoxygenated blood :: pulmonary veins :
   **A.** type A blood
   **B.** type B blood
   **C.** oxygenated blood
   **D.** deoxygenated blood

**INTERPRETING GRAPHICS:** The model below shows a cross section of the heart. Use the model to answer the question that follows.

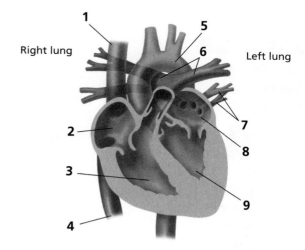

6. Which numbers point to vessels that bring blood into the heart?
   **F.** 1, 4, and 7
   **G.** 1, 5, and 6
   **H.** 4, 5, and 6
   **J.** 5 and 6 only

## SHORT RESPONSE

Even a small increase or decrease in blood volume has an effect on blood pressure. When an accident victim suffers significant blood loss, the person is transfused with plasma rather than whole blood.

Why is plasma effective in meeting the immediate threat to life?

## EXTENDED RESPONSE

Polio is a disease that paralyzes muscles by affecting the nerves that make the muscles move.

*Part A* List muscles involved in breathing.

*Part B* Explain how polio might affect breathing.

**Test TIP** Slow, deep breathing helps a person relax. If you suffer from test anxiety, focus on your breathing in order to calm down.

# Measuring Lung Volumes and CO₂ Production

## OBJECTIVES

- Use indirect measurement to determine lung capacity.
- Determine the effect of exercise on breathing rate and CO₂ production.

## PROCESS SKILLS

- measuring
- hypothesizing
- collecting data
- analyzing data
- experimenting

## MATERIALS

- safety goggles
- lab apron
- disposable gloves
- 1 L bromothymol indicator solution
- drinking straws
- 100 mL Erlenmeyer flasks, 2 per group
- 100 mL graduated cylinders
- marker
- plastic wrap
- spirometer
- stopwatch or clock with second hand

## Background

1. A spirometer is an instrument used to measure the volume of air a person can breathe.
2. Compare the diagram of a spirometer on the right with the spirometer you will be using to complete this investigation. The marking pen creates a line that can be compared with the scale on the left side to measure liters of air.
3. Tidal volume is the volume of air inhaled or exhaled during a normal breath.
4. Lung capacity is the total volume of air that the lungs can hold. Total lung capacity is 5 to 6 L. What factors might increase or reduce lung capacity?
5. Expiratory reserve volume is the amount of air that can be forcefully exhaled after a normal exhalation.
6. Vital capacity is the maximum amount of air that can be inhaled or exhaled.

7. Carbon dioxide is soluble in water. You can determine the relative amount of $CO_2$ in your breath by using an indicator to react with the $CO_2$. Higher $CO_2$ levels will react with the indicator solution faster.

## PART A  Tidal Volume, Expiratory Volume, and Vital Capacity

1. Make a data table in your notebook like the one shown on the next page (Part A Lung Volumes).
2. Place a clean mouthpiece in the end of the spirometer. **CAUTION  Many diseases are spread by body fluids, such as saliva. Do NOT share a mouthpiece with anyone.** Inhale a normal breath. Hold your nose, then exhale a normal breath into the spirometer. Record your data in the table.
3. Measure your expiratory reserve volume by first breathing a normal breath and exhaling normally. Then put the spirometer tube to your mouth as you forcefully exhale whatever air is left in your lungs. Be sure to force out as much air as possible. Record your data in the table.

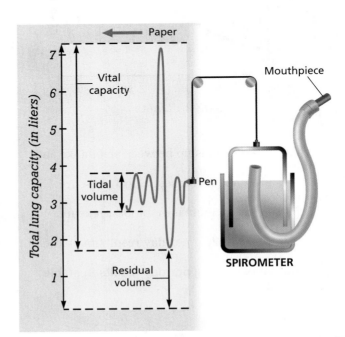

**SPIROMETER**

## PART A  Lung Volumes

| | Average for young adult males | Average for young adult females | Average for athletes | Your readings |
|---|---|---|---|---|
| Tidal volume | 500 mL | | | |
| Expiratory reserve volume | 100 mL | | | |
| Vital capacity | 4,600 mL | | | |

4. The table includes values for young adult males. The average volumes for young adult females are 20–25 percent lower than those of males. Calculate the average volumes for young adult females. Athletes can have volumes that are 30–40 percent greater than the average for their gender. Calculate the average volumes for athletes.

5. Dispose of your mouthpiece in the designated waste container.

### PART B Breathing Rate and $CO_2$ Production

6. Discuss with your partners the use of bromothymol blue as an indicator of $CO_2$. Develop a hypothesis that describes a relationship between air volume exhaled during rest or exercise and the volume of $CO_2$ exhaled.

7. Make a data table in your notebook like the one on this page, titled "Part B $CO_2$ Production".

8. Label two flasks as 1 and 2.

9. CAUTION Wear safety goggles at all times during this procedure. If you get the indicator solution on your skin or clothing, wash it off at the sink while calling to your teacher. If you get the indicator solution in your eyes, immediately flush it out at the eyewash station while calling to your teacher.

10. Add 100 mL of indicator solution to each flask. Cover the mouth of each flask with plastic wrap.

11. Remove the plastic wrap from flask 1. Begin the stopwatch. Blow gently through one straw into flask 1 until the solution turns a yellowish color, exhaling slowly so that the solution does not bubble up. CAUTION Be careful not to inhale the solution or get it in your mouth. Stop the stopwatch.

12. Record in your data table the time in seconds that it took to see a color change in flask 1.

13. Exercise by jogging in place or doing jumping jacks for 2 min. Begin the stopwatch immediately. Blow gently through a new straw into flask 2 until the solution becomes the same yellowish color as the solution in flask 1. Stop the stopwatch.

14. In your data table, record the amount of time in seconds that it took to get the same yellow color in flask 2 as you got in flask 1.

15. Calculate the difference in the amount of time it took to see a color change in the two flasks. What can you infer about the amount of $CO_2$ you exhaled before and after exercise?

16. Clean up your materials. Pour the solutions down the sink, and rinse the sink thoroughly with water. Wash your hands before leaving the lab.

## Analysis and Conclusions

1. How did your tidal volume compare with that of your classmates?

2. What are the independent and dependent variables in Part B? How did you vary the independent variable and measure changes in the dependent variable?

3. Why were the flasks covered with plastic wrap?

4. Do your data support your hypothesis from Part B? Explain your answers.

5. How do you know whether you produced more carbon dioxide before or after you exercised?

6. What were some of the possible sources of error in your experiment?

| PART B $CO_2$ Production | |
|---|---|
| Time for color change in flask 1 | |
| Time for color change in flask 2 | |
| Difference in time between flask 1 and flask 2 | |

## Further Inquiry

Design an experiment to determine whether exercise affects heart rate in the same way it affects breathing rate and tidal volume.

# THE BODY'S DEFENSE SYSTEMS

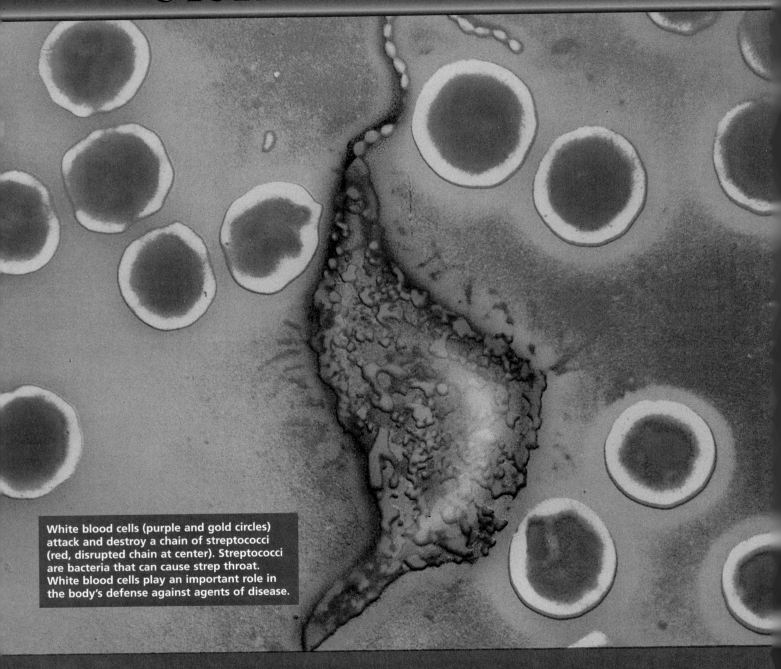

White blood cells (purple and gold circles) attack and destroy a chain of streptococci (red, disrupted chain at center). Streptococci are bacteria that can cause strep throat. White blood cells play an important role in the body's defense against agents of disease.

# NONSPECIFIC DEFENSES

*When a type of virus called a rhinovirus enters the human body, it can cause the common cold. Diseases, such as colds, that are caused by agents that have invaded the body are called* **infectious diseases.** *This section explains how the human body identifies the agents that cause infectious diseases and defends itself against these agents.*

## IDENTIFYING PATHOGENS

A **pathogen** is any agent that causes disease. Robert Koch (KAWHK) (1843–1910), a German doctor, was the first person to establish a step-by-step procedure for identifying the particular pathogen that causes an infectious disease. In the 1870s, Koch studied anthrax, a disease of cattle that can spread to people. Koch observed that cattle with the illness had swarms of bacteria in their blood. He hypothesized that these bacteria caused anthrax.

To test his hypothesis, Koch isolated rod-shaped bacteria from a cow with anthrax and grew colonies of the bacteria to be sure he had isolated a single species. Then, he injected healthy cows with these bacteria. The cows developed anthrax. Koch found that the blood of these cows contained the same rod-shaped bacteria as the first cow. Furthermore, healthy cows that he had not injected lacked this type of bacteria. Koch concluded that the isolated species of bacterium causes anthrax. Through these studies, he developed **Koch's postulates,** which are "rules" for determining the cause of a disease. Figure 47-1 illustrates these postulates.

**FIGURE 47-1**

By applying the four principles of Koch's postulates, scientists can identify the pathogen that causes an infectious disease.

**KOCH'S POSTULATES**

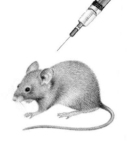

**1.** The pathogen must be present in an animal that has the disease and absent in healthy animals.

**2.** The pathogen must be isolated from the sick animal and grown in a laboratory.

**3.** When the isolated pathogen is injected into a healthy animal, the animal must develop the disease.

**4.** The pathogen should be taken from the second animal and grown in the laboratory. The pathogen cultured from the second animal should be the same as the pathogen cultured from the first animal.

## TABLE 47-1 *Pathogens Responsible for Some Human Diseases*

| Disease | Pathogen | Method of transmission |
|---|---|---|
| Botulism | *Clostridium botulinum* (bacterium) | contaminated food |
| Lyme disease | *Borrelia burgdorferi* (bacterium) | tick bites |
| AIDS | HIV (human immunodeficiency virus) | sexual contact, contaminated needles, contact with contaminated fluids from a mother to a fetus or infant |
| Severe acute respiratory syndrome (SARS) | coronavirus (virus) | person-to-person contact, indirect contact through pathogens in air or on objects (from coughs or sneezes) |
| Amebic dysentery | *Entamoeba histolytica* (protist) | contaminated food and water |
| Athlete's foot | *Tinea* (fungus) | contact with contaminated surfaces, person-to-person contact |
| Head lice | Lice (invertebrate parasite) | person-to-person contact, sharing personal items |

Scientists have used Koch's postulates to identify thousands of pathogens. Many human diseases are caused by bacteria, viruses, protists, fungi, and invertebrates. Pathogens can spread to humans in five main ways—through air, food, water, person-to-person contact, and the bites of animals. Table 47-1 lists examples of pathogens that cause different human diseases and the means by which each is commonly transmitted.

## FIGURE 47-2

The passages of the respiratory system are lined with cells that are covered with beating cilia (purplish strands). Pathogens (bluish circles) that become trapped in mucus secreted by these cells are swept upward, away from the lungs. (5,325×)

# FIRST LINE OF DEFENSE: BARRIERS

The body's nonspecific defenses help protect the body against any pathogen, regardless of the pathogen's identity. Nonspecific defenses include the skin and mucous membranes. **Mucous** (MYOO-kuhs) **membranes** are epithelial tissues that protect the interior surfaces of the body that may be exposed to pathogens.

Most pathogens must enter the body to cause disease. The skin serves as a physical barrier to pathogens. Any break in the skin may allow pathogens to enter the body. In addition, the skin also releases sweat, oils, and waxes. These substances contain chemicals that are toxic to many pathogens. For example, sweat contains *lysozyme,* an enzyme that destroys some bacteria.

Mucous membranes serve as a barrier and secrete *mucus,* a sticky fluid that traps pathogens. Mucous membranes line the respiratory and digestive systems, the urethra, and the vagina. The passages of the respiratory tract are lined with cells that are covered with beating cilia, as shown in Figure 47-2. These cilia sweep mucus and pathogens up to the pharynx, where they are swallowed. Most swallowed pathogens are destroyed in the stomach by acids.

# SECOND LINE OF DEFENSE: NONSPECIFIC IMMUNITY

If a pathogen gets past the skin and the mucous membranes, there is a second line of nonspecific defense inside the body—nonspecific immunity. Nonspecific immunity includes the inflammatory response, the temperature response, and proteins. Like the barriers of the first line of defense, these second-line defenses are nonspecific—they work the same way against any pathogen.

## Inflammatory Response

Any pathogen that gets past the skin or mucous membranes will stimulate the **inflammatory response,** a series of events that suppress infection and speed recovery. An example is shown in Figure 47-3. When cells are damaged, whether through a cut on the skin or invasion by pathogens, some of the damaged cells release histamine (HIS-tuh-MEEN), as described in step ❶. **Histamine** is a substance that increases blood flow to the injured area and increases the permeability of surrounding capillaries. The changes caused by histamine result in redness, swelling, warmth, and pain. If blood vessels have been damaged, platelets begin the blood-clotting process, sealing off surrounding tissues and stopping pathogens from entering the rest of the body.

White blood cells fight pathogens that have entered the body. In step ❷, fluids and white blood cells called *phagocytes* pass through the capillary walls to the injured area. **Phagocytes** ingest and destroy pathogens and foreign matter, as shown in step ❸. Phagocytes and some other types of white blood cells are attracted to the site of injury by histamine.

## Eco Connection

### Agriculture and Human Diseases

The beginning of farming and herding about 10,000 years ago changed the nature of human diseases. When humans began to keep herds of domesticated animals, such as cattle and sheep, humans were exposed to the pathogens that infect these animals. Some of these pathogens then began infecting humans. Measles, tuberculosis, smallpox, and flu are among the diseases that may have been transmitted to humans from domesticated animals.

**FIGURE 47-3**

Injury to cells triggers an inflammatory response.

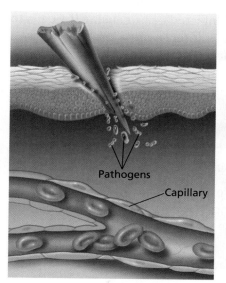

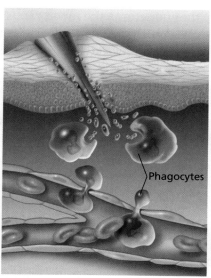

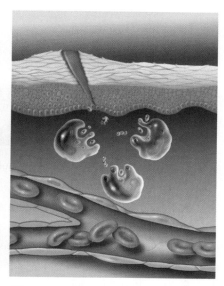

❶ An injury may allow pathogens to get past the barrier of the skin. Injured cells release chemical messengers, such as histamine.

❷ Nearby capillaries respond by swelling and leaking fluid. Phagocytes pass through capillary walls and attack the pathogens.

❸ Phagocytes destroy the pathogens, and the injury begins to heal.

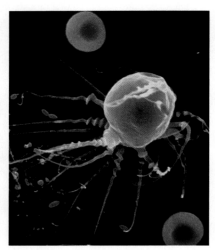

The **neutrophil** (NOO-troh-fil) is the most abundant type of phago-cyte in the body. Neutrophils circulate through blood vessels, and they can squeeze through capillary walls to reach the infection site. Once there, neutrophils ingest pathogens they encounter. Another type of phagocyte is the **macrophage** (MAK-roh-FAYJ), shown in Figure 47-4. Macrophages engulf pathogens and cellular debris. Some are stationed in body tissues, waiting for pathogens, while others seek out pathogens.

**Natural killer cells** are large white blood cells that attack pathogen-infected cells—not the pathogens themselves. Natural killer cells are effective at killing cancer cells and virus-infected cells. A natural killer cell pierces the cell membrane of its target cell, allowing water to rush in and causing the cell to burst.

## Temperature Response

When the body begins to fight pathogens, body temperature may increase several degrees. A rise in body temperature above the normal 37°C (98.6°F) is called a *fever.* Fever is a symptom of illness that shows the body is responding to an infection. Some pathogens trigger fever, as do chemicals released by macrophages. A moder-ate fever may slow bacterial and viral growth and promote white blood cell activity. However, very high fever is dangerous because extreme heat can destroy important cellular proteins. Temperatures greater than 39°C (103°F) can be dangerous, and those greater than 41°C (105°F) can lead to death.

## Proteins

Proteins also provide nonspecific defenses. About 20 different pro-teins make up the **complement system.** Complement proteins cir-culate in the blood and become active when they encounter certain pathogens. Some of these proteins form a ring-shaped structure that punctures the membranes of infected cells, causing the cells to die. Another nonspecific defense is **interferon,** a protein released by cells infected with viruses. Interferon causes nearby cells to make a protein that helps them resist viral infection.

## SECTION 1 REVIEW

1. Explain how Koch tested his hypothesis about the cause of anthrax.

2. How does the body's first line of defense function?

3. What role does greater permeability of capillar-ies play in the inflammatory response?

4. How do natural killer cells differ from macrophages?

5. What is the role of interferon?

**CRITICAL THINKING**

6. **Analyzing Information** Scientists can't always apply all of Koch's postulates to determine the cause of a disease. Explain why.

7. **Forming Reasoned Opinions** Should a fever always be treated? Why or why not?

8. **Inferring Relationships** Explain how cold symptoms show that the body is using both lines of nonspecific defenses to fight pathogens.

# Specific Defenses: The Immune System

*Although the nonspecific defenses usually keep pathogens from harming the body, a pathogen sometimes breaks through. In response, the body begins its third line of defense—a response aimed specifically at the pathogen.*

## SECTION 2

### OBJECTIVES

- **Identify** and describe the parts of the immune system.
- **Explain** how the immune system recognizes pathogens.
- **Compare** the actions of T cells and B cells in the immune response.
- **Relate** vaccination to immunity.
- **Distinguish** between allergy, asthma, and autoimmune disease.

### VOCABULARY

immune system
lymphocyte
thymus
spleen
B cell
T cell
antigen
immune response
helper T cell
cell-mediated immune
 response
cytotoxic T cell
humoral immune response
plasma cell
antibody
memory cell
immunity
vaccination
allergy
asthma
autoimmune disease

## THE IMMUNE SYSTEM

The **immune system,** the cells and tissues that recognize and attack foreign substances in the body, provides the body's specific defenses. The immune system fights pathogens and helps to stop the growth and spread of cancers. The immune system is made up of several tissues and white blood cells. The components of the immune system, shown in Figure 47-5, are found throughout the body. The tissues include the bone marrow, thymus, lymph nodes, spleen, tonsils, and adenoids. The white blood cells of the immune system are called **lymphocytes** (LIM-foh-sietz).

Each part of the immune system plays a special role in defending the body against pathogens. *Bone marrow,* the soft material found inside long bones, such as the femur, makes the billions of new lymphocytes needed by the body every day. The **thymus,** a gland located above the heart, helps produce a special kind of lymphocyte.

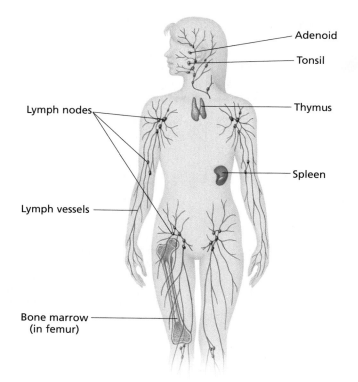

Adenoid
Tonsil
Thymus
Lymph nodes
Spleen
Lymph vessels
Bone marrow
(in femur)

**FIGURE 47-5**

The cells and tissues of the immune system recognize and attack foreign substances in the body.

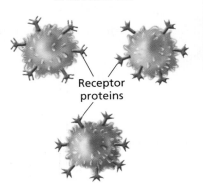
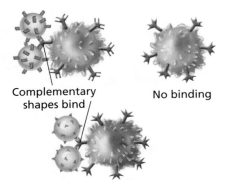

How do lymphocytes identify antigens? A lymphocyte has unique receptor proteins all over the surface of its cell membrane, as shown in Figure 47-6b. These receptor proteins recognize and bind to antigens that match their three-dimensional shape, as shown in Figure 47-6c. The surface of a bacterial cell, for instance, can be covered with many different kinds of molecules, each of which can function as an antigen and cause lymphocytes to react. All of the receptors on an individual lymphocyte are the same shape or type and thus bind to the same type of antigens.

The body can defend itself against an enormous number of different pathogens, because the immune system makes billions of different kinds of lymphocytes. Each kind of lymphocyte carries unique receptors. The specificity of the immune response is due to the specificity of the antigen receptors on the lymphocytes. For example, when a cold virus enters the body, lymphocytes with receptors that match the antigens of that cold virus respond. Lymphocytes with other kinds of receptors, such as those that bind to a flu virus, do not respond.

## IMMUNE RESPONSE

An immune response is a two-part assault on a pathogen. Both parts, the cell-mediated immune response and the humoral immune response, occur at the same time and require a specialized lymphocyte called a **helper T cell.** Steps ❶, ❷, and ❸ of Figure 47-7 on the next page show how an immune response is initiated. The first step occurs when a macrophage engulfs a pathogen. The macrophage then displays fragments of the pathogen's antigens on the surface of its own cell membrane. When the macrophage binds to a helper T cell with a receptor matching this antigen, the macrophage releases a cytokine called *interleukin-1* (in-tuhr-LOO-kin). *Cytokines* are proteins that can affect the behavior of other immune cells. The release of interleukin-1 by the macrophage activates more helper T cells, which then release a second cytokine, interleukin-2.

### Cell-Mediated Immune Response

More than one type of T cell carries out the **cell-mediated immune response.** Interleukin-2 stimulates the further production of helper T cells. The increase in helper T cells produces an increase in interleukin-2, which allows T cells to divide even faster. Interleukin-2 is also responsible for stimulating the production of **cytotoxic** (siet-oh-TAHKS-ik) **T cells** (sometimes called killer T cells), which recognize and destroy cells that have been infected by the pathogen. Invaded cells are recognizable because they usually have some of the pathogen's antigens on their surface, as shown in Figure 47-7. The cytotoxic T cells produced have receptors that match the antigen. Cytotoxic T cells usually kill by making a hole in the cell membrane of their target. Cytotoxic T cells can also kill cancer cells and attack parasites and foreign tissues.

**Word Roots and Origins**

*cytokine*

from the Greek *kytos,* meaning "hollow vessel" or "cell," and *kinesis,* meaning "movement"

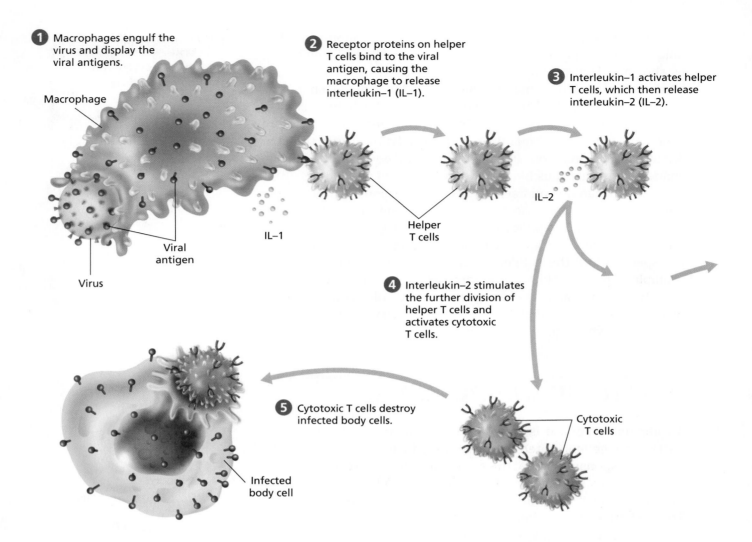

**1** Macrophages engulf the virus and display the viral antigens.

Macrophage

Viral antigen

Virus

IL–1

**2** Receptor proteins on helper T cells bind to the viral antigen, causing the macrophage to release interleukin–1 (IL–1).

Helper T cells

**3** Interleukin–1 activates helper T cells, which then release interleukin–2 (IL–2).

IL–2

**4** Interleukin–2 stimulates the further division of helper T cells and activates cytotoxic T cells.

**5** Cytotoxic T cells destroy infected body cells.

Cytotoxic T cells

Infected body cell

**FIGURE 47-7**

The immune response is a two-part assault on a pathogen: the cell-mediated immune response and the humoral immune response. Both responses occur at the same time and are triggered when a macrophage engulfs a pathogen, thus activating helper T cells (steps **1** through **3**). The cell-mediated immune response is shown in steps **4** and **5**, and the humoral immune response is shown in steps **6** through **9** on the next page.

One other type of T cell that plays a part in cell-mediated immunity is *suppressor T cells*. Suppressor T cells are not well understood but are thought to help shut down the immune response after the pathogen has been cleared from the body. The cell-mediated immune response is shown in steps **4** and **5** in Figure 47-7 above.

## Humoral Immune Response

The **humoral** (HYOO-muhr-uhl) **immune response** involves the action of B cells and occurs at the same time the cell-mediated immune response occurs. Like the cell-mediated immune response, the humoral immune response is triggered when macrophages engulf pathogens, stimulating helper T cells. The release of interleukin-2 stimulates B cells that have receptors that are complementary to the antigen to divide and change into plasma cells. **Plasma cells** are highly specialized cells that make defensive proteins called *antibodies* that are released into the blood. An **antibody** binds to a specific antigen or inactivates or destroys toxins. Antibodies are Y-shaped molecules. The two arms of each Y are identical, and each arm has a receptor that can attach to a specific antigen. A plasma cell can make up to 30,000 antibody molecules per second.

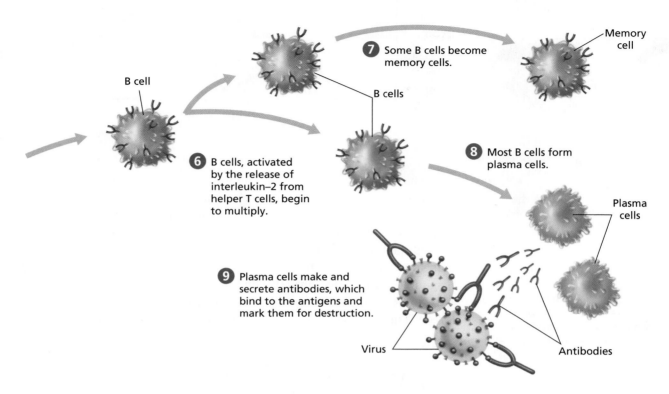

**B cell**

**7** Some B cells become memory cells.

**Memory cell**

**B cells**

**6** B cells, activated by the release of interleukin–2 from helper T cells, begin to multiply.

**8** Most B cells form plasma cells.

**Plasma cells**

**9** Plasma cells make and secrete antibodies, which bind to the antigens and mark them for destruction.

**Virus**

**Antibodies**

Antibodies bind to pathogens but do not destroy them directly. Instead, antibodies either inactivate the pathogen or cause its destruction by the nonspecific defenses. For example, by attaching to the surface proteins of a virus, antibodies prevent the virus from entering a cell, thereby blocking its reproduction. Antibodies also cause pathogens to clump together, which helps macrophages to engulf the pathogens. Antigen-antibody binding also activates the complement system. The complement proteins can then create holes in the membranes of the pathogen's cells, causing them to burst. The humoral immune response is shown in steps **6** through **9** in Figure 47-7 above.

## Primary and Secondary Immune Responses

Although the immune response stops once the body has overcome an infection, some memory cells remain in the body. **Memory cells** are lymphocytes that will not respond the first time that they meet with an antigen or an invading cell but will recognize and attack that antigen or invading cell during later infections.

Memory cells are the body's long-term protection against reinfection by a pathogen. Memory cells often remain effective throughout an individual's life. Because of memory cells, a person will get most diseases only once. When exposed to a pathogen a second time, memory cells immediately recognize it and begin to divide rapidly. They eliminate the pathogen before it can produce serious illness.

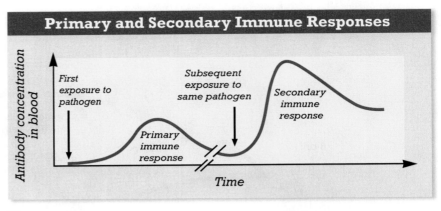

## Primary and Secondary Immune Responses

Antibody concentration in blood

First exposure to pathogen

Primary immune response

Subsequent exposure to same pathogen

Secondary immune response

Time

**(b)**

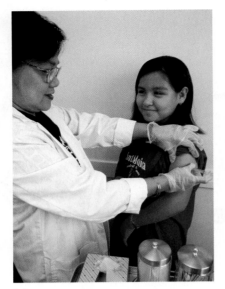

**(a)**

**FIGURE 47-8**

(a) Vaccinations take advantage of the production of memory cells and the secondary immune response.
(b) Compare the production of antibodies during the primary and secondary immune responses that are shown on the graph.

## Quick Lab

### Organizing the Immune Response

**Materials** paper, pencil

**Procedure** Create a diagram or a flowchart that outlines the steps involved in an immune response. Label the cells and the steps.

**Analysis** What are helper T cells? How is a cell-mediated response different from a humoral response?

The first time the body encounters an antigen, the immune response is called a *primary immune response*. The response of memory cells to a later infection by the same pathogen is called a *secondary immune response*. The secondary immune response is much faster and more powerful, producing many more antibodies, as shown in the graph above. Recall that memory cells protect only against pathogens already encountered. Colds and flu are an exception, because rhinoviruses and flu viruses mutate at a high rate. Therefore, these viruses are always presenting new antigens.

# IMMUNITY AND VACCINATION

**Immunity** is the ability to resist an infectious disease. A person who is resistant to a pathogen is said to be immune to it. One way for the body to gain immunity to a pathogen is to be infected by it, undergo a primary immune response, and survive the disease it causes. Another, safer way is through **vaccination** (vak-suh-NAY-shuhn), the introduction of antigens into the body to cause immunity. Vaccination usually involves an injection of a vaccine under the skin, as shown in Figure 47-8a.

## Vaccines

A *vaccine* is a solution that contains a dead or weakened pathogen or material from a pathogen. However, the antigens are still present, so the body produces a primary immune response to the antigens in the vaccine. The memory cells that remain after the primary immune response can provide a quick secondary immune response if the antigen ever enters the body again.

Some of the diseases that have been controlled through the use of vaccines are polio, measles, mumps, tetanus, and diphtheria. An intensive worldwide vaccination campaign has eliminated smallpox. Sometimes, the protection provided by vaccines wears off over time. So, doctors recommend *booster shots* to restore immunity against some diseases, such as tetanus and polio.

# MILESTONES IN Vaccine Development

*Centuries ago, Asian physicians sought to understand immunity by exposing healthy people to material from the sores of smallpox victims. This technique, called* variolation, *had limited success but a huge historical impact. In the early 1700s, a British woman saw the technique being used in Turkey and described it to British doctors, who tried it on children. One of those children was Edward Jenner, the inventor of vaccination.*

## Timeline

**Before 1700** Asian physicians use variolation.

**1796** Jenner uses cowpox to immunize against smallpox.

**1885** Pasteur treats rabies with vaccination.

**1940s** Vaccines for diphtheria, pertussis, tetanus, and smallpox are used routinely.

**1955** An injectable polio vaccine is introduced by Jonas Salk.

**1964** A vaccine for measles is released.

**1967** A mumps vaccine is introduced.

**1986** Recombinant vaccines are developed.

**1990s and later** Researchers seek an effective vaccine for HIV and other pathogens.

As a country doctor in the late 1700s, Edward Jenner was investigating cowpox, a relatively harmless disease. He knew that milkmaids often contracted cowpox from cows. He had also heard that milkmaids who had cowpox were immune to smallpox. Jenner saw a connection, and he hypothesized that exposure to the pathogen that causes cowpox would give a person immunity to the smallpox pathogen also. In 1796, Jenner tested his hypothesis.

Jenner took matter from the cowpox sore of a milkmaid and injected it into an 8-year-old boy. Two months later, Jenner injected material from a sore of a smallpox patient. The boy remained healthy, even after several more injections. Jenner's experiment would be considered unethical today, but his observations led to millions of lives being saved through vaccination.

Science and medicine advanced slowly before the 20th century, and vaccination caught on only after scientists understood that germs cause disease. Louis Pasteur succeeded in vaccinating sheep against anthrax in 1881. In 1885, he injected a boy with killed rabies virus to save him from contracting the disease. This event helped explain vaccination, and soon scientists around the world began searching for the agents of disease and creating vaccines. By the early 1970s, vaccines had been developed for diphtheria, pertussis, tetanus, mumps, polio, measles, and rubella. In the United States, these illnesses have been virtually eliminated through vaccination.

Researchers soon discovered that the immune system can recognize a tiny piece of a pathogen and still form antibodies. By 1986, scientists had developed a recombinant hepatitis B vaccine by using harmless organisms altered to make a protein from the virus. The new vaccine cannot actually cause the disease, a rare but dangerous side effect of previous vaccines.

Vaccine research now focuses on conquering pathogens that have caused new outbreaks of disease around the world. These pathogens include HIV, the West Nile virus, the Ebola virus, and the coronavirus that causes SARS. In addition, researchers are working to improve existing vaccines, such as those for smallpox and anthrax.

## Review

1. Why is it unnecessary for a vaccine to contain a whole pathogen?
2. **Critical Thinking** How can a person be immune to smallpox after exposure to cowpox?
3. **Critical Thinking** Do you think Pasteur's injection of rabies virus into a child would be considered unethical today?

**internet** connect

www.scilinks.org
**Topic:** Vaccines
**Keyword:** HM61590

SCI LINKS. Maintained by the National Science Teachers Association

# PROBLEMS OF THE IMMUNE SYSTEM

Sometimes, the immune system reacts to otherwise harmless antigens in ways that can be harmful. Three examples of such problems of the immune system are allergies, asthma, and autoimmune diseases.

## Allergies

An **allergy** is a physical response to an antigen. The antigen can be a common substance that produces little or no response in the general population. Antigens that can trigger allergic reactions include pollen, animal dander (flakes of skin), dust mites, food, and fungal spores. Allergic symptoms are generally mild, including a runny nose, sneezing, watery eyes, or itchy swellings of the skin. However, some people have extreme and life-threatening reactions to allergies. Many of the symptoms of allergy result from the release of histamine by cells that are exposed to the antigen. Drugs called *antihistamines* help counteract the effects of histamine and can relieve some symptoms of allergies.

## Asthma

Allergies can also trigger **asthma,** a respiratory disorder that causes the bronchioles (airways of the lungs) to narrow. Asthma attacks occur when the muscles covering the bronchioles overreact to substances in the air, as shown in Figure 47-9. Substances that can cause asthma attacks include cigarette smoke and allergens such as animal dander. During an asthma attack, the lining of the bronchioles and other respiratory tissues may also swell and become inflamed, making breathing difficult. Other symptoms of asthma include shortness of breath, wheezing, and coughing. Asthma attacks are serious. Thousands of people in the United States die from asthma each year.

**FIGURE 47-9**

During an asthma attack, the muscles that encircle the airways of the lung (bronchioles) constrict, and inflammation of the respiratory tissues causes swelling and extra mucus to be produced in the airways. These reactions can make breathing difficult.

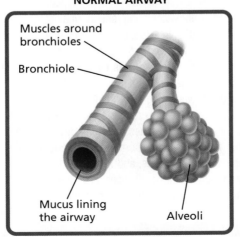

**NORMAL AIRWAY**

Muscles around bronchioles

Bronchiole

Mucus lining the airway

Alveoli

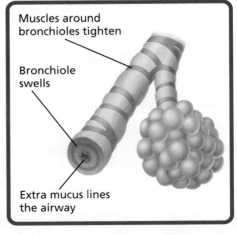

**AIRWAY UNDER ASTHMA ATTACK**

Muscles around bronchioles tighten

Bronchiole swells

Extra mucus lines the airway

**TABLE 47-2** *Autoimmune Diseases, Target Tissues, and Symptoms*

| Disease | Tissues affected | Symptoms |
| --- | --- | --- |
| Systemic lupus erythematosus | Connective tissue throughout the body | Facial rash, painful joints, fever, fatigue, kidney problems, weight loss |
| Type 1 diabetes | Insulin-producing cells in pancreas | Excessive urine production, excessive thirst, weight loss, fatigue, confusion |
| Rheumatoid arthritis | Joints | Painful, crippling inflammation of the joints |
| Psoriasis | Skin | Dry, scaly, red skin patches |
| Scleroderma | Multiple organs | Hardening and stiffening of the skin |
| Crohn's disease | Digestive system | Abdominal pain, nausea, vomiting, weight loss |

## Autoimmune Diseases

A disease in which the immune system attacks the organism's own cells is called an **autoimmune** (awt-oh-i-MYOON) **disease.** Lymphocytes that recognize and react to the body's own cells are usually eliminated during development, before they become functional. This removal of certain lymphocytes prevents an attack directed at the body's own tissues. However, in rare cases the immune system does respond to the body's own cells, attacking them as if they were pathogens. An autoimmune disease results.

Autoimmune diseases affect organs and tissues in various areas of the body. Multiple sclerosis is an autoimmune disease of the nervous system that affects mainly young adults. In this disease, T cells attack and slowly destroy the insulating material surrounding nerve cells in the brain, in the spinal cord, and in the nerves leading from the eyes to the brain. Symptoms include weakness, unsteadiness, tingling or burning sensations, and blurred vision. In severe cases, paralysis, blindness, and even death can result. Scientists are still searching for the causes of multiple sclerosis and other autoimmune diseases. Table 47-2 lists some other autoimmune diseases and describes their effects on the body.

internet connect

www.scilinks.org
Topic: Autoimmune Diseases
Keyword: HM60125

SCI
LINKS. Maintained by the National Science Teachers Association

---

## SECTION 2 REVIEW

1. Describe the functions of the spleen and of the bone marrow.

2. What is an antigen?

3. How does the role of B cells in the immune response differ from that of helper T cells?

4. Explain how vaccination stimulates immunity to a disease.

5. Name one similarity and one difference between autoimmune diseases and allergies.

**CRITICAL THINKING**

6. **Recognizing Relationships** Explain how B cells depend on T cells.

7. **Evaluating an Argument** "A person who has just recovered from a cold cannot get the flu." Is this statement true? Explain your reasoning.

8. **Forming Reasoned Opinions** Would vaccine research be useful in preventing autoimmune diseases? Explain your reasoning.

- **Describe** the relationship between HIV and AIDS.
- **Distinguish** between the three phases of HIV infection.
- **Identify** the two main ways that HIV is transmitted.
- **Determine** how the evolution of HIV affects the development of vaccines and treatment.

VOCABULARY

AIDS
HIV
opportunistic infection

# HIV AND AIDS

*The immune system normally provides protection against infectious diseases. The importance of the immune system can be seen in diseases in which the immune system does not function properly. One of the deadliest of these diseases is* **AIDS** *(acquired immunodeficiency syndrome), in which the immune system loses its ability to fight off pathogens and cancers. AIDS was recognized as a disease in 1981. Since then, it has killed more than 22 million people worldwide.*

## THE COURSE OF HIV INFECTION

AIDS results from infection by the human immunodeficiency virus, or **HIV.** Once HIV has entered the bloodstream, HIV binds to CD4, a receptor protein on the surface of some cells. To enter a cell, HIV must also bind to an associated protein, or co-receptor. Macrophages, which have the CD4 receptor and a co-receptor called CCR5, are often the first cells of the immune system infected with HIV. The virus replicates inside the macrophages, and new viruses are released through "budding." This process does not destroy the macrophages. Viral replication of HIV results in many mutations. Eventually, a mutation may enable the virus to recognize other co-receptors, such as those found on helper T cells.

After release from macrophages, HIV attaches to and enters helper T cells. After viral replication, the new viruses are released from the T cell, as shown in Figure 47-10. These viruses then attach to other helper T cells, where the process repeats. Unlike macrophages, helper T cells are destroyed. Eventually, HIV kills enough helper T cells to cripple the immune system, leading to AIDS. HIV infection doesn't progress to AIDS on a specific timetable, but people tend to go through three phases of infection.

### Phase I

Phase I of HIV infection is called the *asymptomatic stage,* because there are few or no symptoms. However, the amount of virus increases due to replication, as shown in Figure 47-11. The immune system begins an attack, and plasma cells make antibodies to fight the virus. However, it may take several weeks for the amount of anti-HIV antibodies to become large enough to result in a positive HIV test. HIV-infected people may feel well during phase I but can still infect other people. Phase I can last for up to 10 years or more.

**FIGURE 47-10**

An HIV-infected helper T cell (grey mass) releases hundreds of new virus particles (red dots). (SEM 5,600×)

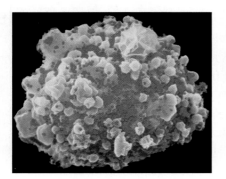

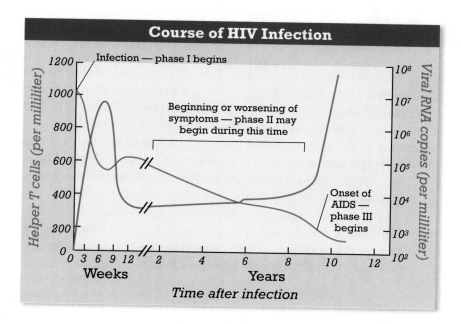

**Course of HIV Infection**

**FIGURE 47-11**

This graph shows an example of how the course of HIV infection can proceed. The course of HIV infection depends on both the numbers of virus particles and the numbers of helper T cells in the blood.

## Phase II

The beginning or worsening of symptoms marks the start of the second phase of HIV infection. B cells continue to make a large amount of antibody against HIV. However, as shown in Figure 47-11, the number of T cells drops steadily as the virus continues to replicate. As the immune system fails, lymph glands become swollen, and fatigue, weight loss, fever, or diarrhea develop or worsen. Some infected people may notice mental changes, such as forgetfulness and abnormal thinking patterns.

## Phase III

In phase III, the number of helper T cells drops so low that they can no longer stimulate B cells and cytotoxic T cells to fight invaders. As a consequence, the amount of anti-HIV antibody falls, and HIV levels rise dramatically. The virus continues destroying the few helper T cells remaining. AIDS is diagnosed when the helper T-cell count drops to 200 cells per milliliter of blood or lower (a normal amount is 600 to 700 helper T cells per milliliter).

AIDS may also be diagnosed if an opportunistic infection has developed. **Opportunistic infections** are illnesses caused by pathogens that produce disease in people with weakened immune systems. These organisms usually do not create problems in people with a healthy immune system. Opportunistic infections include pneumocystis pneumonia, tuberculosis, and a rare infection of the brain called *toxoplasmosis*. Rare cancers such as Kaposi's sarcoma, which causes purplish-red blotches on the skin, can also signal the onset of AIDS.

Drug therapy can slow the progress from HIV infection to AIDS. But AIDS is fatal. Few individuals live more than two years after an AIDS diagnosis. It is important to note that HIV itself does not cause death. Rather, death results from the weakened immune system's inability to fight opportunistic infections and cancers.

# TRANSMISSION OF HIV

HIV is transmitted by the transfer of body fluids containing HIV or HIV-infected cells. The most common means of infection is sexual contact with an infected person. The second most common means is the use of syringes and hypodermic needles that have been contaminated with blood containing HIV. People who inject intravenous drugs and who share needles are at very high risk of infection. HIV can also be transmitted from an infected mother to her infant before or during birth or through breast-feeding.

HIV is not transmitted through casual contact, such as shaking hands. HIV is apparently not transmitted through the air, in water, on toilet seats, or through insect bites. The likelihood of infection through a blood transfusion is extremely low.

## FIGURE 47-12

A scientist studies blood samples as part of the search for a treatment or vaccine for HIV.

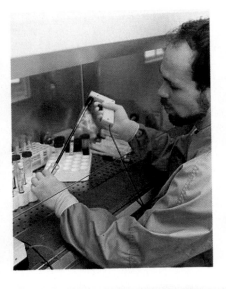

# VACCINES AND TREATMENTS

Scientists trying to create vaccines and treatments for HIV, such as the scientist shown in Figure 47-12, must contend with its rapid rate of evolution. The genes that code for the virus's surface proteins mutate frequently. As a result, new variants of the virus with slightly different surface proteins are constantly appearing. To produce effective immunity, a vaccine against HIV must stimulate the immune system to respond to many variants of the virus. Although researchers are developing and testing several vaccines against HIV, none has yet proven effective.

In addition, HIV can quickly become resistant to drugs. Scientists now treat patients with a combination of three drugs. Because mutations are random, mutations that create resistance to all three drugs are not likely to occur. However, this therapy often requires patients to take 50 or more pills a day. Many HIV-infected patients find the plan difficult and expensive. Nevertheless, the multidrug treatment is the most effective plan currently available. Because there is not yet a vaccine or cure for HIV infection, the only way to prevent HIV infection is to avoid high-risk behaviors.

## SECTION 3 REVIEW

1. Describe the relationship between HIV and AIDS.

2. State the developments during the course of HIV infection that can lead to a diagnosis of AIDS.

3. List two ways that HIV can be transmitted and two ways that it cannot.

4. Why have scientists been unable to develop an effective vaccine for HIV?

**CRITICAL THINKING**

5. **Recognizing Factual Accuracy** Evaluate the statement "HIV infection causes death."

6. **Analyzing Current Research** Explain how research on co-receptor blocking might affect the search for a treatment for HIV infection.

7. **Comparing Concepts** Identify one similarity and one difference between HIV and a cold virus.

# CHAPTER HIGHLIGHTS

**Nonspecific Defenses**

- A pathogen is any agent that causes a disease. Robert Koch developed four basic steps, or postulates, for identifying the pathogen responsible for a disease.

- The skin and mucous membranes are nonspecific defenses that keep pathogens out of the body.

- The skin acts as an external barrier to pathogens and also releases substances that are toxic to pathogens.

- The mucous membranes protect the interior surfaces of the body and secrete mucus, a sticky fluid that traps pathogens.

- Injury to cells triggers an inflammatory response. Injured cells release chemical messengers that attract phagocytes through the capillary walls. Phagocytes then destroy the pathogens.

- White blood cells fight pathogens. Two types of phagocytes (neutrophils and macrophages) ingest pathogens. Natural killer cells pierce the cell membranes of infected cells.

- Nonspecific defenses also include an elevation in temperature (fever) and the activation of proteins such as the complement system and interferon.

**Vocabulary**

| | | | |
|---|---|---|---|
| infectious disease (p. 957) | inflammatory | neutrophil (p. 960) | complement |
| pathogen (p. 957) | response (p. 959) | macrophage (p. 960) | system (p. 960) |
| Koch's postulates (p. 957) | histamine (p. 959) | natural killer cell (p. 960) | interferon (p. 960) |
| mucous membrane (p. 958) | phagocyte (p. 959) | | |

**SECTION 2** **Specific Defenses: The Immune System**

- The immune system consists of the cells and tissues that recognize and attack foreign substances in the body.

- Lymphocytes must be able to recognize foreign invaders and tell them apart from the cells of the body. Receptor proteins on a lymphocyte's plasma membrane allow the lymphocyte to recognize the invaders' antigens.

- The reaction of the body against an antigen is called an *immune response*. An immune response is a two-part assault on a pathogen: the cell-mediated immune response and the humoral immune response.

- Memory cells that remain after a primary response to an antigen allow a rapid secondary immune response if that antigen appears again. Vaccinations take advantage of the production of memory cells and the secondary immune response.

- An allergy is a physical response to an antigen that causes little or no response in the general population. Allergies can trigger asthma, a respiratory disorder that causes the bronchioles to narrow. An autoimmune disease is a disease in which the immune system attacks the organism's own cells.

**Vocabulary**

| | | | |
|---|---|---|---|
| immune system (p. 961) | antigen (p. 962) | humoral immune | vaccination (p. 966) |
| lymphocyte (p. 961) | immune response (p. 962) | response (p. 964) | allergy (p. 968) |
| thymus (p. 961) | helper T cell (p. 963) | plasma cell (p. 964) | asthma (p. 968) |
| spleen (p. 962) | cell-mediated immune | antibody (p. 964) | autoimmune |
| B cell (p. 962) | response (p. 963) | memory cell (p. 965) | disease (p. 969) |
| T cell (p. 962) | cytotoxic T cell (p. 963) | immunity (p. 966) | |

**SECTION 3** **HIV and AIDS**

- AIDS results from infection by HIV. HIV can replicate inside macrophages and helper T cells.

- The course of HIV infection usually has three phases: phase I, the asymptomatic phase; phase II, the beginning or worsening of symptoms; and phase III, AIDS.

- HIV is transmitted mainly through sexual contact and the use of HIV-contaminated needles.

- Because its genes mutate often, HIV can quickly become resistant to medication. The rapid evolution of HIV also makes it difficult to develop an effective vaccine.

**Vocabulary**

| | | |
|---|---|---|
| AIDS (p. 970) | HIV (p. 970) | opportunistic infection (p. 971) |

## USING VOCABULARY

1. For each pair of terms, explain how the meanings of the terms differ.
   a. *macrophage* and *natural killer cell*
   b. *B cell* and *T cell*
   c. *antigen* and *antibody*
   d. *allergy* and *asthma*

2. Explain the relationship between HIV and AIDS.

3. Use the following terms in the same sentence: *cell-mediated immune response, helper T cell, cytotoxic T cell,* and *interleukin-2.*

4. **Word Roots and Origins** The word *pathogen* is derived from the Greek *pathos,* which means "suffering" or "disease," and *-gen,* which means "to produce." Using this information, explain why the term *pathogen* is a good name for an infectious agent.

## UNDERSTANDING KEY CONCEPTS

5. **Describe** the steps that must be followed to prove that a particular pathogen is responsible for a disease.

6. **Compare** the function of the mucous membranes with that of the skin.

7. **Summarize** the steps of the inflammatory response.

8. **Name** the chemical messenger that increases the permeability of the capillaries surrounding an injury.

9. **Identify** the roles that white blood cells play in the second line of nonspecific defenses.

10. **Explain** how fever and protein production help defend against infection.

11. **Name** one function of the thymus.

12. **Describe** how lymphocytes recognize and bind to pathogens.

13. **Explain** the role that helper T cells play in the immune response.

14. **Name** the type of cell that produces antibodies and releases them into the blood.

15. **Explain** the function of antibodies.

16. **State** the role that memory cells play in providing immunity against disease.

17. **Relate** vaccination to immunity.

18. **Describe** the cause of autoimmune diseases.

19. **Name** the point at which phase III in the course of HIV infection begins.

20. **List** two main ways HIV is usually transmitted.

21. **Identify** the problem scientists have encountered when trying to develop a vaccine against HIV.

22. **CONCEPT MAPPING** Use the following terms to create a concept map: *pathogen, macrophage, helper T cell, cytotoxic T cell, B cell, plasma cell,* and *antibody.*

## CRITICAL THINKING

23. **Making Comparisons** Scientists created an effective vaccine for smallpox but have not been able to do so for HIV. What does this suggest about the rate of evolution of the smallpox virus?

24. **Relating Concepts** Cytotoxic T cells attack and destroy some kinds of cancer cells. What can you conclude about the surface proteins of these cancer cells?

25. **Interpreting Graphics** The graph below shows the amount of HIV in the blood of an infected person over time. Use the graph to answer the following questions:
    a. What caused the peak in viral concentration at point a?
    b. Why did the level of virus drop between points a and b?
    c. Describe what is happening to both the virus and the immune system at points c and d.

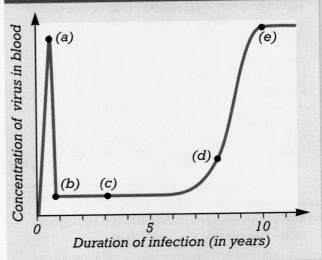

**Virus Concentration in HIV Infection**

26. **Inferring Relationships** People who are severely burned often die from infection. Use what you know about disease transmission to explain why this situation is common.

# Standardized Test Preparation

**DIRECTIONS:** Choose the letter of the answer choice that best answers the question.

1. Which of the following is part of the nonspecific defenses?
   A. the inflammatory response
   B. the primary immune response
   C. the humoral immune response
   D. the secondary immune response

2. Which of the following statements is false?
   F. Autoimmune diseases can be fatal.
   G. Autoimmune diseases are a type of cancer.
   H. Multiple sclerosis is an autoimmune disease.
   J. Autoimmune diseases target the body's cells.

3. Which of the following is the most common means of HIV transmission?
   A. receiving a blood transfusion
   B. performing experiments with HIV
   C. shaking hands with a person who has AIDS
   D. having sexual contact with an HIV-infected person

**INTERPRETING GRAPHICS:** The image below shows two kinds of structures involved in an immune response. Use the image to answer the questions that follow.

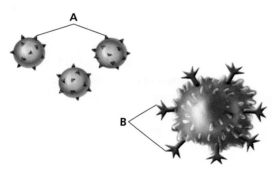

4. What are the structures labeled *A*?
   F. antigens
   G. interferons
   H. interleukins
   J. receptor proteins

5. What are the structures labeled *B*?
   A. antigens
   B. interferons
   C. interleukins
   D. receptor proteins

6. Why do structures *A* and *B* interact with each other?
   F. Both are viral proteins.
   G. Both are "nonself" structures.
   H. They are complementary shapes.
   J. They are produced by the same cells.

**DIRECTIONS:** Complete the following analogy.

7. T cell : cell-mediated :: B cell :
   A. humoral
   B. infectious
   C. secondary
   D. inflammatory

**INTERPRETING GRAPHICS:** The graph below shows the number of helper T cells over time from the onset of HIV infection. Use the graph to answer the question that follows.

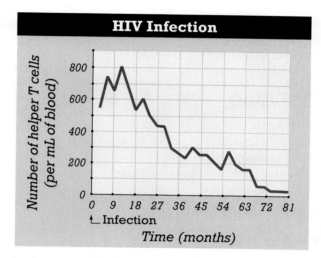

8. About how many months after infection did the number of T cells first drop below 200/mL?
   F. 18
   G. 39
   H. 51
   J. 58

## SHORT RESPONSE

A person infected with HIV today might not test positive for HIV antibodies for up to 6 months.

Explain why an HIV antibody test may not be positive until several weeks after a person's exposure to HIV.

## EXTENDED RESPONSE

The inflammatory response results from cell injury.

*Part A* Explain the role of histamine in the inflammatory response.

*Part B* Explain the usefulness of having more than one type of white blood cell respond in the inflammatory response.

**Test TIP** Whenever possible, highlight or underline numbers or words that are critical to correctly understanding a question.

# Simulating Disease Transmission

## OBJECTIVES

- Simulate the transmission of a disease.
- Determine the original carrier of the disease.

## PROCESS SKILLS

- organizing data
- analyzing data
- identifying
- modeling

## MATERIALS

- lab apron
- safety goggles
- disposable gloves
- dropper bottle of unknown solution
- large test tube
- indophenol indicator

## Background

1. What are the five main ways that human diseases can be transmitted?
2. How does a cold or flu spread from person to person?
3. How does the body fight invading viruses?
4. Why has the transmission of HIV become a great concern worldwide?
5. Why is a person with AIDS less able to combat infections than a person who does not have AIDS?

## PART A Simulating the Transmission of a Disease

1. This investigation will involve the class in a simulation of disease transmission. After the simulation, you will try to identify the original infected person in the closed class population.
2. In your lab report, construct a data table similar to Table A.
3. **CAUTION Put on a lab apron, goggles, and disposable gloves.**
4. **CAUTION If you get any solution used in this investigation on your skin or clothing, wash it off at the sink while calling to your**

### TABLE A  LIST OF PARTNERS' NAMES

| Round number | Partner's name |
|---|---|
| 1 | |
| 2 | |
| 3 | |

teacher. **If you get any solution used in this investigation in your eyes, immediately flush your eyes with water at the eyewash station while calling to your teacher.** You have been given a dropper bottle of unknown solution and a clean test tube. The solution in the dropper bottle represents the pathogens that you carry. Handle the unknown solution with care because it is not simply water.

5. When your teacher says to begin, transfer three dropperfuls of your solution to your clean test tube. Then, replace the lid on the dropper bottle, and do not re-open it until Part B of this investigation.

6. Select one person to be your partner. Let one partner pour the contents of his or her test tube into the other partner's test tube. Then, pour half the solution back into the first test tube. You and your partner now share pathogens of any possible transmittable disease that either of you might have had. Record the name of your first partner (Round 1) in your data table in your lab report.

7. For Round 2, wait for your teacher's signal, and then find a different partner and exchange solutions in the same manner as you did in step 6. Record the name of your second partner (Round 2) in your lab report. Do not exchange solutions with the same person more than once. Repeat this procedure again for Round 3.

8. After all rounds are finished, your instructor will ask you to add one dropperful of indophenol indicator to your test tube to see if the fluids in your test tube have become infected. Infected solutions will be colorless or light pink. All uninfected solutions will appear blue. Record the outcome of your tests in your lab report.

## TABLE B  PATH OF DISEASE TRANSMISSION

| Name of infected person | Names of infected person's partners | | |
|---|---|---|---|
| | Round 1 | Round 2 | Round 3 |
| | | | |
| | | | |
| | | | |
| | | | |
| | | | |

## PART B  Tracing the Source of the Disease

**9.** If you are an infected person, give your name to your teacher. As names of infected people are written on the chalkboard or on the overhead projector, record them in your lab report in a table similar to Table B shown above.

**10.** Try to trace the original source of the infection, and then determine the transmission route of the disease. In your table, cross out the names of all the uninfected partners in Rounds 1, 2, and 3. There should be only two people in Round 1 who were infected. One of these people was the original carrier.

**11.** Draw a diagram that shows the transmission route of the disease through all three rounds. Your diagram may look something like the chart below. Include your diagram in your lab report.

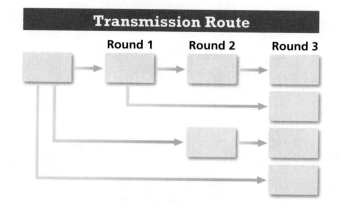

**Transmission Route**

Round 1    Round 2    Round 3

**12.** In your diagram, insert the names of the two people in Round 1 who were infected and the names of their partners in Rounds 2 and 3.

**13.** To test whether a person was the original disease carrier, pour a sample from his or her dropper bottle into a clean test tube, and add indophenol indicator.

**14.** Clean up your materials, and wash your hands before leaving the lab.

## Analysis and Conclusions

**1.** What might the clear fluid in each student's dropper bottle represent?

**2.** Does the simulated disease have any apparent symptoms?

**3.** What chemical is added to the test tubes when the rounds are completed?

**4.** What color indicates a positive result?

**5.** What color indicates a negative result?

**6.** Who was the original disease carrier?

**7.** After the three rounds, how many students were infected? Express this as a percentage of the number of students in the class.

**8.** If an epidemic occurred in your community, how might public-health officials work to stop the spread of the disease?

## Further Inquiry

A public-health official is sent to investigate an outbreak of a new disease. Devise an experiment to allow the official to determine whether the disease has been caused by the passing of pathogens from person to person or by environmental conditions.

# CHAPTER 48

# DIGESTIVE AND EXCRETORY SYSTEMS

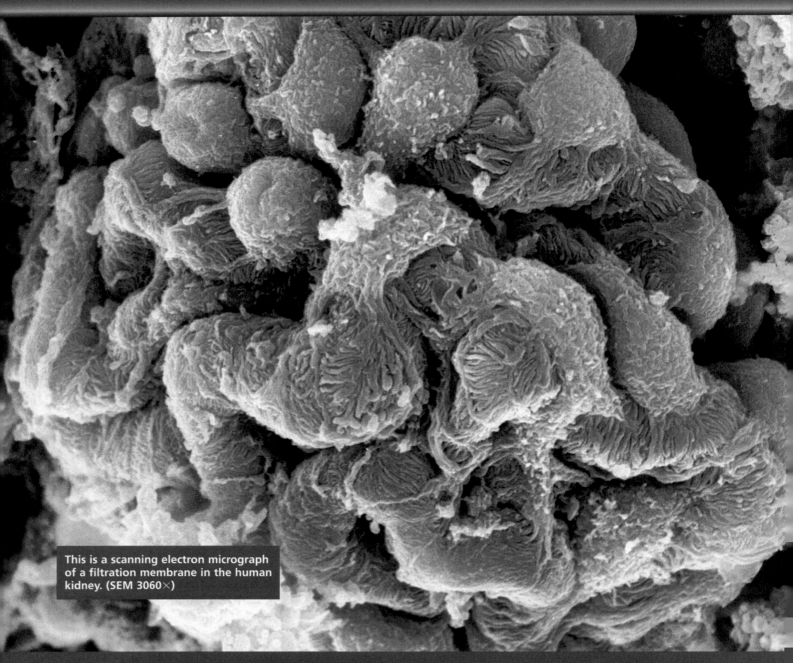

This is a scanning electron micrograph of a filtration membrane in the human kidney. (SEM 3060×)

# NUTRIENTS

*Carrots, fish, eggs, hamburgers, blackberries, cow's milk—the human body is able to convert each of these foods into nutrients that body cells need to function, grow, and replicate. In this section, you will learn what nutrients the human body needs and how it uses those nutrients to carry out life processes.*

## SIX CLASSES OF NUTRIENTS

Organisms that do not carry out photosynthesis must obtain energy from nutrients in the food they consume. A **nutrient** is a substance required by the body for energy, growth, repair, and maintenance. All foods contain at least one of six basic nutrients: carbohydrates, proteins, lipids, vitamins, minerals, and water. Few foods contain all six nutrients. Most foods contain a concentration of just one or two.

Nutritionists classify foods into six groups—meat, milk, fruits, vegetables, breads and cereals, and fats, oils, and sweets—based on nutrient similarity. Each nutrient plays a different role in keeping an organism healthy. The USDA Food Guide Pyramid, shown in Figure 48-1, shows the number of servings from each food group needed for a balanced diet.

Some nutrients provide energy for powering cellular processes. The energy available in food is measured in kilocalories, or Calories, which is equal to 1,000 calories. A *calorie* is the amount of heat energy required to raise the temperature of 1 g of water 1°C (1.8°F). The greater the number of calories in a quantity of food, the more energy the food contains.

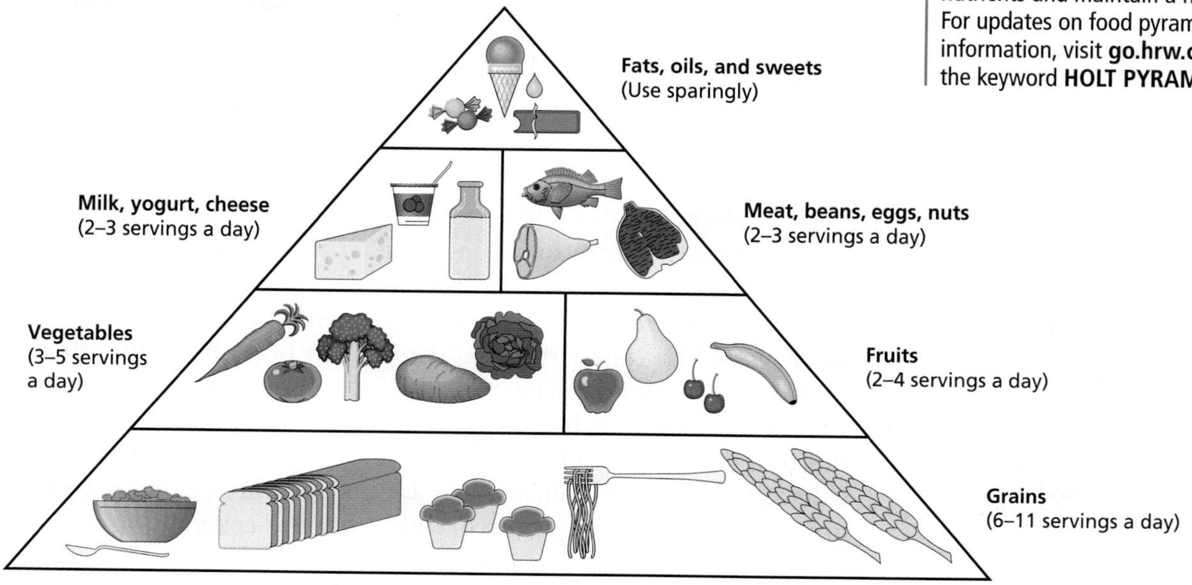

### OBJECTIVES

- **Relate** the role of each of the six classes of nutrients in maintaining a healthy body.
- **Describe** each of the parts of the USDA Food Guide Pyramid.
- **Identify** foods containing each of the organic nutrients.
- **Explain** the importance of vitamins, minerals, and water in maintaining the body's functions.
- **Identify** three disorders associated with improper nutrition.

### VOCABULARY

nutrient
vitamin
mineral
dehydration

**FIGURE 48-1**

The USDA Food Guide Pyramid lists the daily number of servings needed from each food group to obtain a variety of nutrients and maintain a healthy diet. For updates on food pyramid information, visit **go.hrw.com** and enter the keyword **HOLT PYRAMID**.

Fats, oils, and sweets
(Use sparingly)

Milk, yogurt, cheese
(2–3 servings a day)

Meat, beans, eggs, nuts
(2–3 servings a day)

Vegetables
(3–5 servings a day)

Fruits
(2–4 servings a day)

Grains
(6–11 servings a day)

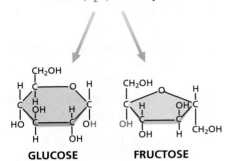

**SUCROSE**

+

Water (H$_2$O) and enzyme

**GLUCOSE**     **FRUCTOSE**

**FIGURE 48-2**

The hydrolysis of a disaccharide requires water and an enzyme. When sucrose is hydrolyzed, two monosaccharides are formed—glucose and fructose. These monosaccharides are then transported through cell membranes to be used by cells.

**Word Roots and Origins**

*hydrolysis*

from the Greek *hydro,* meaning "water," and *lysis,* meaning "dissolve"

# CARBOHYDRATES, PROTEINS, AND LIPIDS

The three nutrients needed by the body in the greatest amounts—carbohydrates, proteins, and lipids—are organic compounds. *Organic compounds* are compounds containing the elements carbon, hydrogen, and oxygen.

## Carbohydrates

*Carbohydrates* are organic compounds composed of carbon, hydrogen, and oxygen. Carbohydrates are broken down in aerobic respiration to provide most of the body's energy. Although proteins and fats also supply energy, the body most easily uses the energy provided by carbohydrates. Carbohydrates contain sugars that are quickly converted into the usable energy ATP, but proteins and fats must go through many chemical processes before the body can use them to make ATP.

The fructose and glucose (also known as dextrose) in fruit and honey are simple sugars, or *monosaccharides*. These sugars can be absorbed directly into the bloodstream and made available to cells for use in cellular respiration. Sucrose (table sugar), maltose, and lactose (milk sugar) are *disaccharides*. Disaccharides are sugars that consist of two chemically linked monosaccharides. Before disaccharides can be used by the body for energy they must be split into two monosaccharides in a process called *hydrolysis*. Figure 48-2 shows how sucrose is hydrolyzed to produce glucose and fructose.

*Polysaccharides* are complex molecules that consist of many monosaccharides bonded together. The starch found in many grains and vegetables is a polysaccharide made up of long chains of glucose molecules. During digestion, the enzymes hydrolyze these long chains into individual glucose units.

Many foods we get from plants contain cellulose, a polysaccharide that forms the walls of plant cells. The body cannot break down cellulose into individual component sugars. Nevertheless it is an extremely important part of the human diet. Cellulose and other forms of fiber help move the food along by stimulating contractions of the smooth muscles that form the walls of the digestive organs.

## Proteins

The major structural and functional material of body cells are *proteins.* Proteins consist of long chains of amino acids. Proteins from food must be broken down into amino acids in order for the body to grow and to repair tissues. The human body uses 20 different amino acids to build the proteins it needs. The body can make many of these amino acids, but it cannot produce all of them in the quantities that it needs. Amino acids that must be obtained from food are called *essential amino acids*. Ten amino acids are essential to children and teenagers for growth. Only eight are essential to adults.

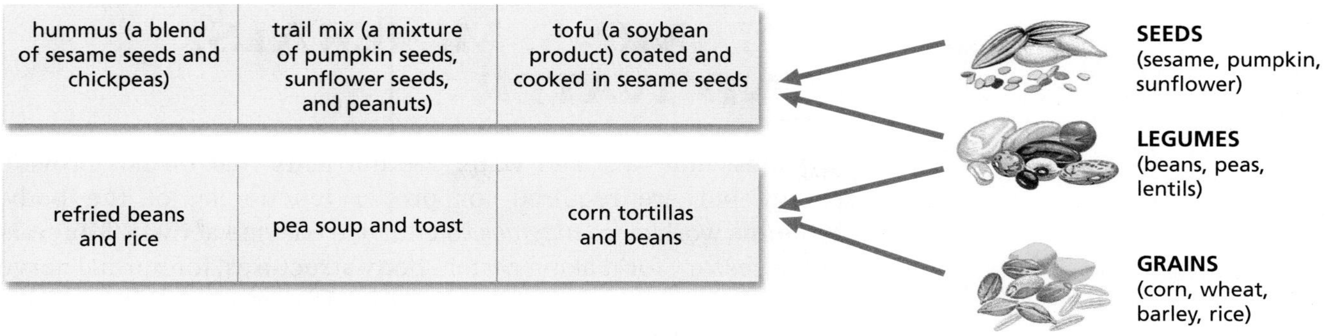

| hummus (a blend of sesame seeds and chickpeas) | trail mix (a mixture of pumpkin seeds, sunflower seeds, and peanuts) | tofu (a soybean product) coated and cooked in sesame seeds |
|---|---|---|

| refried beans and rice | pea soup and toast | corn tortillas and beans |
|---|---|---|

**SEEDS** (sesame, pumpkin, sunflower)

**LEGUMES** (beans, peas, lentils)

**GRAINS** (corn, wheat, barley, rice)

**FIGURE 48-3**

The combination of legumes, seeds, and grains furnishes all the essential amino acids.

Most of the foods we get from plants contain only small amounts of certain essential amino acids. Eating certain combinations of two or more plant products, such as those shown in Figure 48-3, can ensure an adequate supply of all the essential amino acids. Most animal products, such as eggs, milk, fish, poultry, and beef, contain larger amounts of all the essential amino acids.

## Lipids

*Lipids* are organic compound that are insoluble in water. They include fats, oils, and waxes. Lipids are used to make cell membranes and steroid hormones and to store energy.

The most common fats are *triglycerides* which are used for energy and to build cell membranes and other cell parts. The body stores excess fat from the diet. Excess carbohydrates and protein may also be converted to fat for storage. Stored fats are beneficial unless they are excessive. A light layer of body fat beneath the skin provides insulation in cold weather. Fat surrounding vulnerable organs, such as the kidneys and liver, acts as protective padding. Most important, fat reserves are a concentrated source of energy.

To use fats, the body must first break down each fat molecule into *glycerol* and *fatty acids*. The glycerol molecule is the same in all fats, but the fatty acids differ in both structure and composition. The body converts some fatty acids to other fatty acids, depending on which one the body needs at the time.

Scientists classify fats as saturated or unsaturated, based on structural differences in their fatty acids. A *saturated fatty acid* has all its carbon atoms connected by single bonds and thus contains as many hydrogen atoms as possible. An *unsaturated fatty acid* has at least one double bond between carbon atoms. If there are two or more double bonds, as shown in Figure 48-4, the fatty acid is called *polyunsaturated*. Although lipids are essential nutrients, too much fat in the diet is known to harm several body systems. A diet high in saturated fats is linked to heart disease and to high levels of blood-cholesterol. High cholesterol contributes to atherosclerosis, or build-up of fatty deposits within vessels. A diet high in fat also contributes to obesity, and can lead to late-onset diabetes. Diabetes is the leading cause of kidney failure, blindness, and amputation in adults.

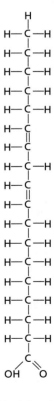

**Linoleic acid**

**FIGURE 48-4**

The structure of linoleic acid, a fatty acid in margarine, is shown in this figure. Notice the two double bonds between carbon atoms.

# VITAMINS, MINERALS, AND WATER

Vitamins, minerals, and water are nutrients that do not provide energy but are required for proper functioning of the body. **Vitamins** work as *coenzymes* to enhance enzyme activity. **Minerals** are necessary for making certain body structures, for normal nerve and muscle function, and for maintaining osmotic balance. Water transports gases, nutrients, and waste; is a reagent in some of the body's chemical reactions; and regulates body temperature. Table 48-1 summarizes the sources of vitamins and their functions.

## TABLE 48-1 *Food Sources of Vitamins*

| Vitamins | Best sources | Essential for | Deficiency diseases and symptoms |
|---|---|---|---|
| Vitamin A (carotene; fat soluble) | fish-liver oils, liver and kidney, green and yellow vegetables, yellow fruit, tomatoes, butter, egg yolk | growth, health of the eyes, and functioning of the cells of the skin and mucous membranes | retarded growth, night blindness, susceptibility to infections, changes in skin, defective tooth formation |
| Vitamin $B_1$ (thiamin; water soluble) | meat, soybeans, milk, whole grains, legumes | growth; carbohydrate metabolism; functioning of the heart, nerves, muscles | beriberi—loss of appetite and weight, nerve disorders, and faulty digestion |
| Vitamin $B_2$ (riboflavin; water soluble) | meat, fowl, soybeans, milk, green vegetables, eggs, yeast | growth, health of the skin, eyes, and mouth, carbohydrate metabolism, red blood cell formation | retarded growth, dimness of vision, inflammation of the tongue, premature aging, intolerance to light |
| Vitamin $B_3$ (niacin; water soluble) | meat, fowl, fish, peanut butter, potatoes, whole grains, tomatoes, leafy vegetables | growth; carbohydrate metabolism; functioning of the stomach, intestines, and nervous system | pellagra—smoothness of the tongue, skin eruptions, digestive disturbances, and mental disorders |
| Vitamin $B_6$ (pyridoxine; water soluble) | whole grains, liver, fish | protein metabolism, production of hemoglobin, health of the nervous system | dermatitis, nervous disorders |
| Vitamin $B_{12}$ (cyanocobalamin; water soluble) | liver, fish, beef, pork, milk, cheese | red blood cell formation, health of the nervous system | a reduction in number of red blood cells, pernicious anemia |
| Vitamin C (ascorbic acid; water soluble) | fruit (especially citrus), tomatoes, leafy vegetables | growth, strength of the blood vessels, development of teeth, health of gums | scurvy—sore gums, hemorrhages around the bones, and tendency to bruise easily |
| Vitamin D (calciferol; fat soluble) | fish-liver oil, liver, fortified milk, eggs, irradiated foods | growth, calcium and phosphorus metabolism, bones and teeth | rickets—soft bones, poor development of teeth, and dental decay |
| Vitamin E (tocopherol; fat soluble) | wheat-germ oil, leafy vegetables, milk, butter | normal reproduction | anemia in newborns |
| Vitamin K (naphthoquinone; fat soluble) | green vegetables, soybean oil, tomatoes | normal clotting of the blood, liver functions | hemorrhages |

## Vitamins

Vitamins are small organic molecules that act as coenzymes. Coenzymes activate enzymes and help them function. Because vitamins generally cannot be synthesized by the body, a diet should include the proper daily amounts of all vitamins. Like enzymes, coenzymes can be reused many times. Thus, only small quantities of vitamins are needed in the diet.

Vitamins dissolve in either water or fat. The fat-soluble vitamins include vitamins A, D, E, and K. The water-soluble vitamins are vitamin C and the group of B vitamins. Because the body cannot store water-soluble vitamins, it excretes surplus amounts in urine. Fat-soluble vitamins are absorbed and stored like fats. Unpleasant physical symptoms and even death can result from storing too much or having too little of a particular vitamin.

The only vitamin that the body can synthesize in large quantities is vitamin D. This synthesis involves sunlight converting cholesterol to vitamin D precursors in the skin. People who do not spend a lot of time in the sun can get their vitamin D from food.

## Minerals

Minerals are naturally occurring inorganic substances that are used to make certain body structures, to carry out normal nerve and muscle function, and to maintain osmotic balance. Some minerals, such as calcium, magnesium, and iron, are drawn from the soil and become part of plants. Animals that feed on plants extract the minerals and incorporate them into their bodies. Table 48-2 lists the primary sources and functions of a few of the minerals considered most essential to human beings. Iron, for example, is necessary for the formation of red blood cells, and potassium maintains the body's acid-base balance and aids in growth. Both are found in certain fruits and vegetables. Excess minerals are excreted through the skin in perspiration and through the kidneys in urine.

### TABLE 48-2  *Food Sources of Minerals*

| Minerals | Source | Essential for |
|---|---|---|
| Calcium | milk, whole-grain cereals, vegetables, meats | deposition in bones and teeth; functioning of heart, muscles, and nerves |
| Iodine | seafoods, water, iodized salt | thyroid hormone production |
| Iron | leafy vegetables, liver, meats, raisins, prunes | formation of hemoglobin in red blood cells |
| Magnesium | vegetables | muscle and nerve action |
| Phosphorus | milk, whole-grain cereals, vegetables, meats | deposition in bones and teeth; formation of ATP and nucleic acids |
| Potassium | vegetables, citrus fruits, bananas, apricots | maintaining acid-base balance; growth; nerve action |
| Sodium | table salt, vegetables | blood and other body tissues; muscle and nerve action |

FIGURE 48-5

Athletes drink water to replace water lost through perspiration. Excess water loss can lead to a condition called dehydration.

## Water

Water accounts for over half of your body weight. Most of the reactions that maintain life can take place only in water. Water makes up more than 90 percent of the fluid part of the blood, which carries essential nutrients to all parts of the body. It is also the medium in which waste products are carried away from body tissues.

Water also helps regulate body temperature. It absorbs and distributes heat released in cellular reactions. When the body needs to cool, perspiration—a water-based substance—evaporates from the skin, and heat is drawn away from the body. Usually, the water lost through your skin, lungs, and kidneys is easily replaced by drinking water or consuming moist foods. People, like the athletes in Figure 48-5, must drink water to avoid **dehydration**—excess water is lost and not replenished. Water moves from intercellular spaces to the blood by osmosis. Eventually, water will be drawn from the cells themselves. As a cell loses water, the cytoplasm becomes more concentrated until the cell can no longer function.

## SECTION 1 REVIEW

1. Summarize the major role of each of the organic nutrients in the body's function.

2. Describe the type of information the USDA Food Guide pyramid provides.

3. Identify a food that is high in carbohydrates, another that is high in proteins, and a third that is high in lipids.

4. Identify the role that minerals play in maintaining a healthy body.

5. Explain the importance of water to the body.

6. Identify disorders caused by a diet high in saturated fats.

**CRITICAL THINKING**

7. **Predicting Results** What might be the health consequences of a diet consisting of only water and rice?

8. **Justifying Conclusions** Why would large doses of vitamin $B_2$ be less harmful than large doses of vitamin A?

9. **Applying Information** Caffeine tends to increase the discharge of urine. Should an athlete drink a caffeinated beverage before a big game? Explain your answer.

# DIGESTIVE SYSTEM

*B*efore your body can use the nutrients in the food you consume, the nutrients must be broken down physically and chemically. The nutrients must be absorbed, and the wastes must be eliminated.

## THE GASTROINTESTINAL TRACT

The process of breaking down food into molecules the body can use is called **digestion.** Digestion occurs in the **gastrointestinal tract,** or digestive tract, a long, winding tube which begins at the mouth and winds through the body to the anus. The gastrointestinal tract, shown in Figure 48-6, is divided into several distinct organs. These organs carry out the digestive process. Along the gastrointestinal tract are other organs that are not part of the gastrointestinal tract, but that aid in digestion by delivering secretions into the tract through ducts.

### OBJECTIVES

- **List** the major organs of the digestive system.
- **Distinguish** between mechanical digestion and chemical digestion.
- **Relate** the structure of each digestive organ to its function in mechanical digestion.
- **Identify** the source and function of each major digestive enzyme.
- **Summarize** the process of absorption in both the small and large intestine.

### VOCABULARY

digestion
gastrointestinal tract
saliva
pharynx
epiglottis
peristalsis
gastric fluid
ulcer
cardiac sphincter
chyme
pyloric sphincter
gallbladder
villus
colon

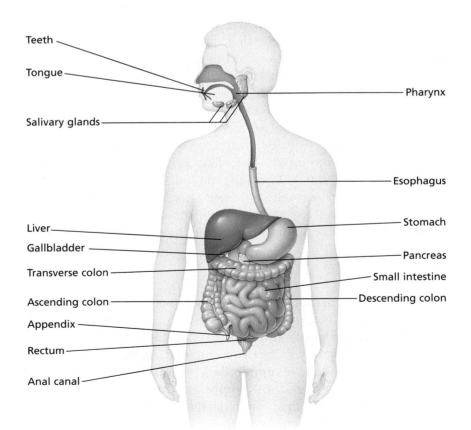

Teeth
Tongue
Salivary glands
Pharynx
Esophagus
Liver
Gallbladder
Transverse colon
Ascending colon
Appendix
Rectum
Anal canal
Stomach
Pancreas
Small intestine
Descending colon

**FIGURE 48-6**

The digestive system is made up of the gastrointestinal tract, salivary glands, the liver, gallbladder, and pancreas. These organs break down food into nutrients that can be absorbed into the bloodstream.

FIGURE 48-7

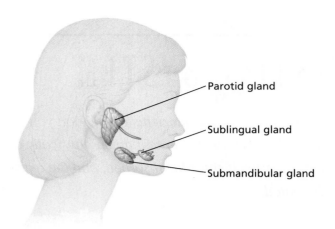

Parotid gland

Sublingual gland

Submandibular gland

# THE MOUTH AND ESOPHAGUS

Digestion includes the mechanical and chemical breakdown of food into nutrients, the absorption of nutrients, and the elimination of waste. In the mechanical phase, the body physically breaks down chunks of food into small particles. Mechanical digestion increases the surface area on which digestive enzymes can act.

## Mouth

When you take a bite of food, you begin the mechanical phase of digestion. *Incisors*—sharp front teeth—cut the food. Then, the broad, flat surfaces of *molars,* or back teeth, grind it up. The tongue helps keep the food between the chewing surfaces of the upper and lower teeth by manipulating it against the *hard palate,* the bony, membrane-covered roof of the mouth. This structure is different from the *soft palate,* an area located just behind the hard palate. The soft palate is made of folded membranes and separates the mouth cavity from the nasal cavity.

Chemical digestion involves a change in the chemical nature of the nutrients. Salivary glands produce **saliva** (suh-LIE-vuh), a mixture of water, mucus, and a digestive enzyme called *salivary amylase.* Besides the many tiny salivary glands located in the lining of the mouth, there are three pairs of larger salivary glands, as shown in Figure 48-7. The salivary amylase begins the chemical digestion of carbohydrates by breaking down some starch into the disaccharide maltose.

## Esophagus

After food has been thoroughly chewed, moistened, and rolled into a *bolus,* or ball, it is forced into the pharynx by swallowing action. The **pharynx,** an open area that begins at the back of the mouth, serves as a passageway for both air and food. As Figure 48-8 shows, a flap of tissue called the **epiglottis** (EP-uh-GLAHT-is) prevents food from entering the trachea, or windpipe, during swallowing. Instead, the bolus passes into the esophagus, a muscular tube approximately 25 cm long that connects the pharynx with the stomach.

FIGURE 48-8

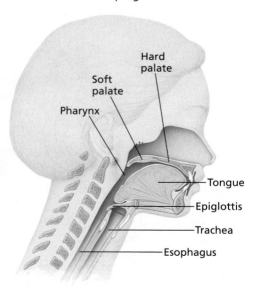

Hard palate

Soft palate

Pharynx

Tongue

Epiglottis

Trachea

Esophagus

The esophagus has two muscle layers: an inner circular layer that wraps around the esophagus and an outer longitudinal layer that runs the length of the tube. As you can see in Figure 48-9, alternating contractions of these muscle layers push the bolus through the esophagus and into the stomach. This series of rhythmic muscular contractions and relaxations is called **peristalsis.**

# STOMACH

The stomach, an organ involved in both mechanical and chemical digestion, is located in the upper left side of the abdominal cavity, just below the diaphragm. It is an elastic bag that is J-shaped when full and that lies in folds when empty. You have probably heard your stomach "growl" when it has been empty for some time. These sounds are made by the contraction of smooth muscles that form the walls of the stomach.

## Mechanical Digestion

The walls of the stomach have several layers of smooth muscle. As you can see in Figure 48-10, there are three layers of muscle—a circular layer, a longitudinal layer, and a diagonal layer. When food is present, these muscles work together to churn the contents of the stomach. This churning helps the stomach carry out mechanical digestion.

The inner lining of the stomach is a thick, wrinkled mucous membrane composed of epithelial cells. This membrane is dotted with small openings called gastric pits. *Gastric pits,* which are shown in Figure 48-10, are the open ends of gastric glands that release secretions into the stomach. Some of the cells in gastric glands secrete mucus, some secrete digestive enzymes, and still others secrete hydrochloric acid. The mixture of these secretions forms the acidic digestive fluid.

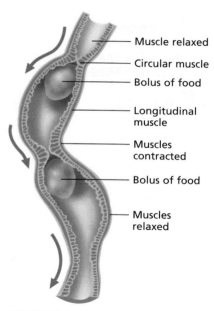

**FIGURE 48-9**

Peristalsis is so efficient at moving materials down the esophagus that you can drink while standing on your head. The smooth muscles move the water "up" the esophagus, against the force of gravity.

**FIGURE 48-10**

Each of the muscle layers of the stomach is oriented in a different direction. The pH of the stomach is normally between 1.5 and 2.5, making it the most acidic environment in the body. Mucous cells lining the stomach wall protect the organ from damage.

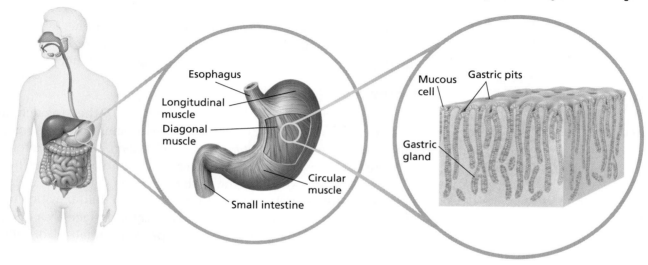

## Chemical Digestion

**Gastric fluid** carries out chemical digestion in the stomach. An inactive stomach secretion called *pepsinogen* is converted into a digestive enzyme called *pepsin* at a low pH. Chemical digestion of proteins starts in the stomach when pepsin splits complex protein molecules into shorter chains of amino acids called *peptides*. Hydrochloric acid in the stomach not only ensures a low pH but also dissolves minerals and kills bacteria that enter the stomach along with food.

Mucus secreted in the stomach forms a coating that protects the lining from hydrochloric acid and from digestive enzymes. In some people, the mucous coating of the stomach tissue breaks down, allowing digestive enzymes to eat through part of the stomach lining. The result is called an **ulcer.** The breakdown of the mucous layer is often caused by bacteria that destroy the epithelial cells, which form the mucous layer.

## Formation of Chyme

The **cardiac sphincter** (SFINGK-tuhr) is a circular muscle located between the esophagus and the stomach. After the food enters the stomach, the cardiac sphincter closes to prevent the food from re-entering the esophagus. Food usually remains in the stomach for three to four hours. During this time, muscle contractions in the stomach churn the contents, breaking up food particles and mixing them with gastric fluid. This process forms a mixture called **chyme** (KIEM).

Peristalsis forces chyme out of the stomach and into the small intestine. The **pyloric** (pie-LOHR-ik) **sphincter,** a circular muscle between the stomach and the small intestine, regulates the flow of chyme. Each time the pyloric sphincter opens, about 5 to 15 mL (about 0.2 to 0.5 oz) of chyme moves into the small intestine, where it mixes with secretions from the liver and pancreas.

**FIGURE 48-11**

The liver is the body's largest internal organ, weighing about 1.5 kg (3 lb). If a small portion is surgically removed because of disease or injury, the liver regenerates the missing section.

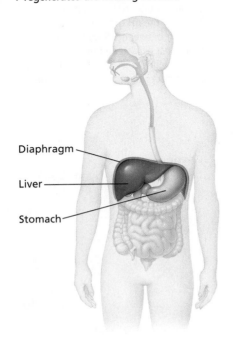

Diaphragm
Liver
Stomach

# THE LIVER, GALLBLADDER, AND PANCREAS

Several of the organs involved in digestion do not come directly in contact with food. The liver, gallbladder, and pancreas work with the digestive system to perform several important functions.

## Liver

The liver is a large organ located to the right of the stomach, as shown in Figure 48-11. The liver performs numerous functions in the body, including storing glucose as glycogen, making proteins, and breaking down toxic substances, such as alcohol. The liver also secretes bile, which is vital to the digestion of fats. Bile breaks fat globules into small droplets, forming a milky fluid in which fats are suspended. This process exposes a greater surface area of fats to the action of digestive enzymes and prevents small fat droplets from rejoining into large globules.

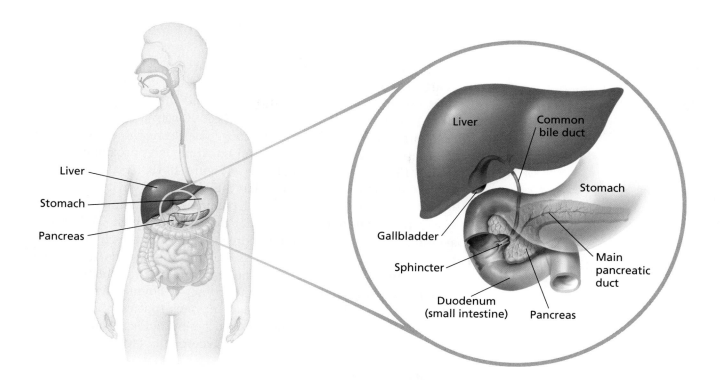

## Gallbladder

The bile secreted by the liver passes through a Y-shaped duct, as shown in Figure 48-12. The bile travels down one branch of the Y-shaped duct and then up the other branch to the **gallbladder,** a saclike organ that stores and concentrates bile. When chyme is present in the small intestine, the gallbladder releases bile through the common bile duct into the small intestine.

## Pancreas

As shown in Figure 48-12, the pancreas is an organ that lies behind the stomach, against the back wall of the abdominal cavity. The pancreas is a gland that serves several important functions. The pancreas acts as an endocrine gland, producing hormones that regulate blood sugar levels. As part of the digestive system, the pancreas serves two roles. It produces sodium bicarbonate, which neutralizes stomach acid. The pH of stomach acid is about 2. Pancreatic fluid raises the pH of the chyme from an acid to a base.

Neutralizing stomach acid is important in order to protect the interior of the small intestine and to ensure that the enzymes secreted by the pancreas can function. Many enzymes in the pancreatic fluid are activated by the higher pH. The pancreas produces enzymes that break down carbohydrates, proteins, lipids, and nucleic acids. These enzymes hydrolyze disaccharides into monosaccharides, fats into fatty acids and glycerol, and proteins into amino acids. Pancreatic fluid enters the small intestine through the pancreatic duct, which joins the common bile duct just before it enters the intestine.

**FIGURE 48-12**

Cholesterol deposits known as *gallstones* can form in the ducts leading from the liver and gallbladder to the small intestine. If the gallstones interfere with the flow of bile, they must be removed, along with the gallbladder in some cases.

# SMALL INTESTINE

If the small intestine were stretched to its full length, it would be nearly 7 m (about 21 ft) long. The *duodenum,* the first section of this coiled tube, makes up only the first 25 cm (about 10 in.) of that length. The *jejunum* (jee-JOO-nuhm), the middle section, is about 2.5 m (about 8 ft) long. The *ileum,* which makes up the remaining portion of the small intestine, is approximately 4 m (about 13 ft) in length. As shown in Figure 48-13, the entire length of the small intestine lies coiled in the abdominal cavity.

Secretions from the liver and pancreas enter the duodenum, where they continue the chemical digestion of chyme. When the secretions from the liver and pancreas, along with the chyme, enter the duodenum, they trigger intestinal mucous glands to release large quantities of mucus. The mucus protects the intestinal wall from protein-digesting enzymes and the acidic chyme. Glands in the lining of the small intestine release enzymes that complete digestion by breaking down peptides into amino acids, disaccharides into monosaccharides, and fats into glycerol and fatty acids.

## Absorption

During *absorption,* the end products of digestion—amino acids, monosaccharides, glycerol, and fatty acids—are transferred into the circulatory system through blood and lymph vessels in the lining of the small intestine. The structure of this lining provides a huge surface area for absorption to take place. The highly folded lining of the small intestine is covered with millions of fingerlike projections called **villi** (singular, *villus*), which are shown in Figure 48-13. The cells covering the villi, in turn, have extensions on their cell membranes called *microvilli.* The folds, villi, and microvilli give the small intestine a surface area of about 250 m$^2$ (about 2,685 ft$^2$), or roughly the area of a tennis court. Nutrients are absorbed through this surface by means of diffusion and active transport.

**FIGURE 48-13**

Although the small intestine is nearly 7 m long, only the first 25 cm are involved in digesting food. The rest is involved in the absorption of nutrients. Villi, as shown in the SEM (137×) and the diagram, expand the surface area of the small intestine to allow greater absorption of nutrients.

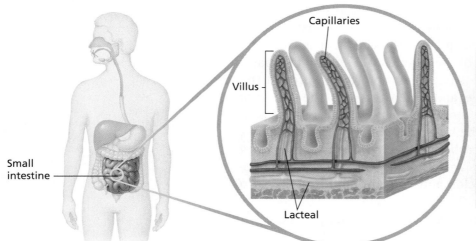

Capillaries

Villus

Lacteal

Small intestine

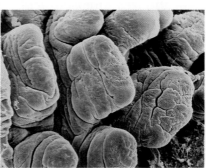

SEM of intestinal villi

Inside each of the villi are capillaries and tiny lymph vessels called *lacteals* (LAK-tee-uhlz). The lacteals can be seen in Figure 48-13. Glycerol and fatty acids enter the lacteals, which carry them through the lymph vessels and eventually to the bloodstream through lymphatic vessels near the heart. Amino acids and monosaccharides enter the capillaries and are carried to the liver. The liver neutralizes many toxic substances in the blood and removes excess glucose, converting it to glycogen for storage. The filtered blood then carries the nutrients to all parts of the body.

# LARGE INTESTINE

After absorption in the small intestine is complete, peristalsis moves the remaining material on to the large intestine. The large intestine, or **colon,** is the final organ of digestion. Study Figure 48-14 to identify the four major parts of the colon: *ascending colon, transverse colon, descending colon*, and *sigmoid colon.* The sigmoid colon leads into the very short, final portions of the large intestine called the *rectum* and the *anal canal.*

Most of the absorption of nutrients and water is completed in the small intestine. About 9 L (9.5 qt) of water enter the small intestine daily, but only 0.5 L (0.53 qt) of water is present in the material that enters the large intestine. In the large intestine, only nutrients produced by bacteria that live in the colon, as well as most of the remainder of the water, are absorbed. Slow contractions move material in the colon toward the rectum. Distension of the colon initiates contractions that move the material out of the body. As this matter moves through the colon, the absorption of water solidifies the mass. The solidified material is called *feces.*

As the fecal matter solidifies, cells lining the large intestine secrete mucus to lubricate the intestinal wall. This lubrication makes the passing of the feces less abrasive. Mucus also binds together the fecal matter, which is then eliminated through the anus.

**FIGURE 48-14**

This X ray shows the large intestine, or colon. The ascending colon is on the left. The transverse colon crosses the abdominal cavity. The descending colon can be seen on the right. The sigmoid colon is the small section that leads to the anal canal.

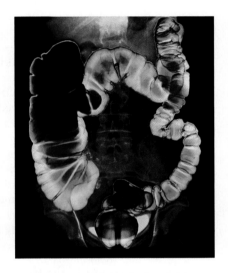

## SECTION 2 REVIEW

1. Sequence the organs that are involved in each step of digestion.

2. Explain the difference between mechanical digestion and chemical digestion.

3. Describe the processes involved in mechanical digestion.

4. Identify the source and function of each class of digestive enzymes.

5. Explain how the small intestine and large intestine are related to the function of absorption.

**CRITICAL THINKING**

6. **Applying Information** Which of the six basic nutrients might a person need to restrict after an operation to remove the gallbladder? Why?

7. **Predicting Results** Explain how the gastrointestinal tract would be affected if the pancreas were severely damaged.

8. **Forming Reasoned Opinions** Considering the stomach's role in the digestive system, is it possible for a person to digest food without a stomach? Explain your answer.

# Science in Action

## Can Saris Prevent Cholera?

Health authorities in Bangladesh urge villagers to boil surface water before drinking it, but a severe shortage of wood makes this process impossible for most people. Millions of people therefore must still use surface water and are at risk of cholera. However, scientist Rita Colwell came up with a method to filter out disease-causing organisms with an item available even in the poorest homes.

**Dr. Rita Colwell**

### HYPOTHESIS: Simple Filtration Methods Will Reduce the Incidence of Cholera

Cholera is a severe disease that causes thousands of deaths each year. Symptoms of cholera include abdominal cramps, nausea, vomiting, dehydration, and shock. If untreated, death may occur after severe fluid and electrolyte loss. The responsible agent is a comma-shaped bacterium called *Vibrio cholerae.* In certain developing regions around the world where people must obtain untreated drinking water from streams and lakes, *V. cholerae* infection can occur.

Dr. Colwell, one of the world's leading cholera researchers, observed that *V. cholerae* lives in association with microscopic copepods, which are a type of zooplankton. Dr. Colwell also showed that cholera outbreaks occurred seasonally in association with temperature changes and blooms of the copepod organisms.

Dr. Colwell and her colleagues knew that villagers often strained flavored beverages through a piece of fine cloth cut from an old, discarded sari, a woman's long flowing garment. Colwell came up with a hypothesis: Straining drinking water through an old piece of sari cloth could remove copepods and the associated cholera bacteria and prevent cases of cholera.

### METHODS: Compare Filtration Methods

Colwell's team chose 142 villages in Bangladesh where people use untreated river or pond water for drinking and have high rates of cholera. They assigned over 45,000 participants to three groups. The

control group would continue to use unfiltered, untreated water. One experimental group would collect water in jars by tying four layers of sari cloth over the opening. The other experimental group would collect water in containers covered by filter fabric designed to remove copepod-sized organisms. Field workers collected medical data on cholera cases during the study period.

### RESULTS: Cholera Cases Are Reduced

The team compared the incidence of cholera for the control group with that of the two experimental groups. They found that the control group had the usual number of cholera cases (about 3 per 1,000 people per year). However, using either nylon filtration cloth or sari cloth cut the number of cases in half. Interestingly, old cloth worked better than new cloth because older fibers soften, the pore size is reduced, and more copepods and attached bacteria are trapped in the pores.

### CONCLUSION: Saris Can Reduce the Incidence of Cholera

Rita Colwell and her team concluded that saris are a simple, practical solution to a serious global problem. They are currently looking at ways to expand this filtration idea to other parts of the world. Women don't wear saris everywhere, but old cloth is available in virtually every home.

### REVIEW

1. Identify the relationship between copepods, *V. cholerae,* and drinking water.

2. Explain the reason that the age of the saris made a difference in filtration.

3. **Critical Thinking** If the *V. cholerae* bacteria were not associated with copepods, would this filtration have been successful? Explain your reasoning.

**internet** connect

**www.scilinks.org**
**Topic: Disease Prevention**
**Keyword: HM60414**

SCiLINKS. Maintained by the National Science Teachers Association

# URINARY SYSTEM

*The body must rid itself of the waste products of cellular activity. The process of removing metabolic wastes, called **excretion**, is just as vital as digestion in maintaining the body's internal environment. Thus, the urinary system not only excretes wastes but also helps maintain homeostasis by regulating the content of water and other substances in the blood.*

**SECTION 3**

### OBJECTIVES

- **Identify** the major parts of the kidney.
- **Relate** the structure of a nephron to its function.
- **Explain** how the processes of filtration, reabsorption, and secretion help maintain homeostasis.
- **Summarize** the path in which urine is eliminated from the body.
- **List** the functions of each of the major excretory organs.

### VOCABULARY

excretion
renal cortex
renal medulla
renal pelvis
urea
ammonia
urine
nephron
Bowman's capsule
glomerulus
renal tubule
filtration
reabsorption
secretion
loop of Henle
ureter
urinary bladder
urethra

## KIDNEYS

The main waste products that the body must eliminate are carbon dioxide, from cellular respiration, and nitrogenous compounds, from the breakdown of proteins. The lungs excrete most of the carbon dioxide, and nitrogenous wastes are eliminated by the kidneys. The excretion of water is necessary to dissolve wastes and is closely regulated by the kidneys, the main organs of the urinary system.

Humans have two bean-shaped kidneys, each about the size of a clenched fist. The kidneys are located one behind the stomach and the other behind the liver. Together, they regulate the chemical composition of the blood.

### Structure

Figure 48-15 shows the three main parts of the kidney. The **renal cortex,** the outermost portion of the kidney, makes up about a third of the kidney's tissue mass. The **renal medulla** is the inner two-thirds of the kidney. The **renal pelvis** is a funnel-shaped structure in the center of the kidney. Also, notice in Figure 48-15 that blood enters the kidney through a renal artery and leaves through a renal vein. The renal artery transports nutrients and wastes to the kidneys. The nutrients are used by kidney cells to carry out their life processes. One such process is the removal of wastes brought by the renal artery.

The most common mammalian metabolic waste is **urea** (yoo-REE-uh), a nitrogenous product made by the liver. Nitrogenous wastes are initially brought to the liver as **ammonia,** a chemical compound of nitrogen so toxic that it could not remain long in the body without harming cells. The liver removes ammonia from the blood and converts it into the less harmful substance urea. The urea enters the bloodstream and is then removed by the kidneys.

# NEPHRONS

The substances removed from the blood by the kidneys—toxins, urea, water, and mineral salts—form an amber-colored liquid called **urine.** Urine is made in structures called **nephrons** (NEF-RAHNZ), the functional units of the kidney. Nephrons are tiny tubes in the kidneys. One end of a nephron is a cup-shaped capsule surrounding a tight ball of capillaries that retains cells and large molecules in the blood and passes wastes dissolved in water through the nephron. The cup-shaped capsule is called **Bowman's capsule.** Within each Bowman's capsule, an arteriole enters and splits into a fine network of capillaries called a **glomerulus** (gloh-MER-yoo-luhs).

Take a close look at the structure of the nephron, shown in Figure 48-15. Notice the close association between a nephron of the kidney and capillaries of the circulatory system. Initially, fluid passes from the glomerulus into a Bowman's capsule of the nephron. As the fluid travels through the nephron, nutrients that passed into the Bowman's capsule are reabsorbed into the bloodstream. What normally remains in the nephron are waste products and some water, which form urine that passes out of the kidney.

Each kidney consists of more than a million nephrons. If they were stretched out, the nephrons from both kidneys would extend for 80 km (50 mi). As you read about the structure of a nephron, locate each part in Figure 48-15.

**FIGURE 48-15**

The outer region of the kidney, the renal cortex, contains structures that filter blood brought by the renal artery. The inner region, or renal medulla, consists of structures that carry urine, which empties into the funnel-shaped renal pelvis. The renal vein transports the filtered blood back to the heart.

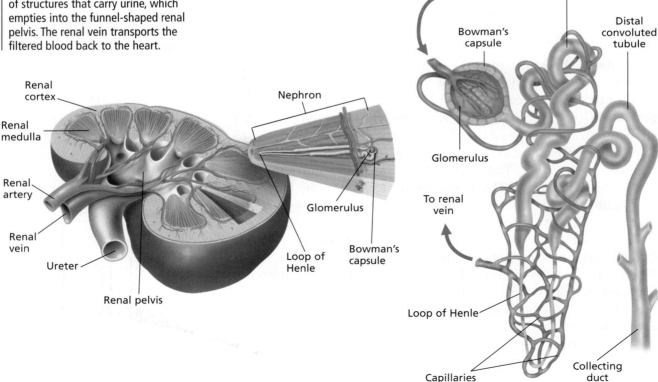

Each nephron has a cup-shaped structure, called a Bowman's capsule, that encloses a bed of capillaries. This capillary bed, called a glomerulus, receives blood from the renal artery. Fluids are forced from the blood through the capillary walls and into the Bowman's capsule. The material filtered from the blood then flows through the **renal tubule,** which consists of three parts: the proximal convoluted tubule, the loop of Henle, and the distal convoluted tubule. Blood remaining in the glomerulus then flows through a network of capillaries. The long and winding course of both the renal tubule and the surrounding capillaries provides a large surface area for the exchange of materials.

As the filtrate flows through a nephron, its composition is modified by the exchange of materials among the renal tubule, the capillaries, and the extracellular fluid. Various types of exchanges take place in the different parts of the renal tubule. To understand how the structure of each part of the nephron is related to its function, we will examine the three major processes that take place in the nephron: filtration, reabsorption, and secretion. Figure 48-16 shows the site of each of these processes in the nephron.

**Word Roots and Origins**

*glomerulus*

from the Latin *glom,* meaning "little ball of yarn"

# FILTRATION

Materials from the blood are forced out of the glomerulus and into the Bowman's capsule during a process called **filtration.** Blood in the glomerulus is under relatively high pressure. This pressure forces water, urea, glucose, vitamins, and salts through the thin capillary walls of the glomerulus and into the Bowman's capsule. About one-fifth of the fluid portion of the blood filters into the Bowman's capsule. The rest remains in the capillaries, along with proteins and cells that are too large to pass through the capillary walls. In a healthy kidney, the filtrate—the fluid that enters the nephron—does not contain large protein molecules.

**internet** connect

www.scilinks.org
**Topic: Excretory System**
**Keyword: HM60553**

SC*LINKS.* Maintained by the National Science Teachers Association

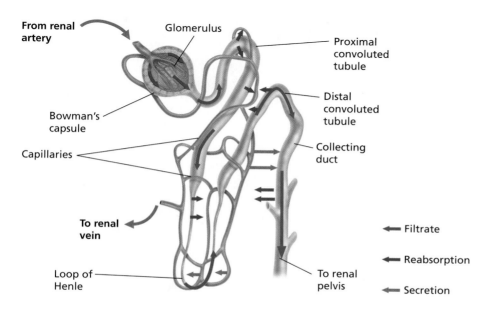

From renal artery

Glomerulus

Proximal convoluted tubule

Distal convoluted tubule

Bowman's capsule

Collecting duct

Capillaries

To renal vein

Loop of Henle

To renal pelvis

← Filtrate

← Reabsorption

← Secretion

**FIGURE 48-16**

Color-coded arrows indicate where in the nephron the filtrate travels, and where reabsorption and secretion occur.

According to data from the U.S. Environmental Protection Agency, indoor areas, where we spend up to 90 percent of our time, contain substances that may be hazardous to our health. Because of their function in excretion, kidneys often are exposed to hazardous chemicals that have entered the body through the lungs, skin, or gastrointestinal tract. Household substances that, in concentration, can damage kidneys include paint, varnishes, furniture oils, glues, aerosol sprays, air fresheners, and lead.

Many factors in our environment are difficult to control, but the elimination of pollutants from our indoor living areas is fairly simple. The four steps listed below may help reduce the effects of many indoor pollutants.

1. Identify sources of pollutants in your home.
2. Eliminate the sources, if possible.
3. Seal off those sources that cannot be eliminated.
4. Ventilate to evacuate pollutants and bring in fresh air.

# REABSORPTION AND SECRETION

The body needs to retain many of the substances that were removed from the blood by filtration. Thus, as the filtrate flows through the renal tubule, these materials return to the blood by being selectively transported through the walls of the renal tubule and into the surrounding capillaries. This process is called **reabsorption.** Most reabsorption occurs in the proximal convoluted tubule. In this region, about 75 percent of the water in the filtrate returns to the capillaries by osmosis. Glucose and minerals, such as sodium, potassium, and calcium, are returned to the blood by active transport. Some additional reabsorption occurs in the distal convoluted tubule.

When the filtrate reaches the distal convoluted tubule, some substances pass from the blood into the filtrate through a process called **secretion.** These substances include wastes and toxic materials. The pH of the blood is adjusted by hydrogen ions that are secreted from the blood into the filtrate.

## Formation of Urine

The fluid and wastes that remain in the distal convoluted tubule form urine. The urine from several renal tubules flows into a collecting duct. Notice in Figure 48-17 that the urine is further concentrated in the collecting duct by the osmosis of water through the wall of the duct. This process allows the body to conserve water. In fact, osmosis in the collecting duct, together with reabsorption in other parts of the tubule, returns to the blood about 99 of every 100 mL (about 3.4 oz) of water in the filtrate.

**FIGURE 48-17**

The sodium chloride that is actively transported out of the loop of Henle makes the extracellular environment surrounding the collecting duct hypertonic. Thus, water moves out of the collecting duct by osmosis into this hypertonic environment, increasing the concentration of urine.

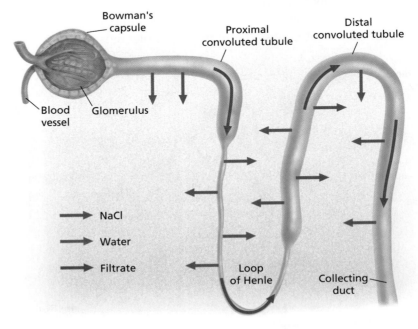

**FORMATION OF URINE**

## The Loop of Henle

The function of the **loop of Henle** (HEN-lee) is closely related to that of the collecting duct. Water moves out of the collecting duct because the concentration of sodium chloride is higher in the fluid surrounding the collecting duct than it is in the fluid inside the collecting duct. This high concentration of sodium chloride is created and maintained by the loop of Henle. Cells in the wall of the loop transport chloride ions from the filtrate to the fluid between the loops and the collecting duct. Positively charged sodium ions follow the chloride ions into the fluid. This process ensures that the sodium chloride concentration of the fluid between the loops and the collecting duct remains high and thus promotes the reabsorption of water from the collecting duct.

# ELIMINATION OF URINE

Urine from the collecting ducts flows through the renal pelvis and into a narrow tube called a **ureter** (yoo-REET-uhr). A ureter leads from each kidney to the **urinary bladder,** a muscular sac that stores urine. Muscular contractions of the bladder force urine out of the body through a tube called the **urethra** (yoo-REE-thruh). Locate the ureters, urinary bladder, and urethra in Figure 48-18.

At least 500 mL (17 oz) of urine must be eliminated every day because this amount of fluid is needed to remove potentially toxic materials from the body and to maintain homeostasis. A normal adult eliminates from 1.5 L (1.6 qt) to 2.3 L (2.4 qt) of urine a day, depending on the amount of water taken in and the amount of water lost through respiration and perspiration.

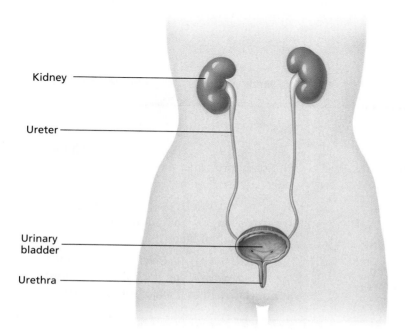

Kidney

Ureter

Urinary bladder

Urethra

## Quick Lab

### Analyzing Kidney Filtration

**Materials** disposable gloves, lab apron, safety goggles, 20 mL of test solution, 3 test tubes, filter, beaker, 15 drops each of biuret and Benedict's solution, 2 drops IKI solution, 3 pipets, wax marker pen

**Procedure**

1. Put on your gloves, lab apron, and safety goggles.

2. Put 15 drops of the test solution into each of the test tubes. Label the test tubes "Protein," "Starch," and "Glucose."

3. Add 15 drops of biuret solution to the test tube labeled "Protein." Record your observations.

4. Add 15 drops of Benedict's solution to the test tube labeled "Glucose." Record your observations.

5. Add two drops of IKI solution to the test tube labeled "Starch." Record your observations.

6. Discard the tested solutions, and rinse your test tubes as your teacher directs.

7. Pour the remaining test solution through a filter into a beaker. Using the test solution from the beaker, repeat steps 3–5.

**Analysis** Which compounds passed through the filter paper? If some did not, explain why. How does the filtration of this activity resemble the activity of the kidney?

**FIGURE 48-18**

Urine travels from each kidney through a ureter to the urinary bladder, where it is stored until it is eliminated from the body through the urethra.

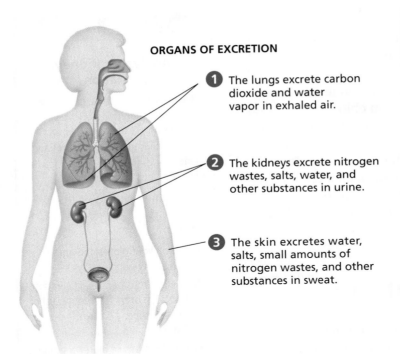

**ORGANS OF EXCRETION**

1 The lungs excrete carbon dioxide and water vapor in exhaled air.

2 The kidneys excrete nitrogen wastes, salts, water, and other substances in urine.

3 The skin excretes water, salts, small amounts of nitrogen wastes, and other substances in sweat.

**FIGURE 48-19**

The lungs, the kidneys, and the skin all function as excretory organs. The main excretory products are carbon dioxide, nitrogen wastes (urea), salts, and water.

# THE EXCRETORY ORGANS

Although the kidneys, lungs, and skin belong to different organ systems, they all have a common function: waste excretion.

The kidneys are the primary excretory organs of the body. They play a vital role in maintaining the homeostasis of body fluids.

The lungs are the primary site of carbon dioxide excretion. The lungs carry out detoxification, altering harmful substances so that they are not poisonous. The lungs are also responsible for the excretion of the volatile substances in onions, garlic, and other spices.

The skin helps the kidneys control the salt composition of the blood. Some salt, water, nitrogen waste and other substances are excreted through perspiration. A person working in extreme heat may lose water through perspiration at the rate of 1 L per hour. This amount of perspiration represents a loss of about 10 to 30 g of salt per day. Both the water and salt must be replenished to maintain normal body functions.

Figure 48-19 summarizes some waste substances and the organ(s) that excrete them. Notice that undigested food is not in the figure. Undigested food is not excreted in the scientific sense; it is eliminated, meaning it is expelled as feces from the body without ever passing through a membrane or being subjected to metabolic processes. The term *excretion* correctly refers to the process during which substances must pass through a membrane to leave the body.

## SECTION 3 REVIEW

1. Illustrate and label the major parts of the kidney.

2. Explain how the structure of a nephron relates to its function.

3. Describe three processes carried out in the kidney that help maintain homeostasis.

4. Identify five of the structures through which urine is eliminated.

5. Explain the function of each of the organs involved in excretion.

**CRITICAL THINKING**

6. **Relating Concepts** Explain why a high concentration of protein in the urine may indicate damaged kidneys.

7. **Recognizing Relationships** Why would there be a decrease in urine output if a person had lost a large amount of blood?

8. **Analyzing Concepts** Given the definition of *excretion,* why do you think the large intestine is not classified as a major excretory organ?

# CHAPTER HIGHLIGHTS

## SECTION 1 · Nutrients

- The human body needs six nutrients—carbohydrates, proteins, lipids, vitamins, minerals, and water—to grow and function.

- Carbohydrates, found in foods such as breads, provide most of the body's energy. The body quickly processes monosaccharides. Cellulose cannot be digested but is needed for fiber.

- Proteins, found in foods such as meats, help the body grow and repair tissues. Essential amino acids must be obtained from foods.

- Lipids, found in foods such as oils, are used to build cell membranes.

- Vitamins act as coenzymes to enhance enzyme function.

- Minerals are inorganic substances used to build red blood cells and bones and for muscle and nerve functions.

- Water helps regulate body temperature and transports nutrients and wastes.

### Vocabulary
| | | | |
|---|---|---|---|
| nutrient (p. 979) | vitamin (p. 982) | mineral (p. 982) | dehydration (p. 984) |

## SECTION 2 · Digestive System

- Mechanical digestion involves the breaking of food into smaller particles. Chemical digestion involves changing the chemical nature of the food substance.

- The mouth, teeth, and tongue initiate mechanical digestion. Chemical digestion of carbohydrates begins in the mouth.

- The esophagus is a passageway through which food passes from the mouth to the stomach by peristalsis.

- The stomach has layers of muscles that churn the food to assist in mechanical digestion. Pepsin in the stomach begins the chemical digestion of proteins.

- Bile assists in the mechanical digestion of lipids. Enzymes secreted by the pancreas complete the digestion of the chyme.

- The digested nutrients are absorbed through the villi of the small intestine.

- The large intestine absorbs water from the undigested mass. The undigested mass is eliminated as feces through the anus.

### Vocabulary
| | | | |
|---|---|---|---|
| digestion (p. 985) | epiglottis (p. 986) | cardiac sphincter (p. 988) | villus (p. 990) |
| gastrointestinal tract (p. 985) | peristalsis (p. 987) | chyme (p. 988) | colon (p. 991) |
| saliva (p. 986) | gastric fluid (p. 988) | pyloric sphincter (p. 988) | |
| pharynx (p. 986) | ulcer (p. 988) | gallbladder (p. 989) | |

## SECTION 3 · Urinary System

- Excretion is the removal of metabolic wastes from the body.

- The kidneys are the main organs of excretion and of the urinary system.

- Nephrons are the functional units of the kidneys. Through filtration, reabsorption, and secretion, they remove wastes and return nutrients and water to the blood.

- The urine passes through a ureter and is stored in the urinary bladder until it is eliminated through the urethra.

- Urine must be eliminated from the body to remove toxic materials and to maintain homeostasis.

- The lungs and the skin also play an important role in the excretion of wastes.

### Vocabulary
| | | | |
|---|---|---|---|
| excretion (p. 993) | ammonia (p. 993) | renal tubule (p. 995) | ureter (p. 997) |
| renal cortex (p. 993) | urine (p. 994) | filtration (p. 995) | urinary bladder (p. 997) |
| renal medulla (p. 993) | nephron (p. 994) | reabsorption (p. 996) | urethra (p. 997) |
| renal pelvis (p. 993) | Bowman's capsule (p. 994) | secretion (p. 996) | |
| urea (p. 993) | glomerulus (p. 994) | loop of Henle (p. 997) | |

## USING VOCABULARY

1. For each set of terms, choose the one that does not belong, and explain why it does not belong.
   a. *carbohydrate, protein, lipid,* and *mineral*
   b. *pharynx, epiglottis, bolus,* and *esophagus*
   c. *cardiac sphincter, gastric pits, renal medulla,* and *pyloric sphincter*
   d. *absorption, filtration, secretion,* and *reabsorption*

2. Use the following terms in the same sentence: *gallbladder, gastric fluid, pepsin,* and *saliva.*

3. **Word Roots and Origins** The word *protein* is derived from the Greek *proteios,* which means "of prime importance." Using this information, explain why the term *protein* is a good name for the nutrient it describes.

## UNDERSTANDING KEY CONCEPTS

4. **Identify** which of the six nutrients needed by the body are organic and which are inorganic.

5. **State** the daily number of servings needed from each food group in the USDA Food Guide pyramid in order to maintain a healthy diet.

6. **Propose** a vegetarian diet that includes all of the nutrients needed by the human body.

7. **Explain** the role of inorganic nutrients in keeping the body healthy.

8. **Name** the nutrient that makes up more than 90 percent of the fluid part of blood.

9. **Name** the nutrient associated with heart disease when it is consumed in high levels.

10. **List** the organs of the digestive system and their functions.

11. **Contrast** the processes involved in mechanical and chemical digestion.

12. **Describe** how the stomach carries out mechanical digestion.

13. **Identify** the source and function of each major digestive enzyme.

14. **Predict** the problems a person might have if his or her small intestine were not functioning properly.

15. **Identify** the function of the large intestine.

16. **Identify** the major parts of the kidney.

17. **Explain** the relationship between Bowman's capsule, the proximal tubule, the loop of Henle, and the distal tubule.

18. **Identify** the processes that occur in the nephron that maintain homeostasis.

19. **Summarize** how urine is stored and eliminated from the body.

20. **Describe** the function of two organs other than kidneys that are also involved in excretion.

21. **CONCEPT MAPPING** Use the following terms to create a concept map that shows the process of digestion: *bile, chemical digestion, chyme, digestion, liver, mechanical digestion, molar, pancreas, saliva, small intestine,* and *stomach.*

## CRITICAL THINKING

22. **Applying Information** In some countries, many children suffer from a type of malnutrition called *kwashiorkor.* They have swollen stomachs and become increasingly thin until they die. Even when given rice and water, these children still die. What type of nutritional deficiency might these children have?

23. **Analyzing Concepts** Why is it important that the large intestine reabsorb water and not eliminate it?

24. **Predicting Patterns** The loop of Henle functions to conserve water by aiding in reabsorption. Its length varies among mammal species. Would you expect the loop of Henle of an animal such as the beaver, which lives in a watery environment, to be longer or shorter than that found in humans? Explain your answer.

25. **Recognizing Relationships** Look at the pictures of the teeth of different animals. What can you tell about the human diet by comparing the teeth of humans with those of other animals shown here?

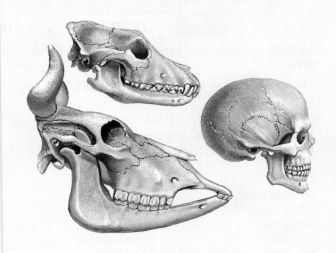

# Standardized Test Preparation

**DIRECTIONS:** Choose the letter of the answer choice that best answers the question.

1. What is the primary function of carbohydrates?
   - **A.** to aid in digestion
   - **B.** to break down molecules
   - **C.** to regulate the flow of chyme
   - **D.** to supply the body with energy

2. How can dehydration best be prevented?
   - **F.** by perspiring
   - **G.** by inhaling air
   - **H.** by drinking water
   - **J.** by not drinking water

3. Why is the epiglottis important?
   - **A.** It regulates the flow of chyme.
   - **B.** It prevents food from going down the trachea.
   - **C.** It separates the pharynx from the nasal cavity.
   - **D.** It is the passage through which food travels to the stomach.

**INTERPRETING GRAPHICS:** The graph below shows the approximate length of time food spends in each digestive organ. Use the graph below to answer the following question.

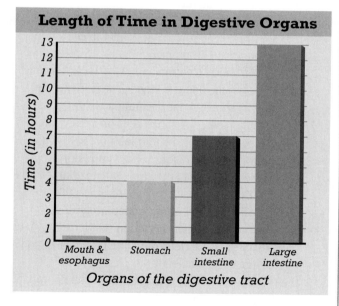

**Length of Time in Digestive Organs**

Time (in hours) vs. Organs of the digestive tract (Mouth & esophagus, Stomach, Small intestine, Large intestine)

4. Bile breaks up large fat droplets. Approximately how long is the food in the digestive tract before it comes into contact with bile?
   - **F.** 4 hours
   - **G.** 7 hours
   - **H.** 11 hours
   - **J.** 13 hours

**DIRECTIONS:** Complete the following analogy.

5. lung : alveolus :: kidney :
   - **A.** ureter
   - **B.** nephron
   - **C.** microvillus
   - **D.** glomerulus

**INTERPRETING GRAPHICS:** The figure below shows a cross section of a kidney. Use the figure to answer the question that follows.

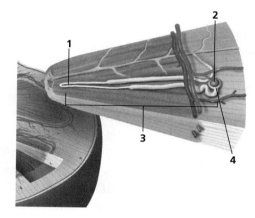

6. Which part of the model represents the loop of Henle?
   - **F.** 1
   - **G.** 2
   - **H.** 3
   - **J.** 4

## SHORT RESPONSE

The liver and pancreas are accessory organs of the gastrointestinal tract.

In what two ways do the liver and pancreas differ from other digestive organs?

## EXTENDED RESPONSE

When a person's kidneys stop functioning, urea builds up in the blood. For the urea to be removed, the person must be attached to a mechanical kidney, also called a dialysis machine.

*Part A* What would happen if the person did not have the urea removed from his or her blood?

*Part B* Using your understanding of how a normal kidney functions, suggest a design for the major components of a dialysis machine.

**Test TIP** Study of the digestive and urinary systems is often aided by drawing flowcharts of the processes described.

# Modeling Human Digestion

## OBJECTIVES

- Test a model of digestion in the human stomach.

## PROCESS SKILLS

- modeling
- hypothesizing
- observing
- predicting
- inferring

## MATERIALS

- safety goggles
- lab apron
- glass-marking pencil
- 5 test tubes with stoppers
- test-tube rack
- scalpel
- cooked egg white
- balance
- 10 mL graduated cylinder
- 1% pepsin solution
- 0.2% hydrochloric acid
- 1% sodium bicarbonate
- distilled water
- red and blue litmus paper
- lined paper
- disposable gloves

## Background

1. How is food changed from the chunks you chew with your teeth to the chyme absorbed in your small intestine?
2. What type of organic compound does the enzyme pepsin digest?

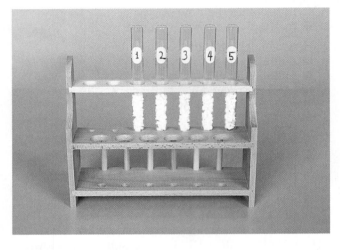

**PART A** Setting Up

1. Label five test tubes 1, 2, 3, 4, and 5, and place them in a test-tube rack.
2. **CAUTION** **Always cut in a direction away from your body.** Use a scalpel to cut a firm, cooked egg white into fine pieces.
3. Using the balance, measure and place equal amounts (about 6 g) of the fine egg white sample into each test tube, as shown in the illustration above.
4. **CAUTION** **Put on safety goggles and a lab apron. If you get hydrochloric acid solution on your skin or clothes, wash it off at the sink while calling to your teacher. If you get any solutions in this investigation in your eyes, immediately flush them out at the eyewash station while calling to your teacher.** Use a clean graduated cylinder to add the solutions listed below to the test tubes. Rinse the cylinder between additions so that you do not contaminate the samples.
   - test tube 1—10 mL of water
   - test tube 2—10 mL of pepsin solution
   - test tube 3—10 mL of hydrochloric acid
   - test tube 4—5 mL of pepsin solution and 5 mL of sodium bicarbonate solution
   - test tube 5—5 mL of pepsin and 5 mL of hydrochloric acid

## DEGREE OF DIGESTION OF EGG WHITE UNDER VARYING CONDITIONS

| Test-tube number | Contents | pH | Degree of digestion |
|---|---|---|---|
| 1 | egg white<br>10 mL water | | |
| 2 | egg white<br>10 mL 1% pepsin solution | | |
| 3 | egg white<br>10 mL 0.2% hydrochloric acid solution | | |
| 4 | egg white<br>5 mL 1% pepsin solution<br>5 mL 1% sodium bicarbonate solution | | |
| 5 | egg white<br>5 mL 1% pepsin solution<br>5 mL 0.2% hydrochloric acid solution | | |

**5.** Stopper and gently shake each test tube.

**6.** In your lab report, make a data table like the one shown above.

**7.** In your lab report, write a hypothesis which predicts which test tube will show the most digestion after 48 hours. Explain your reasoning.

**8.** Label your test-tube rack with your initials. Store the test-tube rack for 48 hours at room temperature. Leave a note on the rack cautioning others not to spill the acids or bases.

**9.**   Clean up your lab materials, and wash your hands before leaving the lab.

### PART B Recording the Results

**10.** After 48 hours, measure the pH of each solution with red and blue litmus paper. Record your results in the data table you created in your lab report.

**11.** Look for the egg white in each test tube. In your data table, describe the degree to which the egg white has broken down and dissolved in each test tube.

**12.**   Clean up your lab materials, and wash your hands before leaving the lab.

### Analysis and Conclusions

**1.** What conditions caused the greatest digestion of cooked egg white?

**2.** Which test tube best modeled the chemical composition in the human stomach?

**3.** What information do test tubes 1, 2, and 3 give you? What do they control?

**4.** Compare test tubes 4 and 5. What can you conclude about the effects of the chemical environment on the activity of pepsin?

**5.** List some other foods that pepsin is likely to digest.

**6.** Do you think that pepsin would digest butter? Explain your answer.

### Further Inquiry

Design an experiment to test the digestion of a food containing carbohydrates, such as a potato or an apple.

# CHAPTER 49 — NERVOUS SYSTEM AND SENSE ORGANS

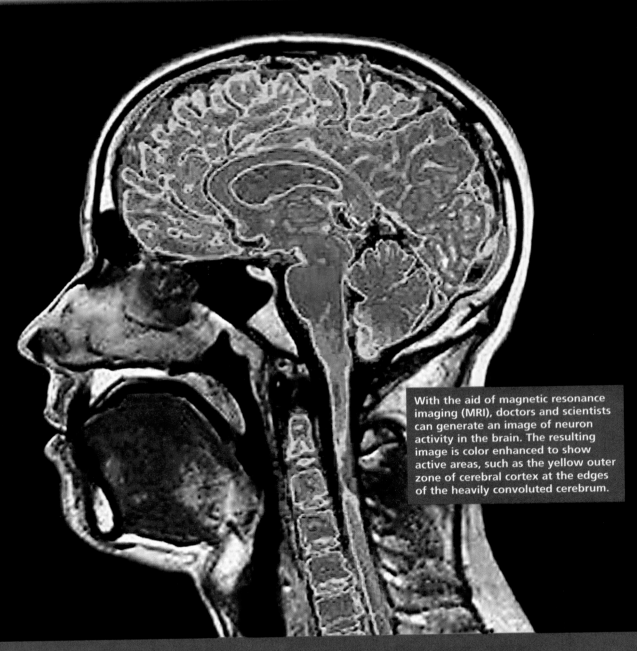

With the aid of magnetic resonance imaging (MRI), doctors and scientists can generate an image of neuron activity in the brain. The resulting image is color enhanced to show active areas, such as the yellow outer zone of cerebral cortex at the edges of the heavily convoluted cerebrum.

SCIENTIFIC AMERICAN

For project ideas from *Scientific American*, visit go.hrw.com and type in the keyword **HM6SAM**.

# NEURONS AND NERVE IMPULSES

*The **nervous system,** a complex network of cells that communicate with one another, controls mental and physical activities and maintains homeostasis. The ability of the nervous system to monitor and respond to the environment, both external and internal, depends on the transmission of signals within a neuron and from a neuron to another cell.*

## NEURON STRUCTURE

A **neuron** is a nerve cell. The nucleus of a neuron and most of its organelles are located in the *cell body.* Extending from the cell body in different directions are membrane-covered extensions of the cell called **dendrites.** Dendrites receive information from other neurons or other cells and carry the information toward the cell body. Another cell extension, the **axon,** is a long, membrane-bound projection that transmits information away from the cell body in the form of electrical signals called **action potentials.** A neuron may have a single axon or branching axons that contact several other cells. The end of an axon is called the **axon terminal.** It may contact and communicate with a muscle cell, a gland cell, or another neuron.

The axons of many neurons are covered with a lipid layer known as the **myelin** (MIE-uh-lin) **sheath.** The myelin sheath insulates the axon much as a rubber coating insulates an electrical cord. The myelin sheath speeds up transmission of action potentials along the axon. In neurons that are not part of the brain or spinal cord, cells called *Schwann cells* surround the axon and produce myelin. Gaps in the myelin sheath along the length of the axon are called *nodes of Ranvier* (RAHN-vee-ay).

Neurons communicate with other neurons and other cells at special junctions called **synapses.** Neurons usually do not touch each other or other cells. Instead, a small gap, called a *synaptic cleft,* is present between the axon terminal and the receiving cell. At a synapse, the transmitting neuron is called a *presynaptic neuron.* The receiving cell is called a *postsynaptic cell.*

Electrical activity in the neuron usually causes the release of chemicals called **neurotransmitters** into the synaptic cleft. Often, neurotransmitters cause electrical activity in another neuron. Thus, the signaling activity of the nervous system is made up of electrical activity within neurons and chemical flow between neurons.

## OBJECTIVES

- **Describe** the structure of a neuron.
- **Summarize** the electrical and chemical conditions that characterize a resting potential.
- **Outline** the electrical and chemical changes that occur during an action potential.
- **Explain** the role of neurotransmitters in transmitting a signal across a synapse.

## VOCABULARY

nervous system
neuron
dendrite
axon
action potential
axon terminal
myelin sheath
synapse
neurotransmitter
membrane potential
resting potential
refractory period

### Word Roots and Origins

*synapse*

from the Greek *synaptein,* meaning "to fasten together"

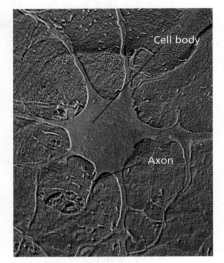

**FIGURE 49-1**

Neurons transmit information throughout the body via chemical and electrical signals. This stellate neuron is named for its starlike shape. (SEM, 26,000×)

**FIGURE 49-2**

Neurons consist of dendrites, which bring signals toward the cell body, and axons, which carry signals away from the cell body. At the tip of the axon, the axon terminal makes contact with a target cell, such as a muscle cell, gland cell, or other neuron, at a synapse.

# NERVE IMPULSES

About 200 years ago, scientists removed muscle from dead animals and passed electric current through it. The scientists discovered that the current caused the muscle to contract just as it did in life. Since then, scientists have learned a great deal about neuron structure, shown in Figure 49-1 and Figure 49-2, and how neurons affect other parts of the body, such as muscles. Scientists have also learned that neuron function is dependent on electrical activity.

All cells, including neurons, have an electrical charge inside the cell that is different from the electrical charge outside the cell. A difference in the electrical charge across the cell membrane is called a **membrane potential.** Membrane potentials are produced by the movement of ions across the cell membrane. The movement of ions depends on the ability of the ions to diffuse through the cell membrane, the concentrations of ions inside and outside the cell, and the electrical charge of the ions. As with batteries, membrane potential is expressed as voltage.

Ions diffuse across a neuron's cell membrane by passing through proteins that act as ion channels. Each type of channel allows only specific ions to pass. Certain channels are voltage gated—that is, whether these channels are open or closed depends on the membrane potential. Even a small change in membrane potential can affect the permeability of the cell membrane to certain ions. As ions move into or out of the neuron, they, in turn, affect the membrane potential.

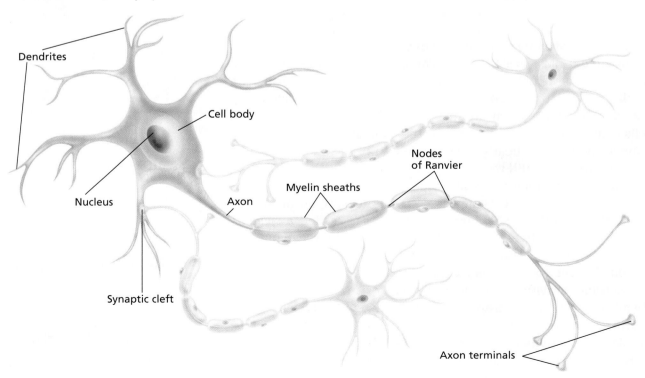

## Resting Potential

A neuron is at rest when it is not receiving or sending a signal. In a neuron at rest, the concentration of negatively charged proteins and positively charged potassium ions, $K^+$, is greater inside the cell than outside. In contrast, the concentration of sodium ions, $Na^+$, is greater outside the cell than inside. The concentrations of $Na^+$ and $K^+$ ions are partly due to the action of the *sodium-potassium pump*, which actively moves $Na^+$ out of cells while moving $K^+$ in.

The cell membrane is permeable to some ions but not to others. $Na^+$ ions do not readily diffuse through the membrane. So, they accumulate outside the cell. Negatively charged proteins remain inside the cell because they are too large to exit. $K^+$ ions, however, pass freely through the membrane and tend to diffuse out of the cell. This exit of positively charged $K^+$ ions and the retention of negatively charged proteins eventually cause the interior of the neuron to become negatively charged with respect to the exterior. This charge difference is called the **resting potential** of the membrane. In most neurons, the resting potential is about −70 millivolts.

## Action Potential

When a dendrite or cell body is stimulated, the permeability of the neuron's membrane changes suddenly. At the point of stimulation, the cell membrane becomes permeable to $Na^+$ ions. The rush of $Na^+$ ions into the cell opens voltage-gated channels in the membrane that allow even more $Na^+$ ions into the neuron. As a result, the interior of the neuron's cell body becomes more positively charged than the exterior. This reversal of polarity across the membrane begins an action potential, shown in Figure 49-3. The action potential starts where the cell body joins the axon.

**FIGURE 49-3**

❶ At resting potential, a neuron's interior is negatively charged with respect to the extracellular fluid around the cell. ❷ The passage of an action potential over the membrane of the axon reverses this polarity, and the interior of the axon becomes more positively charged for a brief time.

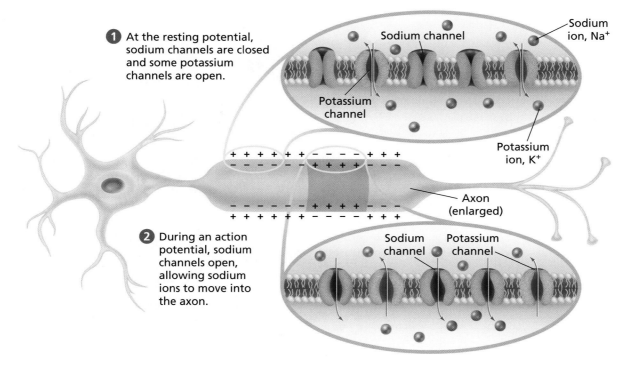

❶ At the resting potential, sodium channels are closed and some potassium channels are open.

Sodium channel

Sodium ion, $Na^+$

Potassium channel

Potassium ion, $K^+$

Axon (enlarged)

❷ During an action potential, sodium channels open, allowing sodium ions to move into the axon.

Sodium channel

Potassium channel

Voltage-gated channels exist along the length of the axon. As a neuron is stimulated and the first small segment of the axon becomes more positively charged, the change in voltage opens channels in the next segment of axon membrane. As before, $Na^+$ ions enter, driving the voltage in a positive direction and opening channels in the next segment of axon. In this way, positive charges pass down the axon membrane like dominoes falling in a row. Axon potentials usually travel in one direction only—away from the cell body, where they begin, and toward the axon terminal.

Shortly after they open, the voltage-gated channels for $Na^+$ ions close. Then, voltage-gated channels for $K^+$ ions open. The result is an abrupt outward flow of $K^+$ ions. The exterior of the cell again becomes positively charged with respect to the interior of the cell. This change in charge signals the end of the action potential. However, the neuron cannot generate another action potential until resting potential is restored. This period, during which the neuron cannot send a signal, is called the **refractory period.**

After the action potential, the concentration of $Na^+$ ions inside the cell is higher than when the cell is at rest, and the concentration of $K^+$ ions inside the cell is lower. Ion channels and the sodium-potassium pump help reestablish the resting concentrations of $Na^+$ ions and $K^+$ ions. $Na^+$ ions are moved out across the cell membrane, while $K^+$ ions are moved in across the membrane. Once the original ion concentrations are restored, the neuron is ready for the next action potential. Restoration of resting potential comes at a price. Neurons need a continuous supply of ATP to keep the sodium-potassium pump operating. In fact, neurons consume a great deal of the body's daily energy.

**FIGURE 49-4**

The presynaptic neuron releases neurotransmitter molecules into the synaptic cleft. These molecules bind to receptor proteins in the postsynaptic membrane, opening ion channels. Positive ions entering through these channels cause the membrane potential of the postsynaptic neuron to become more positive. If the membrane potential becomes sufficiently positive, the postsynaptic neuron will generate an action potential, continuing the signal.

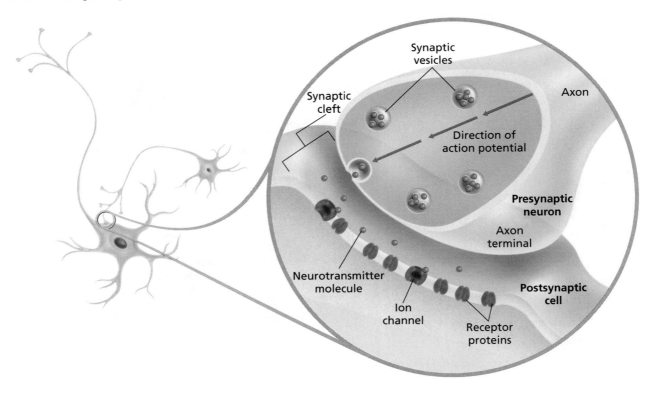

Synaptic vesicles

Synaptic cleft

Axon

Direction of action potential

Presynaptic neuron

Axon terminal

Neurotransmitter molecule

Ion channel

Receptor proteins

Postsynaptic cell

# COMMUNICATION BETWEEN NEURONS

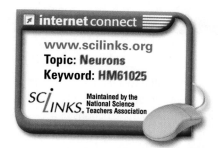

A neuron can communicate with another cell across the synaptic cleft only after an action potential reaches the axon terminal. Vesicles that contain neurotransmitters are stored in the axon terminal. When an action potential reaches the axon terminal of the presynaptic neuron, the vesicles fuse with the presynaptic membrane. This fusion releases neurotransmitters into the synaptic cleft. The neurotransmitters quickly diffuse across the synaptic cleft and bind to receptor proteins embedded in the membrane of the postsynaptic cell. This process is shown in Figure 49-4 on the previous page.

The interaction of neurotransmitter and receptor molecules changes the permeability of the postsynaptic membrane by affecting chemically gated ion channels. The opening of $Na^+$ channels in the postsynaptic membrane causes the membrane potential of the neuron to become more positive. If this change in membrane potential is great enough, a new action potential is generated in the receiving neuron. So, the electrical signal continues. However, the release of neurotransmitters may cause the opening of too few $Na^+$ channels in the postsynaptic membrane or may cause the opening of other channels that allow negatively charged ions into the cell. As a result, the membrane potential of the receiving neuron will not become positive enough or may become more negative. No action potential will be generated in the receiving neuron, and the nervous signal will terminate.

Neurotransmitters do not remain in the synaptic cleft indefinitely. Instead, most neurotransmitters are cleared from the synaptic cleft shortly after they are released. Many presynaptic neurons reabsorb neurotransmitters and use them again. At other synapses, neurotransmitters are broken down by enzymes. The reabsorption or breakdown of neurotransmitters ensures that their effect on postsynaptic cells is not prolonged.

## SECTION 1 REVIEW

1. Describe the structure of a neuron.

2. Define the resting potential of a neuron membrane, and give its typical voltage.

3. What is an action potential?

4. How does a nerve signal transmit from one neuron to the next?

5. Why does the nervous system consume a large amount of energy?

6. Describe two possible effects that neurotransmitters may have at a synapse.

**CRITICAL THINKING**

7. **Applying Information** What functional advantage does a neuron with several dendrites have over a neuron with only one dendrite?

8. **Analyzing Models** Examine the model for synapse function in Figure 49-4. Predict what would happen if excess neurotransmitters were not removed from the synaptic cleft.

9. **Calculating Information** What is the difference in voltage between a 9V battery and the resting potential of a single human neuron, −70mV?

## OBJECTIVES

- **Identify** the two main parts of the central nervous system.
- **Summarize** the functions of the major parts of the brain.
- **Describe** the roles of the sensory and motor divisions of the peripheral nervous system.
- **Distinguish** between the somatic and autonomic nervous systems.

## VOCABULARY

central nervous system
peripheral nervous system
cerebrum
cerebral cortex
brain stem
thalamus
hypothalamus
medulla oblongata
cerebellum
nerve
sensory receptor
motor neuron
interneuron
somatic nervous system
reflex
autonomic nervous system

# STRUCTURE OF THE NERVOUS SYSTEM

*The nervous system is a highly organized network of cells that detect changes, communicate with each other, and control physical activity, brain function, and metabolic processes. The nervous system includes two major divisions: the central nervous system and the peripheral nervous system.*

## ORGANIZATION OF THE NERVOUS SYSTEM

As shown in Figure 49-5, the brain and spinal cord make up the **central nervous system.** The *brain* is the control center of the nervous system, and the *spinal cord* carries nerve signals between the body and the brain. The brain interprets nerve signals from the body and sends response signals that pass through the spinal cord to the body.

The **peripheral nervous system** consists of neurons that have cell bodies that are not included in the brain and spinal cord. Some peripheral neurons collect information from the body and transmit it toward the central nervous system. These neurons are called *afferent neurons.* Other peripheral neurons transmit information away from the central nervous system. These neurons are known as *efferent neurons.*

## BRAIN

The brain oversees daily operations of the body and interprets vast amounts of information. The average adult human brain weighs 1.4 kg (about 3.1 lb), or about 2 percent of total body weight. Despite its relatively small mass, the brain contains about 100 billion neurons. Functioning as a unit, these neurons make up one of the most complex structures on Earth. Scientists have learned a great deal about the brain, but because the brain is so complex, much remains to be discovered.

The brain is responsible for many of the qualities that make each person unique—thoughts, feelings, memories, talents, and emotions. However, much of the brain is dedicated to running the body and maintaining homeostasis.

**internet** connect

**www.scilinks.org**
**Topic:** Central Nervous System
**Keyword:** HM60246

**SCI**
**LINKS.** Maintained by the National Science Teachers Association

# Cerebrum

Through painstaking study, scientists have established how and where various functions are localized in the brain. The largest portion of the human brain is the **cerebrum** (SER-ee-bruhm). The cerebrum is easily identified by its highly folded outer layer. It is composed of two *cerebral hemispheres,* as shown in Figure 49-6. The two cerebral hemispheres are connected by the *corpus callosum* (KAWR-puhs kuh-LOH-suhm). The corpus callosum is a band of axons that lies deep in the central groove that separates the right hemisphere from the left hemisphere. Other grooves separate each hemisphere into four lobes: the frontal, parietal (puh-RIE-uh-tuhl), temporal, and occipital (ahk-SIP-i-tuhl) lobes.

The folded outer layer of the cerebrum is the **cerebral cortex,** which contains 10 to 20 percent of the brain's total number of neurons. The many folds allow the surface area of the cortex to fit within the skull. As shown in Figure 49-6, different parts of the cerebral cortex control information and sensations from the body and motor responses. For example, the area of the cortex that interprets touch information lies in the parietal lobe.

Some functions are not symmetrically localized in the cerebrum. Brain centers involved in speech and language reside primarily in the left hemisphere. Brain centers involved in processing spatial information and certain kinds of reasoning are located primarily in the right hemisphere. These functions are located variably in left-handed people.

Below the folded surface of the cerebral cortex lies the *white matter,* which is composed of myelinated axons. These axons link specific regions of the cortex with each other and with other neural centers. Because of the crossover of these axons as they enter the brain from the body, many impulses originating in the right half of the body are processed in the left half of the brain, and vice versa.

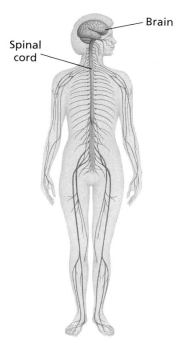

**FIGURE 49-5**

The central nervous system includes the brain and spinal cord, shown in orange. The peripheral nervous system, shown in violet, includes all other nervous tissue in the body.

**FIGURE 49-6**

(a) A view of the top of the brain shows the left and right cerebral hemispheres. (b) Each cerebral hemisphere of the brain has four lobes. Control centers for various functions are located in different areas of the brain.

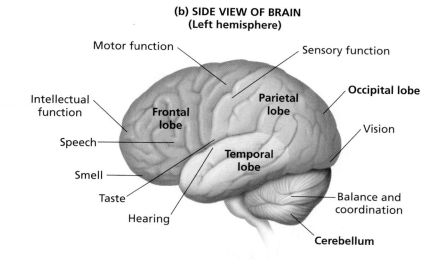

**(a) TOP VIEW OF BRAIN**

Frontal lobe

Parietal lobe

Occipital lobe

Left hemisphere   Right hemisphere

**(b) SIDE VIEW OF BRAIN**
**(Left hemisphere)**

Motor function   Sensory function

Intellectual function   Parietal lobe   **Occipital lobe**

**Frontal lobe**

Speech   Vision

Smell   **Temporal lobe**

Taste   Balance and coordination

Hearing   **Cerebellum**

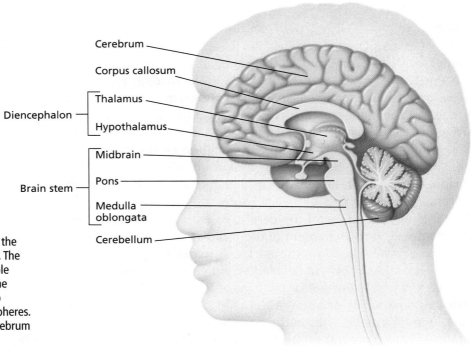

Cerebrum

Corpus callosum

Thalamus

Diencephalon

Hypothalamus

Midbrain

Brain stem

Pons

Medulla oblongata

Cerebellum

A side view through the center of the brain shows the right hemisphere. The convoluted cerebral cortex is visible along the front, rear, and top of the brain, where it folds into the deep groove separating the two hemispheres. The structures lying below the cerebrum are shown in cross section.

## Diencephalon

The **brain stem,** shown in Figure 49-7, lies below the cerebrum and links it to the spinal cord. The *diencephalon* (DIE-uhn-SEF-uh-lahn) lies between the cerebrum and the brain stem and contains relay centers for information entering and exiting the brain. The uppermost relay center is the **thalamus** (THAL-uh-muhs). It directs most incoming sensory signals to the proper region of the cerebral cortex. The **hypothalamus** helps maintain homeostasis. It also directly and indirectly controls much of the body's hormone production.

A set of brain structures called the *limbic system* includes parts of the thalamus and hypothalamus, centers in the temporal lobes, and some deeper parts of the cerebral cortex. The limbic system helps govern emotion, memory, and motivation.

## Brain Stem

Below the diencephalon, the brain stem narrows. This region has three main divisions: midbrain, pons, and medulla oblongata. The *midbrain* relays visual and auditory information. The *pons* relays communications between the cerebral hemispheres and the cerebellum. The **medulla oblongata** (mi-DUHL-uh AHB-lahn-GAHT-uh) serves as both a relay center and a control center for heart rate, respiration rate, and other homeostatic activities.

Lying throughout the brain stem is a diffuse network of neurons called the *reticular formation*. The reticular formation helps control respiration and circulation and helps separate signals that demand attention from those that are unimportant. Learning can modify some functions of the reticular formation. For example, a person can learn to sleep through the noise of a radio but awaken at the sound of a doorbell.

## Cerebellum

Below and behind the cerebral hemispheres lies the **cerebellum** (SER-uh-BEL-uhm), which helps coordinate muscle action. The surface of the cerebellum is highly folded. The cerebellum receives sensory impulses from muscles, tendons, joints, eyes, and ears, as well as input from other brain centers. It processes information about body position and controls posture by keeping skeletal muscles in a constant state of partial contraction. The cerebellum coordinates rapid and ongoing movements. It acts with the brain stem and with the cerebral cortex to coordinate skeletal muscles.

# SPINAL CORD

The spinal cord, shown in Figure 49-8, is a column of nervous tissue that starts at the medulla oblongata. The spinal cord runs down through the vertebral column, carrying nerve signals back and forth like a superhighway. The spinal cord has an outer sheath of white matter. The rigid inner core is made up of *gray matter,* which is composed of dendrites, unmyelinated axons, and the cell bodies of neurons.

# PERIPHERAL NERVOUS SYSTEM

The central nervous system constantly interacts with the peripheral nervous system via 12 pairs of cranial nerves that connect the brain with the head and neck and 31 pairs of spinal nerves that connect the central nervous system with the rest of the body. **Nerves** are the bundled axons and dendrites of neurons found outside the central nervous system. Each spinal nerve has a *dorsal root* and a *ventral root.* The dorsal roots carry signals into the central nervous system from various **sensory receptors.** These neurons are specialized to detect a stimulus such as light, pressure, or heat. The ventral roots contain the axons of **motor neurons,** which carry information from the central nervous system to muscles and glands. The spinal cord has **interneurons,** which relay information between other neurons.

# SENSORY DIVISION

The sensory division of the peripheral nervous system contains sensory receptors and the interneurons that connect them to the central nervous system. Sensory receptors receive information from the body's external and internal environments. Spinal and cranial nerves send sensory information to the central nervous system.

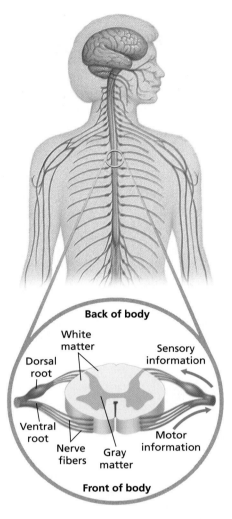

**FIGURE 49-8**

The spinal cord, shown in cross section, carries information toward and away from the brain. Sensory information from the body enters the spinal cord through the dorsal roots. Instructions to the body's muscles and many glands come from motor neurons that exit the spinal cord through the ventral roots.

# MOTOR DIVISION

The motor division of the peripheral nervous system lets the body react to sensory information. The motor division is made up of two independent systems—the somatic nervous system and the autonomic nervous system.

## Somatic Nervous System

Within the peripheral nervous system's motor division, the **somatic nervous system** contains motor neurons that control the movement of skeletal muscles. The somatic system is voluntary—that is, skeletal muscles can be moved at will. The somatic system can also operate without conscious control, as it does when helping to maintain balance.

The peripheral nervous system relays signals in **reflexes,** which are involuntary and often self-protective movements. The patellar reflex is shown in Figure 49-9. A tap on the tendon below the patella stimulates sensory receptors in the quadriceps muscle. The receptors send impulses to the spinal cord. These impulses activate motor neurons that lead back to the quadriceps. As a result, the quadriceps contracts. The impulses also activate interneurons that have an inhibitory, or calming, effect on the motor neurons of the hamstring muscles in the rear thigh. The contraction of the quadriceps coupled with the relaxation of the hamstrings extends the lower leg. This type of reflex is a *spinal reflex*. It involves only neurons in the body and bypasses the brain.

## Word Roots and Origins

**somatic**

from the Greek *somatikos,* meaning "of the body"

**FIGURE 49-9**

In the patellar, or knee-jerk, reflex, a sensory receptor (red) that detects stretch in the quadriceps muscle sends signals to the spinal cord. The sensory receptor has an axon with two branches. One branch stimulates motor neurons (green) in the quadriceps, causing the muscle to contract and extend the leg. The other branch stimulates an interneuron, which inhibits motor neurons (blue) in the hamstrings at the back of the leg. This inhibition releases the hamstring, allowing the forward kick of the leg.

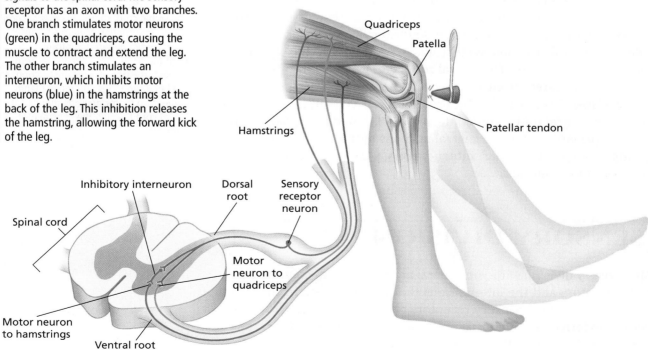

## TABLE 49-1 Effects of Sympathetic and Parasympathetic Divisions on Various Organs

| Organ | Effect of sympathetic division | Effect of parasympathetic division |
|---|---|---|
| Eyes | Pupils dilate | Pupils constrict |
| Heart | Heart rate increases | Heart rate decreases |
| Blood vessels | Blood vessels to skeletal muscles dilate | Little or no effect |
| Adrenal glands | Glands secrete hormones | Glands inactive |
| Intestines | Gastric secretions decrease | Gastric secretions increase |

## Autonomic Nervous System

Also within the peripheral nervous system's motor division is the **autonomic nervous system.** This system controls internal body conditions by regulating smooth muscles in blood vessels and organs. The autonomic nervous system controls respiration, heartbeat, digestion, and other aspects of homeostasis.

The autonomic system has two subdivisions—the *sympathetic division* and the *parasympathetic division*. These subdivisions stimulate or inhibit body systems, as shown in Table 49-1. Physical or emotional stress can activate the sympathetic division. For example, the threat of a physical attack causes the sympathetic division to redirect blood away from the digestive organs and toward the heart and skeletal muscles. The parasympathetic division controls the internal environment during routine conditions. After a threat has passed, the parasympathetic division signals organs to resume normal activity. Blood flow to the heart and skeletal muscles decreases. Under normal conditions, both systems are usually activated to some degree.

## SECTION 2 REVIEW

1. Name the two main organs of the central nervous system.

2. Draw a cross section of the human brain, and label the structures and functions of the cerebrum, diencephalon, brain stem, and cerebellum.

3. Name two divisions of the peripheral nervous system, and describe their roles.

4. How do the somatic nervous system and the autonomic nervous system differ?

5. Describe the two divisions of the autonomic nervous system.

**CRITICAL THINKING**

6. **Applying Information** One division of the autonomic nervous system increases energy use, and the other division conserves energy. Which division does each? Explain your answer.

7. **Analyzing Models** Examine the patellar reflex shown in Figure 49-9, and determine what would happen if the hamstring neuron were damaged.

8. **Making Inferences** Strokes damage neurons in the brain. How can a doctor tell which areas of the brain have been affected by a stroke?

## OBJECTIVES

- **List** the stimuli to which each of the five types of sensory receptors respond.
- **Identify** the parts of the ear responsible for hearing and for maintaining balance.
- **Describe** the structure of the eye and the roles of rods and cones in vision.
- **Discuss** how taste and smell are detected.
- **Compare** the detection of touch, temperature, and pain.

## VOCABULARY

sense organ
auditory canal
tympanic membrane
Eustachian tube
cochlea
semicircular canal
retina
cornea
pupil
iris
lens
rod
cone
taste bud
papilla
olfactory receptor

# SENSORY SYSTEMS

*Humans are affected by both internal and external stimuli. Humans are able to distinguish among the many different types of stimuli by means of a highly developed system of organs. Sensory systems integrate the functions of the peripheral nervous system and the central nervous system to respond to stimuli.*

## PERCEPTION OF STIMULI

To survive, organisms must detect changes in the environment and react appropriately to the changes. To detect changes in the environment, humans and other organisms have highly developed **sense organs**—eyes, ears, nose, mouth, and skin—that receive stimuli. The sensory division of the peripheral nervous system gathers information about the body's internal and external environment.

### Receptors and Sense Organs

A sensory receptor is a neuron that detects stimuli. There are many kinds of sensory receptors. These receptors can be categorized based on the type of stimuli to which they respond.
- *Mechanoreceptors* respond to movement, pressure, and tension.
- *Photoreceptors* respond to variations in light.
- *Chemoreceptors* respond to chemicals.
- *Thermoreceptors* respond to changes in temperature.
- *Pain receptors* respond to tissue damage.

Sensory receptors are found in higher concentrations in the sense organs than in other parts of the body. When the sensory receptors of a particular sense organ receive appropriate stimulation, they convert the stimulus into electrical signals, or action potentials. These electrical signals are sent to specific regions of the brain. The action potentials generated by the different sense organs are electrically similar. So, how can a person know if the stimulation is a blue sky or a loud noise? The regions of the brain where the action potentials are interpreted vary according to the type of stimulus.

The brain has a specific region for each sense. Thus, signals received by the vision region of the occipital lobe are interpreted by the brain as images, even if the actual stimulus was something else. For example, a blow to the eye makes a person "see stars." The pressure of the blow stimulates visual neurons. The brain interprets this pressure as an image.

# HEARING AND BALANCE

The ear performs two main functions: detecting sound and maintaining balance. The fleshy structure of the external ear directs sound vibrations into the ear. As Figure 49-10 shows, the **auditory canal** connects the external ear with the **tympanic** (tim-PAN-ik) **membrane,** or *eardrum*. Vibrations in the air of the auditory canal cause the tympanic membrane to vibrate. Air pressure in the chamber beyond the tympanic membrane, the middle ear, is regulated by the amount of air passing through the Eustachian tube to the middle ear. The **Eustachian** (yoo-STAY-kee-uhn) **tube** is an opening to the throat that equalizes the pressure on both sides of the tympanic membrane during a sudden change in atmospheric pressure, such as occurs when an airplane takes off or lands.

The vibrating tympanic membrane sets in motion three small bones of the middle ear: the hammer, the anvil, and the stirrup. The stirrup transfers vibrations to a membrane called the *oval window*. The oval window separates the middle ear from the inner ear. The inner ear contains the **cochlea** (KAHK-lee-uh), a coiled tube consisting of three fluid-filled chambers that are separated by membranes. The middle chamber contains the *organ of Corti,* which is the organ of hearing. The organ of Corti rests on the bottom membrane in the cochlea and contains mechanoreceptors known as *hair cells*. Vibrations of fluid in the cochlea move the bottom membrane and cause the hair cells to bend against a second membrane, which covers the hair cells. The bending of hair cells activates ion channels. The resulting change in the electric potential of the hair cells causes the release of neurotransmitters. The neurotransmitters stimulate neurons in the auditory nerve. Action potentials are sent to the auditory region of the brain stem, then to the thalamus, and finally to the auditory cortex, which interprets sound.

**Word Roots and Origins**

*tympanic*

from the Greek *tympanon,* meaning "drum"

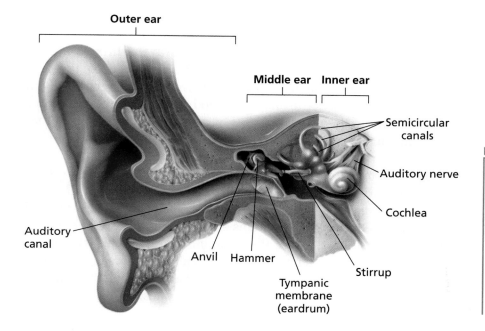

Outer ear

Middle ear    Inner ear

Semicircular canals

Auditory nerve

Cochlea

Auditory canal

Anvil    Hammer

Stirrup

Tympanic membrane (eardrum)

**FIGURE 49-10**

Sound waves, which are vibrations in the air, cause the tympanic membrane to move back and forth. This motion causes the small bones of the middle ear to move as well, transferring vibrations to the oval window. Mechanoreceptors in the inner ear translate these vibrations to action potentials. These, in turn, travel through the auditory nerve to auditory processing centers in the brain.

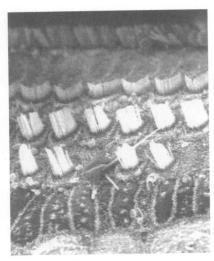

**FIGURE 49-11**

Hair cells are arranged in orderly rows inside the organ of Corti in the middle chamber of the cochlea. In the damaged section shown here, the hair cells in the top and center rows are relatively intact. Many of the hair cells of the bottom row, however, are frayed and bent. The cluster of hair cells in the middle of the bottom row has been completely destroyed.

## Quick Lab

### Observing a Lens

**Materials** beaker, water, newspaper, 4 drops cooking oil

**Procedure** Observe the newspaper through the sides of an empty beaker. Fill the beaker with water, and observe the newspaper through the water. Add four drops of oil to the top of the water. Observe the newspaper through the oil drops and water. Note any difference in print size.

**Analysis** Infer why the print size changes when the newspaper is viewed through water. Which structure of the eye does the oil on the water represent?

The hair cells that line the cochlea are delicate and vulnerable. Repeated or sustained exposure to loud noise destroys hair cells in the organ of Corti. Once destroyed, hair cells do not generally regenerate, and the sound frequencies they interpret are no longer heard. Figure 49-11 shows rows of hair cells in a damaged section of the organ of Corti. Hair cells that respond to high-frequency sound are especially vulnerable to destruction. The loss of these cells typically leads to difficulty understanding human voices. Much of this type of permanent hearing loss is avoidable by reducing exposure to loud noises, such as machine noise and loud music.

Besides detecting sound, the ear also helps maintain balance. Balance is maintained by mechanoreceptors in the three **semicircular canals** of the inner ear. The semicircular canals are filled with fluid. Their interiors are lined with hair cells that have tiny particles of calcium carbonate on top of them. When the head moves, the hair cells are bent by the action of gravity or inertia on the calcium carbonate particles. The brain decodes how far and in what direction the hair cells bend. It interprets the head's motion and orientation in space and sends out the proper orders to help the body maintain balance.

# VISION

The eyes are specialized organs that detect light and transmit signals to visual processing areas of the brain. The eye is basically a hollow sphere filled with a clear fluid. The structures of the eye act together to focus light on the **retina,** the light-sensitive inner layer of the eye.

Light passes first through a clear, protective layer called the **cornea.** Light then passes through the **pupil,** the opening to the interior of the eye. The pupil becomes larger when light is dim and smaller when light is bright. Muscles in the pigmented **iris** that surrounds the pupil control these involuntary responses.

After light passes through the pupil, it travels through a crystalline structure called the **lens.** Muscles attached to the lens adjust the shape of the lens to bend the rays of the incoming light. This bending focuses the image formed by the light onto the retina.

Lying within the retina are rods and cones, photoreceptors that translate light energy into electrical signals that can be interpreted by the brain. **Rods** contain rhodopsin, a light-sensitive pigment that allows the rods to respond to dim light. **Cones** in the retina are stimulated by bright light. The cones initiate the production of sharp images and respond to different colors. Humans have three kinds of cones. Each kind of cone contains a pigment that absorbs different wavelengths of light. When the brain integrates signals from these three kinds of cones, a person perceives all the colors in the visible spectrum. Colorblindness, which is the inability to distinguish certain colors, is caused by faulty or missing cones.

Each photoreceptor responds to light from a single location in the visual field. Signals from the stimulated photoreceptors in the deepest layer of the retina travel to neurons on the surface of the retina. From these neurons, millions of axons, which form the optic nerve, exit the eye. The optic nerve carries visual information in the form of action potentials from the retina to the thalamus. The cortex of the occipital lobe ultimately processes visual information into meaningful patterns of shape and color. Figure 49-12 shows the structure of the eye.

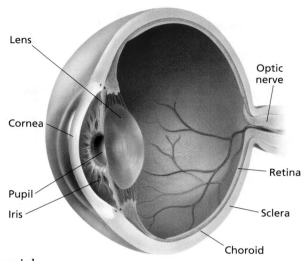

**FIGURE 49-12**

Light entering the eye travels through the cornea, the pupil, and the lens to the retina, which contains millions of photoreceptors. Activation of these specialized sensory receptors sends a signal through the optic nerve to the optic centers of the brain—first to the thalamus and eventually to the visual cortex in the occipital lobe.

# TASTE AND SMELL

People perceive variations in tastes and odors because of specialized chemoreceptors. The chemoreceptors for taste are clustered in **taste buds.** Most of the 10,000 taste buds are embedded between bumps called **papillae** (puh-PIL-ee) on the tongue. Additional taste buds are found in the throat and on the roof of the mouth. Chemicals from food dissolved in saliva enter a taste bud through a small opening. The chemicals bind to receptors and stimulate the neurons that line the inner surface of the taste buds. As shown in Figure 49-13, taste signals travel through a relay in the brain stem, to the thalamus, and finally to the cortex for interpretation.

Receptors in the nasal passages detect chemicals in the air. Specialized chemoreceptors called **olfactory** (ahl-FAK-tuh-ree) **receptors** are located in the mucous lining of the epithelium in the nasal passages. The binding of odor molecules to specific receptor molecules in the olfactory receptors stimulates the receptors. Signals from olfactory receptors travel to the olfactory bulb, a structure of the limbic system. Then, signals travel to olfactory areas of the cortex and to the *amygdala,* another limbic structure.

**FIGURE 49-13**

Taste and smell are chemical senses. Sensory receptors in the mouth and nasal passages bind to molecules from the environment, initiating neural signals that travel to the brain.

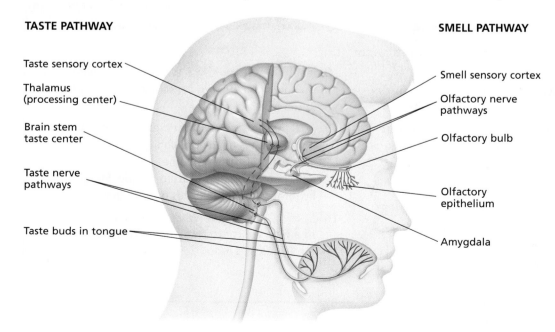

**TASTE PATHWAY**

Taste sensory cortex
Thalamus (processing center)
Brain stem taste center
Taste nerve pathways
Taste buds in tongue

**SMELL PATHWAY**

Smell sensory cortex
Olfactory nerve pathways
Olfactory bulb
Olfactory epithelium
Amygdala

# PRESSURE AND TEMPERATURE

Mechanoreceptors located throughout the skin make it possible to sense touch, pressure, and tension. In humans, touch receptors are concentrated in the face, tongue, and fingertips. Body hair also helps humans sense touch because bending a hair stimulates large numbers of mechanoreceptors found at the base of hair follicles in the skin.

Two types of specialized thermoreceptors in skin monitor temperature. Cold receptors are most sensitive to temperatures below 20°C. Heat receptors respond to temperatures between about 30°C and 45°C.

Pain receptors are sensory neurons located in the base of the epidermis and throughout the interior of the body. Mechanical, thermal, electrical, and chemical energy stimulate pain receptors. The type and number of pain receptors vary at different locations throughout the body. For example, the hands and mouth have high concentrations of pain receptors.

Sensory input from the surface of the body travels to the spinal cord in an orderly way. For example, sensory input from the shoulders enters dorsal root sections of the upper spinal cord. Input from the lower body enters the dorsal root sections of the lower spinal cord. Damage to a specific portion of the spinal cord results in sensory problems limited to a well-defined area of the body. This isolation of sensory problems illustrates how function is mapped throughout the nervous system. Specific areas of the brain's sensory cortex and motor cortex likewise correspond to specific body parts. Damage to specific areas of the cortex can result in isolated problems, such as numbness in part of one hand.

## SECTION 3 REVIEW

1. Distinguish between the five types of sense receptors.

2. How does the sensory perception system distinguish between different types of stimuli?

3. Draw the structures of the ear. Label the structures, and identify the role of each in hearing or balance.

4. Describe the detection of light.

5. What are the roles of rods and cones in vision?

6. Which mechanisms do the senses of taste and smell have in common?

7. What is the role of skin in sensing the external environment?

### CRITICAL THINKING

8. **Applying Information** Why might an injury to the lower spinal cord cause a loss of sensation in the legs?

9. **Analyzing Models** Experiments show that peripheral vision, or the ability to see to the side without turning the head, is greater in deaf people than in hearing people. Suggest a hypothesis to explain this observation.

10. **Making Inferences** What is the importance of a high concentration of pain receptors in the hands and mouth?

# DRUGS AND THE NERVOUS SYSTEM

*Drugs* are substances that cause a change in a person's physical or psychological state. Though many drugs are legal and available to the public, other drugs are illegal. Drugs, whether legal or illegal, can be misused or abused.

## PSYCHOACTIVE DRUGS

Natural or human-made chemical compounds can alter nervous system function. A **psychoactive drug** is a drug that alters the functioning of the central nervous system. The psychoactive drug cocaine comes from the plant shown in Figure 49-14. Many prescribed medications are psychoactive drugs, as is caffeine, which is found in coffee and many soft drinks.

### Addiction and Tolerance

The abuse of psychoactive drugs alters the normal functioning of neurons and synapes. Psychoactive drug abuse often leads to **dependence.** Dependence is a state in which a person relies on a drug physically or emotionally in order to function. Dependence often results in **addiction,** a condition in which a person can no longer control his or her drug use.

With repeated exposure to a drug, a person addicted to the drug develops tolerance to the drug. **Tolerance** is a characteristic of drug addiction in which larger and larger amounts of the drug are needed to achieve the desired sensation. This increase in the *effective dose,* the dose that causes the desired feeling, can be a deadly situation for the users of some drugs. As tolerance increases and the effective dose rises, the addict approaches a *lethal dose*—the amount of drug that will kill the user.

Without the drug, addicts go through **withdrawal,** a physical and emotional response to the drug's absence. The severity of drug dependence is evident in recovering addicts who experience withdrawal when they stop taking an addictive drug. Withdrawal symptoms vary depending on which type of drug was abused and how long it was abused. Symptoms may include vomiting, headache, insomnia, breathing difficulties, depression, mental instability, and seizures. Withdrawal from some drugs, such as alcohol and barbiturates, can be life threatening. Addicts undergoing withdrawal from these drugs are often hospitalized so that doctors can monitor their responses.

**FIGURE 49-14**

The psychoactive and highly addictive drug cocaine comes from the coca plant, *Erythroxylum coca.*

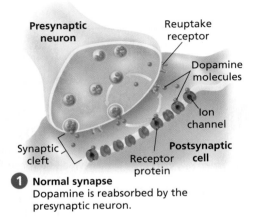

Normal synapse
**1** **Normal synapse**
Dopamine is reabsorbed by the
presynaptic neuron.

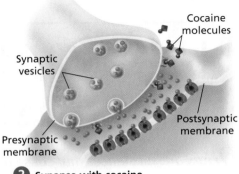

**2** **Synapse with cocaine**
Cocaine blocks the reabsorption
of dopamine.

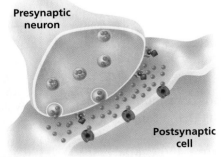

**3** **Overstimulated postsynaptic cell**
The number of receptor proteins on the
postsynaptic cell decreases.

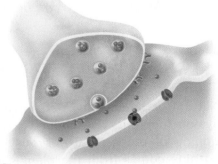

**4** **Cocaine removed from synapse**
Dopamine release returns to normal, but
the postsynaptic cell is understimulated.

**FIGURE 49-15**

**1** At a normal synapse, dopamine
is reabsorbed by reuptake receptors.
**2** Cocaine binds and blocks reuptake
receptors, causing dopamine molecules
to remain longer in the synaptic cleft.
**3** The excess dopamine overstimulates
the postsynaptic neuron, which
responds by reducing its number of
receptor proteins. **4** In the absence of
the drug, dopamine release returns to
normal, but the postsynaptic cell is
understimulated due to a lack of
receptors.

## Neural Changes

Cocaine is a highly addictive **stimulant,** a drug that generally
increases the activity of the central nervous system. Though illegal,
cocaine is still abused by many people. The excitatory effect sought
by cocaine users is due to the drug's action on neurons in the brain.

Figure 49-15 summarizes the effect cocaine addiction has on the
brain. Cocaine affects dopamine (DOH-pah-MEEN) receptors in the
limbic system. The receptors play an important role in the sensation of pleasure. Recall that neurotransmitters secreted into the
synaptic cleft send signals from one neuron to the next. In many
kinds of neurons, *reuptake receptors* bind, or reabsorb, the neurotransmitter molecules in the synaptic cleft and move them back
into the presynaptic cell for later use. Cocaine molecules bind to
these presynaptic reuptake receptors. As a result, the reabsorption
of neurotransmitter molecules is blocked. Rather than being
removed, the neurotransmitter molecules remain for a long time
in the synaptic cleft. The excess neurotransmitters abnormally
excite the postsynaptic neurons, providing the sensation cocaine
abusers seek.

In response to the surplus neurotransmitter molecules that
cocaine causes, postsynaptic neurons make fewer neurotransmitter receptors. As a result, normal levels of neurotransmitter molecules are no longer sufficient to stimulate the postsynaptic neuron
in the absence of cocaine because this neuron has reduced numbers of receptors.

## TABLE 49-2 *Psychoactive Drugs of Abuse*

| Type of drug | Examples | Psychoactive effects | Risks of use |
| --- | --- | --- | --- |
| Depressants | alcohol, barbiturates (sedatives), tranquilizers | decreased activity of the central nervous system, impaired judgment, loss of motor control, confusion, sedation | drowsiness, depression, liver damage, brain or nerve damage, respiratory failure, coma |
| Stimulants | amphetamines, cocaine, crack, nicotine | increased activity of the central nervous system, temporary feeling of exhilaration, irritability, anxiety, elevated blood pressure, increased heart rate | insomnia, paranoia, delusions, loss of coordination, brain damage, respiratory paralysis, irregular heartbeat, cardiac arrest |
| Narcotics | codeine, heroin, morphine, opium | temporary feeling of euphoria, impaired reflexes, impaired sensory perception, sedation | coma, respiratory failure |
| Hallucinogens | LSD, MDMA (Ecstasy), PCP, peyote (mescaline), psilocybe mushroom | sensory distortion, hallucinations, delusions, anxiety, slurred speech, numbness, bizarre or violent behavior | depression, paranoia, aggressive behavior, brain damage |
| Tetrahydro-cannabinol (THC) | hashish, marijuana | temporary feeling of euphoria, short-term memory loss, impaired judgment, hallucinations | lung damage, loss of motivation |
| Inhalants | aerosols, ether, glue, nitrous oxide, paint thinner | disorientation, confusion, memory loss, sedation | brain damage, spasms, liver and kidney damage, cardiorespiratory failure |

# DRUGS AND ABUSE

The possession of psychoactive drugs is often illegal. Table 49-2 lists types of abused psychoactive drugs.

## Alcohol

For people age 21 and older, alcohol is a legal drug. Alcohol is a **depressant,** a drug that decreases the activity of the central nervous system. Alcohol increases circulation to the skin, decreases blood flow to internal organs, and lowers body temperature. Alcohol causes the kidneys to excrete more water, which can cause dehydration. As drinking continues, judgment and coordination become impaired, speech slurs, and reaction time lengthens. Respiration rate slows after an initial increase. High doses of alcohol can cause death by respiratory failure. The severity of these effects depends largely on **blood alcohol concentration** (BAC), a measurement of the amount of alcohol in the blood. A BAC of 0.30 or greater can cause unconsciousness, and a BAC of 0.50 can be fatal.

Alcohol is a factor in nearly 50 percent of fatal car crashes involving young people. Alcohol can contribute to harmful drug interactions. For example, when alcohol is combined with another depressant, the cumulative effects can slow the respiratory systems to the point of death. Alcohol consumed during pregnancy can lead to *fetal alcohol syndrome,* as shown in Figure 49-16.

**FIGURE 49-16**

This child shows some of the physical abnormalities associated with fetal alcohol syndrome. Children born with fetal alcohol syndrome often have physical, mental, behavioral, and learning disabilities.

**FIGURE 49-17**

Nicotine is a stimulant found in the leaves of the tobacco plant.

# Tobacco

Tobacco products are legal for people age 18 and older. **Nicotine** is the major drug found in tobacco, shown in Figure 49-17. Nicotine is a highly addictive stimulant. When a person chews tobacco or inhales its smoke, nicotine is absorbed into the bloodstream through the mouth and lungs. It is then quickly transported throughout the body and, in pregnant women, to the fetus.

Nicotine mimics the action of a neurotransmitter called *acetylcholine* (AS-i-TIL-KOH-leen). Acetylcholine plays a role in many of the body's everyday activities. Nicotine increases blood pressure and heart rate. Nicotine decreases the oxygen supply to body tissues and the blood supply to the hands and feet. Nicotine is also a poison—60 mg of nicotine is a lethal dose for an adult.

Nicotine is not the only harmful substance found in tobacco. Burning tobacco produces *tars,* complex mixtures of chemicals and smoke particles. Tars coat and paralyze the cilia that line air passages and normally sweep particles and debris from those passageways. Tars irritate the nose, throat, trachea, and bronchial tubes, causing sore throat and coughing. Tars disrupt lung cells, reducing breathing capacity and increasing the risk of respiratory infections.

The long-term use of tobacco products has several effects. In the United States, smoking-related illnesses cause more than 400,000 deaths each year. About 25 percent of all heart attacks are associated with the use of tobacco. Smoking causes lung cancer, one of the most common forms of cancer. Many smokers contract *chronic bronchitis* (brahn-KIET-is), an inflammation of the bronchi and bronchioles, or **emphysema** (EM-fuh-SEE-muh), a degenerative lung disease in which alveoli lose their elasticity and eventually rupture.

People who chew tobacco and use snuff have higher rates of lip, gum, and mouth cancer than people who don't use smokeless tobacco. Pregnant women who smoke are twice as likely as nonsmoking mothers to suffer miscarriages. Their babies tend to have lower birth weights than babies of nonsmokers and are twice as likely to die in the first few months of life.

## SECTION 4 REVIEW

1. What is the relationship between addiction and tolerance?

2. Describe the physiological mechanism of cocaine addiction.

3. What are six types of psychoactive drugs?

4. How does a stimulant differ from a depressant?

5. What are some of the effects of alcohol use?

6. What is blood alcohol concentration (BAC)?

7. How do tobacco products affect the body?

**CRITICAL THINKING**

8. **Recognizing Relationships** What do all psychoactive drugs have in common?

9. **Analyzing Models** Examine the model for cocaine addiction shown in Figure 49-15. How does this model illustrate the phenomenon of tolerance?

10. **Applying Concepts** Why are long-term drug abusers, who have built up a large degree of tolerance, endangered by their effective dose?

# CHAPTER HIGHLIGHTS

**Neurons and Nerve Impulses**

- Neurons are specialized cells that rapidly transmit information as electrical signals throughout the body.
- In a neuron at rest, the inside of the cell has a negative charge relative to the outside.

- During an action potential, the polarity of the membrane is reversed briefly as Na⁺ ions diffuse into the neuron through voltage-gated channels.
- When an action potential reaches the presynaptic membrane, neurotransmitters are released into the synapse.

### Vocabulary

| | | | |
|---|---|---|---|
| nervous system (p. 1005) | axon (p. 1005) | myelin sheath (p. 1005) | membrane potential (p. 1006) |
| neuron (p. 1005) | action potential (p. 1005) | synapse (p. 1005) | resting potential (p. 1007) |
| dendrite (p. 1005) | axon terminal (p. 1005) | neurotransmitter (p. 1005) | refractory period (p. 1008) |

## SECTION 2 — Structure of the Nervous System

- The nervous system has two divisions—the central nervous system (CNS) and peripheral nervous system (PNS).
- The CNS is made up of the brain and spinal cord. The PNS is made of neurons with cell bodies that are not part of the brain and spinal cord.

- The sensory division of the PNS contains sensory neurons and interneurons that connect to the CNS. The motor division allows the body to react to sensory information.
- The somatic nervous system controls skeletal muscles and is under voluntary control. The autonomic nervous system controls internal body conditions.

### Vocabulary

| | | | |
|---|---|---|---|
| central nervous system (p. 1010) | cerebral cortex (p. 1011) | cerebellum (p. 1013) | somatic nervous system (p. 1014) |
| peripheral nervous system (p. 1010) | brain stem (p. 1012) | nerve (p. 1013) | reflex (p. 1014) |
| cerebrum (p. 1011) | thalamus (p. 1012) | sensory receptor (p. 1013) | autonomic nervous system (p. 1015) |
| | hypothalamus (p. 1012) | motor neuron (p. 1013) | |
| | medulla oblongata (p. 1012) | interneuron (p. 1013) | |

## SECTION 3 — Sensory Systems

- The ear converts sound into electrical signals that are interpreted by the brain.
- Photoreceptors in the eyes convert light into electrical signals that are interpreted by the brain.

- Stimulation of neurons in taste buds is interpreted as taste. Olfactory receptors in the nasal passages transmit signals to the brain, where they are interpreted as odor.

### Vocabulary

| | | | |
|---|---|---|---|
| sense organ (p. 1016) | cochlea (p. 1017) | pupil (p. 1018) | cone (p. 1018) |
| auditory canal (p. 1017) | semicircular canal (p. 1018) | iris (p. 1018) | taste bud (p. 1019) |
| tympanic membrane (p. 1017) | retina (p. 1018) | lens (p. 1018) | papilla (p. 1019) |
| Eustachian tube (p. 1017) | cornea (p. 1018) | rod (p. 1018) | olfactory receptor (p. 1019) |

## SECTION 4 — Drugs and the Nervous System

- Psychoactive drugs affect the CNS. Dependence is a physical or psychological need for a drug. Tolerance is a characteristic of addiction in which larger and larger amounts of the drug are needed.

- Drug addiction involves physiological changes in neurons.
- Alcohol is an addictive depressant that widely affects the CNS. Nicotine is an addictive stimulant found in tobacco products.

### Vocabulary

| | | | |
|---|---|---|---|
| drug (p. 1021) | tolerance (p. 1021) | depressant (p. 1023) | nicotine (p. 1024) |
| psychoactive drug (p. 1021) | withdrawal (p. 1021) | blood alcohol concentration (p. 1023) | emphysema (p. 1024) |
| dependence (p. 1021) | stimulant (p. 1022) | | |
| addiction (p. 1021) | | | |

# CHAPTER REVIEW

## USING VOCABULARY

1. For each pair of terms, explain the relationship between the terms.
   a. *stimulant* and *depressant*
   b. *motor neuron* and *sensory receptor*
   c. *brain stem* and *diencephalon*
   d. *resting potential* and *action potential*

2. Use each of the following terms in a separate sentence: *neuron, dendrite, myelin sheath,* and *synapse*.

3. Use each of the following terms in a separate sentence: *thalamus, hypothalamus, pons,* and *medulla oblongata*.

4. **Word Roots and Origins** The word *pons* is derived from the Latin *pons,* which means "bridge." Using this information, explain how *pons* is an appropriate term for the part of the brain it describes.

## UNDERSTANDING KEY CONCEPTS

5. **Discuss** the structure of a neuron.

6. **Describe** the chemical conditions within a neuron during resting potential and during action potential.

7. **Explain** how action potentials are transmitted from a neuron to another cell.

8. **Describe** the roles of the two main organs of the central nervous system.

9. **Define** the roles of four portions of the brain.

10. **Summarize** the roles of the sensory and motor divisions of the peripheral nervous system.

11. **Relate** the relationship between motor neurons, interneurons, and sensory receptors.

12. **Describe** the role of chemoreceptors in taste and smell.

13. **List** five different types of sensory receptors in the human body.

14. **Identify** the parts of the ear responsible for hearing and for balance.

15. **Compare** how rods and cones respond to light.

16. **Describe** how the eye receives light stimulus and sends a signal to the brain.

17. **State** the type of receptors that function in taste and smell.

18. **Explain** the role of skin in sensing touch, temperature, and pain.

19. **Relate** addiction and tolerance.

20. **Describe** the process of cocaine addiction.

21. **Identify** six types of psychoactive drugs.

22. **Identify** the effects of alcohol and tobacco on the body.

23. **CONCEPT MAPPING** Use the following terms to create a concept map that describes the effect of drugs on the nervous system: *psychoactive drugs, depressants, alcohol, stimulants, impaired judgment, confusion, increased heart rate, increased blood pressure, addiction,* and *nicotine*.

## CRITICAL THINKING

24. **Analyzing Data** Epilepsy affects one out of every 200 Americans. Brain neurons normally produce small bursts of action potentials in varying patterns. During an epileptic seizure, large numbers of brain neurons send rapid bursts of action potentials simultaneously. The body of an individual having a seizure may grow rigid and jerk or convulse. From what you know about the brain's control of muscles and posture, how might you explain these symptoms?

25. **Making Predictions** Predict what could happen to the nervous system if a person has an imbalance of electrolytes, the ion-containing fluids of the body.

26. **Inferring Relationships** People who suffer from vertigo feel dizzy and disoriented in certain situations. What is the relationship between vertigo and the semicircular canals?

27. **Interpreting Graphics** The diagram below shows the brain of a fish. How does the cerebrum of a fish differ from the cerebrum of a human? The fish's brain has large olfactory bulbs. What does this indicate about the relative importance of the sense of smell to the fish?

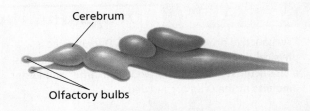

Cerebrum

Olfactory bulbs

# Standardized Test Preparation

**DIRECTIONS:** Choose the letter of the answer choice that best answers the question.

1. Which of the following is true about the cerebral cortex?
   A. It is located deep in the brain.
   B. It is the folded outer covering of the brain.
   C. It is part of the peripheral nervous system.
   D. It is the lobed, highly folded structure located at the back of the brain.

2. When a neuron is at resting potential, which of the following is true?
   F. Both sides of the cell are equally charged.
   G. The inside of the cell is less positive.
   H. The polarity across the membrane reverses.
   J. The outside of the cell is less positive.

3. Which of the following stimuli affects mechanoreceptors?
   A. heat
   B. light
   C. pressure
   D. chemicals

**INTERPRETING GRAPHICS:** The graph below shows the change in voltage during an action potential. Use the graph to answer the questions that follow.

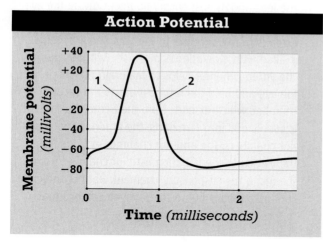

4. How long does the action potential last?
   F. 1 ms
   G. 1.5 ms
   H. 3 ms
   J. 30 ms

5. Which point on the graph represents when the voltage-gated sodium channels are open?
   A. 1
   B. 2
   C. 1 and 2
   D. There is not enough information to determine the answer.

**DIRECTIONS:** Complete the following analogy.

6. stimulant : nicotine :: depressant :
   F. alcohol
   G. cigarettes
   H. neurotransmitters
   J. tetrahydrocannabinol (THC)

**INTERPRETING GRAPHCS:** The diagram below shows a neuron. Use the diagram to answer the questions that follow.

7. Which number indicates the structure from which the neuron receives information from other neurons?
   A. 1
   B. 2
   C. 3
   D. 4

8. Which number indicates the structure that increases the speed of action potentials?
   F. 1
   G. 2
   H. 3
   J. 4

## SHORT RESPONSE

The effect of a drug on the body varies with the size of the dose and an individual's tolerance to the drug.

Explain the difference between the effective dose and the lethal dose of a drug.

## EXTENDED RESPONSE

Both alcohol and tobacco can have a negative effect on human health.

*Part A* Susan is addicted to alcohol. Predict what might happen if she quit drinking.

*Part B* Mark smokes a pack of cigarettes a day. Describe some of the health risks Mark faces if he continues to smoke for a long period of time.

**Test *TIP*** Choose an answer to a question based both on what you already know and on any information presented in the question.

# Dissecting a Sheep's Eye

## OBJECTIVES

- Describe the main external and internal structures of a sheep's eye.
- Name the various structures associated with sight.

## PROCESS SKILLS

- observing
- identifying
- comparing and contrasting

## MATERIALS

- safety goggles
- disposable gloves
- lab apron
- preserved sheep's eye
- dissection tray
- scalpel
- tweezers
- fine scissors
- blunt probe

## Background

1. The sheep's eye is very similar to the human eye, as shown in the diagram below. The wall of the eyeball is made up of three layers. The outer layer, the sclera, is a tough tissue that forms the white of the eye. At the front of the eye, the sclera becomes thin and transparent to form the cornea.

2. The middle layer, the choroid, is dark and rich with blood vessels. At the front of the eye behind the cornea, the choroid is modified into the iris and the ciliary body. The pigment in the iris determines eye color. The opening in the center of the iris is the pupil. What is the function of the pupil?

3. The inner layer, the retina, is sensitive to light. What are the photoreceptors in the retina called?

4. Directly behind the iris is the elastic, transparent lens. The suspensory ligament attaches the ciliary muscle, the main part of the ciliary body, to the lens. This ring of muscle changes the shape of the lens to focus on near and far objects.

5. The lens and its suspensory ligament divide the eye into two chambers. The large vitreous chamber extends from the retina to the lens and ligaments. It is filled with a gelatinous mass, the vitreous humor. The vitreous humor helps to maintain the shape of the eye and hold the retina in place. The second chamber, which extends from the iris to the cornea, is subdivided into two parts, the anterior and posterior chambers. The anterior chamber extends from the cornea to the iris; the posterior chamber from the iris to the suspensory ligament. Both chambers contain aqueous humor, a watery substance that bathes the front part of the eye.

6. Ganglion cells form synapses with bipolar cells, which, in turn, synapse with rods and cones. In the retina, the axons of ganglion cells bundle together at the optic nerve. The region of the retina where its nerve fibers and blood vessels enter the optic nerve is the small optic disk, which contains no rods or cones. Why is the optic disk also called the blind spot?

7. A very short distance away is a yellowish spot, the fovea. It is the site of sharpest vision because it has a high concentration of photoreceptors.

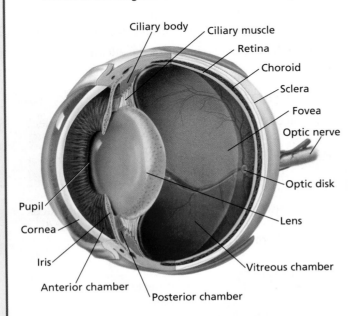

Ciliary body · Ciliary muscle · Retina · Choroid · Sclera · Fovea · Optic nerve · Optic disk · Lens · Vitreous chamber · Posterior chamber · Anterior chamber · Iris · Cornea · Pupil

## Procedure

1.   Put on safety goggles, gloves, and a lab apron.

2.  **CAUTION  Use extreme care when handling all sharp and pointed instruments, such as scalpels.**

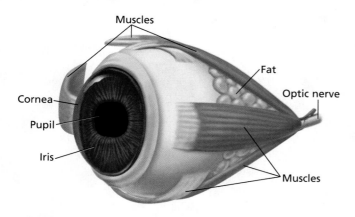

Locate the six main muscles on the outside of the eye, as shown in the diagram above. These muscles move the eye. Use a scalpel to carefully cut the muscles near the eye. This will expose the sclera.

3. Observe the fatty tissue that cushions the eye in its socket, especially around the optic nerve. This fatty tissue helps to prevent shock. With a tweezer and scalpel, remove the fatty tissue. This will expose the optic nerve more fully.

4. Using a scalpel, carefully cut the sclera about 1 cm behind the cornea. Using fine scissors, extend the cut to make a flap that you can lift, as shown in the diagram below.

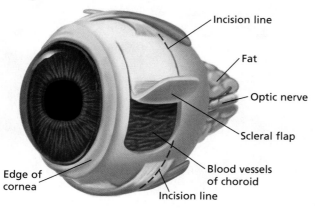

5. With forceps, carefully remove the sclera in this area and observe the dark choroid layer immediately below the sclera.

6. Next, use a scalpel to make an incision through the eye. Following along the incision you made in step 4, cut almost completely around the eye. You have separated the eye into an anterior and a posterior portion.

7. In the posterior section, observe the whitish retina. It is probably shriveled and may have fallen into the vitreous chamber.

8. In the anterior section, use a blunt probe to expose the lens. In a preserved eye, the lens is no longer clear.

9. In the anterior section, also locate the ciliary muscle and as many other structures as possible.

10. When you have finished your dissection, remove the specimen from the dissecting tray. Dispose of your materials according to the directions from your teacher.

11. Clean up your work area, and wash your hands before leaving the lab.

## Analysis and Conclusions

1. How is the lens different from the other structures of the eye?

2. How does the nature of the sclera and choroid change as they reach the front part of the eye?

3. How does the vitreous chamber differ from the anterior and posterior chambers?

4. What would be the result of the cornea becoming cloudy during an animal's lifetime?

5. Sometimes, the retina of the eye becomes detached. Why is it important that the retina be reattached, if possible?

## Further Inquiry

You see light if the vision center of your cerebrum is stimulated electrically. Scientists are trying to find out which brain cells are involved in forming images in our brains. How might scientists someday use this knowledge to help blind people see?

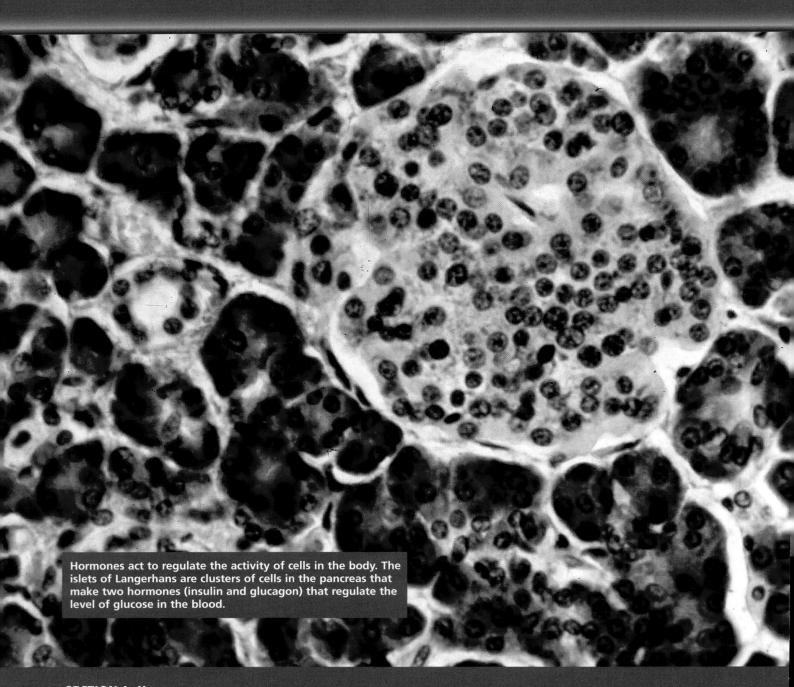

Hormones act to regulate the activity of cells in the body. The islets of Langerhans are clusters of cells in the pancreas that make two hormones (insulin and glucagon) that regulate the level of glucose in the blood.

**SECTION 1** *Hormones*

**SECTION 2** *Endocrine Glands*

# HORMONES

*Chemical messengers are substances that carry messages and instructions to cells. Hormones (HOHR-MOHNZ) and neurotransmitters are both chemical messengers that coordinate the body's activities. Hormones, however, are part of the endocrine system, while neurotransmitters are part of the nervous system. Hormones are often slower acting and have longer effects than neurotransmitters.*

### OBJECTIVES

- **State** the major functions of hormones.
- **Differentiate** between endocrine and exocrine glands.
- **Compare** the structure of amino acid–based hormones with the structure of steroid hormones.
- **Compare** how amino acid–based hormones act on their target cells with how steroid or thyroid hormones act on their target cells.
- **Relate** how neuropeptides and prostaglandins act like hormones.

### VOCABULARY

hormone
endocrine gland
endocrine system
exocrine gland
amino acid–based hormone
steroid hormone
target cell
receptor
second messenger
neuropeptide
prostaglandin

## FUNCTION AND SECRETION

Hormones influence almost every cell and organ in our bodies. **Hormones** are substances secreted by cells that act to regulate the activity of other cells in the body. Hormones have many functions. For example, hormones regulate growth, development, behavior, and reproduction. They also maintain homeostasis, regulate metabolism and water and mineral balance, and respond to external stimuli.

Hormones are made and secreted by endocrine (EN-doh-KRIN) glands. **Endocrine glands** are ductless organs that secrete hormones either into the bloodstream or the fluid around cells (extracellular fluid). Specialized cells in the brain, stomach, small intestine, liver, heart, and other organs also make and release hormones. The endocrine glands and specialized cells that secrete hormones are collectively called the **endocrine system.**

Some endocrine glands, such as the pancreas, are also exocrine (EKS-oh-KRIN) glands. **Exocrine glands** secrete substances through ducts (tubelike structures). These substances can include water, enzymes, and mucus. The ducts transport the substances to specific locations inside and outside the body. Sweat glands, mucous glands, salivary glands, and other digestive glands are examples of exocrine glands.

## TYPES OF HORMONES

Hormones can be grouped into two types based on their structure: amino acid–based hormones and steroid (STIR-OYD) hormones. **Amino acid–based hormones** are hormones made of amino acids. An amino acid–based hormone can be either a single modified amino acid or a protein made of 3 to 200 amino acids. Most amino acid–based hormones are water soluble. **Steroid hormones** are lipid hormones that the body makes from cholesterol. Steroid hormones are fat soluble.

### Word Roots and Origins

*hormone*

from the Greek *hormon,* meaning "to excite"

## Quick Lab

### Observing Solubilities

**Materials** 100 mL beakers (4), water, gelatin, cooking oil, vitamin E capsule, dissecting pin, spoon

**Procedure**

1. Put 75 mL of water into a beaker. Place 2.5 g of gelatin (protein) into the beaker. Stir. Does the gelatin dissolve? Record your observations.

2. Put 75 mL of oil into a beaker. Repeat the procedure in step 1 using oil instead of water.

3. Repeat steps 1 and 2 using the contents of a vitamin capsule (fat) instead of gelatin.

**Analysis** Which substance is fat soluble? Which substance is water soluble? Relate the solubilities of hormones to whether they enter their target cells or work outside them.

FIGURE 50-1

❶ Amino acid–based hormones, such as glucagon, bind to receptor proteins on the cell membrane. ❷ The binding activates an enzyme, which converts ATP to cyclic AMP. ❸ Cyclic AMP starts a cascade of enzyme activations. ❹ Eventually, glycogen is broken down to individual glucose molecules.

# HORMONE ACTION

The body produces many different hormones, but each hormone affects only its target cells. **Target cells** are specific cells to which a hormone travels to produce a specific effect. Target cells have **receptors**—proteins that bind specific signal molecules that cause the cell to respond. Each receptor binds to a specific hormone. When a hormone binds to a receptor, the binding triggers events that lead to changes within the cell. Receptors can be found on the cell membrane, in the cytoplasm, or in the nucleus of a cell.

## Amino Acid–Based Hormones

Most amino acid–based hormones bind to receptor proteins on the cell membrane. Thus, the hormone acts as a "first messenger." As the example in Figure 50-1 shows, the resulting hormone-receptor complex activates an enzyme that converts ATP to cyclic AMP (cAMP). Cyclic AMP, in turn, activates additional enzymes and proteins inside the cell. Thus, the hormone acts as a "first messenger" and cAMP acts as a "second messenger." A **second messenger** is a molecule that initiates changes inside a cell in response to the binding of a specific substance to a receptor on the outside of a cell. In addition to cAMP, cells have other second messengers.

## Steroid and Thyroid Hormones

Because steroid and thyroid hormones are fat soluble, they diffuse through the cell membranes of their target cells and bind to receptors in the cytoplasm or nucleus. The hormone-receptor complexes cause the cells to activate existing enzymes or to initiate synthesis of new enzymes or proteins. Figure 50-2 shows how a hormone-receptor complex binds to DNA, activates transcription of mRNA, and stimulates production of new proteins. The proteins cause changes in the target cell.

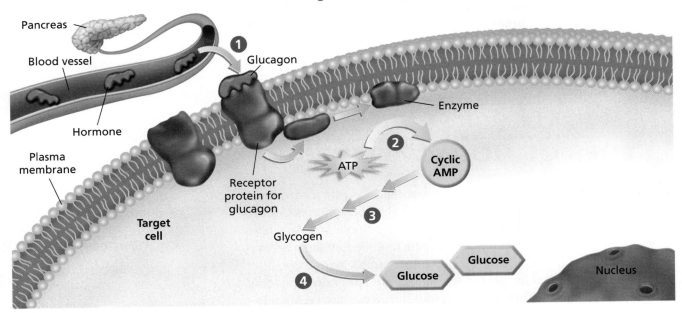

Pancreas

Blood vessel

Hormone

Plasma membrane

Target cell

Glucagon

❶

Enzyme

❷

ATP

Cyclic AMP

Receptor protein for glucagon

❸

Glycogen

❹

Glucose

Glucose

Nucleus

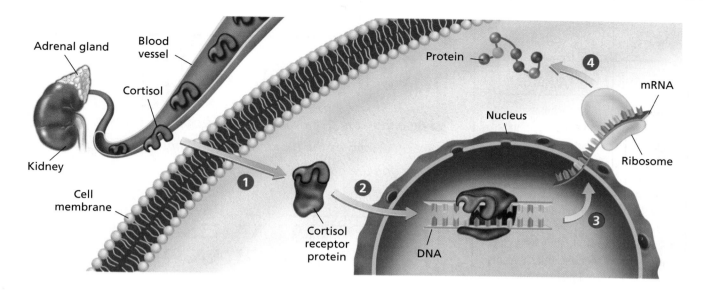

Adrenal gland
Blood vessel
Cortisol
Kidney
Cell membrane
Protein
mRNA
Nucleus
Ribosome
Cortisol receptor protein
DNA

# OTHER TYPES OF HORMONES

Many other chemical messengers are now classified as hormones. These substances include neuropeptides and prostaglandins (PRAHS-tuh-GLAN-dinz).

**Neuropeptides** are hormones secreted by the nervous system. Unlike neurotransmitters, neuropeptides tend to affect many cells near the nerve cells that release them. One group of neuropeptides, called *endorphins* (en-DAWR finz), regulate emotions, influence pain, and affect reproduction. Another group of neuropeptides, *enkephalins* (en-KEF-uh-linz), inhibit pain messages traveling toward the brain.

**Prostaglandins** are modified fatty acids that are secreted by most cells. Prostaglandins accumulate in areas where tissues are disturbed or injured. Some prostaglandins reduce blood pressure; others raise blood pressure. Some prostaglandins cause smooth muscle to relax; others cause smooth muscle to contract. Some prostaglandins cause fever. Aspirin and acetaminophen reduce fever and decrease pain by inhibiting prostaglandin synthesis.

**FIGURE 50-2**

❶ Steroid hormones, such as cortisol, diffuse through the cell membrane and attach to receptors in the cytoplasm of the cell. ❷ The hormone-receptor complex enters the nucleus and binds to DNA. ❸ Genes are activated. ❹ Proteins are made that become active in cells.

**internet** connect

www.scilinks.org
**Topic:** Hormones
**Keyword:** HM60758

SCLINKS. Maintained by the National Science Teachers Association

## SECTION 1 REVIEW

1. Name four functions of hormones.

2. How do endocrine glands differ from exocrine glands?

3. Explain how most amino acid–based hormones affect their target cells.

4. Explain how steroid and thyroid hormones affect their target cells.

5. Why are neuropeptides and prostaglandins now classified as hormones?

### CRITICAL THINKING

6. **Applying Information** Why can steroid and thyroid hormones, but not amino acid–based hormones, move across cell membranes?

7. **Organizing Information** Which types of hormones, amino acid–based, steroid, or thyroid, activate transcription and translation of a gene?

8. **Recognizing Relationships** Why are both hormones and neurotransmitters considered chemical messengers?

## OBJECTIVES

- **Identify** the relationship between the hypothalamus and the pituitary gland in the release of hormones.
- **List** the functions of the major endocrine glands and hormones.
- **Explain** the role of feedback mechanisms in maintaining homeostasis.
- **Compare** how negative feedback and positive feedback mechanisms are used to regulate hormone levels.
- **Summarize** how antagonistic hormones work as pairs to maintain homeostasis.

## VOCABULARY

hypothalamus
pituitary gland
thyroid gland
adrenal gland
epinephrine
norepinephrine
cortisol
gonad
puberty
luteinizing hormone
follicle-stimulating hormone
estrogen
progesterone
androgen
testosterone
insulin
diabetes mellitus
melatonin
negative feedback
positive feedback

**FIGURE 50-3**

Endocrine glands are located throughout the body. All of these glands contain cells that secrete hormones. In addition to the organs shown, many other organs secrete hormones.

# ENDOCRINE GLANDS

*The endocrine glands regulate many vital processes. This section discusses the major hormones that endocrine glands make and the effects of these hormones.*

## HYPOTHALAMUS AND PITUITARY GLAND

As shown in Figure 50-3, endocrine glands are located throughout the body. Two organs, the hypothalamus (HIE-poh-THAL-uh-muhs) and the pituitary (pi-TOO-uh-TER-ee) gland, control the initial release of many hormones.

The **hypothalamus** is the area of the brain that coordinates many activities of the nervous and endocrine systems. It receives information from other brain regions and then responds to these signals as well as to blood concentrations of circulating hormones. The hypothalmus responds by issuing instructions in the form of hormones to the pituitary gland. As shown in Figure 50-4, the **pituitary gland** is suspended from the hypothalamus by a short stalk. The hypothalamus produces hormones that are stored in the pituitary gland or that regulate the pituitary gland's activity.

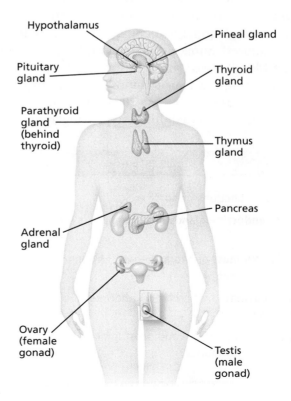

Hypothalamus
Pineal gland
Pituitary gland
Thyroid gland
Parathyroid gland (behind thyroid)
Thymus gland
Adrenal gland
Pancreas
Ovary (female gonad)
Testis (male gonad)

Two hormones—oxytocin (AHKS-ee-TOH-sin) and antidiuretic (AN-TIE-DIE-yoo-RET-ik) hormone (ADH)—are made by nerve cells in the hypothalamus. These nerve cells that secrete hormones are called *neurosecretory cells*. The axons of the neurosecretory cells in the hypothalamus extend into the posterior lobe of the pituitary, as shown in Figure 50-4b. Oxytocin and ADH are transported through these axons into the posterior pituitary, where they are stored for eventual release into the bloodstream.

As shown in Figure 50-4b, a special system of blood vessels connects the hypothalamus with the anterior pituitary. Nerve cells in the hypothalamus secrete releasing and release-inhibiting hormones that travel to the anterior pituitary through the blood vessels. *Releasing hormones* stimulate the anterior pituitary to make and secrete hormones. *Release-inhibiting hormones* inhibit production and secretion of anterior-pituitary hormones.

Some anterior-pituitary hormones, such as prolactin and growth hormone, are regulated through both a releasing hormone and a release-inhibiting hormone. Other hormones regulated by releasing hormones, such as follicle–stimulating hormone, thyroid-stimulating hormone, and adrenocorticotropic hormone (ACTH), in turn stimulate other endocrine glands. Table 50-1 summarizes the function of the hormones secreted by the pituitary gland.

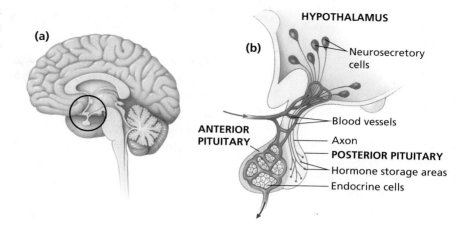

(a)

(b) HYPOTHALAMUS

Neurosecretory cells

Blood vessels

ANTERIOR PITUITARY

Axon

POSTERIOR PITUITARY

Hormone storage areas

Endocrine cells

**FIGURE 50-4**

Neurosecretory cells in the hypothalamus produce hormones that affect the pituitary gland. The area of the brain where the hypothalamus and pituitary gland are found is circled in (a). The hypothalamus regulates the posterior pituitary through axons and the anterior pituitary through blood vessels, as shown in (b). (Blood vessels in the posterior pituitary have been omitted in order to show axon projections.)

**TABLE 50-1** *Hormones Secreted by the Pituitary Gland*

| Hormone | Target | Major function |
|---|---|---|
| Adrenocorticotropic hormone (ACTH) | adrenal cortex | stimulates secretion of cortisol and aldosterone by the adrenal cortex |
| Antidiuretic hormone (ADH) | kidney tubules | stimulates reabsorption of water by kidneys, reducing the concentration of solutes in the blood |
| Follicle-stimulating hormone (FSH) | ovaries in females; testes in males | stimulates egg production in females; stimulates sperm production in males |
| Growth hormone (GH) | muscle and bone | regulates development of muscles and bones |
| Luteinizing hormone (LH) | ovaries in females; testes in males | stimulates progesterone and estrogen production; initiates ovulation in females; stimulates testosterone production in males |
| Oxytocin | uterine muscles and mammary glands | initiates uterine contractions during childbirth; stimulates flow of milk from breasts during lactation |
| Prolactin (PRL) | mammary glands | stimulates milk production in breasts during lactation |
| Thyroid-stimulating hormone (TSH) | thyroid gland | regulates secretion of the thyroid hormones—thyroxine and triiodothyronine |

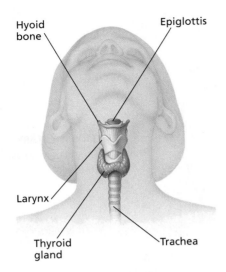

Hyoid bone
Epiglottis
Larynx
Thyroid gland
Trachea

**FIGURE 50-5**

The thyroid gland is located under the larynx and on the trachea.

# THYROID GLAND

The two lobes of the **thyroid** (THIE-ROYD) **gland** are located near the lower part of the larynx, as shown in Figure 50-5. The thyroid gland produces and secretes the hormones thyroxine (thie-RAHKS-een) and triiodothyronine (TRIE-ie-oh-DOH-THIE-roh-NEEN). Both of these hormones are derived from the same amino acid and are synthesized with iodine atoms. Thyroid-stimulating hormone (TSH) regulates the release of the thyroid hormones. Release of TSH from the anterior pituitary is regulated primarily by a releasing hormone as well as release-inhibiting hormones secreted by the hypothalamus.

The thyroid hormones help maintain normal heart rate, blood pressure, and body temperature. They stimulate enzymes that are associated with glucose oxidation and oxygen consumption, generating heat and increasing cellular metabolic rates. They also promote carbohydrate usage over fat usage for energy.

The thyroid gland is important to human development because thyroid hormones promote the development of many of the body's systems. The thyroid gland also produces calcitonin (KAL-sih-TOH-nin), a hormone that stimulates the transfer of calcium ions from blood to bone, where the calcium ions can be used to generate bone tissue. Calcitonin acts to decrease blood calcium levels.

Abnormal thyroid activity can be detrimental to the body's metabolism. Overproduction of the thyroid hormones is called hyperthyroidism (HIE-puhr-THIE-royd-iz-uhm). Symptoms of hyperthyroidism include overactivity; weight loss; and high blood pressure, heart rate, and body temperature. Hyperthyroidism can be treated with medication or by surgical removal of part of the thyroid gland.

Thyroid-hormone deficiency is known as *hypothyroidism* (HIE-poh-THIE-royd-iz-uhm). Symptoms of hypothyroidism include growth retardation, lethargy, weight gain, and low heart rate and body temperature. Hypothydroidism can also cause cretinism (KREET-uhn-IZ-uhm), a form of mental retardation, if the hypothyroidism occurs during fetal and childhood development. If hypothyroidism is caused by iodine deficiency, then goiter (GOY-tuhr), or swelling of the thyroid gland, results. Goiters resulting from iodine deficiency are now rare in the United States because iodine is added to commercially available table salt. Hypothyroidism can be treated with supplementary thyroxine.

# ADRENAL GLANDS

One **adrenal gland** (uh-DREE-nuhl gland) is located above each kidney, as shown in Figure 50-6. Each adrenal gland has an inner core, the medulla, and an outer layer, the cortex. The medulla and cortex function as separate endocrine glands. Secretion of hormones in the medulla is controlled by the nervous system, whereas hormones in the anterior pituitary regulate secretion of hormones in the cortex.

## Adrenal Medulla

The adrenal medulla produces two amino acid–based hormones: **epinephrine** (EP-uh-NEF-rin) and **norepinephrine** (NAWR-EP-uh-NEF-rin), also known as adrenaline (uh-DREN-uh-lin) and noradrenaline (NOR-uh-DREN-uh-lin), respectively. These hormones orchestrate the nervous system's reaction to stress and its "fight-or-flight" response to danger. When a person is stressed, the medulla secretes epinephrine and norepinephrine into the bloodstream. These hormones increase heart rate, blood pressure, blood glucose level, and blood flow to the heart and lungs. Epinephrine and norepinephrine also stimulate enlargement of the bronchial tubes and dilation of the pupils.

## Adrenal Cortex

The adrenal cortex responds to adrenocorticotropic (uh-DRE-noh-KOHR-ti-koh-TROH-pik) hormone (ACTH), which is secreted by the anterior pituitary. Stress causes the hypothalamus to secrete ACTH-releasing hormone. ACTH then stimulates the adrenal cortex to produce the steroid hormone cortisol (KOHRT-uh-SAWL) and aldosterone. **Cortisol** promotes the production of glucose from proteins making usable energy available to cells. Aldosterone (al-DAHS-tuh-ROHN), helps raise blood pressure and volume by stimulating salt and water retention by the kidneys.

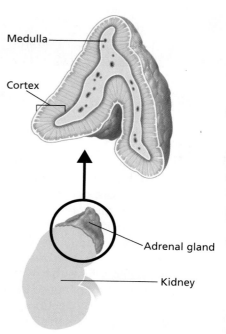

**FIGURE 50-6**

The adrenal glands, located above each kidney, consist of an inner medulla and an outer cortex. Epinephrine and norepinephrine are produced in the medulla. Cortisol and aldosterone are produced in the cortex.

# GONADS

**Gonads**—the ovaries in females and the testes in males—are gamete-producing organs that also produce a group of steroid sex hormones. Sex hormones regulate body changes that begin at puberty. **Puberty** (PYOO-buhr-tee) is the adolescent stage during which the sex organs mature and secondary sex characteristics, such as facial hair, appear. During puberty in males, sperm production begins, the voice deepens, the chest broadens, and hair grows on the body and face. In females, the menstrual cycle begins, the breasts grow, and the hips widen.

When secreted by the anterior pituitary, the hormones **luteinizing** (LOO-tee-in-IZE-ing) **hormone (LH)** and **follicle-stimulating** (FOL-uh-kuhl STIM-yoo-LAYT-ing) **hormone (FSH)** stimulate secretion of sex hormones from the gonads. In females, LH and FSH stimulate secretion of **estrogen** (ES-truh-jen) and **progesterone** (proh-JES-tuh-ROHN) from the ovaries. In preparation for a possible pregnancy, these sex hormones cause the monthly release of an egg by an ovary and buildup of the uterine lining. Estrogen also regulates female secondary sex characteristics. In males, LH stimulates the testes to secrete a group of sex hormones called **androgens** (AN-druh-jenz). **Testosterone** (tes-TAHS-tuh-rohn) is an androgen that regulates male secondary sex characteristics. Along with FSH, testosterone also stimulates sperm production.

# EARLY ONSET OF PUBERTY IN GIRLS

Until a few decades ago, girls began puberty at about age 11 and completed puberty by about age 13. Now, it is more common to see puberty in girls beginning at about 9 and 10 years of age and sometimes as early as 6 or 7 years of age. Researchers are investigating why puberty starts earlier in girls than it used to and what type of implications this may have for a person's health.

### What is Causing the Early Onset of Puberty?

Genetics is one of several factors that influence the onset of puberty in girls. One study showed that girls with two copies of a specific version of a gene that breaks down testosterone began puberty earlier than girls with a different version of the gene.

Some researchers hypothesize that the increasing prevalence of obesity in young girls could be one factor triggering puberty. These researchers found that girls who were overweight or obese started puberty earlier than girls who were not.

Other researchers hypothesize that pollutants could be triggering the onset of early puberty. For example, there are pollutants called *hormone mimics* that behave like natural hormones. Some pollutants, called *hormone disrupters*, prevent natural hormones from functioning normally.

Most hormone disrupters interfere with the sex hormones. Such hormone disrupters prevent normal production of testosterone in males or increase the chances of sexual abnormality in females. Examples of hormone disrupters include phthalate *(THAH-late)* esters (found in plastic toys, vinyl flooring, and cosmetics), and bisphenol A and polybrominated biphenyls (used to make plastic food and drink containers).

### Does Early Puberty Affect a Person's Health?

Researchers have studied the effect of early puberty on a person's health. One study investigated 1,811 sets of female twins in which one or both of the twins developed breast cancer as adults. The twin who entered puberty first was five times more likely to develop breast cancer first. The link was stronger if menstruation started earlier than average. As a result of these and other findings, many scientists and physicians are calling for more research to determine the causes of early puberty.

## REVIEW

1. What are three hypotheses for the early onset of puberty?
2. **Applying Information** If humans are increasingly exposed to pollutants that act as hormone mimics or hormone disrupters, what are some possible results?
3. **Supporting Reasoned Opinions** Do you think government research agencies should fund research investigating the effects of hormone mimics and hormone disrupters on the onset of puberty? Explain.

*Many factors influence the age at which a girl begins puberty. Researchers are studying why girls today are starting puberty earlier than girls 30 years ago and what effect this may have on their health.*

internet connect

www.scilinks.org
**Topic: Hormones and Body Fat**
**Keyword: HM60759**

SCLINKS. Maintained by the National Science Teachers Association

# PANCREAS

The pancreas mostly contains exocrine cells, but specialized cells in the pancreas called the *islets of Langerhans* (LANG-uhr-HANZ) function as an endocrine gland. Shown in Figure 50-7, these endocrine cells secrete two amino acid–based hormones that regulate the level of sugar in the blood. **Insulin** (IN-suh-lin) lowers the blood sugar level by stimulating body cells, especially muscles, to store glucose or use it for energy. In contrast, glucagon (GLOO-kuh-gahn) stimulates release of glucose into the bloodstream by liver cells.

Insulin deficiency causes **diabetes mellitus** (die-uh-BEET-eez muh-LIET-uhs), a condition in which cells are unable to obtain glucose, resulting in abnormally high blood glucose concentrations. In type I diabetes the immune system attacks the insulin-producing islet cells. The cells die. Type I generally is treated with daily injections of insulin into the blood and sometimes with islet cell transplant. Type II diabetes usually occurs after age 40, and it is more common than type I. Type II is caused by insufficient insulin or less responsive target cell receptors. Although type II is hereditary, its onset correlates with obesity and an inactive lifestyle. Type II diabetes can often be controlled through exercise and diet. In diabetes, excess glucose inhibits water reabsorption by the kidneys, producing large amounts of urine. Dehydration and kidney damage can result. Lack of insulin can lead to acid-base and electrolyte imbalances. These changes may result in nausea, rapid breathing, heart irregularities, depression of the nervous system, coma, or even death.

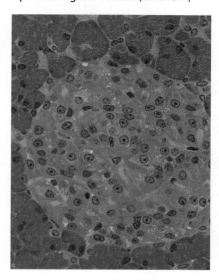

**FIGURE 50-7**

A cross section of pancreatic tissue shows the islets of Langerhans (lightly colored region). These endocrine cells are surrounded by exocrine cells that produce digestive fluids. (LM 315×)

**TABLE 50-2** *Summary of Major Endocrine Glands and Their Functions*

| Glands | Hormone | Function |
|---|---|---|
| Adrenal cortex | aldosterone<br>cortisol | promotes salt and water retention<br>promotes production of glucose from proteins |
| Adrenal medulla | epinephrine, norepinephrine | initiate body's response to stress and the "fight-or-flight" response to danger |
| Ovaries | estrogen<br>progesterone | regulates female secondary sex characteristics<br>maintains growth of uterine lining |
| Pancreas (islets of Langerhans) | glucagon<br>insulin | stimulates release of glucose<br>stimulates absorption of glucose by cells |
| Parathyroid glands | parathyroid hormone | increases blood calcium concentration |
| Pineal gland | melatonin | regulates sleep patterns |
| Pituitary gland | see Table 50-1 | see Table 50-1 |
| Testes | androgens (testosterone) | regulate male secondary sex characteristics; stimulate sperm production |
| Thymus gland | thymosin | stimulates T-cell maturation |
| Thyroid gland | thyroxine, triiodothyronine<br>calcitonin | regulate metabolism and development<br>decreases blood calcium concentration |

Excessive insulin causes *hypoglycemia* (HIE-poh-glie-SEE-mee-uh), a disorder in which glucose is stored, rather than being properly delivered to body cells. This leads to a lowered blood glucose concentration and subsequent release of glucagon and epinephrine. Symptoms of hypoglycemia include lethargy, dizziness, nervousness, overactivity, and in extreme cases, unconsciousness and death.

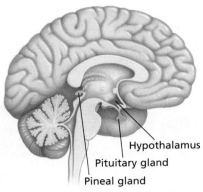

**FIGURE 50-8**

The pineal gland, located near the base of the brain, secretes the hormone melatonin at night.

# OTHER ENDOCRINE GLANDS

There are several other glands in the endocrine system, including the thymus gland, the pineal gland, and the parathyroid glands. There are also specialized endocrine cells in the brain, stomach, small intestine, liver, and other organs. The major endocrine glands and their functions are listed in Table 50-2.

## Thymus Gland

The thymus (THIE-muhs) gland, located beneath the sternum and between the lungs, plays a role in the development of the immune system. The thymus gland secretes *thymosin* (THIE-moh-sin), an amino acid–based hormone that stimulates maturation of T cells, which help defend the body from pathogens.

## Pineal Gland

The pineal (PIEN-ee-uhl) gland is located near the base of the brain, as shown in Figure 50-8. It secretes the hormone melatonin. **Melatonin** (mel-uh-TOH-nin) concentrations increase sharply at night and decrease dramatically during the day. This cyclic release of melatonin suggests that it helps regulate sleep patterns.

## Parathyroid Glands

As Figure 50-9 shows, the four parathyroid glands are embedded in the back of the thyroid gland, two in each lobe. These glands secrete *parathyroid hormone,* which stimulates the transfer of calcium ions from the bones to the blood. Thus, parathyroid hormone has the opposite effect of calcitonin. A proper balance of calcium ions is necessary for cell division, muscle contraction, blood clotting, and neural signaling.

**FIGURE 50-9**

As shown from this back view of the head, the four parathyroid glands are located on the posterior side of the thyroid gland. They secrete a hormone that regulates the concentration of calcium ions in the blood.

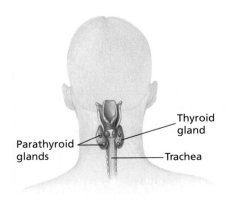

## Digestive Cells

Endocrine cells within the walls of some digestive organs also secrete a variety of hormones that control digestive processes. For example, when food is eaten, endocrine cells in the stomach lining secrete *gastrin* (GAS-trin), a hormone that stimulates other stomach cells to release digestive enzymes and hydrochloric acid. Endocrine cells of the small intestine release *secretin* (si-KREE-tin), a hormone that stimulates the release of various digestive fluids from the pancreas.

# FEEDBACK MECHANISMS

Homeostasis is defined as a stable internal environment. The endocrine system plays an important role in the maintenance of homeostasis because hormones regulate the activities of cells, tissues, and organs throughout the body. To maintain homeostasis, feedback mechanisms control hormone secretion. A feedback mechanism is one in which the last step in a series of events controls the first. Feedback mechanisms can be negative or positive. Most hormone systems use negative feedback.

## Negative Feedback

In **negative feedback,** the final step in a series of events inhibits the initial signal in the series. An example of negative feedback in regulating the levels of thyroid hormones is shown in Figure 50-10. When the hypothalamus detects low levels of thyroid hormones, it secretes a hormone called thyrotropin releasing hormone (TRH) to the anterior pituitary. TRH stimulates the anterior pituitary to secrete thyroid-stimulating hormone (TSH) into the bloodstream. TSH stimulates the thyroid gland to secrete thyroid hormones. When the thyroid hormone levels are high, two major negative feedback loops operate, as shown by the negative signs in Figure 50-10. In one loop, the thyroid hormones act on the hypothalamus to inhibit the release of TRH. In the second loop, the thyroid hormones act on the anterior pituitary to inhibit the release of TSH. The result is that the level of thyroid hormones in the blood decreases. In turn, this decrease causes the amount of negative feedback inhibition to decline. The interplay of these mechanisms helps to keep the concentration of thyroid hormones relatively stable.

**FIGURE 50-10**

The thyroid hormones regulate cellular metabolic rates through several negative feedback mechanisms. Two are shown. High concentrations of thyroid hormones inhibit the hypothalamus from releasing TRH and the anterior pituitary from releasing TSH.

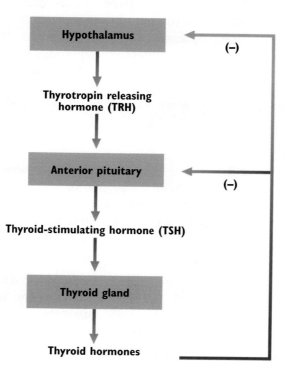

FIGURE 50-11

In negative feedback, a secondary substance (A) inhibits production of the initial stimulating substance (B). In positive feedback, a secondary substance (A) stimulates production of the initial stimulating substance (B).

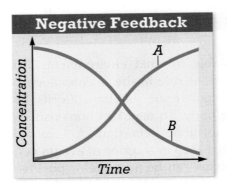

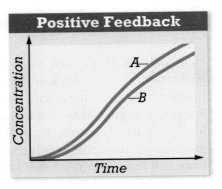

## Positive Feedback

When hormones are regulated by **positive feedback,** release of an initial hormone stimulates release or production of other hormones or substances, which stimulate further release of the initial hormone. For example, increased estrogen concentrations stimulate a surge in luteinizing hormone secretion prior to ovulation. Figure 50-11 illustrates the difference between negative and positive feedback systems.

## Antagonistic Hormones

A number of hormones work together in pairs to regulate the levels of critical substances. These hormones are referred to as *antagonistic hormones* because their actions have opposite effects.

Glucagon and insulin are examples of antagonistic hormones. They maintain a specific level of blood glucose in the blood. When the level of glucose in the blood is high, such as after eating a meal, insulin triggers the transfer of glucose from the blood into the body cells for storage or immediate use. In contrast, when the level of glucose in the blood is low, such as between meals, glucagon promotes the release of glucose into the blood from storage sites in the liver and elsewhere. Together, insulin and glucagon ensure that the level of glucose in the blood is maintained. Calcitonin and parathyroid hormone are other examples of antagonistic hormones.

### Word Roots and Origins

*antagonistic*

from the Greek *anti,* meaning "against" and *agonizesthai,* meaning "to contend for a prize"

---

## SECTION 2 REVIEW

1. How do the hypothalamus and the pituitary gland interact to control the release of some of the hormones in the endocrine system?

2. List six major endocrine glands and the function of these glands.

3. How do feedback mechanisms help maintain homeostasis?

4. How do negative feedback mechanisms differ from positive feedback mechanisms?

5. Compare the effects of glucagon and insulin on blood glucose levels.

**CRITICAL THINKING**

6. **Relating Concepts** A classmate states that hormones from the adrenal medulla, but not from the adrenal cortex, are secreted in response to stress. Do you agree? Explain.

7. **Applying Information** Why might overactive parathyroid glands cause bone problems?

8. **Evaluating Models** Dietary iodine is needed for the body to make thyroid hormones. How would lack of dietary iodine affect the negative feedback of the thyroid hormones?

# CHAPTER HIGHLIGHTS

## SECTION 1  Hormones

- Hormones are chemical messengers secreted by cells that act to regulate the activity of other cells.

- Hormones have many functions, including regulation of growth; maintenance of homeostasis; and regulation of energy production, use, and storage.

- Ductless glands called endocrine glands make most of the body's hormones. Specialized cells in the brain, stomach, and other organs also make and release hormones. Exocrine glands secrete nonhormonal chemicals into specific body locations.

- Amino acid–based hormones bind to cell-membrane receptors of their target cells, activating a second messenger that then activates or deactivates enzymes in a cascade fashion.

- Steroid and thyroid hormones bind to receptors inside the cell. The hormone-receptor complex binds to DNA in the nucleus and turns genes either on or off.

- Similar to hormones, neuropeptides and prostaglandins act on nearby cells to regulate cellular activities.

### Vocabulary

| | | | |
|---|---|---|---|
| hormone (p. 1031) | exocrine gland (p. 1031) | steroid hormone (p. 1031) | second messenger (p. 1032) |
| endocrine gland (p. 1031) | amino acid–based | target cell (p. 1032) | neuropeptide (p. 1033) |
| endocrine system (p. 1031) | hormone (p. 1031) | receptor (p. 1032) | prostaglandin (p. 1033) |

## SECTION 2  Endocrine Glands

- The hypothalamus and pituitary gland serve as the major control centers for the release of many hormones.

- The thyroid gland secretes thyroid hormones that regulate metabolism and development and calcitonin that helps regulate blood calcium levels.

- The adrenal glands secrete epinephrine, norepinephrine, cortisol, aldosterone, and other hormones that help regulate metabolism, the body's responses to stress and danger, and water balance.

- The gonads secrete estrogen and progesterone in females and androgens, including testosterone, in males. These hormones regulate reproductive functions.

- The islets of Langerhans of the pancreas secrete glucagon and insulin, which regulate blood glucose levels.

- Other endocrine glands include the thymus gland, the pineal gland, the parathyroid glands, and endocrine cells of the digestive system.

- Feedback mechanisms help maintain homeostasis.

- In negative feedback, the final product in a series inhibits the first step. Many hormones use negative feedback systems because they prevent excess accumulation of a hormone product.

- In positive feedback, the final product in a series stimulates the first step.

- Antagonistic hormones, such as glucagon and insulin, work together to regulate the levels of critical substances.

### Vocabulary

| | | | |
|---|---|---|---|
| hypothalamus (p. 1034) | cortisol (p. 1037) | estrogen (p. 1037) | melatonin (p. 1040) |
| pituitary gland (p. 1034) | gonad (p. 1037) | progesterone (p. 1037) | negative feedback (p. 1041) |
| thyroid gland (p. 1036) | puberty (p. 1037) | androgen (p. 1037) | positive feedback (p. 1042) |
| adrenal gland (p. 1036) | luteinizing hormone (p. 1037) | testosterone (p. 1037) | |
| epinephrine (p. 1037) | follicle-stimulating | insulin (p. 1039) | |
| norepinephrine (p. 1037) | hormone (p. 1037) | diabetes mellitus (p. 1039) | |

# CHAPTER REVIEW

## USING VOCABULARY

1. For each set of terms, choose the one that does not belong, and then explain why it does not belong.
   a. *insulin, prostaglandin, glucagon*
   b. *oxytocin, epinephrine, antidiuretic hormone*
   c. *aldosterone, cortisol, glucagon*

2. Explain the relationship between the following pairs of terms:
   a. *target cells* and *receptors*
   b. *pituitary gland* and *thyroid gland*
   c. *exocrine gland* and *endocrine gland*

3. Use the following terms in the same sentence: *estrogen, progesterone,* and *testosterone.*

4. **Word Roots and Origins** In Greek, the word *hormon* means "to excite." Why was the name *hormones* chosen for these molecules?

## UNDERSTANDING KEY CONCEPTS

5. **Identify** four major functions of hormones.

6. **Differentiate** how endocrine glands differ from exocrine glands.

7. **Sequence** the steps that occur when most amino acid–based hormones act on their target cells.

8. **Sequence** the steps that occur when a steroid or thyroid hormone acts on its target cell.

9. **Describe** why neuropeptides and prostaglandins are hormones.

10. **Describe** two ways in which the endocrine system and the nervous system are similar.

11. **Discuss** how the hypothalamus and the pituitary gland interact to control the release of many hormones.

12. **Summarize** the major functions of the thyroid hormones.

13. **Name** the two hormones in the adrenal medulla that are released when a person experiences stress.

14. **State** the two hormones that stimulate secretion of the sex hormones from the gonads.

15. **Summarize** the nonhereditary factors that are associated with the onset of type II diabetes.

16. **Describe** how the hormone gastrin helps in the process of digestion.

17. **Summarize** the role of feedback mechanisms in maintaining homeostasis.

18. **Explain** why positive feedback is not an efficient way to control hormone levels.

19. **Explain** how negative feedback regulates the level of thyroid hormones.

20. **Describe** how insulin and glucagon work together as antagonistic hormones to control the level of glucose in the blood.

21. **CONCEPT MAPPING** Use the following terms to create a concept map that describes the endocrine system: *hypothalamus, pituitary gland, thyroid gland, hormones, adrenal glands, pancreas,* and *target cell.*

## CRITICAL THINKING

22. **Making Comparisons** Why might damage to the pituitary gland be considered far more serious than damage to one of the other endocrine glands?

23. **Inferring Relationships** Describe the importance of "fit" between a receptor protein and a hormone.

24. **Analyzing Graphics** Identify and describe the type of feedback mechanism operating in the diagram shown below.

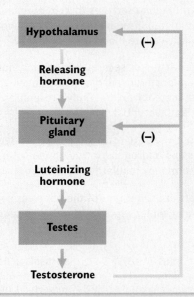

# Standardized Test Preparation

**DIRECTIONS:** Choose the letter of the answer choice that best answers the question.

1. What are the chemical messengers of the endocrine system called?
   - **A.** neurons
   - **B.** hormones
   - **C.** blood cells
   - **D.** carbohydrates

2. $X$ and $Y$ are hormones. $X$ stimulates the secretion of Y, which exerts negative feedback on the cells that secrete $X$. Suppose the level of Y decreases. What should happen immediately afterwards?
   - **F.** Less $X$ is secreted.
   - **G.** More $X$ is secreted.
   - **H.** Secretion of $Y$ stops.
   - **J.** Secretion of $X$ stops.

3. Endocrine glands
   - **A.** function only after puberty.
   - **B.** function only before puberty.
   - **C.** release products through ducts.
   - **D.** release products into the bloodstream.

**INTERPRETING GRAPHICS:** Study the figure below to answer the following questions.

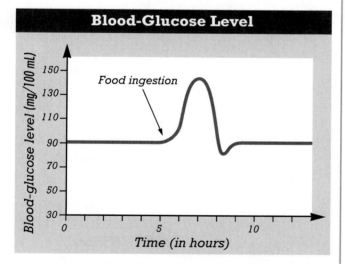

4. What happens after food is eaten?
   - **F.** Blood glucose levels increase.
   - **G.** Blood glucose levels decrease.
   - **H.** Blood glucose levels remain the same.
   - **J.** Blood glucose levels decrease and then increase.

5. Which hormones are primarily responsible for the changes in blood glucose levels about 2 hours after food is eaten?
   - **A.** insulin
   - **B.** estrogen and progesterone
   - **C.** epinephrine and norepinephrine
   - **D.** aldosterone and parathyroid hormones

**DIRECTIONS:** Complete the following analogy:

6. neurotransmitters : nervous system :: hormones :
   - **F.** feedback system
   - **G.** endocrine system
   - **H.** circulatory system
   - **J.** respiratory system

**INTERPRETING GRAPHICS:** The table below gives the relative levels of thyroid-stimulating hormone (TSH) during a 12 hour period. Use the table below to answer the question that follows.

| Time (hours) | Blood level of thyroid-stimulating hormone |
|---|---|
| 0 | normal |
| 4 | high |
| 8 | normal |
| 12 | low |

7. Thyroid-stimulating hormone (TSH) is a hormone that stimulates the release of the thyroid hormones from the thyroid gland. At what time would you expect thyroid hormone levels to be at their lowest?
   - **A.** 0 hours
   - **B.** 4 hours
   - **C.** 8 hours
   - **D.** 12 hours

## SHORT RESPONSE

The pancreas is an organ that carries out many functions related to digestion.

Explain why the pancreas is considered to be both an exocrine gland and an endocrine gland.

## EXTENDED RESPONSE

The endocrine system is involved in maintaining homeostasis. Many of the activities regulated by the endocrine system require maintaining a critical substance at levels that do not vary much.

*Part A* Explain how pairs of hormones are involved in regulating levels of critical substances.

*Part B* Describe a specific example of a pair of hormones that work together to maintain the level of a critical substance.

**Test TIP** Sometimes, only one part of a graph or table is needed to answer a question. In such cases, focus only on that information to answer the question.

# Observing the Effects of Thyroxine on Frog Metamorphosis

## OBJECTIVES

- Observe the effects of the hormone thyroxine on the development of tadpoles.

## PROCESS SKILLS

- observing
- measuring
- comparing and contrasting
- organizing data
- inferring

## MATERIALS

- safety goggles
- protective gloves
- lab apron
- glass-marking pencil
- six 600 mL beakers
- pond water
- 10 mL graduated cylinder
- 0.01% thyroxine solution
- strained spinach
- graph paper marked in 1 mm squares
- Petri dish
- small fish net
- 9 tadpoles with budding hind legs
- 3 pencils in different colors

## Background

1. What is a hormone?
2. What is metamorphosis?
3. Describe the stages of frog development.
4. What are the effects of thyroxine in humans?
5. What effects do you predict the hormone thyroxine will have on tadpole growth and development?

## PART A  Setting Up the Experiment

1. In your lab report, make a data table similar to the one shown on the facing page.
2. Use a glass-marking pencil to label three beakers "A" "B" and "C". Also, write your initials on the beakers.

3. Add 500 mL of pond water to each beaker.
4. **CAUTION  Put on a lab apron and safety goggles. If you get thyroxine on your skin or clothing, rinse with water while calling to your teacher. If you get thyroxine in your eyes, immediately flush them with water at the eyewash station while calling to your teacher.**
5. Use a graduated cylinder to measure 10 mL of thyroxine solution. Add the 10 mL of solution to beaker A. Measure and add 5 mL of thyroxine solution to beaker B.
6. Add equal amounts (about 1 mL) of strained spinach to beakers A, B, and C.
7. Place a sheet of graph paper, ruled side up, under a Petri dish.
8. **CAUTION  You will be working with live animals. Handle them with care, and follow directions carefully.** Catch a tadpole with a fish net, and place the tadpole in the Petri dish. Measure the tadpole's total length, tail length, and body length in millimeters by counting the number of squares that it covers on the graph paper. Then, place the tadpole in beaker A.

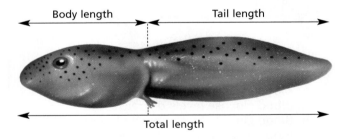

Body length | Tail length

Total length

9. Repeat step 8 with two more tadpoles. Average the total length, tail length, and body length of the three tadpoles that you placed in beaker A. In your data table, record the average measurements under the column labeled "Beaker A."

10. Repeat step 8 with three more tadpoles, this time placing the tadpoles in beaker B. Average the total length, tail length, and body length of the three tadpoles. Record your average measurements in your data table under "Beaker B."

11. Repeat step 8 with three more tadpoles. Place these three tadpoles in beaker C. Average the total length, tail length, and body length of the three tadpoles. Record your average measurements in your data table under "Beaker C." You should have measured a total of nine tadpoles and placed three in each beaker.

12. Clean up your materials, and wash your hands before leaving the lab.

## PART B Observing the Effects of Thyroxine on Tadpoles

13. Feed each beaker of tadpoles 1 mL of spinach every other day. Be careful not to overfeed the tadpoles. Change the water in the beakers every 4 days, adding thyroxine solution in the original amounts to beakers A and B. Label the beakers, and do not mix up the tadpoles during the water changes.

14. Measure the tadpoles once a week for 3 weeks, and average the length of the tadpoles in each beaker. Record the average lengths in your data table.

15. Calculate the average growth per week for each set of three tadpoles. For example, the average growth in total length during the second week is equal to the average total length at the end of week 2 minus the average total length at the end of week 1. Record your values in the appropriate spaces of your data table.

16. Graph your data using a different colored pencil for the tadpoles in each beaker. Label the horizontal axis "Time in weeks," and label the vertical axis "Length in centimeters." You should have three graphs. Each graph should include the changes in average total length, average tail length, and average body length for one group of tadpoles.

17. Clean up your materials, and wash your hands before leaving the lab.

## Analysis and Conclusions

1. Did this investigation include a control group? If so, describe it. If not, suggest a possible control that you could have used.

2. Why are three tadpoles used for each beaker rather than just one?

3. According to the data that you collected in this investigation, what is the effect of thyroxine on tadpole metamorphosis?

4. Which concentration of thyroxine solution caused the greatest visible change in the tadpoles?

5. How do average body length and tail length change during metamorphosis?

## Further Inquiry

Iodine, typically in the form of iodide, is needed to make thyroxine. Design—but do not conduct—an experiment that shows the effect of adding iodine to water that contains tadpoles. **CAUTION: Iodine is a highly poisonous substance.**

### MEASUREMENT OF TADPOLE GROWTH

|  | Beaker A | | | Beaker B | | | Beaker C | | |
|---|---|---|---|---|---|---|---|---|---|
|  | Average total length | Average tail length | Average body length | Average total length | Average tail length | Average body length | Average total length | Average tail length | Average body length |
| Initial |  |  |  |  |  |  |  |  |  |
| End of week 1 |  |  |  |  |  |  |  |  |  |
| End of week 2 |  |  |  |  |  |  |  |  |  |
| End of week 3 |  |  |  |  |  |  |  |  |  |

# REPRODUCTIVE SYSTEM

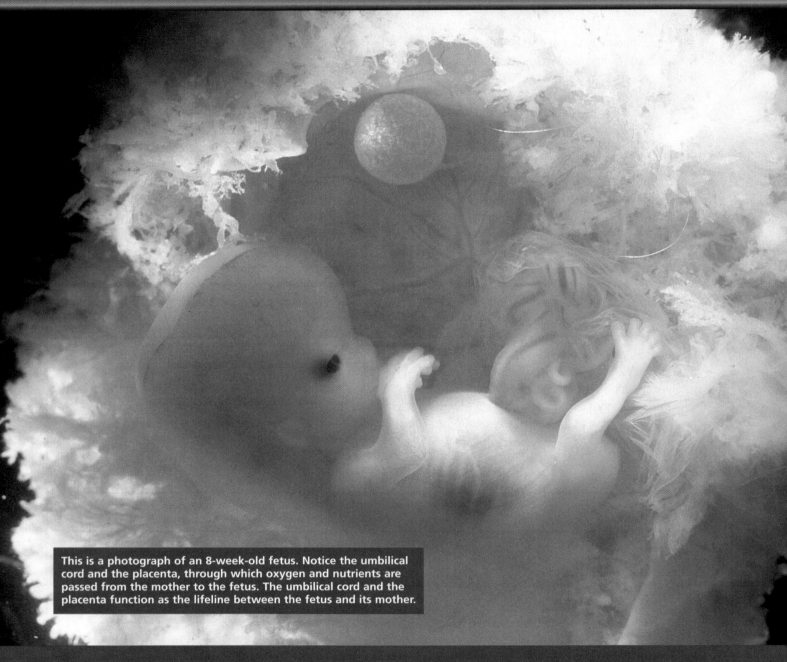

This is a photograph of an 8-week-old fetus. Notice the umbilical cord and the placenta, through which oxygen and nutrients are passed from the mother to the fetus. The umbilical cord and the placenta function as the lifeline between the fetus and its mother.

**SECTION 1** *Male Reproductive System*

**SECTION 2** *Female Reproductive System*

**SECTION 3** *Gestation*

# MALE REPRODUCTIVE SYSTEM

*The gonads—testes and ovaries—are endocrine glands that secrete sex hormones. However, the primary function of the gonads is not to produce hormones but to produce and store gametes—sperm and eggs. Other organs in the male reproductive system prepare sperm for the possible fertilization of an egg.*

### OBJECTIVES

- **Identify** the major structures of the male reproductive system.
- **Describe** the function of each structure of the male reproductive system.
- **Relate** the structure of a human sperm cell to its function.
- **Trace** the path that sperm follow in leaving the body.

### VOCABULARY

testis
seminiferous tubule
scrotum
epididymis
vas deferens
seminal vesicle
prostate gland
bulbourethral gland
semen
penis
ejaculation

## MALE REPRODUCTIVE STRUCTURES

Sexual reproduction involves the formation of a diploid zygote from two haploid gametes through fertilization. The roles of a male in sexual reproduction are to produce sperm cells and to deliver the sperm cells to the female reproductive system to fertilize an egg cell.

The male reproductive system contains two egg-shaped testes. The **testes** (TES-TEEZ) (singular, *testis*) are the gamete-producing organs of the male reproductive system. Each testis, which is about 4 cm (1.5 in.) long and 2.5 cm (1 in.) in diameter, has about 250 compartments. As shown in Figure 51-1, these compartments contain many tightly coiled tubules, called **seminiferous** (SEM-uh-NIF-uhr-uhs) **tubules.** Each seminiferous tubule is approximately 80 cm (32 in.) long. If all of the tubules in both testes were stretched out end to end, they would extend about 500 m (1,640 ft). Sperm form through meiosis in the specialized lining of this extensive network of tubules.

The testes develop within the abdominal cavity. Before a male is born, the testes leave this cavity and descend into an external sac called the **scrotum** (SKROHT-uhm). The temperature within the scrotum is about 2°C to 3°C cooler than the temperature inside the abdomen. Normal body temperature, 37°C, is too high to allow sperm to complete development. The slightly cooler temperature of the scrotum is necessary for the development of normal sperm.

**FIGURE 51-1**

Sperm are formed continuously within the seminiferous tubules, which make up the bulk of each testis. Before leaving the body, sperm mature and are stored in each epididymis.

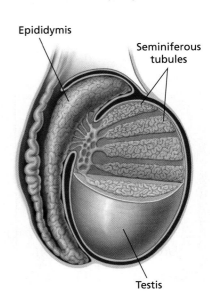

Epididymis

Seminiferous tubules

Testis

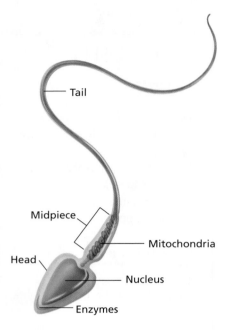

- Tail

- Midpiece
    - Mitochondria
- Head
    - Nucleus
    - Enzymes

**FIGURE 51-2**

A mature sperm is an elongated cell with three distinct parts (a head, a midpiece, and a tail), all of which are enclosed by a cell membrane.

# FORMATION OF SPERM

Males begin to produce sperm during puberty, the adolescent stage of development when changes in the body make reproduction possible. Two hormones released by the anterior pituitary regulate the functioning of the testes. Luteinizing hormone (LH) stimulates secretion of the sex hormone testosterone. Testosterone is the main androgen (male sex hormone) produced by the testes. Cells located between the seminiferous tubules secrete testosterone. Follicle-stimulating hormone (FSH), along with testosterone, stimulates sperm production in the seminiferous tubules. A male will continue to produce sperm as long as his testosterone level is high enough—usually for most of his life.

The formation of gametes in humans involves the process of meiosis. Meiosis results in a reduction of the number of chromosomes from the diploid ($2n$) number to the haploid ($1n$) number. As the cells that produce sperm within the testes undergo meiosis, their chromosome number drops from 46 to 23. Four sperm cells result from each cell that begins meiosis. These immature sperm then undergo significant changes that prepare the sperm for passage through the female reproductive system.

The structure of a mature sperm is shown in Figure 51-2. Notice that a mature sperm consists of three regions—a head, a midpiece, and a tail, or flagellum. The tip of the head region contains enzymes. During fertilization, these enzymes help the sperm penetrate the protective layers that surround an egg cell. Also located in the head region are the 23 chromosomes that will be delivered to the egg. The midpiece is packed with mitochondria. These mitochondria supply the energy that is required for sperm to reach an egg. The tail consists of a single, powerful flagellum that propels the sperm.

## Path of Sperm Through the Male Body

Mature sperm move through and past several other male reproductive structures, some of which further prepare the sperm for a possible journey through the female reproductive system. The path taken by sperm as they exit the body is shown in Figure 51-3.

Sperm move from the seminiferous tubules in the testes to the **epididymis** (EP-uh-DID-i-mis), a long, coiled tubule that is closely attached to each testis. Within each epididymis, a sperm matures and gains the ability to swim as its flagellum completes development. Although most sperm remain stored in each epididymis, some leave the epididymis and pass through the **vas deferens** (vas DEF-uh-RENZ), a duct that extends from the epididymis. Smooth muscles that line each vas deferens contract to help move sperm along as they exit the body. Each vas deferens enters the abdominal cavity, where it loops around the urinary bladder and merges with the urethra. The urethra is the duct through which urine exits the urinary bladder. Thus, in a male, both urine and sperm exit the body through the urethra, but not at the same time.

In the urethra, sperm mix with fluids that are secreted by three exocrine glands—the seminal vesicles, the prostate gland, and the bulbourethral (buhl-boh-yoo-REE-thruhl) glands. Ducts that extend from these glands connect with the urethra. The glands secrete fluids that nourish and protect the sperm as they move through the female reproductive system. The **seminal vesicles,** which lie between the bladder and the rectum, produce a fluid rich in sugars that sperm use for energy. The **prostate** (PRAHS-tayt) **gland,** which is located just below the bladder, secretes an alkaline fluid that neutralizes the acids in the female reproductive system. Before sperm leave the body, the **bulbourethral glands** secrete an alkaline fluid that neutralizes traces of acidic urine in the urethra. Together, sperm and these secretions form a fluid called **semen** (SEE-muhn). To help sperm move through the female reproductive system, semen also contains prostaglandins that stimulate contractions of smooth muscles that line the female reproductive tract.

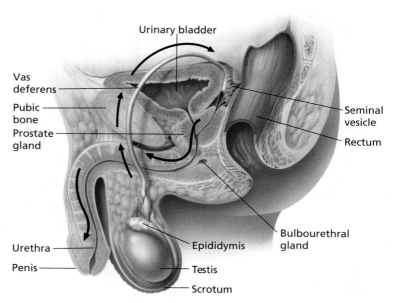

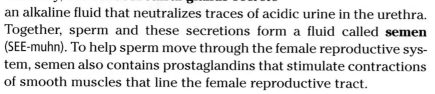

**FIGURE 51-3**

The male reproductive system consists of several internal and external structures. Arrows indicate the path taken by sperm as they leave the body.

## Delivery of Sperm

The urethra passes through the **penis,** the organ that deposits sperm in the female reproductive system. When a male becomes sexually aroused, the spongy tissue in the penis, which is shown in Figure 51-4, fills with blood. This causes the penis to become erect, enabling it to deposit sperm. Semen is forcefully expelled from the penis by contractions of the smooth muscles that line the urethra. This process is called **ejaculation** (ee-JAK-yoo-LAY-shun). Each ejaculation expels 3 to 4 mL (0.10 to 0.14 fl oz) of semen. Sperm make up only 10 percent of this volume. Although a single ejaculation can expel 300 million to 400 million sperm, very few of these sperm reach the site of fertilization. Most sperm are killed by the acidic environment of the female reproductive tract.

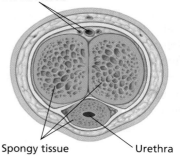

**FIGURE 51-4**

When the spaces in the spongy tissue of the penis fill with blood, the penis becomes erect.

## SECTION 1 REVIEW

1. Explain why the testes are found in the scrotum and not inside the male body.

2. Describe a mature sperm.

3. Describe the path that sperm take in exiting the body.

4. What is the function of the vas deferens?

5. Which structures in a male produce fluids that mix with sperm to form semen?

**CRITICAL THINKING**

6. **Applying Information** Why are so many sperm produced by the male reproductive system?

7. **Making Comparisons** In what way are sperm different from the body's other cells?

8. **Analyzing Concepts** The wearing of tight underwear has been linked to low sperm counts in some men. Explain how such clothing could lead to low sperm counts.

## OBJECTIVES

- **Identify** the major structures of the female reproductive system.
- **Describe** the function of each structure of the female reproductive system.
- **Describe** how eggs are produced.
- **Summarize** the stages of the ovarian cycle.

## VOCABULARY

ovary
fallopian tube
uterus
cervix
vagina
vulva
labium
ovum
ovarian cycle
menstrual cycle
follicular phase
follicle
ovulation
corpus luteum
luteal phase
menstruation
menopause

# FEMALE REPRODUCTIVE SYSTEM

*Like the testes, the female gonads—ovaries—are endocrine glands that produce gametes. The female reproductive system prepares the female gametes—eggs—for possible fertilization. It also contains structures that enable fertilization to occur and that house and nourish a developing baby.*

## FEMALE REPRODUCTIVE STRUCTURES

The female reproductive system contains two almond-shaped ovaries that are located in the lower abdomen. The **ovaries** (OH-vuh-reez) are the gamete-producing organs of the female reproductive system. Eggs mature near the surface of the ovaries, which are about 3.5 cm (1.4 in.) long and 2 cm (0.8 in.) in diameter. A mature egg is released into the abdominal cavity, where it is swept by cilia into the opening of a nearby **fallopian** (fuh-LOH-pee-uhn) **tube,** or uterine tube. Smooth muscles lining the fallopian tube contract rhythmically and move the mature egg down the tub. The fallopian tube leads to the uterus (YOOT-uhr-uhs), as shown in Figure 51-5. The **uterus** is a hollow, muscular organ about the size of a small fist. If an egg is fertilized, it will develop in the uterus.

**FIGURE 51-5**

Ovaries are the gamete-producing organs of the female reproductive system. The uterus nurtures the fetus during pregnancy.

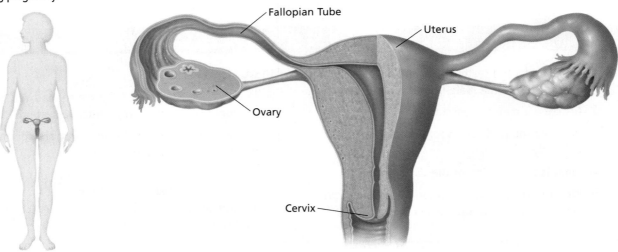

Fallopian Tube

Uterus

Ovary

Cervix

The lower entrance to the uterus is called the **cervix** (SUHR-VIKS). A sphincter muscle in the cervix controls the opening to the uterus. Leading from the cervix to the outside of the body is a muscular tube called the **vagina** (vuh-JIE-nuh), as shown in Figure 51-6. The vagina receives sperm from the penis; it is also the channel through which a baby passes during childbirth. The external structures of the female reproductive system are collectively called the **vulva** (VUHL-vuh). The vulva includes the **labia** (LAY-bee-uh) (singular, *labium*), folds of skin and mucous membranes that cover and protect the opening to the female reproductive system.

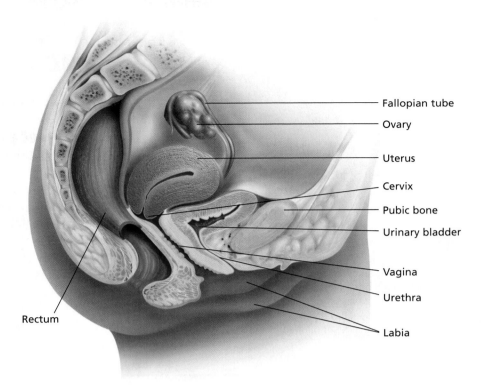

Rectum
Fallopian tube
Ovary
Uterus
Cervix
Pubic bone
Urinary bladder
Vagina
Urethra
Labia

**FIGURE 51-6**

The female reproductive system consists of several internal and external structures that enable fertilization and development.

# FORMATION OF EGGS

A female is born with more than 400,000 eggs in her ovaries. These eggs are immature and cannot be fertilized. Typically, a female will release 300 to 400 mature eggs during her lifetime, averaging one egg about every 28 days from puberty to about age 50. Thus, less than 1 percent of her eggs will mature.

Like sperm formation, egg formation occurs through meiosis. So, each mature egg cell has 23 chromosomes (the haploid number). Unlike sperm formation—in which four functional sperm result from each cell that begins meiosis—egg formation results in one functional egg from each cell that begins meiosis. All immature eggs begin meiosis but stall in prophase I until the female reaches puberty, when the sex hormones stimulate egg maturation. Then, every 28 days these hormones signal 10 to 20 immature eggs to resume meiosis. Generally, only one of these eggs completes meiosis I and is released from an ovary. Meiosis I produces two haploid cells. One cell receives most of the cytoplasm and can go on to become a mature egg. The second haploid cell, or first polar body, contains a very small amount of cytoplasm. In humans, the first polar body usually dies without dividing again. Meiosis II is not completed unless a sperm fertilizes the egg. If fertilized, the egg completes the final meiotic division by dividing into a mature egg and a second polar body. The mature egg, or **ovum** (OH vuhm), retains most of the cytoplasm, which provides nutrients for the egg through the early stages of development. The second polar body dies. An ovum, shown in Figure 51-7, is about 75,000 times larger than a sperm and is visible to the unaided eye.

**FIGURE 51-7**

This ovum is being approached by a single sperm. Notice the tremendous size difference between the egg and the sperm.

# PREPARATION FOR PREGNANCY

Each month, the female reproductive system prepares and releases an ovum in a series of events called the **ovarian cycle.** During this time, an egg matures and enters a fallopian tube, where it is able to fuse with a sperm. If the egg does not fuse with a sperm, the egg degenerates. The ovarian cycle has three stages: the follicular phase, ovulation, and the luteal phase. These stages are regulated by hormones secreted by the endocrine system. While the ovarian cycle occurs, the **menstrual** (MEN-struhl) **cycle** prepares the uterus for a possible pregnancy. For most women, the ovarian and menstral cycles last about 28 days. Figure 51-8 summarizes the stages of the ovarian and menstrual cycles.

## Follicular Phase

An immature egg cell completes its first meiotic division during the **follicular** (fuh-LIK-yoo-luhr) **phase.** This phase begins when the hypothalamus secretes a releasing hormone that stimulates the anterior pituitary to secrete follicle-stimulating hormone (FSH). FSH stimulates cell division in a **follicle,** a layer of cells that surrounds an immature egg. Follicle cells supply nutrients to the egg. They also secrete estrogen, which stimulates mitotic divisions of cells in the lining of the uterus, causing the lining to thicken. The follicular phase lasts approximately 14 days. During this time, the estrogen level in the blood continues to rise until it reaches a peak and the egg moves to the surface of the ovary. The elevated estrogen level acts as a positive feedback mechanism by stimulating the anterior pituitary to secrete luteinizing hormone (LH), which initiates the next stage of the menstrual cycle.

## Ovulation

The sharp rise in the LH level that occurs midway through the ovarian cycle causes the follicle to rupture and release its egg. The release of an egg from a ruptured follicle is called **ovulation** (AHV-yoo-LAY-shuhn). Following ovulation, an egg is swept into a fallopian tube, where it awaits fertilization as it travels through the tube toward the uterus. The egg has enough stored nutrients to survive about 24 hours.

## FIGURE 51-8

During the 28-day ovarian and menstrual cycles, an egg matures and is released by an ovary, and the uterus prepares for a possible pregnancy. The events of the menstrual cycle are regulated by hormones that are produced by the anterior pituitary and the ovaries.

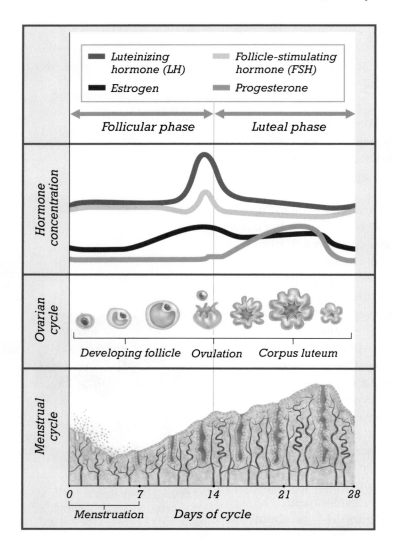

## Luteal Phase

The cells of the ruptured follicle grow larger and fill the cavity of the follicle, forming a new structure called a **corpus luteum** (KAWR-puhs LOOT-ee-uhm). Thus, this stage of the ovarian cycle is called the **luteal** (LOOT-ee-uhl) **phase.** The corpus luteum begins to secrete large amounts of progesterone and estrogen. Progesterone stimulates growth of blood vessels and storage of fluids and nutrients in the lining of the uterus during the menstrual cycle. This stimulation causes the uterine lining to become thicker. In addition, increased levels of estrogen and progesterone acts as a negative feedback mechanism by causing the pituitary gland to stop secreting LH and FSH. The luteal phase lasts about 14 days. During this time, estrogen and progesterone levels in the blood rise, while the FSH and LH levels drop.

## Menstruation

If an egg is fertilized, the resulting zygote attaches to the lining of the uterus, where it will develop for the next nine months. A hormone that is produced early in pregnancy stimulates the corpus luteum to continue producing estrogen and progesterone, and the thickened lining of the uterus is maintained. If the egg is not fertilized, the corpus luteum stops producing sex hormones, which marks the end of the ovarian cycle. Without estrogen and progesterone to maintain the thickened uterine lining, the lining begins to slough off. In this stage of the menstrual cycle, called **menstruation** (MEN-STRAY-shuhn), the lining of the uterus and blood from ruptured blood vessels are discharged through the vagina. Menstruation lasts the first five to seven days of the follicular phase.

Menstruation continues in most women until about age 50. At this time, a woman no longer ovulates. Most of a woman's follicles have either matured and ruptured or degenerated. Without follicles, the ovaries cannot secrete enough estrogen and progesterone to continue the menstrual cycle, and menstruation ceases. This stage is called **menopause** (MEN-uh-PAWZ).

**internet** connect

www.scilinks.org
**Topic:** Female
      Reproductive
      System
**Keyword:** HM60567

SCLINKS. Maintained by the National Science Teachers Association

---

## SECTION 2 REVIEW

1. Identify the main female reproductive organs.

2. What is the function of the uterus?

3. How are eggs and sperm similar, and how are they different?

4. How do high levels of estrogen and progesterone during the luteal phase of the ovarian cycle affect the uterus?

5. What role does luteinizing hormone (LH) play in the ovarian cycle?

6. What is the corpus luteum?

**CRITICAL THINKING**

7. **Predicting Results** What might happen if two or more eggs were released from the ovaries at the same time?

8. **Relating Concepts** A 48-year-old woman stops having menstrual periods. She thinks she may be pregnant. What is another possible explanation?

9. **Making Comparisons** Which male and female reproductive organs are similar to one another in function?

- **Sequence** the events of fertilization, cleavage, and implantation.
- **Describe** the three stages of pregnancy.
- **Summarize** the development of an embryo during pregnancy.
- **Discuss** the effects of unnecessary drug use on development.
- **Describe** the changes in a mother's body during birth.

VOCABULARY

gestation
blastocyst
implantation
pregnancy
trimester
embryo
amniotic sac
chorionic villus
placenta
umbilical cord
human chorionic gonadotropin
fetus
labor
afterbirth

**FIGURE 51-9**
Several sperm surround this ovum, but only one will be able to fertilize it. (SEM 1165×)

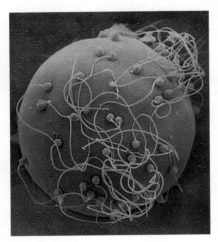

# GESTATION

*A new individual is produced when a sperm fertilizes an egg, resulting in the formation of a zygote. During a nine-month period, a series of changes transforms a single cell into a complex organism made of trillions of cells—a human.*

## FERTILIZATION

Recall that with one ejaculation, a male releases hundreds of millions of sperm into the vagina of a female. Once sperm are released, they swim through the vagina, cervix, and uterus and, finally, up the fallopian tubes. If ovulation occurs anytime from 72 hours before to 48 hours after ejaculation, sperm may encounter an egg in one of the fallopian tubes. Fertilization occurs when a sperm and an egg fuse and form a zygote. From this point, human development takes about nine months—a period known as **gestation** (jes-TAY-shuhn).

An egg in a fallopian tube is encased in a jellylike substance and surrounded by a layer of cells from the follicle of the ovary. As shown in Figure 51-9, several sperm may attach to an egg and attempt to penetrate its outer layers. Recall that the head of a sperm contains digestive enzymes. These enzymes break down an egg's outer layers and enable the cell membrane that surrounds the head of the sperm to fuse with the egg's cell membrane. The sperm's nucleus and midpiece then enter the cytoplasm of the egg. The tail of the sperm remains outside the egg. Usually, only one sperm is successful in penetrating an egg. Electrical changes that occur in an egg's cell membrane after a sperm enters the egg help keep other sperm from penetrating the egg.

After a sperm enters an egg, the egg completes meiosis II, and the sperm's nucleus fuses with the egg's nucleus. The diploid cell that results from this fusion is called a *zygote*. Recall that each gamete contains 23 chromosomes, the haploid $(1n)$ number. Thus, fusion of a sperm nucleus and an egg nucleus causes a zygote to have 46 chromosomes, thus restoring the diploid $(2n)$ number.

### Cleavage and Implantation

Immediately following fertilization and while still in the fallopian tube, the zygote begins a series of mitotic divisions known as *cleavage*. The resulting cells do not increase in size during these cell divisions. Cleavage produces a ball of cells called a *morula* (MAWR-yoo-luh), which is not much larger than the zygote. Cells of the morula divide and release a fluid, resulting in a blastocyst. A **blastocyst** (BLAS-toh-SIST) is a ball of cells with a large, fluid-filled cavity.

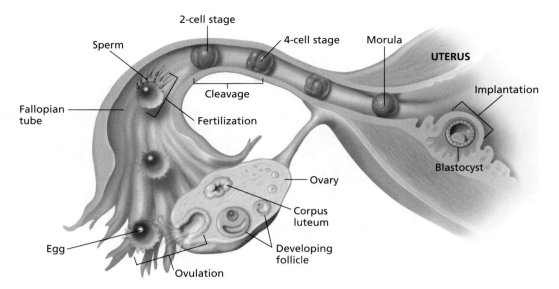

2-cell stage

4-cell stage

Morula

Sperm

**UTERUS**

Implantation

Cleavage

Fallopian tube

Fertilization

Blastocyst

Ovary

Corpus luteum

Egg

Developing follicle

Ovulation

As shown in Figure 51-10, the morula has become a blastocyst by the time it reaches the uterus. In the uterus, the blastocyst attaches to the thickened uterine lining. The blastocyst then releases an enzyme that breaks down the epithelial tissue that lines the uterus and burrows into the thickened lining. The process in which the blastocyst burrows and embeds itself into the lining of the uterus is called **implantation** (IM-plan-TAY-shuhn). Pregnancy begins at implantation, which occurs about a week after fertilization.

# PREGNANCY

After implantation, the blastocyst slowly takes on the recognizable features of a human infant. This nine-month period of development is called *gestation,* or **pregnancy.** Pregnancy is divided into three equal periods, or **trimesters.** Significant changes occur during each trimester.

### First Trimester

The most dramatic changes in human development take place during the first trimester. For the first eight weeks of pregnancy, the developing human is called an **embryo.** Throughout the first two to three weeks following fertilization, a developing human embryo resembles the embryos of other animals. The embryo develops from the mass of cells on the inner surface of the blastocyst. At first, all of the cells in the mass look alike. But the cells soon reorganize, first into two and then into three distinct types of cells, forming the primary germ layers: the ectoderm, mesoderm, and endoderm. Different parts of the body develop from each of the primary germ layers.

Four membranes that aid the development of the embryo also form during the first trimester. One of these membranes, called the *amnion* (AM-nee-uhn), forms the fluid-filled **amniotic** (AM-nee-AHT-ik) **sac,** which surrounds the developing embryo.

**FIGURE 51-10**

The earliest stages of development occur within a fallopian tube as a zygote travels toward the uterus. It takes about a week for the zygote to travel from the fallopian tube to the uterine lining.

## Quick Lab

### Summarizing Vocabulary

**Materials** pencil, paper, dictionary

**Procedure** Write and define the following list of words: *ovary, ovum, follicle, gestation, morula, blastocyst, amnion, chorion, umbilical, uterus, corpus,* and *luteum.* Identify the roots and meanings of the roots for each word.

**Analysis** Do any of the meanings of the words surprise you? Explain. How does knowing the roots and meanings of the words help you remember them?

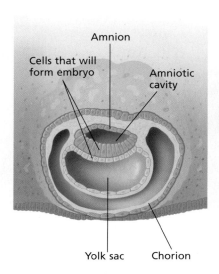

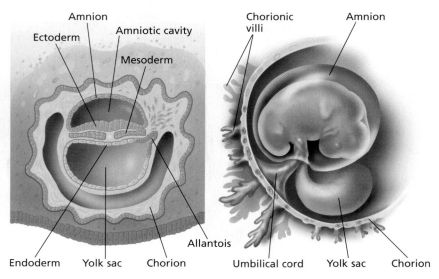

(a) **9-Day Blastocyst**

(b) **16-Day Embryo**

(c) **4-Week Embryo**

**FIGURE 51-11**

(a) An embryo develops from the mass of cells on one side of a blastocyst. (b) The primary germ layers develop by the third week of pregnancy, and the four embryonic membranes form. (c) By the end of the first month of pregnancy, all of the embryonic membranes are formed.

**FIGURE 51-12**

About two weeks after fertilization, the placenta begins to develop. The mother nourishes the developing embryo through the placenta for the duration of the pregnancy.

The fluid in the amniotic sac cushions the embryo from injury and keeps it moist. A second membrane forms the *yolk sac.* Although it does not contain yolk, the yolk sac is an important structure because it is where the first blood cells originate. A third membrane, called the *allantois* (uh-LAN-toh-is), forms near the yolk sac. The fourth membrane, the *chorion* (KAWR-ee-AHN), surrounds all of the other membranes. As shown in Figure 51-11, one side of the chorion forms small, fingerlike projections called **chorionic villi** (KAWR-ee-AHN-ik VIL-IE), which extend into the uterine lining. Blood vessels that form within the chorionic villi originate in the allantois.

Together, chorionic villi and the portion of the uterine lining that they invade form a close-knit structure called the placenta. The **placenta** is the structure through which the mother nourishes the embryo. Nutrients, gases, pathogens, drugs, and other substances can pass from the mother to the embryo through the placenta.

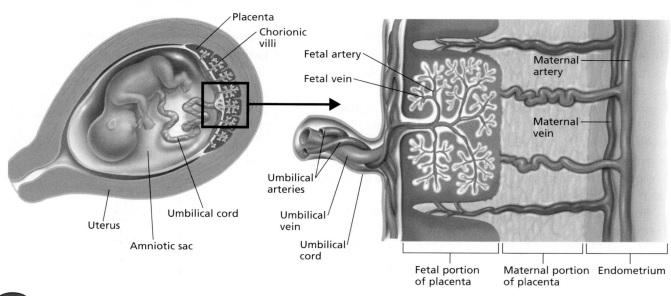

Thus, women should abstain from alcohol and avoid all unnecessary drugs throughout pregnancy. Alcohol use by women, especially during early pregnancy, is the leading cause of birth defects, such as fetal alcohol syndrome (FAS). FAS can result in severe mental, behavioral, and physical retardation.

The embryo is attached to the placenta by the **umbilical** (uhm-BIL-i-kuhl) **cord,** which contains arteries and veins that carry blood between the embryo and the placenta. As Figure 51-12 shows, blood from the mother and fetus never mixes. Materials such as nutrients and wastes are exchanged across the placenta.

A developing placenta begins to secrete a hormone called **human chorionic gonadotropin** (HCG) early in the second week after fertilization. In the early stages of pregnancy, HCG stimulates the corpus luteum to continue producing sex hormones, and thus the uterine lining and the embryo are retained. Otherwise, the corpus luteum will stop producing estrogen and progesterone, and menstruation will occur. As the placenta grows, it begins to secrete large amounts of progesterone and estrogen, which take over maintenance of the uterine lining. Production of estrogen and progesterone throughout pregnancy prevents the release of FSH and LH, and eggs are not released.

The brain, spinal cord, and the rest of the nervous system begin to form in the third week. The heart begins to beat at 21 days. By the fifth week, arms, legs, eyes, and ears have begun to develop. At six weeks, the fingers and toes form, and the brain shows signs of activity. The embryo also begins to move, although the mother cannot yet feel it. From eight weeks until birth, the developing child is called a **fetus** (FEET-uhs). The fetus is only about 5 cm (2 in.) long when the first trimester ends, but all of its organ systems have begun to form, as shown in Figure 51-13.

## Second Trimester

During the second trimester, the mother's uterus enlarges. The fetus's heartbeat can be heard, its skeleton begins to form, and a layer of soft hair called *lanugo* grows over its skin. The fetus also begins to wake and sleep. The mother may feel the fetus move. The fetus swallows and sucks its thumb. It can make a fist, hiccup, kick its feet, and curl its toes. By the end of the second trimester, the fetus is about 34 cm (13.4 in.) long and about 900g (2 lb) in weight.

**Word Roots and Origins**

*fetus*

from the Latin *fetus,* meaning "offspring"

**FIGURE 51-13**

By 12 weeks, the fetus's arms and legs are developing, and 20 buds for future teeth appear. By week 21, eyelashes, eyebrows, and fingernails have formed, and the skin is covered with fine hair called *lanugo*. By eight months, the fetus's bones have hardened, lanugo has disappeared, and body fat is developing.

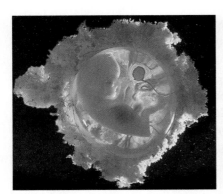

**12 weeks**

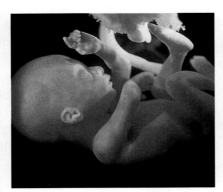

**21 weeks**

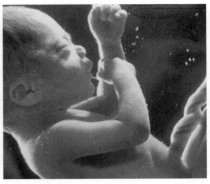

**Eight months**

## Third Trimester

In the third trimester, the fetus grows quickly and undergoes changes that will enable it to survive outside the mother. The fetus can see light and darkness through the mother's abdominal wall, and it can react to music and loud sounds. During the last half of this trimester, the fetus develops fat deposits under its skin. These fat deposits, which make the fetus look rounded and less wrinkled, insulate the body so that it can maintain a steady body temperature.

# BIRTH

Birth occurs about 270 days (38 weeks) after fertilization. Prostaglandins produced by the fetal membranes and hormones produced by both the fetus and the mother initiate childbirth. High levels of estrogen, prostaglandins, and oxytocin, a pituitary hormone, cause the smooth muscles of the uterus to contract. The amniotic sac breaks, and the amniotic fluid flows out through the vagina, a process called "breaking water." Muscles in the cervix and vagina relax, enabling the cervix and vagina to enlarge and allowing the fetus to pass through them. The muscular contractions and other events that lead up to childbirth are called **labor.**

During childbirth, contractions of the uterus push a fetus through the cervix, vagina, and body, as shown in Figure 51-14. The placenta, amnion, and uterine lining, collectively called **afterbirth,** are expelled shortly after the baby is born. Following birth, the newborn baby's lungs expand for the first time as the baby begins to breathe on its own. The umbilical cord is tied and cut. Umbilical arteries and veins close off within 30 minutes after birth. This and other changes in the baby's blood vessels lead to the completion of cardiopulmonary and renal circulation, which allows the baby to function independently of the mother. The newborn baby's respiratory and excretory systems soon become fully functional.

**FIGURE 51-14**

During childbirth, the fetus passes through the greatly enlarged cervix and vagina.

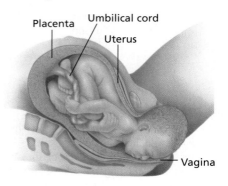

Placenta
Umbilical cord
Uterus
Vagina

---

## SECTION 3 REVIEW

1. How is a zygote formed?

2. What is the process of implantation?

3. How is a fetus nourished during development?

4. Summarize the changes in a mother's body during pregnancy.

5. How can alcohol affect a fetus?

6. What changes occur in a fetus during the third trimester of pregnancy?

7. Summarize the changes in a mother's body that take place during birth.

**CRITICAL THINKING**

8. **Recognizing Relationships** Why is it important for a pregnant woman to eat healthfully and to avoid unhealthy substances?

9. **Applying Information** When blood type A is mixed with blood type B, agglutination, or the formation of clots, occurs. Consider a mother with blood type A carrying a fetus with blood type B. Will agglutination be a problem? Explain.

10. **Predicting Results** Why must a blastocyst be implanted in the uterus and not elsewhere?

# CHAPTER HIGHLIGHTS

**Male Reproductive System**

- The male reproductive structures include two testes, two epididymides, two vasa deferenta, the urethra, and the penis.

- The testes are contained in the scrotum, where the cooler temperature allows normal sperm development.

- Sperm form in the seminiferous tubules of the testes. Meiosis reduces the number of chromosomes in sperm to 23.

- A mature sperm consists of a head, which contains the nucleus and chromosomes; a midpiece, which contains mitochondria; and a tail, which consists of a flagellum.

- Sperm take the following path to exit the body: seminiferous tubules of the testes ⟶ epididymis ⟶ vas deferens ⟶ urethra.

- Fluids that are secreted by various exocrine glands are mixed with sperm to produce semen.

### Vocabulary

testis (p. 1049)
seminiferous tubule (p. 1049)
scrotum (p. 1049)
epididymis (p. 1050)
vas deferens (p. 1050)
seminal vesicle (p. 1051)
prostate gland (p. 1051)
bulbourethral gland (p. 1051)
semen ( p. 1051)
penis (p. 1051)
ejaculation (p. 1051)

---

**SECTION 2** **Female Reproductive System**

- The female reproductive structures include two ovaries, two fallopian tubes, the uterus, the cervix, the vagina, two labia, and the vulva.

- Eggs form in ovaries. Meiosis reduces the chromosome number in eggs to 23. Eggs are about 75,000 times larger than sperm are.

- Starting at puberty, the ovarian and menstrual cycles occur approximately every 28 days.

- The ovarian cycle consists of three phases: follicular phase, ovulation, and luteal phase.

- In the follicular phase, FSH causes a follicle to grow. Estrogen produced by the follicle causes an egg to mature and the uterine lining to build up.

- Ovulation occurs midway through the ovarian cycle, when LH causes the follicle to rupture and release its egg.

- In the luteal phase, the follicle becomes a corpus luteum. The corpus luteum secretes progesterone, which stimulates further buildup of the uterine lining.

- Menstruation occurs at the end of the menstrual cycle, when a corpus luteum stops secreting hormones.

### Vocabulary

ovary (p. 1052)
fallopian tube (p. 1052)
uterus (p. 1052)
cervix (p. 1053)
vagina (p. 1053)
vulva (p. 1053)
labium (p. 1053)
ovum (p. 1053)
ovarian cycle (p. 1054)
menstrual cycle (p. 1054)
follicular phase (p. 1054)
follicle (p. 1054)
ovulation (p. 1054)
corpus luteum (p. 1055)
luteal phase (p. 1055)
menstruation (p. 1055)
menopause (p. 1055)

---

**SECTION 3** **Gestation**

- Fertilization occurs in a fallopian tube. Pregnancy begins when a blastocyst implants itself in the lining of the uterus.

- The three primary germ layers—the ectoderm, mesoderm, and endoderm—form early in embryonic development. Four membranes—the amnion, yolk sac, allantois, and chorion—also form early in embryonic development.

- Nutrients, gases, and other substances pass through the placenta by diffusion from the mother to the fetus.

- For the first eight weeks of pregnancy, the developing human is a called an *embryo.* From the eighth week until birth, a developing human is known as a *fetus.*

- Unnecessary drug use can negatively affect an embryo or fetus.

- During childbirth, contractions of the uterus initiated by prostaglandins and oxytocin push the baby from the mother's body through the vagina.

### Vocabulary

gestation (p. 1056)
blastocyst (p. 1056)
implantation (p. 1057)
pregnancy (p. 1057)
trimester (p. 1057)
embryo (p. 1057)
amniotic sac (p. 1057)
chorionic villus (p. 1058)
placenta (p. 1058)
umbilical cord (p. 1059)
human chorionic
  gonadotropin (p. 1059)
fetus (p. 1059)
labor (p. 1060)
afterbirth (p. 1060)

# CHAPTER REVIEW

## USING VOCABULARY

1. Name the male and female gamete-producing organs.

2. Explain the differences between sperm and semen.

3. Explain the relationships between the following terms: *menstrual cycle, menstruation,* and *menopause.*

4. **Word Roots and Origins** The word *blastocyst* is derived from the Greek *blastos,* which means "bud," and *kustis,* which means "liquid-filled sac." Using this information, explain why the term *blastocyst* is a good name for the biological structure that the term describes.

## UNDERSTANDING KEY CONCEPTS

5. **Name** the sac of skin that houses the testes.

6. **Identify** the organ that deposits sperm in the female reproductive system.

7. **Explain** how semen is formed.

8. **Describe** the structure of a mature human sperm cell.

9. **Sequence** the path that sperm follow in leaving the body.

10. **Identify** four major parts of the female reproductive system.

11. **Identify** the function of the uterus.

12. **State** where eggs are produced.

13. **Compare** the formation of sperm to the formation of eggs.

14. **Describe** the function of the labia.

15. **Predict** in which period of the ovarian cycle that fertilization is most likely to occur.

16. **Identify** the part of the menstrual cycle that does not occur if implantation takes place.

17. **Explain** how a sperm penetrates an egg during fertilization.

18. **Describe** the processes of cleavage and implantation.

19. **Discuss** how the developing fetus receives nourishment.

20. **List** the differences between an embryo and a fetus.

21. **Summarize** the effects of drug use on development.

22. **Outline** fetal development during the second trimester.

23. **State** the changes the cervix undergoes during childbirth.

24. **CONCEPT MAPPING** Use the following terms to create a concept map that shows the ovarian and menstrual cycles: *corpus luteum, estrogen, follicle, hormones, follicular phase, menstrual cycle, luteal phase, ovarian cycle, ovulation, ovum, progesterone,* and *uterus.*

## CRITICAL THINKING

25. **Predicting Results** What do you think might happen if more than one sperm were able to penetrate the cell membrane of an egg?

26. **Evaluating Differences** A human female produces, on average, only one mature egg every 28 days. In contrast, a female salmon lays 50 million eggs at each spawning. Hypothesize why there is such a great difference in egg production between the two species.

27. **Recognizing Relationships** Women who consume tobacco, alcoholic beverages, or other drugs or harmful substances during pregnancy are at high risk of giving birth to infants who are addicted to drugs, have severe birth defects, or tend to develop learning disabilities. Explain.

28. **Interpreting Graphics** What is the fetus doing in the photograph below? Suggest an adaptive advantage for this activity.

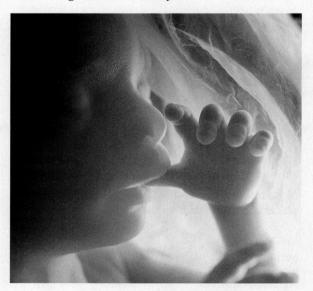

# Standardized Test Preparation

**DIRECTIONS:** Choose the letter of the answer choice that best answers the question.

1. Which of the following is the correct pathway for sperm as it exits the body?
   **A.** the testes to the penis to the epididymis
   **B.** the urethra to the vas deferens to the testes
   **C.** the epididymis to the vas deferens to the urethra
   **D.** the testes to the vas deferens to the epididymis

2. Which of the following is true about follicle-stimulating hormone?
   **F.** It is secreted by the follicle.
   **G.** It is secreted by the pituitary gland.
   **H.** It promotes contractions of the uterus.
   **J.** It stimulates the development of the placenta.

3. Which of the following help form the placenta and umbilical cord?
   **A.** the amnion and chorion
   **B.** the amnion and yolk sac
   **C.** the chorion and yolk sac
   **D.** the chorion and allantois

4. By the end of the first trimester, which of the following has occurred in the fetus?
   **F.** The fetus has a full head of hair.
   **G.** The fetus uses its lungs to breathe.
   **H.** The brain of the fetus is fully developed.
   **J.** All of the organs of the fetus have begun to form.

**INTERPRETING GRAPHICS:** Study the image of the sperm cell below to answer the questions that follow.

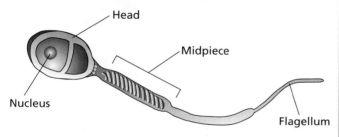

5. Where are the enzymes that help the sperm penetrate the ovum found?
   **A.** in the head
   **B.** in the nucleus
   **C.** in the midpiece
   **D.** in the flagellum

6. Where are the mitochondria that supply the energy that sperm need for movement found?
   **F.** in the head
   **G.** in the nucleus
   **H.** in the midpiece
   **J.** in the flagellum

**DIRECTIONS:** Complete the following analogy.

7. testis : ovary :: vas deferens :
   **A.** sperm
   **B.** urethra
   **C.** fallopian tube
   **D.** prostate gland

**INTERPRETING GRAPHICS:** The image below shows an ovary. Use the image to answer the question that follows.

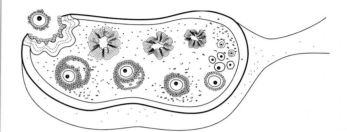

8. What event is illustrated by this figure?
   **F.** ovulation
   **G.** ejaculation
   **H.** fertilization
   **J.** menstruation

## SHORT RESPONSE

Sperm are able to survive for around 48 hours in a female even though they have very little cytoplasm to provide nutrients. Explain why you think sperm can survive with few nutrients.

## EXTENDED RESPONSE

During the 1950s, a number of women were prescribed thalidomide, a drug to relieve morning sickness. These women gave birth to babies with serious limb defects. Scientists later discovered that thalidomide caused limb defects in fetuses.

*Part A* Do you think it is safe for a woman to take thalidomide during her first and second trimesters of pregnancy? Explain your answer.

*Part B* Do you think it is safe for a woman to take thalidomide during the third trimester of her pregnancy? Explain your answer.

**Test TIP** If at first you are unsure of the correct answer to a question, start by crossing out answers you know are wrong. Reducing the number of answer choices in this way may help you choose the correct answer.

# Observing Embryonic Development

- Identify the stages of early animal development.
- Describe the changes that occur during early development.
- Compare the stages of human embryonic development with those of echinoderm embryonic development.

- observing
- comparing and contrasting
- making drawings
- drawing conclusions

- prepared slides of sea-star development, including
  unfertilized egg
  zygote
  2-cell stage
  4-cell stage
  8-cell stage
  16-cell stage
  32-cell stage
  64-cell stage
  blastula
  early gastrula
  middle gastrula
  late gastrula
  young sea-star larva
- compound light microscope
- paper and pencil

## Background

1. Most members of the animal kingdom (including sea stars and humans) begin life as a single cell—the fertilized egg, or zygote.
2. The early stages of development are quite similar in different species. Cleavage follows fertilization. During cleavage, the zygote divides many times without growing. The new cells migrate and form a hollow ball of cells called a *blastula.* The cells then begin to organize into the three primary germ layers: endoderm, mesoderm, and ectoderm. During this process, the developing organism is called a *gastrula.*
3. The early stages of mammalian development are difficult to study because mammalian eggs are tiny and are not produced in great numbers. In addition, mammalian embryos develop within the mother's body. In the laboratory, it is difficult to replicate the internal conditions of the mother's body. Because the early stages of echinoderm development are similar to those of human development, and because echinoderm development is easier to study in the laboratory than human development, you will observe the early developmental stages of an echinoderm—the sea star—in this investigation.

2-cell stage

4-cell stage

8-cell stage

64-cell stage

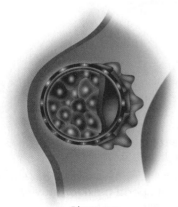
Blastocyst

4. As development continues, the cells continue to specialize as they become part of specific tissues and complex structures. Ectoderm forms the epidermis and nerve tissue. Mesoderm forms muscle, connective tissue, and vascular organs. Endoderm forms the lining of the digestive, urinary, and respiratory tracts.

5. Similarities and differences in early stages of development reflect evolutionary relationships between species.

## Procedure

1. Obtain a set of prepared slides that show sea-star eggs at different stages of development. Choose slides labeled unfertilized egg, zygote, 2-cell stage, 4-cell stage, 8-cell stage, 16-cell stage, 32-cell stage, 64-cell stage, blastula, early gastrula, middle gastrula, late gastrula, and young sea-star larva. (Note: *Blastula* is the general term for the embryonic stage that results from cleavage. In mammals, a blastocyst is a modified form of the blastula.)

2. Examine each slide using a compound light microscope. Using the microscope's low-power objective first, focus on one good example of the developmental stage listed on the slide's label. Then switch to the high-power objective, and focus on the image with the fine adjustment.

3. In your lab report, draw a diagram of each developmental stage that you examine (in chronological order). Label each diagram with the name of the stage it represents and the magnification used. Record your observations as soon as they are made. Do not redraw your diagrams. Draw only what you see; lab drawings do not need to be artistic or elaborate. They should be well organized and include specific details.

4. Compare your diagrams with the diagrams of human embryonic stages shown on previous page.

5. Clean up your materials and wash your hands before leaving the lab.

## Analysis and Conclusions

1. Compare the size of the sea-star zygote with that of the blastula. At what stage does the embryo become larger than the zygote?

2. At what stage do all of the cells in the embryo not look exactly like each other?

3. How do cell shape and size change during successive stages of development?

4. Do the cell nuclei stay the same size, get larger, or get smaller as the stages progress?

5. Compare the number of chromosomes in a fertilized sea-star egg with the number of chromosomes in one cell of each of the following phases: 2-cell stage, blastula, gastrula, and adult stage.

6. From your observations of changes in cellular organization, why do you think the blastocoel (the space in the center of the hollow sphere of cells of a blastula) is important during embryonic development?

7. Label the endoderm and ectoderm in your drawing of the late gastrula stage. What do these two tissue types eventually develop into?

8. How are the symmetries of a sea-star embryo and a sea-star larva different from the symmetry of an adult sea star? Would you expect to see a similar change in human development?

9. What must happen to the sea-star gastrula before it becomes a mature sea star?

10. How do your drawings of sea-star embryonic development compare with those of human embryonic development? Based on your observations, in what ways do you think sea-star embryos could be used to study early human development?

11. Describe one way that the cleavage of echinoderms and mammals is alike.

12. Describe two ways in which cleavage in echinoderms differs from cleavage in mammals.

13. Why are sea-star eggs a good choice for the study of embryonic development in humans?

## Further Inquiry

Using the procedure that you followed in this investigation, compare embryonic development in other organisms with embryonic development in sea stars. Which types of organisms would you expect to develop similarly to sea stars? Which types of organisms would you expect to develop differently from sea stars?

It is your responsibility to protect yourself and other students by conducting yourself in a safe manner while in the laboratory. You will avoid accidents in the laboratory by following directions, handling materials carefully, and taking your work seriously. Read the following general safety guidelines before attempting to work in the laboratory. Make sure that you understand all safety guidelines before entering the laboratory. If necessary, ask your teacher for clarification of laboratory rules and procedures.

# General Guidelines for Laboratory Safety

**Do not perform experiments not specifically assigned by your teacher.** Do not attempt any laboratory procedure without your teacher's direction, and do not work in the laboratory by yourself.

**Familiarize yourself with the experiment and all safety precautions before entering the lab.** Be aware of the potential hazards of the required materials and procedures. Ask your teacher to explain any confusing parts of an experiment before you begin.

**Before beginning work, tie back long hair, roll up loose sleeves, and put on any required personal protective equipment as directed by your teacher.** Avoid or confine loose clothing that could knock things over, catch on fire, or absorb chemical solutions. Nylon and polyester fabrics burn and melt more readily than cotton fabrics do. Do not wear open-toed shoes, sandals, or canvas shoes in the lab.

**Always wear a lab apron and safety goggles in the lab.** Wear this equipment at all times, even if you are not working on an experiment at the time. Laboratories contain chemicals that can damage your clothing, skin, and eyes. If your safety goggles cloud up or are uncomfortable, ask your teacher for help. Lengthening the strap

slightly, washing the goggles with soap and warm water, or using an anti-fog spray may help alleviate the problems.

**Do not wear contact lenses in the lab.** Even if you are wearing safety goggles, chemicals could get between contact lenses and your eyes and cause irreparable eye damage. If your doctor requires that you wear contact lenses instead of glasses, then you should wear eye-cup safety goggles—similar to goggles that are worn for underwater swimming—in the lab. Ask your doctor or your teacher how to use eye-cup safety goggles to protect your eyes.

**Know the location of all safety and emergency equipment used in the laboratory before you begin a lab.** Ask your teacher where the nearest eyewash stations, safety blankets, safety shower, fire extinguisher, first-aid kit, and chemical spill kit are located.

**Immediately report any accident, incident, or hazard—no matter how trivial—to your teacher.** Any incident involving bleeding, burns, fainting, chemical exposure, or ingestion should also be reported immediately to the school nurse or to a physician.

**In case of fire, alert the teacher and leave the laboratory.** Follow standard school fire safety procedures.

**Do not fool around in the lab.** Take your lab work seriously, and behave appropriately in the lab. Be aware of your classmates' safety as well as your own at all times.

**Do not have or consume food, chew gum, or drink in the laboratory.** Do not store food in the laboratory. Keep your hands away from your face. Do not apply cosmetics in the laboratory. Some hair-care products and nail polish are highly flammable.

**Keep your work area neat and uncluttered.** Have only books and other materials that are needed to conduct the experiment in the laboratory.

**Clean your work area at the conclusion of each lab period as your teacher directs.** Dispose of broken glass, chemicals, and other laboratory waste products in separate, special containers. Dispose of waste materials as directed by your teacher.

**Wash your hands with soap and water after each lab period.** Also wash your hands before each lab period to avoid contamination.

# Key to Safety Symbols and Their Precautions

Before you begin working in the laboratory, familiarize yourself with the following safety symbols that are used in this textbook and the guidelines that you should follow when you see these symbols.

## EYE SAFETY

◆ **Wear approved safety goggles as directed.** Goggles should always be worn in the laboratory, especially when you are working with a chemical, a chemical solution, a heat source, or a mechanical device.

◆ **In case of eye contact, do the following:** Go to an eyewash station immediately, and flush your eyes (including under the eyelids) with running water for at least 15 minutes. Hold your eyelids open with your thumb and fingers, and roll your eyeball around. While doing this, have another student notify your teacher.

◆ **Do not wear contact lenses in the laboratory.** Chemicals can be drawn up under the contact lens and into the eye. If you must wear contacts, tell your teacher. You must also wear approved eye-cup safety goggles to protect your eyes.

◆ **Do not look directly at the sun through any optical device or lens system or reflect direct sunlight to illuminate a microscope.** Such actions concentrate light rays to an intensity that can severely burn your retina and that may cause blindness.

## HAND SAFETY

◆ **Do not cut objects while holding them in your hand.** Dissect specimens in a dissecting tray.

◆ **Wear protective gloves when working with an open flame, chemicals, solutions, or wild or unknown plants.**

## SAFETY WITH GASES

◆ **Do not inhale any gas or vapor unless directed to do so by your teacher.** Do not breathe pure gases. If your teacher directs you to note the odor of a gas, do so by waving the fumes toward you with your hand.

◆ **Handle materials prone to emit vapors or gases in a well-ventilated area.** This work should be done in an approved chemical fume hood.

## SHARP-OBJECT SAFETY

◆ **Use extreme care when handling all sharp and pointed instruments, such as scalpels, scissors, sharp probes, and knives.**

◆ **Do not use double-edged razor blades in the laboratory.**

◆ **Do not cut objects while holding them in your hand.** Cut objects on a suitable work surface. Always cut in a direction away from your body.

## CLOTHING PROTECTION

◆ **Wear an apron or laboratory coat at all times in the laboratory to prevent chemicals or solutions from contacting skin or clothes.**

## ANIMAL CARE AND SAFETY

◆ **Do not touch or approach wild animals.** When working in the field, be aware of poisonous or dangerous animals in the area.

◆ **Always obtain your teacher's permission before bringing any animal (including pets) into the school building.**

◆ **Handle animals only as your teacher directs.** Mishandling or abusing any animal will not be tolerated.

### GLASSWARE SAFETY

◆ **Inspect glassware before use; do not use chipped or cracked glassware.** Use heat-resistant glassware for heating materials or storing hot liquids.

◆ **Do not attempt to insert glass tubing into a rubber stopper without specific instruction from your teacher.**

◆ **Immediately notify your teacher if a piece of glassware breaks. Do not attempt to clean up broken glass unless directed to do so by your teacher.**

### HEATING SAFETY

◆ **Be aware of any source of flames, sparks, or heat (open flames, electric heating coils, hot plates, etc.) before working with flammable liquids or gases.**

◆ **When heating chemicals or reagents in a test tube, do not point the test tube toward anyone.**

◆ **Avoid using open flames.** If possible, work only with hot plates that have an on/off switch and an indicator light. Do not leave hot plates unattended. Do not use alcohol lamps. Turn off hot plates and open flames when they are not in use.

◆ **Know the location of laboratory fire extinguishers and fire-safety blankets.**

◆ **Use tongs or other appropriate, insulated holders when heating objects.** Heated objects often do not appear to be hot. Thus, do not pick up an object with your hand if the object could be warm.

◆ **Keep flammable substances away from heat, flames, and other ignition sources.**

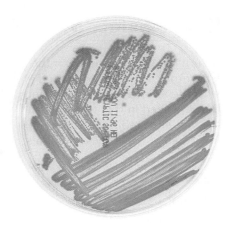

### HYGIENIC CARE

◆ **Keep your hands away from your face and mouth while working in the laboratory.**

◆ **Wash your hands thoroughly before leaving the laboratory.**

◆ **Remove contaminated clothing immediately.** If you spill caustic substances on your skin or clothing, use the safety shower or a faucet to rinse. Remove affected clothing while under the shower, and call to your teacher. (It may be temporarily embarrassing to remove clothing in front of your classmates, but failing to rinse a chemical off your skin could cause permanent damage.)

◆ **Launder contaminated clothing separately.**

◆ **Use the proper technique demonstrated by your teacher when handling bacteria or similar microorganisms.** Do not open Petri dishes to observe or count bacterial colonies.

## PROPER WASTE DISPOSAL

◆ **Clean and decontaminate all work surfaces and personal protective equipment after each lab period as directed by your teacher.**

◆ **Dispose of all sharp objects (such as broken glass) and other contaminated materials (biological or chemical) in special containers as directed by your teacher.**

## ELECTRICAL SAFETY

◆ **Do not use equipment with frayed electrical cords or loose plugs.**

◆ **Fasten electrical cords to work surfaces with tape.** This will prevent tripping and will ensure that equipment cannot fall off the table.

◆ **Do not use electrical equipment near water or with wet hands or clothing.**

◆ **Hold the rubber cord when you plug in or unplug equipment. Do not touch the metal prongs of the plug, and do not unplug equipment by pulling on the cord.**

## PLANT SAFETY

◆ **Do not ingest any plant part used in the laboratory (especially commercially sold seeds).** Do not touch any sap or plant juice directly. Always wear gloves.

◆ **Wear disposable polyethylene gloves when handling any wild plant.**

◆ **Wash hands thoroughly after handling any plant or plant part (particularly seeds).** Avoid touching your face and eyes.

◆ **Do not inhale or expose yourself to the smoke of any burning plant.** Smoke contains irritants that can cause inflammation in the throat and lungs.

◆ **Do not pick wildflowers or other wild plants unless your teacher instructs you otherwise.**

## CHEMICAL SAFETY

◆ **Always wear appropriate protective equipment.** Always wear eye goggles, gloves, and a lab apron or lab coat when working with any chemicals or chemical solutions.

◆ **Do not taste, touch, or smell any substance or bring it close to your eyes, unless specifically instructed to do so by your teacher.** If your teacher directs you to note the odor of a substance, do so by waving the fumes toward you with your hand. Do not pipette any substance by mouth; use a suction bulb as directed by your teacher.

◆ **Always handle chemicals and solutions with care.** Check the labels on bottles, and observe safety procedures. Do not return unused chemicals or solutions to their original containers. Return unused reagent bottles or containers to your teacher.

◆ **Do not mix any chemicals unless specifically instructed to do so by your teacher.** Two harmless chemicals can be poisonous if combined.

◆ **Do not pour water into a strong acid or strong base.** The mixture can produce heat and splatter.

◆ **Report any spill immediately to your teacher.** Do not clean up spills yourself unless your teacher instructs you otherwise.

Microscopes are tools that extend human vision by making enlarged images of objects. Scientists use microscopes to see very small objects, such as microorganisms, cells and even cell parts. Microscopes help scientists reveal details that might otherwise be difficult, or even impossible to see.

## Parts of the Compound Light Microscope

- The **eyepiece** magnifies the image, usually 10×.

- The **low-power objective** further magnifies the image, up to 4×.

- The **high-power objectives** further magnify the image, from 10× to 43×.

- The **nosepiece** holds the objectives and can be turned to change from one objective to another.

- The **body tube** maintains the correct distance between the eyepiece and the objectives. This distance is usually about 25 cm (10 in.), the normal distance for reading and viewing objects with the naked eye.

- The **coarse adjustment** moves the body tube up and down in large increments to allow gross positioning and focusing of the objective lens.

- The **fine adjustment** moves the body tube slightly to bring the image into sharp focus.

- The **stage** supports a slide.

- The **stage clips** secure the slide in position for viewing.

- The **diaphragm** (not labeled), located under the stage, controls the amount of light that is allowed to pass through the object being viewed.

- The **light source** provides light for viewing the image. It can be either a light reflected with a mirror or an incandescent light from a small lamp. NEVER use reflected direct sunlight as a light source.

- The **arm** supports the body tube.

- The **base** supports the microscope.

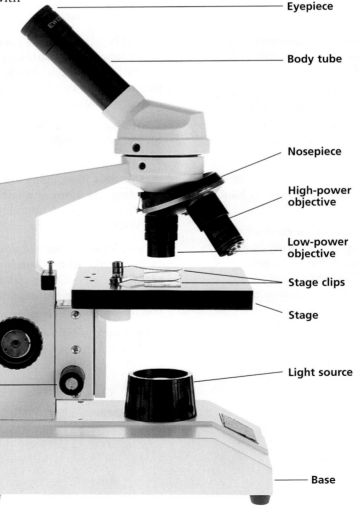

Eyepiece

Body tube

Nosepiece

High-power objective

Low-power objective

Arm

Stage clips

Stage

Coarse adjustment

Fine adjustment

Light source

Base

# Proper Handling and Use of the Compound Light Microscope

1. Carry the microscope to your lab table by using both hands, one supporting the base and the other holding the arm of the microscope. Hold the microscope close to your body.

2. Place the microscope on the lab table at least 5 cm (2 in.) from the edge of the table.

3. Check to see what type of light source the microscope has. If the microscope has a lamp, plug it in and make sure that the cord is out of the way. If the microscope has a mirror, adjust it to reflect light through the hole in the stage.

   **CAUTION** If your microscope has a mirror, do not use direct sunlight as a light source. Using direct sunlight can damage your eyes.

   **CAUTION** If your microscope has a lamp, be careful not to touch the bulb of the lamp. The bulb can get very hot.

4. Adjust the revolving nosepiece so that the low-power objective is in line with the body tube.

5. Place a prepared slide over the hole in the stage, and secure the slide with the stage clips.

6. Look through the eyepiece, and move the diaphragm to adjust the amount of light that passes through the specimen.

7. Now look at the stage at eye level, and slowly turn the coarse adjustment to raise the stage until the objective almost touches the slide. Do not allow the objective to touch the slide.

8. While looking through the eyepiece, turn the coarse adjustment to lower the stage until the image is in focus. Never focus objectives downward. Use the fine adjustment to attain a sharply focused image. Keep both eyes open while viewing a slide.

9. Make sure that the image is exactly in the center of your field of vision. Then, switch to the high-power objective. Focus the image with the fine adjustment. Never use the coarse adjustment at high power.

10. When you are finished using the microscope, remove the slide. Clean the eyepiece and objectives with lens paper, and return the microscope to its storage area.

# Procedure for Making a Wet Mount

1. Use lens paper to clean a glass slide and coverslip.

2. Place the specimen that you wish to observe in the center of the slide.

3. Using a medicine dropper, place one drop of water on the specimen.

4. Position the coverslip so that it is at the edge of the drop of water and at a 45° angle to the slide. Make sure that the water runs along the edge of the coverslip.

5. Lower the coverslip slowly to avoid trapping air bubbles.

6. If a stain or solution will be added to a wet mount, place a drop of the staining solution on the microscope slide along one side of the coverslip. Place a small piece of paper towel on the opposite side of the coverslip.

7. As the water evaporates from the slide, add another drop of water by placing the tip of the medicine dropper next to the edge of the coverslip, just as you would if you were adding stains or solutions to a wet mount. If you have added too much water, remove the excess by using the corner of a paper towel as a blotter. Do not lift the coverslip to add or remove water.

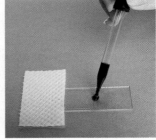

Scientists throughout the world use the Système International d'Unités, or International System of Units. It is usually referred to simply as SI. You will often use SI units to express the measurements that you will make in the laboratory. Most measurements in this book are expressed in SI units.

SI is a decimal system; that is, all relationships between SI units are based on powers of 10. Most units have a prefix that indicates the relationship of that unit to a base unit. For example, the SI base unit for length is the meter. A meter equals 100 centimeters (cm), or 1,000 millimeters (mm). A meter also equals 0.001 kilometers (km). Table 1 summarizes the prefixes and abbreviations that are commonly used to represent SI units.

### TABLE 1   Some SI Prefixes

| Prefix | Abbreviation | Factor of base unit |
|--------|--------------|---------------------|
| giga- | G | 1,000,000,000 |
| mega- | M | 1,000,000 |
| kilo- | k | 1,000 |
| hecto- | h | 100 |
| deka- | da | 10 |
| deci- | d | 0.1 |
| centi- | c | 0.01 |
| milli- | m | 0.001 |
| micro- | μ | 0.000001 |
| nano- | n | 0.000000001 |
| pico- | p | 0.000000000001 |

## SI Units

### BASE UNITS

Seven fundamental quantities are represented by base units in SI. These base units include familiar quantities, such as length, mass, and time. These base quantities, their units, and their symbols are given in Table 2.

### TABLE 2   SI Base Units

| Base quantity | Unit | Symbol |
|---------------|------|--------|
| Length | meter | m |
| Mass | kilogram | kg |
| Time | second | s |
| Electric current | ampere | A |
| Thermodynamic temperature | kelvin | K |
| Amount of substance | mole | mol |
| Luminous intensity | candela | cd |

### DERIVED UNITS

The base units in Table 2 cannot be used to express measurements such as the surface area of a wildlife preserve or the speed of a running cheetah. Therefore, other important quantities, such as area, volume, and velocity, are expressed in derived units. Derived units are mathematical combinations of one or more base units.

### TABLE 3   SI-Derived Units Often Used in Biology

| Derived quantity | Unit | Symbol |
|------------------|------|--------|
| Area | square meter | $m^2$ |
| Volume | cubic meter | $m^3$ |
| Mass density | kilogram per cubic meter | $kg/m^3$ |
| Specific volume | cubic meter per kilogram | $m^3/kg$ |
| Velocity | meter per second | m/s |
| Celsius temperature | degree Celsius | °C |

Table 3 lists some derived units that you may encounter in your study of biology. Like base units, derived units can be expressed by using prefixes. In the lab, you will often express volume measurements in cubic centimeters ($cm^3$). Graduated cylinders are calibrated in milliliters or cubic centimeters. A square meter equals 10,000 square centimeters ($cm^2$). Large area measurements are often expressed in hectares (ha). A hectare equals 10,000 square meters ($m^2$).

### UNITS ACCEPTED FOR USE WITH SI

Certain units of measure that are not SI units are still acceptable for use with SI units. They are the minute, hour, and day (units of time); the liter (a unit of volume); and the metric ton (a unit of mass). These units are listed in Table 4.

| TABLE 4 | *Examples of Units Accepted for Use with SI* | |
|---|---|---|
| **Unit** | **Symbol** | **Value in SI units** |
| Minute | min | 1 min = 60 s |
| Hour | h | 1 h = 3,600 s |
| | | 1 h = 60 min |
| Day | d | 1 d = 24 h |
| Liter | L | 1 L = 0.001 mg$^3$ |
| Metric ton | t | 1 t = 1,000 kg |

# Equivalent Measurements and Conversions

Conversion between SI units requires a conversion factor. For example, to convert from meters to centimeters, you need to know the relationship between meters and centimeters.

$$1 \text{ cm} = 0.01 \text{ m} \quad \text{or} \quad 1 \text{ m} = 100 \text{ cm}$$

If you needed to convert a lab measurement of 15.5 centimeters to meters, you could do either of the following:

$$15.5 \text{ cm} \times \frac{1 \text{ m}}{100 \text{ cm}} = 0.155 \text{ m}$$

or

$$15.5 \text{ cm} \times \frac{0.01 \text{ m}}{1 \text{ cm}} = 0.155 \text{ m}$$

The following are some measurement equivalents for length, area, mass, and volume.

### LENGTH

| | |
|---|---|
| 1 kilometer (km) | = 1,000 m |
| 1 meter (m) | = base unit of length |
| 1 centimeter (cm) | = 0.01 m |
| 1 millimeter (mm) | = 0.001 m |
| 1 micrometer (µm) | = 0.000001 m |

### AREA

| | |
|---|---|
| 1 square kilometer (km$^2$) | = 100 ha |
| 1 hectare (ha) | = 10,000 m$^2$ |
| 1 square meter (m$^2$) | = 10,000 cm$^2$ |
| 1 square centimeter (cm$^2$) | = 100 mm$^2$ |

### MASS

| | |
|---|---|
| 1 kilogram (kg) | = base unit of mass |
| 1 kg | = 1,000 grams (g) |
| 1 gram (g) | = 0.001 kg |
| 1 milligram (mg) | = 0.001 g |
| 1 microgram (µg) | = 0.000001 g |

### LIQUID VOLUME

| | |
|---|---|
| 1 kiloliter (kL) | = 1,000 L |
| 1 liter (L) | = base unit of liquid volume |
| 1 milliliter (mL) | = 0.001 L |
| 1 mL | = 1 cm$^3$ |

**NOTE:** When measuring liquid volume in a graduated cylinder, read the measurement at the bottom of the meniscus, or curve.

### TEMPERATURE

In this textbook, the Celsius scale is used to express temperature measurements. In degrees Celsius, 0° is the freezing point of water, and 100° is the boiling point of water. You can use the scale shown below to convert between the Celsius scale and the Fahrenheit scale.

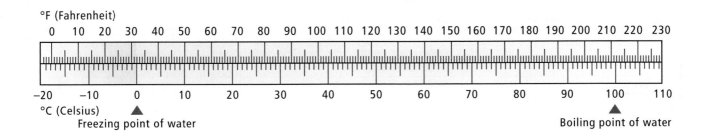

°F (Fahrenheit)
0 10 20 30 40 50 60 70 80 90 100 110 120 130 140 150 160 170 180 190 200 210 220 230

−20 −10 0 10 20 30 40 50 60 70 80 90 100 110
°C (Celsius)
▲ Freezing point of water    ▲ Boiling point of water

Part of learning biology involves learning many new words. By breaking down some of the words, you can more easily understand their meaning. The table below provides a simple definition and example of some common prefixes, suffixes, and word roots. Refer to this table as you explore each chapter in this textbook.

## WORD PREFIXES, SUFFIXES, AND WORD ROOTS

| Prefix, suffix, or word root | Definition | Example |
| --- | --- | --- |
| a- | not, without | asymmetrical: not symmetrical |
| ab- | away, apart | abduct: move away from the middle |
| -able | able | viable: able to live |
| ad- | to, toward | adduct: move toward the middle |
| amphi- | both | amphibian: type of vertebrate that lives both on land and in water |
| ante- | before | anterior: front of an organism |
| anti- | against | antibiotic: substance, such as penicillin, capable of killing bacteria |
| arche- | ancient | Archaeopteryx: a fossilized bird |
| arthro- | joint | arthropod: jointed-limbed organism belonging to the phylum Arthropoda |
| auto- | self, same | autotrophic: able to make its own food |
| bi- | two | bivalve: mollusk with two shells |
| bio- | life | biology: the study of life |
| blast- | embryo | blastula: hollow ball stage in the development of an embryo |
| carcin- | cancer | carcinogenic: cancer-causing |
| cereb- | brain | cerebrum: part of the vertebrate brain |
| chloro- | green | chlorophyll: green pigment in plants needed for photosynthesis |
| chondro- | cartilage | Chondrichthyes: cartilaginous fish |
| chromo- | color | chromatin: plant pigment that absorbs different-colored wavelengths |
| -cide | kill | insecticide: a substance that kills insects |
| circ- | around | circulatory: system for moving fluids through the body |
| co-, con- | with, together | conjoined twins: identical twins physically joined by a shared portion of anatomy at birth |
| -cycle | circle | pericycle: layer of plant cells |
| cyt- | cell | cytology: the study of cells |
| de- | remove | dehydration: removal of water |
| derm- | skin | dermatology: study of the skin |
| di- | two | diploid: full set (which is two sets) of chromosomes |
| dia- | through | dialysis: separating molecules by passing them through a membrane |
| ecol- | dwelling, house | ecology: the study of living things and their environments |
| ecto- | outer, outside | ectoderm: outer germ layer of developing embryo |
| -ectomy | removal | appendectomy: removal of the appendix |
| endo- | inner, inside | endoplasm: cytoplasm within the cell membrane |
| epi- | upon, over | epiphyte: plant growing upon another plant |
| ex-, exo- | outside of | exobiology: the search for life elsewhere in the universe |
| gastro- | stomach | gastropod: type of mollusk |
| -gen | type | genotype: genes in an organism |
| -gram | write or record | climatogram: depicting the annual precipitation and temperature for an area |
| hemi- | half | hemisphere: half of a sphere |
| hetero- | different | heterozygous: different alleles inherited from parents |
| hist- | tissue | histology: the study of tissues |

| Prefix, suffix, or word root | Definition | Example |
|---|---|---|
| homeo- | the same | homeostasis: maintaining a constant condition |
| hydro- | water | hydroponics: growing plants in water instead of soil |
| hyper- | above, over | hypertension: blood pressure higher than normal |
| hypo- | below, under | hypothalamus: part of the brain located below the thalamus |
| -ic | of or pertaining to | hypodermic: pertaining to under the skin |
| inter- | between, among | interbreed: breed within a family or strain |
| intra- | within | intracellular: inside a cell |
| iso- | equal | isogenic: having an identical set of genes |
| -ist | someone who practices or deals with something | biologist: someone who studies life |
| -logy | study of | biology: the study of life |
| macro- | large | macromolecule: large molecule, such as DNA or a protein |
| mal- | bad | malnourishment: poor nutrition |
| mega- | large | megaspore: larger of two types of spores produced by some ferns and flowering plants |
| meso- | in the middle | mesoglea: jellylike material found between outer and inner layers of coelenterates |
| meta- | change | metamorphosis: change in form |
| micro- | small | microscopic: too small to be seen with unaided eye |
| mono- | one, single | monoploid: one set of alleles |
| morph- | form | morphology: study of the form of organisms |
| neo- | new | neonatal: newborn |
| nephr- | kidney | nephron: functional unit of the kidneys |
| neur- | nerve or sinew | neurotransmitter: chemical released by a neuron |
| oo- | egg | oogenesis: gamete formation in female diploid organisms |
| -oma | swelling | carcinoma: cancerous tumor |
| org- | living | organism: living thing |
| orth- | straight | orthodontics: the practice of straightening teeth |
| pachy- | thick | pachyderm: thick-skinned animal, such as an elephant |
| para- | near, on | parasite: organism that lives on and gets nutrients from another organism |
| path- | disease | pathogen: disease-causing agent |
| peri- | around | pericardium: membrane around the heart |
| photo- | light | phototropism: bending of plants toward light |
| phyto- | plants | phytoplankton: plankton that consists of plants |
| -pod | foot | pseudopod: false foot that projects from the main part of an amoeboid cell |
| poly- | many | polypeptide: sequence of many amino acids joined together to form a protein |
| pre- | before | prediction: a forecast of events before they take place |
| -scope | instrument used to see something | microscope: instrument used to see very small objects |
| semi- | partially | semipermeable: allowing some particles to move through |
| -some | body | chromosome: structure found in eukaryotic cells that contains DNA |
| sub- | under | substrate: molecule on which an enzyme acts |
| super-, supra- | above | superficial: on or near the surface of a tissue or organ |
| syn- | with | synapse: junction of a neuron with another cell |
| -tomy | to cut | appendectomy: operation in which the appendix is removed |
| trans- | across | transformation: the transfer of genetic material from one organism to another |
| ur- | referring to urine | urology: study of the urinary tract |
| visc- | organ | viscera: internal organs of the body |

## Key:

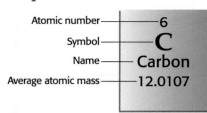

Atomic number — 6
Symbol — **C**
Name — Carbon
Average atomic mass — 12.0107

**Metals**
- Alkali metals
- Alkaline-earth metals
- Transition metals
- Other metals

**Nonmetals**
- Halogens
- Noble gases
- Other nonmetals

- Hydrogen
- Semiconductors
  (also known as *metalloids*)

- Essential to plants
- Found in the atmosphere
- Found in humans

Hydrogen is a component of all organic molecules and water. As an ion, hydrogen influences the pH of cellular and body fluids.

| | | | | | | | | |
|---|---|---|---|---|---|---|---|---|
| **1** **H** Hydrogen 1.007 94 | | | | | | | | |

Magnesium activates plant and animal enzymes and is a component of chlorophyll.

Cobalt is a component of the vitamin B$_{12}$, which is needed for maturation of red blood cells.

**Group 1** **Group 2**

Sodium is important in nerve function and muscle contraction and helps maintain water balance.

Manganese activates plant and animal enzymes.

Molybdenum plays a role in nitrogen fixation and is a component of some enzymes.

Iron is a component of hemoglobin and certain enzymes.

| 3 **Li** Lithium 6.941 | 4 **Be** Beryllium 9.012 182 |
| 11 **Na** Sodium 22.989 770 | 12 **Mg** Magnesium 24.3050 |

**Group 3** **Group 4** **Group 5** **Group 6** **Group 7** **Group 8** **Group 9**

Potassium is critical for plant protein synthesis and is important in animal nerve function.

| Period | | | | | | | | |
|---|---|---|---|---|---|---|---|---|
| 19 **K** Potassium 39.0983 | 20 **Ca** Calcium 40.078 | 21 **Sc** Scandium 44.955 910 | 22 **Ti** Titanium 47.867 | 23 **V** Vanadium 50.9415 | 24 **Cr** Chromium 51.9961 | 25 **Mn** Manganese 54.938 049 | 26 **Fe** Iron 55.845 | 27 **Co** Cobalt 58.933 200 |
| 37 **Rb** Rubidium 85.4678 | 38 **Sr** Strontium 87.62 | 39 **Y** Yttrium 88.905 85 | 40 **Zr** Zirconium 91.224 | 41 **Nb** Niobium 92.906 38 | 42 **Mo** Molybdenum 95.94 | 43 **Tc** Technetium (98) | 44 **Ru** Ruthenium 101.07 | 45 **Rh** Rhodium 102.905 50 |
| 55 **Cs** Cesium 132.905 43 | 56 **Ba** Barium 137.327 | 57 **La** Lanthanum 138.9055 | 72 **Hf** Hafnium 178.49 | 73 **Ta** Tantalum 180.9479 | 74 **W** Tungsten 183.84 | 75 **Re** Rhenium 186.207 | 76 **Os** Osmium 190.23 | 77 **Ir** Iridium 192.217 |
| 87 **Fr** Francium (223) | 88 **Ra** Radium (226) | 89 **Ac** Actinium (227) | 104 **Rf** Rutherfordium (261) | 105 **Db** Dubnium (262) | 106 **Sg** Seaborgium (266) | 107 **Bh** Bohrium (264) | 108 **Hs** Hassium (277) | 109 **Mt** Meitnerium (268) |

Calcium is part of the structure of bones and teeth, is involved in blood clotting, triggers muscle contraction, and is needed to maintain plant cell walls and membranes.

\* The systematic names and symbols for elements greater than 110 will be used until the approval of trivial names by IUPAC.

| 58 **Ce** Cerium 140.116 | 59 **Pr** Praseodymium 140.907 65 | 60 **Nd** Neodymium 144.24 | 61 **Pm** Promethium (145) | 62 **Sm** Samarium 150.36 |
| 90 **Th** Thorium 232.0381 | 91 **Pa** Protactinium 231.035 88 | 92 **U** Uranium 238.028 91 | 93 **Np** Neptunium (237) | 94 **Pu** Plutonium (244) |

**internet** connect
**go.hrw.com**
Topic: Periodic Table
Go To: go.hrw.com
Keyword: HOLT PERIODIC

Visit the HRW Web site for updates on the periodic table.

Boron is used by plants during photosynthesis.

Zinc is required by plants to make chlorophyll and by humans to maintain a healthy digestive system.

Copper is needed to metabolize iron.

Nickel is an important cofactor for plants to help them metabolize nitrogenous foods.

Nitrogen is a component of amino acids, hormones, and coenzymes.

Carbon forms the backbone of all organic molecules.

Oxygen is needed for aerobic respiration and is a component of all organic compounds.

Fluorine maintains bone structure.

Phosphorus is a component of nucleic acids, phospholipids, ATP, and coenzymes.

Chlorine is found as a negative ion and helps the human body maintain a balanced pH.

Sulfur is a component of some amino acids.

Iodine is used to make thyroid hormones.

**Group 18**

| 2 He Helium 4.002 602 |

**Group 13** | **Group 14** | **Group 15** | **Group 16** | **Group 17**

| 5 B Boron 10.811 | 6 C Carbon 12.0107 | 7 N Nitrogen 14.0067 | 8 O Oxygen 15.9994 | 9 F Fluorine 18.998 4032 | 10 Ne Neon 20.1797 |

| 13 Al Aluminum 26.981 538 | 14 Si Silicon 28.0855 | 15 P Phosphorus 30.973 761 | 16 S Sulfur 32.065 | 17 Cl Chlorine 35.453 | 18 Ar Argon 39.948 |

**Group 10** | **Group 11** | **Group 12**

| 28 Ni Nickel 58.6934 | 29 Cu Copper 63.546 | 30 Zn Zinc 65.409 | 31 Ga Gallium 69.723 | 32 Ge Germanium 72.64 | 33 As Arsenic 74.921 60 | 34 Se Selenium 78.96 | 35 Br Bromine 79.904 | 36 Kr Krypton 83.798 |

| 46 Pd Palladium 106.42 | 47 Ag Silver 107.8682 | 48 Cd Cadmium 112.411 | 49 In Indium 114.818 | 50 Sn Tin 118.710 | 51 Sb Antimony 121.760 | 52 Te Tellurium 127.60 | 53 I Iodine 126.904 47 | 54 Xe Xenon 131.293 |

| 78 Pt Platinum 195.078 | 79 Au Gold 196.966 55 | 80 Hg Mercury 200.59 | 81 Tl Thallium 204.3833 | 82 Pb Lead 207.2 | 83 Bi Bismuth 208.980 38 | 84 Po Polonium (209) | 85 At Astatine (210) | 86 Rn Radon (222) |

| 110 Ds Darmstadtium (281) | 111 Uuu* Unununium (272) | 112 Uub* Ununbium (285) | 113 Uut* Ununtrium (284) | 114 Uuq* Ununquadium (289) | 115 Uup* Ununpentium (288) |

A team at Lawrence Berkeley National Laboratories reported the discovery of elements 116 and 118 in June 1999. The same team retracted the discovery in July 2001. The discovery of elements 113, 114, and 115 has been reported but not confirmed.

| 63 Eu Europium 151.964 | 64 Gd Gadolinium 157.25 | 65 Tb Terbium 158.925 34 | 66 Dy Dysprosium 162.500 | 67 Ho Holmium 164.930 32 | 68 Er Erbium 167.259 | 69 Tm Thulium 168.934 21 | 70 Yb Ytterbium 173.04 | 71 Lu Lutetium 174.967 |

| 95 Am Americium (243) | 96 Cm Curium (247) | 97 Bk Berkelium (247) | 98 Cf Californium (251) | 99 Es Einsteinium (252) | 100 Fm Fermium (257) | 101 Md Mendelevium (258) | 102 No Nobelium (259) | 103 Lr Lawrencium (262) |

The atomic masses listed in this table reflect the precision of current measurements. (Values listed in parentheses are the mass numbers of those radioactive elements' most stable or most common isotopes.)

The classification system used in this book is based on both the commonly recognized six-kingdom system and the newer, three-domain system. A **kingdom** is a group of related phyla, whereas a **domain** is a larger-scale grouping that can encompass kingdoms. In the three-domain system, all living organisms are classified into one of three domains based on cellular similarities. Two of the three domains consist of prokaryotes, and one domain consists of eukaryotes. The table below compares the two systems of classification.

The domain **Bacteria** aligns with the kingdom Eubacteria. The domain **Archaea** aligns with the kingdom Archaebacteria. Both archaea and bacteria are prokaryotic microbes, although the two groups differ significantly.

The third domain, **Eukarya,** consists of all of the eukaryotic organisms. The four kingdoms that align with the domain Eukarya are Animalia (animals), Plantae (plants), Fungi (fungi), and Protista (protists).

The information on the following pages is conveniently organized into commonly recognized subgroups. However, not all of the existing subgroups are presented here, and all classifications are sometimes debated and revised by the scientific community. For example, biologists have proposed several new kingdoms to replace Protista, because the subgroups of Protista are no longer thought to be strongly related. Also, scientists are still uncertain about the number of species in each group.

| PROKARYOTES | | EUKARYOTES | | | |
|---|---|---|---|---|---|
| Domain Bacteria | Domain Archaea | Domain Eukarya | | | |
| Kingdom Eubacteria | Kingdom Archaebacteria | Kingdom Protista | Kingdom Fungi | Kingdom Plantae | Kingdom Animalia |

# DOMAIN BACTERIA

All bacteria are prokaryotic and lack membrane-bound organelles. Most are unicellular and reproduce by fission. Most species are heterotrophic, but some are photosynthetic or chemosynthetic. More than 4,000 living, described species of bacteria exist.

## Proteobacteria

**Alpha Proteobacteria**   many species, such as *Rhizobium* sp., are parasitic or mutualistic bacteria that live within eukaryotic hosts

**Beta Proteobacteria**   diverse modes of nutrition; some species, such as *Nitrosomonas* sp., are important in the nitrogen cycle

**Gamma Proteobacteria**   some species are photosynthetic; some species derive energy by reducing ammonia and hydrogen sulfide; some species, such as *Escherichia coli,* are enteric

**Delta Proteobacteria**   some species, such as *Bdellovibrio* sp., are predators of other bacteria

**Epsilon Proteobacteria**   many species, such as *Helicobacter pylori,* are pathogenic

## Gram-Positive Bacteria

Most, but not all, members of this diverse group are Gram-positive. One subgroup, the actinomycetes, is the source of many antibiotics. Many species, including actinomycetes, can cause disease.

## Spirochetes

These long, spiral cells have flagellated ends. Some cause serious diseases such as syphilis.

## Chlamydia

This group includes obligate internal parasities. Some cause diseases.

## Cyanobacteria

This group includes photosynthetic bacteria which are common on land and in water. The chloroplasts of some protists probably evolved from cyanobacteria.

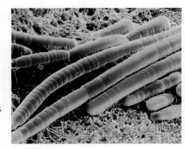

*Lyngbya sp.,*
a cyanobacterium

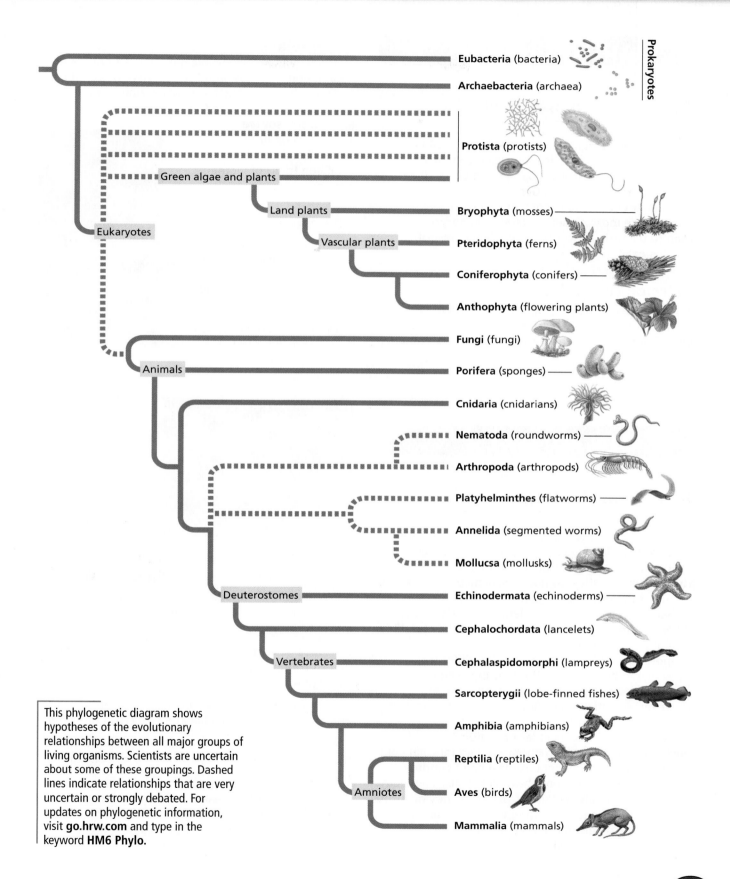

**Eubacteria** (bacteria)

**Archaebacteria** (archaea)

**Protista** (protists)

Green algae and plants

Land plants

**Bryophyta** (mosses)

Vascular plants

**Pteridophyta** (ferns)

**Coniferophyta** (conifers)

**Anthophyta** (flowering plants)

Eukaryotes

**Fungi** (fungi)

Animals

**Porifera** (sponges)

**Cnidaria** (cnidarians)

**Nematoda** (roundworms)

**Arthropoda** (arthropods)

**Platyhelminthes** (flatworms)

**Annelida** (segmented worms)

**Mollucsa** (mollusks)

Deuterostomes

**Echinodermata** (echinoderms)

**Cephalochordata** (lancelets)

Vertebrates

**Cephalaspidomorphi** (lampreys)

**Sarcopterygii** (lobe-finned fishes)

**Amphibia** (amphibians)

**Reptilia** (reptiles)

Amniotes

**Aves** (birds)

**Mammalia** (mammals)

This phylogenetic diagram shows hypotheses of the evolutionary relationships between all major groups of living organisms. Scientists are uncertain about some of these groupings. Dashed lines indicate relationships that are very uncertain or strongly debated. For updates on phylogenetic information, visit **go.hrw.com** and type in the keyword **HM6 Phylo.**

## DOMAIN ARCHAEA

# Kingdom Archaebacteria

This kingdom is made up of prokaryotes called *archaea*. Many archaea live in extreme environments. They differ from eubacteria in cell wall and cell membrane structure. Genetic similarities between archaea and eukaryotes suggest that archaea are more closely related to eukaryotes than to bacteria. Fewer than 100 living, described species exist.

## Extreme Halophiles

Extreme halophiles inhabit environments of very high salinity, such as the Dead Sea and Great Salt Lake (salinity 15 to 20 percent). Many are aerobic.

### Methanogens

Methanogens are anaerobic methane producers that inhabit soil, swamps, and the digestive tracts of animals—particularly the tracts of grazing mammals such as cattle. Most use $CO_2$ as a carbon source. Methanogens produce nearly 2 trillion kilograms (2 billion tons) of methane gas annually.

### Thermoacidophiles

Thermoacidophiles inhabit hot, acidic areas, tolerate extreme heat, and require sulfur. Most are anaerobic.

This undersea hydrothermal vent is home to thermoacidophiles.

## DOMAIN EUKARYA

# Kingdom Protista

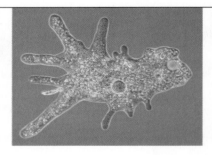

*Amoeba proteus,* an amoeba

Kingdom Protista is a diverse group of eukaryotes that are not plants, fungi, or animals. Traditionally, species have been classified in Protista whenever their characteristics do not clearly match with those of one of the other eukaryotic kingdoms.

Because protists are not defined clearly, are so diverse, and are so poorly understood, the classification of protists is problematic. Many scientists have proposed groupings and names that differ from those listed here. In fact, three or more new kingdoms have been proposed to replace Protista. However, scientists have not yet clearly favored any particular new system.

Protists can be unicellular or multicellular. Most have chromosomes, mitochondria, and internal compartments. Some have chloroplasts and conduct photosynthesis, and some have cell walls. They may reproduce sexually, asexually, or both. They occur in many environments, including water, soil, and inside of other organisms. More than 40,000 living, described species exist.

## Animal-like Protists (includes Protozoa and Sarcomastigophora)

**Sarcodina or Rhizopoda** amoebas; unicellular, heterotrophic, and amorphous; move by using cytoplasmic extensions, or *pseudopodia*

**Radiozoa or Actinipoda** radiolarians; unicellular, heterotrophic, and marine; have pored shells through which cytoplasmic threads project

**Ciliophora** ciliates; unicellular, heterotrophic, and complex; have rows of cilia and two types of nuclei

**Mastigophora or Kinetoplastida** mastigophorans; have at least one flagellum; most are unicellular and heterotrophic; some cause disease

**Apicomplexa or Sporozoa** unicellular, heterotrophic, and spore-forming; have complex life cycles; adults are nonmotile parasites; undergo asexual and sexual reproduction

# Kingdom Protista, *continued*

## Plantlike Protists

**Chlorophyta**   green algae; unicellular, colonial, multicellular, and photosynthetic; contain chlorophylls *a* and *b;* their chloroplasts are similar to those of plants; scientists think that plants descended from green algae

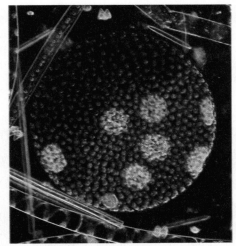

*Volvox* sp., a green alga

**Euglenophyta**   euglenoids; unicellular, photosynthetic, and heterotrophic; reproduce asexually; most species live in fresh water; chloroplasts resemble the chloroplasts of green algae and may have evolved from the same symbiotic bacteria from which green algae chloroplasts evolved; some are considered to be animal-like and are classified in Euglenozoa

**Bacillariophyta**   diatoms; unicellular and photosynthetic; secrete a unique shell that is made of opaline silica and that resembles a lidded box; have chloroplasts that resemble the chloroplasts of brown algae; contain chlorophylls *a* and *c* and fucoxanthin

**Phaeophyta**   brown algae; multicellular and photosynthetic; contain chlorophylls *a* and *c* and fucoxanthin (the source of their brownish color)

**Dinoflagellata**   unicellular; heterotrophic and autotrophic species; most species are marine and are enclosed by two cellulose plates; most species contain carotenoids and chlorophylls *a* and *c.;* sometimes grouped in Alveolata with the animal-like protist groups Apicomplexa and Ciliata

*Corallina* sp., a red alga

**Rhodophyta**   red algae; multicellular and photosynthetic; most are marine and contain chlorophyll *a* and phycobilins; chloroplasts probably evolved from symbiotic cyanobacteria

## Funguslike Protists

**Myxomycota**   plasmodial slime molds; heterotrophic; individuals stream as part of a multinucleate mass of cytoplasm; can produce spores that give rise to new individuals; sometimes grouped with other slime molds in Mycetozoa within Protozoa

**Oomycota or Pseudofungi**   water molds, white rusts, and downy mildews; unicellular heterotrophs; parasites or decomposers; cell walls consist of cellulose; sometimes grouped in Stramenopila with Bacillariophyta, Chrysophyta, and Phaeophyta

**Dictyostelida**   cellular slime molds; heterotrophic cells that take on different forms depending on food availability; cells are usually amoeba-shaped but may aggregate into a moving mass called a *slug;* a slug may produce spores

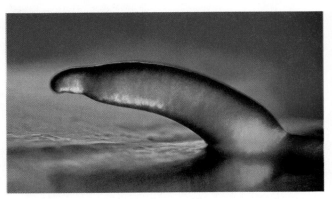

*Dictyostelium* sp., a cellular slime mold

# Kingdom Fungi

Fungi are heterotrophic by absorption and eukaryotic. Most are multicellular and are composed of filaments called *hyphae.* Although all fungi that are yeasts are unicellular, some are dimorphic, or have both hyphal and unicellular stages. Hyphae are multinucleate, have divisions called *septae* between cells, and have chitinous cell walls. Most fungi reproduce sexually and asexually. Some lack a sexual stage or are difficult to classify and are labeled *Fungi Imperfecti,* or *Deuteromycetes.* About 70,000 living, described species of fungi exist.

## Phylum Zygomycota

Zygomycetes, such as bread molds, usually lack septae. Some are terrestrial. Some are parasitic. Fusion of hyphae leads to formation of a zygote, which divides by meiosis when it germinates.

## Phylum Ascomycota

Ascomycetes—such as brewer's and baker's yeasts, molds, morels, and truffles—include terrestrial, marine, and freshwater species. Septae are usually perforated. Fusion of the hyphae forms a dense, interwoven mass that contains characteristic microscopic reproductive structures called *asci* (singular, *ascus*). Many fungi formerly classified as Deuteromycetes are now classified as Ascomycota.

## Phylum Basidiomycota

Basidiomycetes reproduce sexually. Hyphae usually have incomplete septae. Fusion of the hyphae forms a *mushroom,* a densely interwoven structure that contains characteristic microscopic reproductive structures called *basidia* (singular, *basidium*). Basidiomycota includes mushrooms, toadstools, shelf fungi, rusts, and smuts.

*Morchella* sp., a mushroom

# Kingdom Plantae

Plants are multicellular eukaryotes whose cell walls contain cellulose. Most are autotrophic and terrestrial and contain tissues and organs. Plants contain chlorophylls *a* and *b* in plastids and have a life cycle in which sexual and asexual reproduction alternate. About 280,000 living, described species exist.

## Phylum Bryophyta

Bryophytes, or mosses, are nonvascular plants whose gametophytes are larger than their sporophytes. The sporophytes grow on the gametophytes. Bryophytes have simple conducting tissue and lack roots, stems, and leaves.

*Marchantia* sp., a liverwort

## Phylum Hepatophyta

Hepatophytes, or liverworts, are nonvascular plants whose gametophytes are larger than their sporophytes. The sporophytes grow on the gametophytes and lack stomata, roots, stems, and leaves.

## Phylum Anthocerophyta

Anthocerophytes, or hornworts, are nonvascular plants whose gametophytes are larger than their sporophytes. The sporophytes grow on the gametophytes, have stomata, and lack roots, stems, and leaves.

*Dicksonia antartica,* a fern        *Ginko biloba,* a ginkophyte

## Phylum Pteridophyta

Pteridophytes, or ferns, are seedless vascular plants whose sporophytes are larger than their small, flat, independent gametophytes. The sporophytes have roots and stems. The lower surfaces of the leaves produce spores.

## Phylum Lycophyta

Lycophytes, such as club mosses, are seedless vascular plants whose sporophytes are larger than their small, flat, independent gametophytes. The sporophytes resemble the gametophytes of mosses; they produce spores in cones and have roots, stems, and leaves.

## Phylum Sphenophyta

Sphenophytes, such as horsetails, are seedless vascular plants whose sporophytes are larger than their small, flat, independent gametophytes. The sporophytes produce spores in cones and have roots, leaves, and jointed stems.

## Phylum Psilotophyta

Psilophytes, such as whisk ferns, are seedless vascular plants whose sporophytes are larger than their small, flat, independent gametophytes. The sporophytes lack leaves, have roots and stems, and produce spores in sporangia at stem tips.

## Phylum Coniferophyta

Conifers are gymnosperms such as pines, spruces, firs, larches, and yews. Most have sporophytes that are evergreen trees or shrubs that have needlelike or scalelike leaves. Microscopic gametophytes develop from spores produced within cones on the sporophytes.

## Phylum Cycadophyta

Cycads are gymnosperms and seed-bearing vascular plants. The sporophytes are evergreen trees and shrubs that have palmlike leaves. Microscopic gametophytes develop from spores produced in cones on separate sporophytes.

## Phylum Ginkgophyta

Ginkgophyta contains one species: a gymnosperm called *Ginkgo biloba.* The sporophyte is a deciduous tree that has fan-shaped leaves and fleshy seeds. Microscopic gametophytes develop from spores produced on separate sporophytes.

## Phylum Gnetophyta

Gnetophytes are gymnosperms and seed-bearing vascular plants whose sporophytes are shrubs or vines that have some angiosperm features. Microscopic gametophytes develop from spores produced in cones on the sporophytes.

## Phylum Anthophyta

Anthophytes are angiosperms, or flowering plants, and are seed-bearing vascular plants whose sporophytes are flowering trees, shrubs, herbs, or vines. Microscopic gametophytes develop from spores produced in flower reproductive structures.

**Class Monocotyledones** monocots; embryos have one cotyledon; flower parts in multiples of three; leaf veins parallel; includes grasses, sedges, lilies, irises, palms, and orchids

**Class Dicotyledones** dicots; embryos have two cotyledons; flower parts in multiples of two, four, or five; includes most flowering plants, such as daisies, legumes, hardwood trees, shrubs, and vines

*Helianthus annuus,* a dicot

## DOMAIN EUKARYA, *continued*

# Kingdom Animalia

Animals are multicellular, eukaryotic, and heterotrophic organisms. Most obtain nutrition by ingestion and have specialized tissues. Many have complex organs and organ systems. None have cell walls or chloroplasts. Most undergo sexual reproduction. They are aquatic or terrestrial. More than 1 million living, described species exist.

## Phylum Porifera

Poriferans, or sponges, are asymmetrical and lack tissues and organs. Their body wall consists of two layers of interdependent cells. Poriferans undergo sexual and asexual reproduction. Most are marine.

## Phylum Cnidaria

Cnidarians are radially symmetrical and are marine or freshwater. Most are gelatinous and have distinct tissues and a baglike body of two cell layers.

**Class Hydrozoa**   hydras
**Class Cubozoa**   box jellies
**Class Scyphozoa**   jellyfish
**Class Anthozoa**   sea anemones and corals

*Cribrinopsis fernadli*, a sea anemone

## Phylum Ctenophora

Ctenophores, or comb jellies, are radially symmetrical, marine, transparent, and gelatinous.

## Phylum Platyhelminthes

Flatworms are bilaterally symmetrical.

**Class Turbellaria**   planarians
**Classes Trematoda and Monogenea**   flukes
**Class Cestoda**   tapeworms

## Phylum Nematoda

Nematodes, or roundworms, are parasitic, unsegmented, long, and slender pseudocoelomates.

## Phylum Rotifera

Rotifers are free-living, aquatic pseudocoelomates.

## Phylum Mollusca

Mollusks are soft-bodied protostomes whose three-part body consists of a foot, a visceral mass, and a mantle. They are terrestrial, freshwater, or marine.

**Class Polyplacophora**   chitons
**Class Gastropoda**   gastropods
**Class Bivalvia**   bivalves
**Class Cephalopoda**   cephalopods

## Phylum Annelida

Annelids are serially segmented, bilaterally symmetrical protostomes.

**Class Polychaeta**   bristle worms
**Class Oligochaeta**   earthworms
**Class Hirudinea**   leeches

## Phylum Arthropoda

Arthropods are bilaterally symmetrical, segmented protostomes that are aerial, terrestrial, or aquatic and have paired, jointed appendages and a chitinous exoskeleton.

**Subphylum Chelicerata**   includes arachnids
**Subphylum Crustacea**   crustaceans
**Subphylum Myriapoda**   centipedes and millipedes
**Subphylum Hexapoda**   insects and parainsecta

## Phylum Echinodermata

Echinoderms are marine deuterostomes. Adults have radial symmetry and a five-part body plan. Most have a water-vascular system and tube feet.

**Class Crinoidea**   sea lilies and feather stars
**Class Ophiuroidea**   brittle stars and basket stars
**Class Echinoidea**   sea urchins and sand dollars
**Class Holothuroidea**   sea cucumbers
**Class Asteroidea**   sea stars

## Phylum Chordata

Chordates are bilaterally symmetrical, aquatic or terrestrial deuterostomes that have a notochord, a dorsal nerve cord, pharyngeal slits, and a tail.

*Ambystoma cingulatum,* a vertebrate

**Subphylum Urochordata**   tunicates
**Subphylum Cephalochordata**   lancelets
**Subphylum Vertebrata**   vertebrates

## The Geologic Time Scale

| Era | Period | Epoch | Beginning of interval (mya*) | Characteristics from geologic and fossil evidence |
|---|---|---|---|---|
| Cenozoic | Quaternary | Holocene | 0.0115 | The last glacial period ends; complex human societies develop. |
| | | Pleistocene | 1.8 | Woolly mammoths, rhinos, and humans appear. |
| | Tertiary | Pliocene | 5.3 | Large carnivores (bears, lions, wolves) appear. |
| | | Miocene | 23.0 | Grazing herds are abundant; raccoons and wolves appear. |
| | | Oligocene | 33.9 | Deer, pigs, horses, camels, cats, and dogs appear. |
| | | Eocene | 55.8 | Horses, flying squirrels, bats, and whales appear. |
| | | Paleocene | 65.5 | Age of mammals begins; first primates appear. |
| Mesozoic | Cretaceous | | 146 | Flowering plants and modern birds appear; mass extinctions mark the end of the Mesozoic Era. |
| | Jurassic | | 200 | Dinosaurs are the dominant life-form; primitive birds and flying reptiles appear. |
| | Triassic | | 251 | Dinosaurs appear; ammonites are common; cycads and conifers are abundant; and mammals appear. |
| Paleozoic | Permian | | 299 | Pangaea comes together; mass extinctions mark the end of the Paleozoic Era. |
| | Carboniferous | Pennsylvanian Period | 318 | Giant cockroaches and dragonflies are common; coal deposits form; and reptiles appear. |
| | | Mississippian Period | 359 | Amphibians flourish; brachiopods are common in oceans; and forests and swamps cover most land. |
| | Devonian | | 416 | Age of fishes begins; amphibians appear; and giant horsetails, ferns, and cone-bearing plants develop. |
| | Silurian | | 444 | Eurypterids, land plants, and animals appear. |
| | Ordovician | | 488 | Echinoderms appear; brachiopods increase; trilobites decline; graptolites flourish; atmosphere reaches modern $O_2$-rich state. |
| | Cambrian | | 542 | Shelled marine invertebrates appear; trilobites and brachiopods are common. First vertebrates appear. |
| Precambrian time | | | 4,600 | The Earth forms; continental shields appear; fossils are rare; and stromatolites are the most common organism. |

*millions of years ago

| Sound symbol | Key word(s) | Phonetic respelling |
|---|---|---|
| *a* | map | M<u>A</u>P |
| *ay* | face<br>day | F<u>AY</u>S<br>D<u>AY</u> |
| *ah* | father<br>cot | F<u>AH</u>-thuhr<br>K<u>AH</u>T |
| *aw* | caught<br>law | K<u>AW</u>T<br>L<u>AW</u> |
| *ee* | eat<br>ski | <u>EE</u>T<br>SK<u>EE</u> |
| *e* | wet<br>rare | W<u>E</u>T<br>R<u>E</u>R |
| *oy* | boy<br>foil | B<u>OY</u><br>F<u>OY</u>L |
| *ow* | out<br>now | <u>OW</u>T<br>N<u>OW</u> |
| *oo* | shoot<br>suit | SH<u>OO</u>T<br>S<u>OO</u>T |
| *u* | book<br>put | B<u>U</u>K<br>P<u>U</u>T |
| *uh* | sun<br>cut | S<u>UH</u>N<br>K<u>UH</u>T |
| *i* | lip | L<u>I</u>P |
| *ie* | tide<br>sigh | T<u>IE</u>D<br>S<u>IE</u> |
| *oh* | over<br>coat | <u>OH</u>-vuhr<br>K<u>OH</u>T |
| *yoo* | yule<br>globule | <u>YOO</u>L<br>GLAH-b<u>yoo</u>l |
| *yu* | cure | K<u>YU</u>R |
| *uhr* | paper<br>fern | PAY-p<u>uhr</u><br>F<u>UHR</u>N |
| *k* | card<br>kite | <u>K</u>AHRD<br><u>K</u>IET |
| *s* | cell<br>sit | <u>S</u>EL<br><u>S</u>IT |
| *y* | yes | <u>Y</u>ES |
| *j* | job | <u>J</u>AHB |
| *g* | got | <u>G</u>AHT |
| *zh* | pleasure | PLE-<u>zh</u>uhr |

Each page number provided indicates where the word is defined and not necessarily where it is first used. Remember to refer to the index for more page numbers if further investigation is needed.

—————— **A** ——————

**abdomen** in arthropods, the posterior tagma; in vertebrates, the region that comprises the posterior part of the coelom and the viscera; the internal organs other than the heart, lungs, thymus (728)

**abdominal cavity** the hollow part of the body that is below the diaphragm and above the pelvis; contains the organs of digestion, excretion, and reproduction (910)

**abiotic factor** an environmental factor that is not associated with the activities of living organisms (363)

**abscisic acid** a hormone in plants that helps regulate the growth of buds and the germination of seeds (abbreviation, ABA) (635)

**abscission** the separation of leaves or other plant structures by the formation of a layer of cells that develops on the base of the plant structure when the structure is ready to fall (634)

**absolute age** the numeric age of an object or event, often stated in years before the present, as established by an absolute-dating process, such as radiometric dating (303)

**accessory pigment** a pigment that absorbs light energy and transfers it to chlorophyll in photosynthesis (511)

**acclimation** an organism's change in response to a change in the organism's environment (364)

**acetyl-CoA** acetyl coenzyme A, a compound that is synthesized by cells and that plays a major role in metabolism (138)

**acid** any compound that increases the number of hydronium ions when dissolved in water; acids turn blue litmus paper red and react with bases and some metals to form salts (43)

**acid precipitation** precipitation, such as rain, sleet, or snow, that contains a high concentration of acids, often because of the pollution of the atmosphere (441)

**acoelomate** an animal that lacks a coelom, or body cavity (665)

**actin** a protein that makes up the thin filaments of muscle fibers and that functions in the contraction and relaxation of muscle (919)

**action potential** a sudden change in the polarity of the membrane of a neuron, gland cell, or muscle fiber that facilitates the transmission of electrical impulses (1005)

**activation** in genetics, the initiation of transcription of a particular gene (219)

**activation energy** the minimum amount of energy required to start a chemical reaction (36)

**active site** the site on an enzyme that attaches to a substrate (57)

**active transport** the movement of chemical substances, usually across the cell membrane, against a concentration gradient; requires cells to use energy (103)

**adaptation** the process of becoming adapted to an environment; an anatomical, physiological, or behavioral trait that improves an organism's ability to survive and reproduce (12, 300)

**adaptive radiation** an evolutionary pattern in which many species evolve from a single ancestral species (309)

**addiction** the condition in which a person can no longer control his or her drug use (1021)

**adhesion** the attractive force between two bodies of different substances that are in contact with each other (41)

**adrenal gland** one of the two endocrine glands located above each kidney (1036)

**adventitious root** a root that occurs in an unusual position, such as on stems or leaves (588)

**aerobic respiration** the process in which pyruvic acid is broken down and NADH is used to make a large amount of ATP; the part of respiration that is carried out in the presence of oxygen (131)

**aflatoxin** a toxic fungal poison that causes liver cancer; found as contaminants in peanuts and corn; produced by a species of the genus *Aspergillus* (535)

**afterbirth** the remains of the placenta and the membranes, which are expelled from the mother's body following birth (1060)

**agar** a gel-like polysaccharide compound used for culturing microbes; extracted from certain red algae (518)

**age structure** the classification of members of a population into groups according to age or the distribution of members of a population in terms of age groups (384)

**Agent Orange** a mixture of plant hormones that has been used to cause plants to lose their leaves; has been used in military campaigns to defoliate large areas of forest (633)

**aggressive behavior** threatening behavior or physical conflict between animals (893)

**agricultural revolution** the change from a hunting and gathering society to an agricultural society that began about 10,000 years ago (390)

**agriculture** the raising of crops and livestock for food or for other products that are useful to humans (545)

**AIDS** acquired immune deficiency syndrome, a disease caused by HIV; an infection that results in an ineffective immune system (970)

**albumen** the white of an egg, composed primarily of the protein albumin (823)

**alcoholic fermentation** the anaerobic process by which yeasts and other microorganisms break down sugars to form carbon dioxide and ethanol (135)

**algae** autotrophic eukaryotic organisms that convert the sun's energy into food through photosynthesis but that do not have roots, stems, or leaves (singular, *alga*) (510)

**algal bloom** a vast increase in the concentration of algae and cyanobacteria in a body of eutrophic water which causes harmful changes in the water; some species of algae produce toxins that kill other sea life (517)

**alginate** a polysaccharide derivative of alginic acid that is found in brown algae and that has many industrial uses including thickening agent in foods and a dental impression agent (518)

**allantois** a membranous sac that acts as an organ of respiration and nutrition for the embryo; in humans, its blood vessels become the blood vessels of the umbilical cord (823)

**allele** one of the alternative forms of a gene that governs a characteristic, such as hair color (178)

**allele frequency** the proportion of gene copies in a population that are a given allele, expressed as a percentage (318)

**allergy** a physical response to an antigen, which can be a common substance that produces little or no response in the general population (968)

**alternation of generations** the alternation of sexual reproduction and asexual reproduction in certain plants and animals (565)

**altricial** describes organisms that are not very developed when born and that require care or nursing (849)

**altruistic behavior** self-sacrificing behavior that benefits another individual (754)

**alveolus** any of the tiny air cells of the lungs where oxygen and carbon dioxide are exchanged (plural, *alveoli*) (826, 947)

**amino acid** an organic molecule that contains a carboxyl and an amino group and that makes up proteins; a protein monomer (56, 664)

**amino acid–based hormone** a hormone that is made up of simple amino acids, peptides, or proteins (1031)

**ammonia** a colorless gas that has an alkaline reaction in water; forms in nature as an end product of animal metabolism (formula, $NH_3$) (993)

**ammonification** the formation of ammonia compounds in the soil by the action of bacteria on decaying matter (374)

**amniocentesis** a procedure used in fetal diagnosis in which amniotic fluid is removed from the uterus of the pregnant woman (245)

**amnion** in mammals, birds, and reptiles, the membrane that contains a developing embryo and its surrounding fluid (823)

**amniotic egg** a type of egg that is produced by reptiles, birds, and egg-laying mammals and that contains a large amount of yolk; usually surrounded by a leathery or hard shell within which the embryo and its embryonic membranes develop (823)

**amniotic sac** the sac formed by the amnion (1057)

**amoebocyte** within the body wall of a sponge, a specialized cell that crawls about and delivers nutrients from the choanocytes to the rest of the body cells (674)

**amoeboid movement** a characteristic movement of protozoa that occurs because of the formation of pseudopodia (506)

**amplexus** the copulatory embrace of amphibians (810)

**ampulla** on the upper end of a tube foot of an echinoderm, a bulblike sac that forces water into the tube foot and causes the tube foot to expand (766)

**anaerobic** describes a process that does not require oxygen (131)

**anal pore** in protozoa, an opening from which wastes are eliminated (508)

**analogous structure** an anatomical structure in one species that is similar in function and appearance, but not in evolutionary origin, to another anatomical structure in another species (305)

**anaphase** a phase of mitosis and meiosis in which the chromosomes separate (157)

**androgen** a hormone that is secreted by the testes and that controls secondary male characteristics (1037)

**angiosperm** a flowering plant that produces seeds within a fruit (565)

**animal** a multicellular, heterotrophic organism that lacks cell walls and that is usually characterized by movement and sexual reproduction; a member of Kingdom Animalia (651)

**Animalia** in a traditional taxonomic system, a kingdom made up of complex, multicellular organisms that lack cell walls, are usually able to move around, and possess specialized sense organs that help them quickly respond to their environment (350)

**annual ring** in secondary xylem (wood), the growth ring formed in one season (595)

**antenna** a feeler that is on the head of an invertebrate, such as a crustacean or an insect, and that senses touch, taste, or smell (728)

**antennule** in crustaceans, a second pair of antennae, usually smaller than the first (728)

**anterior** the front part of a body or structure (655)

**anther** in flowering plants, the tip of a stamen, which contains the pollen sacs where grains form (613)

**antheridium** a reproductive structure that produces male sex cells in flowerless and seedless plants (532, 609)

**anthropoid primate** one of a subgroup of primates that includes monkeys, apes, and humans (876)

**antibiotic** a substance that inhibits the growth of or kills microorganisms (465)

**antibiotic resistance** the ability of a population of bacteria to survive the lethal effects of an antibiotic (473)

**antibody** a protein that reacts to a specific antigen or that inactivates or destroys toxins (941, 964)

**anticodon** a region of tRNA that consists of three bases complementary to the codon of mRNA (208)

**antigen** a substance that stimulates an immune response (943, 962)

**aorta** the main artery in the body; it carries blood from the left ventricle to systemic circulation (935)

**aortic arch** a muscular blood vessel that links the blood vessels from the dorsal and ventral parts of an animal's body (715)

**aphotic zone** the deeper parts of the ocean, where there is so little light that plants cannot carry out photosynthesis (423)

**apical dominance** the inhibition of lateral bud growth on the stem of a plant by auxin produced in the terminal bud (633)

**apical meristem** the growing region at the tips of stems and roots in plants (586)

**apical organ** in ctenophores, a sensory structure that enables the animal to sense its orientation in water; in annelids, a ciliated plate located at the back of the larva (682)

**aposematic coloration** in animals, bright coloration that warns predators that a potential prey animal is poisonous (896)

**appendage** a structure that extends from the main body, such as a limb, tentacle, fin, or wing (723)

**appendicular skeleton** the bones of the arms and legs, along with scapula, clavicle, and pelvis (911)

**aqueous solution** a solution in which water is the solvent (42)

**arachnid** an arthropod that has eight legs and no wings or antennae; a spider, scorpion, mite, or tick (731)

**archaea** prokaryotes, most of which are known to live in extreme environments; differentiated from other prokaryotes by genetic differences and differences in the make up of their cell walls (singular, *archaeon*) (289, 347)

**Archaea** in a modern taxonomic system, a domain made up of prokaryotes that can live in extreme environments and that are differentiated from other prokaryotes by various important chemical differences; this domain aligns with the traditional kingdom Archaebacteria (347)

**Archaebacteria** in a traditional taxonomic system, a kingdom made up of prokaryotes that can live in extreme environments; differentiated from other prokaryotes by various important chemical differences; biologists more recently prefer to classify these organisms as Domain Archaea (348)

**archegonium** a female reproductive structure of small, nonvascular plants that produces a single egg and in which fertilization and development take place (609)

**archenteron** the primitive gastric cavity of an embryo (664)

**artery** a blood vessel that carries blood away from the heart to the body's organs (936)

**arthropod** a member of the phylum Arthropoda, which includes invertebrate animals such as insects, crustaceans, and arachnids; characterized by having segmented bodies and paired appendages (723)

**artificial selection** the selective breeding of organisms (by humans) for specific desirable characteristics (310)

**ascocarp** the reproductive portion of an ascomycete (532)

**ascogonium** the female sexual organ or cell in ascomycetes (532)

**ascospore** a spore produced in an ascus by ascomycetes (532)

**ascus** the spore sac where ascomycetes produce ascospores (532)

**asexual reproduction** reproduction that does not involve the union of gametes and in which a single parent produces offspring that are genetically identical to the parent (155)

**aspirin** the common name of acetylsalicylic acid, a pain reliever (548)

**assortative mating** sexual reproduction in which males and females do not breed randomly (323)

**asteroid-impact hypothesis** an explanation for the mass extinction of most of the dinosaurs; holds that a giant asteroid struck Earth and caused catastophic climate change about 66 million years ago (821)

**asthma** a lung disorder characterized by labored breathing due to narrowing of the bronchioles; associated with shortness of breath, wheezing, and coughing; and caused by a reaction to certain irritants (968)

**atherosclerosis** a disease characterized by the buildup of fatty materials on the interior walls of the arteries (938)

**atom** the smallest unit of an element that maintains the chemical properties of that element (32)

**atomic number** the number of protons in the nucleus of an atom; the atomic number is the same for all atoms of an element (32)

**ATP (adenosine triphosphate)** an organic molecule that acts as the main energy source for cell processes; composed of a nitrogenous base, a sugar, and three phosphate groups (54)

**atriopore** an opening from the atrial cavity to the exterior in certain fish (770)

**atrium** a chamber that receives blood that is returning to the heart (933)

**auditory canal** the tube through which air enters the ear (1017)

**australopithecine** one of a subfamily of early hominids that lived between 4.2 million and 1 million years ago; includes the genus *Australopithecus* and possibly the genus *Paranthropus* (877)

**autoimmune disease** a disease in which the immune system attacks the organism's own cells (969)

**autonomic nervous system** the part of the nervous system that controls involuntary actions (1015)

**autosome** any chromosome that is not a sex chromosome (152, 236)

**autotomy** the ability of an organism to drop a body part and, usually, to regenerate a new one (832)

**autotroph** an organism that produces its own nutrients from inorganic substances or from the environment instead of consuming other organisms (113, 469)

**AV node (atrioventricular node)** a mass of specialized cardiac muscle that is located between the right atrium and right ventricle and that generates electrical impulses that cause the ventricles of the heart to contract (935)

**axial skeleton** the bones of the skull, ribs, vertebral column, and sternum (911)

**axon** an elongated extension of a neuron that carries impulses away from the cell body (1005)

**axon terminal** the end of an axon (1005)

## B

**B cell** a white blood cell that matures in bones and makes antibodies (962)

**bacillus** a rod-shaped bacterium (463)

**Bacteria** in a modern taxonomic system, a domain made up of prokaryotes that usually have a cell wall and that usually reproduce by cell division; this domain aligns with the traditional kingdom Eubacteria (347)

**bacteriophage** a virus that infects bacteria (195, 486)

**baleen** the thin plates of keratin that hang from the mouth of some whales; used to filter out water but to retain solids when whales feed (865)

**bark** a tissue of dead cells that forms on the exterior of woody plants for protection (595)

**base** any compound that increases the number of hydroxide ions when dissolved in water; bases turn red litmus paper blue and react with acids to form salts (44)

**base pairing rules** the rules stating that cytosine pairs with guanine and adenine pairs with thymine in DNA, and that adenine pairs with uracil in RNA (198)

**base unit** one of the fundamental units of measurement that describes length, mass, time, and other quantities and from which other units are derived (23)

**basidiocarp** the part of a basidiomycete that produces spores (531)

**basidiospore** an asexual spore formed by a basidium (531)

**basidium** a structure that produces asexual spores in basidiomycetes (531)

**behavior** an action that an individual carries out in response to a stimulus or to the environment (887)

**bell curve** on a graph of the frequency of some variable, a curve that first rises and then falls and thus forms a symmetric bell-shaped curve (317)

**benthic zone** the bottom region of oceans and bodies of fresh water (424)

**biennial** a plant that has a two-year life cycle (642)

**bilateral symmetry** a condition in which two equal halves of a body mirror each other (655)

**binary fission** a form of asexual reproduction in single-celled organisms by which one cell divides into two cells of the same size (154, 504)

**binomial nomenclature** a system for giving each organism a two-word scientific name that consists of the genus name followed by the species name (339)

**biodiversity** the variety of organisms considered at all levels, from populations to ecosystems (337, 438)

**biodiversity hotspot** region of the biosphere that has been identified by conservationists as having high species diversity and as being highly threatened by human impacts (449)

**bioethics** the study of ethical issues related to DNA technology (270)

**biogenesis** the scientific principle that living organisms come only from other living organisms (279)

**biogeochemical** cycle the circulation of substances through living organisms from or to the environment (371)

**biogeography** the study of the geographical distribution of living organisms and fossils on Earth (305)

**bioindicator** a species that is especially sensitive to ecological change and thus can serve as an indicator of environmental conditions (447)

**bioinformatics** a technology that combines biological science, computer science, and information technology to enable the discovery of new biological insights and unifying principles (263)

**biological magnification** the accumulation of increasingly large amounts of toxic substances within each successive link of the food chain (442)

**biological molecule** chemical compound that provides physical structure and brings about movement, energy use, and other cellular functions (7)

**biological species concept** the concept that a species is a population of organisms that can interbreed but cannot breed with other populations (327)

**biology** the study of life (5)

**bioluminescence** the production of light by means of a chemical reaction in an organism (513, 682)

**biomass** any organic material that has been produced in an ecosystem (366)

**biome** a large region characterized by a specific type of climate and certain types of plant and animal communities (417)

**bioremediation** the biological treatment of hazardous waste by natural or genetically engineered microorganisms (476)

**biosphere** the part of Earth where life exists; includes all of the living organisms on Earth (361, 437)

**biotic factor** an environmental factor that is associated with or results from the activities of living organisms (363)

**bipedalism** in hominids, the condition of being adapted to walk primarily upright on two legs (876)

**bipinnaria** the larva of starfish (767)

**birth rate** the number of births that occur in a period of time in a given area (383)

**bivalve** an aquatic mollusk that has a shell divided into two halves connected by a hinge, such as a clam, oyster, or mussel (708)

**blade** the broad, flat portion of a typical leaf (600)

**blastocyst** the modified blastula stage of mammalian embryos (1056)

**blastopore** an opening that develops in the blastula (664)

**blastula** the stage of an embryo before gastrulation (664)

**blood alcohol concentration** a measurement of the amount of alcohol in a person's blood (abbreviation, BAC) (1023)

**blood pressure** the force that blood exerts on the walls of the arteries (936)

**blood type** a classification of blood that depends on the type of antigen present on the surface of the red blood cell (943)

**bolting** the premature production of flowers and seeds, especially during the first year of a biennial plant (642)

**bone marrow** soft tissue inside bones where red and white blood cells are produced (913)

**book lung** in spiders and scorpions, an organ for respiration that has parallel folds that resemble the pages of a book (732)

**Bowman's capsule** the cup-shaped structure of the nephron of a kidney that encloses the glomerulus and in which filtration takes place (994)

**brainstem** the stemlike portion of the brain that connects the cerebral hemispheres with the spinal cord and that maintains the necessary functions of the body, such as breathing and circulation (1012)

**bronchiole** a small air passage that branches from the bronchi within the lungs (947)

**bronchus** one of the two tubes that connect the lungs with the trachea (947)

**brood patch** on the abdomen of birds, a thickened, featherless patch of skin that is used for incubating eggs (848)

**bryophyte** a plant that has no vascular tissue and absorbs nutrients and water from the soil through rootlike hairs; examples include mosses and liverworts (567)

**bud** a shoot or flower that has immature leaves folded in the growing tip (593)

**bud scale** a modified leaf that forms a protective covering for a bud until it opens (593)

**budding** asexual reproduction in which a part of the parent organism pinches off and forms a new organism (528)

**buffer** a solution made from a weak acid and its conjugate base that neutralizes small amounts of acids or bases added to it (44)

**bulbourethral gland** one of the two glands in the male reproductive system that add fluid to the semen during ejaculation (1051)

## C

**C₄ pathway** a carbon-fixing process in which carbon dioxide is bound to a compound to form a four-carbon intermediate (122)

**Calvin cycle** a biochemical pathway of photosynthesis in which carbon dioxide is converted into glucose using ATP (120)

**CAM pathway** a water-conserving, carbon-fixing process; CAM plants take in carbon at night and fix it into various organic compounds and release it during the day (122)

**cancer** a tumor in which the cells begin dividing at an uncontrolled rate and become invasive (225)

**canine** a sharp tooth located on either side of both jaws (865)

**canopy** the layers of treetops that shade the forest floor (419)

**capillarity** the attraction between molecules that results in the rise of a liquid in small tubes (41)

**capillary** a tiny blood vessel that allows an exchange between blood and cells in tissue (936)

**capsid** a protein sheath that surrounds the nucleic acid core in a virus (484)

**capsule** in mosses, the part that contains spores; in bacteria, a protective layer of polysaccharides around the cell wall (468)

**carapace** a shieldlike plate that covers the cephalothorax of some crustaceans and reptiles (728, 830)

**carbohydrate** any organic compound that is made of carbon, hydrogen, and oxygen and that provides nutrients to the cells of living things (55)

**carbon cycle** the movement of carbon from the nonliving environment into living things and back (372)

**carbon fixation** the synthesis of organic compounds from carbon dioxide, such as in photosynthesis (120)

**carcinogen** a cancer-causing substance (226)

**carcinoma** a malignant tumor that grows in the skin or in the tissues that line organs (228)

**cardiac muscle** the type of involuntary muscle found in the heart (907)

**cardiac sphincter** a circular muscle located between the esophagus and the stomach (988)

**cardiovascular system** a collection of organs that transport blood throughout the body; the organs in this system include the heart, the arteries, and the veins (933)

**carnivore** an organism that eats animals (367)

**carotenoid** a class of pigments that are present in the thylakoid membrane of plants and that aid in photosynthesis (115)

**carpel** the structure where the ovule is in flowering plants (613)

**carrageenan** a sticky polysaccharide that coats the cell walls of certain species of red algae and that is used in the food industry to control the texture of many food products (518)

**carrier** in genetics, an individual who has one copy of a recessive autosomal allele that causes disease in the homozygous condition (242)

**carrier protein** a protein that transports substances across a cell membrane (101)

**carrying capacity** the largest population that an environment can support at any given time (387)

**cartilage** a flexible and strong connective tissue (784)

**catalyst** a substance that changes the rate of a chemical reaction without being consumed or changed significantly (36)

**cecum** in some herbivorous animals, a sac usually found at the beginning of the large intestine that acts as a fermentation chamber for plant materials (866)

**cell** in biology, the smallest unit that can perform all life processes; cells are covered by a membrane and contain DNA and cytoplasm (7, 69)

**cell differentiation** the process by which a cell becomes specialized for a specific structure or function (223)

**cell division** the formation of two cells from one existing cell (8)

**cell plate** the precursor of a new plant cell wall that forms during cell division and divides a cell into two (7, 158)

**cell theory** the theory that states that all living things are made up of one or more cells, that cells are the basic units of organisms, that each cell in a multicellular organism has a specific job, and that cells come only from existing cells (70)

**cell wall** a rigid structure that surrounds the cell membrane and provides support to the cell (88)

**cell-mediated immune response** an immune response that functions to defend cells against invasion by foreign cells and that depends on the action of T cells (963)

**cellular respiration** the process by which cells obtain energy from carbohydrates; atmospheric oxygen combines with glucose to form water and carbon dioxide (131)

**cellular slime mold** a type of protist that lives as an individual haploid amoeboid cell that gathers with other such cells in a

# Glossary

dense structure called a pseudoplasmodium when nutrients become scarce (514)

**central nervous system** the brain and the spinal cord; its main function is to control the flow of information in the body (1010)

**central vacuole** in some protists and in most plant cells, a large, fluid-filled organelle that stores water, enzymes, metabolic wastes, and other materials (88)

**centriole** an organelle that is composed of two short microtubules at right angles to each other and that has an active role in mitosis (85)

**centromere** the region of the chromosome that holds the two sister chromatids together during mitosis (152)

**cephalization** the concentration of nerve tissue and sensory organs at the anterior end of an organism (655)

**cephalopod** a marine mollusk that has tentacles extending from the head; an octopus, squid, cuttle-fish, or nautilus (710)

**cephalothorax** in arachnids and some crustaceans, the body part made up of the head and the thorax (728)

**cereal** any grass that produces grains that can be used for food, such as rice, wheat, corn, oats, or barley (546)

**cerebellum** a posterior portion of the brain that coordinates muscle movement and controls subconscious activities and some balance functions (1013)

**cerebral cortex** the gray, outer portion of the cerebrum that controls the higher mental functions, general movement, organ function, perception, and behavioral reactions (1011)

**cerebral ganglion** one of a pair of nerve-cell clusters that serve as a primitive brain at the anterior end of some invertebrates, such as annelids (691)

**cerebrum** the upper part of the brain that receives sensation and controls movement (1011)

**cervix** the neck of the uterus (1053)

**chaparral** a type of vegetation that includes broad-leafed evergreen shrubs and that is located in areas with hot, dry summers and mild, wet winters (421)

**chelicera** in some arthropods, either of a pair of pincerlike appendages used to attack prey (724)

**cheliped** in arthropods, one of the pair of appendages that have claws (728)

**chemical bond** the attractive force that holds atoms or ions together (33)

**chemical reaction** the process by which one or more substances change to produce one or more different substances (36)

**chemiosmosis** in chloroplasts and mitochondria, a process in which the movement of protons down their concentration gradient across a membrane is coupled to the synthesis of ATP (118)

**chemoreception** the ability to detect chemicals in the environment (783)

**chemosynthesis** the production of carbohydrates through the use of energy from inorganic molecules instead of light (289, 366)

**chemotaxis** in prokaryotes and protists, the movement toward or away from a chemical stimulus, such as the movement toward food or away from a toxin (517)

**chemotroph** an organism that gets its energy from chemicals taken from the environment (469)

**chemotropism** the tendency of an organism or a part of an organism to grow toward or away from a chemical stimulus (638)

**chitin** a carbohydrate that forms part of the exoskeleton of arthropods and other organisms, such as insects, crustaceans, fungi, and some algae (527, 715, 723)

**chlorofluorocarbon** a type of hydrocarbon in which some or all of the hydrogen atoms are replaced by chlorine and fluorine; used in coolants for refrigerators and air conditioners and in cleaning solvents (abbreviation, CFC) (440)

**chlorophyll** a green pigment that is present in most plant cells, that gives plants their characteristic green color, and that reacts with sunlight, carbon dioxide, and water to form carbohydrates (89, 115)

**chloroplast** an organelle found in plant and algae cells where photosynthesis occurs (89, 114)

**choanocyte** any of the flagellate cells that line the cavities of a sponge (673)

**chordate** an animal that at some stage in its life cycle has a dorsal nerve, a notochord, and pharyngeal pouches; examples include mammals, birds, reptiles, amphibians, fish, and some marine lower forms (654)

**chorion** the outer membrane that surrounds an embryo (823)

**chorionic villi** fingerlike projections of the chorion that extend into the uterine lining (singular, *chorionic villus*) (1058)

**chorionic villi sampling** a procedure in which the chorionic villi to are analyzed to diagnose fetal genotypes (246)

**chromatid** one of the two strands of a chromosome that become visible during meiosis or mitosis (152)

**chromatin** the material that makes up both mitotic and interphase chromosomes; a complex of proteins and DNA strands that are loosely coiled such that translation and transcription can occur (152)

**chromosome** in a eukaryotic cell, one of the structures in the nucleus that are made up of DNA and protein; in a prokaryotic cell, the main ring of DNA (79, 151)

**chromosome map** a diagram of gene positions on a chromosome (238)

**chronic bronchitis** a long-term inflammation of the bronchi (1024)

**chyme** the mixture formed in the stomach from digested food particles and gastric fluid (988)

**cilium** a hairlike structure arranged in tightly packed rows that projects from the surface of some cells (plural, *cilia*) (85, 507)

**circadian rhythm** a biological daily cycle (898)

**cirrus** in arthropods, one of several long, curved, hair-shaped appendages (plural, *cirri*) (727)

**citric acid** a six-carbon compound formed in the Krebs cycle (138)

**clade** a taxonomic grouping that includes only a single ancestor and all of its descendants (343)

**cladistics** a phylogenetic classification system that uses shared derived characters and ancestry as the sole criterion for grouping taxa (342)

**cladogram** a diagram that is based on patterns of shared, derived traits and that shows the evolutionary relationships between groups of organisms (343)

**class** in a traditional taxonomic system, the category contained within a phylum or division and containing orders (339)

**classical conditioning** a type of learning in which an animal learns to produce a specific response to a predictive stimulus in anticipation of receiving external reinforcement (890)

**cleavage** in biological development, a series of cell divisions that occur immediately after an egg is fertilized (664)

**climax community** a community that, after a process of ecological sucession, has reached a generally stable state (410)

**clitellum** in leeches and earthworms, a thick depression of the body wall that functions in reproduction (715)

**cloaca** in all vertebrates except mammals and reptiles, a chamber in the intestine that receives materials from the digestive, reproductive, and excretory systems (698)

**clone** an organism that is produced by asexual reproduction and that is genetically identical to its parent; to make a genetic duplicate (258, 623)

**cloning by nuclear transfer** the introduction of the nucleus of a somatic (body) cell into an egg cell that has been stripped of its genetic material for the purpose of cloning a whole organism (268)

**closed circulatory system** a circulatory system in which the heart circulates blood through a network of vessels that form a closed loop; the blood does not leave the blood vessels, and materials diffuse across the walls of the vessels (658)

**cnidocyte** a stinging cell of a cnidarian (677)

**coacervate** a mass of droplets of colloidal susbstances, such as lipids, amino acids, and sugars, that are held together by electrostatic attraction (286)

**coccus** a sphere-shaped bacterium (463)

**cochlea** a coiled tube that is found in the inner ear and that is essential to hearing (1017)

**codominance** a condition in which both alleles for a gene are fully expressed (184, 244)

**codon** in DNA, a three-nucleotide sequence that encodes an amino acid or signifies a start signal or a stop signal (207)

**coelom** a body cavity that is completely lined by mesoderm and that contains the internal organs of an animal (665)

**coenocytic** describes filaments that do not have cell walls (528)

**coevolution** the evolution of two or more species that is due to mutual influence, often in a way that makes the relationship more mutually beneficial (310)

**cohesion** the force that holds molecules of a single material together (41)

**cohesion-tension theory** an explanation for the movement of water up the stem xylem of tall plants; states that water is pulled up the xylem vessels by the cohesive force between the water molecules and the adhesion of the water molecules to the rigid vessel walls (597)

**collenchyma** a group of elongated, thick-walled plant cells that support the growth of leaves and stems (583)

**colloblast** a cell that is found on the tentacles of a ctenophore and that secretes a sticky substance (682)

**colon** a section of the large intestine (991)

**colonial organism** a collection of genetically identical cells that are permanently associated but in which little or no integration of cell activities occurs (76)

**columella** the axis of the cochlea in the ear bones of some animals (809)

**commensalism** a relationship between two organisms in which one organism benefits and the other is unaffected (403)

**communication** a transfer of a signal or message from one animal to another that results in some type of response (896)

**community** a group of various species that live in the same habitat and interact with each other (362)

**compact bone** the layer of bone that is just beneath the periosteum and that gives that bone its strength and rigidity (913)

**companion cell** a specialized parenchyma cell that assists in transport and that gives rise to sieve tubes in angiosperms (585)

**complement system** a system of proteins that circulate in the bloodstream and that combine with antibodies to protect against antigens (960)

**complementary base pair** the nucleotide bases in one strand of DNA or RNA that are paired with those of another strand; adenine pairs with thymine or uracil, and guanine pairs with cytosine (198)

**complete dominance** a relationship in which one allele is completely dominant over another (184)

**complete metamorphosis** an animal life cycle in which the individual undergoes two major stages of development (larva, pupa) between the egg stage and the adult stage (748)

**complex character** a character such as skin color that is influenced strongly by both genes and the environment (243)

**compound** a substance made up of atoms of two or more different elements joined by chemical bonds (33)

**compound eye** an eye composed of many light detectors separated by pigment cells (723)

**compound leaf** a type of leaf in which the blade is divided into leaflets (600)

**compound light microscope** a microscope that uses light to illuminate a specimen that is then magnified by two lenses (21)

**concentration** the amount of a particular substance in a given quantity of a mixture, solution, or ore (42)

**concentration gradient** a difference in the concentration of a substance across a distance (97)

**condensation reaction** a chemical reaction in which two or more molecules combine to produce water or another simple molecule (53)

**cone** in plants, a seed-bearing structure; in animals, a photoreceptor within the retina that can distinguish colors and is very sensitive to bright light (572, 1018)

**conidiophore** a type of hypha that bears asexual spores called conidia (528)

**conidium** an asexual spore produced in certain fungi (528)

**coniferous tree** a tree belonging to a group of tree species that bear their seeds in cones and tend to be evergreen (419)

**conjugation** in algae and fungi, an exchange of genetic material that occurs between two temporarily joined cells; in prokaryotes, the process by which two organisms bind together and one cell transfers DNA to the other cell through a structure called a sex pilus (471, 504)

**connective tissue** a tissue that has a lot of intracellular substance and that connects and supports other tissues (908)

**conservation biology** a branch of biology that is the study of the management of natural resources and the preservation of biodiversity (446)

**constrictor** a snake that kills its prey by crushing and suffocating it (833)

**consumer** an organism that eats other organisms or organic matter instead of producing its own nutrients or obtaining nutrients from inorganic sources (367)

**contractile vacuole** in protists, an organelle that accumulates water and then releases it periodically to maintain osmotic pressure (99, 508)

**control group** in an experiment, a group that serves as a standard of comparison with another group to which the control group is identical except for one factor (15)

**convergent evolution** the process by which unrelated species become more similar as they adapt to the same kind of environment (309)

**coral reef** a limestone ridge found in tropical climates and composed of coral fragments that are deposited around organic remains (681)

**cork** the outer layer of bark of any woody plant (586)

**cork cambium** a layer of tissue under the cork layer where cork cells are produced (586)

**cornea** a transparent membrane that forms the front portion of the eyeball (1018)

**corpus luteum** the structure that forms from the ruptured follicle in the ovary after ovulation; it releases hormones (1055)

**cortex** in plants, the primary tissue located in the epidermis; in animals, the outermost portion of an organ (589, 993)

**cortisol** a hormone that regulates certain phases of carbohydrate, protein, and water metabolism; affects muscle tone; increases gastric secretion; and alters tissue response to injury (1037)

**cotyledon** the embryonic leaf of a seed (576)

**countercurrent flow** in fish gills, an arrangement whereby water flows away from the head and blood flows toward the head (791)

**courtship** an animal behavior that functions to attract mates (895)

**covalent bond** a bond formed when atoms share one or more pairs of electrons (33)

**cranial cavity** the area of the skull within which the brain rests (910)

**cranium** the skeleton of the head, especially the portion of the skull where the brain is enclosed (779)

**crista** one of the many foldings of the inner membrane of mitochondria (80)

**critical night length** a minimum amount of darkness required per solar day by some plant species in order to flower (640)

**crop** in the digestive systems of birds and some invertebrates, a sac or pouch that temporarily stores food (714, 846)

**crop milk** a nutritious milklike fluid secreted by the crop of pigeons and doves to feed their young (853)

**crossing-over** the exchange of genetic material between homologous chromosomes during meiosis; can result in genetic recombination (162)

**cross-pollination** a reproductive process in which pollen from one plant is transferred to the stigma of another plant (174)

**cryptosporidiosis** a diarrheal disease caused by the protist *Cryptosporidium parvum*, which is spread by contact with fecally contaminated water (520)

**cutaneous respiration** in animals, respiration through the skin (806)

**cuticle** a waxy or fatty and watertight layer on the external wall of epidermal cells (563, 584, 695)

**cutting** a root, stem, or leaf that is cut from a living plant and that can produce a new plant (624)

**cyanobacteria** a group of bacteria that can carry out photosynthesis (singular, *cyanobacterium*); formerly called blue-green algae (289)

**cyst** a cavity or cell that contains embryos or bacteria in a resting stage (694)

**cytokinesis** the division of the cytoplasma of a cell; cytokinesis follows the division of the cell's nucleus by mitosis or meiosis (155)

**cytokinin** a plant hormone that affects cell division, plant metabolism, and the synthesis of RNA and proteins (635)

**cytolysis** the bursting of a cell (100)

**cytoplasm** the region of the cell within the membrane that includes the fluid, the cytoskeleton, and all of the organelles except the nucleus (74)

**cytoskeleton** the cytoplasmic network of protein filaments and tubes that plays an essential role in cell movement, shape, and division (84)

**cytosol** the soluble portion of the cytoplasm, which includes molecules and small particles, such as ribosomes, but not the organelles covered with membranes (74)

**cytotoxic T cell** a type of T cell that recognizes and destroys infected cells and cancer cells (963)

— **D** —

**2,4-D** a synthetic plant hormone that is used as a weedkiller (633)

**death rate** the number of deaths occurring in a period of time (383)

**decapod** a crustacean that has five pairs of legs; examples include shrimp, crabs, and lobsters (728)

**deciduous tree** a tree that sheds and regrows its leaves in response to seasonal changes (419)

**decomposer** an organism that feeds by breaking down organic matter from dead organisms; examples include bacteria and fungi (367)

**dehydration** a condition resulting from excessive water loss (984)

**deletion** the loss of a part of DNA from a chromosome (239)

**demographic transition** the general pattern of demographic change from high birth and death rates to low birth and death rates, as observed in the history of more-developed countries (392)

**dendrite** a cytoplasmic extension of a neuron that receives stimuli (1005)

**denitrification** the liberation of nitrogen from nitrogen-containing compounds by bacteria in the soil (374)

**density-dependent factor** a variable affected by the number of organisms present in a given area (388)

**density-independent factor** a variable that affects a population regardless of the population density, such as climate (388)

**deoxyribose** a five-carbon sugar that is a component of DNA nucleotides (197)

**dependence** the state in which a person relies on a drug physically or emotionally in order to function (1021)

**dependent variable** in an experiment, the factor that changes as a result of manipulation of one or more other factors; also called a *responding variable* (15)

**depressant** a drug that reduces functional activity and produces muscular relaxation (1023)

**derived character** a feature that evolved only within a particular taxonomic group (342)

**dermis** the layer of skin below the epidermis (925)

**desert** a region that has little or no vegetation, long periods without rain, and extreme temperatures; usually found in warm climates (422)

**detritivore** a consumer that feeds on dead organisms or on the parts or wastes of other organsims (367)

**deuterostome** an organism whose embryonic blastopore develops into an anus, whereas its mouth develops from a second opening at the opposite end of the archenteron; usually characterized by an embryo that undergoes indeterminate, radial cleavage (665)

**developed country** a modern, industrialized country in which people are generally better educated and healthier and live longer than people in developing countries do (391)

**developing country** a country in which the society is less modern and less industrialized and in which inhabitants are generally poorer than they are in developed countries (391)

**development** the gene-directed process by which an organism matures (8)

**diabetes mellitus** a serious disorder in which cells are unable to obtain glucose from the blood; caused by a deficiency of insulin or lack of response to insulin (1039)

**diaphragm** a dome-shaped muscle that is attached to the lower ribs and that functions as the main muscle in respiration (865, 910, 949)

**diatom** a unicellular alga that has a double shell that contains silica (512)

**diatomaceous earth** a soft, fine, porous deposit that is composed mainly of the skeletons of diatoms (518)

**dicot** a dicotyledonous plant; an angiosperm that has two cotyledons, net venation, and flower parts in groups of four or five (576)

**differentiation** the structural and functional specialization of cells during an organism's development (652)

**diffusion** the movement of particles from regions of higher density to regions of lower density (97)

**digestion** the breaking down of food into chemical substances that can be used to obtain energy (985)

**digestive gland** any gland that secretes a substance to help transform food into substances that the body can use (729)

**dihybrid cross** a cross between individuals that have different alleles for the same gene (185)

**dimorphism** the ability of some organisms, such as fungi, to exist in two forms, depending in general on the temperature and availability of nutrients (528)

**dinosaur** one of a varied group of mostly-extinct reptiles that lived from about 235 million years ago to about 66 million years ago (819)

**diploid** a cell that contains two haploid sets of chromosomes (153)

**directional selection** a type of natural selection in which the most extreme form of a trait is favored and becomes more common (325)

**disaccharide** a sugar formed from two monosaccharides (56)

**dispersion** in ecology, the pattern of distribution of organisms in a population (382)

**disruptive selection** a type of natural selection in which two extreme forms of a trait are selected (324)

**disturbance** in ecology, an event that changes a community by removing or destroying organisms or altering resource availability (407)

**divergent evolution** the process by which two or more related but reproductively isolated populations become more and more dissimilar (309)

**division** in a traditional taxonomic system for plants, the category contained within a kingdom and containing classes (339)

**DNA (deoxyribonucleic acid)** the material that contains the information that determines inherited characteristics (60)

**DNA fingerprint** the pattern of bands that results when an individual's DNA sample is radiolabeled and exposed to X rays after being fragmented, replicated, and separated (257)

**DNA polymerase** an enzyme that catalyzes the formation of the DNA molecule (200)

**DNA replication** the process of making a copy of DNA (200)

**DNA vaccine** a vaccine that is made from the DNA of a pathogen and that does not have disease-causing capabilities (269)

**domain** in a modern taxonomic system, the broadest category; the category that contains kingdoms (11, 339)

**dominance hierarchy** in competitive animal groups, a ranking of individuals from most dominant to most subordinate (894)

**dominant** describes the allele that is fully expressed when carried by only one of a pair of homologous chromosomes (177)

**dormancy** a state in which seeds, spores, bulbs, and other reproductive organs stop growth and development and reduce their metabolism, especially respiration (365, 621)

**dorsal** lying on or near the back (655)

**dorsal nerve chord** a neural tube dorsal to the notochord (654)

**double fertilization** the process by which one of the two sperm nuclei fuses with the egg nucleus to produce a diploid zygote and the other fuses with the polar nuclei to produce a triploid endosperm (617)

**drone** a male bee that develops from an unfertilized egg and functions only to fertilize eggs from the queen (752)

**drug** any substance that causes a change in an organism's physical or psychological state (1021)

**duodenum** the first section of the small intestine (807)

## E

**echinoderm** a radially symmetrical marine invertebrate that has an endoskeleton, such as a starfish, a sea urchin, or a sea cucumber (761)

**echolocation** the process of using reflected sound waves to find objects; used by animals such as bats (866)

**ecological model** a model that represents or describes the relationships between the components of an ecological system (360)

**ecological succession** a gradual process of change and replacement in a community (408)

**ecology** the study of the interactions between organisms and the other living and nonliving components of their environment (11, 359)

**ecosystem** a community of organisms and their abiotic environment (11, 362)

**ecotourism** a form of tourism that supports the conservation and sustainable development of ecologically unique areas (450)

**ectoderm** the outermost of the three germ layers of an embryo that develops into the epidermis and epidermal tissues, the nervous system, external sense organs, and the mucous membranes lining the mouth and anus (664)

**ectotherm** an organism that needs sources of heat outside of itself (828)

**ejaculation** the expulsion of seminal fluids from the urethra of the penis during sexual intercourse (1051)

**elapid** a venomous snake that has two small, fixed fangs in the front of the mouth (833)

**electron** a subatomic particle that has a negative charge (32)

**electron transport chain** a series of molecules, found in the inner membranes of mitochondria and chloroplasts, through which electrons pass in a process that causes protons to build up on one side of the membrane (117)

**element** a substance that cannot be separated or broken down into simpler substances by chemical means; all atoms of an element have the same atomic number (31)

**elephantiasis** a disease in humans that is caused by filarial worms and that is characterized by fluid accumulation that results in thickened skin around swollen extremities (697)

**embryo** an organism in an early stage of development of plants and animals; in humans, a developing individual is referred to as an embryo from the second through the eighth week of pregnancy (1057)

**embryo sac** in plants, the female gametophyte that develops from a megaspore; contains the ovum that fuses with a sperm nucleus during fertilization to form an embryo and seven other cells, including the polar bodies that fuse with another sperm nucleus to form endosperm (614)

**emerging disease** a disease that is caused by new or reappearing infectious agents that typically exist in animal populations (491)

**emigration** the movement of an individual or group out of an area (321, 385)

**emphysema** a degenerative lung disease that is characterized by the breakdown of alveoli, which reduces the area available for gas exchange (1024)

**endocrine gland** a ductless gland that secretes hormones into the blood or extracellular fluid (1031)

**endocrine system** a collection of glands and groups of cells that secrete hormones that regulate growth, development, and homeostasis; includes the pituitary, thyroid, parathyroid, and adrenal glands, the hypothalamus, the pineal body, and the gonads (1031)

**endocytosis** the process by which a cell membrane surrounds a particle and encloses the particle in a vesicle to bring the particle into the cell (105)

**endoderm** the innermost germ layer of the animal embryo; develops into the epithelium of the pharynx, respiratory tract, digestive tract, bladder, and urethra (664)

**endodermis** the single layer of cells that surrounds the vascular tissue in the roots and in some stems of plants; the innermost layer of cortex in seed plants (589)

**endoplasmic reticulum** a system of membranes that is found in a cell's cytoplasm and that assists in the production, processing, and transport of proteins and in the production of lipids (81)

**endoskeleton** an internal skeleton made of bone and cartilage (660)

**endospore** a thick-walled protective spore that forms inside a bacterial cell and resists harsh conditions (469)

**endosymbiosis** a mutually beneficial relationship in which one organism lives within another; a theory that eukaryotic cells originated through endosymbiotic relationships between ancient prokaryotic cells (290)

**endotherm** an animal that can generate body heat through metabolism and can maintain a constant body temperature despite temperature changes in the animal's environment (828)

**endothermy** in animals, the characteristic of maintaining a high, constant body temperature through regulation of metabolism and heat loss (861)

**endotoxin** a toxin that occurs in the outer membrane of Gram negative bacteria and that is released when the bacterial cell breaks apart (472)

**energy** the capacity to do work (35)

**enhancer** a DNA sequence that recognizes certain transcription factors that can stimulate transcription of nearby genes (222)

**enterocoely** in deuterostomes, the method of coelom formation in which the embryonic mesoderm develops from pouches within the archenteron (666)

**entomology** the study of insects and other terrestrial arthropods (742)

**envelope** a membranelike layer that covers the capsids of some viruses (484)

**enzyme** a type of protein or RNA molecule that speeds up metabolic reactions in plant and animals without being permanently changed or destroyed (36, 57)

**epicotyl** the portion of the stem of a plant embryo that is between the cotyledons and the first true leaves (620)

**epidermis** the outer surface layer of cells of a plant or animal (584, 676, 924)

**epididymis** the long, coiled tube that is on the surface of a testis and in which sperm mature (1050)

**epiglottis** a structure that hangs at the entrance of the larynx and prevents food from entering the larynx and the trachea while swallowing (947, 986)

**epinephrine** a hormone that is released by the adrenal medulla and that rapidly stimulates the metabolism in emergencies, decreases insulin secretion, and stimulates pulse and blood pressure; also called *adrenaline* (1037)

**epiphyseal plate** the point at which bones elongate during growth; it is found at joint ends of long bones, is composed of cartilage, and becomes an epiphyseal line in mature bone (914)

**epiphyte** a plant that uses another plant for support, but not for nourishment (419)

**epithelial tissue** a tissue that is composed of a sheet of cells and that covers a body surface or lines a body cavity (908)

**equilibrium** in biology, a state that exists when the concentration of a substance is the same throughout a space (97)

**erythrocyte** a red blood cell (940)

**estrogen** a hormone that regulates the sexual development and reproductive function of females (1037)

**estuary** an area where fresh water from rivers mixes with salt water from the ocean; the part of a river where the tides meet the river current (425)

**ethephon** a chemical used as a growth regulator for fruit (634)

**ethologist** a person who specializes in the scientific study of animal behavior (887)

**ethylene** a gaseous plant hormone that plays a role in the ripening of fruits (634)

**Eubacteria** in a traditional taxonomic system, a kingdom that contains all prokaryotes except Kingdom Archaebacteria (Domain Archaea); biologists more recently prefer to classify these organisms as Domain Bacteria (348)

**euchromatin** a region of DNA that is uncoiled and undergoing active transcription into RNA (220)

**euglenoid** a flagellated unicellular algae (513)

**Eukarya** in a modern taxonomic system, a domain made up of all eukaryotes; aligns with the traditional kingdoms Protista, Fungi, Plantae, and Animalia (348)

**eukaryote** an organism made up of cells that have a nucleus enclosed by a membrane, multiple chromosomes, and a mitotic cycle; eukaryotes include animals, plants, and fungi but not bacteria or archaea (75)

**Eustachian tube** a channel that connects the middle ear to the mouth cavity (1017)

**eutrophic lake** a lake that contains a large amount of decaying organic matter and lacks oxygen as a result (427)

**evolution** a heritable change in the characteristics within a population from one generation to the next; the development of new types of organisms from preexisting types of organisms over time (12, 297)

**excretion** the process of eliminating metabolic wastes (993)

**excurrent siphon** a tube through which water exits the mantle cavity of a bivalve (709)

**exocrine gland** a gland that discharges its secretions through a duct (925, 1031)

**exocytosis** the process by which a substance is released from the cell through a vesicle that transports the substance to the cell surface and then fuses with the membrane to let the substance out (106)

**exon** in a structural gene, one of the segments that are ultimately transcribed and translated when the gene is expressed (220)

**exoskeleton** a hard, external, supporting structure that develops from the ectoderm (658)

**exotoxin** a potent, extracellular toxin secreted by some gram positive bacteria (472)

**experiment** a procedure that is carried out under controlled conditions to discover, demonstrate, or test a fact, theory, or general truth (13)

**experimental group** in an experiment, a group that is identical to a control group except for one factor and that is compared with the control group (15)

**expiration** the process in which air is forced out of the lungs (950)

**exponential model** a model of population growth in which a constant and unlimited growth rate results in geometric increases in population size (386)

**extensor** a muscle that extends a joint (921)

**external fertilization** the union of gametes outside the bodies of the parents, as in many fishes and amphibians (784)

**external respiration** the exchange of gases between the atmosphere and the lungs (946)

**extinction** the death of every member of a species (442)

**eyepiece** the part of a compound light microscope that magnifies an image, usually 10 times, also called an *ocular lens* (21)

**eyespot** an organ that is covered by pigment in some invertebrates and protozoa and that detects changes in the quantity and quality of light (691)

## F

**$F_1$ generation** the first generation of offspring obtained from an experimental cross of two organisms (175)

**$F_2$ generation** the second generation of offspring, obtained from an experimental cross of two organisms; the offspring of the $F_1$ generation (175)

**facilitated diffusion** the transport of substances through a cell membrane along a concentration gradient with the aid of carrier proteins (101)

**facultative anaerobe** an organism that can live with or without oxygen (470)

**FAD** flavin adenine dinucleotide, a compound that acts as a hydrogen acceptor in dehydrogenation reactions (139)

**fall color** change in the color of deciduous tree leaves in the fall in response to changes in average temperature and day length (642)

**fallopian tube** a tube through which eggs move from the ovary to the uterus (1052)

**family** in a traditional taxonomic system, the category contained within an order and containing genera (339)

**fatty acid** an organic acid that is contained in lipids, such as fats or oils (59)

**feather** in birds, a modified scale that provides lift for flight and conserves body heat (844)

**fermentation** the breakdown of carbohydrates by enzymes, bacteria, yeasts, or mold in the absence of oxygen (133)

**fertilization** the union of a male and female gamete to form a zygote (663)

**fertilizer** a compound that improves the quality of the soil to produce plants (548)

**fetus** a developing human during the period from the eight week after fertilization until birth (1059)

**fibrin** a protein that forms a network of fibers during blood clotting (942)

**fibrous root system** a system of adventitious roots of approximately equal diameter that arise from the base of the stem of a plant (587)

**fiddlehead** the tightly coiled new leaves of a fern (572)

**filament** in flowers, the part of a stamen that supports the anther (613)

**filarial worm** one of a group of nematodes that cause diseases such as elephantiasis in humans and heartworm disease in dogs and cats (697)

**filter feeding** in an aquatic animal, a method of feeding in which the animal traps organic material that is floating in the surrounding water (674)

**filtration** the process of separating dissolved substances, such as impurities in the blood by passing them through a porous material; occurs between the glomerulus and the Bowman's capsule in the nephrons of a kidney (995)

**fitness** in evolutionary theory, a measure of an individual's hereditary contribution to the next generation (301)

**fixed action pattern behavior** an innate behavior that is characteristic of certain species (888)

**fixed joint** a joint at which no movement occurs; examples include the joints between the bones of the skull (915)

**flagellum** a long, hairlike structure that grows out of a cell and enables the cell to move (plural, *flagella*) (85, 508)

**flame cell** in a flatworm, a cell that has flagella or cilia that move waste products through the body (690)

**flexor** a muscle that bends a joint (921)

**fluke** a parasitic flatworm of the class Trematoda or Monogenea (691)

**follicle** a small, narrow cavity or sac in an organ or tissue, such as the ones on the skin that contain hair roots or the ones in the ovaries that contain the developing eggs (844, 1054)

**follicle-stimulating hormone** a gonadotropin that stimulates sperm production in the male and the growth and maturation of the ovarian follicles in the female (abbreviation, FSH) (1037)

**follicular phase** the stage in which an immature egg completes its first meiotic division (1054)

**food chain** the pathway of energy transfer through various stages as a result of the feeding patterns of a series of organisms (368)

**food web** a diagram that shows the feeding relationships among organisms in an ecosystem (368)

**fossil** the trace or remains of an organism that lived long ago, most commonly preserved in sedimentary rock (302)

**fracture** an injury in which the tissue of a bone is broken (913)

**fragmentation** in fungi, a reproductive process in which septate hypha dry and shatter and individual cells that act as spores are released (528)

**frameshift mutation** a mutation, such as the insertion or deletion of a nucleotide in a coding sequence, that results in the misreading of the code during translation because of a change in the reading frame (240)

**freshwater wetland** an area of land that is covered in fresh water for at least part of each year (428)

**frond** the leaf of a fern or palm (572)

**fruit** a mature plant ovary; the plant organ in which the seeds are enclosed (547)

**fruiting body** a part of a plant, fungus, or protist that produces seeds or spores (514)

**functional group** the portion of a molecule that is active in a chemical reaction and that determines the properties of many organic compounds (52)

**Fungi** in a traditional taxonomic system, a kingdom made up of nongreen, eukaryotic organisms that get food by breaking down organic matter and absorbing the nutrients, reproduce by means of spores, and have no means of movement (349)

**furcula** in birds, the fused pair of collarbones; commonly called the wishbone (842)

## G

**gallbladder** a sac-shaped organ that stores bile produced by the liver (988)

**gametangium** a cell or an organ that produces gametes (510, 530)

**gamete** a haploid reproductive cell that unites with another haploid reproductive cell to form a zygote (155)

**gametocyte** a cell that is not differentiated and that develops into a gamete (519)

**gametophyte** in alternation of generations, the phase in which gametes are formed; a haploid individual that produces gametes (565)

**ganglion** a cluster of nerve cells (plural, *ganglia*) (706)

**gasohol** a mixture of gasoline and alcohol that is used as a fuel (551)

**gastric fluid** a liquid secreted by gastric glands in the stomach (988)

**gastrodermis** in cnidarians, the layer of cells surrounding the digestive tract (676)

**gastrointestinal tract** the digestive tract from the mouth to the anus, including the stomach and intestines (985)

**gastropod** a mollusk that has a well-developed head and a flattened foot, such as a snail, slug, or conch (707)

**gastrovascular cavity** a cavity that serves both digestive and circulatory purposes in some cnidarians (676)

**gastrula** the embryo in the stage of development after the blastula; contains the embryonic germ layers (664)

**gastrulation** the transformation of the blastula into the gastrula or the formation of the embryonic germ layers (664)

**gel electrophoresis** a technique used to separate nucleic acids or proteins according to size and charge in an agarose or acrylamide gel (257)

**gemmule** an asexual reproductive structure produced by some freshwater sponges (675)

**gene** a short segment of DNA that contains the instructions for a single trait (9)

**gene expression** the activation, or "turning on" of a gene that results in transcription and the production of mRNA (217)

**gene flow** the movement of genes into or out of a population due to interbreeding (321)

**gene pool** all of the genes of the reproductively active members of a population (9, 318)

**gene therapy** a technique that places a gene into a cell to correct a hereditary disease or to improve the genome (248, 267)

**generative cell** in a pollen grain, the cell that divides mitotically and forms two sperm cells (615)

**genetic code** the rule that describes how a sequence of nucleotides, read in groups of three consecutive nucleotides (triplets) that correspond to specific amino acids, specifies the amino acid sequence of a protein (207)

**genetic counseling** the process of testing and informing potential parents about their genetic makeup and the likelihood that they will have offspring with genetic defects or hereditary diseases (247)

**genetic disorder** an inherited disease or disorder that is caused by a mutation in a gene or by a chromosomal defect (242)

**genetic diversity** the amount of variation in the genetic material within all members of a popualtion (438)

**genetic drift** the random change in allele frequency in a population (322)

**genetic engineering** a technology in which the genome of a living cell is modified for medical or industrial use (258)

**genetic recombination** the regrouping of genes in an offspring that results in a genetic makeup that is different from that of the parents (162)

**genetics** the science of heredity and of the mechanisms by which traits are passed from parents to offspring (173)

**genome** the complete genetic material contained in an individual (210, 217)

**genotype** the entire genetic makeup of an organism; also the combination of genes for one or more specific traits (180)

**genotypic ratio** the ratio of the genotypes that appear in offspring (183)

**genus** in a traditional taxonomic system, the category contained within a family and containing species (plural, *genera*) (339)

**geographic isolation** the physical separation of populations due to geographic barriers that prevent interbreeding (327)

**germ layer** one of the layers of tissue that develop in the embryos of all animals except sponges (655)

**germ-cell mutation** mutation that occurs in an organism's gametes (239)

**germinate** to begin to grow from an embryo into a mature form (572)

**gestation** in mammals, the process of carrying young from fertilization to birth (1056)

**giardiasis** a diarrheal illness caused by the parasitic protozoan *Giardia lamblia* and characterized by intestinal cramping and diarrhea (1056)

**gibberellin** a plant hormone that stimulates growth of stems and leaves (633)

**gill** in aquatic animals, a respiratory structure that consists of many blood vessels surrounded by a membrane that allows for gas exchange (658)

**gill arch** one of the jointed and cartilaginous or bony structures behind the jaws in fish and larval amphibians (781)

**gizzard** an enlargement of the digestive tract of some invertebrates, such as annelids and insects, that grinds food; a muscular region in the digestive tract of birds that grinds and softens food (714, 846)

**glomerulus** a cluster of capillaries that is enclosed in a Bowman's capsule in a nephron of the kidney, where blood is filtered (994)

**glycocalyx** a bacterial capsule that is made of a fuzzy coat of sticky sugars (468)

**glycolysis** the anaerobic breakdown of glucose to pyruvic acid, which makes a small amount of energy available to cells in the form of ATP (132)

**Golgi complex** cell organelle that helps make and package materials to be transported out of the cell (82)

**gonad** an organ that produces gametes (1037)

**gradualism** a model of evolution in which gradual change over a long period of time leads to biological diversity (330)

**grafting** a technique in which a portion of one plant is attached to the root or shoot of another plant and grows there (624)

**Gram-negative bacterium** a bacterium that, in the Gram stain process, is stained reddish-pink and that has a small amount of peptidoglycan in its cell wall (463)

**Gram-positive bacterium** a bacterium that, in the Gram stain process, is stained purple and that has a large amount of peptidoglycan in its cell wall (463)

**granum** a stack of thylakoids in a chloroplast (plural, *grana*) (114)

**gravitropism** the growth of a plant in a particular direction in response to gravity (638)

**great ape** an ape whose face has little hair and whose hands have nails and complex fingerprints, such as an orangutan, gorilla, or chimpanzee (876)

**green gland** an excretory organ of some crustaceans that is located at the base of the antennae (730)

**greenhouse effect** the warming of the surface and lower atmosphere of Earth that occurs when carbon dioxide, water vapor, and other gases in the air absorb and reradiate infrared radiation (436)

**gross primary productivity** the rate at which organic matter is assimilated by plants and other producers during a period of time over a certain area (366)

**groundwater** the water that is beneath the Earth's surface (371)

**growth rate** an expression of the increase in the size of an organism or population over a given period of time (385)

**growth retardant** a chemical that prevents growth, especially the growth of vegetation (635)

**guard cell** one of a pair of specialized cells that border a stoma and regulate gas exchange (602)

**gullet** in protozoa, an opening into which the mouth pore opens (508)

**gymnosperm** a woody, vascular seed plant whose seeds are not enclosed by an ovary or fruit (565)

## H

**habitat** the place where an organism usually lives (363)

**habituation** a type of learning in which an animal learns to ignore a frequent, harmless stimulus (889)

**half-life** the time required for half of a sample of a radioactive isotope to break down by radioactive decay to form a daughter isotope (283)

**halophile** an organism that can grow in, or favors environments that have very high salt concentrations (462)

**haploid** describes a cell, nucleus, or organism that has only one set of unpaired chromosomes (153)

**Hardy-Weinberg principle** the principle that states that the frequency of alleles in a population does not change over generations unless outside forces act on the population (320)

**Haversian canal** a channel containing blood vessels in compact bone tissue (913)

**hay fever** a pollen allergy that results in sneezing, a runny nose, and watering eyes (556)

**helicase** an enzyme that separates DNA strands (200)

**helper T cell** a white blood cell necessary for B cells to develop normal levels of antibodies (963)

**hemocoel** the blood-filled space or body cavity of some invertebrates (707)

**hemoglobin** the oxygen-carrying protein in red blood cells (940)

**hemolymph** the fluid that circulates through the body of an animal that has an open circulatory system (707)

**herbivore** an organism that eats only plants (367)

**heredity** the passing of genetic traits from parent to offspring (173)

**hermaphrodite** an organism that has both male and female reproductive organs (659, 675)

**heterospory** the production of two or more kinds of asexual spores (611)

**heterotroph** an organism that obtains organic food molecules by eating other organisms or their byproducts and that cannot synthesize organic compounds from inorganic materials (113, 469)

**heterozygous** describes an individual that has two different alleles for a trait (181)

**hibernation** a period of inactivity and lowered body temperature that some animals undergo in winter as a protection against cold weather and lack of food (898)

**hilum** on a plant seed, a scar that marks where the seed was attached to the ovary wall (620)

**histamine** a chemical that stimulates the autonomous nervous system, secretion of gastric juices, and dilation of capillaries (959)

**histone** a type of protein molecule found in the chromosomes of eukaryotic cells but not prokaryotic cells (151)

**HIV** human immunodeficiency virus, the virus that causes AIDS (970)

**homeobox** a DNA sequence within a homeotic gene that regulates development in animals (224)

**homeostasis** the steady-state physiological condition of the body (8)

**homeotic gene** a gene that controls the development of a specific adult structure (223)

**hominid** a member of the family Hominidae of the order Primates; characterized by bipedalism, relatively long lower limbs, and lack of a tail; examples include humans and their ancestors (877)

**homologous chromosomes** chromosomes that have the same sequence of genes, that have the same structure, and that pair during meiosis (152)

**homologous structures** anatomical structures in one species that, compared to other anatomical structures in another species, originated from a single anatomical structure in a common ancestor of the two species (305)

**homospory** the production of only one kind of spore (610)

**homozygous** describes an individual that has identical alleles for a trait on both homologous chromosomes (181)

**hookworm** a parasitic roundworm found in the intestines of mammals (696)

**hormone** a substance that is secreted by cells and that that acts to regulate the activity of other cells in the body (1031, 631)

**hornwort** a member of the phylum Anthocerophyta, a unique group of bryophytes that grow close to the ground in moist, shady areas and that are characterized by long, thin, photosynthetic sporophytes (569)

**human** a member of the genus *Homo* of the family Hominidae; includes modern humans and closely related extinct species (879)

**human chorionic gonadotropin** a hormone that is secreted by the placenta and that stimulates ovulation and secretion of progesterone or testosterone (abbreviation, HCG) (1059)

**Human Genome Project** a worldwide scientific research effort to map and sequence the human genome (261)

**humoral immunity** a type of immune response that is produced by the action of antibodies within body fluids (964)

**hunter-gatherer lifestyle** a way of life in which people obtain their food by hunting and gathering wild animals and plants (390)

**Huntington's disease** a rare hereditary disease of the brain characterized by involuntary movements of the limbs or face, decreasing mental abilities, and eventual death (245)

**hydrogen bond** the intermolecular force occurring when a hydrogen atom that is bonded to a highly electronegative atom of one molecule is attracted to two unshared electrons of another molecule (40)

**hydrolysis** a chemical reaction between water and another substance to form two or more new substances; a reaction between water and a salt to create an acid or a base (53)

**hydronium ion** an ion consisting of a proton combined with a molecule of water; $H_3O^+$ (43)

**hydroxide ion** the $OH^-$ ion (43)

**hypertension** a condition of high blood pressure (936)

**hypertonic** describes a solution whose solute concentration is higher than the solute concentration inside a cell (98)

**hypha** a nonreproductive filament of a fungus (527)

**hypocotyl** the portion of the stem of a plant embryo that is between the cotyledons and the embryonic root (620)

**hypothalamus** the region of the brain that coordinates the activities of the nervous and endocrine systems and that controls many body activities related to homeostasis (1012, 1034)

**hypothesis** in science, an idea or explanation that is based on observations and that can be tested (13)

**hypotonic** describes a solution whose solute concentration is lower than the solute concentration inside a cell (98)

## I

**ileum** the middle portion of the small intestine where many nutrients are absorbed (807)

**immigration** the movement of an individual or group into an area (321, 385)

**immune response** the reaction of the body against an antigen (962)

**immune system** the cells and tissues that recognize and attack foreign substances in the body (961)

**immunity** the ability to resist an infectious disease (966)

**implantation** the process by which the newly fertilized egg in the blastocyst stage embeds itself in the lining of the uterus (1057)

**imprinting** learning that occurs early and quickly in a young animal's life and that cannot be changed once learned (891)

**inbreeding** the crossing or mating of plants or animals with close relatives (389)

**incisor** any of the four cutting teeth located between the canines in the upper and lower jaws (865)

**incomplete dominance** a condition in which a trait in an individual is intermediate between the phenotype of the individual's two parents because the dominant allele is unable to express itself fully (184, 244)

**incomplete metamorphosis** an animal life cycle in which the individual undergoes gradual development through several nymph stages after the egg stage and before the adult stage (748)

**incurrent siphon** a tube through which water enters the body of a bivalve (709)

**independent assortment** the random distribution of the pairs of genes on different chromosomes to the gametes (162)

**independent variable** in an experiment, the factor that is deliberately manipulated, also called the *manipulated variable* (15)

**inducer** a substance that combines with and inactivates a repressor which allows the transcription of a gene (219)

**infectious disease** a disease that is caused by pathogenic bacteria, viruses, fungi, or protists (957)

**inflammatory response** a protective response of tissues affected by disease or injury, characterized by redness, swelling, and pain (959)

**ingestion** the process of taking in food (652)

**innate behavior** an inherited behavior that does not depend on the environment or experience (752, 888)

**insertion** in anatomy, the point at which a muscle is attached to a moving bone (921)

**insertion mutation** a mutation in which one or more nucleotides are added to a gene (240)

**inspiration** the process of taking air from the outside of the body into the lungs (949)

**insulin** a hormone that is produced by a group of specialized cells in the pancreas and that lowers blood glucose levels (1039)

**integument** the outer, protective covering of a body, a body part, an ovule, or a sporangium (612, 660)

**interdependence** the dependence of every organism on its connections with other living and nonliving parts of its environment (359)

**interferon** a protein that is produced by cells infected by a virus and that can protect uninfected cells from reproduction of the virus (960)

**intermediate host** a host that gives food and shelter to immature stages of a parasite (693)

**internal fertilization** fertilization of an egg by sperm that occurs inside the body of a female (786)

**internal respiration** the exchange of gases between the blood and the cells of the body (946)

**interneuron** a neuron located between the afferent neuron and the final neuron in a neural chain (1013)

**internode** the part of a plant stem between two consecutive nodes (593)

**interphase** a period between two mitotic or meiotic divisions during which the cell grows, copies its DNA, and synthesizes proteins (155)

**interspecific competition** a relationship between two species in which both species compete for limited resources such that both species are negatively affected by the relationship (401)

**intertidal zone** an area along ocean shorelines that lies between low and high water lines (423)

**intron** a segment of a structural gene that is transcribed but not translated (220)

**inversion** a reversal in the order of the genes, or of a chromosome segment, within a chromosome (239)

**invertebrate** an animal that does not have a backbone (651)

**involuntary muscle** a muscle whose movement cannot be controlled voluntarily, such as the cardiac muscle (918)

**ion** an atom, radical, or molecule that has gained or lost one or more electrons and has a negative or positive charge (34)

**ion channel** a complex of protein molecules in a cell membrane that form a pore through which ions can pass (102)

**ionic bond** the attractive force between oppositely charged ions, which form when electrons are transferred from one atom to another (34)

**iris** the colored, circular part of the eye (1018)

**isopod** a crustacean that has seven pairs of identical legs and no carapace; examples include sowbugs and pill bugs (727)

**isotonic** describes a solution whose solute concentration is equal to the solute concentration inside a cell (99)

**isotope** an atom that has the same number of protons (or the same atomic number) as other atoms of the same element do but that has a different number of neutrons (and thus a different atomic mass) (32, 282)

---

**J**

**Jacobson's organ** an olfactory sac that opens into the mouth and is highly developed in reptiles (827)

**joint** a place where two or more bones meet (915)

---

**K**

**karyotype** a micrograph of the array of chromosomes visible in a cell during metaphase; a graphical display that shows an individual's chromosomes arranged in homologous pairs and in order of diminishing size (153)

**keratin** a hard protein that forms hair, bird feathers, nails, and horns (824, 924)

**keystone species** a species that is critical to the functioning of the ecosystem in which it lives because it affects the survival and abundance of many other species in its community (443)

**kidney** one of the organs that filter water and wastes from the blood, excrete products as urine, and regulate the concentration of certain substances in the blood (661)

**kilocalorie** a unit of energy equal to 1,000 calories (135)

**kin selection** a mechanism for increasing the frequency of one's genes in a population by helping increase the reproductive success of relatives (754, 879)

**kingdom** in a traditional taxonomic system, the highest taxonomic category, which contains a group of similar phyla (11, 339)

**Koch's postulates** a four-stage procedure that Robert Koch formulated for identifying a specific pathogen as the cause of a specific disease (957)

**Krebs cycle** a series of biochemical reactions that convert pyruvic acid into carbon dioxide and water; it is the major pathway of oxidation in animal, bacterial, and plant cells, and it releases energy (138)

---

**L**

**labium** in some animals, one of a pair of lips around the mouth; also, in some female animals, one of two pairs of folds of skin and mucous membranes that cover and protect the openings of the vulva; in insects, a mouthpart that functions as a lower lip (plural, *labia*) (746, 1053)

**labor** the process by which the fetus and the placenta come out of the uterus (1060)

**labrum** in arthropods, a mouthpart that functions as an upper lip (746)

***lac* operon** a gene system whose operator gene and three structural genes control lactose metabolism in *E. coli* (218)

**lactic acid fermentation** the chemical breakdown of carbohydrates that produces lactic acid as the main end product (134)

**larva** an independent and immature form of an organism that is morphologically different from the adult form (659)

**larynx** the area of the throat that contains the vocal cords and produces vocal sounds (947)

**lateral line** a faint line visible on both sides of a fish's body that runs the length of the body and marks the location of sense organs that detect vibrations in water (783)

**lateral meristem** dividing tissue that runs parallel to the long axis of a stem or a root (586)

**law of independent assortment** the law that states that genes separate independently of one another in meiosis (178)

**law of segregation** Mende's law that states that the pairs of homologous chromosomes separate in meiosis so that only one chromosome from each pair is present in each gamete (177)

**layering** the process of causing roots to form on stems or branches of a plant that are covered with soil (624)

**leaflet** one segment of a compound leaf (600)

**learning** the development of behaviors through experience or practice (889)

**legume** any plant of the family Leguminosae (Fabaceae), such as a bean, pea, or lentil; the name for the type of fruit produced by members of this family (547)

**lens** a convex transparent structure in the eye that focuses light on the retina (1018)

**lethal mutation** a gene or chromosomal mutation that influences the development of an organism in such a way that the organism cannot survive (239)

**leukemia** a progressive, malignant disease of the blood-forming organs (228)

**leukocyte** a white blood cell (941)

**lichen** a mass of cells formed by a fungus in symbiosis with a photosynthetic partner (usually a cyanobacterium or green algae); lichen typically grow on nutrient-poor surfaces, such as rocks and tree bark (533)

**life expectancy** the average length of time that an individual is expected to live (383)

**ligament** a type of connective tissue that holds together the bones in a joint (915)

**light reactions** the initial reactions in photosynthesis, which are triggered by the absorption of light by photosystems I and II and include the passage of electrons along the electron transport chains, the production of NADPH and oxygen gas, and the synthesis of ATP through chemiosmosis (114)

**limiting factor** an environmental factor that prevents an organism or population from reaching its full potential of distribution or activity (386)

**linked gene** one of a pair of genes that tend to be inherited together (238)

**lipid** a large, nonpolar organic molecule, including fats and steroids; lipids store energy and make up cell membranes (59)

**liverwort** a member of the phylum Hepatophyta, a unique group of bryophytes that grow close to the ground in moist, shady areas and that are characterized by unique structures on the gametophytes (568)

**lobe-finned fish** a kind of fish that has fleshy fins that are supported by a series of bones; living species include lungfishes and the coelocanth (787)

**logistic model** a model of population growth that assumes that finite resource levels limit population growth (387)

**loop of Henle** in the kidney, the long, U-shaped part of a nephron that reabsorbs water and salts from the urine collected by the glomerulus (997)

**lung** the central organ of the respiratory system in which oxygen from the air is exchanged with carbon dioxide from the blood (660, 946)

**luteal phase** the menstrual stage in which the corpus luteum develops (1055)

**luteinizing hormone** a hormone that stimulates ovulation and progesterone secretion by the corpus luteum in the female and testosterone secretion in the male (abbreviation, LH) (1037)

**lymph** the fluid that is collected by the lymphatic vessels and nodes (939)

**lymphatic system** a collection of organs whose primary function is to collect extracellular fluid and return it to the blood; the organs in this system include the lymph nodes and the lymphatic vessels (933)

**lymphocyte** a type of white blood cell that exists in two primary forms, T cells and B cells (961)

**lymphoma** a tumor in the lymphoid tissues (228)

**lysis** the disintegration of a cell by disruption of the plasma membrane (486)

**lysogenic cycle** a method of viral replication in which a viral genome is replicated as a provirus without destroying the host cell (487)

**lysosome** a cell organelle that contains digestive enzymes and that buds from the Golgi apparatus (82)

**lytic cycle** a method of viral replication that results in the destruction of a host cell and the release of many new virus particles (486)

--- **M** ---

**macromolecule** a very large organic molecule, usually a polymer, composed of hundreds or thousands of atoms (53)

**macronucleus** in many protozoans, the larger of two types of cell nuclei and the one that contains multiple copies of DNA (508)

**macronutrient** an element required in relatively large amounts (590)

**macrophage** an immune system cell that engulfs pathogens and other materials (960)

**madreporite** the porous structure through which water enters and exits the water-vascular system of echinoderms (766)

**magnification** the increase of an object's apparent size by using lenses or mirrors (22)

**malaria** an infectious tropical disease caused by a protozoan and transmitted to humans by a mosquito; it produces high fevers, chills, sweating, and anemia (519)

**Malpighian tubule** an excretory tube that opens into the back part of the intestine of most insects and certain arthropods (732)

**mammary gland** a gland that is located in the chest of a female mammal and that secretes milk (861)

**mandible** in some arthropods, a jawlike mouthpart used to pierce and suck food; in vertebrates, the lower part of the jaw (724)

**mantle** in biology, a layer of tissue that covers the body of many invertebrates (706)

**mantle cavity** the space between the mantle and body mass in mollusks and brachiopods (706)

**map unit** in chromosome mapping, an increment of 1 percent in the frequency of crossing-over (238)

**marsupial** a mammal that lacks a true placenta and gives birth to relatively undeveloped young, and then carries and nourishes the young in a pouch (863)

**mass** a measure of the amount of matter in an object; a fundamental property of an object that is not affected by the forces that act on the object, such as the gravitational force (31)

**mass number** the sum of the numbers of protons and neutrons in the nucleus of an atom (32, 283)

**mastax** the muscular pharynx in rotifers (698)

**matrix** an extracellular substance that gives connective tissue its strength and flexibility; can be solid, semisolid, or liquid (908)

**matter** anything that has mass and takes up space (31)

**medulla** the innermost portion of an organ, such as the kidney (993)

**medulla oblongata** in fish, the posterior brain lobes that regulate the internal organs; in humans, the lower portion of the brain stem, which regulates circulation, respiration, and certain special senses (1012)

**medusa** a free-swimming, jellyfish-like, and often umbrella-shaped sexual stage in the life cycle of a cnidarian; also a jellyfish or a hydra (676)

**megaspore** the larger of the two types of spores produced by heterosporous plants; develops into a female gametophyte (611)

**meiosis** a process in cell division during which the number of chromosomes decreases to half the original number by two divisions of the nucleus, which results in the production of sex cells (gametes or spores) (155)

**melanin** a pigment that helps determine skin color (924)

**melatonin** a hormone that is produced by the pineal gland during the night and that helps regulate certain biorhythms, such as sleep patterns (1040)

**membrane potential** the difference in electric potential between the two sides of a cell membrane (1006)

**memory cell** an immune system B cell or T cell that does not respond the first time that it meets with an antigen or an invading cell but that recognizes and attacks the antigen or invading cell during subsequent infections (965)

**menopause** the termination of the menstrual cycle; occurs between the ages of 45 and 55 (1055)

**menstrual cycle** the female reproductive cycle, characterized by a monthly change of the lining of the uterus and the discharge of blood (1054)

**menstruation** the discharge of blood and discarded tissue from the uterus during the menstrual cycle (1055)

**meristem** a region of undifferentiated plant cells that are capable of dividing and developing into specialized plant tissues (586)

**merozoite** the infective stage of the plasmodial life cycle; infects red blood cells of the host organism (519)

**mesentery** a membrane that attaches the small intestine to the abdominal wall (807)

**mesoderm** in an embryo, the middle layer of cells that gives rise to muscles, blood, and various systems (664)

**mesoglea** in cnidarians, the jellylike material located between the ectoderm and the endoderm (676)

**mesophyll** in leaves, the tissue between epidermal layers, where photosynthesis occurs (600)

**metabolism** the sum of all chemical processes that occur in an organism (8, 36)

**metamorphosis** a phase in the life cycle of many animals during which a rapid change from the immature organism to the adult takes place; an example is the change from larva to adult in insects (748)

**metaphase** one of the stages of mitosis and meiosis, during which all of the chromosomes move to the cell's equator (157)

**metastasis** the spread of cancer cells beyond the original site of growth (226)

**methanogen** a microorganism that produces methane gas (462)

**metric system** a decimal-based standard system of measurement that is used by scientists; similar to the *Systeme Internationale* (abbreviation, *SI*) (23)

**microevolution** a change in the collective genetic material of a population (317)

**microfilament** a fiber found inside eukaryotic cells that is composed mainly of the protein actin and that has a role in cell structure and movement (84)

**micronucleus** the smaller, reproductive nucleus found in some protozoans (508)

**micronutrient** a chemical needed in very small amounts for plant growth, such as manganese, iron, and zinc (590)

**micropyle** the small opening in the wall of an ovule through which a pollen tube enters the ovule (612)

**microsphere** a microscopic spherical structure composed of many protein molecules that are organized as a membrane (286)

**microspore** the smaller of the two types of spores produced by most plants that develops into the male gametophyte (611)

**microtubule** one of the small, tubular fibers composed of the protein tubulin that are found in the cytoplasm of eukaryotic cells, that compose the cytoskeleton, and that play a role in cell structure and movement (84)

**migration** in general, any movement of individuals or populations from one location to another; specifically, a periodic group movement that is characteristic of a given population or species (365, 898)

**mimicry** a defense in which one organism resembles another that is dangerous or poisonous (896)

**mineral** a class of nutrients that are inorganic compounds and that are necessary for certain body processes, such as enzyme activity and bone formation (982)

**mitochondrial matrix** the fluid that is inside the inner membrane of a mitochondrion (137)

**mitochondrion** in eukaryotic cells, the cell organelle that is surrounded by two membranes and that is the site of cellular respiration, which produces ATP (plural, *mitochondria*) (80)

**mitosis** in eukaryotic cells, a process of cell division that forms two new nuclei, each of which has the same number of chromosomes (155)

**molar** a large tooth that is located in the back of the mouth and that is used to grind and crush food (865)

**mold** in biology, a fungus that grows in the form of a tangled mass of filaments (527)

**molecular genetics** the study of the structure of nucleic acids and the function and regulation of genes (178)

**molecule** a group of atoms that are held together by chemical forces; a molecule is the smallest unit of matter that can exist by itself and retain all of a substance's chemical properties (33)

**molting** the shedding of an exoskeleton, skin, feathers, or hair to be replaced by new parts (724)

**monocot** a monocotyledonous plant; a plant that produces seeds that have only one cotyledon (576)

**monohybrid cross** a cross between individuals that involves one pair of contrasting traits (182)

**monomer** a simple molecule that can combine with other like or unlike molecules to make a polymer (53)

**monosaccharide** a simple sugar that is the basic subunit, or monomer, of a carbohydrate (55)

**monotreme** a mammal that lays eggs (863)

**morphology** the study of the structure and form of an organism (326)

**motor neuron** a nerve cell that conducts nerve impulses from the central nervous system to the muscles and glands (1013)

**mouth pore** in protozoa, an opening into which the oral groove opens (508)

**movable joint** a joint at which a wide range of motion occurs; examples include ball-and-socket, hinge, pivot, saddle, and gliding joints (915)

**mRNA (messenger RNA)** a single-stranded RNA molecule that encodes the information to make a protein (205)

**mucous gland** a gland in the skin of an amphibian that produces lubricants to keep the skin moist (804)

**mucous membrane** the layer of epithelial tissue that covers internal surfaces of the body and that secretes mucus (958)

**multicellular** describes a tissue, organ, or organism that is made of many cells (7)

**multiple alleles** more than two alleles (versions of the gene) for a genetic trait (244)

**multiple fission** a form of cell division that produces more than two cells (504)

**muscle fatigue** the physiological inability of a muscle to contract (922)

**muscle fiber** a multinucleate muscle cell, especially of skeletal or cardiac muscle tissue (917)

**muscle tissue** the tissue made of cells that can contract and relax to produce movement (907)

**mutation** a change in the nucleotide-base sequence of a gene or DNA molecule (202)

**mutualism** a relationship between two species in which both species benefit (403)

**mycelium** the mass of fungal filaments, or hyphae, that forms the body of a fungus (527)

**mycology** the study of fungi (527)

**mycorrhiza** a symbiotic association between fungi and plant roots (533)

**myelin sheath** a layer of fatty material that surrounds certain nerve fibers and that acts as an electrical insulator (1005)

**myofibril** a bundle of threadlike structures found within a striated muscle cell and mostly made up of actin and myosin (919)

**myosin** the most abundant protein in muscle tissue and the main constituent of the thick filaments of muscle fibers (919)

## N

**NAD$^+$ (nicotinamide adenine dinucleotide)** an organic molecule that serves as an electron carrier by being oxidized to NAD$^+$ and reduced to NADH (133)

**NADH** the reduced form of NAD$^+$; an electron-carrying molecule that functions in cellular respiration (131)

**naphthalene acetic acid** a synthetic plant hormone that is used to promote root formation on stems and leaf cuttings (abbreviation, NAA) (632)

**nastic movement** a type of plant response that is independent of the direction of a stimulus (638)

**natural killer cell** a type of white blood cell that is present in individuals who have not been immunized and that kills a variety of cells (960)

**natural selection** the process by which individuals that are better adapted to their environment survive and reproduce more successfully than less well adapted individuals do; a theory to explain the mechanism of evolution (12, 300)

**nauplius** the free-swimming larva of most crustaceans (726)

**nectar** a sugar-containing fluid secreted by flowers to attract birds or insects for pollination (616)

**negative feedback** a mechanism of homeostasis whereby a step in a series of events inhibits the initial signal in the series (1041)

**nematocyst** in cnidarians, a stinging cell that is used to inject a toxin into prey (677)

**nephridium** a tubule through which some invertebrates eliminate wastes (715)

**nephron** the functional unit of the kidney (994)

**neritic zone** a shallow marine environment that is near the shore or over the continental shelf and that is rich in minerals and nutrients produced by biotic activity (423)

**nerve** a collection of nerve fibers through which impulses travel between the central nervous system and other parts of the body (1013)

**nerve net** in cnidarians, a network of nerve cells that lacks a central control; impulses pass in any or all directions to produce a generalized response (677)

**nervous system** the structures that control the actions and reactions of the body in response to stimuli from the environment; a body system formed by billions of specialized nerve cells (1005)

**nervous tissue** the tissue of the nervous system, which consists of neurons, their supporting cells, and connective tissue (907)

**net primary productivity** the rate at which biomass accumulates in an ecosystem (366)

**net venation** a nonparallel, branching network of veins that is typical of the leaves of dicots (576, 600)

**neuron** a nerve cell that is specialized to receive and conduct electrical impulses (907, 1005)

**neuropeptide** a hormone secreted by the nervous system (1033)

**neurotransmitter** a chemical substance that transmits nerve impulses across a synapse (1005)

**neutron** a subatomic particle that has no charge and that is located in the nucleus of an atom (32)

**neutrophil** a large leukocyte that contains a lobed nucleus and many cytoplasmic granules (960)

**niche** the unique position occupied by a species, both in terms of its physical use of its habitat and its function within an ecological community (365)

**nicotine** a toxic, addictive alkaloid that is derived from tobacco and that is one of the major contributors to the harmful effects of smoking (1024)

**nictitating membrane** a third eyelid found under the lower eyelid of many vertebrates, including birds, reptiles, and amphibians (809)

**nitrification** the process by which nitrites and nitrates are produced by bacteria in the soil (374)

**nitrogen cycle** the process in which nitrogen circulates among the air, soil, water, plants, and animals in an ecosystem (373)

**nitrogen fixation** the process by which gaseous nitrogen is converted into nitrates, compounds that organisms can use to make amino acids and other nitrogen-containing organic molecules (373)

**nitrogen-fixing bacterium** a bacterium that converts atmospheric nitrogen into ammonia (373)

**nitrogenous base** an organic base that contains nitrogen, such as a purine or pyrimidine; a subunit of a nucleotide in DNA and RNA (197)

**node** in biology, a joint between two adjacent sections in the stem of a plant where buds form and leaves or branches start to grow; usually marked by a knot or swelling (593)

**nondisjunction** the failure of homologous chromosomes to separate during meiosis I or the failure of sister chromatids to separate during mitosis or meiosis II (239)

**nonvascular plant** the three groups of plants (liverworts, hornworts, and mosses) that lack specialized conducting tissues and true roots, stems, and leaves (564)

**norepinephrine** a chemical that is both a neurotransmitter produced by the sympathetic nerve endings in the autonomic nervous system and a hormone secreted by the adrenal medulla to stimulate the functions of the circulatory and respiratory systems especially (1037)

**nosepiece** the part of a compound light microscope that holds the objective lenses in place above the specimen (22)

**notochord** in the embryos of all chordates and in many adult chordates, a firm, flexible rod of tissue that is located in the dorsal part of the body (654)

**nuclear envelope** the double membrane that surrounds the nucleus of a eukaryotic cell (79)

**nucleic acid** an organic compound, either RNA or DNA, whose molecules are made up of one or two chains of nucleotides and carry genetic information (60)

**nucleolus** the part of the eukaryotic nucleus where ribosomal RNA is synthesized (79)

**nucleotide** in a nucleic-acid chain, a subunit that consists of a sugar, a phosphate, and a nitrogenous base (60, 197)

**nucleus** in physical science, an atom's central region, which is made up of protons and neutrons (32)

**nucleus** in a eukaryotic cell, a membrane-bound organelle that contains the cell's DNA and that has a role in processes such as growth, metabolism, and reproduction (74)

**nut** a dry fruit that has one seed and a hard shell; cultivated as a food crop (547)

**nutrient** a substance or compound that provides nourishment (or food) or raw materials needed for life processes (979)

**nyctinastic movement** a nastic movement that occurs in a plant in response to cycles of dark and light (639)

**nymph** an immature stage of some insects that is similar in function and structure to the adult (748)

——————— O ———————

**objective lens** the part of a compound light microscope that is located directly above the specimen and that magnifies the image of the specimen (21)

**obligate anaerobe** an organism that needs the absence of oxygen in order to live (470)

**observation** the process of obtaining information by using the senses; the information obtained by using the senses (13)

**oceanic zone** the regions of the open sea that lie beyond and between the continental shelves (424)

**ocular lens** the part of a compound light microscope that magnifies an image, usually 10 times, also called the *eyepiece* (21)

**oil gland** an exocrine gland that secretes an oily substance called sebum; also known as a *sebaceous gland* (925)

**olfactory receptor** a cell found in the nasal passages that is stimulated by certain substances, produces nerve impulses, and gives rise to the sense of smell (1019)

**oligotrophic lake** a lake that lacks organic nutrients and, as a result, contains high levels of dissolved oxygen in its lower layer (427)

**omnivore** an organism that eats a variety of other organisms, including animals and plants (367)

**oncogene** a gene that induces cancer, or uncontrolled cell proliferation (225, 491)

**oogenesis** the production, growth, and maturation of an egg, or ovum (164)

**open circulatory system** a type of circulatory system in which the circulatory fluid is not contained entirely within vessels; a heart pumps fluid through vessels that empty into spaces called sinuses (658)

**operant conditioning** a type of learning in which specific animal behaviors are deterred or reinforced by external actions upon the animal; usually refers to a controlled experimental situation (889)

**operator** a short sequence of viral or bacterial DNA to which a repressor binds to prevent transcription (mRNA synthesis) of the adjacent gene in an operon (218)

**operculum** in fish, a hard plate that is attached to each side of the head, that covers gills, and that is open at the rear (788)

**operon** a unit of gene regulation and transcription in bacterial DNA that consists of a promoter, an operator, and one or more structural genes (218)

**opportunistic infection** an infection caused by a microorganism that normally does not cause disease but that becomes pathogenic if the patient's immune system is weakened (971)

**opposable thumb** in primates, a thumb that can touch and move in opposition to the other fingers of the hand (876)

**optic tectum** the largest part of the midbrain of a fish; receives and processes information from the fish's visual, auditory, and lateral-line systems (792)

**optimality hypothesis** a prediction of the ratio of the energy expended to the energy gained as an animal searches for food; holds that animals tend to behave in a way that maximizes food intake while minimizing efforts to find food and avoiding danger (893)

**oral groove** a depressed region around the mouth of some ciliate protozoans, such as paramecia (508)

**orbital** a region in an atom where there is a high probability of finding electrons (32)

**order** in a traditional taxonomic system, the category contained within a class and containing families (339)

**organ** a collection of tissues that carry out a specialized function of the body (7, 76, 909)

**organelle** one of the small bodies that are found in the cytoplasm of a cell and that are specialized to perform a specific function (7, 75)

**organic compound** a covalently bonded compound that contains carbon, excluding carbonates and oxides (51)

**organism** an independent individual that possesses all characteristics of life (7)

**organization** the high degree of order within an organism's internal and external parts and in its interactions with the living world (6)

**origin** in anatomy, the point at which a muscle attaches to a stationary bone (921)

**ornithologist** a person who specializes in the scientific study of birds (849)

**osculum** an opening in a sponge's body through which water exits (673)

**osmosis** the diffusion of water or another solvent from a more dilute solution (of a solute) to a more concentrated solution (of the solute) through a membrane that is permeable to the solvent (98)

**ossicle** one of the small, calcium carbonate plates that make up the endoskeleton of an echinoderm (762)

**ossification** the process by which cartilage is converted into bone (914)

**osteoarthritis** a degenerative joint disease in which the cartilage covering the surface of the bones becomes thinner and rougher (916)

**osteocyte** a bone cell (913)

**ostium** one of the small openings in a sponge's body through which water enters (673)

**ovarian cycle** a series of hormone-induced changes in which the ovaries prepare and release a mature ovum each month (1054)

**ovary** in the female reproductive system of animals, an organ that produces eggs; in flowering plants, the lower part of a pistil that produces eggs in ovules (575, 613, 1052)

**oviduct** the tube that leads from an ovary to the uterus (848)

**oviparity** in egg-laying amniotes, a reproductive method in which the female's reproductive tract encloses each egg in a tough, protective shell (829)

**oviparous** describes organisms that produce eggs that develop and hatch outside the body of the mother (863)

**ovipositor** in many female insects, a structure that is at the end of the abdomen and that is used to lay eggs (748)

**ovoviviparity** in amniotes, a reproductive method wherein shelled eggs are produced, develop, and sometimes hatch inside the body of the mother (829)

**ovoviviparous** describes organisms that produce eggs that develop and hatch inside the body of the mother (829)

**ovulation** the release of an ovum from a follicle of the ovary (1054)

**ovule** a structure in the ovary of a seed plant that contains an embryo sac and that develops into a seed after fertilization; in gymnosperms the ovule is found in the carpel and is structurally simple and naked (612)

**ovum** a mature egg cell (1053)

**oxaloacetic acid** a four-carbon compound of Krebs cycle that combines with acetyl CoA to form citric acid (138)

**oxidation reaction** a chemical reaction in which a reactant loses one or more electrons such that the reactant becomes more positive in charge (37)

**oxygen debt** the extra amount of oxygen that must be taken in by the body to replenish the muscles' oxygen reserves and to allow for the breakdown of lactic acid within the muscles, especially after strenuous activity (922)

**ozone** a gas molecule that is made up of three oxygen atoms (289)

**ozone layer** the layer of the atmosphere at an altitude of 15 to 40 km in which ozone absorbs ultraviolet solar radiation (436)

### P

**P generation** parental generation, the first two individuals that mate in a genetic cross (175)

**palisade mesophyll** in plants, the layer of vertically elongated cells that contains chloroplasts, that is located beneath the upper epidermis of leaves, and that participates in photosynthesis (600)

**papilla** one of the bumps of tissue on the tongue, between which taste buds are embedded (plural, *papillae*)(1019)

**parallel venation** a parallel arrangement of veins; typical of the leaves of monocots (576, 600)

**parapodium** in polychaete annelid worms, one of the two flap-shaped appendages that are used for locomotion or gas exchange (713)

**parasitism** a relationship between two species in which one species, the parasite, benefits from the other species, the host, which is harmed (403)

**parenchyma** in higher plants, the fundamental tissue that is composed of thin-walled living cells that function in photosynthesis and storage (583)

**parthenogenesis** a type of reproduction in which unfertilized eggs develop into adults (698)

**passive transport** the movement of substances across a cell membrane without the use of energy by the cell (97)

**pathogen** a virus, microorganism, or other organism that causes disease; an infectious agent (957)

**pathology** the scientific study of disease (472)

**PCR (polymerase chain reaction)** a molecular biology technique that is used to make many copies of selected segments of DNA (256)

**pedicellaria** on the surface of some echinoderms, very small pincers that are used for protection against ectoparasites (765)

**pedigree** a diagram that shows the occurrence of a genetic trait in several generations of a family (241)

**pedipalp** one of the second pair of appendages that are beside the mouth of an arachnid and that are used for chewing and handling prey (731)

**peer review** the process in which experts in a given field examine the results and conclusions of a scientist's study before that study is accepted for publication (19)

**pelagic zone** the upper, central, or open region of a body of water (424)

**pellicle** a protective envelope of nonliving material that covers many protozoans (508)

**pelvic cavity** the hollow part of the body that is below the abdominal cavity and that contains the organs of the reproductive and excretory systems (910)

**penis** the male organ that transfers sperm to the female reproductive tract during sexual intercourse and that carries urine out of the body (1051)

**peptide bond** the chemical bond that forms between the carboxyl group of one amino acid and the amino group of another amino acid (57)

**peptidoglycan** a protein-carbohydrate compound that makes the cell walls of bacteria rigid (462)

**pericycle** in plants, the outer portion of the central cylinder of vascular tissue (590)

**periosteum** a white, double-layered membrane that covers the entire surface of bone except for the joint surfaces, it is richly supplied with nerve fibers and blood vessels (912)

**peripheral nervous system** all of the parts of the nervous system except for the brain and the spinal cord (the central nervous system); includes the cranial nerves and nerves of the neck, chest, lower back, and pelvis (1010)

**peristalsis** the series of rhythmic muscular contractions that move food through the digestive tract (987)

**permafrost** in arctic regions, the permanently frozen layer of soil or subsoil (418)

**pesticide** a poison used to destroy pests, such as insects, rodents, or weeds; examples include insecticides, rodenticides, and herbicides (548)

**petal** one of the usually brightly colored, leaf-shaped parts that make up one of the rings of a flower (613)

**petiole** the stalk that attaches a leaf to the stem of a plant (600)

**pH scale** a range of values that are used to express the acidity or alkalinity (basicity) of a system; each whole number on the scale indicates a tenfold change in acidity; a pH of 7 is neutral, a pH of less than 7 is acidic, and a pH of greater than 7 is basic (44)

**phagocyte** a cell that ingests and destroys (digests) foreign matter or microorganisms (105, 941, 959)

**phagocytosis** the process by which a cell engulfs large particles or whole cells, either as a defense mechanism or as a means to obtain food (105)

**pharyngeal pouch** one of the lateral sacs that branch from the pharynx of chordate embryos and that may open to the outside as gill slits in adult fishes and invertebrate chordates (654)

**pharynx** in flatworms, the muscular tube that leads from the mouth to the gastrovascular cavity; in animals with a digestive tract, the passage from the mouth to the larynx and esophagus (690, 947)

**phenotype** an organism's appearance or other detectable characteristic that results from the organism's genotype and the environment (180)

**phenotype frequency** the ratio of individuals with a particular phenotype to the total number of individuals in a population (319)

**phenotypic ratio** the ratio of phenotypes produced by a cross (183)

**pheromone** a substance that is released by the body and that causes another individual of the same species to react in a predictable way (751, 896)

**phloem** in vascular plants, the tissue that carries organic and inorgnaic nutrients in any direction, depending on the plant's needs (564)

**phospholipid** a lipid that contains phosphorus and that is a structural component in cell membranes (59)

**phospholipid bilayer** a double layer of phospholipids that makes up plasma and organelle membranes (77)

**phosphorus cycle** the cyclic movement of phosphorus in different chemical forms from the environment to organisms and then back to the environment (374)

**photic zone** the area of an aquatic system that receives enough light for photosynthesis to occur (423)

**photoperiodism** the response of plants to seasonal changes in the relative length of nights and days (640)

**photosynthesis** the process by which plants, algae, and some bacteria use sunlight, carbon dioxide, and water to produce carbohydrates and oxygen (113)

**photosystem** in the thylakoid membranes of chloroplasts, a cluster of chlorophyll and other pigment molecules that harvest light energy for the light reactions of photosynthesis (116)

**phototroph** an organism that gets its energy from sunlight (469)

**phototropism** a plant growth movement that occurs in response to the direction of a source of light (636)

**phylogenetic diagram** a branching diagram that models the relationships by ancestry between different species or other taxonomic groups (341)

**phylogenetics** the analysis of evolutionary, or ancestral, relationships between taxa (341)

**phylogeny** the evolutionary history of a species or taxonomic group; the relationships by ancestry among species or taxonomic groups (307)

**phylum** in a traditional taxonomic system for organisms other than plants, the category contained within a kingdom and containing classes (339)

**phytochrome** a protein pigment that regulates flowering in plants in response to light absorption and seed germination (641)

**phytoplankton** the microscopic, photosynthetic organisms that float near the surface of marine or fresh water and that are the basic source of food in many aquatic ecosystems; examples include algae and cyanobacteria (510)

**pigment** a substance that gives another substance or a mixture its color (115)

**pilus** a short, thick hair-like protein structure that allows a bacterium to attach to other bacteria and surfaces (plural, *pili*) (468)

**pinniped** an aquatic, fin-footed, carnivorous animal, such as a sea lion, walrus, or seal (872)

**pinocytosis** a method of active transport across the cell membrane in which the cell takes in extracellular fluids (105)

**pinworm** a nematode worm parasite that lives in the intestine of humans and animals; females lay their eggs around the anus, which causes itching (697)

**pioneer species** a species that colonizes an uninhabited area and that starts an ecological cycle in which many other species become established (408)

**pistil** the female reproductive part of a flower that produces seeds and consists of an ovary, style, and stigma, made of one or more fused carpels (614)

**pit** in plants, the thin, porous areas of a thracheid cell wall (585)

**pith** the tissue that is located in the center of the stem of most vascular plants and that is used for storage (594)

**pituitary gland** an endocrine gland that is located at the base of the brain, stores and releases hormones produced by the hypothalamus, and secretes hormones under the control of the hypothalamus (1034)

**placenta** the structure that attaches a developing fetus to the uterus and that enables the exchange of nutrients, wastes, and gases between the mother and the fetus (829, 863, 1058)

**placental mammal** a mammal that nourishes its unborn offspring through a placenta inside its uterus (863)

**placoid scale** one of the hard scales that resemble vertebrate teeth and cover skin of sharks and rays (784)

**plankton** the mass of mostly microscopic organisms that float or drift freely in the waters of aquatic (freshwater and marine) environments (424)

**plant hormone** organic chemical messengers that affect a plant's ability to respond to its environment (631)

**Plantae** in a traditional taxonomic system, a kingdom made up of eukaryotic, multicellular organisms that have cell walls made mostly of cellulose, that have pigments that absorb light, and that supply energy and oxygen to themselves and to other life-forms through photosynthesis (350)

**planula** the free-swimming, ciliated larva of a cnidarian (680)

**plasma** in biology, the liquid component of blood (940)

**plasma cell** a type of white blood cell that produces antibodies (964)

**plasma membrane** or cell membrane, the cell's outer boundary (74)

**plasmid** a circular DNA molecule that is usually found in bacteria and that can replicate independent of the main chromosome (259, 468)

**plasmodial slime mold** a type of protist that has ameboid cells, flagellated cells, and a plasmodial feeding stage in its life cycle (514)

**plasmolysis** the contraction or shrinking of the cell membrane of a plant cell in a hypertonic solution in response to the loss of water by osmosis (100)

**plastid** an organelle of plant cells that contains specific substances and performs specific functions for the cell; examples include chloroplasts and chromoplasts (89)

**plastron** the bottom, or ventral, portion of a turtle's shell (830)

**platelet** a fragment of a cell that is needed to form blood clots (942)

**plumule** the developing shoot above the cotyledons in plant embryos; consists of the epicotyl and young leaves (620)

**point mutation** a mutation in which only one nucleotide or nitrogenous base in a gene is changed (240)

**polar** describes a molecule with opposite charges on opposite ends (39)

**polar body** a short-lived product of the formation of gametes by meiosis (164)

**polar nucleus** one of the two haploid nuclei in the embryo sac of a seed plant that fuse with a male gamete to form the triploid cell that develops into the endosperm (plural, *polar nuclei*) (613)

**pollen grain** the structure that contains the male gametophyte of seed plants (612)

**pollen tube** a tubular structure that grows from a pollen grain, enters the embryo sac, and allows the male reproductive cells to move to the ovule (612)

**pollination** the transfer of pollen from the male reproductive structures (the anthers) to the tip of a female reproductive structure (the pistil) of a flower in angiosperms or to the ovule in gymnosperms (174, 612)

**polygenic** describes a characteristic that is influenced by many genes (242)

**polymer** a large molecule that is formed by more than five monomers, or small units (53)

**polyp** a form of a cnidarian that has a cylindrical, hollow body and that is usually attached to a rock or to another object (676)

**polypeptide** a long chain of several amino acids (57)

**polysaccharide** one of the carbohydrates made up of long chains of simple sugars; polysaccharides include starch, cellulose, and glycogen (56)

**population** a group of organisms of the same species that live in a specific geographical area and interbreed (362, 381)

**population density** the number of individuals of the same species that live in a given unit of area (382)

**population genetics** the study of the frequency and interaction of alleles and genes in populations (317)

**positive feedback** the release of an initial hormone that stimulates release or production of other hormones or substances, which stimulate further release of the initial hormone (1042)

**posterior** in animals with bilateral symmetry, refers to the end of the body that is opposite the head; rear (655)

**preadaptation** an adaptation in an ancestral group that evolves through natural selection to allow new functions in a descendant group (799)

**precocial** describes a species of birds or mammals whose young are born at an advanced stage of development, with open eyes and the ability to walk and run almost immediately (849)

**predation** a relationship between two species in which one species, the predator, feeds on the other species, the prey (399)

**prediction** a statement made in advance that expresses the results that will be obtained from testing a hypothesis if the hypothesis is supported; the expected outcome if a hypothesis is accurate (13)

**preen gland** in birds, a special gland that secretes oil that a bird spreads over its feathers to clean and waterproof them (844)

**pregnancy** the period of time between implantation and birth (1057)

**prehensile appendage** an appendage that can grasp objects, as in a primate's hand, foots, or tail (875)

**premolar** one of the eight teeth that are located between the molars and the canines (865)

**pre-mRNA** precursor mRNA; the first strand of mRNA produced by gene transcription that contains both introns and exons (221)

**pressure-flow hypothesis** an explanation for the movement of carbohydrates in the phloem of plants; holds that carbohydrates are actively transported into sieve tubes (596)

**primary electron acceptor** in chloroplasts, an acceptor of electrons lost from chlorophyll a; found in the thylakoid membrane (117)

**primary host** the host from which an adult parasite gets its nourishment and in which reproduction occurs (692)

**primary succession** succession that begins in an area that previously did not support life (408)

**primer** a short, single-stranded fragment of DNA or RNA that is required for the initiation of DNA replication (256)

**prion** an infectious particle that consists only of a protein and that does not contain DNA or RNA (494)

**probability** the likelihood that a possible future event will occur in any given instance of the event; the mathematical ratio of the number of times one outcome of any event is likely to occur to the number of possible outcomes of the event (181)

**probe** a strand of RNA or single-stranded DNA that has been labeled with a radioactive element or fluorescent dye

and that is used to bind with and identify a specific gene in genetic engineering (259)

**producer** an organism that can make organic molecules from inorganic molecules; a photosynthetic or chemosynthetic autotroph that serves as the basic food source in an ecosystem (366)

**product** a substance that forms in a chemical reaction (36)

**progesterone** a steroid hormone that is secreted by the corpus luteum of the ovary, that stimulates changes in the uterus to prepare for the implantation of a fertilized egg, and that is produced by the placenta during pregnancy (1037)

**proglottid** one of the many body sections of a tapeworm; contains reproductive organs (693)

**prokaryote** a single-celled organism that has no nucleus and has no membrane-bound organelles; examples include bacteria and archaea (75, 461)

**promoter** a nucleotide sequence on a DNA molecule to which an RNA polymerase molecule binds, which initiates the transcription of a specific gene (206)

**propagation** the production of new individuals (618)

**prophage** the viral genome (DNA) of a bacteriophage that has entered a bacterial cell, has become attached to the bacterial chromosome, and is replicated with the host bacterium's DNA (487)

**prophase** the first stage of mitosis and meiosis in cell division; characterized by the condensation of the chromosomes and the dissolution of the nuclear envelope (156)

**prostaglandin** a type of hormone that is synthesized in the body tissues and that usually acts locally; prostaglandins have a variety of effects, such as the dilatation of blood vessels, the contraction and relaxation of smooth muscle, and the regulation of the kidney function (1033)

**prostate gland** a gland in males that contributes to the seminal fluid (1051)

**protease inhibitor** a type of drug that blocks the synthesis of new viral capsid and that is used to treat diseases such as AIDS (491)

**protein** an organic compound that is made of one or more chains of amino acids and that is a principal component of all cells (56)

**protein synthesis** the formation of proteins by using information contained in DNA and carried by mRNA (204, 207)

**proteome** an organism's complete set of proteins (262)

**proteomics** the study of all of an organism's proteins, including its identity, structure, interaction, and abundance (264)

**protist** an organism that is classified a a member of the kingdom Protista; generally, a single-celled or simple multicellular eukaryote that cannot be readily classified as either plant, animal, or fungus (501)

**Protista** in a traditional taxonomic system, a kingdom made up of mostly one-celled eukaryotic organisms that are not readily classified as either plants, animals, or fungi (349)

**proton** a subatomic particle that has a positive charge and that is located in the nucleus of an atom; the number of protons of the nucleus is the atomic number, which determines the identity of an element (32)

**proto-oncogene** a gene that regulates normal cell division but that can become a cancer-causing oncogene as a result of mutation or recombination (225, 491)

**protostome** an organism whose embryonic blastopore develops into the mouth, whose coelom arises by schizocoely, and whose embryo has determinate cleavage (665)

**proventriculus** the first of the two chambers in the stomach of a bird (846)

**provirus** viral DNA that has attached to a host cell's chromosome and that is replicated with the chromosome's DNA (485)

**pseudocoelom** the type of body cavity, derived from the blastocoel and referred to as a "false body cavity," that forms between the mesoderm and the endoderm in rotifers and roundworms (665)

**pseudopodium** a retractable, temporary cytoplasmic extension that functions in food ingestion and movement in certain amoeboid cells (506)

**psychoactive drug** a drug or medicine that affects and changes the functioning of the central nervous system (1021)

**puberty** the stage of human life in which menstruation begins in females, sperm production begins in males, and secondary sex characteristics begin to appear (1037)

**pulmonary circulation** the flow of blood from the right ventricle of the heart to the lungs and back to the left atrium of the heart through the network of pulmonary arteries, capillaries, and veins (805, 937)

**pulmonary respiration** in animals, respiration through the lungs (806)

**pulse** the rhythmic pressure of the blood against the walls of a vessel, particularly an artery (935)

**punctuated equilibrium** a model of evolution in which short periods of drastic change in species, including mass extinctions and rapid speciation, are separated by long periods of little or no change (330)

**Punnett square** a graphic used to predict the results of a genetic cross (182)

**pupa** the immobile, nonfeeding stage between the larva and the adult of insects that have complete metamorphosis; as a pupa, the organism is usually enclosed in a cocoon or chrysalis and undergoes important anatomical changes (749)

**pupil** the opening that is located in the center of the iris of the eye and that controls the amount of light that enters the eye (1018)

**purine** a nitrogenous base that has a double-ring structure; one of the two general categories of nitrogenous bases found in DNA and RNA; either adenine or guanine (198)

**pygostyle** in birds, the fused terminal vertebrae of the spine; supports the tail feathers (845)

**pyloric sphincter** the circular muscle that controls the flow of chyme from the stomach to the small intestine (988)

**pyrimidine** a nitrogenous base that has a single-ring structure; one of the two general categories of nitrogenous bases found in DNA and RNA; thymine, cytosine, or uracil (198)

**pyruvic acid** the three-carbon compound that is produced during glycolysis and needed for both the aerobic and anaerobic pathways of cellular respiration that follow glycolysis (131)

---

## Q

**queen bee** the mature, fertile female that lays eggs in a colony of bees (752)

**queen factor** a pheromone that is produced by a queen bee and that prevents other female larvae from developing into queens (753)

---

## R

**radial symmetry** a body plan in which the parts of an animal's body are organized in a circle around a central axis (655)

**radicle** in plants, the embryonic, or primary, root (620)

**radioactive decay** the disintegration of an unstable atomic nucleus into one or more different nuclides, accompanied by the emission of radiation, the nuclear capture or ejection of electrons, or fission (283)

**radioactive isotope** an isotope that has an unstable nucleus and that emits radiation (283)

**radiometric dating** a method of determining the absolute age of an object by comparing the relative percentages of a radioactive (parent) isotope and a stable (daughter) isotope (282)

**radula** a rasping, tonguelike organ that is covered with chitinous teeth and that is used for feeding by many mollusks (706)

**ray-finned fish** a kind of fish whose fins are supported by long, segmented, and flexible bony elements called rays (788)

**reabsorption** the process in the kidneys by which materials return to the blood from the nephrons (996)

**reactant** a substance or molecule that participates in a chemical reaction (36)

**reasoning** a type of problem solving that requires the ability to solve a problem

that has not been encountered previously (890)

**receptacle** the enlarged tip of a flower stalk to which the flower is attached (613)

**receptor** a specialized sensory nerve that responds to specific types of stimuli (1032)

**recessive** describes a trait or an allele that is expressed only when two recessive alleles for the same characteristic are inherited (177)

**recombinant DNA** DNA molecules that are artificially created by combining DNA from different sources (258)

**red blood cell** a disc-shaped cell that has no nucleus, that contains hemoglobin, and that transports oxygen in the circulatory system (940)

**red tide** a population explosion of certain marine dinoflagellates that causes the water to turn a red or red-brown color and to contain poisonous alkaloids produced by the dinoflagellates (513)

**redox reaction** a reaction in which electrons are transferred between atoms; also known as an oxidation-reduction reaction (37)

**reduction reaction** a chemical change in which electrons are gained, either by the removal of oxygen, the addition of hydrogen, or the addition of electrons (37)

**reflex** an involuntary and almost immediate movement in response to a stimulus (1014)

**refractory period** a short period of time after the stimulation of a nerve during which the nerve cannot be stimulated (1008)

**regeneration** the regrowth of missing tissues or organs (675)

**regulator gene** a genetic unit that regulates or suppresses the activity of one or more structural genes (219)

**relative age** the age of an object in relation to the ages of other objects (302)

**renal tubule** the long, tubular portion of a nephron that produces and that takes urine to the renal pelvis of a kidney (995)

**replication fork** a Y-shaped point that results when the two strands of a DNA double helix separate so that the DNA molecule can be replicated (200)

**repressor protein** a regulatory protein that binds to an operator and blocks transcription of the genes of an operon (219)

**reproduction** the process of producing offspring (9)

**reproductive isolation** the inability of members of a population to successfully interbreed with members of another population of the same or a related species (328)

**resolution** in microscopes, the ability to form images with fine detail (22)

**respiratory system** a collection of organs whose primary function is to take in oxygen and expel carbon dioxide; the organs of this system include the lungs, the throat, and the passageways that lead to the lungs (946)

**resting potential** the electric potential across the cell membrane of a nerve cell or muscle cell when the cell is not active (1007)

**restoration biology** the science of rehabilitating, replacing, or acquiring the equivalent of any natural resources that have been injured, destroyed, or lost (446)

**restriction enzyme** an enzyme that destroys foreign DNA molecules by cutting them at specific sites (257)

**retina** the light-sensitive inner layer of the eye, which receives images formed by the lens and transmits them through the optic nerve to the brain (1018)

**retrovirus** a virus that contains single-stranded RNA and produces a reverse transcriptase, which converts RNA to DNA (486)

**reverse transcriptase** an enzyme that catalyzes the formation of DNA from an RNA template (486)

**Rh factor** one of several blood-group antigens carried on the surface of red blood cells (944)

**rheumatoid arthritis** a chronic immune-system disorder that causes stiff and painful joints (916)

**rhizoid** a rootlike structure in nonvascular plants, such as mosses or liverworts, that holds the plants in place and aids in absorption (530)

**rhizome** a horizontal, underground stem that provides a mechanism for asexual reproduction (572)

**ribose** a five-carbon sugar present in RNA (205)

**ribosome** a cell organelle composed of RNA and protein; the site of protein synthesis (79)

**ribozyme** a type of RNA that can act as an enzyme (288)

**RNA (ribonucleic acid)** a natural polymer that is present in all living cells and that plays a role in protein synthesis (60, 204)

**RNA polymerase** an enzyme that starts (catalyzes) the formation of RNA by using a strand of a DNA molecule as a template (206)

**rod** one of the two types of light-detecting cells in the eye; rods can detect dim light and play a major role in noncolor and night vision (1018)

**root cap** the protective layer of cells that covers the tip of a root (588)

**root crop** a plant root or underground stem that is rich in carbohydrates and can serve as the major part of a diet (547)

**root hair** an extension of the epidermis of a root that increases the root's surface area for absorption (588)

**rotifer** a member of the phylum Rotifera, which consists of small, aquatic invertebrates whose ring of cilia around the mouth makes the animal look like a spinning wheel (698)

**roundworm** a member of the phylum Nematoda, which consists of animals that have smooth skin and a long, cylindrical, and unsegmented body that tapers at both ends (695)

**royal jelly** a high-protein substance secreted by worker bees and fed to a queen bee and female larvae that develop into queen bees (752)

**rRNA (ribosomal RNA)** an organelle that contains most of the RNA in the cell and that is responsible for ribosome function (205)

**rumen** the first of the four compartments in the stomach of a ruminant mammal (866)

---

# S

---

**saliva** the watery fluid that is secreted by the salivary glands of the mouth, that softens and moistens food, and that begins digestion (986)

**sarcoma** a malignant tumor that grows in bone or muscle tissue (228)

**sarcomere** the basic unit of contraction in skeletal and cardiac muscle (919)

**saturated solution** a solution that cannot dissolve any more solute under the given conditions (42)

**savanna** a plain full of grasses and scattered trees and shrubs; found in tropical and subtropical habitats and mainly in regions with a dry climate, such as East Africa (421)

**scanning electron microscope** a microscope that produces an enlarged, three-dimensional image of an object by using a beam of electrons rather than light (abbreviation, *SEM*) (22)

**schistosomiasis** a disease that is caused by a parasitic blood fluke of the genus *Schistosoma* and that affects the skin, intestines, liver, vascular system, or other organs (693)

**schizocoely** the method of coelom formation in protosomes in which the embryonic mesoderm splits into two layers (666)

**scientific methods** the series of steps followed to solve problems, including collecting data, formulating a hypothesis, testing the hypothesis, and stating conclusions (13)

**sclerenchyma** a type of plant tissue composed of cells that have thickened secondary cell walls that function in plant support (584)

**scolex** the head of a tapeworm, which has hooks and suckers to adhere to the host tissues (693)

**scrotum** the sac that contains the testes in most male mammals (1049)

**sebum** the oily secretion of the sebaceous glands (925)

**second messenger** a molecule that is generated when a specific substance attaches to a receptor on the outside of a cell membrane, which produces a change in cellular function (1032)

**secondary succession** the process by which one community replaces another

community that has been partially or totally destroyed (408)

**secretion** the process by which the glands of the body release their substances; a substance produced by a gland; the process by which substances pass from the blood into the kidneys (996)

**seed** a plant embryo that is enclosed in a protective coat (563)

**seed coat** the protective, outer covering of a seed (620)

**seed plant** a plant that produces seeds (565)

**seedling** a young plant grown from a seed (572)

**segmentation** the division of the body of an organism into a series of similar parts (657)

**self-pollination** the transfer of pollen grains from an anther to the stigma of the same flower or to the stigma of another flower on the same plant (174)

**semen** the fluid that contains sperm and various secretions produced by the male reproductive organs (1051)

**semicircular canal** the fluid-filled canal in the inner ear that helps maintain balance and coordinate movements (1018)

**semi-conservative replication** in each new DNA double helix, one strand is from the original molecule, and one strand is new (200)

**semimovable joint** a joint at which limited movement occurs; examples include the joints between the bones of the vertebral column (915)

**seminal receptacle** a saclike organ of female or hermaphroditic invertebrates that stores sperm (715)

**seminal vesicle** one of two glandular structures in male vertebrates that hold and secrete seminal fluid (1051)

**seminiferous tubule** one of the many tubules in the testis where sperm are produced (1049)

**sense organ** an organ that receives stimuli and gives rise to the senses such as sight, smell, hearing, and pain (1016)

**sensitive period** in an animal's development, the specific phase during which imprinting occurs (891)

**sensory receptor** a specialized structure that contains the ends of sensory neurons and that responds to specific types of stimuli (1013)

**sepal** in a flower, one of the outermost rings of modified leaves that protect the flower bud (613)

**septum** a dividing wall, or partition, such as the wall between adjacent cells in a fungal hypha, the internal wall between adjacent segments of an annelid, and the thick wall between the right and left chambers of the heart (plural, *septa*) (527, 825, 933)

**sessile** describes an organism that remains attached to a surface for its entire life and does not move (673)

**seta** one of the external bristles or spines that project from the body of an animal (plural, *setae*) (713)

**sex chromosome** one of the pair of chromosomes that determine the sex of an individual (152, 236)

**sex-influenced trait** an autosomal trait that is influenced by the presence of male or female sex hormones (245)

**sex-linked trait** a trait that is determined by a gene found on one of the sex chromosomes, such as the X chromosome or the Y chromosome in humans (237)

**sexual reproduction** reproduction in which gametes from two parents unite (164)

**sexual selection** an evolutionary mechanism by which traits that increase the ability of individuals to attract or acquire mates appear with increasing frequency in a population; selection in which a mate is chosen on the basis of a particular trait or traits (323, 894)

**shared character** a feature that is shared by all members of a particular group of organisms (342)

**shell** the cell wall of a diatom (512)

**sieve plate** a region that connects two sieve cells and that has one or more sieve areas, which consist of clusters of pores through which the cytoplasm of the cells is connected and through which materials are transported (585)

**sieve tube** in the phloem of a flowering plant, a conducting tube that is made up of a series of sieve-tube members stacked end to end (585)

**sieve-tube member** one of the component cells of a sieve tube, which is found mainly in flowering plants (585)

**simple leaf** a leaf that has an undivided blade (600)

**single nucleotide polymorphism** a unique area of DNA where individuals differ by a single nucleotide; important in mapping the genome (abbreviation, SNP) (262)

**sink** any place where a plant stores or uses organic nutrients, such as sugar or starches (596)

**sinoatrial node** a mass of cardiac muscle cells that lies at the junction of the superior vena cava with the right atrium and that initiates and regulates contraction of the heart (abbreviation, *SA node*) (935)

**skeletal muscle** a voluntary muscle that is attached to the bones and that moves parts of the body (907)

**skeleton** the bones of a human or animal body that form the framework of the body, support the muscles and organs, and protect the inner organs (911)

**smog** urban air pollution composed of a mixture of smoke and fog produced from industrial pollutants and burning fuels (440)

**smooth muscle** the elongated muscle that is not under voluntary control and that is found in the digestive tract, blood vessels, glands, and hair follicles, but not in the heart (907)

**social behavior** the interaction between animals of the same species that are not related or are only distant relatives (897)

**social insect** an insect that lives in a large community, such as an ant or a bee (752)

**sodium-potassium pump** a carrier protein that uses ATP to actively transport sodium ions out of a cell and potassium ions into the cell (103)

**solar tracking** the movement of leaves or flowers in response to the sun's movement across the sky (637)

**solute** in a solution, the substance that dissolves in the solvent (42)

**solution** a homogeneous mixture throughout which two or more substances are uniformly dispersed (42)

**solvent** in a solution, the substance in which the solute dissolves (42)

**somatic nervous system** the portion of the neural structure that provides nerve connections to the skin, skeleton, and muscles of the body, but not to the viscera, blood vessels, and glands (1014)

**somatic-cell mutation** a mutation that occurs in a body cell (239)

**sorus** a cluster of spores or sporangia (611)

**source** a part of a plant that makes sugars and other organic compounds and from which these compounds are transported to other parts of the plant (596)

**spawning** a method of reproduction in fish, amphibians, mollusks, and crustaceans in which eggs or sperm are deposited into water (792)

**specialization** the evolutionary adaptation of a cell, organ, organism, or population for a particular function or environment (651)

**speciation** the formation of new species as a result of evolution (326)

**species** a group of organisms that are closely related and can mate to produce fertile offspring; also the level of classification below genus and above subspecies (339)

**species diversity** an index that combines the number and relative abundance of different species in a community (438)

**species evenness** a measure of the relative adundance of each species in an ecological community (405)

**species richness** the number of different species in an area or community (405)

**species-area effect** a pattern in which the number of species in an area increases as the area increases (406)

**spermatid** an immature sperm cell that has almost completed its development (164)

**spermatogenesis** the process by which male gametes form (164)

**spicule** a needle of silica or calcium carbonate in the skeleton of some sponges (673)

**spinal cavity** the hollow part of the body that contains the spinal cord (910)

**spindle fiber** one of the microtubules that extend across a dividing eukaryotic cell; assists in the movement of chromosomes (156)

**spinneret** an organ that spiders and certain insect larvae use to produce silky threads for webs and cocoons (732)

**spiracle** an external opening in an insect or arthropod, used in respiration (732)

**spirillum** a spiral-shaped bacterium (463)

**spleen** the largest lymphatic organ in the body; serves as a blood reservoir, disintegrates old red blood cells, and produces lymphocytes and plasmids (962)

**sponge** an aquatic invertebrate of the phylum Porifera that attaches to stones or plants and that has a porous structure and a tough, elastic skeleton (673)

**spongin** a fibrous protein that contains sulfur and composes the fibers of the skeleton of some sponges (673)

**spongy bone** less-dense bone tissue that has many open spaces (913)

**spongy mesophyll** inside a leaf, the tissue that is made up of loosely arranged parenchyma cells that contain chloroplasts and are surrounded by air spaces that promote the diffusion of oxygen, carbon dioxide, and water throughout the leaf (600)

**spontaneous generation** an early and now disproved theory that living organisms come to life spontaneously from nonliving material (279)

**sporangiophore** a plant or fungal structure that bears a sporangium or spores (528)

**sporangium** a specialized sac, case, capsule, or other structure that produces spores (528)

**spore** a reproductive cell or multicellular structure that is resistant to environmental conditions and that can develop into an adult without fusion with another cell (563)

**sporophyte** in plants and algae that have alternation of generations, the diploid individual or generation that produces haploid spores (565)

**sporozoite** a sporozoan that has been released from the oocyst and is ready to penetrate a new host cell (519)

**stability** the tendency of a community to maintain a relatively constant structure (407)

**stabilizing selection** a type of natural selection in which the average form of a trait is favored and becomes more common (324)

**stage** a platform of a compound light microscope that supports the slide holding the specimen (21)

**stamen** the male reproductive structure of a flower that produces pollen and consists of an anther at the tip of a filament (613)

**staphylococcus** a coccus that grows with others in grapelike clusters; examples include cocci of the species *Staphlococcus aureus* (463)

**sternum** in birds, the large, keel-shaped pectoral bone to which flight muscles attach; commonly called the breastbone (845)

**steroid** a type of lipid that consists of four carbon rings to which various functional groups are attached and that usually has a physiological action (60)

**steroid hormone** a type of hormone that is derived from the steroid cholesterol; various steroid hormones are secreted by the adrenal cortex, testis, ovary, and placenta (1031)

**stigma** the expanded apex of a pistil, supported by the style; the part of the pistil that receives the pollen (613)

**stimulant** a drug that increases the activity of the body or the activity of some part of the body (1022)

**stolon** in plants, a creeping stem that can develop roots and shoots at its nodes or at its tip to form new individuals; the creeping hypha of some fungi that gives rise to new individuals (530)

**stoma** one of many openings in a leaf or a stem of a plant that enable gas exchange to occur (plural, *stomata*) (121)

**strata** layers of rock (singular, *stratum*) (298)

**streptococcus** a coccus that grows with others in chains; examples include cocci of the disease-causing species *Streptococcus mutans* (463)

**strobilus** a conelike structure of sporangia-bearing leaves (571)

**stroma** in plants, the solution that surrounds the thylakoids in a chloroplast (114)

**structural gene** a gene that codes for a product, such as an enzyme, protein, or RNA, rather than serving as a regulator (218)

**style** in plants, the slender, upper part of the pistil (613)

**subspecies** a taxonomic classification below species that groups organisms that live in different geographical areas, differ morphologically from other populations of the species, but can interbreed with other populations of the species (339)

**substitution** a mutation in which a nucleotide or a codon in DNA is replaced with a different nucleotide (240)

**substrate** a part, substance, or element that lies beneath and supports another part, substance, or element; the reactant in reactions catalyzed by enzymes (57)

**superposition** a principle that states that younger rocks lie above older rocks if the layers have not been disturbed (302)

**surface area–to-volume ratio** the relationship of a cell's outer surface area to its volume (73)

**survivorship curve** a graph of the mortality data of a population; indicates the probability that individuals will survive to any given age (384)

**sustainability** the condition in which human needs are met in such a way that a human population can survive indefinitely (444)

**sweat gland** an exocrine gland that secretes sweat; these glands are distributed over the skin surface of most of the body (925)

**swim bladder** in bony fishes, a gas-filled sac that is used to control buoyancy (787)

**swimmeret** in some crustaceans, an abdominal appendage modified to allow movement, respiration, or the carrying of eggs (728)

**symbiosis** a relationship in which two different organisms live in close association with each other (403)

**symmetry** a body arrangement in which parts that lie on opposite sides of a central line are identical (654)

**synapse** the junction at which the end of the axon of a neuron meets the end of a dendrite or the cell body of another neuron or meets another cell (1005)

**synapsid** a lineage of amniotes that gave rise to mammals; characterized by skulls that have a single opening in a bone behind the eye socket (862)

**synapsis** the pairing of homologous chromosomes during meiosis (161)

**synovial fluid** the transparent fluid that lubricates joints (915)

**syrinx** the sound-producing organ of birds (853)

**systematics** the classification of living organisms in terms of their natural relationships; it includes describing, naming, and classifying the organisms (341)

**systemic circulation** the movement of blood from the heart to all parts of the body and back to the heart (805, 937)

—————————— **T** ——————————

**T cell** a cell that derives from the thymus and that participates in many immune reactions mediated by cells (962)

**tadpole** the aquatic, fishlike larva of a frog or toad (802)

**tagma** in arthropods, a structure that is composed of several fused body segments and that is typically specialized for a specific function (plural, *tagmata*) (724)

**taiga** a region of evergreen, coniferous forest below the arctic and subarctic tundra regions (420)

**taproot** a root that develops from the radicle of a plant embryo, grows vertically downward, and forms branches called lateral roots (587)

**target cell** a specific cell to which a hormone is directed to produce a specific effect (1032)

**taste bud** one of many oval concentrations of sensory nerve endings on the tongue, palate, and pharynx (1019)

**taxon** any particular group within a taxonomic system (338)

**taxonomy** the science of describing, naming, and classifying organisms (338)

**tegument** the external skin of an organism; on the external surface of a parasitic invertebrate, a layer that counters the defenses of the host's body (692)

**telomere** a repeated DNA sequence that is found at the end of chromosomes and that shortens with each cell division (268, 303)

**telophase** the final stage of mitosis or meiosis, during which a nuclear membrane forms around each set of new chromosomes (157)

**telson** the unpaired, terminal abdominal segment of crustaceans (729)

**temperate deciduous forest** a region of forest that has pronounced seasons, moderate temperatures, and moderate precipitation; characterized by trees that shed their leaves in the fall (420)

**temperate grassland** a region that has cold winters and rainfall that is intermediate between that of a forest and a desert; characterized by extensive grasses and few trees (421)

**temperate virus** a virus whose replication includes the lysogenic cycle (487)

**tendon** a tough connective tissue that attaches a muscle to a bone or to another body part (921)

**tendril** an organ of climbing plants that grows in spiral form and wraps around another body to help support the plant (599)

**tension-cohesion theory** the theory that water moves up the stem of a plant because of the strong attraction between water molecules (462)

**tentacle** a flexible appendage with which an animal feeds itself, grasps objects, or feels its environment (676)

**termination signal** a specific sequence of nucleotides that marks the end of a gene (206)

**territory** an area that is occupied by one animal or a group of animals that do not allow other members of the species to enter (894)

**test** in some protists and invertebrates, a protective covering that the organism secretes or builds around itself (507, 763)

**test cross** the crossing of an individual of unknown genotype with a homozygous recessive individual to determine the unknown genotype (183)

**testes** the primary male reproductive organs, which produce sperm cells and testosterone (singular, *testis*) (1049)

**testosterone** a hormone that regulates male secondary sex characteristics and the production of sperm cells (1037)

**tetrad** the four chromatids in a pair of homologous chromosomes that come together as a result of synapsis during meiosis (161)

**thalamus** the part of the brain that directs incoming sensory and motor signals to the proper region (1012)

**thallus** the body type of an algae, fungus, or plant that is not differentiated into roots, stems, or leaves (510)

**theory** an explanation for some phenomenon that is based on observation, experimentation, and reasoning; that is supported by a large quantity of evidence; and that does not conflict with any existing experimental results or observations (17)

**therapsid** a lineage of synapsids that were abundant during the late Permian period and gave rise to mammals; characterized by limbs positioned directly beneath the body; some may have been endothermic (862)

**thermoacidophile** an organism that grows well in a warm, acidic environment (462)

**thermoregulation** the processes by which the body regulates its internal temperature (828)

**thigmonastic movement** a nastic movement that occurs in a plant in response to touch (638)

**thigmotropism** a response of an organism or part of an organism to touch, such as the coiling of a vine around an object (637)

**thoracic cavity** the part of the human body cavity that is between the neck and the abdomen and that contains the heart and the lungs (910)

**thorax** in higher vertebrates, the part of the body between the neck and the abdomen; in other animals, the body region behind the head; in anthropods, the mid-body region (728)

**thylakoid** a membrane system found within chloroplasts that contains the components for photosynthesis (89, 114)

**thymus** the gland that produces T lymphocytes (961)

**thyroid gland** an endocrine gland that is located at the base of the neck and that produces secretions important in regulating many aspects of metabolism and mineral balance (1036)

**tissue** a collection of specialized cells and cell products that perform a specific function (7, 76)

**tissue culture** the technique for growing living cells in an artificial medium (624)

**tolerance** the condition of drug addiction in which greater amounts of a drug are needed to achieve the desired effect (1021)

**tolerance curve** a graph of the performance of an organism versus the value of an environmental vairable (363)

**trachea** in insects, myriapods, and spiders, one of a network of air tubes; in vertebrates, the tube that connects the larynx to the lungs (732, 947)

**tracheid** a thick-walled, cylindrical cell with tapered ends that is found in xylem and that provides support and conducts water and nutrients (585)

**trait** a genetically determined variant of a characteristic (173)

**transcription** the process of forming a nucleic acid by using another molecule as a template; particularly the process of synthesizing RNA by using one strand of a DNA molecule as a template (204)

**transcription factor** a regulatory protein that binds to DNA and stimulates the transcription of certain genes (222)

**transduction** the transfer of a bacterial gene from one bacterium to another through a bacteriophage (471)

**transformation** the transfer of genetic material in the form of DNA fragments from one cell to another or from one organism to another (194, 471)

**translation** the portion of protein synthesis that takes place at ribosomes and that uses the codons in mRNA molecules to specify the sequence of amino acids in polypeptide chains (204)

**translocation** the movement of a segment of DNA from one chromosome to another, which results in a change in the position of the segment; also the movement of soluble nutrients from one part of a plant to another (239, 596)

**transmission electron microscope** a microscope that transmits a beam of electrons through a very thin slice of specimen and that can magnify up to 200,000 times (abbreviation, *TEM*) (22)

**transpiration** the process by which plants release water vapor into the air through stomata; also the release of water vapor into the air by other organisms (372, 597)

**trichinosis** a disease that is caused by a parasitic roundworm of the genus *Trichinella* that results from eating the larvae in undercooked meat and that is characterized by diarrhea, fever, abdominal and muscle pain, and affliction of the lungs, nervous system, and heart (697)

**trichomoniasis** a common sexually transmitted infection that is caused by the mastigophoran *Trichomonas vaginalis*; symptoms include discolored discharge, genital itching, and an urge to urinate (520)

**triglyceride** a lipid made of three fatty acid molecules and one glycerol molecule (175)

**trilobite** a member of the class Trilobita; an extinct type of arthropods that is characterized by many body segments each of which had one pair of appendages (724)

**trimester** one of the three equal periods of about 12 weeks into which the human gestation period is divided (1057)

**tRNA (transfer RNA)** an RNA molecule that transfers amino acids to the growing end of a polypeptide chain during translation (205)

**trochophore** a free-swimming, ciliated larva of many worms and some mollusks (705)

**trophic level** an organism's relative position in a sequence of energy transfers in a food chain or food pyramid, examples include producers and primary, secondary, and tertiary consumers (368)

**tropical forest** a region of forest or jungle that located near the equator and that is characterized by large amounts of rain and little variation in temperature (419)

**tropism** the movement of all or part of an organism in response to an external stimulus, such as light or heat; move-

ment is either toward or away from the stimulus (636)

**true-breeding** describes organisms or genotypes that are homozygous for a specific trait and thus always produce offspring that have the same phenotype for that trait (175)

**tube cell** the cell of a pollen grain that gives rise to the pollen tube (615)

**tube foot** one of many small, flexible, fluid-filled tubes that project from the body of an echinoderm and that are used in locomotion, feeding, gas exchange, and excretion (762)

**tumor** a growth that arises from normal tissue but that grows abnormally in rate and structure and lacks a function (225)

**tumor suppressor gene** a gene that suppresses tumor formation but that, when mutated, causes a loss in cell function, which results in tumor formation (225)

**tundra** a treeless plain that is located in the Arctic or Antarctic and that is characterized by very low winter temperatures; short, cool summers; and vegetation that consists of grasses, lichens, and perennial herbs (418)

**turgor pressure** the pressure that is exerted on the inside of cell walls and that is caused by the movement of water into the cell (100)

**two-dimensional gel electrophoresis** a laboratory method that separates proteins according to their isoelectric points and molecular weights (264)

**tympanic membrane** the eardrum (809, 1017)

**tympanum** a sound-sensing membrane on the abdomen of an insect (747)

**typhlosole** in some animals, an infolding of the intestinal wall that increases the surface area available for digestion (714)

--- U ---

**ulcer** a lesion of the surface of the skin or a mucous membrane; sometimes occurs in the digestive system (988)

**umbilical cord** the structure that connects an embryo and then the fetus to the placenta and through which blood vessels pass (1059)

**ungulate** a hoofed mammal (872)

**unicellular** describes an organism that consists of a single cell (7)

**urban ecology** the study of ecology in areas that are densely populated by humans (452)

**urea** the principal nitrogenous product of the metabolism of proteins that forms in the liver from amino acids and from compounds of ammonia and that is found in urine and other body fluids (993)

**ureter** one of the two narrow tubes that carry urine from the kidneys to the urinary bladder (997)

**urethra** the tube that carries urine from the urinary bladder to the outside of the body (997)

**urinary bladder** a hollow, muscular organ that stores urine (997)

**urine** the liquid excreted by the kidneys, stored in the bladder, and passed through the urethra to the outside of the body (994)

**uropod** a flattened posterior appendage in some crustaceans (729)

**uterus** in female mammals, the hollow, muscular organ in which a fertilized egg is embedded and in which the embryo and fetus develop (1052)

— **V** —

**vaccination** the administration of treated microorganisms or material from a pathogen into humans or animals to induce an immune response (966)

**vagina** the female reproductive organ that connects the outside of the body to the uterus and that receives sperm during reproduction (1053)

**valve** a fold of membranes that controls the flow of a fluid (934)

**variable** a factor that changes in an experiment in order to test a hypothesis (937)

**vas deferens** a duct through which sperm move from the epididymis to the ejaculatory duct at the base of the penis (plural, *vasa deferentia*) (848, 1050)

**vascular cambium** in a plant, the lateral meristem that produces secondary xylem and phloem (586)

**vascular plant** a plant that has has true roots, stems, and leaves and a vascular system composed of xylem and phloem which are specialized tissues that conduct materials from one part of the plant to another (564)

**vascular tissue** the specialized conducting tissue that is found in higher plants and that is made up mostly of xylem and phloem (564)

**vector** in biology, any agent, such as a plasmid or a virus, that can incorporate foreign DNA and transfer that DNA from one organism to another; an intermediate host that transfers a pathogen or a parasite to another organism (258, 489)

**vegetable** a plant part that is used as food but that is not classified botanically as a fruit (547)

**vegetative propagation** the growth of plants by some means of asexual reproduction (623)

**vegetative reproduction** a type of asexual reproduction in which new plants grow from nonreproductive plant parts (623)

**vein** in plants, a bundle of vascular tissue that transports fluids and nutrients; in animals, a vessel that carries blood to the heart (576, 600, 937)

**venation** the arrangement of veins in a leaf (600)

**vent** in some animals, the body opening to which the cloaca is connected and through which wastes exit (807)

**ventral** the lower or abdominal part of an organism (655)

**ventricle** one of the two large muscular chambers that pump blood out of the heart (933)

**vernalization** in plants, the exposure of seeds or seedlings to a period of cold (642)

**vertebra** one of the 33 bones in the spinal column (backbone) (660, 779)

**vertebrate** an animal that has a backbone; includes mammals, birds, reptiles, amphibians, and fish (651)

**vesicle** a small cavity or sac that contains materials in a eukaryotic cell; forms when part of the cell membrane surrounds the materials to be taken into the cell or transported within the cell (105)

**vessel** in plants, a tubelike structure in the xylem that is composed of connected cells that conduct water and mineral nutrients; in animals, a tube or duct that carries blood or another bodily fluid (585)

**vessel element** in plants, one of the cellular components of a xylem vessel (585)

**vestigial structure** a structure in an organism that is reduced in size and function and that may have been complete and functional in the organism's ancestors (306)

**villus** one of the many tiny projections from the cells in the lining of the small intestine; increases the surface area of the lining for absorption (plural, *villi*) (990)

**viper** a venomous snake that has two large, mobile fangs at the front of the mouth (833)

**viroid** an infectious agent that is made up of a short, circular, single strand of RNA that does not have a capsid; the smallest known particle that is able to replicate (494)

**virulent** describes a microorganism that causes disease and that is highly infectious; strictly, refers only to viruses that reproduce by the lytic cycle (193, 486)

**virus** a nonliving, infectious particle composed of a nucleic acid and a protein coat; it can invade and destroy a cell (483)

**visceral mass** the central section of a mollusk's body that contains the mollusk's organs (706)

**vitamin** an organic compound that participates in biochemical reactions and that builds various molecules in the body; some vitamins are called coenzymes and activate specific enzymes (982)

**viviparity** in amniotes, a reproductive method in which eggs that lack shells are produced and develop inside the body of the mother, who then gives birth to the offspring (829)

**viviparous** an organism whose offspring develop within the mother's body and are born alive (863)

**voluntary muscle** a muscle whose movement can be consciously controlled (917)

**vulva** the external part of the female reproductive organs (1053)

— **W** —

**water cycle** the continuous movement of water between the atmosphere, the land, and the oceans (371)

**water mold** a funguslike protist that is composed of branching filaments of cells (514)

**water vascular system** a system of canals filled with a watery fluid that circulates throughout the body of an echinoderm (762)

**wax** a type of structural lipid consisting of a long fatty-acid chain that is joined to a long alcohol chain (60)

**weed** undesirable plants that often crowd out crop plants or native plant species (556)

**white blood cell** a type of cell in the blood that destroys bacteria, viruses, and toxic proteins and helps the body develop immunities (941)

**withdrawal** uncomfortable physical and psychological symptoms produced when a physically dependent drug user stops using drugs (1021)

**wood** secondary xylem produced in gymnosperm and dicot stems (594)

**worker bee** a bee that does not reproduce but that works for the community by collecting food and maintaining the hive (752)

— **X** —

**xylem** the type of tissue in vascular plants that provides support and conducts water and nutrients from the roots (564)

— **Y** —

**yeast** a very small, unicellular fungus that ferments carbohydrates into alcohol and carbon dioxide; used to ferment beer and to leven bread and used as a source of vitamins and proteins (527)

**yolk sac** the membrane that is attached to a vertebrate embryo and that encloses the yolk and thus stores energy reserves for the developing embryo (823)

— **Z** —

**Z line** the line formed by the attachment of actin filaments between two sarcomeres of a muscle fiber in striated muscle cells (919)

**zoonosis** a disease that can pass from animals to humans; an example is Lyme disease, which can be passed from deer to humans through infected ticks (474)

**zygosporangium** in members of the phylum Zygomycota, a sexual structure that is formed by the fusion of two gametangia and that contains one or more zygotes that resulted from the fusion of gametes produced by the gametangia (531)

**zygote** the cell that results from the fusion of gametes; a fertilized egg (652)

# Index

# Index

## Academic Reviewers

*(continued from p. iv)*

**Chris C. Nice**
*Assistant Professor*
Department of Biology
Texas State University—San Marcos
San Marcos, Texas

**Eva Oberdörster, Ph.D.**
*Lecturer*
Biology Department
Southern Methodist University
Dallas, Texas

**Jane Packard**
*Associate Professor, Ethology*
Department of Wildlife and Fisheries Sciences
Texas A&M University
College Station, Texas

**Barron Rector, Ph.D.**
*Assistant Professor and Extension Range Specialist*
Texas Agricultural Extension Service
Texas A&M University
College Station, Texas

**Dork Sahagian**
*Research Professor of Earth Science*
Institute for the Study of Earth, Oceans, and Space
University of New Hampshire
Durham, New Hampshire

**Miles R. Silman, Ph.D.**
*Associate Professor of Biology*
Department of Biology
Wake Forest University
Winston-Salem, North Carolina

**Richard D. Storey, Ph.D.**
*Professor of Biological Sciences and Chancellor*
University of Montana—Western
Dillon, Montana

**Gerald Summers**
*Associate Professor*
Division of Biological Sciences
University of Missouri
Columbia, Missouri

**Mary K. Wicksten, Ph.D.**
*Professor of Biology*
Department of Biology
Texas A&M University
College Station, Texas

## Teacher Reviewers

**Robert S. Akeson**
*Teacher*
Boston Latin School
Boston, Massachusetts

**Shahira Badran**
*Biology-Chemistry Teacher 9–12*
Science Department
Somerville High School
Somerville, Massachusetts

**Robert Baronak**
*High School Biology Teacher*
Science
Donegal High School
Mount Joy, Pennsylvania

**Kelcey Burris**
*Chairperson*
Science Department
Palmetto Ridge High School
Naples, Florida

**Ellen F. Cohen**
*Science Department Chair*
Marjory Stoneman Douglas High School
Parkland, Florida

**Brenda Crouch, Ed.S.**
*Chairperson*
Science Department
Marianna High School
Marianna, Florida

**Alonda Droege**
*Science Teacher*
Science Department
Highline High
Burien, Washington

**Alan Eagy**
*Biology Teacher*
Columbia Gorge High School
The Dalles, Oregon

**Benjamin D. Ebersole**
*Biology/Chemistry Teacher*
Science Department
Donegal School District
Mount Joy, Pennsylvania

**Yolanda Michelle Harman**
*Science Chairperson*
Northern Garrett High School
Accident, Maryland

**Jason Hook**
*Science and Technology Teacher*
Magnet Science Department
Kealing Middle School
Austin, Texas

**Jo Ann Lane**
*Science Department Chair*
St. Ignatius High School
Cleveland, Ohio

**Thomas E. Manerchia**
*Adjunct Faculty*
Science
Neumann College
Aston, Pennsylvania

**Amy K. Ragan**
*Science Department Chair*
Cedar Park High School
Cedar Park, Texas

**Denice Sandefur**
*Life Science Teacher*
Nucla High School
Nucla, Colorado

**Robert F. Siggens**
*K–12 Science Supervisor*
Somerville Public Schools
Somerville, Massachusetts

**Dale Simon**
*Biology Teacher*
Science Department
Central High School
Camp Point, Illinois

**Joe Stanaland**
*AP Biology Teacher*
Lake Travis High School
Austin, Texas

**Peter Upperco**
*Teacher and Science Multimedia Specialist*
Biology
Miami Senior High School
Miami, Florida

# Acknowledgments

## Teacher Reviewers
(*continued*)

**Albert C. Wartski**
*Biology Teacher*
Science Department
Chapel Hill High School
Chapel Hill, North Carolina

**Emily Wise**
*Biology Department*
University of Nebraska
Omaha, Nebraska

**Tyson R. Yager**
*Science Teacher*
Wichita High School East
Wichita, Kansas

**Kathy A. Yorks**
*Teacher*
Science
Keystone Central School District
Central Mountain High School
Mill Hall, Pennsylvania

## Staff Credits

**Editorial**
Mark Grayson, *Executive Editor*
Laura Juárez de Ku, *Senior Editor*
Debbie Starr, *Managing Editor*

**Editorial Development Team**
Anne Bunce
Helene Engler-Chaouat
Amy Fry
Marcela Garza
Niamh Gray-Wilson
Frieda Gress
Betsy Roll

**Copyeditors**
Dawn Marie Spinozza, *Copyediting
  Manager*
Simon Key
Jane A. Kirschman
Kira J. Watkins

**Editorial Support Staff**
Kristina Bigelow
Suzanne Krejci
Shannon Oehler

**Online Products**
Robert V. Tucek, *Executive Editor*
Wesley M. Bain

**Production**
Eddie Dawson, *Senior Production
  Manager*
Beth Sample, *Project Manager*

**Book Design**
Kay Selke, *Director of Book Design*
Bruce Albrecht
Peter D. Reid
Holly Whittaker

**Media Design**
Richard Metzger, *Design Director*
Chris Smith

**Image Acquisitions**
Curtis Riker, *Director*
Jeannie Taylor, *Photo Research
  Manager*
Elaine Tate, *Art Buyer Supervisor*
Diana Goetting

**Cover**
Kay Selke, *Director of Book Design*

**Publishing Services**
Carol Martin, *Director*

**Graphic Services**
Bruce Bond, *Director*
Katrina Gnader
Cathy Murphy
Nanda Patel
JoAnn Stringer

**Technology Services**
Laura Likon, *Director*
Juan Baquera, *Technology Services
  Manager*
Jeff Robinson, *Ancillary Design
  Manager*
Sara Buller
Lana Kaupp
Margaret Sanchez
Patty Zepeda

**EMedia**
Kate Bennett, *Director*
Armin Gutzmer, *Director of
  Development*
Ed Blake, *Design Director*
Kimberly Cammerata, *Design
  Manager*
Lydia Doty, *Senior Project Manager*
Marsh Flournoy, *Technology Project
  Manager*
Tara F. Ross, *Senior Project Manager*
Melanie Baccus
Cathy Kuhles
Michael Rinella

**Manufacturing/Inventory**
Ivania Quant Lee, *Inventory
  Supervisor*
Wilonda Ieans
Jevara Jackson
Kristen Quiring

**Student and Teacher Edition
  Development and Production**
Anthology, Inc., Arlington Heights,
  Illinois

**Ancillary Development and
  Production**
Navta Associates, Inc., Chicago,
  Illinois

# Image Credits


**Abbreviation Code**
AA/ES = Animals Animals/Earth Scenes; BPA = Biophoto Associates; BPS = Biological Photo Service; CB = Corbis; CMS = Custom Medical Stock Photo; FH = Fran Heyl Associates; GH = Grant Heilman Photography; GT = Getty Images; HRW = Holt, Rinehart and Winston staff photograph; JS/FS = Jeff Smith/FOTOSMITH; MP = Minden Pictures; NASC = National Audubon Society Collection; OSF = Oxford Scientific Films; PA = Peter Arnold, Inc.; PH = Phototake NYC; PR = Photo Researchers; RLM = Robert & Linda Mitchell; SPL = Science Photo Library; SS = Science Source; VU = Visuals Unlimited

**Cover:** © Manfred Danegger/Okapai/PR; **ii** (t) © Jerry Gleason, University of Oregon, Department of Biology; **ii** (b) Photograph by Chris Bratt; **iii** © Lee D. Simon/PR; **iv** © Manoj Shah/AA/ES; **vi** (t) © A. Kerstitch/VU; **vii** © David M. Phillips/VU; **viii** (cl) © Oliver Meckes/PR; **viii** (tl) © Oliver Meckes/PR; **ix** (t) © Art Wolfe/GT; **ix** (b) © Terry Donnelly/GT; **x** (t) © R.Toms, OSF/AA/ES; **xi** © Michael Sewell/PA; **xii** (b) © Kevin Schafer; **xiii** (b) Telegraph Color Library/GT; **xiii** (t) © Edward S. Ross/PH; **xiv** (t) © Kevin Schafer/Martha Hill; **xiv** (b) © Roy Morsch/CB; **xvi** © Lester Lefkowitz/CB; **xviii** (bl) © JS/FS; **xix** © JS/FS; **Unit 1: 2** © E.R. Degginger; **2–3** (bkgd) Planet Art; **3** (b) © Tim Davis/GT; **3** (tr) © Frans Lanting/MP; **3** (tc) © Luiz C. Marigo/PA; **3** (tl) © GT; **Chapter 1: 4** Art Wolfe; **5** © Tim Fuller; **6** (l) © W. Perry Conway/CB; **7** (c) © Don W. Fawcett/VU; **8** (bl) © Dr. K.S. Kim/PA; **9** (tr) © A. Kerstitch/VU; **11** © Gunter Ziesler/PA; **12** (t) © Jim Brandenburg/MP; **12** (b) © Joe McDonald/CB; **13** © Heidi Jo/Alamy; **14** (l) © Ron Austing; Frank Lane Picture Agency/CB; **15** (r) © Jerry Gleason, University of Oregon; **17** Courtesy of Society of Mexican American Engineers and Scientists, Inc.; **19** Peter Van Steen/HRW; **20** © Jeff Greenberg/PhotoEdit; **20** (tcl) © Michael Freeman/CB; **20** (l) © Digital Art/CB; **20** (tcr) © Royalty-Free/CB; **21** CENCO; **22** (t) Robert Brons/BPS; **22** (c) Microworks/PH; **22** (b) VU/Karl Aufderheide; **24** (tl) HRW; **26** (bl) © E. White/VU; **26** (br) © Jerome Paulin/VU; **28** © JS/FS; **Chapter 2: 30** © Fred Bavendam/GT; **35** (br) Sergio Purtell/HRW; **36** (t) © Ed Reschke/PA; **38** (tr) © European PressPhoto Agency, PA/NASA; **38** (cr) Courtesy NASA/JPL/Cornell University; **41** (tr) © Barry L. Runk/GH; **42** (t) © Allen & Larimer/Brand X Pictures/PictureQuest; **43** (l) © 1994 NYC Parks Photo Archive/Fundamental Photographs; **43** (r) © 1994 Kristen Brochmann/Fundamental Photographs; **48** © HRW/Sam Dudgeon; **Chapter 3: 50** © Robert Lubeck/AA/ES; **53** Peter Dean/GH; **56** SuperStock; **58** (l) © Digital Art/CB; **58** (tcr) © Royalty-Free/CB; **58** (tcl) © Michael Freeman/CB; **58** Jonathan Nourok/PhotoEdit/PictureQuest; **Unit 2: 66** (l) © Dr. Gopal Murti/PH; **66–67** (bkgd) © BPA/PR; **67** (l) © Don Fawcett/E. Shelton/PR; **67** (tc) © Barry L. Runk/Rannels/GH; **67** (cr) © FH; **67** (c) © Don W. Fawcett/VU; **Chapter 4: 68** © Dr. Gopal Murti/PR; **69** (bl) © Bettmann/CB; **69** (bc) © Bettmann/CB; **69** (r) © RLM; **70** (tl) © Bettmann/CB; **70** (tc) © Andrew Syred/SPL; **70** (tr) © A. Rakosy/CMS; **72** (bl) David McCarthy/SPL; **72** (tl) Andrew Syred/SPL; **72** (bc) Dr. Yorgos Nikas/SPL; **72** (tr) Dr. Tony Brain/SPL; **72** (br) © Laude Nuridsany & Marie Perennou/SPL; **74** (bl) Prof. Aaron Pollack, Hadassah University, Hospital/SPL; **74** (br) © Don W. Fawcett/PR; **75** (br) © Dr. Dennis Kunkel/PH; **76** (tl) © Carolina Biological/VU; **80** (tr) © Don Fawcett/VU; **81** (r) © R. Bolender-D. Fawcett/VU; **82** (tr) © R. Bolender-D. Fawcett/VU; **85** (br) © Professor Jan de May/PH; **85** (tc) © David M. Phillips/VU; **85** (tl) © David M. Phillips/VU; **85** (tr) © David M. Phillips/VU; **86** © SPL; **86** (br) © The Nobel Foundation, 1974; **88** © Dr. Jeremy Burgess/SPL/SS/PR; **89** (r) © PR; **92** © Don W. Fawcett/VU; **94** © Sergio Purtell/FOCA; **95** © Runk/Schoenberger/GH; **Chapter 5: 96** © FH; **99** (tr) © M. Abbey/VU; **99** (br) © M. Abbey/VU; **100** (tl) © Runk/Schoenberger/GH; **100** (tr) © Runk/Schoenberger/GH; **100** (bl) © David M. Phillips/VU; **100** (bc) © David M. Phillips/VU; **100** (br) © David M. Phillips/VU; **106** (l) © Professor Birgit H. Satir; **110** Ward's Natural Science; **Chapter 6: 112** © Grant Heilman/GH; **119** (tr) Courtesy of Dr. Darius Kuciauskas; **119** (bl) Courtesy of Dr. Darius Kuciauskas; **121** (l) © Dr. Jeremy Burgess, SS/PR; **121** (r) © Dr. Jeremy Burgess, SS/PR; **128** © HRW/Sam Dudgeon; **129** © HRW/Sam Dudgeon; **Chapter 7: 130** © Frans Lanting/MP; **132** (t) © Rod Planck/PR; **134** © John Colwell/GH; **135** © SciMAT/PR; **141** (bl) © Dr. Gopal Murti/PR; **141** (tcl) © Michael Freeman/CB; **141** (l) © Digital Art/CB; **141** (tcr) © Royalty-Free/CB; **143** (tr) Sam Dudgeon/HRW; **148** © WARD'S Natural Science; **Chapter 8: 150** © CNRI/SPL/PR; **152** © Gunther F. Bahr/AFIP/GT; **153** © CNRI/PH; **157** (t) © David M. Phillips/VU; **157** (br) © David M. Phillips/VU; **158** (tl) © R. Calentine/VU; **160** © Associated Press, AP; **160** (tcl) © Michael Freeman/CB; **160** (l) © Digital Art/CB; **160** (tcr) © Royalty-Free/CB; **163** (b) © David M. Phillips/PR; **166** © David M. Phillips/VU; **168** © John D. Cunningham/VU; **Unit 3: 170** (b) © Schafer & Hill/GT; **170–171** (bkgd) From The Double Helix by James Watson; **171** (c) Morgan-Cain & Associates; **171** (tl) © Mark Joseph/GT; **171** (tc) © David Scharf; **171** (br) Steve Roberts; **171** (b) © James H. Robinson; **Chapter 9: 172** © James H. Robinson; **173** Culver Pictures; **179** (tr) © AP/Wide World Photos; **179** (br) © Gregory G. Dimijian/PR; **180** (br) © Christian Grzimek, OKAPIA/PR; **180** (bl) © Jane Grushow/GH; **Chapter 10: 192** © 1991 Richard Megna, Fundamental Photographs, NYC; **193** Mr. Joseph B. Haulenbeek/1943 Rockefeller University Press; **196** © SS/PR; **197** (t) © SPL/PR; **197** (c) © Rosalind Franklin, SS/PR; **200** © Educational Images/CMS; **202** © Triller-Berretti/Barts Medical Library/PH; **203** David Young-Wolff/PhotoEdit; **203** (tcl) © Michael Freeman/CB; **203** (l) © Digital Art/CB; **203** (tcr) © Royalty-Free/CB; **210** © O.L. Miller, B.R. Beatty, D.W. Fawcett/VU; **214** (l) © JS/FS; **214** (r) © JS/FS; **215** © JS/FS; **Chapter 11: 216** © David Scharf; **224** (l) © Oliver Meckes/PR; **224** (bl) © Volker Steger/PR; **224** (r) © Oliver Meckes/PR; **226** Bob Thomason/GT; **227** (t) © Volker Steger/PR; **227** (tc) © Sinclair Stammers/SPL; **227** (bc) © James King-Holmes/SPL; **227** (b) © Dr. Yorgos Nikas/SPL; **228** (b) © Martin M. Rotker, SS/PR; **228** (tl) VU; **Chapter 12: 234** © BPA, SS/PR; **235** © 1991 Kay Chernush for HHMI; **236** (tl) © J. Cavallini/CMS; **236** (tr) © J. Cavallini/CMS; **239** (br) © Tim Fuller; **239** (b) CMS; **242** © John Henley/CB; **244** (c) Barraquer Ophthalmological Center, Barcelona; **245** (b) © J. Cavallini/CMS; **247** Peter Van Steen/HRW; **248** © 1991 Kay Chernush for HHMI; **Chapter 13: 254** © Science VU/VU; **258** (b) Dr. Brant Weinstein; **258** (t) © Andrew Brookes/CB; **261** © TEK IMAGE/PR; **262** (bc) © National Portrait Gallery, Smithsonian Institution/Art Resource, NY.; **262** (b) © FH; **262** (t) © Carolina Biological Supply Company/PH; **262** (tc) © Stephen Kron/University of Chicago; **262** (b) © PhotoDisc/GT; **263** TGen; **264** © University of Newcastle Upon Tyne/PR; **265** © Alfred Pasieka/ PR; **265** (tcl) © Michael Freeman/CB; **265** (l) © Digital Art/CB; **265** (tcr) © Royalty-Free/CB; **266** (l) © Journal of Mechanisms of Development, March 2003; **267** Courtesy The University of Florida; **269** (tr) © Roslin Institute/PH; **272** Courtesy of Cellmark Diagnostics, Inc., Germantown, Maryland; **274** (cl) © Sergio Purtell/FOCA; **274** (cr) © Sergio Purtell/FOCA; **Unit 4: 276** (c) © Tui DeRoy/Bruce Coleman, Inc.; **276** (br) © Bettmann/CB; **276–277** (bkgd) Iconographic Encyclopedia of Science, Art and Literature (1851); **277** (b) © Cabisco/VU; **277** (tl) © Nanci Kahn/Institute of Human Origins; **277** (tc) Smithsonian Institution, Washington, DC; **Chapter 14: 278** © Douglas Peebles; **284** © Kenneth Garrett; **286** © Sidney Fox/VU; **289** (t) © Henry C. Aldrich, University of Florida; **289** (cr) © Microfield Scientific Ltd/SPL; **289** (br) © Georgette Douwma/SPL; **294** © WARD'S Natural Science; **Chapter 15: 296** © Tui DeRoy/Bruce Coleman, Inc.; **297** Portrait of Charles Darwin, 1840 by George Richmond (1809–96), Downe House, Downe, Kent, UK/The Bridgeman Art Library, New York/London; **298** (tl) © Peter Finger/CB; **299** (tr) © RO-MA Stock/Index Stock Imagery; **299** (tl) © Wolfgang Kaehler/CB; **299** (tc) © Sandro Vannini/CB; **302** (cr) © RLM; **302** (l) © E.R. Degginger/AA/ES; **302** (bc) © Dr. Ed Degginger/Color-Pic; **302** (br) © Layne Kennedy/CB; **304** (b) Courtesy of Betsy Webb, Pratt Museum, Homer, Alaska; **304** (br) Courtesy of Betsy Webb, Pratt Museum, Homer, Alaska; **304** (t) Courtesy of Research Casting International and Dr. J. G. M. Thewissen; **304** (tc) Courtesy of Research Casting International and Dr. J. G. M. Thewissen; **304** (bc) © 1998 Philip Gingerich/Courtesy of the Museum of Paleontology, The University of Michigan; **304** (cl) © 1998 Philip Gingerich/Courtesy of the Museum of Paleontology, The University of Michigan; **306** (tl) Courtesy of Dr. Michael Richardson; **306** (cl) Courtesy of Dr. Michael Richardson; **306** (bl) Courtesy of Dr. Michael Richardson; **307** (t) © Ron Kimball/Ron Kimball Stock; **307** (tr) © Carl & Ann Purcell/CB; **307** (cl) © SuperStock; **307** (cr) © Martin B. Withers; Frank Lane Picture Agency/CB; **307** (bl) © Martin Ruegner/Alamy Photos; **307** (br) © James D. Watt/Stephen Frink Collection/Alamy Photos; **308** (bl) Courtesy of Dr. Johnathan Losos; **308** (bc) Courtesy of Dr. Johnathan Losos; **308** (br) Courtesy of Dr. Johnathan Losos; **310** © Fritz Prenzel/AA/ES; **Chapter 16: 316** © Art Wolfe/GT; **318** HRW/Sam Dudgeon; **320** © Art Wolfe/GT; **320** © Art Wolfe/GT; **322** © Ralph Reinhold/AA/ES; **323** © Art Wolfe/GT; **327** (t) © Tom McHugh, Steinhart Aquarium/PR; **327** (b) © Tom McHugh, Steinhart Aquarium/PR; **328** (t) © Michael & Patricia Fogden/CB; **328** (b) © Royalty-Free/CB; **329** (t) © Zigmund Leszczynski/AA/ES; **329** (b) © Barry L. Runk/GH; **Chapter 17: 336** © Nigel J. Dennis/PR; **337** © PIERRE PERRIN/CB SYGMA; **338** (bl) © Nigel J. Dennis/PR; **338** (bc) © Niall Benvie/CB; **340** (t) © SPL/PR; **340** (tc) © Rare Book & Special Collections, University of Sydney Library; **340** (bc) SPL/PR; **340** (b) © Bill Wiegand/University of Illinois; **348** (l) © Gary D. Gaugler/PR; **348** (cl) © Wolfgang Baumeister/PR; **348** (tc) © Dr. Dennis Kunkel/PR; **348** (bc) © Rod Planck/PR; **348** (tr) © Adam Jones/PR; **348** (br) © Myron Jay Dorf/CB; **Unit 5: 356** © Fred Bavendam; **356–357** (bkgd) Planet Art; **357** (tr) © DRA/Still Pictures/PA; **357** (bc) © Art Wolfe/GT; **357** (cl) © Doug Wechsler/AA/ES; **357** (tl) © Tom Edwards/AA/ES; **Chapter 18: 358** © DRA/Still Pictures/PA; **362** © Ralph A. Clevenger/CB; **363** (tr) © Color-Pic/AA/ES; **363** (br) © E.R. Degginger/AA/ES; **364** (br) © International Canopy Network/Evergreen State College; **367** (b) © Darrell Gulin/CB; **370** (t) University Archives. Department of Rare Books and Special Collections. Princeton University Library; **370** (tr) © Bettmann/CB; **370** (cr) © Sergio Dorantes/CB; **Chapter 19: 380** © Flip Nicklin/MP; **381** © Robert Laird/GT; **382** © Mitsuaki Iwago/MP; **383** (tc) © Robert W. Hernandez/PR; **383** (tl) © Michael Fogden/AA/ES; **383** (tr) © Jack Wilburn/AA/ES; **388** (cl) © Tom J. Ulrich/VU; **389** (cl) © Manoj Shah/AA/ES; **396** (cl) © Stephen Kron/University of Chicago; **396** Dr. David P. Frankhauser URL:http://biology.clc.uc.edu/Frankhauser; **396** (cr) © Stephen Kron/University of Chicago; **Chapter 20: 398** © Franklin J. Viola; **399** © Charles and Elizabeth Schwartz Trust/AA/ES; **400** (l) © Doug Wechsler/AA/ES; **400** (r) © John Netherton/AA/ES; **401** (l) © Suzanne L. Collins & Joseph T. Collins, NASC/PR; **401** (r) © E.R. Degginger; **403** © C. James Webb/PH; **404** © Patty Murray/AA/ES; **407** (b) © Scott Smith/Dembinsky Photo Associates; **407** (t) © Terry Donnelly/GT; **408** (l) © Larry Nielsen/PA; **408** (r) © Patty Murray/AA/ES; **409** (l) © Ken M. Johns, NASC/PR; **409** (c) © Glenn M. Oliver/VU; **409** (r) © E.R. Degginger; **410** © Kirtley Perkins/VU; **415** (t) © Runk/Schoenberger/GH; **415** (b) © RLM; **Chapter 21: 416** © Art Wolfe/GT; **418** © Galen Rowell/CB; **419** (t) © Ray Pfortner/PA; **420** (br) © E.R. Degginger; **420** (tl) © Art Wolfe/GT; **421** (tr) © Jim Brandenburg/MP; **421** (cr) © Art Wolfe/GT; **421** (b) © Coco McCoy/Rainbow; **422** © Philip and Karen Smith/GT; **424** (tl) © Norbert Wu/PA; **424** (b) © Fred Bavendam; **425** (tr) © Kim R. Reisenbichler for MBARI; **425** (br) © C.C. Lockwood/AA/ES; **426** (b) © Stephen Frink/CB; **426** (inset) Florida Keys National Marine Sanctuary; **426** (tcl) © Michael Freeman/CB; **426** (l) © Digital Art/CB; **426** (tcr) © Royalty-Free/CB; **427** (l) © R.Toms, OSF/AA/ES; **427** (r) © Adam Jones/PR; **428** © Brian Miller/AA/ES; **430** © Kim R. Reisenbichler for MBARI; **Chapter 22: 434** © H. Ray-Operation Migration Inc.; **437** © Roger Ressmeyer/CB; **440** © NOAA; **443** © Jeff Foott/Bruce Coleman, Inc.; **445** (t) © Darrell Gulin/CB; **445** (tc) © Bettmann/CB; **445** (bc) © Linda A. Cicero/Stanford News Service; **445** (b) © Todd A. Gipstein/CB; **446** Courtesy of Cliff Lerner/HRW; **447** (br) © David Thompson; **447** (bl) Photo by Mark Trabue; **448** (tl) © Tom McHugh/PR; **448** (tc) © Sally A. Morgan/CB; **448** (tr) © Tom McHugh/PR; **448** (bl) © Merlin D. Tuttle/Bat Conservation International; **448** (br) © S. Cordier/Jacana/PR; **450** (b) © Underwood & Underwood/CB; **450** (t) Peter Van Steen/HRW; **451** (br) © Stuart Westmorland/CB; **451** (bl) © GT; **457** © JS/FS; **Unit 6: 458** (c) © Manfred Danegger/OKAPIA/PR; **458–459** (bkgd) © BPA/PR; **459** (c) © M. Abbey/VU; **459** (tr) © 1997 Kent Wood; **459** (tl) © FH; **459** (br) © Hank Morgan/PR; **Chapter 23: 460** © David McCarthy/PR; **462** Woods Hole Oceanographic Institute; **463** (tl) © FH; **463** (tc) © G. Shih-R. Kessel/VU; **463** (bl) Science VU/VU; **463** (br) © George J. Wilder/VU; **463** (tr) © John D. Cunningham/VU; **464** (t) Courtesy of James E. Rogers, PhD.; **464** (br) © E. Weber/VU; **464** (bl) © E. Weber/VU; **465** (tr) © Scott Camazine/PR; **465** (br) © CMS; **466** © Rakosky/CMS; **469** (tr) © A.B. Dowsett/PR; **470** (tl) Courtesy of Thomas D. Brock, University of Wisconsin, Madison; **470** (bl) Courtesy Thomas D. Brock, University of Wisconsin, Madison; **475** (tl) © Bettmann/CB; **475** (cl) © Bettmann/CB; **475** (bl) © CMS; **475** (bc) © GT; **476** (tl) © Alan & Linda Detrick/PR; **476** (bl) © Natalie Fobes/CB; **478** (br) © A.M. Siegelman/VU; **480** (bl) © JS/FS; **Chapter 24: 482** © Hans Gelderblom/GT; **483** © Norm Thomas/PR; **484** (tl) © Dr. O. Bradfute/PA; **484** (tc) © E.O.S./Gelderglom/PR; **484** (tr) © NIBSC/SPL/PR; **486** Agricultural Research Service/USDA; **489** © SIU/VU; **491** © Brad Rickerby/Bruce Coleman, Inc.; **492** © Barts Medical Library/PH; **493** (b) © Rachel T. Noble, Ph.D.; **493** (tr) © Michael Freeman/CB; **493** (r) © Digital Art/CB;

**493** (tc) © Royalty-Free/CB; **494** © Germain Rey/Liaison Agency; **498** © JS/FS; **499** © Norm Thomas/PR; **Chapter 25: 500** © Eric Grave/PH; **501** © BPA/PR; **503** (tl) © M. Abbey/VU; **503** (cr) © Gregory Ochocki/PR; **503** (cl) © RLM; **503** (tr) Matt Meadows/PA; **504** (tr) Microfield Scientific Ltd/SPL/PR; **505** (b) © Sinclair Stammers/PR; **505** (t) Ben Barnhart; **506** (br) © Dennis Kunkel/PH; **506** (bl) © Michael Abbey/PR; **507** (bl) © Robert Brons/GT; **508** © Eye of Science/PR; **509** (b) Tetsu Yamazaki/International Stock Photography; **509** (t) Centers for Disease Control; **510** Dr. E.R. Degginger; **511** © Doug Wechsler/AA/ES; **512** (b) © Anne Wertheim/AA/ES; **512** (t) © Gregory Ochocki/PR; **513** (t) © Roland Birke/PA; **514** (t) David M. Dennis/Tom Stack & Associates; **514** (b) Matt Meadows/PA; **515** Fred Rhoades/Mycena Consulting; **517** (b) Carolina Biological Supply Company/PH; **517** (tr) J.A.L. Cooke/OSF/AA/ES; **518** © Royalty-Free/CB; **520** © Professors P.M. Motta & F.M. Magliocca/SPL/PR; **522** (l) © RLM; **522** (l) Courtesy of Richard Trimer, Rutgers University; **522** (r) © RLM; **522** (r) © M. Abbey/VU; **524** © RLM; **525** © Herb Charles Ohlmeyer/FH; **Chapter 26: 526** Manfred Danneger/OKAPIA/PR; **528** (t) © University of Texas Medical Mycology Research Center; **528** (b) © J. Forsdyke, SPL/PR; **532** (b) © Rod Planck/PR; **533** (b) © Grant Heilman/GH; **534** © SPL/PR; **535** © E.R. Degginger; **536** (t) © François Ducasse/PR; **536** (b) © Dr. Paul A. Zahl/PR; **540** © JS/FS; **541** © JS/FS; **Unit 7: 542** © Pal Hermansen/GT; **542–543** (bkgd) Planet Art; **543** (c) © Kurt Coste/GT; **543** (tl) © Frans Lanting/MP; **543** (cr) © RLM; **543** (tr) William E. Ferguson; **Chapter 27: 544** © Yann Layma/GT; **545** © GT; **547** (t) © Peter Holden/VU; **547** (b) © Michel Viard/PA; **549** (tr) © Jim Strawser/GH; **549** (tl) © E.R. Degginger; **549** (b) © RLM; **551** (tl) © Patrick Bennett/CB; **551** (b) Mark Philbrick/Brigham Young University; **552** © H. Richard Johnston/GT; **553** (t) © akg-images; **553** (tc) © Paroli Galperti/CuboImages srl; **553** (bc) © Royalty-Free/CB; **553** (b) © E.R. Degginger; **554** © Frans Lanting/MP; **555** (t) © Bob Gibbons, NASC/PR; **555** (b) © RLM; **556** © Martha Cooper/PA; **560** (t) © WARD'S Natural Science; **560** (b) © WARD'S Natural Science; **Chapter 28: 562** © Michael Sewell/PA; **567** © Ed Reschke/PA; **568** (bl) © L. West/PR; **568** (br) © RLM; **568** (t) © Stephanie Maze/CB; **569** © Henry Robison/VU; **570** © RLM; **571** © Runk/Schoenberger/GH; **572** (t) © Tom Dietrich/GT; **572** (b) © Tom Till/GT; **573** (t) © Lefever/Grushow/GH; **573** (b) © E. Webber/VU; **574** (b) © David Cavagnaro/VU; **575** (t) © RLM; **575** (b) © Frans Lanting/MP; **578** © Willard Clay/GT; **580** (t) © Pat Anderson/VU; **580** (b) © David Sieren/VU; **581** (l) © Runk/Schoenberger/GH; **581** (r) © E.R. Degginger; **Chapter 29: 582** © Sally A. Morgan; Ecoscene/CB; **582** © Jack Dykinga; **587** (bl) © Dwight R. Kuhn; **587** (br) © R. Calentine/VU; **588** (cl) © RLM; **588** (tl) © Jane Grushow/GH; **588** (tr) © Brian Rogers/VU; **588** (bl) © Runk/Rannels/GH; **589** (br) © Runk/Schoenberger/GH; **589** (t) © RLM; **589** (bl) © Stan Elems/VU; **590** © Dwight R. Kuhn; **592** (c) © William E. Ferguson; **592** (bl) © William E. Ferguson; **592** (br) © Gregory Ochocki/PR; **594** (tl) © Carolina Biological Supply/PH; **594** (cl) © Ken Wagner/PH; **595** (br) © Albert Copley/VU; **595** (l) © Runk/Schoenberger/GH; **598** (tr) © Dr. Michael A. Huffman/The Primate Research Institute at Kyoto University; **598** (br) © Dr. Michael A. Huffman/The Primate Research Institute at Kyoto University; **599** (bl) © Donald Specker/AA/ES; **599** (bc) © E.R. Degginger; **599** (br) © John Pontier/AA/ES; **600** (tl) © John Kaprielian/PR; **600** (cl) © E.R. Degginger; **600** (bl) © JS/FS; **601** (br) © Michael Fogden/DRK Photo; **602** (tl) © P. Dayanandan/PR; **602** (tr) © P. Dayanandan/PR; **604** © Gerlach Nature Photography/AA/ES; **606** © Ed Reschke/PA; **607** (bl) © RLM; **607** (cl) PH; **607** (tl) © Carolina Biological Supply/PH; **Chapter 30: 608** © Dr. Jeremy Burgess, SPL/PR; **612** © RLM; **616** © Michael Fogden/DRK Photo; **618** © Dick Canby/DRK Photo; **621** © Runk/Schoenberger/GH; **623** © Runk/Schoenberger/GH; **624** © Rosenfeld Images Ltd., SPL/PR; **626** © Runk/Schoenberger/GH; **628** © JS/FS; **Chapter 31: 630** © Sally A. Morgan; Ecoscene/CB; **633** © Stefan Eberhard/FH; **634** (tr) © E.R. Degginger; **634** (bl) Courtesy of Valent BioSciences Corporation; **636** © Cathlyn Melloan/GT; **637** David Newman/VU; **638** (tl) © Runk/Schoenberger/GH; **638** (bl) © Christi Carter/GH; **638** (br) © Christi Carter/GH; **639** (tl) © Tom McHugh/PR; **639** (tr) © Tom McHugh/PR; **642** © Pal Hermansen/GT; **644** © David Newman/VU; **Unit 8: 648** Kevin Schafer; **648–649** (bkgd) © BPA/PR; **649** (c) © Mark Moffett/MP; **649** (tl) © E.R. Degginger; **649** (tc) © CNRI/SPL/PR; **649** (tr) © Jack Dykinga; **Chapter 32: 650** © Kevin Schafer; **652** © Merlin D. Tuttle, Bat Conservation International/PR; **654** © Fred Bruemmer/DRK Photo; **654** (b) Peter Van Steen/HRW; **657** © S.J. Krasemann/PA; **658** © Phil Degginger/GT; **660** (t) © Stephen J. Krasemann/DRK Photo; **660** (b) © Stephen J. Krasemann/PR; **662** (t) © Hulton-Deutsch Collection/CB; **662** (tc) Courtesy of Dr. Michael Richardson; **662** (bc) © Dr. Yorgos Nikas/PR; **662** (b) © MC LEOD MURDO/CB SYGMA; **663** © David Philips/The Population Council/PR; **Chapter 33: 672** © Azure Computer & Photo Services/AA/ES; **678** (l) © Robert Brons/BPS/GT; **678** (r) © Runk/Schoenberger/GH; **679** (tr) © Runk/Schoenberger/GH; **681** (tr) © Neil McDaniel/PR; **681** (tc) © Fred Bavendam; **681** (bl) © Stuart Westmorland/GT; **682** © Andrew J. Martinez/PR; **686** (bl) © Carolina Biological Supply/PH; **Chapter 34: 688** © RLM; **689** © Milton Love/PA; **692** © CNRI/SPL/PR; **696** (tl) © C. James Webb/PH; **696** (br) © Peter Arnold/PA; **697** © Andrew Syred/SPL/PR; **700** © A.M. Siegelman/VU; **702** © T.E. Adams/VU; **Chapter 35: 704** © Franklin J. Viola; **706** (bl) © Andrew Syred, SS/PR; **708** (tl) © Hal Beral/VU; **708** (bl) © David & Hayes Norris/PR; **710** © Andrew Martinez/PR; **711** © Rudie Kuiter/OSF/AA/ES; **712** © St. Bartholomew's Hospital/SPL/PR; **712** (tcl) © Michael Freeman/CB; **712** (l) © Digital Art/CB; **712** (tcr) © Royalty-Free/CB; **713** © Marty Snyderman/VU; **716** © RLM; **Chapter 36: 722** © Color-Pic/AA/ES; **724** © RLM; **727** (tl) © OSF/AA/ES; **727** (tc) Photo by I. Dutchner, Courtesy Dept. of Library Services, American Museum of Natural History; **727** (tr) © RLM; **732** (tl) © RLM; **732** (bl) © Sturgis McKeever/PR; **733** (t) © RLM; **733** (b) © RLM; **734** (tl) © Thomas Gula/VU; **734** (tc) © Edward S. Ross/PH; **739** © JS/FS; **Chapter 37: 740** © Raymond Mendez/AA/ES; **741** (br) © WHM Bildarchiv/PA; **741** (bl) © Bruce Davidson/naturepl.com; **742** Courtesy Dr. Gene J. Paull; **744** (tl) © RLM; **744** (tr) © RLM; **750** (tl) © James C. Cokendolpher/FH; **750** (cl) © Color-Pic/AA/ES; **751** © Tom McHugh/PR; **758** © Stephen Dalton/PR; **Chapter 38: 760** © Fred Bavendam; **762** (bl) F. Stuart Westmorland/PR; **762** (br) © Fred Bavendam; **763** (t) © Clay Wiseman/AA/ES; **763** (br) © Fred Bavendam; **764** (tc) © Steven David Miller/AA/ES; **764** (bl) © E.R. Degginger; **764** (br) © Daniel W. Gotshall/VU; **766** © Fred Winner/Jacana/PR; **767** © Fred McConnaughey/PR; **769** (bl) © G.I. Bernard/OSF/AA/ES; **770** (tl) © Fred Bavendam; **774** © Pat O'Hara/GT; **Unit 9: 776** © Art Wolfe; **776–777** (bkgd) Planet Art; **777** (c) © Frans Lanting/MP; **777** (tr) © Art Wolfe/GT; **777** (tc) © S.J. Krasemann/PA; **777** (tl) © Fred Bavendam; **Chapter 39: 778** © Stuart Westmorland/GT; **783** (br) © William E. Ferguson; **784** (bl) © Meckes/Ottawa/PR; **784** (tl) © Hans Reinhard/Okapia/NASC/PR; **785** (br) © Fred Bavendam; **787** (bl) Steinhart Aquarium/Tom McHugh/PR; **787** (br) © Tom McHugh/PR; **792** (bl) © Fred Bavendam; **797** © M. Gibbs/AA/ES; **Chapter 40: 798** © William J. Weber/VU; **801** (bl) © RLM; **801** (br) © RLM; **802** (bl) © Suzanne L. & Joseph T. Collins/PR; **802** (br) © Suzanne L. & Joseph T. Collins/PR; **803** (tl) © Zigmund Leszczynski/AA/ES; **803** (tr) © Juan Manuel Renjifo/AA/ES; **809** © Chris Mattison; Frank Lane Picture Agency/CB; **810** (bl) Telegraph Color Library/GT FPG International; **811** (bl) Stephen Dalton/NHPA; **812** © Michael Fogden/DRK Photo; **816** © Runk/Schoenberger/GH; **817** © Dwight R. Kuhn; **Chapter 41: 818** © Kevin Schafer/Martha Hill; **824** © Zigmund Leszczynski/AA/ES; **827** (br) © Zigmund Leszczynski/AA/ES; **828** (bl) © RLM; **829** © Roger de la Harpe/AA/ES; **830** (bl) © McDonald Wildlife Photography/AA/ES; **830** (br) © Victoria McCormick/AA/ES; **831** (bl) © Beth Davidow/VU; **831** (br) © E.R. Degginger; **832** (bl) © Michael Dick/AA/ES; **832** (br) © Zigmund Leszczynski/AA/ES; **833** (tl) © E.R. Degginger; **833** (tr) © Breck P. Kent/AA/ES; **834** (bl) © Tom J. Ulrich/VU; **834** (tl) © Michael Fogden/DRK Photo; **834** (tr) © Michael Fogden/DRK Photo; **834** (tc) © Michael Fogden/DRK Photo; **838** © JS/FS; **Chapter 42: 840** © Art Wolfe/GT; **843** (tl) © James L. Amos/PR; **849** © Color-Pic/AA/ES; **850** (b) © Fred Bruemmer/DRK Photos; **850** (tcl) © Michael Freeman/CB; **850** (l) © Digital Art/CB; **850** (tcr) © Royalty-Free/CB; **851** (cl) © Tom Edwards/AA/ES; **851** (cr) © Gary Meslaros/VU; **851** (bl) © Neal & Mary Mishler/GT; **851** (br) © Gerlach Nature Photography/AA/ES; **852** (bl) © Tony Tilford/OSF/AA/ES; **852** (tl) © Carl R. Sams II/PA; **853** (tr) © Frans Lanting/MP; **853** (br) © S. Maslowski/VU; **854** © Joe McDonald/VU; **858** © WARD'S Natural Science; **859** (cl) © WARD'S Natural Science; **859** (bl) © WARD'S Natural Science; **Chapter 43: 860** © Art Wolfe; **861** © Paul A. Souders/CB; **862** (bl) Bernd Wolter Design GmbH, Heide 3, 31547 Rehburg-Loccum; **865** (b) © Michael T. Sedam/CB; **866** © Art Wolfe/GT; **867** © Robert Maier/AA/ES; **869** (tl) © Tom McHugh/PR; **869** (tr) © Tom McHugh/PR; **870** (b) © S.J. Krasemann/PA; **870** (t) © George D. Lepp/CB; **871** (cr) © Art Wolfe/GT; **871** (br) © Sturgis McKeever/PR; **872** (cl) © S.J. Krasemann/PA; **872** (bl) © Ruth Cole/AA/ES; **873** (tl) © Fred Felleman/GT; **873** (cl) © Douglas Faulkner/PR; **875** © Tim Davis/PR; **876** (tl) © Adam Jones/PR; **877** © John Reader/SPL/PR; **878** (c) © 1994 David L. Brill/Artifact Credit: Original housed in Transvaal Museum, Pretoria; **878** (r) © 1995 David L. Brill/Artifact Credit National Museums of Kenya, Nairobi; **878** (l) © Patrick Robert/CB; **879** (b) © 1985 David L. Brill/FOSSIL CREDIT: National Museums of Kenya, Nairobi; **879** (t) © 1985 David L. Brill/FOSSIL CREDIT: Musee De líHomme, Paris; **884** (bl) © Phil Degginger/Color-Pic, Inc; **884** (br) © David Austen/GT; **Chapter 44: 886** © Roy Morsch/CB; **887** © E.S. Ross/VU; **888** (t) © Robin Brandt/Natural Selection; **888** (b) © Ed Reschke/PA; **889** © Omikron/SS/PR; **890** © Tim Davis/GT; **891** Thomas McAvoy/LIFE Magazine © TIME Inc.; **892** (t) © Credit Associated Press, AP Photographer ELAINE THOMPSON, Staff; **892** (b) © Jeffrey Greenberg/PR; **893** (tl) © Theo Allofs/CB; **894** © Michael & Patricia Fogden/CB; **895** © The Image Bank/GT; **896** (t) © Bios/PA; **896** (b) © Scott Camazine/PR; **897** (t) © Gallo Images/CB; **897** (br) Richard R. Hansen/PR; **898** © George D. Lepp/GT; **900** (bl) Thomas McAvoy/LIFE Magazine © TIME Inc.; **900** (br) Ed Reschke/PA; **901** (l) Bios/PA; **901** (tr) Thomas McAvoy/LIFE Magazine © TIME Inc.; **902** HRW/Sam Dudgeon; **Unit 10: 904** © David Young Wolff/GT; **904–905** (bkgd) Planet Art; **905** (c) Professors P.M. Motta & S. Correr/SPL/PR; **905** (tl) © Image Shop/PH; **905** (tc) © Nestle/Petit Format/PR; **905** (tr) © Terry Vine/GT; **Chapter 45: 906** © U.H.B. Trust/GT; **913** (tr) © Andrew Syred/GT; **918** (bl) © John D. Cunningham/VU; **918** (c) © David M. Phillips/VU; **918** (br) © Eric Grave, SS/PR; **918** (t) Courtesy of Sharon Killian; **922** © David Madison 2000; **923** (t) © CNRI/PH; **923** (b) © U.H.B. Trust/GT; **923** (tcl) © Michael Freeman/CB; **923** (l) © Digital Art/CB; **923** (tcr) © Royalty-Free/CB; **925** © David Madison 2000; **Chapter 46: 932** © Oliver Meckes/PR; **936** (b) © Ed Reschke/PA; **940** © Andrew Syred/GT; **941** © Biology Media/PR; **942** (tl) © A.B. Dowsett/SPL/PR; **942** (tr) © NIBSC/SPL/PR; **943** (t) © ISM/PH; **943** (b) © ISM/PH; **945** (t) © CB; **945** (bc) © PIX INC/GT; **945** (b) © The Image Bank/GT; **945** (tc) © Bettmann/CB; **Chapter 47: 956** Omikron/PR; **957** (br) © CNRI/SPL/PR; **957** (cl) © Hank Morgan/PR; **958** © Prof. P. Motta/Dept. of Anatomy/University "La Sapienza," Rome/SPL/PR; **960** © Dr. Dennis Kunkel/PH; **966** (tl) Michael Newman/PhotoEdit; **967** (t) Wood River Gallery/Picture Quest; **967** (bl) © Bettmann/CB; **967** (cl) © Bettmann/CB; **967** (b) © Oliver Meckes/Gelderblom/PR; **970** © Nibsc/PR; **972** © Associated Press, AP; **Chapter 48: 978** (c) © John Kennedy/BPS/GT; **982** Russell Diane/HRW; **983** © Sergio Purtell/FOCA CO., NY., NY; **984** © Michael Newman/PhotoEdit Inc.; **990** (bl) © Prof. P. Motta/Dept of Anatomy/University "La Sapienza," Rome/SPL/PR; **991** © Scott Camazine/PR; **992** (t) Photo by Sam Kittner, courtesy of Rita Colwell/National Science Foundation; **992** (b) Anwar Huq, UMBI; **1002** (bl) © JS/FS; **1002** (tr) © JS/FS; **Chapter 49: 1004** © Lester Lefkowitz/CB; **1006** (tl) © Dr. David Scott/PH; **1018** (tl) Courtesy of Professor Dr. G. Reiss, Dept. of Cell Biology/Electron Microscopy, Hannover Medical School, Germany; **1021** (b) © Gregory G. Dimijian/PR; **1023** (b) © George Steinmetz; **1024** (t) © Scott Camazine/PR; **1024** (t) © Jim Strawser/GH; **Chapter 50: 1030** © Educational Images/CMS; **1038** (b) © Bob Rowan; Progressive Image/CB; **1038** (tcl) © Michael Freeman/CB; **1038** (l) © Digital Art/CB; **1038** (tcr) © Royalty-Free/CB; **1039** © Carolina Biological Supply/PH; **Chapter 51: 1048** © Lennert Nilsson/Albert Bonniers Forlagen AB, from *A Child Is Born*, Dell Publishing Company; **1053** (b) © David M. Phillips/PR; **1056** © David M. Phillips/PR; **1059** (bl) © Lennert Nilsson/Albert Bonniers Forlag; **1059** (bc) © D. Bromhall/OSF/AA/ES; **1059** (br) © Petit Format/Nestle/PR; **1062** © Lennert Nilsson/Albert Bonniers Forlagen AB, from *A Child Is Born*, Dell Publishing Company; **1066** © JS/FS; **1067** (bl) Sergio Purtell/Foca; **1067** (br) Sergio Purtell/Foca; **1068** © JS/FS; **1069** (t) Sergio Purtell/Foca; **1069** (b) © Digital Vision/GT; **1070** Sergio Purtell/Foca; **1071** (bl) Sergio Purtell/Foca; **1071** (br) Sergio Purtell/Foca; **1073** Charles D. Winters; **1078** © MICROFIELD SCIENTIFIC LTD/SPL; **1080** (tr) Woods Hole, Oceanographic Institute; **1080** (r) © Michael Abbey/PR; **1081** (l) Anne Wertheim/AA/ES; **1081** (r) © Carolina Biological Supply/PH; **1081** (t) © RLM; **1082** (bl) © Dr. Paul A. Zahl/PR; **1082** (cr) © RLM; **1083** (tl) © Tom Till/GT; **1083** (tr) © E. Webber/VU; **1083** (br) © David Newman/VU; **1084** (cl) © Neil McDaniel/PR; **1084** (br) © Suzanne L. & Joseph T. Collins/PR

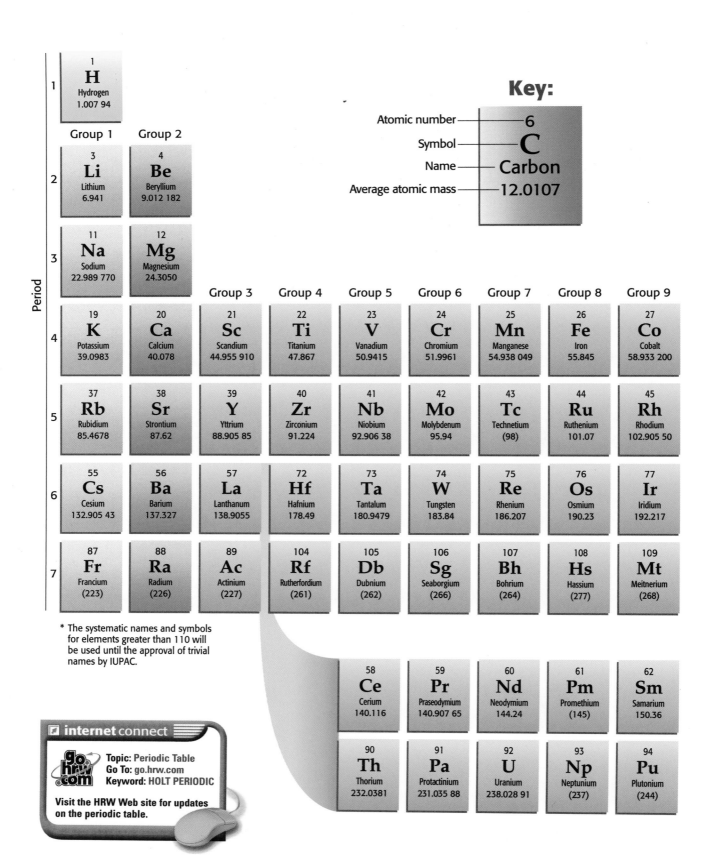

**Key:**

Atomic number — 6
Symbol — C
Name — Carbon
Average atomic mass — 12.0107

| Period | | | |
|---|---|---|---|

**Period 1**

1
**H**
Hydrogen
1.007 94

Group 1 / Group 2

**Period 2**

3
**Li**
Lithium
6.941

4
**Be**
Beryllium
9.012 182

**Period 3**

11
**Na**
Sodium
22.989 770

12
**Mg**
Magnesium
24.3050

Group 3 | Group 4 | Group 5 | Group 6 | Group 7 | Group 8 | Group 9

**Period 4**

19 **K** Potassium 39.0983
20 **Ca** Calcium 40.078
21 **Sc** Scandium 44.955 910
22 **Ti** Titanium 47.867
23 **V** Vanadium 50.9415
24 **Cr** Chromium 51.9961
25 **Mn** Manganese 54.938 049
26 **Fe** Iron 55.845
27 **Co** Cobalt 58.933 200

**Period 5**

37 **Rb** Rubidium 85.4678
38 **Sr** Strontium 87.62
39 **Y** Yttrium 88.905 85
40 **Zr** Zirconium 91.224
41 **Nb** Niobium 92.906 38
42 **Mo** Molybdenum 95.94
43 **Tc** Technetium (98)
44 **Ru** Ruthenium 101.07
45 **Rh** Rhodium 102.905 50

**Period 6**

55 **Cs** Cesium 132.905 43
56 **Ba** Barium 137.327
57 **La** Lanthanum 138.9055
72 **Hf** Hafnium 178.49
73 **Ta** Tantalum 180.9479
74 **W** Tungsten 183.84
75 **Re** Rhenium 186.207
76 **Os** Osmium 190.23
77 **Ir** Iridium 192.217

**Period 7**

87 **Fr** Francium (223)
88 **Ra** Radium (226)
89 **Ac** Actinium (227)
104 **Rf** Rutherfordium (261)
105 **Db** Dubnium (262)
106 **Sg** Seaborgium (266)
107 **Bh** Bohrium (264)
108 **Hs** Hassium (277)
109 **Mt** Meitnerium (268)

\* The systematic names and symbols for elements greater than 110 will be used until the approval of trivial names by IUPAC.

58 **Ce** Cerium 140.116
59 **Pr** Praseodymium 140.907 65
60 **Nd** Neodymium 144.24
61 **Pm** Promethium (145)
62 **Sm** Samarium 150.36

90 **Th** Thorium 232.0381
91 **Pa** Protactinium 231.035 88
92 **U** Uranium 238.028 91
93 **Np** Neptunium (237)
94 **Pu** Plutonium (244)